10142

Short Story Criticism

Guide to Gale Literary Criticism Series

For criticism on	Consult these Gale series
Authors now living or who died after December 31, 1959	*CONTEMPORARY LITERARY CRITICISM (CLC)*
Authors who died between 1900 and 1959	*TWENTIETH-CENTURY LITERARY CRITICISM (TCLC)*
Authors who died between 1800 and 1899	*NINETEENTH-CENTURY LITERATURE CRITICISM (NCLC)*
Authors who died between 1400 and 1799	*LITERATURE CRITICISM FROM 1400 TO 1800 (LC)* *SHAKESPEAREAN CRITICISM (SC)*
Authors who died before 1400	*CLASSICAL AND MEDIEVAL LITERATURE CRITICISM (CMLC)*
Black writers of the past two hundred years	*BLACK LITERATURE CRITICISM (BLC)*
Authors of books for children and young adults	*CHILDREN'S LITERATURE REVIEW (CLR)*
Dramatists	*DRAMA CRITICISM (DC)*
Hispanic writers of the late nineteenth and twentieth centuries	*HISPANIC LITERATURE CRITICISM (HLC)*
Native North American writers and orators of the eighteenth, nineteenth, and twentieth centuries	*NATIVE NORTH AMERICAN LITERATURE (NNAL)*
Poets	*POETRY CRITICISM (PC)*
Short story writers	*SHORT STORY CRITICISM (SSC)*
Major authors from the Renaissance to the present	*WORLD LITERATURE CRITICISM, 1500 TO THE PRESENT (WLC)*

ISSN 0895-9493

Volume 17

Short Story Criticism

Excerpts from Criticism of the
Works of Short Fiction Writers

Drew Kalasky, Editor

Margaret Haerens
Jeff Hill
Jane Kelly Kosek
Thomas Ligotti
Lynn M. Spampinato
Lawrence J. Trudeau
Associate Editors

 *Gale Research Inc.*

An International Thomson Publishing Company

I⊤P

NEW YORK • LONDON • BONN • BOSTON • DETROIT • MADRID
MELBOURNE • MEXICO CITY • PARIS • SINGAPORE • TOKYO
TORONTO • WASHINGTON • ALBANY NY • BELMONT CA • CINCINNATI OH

STAFF

Drew Kalasky, *Editor*

Margaret Haerens, Jeff Hill, Jane Kelly Kosek, Thomas Ligotti, Lynn M. Spampinato,
Lawrence J. Trudeau, *Associate Editors*

Martha Bommarito, Debra A. Wells, *Assistant Editors*

Marlene H. Lasky, *Permissions Manager*
Margaret A. Chamberlain, Linda M. Pugliese, *Permissions Specialists*

Susan Brohman, Diane Cooper, Maria L. Franklin, Pamela A. Hayes, Arlene Johnson, Josephine M. Keene,
Michele Lonoconus, Maureen Puhl, Shalice Shah, Kimberly F. Smilay, Barbara A. Wallace, *Permissions Associates*

Edna Hedblad, Tyra Y. Phillips, *Permissions Assistants*

Victoria B. Cariappa, *Research Manager*
Barbara McNeil, *Research Specialist*

Frank Vincent Castronova, Eva M. Felts, Mary Beth McElmeel, Donna Melnychenko,
Tamara C. Nott, Tracie A. Richardson, Norma Sawaya, *Research Associates*

Alicia Noel Biggers, Maria E. Bryson, Julia C. Daniel, Shirley Gates,
Michele P. Pica, Amy Terese Steel, Amy Beth Wieczorek, *Research Assistants*

Mary Beth Trimper, *Production Director*
Mary Kelley, *Production Associate*

Cynthia Baldwin, *Product Design Manager*
Barbara J. Yarrow, *Graphic Services Supervisor*
Sherrell Hobbs, *Macintosh Artist*
Willie F. Mathis, *Camera Operator*

Library of Congress Catalog Card Number 88-641014
ISBN 0-8103-9281-X
ISSN 0895-9439

Printed in the United States of America
Published simultaneously in the United Kingdom
by Gale Research International Limited
(An affiliated company of Gale Research Inc.)
10 9 8 7 6 5 4 3 2 1

Contents

Preface   vii

Acknowledgments   xi

Preface

A Comprehensive Information Source
on World Short Fiction

S *hort Story Criticism (SSC)* presents significant passages from criticism of the world's greatest short story writers and provides supplementary biographical and bibliographical materials to guide the interested reader to a greater understanding of the authors of short fiction. This series was developed in response to suggestions from librarians serving high school, college, and public library patrons, who had noted a considerable number of requests for critical material on short story writers. Although major short story writers are covered in such Gale series as *Contemporary Literary Criticism (CLC), Twentieth-Century Literary Criticism (TCLC), Nineteenth-Century Literature Criticism (NCLC),* and *Literature Criticism from 1400 to 1800 (LC),* librarians perceived the need for a series devoted solely to writers of the short story genre.

Coverage

SSC is designed to serve as an introduction to major short story writers of all eras and nationalities. Since these authors have inspired a great deal of relevant critical material, *SSC* is necessarily selective, and the editors have chosen the most important published criticism to aid readers and students in their research.

Approximately eight to ten authors are included in each volume, and each entry presents a historical survey of the critical response to that author's work. The length of an entry is intended to reflect the amount of critical attention the author has received from critics writing in English and from foreign critics in translation. Every attempt has been made to identify and include excerpts from the most significant essays on each author's work. In order to provide these important critical pieces, the editors sometimes reprint essays that have appeared elsewhere in Gale's Literary Criticism Series. Such duplication, however, never exceeds twenty percent of an *SSC* volume.

Organization

An *SSC* author entry consists of the following elements:

- The **Author Heading** cites the name under which the author most commonly wrote, followed by birth and death dates. If the author wrote consistently under a pseudonym, the pseudonym will be listed in the author heading and the author's actual name given in parentheses on the first line of the biographical and critical introduction.

- The **Biographical and Critical Introduction** contains background information designed to introduce a reader to the author and the critical debates surrounding his or her work.

- A **Portrait of the Author** is included when available. Many entries also contain illustrations of materials pertinent to an author's career, including holographs of manuscript pages, title pages, dust jackets, letters, or representations of important people, places, and events in the author's life.

- The list of **Principal Works** is chronological by date of first publication and lists the most important works by the author. The first section comprises short story collections, novellas, and novella collections. The second section gives information on other major works by the author. For foreign authors, the editors have provided original foreign-language publication information and have selected what are considered the best and most complete English-language editions of their works.

- **Criticism** is arranged chronologically in each author entry to provide a useful perspective on changes in critical evaluation over the years. All short story, novella, and collection titles by the author featured in the entry are printed in boldface type to enable a reader to ascertain without difficulty the works discussed. Also for purposes of easier identification, the critic's name and the publication date of the essay are given at the beginning of each piece of criticism. Unsigned criticism is preceded by the title of the journal in which it appeared.

- Critical essays are prefaced with **Explanatory Notes** as an additional aid to students and readers using *SSC*. An explanatory note may provide useful information of several types, including: the reputation of the critic, the intent or scope of the critical essay, and the orientation of the criticism (biographical, psychoanalytic, structuralist, etc.).

- A complete **Bibliographical Citation,** designed to help the interested reader locate the original essay or book, precedes each piece of criticism.

- The **Further Reading List** appearing at the end of each author entry suggests additional materials on the author. In some cases it includes essays for which the editors could not obtain reprint rights. Boxed material following the further reading list provides references to other biographical and critical sources on the author in series published by Gale.

Beginning with volume six, *SSC* contains two additional features designed to enhance the reader's understanding of short fiction writers and their works:

- Each *SSC* entry now includes, when available, **Comments by the Author** that illuminate his or her own works or the short story genre in general. These statements are set within boxes or bold rules to distinguish them from the criticism.

- A **Select Bibliography of General Sources on Short Fiction** is included as an appendix. This listing of materials for further research provides readers with a selection of the best available general studies of the short story genre.

Other Features

A **Cumulative Author Index** lists all the authors who have appeared in *SSC, CLC, TCLC, NCLC, LC,* and *Classical and Medieval Literature Criticism (CMLC),* as well as cross-references to other Gale series. Users will welcome this cumulated index as a useful tool for locating an author within the Literary Criticism Series.

A **Cumulative Nationality Index** lists all authors featured in *SSC* by nationality, followed by the number of the *SSC* volume in which their entry appears.

A **Cumulative Title Index** lists in alphabetical order all short story, novella, and collection titles contained in the *SSC* series. Titles of short story collections, separately published novellas, and novella collections are printed in italics, while titles of individual short stories are printed in roman type with quotation marks.

Each title is followed by the author's name and corresponding volume and page numbers where commentary on the work is located. English-language translations of original foreign-language titles are cross-referenced to the foreign titles so that all references to discussion of a work are combined in one listing.

Citing *Short Story Criticism*

When writing papers, students who quote directly from any volume in the Literary Criticism Series may use the following general forms to footnote reprinted criticism. The first example pertains to material drawn from periodicals, the second to material reprinted from books:

[1]Henry James, Jr., "Honoré de Balzac," *The Galaxy 20* (December 1875), 814-36; excerpted and reprinted in *Short Story Criticism,* Vol. 5, ed. Thomas Votteler (Detroit: Gale Research, 1990), pp. 8-11.

[2]F. R. Leavis, *D. H. Lawrence: Novelist* (Alfred A. Knopf, 1956); excerpted and reprinted in *Short Story Criticism,* Vol. 4, ed. Thomas Votteler (Detroit: Gale Research, 1990), pp. 202-06.

Comments

Readers who wish to suggest authors to appear in future volumes, or who have other suggestions, are invited to contact the editors by writing to Gale Research Inc., Literary Criticism Division, 835 Penobscot Building, Detroit, MI 48226-4094.

Acknowledgments

The editors wish to thank the copyright holders of the excerpted criticism included in this volume and the permissions managers of many book and magazine publishing companies for assisting us in securing reprint rights. We are also grateful to the staffs of the Detroit Public Library, the Library of Congress, the University of Detroit Mercy Library, Wayne State University Purdy/Kresge Library Complex, and the University of Michigan Libraries for making their resources available to us. Following is a list of the copyright holders who have granted us permission to reprint material in this volume of *SSC*. Every effort has been made to trace copyright, but if omissions have been made, please let us know.

COPYRIGHTED EXCERPTS IN *SSC*, VOLUME 17, WERE REPRINTED FROM THE FOLLOWING PERIODICALS:

America, v. 169, July 31-August 7, 1993 for a review of "The Collected Stories" by Eamon Grennan. Copyright © 1993. All rights reserved. Reprinted with permission of America Press, Inc., 106 West 56th Street, New York, NY 10019 and the author.—*The American Book Review,* v. 10, January, 1989. © 1989 by *The American Book Review.* Reprinted by permission of the publisher.—*The American Scholar,* v. 21, Winter, 1951-52. Copyright 1952, renewed 1980 by the United Chapters of the Phi Betta Kappa Society. Reprinted by permission of the publishers.—*Arizona Quarterly,* v. 41, Summer, 1985 for "'Bartleby the Scrivener': A Simple Reading" by Michael Murphy. Copyright © 1985 by Arizona Board of Regents. Reprinted by permission of the publisher and the author.—*Best Sellers,* v. 38, April, 1978; v. 45, August 1985. Copyright © 1978, 1985 Helen Dwight Reid Educational Foundation. Both reprinted by permission of the publisher.—*Book World—The Washington Post,* May 16, 1976; August 22, 1982; May 20, 1984; June 16, 1985; August 26, 1990. © 1976, 1982, 1984, 1985, 1990, *The Washington Post.* All reprinted with permission of the publisher.—*Booklist,* v. 89. July, 1993. Copyright © 1993 by the American Library Association. Reprinted by permission of the publisher.—*Bulletin of Hispanic Studies,* v. LII, 1975. © copyright 1975 Liverpool University Press. Reprinted by permission of the publisher.—*Chasqui,* v. XX, November, 1991. Reprinted by permission of the publisher.—*Chicago Tribune—Books,* August 21, 1988. © copyrighted 1988, Chicago Tribune Company. All rights reserved. Used with permission.—*The Christian Science Monitor,* November 4, 1971. © 1971 The Christian Science Publishing Society. All rights reserved. Reprinted by permission from *The Christian Science Monitor.*—*College Literature,* v. II, Winter, 1975. Copyright © 1975 by West Chester University. Reprinted by permission of the publisher.—*Commonweal,* v. CXIV, September 11, 1987. Copyright © 1987 Commonweal Foundation. Reprinted by permission of Commonweal Foundation.—*Critique: Studies in Modern Fiction,* v. XIII, 1970; v. XXII, 1981. Copyright © 1970, 1981 Helen Dwight Reid Educational Foundation. Both reprinted with permission of the Helen Dwight Reid Educational Foundation, published by Heldref Publications, 1319 18th Street, N. W., Washington, DC 20036-1802.—*Delta,* England, v. 6, May, 1978 for "The 'Incurable Disorder' in 'Bartleby the Scrivener'" by Thomas P. Joswick. Reprinted by permission of the author. —*Dispositio,* vs. V-VI, Otoño-Invierno, 1980-81. Reprinted by permission of the publisher.—*Fantasy & Science Fiction,* v. 64, February, 1983 for a review of "Different Seasons" by Algis Budrys. Reprinted by permission of the author.—*The Georgia Review,* v. XLII, Winter, 1988. Copyright, 1988, by the University of Georgia. Reprinted by permission of the publisher.—*Interview,* v. 18, January, 1988. © Copyright 1988 by *Interview* magazine. All rights reserved. Reprinted by permission of the publisher.—*Irish Literary Supplement,* v. 12, Fall, 1993. Copyright © 1993, *Irish Literary Supplement.* Reprinted by permission of the publisher.—*Japan Quarterly,* v. XVIII, July-September, 1971. © 1971, by the Asahi Shimbun. Reprinted by permission of the publisher.—*Journal of the Short Story in English,* n. 13, Autumn, 1989. © Universite d'Angers, 1989. Reprinted by permission of the

LIV, December 4, 1971. © 1969, 1971 *Saturday Review* magazine. Both reprinted by permission of the publisher./ v. XLVIII, May 8, 1965. © 1965, renewed 1993, *Saturday Review* magazine. Reprinted by permission of the publisher. —*The Sewanee Review,* v. LXI, Autumn, 1953 for "Melville's Parable of the Walls" by Leo Marx. Copyright 1953, renewed 1981, by The University of the South. Reprinted with the permission of the editor of *The Sewanee Review* and the author.—*South Atlantic Quarterly,* v. LXI, Autumn, 1962. Copyright © 1962, renewed 1990 by Duke University Press, Durham, NC. Reprinted by permission of the publisher.—*Southwest Review,* v. 74, Summer, 1989 for "The Asymmetrical Garden: Discovering Yasunari Kawabata" by Thom Palmer. © 1989 Southern Methodist University. Reprinted by permission of the author.—*Studies in Short Fiction,* v. V, 1968; v. 24, Summer, 1987; v. 27, Winter, 1990; v. 31, Winter, 1994. Copyright 1968, 1987, 1990, 1994 by Newberry College. All reprinted by permission of the publisher./ v. III, Fall, 1965. Copyright 1965, renewed 1993 by Newberry College. Reprinted by permission of the publisher.—*Sub-Stance,* n. 41, 1983. Copyright © Sub-Stance, Inc. 1983. Reprinted by permission of the publisher.—*The Times Literary Supplement,* n. 3976, June 16, 1978; n. 4143, August 27, 1982; n. 4302, September 13, 1985. © The Times Supplements Limited 1978, 1982, 1985. All reproduced from *The Times Literary Supplement* by permission.—*TriQuarterly, 16,* n. 16, Fall, 1969. © 1969 by *TriQuarterly,* Northwestern University.—*The Village Voice,* v. XX, November 3, 1975 for "Borges Disciple" by Nathan Rosenstein; v. XXV, September 17-23, 1980 for "Gordimer Confined" by Vivian Gornick. Copyright © The Village Voice, Inc., 1975, 1980. Both reprinted by permission of *The Village Voice* and the respective authors. —*The Virginia Quarterly Review,* v. 67, Autumn, 1991. Copyright, 1991, by *The Virginia Quarterly Review,* The University of Virginia. Reprinted by permission of the publisher.—*VLS,* n. 28, September, 1984 for "The Politics of Good Intention" by Melvyn Hill. Copyright © 1984 News Group Publications, Inc. Reprinted by permission of *The Village Voice* and the author.—*World Literature Today,* v. 61, Autumn, 1987; v. 67, Winter, 1993. Copyright 1987, 1993 by the University of Oklahoma Press. Both reprinted by permission of the publisher.

COPYRIGHTED EXCERPTS IN *SSC*, VOLUME 17, WERE REPRINTED FROM THE FOLLOWING BOOKS:

Barbey, d'Aurevilly, Jules. From *The She-Devils (Les Diaboliques).* Translated by Jean Kimber. Oxford University Press, London, 1964. English translation and introduction © Oxford University Press 1964. Reprinted by permission of the publisher.—Bernheimer, Charles. From *Figures of Ill Repute: Representing Prostitution in Nineteenth-Century France.* Cambridge, Mass.: Harvard University Press, 1989. Copyright © 1989 by the President and Fellows of Harvard College. All rights reserved. Excerpted by permission of the publisher and the author.—Bickley, R. Bruce, Jr. From *The Method of Melville's Short Fiction.* Duke University Press, 1975. Copyright © 1969, 1975 by Duke University Press, Durham, NC. Reprinted with permission of the publisher.—Biddle, Arthur W. From "The Mythic Journey in 'The Body'," in *The Dark Descent: Essays Defining Stephen King's Horrorscope.* Edited by Tony Magistrale. Greenwood Press, 1992. Copyright © 1992 by Anthony S. Magistrale. All rights reserved. Reprinted by permission of Greenwood Publishing Group, Inc., Westport, CT. —Birkerts, Sven. From *An Artificial Widerness: Essays on 20th-Century Literature.* Morrow, 1987. Reprinted by permission of William Morrow and Company, Inc. In the British Commonwealth by the author.—Blair, Walter. From "Dashiell Hammett: Themes and Techniques," in *Essays on American Literature in Honor of Jay B. Hubbell.* Edited by Clarence Gohdes. Duke University Press, 1967. Copyright © 1967 by Duke University Press, Durham, NC. Reprinted with permission of the publisher.—Borges, Jorge Luis and Adolfo Bioy-Casares. From *Six Problems for Don Isidro Parodi.* Translated by Norman Thomas di Giovanni. E. P. Dutton, 1981. Copyright © 1980, 1981 by Jorge Luis Borges, Adolfo Bioy-Casares, and Norman Thomas di Giovanni. All rights reserved.—Bradbury, Nicola. From "High Ground," in *Re-reading the Short Story.* Edited by Clare Hanson. Macmillan Press, 1989. © Clare Hanson 1989. All rights reserved. Reprinted by permission of Macmillan London and Basingstoke. —Brown, Terence. From "John McGahern's 'Nightlines': Tone, Technique and Symbolism," in *The Irish Short Story.* Edited by Patrick Rafroidi and Terence Brown. Colin Smythe, 1979. Copyright © 1979, by Presses Universitaires de Lille (C.E.R.I.U.L.) and Colin Smythe Ltd. All rights reserved. Reprinted by permission of the publisher.—Colleran, Jeanne. From "Archive of Apartheid: Nadine Gordimer's Short Fiction at the End of the Interregnum," in *The Later Fiction of Nadine Gordimer.* Edited by Bruce King. St. Martin's Press, 1993, The Macmillan Press Ltd., 1993. © The Macmillan Press Ltd 1993. Editorial matter, selection and Introduction © Bruce King 1993. All rights reserved. Reprinted by

the Scandalmongers: Essays in Criticism. University of Oklahoma Press, 1965. Copyright 1965 by the Unversity of Oklahoma Press, Publishing Division of the University. Reprinted by permission of the publisher.—Winter, Douglas E. From Stephen King: The Art of Darkness. New American Library, 1984. Copyright © 1984 by Douglas E. Winter. All rights reserved. Used by permission of Dutton Signet, a Division of Penguin Books USA Inc., New York.

PHOTOGRAPHS AND ILLUSTRATIONS APPEARING IN *SSC,* VOLUME 17, WERE RECEIVED FROM THE FOLLOWING SOURCES:

Cover of *El lado de la sombra,* by Adolfo Bioy Casares. Tusquets, 1991: **p. 61;** Photograph by David Goldblatt: **pp. 150, 167;** The Granger Collection, New York: **pp. 197, 219;** UPI/Bettmann Newsphotos: **p. 228;** Harold Strauss and Alfred A. Knopf, Inc., N.Y.: **p. 233;** Consulate General of Japan, New York: **p. 248;** ©1987 Thomas Victor: **p. 260.**

Jules Amédée Barbey d'Aurevilly

1808-1889

French critic, novelist, short story writer, and poet.

INTRODUCTION

An eccentric character who ignored the literary fashions of his time, Barbey gained recognition as literary critic on *Le constitutionnel*, for which he wrote criticism that rang with striking invective and prejudice. He detested all things common, an attitude that permeated his religion, politics, fiction, and lifestyle. A dogmatic Catholic, he defended traditional morality while simultaneously offending, with perverse novels and stories, the church he claimed to love. *Les diaboliques* (*The Diaboliques*), a collection of six short stories, is his masterpiece, a work that best displays his recurring concern with dark passions and their manifestations, such as illicit love, cruelty, sadism, vengeance, violence, murder, depravity, and diabolism.

Biographical Information

Born into an aristocratic family at Saint-Sauveur-le-Vicomte in the region of Normandy, Barbey made the idea of nobility and distinction his driving obsession. He was not only a dandy, but also the historian and theoretician of dandyism. He studied in Paris, where he acquiesced to his father's wishes by obtaining a law degree. Although his principal inclination was to political journalism, Barbey became a critic, contributing analyses of art, drama, fashion, and contemporary literature to a number of periodicals, and eventually succeeded the accomplished man of letters Charles Sainte-Beuve as the literary critic for *Le constitutionnel*. Upon publication of *The Diaboliques*, the Church pronounced the collection immoral, seized all unsold copies, and threatened Barbey with litigation. Consequently, he contacted influential friends in the hopes of forestalling a public trial. The case was dropped the following year, but he did not attempt to republish the book until eight years later. Toward the end of his life, Barbey finally received some of the respect and understanding he had sought throughout his career, appropriately enough from an elite group of literati rather than the public.

Major Works of Short Fiction

"Le rideau cramoisi" ("The Crimson Curtain"), a story in *The Diaboliques* known for its mystery and ominous tone, tells the tale of two gentlemen on a coach that has broken down at night in a little town. The sight of a crimson curtain in the window of a nearby house provokes one of the passengers to relate the story of his experiences as a young man in that very house—an account recollecting deception, suppressed emotions, secret assignations, sexual consummation, an enigmatic death, and a sudden, shameful flight. In the tale "La vengeance d'une femme"

("A Woman's Revenge"), a prostitute tells a client of her prior life as a duchess. She explains that in retaliation for the brutal murder of her lover by her husband, the duke, she has become a whore, debasing her husband's glorious family name by revealing her identity and her husband's deed to each of her patrons. Another story from *The Diaboliques*, "Le bonheur dans le crime" ("Happiness in Crime"), consists of a discussion between two gentlemen who have espied a strikingly handsome couple walking. The couple, as the reader learns from the men, are a count and his former chambermaid, the two of whom poisoned the countess; the lovers now live happily without regard for the suspicions of the townspeople.

Critical Reception

Contemporaries of Barbey tended to concentrate on the lurid subject matter and irreligious tenor of *The Diaboliques*. Some readers perceived the women in his stories as instruments of Satan, leading men to moral corruption with no hope for salvation. Others claimed that the stories betray a prurient intent on the part of the author, belying his claim to Christian morality. More recently, commentators have suggested that several of the protagonists in

The Diaboliques are daring individuals unfettered by fear and ethics. Much current discussion of the stories, however, approaches the collection through postmodern analysis of narrative: the foremost issue is the structure of the stories, which are related by means of a framing narrative that contains one or more subnarratives, prompting debate about the tales as metafictional commentary on the nature of storytelling.

PRINCIPAL WORKS

Short Fiction

Les diaboliques [*The Diaboliques*]   1874
"Le cachet d'onyx," "Léa" (1831-1833)   1919

Other Major Works

L'amour impossible   (novel)   1841
Du dandysme et de Georges Brummel [*Of Dandyism and of George Brummell*]   (essay)   1845
Une vieille maîtresse. 3 vols. [*An Old Mistress*]   (novel)   1851
*L'ensorcelée. 2 vols. [*The Bewitched*]   (novel)   1854
Poésies   (poetry)   1854
Le XIXe siecle: Les oeuvres et les hommes. 26 vols. [*Works and Men, 1860-1895*]   (criticism)   1860-1909
*Le chevalier des Touches   (novel)   1864
*Un prêtre marié. 2 vols. [*A Married Priest*]   (novel)   1865
Poésies   (poetry)   1870
Goethe et Diderot   (criticism)   1880
Une histoire sans nom [*A Story without a Name*]   (novel)   1882
Une page d'histoire   (novel)   1882
Ce qui ne meurt pas [*What Never Dies*]   (novel)   1883
Amaïdée. Poème en prose   (poem)   1890
Les oeuvres complètes. 17 vols.   (novels, short stories, poetry, letters, and memoranda)   1926-27

*These novels are commonly referred to as the Normandy novels or the Normandy cycle.

CRITICISM

Jules Barbey d'Aurevilly   (essay date 1874)

SOURCE: A preface to *The She-Devils (Les Diaboliques),* translated by Jean Kimber, Oxford University Press, London, 1964, pp. xvii-xviii.

[*In the following essay, which originally accompanied the first edition of his short fiction collection, Barbey discusses the intent of the stories in* The Diaboliques.]

Here are the first six. . . .

If the public likes them, and finds them to its taste, I shall shortly publish the other six, for there are a dozen of these tales in all.

Naturally, with a title such as *Les Diaboliques*, they cannot lay claim to being a book of prayer or of model Christianity. They are none the less the work of a Christian moralist, but a moralist who prides himself on truthful, if extremely bold, observation, and who believes—this is his own very individual poetic credo—that powerful painters can paint anything, and that their painting is always sufficiently moral when it is tragic and when it inspires horror for what it represents. Only the cold and cynical are immoral. Now the present author, who believes in the Devil and his works, does not laugh at them, and he tells pure souls about them in order to put the fear of Hell into them.

After reading these *Diaboliques* I doubt if anybody will feel inclined to imitate them, and the whole morality of the book consists in that fact.

So much for the honour of the book. Now another question: why has the author given these little tragedies the high-sounding name of *Les Diaboliques*? Is it the stories themselves which are diabolical or the heroines?

Unfortunately these stories are all true. Nothing in them has been invented. The author has not named the characters, that is all. He has masked them, and removed the names from their linen. . . . 'The alphabet belongs to me,' Casanova used to say when people criticized him for not using his own name. A novelist's alphabet consists of the lives of all who have known passion and adventure, and it is simply a matter of arranging, with the discretion of a consummate art, the letters of that alphabet. Besides, despite the piquancy of these necessarily disguised stories, there are sure to be some people, excited by this title of *Les Diaboliques*, who will not consider them as diabolical as they seem to wish to appear. These people will expect inventions, complications, affectations, refinements, all the *tremolo* of the modern melodrama which is insinuating itself everywhere, even into the novel. They will be wrong, those charming souls! *Les Diaboliques* is not about devilry but diabolism: it is a collection of true stories of this age of progress, this period of such *divine* civilization that when they are written down it seems as if it was the Devil who had dictated them. . . . The Devil is like God. Manichaeism, which was the source of the greatest heresies of the Middle Ages, is not as stupid as all that. Malebranche once said that God could be recognized by 'the use of the simplest means'. The Devil too.

As for the women in these stories, why should it not be they that are *Les Diaboliques*? Is there not enough diabolism in their persons to merit that sweet name? Diabolical? There is not a single one here who is not diabolical to some degree. There is not a single one of them to whom a man could seriously say: 'Angel!' without exaggeration. Like the Devil, who was also an angel, but a fallen one, if they are angels then it is after his fashion—head down and . . . the rest up. There is not one of them who is pure, virtuous, or innocent. Even leaving aside their vices, they are not exactly rich in virtues and moral sentiments. They too could therefore reasonably be called *Les Diaboliques*. . . . The present author has set out to make a little museum of these ladies—pending the time when he can make the even smaller museum of the ladies who form a complement and a contrast to them in society, for everything is double. Art has two lobes, like the brain. Nature is like those women who have one blue eye and one black. Here is the black eye . . . drawn in the ink of easy virtue.

Later on, perhaps, the author may depict the blue eye. After *Les Diaboliques*, *Les Célestes* . . . if there is a blue pure enough for the purpose.

But is there?

William Aspenwall Bradley   (essay date 1910)

SOURCE: "Barbey d'Aurevilly: A French Disciple of Walter Scott," in *The North American Review*, Vol. 192, No. 3, September, 1910, pp. 473-85.

[*An author, translator, and editor, Bradley was the most successful American literary agent in Paris during the 1920s and 1930s. He represented, at various times, such American authors as John Dos Passos, Claude McKay, Henry Miller, Katherine Anne Porter, Ezra Pound, Edith Wharton, and Thornton Wilder, and passionately championed French literature in America. In the following excerpt, Bradley offers a positive general assessment of Barbey's fiction.*]

> Barbey d'Aurevilly is one of the most original figures of the nineteenth century. It is probable that he will long excite curiosity, that he will long remain one of those singular and, as it were, subterranean writers, who are the veritable life of French literature. Their altar is at the bottom of a crypt, but the faithful descend to it willingly, while the temple of the great saints opens to the sun its ennui and its void. . . . Barbey d'Aurevilly is not one of those men who impose themselves on the banal admiration. He is complex and capricious. Some hold him to be a Christian writer . . . others denounce his immorality and his diabolical audacity. There is all of that in him: whence arose contradictions that were not solely successive. [M. Remy de Gourmont]

It is owing to this *malentendu* that even in France [Barbey] is relatively little read, and only in a circle whose opinions are not shaped by ecclesiastical authority and the official criteria of the libraries which have tended silently to suppress him. For the public at large he has remained principally a fantastic figure who believed in the Devil—perhaps worshipped him—and who not only wrote a book about Beau Brummel, but exemplified the philosophy of "dandysme" in his own person to the delight of the Boulevards.

It is thus that Anatole France has portrayed d'Aurevilly as a fanciful memory of his own childhood, while he himself was still viewing the world framed by the door of an old bookshop on the quays of the Seine; and it is probable that this half legendary evocation by one who has in a high degree the fatal faculty of fixing values, will survive the efforts of the friends of the critic and novelist—he died as recently as 1889, though he was born in 1808—to establish for him a definite and recognized place in the literature of the last century. . . .

D'Aurevilly is anything but impersonal. He cannot keep himself out of his stories, all of which in their main actions express rather his idealized vision than his direct observation of life. His whole personality is flamboyant; and his style is like a flame flashing from a volcano that from time to time erupts and spurts streams of fiery lava in every direction. Hence is explained his lack of sympathy with the Parnassian poets. Baudelaire himself was very far from being a Parnassian. He put passion into his pursuit of the exotic, the macabre, the sinister and into his portrayal of delicate shades of corruption. This also was the range of d'Aurevilly's subjects. Here in both is to be found the very essence of that "demoniac tendency" which Baudelaire notes as an essential characteristic in modern art. In him it remains resolved in its metaphysical state. In d'Aurevilly it takes a theological turn and produces the devil.

Personally, however, I feel that too much stress has perhaps been laid upon the diabolism of this writer. Whatever interest it may possess in itself, it has little to do with the actual *procédés* of his art. There is not one of his stories the design of which, however much it might justify acceptance of the devil as a factor in human affairs, in any way absolutely requires his interposition as a kind of infernal *deus ex machinâ*. That is, you may take the devil or leave him, as you like. The author is merely engaged in painting human passions and their effects, and while he may hold his own opinion as to the origin of the element of corruption they contain, you may have yours, and he will take no unfair advantage of you or attempt to convert you to his cult. . . . As for Barbey's choice of subjects, it must always be remembered that he was a romantic writer. For him, as for Byron, the criminal was fascinating because of his force and strange distinction; also because he was at war with society and set at naught the conventional moral code. Powerful, he was "only half a monster." In him something of the passion and self-reliance of the primitive man is displayed, and he may readily be made to seem heroic, superhuman. It was such a sentiment that made Stendhal in Italy welcome manifestations of atrocious crime because they proved that that country could still produce "characters." D'Aurevilly's books abound in Byronic figures, and they include women as well as men. There is this difference, however, that, while Byron's criminals derive much of their romantic suggestion from the exotic coloring of their expoits, which are commonly little more than ordinary acts of murder and rapine, d'Aurevilly's derive theirs rather from the secrecy, or from the peculiar violence and perversity, of their acts. Here he possesses a distinct advantage as a Catholic writer. For not only does the spiritual significance of crime become immeasurably deepened and intensified when it is regarded as sin, but the casuistry of the Catholic conscience, developed through the secular experience of the confessional, suggests varieties and subtleties of wrong-doing that the less completely evolved legal and social conscience cannot compete with.

But there is also another distinction to be made. D'Aurevilly has drawn one type that is altogether different from any to be found in Byron. This is the absolute criminal. A great crime is ordinarily represented as entailing a moral crisis. Remorse, mingled with Satanic pride, is the very key-note of Byron's criminals, as it is of Lucifer. Nothing, indeed, is more difficult to draw than a human being from whom all sense of guilt is eliminated. Such a character—we may take the Marquise in *Les Liaisons Dangereuses* as an example—is likely to suffer in its sense of reality, unless, indeed, as in Feuillet's *La Morte*, it is presented as frankly pathological. D'Aurevilly presents two such individuals, strangely instinct with life and artistic truth, in one of the stories in **Les Diaboliques**, where he depicts the passion of a man and a woman who deliberately put out of their way the obstacle to their union. The situation is the same as that in one of the episodes of *Pippa Passes*, but the moral issues are wholly different. Having attained their end, there is no after-weakening, no moral deterioration on either side, only the serene enjoyment of a happiness in no wise affected by the nature of the acts through which it was acquired. The implied moral of the story would evidently seem to be that, as Maeterlinck says in *Les Trésor des Humbles*, "the soul may retain its innocence even in the midst of a great crime." There is, however, on d'Aurevilly's part, no attempt to draw a moral, to establish a mystical law. He presents his man and woman frankly as exceptions, and it is just because they are exceptional, and because the incident is precisely a singular and disconcerting paradox of criminal psychology, that they interest him and the reader. These people, one feels, live in a region "beyond good and evil." Thus in them d'Aurevilly anticipates the theory of the Superman. That, being of the elect who win the right to a special moral standard by living up to the full level of their passions, they are, from d'Aurevilly's point of view, the elect of the devil rather than of nature, constitutes the only divergence from Nietzsche's idea. And this is merely a superficial difference, after all. If the German is a Greek at heart, d'Aurevilly is a child of the early Renaissance. He is, as it were, a Pollaiuolo of the pen. He is absorbed and fascinated by manifestations of power and forms of personal distinction. The devil still terrifies him. This shows itself in contortion and grimace. But he is already beginning to feel the fiend dissolving into the complexity of natural forces and to interpret these physically and psychologically. Meanwhile the pagan finds, or believes to find, a certain support in the primitive Christian—a justification for the broad and liberal representation of life to which he is drawn. The plea which he makes in the preface to *L'Ensorcelée* is ingenious and characteristic:

> As for the manner [he says] in which the author . . . has described the effects of passion and sometimes spoken its language, he has used that great Catholic breadth which does not fear to touch the human passions, when this creates terror at its consequences. A novelist, he has accomplished his task of novelist which is to paint the heart of man in strife with sin, and he has painted it without embarrassment and false shame. It would please unbelievers to have the things of the imagination and the heart—that is to say, the novel and the drama—at least half of the human soul, forbidden to Catholics, under the pretext that Catholicism is too severe to oc-

cupy itself with this sort of subject. . . . On this count a Catholic Shakespeare would not be possible, and Dante even would have passages that would have to be suppressed.

Here one is reminded of Francis Thompson's plea in the proem to his "Shelley" for a larger Catholic view of the nature and functions of poetry. Such pleas, however, have never been heeded by the Church since it has been necessary to make them at all. Certainly history would seem to show that a Catholic Shakespeare is impossible, since he has never appeared, while the distance of Dante merely serves to show how far Catholicism has travelled since pre-Reformation days when the Church still conserved the traditions of paganism. If d'Aurevilly actually believed that his profession of an edifying purpose would set him right with Christian orthodoxy he was sorely mistaken, and he might as well have made full profession of paganism. It is one thing to accept the devil (which must to-day be done very softly and apologetically by all creeds) and another to accord him a seat in the sanctuary. Hence like another but unrepentant Tannhäuser, d'Aurevilly was dismissed from the conclave and left free to return to the Horselberg of his imagination. And for him no staff has ever broken into miraculous blossom. *Les Diaboliques*, in which, indeed, the flimsy pretext of a moral intention is more or less abandoned, was prosecuted on its appearance, being the third of the famous trilogy of works thus treated in France during the nineteenth century. The other two were, of course, *Madame Bovary* and *Fleurs du Mal*. The author was discharged, but public sentiment has never quite acquitted him of crime in the execution of that daring but profoundly beautiful and artistic work. . . .

All that was truly Satanic in Barbey's soul insinuated itself into words which writhe like a nest of snakes and hiss like the coil of a whip wielded by one of his Chouan heroes. Wherever it falls, this lash, wrapping itself around the firm flesh of a fact, leaves a livid line or a trail of blood.

—*William Aspenwall Bradley*

[A] heroicizing tendency, if I may call it so, finds, perhaps, its most exalted expression in one of the stories in **Les Diaboliques**, where its almost dazzling purity is enhanced by the murky and infernal fires which light that book of strange passions and perversities. A group of old Napoleonic soldiers, brutal atheists of the Age of Reason and the bivouac, feast together regularly on the Friday of each week to publish their defiance of all religion. Harmless enough they are, with all their swaggering bluster, these old Jacobins and *grognards*. On the present occasion, however, one of the *convives* tells the story of a young girl of the Vendée who had served as the agent of the proscribed priests. When she was captured she was found to carry the sacramental wafers concealed upon her person. Seizing these, her captors cast them to the swine. This story is received with great gusto, and is roundly applauded by the majority of the listeners, who glory in the outrage to the most precious symbols of the Christian faith, and indulge in gross witticisms at the girl's expense. But there is one man at the table who, younger and less hardened than the rest, flashes out in protest. How can they miss, he asks, the true tragic significance of the story they have just heard? For them, since they professed not to believe in the validity of the sacraments, there could be no sacrilege in their insult. Not so for the girl. Why did they treasure their medals they had won on the field of honor? Was it not because these were the very incarnation of the Emperor, and because, in wearing them, they thus bore him above their hearts? Then, instead of covering her with their slime, they should understand and pity the poor child who carried concealed within her breast the divine body of her Lord, and for whom, therefore, the act of her captors was of the last horror. *Sava indignatio* can rarely have found a more superb denunciatory gesture than in this speech which glorifies, with supreme tenderness and beauty, the figure of a simple peasant girl who, in her humble act of piety and devotion, is one with the heroic maid. . . .

[Sir Walter] Scott employs apparitions and invokes supernatural forces, and does this far more artificially than does d'Aurevilly, who . . . always leaves a psychologic loophole of escape for the incredulous. Among other modern story-tellers, Mr. Watts-Dunton has given an admirable example of this *genre* in his "Aylwin," with all the familiar machinery of the curse and its effects. In this instance, however, the occult acquires a special spiritual significance in itself apart from the imaginative use that is made of it. While not interpreted in the spirit of gross popular superstition, it is, nevertheless, conceived as possessing a certain character of truth for those who read all physical phenomena in a spiritual sense. In the same way d'Aurevilly may also be regarded as an apostle of "the renascence of wonder." And though he may solemnly cite "the irrefragable attestation" of the Church as his ultimate authority, one may nevertheless feel that if he does not dismiss the marvellous with the contemptuous scorn of the cultivated, the real reason is because, for him, the marvellous is not restricted to any particular manifestations, but pervades all life.

The important thing for us to note at this point is, however, not that he professed a sort of philosophical belief in the potency of gypsy charms and incantations, but that he described the gypsies; not that he assumed as a fact "the intervention of occult and evil powers in the struggles of humanity," but that he portrayed the lives of those for whom such intervention was a vital part of their religious belief. He is as much dominated by his human material as by his imaginative motives and spiritual conceptions. He had a set purpose in his stories, over and above the poetical representation of life in the abstract as a conflict for man's soul. This was to bring into literature the moral and social life of those remnants of the old Norman race which persisted, after so many centuries, in out-of-the-way corners

of the land wrested by Rollo and his freebooters from the French. He carries out this purpose with singular completeness, and with an insight born of perfect racial sympathy. Into his portraits he puts all his intimate knowledge of the people, and aims to incorporate in them every distinctive trait, even to the precise shape of their speech—thus anticipating Maupassant in the same general locality—the style of their dress, and their physical characteristics. The racial traits are always kept clear and continuous even in the most highly individualized creations and through all classes of society, so that his characters, high and low, seem to constitute a single family. And with the people he gives, at the same time, the environment in which they live, which has moulded them. D'Aurevilly's sensibility to landscape impressions, especially in the broad, grandiose and mysterious aspects of nature and of nature saturated with human associations and sentiment, is extraordinarily great. . . .

His books are filled with the spirit of a peculiar past, and with impressions of things seen and felt with marvellous emotional responsiveness and freshness of poetic insight. The full measure of his originality may be perceived in his style, which is like that of no other French writer, though its framework is the rhetoric of romanticism. Thus it is elaborate, ornate and often tortuously involved, but it is at the same time nervous, sinuous and expressive in every phrase. There is in its slow and measured movement a note of *hauteur* and hatred of the vulgar, yet the intensity of the life that inhabits it is shown by the power it possesses of generating images. In these, the material for which is supplied not merely by wide reading, but by a penetrating observation of the minute and curious concrete facts of physical life, the sensibility of the man is completely incorporated. All that was truly Satanic in his soul insinuated itself into words which writhe like a nest of snakes and hiss like the coil of a whip wielded by one of his Chouan heroes. Wherever it falls, this lash, wrapping itself around the firm flesh of a fact, leaves a livid line or a trail of blood. It is this style that imparts most life to d'Aurevilly's books to-day, and will cause them to be read most eagerly in the future by all for whom the perfect crystallization of a rare and exotic personality always presents an irresistible appeal.

Edmund Gosse   (essay date 1913)

SOURCE: "Jules Barbey d'Aurevilly," in *French Profiles,* revised edition, William Heinemann, 1913, pp. 87-102.

[*Gosse was an eminent man of letters during the late nineteenth century. In the following excerpt, he comments on Barbey's stories and novels, concluding that Barbey was a "fervid, sumptuous, magnificently puerile" writer whose prospect of securing a prominent place in literature is "improbable."*]

Those who can endure an excursion into the backwaters of literature may contemplate, neither too seriously nor too lengthily, the career and writings of Barbey d'Aurevilly. Very obscure in his youth, he lived so long, and preserved his force so consistently, that in his old age he became, if not quite a celebrity, most certainly a notoriety. At the close of his life—he reached his eighty-first year—he was still to be seen walking the streets or haunting the churches of Paris, his long, sparse hair flying in the wind, his fierce eyes flashing about him, his hat poised on the side of his head, his famous lace frills turned back over the cuff of his coat, his attitude always erect, defiant, and formidable. Down to the winter of 1888 he preserved the dandy dress of 1840, and never appeared but as M. de Pontmartin has described him, in black satin trousers, which fitted his old legs like a glove, in a flapping, brigand wideawake, in a velvet waistcoat, which revealed diamond studs and a lace cravat, and in a wonderful shirt that covered the most artful pair of stays. In every action, in every glance, he seemed to be defying the natural decay of years, and to be forcing old age to forget him by dint of spirited and ceaseless self-assertion. He was himself the prototype of all the Brassards and Mesnilgrands of his stories, the dandy of dandies, the mummied and immortal beau.

His intellectual condition was not unlike his physical one. He was a survival—of the most persistent. The last, by far the last, of the Romantiques of 1835, Barbey d'Aurevilly lived on into an age wholly given over to other aims and ambitions, without changing his own ideals by an iota. He was to the great man who began the revival, to figures like Alfred de Vigny, as Shirley was to the early Elizabethans. He continued the old tradition, without resigning a single habit or prejudice, until his mind was not a whit less old-fashioned than his garments. Victor Hugo, who hated him, is said to have dedicated an unpublished verse to his portrait:

> Barbey d'Aurevilly, formidable imbécile,

But *imbécile* was not at all the right word. He was absurd; he was outrageous; he had, perhaps, by dint of resisting the decrepitude of his natural powers, become a little crazy. But imbecility is the very last word to use of this mutinous, dogged, implacable old pirate of letters. . . .

Barbey d'Aurevilly undertook to continue the work of Chateaubriand, and he gave his full attention to a development of the monarchical neo-catholicism which that great inaugurator had sketched out. He was impressed by the beauty of the Roman ceremonial, and he determined to express with poetic emotion the mystical majesty of the symbol. It must be admitted that, although his work never suggests any knowledge of or sympathy with the spiritual part of religion, he has a genuine appreciation of its externals. It would be difficult to point to a more delicate and full impression of the solemnity which attends the crepuscular light of a church at vespers than is given in the opening pages of **"A un Dîner d'Athées."** In *L'Ensorcelée* (1854), too, we find the author piously following a chanting procession round a church, and ejaculating, "Rien n'est beau comme cet instant solennel des cérémonies catholiques." Almost every one of his novels deals by preference with ecclesiastical subjects, or introduces some powerful figure of a priest. But it is very difficult to believe that his interest in it all is other than histrionic or phenomenal. He likes the business of a priest, he likes the furniture of a church, but there, in spite of his vehement protestations, his piety seems to a candid reader to have begun and ended.

> **D'Aurevilly's whim is to see Satanism everywhere, and to consider it a matter of mirth; he is like a naughty boy, giggling when a rude man breaks his mother's crockery. He loves to play with dangerous and forbidden notions.**
>
> —*Edmund Gosse*

For a humble and reverent child of the Catholic Church, it must be confessed that Barbey d'Aurevilly takes strange liberties. The mother would seem to have had little control over the caprices of her extremely unruly son. There is scarcely one of these ultra-catholic novels of his which it is conceivable that a pious family would like to see lying upon its parlour table. The Devil takes a prominent part in many of them, for d'Aurevilly's whim is to see Satanism everywhere, and to consider it matter of mirth; he is like a naughty boy, giggling when a rude man breaks his mother's crockery. He loves to play with dangerous and forbidden notions. In *Le Prêtre Marié* (which, to his lofty indignation, was forbidden to be sold in Catholic shops) the hero is a renegade and incestuous priest, who loves his own daughter, and makes a hypocritical confession of error in order that, by that act of perjury, he may save her life, as she is dying of the agony of knowing him to be an atheist. This man, the Abbé Sombreval, is bewitched, is possessed of the Devil, and so is Ryno de Marigny in *Une Vieille Maîtresse,* and Lasthénie de Ferjol in *Une Histoire sans Nom.* This is one of Barbey d'Aurevilly's favourite tricks, to paint an extraordinary, an abnormal condition of spirit, and to avoid the psychological difficulty by simply attributing it to sorcery. But he is all the time rather amused by the wickedness than shocked at it. In **"Le Bonheur dans le Crime"**—the moral of which is that people of a certain grandeur of temperament can be absolutely wicked with impunity—he frankly confesses his partiality for "la plaisanterie légèrement sacrilège," and all the philosophy of d'Aurevilly is revealed in that rash phrase. It is not a matter of a wounded conscience expressing itself with a brutal fervour, but the gusto of conscious wickedness. His mind is intimately akin with that of the Neapolitan lady, whose story he was perhaps the first to tell, who wished that it only were a sin to drink iced sherbet. Barbey d'Aurevilly is a devil who may or may not believe, but who always makes a point of trembling.

The most interesting feature of Barbey d'Aurevilly's temperament, as revealed in his imaginative work, is, however, his pre-occupation with his own physical life. In his youth, Byron and Alfieri were the objects of his deepest idolatry; he envied their disdainful splendour of passion; and he fashioned his dream in poverty and obscurity so as to make himself believe that he was of their race. He was a Disraeli—with whom, indeed, he has certain relations of style—but with none of Disraeli's social advantages, and with a more inconsequent and violent habit of imagination. Unable, from want of wealth and position, to carry his dreams into effect, they became exasperated and intensified, and at an age when the real dandy is settling down into a man of the world, Barbey d'Aurevilly was spreading the wings of his fancy into the infinite azure of imaginary experience. He had convinced himself that he was a Lovelace, a Lauzun, a Brummell, and the philosophy of dandyism filled his thoughts far more than if he had really been able to spend a stormy youth among marchionesses who carried, set in diamonds in a bracelet, the ends of the moustaches of viscounts. In the novels of his maturity and his old age, therefore, Barbey d'Aurevilly loved to introduce magnificent aged dandies, whose fatuity he dwelt upon with ecstasy, and in whom there is no question that he saw reflections of his imaginary self. No better type of this can be found than that Vicomte de Brassard, an elaborate, almost enamoured, portrait of whom fills the earlier pages of what is else a rather dull story, **"Le Rideau Cramoisi."** The very clever, very immoral tale called **"Le Plus Bel Amour de Don Juan"**—which relates how a superannuated but still incredibly vigorous old beau gives a supper to the beautiful women of quality whom he has known, and recounts to them the most piquant adventure of his life—is redolent of this intense delight in the prolongation of enjoyment by sheer refusal to admit the ravages of age. . . .

It is . . . in his novels that Barbey d'Aurevilly displays his talent in its most interesting form. His powers developed late; and perhaps the best constructed of all his tales is *Une Histoire sans Nom,* which dates from 1882, when he was quite an old man. In this, as in all the rest, a surprising narrative is well, although extremely leisurely, told, but without a trace of psychology. It was impossible for d'Aurevilly to close his stories effectively; in almost every case, the futility and extravagance of the last few pages destroys the effect of the rest. Like the Fat Boy, he wanted to make your flesh creep, to leave you cataleptic with horror at the end, but he had none of Poe's skill in producing an effect of terror. In **"Le Rideau Cramoisi"** (which is considered, I cannot tell why, one of his successes) the heroine dies at an embarrassing moment, without any disease or cause of death being suggested—she simply dies. But he is generally much more violent than this; at the close of **"A un Dîner d'Athées,"** which up to a certain point is an extremely fine piece of writing, the angry parents pelt one another with the mummied heart of their only child; in **"Le Dessous des Cartes,"** the key of all the intrigue is discovered at last in the skeleton of an infant buried in a box of mignonette. If it is not by a monstrous fact, it is by an audacious feat of anti-morality, that Barbey d'Aurevilly seeks to harrow and terrify our imaginations. In **"Le Bonheur dans le Crime,"** Hauteclaire Stassin, the woman-fencer, and the Count of Savigny, pursue their wild intrigue and murder the Countess slowly, and then marry each other, and live, with youth far prolonged (d'Aurevilly's special idea of divine blessing), without a pang of remorse, without a crumpled rose-leaf in their felicity, like two magnificent plants spreading in the violent moisture of a tropical forest.

On the whole, it is as a writer, pure and simple, that Barbey d'Aurevilly claims most attention. His style, which Paul de Saint-Victor (quite in his own spirit) described as a mixture of tiger's blood and honey, is full of extravagant beauty. He has a strange intensity, a sensual and fantastic force, in his torrent of intertwined sentences and preposterous exclamations. The volume called **Les Diaboliques**, which contains a group of his most characteristic stories, published in 1874, may be recommended to those who wish, in a single example, compendiously to test the quality of Barbey d'Aurevilly. He has a curious love of punning, not for purposes of humour, but to intensify his style: "Quel oubli et quelle oubliette" (**"Le Dessous des Cartes"**), "boudoir fleur de pêcher ou de péché" (**"Le Plus bel Amour"**), "renoncer à l'amour malpropre, mais jamais à l'amour propre" (**"A un Dîner d'Athées"**). He has audacious phrases which linger in the memory: "Le Profil, c'est l'écueil de la beauté" (**"Le Bonheur dans le Crime"**); "Les verres à champagne de France, un lotus qui faisait [les Anglais] oublier les sombres et religieuses habitudes de la patrie"; "Elle avait l'air de monter vers Dieu, las mains toutes pleines de bonnes oeuvres" (*Memoranda*).

That Barbey d'Aurevilly will take any prominent place in the history of literature is improbable. He was a curiosity, a droll, obstinate survival. We like to think of him in his incredible dress, strolling through the streets of Paris, with his clouded cane like a sceptre in one hand, and in the other that small mirror by which every few minutes he adjusted the poise of his cravat, or the studious tempest of his hair. He was a wonderful old fop or beau of the forties handed down to the eighties in perfect preservation. As a writer he was fervid, sumptuous, magnificently puerile; I have been told that he was a superb talker, that his conversation was like his books, a flood of paradoxical, flamboyant rhetoric. He made a gallant stand against old age, he defied it long with success, and when it conquered him at last, he retired to his hole like a rat, and died with stoic fortitude, alone, without a friend to close his eyelids. It was in a wretched lodging high up in a house in the Rue Rousselet, all his finery cast aside, and three melancholy cats the sole mourners by his body, that they found, on an April morning of 1889, the ruins of what had once been Barbey d'Aurevilly.

The New York Times Book Review (essay date 1925)

SOURCE: "Barbey D'Aurevilly," in *The New York Times Book Review,* March 29, 1925, pp. 16, 22.

[*In the following excerpt, the critic finds Barbey's stories in* The Diaboliques *derivative.*]

In spite of Lamartine's fine title for him—"the Duc de Guise of Literature"—the French church militant has shown no disposition to claim Barbey d'Aurevilly as an asset. An aura of disreputability has always clung around his truculent professions of faith, mingled as they were with "hysteria, sadism and diablerie." It has always been hard to resist a suspicion that, for a man of so many attitudes, they were only one pose the more. Something of the old suspicion must also attach to a personal legend so sedulously created in advance and adorned so lavishly with arabesques of eccentricity. His titles to nobility, to begin with, were fictitious ones. Sir Edmund Gosse, in his prefatory study to [a] translation of *Les Diaboliques*, repeats the unkind legend that the father of this swashbuckling mousquetaire was a butcher at Valognes. His famous dandyism was an equally synthetic affair, to which the pen of Aubrey Beardsley alone could do full justice. There was no sartorial tradition for the tight plum-colored trousers braided with gold, the crimson hatbrim and the ruffles which he flourished in the face of a drab world.

That Barbey, for all his eccentricities, was no fool, there is abundant testimony. The man who branded Zola with the searing phrase "he went to the dungheap 'pour y ajouter,' " who offered Huysmans his choice between the muzzle of a pistol or the foot of the cross, who commiserated Baudelaire on his skepticism ("No belief in God. What a pity! I think He would have liked you.") is not to be dismissed with any such snap judgment as Hugo's "formidable imbecile." Personally and socially he was "a great creature," brilliant and dangerous in controversy, a zealous seeker in the tragic byways of French history, and, as his letters to the "blond child" whose affection sweetened his lonely poverty are proof, singularly winning and affectionate to those whom he took into his heart. Best of all, he was unworldly and poor by deliberate choice. If he has any spiritual descendants in France today they are not easily discernible.

Of the six stories contained in *The Diaboliques,* . . . by far the most powerful is **"The Crimson Curtain."** The situation with which it opens is, it is safe to say, unprecedented. Two men, a ruined officer of the Grande Armée and a fellow-traveler, who narrates the tale, find themselves, at dead of night, and by one of those intolerable coincidences which life sometimes springs upon the unwary, the sole waking inhabitants of a little country town, in which the only sign of life is a solitary lamp burning behind a red curtain. While the accident to the diligence is being repaired, the soldier relates a dreadful incident of his youth of which this very room was the theatre. It is an appalling story that he tells—one of those tragic dilemmas which have three issues for escape—death, dishonor or flight. And, breathlessly as we follow the narrative, we are conscious that, at every moment, the lurid square of red is looking down upon road and coach like an accusing and bleeding eye. The mishap is repaired, the horses harnessed afresh and the coach rolls away. As it leaves the square a woman's silhouette appears against the curtain. In a stroke what would have remained a masterpiece of sheer horror is reduced to the level of the commonplace supernatural. Sir Edmund Gosse notes that "it was impossible for d'Aurevilly to close his stories effectively."

None of the other stories equals **"Le Rideau Cramoisi"** in power. In **"The Greatest Love"** a quite ordinary piece of "gauloiserie" is given a Sardanapalian setting of "dazzling bosoms, beating in majestic swell above liberally cut corsages . . . naked shoulders, arms of every type of beauty," the voluptuous hotchpotch of the attorney's clerk "dreaming his sultanas" in Flaubertian phrase. **"Happiness in Crime"** called for a skill in psychology which Barbey never possessed. What stays with us is the vision of a

mistress who is poisoning the wife who stands in her way, and fencing in between times with her lover in a deserted pavilion of his chateau. In its revolting sadism **"A Dinner of Atheists"** is a striking example of Barbey's hunt for the unforgivable sin, the vertiginous attraction that depths of wickedness hitherto unimagined always held for him.

Power of a sort Barbey undoubtedly possessed. It is rather remarkable that he could perceive no affinity in Poe. But it is a power that, to quote Abbé Bethléem, defeats its own end by being "violent, excessive and unjust." The last of the Romantics, he comes to his task with no sense that he is using discredited or discarded material. Volcanic Don Juans, apostate priests, voluptuous duchesses culled from mildewed books of beauty, blasphemers sold to the devil in advance, plumes waving over doomed foreheads, sorceries and mummied hearts—it is the very ragbag of Byronism into which he dips his ringed and aging hand. There is something of de Vigny in him, but it is mash from which the de Vigny wine has been drawn. His skill for portraiture has caused him to be compared with Saint-Simon. But it is portraiture of the elaborate and overloaded sort, quite in place where the facts of a life are history, but an incongruity in stories whose structure is slight and whose dénouements are arbitrary. Sir Edmund Gosse's word on his endings has already been quoted. Perhaps there is no surer sign that the equipment of a true novelist is lacking than this inability to deliver characters from the quandaries to which an unbridled imagination has committed them. . . .

The growing attention paid [d'Aurevilly's] work may be an act of tardy justice. On the other hand, it may be only one symptom more of a growing depravity of taste, a new penchant for the preposterous and overweening that many seem to think they perceive in modern French letters, and which is largely due to the absence of any critical authority approaching these men in weight and finality.

Brian G. Rogers   (essay date 1965)

SOURCE: "Two Short Stories by Barbey d'Aurevilly," in *The Modern Language Review,* Vol. LX, No. 1, 1965, pp. 516-19.

[*In the following excerpt, Rogers studies Barbey's uncollected early stories "Le cachet d'onyx" and "Léa" as initial attempts to use themes and a style that recur in his subsequent fiction.*]

More than his early novels, Barbey d'Aurevilly's first two short stories provide us with the key to the fictional world that is epitomized by the *Diaboliques.* Although they have never been available in the Bernouard edition of his collected fiction, a current edition of his most famous short stories in 1962 reprinted them for the first time since 1919 as 'Deux autres Diaboliques', and both clearly establish a direction leading from the first full-length novel, *Ce qui ne meurt pas,* to the works of Barbey's maturity. Both fully illustrate the intimate ties between the man and his work; they are the first examples of his personal response to literary sources and to scenes of physical violence; both embroider richly on Barbey's dominant preoccupation: the theme of passion; and both exist in a world which has no place for the conventional moral standards of the nine-teenth century, though they were written partially to carve out a niche in its society for the still struggling author. Both betray, too, like many of the novels, signs of hasty composition; in form each is reducible to a single impor-tant scene, and, in style, to a hyperbolic formula. In short, **'Le Cachet d'onyx'** and **'Léa'**, written in 1831 and 1832, set the atmosphere which pervades the whole of Barbey d'Aurevilly's strange and highly personal world of fiction.

'Le Cachet d'onyx' begins as an expression of Barbey's self-identification with certain literary sources. Written when he was twenty-three, the first story reflects his recent introduction, through his liaison with Louise de Costils, into the world of passion and jealousy. It rarely manages to free itself from the Shakespearean theme which triggers it off, and mostly provides a commentary on it; but to-wards the end, a flash of genuine inspiration provides the basis for a single scene of great visual intensity, whose slowly-gathering momentum and eventual explosion are characteristic of much of Barbey's fiction. The story is cast in three sections: a conventional evocation of a literary fig-ure, Othello, followed by a subsidiary illustration of his jealous passion in the story of Dorsay and Hortense de . . . , and finally the rapid transformation of both source and illustration in a scene which, though hastily prepared and rapidly drawn, nevertheless stands out in retrospect as the main substance of the story.

'Othello vous paraît donc bien horrible, douce Maria?', is Barbey's opening remark. He determines to substitute a feeling of pity in his imaginary listener to replace her hor-ror of 'ce diable noir'. A wordy exordium follows, plead-ing for compassion and understanding, but it is reasoned rather than felt, broken in style and rhythm, and draws heavily on other literary examples. As a critical apprecia-tion of Shakespeare's treatment of jealousy, **'Le Cachet d'onyx'** is hardly satisfactory, with its banal injunctions to weep over misfortune, although as a personal response to the theme of passion in general it is more promising, and contains passages of genuine feeling:

> Il n'est pas besoin d'être Africain, d'avoir du sang liquéfié sous une peau noire et plein ses larges veines; il n'est pas besoin d'avoir du lion et du tigre dans sa nature pour être jaloux et se venger. Il ne faut qu'assez d'intelligence pour comprendre le mot *trahison*.

Neither approach achieves sustained expression, however, and only by creating characters and a situation designed to illustrate his remarks does Barbey take the next step forward.

It is characteristic that such illustration is based on real events and people. The characters Barbey chooses are Dorsay, a celebrated dandy who modelled himself on Brummell, and a well-known society lady whose real name had to be suppressed. The situation is typical of many that Barbey must have known: the cooling-down of a love-affair, and its different results on the separating partners. Their meeting, adultery and parting are briefly told, the characters sketched in and a background suggest-ed. But Barbey is still too close to the centre of his subject to give depth to the story. He is too ready to turn to Shake-

speare, Byron, Sheridan, Mme de Stael, and Rousseau for inspiration, and not sufficiently skilled in manipulating his figures to make external parallels unnecessary. The style is exaggerated or platitudinous, and the central theme sev-eral times in danger of being lost under a mass of digres-sions.

Then, suddenly, in the midst of the discussion, the narra-tive slows almost to a halt, only to give way to a scene which emerges triumphantly from behind the literary as-sociations, personal reminiscences and platitudinous mor-alizing—a scene which is the epitome of Barbey d'Aurevilly's personal approach to fictional composition. Having established his characters' social and 'historical' reality by basing them on fact, he lets his imagination transform this pair of ordinary lovers into a couple whose rôle it is to re-enact symbolically and realistically the whole drama of passion. This scene, in which the charac-ters abandon themselves to the worst excesses of jealousy, marks Barbey d'Aurevilly's determination to replace the reality of others with his own. In the final page and a half of **'Le Cachet d'onyx'**, he infuses into his original, enthusi-astic contact with literature a violent and personal concep-tion of passion, and embodies both in a surge of creative activity whose therapeutic and cathartic effects on him are described at length in his correspondence. Style and mood undergo a transformation, a fresh, decisive tone emerges, and the action, stripped to its essentials, is described with a hardness characteristic of his best works:

> Il prit sur la table à écrire la cire argent et azur et un cachet. Jamais bourreau ne s'était servi d'instruments plus mignons. Le cachet, où était artistiquement gravée une mystérieuse devise d'amour, était un superbe onyx que lui, Dorsay, avait donné à Hortense dans un temps où la de-vise ne mentait pas. Il présenta à la flamme de la bougie la cire odorante, qui se fondit toute bouillonnante, et dont il fit tomber les gouttes là où l'amour avait épuisé tout ce qu'il avait de nec-tar et de parfums.

> La victime poussa un cri d'agonie et se souleva pour retomber. Dorsay, intrépide et la main as-surée imprima sur la cire bleue et pailletée qui s'enfonçait dans les chairs brulées le charmant cachet à la devise d'amour!

The story comes vividly, cruelly to life, an imaginative re-sponse is awakened, and Barbey's first question takes on a new and sinister meaning: 'Eh bien, Maria, est-ce qu'à présent vous n'aimez pas Othello?'

'Léa', the second story, benefits from a care in design ab-sent from **'Le Cachet d'onyx'**. It is the telling, in reverse, of the Sleeping Beauty legend, and could hardly be a more significant illustration of Barbey's favourite equation of passion and death. In the fairy-tale, the Prince, overcom-ing great obstacles, penetrates into the Princess's castle and wakens her with a kiss. But in Barbey's universe of violent, destructive emotions, the story undergoes a sinis-ter transformation. Reginald and Amédée, two life-long friends, return from Italy at the request of the latter's mother, who informs them that his sister Léa is gravely ill. She is suffering from an incurable illness—Barbey is not more specific—which forbids the slightest emotional disturbance. She has consequently been brought up in a state of unawareness, living, like the Princess, in an incomplete, twilight world. Reginald, who lives with them, falls in love with her, and his passion grows as he succumbs to the mysterious attraction of her situation. Despite warnings, he finally reveals his feelings to her; their proximity and her ignorance inflame him until, in the climax of the story, Réginald kisses her. The Prince in the legend brings back to life the eternally sleeping Princess with a kiss, but at the touch of Barbey's hero, Léa's state of emotional purity and insensibility vanishes, and she dies without a word.

The re-telling in symbolic terms of the Sleeping Beauty legend is probably the clearest blue-print we possess of certain of Barbey's ideas; in its simplest terms it is the illustration of the theory that man's nervous and physical constitutions are intimately related, and that the effects of violent passion rebound fatally from one to the other. It is one of the keys to Barbey's world of mysterious, hidden motives. When Mme de Saint-Severin, Léa's mother, explains her daughter's precarious situation, she introduces us to the first of a long line of heroines whose surrender to passion makes them hover uncertainly between life and death. Calixte, in *Un prêtre marié*, the daughter in '**Le rideau cramoisi**', are two of Léa's elder sisters, reflections of an archetypal image which expresses one of Barbey's most recurrent preoccupations. Reginald's reaction to this curious situation is, in reality, a detailed exposition of Barbey's own fascination with a theme he constantly reintroduces. It awakens in him a flood of emotion and suggests a rich source of inspiration.

The autobiographical element in the novels of Barbey d'Aurevilly is always strong, and already, in 'Léa', much of his subject matter revolves around a fictional projection of himself.

—*Brian G. Rogers*

Yet, despite the lethal aspects of passion, Barbey justifies it wholeheartedly. The aim of '**Le Cachet d'onyx**' is to plead its cause. It is not Desdemona whom we should pity, but Othello, the real victim of passion. All the more pitiful, too, in Barbey's eyes, because he is completely innocent. 'Il ne faut qu'assez d'intelligence pour comprendre le mot *trahison*', he explains; 'Eh bien, quand, avec ce peu d'intelligence on a de l'amour aussi, comme Othello, qui oserait appeler coupable celui-là qui est jaloux et qui se venge!' The criterion invoked springs from the laws of passion alone, answerable, for Barbey, to no other code. 'Weep for Othello!', he exclaims in his first story, 'la vengeance d'Othello ne fut point d'un monstre'. Barbey's ar-

guments for passion existing *per se* are not only the basis of the two early short stories but remain constant and unaltered throughout all his subsequent writings. For here, in embryonic form, the author's interest in the causes, development and consequences of passion gradually unfolds. If passion is the beginning, violent action is inevitably the end, and the construction of most of his later novels and stories hinges upon the train of action leading from one to the other. The author's task is to uncover the 'dessous de cartes', the mysterious connections linking and explaining motives and actions. Not for nothing did he call the first of the *Diaboliques* '**Le dessous de cartes d'une partie de whist**'. Barbey savours words like 'crime', 'atrocity', 'scandal', 'passion', not for their moral, or immoral implications, but because they set up in him a familiar imaginative response, that sends him searching from scene to scene for hidden emotional links. There is, therefore, no hint of disapproval in the list of possible discoveries he may make, but a stylistic enrichment, on the contrary, a positive, enthusiastic relish at the thought of the ravages of passion: 'Vous ne savez pas ce que c'est qu'une âme, ce que c'est qu'une passion, ce que c'est que cet ouragan, cette trombe qui tourbillonne dans les anfractuosités d'une poitrine d'homme, et qui finit par les briser'.

The autobiographical element in the novels of Barbey d'Aurevilly is always strong, and already, in '**Léa**', much of his subject matter revolves around a fictional projection of himself. One of the heroes is called Amédée, Barbey's own Christian name, and this character's close friendship with Reginald recalls the author's with Maurice de Guérin.

In style, too, both stories present obvious affinities with the later works. The quality of Barbey's style is normally directly proportionate to the degree and intensity of the imaginative response at the root of their inspiration. When aroused, Barbey writes naturally in a style which is rapid, unconsciously rhythmical, powerful but sometimes careless. His best passages reproduce an emotional excitement immediately recognizable, and that describing Reginald's sickening sense of frustration at Léa's incomprehension is characteristic of a manner he never lost. 'Chez moi', he explained much later, 'la phrase sort du fond, la phrase n'est pas une girouette piquée sur ma pensée et qui tourne selon le vent'. But should his imagination fail, or his inspiration run dry, as in the opening sections of '**Le Cachet d'onyx**', his style becomes correspondingly turgid, pedestrian and aimless. It is this lack of balance between a heavy, pompous, artificial means of expression—the result of a divorce between inspiration and style—and a brilliant, rapid manner—the surface reverberation of an underlying imaginative response to a theme—it is this lack of balance that is reflected most clearly in '**Le Cachet d'onyx**' and '**Léa**'. Both, however, suggest something of the crystalline purity of some of the later works. In the closing scene of each story, a hard precision occasionally makes an appearance, recalling some of the most hallucinating scenes in *L'Ensorcelée* and *Le Chevalier des Touches*. When Mme de Saint-Séverin discovers Reginald beside the body of her daughter, her words take on a bite which clearly points to the style of the *Diaboliques*:

Elle regarda alors ce qui lui restait, la pauvre mère, mais quand elle fixa sur Reginald ses yeux qui s'étaient remplis de larmes au mot consolant de son fils, ils s'affilèrent comme deux pointes de poignard. Elle se dressa de toute sa hauteur, et, d'une voix qu'il ne dut pas oublier quand il l'eut entendue, elle lui cria aux oreilles: 'Reginald tu es un parjure!'

Elle s'était aperçue qu'il avait les lèvres sanglantes.

'Le Cachet d'onyx' and 'Léa' are Barbey d'Aurevilly's first attempts to use themes and methods to which he constantly returned. The equating of passion with death and degradation, and the eulogy of passion *quand même* find echoes in *Ce qui ne meurt pas, Une vieille maîtresse, l' Amour impossible,* the Normandy novels, and most of the *Diaboliques.* Biographical and stylistic affinities are equally striking between 'Le Cachet d'onyx' and 'Léa', and the rest of his work. In only one major respect is there any difference between Barbey's outlook in his first attempts at fictional composition and that prevailing in the more mature novels—the question of background. Once he had substituted the mysterious Cotentin background for the vague settings of 'Le Cachet d'onyx' and 'Léa', he was able to pursue his researches into the effects of passion with much greater effect and vigour.

Anatole France's personal recollection of Barbey:

My grandmother, who knew [M. d'Aurévilly] slightly, and whom he greatly astonished, used to point him out to me in our walks, as a curiosity. This gentleman, wearing over his ear a hat with crimson velvet edges, with his figure encased in an overcoat with puffed skirts, tapping the gold stripe on his tight trousers with a whip as he walked, inspired no reflections in my mind, for I had no natural tendency to seek out the cause of things. I used to look at him, and no thought troubled the limpidity of my stare. I was simply pleased that there should be anyone so easy to recognize. M. d'Aurévilly was certainly that. I instinctively felt a sort of affection for him. I related him, in my sympathies, with a pensioner who walked with sticks on two wooden legs, and used to bid me good morning, his nose all snuffy; with an old mathematical professor, red-faced and one-armed, whose bearded visage smiled at my nurse like a satyr's, and with a very old man who had always worn bed-ticking since the tragic death of his son. For me these four individuals possessed, apart from others, the advantage of being perfectly distinct, and it gave me pleasure to distinguish them. Even to-day I cannot quite disentangle M. d'Aurévilly from the memory of the professor, the invalid and the madman, whom he has gone to rejoin in the land of shades. They formed, for me, all four, part of the monuments of Paris, like the stone horses on the Pont d'Iéna. There was this difference, that they moved, and the statues did not.

Anatole France, in his On Life & Letters, *translated by D.B. Stewart, 1922.*

Brian G. Rogers   **(essay date 1967)**

SOURCE: "The *Diaboliques,*" in *The Novels and Stories of Barbey d'Aurevilly,* Librairie Droz, 1967, pp. 107-35.

[*In the following excerpt, Rogers asserts that the stories in* The Diaboliques *are interrelated and also evince connections to Barbey's earlier novels such as* What Never Dies *and* Une vieille maîtresse.]

Les Diaboliques is a collection of six stories varying in length and intensity, but all so unusual in tone and content that they aroused comment and controversy as soon as they were published. Each is related both to its companions, and to [Barbey d'Aurevilly's] earlier novels; all six, 'Le Rideau cramoisi,' 'Le Plus Bel Amour de Don Juan,' 'Le Bonheur dans le crime,' 'Le Dessous de cartes d'une partie de whist,' 'A un Dîner d'athées' and 'La Vengeance d'une femme,' fit into a coherent framework conceived over a period of twenty years, and introduce a series of climaxes similar to those of each of the novels. [The critic adds in a footnote: 'The first story to be written was **"Le Dessous de cartes d'une partie de whist"** (1850), the second **"Le Rideau cramoisi"** (1866), and the third **"Le Plus Bel Amour de Don Juan"** (1867). It is not known what the order of composition of the three remaining stories was, although **"A un Dîner d'athées"** is known to have been completed in 1872'.] The *Diaboliques* crown Barbey's fictional writings, and by their strategy reveal them to be interdependent and interlocking.

Each story is one of a set of mounting climaxes, the conclusions, as it were, of six unwritten full-length novels; the formal structure of the novels, which virtually come to an end with the *Diaboliques,* is reproduced with growing intensity in each section of this 'final' work, and Barbey d'Aurevilly's sole collection of short stories represents his ultimate excursion into the field of climactic narrative based on a single device, in the manipulation of which he excelled, and to which he lent a new and characteristically personal meaning. If stories, on the one hand, and novels, on the other, are interrelated, the *Diaboliques* act as a 'sounding-board' in which all the themes in Barbey's writings reverberate. The actors in the later stories of the collection inherit the accumulated tension already built up in the earlier ones, just as characters in those provide the groundwork for what is subsequently developed in the *Diaboliques.* The strategy of the latter resides in the substitution for the series of accumulated scenes, so common in *Une Vieille Maîtresse, Le Chevalier des Touches* and *L'Ensorcelée,* of entire, self-contained stories; and carefully positioned at points along the mounting crescendo formed by the *Diaboliques* as a whole are all the vital themes of the novels—restated, re-shaped and reconsidered. They sum up the author's final pronouncements on all the obsessions, fancies, dreams, disillusions and psychological enquiries which make up the three first novels and the Normandy cycle, and provide a unique counterpoint to the interconnected crescendos. Thus the *Diaboliques* constitute a commentary on the novels of Barbey d'Aurevilly, highlighting and developing to their natural, albeit sometimes horrifying, conclusions his preoccupation with the motives and stresses at work behind emotional relationships of all kinds, in short, with their 'dessous de cartes', the title, significantly, of the first of the stories to be completed.

'Le Rideau cramoisi' begins like a Rossini crescendo, with barely the slightest hint of coming momentum, moving calmly, almost ponderously, from anecdote to anecdote. . . . Soon a visual scene replaces the first-person narrator's observations, which prepares for the introduction of the main events, unfolded by a second narrator, the 'seule personne' sharing the 'coupé' with the author. As he begins his story, the familiar upward curve of interest appears in the narrative. A forced halt in a deserted town in the early morning provides the starting point for one of Barbey's most successful tales; the mastery of tension and suspense already apparent in *Le Chevalier des Touches* is again brought into play to heighten a growing sense of anticipation, and emphasises the unusual nature of the events to be unfolded. Just as the sleeping town from which the Chouan leader was abducted undergoes a 'magical' transformation [in *Le Chevalier des Touches*], so, in **'Le Rideau cramoisi'**, the waiting coach, stranded between two rows of shuttered houses, with its motionless horses and two conversing passengers, freezes into an 'enchanted' tableau, which marks the beginning of an increase in tension. . . . Even the old woman of Coutances [in the novel], pouring water from an upstairs window so slowly that it appeared like a frozen cataract in the moonlight, has her counterpart when the silence is broken by a 'coup de balai, monotone et lassé, de quelqu'un (. . .) qui balayait la grande cour de cet hôtel muet.' Reminiscences of earlier novels, recast and adapted to suit different circumstances, begin to make their appearance. In *Le Chevalier des Touches,* for example, Mlle de Percy's story depends on a sustained conversational flow distributed among a number of secondary characters; in **'Le Rideau cramoisi'**, Brassard's tale is supported in a similar way by the repetition, not of conversational interjections, but of a single, isolated detail introduced at first casually, then deliberately accentuated until it becomes the focal point of the story, occupying the centre of interest while the coach, its passengers and the relay town all fade into the background. Its first appearance sparks off the story; glancing out of the coach, the passengers notice a solitary house in the closely shuttered street showing a dim but arresting light. . . . With every subsequent reappearance of the crimson curtain, shedding its red glow over the waiting coach, a further stage in the story is unfolded, and the Vicomte de Brassard relates how he met, loved and helped cause the death of a young girl who used to visit him in the room with the crimson curtain, the unexpected sight of which suddenly calls to mind this episode in his youth.

'Le Rideau cramoisi' does more than announce the series of the *Diaboliques* through its characteristic form; it provides an introduction, in the portrait of Mlle Alberte, Brassard's mistress, to the six heroines of the work, the common ancestor of all of whom is traceable through Vellini [of *Une Vieille Maîtresse*], Mme de Gesvres and Mme de Scudemor [of *Ce qui ne meurt pas*], to the archetypal figure of the victim in **'Le Cachet d'onyx'**. While their physical characteristics vary, they form, in a series of six portraits, a composite picture embodying Barbey's views on women, passion, their secret motives and physical degradation and death, the latter often being the symbols of a deeper, moral disintegration. The many-sided portrait first begins to take shape in the person of Alberte; like all of Barbey d'Aurevilly's heroines, she is, on the surface, a beautiful young woman: the first impression gained is one of a graceful young girl, whose charm and virtue are immediately, externally apparent. When Brassard, through whose eyes the reader relives the story, first meets her, he sees:

> (. . .) une grande personne qui, debout et sur la pointe des pieds, suspendait par les rubans son chapeau à une patère, comme une femme parfaitement chez elle et qui (venait) de rentrer. Cambrée à outrance, comme elle l'était, pour accrocher son chapeau à cette patère placée très haut, elle déployait la taille superbe d'une danseuse qui se renverse (. . .)

As the story unfolds, her external characteristics, like the setting of the story itself, melt into the background, and, as each does so, the tangible world of recognisable reality disappears. The town gives way to the claustrophobic room in which Brassard meets Alberte, while Alberte herself turns into a creature of unsuspected depth, —an enigma, which is part of all the subsequent narratives. She seems to bear no relation either to her parents, to whom she is utterly dissimilar, or to the town in which she suddenly appears; reserved and impassive, like Mme de Scudemor in *Ce qui ne meurt pas,* but, underneath her frigid exterior, surprisingly tempestuous, like Vellini in *Une Vieille Maîtresse,* Alberte, the 'danseuse', 'cette calme et insolente fille, à l'air si déplacé d'Infante', is a further incarnation of the author's ideal of the eternal seductress; she becomes, like the daughter in **'Le Plus Bel Amour de Don Juan'**, the Comtesse de Stasseville in **'Le Dessous de cartes d'une partie de whist'**, and La Rosalba in **'A un Dîner d'athées'**, a living example of 'le mensonge attribué aux femmes'—'la force de masque qu'elles peuvent mettre à leurs plus violentes ou leurs plus profondes émotions'. Over the dinner table, on her first evening home, she ignores her parents' guest, avoids speaking to him, scarcely acknowledges his existence. Then later, while trimming the lamp in the centre of the table, she takes hold of Brassard's hand below the cloth, unmistakably giving herself to him on the one hand, but maintaining complete self-possession on the other. Her apparently two-sided nature is summed up in the following scene:

> Honteux, pourtant—explains Brassard—d'être moins homme que cette fille hardie qui s'exposait à se perdre, et dont un incroyable sangfroid couvrait l'égarement, je mordis ma lèvre au sang dans un effort surhumain, pour arrêter le tremblement du désir, qui pouvait tout révéler à ces pauvres gens sans défiance, et c'est alors que mes yeux cherchèrent l'autre de ces deux mains que je n'avais jamais remarquées, et qui, dans ce périlleux moment, tournait froidement le bouton d'une lampe qu'on venait de mettre sur la table, car le jour commençait de tomber . . .

The essence of Alberte's character lies in a curious amalgam of impassivity and voluptuousness, and reappears in differing degrees in all the heroines of the *Diaboliques.*

The relationship developing between Brassard and Alberte is founded on the combination of abandon and frigidity in the latter and is governed, right up to its tragic conclusion, by the laws of this paradoxical compound. Even the climax of their love-affair, like that of their first contact, is constructed from these two elements, and the last scene in the crimson-curtained room is the exact, macabre reversal of that with which the relationship began. Instead of revealing unexpectedly, as she does there, a passionate amoral nature beneath a frigidly moral exterior, Alberte one night finds her rôle tragically reversed. A comparison between the first episode in which the duality of her nature is revealed, and the second in which this duality is cruelly underlined, emphasises Barbey's previously stated views on the equation of passion and death better than any argument. In the final scene, Barbey's world is turned upside down, all is reversed; the voluptuous part of the heroine reveals an unexpected, uncompromising rigidity as, with consummate art, the author transforms a sensuous description of love-making into the evocation of a stiffening corpse:

> Je la regardai comme elle était, liée à moi, sur le canapé bleu, épiant le moment où ses yeux, disparus sous les larges paupières, me remontreraient leurs beaux orbes de velours noir et de feu; où ses dents, qui se serraient et grinçaient à briser leur émail au moindre baiser appliqué brusquement sur son cou et traîné longuement sur ses épaules, laisseraient, en s'entr'ouvrant, passer son souffle. Mais ni les yeux ne revirent, ni les dents ne se desserrèrent . . . Le froid des pieds d'Alberte était monté jusque dans ses lèvres et sous les miennes . . . Quand je sentis cet horrible froid, je me dressai à mi-corps pour mieux la regarder; je m'arrachai en sursaut de ses bras, dont l'un tomba sur elle et l'autre pendit à terre, du canapé sur lequel elle était couchée. Effaré, mais lucide encore, je lui mis la main sur le cœur . . . Il n'y avait rien! rien au pouls, rien aux tempes, rien aux artères carotides, rien nulle part . . . que la mort qui était partout et déjà avec son épouvantable rigidité!

The combination of impassivity and passion, the psychological impetus of the love-affair, is given a sudden twist, and the climax of the first of the *Diaboliques* equates death and passion in a more dramatic way than ever before.

The rest of the story tails off neatly, if ambiguously, after this scene. Almost imperceptibly the opening setting returns—coach, deserted street and sleeping town—and the crimson curtain glows on dully in the night, a single, barely noticeable light as the coach moves on its way. 'Et après?' —demands the author of Brassard, when the latter relapses into silence. 'Eh bien, voilà, —répondit-il, —il n'y a pas d'après,' and the first story comes to an end without an explanation of the unexpected substitution of a corpse for a symbol of passion.

In comparison with 'Le Rideau cramoisi', the second tale—'Le Plus Bel Amour de Don Juan'—is a lightweight piece. Like 'Le Cachet d'onyx' it is woven around a literary theme, Don Juan's defiant invitation to the Commander to dine with him. In the world of Barbey d'Aurevilly, however, events are reversed, circumstances turned upside

down; in this version of the legend, Don Juan's former conquests, symbolised by twelve fashionable women from the 'faubourg Saint-Germain', themselves invite their seducer to supper in a sumptuous boudoir recalling his affairs with each of them. Juan, moreover, is approaching middle age and it is he, not the Commander, who heralds the approach of punishment in the next world. They sit down together in the luxurious apartment, forming a tableau which provides, in turn, a setting for the telling of Don Juan's most 'successful' love affair. That it is to be no ordinary revelation is clear from the portrait of the ageing seducer, and the festival planned by his former mistresses turns out to be one of Barbey's wryest, most paradoxical jokes at their, and the readers', expense. . . . After the cold stillness of the first story, the opening of the second comes as a complete change. Whereas the characters in the former are young and inexperienced, the thirteen figures around the dinner table in the latter display a sumptuous physical maturity—'une mer de chairs lumineuses et vivantes'. . . . Over them hangs an equally sumptuous atmosphere of sacrilege and profanation. On the threshold of Hell, these thirteen, twelve and one outsider, assemble for the last supper, against a background of flippant, though carefully meditated sacrilegious small-talk. From this setting emerges the second of the *Diaboliques*, a small anecdote well told, the negative, as it were, of its setting.

Not only is Juan's lengthy career dubbed by the assembly 'l'Adoration perpétuelle', but his most successful love affair is clothed in the terminology of the most important Catholic sacrament. Warming to his story, the hero explains that in the beginning of his memorable liaison he performed the functions of an anointed priest, transforming the rehearsal of 'true communion' into a magnificent ceremony. . . . But in the middle of this 'divine service', an unforeseen development marked this adventure out from all the others.

The story is barely twenty pages long, and the climax comes almost at once. His mistress's thirteen-year-old daughter had taken a dislike to him from the beginning and, like Mlle Alberte, avoided all contact with him. Like the latter, she reveals a deeply passionate nature behind her façade of indifference, which Barbey associates with the whole question of religiosity and sacrilege previously examined in *L'Ensorcelée* and *Un Prêtre marié*. Most of all 'Le Plus Bel Amour de Don Juan' is the companion piece to 'Le Rideau cramoisi'; two analogous situations are treated from different points of view, and a central problem is examined in two different moods, but the shock resulting from them both is the same. One day, the girl, religious to the point of superstition, turns her back on her faith, rejects her mother and her confessor, and admits to being pregnant with Juan's child. In 'Le Rideau cramoisi' passion is associated with death, in 'Le Plus Bel Amour' with sacrilege; but so brief is the anecdote, so sudden its conclusion and so neatly is its climax reversed that the tale, with its wryly humorous epilogue, punctures the 'bulle de savon'—albeit of brilliant colouring—that it really is. In a rare passage in which Barbey d'Aurevilly seems genuinely to be laughing at himself and his readers, he deflates his story of passion and sacrilege, and transports us back from his fantasy world of nightmares to the real world of his 'heroine', who is, after all, only thirteen years old. Taxed by her discomfited mother to reveal the father of her child, she confesses to the circumstances of its 'immaculate' conception in her mother's drawing room, after Juan had spent the evening there. In truly tragi-comic style, her distraught avowal of her crime is solemnly transcribed:

> —Mère, c'était un soir. Il était dans le grand fauteuil qui est au coin de la cheminée, en face de la causeuse. Il y resta longtemps, puis il se leva, et moi j'eus le malheur d'aller m'asseoir après lui dans ce fauteuil qu'il avait quitté. Oh! maman!. . . c'est comme si j'étais tombée dans du feu. Je voulais me lever, je ne pus pas . . . le cœur me manqua! et je sentis . . . tiens! là, maman. . . que ce que j'avais . . . c'était un enfant!

Juan's twelve conquests remain silent after the tale is finished, and the story makes a faintly disturbing, unpleasant impression, despite the obvious flippancy and purely verbal brilliance of its sacrilegious tone. Despite Barbey's disclaimer at the end, it is an impression which remains and is confirmed in the third, more extended tale, **'Le Bonheur dans le crime'**.

An account of murder and adultery in Normandy, **'Le Bonheur dans le crime'** is roughly two and a half times as long as **'Le Plus Bel Amour de Don Juan'**, and is designed to throw into relief Barbey's continued fascination with the unacknowledged motives behind apparently normal behaviour. The plot is simple: the daughter of a retired army sergeant falls in love with, and eventually marries a local aristocrat, after plotting with him to poison his wife. The plan succeeds and they live on in the murdered wife's château, the epitome of marital bliss and contentment. Its main interest lies in the portrait of Hauteclaire Stassin, the third—if we count the enigmatic daughter of **'Le Plus Bel Amour de Don Juan'**—in the series of characters who cover their emotions with a mask. With his usual irony Barbey presents the couple at the summit of their career, their past forgotten by all but a few observers, a pair of brilliant masks, no longer assumed but sincerely worn—a modern Philemon and Baucis.

Like many of his heroines, Hauteclaire Stassin is a woman of great beauty; the author and a friend who remembers the past history of the Count and Countess de Savigny, as Hauteclaire and her lover now are, are confronted with the couple by chance while walking in the Jardin des Plantes. 'Je ne la voyais alors que de profil', he remarks, struck by her beauty, 'mais le profil, c'est l'écueil de la beauté ou son attestation la plus éclatante. Jamais, je crois, je n'en avais vu de plus pur et de plus altier'. Like many of his heroines, too, she has something in her character which sets her apart from ordinary people; not only does her husband remind the author of a 'mignon du temps de Henri III', but she seems to belong to a race of almost God-like people, transformed like Philemon and Baucis into immortals by some secret knowledge or power. . . . The bulk of the story is taken up with the revelation of their secret. The author's friend, once the Savigny family's physician, begins to tell in retrospect the events leading to their marriage, the death of the first Countess de Savigny

and Hauteclaire's change in status. Concerned primarily with the existence of motives, and illogical, emotional trains of reasoning functioning behind the façade of social, religious and 'moral' masks, Barbey describes a couple sufficiently strong-willed to realise their ambitions, to turn their personalities inside out. Normally, the lesson of all Barbey's novels is that the effort to repress feeling and memory inevitably rebounds on the individual, either morally or physically, and ends in disaster. But for once we are presented with two people sufficiently lucid and ruthless to acknowledge their real feelings, and to transform themselves into what they have always desired to be. The complete opposites of Barbey himself, Hauteclaire and her husband achieve the happiness which Barbey never found, but it is significant that they are the only examples of complete self-realisation in his work. Creatures such as they are rare, Savigny and his wife are unique in Barbey d'Aurevilly's fictional world and the impression they cause at the beginning of the story is enough to incite the strongest curiosity. . . . There is no attempt to chronicle, as Balzac might, the social phenomenon represented by Hauteclaire Stassin's transformation from an enigmatic girl, working in her father's fencing-school in Normandy, to the Countess de Savigny. On the contrary, it is the unshakeable willpower and determination of his heroine which occupies Barbey's attention. The tale is in essence the peeling-off of the mask which separates the sergeant's daughter from the Countess.

As a young girl there is little to distinguish Hauteclaire from many of Barbey's other heroines. She is enigmatic, and the same undercurrents of passion are apparent in her character as those described in **'Le Rideau cramoisi'** and **'Le Plus Bel Amour de Don Juan'**. The mask that her profession as a fencing instructress obliges her to wear is symbolic of the mask behind which she hides her deepest feelings. . . . No less symbolic is her first encounter with Savigny, during the course of which the kernel of the master couple's future relationship is announced:

> (Savigny) la regarda donner sa leçon, et lui demanda de croiser le fer avec elle. Mais il ne fut point le Tancrède de la situation, le comte de Savigny! Mlle Hauteclaire Stassin plia à plusieurs reprises son épée en faucille sur le cœur du beau Serlon, et elle ne fut pas touchée une seule fois.

Hauteclaire begins to emerge from her chrysalis—in Barbey's terms, to shed her mask.

The second stage in the transformation, the substitution of Barbey's ideal, passionate universe for normal reality, occurs when Hauteclaire is taken secretly to the Savigny castle and disguised as the Countess's personal maid. Part of her mask is now laid aside, and the doctor, who has taken over the narration, visiting the Countess to treat a malingering illness, recognises in the efficient helper at her bedside the fencing instructor's daughter. He can elicit no sign of recognition from her, although it is clear that she knows her disguise has been penetrated. The discarding of the chrysalis is not performed without anguish to Hauteclaire; her new identity, not the woman behind the series of disguises, but that formed by the free expression of her

The lesson of all Barbey's novels is that the effort to repress feeling and memory inevitably rebounds on the individual, either morally or physically, and ends in disaster.

—Brian G. Rogers

innermost personality, liberated from all 'normal' inhibitions, struggles for a moment before completely shedding its mask. From this moment, the portrait of Hauteclaire comes to life; Barbey excels in painting the almost hidden feelings which obsess his characters in a slight trembling of a hand, or an imperceptibly stiffened walk. In the scene describing the doctor's growing awareness of Hauteclaire's functions and intentions at the dying Countess's bedside, an electric shock passes between Hauteclaire and himself; for a moment her will-power is fully exerted to repress the desire to acknowledge the latter's shocked signal of complicity, but the moment passes, and from then onwards Hauteclaire's transformation is assured. . . . The narrator's curiosity centres on the personality slowly emerging from behind its façade: '(. . .) les sentiments qu'il y avait au fond de cet adultère, quels étaient-ils? . . . Quelle était la situation respective de ces deux êtres l'un vis-à-vis de l'autre? . . . Cette inconnue de mon algèbre, ie tenais à la dégager'.

The Countess dies, and despite the scandal caused by her 'maid's' accidental substitution of poison for medicine, the latter's mask ceases to hide the future Countess de Savigny. She is gradually completely revealed as the incarnation of a passion so strong that it takes no account of public opinion, crime, adultery or murder. The tale moves bodily into the realm of pathological fantasy, as Hauteclaire emerges, a more consummate and sophisticated Vellini, not suffering from the boredom, caprices and regrets of her ancestor in *Une Vieille Maîtresse,* although their resemblance is striking. Where they differ is in Hauteclaire's complete absence of remorse or conscience, a peculiarity she shares with Sombreval in *Un Prêtre marié.* Her amoral, passionate nature asserts itself so completely as to wipe out the memory of the original Hauteclaire: one day, visiting the Count, the doctor meets her on the stairs; in his eyes she has become a different person, the person that lay dormant behind all her previous masks, and in the recesses of Barbey's own imagination:

> En descendant les marches de son escalier, ses jupes flottant en arrière sous les souffles d'un mouvement rapide, elle semblait descendre du ciel. Elle était sublime d'air heureux (. . .) Femme de chambre, elle l'était encore ce jour-là, de tenue, de mise, de tablier blanc mais l'air heureux de la plus triomphante et despotique maîtresse avait remplacé l'impassibilité de

l'esclave. Cet air-là ne l'a point quittée. Je viens de le revoir, et vous avez pu en juger. Il est plus frappant que la beauté même du visage sur lequel il resplendit.

The secret of her 'immortal' beauty is revealed, the perspectives of Barbey's dream-world widened in the rhapsody her crime occasions from the author, and this modern Philemon and Baucis, almost Nietzschean in their concentrated strength of mind, pass out of sight, their past history satisfactorily unravelled, the story brought dramatically to a close.

Hauteclaire's story throws light on all the heroines of the *Diaboliques,* on those of the novels which precede and prepare for them. Strategically placed as the third of the six tales, **'Le Bonheur dans le crime'** represents the fullest development of the Aurevillian hero and heroine and provides a yardstick by which the central characters of other stories and novels can be measured. Only Vellini and the Duchesse de Sierra-Leone come near to matching the consistency with which Hauteclaire sets about conducting her affairs; but in *Une Vieille Maîtresse* there is less emphasis on the emergence of suppressed or dormant passion, more on the romantic wildness of the actual character, while in **'La Vengeance d'une femme'** the central character dies.

In this story, Barbey finds a successful formula for shaping the narrative around the emergence of forgotten or hidden facts, regulating the mechanics of the plot in **'Le Bonheur dans le crime'** and in the story into which it leads, transmitting to the latter the tension and suspense contained in

Caricature of Barbey as a dandy.

15

its surprising climax. **'Le Dessous de cartes d'une partie de whist'** is the continuation of **'Le Bonheur dans le crime'**, although, as might be expected, the author reserves further shocks for his readers.

The fourth story illustrates better than any of the others Barbey d'Aurevilly's concern with emotions, and the dividing-line between what is revealed and what remains hidden in the make-up of human beings. It is a consummate exercise in the revelation of the Dante-like inner existence of his major characters.

There is practically no story or plot. Instead, a fixed situation is presented—just as the 'complete' figures of Hauteclaire and Savigny are presented at the beginning of **'Le Bonheur dans le crime'**; from this, the author draws conclusions, reveals significant facts from a retrospective viewpoint and ultimately returns to the original setting, in which no action has taken place, but which has been subjected to an 'X-ray' examination for hints of unsuspected, uncharted diseases at work below the surface. The major feat of **'Le Dessous de cartes d'une partie de whist'** is dramatically to command interest when no action in the normal sense of the word is observed or recorded.

The setting, a game of whist in a small provincial town, is neither striking nor original; its use is partially due to Barbey's wish to pun on the term 'dessous de cartes', which in the context has two separate, obvious meanings, partially to childhood memories. The intention of the story is to reveal the underside of the cards on the whist table, a process which involves turning each of the characters inside out, and exposing their secret lives. The result can be likened to a medieval diagram of the world, with its sphere reserved for humans, and below it, encircled by fire, a sphere reserved for the damned. But as might be expected in a work, the title of which indicates a predominant interest in Hell, the diagram shows no corresponding Heaven. As the narrative unfolds, the point of the diagram becomes clear: two of the figures seated around the whist table belong to the underworld of the damned. They have provided themselves, like Hauteclaire Stassin, with masks preventing their recognition, and the 'action' of **'Le Dessous de cartes'** is simply the slow chipping-away of the masks which conceal their true identity and nature. The first of these two characters is significantly named Marmor de Karkoël, the second—one of the author's most forceful creations—Mme de Stasseville.

The first sphere, that reserved for the living, is a stagnant town whose inhabitants, predominantly aristocratic, have evolved a complicated, stylised form of existence. They gather in elegant 'hôtels' to indulge their one acknowledged passion, whist. The strictness with which the rules of this game are observed almost turns them into symbolic characters, solemnly treading out the measures of a long-established ritual, frigid, silent and uncommunicative. Into this setting move two 'alien' figures about whom little is known, who observe the rules of the society which adopts them but who, unsuspected by their new partners, fashion themselves masks behind which they indulge in a simultaneous, but totally different game. They come separately, appear not to know each other; like the other characters in the game, they are admirable, beautiful and ele-

gant, only their pasts remain a mystery. Both sum up the relationship of all Barbey d'Aurevilly's main characters to their surroundings. In direct contrast to the Norman peasants who emanate naturally from their environment, personifications of the places in which they live, the main characters seem not to belong to the 'real' world of the living at all. 'Immortels' or 'Diaboliques', they all constitute an enigma, like Marmor, who is 'une espèce de muet'. . . . Mme de Stasseville is a 'nature stagnante'. . . . Yet both form part of the society and conform externally to its rules, spending their time playing boston or whist in a 'trou à nobles' with 'de vieilles filles qui avaient vu la Chouannerie, et de vieux chevaliers, héros inconnus, qui avaient délivré Destouches.'

A closer examination of this formal pattern reveals more of the external signs of undetected emotional disturbance which Barbey is expert in deciphering. Marmor, a brilliant exponent at cards, is received in virtually every household in the town except one, that of Mme de Stasseville. The relationship of these two figures immediately attracts the author's attention. . . . Although Marmor, as his name indicates, is naturally reserved and silent, Mme de Stasseville is not, and it is she who provides, under Barbey's magnifying glass, the first unmistakeable signs of an inner emotional disequilibrium. The closer the observer looks, the more apparent the indications become; Mme de Stasseville alters with the change of perspective until she is revealed as a person whose external, highly-strung nature conceals a fund of repressed emotions, the extent of which can scarcely be imagined. . . . Unsuspected links now become apparent, upsetting the formal pattern of the fossilized, 'symbolic' society with its clearly marked lines and definitions; the second sphere of action begins to be sensed—the world of the damned, to which, as Barbey probes behind her mask, it is evident that Mme de Stasseville, and probably Marmor, too, belongs. The author concludes that she is a 'Diabolique', belonging to the 'depths' of passion . . . , convinced, too, that her world, Barbey's world, is one of lies and double meanings, hypocrisy and masks, and that she and those like her, Mme de Scudemor, Vellini, Mme de Gesvres, Jeanne Le Hardouey and the others are happy only there, 'l'aimant jusqu'au mensonge, car le mensonge, c'est du mystère redoublé, des voiles épaissis, des ténèbres faites à tout prix'.

Spurred on by his discoveries, tension mounting characteristically the while, the narrator again alters his angle of vision. Immediately two seemingly inexplicable scenes are enacted before his eyes, the first concerning Marmor, the second Mme de Stasseville. The former is one day surprised by a visit from the narrator, who finds him inserting poison into a ring. The unexpectedness and the implications of the action are both emphasised, and a clue to Marmor's true identity discovered. . . . Soon afterwards Mme de Stasseville's daughter is discovered to be suffering from a lingering illness recalling that of the first Countess de Savigny in **'Le Bonheur dans le crime'**. In the second scene Mme de Stasseville betrays a side of her nature until then concealed from public view: in a moment of intense excitement, she takes a bunch of resedas from her dress and breathes in their scent 'avec une sensualité qu'on n'eût, certes, pas attendue d'une femme comme elle, si peu faite pour les rêveuses voluptés.' Her subsequent destruction of the flowers, performed with 'une expression idolâtre et sauvage, les yeux rouverts sur Karkoël (.. .)', reveals all the narrator needs to know about the couple, though he was never able to verify his suspicions at the time. The narrative then transports the reader to a period much later when, returning to the little town many years later, the author discovers that after his departure the whole story became a public talking point, when Marmor de Karkoël disappeared, Mme de Stasseville's daughter died and the latter herself committed suicide. When all the pieces of the jigsaw are assembled, the 'chaos' of the two characters' passionate world is fully revealed. . . . The climax of the story relates how, when the Stasseville house was shut up, the 'jardinière' from the salon, containing the same resedas which the narrator had observed before, was removed and the flowers planted in the garden. 'Et l'on trouva', continues the narrative, 'dans la caisse, devinez quoi! . . . le cadavre d'un enfant qui avait vécu . . .' The author's intuition is proved correct and the uncomfortably close proximity of the 'abyss' which Marmor and Mme de Stasseville reveal, to the apparently fixed and stable world of the little Normandy town is highlighted. This confrontation having been the object of the tale, Barbey now swiftly brings it to a close, with a remark from one of the narrator's audience:

> —Vous m'avez gâté des fleurs que j'aimais, —dit la baronne de Mascranny, en se retournant de trois quarts vers le romancier (.. .) Voilà qui est fini! —ajouta-t-elle; —je ne porterai plus de résédas.

More stylised, perhaps more unreal than any of the previous stories of the *Diaboliques*, **'Le Dessous de cartes d'une partie de whist'** is a résumé of the recurrent pattern of Barbey d'Aurevilly's novels and stories. Rarely is the basis of Barbey's world so clearly or so successfully displayed. As for being unreal, the original publication of the story, preceding that of the *Diaboliques* as a whole, awakened such precise memories in Barbey's cousin Edelestand du Méril in Valognes that the author was forced to alter certain circumstances, which referred to identities too easily recognisable, and Barbey remarks uncomfortably at the beginning that 'les plus beaux romans de la vie (. . . .) sont des réalités qu'on a touchées du coude, ou même du pied, en passant'.

'A un Dîner d'athées' is an extended version of Barbey d'Aurevilly's first short story, **'Le Cachet d'onyx'**. The main elements in this account of excessive jealousy and vengeance remain unchanged, but from their juxtaposition with a sombre religious atmosphere which continues from beginning to end, comes one of Barbey's most striking stories. An opening description and a prologue are added to the original, the latter recounting in detail one of a series of weekly dinners given by an old man in Normandy every Friday; his passion was to collect the most hardened blasphemers, anti-clerics, renegade priests and soldiers of his acquaintance, and dine them regularly whenever his son stayed with him. During one of these 'dîners d'athées,' Mesnilgrand 'fils' relates the story of La Pudica, the fifth in Barbey's series of heroines, another descendant of Vellini, the companion, this time, of a soldier

campaigning in Spain during the Napoleonic wars. In a fit of jealous rage, her protector, Major Ydow, brutally murders her in the same way as Dorsay mutilates his mistress Hortense in **'Le Cachet d'onyx'**. Although more richly embroidered, its series of mounting climaxes more skilfully prepared than before, it is this single theme, with which Barbey began his career as a novelist fifty years before, which contains the crux of the narrative. The element of horror in the first story is intensified in the later version, however, by the atmosphere of blasphemy and sacrilege in which it is set. Before the prologue, a long description of a provincial church on the eve of a Feast day opens the story, which finally closes on the narrator's explanation for his visit there, during which he offered one of the priests in a confessional a macabre relic of La Pudica's immoral career. The mixture of passion and religious feeling reappears in the subsequent account of her death, links the opening scene with the climax, and adds a force to the theme of passion and physical degradation of which there is no hint in **'Le Cachet d'onyx'**.

The opening passage, describing the interior of the gloomy church combines most of the features of Barbey's florid style with his habit of associating the sensual overtones of devotion with passion.

Evoking the obscurity of the long romanesque nave, the author likens the communion of God and man to 'le tête-à-tête en cachette' with a woman of easy virtue. . . . The church is alive with a particular atmosphere, which, whatever its explanation, Barbey catches and reproduces. He senses the shadowy presence of scores of kneeling people . . . , is vividly aware of the slight, almost organic sounds emanating from the silent crowd . . . , and sums up his impression in a striking metaphor:

> Toutes ces bouches qui priaient à voix basse, dans ce grand vaisseau silencieux et sonore, faisaient ce susurrement singulier qui est comme le bruit d'une fourmilière d'âmes, visibles seulement à l'oeil de Dieu.

In the middle of this carefully described atmosphere, the narrator is introduced, the son of Mesnilgrand the atheist. A sensual delight in the mixing of the religious and the sacrilegious, recalling *L'Ensorcelée,* is evident as his progress is followed through the church, surrounded, as it were, by a profane 'halo' marking him out from the kneeling congregation, 'qui (. . .) n'auraient pu le *distinguer* autrement que par je ne dirai pas l'impiété, mais la *non piété* de son attitude.' Mesnilgrand 'fils' gives the priest an object indistinguishable in the darkness and turns to leave when he meets a friend who has followed him, amazed at seeing him enter a church. For a moment the nave rings with their oaths, a brief conversation ensues and the hushed silence is violently disturbed:

> —Que tous les tonnerres de l'enfer te brûlent, Mesnil! —continua *l'autre,* qui paraissait comme enragé. —Vas-tu donc te faire capucin? (. . .) Vas-tu donc manger de la messe? (. . .) Toi, Mesnilgrand, le capitaine de Chamboran, comme un calotin, dans une église!

Then the two friends leave, the passage comes to an end and the prologue itself, the Friday dinner at the Mesnilgrand house, follows on naturally, the second great set-piece leading to the climax of La Pudica's death.

Mesnilgrand's dinners are regarded by the townspeople with superstitious horror, and throughout it the same mixture of sacred and profane recurs. It is as though '(. . .) ils profanaient des hosties et egorgeaient des enfants', and inspired '(. . .) une horreur presque égale à l'horreur que les chrétiens, au Moyen Age, ressentaient pour (les) repas des Juifs'. Everything is done to give the greatest offence to the Church. . . . A lengthy description of the dinner follows, the style in which it is evoked growing progressively excited as the feast continues, culminating in a series of anecdotes told by the guests, each of which is designed to prepare in atmosphere and content the final story about La Pudica. Both this tableau and the one which precedes it contain preparatory elements for the final narrative; the predominantly religious atmosphere of the church, rudely shattered by the oaths of Mesnilgrand and his friend, the overwhelmingly sensual and sacrilegious atmosphere of the feast, with its overtones of religious detail, are the twin supports for the original story of **'Le Cachet d'onyx'** and provide a background for Barbey's most audacious exercise in stylistic ambiguity, the like of which, save for *L'Ensorcelée*, is found nowhere in his work. The orgy gathers momentum and the guests are transformed, on the one hand by wine, on the other hand by the force of Barbey's 'apocalyptic' style, into symbols of impiety. . . . Their conversation turns into a frenzied verbal bacchanale, stories, repartees and anecdotes following thick and fast, each stronger and more daring than the last. Analogies, metaphors, comparisons are heaped indiscriminately on one another, sentences grow longer, and parentheses accumulate: rarely does Barbey's style reach the level it attains in the description of the weekly, 'verbal' orgy. . . . The guests' individual stories grow progressively longer, until the Abbé Reniant, a renegade priest famous for once having fed a box of communion wafers to a herd of pigs recounts a last anecdote, which leads into Mesnilgrand's own, longer narrative. . . . [The] conversations immediately preceding the story of La Pudica are designed to flavour it with their own atmosphere; Joséphine Tesson, a local heroine, recounts the Abbé, concealed the same box of wafers in her bosom, to protect them from the Bleus. The anecdote is told with bombast, and received with enthusiasm, and with its implications in mind, Mesnilgrand tells his own story, with which he was personally involved and to which he adds a further layer of horror.

He recounts how La Pudica was known to share her favours, despite Ydow's jealousy, with whoever in the regiment took her fancy. One day matters came to a head between them in a quarrel at which by accident Mesnilgrand, though hidden from view, was present. At the end of the altercation, recounted with the familiar device of increasing tension, silence ensues, and Ydow kills La Pudica. During the quarrel, however, direct reference is made to the opening description of the church, and Mesnilgrand's presence in the confessional. The quarrel centres on the embalmed heart of La Pudica's child whom Ydow loved and considered his son; when she reveals that he is mistaken, a pitch of intensity is reached in the narrative which culminates in her death. Mesnilgrand reveals to his

audience that he had entered the church to deliver the same heart into the custody of a priest, and in this curious way sets up a train of thought linking the religious atmosphere from the beginning of the tale with the crime on which it ends. Already prepared by the story of Joséphine Tesson, in which religion and sensuality are combined, the association is fully exploited. It is hard to see why the details of this scene are described at such length, unless the complicated structure of the story, resolving into three main scenes—the church, the dinner party, the quarrel—is fully understood. Each separate 'tableau' contains a series of cross-references to the other two, and culminates in a series of allusions recalling those of *Un Prêtre marié*. The killing of La Pudica is presented almost as a demoniac black mass; the half-sensuous half-religious atmosphere of the opening is picked up and reinforced: the heart in its cristal urn recalls the sacrament at the end of the long, gloomy church and its desecration in the earlier anecdote by Abbé Reniant. La Pudica and Ydow themselves are altar and priest—a transformation already hinted at in the original description of Mesnilgrand 'père', 'au milieu de sa table, comme l'Eveque mitré de la messe du Sabbat'. . . . When the 'deux maigres cierges' of the opening are recalled in the final scene, the pattern of the story is revealed: the presentation of the religious atmosphere is juxtaposed with a sacrilegious scene and finally, transformed into a superstitious black mass. The transformation itself is performed with the care for detail, and the feeling for tension and climax which characterise all the stories in the *Diaboliques* and, the climax reached, Barbey d'Aurevilly provides a final, ironical touch which dramatically, if flippantly, brings the narrative to a close. Returning for a moment to the feast, at which, it will be remembered, Mesnilgrand has been telling the Pudica story, the author captures the reaction of his audience in a single, libertine repartee, which sums up the whole affair—

> Eh! mais c'est l'aventure d'Abélard, transposée
> à Héloise! —fit l'abbé Reniant. —Un beau cas de
> chirurgie, —dit le docteur Bleny, —et rare!

'La Vengeance d'une femme' closes the cycle of the *Diaboliques* in its original edition, and confirms its thematic relationship with the Normandy cycle which precedes it. Both are conceived around recurrent obsessions, introduce similar characters and motives, and are interconnected in style and subject. Both are constructed on a principle of mounting climax, the only difference between them being that the *Diaboliques*, with their 'final' treatment of all the previous themes, provide a climax not only to the Normandy novels but to all the fictional writings of Barbey d'Aurevilly.

The narrative is a graduated introduction to the apartment of a Paris prostitute, and culminates in a revelation of her past as she recounts it to the author. Designed around a single scene, **'La Vengeance d'une femme'** is reminiscent of **'Le Dessous de cartes d'une partie de whist'**, in that each is an almost schematic presentation of the author's fascination with appearance and reality. A Parisian dandy's visit to the prostitute serves to juxtapose a social façade with the background it conceals, the contrast achieved between a squalid street behind the Boulevard, and the unexpected history and identity of the prostitute who lives in it being Barbey's most dramatic revelation of 'dessous de cartes'. In parts, the story contains elements of a modern parable, while throughout, especially in the climax, it is permeated with an obsession with physical disease and death linked with the ravages of passion.

Like a 'fantastic' projection of the scene in *Une Vieille Maîtresse* where Vellini leads Marigny down to the 'tombeau du Diable', the prostitute leads her customer away from the fashionable part of the town where they had met, and descends with him into a squalid, overhung network of streets, rarely penetrated by daylight, and symbolic of the 'downward' path both are taking. Their destination, the rue Basse-du-Rempart, deserves its name 'car elle était moins élevée que le sol du boulevard, et formait une excavation toujours mal éclairée et noire'. Its immoral nature is never in doubt:

> (. . .) cette espèce de ravin sombre, où l'on se risquait à peine le jour, était fort mal hantée quand venait la nuit. Le Diable est le Prince des ténèbres. Il avait là une de ses principautés.

There follows a description of the house in which the woman practises her profession: the ugliness of the building, like the character of its surroundings, sums up the life she leads, and the grotesque quality lent by Barbey to this, an extended 'mask', is heightened to set off the revelations of the climax, when façade and mask are torn down, and the secrets they conceal disclosed. A visual parallel to the passage which results might be found in the nightmarish drawings of Victor Hugo. Like one of his fantastic, leaning edifices, the house is described in a sequence which contains the best of Barbey's richly evocative style, and in which overtones of Balzac and Zola are combined with a florid imaginative power characteristic of neither. . . . As the author's eye travels up its crumbling walls, the building undergoes a complete transformation, reminiscent of those . . . in *Le Chevalier des Touches* and '**Le Rideau cramoisi**'. Solidly anchored at its base in the reality of a Paris street, the house becomes a thing of fantasy, a passive witness to crimes unnamed, losing touch with concrete reality and developing a sense and personality of its own:

> Longue perche de maison aveugle, car aucune de ses fenêtres (et les fenêtres sont les yeux des maisons) n'était éclairée, et qui avait l'air de vous raccrocher en tâtonnant dans la nuit!

At the same time as her house undergoes a transformation, so the prostitute turns into somebody else. She reveals after persistent questioning that she is no less than the Duchesse d'Arcos de Sierra-Leone, the wife of a Spanish grandee, one of the most influential men in Spain. After discovering the existence of her young lover, the Duke had had him murdered in a brutal fashion before her eyes, and to avenge him she turned to a life of prostitution in the hope that, by sullying the name of a husband who did not love her, but who was proud of his family name and position, she might die in a street-walker's hospital of venereal disease, the physical degradation of which would rebound on the character of the Duke, and at the same time serve as a perpetual reminder of her continuing attachment to the memory of her lover. The narrative in

which these facts are set out is long and vivid, but the real climax comes when the dandy learns much later of her death and witnesses the accomplishing of her vengeance. The story pivots on two portraits of the heroine, the first displaying the insolent beauty of a young woman, the second the ugliness of her decomposing corpse. The contrast derived from the two tableaux illustrates Barbey's fascination with the physical aspects of death. Young and beautiful at first, . . . she is nevertheless transformed, after her death, into a creature recalling nothing so much as the gloomy decrepit house of the opening pages. It is as though all the characteristics of the crumbling building were transferred to her person. . . .

Nine years after *Les Diaboliques* was published in 1874, Barbey produced *Une Histoire sans nom*, half-novel, half *Diabolique*-like short story, a curious, not wholly successful attempt to combine elements of his earlier works in a new framework. It is little more than the rewriting of *L'Ensorcelée* and *Un Prêtre marié*, condensed and synthesised in a short piece hardly longer than the longest of his short stories. . . .

It is a pity that *Une Histoire Sans nom*, although a work of old age, should set so disappointing a seal on the powerful works that it follows and distorts. Neither its exaggerated plot nor its decadent style, however, can substantially lessen the effect of the four novels which precede it: *Une Vieille Maîtresse*, *L'Ensorcelée*, *Le Chevalier des Touches* and *Un Prêtre marié*, nor that of the well-engineered stories of the *Diaboliques*: '**Le Rideau cramoisi**', '**Le Plus Bel Amour de Don Juan**', '**Le Bonheur dans le crime**', '**Le Dessous de cartes d'une partie de whist**', '**A un Dîner d'athées**' and '**La Vengeance d'une femme**'. It is on these, with parts of *Ce qui ne meurt pas* and *l'Amour impossible* that Barbey d'Aurevilly's reputation as a novelist will stand.

On the autobiographical element of Barbey's fiction:

[Despite] his recourse to the device of the intermediary or second narrator in his story telling, one readily suspects Barbey of portraying personal solitude not from the point of view of the detached observer and connoisseur he would like us to believe he is, but from that of a man all too intimately aware of its perspectives of moral desolation. Long before Georges Bernanos was to paint in his novels the awesome spectacle of the degradation resulting from *ennui*, Barbey d'Aurevilly had created, if not for our edification, at least for our enthrallment, a host of sensational but essentially lonely sinners whose natures and fates offer striking parallels with those of the inveterate dandy that Barbey was.

Will L. McLendon, in "Isolation and Ostracism in the Works of Barbey d'Aurevilly," Forum, Vol. 8, No. 1, Fall-Winter, 1970.

Dzintars Freimanis   (essay date 1970)

SOURCE: "The Motif of the '*Dessous*' in *Les Diaboliques*," in *Romance Notes,* Vol. XI, No. 3, Spring, 1970, pp. 553-56.

[*In the following essay, Freimanis examines the relationship between surface appearances and underlying dark passions in* The Diaboliques.]

Among the six short stories contained in Barbey d'Aurevilly's **Les Diaboliques** there is one that bears the significant title **"Les Dessous de cartes d'une partie de whist."** Only its final pages reveal what has been developing under the surface of events: devastating passion and crime. Such a juxtaposition of the apparent and the hidden is essential to all the **Diaboliques.** The manifestations of the *dessous* offer enough variety to justify their examination.

A certain progression seems evident in the order of the stories. The first one, **"Le Rideau cramoisi,"** announces the theme of the simultaneous existence of overt coldness and hidden passion in an individual. The *vicomte* de Brassard recalls his experiences with Albertine, the daughter of the bourgeois couple with whom he was staying as a young army officer. She was beautiful and seemed to ignore Brassard in a way that was more than disdainful. But then, one evening at supper, in the presence of her unsuspecting parents, she took hold of his hand below the table. The surprise and the sensual pleasure he experienced were beyond comparison. What strikes the reader is the strangeness of the girl's behavior. It seems almost as if, in the character of Albertine, Barbey d'Aurevilly had wanted to create an epitome of the duality he was to show throughout the **Diaboliques**: the constant presence of the *dessus* and the *dessous.* This contrast appears, first, in its literal sense: what goes on above and below the table. A further evidence of Albertine's ambiguous personality is the cold silence she maintains during their intimate moments. For six months they meet in Brassard's room every other night, braving the danger of being discovered by her parents, but never does he succeed in fully reaching the fire below the surface: "Elle me produisait l'effet d'un épais et dur couvercle de marbre qui brûlait, chauffé par en dessous." She has always remained an enigma for him.

The second story, **"Le plus bel amour de Don Juan,"** also deals with a hidden passion, this time in the form of unconscious temptation. Although the narrative offers mere glimpses at the emotions of a thirteen-year-old girl, the reader may feel invited to make his own assumptions about the unknown depths of her soul: in spite of her dislike for her mother's lover, she unwittingly falls in love with him. In her naïveté she believes that her feelings have made her pregnant, and confesses this condition to a priest. Nowhere else in **Les Diaboliques** does one find such a contrast between actual innocence and imagined sin.

A most powerful presentation of clandestine love behind respectable appearances forms the basis for the third story, **"Le Bonheur dans le crime."** To introduce the heroine, the countess Serlon de Savigny, the author first describes a black panther in the *Jardin des Plantes.* It is an example of his technique to proceed by degrees, doubling and sometimes further multiplying his analogies, until the reader is sufficiently prepared for the central character or event. Thus, the woman is preceded by the panther, which in turn is preceded by an evocation of its country of origin—Java, where flowers are supposed to be more fragrant, fruit tastier, animals more beautiful and stronger than in any other land of the world, "une contrée tout à la fois enchantante et empoisonnante." We may interpret this combination of enchantment and poison as a variant of Barbey d'Aurevilly's leitmotif—the deceitful appearance versus the hidden "dessous." The panther possesses a primordial majesty, which makes her superior to all humans except one: the countess de Savigny. "La femme, inconnue, était comme une panthère humaine, dressée devant la panthère animale qu'elle éclipsait." Any notion of sin is ruled out for such a pantherlike woman. Therefore, the *dessous* can grow to its fullest proportions, unhampered by conscience. We have here the exact opposite of **"Le plus bel amour de Don Juan,"** where a sin committed merely in imagination leads to repentance and confession.

The protagonists of **"Le Dessous de cartes d'une partie de whist"** add another dimension to the motif under consideration. The countess du Tremblay de Stasseville and the young Scotsman Marmor de Karkoël, unlike any other characters in **Les Diaboliques,** have no urgent reason to hide their feelings. She is a widow; he is single; except for their different ages, people would find little to blame if their mutual affection were known. Yet they prefer to place it under the mask of indifference and scorn, even long before their final crime. Theirs is a case where hiding ceases to be a mere necessity and becomes an essential part of being a *diabolique.* According to the narrator, "Il y a une effroyable, mais enivrante félicité dans l'idée qu'on ment et qu'on trompe; dans la pensée qu'on *se* sait seul *soi-même,* et qu'on joue à la société une comédie dont elle est la dupe, et dont on se rembourse les frais de mise en scène par toutes les voluptés de mépris."

The main enjoyment to be derived from such hypocrisy, then, is the secret possession of the truth. Yet truth may also become a burden, as in the case of the hardened disbeliever Mesnilgrand in **"A un dîner d'athées."** On one occasion, he is seen entering a church. To explain this strange act, he tells his friends about the affair he had during the war with the beautiful Rosalba, who was the mistress of a major Ydow. In an outburst of rage against her "legitimate" lover, Rosalba told Ydow that the child whom she had born and who had soon died was not his. Deeply hurt, the major broke the urn where he had been keeping the child's embalmed heart and threw it at Rosalba. Eventually, Mesnilgrand took the heart—perhaps that of his own child—and kept it until, years later, he entrusted it to a priest. That is why he entered the church.

The underground secret has now taken on a double form. In the first place, one finds a new aspect of the *diabolique*: under the guise of love and docility, Rosalba had been harboring a deep hatred. In the second place, Mesnilgrand's action shows an inverse development of the motif of the *dessous.* Instead of the usual diabolism of Barbey d'Aurevilly's female characters, which involves some dark passion, Mesnilgrand—the man—has been hiding a possibly incipient faith and repentance.

Hate at its extreme constitutes the *dessous* of the final story, **"La Vengeance d'une femme."** To inflict the most atrocious vengeance on her husband, a Spanish nobleman who failed to see the rare purity of her illicit love and who literally threw her lover's heart to the dogs, the duchess d'Arcos de Sierra-Leone will sully and utterly dishonor his name by becoming a prostitute. She accomplishes her plan and dies in willful self-debasement. We may agree with Barbey d'Aurevilly that the intensity of her feelings is sublime. Here, the author has produced perhaps the most powerful example of his concept of the *diabolique*.

It has been seen that the *dessous* is a constant element in Barbey d'Aurevilly's narrative technique. We are confronted with two parallel courses of action, the one easily observable, the other hidden. The author examines the *dessus* until the tension of the *dessous* breaks the surface. While other authors, too, may have written about concealed truths or hidden passions, few of them have exploited the same motif with the power and depth of a Barbey d'Aurevilly.

On suspense in Barbey's stories:

[Barbey is] expert at creating suspense, leaving the reader in doubt concerning what has really happened, for he likes ending on a query, to allow him to go on imagining the upshot. How does 'The Crimson Curtain' in fact really end? What occurred after the commanding officer had whisked the young lieutenant away from the scene of the tragedy, and what happened when the parents found their daughter dead, and where did they find her? In 'The Story Behind a Game of Whist', whose was the dead infant eventually discovered buried in one of the jardinières? Who loved whom and who killed whom? Did mother and daughter both love Marmor, or only one, and which? Did he poison both, or only the mother to punish her for having killed her daughter? Or did the daughter commit suicide in despair? What interested Barbey d'Aurevilly was the building up of the horror and suspense, creating the atmosphere, and then he left his readers to wind up the story according to their own whim.

Enid Starkie, in the introduction to The She-Devils, *by Jules Barbey d'Aurevilly, translated by Jean Kimber, 1964.*

Eileen Boyd Sivert   (essay date 1979)

SOURCE: "Narration and Exhibitionism in 'Le rideau cramoisi,'" in *The Romanic Review*, Vol. LXX, No. 2, (March, 1979), pp. 146-58.

[*In the following excerpt, Sivert examines aspects of Barbey's narrative technique in "The Crimson Curtain," citing an interplay between voyeurism and exhibitionism in his storytelling.*]

Voyeurism, seen recently [by Marcelle Marini in "Ricochets de lecture: La fantasmique des *Diaboliques*," *Littérature* 10 (1973)] as an organizing principle in Jules Barbey d'Aurevilly's **Les Diaboliques,** logically suggests its apparent opposite, exhibitionism. The connection between these two instinctual drives is developed in Freud's "Instincts and their Vicissitudes" where he shows their common auto-erotic source (the subject looking at his own sexual organ). The instinct of gazing (scoptophilia) and that of exhibitionism, and the dynamic of their interrelationship, can be located in Barbey's fictions where the text plays with two narrators and the reader in such a way that the acts of narrating, writing and reading seem to depend on the same erotic desire that Freud posits as the source of voyeurism and exhibitionism (one exposes oneself in order to see oneself exposed). Both instinctual drives stand out clearly in **Les Diaboliques** because of the structure of the stories, in most of which a character within the narration subsequently himself becomes a narrator and exhibits an episode from his own past to the original narrator. Such narrative organization with its repetitions and variations leads to discussions of literary creation by Barbey himself within the text, and invites an analysis of the shifting relationship between the narrators and then between narrator and reader, a shifting whose consequences threaten the equilibrium of the reader's position. Moreover, precisely at those points where the narrator, usually an admitted voyeur, claims to be intent on viewing the intimacies and dramas which take place behind drawn curtains (as in **"Le Rideau cramoisi"**) Barbey exposes himself and reveals his particular art of narrative creation.

"Le Rideau cramoisi," the first of six **Diaboliques** will be our model for a study of contradictions within narration revealing a double or multiple narrator whose presence invests the age-old topos of *mise en abyme* with a peculiarly dialectical movement rebounding between narrative and textual surface. Not that the problems studied and the conclusions drawn are limited to this particular type of writing; indeed the questions raised suggest possibilities for a more general theory of discourse—a theory which assumes an interplay between voyeurism and exhibitionism on levels of both sex and narration.

Referred to only by the pronoun "je," a semi-anonymous narrator tells **"Le Rideau cramoisi."** He recounts his chance meeting in a coach with an old acquaintance, the Vicomte de Brassard. The first quarter of the story depicts the aging but still robust Brassard and his career as a military man, a dandy and a libertine. When a broken coach wheel forces a stop late at night in a small town, the appearance of one lighted window screened by a double crimson curtain and Brassard's stunned reaction to that window, awaken the narrator's curiosity. Brassard explains by relating an episode from his youth.

The crimson curtain screens the very room in which, as a young officer of seventeen, he was quartered in the home of an elderly bourgeois couple. One month after his arrival the couple's daughter, Alberte, of whose existence Brassard had never been aware, returned home from boarding school. He found her aloof and impassive. Despite her beauty he remained indifferent to her until the evening she seized his hand under the dinner table while she retained her impassive attitude for the benefit of her parents. The next day, however, she refused to answer his written declaration, returned to her former place between her parents at the dinner table, and seemed, once again, to remain unaware of his existence. Following a month of futile attempts by Brassard to force a response from Alberte, she astonished him by entering his room late at night, having slipped past her sleeping parents to join him. After six months of a passionately silent affair—Alberte never answered Brassard's questions, she responded to him with her body—the fear both lovers had felt at the risk they were taking turned to complete terror for Brassard when Alberte died in his embrace and he fled in panic. He never learned what happened behind those curtains after he left, but the experience "mordant sur [sa] vie comme un acide sur de l'acier . . . a marqué à jamais d'une tache noire tous [ses] plaisirs de mauvais sujet."

The title reflects Barbey's narrative method. The light within the room in question is "tamisée par un double rideau cramoisi dont elle traversait mystérieusement l'épaisseur." The interior story of physical and of sexual death (or castration) filters mysteriously through two narrators and each distorts it for his own purposes and—we shall see—is distorted by it. Only one of the two has experienced what is recounted and an intricate play of blocked and blurred perception screens him—as the curtain does—from his own past, making him a voyeur watching a drama lived by his younger self as well as an exhibitionist exposing to the first narrator this younger self and his present reaction to the drama.

The first narrator appears, in the beginning, to correspond to the author, and he makes it very clear that what he is relating is a story. . . . Though his words are filtered through those of the first narrator, when Brassard continues the narration the function of the former changes; as listener he takes the place of the reader within the story. Once again the narrator—this time it is Brassard—stresses story and fiction although he is relating an autobiographical episode. Though Brassard may not be distorting to make a story amusing, his credibility as narrator is brought into question when he narrates himself from an external rather than an internal point of view. For example, many of the actions and feelings of the younger Brassard are preceded by "comme si" suggesting that Brassard the narrator is himself uncertain of the truth or the significance of what he is relating. Brassard compounds this problem in reducing his narrative powers further with constant interruptions: he will never convince his listener of the depth of the sensations he felt, no one could ever understand the experience he is relating. Appearing to excuse himself in advance for an author's inability to achieve what he envisions before writing, Barbey conveys more than modesty. When Brassard says "Non, jamais je ne pourrai vous donner l'idée ce cette sensation et de cet étonnement!" he forcefully makes the point that neither his past experience nor his reaction to that experience, is communicable. At the same time he underlines the necessarily subjective element of any eye-witness description when the narrator is also a participant, and by doing so suggests that the function and purpose of the story must be found somewhere other than in its factual account or shared experience.

Barbey already executes literary criticism by recreating the problem of writer and reader within the text, even though the story within the tale is told, not written. The recounted story undergoes a transformation, however, because Brassard, speaking at night, in a closed carriage, cannot be seen. The listener cannot distinguish facial expressions and so becomes a "reader" of the voice, so that, in a sense, the story told becomes the story written. Intonation does remain, but by virtue of the loss of the speaker-spectator opposition the story loses most of the qualities of oral literature.

Allusions to literary production are obvious and significant. Telling the story in the carriage is a spontaneous reaction to the unexpected sight of the crimson curtain. The setting allows the characters to fall easily into a pattern which corresponds to that of an author and his reader. A public carriage (unlike a drawing room where politeness is required) allows the author to relate as much as he wants and to stop when he wants, while an "audience" can "listen" as long as he pleases or shut the book. . . . Yet the lack of compulsion is only theoretical for both the metaphor and its referent. The crimson curtain sets the narration in motion only because of a broken coach wheel which interrupts the original narrator's description of Brassard—of the present Vicomte de Brassard moving toward the future. The movement of the carriage suggests a forward narration which is impossible for Brassard himself and which he refuses. The arrested carriage serves as a frame—a counterpart to the curtained window—a frame for the narration of a story he attempts to arrest, to fix within a frame of its own as a way of binding together discordant fragments of the past. An invitation to the listener or reader to play a role—though not the form and dimensions of that role—is an outcome of the storyteller-exhibitionist's need to expose himself to another even if, through this other, his desire is to see himself exposed. Exposing his sexual self, Brassard encourages desire on the part of the original narrator who will then continue to participate in the construction of a frame. Complicity of author and reader is so essential to production that the reader, like the itinerant listener, must be manipulated in such a way that he desires participation so that the conversation cannot end, in order that literary production may continue. In our model the desire of the first narrator is transformed. Originally an instigator, he becomes an unwilling listener whose efforts to end the conversation fail, forcing him to continue in the construction of the story.

The author has no more freedom than the reader. A parallel preoccupation with creation within the interior story reveals it to be more compulsive than voluntary and reinforces the obligation of Brassard-narrator to tell his story and of "je" the first narrator, to listen. Brassard the young officer is driven to create. Frustrated by his inability to possess Alberte physically, he does so indirectly by sketching images of her on paper. As an old man he must tell the story, re-create it in order to de-possess himself of Alberte and the death she has shaped within him. The first shift from voyeur to exhibitionist occurs within the interior story when the younger Brassard wants to see Alberte fully—to possess her. When he does, the possibility of being discovered and exposed terrifies him, yet he derives pleasure, indeed sexual pleasure, from this very possibility. While Brassard-narrator seeks to arrest the initial sexual pleasure so he may perceive and possibly relive it as he relates it, he attempts, more importantly, to cure himself of its disastrous effects by exposing it to another. The first narrator, then, an admitted voyeur, has the second as his accomplice since they both "observe" the sexual pleasure and terror of the young soldier, but the relationship shifts when Brassard-narrator becomes a determined exhibitionist, when he begins to dis-cover himself to the original narrator.

The young soldier's preoccupation with creating does not begin in front of Alberte. It is present from the moment he arrives in the town in which he is garrisoned. The town is dead. Animating himself, he lives within a heroic world formed by his own imagination in which he dreams of battlefield victories. This drive to fill a void in the world around him gains force through writing the moment he becomes aware of the possibility of a liaison with Alberte; he writes her a letter. "La seule ressource à ma portée . . . était d'écrire" he says, and when this fails, he simply repeats the same act in another form—he draws. The letter substituted for the active life of the normal military garrison in the same way the sketch of Alberte substitutes for the possession of Alberte.

Though incipiently obvious comparisons of literature and masturbation have become hackneyed, it must be noted that Barbey, with repetition of the word "moi," disperses the convention. Everything surrounding Brassard was caught up in a death-like sleep the night he drew the sketch, alone in his room, from the street which was "silencieuse comme le fond d'un puits" to the curtain "qui tombait devant la fenêtre, perpendiculaire et immobile," and the only noise, the only activity or sign of life "dans ce profond et complet silence, c'était moi qui le faisais," he tells us, "avec mon crayon." The sketch itself depicts "cette diablesse de femme dont [il était] possédé," and the only possibility of reversing that situation is through masturbatory fantasy, through the image he was sketching "Dieu sait avec quelle caresse de main et quelle préoccupation enflamée!"

To be sure the suggestion is not unexpected. Brassard was initially presented in a similar, though less self-conscious, manner. As we have seen, the young officer, forced to create his own pleasure in a town without activity did so easily, finding all the satisfaction he needed in the view of his own body in an officer's uniform. His very name, Brassard, signifies a convergence of his own identity with military trappings. He needed no one to admire him. He dressed for himself and spent his free hours in self-admiration. "Je jouissais solitairement" he tells his listener, "de mes épaulettes et de la dragonne de mon sabre, brillant au soleil, dans quelque coin de Cours désert où, vers quatre heures, j'avais l'habitude de me promener, sans chercher personne pour être heureux." Later, in despair at Alberte's lack of response, he confesses that he no longer thought of his uniform. What seems like a drastic change in the young man's attitude, however, is not. He simply redirected his masturbatory pleasure, exchanging one object for another. The image of Alberte may replace the uniform but the effect is the same.

Any change that does take place is the result of the sketch, not its cause. In the month since Alberte's audacious approach to him, Brassard had done everything in his power to elicit further response. Only when he attempted to possess her by reproducing her image on paper did she appear, hardly different, framed in the doorway of his room, from her image, framed by the edges of his paper. In one sense the Alberte he embraced is an Alberte of his own creation; she never revealed more depth than the surface figure in his drawing. The text has, at this point, already suggested that Alberte materialized within Brassard's room as if from the air. Silently, she appeared at his door as though by magic in what he compares to "la vision la plus surnaturelle." Earlier in the story Brassard had no hint that a daughter existed until she appeared, again as if from nowhere, and he makes it clear that she could not possibly have been conceived by the simple couple he lived with. He insists she must have fallen from the skies in the shape of a joke played upon his elderly bourgeois hosts. With no past she is, in a sense, invented by Brassard.

If Alberte can only be possessed by Brassard as he draws her portrait, then the elder Brassard is willing to do the same on the narrative level in order finally to dispossess himself of her, for Alberte's first appearance in the story is clearly in the form of portraiture rather than dynamic description. Brassard narrates Alberte and recreates her. All movement stops. The significance of the word "suspendait" used in this first description of Alberte shifts from her action (hanging her hat) to her very appearance. Suspended in various attitudes, she is displayed, her body unfolded for view while frozen in a series of poses. The portrait breaks itself up into a group of drawings ("debout et sur la pointe des pieds . . . Cambrée à outrance . . . la taille superbe d'une danseuse qui se renverse. . . . Les bras encore en l'air"). These drawings, which appear to be studies for a finished portrait of Alberte, have the effect of suspending life for a moment, of holding Alberte still within the frame of the room and of the story so that she may be examined and exposed to another. There is an unsuccessful parallel effort within the interior story on the part of the young Brassard who tried "d'arrêter, pour les fixer et les examiner, toutes les idées qui [lui] fouettaient le cerveau comme une toupie cruelle." One reason for his lack of success in halting and examining ideas is the lack of participation by another in this act. He is exposing his ideas—and himself—to himself, so the effort falls into the same category as his earlier masturbatory activity. In the later act of production, Brassard can "fix" his obsessions in a somewhat stable form and possibly attenuate or, at least, mediate their effect as he begins to see them from a point of view other than, but combined with, his own. With the portrait, the elder Brassard continues the act begun as a young man.

The driving force behind compulsive production shared by the author and reader or exhibitionist and voyeur is not, as some would have it, production itself. It is also the expression of some obsession of the author, something he will, consciously or not, clarify and bring back to himself through another. The obsession here is clearly with castration. The story Brassard relates has touched his entire life in the same way Alberte touched him as a youth. He at first hints, then insists that it is his sexual life itself that has been destroyed, describing the story as "un événement, mordant sur [sa] vie comme un acide sur de l'acier, et qui a marqué à jamais d'une tache noire tous [ses] plaisirs de mauvais sujet." We are talking, of course, not about physical but about symbolic castration and, with this destruction of sex, the destruction of communication or union in one sense, and its beginning in another. Brassard's experience with Alberte destroyed the possibility of future satisfactory union for him on a physical level. The story he tells is an attempt to recapture this union on a verbal level.

In *Les Diaboliques*, there is a spirit of revolt against the spiritual order of things, a spirit of concupiscence, the very spirit of evil itself, as well as an atmosphere of mystery and sensuality, a combination of elements best synthesized by Barbey d'Aurevilly and Baudelaire.

—*Armand B. Chartier, in his* Barbey d'Aurevilly, *1977.*

The question of union with another has already entered this discussion in a very problematic way. Implied in the early description of the young Brassard is a certain element of narcissism. He is indifferent to the dull world surrounding him and his pleasures are auto-erotic. Alberte intrudes into Brassard's world by seizing his hand under the table and some kind of communication, difficult though it may be, begins between them when Brassard's desire shifts from himself and settles on Alberte. The problem, of course, is that we have already introduced the possibility that Alberte is transformed, even if temporarily, from a real person to Brassard's own fabrication, and so is not really something outside himself. Where, then, is communication? What is union with oneself? It does seem at some point, though the reader cannot be sure exactly when, Alberte functions for both the young and the old Brassard as if she once again really exists and the reader must allow her to function in the same way. It is no longer a question of having created an image to satisfy his sexual fantasies; he has moved from creation to some kind of contact with another, even if only to return to himself. He is talking about the physical possession of a human being other than himself so that when Alberte dies we are dealing not with a loss of creative powers, but with total and final separation of one human being from another and the beginning of a story.

The problem, like most in this story, exists on several levels of the text. In the narration, the first narrator exists

perhaps even less than Alberte for he is obviously the creation of Barbey. If Brassard-Barbey is telling his story only to this first narrator then we are once again in a clotured world. But as Brassard corresponds to the author, the original narrator, "je," corresponds to the reader and it is with us, the readers of **"Le Rideau cramoisi"** that Barbey is communicating. The reader is repeatedly reminded of his function in the linguistic circuit. References to what is being told, an experience of castration, are syntagmatically linked to the person who is being told: "la circonstance *que je m'en vais vous dire,* et qui m'atteignit comme la foudre. . . ." (my italics). Moreover, references to this castration or "tache noire" are often made by the listener himself. The ambiguity can never be entirely eliminated. The younger Brassard makes Alberte into what he wants her to be and so communicates, through her, with himself. Barbey communicates to an audience outside himself and his work but draws this audience inside the frame and in a sense makes the audience, like Alberte, into what he wants it to be through his already existing listener-reader and his already executed literary criticism.

The themes of castration, physical death, and sexual differentiation or lack of it are closely connected in this story. The metaphor depicting Brassard and Alberte "faisant l'amour sur cette lame de sabre posée en travers d'un abîme" predicts not only Brassard's castration by Alberte, but Alberte's own death, and both of these events are intertwined with a blurring of masculinity and femininity within the two characters. A preliminary indication of sexual non-differentiation comes from the original narrator, from the frame which surrounds Brassard's story and gives it life. The sound of a broom which [the critic Marcelle Marini] claims sets the story in motion comes from "homme ou femme . . . on ne savait; il faisait trop nuit pour bien s'en rendre compte." Within the interior story each character displays actual physical characteristics belonging to the opposite sex. Alberte's hand is "un peu grande, et forte comme celle d'un jeune garçon," "au lieu de nerfs elle [a] sous sa peau fine presque autant de muscles que [Brassard]," while the latter struggles constantly to remind himself "[qu'il était] un homme après tout." Alberte is also the seducer and Brassard the seduced. To underscore the point Barbey recreates Stendhal's famous garden scene from *Le Rouge et le noir,* but here Alberte plays Julien Sorel's role as she seizes the young officer's hand under the table while they dine with her parents. Alberte makes the first move, Alberte's energetic gesture keeps the frightened young man from crying out when she comes to him, Alberte takes him in her arms rather than being taken in his, while Brassard declares himself "honteux . . . d'être moins homme que cette fille hardie."

Young Brassard is a seduced, passive, feminine figure, the antithesis of Brassard-dandy of the narration. Paradoxically within the interior story signs of the dandy are united under the name of Alberte. She dominates herself and her own emotions as easily as she dominates Brassard; she is truly "Mademoiselle Impassible." When he becomes a dandy in his later life, Brassard outwardly regains his place in the world of men by becoming Alberte, contradictory as this may sound, by exhibiting her force, her calm exterior, her perfect self-control, though this exhibition does not necessarily make him a masculine figure. The most important effect of the mask of the dandy is to hide the sexual anguish already present in the young officer before any encounter with Alberte. During this encounter anguish intensifies as he becomes less and less a masculine figure and finally experiences his own sexual death when Alberte dies during sexual intercourse. Communication or physical union with Alberte ends, but when she ceases to respond, Brassard—however much later—begins to write. We have already seen writing cease as communication began; when union with Alberte ends, writing recommences.

Alberte's death is more important as symbol than as fact; after all we have never been sure of her existence. Just as the distinction between masculinity and femininity is blurred, so is that between life and death. In **"Le Rideau"** the two sets of oppositions function together: as signs of femininity become stronger in Brassard so do signs of death. Figures describing his submission to the powers of Alberte are associated with liquids—he makes comparisons to warm baths, to dissolving, to the pumping of liquids and simply to water. Critics have seen death in Barbey's world as inevitably linked to water and so a feminine death, a death without struggle, a suicide. Even when death is the result of the violent aggression of another, the supposed victim is always, to some degree, an accomplice of his executioner. In **"Le Rideau cramoisi"** Brassard's relationship to Alberte is associated with a fluidity which signifies a non-differentiation of the sexes, a blurring of life and death and, as we shall see, an unbreakable link between passion and death which, like fluid, seeps out of the interior story and makes Brassard's later life a lingering suicide.

In Alberte sexual passion leads directly to physical death. While she is associated in the text with figures of coldness, of absence of all feeling, of total emotional and physical self-control, of immobility, rigidity and even frigidity and sterility, the plot depends on the antithesis of coldness in Alberte. It depends on the passion felt first by Bassard in Alberte's hand "pénétrant la mienne, comme un foyer d'où rayonnaient et s'étendaient le long de mes veines d'immenses lames de feu!" while the other hand "ne tremblait pas et faisait son petit travail d'arrangement de la lampe, pour la faire aller, avec une fermeté, une aisance et une gracieuse langeur de mouvement incomparables!" This inseparability of passion and sang-froid which eventually signifies an equivalence between passion and death, describes at first Alberte ("un èpais et dur couvercle de marbre qui brûlait, chauffé par en dessous"), then Brassard. It is both passion and death that Alberte's body evokes in Brassard. The fine line between the two is difficult enough to distinguish before her death, impossible afterward. This "chair qui [lui] faisait bouillonner le sang de désir il n'y avait qu'une heure, et qui maintenant [le] transissait!" will touch every aspect of his life and will effect his sexual death. The crimson curtain, at the same time screen and frame, is the equivalent of the libertine life Brassard ostensibly leads later. The mask disguises but also draws attention to itself. Both signify blood and passion, both hide a "tache noire," a dark stain suggesting sexual absence with which Brassard has been marked.

In his conduct with Alberte, Brassard transgressed society's prohibitions and her resulting death punished them both. He moved from a position of having no interest at all in Alberte to a voluptuous delight in the midst of his terror at having transgressed the prohibition. Curiosity about, desire for, Alberte is punished here, as the original narrator's initial voyeuristic curiosity about Brassard will be punished. While trying to escape the contamination of Alberte's death the young soldier reenacted it. The only objects he took when he ran were his pistols, and his flight from Alberte was a flight toward war, toward battle, toward the kind of killing society will allow and which approximates the prohibited killing he is trying to escape.

The equivalence of death and sex reappears on several levels in Brassard's reaction. His thoughts of suicide were swept away by the obvious sexual desire expressed in the young officer's admission: "Mais que voulez-vous? . . . Je serai franc: j'avais dix-sept ans et j'aimais . . . mon épée." While this hardly needs clarification, it is reinforced by Brassard's earlier expressed desire to "perdre . . . [son] pucelage militaire." Consequently he repeated ritualistic acts of sex and death in an attempt to purify himself and avoid their combination in his own being. The battles, interspaced with sexual adventures, distracted him from the cruel memory of Alberte "sans pouvoir pourtant l'effacer."

Because action fails to efface her memory, storytelling itself becomes a purifying ritual. By telling the story once again in its entirety, by fixing it in words, Brassard attempts to end it. Like Doctor Torty in another of Barbey's *Diaboliques,* Brassard keeps the memory of Alberte, as he explains it, like a bullet that cannot be extracted. He makes a second attempt at purification and, like Torty, lifts away the skin, layer by layer, to expose and, if possible, to remove the bullet, the stain which has poisoned every part of his sexual life. If Alberte's body is eternally accusing, so is the story Brassard tells. But by sharing the story, by becoming an exhibitionist, he can also share the story's effects with the "voyeur," diluting the stain on himself if he cannot eradicate it.

Without the first narrator there is no story. This is not only because he is the source of our information, the second *rideau* through which the light is filtered, but because the exhibitionist must have an audience, one he can touch. Indeed Brassard has no naive illusions about the effect of his story and takes the precaution of raising the carriage window to contain the sound of his voice. He will limit contamination to the original narrator, "je," who is unaware of the danger until it is too late, until he is reduced to a game of pretense "pour ne pas paraître trop pris par son histoire, qui [le] prenait." The function of this first narrator, "je," and his relation to others on several levels of the text establishes the reader's position more clearly. As listener "je" is closely tied to the reader but, even more importantly, he has a paradigmatic equivalent in Brassard's friend Louis de Meung within the interior story. Louis serves as confident to the young Brassard as "je" does to Brassard-narrator, but "je" carries the role to the conclusion Louis escapes. Both listen to the difficulties Brassard relates and both, sensing the danger of contamination, attempt to withdraw by means of insults and laughter. Louis mocks Alberte and tries to destroy her by having Brassard replace her with a town seamstress: "un clou chasse l'autre" he proclaims. The narrator, though, is not a part of the interior story. Like the reader he must respond not to the person Alberte, but to her story. He deals with Brassard on the level of words and descriptions and cannot, as Louis does, offer a real person as a substitute for Alberte. Instead he offers an exchange on the same level Brassard offers Alberte: he combats story with story. These interventions have an importance far beyond that suggested by Jacques Petit [in his edition of Barbey's *Œuvres romanesques complètes*] of breaking up the story to arouse the curiosity of the reader. The original narrator must destroy the power of Alberte and her story if he hopes to escape it. The stories he tells of other women who secretly received love letters or who welcomed lovers in bed while parents were close by, are meant very clearly to render Alberte harmless by comparing her with ordinary women and oft-told stories (words) which belong to the public. His interruptions have no effect on Brassard, however, "que j'avais cru humilier," he says "par une comparaison, dans la personne de son Alberte." Brassard always continues with the story "comme s'il n'avait pas entendu [la] moqueuse observation," and the formal resemblance between the narrator and Louis ends. Louis became discreet at the crucial moment and no longer asked questions. The narrator's game of protection fails as he learns of the castrating effects of the story and is touched by them (particularly so with the use of words like "tranchant" and "coupant" to describe the narration itself). As the dead body seemed to fill up Brassard's entire room to keep him from escaping, the story has the same force within the restricted frame of the dark closed carriage where it is being related, and the last words are those of the first narrator who insists on the lingering effect of "la mystérieuse fenêtre, [qu'il voit] toujours dans [ses] rêves, avec son rideau cramoisi."

Thus exhibitionism must pass to another level, and the story is told once again. On one level the first narrator, or the listener, has played the role of reader throughout Brassard's story—the link between ourselves and him cannot be denied. On another level the first narrator, "je," takes the place of Brassard the exhibitionist, and puts the reader in his own former place, that of voyeur. Exhibitionism as voyeurism turned back upon the self, as a love of gazing at one's own body can be followed on various levels of the text. The younger Brassard's curiosity about Alberte can be seen as a kind of voyeurism which is transformed into a desire to be seen with her. The elder Brassard begins by looking at his younger self, then exposes himself as a youth and as an adult to the original narrator who moves from a position of listener (reader-voyeur) back to his original position as author-exhibitionist of a tale which, though not his own, includes his reactions, particularly his resistance to the words and figures expressed. He then passes these words and figures colored by his own emotions, on to the reader. Not being aware of the possibility of contamination until the end of the story, the reader, like the first narrator, cannot escape its consequences. If we accept Barbey's storytelling metaphor then we must also accept

the role of the listener whose attempts to remain uninvolved are futile.

In the end the vital element of **"Le Rideau cramoisi"** is the frame. The *rideau* itself is one form of this frame, like every other aspect of the story. Everything is structured within a series of frames. The *cadre* of the original narration frames that of Brassard which frames the story of his youth. The edges of Brassard's paper frame his sketch of Alberte as the doorway frames Alberte herself. The carriage surrounds the two storytellers just as the room does the two lovers. Both carriage and room make a picture and frame of their windows. Brassard's narcissism is its own frame: closed mirrored space of Narcissus' pool, water linked to death.

Barbey d'Aurevilly then becomes a meta-exhibitionist. **"Le Rideau cramoisi"** is the *cadre* he seeks and it functions in the same way the other frames do within it, offering protection by hiding or disguising as it exposes. What is to be communicated, no matter how conflicting its elements may be, can be collected, set off by the frame, fixed and so exposed to anyone who must look, and participate. Sexual anguish, fears of castration, dissolving of the limits between man and woman, between life and death—all these things are reconstructed and organized by the frame. Whether or not oppositions can be reconciled, the text does enable frames created on four levels (that of the young Brassard, of Brassard-narrator, of the first narrator, and of Barbey d'Aurevilly) to give them form, and so to create a system of relationships in which these forms may be exhibited, shared and perhaps mediated through writing and reading.

Barbey and escapism:

[In **"Le bonheur dans le crime"**], lasting happiness, combined with passion, is shown to rest on a basis of crime and murder. Somewhere, in Barbey's mind, an ideal 'island' of happiness existed, untouched by the disappointments he met with in his life. It is with this 'paradise' that the protagonists of **"Le bonheur dans le crime"** are intimately associated, 'immortal', dream-like figures, who live, as Barbey would have liked to live had his conscience let him, in a realm divorced from 'reality' altogether.

B. G. Rogers, in his The Novels and Stories of Barbey d'Aurevilly, *1967.*

Angela S. Moger   (essay date 1983)

SOURCE: "Gödel's 'Incompleteness Theorem' and Barbey: Raising Story to a Higher Power," in *Sub-Stance,* No. 41, 1983, pp. 17-30.

[*Below, Moger discusses the significance of "Beneath the Cards of a Game of Whist" as a metafictional text, examining the following features of the story: multiple narrative layers, self-reflexive storytelling devices, emphasis of reportage over action, and structural circularity achieved through inversion of the relationships between narrator and audience, observer and the subject observed.*]

A story, according to conventional wisdom, is the composite of two elements, a hero and his observer, the storyteller; that is, the paradigm for "story" is made up of one who performs significant actions and one who relates that person's exploits. A fiction always entails at least this sequence of two since there is no such thing as a heroic storyteller. But, of course, there is no story without its audience. A message does not exist by reason of its having an addressor; it must have an addressee to come into existence. A story is only constituted when there is someone to hear about the exploits of the hero. The briefest reflection makes us aware that there are more than two steps in the sequence which creates a story: there has to be a third entry in the chain, the receiver who assembles and gives a design to what is dispatched by the sender. That is, the receiver is not merely acted upon; the story assumes a configuration and a meaning insofar as it responds to the values and experience of its audience, the mold into which it must flow in order to take form. The story "takes" to the extent that the receiver (reader or listener) has the "shock of recognition" at some level; that is, the addressee of the narrative message is the model as well as the spectator, the observed as well as the observer. He is, in fact, both figure and ground—ground, indeed, because he is in some sense the figure. Framed stories dramatize this circularity, making it evident that the addressee plays two kinds of roles in the creation of every narrative, and thus compelling us to move beyond the original intuition that a story is the representation of successive steps in a sequence. If we are accustomed to imagining that the diagram for story-qua-story would take the form of an arrow's path, moving along a horizontal axis from left to right, framed narrative, in projecting the listener as protagonist, substitutes a circle for that path. In **"Le Dessous de cartes d'une partie de whist,"** Barbey d'Aurevilly's explicit, rhetorical demonstration of a story which loops back on itself illuminates the profound shift in world view—and thus in concept of narrative—implicit in this passage from depiction of arrow to depiction of loop. Barbey's demonstration entails, among other types of displacement, the neutralization of traditional modes of organizing experience, such as hierarchies and polarities. Throughout **"Le Dessous de cartes,"** indeed, we find all manner of disorienting reversals. One must begin by interrogating the story for some common denominator among these reversals.

The story opens in the drawing room of the baronne de Mascranny where a small circle of distinguished people is gathered. This group of "gens d'esprit" are all practitioners of the dying art of witty conversation, the narrator tells us. He introduces, then, the champion of wit, "le plus étincelant causeur" of this esoteric society, the narrator of the story we read. When the storyteller was just a school boy, a Scotsman came to spend a protracted sojourn in the small provincial town where this internal narrator was born. Marmor de Karkoel is detained by the prominent citizens of the town because of his proficiency at whist, the exclusive occupation and passion of this waning, impoverished aristocracy. The storyteller describes at length the

various personages of this society, especially the implacable and inscrutable comtesse du Tremblay de Stasseville and her beautiful daughter, Herminie. The rest of his story is composed of descriptions of specific whist parties and frequent innuendos concerning the relationship between Marmor and the comtesse du Tremblay. Finally the storyteller reports having learned of the death of the young Herminie, followed shortly thereafter by the death of her mother. From an old gentleman who figured prominently in the whist circle, he has heard, furthermore, that "they say" that Marmor, long since departed, was the lover of mother and daughter. But the most sensational aspect of the hearsay which the raconteur passes on to the members of the baronne de Mascranny's "salon" is that the body of an infant "qui avait vécu" was found under the flowers planted in a huge "jardinière" in Mme de Stasseville's drawing room. At the end of his story, then, the internal narrator assures his audience that no one will ever know whose child it was or the causes of the deaths of the two women. **"Le Dessous de cartes"** ends with a brief description, by the primary narrator, of the impact of the internal story on its audience.

In *Gödel, Escher, Bach: an Eternal Golden Braid*, Douglas Hofstadter comments: "When a figure or 'positive space' (e. g., a human form, or a letter, or a still life) is drawn . . . an unavoidable consequence is that its complementary shape—also called the 'ground,' or 'background', or 'negative space'—has also been drawn." He elaborates further by making a distinction between what he calls "cursively drawable figures" and "recursive figures"; "A 'cursively drawable' figure is one whose ground is merely an accidental by-product of the drawing act. A 'recursive' figure is one whose ground can be seen as a figure in its own right." Hofstadter cites the drawings of the Dutch artist M. C. Escher as perfect examples of recursive figures, ones where both foreground and background are "recognizable forms." If these comments are used to orient a reading of **"Le Dessous de cartes d'une partie de whist,"** perhaps they offer some illumination of two arresting images which spring to mind from its pages.

The first is the characterization by the internal narrator of Barbey's elaborate tale, of the story he is about to tell as one of those *"drames à transpiration rentrée,"* which is quite a provocative notion all by itself. Many pages later, this same person is recalling for his audience of spellbound listeners what Mme la comtesse du Tremblay de Stasseville was like, but his recollection does not proceed from some mental image of the actual person: "Du reste, cette analyse que je fais maintenant de la comtess du Tremblay, sur le souvenir de son image, *empreinte dans ma mémoire comme un cachet d'onyx fouillé par un burin profond sur de la cire . . . ,"* his analysis is based on a memory of her *image,* and that image is, in turn, impressed on his memory like the imprint in wax made by a seal. A seal is the curious case of production by subtraction rather than addition—presence from absence, depth instead of protrusion.

There is an inversion at work in both these remarks which is most distracting. Reality is subjected to a manipulation which surpasses mere reversal; the "opposite" is being exposed, specifically, in the sense that things are being turned inside out. There is a kind of primacy of the "concave" over the "convex," if you will. One could, in fact, using the terminology of Hofstadter, say that the "ground," or "negative space" is here valorized over the "figure." A similar kind of paradox is represented in *our* narrator's insistence on the eloquence of the Countess de Damnaglia's back. She, like our narrator, is seated in the salon of the barrone de Mascranny, listening intently to the "drame" recited by an unnamed member of the group. Our narrator "reads" her opinions and reactions to what is being said not by observing, as would be the conventional approach, the expression on her face or the movements of her hands, but by examining her back closely: "son dos . . . avait une physionomie," he announces; and at key moments, he scrutinizes this "text" and reports as if they were very distinct and revealing messages, the "frémissement nerveux" or the beads of "une sueur légère" which find expression there. There may not be the literal turning inside-out of a body here, but there is an inversion of the usual priority in the matter of which surface of the body is treated as most communicative. Furthermore, to sustain for a moment longer the issue of paradoxes of inversion, our narrator is clearly much more interested in the "impression" (in the literal, as well as the figurative, sense of the word) made by the story *on* the Countess de Damnaglia than he is in the story they are both listening to. We could call that "imprint" of the story on its listener the "negative space" automatically generated by, and implicit in, the "positive space" which is the tale told that listener. Every framed narrative articulates a paradox, and any one is susceptible to the interpretation that it describes the relationship between a "figure" and a "ground"—a story and the context of its reception. The singularity of **"Le Dessous de cartes,"** however, is that it manifests itself explicitly as a "recursive" figure: the surface on which it is "mounted," the context in which it is embedded (what I have called throughout this discussion the "frame"), "can be seen as a figure in its own right." The reader must perceive contained story and containing story as co-present on the same plane. Figure and ground, in Barbey's story, do not signify in the manner of a collage or of a chain—in these structures, there is a perceptible border or limit between distinct elements—but rather, the frame and the framed form a kind of pretzel, a complicated loop where it is not possible to establish where one begins and the other leaves off. Why should this matter? What can a narrative be or say whose configuration is that of a loop, and in what does the "loopiness" of **"Le Dessous de cartes d'une partie de whist"** consist? The question, and indeed, the terminology, bring us back to Hofstadter.

Hofstadter's book discusses the implications, in modern technology and current metaphysical thought, of the work of the Austrian mathematician, Kurt Gödel. In 1931, Gödel published "On Formally Undecidable Propositions of Principia Mathematica and Related Systems," colloquially referred to as "Gödel's Incompleteness Theorem." Ten years before Hofstadter, Piaget gives us a simple summary of Gödel's contribution:

> In the first place, he showed that no consistent formal system sufficiently "rich" to contain elementary arithmetic (for example, the system of

Russell and Whitehead's *Principia Mathematica*), can by its own principles or reasoning . . . *demonstrate* its own consistency; second, that any such system allows for the generation of propositions which are "formally undecidable," or, to use yet another technical expression, that any logical system that might appear capable of serving as foundation for mathematics is "essentially incomplete."

Hofstadter makes a more compressed statement of Gödel's findings: "All consistent axiomatic formulations of number theory include undecidable propositions." How Gödel demonstrated this is perhaps even more pertinent to our subject than what he proved.

Having established a code where numbers could stand for both themselves and for statements of number theory, Gödel showed that a statement *of* number theory could be *about* a statement of number theory, i. e., that it refers to itself. "The exploitation of the notion of mapping is the key to the argument in Gödel's famous paper . . . Gödel showed that metamathematical statements about a formalized arithmetical calculus can indeed be represented by arithmetical formulas *within* the calculus" [Ernest Nagel and James R. Newman, *Gödel's Proof,* 1958]. Once it was shown that mathematical statements can also be metamathematical statements, Gödel was able to demonstrate in just one more step that an axiomatic system like Russell and Whitehead's always generates true propositions not provable or verifiable by the prescribed method, which is therefore incomplete.

> . . . [He] devised a method of representation such that neither the arithmetical formula corresponding to a certain true metamathematical statement about the formula, nor the arithmetical formula corresponding to the denial of the statement, is demonstrable within the calculus. Since one of these arithmetical formulas must codify an arithmetical truth, yet neither is derivable from the axioms, the axioms are incomplete. [*Gödel's Proof*]

The system, in fact, collapsed under the application of its own principles and procedures, engendering propositions it could not account for. "Gödel showed . . . how to construct an arithmetical formula G that represents the meta-mathematical statement: 'the formula G is not demonstrable.' . . . The formula G thus says of itself that it is not demonstrable" [*Gödel's Proof*]. What axiomatic systems really describe, it would seem, is their own insufficiency. Gödel, then, held that most hierarchical systems are characterized by an incompleteness of this type; each level is not self-contained but actually borrows from outside, from some other "set" (as the mathematicians call it), making it possible for it to stand both for itself and for a statement about itself. There is a jumping out of the system which, producing statements which are not accounted for within the system, demonstrates that it is not sufficient in itself.

Hofstadter reminds us that from Epimenides down to modern thinkers like Bach and Escher, men have been preoccupied with the self-reference illustrated by Gödel and thus have chosen to represent reflexivity itself. The drawings of Escher depict, one after another, the doubling back on itself of all seemingly progressive movement. There is an optical illusion whereby monks climbing stairs end up at the point of origination and waterfalls cascade down a few levels only to suddenly arrive at their point of origin, without the eye's being able to detect a circle in the picture. Hofstadter calls this introspective mode a "Strange Loop":

> The "Strange Loop" phenomenon occurs when-
> ever, by moving upwards (or downwards)
> through the levels of some hierarchical system,
> we unexpectedly find ourselves right back where
> we started.

If Gödel is right—if at the crux of consciousness are these "Strange Loops," when the artist wants to capture truth, he too must avoid projecting some tidy hierarchy. But how does the narrative artist represent the Strange Loop? How can he construct a self-referential story, one which is both itself and a statement about itself? How can the writer assemble a "self-swallowing" [Hofstadter] construct whereby we might find ourselves, at the end, right back where we started? Barbey has made, in **"Le Dessous de cartes,"** a narrative proposition which works like Gödel's proof; he borrows from its own premises to show the system he describes as incomplete, and it is the frame which makes it possible for this self-reference to occur. After all, telling a story about game playing (whist) to a group where the game is storytelling constitutes, already, a self-referential loop.

There are many signals that we are not meant to pursue the story dangled before us by the anonymous internal narrator, and he furnishes, as well, formal and thematic cues that there is a significant continuous reciprocity between the presumably separate planes of the frame and the framed. From the moment when the reverse Lancelot—an Englishman introduced into the French "court"—is described, we should, perhaps, realize that paradox is afoot. The irony of this presentation of the foreign card player at the "lists" is, however, critical; he is the true anti-hero. He will never perform any valorous deed (quite the contrary) and, in retrospect, we realize that he replaces, at the first "tournament," a seventy-five-year-old woman! As to the substance of the story told about this Marmor and his fellow players, we finish our reading with more questions than we had at the outset; and we perceive that the unreliability of the paucity of information we *do* have, has been repeatedly underlined. In fact, if the internal narrator were a reporter, his editor would be afraid of libel suits, given how cavalier the documentation is. For example, the narrator persona paints an absolutely compelling picture of the debut of the Black Knight; he gives us a detailed description of the first evening when the Englishman, Hartford, brings Marmor to the "whist de M. de Saint-Albans." It is somewhat disconcerting, then, to read, immediately following this vivid tableau, "Je n'y étais pas." It seems he learned all that has been said from a relative. Then, after Marmor de Karkoel has been on the scene for apparently quite some time, this narrator persona, reporting on a game of whist he saw Marmor play seated in a boat during a salmon fishing expedition, says of himself, "(J)' etais un ecolier en vacances alors." So, he was not

even an adult at the time of the most critical events he claims to transmit with accuracy. A little later in the course of his chronicle, the storyteller admits to having been absent during the dénouement of the drama he has been relaying: "Les deux dernières années de mon éducation s'y écoulèrent sans que je revinsse dans mon pays." One is then offered objective confirmation that he may not have understood what he is reporting and may, indeed, have missed a lot when the chevalier de Tharsis, recalling a curious aspect of Mme de Stasseville's behavior, is reported by this storyteller to have said to the latter "Vous rappelez-vous . . . non! vous étiez trop enfant. . . ." The storyteller himself, then, is repeatedly responsible for discrediting his own narrative authority. As for Tharsis, *his* information—that "*they say*" that Mme de Stasseville and her daughter were both in love with Marmor de Karkoel and that he was suspected of being responsible for both their deaths—acquires the status of backstairs gossip as soon as it is uttered. Tharsis admits that a lot of what he has said was learned from "les femmes de chambre," and his conversation is generously sprinkled with expressions like "à les entendre" and "du moins l'a-t'on fait entendre ici quand on en parlait à voix basse." In other words, he doesn't know anything for sure himself. This extended hearsay amounts to a kind of teasing of the story's audience, especially in view of all the earlier innuendos promising ultimate revelations: " . . . avec des impressions rétrospectives— . . . cette soirée . . . prendra des proportions qui pourront peut-être vous étonner . . ."—"il aurait été curieux de surprendre dans cette femme . . . si ce qu'on a cru depuis et répété tout bas avec épouvante, a daté de ce moment-là"—"Etait-ce un signe, une entente quelconque, une complicité, comme en ont les amants entre eux . . . ?" But what do we know? Is there a single event, other than the fact of the deaths of the Countess and her daughter, which is certain? And what were any of the protagonists of this drama really like? Indeed, the only thing we know about the two central figures is that they were both "indéchiffrable," a strange and startling assertion about a story's principal characters.

The presumed foreground remains obscure while the background, it occurs to us, is constantly protruding. We are told more about those listening to the story than about the people in the story. These listeners are extremely vocal, and it is clear that pains have been taken to carry the mind's eye out into the "spectator section."

> Voulez-vous que je m'arrête? —répondit le con-
> teur, avec une sournoise courtoisie et la petite
> rouerie d'un homme sûr de l'intérêt qu'il a fait
> naître. —Par exemple! —reprit la baronne;
> —est-ce que nous pouvons rester, maintenant,
> l'attention en l'air, avec une moitié d'histoire?
> —Ce serait aussi par trop fatigant! —dit, en dé-
> frisant une de ses longues anglaises d'un beau
> noir bleu, Mlle Laure d'Alzanne, la plus languis-
> sante image de la paresse heureuse, avec le gra-
> cieux effroi de sa nonchalance menacée. —Et dé-
> sappointant en plus! —ajouta gaiment le doc-
> teur. —Ne serait-ce pas comme si un coiffeur,
> après vous avoir rasé un côté du visage, fermait
> tranquillement son rasoir et vous signifiait qu'il
> lui est impossible d'aller plus loin? . . .

Following these protestations to the storyteller, there is one more comment from a member of his audience—*our* narrator characterizes the secondary narrator's resumption of his story: "Je reprends donc, —reprit le conteur avec la simplicité de l'art suprême qui consiste surtout à se bien cacher . . . ." The mind stumbles as it attempts to assign a meaning to this line, for it is self-cancelling. If this comment can be made, the art of the teller has not been well "hidden," but, of course, that art can only be fully appreciated by someone who perceives it as art. Furthermore, what does the comment invite us to make of the story we are reading where little effort is made to sustain any fictional illusion—where, indeed, not only is there an absence of plot (unless it be that absence), but where the narrator's intrusions seem to deliberately stress its irrelevance? Perhaps this comment is an emblematic Strange Loop, bearing, like a cell, information about the code which prevails in the larger organism. This is a statement, after all, which can only be proven by a judgment from without; a trompe l'oeil can only be admired by one who is aware that it is artifice. That is, the proof of the success of the device resides in its not working completely. It must point to itself in some way which defeats the illusion; it must be, in some manner, "incomplete." This is why the narrator's comment is the essence of the Strange Loop. Like Gödel's version of Principia Mathematica, it dismantles itself.

Does the narrative as a whole effect dismantling of what it has assembled? The story's excessive self-reference might serve as a key—the reader is continually drawn out into the frame, both by the distracting comments on the proceedings from without and by the mirroring, in the outer narrative, of detail from the inner narrative. There is an explicit parallel drawn between the Countess Damnaglia and Mme de Stasseville ["On prétend que, comme Mme de Stasseville, la comtesse de Damnaglia a la force de cacher bien des passions et bien du bonheur"]. Among the listeners in the drawing room is a Baronne de Saint-Albin who echoes the Marquis de Saint-Albans of the interior story. For supporting players we have in each story an elderly remnant of the Old Order who enjoys gossip (the vicomte de Rassy and the chevalier de Tharsis) and a secondary female voice contributing provocative non sequiturs (Mlle Sophie de Revistal and Mlle Ernestine de Beaumont). Most important of all, of course, is the mother-daughter pairing; the baronne de Mascranny and her daughter, Sibylle, form a disturbing replica of the comtesse du Tremblay and Herminie. When the baronne de Mascranny takes the story so personally that she destroys a flower from her own corsage declaring, "Voilà qui est fini! . . . je ne porterai plus de résédas," it is evident that we are meant to read the so-called listeners as protagonists, that the "action" of the narrative is situated in the "ground" as much as in the "figure." But these two groups of people repeat each other in a more significant way than any yet mentioned.

In the interior story, the people's lives are devoted to playing whist. They spend much of the day and night engaged in this activity which has no natural outcome, which "yields" nothing. Indeed, the tableau representing the young women of this society seated in the darkened alcoves while barren old age occupies the central position, sitting, fully-lit, at the whist tables, recurs often enough in the text to invite us to make something of it: those who might bear fruit never will, they will remain in the shadows of life while the society to which they belong will dedicate itself to rituals which assign value to the nonreproductive, to games, closed systems which have no issue. Passion and procreation are not connected in this world, a world which functions, in fact, like a card game. The people are all "face" cards (king, queen, jack); the young women are all doomed not to "duplicate" since there are no partners of their own "suit" available. But what of the people in the narrator's esoteric circle? Although the opening of **"Le Dessous de cartes d'une partie de whist"** is a long pronouncement on the value of being witty and telling stories well, there is, performatively, as much value in telling stories as in playing cards. Instead of playing whist, they play wit. Mme de Mascranny's guests are, like M. de Saint-Albans' guests, seated in a circle sparring with each other. Like the whist circle, moreover, this "wit" circle is presented by the author of **"Le Dessous de cartes"** in a manner which insists on the analogy with a deck of cards. A considerable portion of the first paragraph of the story is devoted to the description of the coat of arms of the family of the baronne de Mascranny. Coats of arms are stylized representations of a family; this is as close as we will come to a family in the story since actual biological succession is no more in evidence here than it is among the "whisteurs." Since cards are arbitrary signs taken from coats of arms, we find here again textual confirmation of the interaction of "sets," those told (the countess de Damnaglia et al.) and those told about (the countess de Tremblay de Stasseville).

[*Les Diaboliques*] points up the gap between the superhuman characters of Barbey's fictional universe and what was, for him, the insufferable banality of the contemporary world. Condemn as he might the evil committed by his diabolical men and women, *they* at least had the requisite boldness to live out their passions to the fullest.

—*Armand B. Chartier, in his* Barbey d'Aurevilly, *1977.*

A deck of cards is a semiotic set, valorized from without by whatever definition is applied. The cards have no intrinsic meaning or value. If one looks beneath the sign for something other than the relationship between signs, one finds that there is no referent; there is only the intercommunication. Thus, where Barbey's tale is concerned, since the story at its center is more illusory than real, a series of fragments directing one's attention beyond it to the reflections of those elements in the frame, this interplay itself emerges as sign. But, the very signals which have directed attention to the reciprocity between the two "decks" of "face cards" simultaneously point beyond to another "set." After all, the reader is in a position to glean all of the above because of the existence of a narrator who situates *himself* outside the so-called outer circle—his designation of the countess de Damnaglia's back as his "rempart" defines him as the observer, in turn, of the "wit" players. But then, the all-important coat of arms which initiates a link between wit and whist and us (it is our narrator who brings up the baronne de Mascranny's coat of arms) refers to, and originates with, a group which antedates even the whist players.

Actually, implicit in this story is a hierarchy of sorts. The "Emigres" at the whist tables all have inherited nobility; their coats of arms are signs memorializing the real accomplishments and feats of arms of the earlier generation who actually earned the coat of arms. Nobility had been conferred on them in recognition of brave deeds (crusades, battles, acts of daring). Their idle descendants offer an impoverished version of this valorous activity in their whist tournaments. "Ils élevèrent ce whist jusqu'à la hauteur de la plus difficile et de la plus magnifique escrime," says the storyteller. The tone and diction of the authorial rendering of these "tournaments" inform the reader that an ironical comparison is intended. In fact, the inflated diction of this last comment makes the absence of the true heroes virtually palpable. The next group in the hierarchy, in descending order (in chronological time and in terms of diminution of nobility), is of course, the aristocracy who sit around and talk in each others' drawing rooms and whose titles have been emptied of any significance following the "revolution." Next, after the witty conversationalists who listen to the story of the whist circle, is a fourth group who listen to the story of the wit circle. The chief character of this tier is *our* narrator; and, therefore, the rest of the circle is composed of those who represent a Damnaglia to his telling—us. Those who engage in the activity of story writing and story reading constitute yet another layer in the succession of removals from action to pure semiotic activity; there has been a progression from action in the world to games of moving signs around (card playing and story telling) to pure sign, the literary text. We seem to be very far from the first element of the series, the real heroes, but are we?

Observation of the device at work on the structural level of **"Le Dessous de cartes"** provides confirmation of what we have sensed in that graduated series, a series of pairs,

Illustrations accompanying "Happiness in Crime" and "The Crimson Curtain," respectively, in the 1882 edition of The Diaboliques.

actually: the last tier, the reader, is ultimately coincident with the first element of the sequence. That is, in each tier we find, as well, a representative of the next, a figure who anticipates the subsequent level. The marquis de Saint-Albans, designated as "le seigneur féodal de tous ces nobles," is linked to many of the greatest names of the truly heroic past, as we have seen, and thus has one foot in the society of the true heroes. Then, there is the boy who, growing up in the society of "whisteurs" (he reports that his own father spent much of his time at the tables), constitutes the most prominent member of the new series, the "causeurs." He is described, in fact, as "le plus étincelant causeur de ce royaume de la causerie." (He is *their* Marmor who, in turn, is described as the "meilleur joueur de whist" of the "Trois Royaumes".) He is the best player of the game which occupies this circle: Mme de Mascranny herself, the Countess de Damnaglia, and, of course, the frequenter of this salon who slips in behind the Countess and studies the effect of the story on her and the other players of wit, the narrator who speaks to us. In that capacity, of course, he anticipates the ultimate circle of the story, made up of "author" and readers. This is what we have earlier termed the level of "pure sign" since semiotic manipulation is the only occurrence at this stage of the series—there is *only* the text. A message has no existence without a receiver, so the reader is necessarily called into being (and into the story) as the other member of a pair with the narrator. The question which automatically arises here is: what group does the reader point to? This is complicated, for although the reader is unquestionably the necessary receiver of the sign, he, like the original heroes, is present only by implication in the story. That is, like those illustrious ancestors of the whist players, we exist, after all, without participating in literariness. In this, we rejoin the first group in the series. I am in the world without there having to be a story by Barbey, unlike either Mme de Tremblay or Mme de Mascranny; and in this I make a pair with their forbears who operated in the world, not merely in a narrative universe. The Strange Loop occurs since the reader is on the same level of abstraction as the initial doer. That is, we progress through a hierarchical system or a "series of ordered pairs," to use the mathematical terminology, only to find ourselves "unexpectedly back where we started." This anticipation of the subsequent level characteristic of each stage of the series set up by **"Le Dessous de cartes"** confirms a Gödelian incompleteness since that borrowing from the yet-to-come is what finally creates the loop which has the reader rubbing shoulders with the heroic ancestors of the whist circle. Piaget makes a compelling statement of the implications of this anticipatory borrowing (in all axiomatic systems) which Gödel brings to light; Piaget's translator, moreover, in having recourse to the word "story" in order to render Piaget's "étage," may be offering an unwitting revelation of the ultimate signification of the loop which Barbey substitutes for plot:

> Gödel showed that the construction of a demonstrably consistent relatively rich theory requires not simply an "analysis" of its "presuppositions," but the construction of the next "higher" theory. Previously, it was possible to view theories as layers of a pyramid, each resting on the one below, the theory at ground level being the most secure because constituted by the simplest means, and the whole firmly poised on a self-sufficient base. Now, however, "simplicity" becomes a sign of weakness and the "fastening" of any story in the edifice of human knowledge calls for the construction of the *next higher story* [Moger's emphasis]. To revert to our earlier image, the pyramid of knowledge no longer rests on foundations but hangs by its vertex, an ideal point never reached and, more curious, constantly rising! In short, rather than envisaging human knowledge as a pyramid or building of some sort, we should think of it as a spiral, the radius of whose turns increases as the spiral rises. This means, in effect, that the idea of *structure* as a system of transformations becomes continuous with that of *construction* as a continual formation. [Jean Piaget, *Structuralism,* translated by Chaninah Maschler, 1970]

Finally, the reader of Barbey's story has to rethink his initial assumptions about the meaning of the title. Are the cards of the story face down? Or are they all the same underneath (the value side is, in fact, turned up from the outset: "marquis," "comtesse," "chevalier")? Which side are you getting beneath? It turns out that the concealment/revelation polarity is, after all, not the axis of the story. The mistake is in believing that there is a right-side-up, or, rather, that some kind of truth resides in a given sign. The signified arises from the semiotic network and not from the sign itself. That is, implicit in the concept of cards is inversion since cards are all the same on one side and unique on the other side. It is the fact of rotation and not what gets turned up which matters. We always find ourselves back where we started. There is no underside and topside to the story; it is a mobius strip, a loop which has but a single surface. Thus, the story is never "over"; like the cards, it is in perpetual rotation. "Implicit in the concept of strange loops is the concept of infinity," says Hofstadter, "since what else is a loop but a way of representing an endless process in a finite way?"

While appearing to probe the mystery enveloping Mme du Tremblay and Marmor de Karkoel, Barbey's tale provides, instead, rhetorical illustration that to read a story is to jump into a chain. For his explicit dramatization of a chain stands for the chain implicit in story qua story; hero, agent of significant deeds: teller, celebrant of hero's exploits: listener, recipient of teller's message but capable of decoding it by reason of his similarity to the model. The listener is both "ground," the hollow space into which the story flows, and "figure," the creature who imbues it with a configuration to begin with. A story, in fact, is generated because the listener's role is split into two parts, two parts which exist in a relationship of inverse complementarity, one to the other.

The outset of this discussion consisted of a groping for the nature of the singular form of inversion which recurs continually in the pages of **"Le Dessous de cartes."** When we consider again now the storyteller's peculiar invocation of the onyx seal as a way of conjuring up Mme du Tremblay, we perceive that a seal is the very incarnation of inverse complementarity and that, moreover, Barbey has fashioned a story whose entire process enacts this inverse complementarity. The way this is done has important implications for the ontology of narrative in general.

"Story" promises climax. When one tells a story, one proceeds inductively building toward the climax. The listener is performing not a duplicate task but a complementary deductive one in trying to deduce what the climax is. There is an inverse correspondence in their two roles. The teller, full of the knowledge of the undisplayed climax, unburdens himself like the Ancient Mariner to the empty listener, who is then full of the story when the teller is finally empty.

But what if the teller is telling a story about the telling of a story? To frame a story is to insist on the fact that the end has already happened—the installed narrator signifies a listener who has already learned the end and is retelling it. (If, indeed, reading a story is like playing cards, deciphering a framed story is more like reading the bridge column in the newspaper.) When the teller is a prior listener, the story is not a template, a duplication—some translation must occur. The teller switches from what he received deductively to what he imparts inductively. But each telling is, of course, cumulative. In the second telling, it is not the story which is being retold; it is the first telling which is being retold (the listener is, this time, full of the *telling* of the story). With this second sequence (the first sequence is the basic pair; full teller/empty listener), that is, with the prior listener's telling of the telling, the self-reference of Gödel's proof has been introduced into the inverse complementarity. Any story proposes itself as a mimesis, but a framed story, having at its heart the process of telling about telling, is borrowing from the very imitation of life which it offers, the elements which will invalidate that mimetic system. What starts out as mimesis ends up in a loop. There is the self-conscious conversion of the natural, or rather, the life-like, into the artificial. **"Le Dessous de cartes"** is replete with thematic and rhetorical examples of this narrative "dandyism."

Throughout Barbey's story there is a valorization of the man-made over the natural. That is, activities characterized by human intervention into the natural take precedence over any natural activity. We have commented on the denial of natural succession which is particularly evident in the pages of **"Le Dessous de cartes."** The single instance of procreation is but hearsay (the allegation is that the baby was immediately murdered); and the reader has to wonder if there is something symbolic of this negation of generational succession in the "banishment" of the two daughters who figure in **"Le Dessous de cartes."** Furthermore, there is a similar suggestion implicit in the famous scene of juxtaposition of Mme du Tremblay's most beautiful "possessions," her exquisite daughter and her extraordinary diamond ring—or in the language of the text, the "diamant humain" and the "diamant minéral." Indeed, the parallelism of the mother's memorable response to the questions of two different members of the circle ("Eh! eh! eh! qu'est-ce qui brille?" and "Et, qui est-ce qui tousse?"), "C'est mon diamant et c'est ma fille," seems to establish that she considers them comparable in value, that is, that the girl does not take precedence over the in-

animate object. When, therefore, the rest of this scene is devoted to an elaborate comparison of the scintillating vitality of the diamond and the sickly pallor of the girl, there is at the textual level a devaluation of natural succession which is dramatically underscored by the chief protagonist's obliviousness to the entire discussion of these two "diamonds." The only diamond he is interested in is the one which figures in the realm of stylized generational succession: "Karkoel . . . regardait d'un oeil distrait sa dame de carreau." We have noted certain analogous aspects of card playing and story telling, but this particular scene illuminates another critical parallelism where Barbey's story is concerned. A deck of cards is an artifact modeled on the principle of generation; similarly, **"Le Dessous de cartes"** makes an artifact of the issue of generation in substituting a communicational chain for a genetic chain. Instead of the representation of a family, and of the continuation through time of a family through marriages and births, the thematic material of the story establishes, rather, the pre-eminence of story line over blood line. The story exists not to celebrate fathers and sons but to celebrate narrative generation; the people do not reproduce, they relate and are related. Artificial succession (and fictions which stand for actual families like coats of arms and cards) triumphs everywhere over natural succession. Art takes over for life.

Narrative "generation" (in the two senses of that word, "production" and "succession"), then, as opposed to natural generation—this being the case, there is an amusing irony inherent in the mode of transmission operative in Barbey's story. A framed narrative's inverse complementarity, with its successive pairs of teller and listener, offers a substitute on the structural and referential level for the representation of natural activity. That is to say, in this story so dedicated to the denial of natural generation, the performative substitute bears the same modular form as the device for real (biological) communication between generations. At the chemical heart of natural communication is the DNA, a mechanism whose functioning is duplicated in the principle found at the heart of framed narrative. The grandson has his grandfather's gait and his grandmother's eyes, it seems, because of the sequence of inversely complementary pairs which make up the DNA. In constructing a story where "information" is transmitted by means of a similar pattern, the author communicates a singular vision of the nature of narrative. Implicit in the sequence of pairs where one member of each couple constitutes an anticipation of the subsequent element of the sequence is the proposition that a listener is also a teller, that a story is a process not an entity, that, in fact, all fictions are "recursive" figures. If the story about Marmor and the Countess du Tremblay is the "figure" and the context of its telling, the "ground," we have surely witnessed the extent to which the ground is the figure in its own right; that is, in this narrative "event," there seems to be no "content" but only a "receiver." The narrative fabric is a chevron stripe in alternating rows of black and white. Which is figure and which is ground? Or do they continually alternate in a perpetual rotation of roles which renders meaningless the distinction between figure and ground and all analogous oppositions: form/content, teller/listener, dessus de cartes/dessous de cartes?

In the oscillation of the pairs full teller/empty listener, framed narrative offers itself as a recursive figure, a design where nothing is sure (in the sense of permanently fixed in place or hierarchically established) other than the fact of perpetual motion. If Barbey's unique manipulation of the framed story causes us to perceive the general principle that at the core of narrative communication is the same mechanism which brings about genetic communication, the "mise en abîme" of that inverse complementarity incarnate in the rhetorical system of **"Le Dessous de cartes"** ironizes notions like generational succession and the human hopes rooted in such ideas. We have to qualify our earlier complacency as to the implications of the loop traced by the story. A mobius strip, after all, is more than the guarantee of perpetuity; since the end is coincident with the beginning, cherished illusions based on teleological models are invalidated. End-oriented convictions such as the belief in immortality, in the accessibility and intelligibility of messages (i. e., knowledge), in the meaning or purpose of things, are rendered nonsensical in a stroke. There is no "great design" and nothing to be revealed; there is only the endless shuffling of the cards, endlessly promising and endlessly withholding any disclosure of the "dessous."

Satanism in *The Diaboliques*:

[*The Diaboliques*] signals Barbey's evolution away from a reliance on the *fantastique* to evoke the effects of Satan's presence in the world. Satanism is cast in purely human terms by means of characters who signify absolute evil. These characters are not "bewitched" or "possessed" as were some of their predecessors in previous stories; they are single-mindedly obsessed by a given passion, the consequences of which they are destined to play out to a logical extreme. The equation of passion with satanism could hardly be clearer, yet occult forces do not intervene in human affairs; the pomps and works of Satan originate in the human soul. The meaning is clear: in the human heart reside potentialities which can best be described as "diabolical" and which find full expression in paroxysms of passion.

Armand B. Chartier, in his Barbey d'Aurevilly, *1977.*

Charles Bernheimer (essay date 1989)

SOURCE: "Barbey's Dandy Narratives," in *Figures of Ill Repute: Representing Prostitution in Nineteenth-Century France.* Cambridge, Mass.: Harvard University Press, 1989, pp. 69-88.

[*Bernheimer is an American educator and critic. In the following excerpt, he examines Barbey's conceptions of dandyism, gender roles, and sexuality as they relate to his narrative approach in "A Woman's Revenge" and "At a Dinner of Atheists."*]

The theory of dandyism was set forth in 1844 in a little book called *Du dandysme et de George Brummell* by Bau-

delaire's friend and admirer, Jules Barbey d'Aurevilly. One of the points of Barbey's essay is that a dandy should never allow himself to love, since loving entails becoming a slave to desire. George Brummell . . . escaped such slavery. His triumphs, notes Barbey, "had the insolence of disinterestedness." He always stopped with women "at the limit of gallantry," keeping them under his intellectual dominion by nullifying their sexual attraction. The dandy is the sovereign creation of his own "instantly mobile" intelligence; he is "intellectual even in the kind of beauty he possessed." His manner is saturated with irony, giving him "the look of a sphinx, which fascinates like a mystery and disturbs like a danger." Fascination and danger of the sphinx's ambiguous sexuality: the crouching lion's body is furnished with a male head in Egyptian mythology, a female one in Greek mythology. The dandy has the ability to synthesize the signs of sexual difference in the artifice of his self-creation. Dandies, writes Barbey, are "double and multiple natures, of an undecidable intellectual sex [*d'un sexe intellectuel indécis*], in whom grace is still more graceful as strength and strength appears again as grace."

Dandyism understood in these terms functions both as thematic focus and narrative principle in a number of the stories Barbey collected under the title *Les Diaboliques* (published in 1874, though many of the stories were written much earlier; exact dates are uncertain). Two of these stories, **"La vengeance d'une femme"** (probably written last, around 1870-71) and **"A un dîner d'athées"** (possibly 1867-68) are of particular interest to us since they dramatically cast the dandy's figuration of gender instability against the prostitute's disfiguring sexual animality. The crucial context for this drama, which the analysis of a short fictional form will allow us to trace in some detail, is the question Roland Barthes has identified as central to any narrative act: "Against what can the story be exchanged? What is the 'value' of the story?"

The narrator's remarks introducing **"La vengeance d'une femme"** suggest that the value of the story we are about to read derives from its true reflection of a historical moment of "extreme civilization," when crime has attained "a superior level of intellectuality." Far more sophisticated in their refinement and corruption than the crudely materialistic and sensual crimes of earlier times, modern criminal acts "speak more to the mind," letting no blood flow and massacring only "in the order of feelings and manners." The reader of *Du dandysme* identifies these acts of intelligent and original cruelty as belonging to the hypercivilized domain of dandyism. Indeed, the dandy's irony is almost criminal in its cutting genius, and his autocratic power derives from his callous divorce from passion and sensuality. Thus, the narrator of **"La vengeance"** is claiming that the true story he is about to tell involves a crime committed under the modern aegis of the dandy's sensibility and, by extension, he implies that what has been added to that truth, his own "manner of telling it," is of value to the extent that it shares the same modernity.

Robert de Tressignies, the hero of **"La vengeance d'une femme,"** is a "highly intellectualized" dandy who imagines that he has "reflected enough on his sensations so that he could never be their dupe." He has used this confidence in his perfect self-control to take a step from which Brummell held back: he has become a libertine who is expertly acquainted with "the female animal in all the varieties of her species and race." At the outset of the story, his curiosity is piqued by an unusually attractive prostitute he has observed promenading provocatively up and down the boulevard and he decides to follow her, more to find out what might explain such a beautiful woman's being "a whore of the lowest rank" than to fulfill his skeptical, overindulged lust. Moreover, and psychologically this appears as the determining motive in Tressignies's curiosity, "this woman bore a resemblance for him." He is following the trail of "another woman, seen elsewhere"—the suggestion of an unconscious maternal image will be confirmed later—but the trail takes him into so ugly and vile a neighborhood that he hesitates to enter "this black hole." Subsequently he penetrates a narrow, filthy alleyway and mounts a damp, slimy spiral staircase. Here a fantasized geography of degraded female genitalia is superimposed on an evocation of the corrupt, dirty, ruinous old Paris from which Eugène Sue had saved his heroine Fleur-de-Marie. Tressignies, however, allows himself to be seduced by the artfully presented sensual attractions of the prostitute, with whom intercourse is so terrifyingly intense that he loses his reflexive defensiveness and forgets everything. Her body is an abyss that sucks his soul into it ("Positively, she drew off the soul that was his into the body that was hers"), though his vanity is such that he interprets this castrating loss as a gain, imagining that he has inspired her with a passion greater than she has experienced with any other man.

But then Tressignies suddenly realizes that his partner, in the midst of sexual intimacy, has been absorbed in the contemplation of a man's portrait on her bracelet. Just when he is indulging the romance of his exceptional amorous prowess, he is confronted with the humiliating realization that he is at best a stand-in. His oedipal reading of the situation casts him in a substitute role similar to the one the intriguingly resemblant whore has played in his own fantasy. He angrily imagines "that he *was posing for another*—that he was there on another's account," which does indeed turn out to be the case but in a much more sophisticated scenario than Tressignies's banal triangular script.

The duchess of Sierra Leone now reveals her identity, which confirms the likeness Tressignies sensed from the outset. He had seen the great Spanish duchess only a few years earlier at the height of her prestige, admired her at a distance and dreamed of her thereafter, even loved her in fantasy. That such a fantasy was suffused with admiration for the pure, asexual mother becomes clear in Tressignies's response to the duchess's revelation: he divorces her entirely from the whore he has purchased and is horrified at the idea of touching her body. It is as if the incest taboo had suddenly taken effect, with a most interesting consequence. The duchess's remarkable beauty no longer attracts Tressignies. All he desires now is her story, and that desire is murderous: "He looked at her as if he wanted to witness the dissection of her cadaver. Was she going to revive it for him?" The cadaver is no doubt that of the whore who was "annihilated" in Tressignies's fantasy when the duchess "emerged through her." He attributes to the maternal figure the task of reviving the sexualized, passionately desiring woman as a pure figure of narration. The cadaver of the prostitute will make the mother's story available, so the dandy hopes, in terms that present her degraded sexuality as a fictional invention.

But as the duchess unveils her story, Tressignies realizes that its telling is part of a discourse addressed to a paternal figure and that his desire for narrative has been stimulated only to assist in the communication of that discourse. The duchess now acknowledges Tressignies's exceptional status among her clients, but that recognition has nothing to do with his merits as a lover. It is entirely a function of his suitability, given his having witnessed her earlier existence, to believe a story other clients had dismissed as mad fabulation and to assume a role in disseminating its subversive desire. That destructive rage is directed less against her hated husband's body than against his name, the symbol of the family honor, which is all he really cares about. The duchess's masochistic strategy of revenge is to degrade herself to the level of *fille publique* so as to drag her husband's nominal heritage "in the most vile filth, . . . in refuse, in excrement." She hopes that the story of her shameful debasement will reach the duke through one of her lovers, but, if not, she is counting on her dead body, putrefied with venereal disease, to tell the story of her prostitution. By using her body as a common place of male desire, the duchess is turning the possessive privilege inherent in the father's name against the patriarchal order that name sustains.

Her strategy shows her to be more than Tressignies's match in the intellectual mastery of sensual experience. Indeed, the blasé dandy has been entirely her dupe. Not only has she caused him to lose all self-control in the abyss of her sensuality, she has staged that sensuality as a role in her private play of representations. Tressignies's phallus has been for nothing in her purely ideal pleasure. It was valuable to her only insofar as the could imagine it as seen by the duke's eyes in the portrait on her bracelet. "His image excites my transport," she tells the man whom those transports had, a moment earlier, carried out of himself. The duke's image serves as a sadistic phallus in a masochistic scenario that puts sexuality entirely in the service of the imaginary: "I drove that execrable image into my eyes and into my heart so as to be more pliant under you when you held me." The prostitute, the duchess implies, was a cadaver from the outset. Performing the passionate body's revival, the duchess invents the harlot's sexuality as fiction. But the plot of her revenge drama blocks Tressignies's fantasy of appropriating that fictionality. Not only was her performance put on for another, but the divorce from the sexualized body that it entails has already been dedicated to a second Other's love.

The second Other is Don Esteban, the duke's cousin, with whom the duchess fell in love after some years of unhappy marriage. Their chaste, innocent, sublimated love was a positive version of the imaginary, visual relationship that later binds the duchess in hatred to her husband. The duke came upon the lovers, the duchess recounts, "as we always were, as we spent our life since our love began, tête-à-tête, united only through our eyes, he at my feet as if before the

Virgin Mary, in such profound contemplation that we needed no caresses." This scene, conventional though it may be, fulfills a central fantasy in this text, repeated in Tressignies's perception that the duchess, in telling her story, has "completely effaced the whore, . . . become chaste, [with a bosom] of virginal roundness and firmness." The fantasy is of a preoedipal union modeled on the infant's relation to the nurturant mother. It requires that any incestuous implications be sublimated ("never did Esteban's lips touch mine," declares the duchess) so that a fusion can be imagined that dissolves sexual difference ("We were melted into one another").

Oedipal violence breaks up this "chivalric, romantic" love, however, when the duke takes his brutal revenge by ordering Esteban murdered and his love organ cut out and fed to the dogs. That this organ is the heart rather than the penis is not only a function of literary decorum. The duke had no reason to believe that sexual relations had been consummated between his cousin and his wife. He wanted to degrade the symbolic meaning of the heart by treating the organ as meat. The duchess adopts the same strategy for her counter-revenge: she treats her body as sexual meat, repeatedly consumed by brutes, in order to attack the only symbolic value the duke cherishes, his name, the source of the patriarchal narrative of generational continuity with which he entirely identifies. The prostituted body thus becomes the literalized, reified body, the body that defeats symbolic recuperation by its sheer dead weight.

Tressignies's goal is to reverse this defeat and revive prostitution within a symbolic structure. "By throwing her story between the two of them, [the duchess] had cut, as if with an axe, the momentary bonds of intimacy they had just formed." The story castrates the sexual relation of bodies, but is itself independent of that sexuality. Tressignies now takes advantage of this independence to hoard the story for himself, instead of repeating it as the duchess has requested. Thus, he extricates himself from the oedipal scenario of the duchess's revenge. His attitude toward the narrative, cloistering himself in his room "tête-à-tête" with his memories of the evening, "sealing the story up in the most mysterious corner of his being," suggests that he is trying to recreate with the story a relationship not unlike Esteban's with the duchess. Instead of her eyes, which Esteban had contemplated in rapture, the duchess's story is Tressignies's object of absorbed fascination. He feels himself narcissistically identified with the story, as if its energy alone constituted his interiority: "Thus, he spent hours, leaning against the armrests of his easychair, dreamily turning over within himself the open pages of this hideously powerful poem." It appears that Tressignies has successfully transformed the duchess's promiscuous sexual availability into her narrative availability, as a nurturing maternal source, "strange and all-powerful," to him alone.

One fear still troubles Tressignies, however: the duchess's story could once again function as an axe, this time to divide him from itself. Her prostituted body remains open to others and its promiscuous activity could make available to those others the story he now considers his own.

Thus, when Tressignies emerges from his period of hermetic intimacy with the duchess's story, "he never encountered one of his friends without the fear of hearing him tell, as having happened to him, the adventure that was his own." This fear of oedipal rivalry appears to be the cause of Tressignies's subsequent physical degeneration—he shows no interest in women, loses the dandy's formidable social skills, and finally appears quite sickly—as if by refusing the life of the body he could come closer to the sublimated life of narrative. His sudden disappearance from Paris, "as if through a hole," radicalizes this movement to cancel his physical presence.

But Barbey's story does not end there. Its concluding episode puts the fantasmatic structure of the narrative entirely into the service of Tressignies's regressive desire. He returns to Paris after a year's absence and, at a swank dinner party, witnesses the first public revelation of the duchess's prostitution: a newspaper notice announcing her burial as a common whore is read to the scandalized assembly. Her story of revenge, however, is not yet known, and Tressignies does not tell it. Instead he visits the church of the Salpêtrière hospital where the duchess was buried and requests information from a priest about her final illness. He learns that she had indeed contracted the venereal disease she had wished for and that her body had rotted with decay. The text pays special attention to the gruesome fate of her eyes: one eye had popped out of its socket and fallen at her feet while the other had liquefied and melted. The imagery of castration is evident here and relates specifically to the metaphorical sense in which the duchess's soul was in her eyes. Her love for Esteban had been a communion of souls through the spiritual path of visual contemplation. She had expressed her hatred of the duke by contemplating his portrait imagined as the voyeuristic witness to her prostitution. Now Tressignies alone hears the details that reduce the duchess's eyes to merely physical organs, ripped out of her face by self-inflicted disease. Although it is likely that the story of the duchess's prostitution will eventually reach the duke, at the end of Barbey's narrative this communication has not yet occurred and Tressignies has taken the duke's place. It is he, rather than the mutilator of Esteban, who receives the duchess's posthumous message of her self-mutilation. Thereby he takes imaginary possession of her revenge, of the reified body she had imagined to be symbolically irrecuperable. And the text sustains the fantasy that he turns that revenge against the duchess, drawing her soul into his body.

"La vengeance d'une femme," which is really that of a man, ends with Tressignies exulting in his privileged knowledge of the duchess's plot. He considers himself the only reader qualified to establish the truth of the text she has left behind. Whereas the deluded priest believes that humility prompted her to want the word "repentie" removed from the phrase "fille repentie" in her epitaph, Tressignies's command of her narrative enables him to read this gesture as a final refinement in her masochistic scenario of revenge. The duchess's masochism, which transforms her sexuality into a pleasure-denying instrument of her death drive, now appears to correspond perfectly to Tressignies's sadism. He has succeeded in appropriating her story so that it works fantasmatically to fulfill the dandy's unconscious desire, the repression of female sexuality, and to degrade that sexuality to the point where its castrating power is made to turn against itself. Tressignies gets his wish: he dissects the prostitute's cadaver and is reborn in function of its revival as fiction. This, I think, is the meaning of his departure from and return to Paris: he is revived narratively in terms of an imagined defeat of all oedipal rivals and a fantasized identification with the soul-meaning of the duchess's plot, the dissolution of sexual difference in union with the chaste and virginal mother.

A similar narrative and psychological structure is discernible in **"A un dîner d'athéss."** The main story is introduced by its narrator, Mesnilgrand, after a lengthy description of the society of erstwhile soldiers and officers of Napoleon's army now living in a provincial town, of which the proud, aristocratic Mesnilgrand is the acknowledged leader. The active life of these men is essentially over. The present exists for them as a vehicle to narrate the past, to tell its romantic and heroic story, and thereby to forget the banality of contemporary existence. Mesnilgrand stands out as forcefully in this narrative enterprise as he had once on the field of battle. His eloquence is so extraordinarily intense that it strikes his listeners with a physical impact. Mesnilgrand has transformed his life entirely in the service of representation. After a few initial forays into the local salons, this once passionate lover of women has retired from the social scene, although he continues to dress with the most tasteful elegance, his dandyism having "outlived this defunct, buried life." He spends his days at an occupation as far removed from war as possible, namely landscape painting, and his somewhat dated patrician appearance actually makes him resemble "a walking portrait."

When Mesnilgrand finally tells his story, it becomes apparent that his "transfiguration" from soldier to artistic creator and creation was a response not so much to the loss of his military identity as to the loss of his sexual identity. As in **"La vengeance d'une femme,"** the crucial confrontation here is with a prostitute figure. Unlike the duchess of Sierra Leone, however, Rosalba is not a whore who, subsequent to intercourse, reveals herself to be a mother, but a woman who, even in the midst of the sexual act, is simultaneously mother and whore. Mesnilgrand dwells on this paradox. Rosalba, mistress of a certain captain Ydow, provokes the entire regiment through "the diabolical construction of her being . . . that made her the most madly passionate of courtesans, with the appearance of one of the most celestial madonnas of Raphaël." Happily she satisfies the desire she invites and sleeps with the whole officer corps, maintaining all the while the blushing virginal modesty that makes her given name, with its suggestion of combined red and white, seem allegorical and that earns her the nickname "La Pudica."

Mesnilgrand has his turn with Rosalba, thereby becoming one in a series of Others for whom she remains the same (the regimental view of her position stresses the logic of substitution: "Since she had given herself to [Ydow], she could just as well give herself to another and, why not, everyone could be that other!"). But he experiences his otherness to her, the principle of her sexual openness, as a castrating refusal of his desire. Like Tressignies, who momentarily imagines himself exceptional, Mesnilgrand wants Rosalba to admit to loving him, even though he has no love for her "in the elevated and romantic sense that people give to this word, myself first among them." She, however, refuses to romanticize their affair, to give him any kind of linguistic privilege over her sexuality, to narrativize her body. Physically penetrated, she remains "impenetrable like the sphinx." Stories are circulated about her among her lovers, but "she gave no hold over her openly through her conduct." Her body, which Mesnilgrand calls "her only soul," remains outside any narrative plot.

Although the duchess of Sierra Leone's soul is dramatically not in her body and her deep sensuality is an act whereas Rosalba's is real, the psychological function of sensuality is not dissimilar for the two women. What the male imagines to be his act of taking possession ensures the female's self-possession. The gift of her body, offered in apparently total abandon, turns out to be a gift to herself, of which the male is the easily replaceable vehicle. She denies love at the very moment when sexual delight seems to be its manifest sign. Thus the female body, as apprehended in the male fantasy structure of these two stories, becomes most unreadable when it is physically most open. . . . The more fully the prostitute satisfies male desire, the more completely she destroys the psychological dimension of that satisfaction, that is, its insertion into the male plot of conquest and control. Intercourse with Rosalba, according to Mesnilgrand, denies the very temporality of male experience: "One was always at the beginning with her, even after the conclusion . . . Language dissolves in attempting to express this."

The climax of Mesnilgrand's story, however, dramatizes the dependence of narrative on precisely the erotic female body that it cannot express. Out of what he calls "moral disgust," Mesnilgrand dissociates himself from the castrating Rosalba, "a sphinx that devoured pleasure silently and kept its secret." Just as the duchess absorbed Tressignies's soul into her body, so Rosalba threatens Mesnilgrand with the dissolution of his spiritual superiority. He recaptures his virile strength by abandoning desire and becoming "very calm and very indifferent with all women." Nonetheless, one evening he responds to the renewed call of the flesh and returns to see—that is, to make love to—Rosalba. In the unconscious structure of the story, it seems as if the violent act of sexual revenge that interrupts his erotic encounter actually fulfills his deepest wish. Surprised by the unexpected appearance of Ydow, Rosalba hides Mesnilgrand in a closet, from whose dark, protected space he overhears Ydow verbally abusing her. Ydow is in a jealous rage over a letter of assignation he has found unaddressed on her table and wants to know who the intended recipient is. She refuses to name her lover and goes on to further provoke the captain by declaring that she has never loved him.

Thus far the scene repeats Mesnilgrand's emasculating experience with Rosalba, her insistence on the substitutability of her sex partners, and her denial of romantic feeling. But now she goes a step further to mock the entire symbolic order of male authority associated with the name of the father. She denies that Ydow was the father of her son, who died a few months after birth, lists all the men who could potentially have claimed paternity, and then suddenly names as the actual father the other man in the room, Mesnilgrand, "the only man whom I have ever loved, whom I have ever idolized." Mesnilgrand knows this romantic assertion to be a fiction and hence cannot but doubt his alleged paternity, although his name pronounced in this context "struck him like a shot through [his] closet." Thus, Rosalba repudiates that most cherished of male stories, the history of generations, and, on the basis of the impenetrable interiority of her body, unmans both Ydow, who wants to believe himself the father, and Mesnilgrand, who does not.

Earlier in the story Mesnilgrand had already reflected that "what is most horrible about shared love affairs . . . is the terrible anxiety that prevents you from listening to the voice of nature, stifling it in a doubt that is impossible to dismiss." The voice Mesnilgrand considers natural speaks to a man of his right to possess a woman, control her sexuality, and inscribe her in his genealogical story. By placing her body outside this patriarchal scheme, Rosalba throws the scheme into confusion: paternity becomes a mere fiction, a matter of arbitrary naming. Here, as in **"La vengeance,"** the prostitute figure generates narrative precisely by asserting her independence of it. The father's nomination is her prerogative, which "is impossible to dismiss."

But Barbey cannot allow the subversive power of female fictionalizing to determine the outcome of his narrative. Rosalba's open sexuality must be sealed up so that Mesnilgrand's anxiety can be calmed and he can take possession of her story. By pouring hot wax into his mistress's sexual organs, Ydow is fulfilling both his own and Mesnilgrand's vengeful impulses. Thus, it is no accident that Mesnilgrand bursts out of his closet only *after* the mutilated Rosalba has emitted a cry so wild that it seemed to come out of "the vulva of a she-wolf." This startling phrase suggests that Rosalba's sexuality is bestial and predatory and thus warrants extermination. Mesnilgrand, however, cannot accept his implication in Ydow's act and runs him through the back with a sword. Just at this point, thankfully, a call to arms sounds and the heroic violence of the battlefield displaces and veils the far more troubling arena of sexual violation.

Mesnilgrand never hears of Rosalba again—she is as good as dead, having been rejected from the narrative—but he has taken with him the heart of the child she called his. This heart, lovingly embalmed by Ydow when he thought he was the child's father, served, hideously, as a projectile in his fight with Rosalba. Its fate relates the end of the story to its beginning. After years of carrying the heart around with him like a relic, Mesnilgrand decides to give it to a priest. This accounts for his having been in the church where a scandalized fellow soldier-atheist, Rançonnet, glimpsed him in the text's opening scene. Mesnilgrand's story is a response to Rançonnet's demand to know what he was doing in this religious haunt.

One psychoanalytic interpretation of this ending, offered by Jacques Petit [in *Essais de lectures des "Diaboliques" de Barbey Aurevilly,* 1974], is that Mesnilgrand is returning the phallus (the child's heart) to a maternal refuge (the church). This analysis, however, needs to be nuanced, especially in regard to Petit's conclusion that Mesnilgrand is hereby accepting his own castration. The heart, for Mesnilgrand, is associated above all with anxiety about the potentially fictional status of paternity. He refers to it as "this child's heart about which I had doubts." Earlier he had reflected that uncertainty about the patriarchal status of the phallus in determining the order of nature could drive a man mad: "If you were to think long about that [the shameful partition to which you have ignobly submitted], being big-hearted [*quand on a du coeur*], you would go mad." "Quand on a du coeur" . . . Clearly it is to this metaphorical meaning of "having the heart" that the child's actual organ must be assimilated if the madness generated by the impenetrable abyss of female sexuality is to be controlled. "Heart" in this sense corresponds to Mesnilgrand's "elevated and romantic" interpretation of love. Religion for him has this same romanticizing function of metaphorical elevation. To deposit the child's heart with the church thus is to elevate the whole question of the uncertain origin of paternal authority into the sphere of imaginary representation. Only in this sphere can the priest to whom Mesnilgrand hands over the "indistinguishable object" be called "my father." The father's nomination becomes a male prerogative once the sexual basis of paternity has been eliminated.

In this scene of symbolic restitution, the phallus, veiled, indiscernible, is returned to the father, in name only, whose place is inside the darkened body of the maternal church, itself associated with death. ("At that hour of the day, one feels very strongly that the Christian religion is the daughter of the catacombs"). Physical presence is dissolved in a proliferation of symbolic substitutes. The maternal space, which provides the story's narrative frame, is protective precisely insofar as it sublimates the body and fictionalizes the whole issue of sexual differentiation. The worshippers in the church are described as "souls" rather than as men and women. In the "ghostly twilight" of this edifice, "it was possible to see one another uncertainly and indistinctly, but it was impossible to recognize anyone." This is not the doubt generated by sexual anxiety, but a reassuring confusion that allows sexual difference to be hidden by a veil of uncertainty.

In the unfolding of the *récit,* the description of the church precedes the description of Mesnilgrand's post-Napoleonic life style. In effect, the one appears to derive from the other. Mesnilgrand, who was struck by "the almost tomb-like aspect of the church," at present "asks nothing more of life." In his roles as painter, storyteller, and dandy, he has made life over as representation, image, artifice: "One felt that the artist had passed through the soldier and transfigured him." His having apparently renounced all sexual activity does indeed suggest an acceptance of castration. But his dandyism is more accurately understood as a way of putting the fixity of sexual identity in doubt. We remember that Barbey thought of dandies as having "double and multiple natures, of an undecidable intellectual sex," combining strength with grace. Dandyism multiplies, intellectualizes, and transfigures nature, in particular prostituted female nature. This transfiguration constitutes the essential principle of narrative closure in both the stories we have examined. The artistic transfiguration of Mesnilgrand's soldiership is evident in the way he tells his story, as if he were directing a battle: "Stay in the ranks," he tells Rançonnet. "Let me maneuver my story as I see fit." Mesnilgrand identifies with "the adventure that was his" as intimately as Tressignies does with the story he makes his. In both cases, this identification eliminates the threat that the sexualized female will control the name of the father and thus authorize the story of generations. The goal of Mesnilgrand's narrative maneuvering is a victory over the sexual determinants of the story's violence, through a return of the emblem of doubtful paternity to a symbolic space that eliminates the sexual basis of fatherhood. This return corresponds, I think, to the "one-ness" Baudelaire considers the glory of the man of genius, who has no need to "forget his ego in external flesh" and whose dandified cult of himself allows him to survive all illusions. Barbey's stories suggest the maternal fantasy underlying Baudelaire's insistence on oneness as the basis of a poetic "prostitution of the soul." By emptying sexuality of its physical reference, these stories sustain the fantasy that their narrators have survived their search for happiness in the sexual Other, embodied in the prostitute, and have achieved union with the generative principle of their own narrative activity. This principle is embodied in the dandy, but only in the sense that the dandy's embodiment is a transfiguring disembodiment, of undecidable sex, created in imaginary union with the mother's transformative powers.

A traditional psychoanalytic interpretation would have no trouble finding the "source" in Barbey's biography of the narrative patterns I have traced here. His need for maternal protection can be seen as a response to the coldness his actual mother displayed in his childhood, and his masochistic fascination with the dominating, masculinized female can be shown to have the same origin, via a reversal typical of the psyche ("Maternal love is the castrator of the other love," he [wrote in *Disjecta membra*]). His hostility toward the father, representative of the sexually active male, can be traced back to an unresolved Oedipus complex (which, inversely, also leads him to desire a powerful authority worthy of his rebellion). But a reading along these lines, however fruitful, would focus attention on the eccentricities of individual neurotic symptomatology, whereas what is most remarkable about Barbey's narrative strategies is the degree to which the fantasies they encode are shared by male artists and writers in France in the second half of the nineteenth century.

The prostitute is a key figure in these fantasies. She is imagined as animalistic, intense, a sensual feast for the blasé upper-class male. But almost immediately her sexuality becomes threatening. She is somehow impenetrable even as she gives herself to be penetrated, opaque just when she should be most readable. She asserts her independence of the male plot at the very moment when the male thinks he is inscribing her body into it. This assertion, which stimulates narratively productive castration fears, becomes the object of complex strategies designed to put these fears to rest and achieve narrative closure. One of the most powerful of these strategies is the rhetori-

cal fictionalization of sexual difference. Domination is thus acquired not by the assertion of power within a binary structure but by the destabilization of that structure and its assimilation into the sphere of male artistic invention, where the body becomes "d'un sexe intellectuel indécis." Barbey's texts reveal one of the primary motives for this intellectualization of sexual difference: male anxiety about woman's prerogative to designate paternity and thereby determine genealogy and patronymic lineage. This anxiety inspires a revision of the traditional plot that subverts its biological basis (associated with devastating female sexual power) and that makes of paternity a dandy fiction whose transfigurations inscribe fantasies of maternal union. This revised plot is "something modern that derives from altogether new causes," as Baudelaire wrote of dandyism in 1846.

On the setting of Barbey's fiction:

"The little town of $+++$" is the trite, almost insufferable device exploited by d'Aurevilly to designate some obscure locale, usually in the Cotentin peninsula of his native Normandy. It regularly appears in his works that to give the true name of a town would be an act of daring comparable only to total disrobing in public. The striptease, however, is another matter. Nothing delights him more in his descriptions of locale than to carry suggestion almost, but not quite, to the point of certain identity. Thus in his view of Valognes, which serves as a setting for the **"Dessous de cartes d'une partie de whist"** (**"Behind the Scenes at a Whist Game"**), Barbey paints a town which, he tells us, shall remain nameless (i. e. properly draped); but he at once adds that, after a certain detail he is about to supply, we shall have no trouble recognizing the spot (read: "seeing through the flimsy clothes").

Will L. McLendon, in "Isolation and Ostracism in the Works of Barbey d'Aurevilly," Forum, Vol. 8, No. 1, Fall-Winter, 1970.

Charles J. Stivale   (essay date 1991)

SOURCE: " 'Like the Sculptor's Chisel': Voices 'On' and 'Off' in Barbey d'Aurevilly's *Les Diaboliques,*" in *The Romanic Review,* Vol. LXXXII, No. 3, May, 1991, pp. 317-30.

[*In the following essay, Stivale explores the tension between the framing and imbedded narratives in* The Diaboliques, *focusing especially on the story "The Crimson Curtain."*]

In several persuasive treatises on the novel, Mikhail Bakhtin/V. N. Volosinov have insisted on the need for a dialogic understanding of novelistic prose, and this necessity is perhaps nowhere more acute than in studies on the fiction of the nineteenth-century French novelist, Barbey d'Aurevilly. To consider only the six tales of **Les Diaboliques** (1874), I am interested in examining how their predominant narrative and thematic tensions intersect to produce the dialogical tug-of-war of voices which characterize these texts. Bakhtin calls this the "dialogic interaction with an alien word" which not only is in the object, "a focal point for heteroglot voices among which [the writer's] own must also sound" [*The Dialogic Imagination,* translated by Caryl Emerson and Michael Holquist]. This interaction is also "directed toward an *answer* and cannot escape the profound influence of the answering word that it anticipates" and gives rise to an active, "responsive understanding." Such understanding, says Bakhtin, "establishes a series of complex interrelationships, consonances and dissonances with the word and enriches it with new elements." By studying the directions and misdirections prevalent in these tales from the perspective of narrative voice and its dialogization, I wish to respond to two sets of questions raised in these tales regarding two sets of textual and intertextual processes: on one hand, the interplay of narrative levels and modes of focalization with thematic and discursive strategies in Barbey's work, and on the other hand, the relationship that this narrative interplay suggests for developing a "feminist dialogics" [a term coined by Dale M. Bauer in his *Feminist Dialogics,* 1988].

The first set of questions concerns the primary focus of *Les Diaboliques* in terms of the relationship between the "central" *histoire* and the "marginal" *discours*: do the multi-tiered framing devices for the conversational "ricochets" in these tales serve, as some critics maintain, to direct the reader's attention primarily to each text's seemingly all-important framed *histoire,* to the exclusion of the bothersome, even irritating framing dialogues and digressions? Do these tales constitute, as other critics insist, either a synthetic totality or the subversion, even the destruction, of the *histoire* by "marginal," yet primary, textual effects? These different modes of reading, that we can characterize respectively, following Timothy Unwin ["Barbey d'Aurevilly conteur: Discours et narration dans *Les Diaboliques,*" *Neophilologus* 72, No. 3 (1988)], as "linear," "synthetic" and "peripheral," recall what Bakhtin has identified as the centripetal force of language, tending toward the constitution of a unitary language which is opposed to "the realities of heteroglossia." Unwin concludes that "dans cette tension, cette contradiction" between opposing readings to which these tales give rise, "se trouve peut-être la véritable originalité des *Diaboliques,* car elles renvoient sans cesse à la problématique de l'écriture." From this perspective, certain critics have emphasized the importance of understanding the dialogic unfolding of Barbey's tales in terms of the dynamic relationship between the tales' apparent "peripheries" and "central" *histoires.* Similarly, Bakhtin develops this very emphasis by noting that the centrifugal forces of language, i. e. those of dialogized heteroglossia, carry on their uninterrupted work of "decentralization and disunification" alongside the centripetal forces. Furthermore, says Bakhtin, "the framing context, *like the sculptor's chisel,* hews out the rough outlines of someone else's speech, and carries the image of language out of the raw empirical data of speech life" (my emphasis). In this way, the dialogic perspective insists on the text's inherent socio-ideological tension created by the dynamic interplay between narrative border and center, and I will argue that it is through a "responsive understanding" of such interplay and tensions initiat-

ed within the framing context that the double-voiced relationships in *Les Diaboliques* can be best examined.

At this point, however, another question arises regarding the relationship between text and reader in conceptualizing "dialogics" from a feminist perspective. Using Bakhtin's terms, how does the narrative "object," or story, of *Les Diaboliques* maintain a constant tension in regards to the multiple "answering word" manifested not only as textualized interlocutors and narrators of each tale, but also as reader? I follow recent feminist and narratological studies in maintaining that the reader's understanding of the dialogical interaction depends on a dual process of critical resistance. This dual process confronts the author's narrational ploys that draw from the centripetal forces of language to facilitate a primarily unitary reading (be it "linear," "synthetic" or "peripheral"), and simultaneously appreciates the narrative and socio-ideological constructions developed in these anecdotal dialogues through the textual interplay of conflicting forces of voices "on" and "off." In this respect, recent studies that develop "feminist dialogics" aim precisely at enabling the reader to find "a space of resistance in interpretive communities" [Bauer, *Feminist Dialogics*]. However, as Laurie Finke argues persuasively [in "The Rhetoric of Marginality: Why I Do Feminist Theory," *Tulsa Studies in Women's Literature* 5, No. 2 (Fall 1986)], feminist literary criticism must "enable us to create a position from which we can, as a first step, deconstruct—subvert—the hierarchical center/margin dichotomy," a provisional position "always subject to revision based on the shifting relations between centers and margins of social and critical discourse." As Finke suggests, Bakhtin offers an extremely useful distinction not only for encouraging "creative misreading," but also to enhance our own critical understanding of the dialogical struggle in Barbey's fiction. For, as Bakhtin proposes, *authoritative discourse* and *internally persuasive discourse* may be conceived as forms by which another's discourse strives "to determine the very bases of our ideological interrelations with the world." On one hand, authoritative discourse is, quite simply, "the word of the fathers. Its authority was already *acknowledged* in the past," remaining "sharply demarcated" from other types of discourse. Furthermore, Bakhtin maintains that authoritative discourse's very "inertia," "semantic finiteness and calcification . . . the impermissibility of any free stylistic development in relation to it," all contribute to rendering "the artistic representation of authoritative discourse impossible," its role in the novel being "insignificant" and "incapable of being double-voiced."

Internally persuasive discourse, on the other hand, would presumably be the word of the mothers, and its characteristics seem to support this since it is "denied all privilege, backed by no authority at all, and is frequently not even acknowledged in society." When we acknowledge and assimilate such discourse, Bakhtin argues, it is "tightly interwoven with 'one's own word'," that is, "not so much interpreted by us as it is further, that is, freely, developed, applied to new material, new conditions," entering into "interanimating relationships with new contexts." Furthermore, internally persuasive discourse "enters into an intense interaction, a *struggle* with other internally persuasive discourses," such as the ongoing and constant "struggle within each of us which constitutes our ideological development." Finally, the inherent resistance to such a discourse is the "soil," says Bakhtin, in which "novelistic images, profoundly double-voiced and double-languaged, are born" in that they "seek to objectivize the struggle with all types of internally persuasive alien discourse that had at one time held sway over the author."

Without wishing to follow this line of theorizing in the psychologizing direction that it suggests, I believe that these discursive categories can be usefully deployed by understanding their definitions in a dynamic rather than static way as means of emphasizing the constant dialogic and productive interaction which they entail. Like Barthes's *écriture scriptible* and *plurielle,* which is an ideal category rarely, if ever, attained in literature, both the authoritative and the internally persuasive discourses constitute extremes on an ideal polyphonic spectrum that are actualized in prose in "parsimonious" form. That is, just as "our ideological development," says Bakhtin, "is just such an intense struggle within us for hegemony among various available and verbal points of view," these discourses are locked in ongoing dialogical struggle, each yielding some of the absolute traits in the direction of the other when actualized. Such a productive tension can help us better to discern the narrative interplay at work in all texts, and especially in the tales of *Les Diaboliques,* as strategies of "narrative desire" functioning via diverse textual strategies and thus as much between author and text as between text and reader. I wish to argue that in this contest for authority and persuasion from which "novelistic images . . . are born" [Bakhtin], neither discursive category necessarily "wins" or ultimately dominates these tales, but rather are kept in a state of precarious movement and of curious ambiguity due to the double-voiced nature of their dialogic enunciation. I propose therefore to examine the polyphonic ambiguity and tension in the opening tale of *Les Diaboliques,* "Le Rideau cramoisi," and then to develop in the final section the discursive variations of sexual and textual difference that occur in the five other tales as manifestations of their constitutive, double-voiced oscillation.

In the opening tale, the anonymous, homodiegetic narrator encounters a fellow passenger, the vicomte de Brassard, in a coach while crossing Normandy, and when the coach is forced to halt that night for repairs in a Norman village that the vicomte clearly knows well, the narrator coaxes him to relate the tale of his earlier stay there. The vicomte's tale thus forms the embedded narrative, the voice "on," that constitutes the focus of the diegetic development, i. e. the relations between the youthful vicomte, then only a lieutenant, and the daughter of his host family, the silent Mlle Albertine, known as Alberte, during his stay in their home, culminating in Alberte's apparent death-from-*jouissance* followed by the vicomte's strategic and rapid departure. The ponderous silence of Alberte is linked both to her audacity in initiating their physical relations in her parents' house and to her evident sexual enjoyment (at least as related by the somewhat bewildered vicomte), and these combined traits signal the supposedly "diabolical" nature of her demeanor. This is especially emphasized in the final moments of the vicomte's conver-

sation with the narrator as he notices "l'ombre svelte d'une taille de femme" passing before the crimson curtain he knew so well. As we shall see, that fleeting, final "diabolical" image, broken sharply by the driver's command for departure, "Roulez!," has not only thematic, but dialogical resonances for the voices "on" and "off".

What interests me particularly is the discursive displacement that becomes evident in the dialogic struggle during the tale. Prior to engaging the vicomte, the narrator clearly revels in his own ample verbiage, describing at length his travelling companion, particularly the distinctive characteristics of the vicomte's dandyism and military reputation as a willful captain who renounced his commission in 1830 rather than serve under the Orleanist rule. Once engaged in casual conversation with the vicomte, all of whose initial comments are related indirectly, the narrator continues to cherish his authoritative role, explaining that "un des avantages de la causerie en voiture, c'est qu'elle peut cesser quand on n'a plus rien à se dire, et cela sans embarras pour personne." By contrast, in a *salon,* "la politesse vous fait un devoir de parler," with the frequent result being punishment "de cette hypocrisie innocente par le vide et l'ennui de ces conversations" with idiots. Thus, through his control of narrative discourse, both of its quantity and its mode of focalization, the narrator asserts a decisive authority during the opening segment of the tale. But, once the vicomte echoes the narrator's own fascination with a particular anonymous window, by murmuring "comme s'il se parlait à lui-même, 'On dirait que c'est toujours le même rideau'!," the narrator, a self-proclaimed "chasseur d'histoires," rises to the occasion in order to elicit the vicomte's anecdote that would explain his apparently distracted remark.

We must ask, however, who is in fact the hunter and who is the prey, for the prefatory comments by the vicomte de Brassard are themselves quite enticing. The narrator's questioning reveals that 1) behind the vicomte's memory of the curtain dwells the memory of a woman, 2) that rather than having conquered her, it was the young, inexperienced vicomte who was conquered, and 3) that he fled at this defeat " 'quoique trop tard et . . . avec une peur à me faire comprendre la phrase du maréchal Ney . . . "Je voudrais bien savoir quel est le Jean-f . . . (il lâcha le mot tout au long) qui dit n'avoir jamais eu peur!" ' " This series of repartees, unbeknownst to the narrator, constitutes a verbal engagement which he apparently "wins" with his leading comment, " 'Une histoire dans laquelle vous avez eu cette sensation-là doit être femeusement intéressante, capitaine!' " But even as the vicomte assents to relate this event, it becomes clear that he will do so on and in his own terms, a narrative authority first manifested by his dramatic pause before beginning and by his strategic position in the dark corner of the coach, his face invisible, forcing the narrator, now the vicomte's audience, to focus "à sa voix seule, —aux moindres nuances de sa voix."

The subsequent tale can be read, then, as a dialogical struggle between voices "on" and "off," i. e. between the *raconteur* of the framed, focal tale and the now-displaced narrator. Yet, throughout the exchange, both interlocutors assert varying degrees of authoritative and internally persuasive discourses for mastery of the narrative situation. Since the vicomte has conquered the word, i. e. literally *pris la parole,* wrested it away from the narrator with his direct speech, he is able to assert throughout the ensuing narrative his own authoritative discourse, of both the soldier and the dandy, that contributes to what Jean-Pierre Boucher calls Barbey's "esthétique de la dissimulation et de la provocation" [*Les Diaboliques de Barbey d'Aurevilly,* 1976]. This authority remains parsimonious, however, in that it is shot through with the quite evident and insistent traits of the vicomte's internally persuasive discourse. For the reader (if not the listener) is struck by the terms in which the vicomte's own "defeat," quite literally at the hands of Alberte, is expressed since the crucial scene at the host family's dinner table reveals the vicomte's own vulnerability to surprise attack:

> Au moment où je déliais ma serviette sur mes genoux . . . je sentis une main qui prenait hardiment la mienne par-dessous la table . . . Je n'eus que l'incroyable sensation de cette main jusque sous ma serviette! . . . Tout mon sang, allumé sous cette prise, se précipita de mon coeur dans cette main . . . Je crus que j'allais m'évanouir, que j'allais me dissoudre dans l'indicible volupté causée par la chair tassée de cette main . . . Je fis un mouvement pour retirer ma main de cette folle main qui l'avait saisie, mais qui, me la serrant alors avec l'ascendant du plaisir qu'elle avait conscience de me verser, la garda d'autorité, vaincue comme ma volonté. . . .

In quoting this at length (and it continues for several more paragraphs, shifting the focus from the hand to the foot that Alberte rubs against the vicomte under the table), I present but a small sample of the obsessive emphasis which this dually discursive voice places both on the corporality and on the concomitant madness, and even monstrosity, of his female aggressor. This section of the vicomte's tale thus reveals a crucial juxtaposition of discourses: in contrast to the authoritative discourse so skillfully usurped from the narrator and then forcefully maintained, the quavering internally persuasive discourse emerges as the vicomte's mode of exposition and justification of the fear occasioned not simply by the increasingly "diabolical" actions of Alberte, but also by the displaced tumescence and attendant loss of authority.

As counterpoint to this interplay of discourses are the efforts of the voice "off," i. e. of the narrator's framing context, to express itself, and it is this struggle with the voice "on" that serves, like the "sculptor's chisel," to establish textual contour and nuance within the tale. For the narrator pointedly interrupts the vicomte, the first time "car son histoire me faisait l'effet de tourner un peu vite à une leste aventure de garnison," and in his own answering anecdote, the narrator appears to reassert the authority of the voice "on" by transmitting evidence of his own experience and *savoir-vivre.* Yet, as he breaks into the vicomte's story, the narrator's persuasive discourse emerges to undermine this very will to authority by admitting, in implicit apology to the listener/reader, that he has intruded without "[se] dout[er] de ce qui allait suivre." Nonetheless, intermittently throughout the tale's second half, the narrator attempts to usurp the *parole* of the vicomte who, in turn,

skillfully parries each verbal assault. For example, to the narrator's initial interruption, the vicomte responds "froidement," continuing quite smoothly, "mais laissez-moi vous achever [mon histoire]." To a coarse comment regarding Alberte's apparently easy virtue, the vicomte "reprit comme s'il n'avait pas entendu ma moqueuse observation." Later, despite the narrator's continuing attempts to establish his own authority by expressing impatience and incredulity with successive joking comments, his persuasive discourse again returns as he remarks to the listener/reader that his interventions are explicitly meant to make himself "ne pas paraître trop pris par son histoire, qui me prenait, car, avec les dandys, on n'a guère que la plaisanterie pour se faire un peu respecter." Furthermore, the narrator admits that he is willfully "contrariant" in attempting to match the vicomte's portrayal of Alberte's aplomb with a counterexample. But rather than humiliating the vicomte with an adroit comparison, the narrator is himself taken down a peg by the vicomte's intimate knowledge of details of this very counterexample, also allowing him not only to return deftly to his own story, but to introduce its final phase with a reference to the frightening dénouement.

Here, the "diabolical" elements of Alberte's final visit and subsequent death confront the authoritative discourse of the framed narration (i. e. the vicomte's skillful control of *la parole*) and thereby fortify the internally persuasive emphasis of the diegesis, i. e. the vicomte's exposition of the obsessive details of corporality and monstrosity, even of hallucination, that contribute to the loss of authority in his relations with Alberte. Moreover, this weakening is clearly contagious for once the vicomte completes his tale, "sa forte voix un peu brisée," the narrator "ne songeai[t] plus à plaisanter," and instead is forced to break the silence by asking, " 'Et après?' " The vicomte's explanation of how he was unable, and eventually unwilling, to confirm the suspected fate of Alberte after his rapid departure serves to clarify the ultimately persuasive point of his own tale, notably to justify the foundation of " 'cette peur que je ne voulais pas sentir une seconde fois'." This sentiment, scandalous as much for the dandy as for the soldier, echoes the vicomte's earlier admission that this event " 'a marqué à jamais d'une tache noire tous mes plaisirs de mauvais sujet'." The final remarks also function to transform the narrator's own perceptions of "ce dandy," remarks that persuasively reveal the vicomte as "un homme plus profond qu'il ne paraissait."

However, unbeknownst to either voice, these remarks also prepare the ultimate *coup de grâce,* as it were, to the force of authoritative discourse. This *coup* is dealt initially to the apparent victory of the centripetal, diegetically unifying voice "on" through its dislocation by the invasion of "reality" into the framed narration. For the vicomte's attempts to maintain authority are finally disrupted by the haunting movement of an "ombre svelte" (perhaps of Alberte, perhaps imagined), passing before the crimson curtain, and the discursive displacement is revealed by his final bitter remark, " 'Le hasard est par trop moqueur ce soir'." Then, as the carriage departs, the framing narrator's final comments reveal the impact that this dialogical struggle has had in his own existence. He admits, in the present tense, that the same window with its crimson curtain still continues to haunt his every dream, implicitly suggesting that the "diabolical" invades the dialogical, the authoritative discourse shifting abruptly in the dialogical struggle with the polyphonic need-to-persuade. Yet, this conflict is one that functions in a compensatory manner "between men," to use strategically the term proposed by Eve K. Sedgwick [in *Between Men: English Literature and Male Homosocial Desire,* 1985], i. e. the homosocial bond-in-conflict attempting to palliate dialogically the "diabolical" dis-ease occasioned by contact with the forceful, if silent, presence of (a) woman.

In the analytical model of the double-voiced struggle of discourses in **"Le Rideau cramoisi,"** I have attempted to provide both an understanding of the dynamic nature of this struggle and a dialogical means to confront the tale's inherent "narrative desire," i. e. the "complicity of author and reader [which] is so essential to production that the reader, like the intinerant listener, must be manipulated in such a way that he desires participation" [Eileen Boyd Sivert, "Narration and Exhibitionism in 'Le rideau cramoisi,' " *Romanic Review,* 70, No. 2 (1979)]. This discursive conflict unfolds with varying degrees of complexity in each of *Les Diaboliques,* with lesser or greater dialogical weight vested in the narrator, the voice "off," vis-à-vis the framed tale, or voice "on," and I wish to suggest a brief typology of their progression in terms of the "diabolical" sexual difference implied by the polyphonic discursive development just outlined.

Although quite similar to the opening tale, the dialogical tension in **"Le Bonheur dans le Crime"** arises almost entirely in the duelling discourses of the framed narrator, the docteur Torty. That is, his authoritative, medical discourse is vested in a voyeuristic, pseudo-scientific obsession with observing and, as he believes, thus knowing the "true" nature of the relationship between the mysterious, "diabolical" Hauteclaire de Stassin and her companion and lover, the comte de Savigny. This authoritative impulse reveals, in fact, that the doctor's obsession is itself part of their incomprehensible "bonheur" by dint of his solitary pleasure of observation, constituting an ascetic sexual practice from which the doctor must persuade the listener that he has remained immune, but which the reader comes to understand as the dominant impetus of the internally persuasive discourse.

"A un Dîner d'Athées," despite similarities to the opening tale, presents dual dialogic tensions that interweave in a more complex manner. On one hand, between the narrator of the embedded tale, Mesnilgrand, and his interlocutors, the irreverent guests at the dinner in his home, a struggle for anticlerical, more-blasphemous-than-thou authority ensues. Closely linked to, even resulting from this struggle is Mesnilgrand's impulse to persuade by elucidating convincingly the intense circumstances of the initial sacralizing event (his exceptional visit to a church) which apparently belie his (the framed narrator's) authoritative force. On the other hand, a more marginal, oblique struggle occurs: through moralistic, almost incredulous observations, the framing narrator attempts to assert his own implicitly religious authority, an impulse that is nonethe-

less undermined by his evident fascination, despite himself, with the persuasive force as well as the blasphemous authority of the diverse voices "on," of Mesnilgrand and his companions.

The dialogical structure of **"Le Plus Bel Amour de Don Juan"** is more Balzacian since the framing narrator relates a tale in confidence to a marquise, a tale recounted to him by and about the eponymous Don Juan, the comte Ravila de Ravilès, i. e. the latter's dinner with twelve adoring noble women who persuade him to reveal to them his "plus bel amour." Here, the voice "on" (recounting the anecdote to the women) is itself double-voiced as voice "off" (recounting the tale to the framing narrator) and thus establishes, throughout the tale, an apparent confusion of narrative levels. However, this confusion masks a dialogical struggle for authority and persuasion between voices "off" since it becomes increasingly unclear which voice "off" is, in fact, relating the anecdote at any given moment, i. e. the original, framing narrator to the marquise, on one hand, and on the other, Ravila de Ravilès to the framing narrator. This complexity thus provides the structure of a fierce discursive conflict in which "le 'bon' narrateur, celui qui sait, reste toujours insaisissable" [Marie-Claire Ropars-Wuilleumier, " 'Le plus bel amour de Don Juan': Narration et Signification," *Littérature* 9 (1973)], and in which the boundaries between authority and persuasion remain entirely fluid, if not disappearing altogether.

"Le Dessous de Cartes d'Une Partie de Whist" compounds this dialogic complexity and tension by presenting multiple framed narrators within an embedded tale of silent fascination, ending in the likely murders of an adolescent girl and her illegitimate baby. The dialogical "dessous" of the repressive social scene is recounted through the voice "on" of an authoritative *raconteur* who, like Mesnilgrand among the atheists, must contend with the interlocutors' resistance to his tale, but here, as in **"Le Plus Bel Amour de Don Juan,"** a resistance posed by the various *interlocutrices* in attendance. Moreover, this dialogic interaction is situated within the truly parsimonious authority of the framing narrator whose presence both on the margins of the framed tale and at the edge of the site of its enunciation, the *salon* of the baronne de Mascranny, seems designed to mask the discreetly silent, yet intense relationship between this nearly hidden voice "off," and another listener/observer, the statuesque comtesse de Damnaglia. Yet, this "dessous" of the scene of narration mirrors the multiple "dessous" within the embedded narrative itself: on one hand, the implicit relationship of the *raconteur* as a youth with the embedded tale's protagonist, Marmor de Karkoël, and the effect of the latter's example on the subsequent attitudes of the *raconteur;* on the other hand, the dialogic tension, however parsimonious, existing between the *raconteur*'s voice "on" and the framing narrator's voice "off." It is, however, the latter's gaze that recurrently focusses on, i. e. on the back of the *comtesse,* quivering in silent response to the tale being recounted, and perhaps to the circumstances of its presentation.

What *Les Diaboliques* all share is the final result of dialogic interaction and tension, i. e. silence, at the cost of the suffering, even death, of one, if not several, female bodies. As I suggested briefly for **"Le Rideau cramoisi,"** the dialogical duels within these tales emphasize the homosocial bond that dominates their confrontations, even when occurring in the presence and at the request of women, intermittently silenced in their role of *interlocutrices*. Likewise, the cost of the reader's "desire for narration" is the passive, "readerly" consumption of the focal tale in the role of witness implicitly positioned in relation to the texts' dialogical struggles. But the further cost, of course, is not merely the exclusion, but even the destruction, if not (always) of the reader, then certainly of women. For the docteur Torty in **"Le Bonheur dans le Crime,"** this silence arises from the mystery of happiness in relation to, and even because of, the shared crime of Hauteclaire de Stassin and the comte de Savigny, i. e. the murder of the latter's wife. For Mesnilgrand in **"A un Dîner d'Athées,"** the violent and hideously lethal confrontation between the seductive *La Pudica* and her lover, the major Ydow, inspires the heretofore silent motives that eventually result in Mesnilgrand's incongruously reverent act (entrusting to a priest a dead baby's shrunken heart) that gives rise itself to the dialogic struggles of the voice "on." In **"Le Plus Bel Amour de Don Juan,"** the simultaneously impossible, yet disturbingly elliptical events leading to a young girl's impregnation and death are related by the eponymous framed narrator as "le plus bel amour que j'aie inspiré de ma vie." This perplexing admission, while producing silence among his twelve noble *interlocutrices* first, and then entirely in the framing conversation of the voices "off," results finally in the usurpation of authority through the duchess's mysterious words, " 'Sans cela . . .'," an elliptical remark with which the text ends suggesting the implicit authority of a whole counter-tale. In **"Le Dessous de Cartes d'une Partie de Whist,"** after the departure of the framed tale's focal protagonist, "ce diable de Marmor de Karkoël," the revelation of the tale's dénouement (the triple death of a mother, daughter and smothered infant) is the disturbing diegetic counterpart both of the framed male *raconteur*'s authoritative force in response to the resistance of the attentive, female listeners, and of the silent, scopophilic insistence of the anonymous male narrator's gaze focussing on the back of the "statuesque" comtesse de Damnaglia.

However, it is in **"La Vengeance d'une Femme"** that the voice "on" itself succumbs to this diabolical force of silence, for it is only in this tale that the narratological situations are doubly exceptional, on one hand, with the framing narrator as a conventionally anonymous, heterodiegetic observer and, on the other hand, the framed narrator as *raconteuse*, i. e. the eponymous vengeful woman. It would appear that her voice "on" truly imposes both its authoritative and persuasive forces since the noblewoman's body arouses the client while her voice renders this interlocutor, the apparent protagonist Robert de Tressignies, physically and vocally impotent. Yet, the dialogical interaction is completed in the final pages by the anonymous, heterodiegetic narrator/observer via the focalization of de Tressignies: he (and the reader) discover from a gambler's remarks that the vengeful and authoritative female voice and body, that dared to speak persuasively while enacting an authoritative carnal vengeance, were

buried that very morning after suffering, like Zola's heroine in *Nana,* a hideously disfiguring malady. As Charles Bernheimer suggests [in his *Figures of Ill Repute,* 1989], the putrefaction of this body constitutes the final chapter of "the story of her shameful debasement . . . of her prostitution" which will undoubtedly be recounted to her husband, the duke of Sierra Leone. That is, the duchess's plot (her prostitution and eventual death in scandalous circumstances) is a calculated expression of the internally persuasive discourse aimed at "turning the possessive privilege inherent in the father's name against the patriarchal order that name sustains" [Bernheimer], thus at diminishing traditional authority by means of the ultimate act of "persuasion."

The dialogical interaction itself, the struggle between authoritative and internally persuasive discourses, thus wreaks a cruel vengeance in Barbey d'Aurevilly's tales on those who presume to usurp the authoritative discourse and to persuade too effectively. The conditions for polite attendance to these words, for example, in **"Don Juan,"** are stunned silence, except by one final voice, suggesting what Angela Moger [in an unpublished paper] calls the possible "accession of the female to verbal power." Once the lines of *politesse* are transgressed, as by the framing narrator in **"Le Rideau cramoisi"** as well as by the docteur Torty, Mesnilgrand, and both narrators of **"Le Dessous de Cartes"** in their respective diegetic (and dialogical) relations, the silence is accompanied by a contagious obsession which cannot be relieved, even through the most extreme acts (e. g. Mesnilgrand's) of self-redemption. However, the actions of Alberte as well as of other female characters such as Hauteclaire de Stassin (**"Le Bonheur dans le Crime"**), La Pudica (**"A un Dîner d'Athées"**), and the mothers and daughters of **"Le Plus Bel Amour"** and **"Le Dessous de Cartes,"** however subtle, are all the more passionate, thus "speak" more loudly than words, in a persuasive mode which seems to call for suppression by an authoritative voice, "on" and "off." Like the traveler in **"Le Rideau cramoisi"** who seeks the advantage of silence "quand on n'a plus rien à se dire," effective authoritative speech finally gains this advantage over the most passionately persuasive characters of the framed tales, all the more brutally silenced when, in **"La Vengeance d'une Femme,"** the same voice is manifested as a woman's (verbal and physical) "enunciation." For the effect of such direct dialogical interaction is most clearly seen through the portrayal of the vengeful duchess's usurpation of *la parole.* The "diabolical" vengeance which she seeks and appears to achieve in the final putrefaction of her body is itself countered by the dialogical and diegetic retaliation enacted, respectively, upon her discourse and upon her body, as evidence of a vengeance "which is really that of a man" [Bernheimer], i. e. the authoritative violence perpetrated in *Les Diaboliques*, but not merely toward the persuasive accession to (verbal) power of females. This violence is directed as well toward and through the reading subject's "desire for narration," positioned in a dialogue "between men," but required, as I have argued, to resist such positioning so that the reading act might remain "alive," that is, active and productive. I have attempted to provide an example of such productive resistance that would enable the reading subject to counter the diverse effects of "narrative desire" through a strategy of re-reading, attentive not only to the textual, but the sexual and dialogical means constitutive of the writer's narrative authority and force of duplicity.

FURTHER READING

Criticism

Boyd, Ernest. Introduction to *The Diaboliques,* by Jules Barbey d'Aurevilly, translated by Ernest Boyd, pp. vii-xii. New York: Alfred A. Knopf, 1925.

    Considers *The Diaboliques* in the context of Barbey's life and works.

Chartier, Armand B. "Erotic Horrors: From *Les diaboliques* to *Ce qui ne meurt pas.*" In his *Barbey d'Aurevilly,* pp. 103-43. Boston: Twayne, 1977.

    Surveys the stories in *The Diaboliques.*

Pasco, Allan H. "A Study of Allusion: Barbey's Stendhal in 'Le rideau cramoisi.'" *PMLA* 88, No. 3 (May 1973): 461-71.

    Detailed study of plot and thematic parallels between Barbey's "Le rideau cramoisi" ("The Crimson Curtain") and Stendhal's *Le rouge et le noir* (*The Red and the Black*).

Sivert, Eileen. "Text, Body, and Reader in Barbey d'Aurevilly's *Les diaboliques.*" *Symposium* XXXI, No. 2 (Summer 1977): 151-64.

    Uses "At a Dinner of Atheists" and "A Woman's Revenge" to support the assertion that in *The Diaboliques* "narration is more important than what is narrated." Sivert further contends that the narrative style of the collection simultaneously invites and discourages attempts at interpretation.

Toumayan, Alain. "Barbey d'Aurevilly and Flaubert: Engendering a *Diabolique.*" In *Literary Generations: A Festschrift in Honor of Edward D. Sullivan by His Friends, Colleagues, and Former Students,* edited by Alain Toumayan, pp. 141-49. Lexington, Ky.: French Forum, 1992.

    Maintains that Gustave Flaubert's *Madame Bovary* influenced Barbey's story "Happiness in Crime" and assesses the significance of this connection.

Unwin, T. A. "Barbey d'Aurevilly and Balzac: A Possible Source of 'A un dîner d'athées.'" *Romance Notes,* XXVI, No. 3 (Summer 1986): 237-40.

    Examines similarities and differences between "A un dîner d'athées" ("At a Dinner of Atheists") and several works of short fiction by Honoré de Balzac that may have served as source material for Barbey's story.

Additional coverage of Barbey's life and career is contained in the following sources published by Gale Research: *Dictionary of Literary Biography*, Vol. 119; and *Nineteenth-Century Literature Criticism*, Vol. 1.

Adolfo Bioy Casares
1914-

(Also wrote under the pseudonyms Martín Sacastru and Javier Miranda; joint pseudonyms with Jorge Luis Borges include H[onorio] Bustos Domecq, B. Lynch Davis, and B. Suarez Lynch) Argentine novelist, short story writer, essayist, and screenwriter.

INTRODUCTION

Bioy Casares creates highly imaginative stories blending science fiction, fantasy, and mystery to comment on social and political conditions in Argentina as well as broader themes concerning love, identity, human nature, and the absurdity of the human condition. His innovative and complex plots often incorporate devices common to fantastic fiction, including simultaneity (the occurrence of past, present, and future at the same time), time travel, invisibility, oneiric images, metamorphosis, and other supernatural happenings.

Biographical Information

Bioy Casares was born in Buenos Aires to wealthy parents. His father frequently read gaucho epics to him when he was a boy. At an early age Bioy Casares began to compose stories and poetry that reveal a fascination with the supernatural. His first published work, *Prológo* (1929; *Prologue*), appeared when he was only 15, and was edited by his father and published at his father's expense. One of the most significant events of Bioy Casares's life was meeting the Argentine fantasist Jorge Luis Borges at the home of Victoria Ocampo, a fiction writer and publisher of the literary magazine *Sur*. Bioy Casares was only 17, Borges 32, but the two began a friendship and mentorship. Borges' encouragement led Bioy Casares to transfer from the study of law to philosophy and literature, and ultimately, to choose writing as a career. Rejecting the then-prevalent historical approach to literary criticism, Bioy Casares and Borges in 1936 began a magazine of avant-garde criticism called *Destiempo* (*Out of Time*). Although the magazine did not remain in circulation long, it initiated their collaboration on a variety of projects such as short stories; anthologies of Argentine fantastic fiction, detective stories, and their favorite gaucho poetry; and *Cuentos breves y extraordinarios* (1955; *Extraordinary Tales*), a miscellany of quotes and epigrams by popular writers from classical to modern times. Bioy Casares continues to live and work in Buenos Aires.

Major Works of Short Fiction

In Bioy Casares's short fiction, the characters experience what D. P. Gallagher has described as an "adventure . . . whether plausible or fantastic, in order to reveal their comic puniness." In *Guirnalda con amores* (1959; *A Gar-*

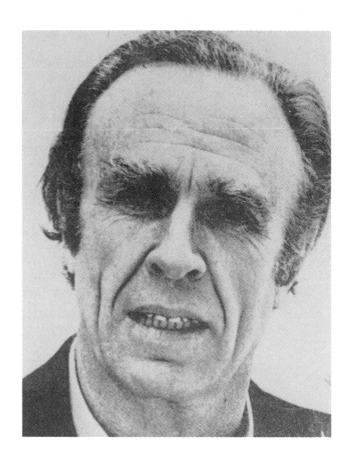

land *of Love*), Bioy Casares deals with issues of identity and presents comic ironies which frequently surround romantic love. Other stories include politics as a subplot to the major drama, as in a collection written with Borges, *Seis problemas para Don Isidro Parodi* (1942; *Six Problems for Don Isidro Parodi*). The protagonist in *Six Problems for Don Isidro Parodi* solves crime mysteries through deductive reasoning from a prison cell, having been framed for a murder committed by a public official. In *Plan de evasión*, (1975; *A Plan for Escape*), set on a small island off the coast of French Guiana, the protagonist Enrique Nevers attempts to observe the activities of the French governor who is stationed on nearby Devil's Island. The novella centers on Nevers's changing perceptions and the disparity between what he knows and what is actually taking place; the governor, in fact, is overseeing a surgical experiment that produces permanent synaesthesia in prisoners on the island. Bioy Casares's interest in film and the medium's capacity for mimicking dreams and fantasy appears in his most famous work, the novella *La invención de Morel* (1940; *The Invention of Morel*), in which the protagonist falls in love with a virtual woman projected by a machine that transforms people into holographic images of themselves. In *The Invention of Morel* Bioy Casares uses his trademark techniques of concise dialogue, brief sentences, and an omniscient narrator who comments on events about which the protagonist is unaware. In the short story "El otro laberinto" collected in *La trama celeste* (1956; *The Celestial Plot*), the metaphysical phenomena of temporal simultaneity and time travel serve as ways to solve the mystery of a death which had taken place centuries in the past. *Crónicas de Bustos Domecq*, (1967; *Chronicles of Bustos Domecq*), described by Clarence Brown as "sheer nonsensical hilarity," features vignettes and fictional essays satirizing modern aesthetic theories and figures from Argentine literary and artistic circles.

Critical Reception

Bioy Casares has not received much attention in English-speaking countries because few of his works have been translated. In addition, publishers of his collaborative works with Borges have tended to emphasize Borges's authorship over that of Bioy Casares. Likewise, most of the critical regard paid to these works is generated by Borges's renown, and commentators therefore focus on Borges's contribution. Initially, critics regarded Bioy Casares's social criticism and satires of Argentine political society as too obscure, but more recent studies of Bioy Casares's fiction praise his inventive plots, sardonic humor, and concise language. He has been the recipient of numerous national and international awards, garnering the prestigious Premio Internacional Literario IILA (Roma) in 1986 for *Historias Fantasticas* and *Historias de amor*. *The Invention of Morel* is generally considered a minor masterpiece and a model of fantastic fiction.

PRINCIPAL WORKS

Short Fiction

Prólogo [*Prologue*] 1929
Diecisiete disparos contra lo porvenir [as Martín Sacastru; *Seventeen Shots against the Future*] 1933
Caos [*Chaos*] 1934
La nueva tormenta; o, La vida multiple de Juan Ruteno 1937
**La invención de Morel* [*The Invention of Morel*] 1940
Seis problemas para Don Isidro Parodi [with Jorge Luis Borges; *Six Problems for Don Isidro Parodi*] 1942
El perjurio de la nieve [*The Perjury of Snow*] 1944
Dos fantasías memorables [with Jorge Luis Borges under the joint pseudonym of Bustos Domecq] 1946
* *La trama celeste* [*The Celestial Plot*] 1948
Historia prodigiosa [*Prodigious History*] 1956
Guirnalda con amores: Cuentos [*A Garland of Love: Stories*] 1959
El lado de la sombra [*The Shady Side*] 1962
Crónicas de Bustos Domecq [with Jorge Luis Borges; *Chronicles of Bustos Domecq*] 1967
El gran serafín 1967
Historias de amor [*Love Stories*] 1972
Historias fantásticas [*Fantastic Stories*] 1972
Plan de evasión [*A Plan for Escape*] 1975

Nuevos cuentos de Bustos Domecq [with Jorge Luis Borges] 1977
El héroe de las mujeres 1978
Historias desaforadas 1987
A Russian Doll, and Other Stories 1992

Other Major Works

Antología de la literatura fantástica [edited with Silvina Ocampo and Jorge Luis Borges; *The Book of Fantasy*] (anthology) 1940; [enlarged edition] 1965
El sueño de los heroes [*The Dream of Heroes*] (novel) 1954
Diario de la guerra del cerdo [*Diary of the War of the Pig*] (novel) 1969
Cuentos breves y extraordinarios [edited with Jorge Luis Borges; *Extraordinary Tales*] (anthology) 1971
Dormir al sol [*Asleep in the Sun*] (novel) 1973
La aventura de un fotógrafo en La Plata [*The Adventures of a Photographer in La Plata*] (novel) 1985

*Translations of *La trama celeste* and *La invención de Morel* were published together as *The Invention of Morel, and Other Stories from "La trama celeste"* in 1964.

CRITICISM

Jorge Luis Borges with Thomas di Giovanni (essay date 1970)

SOURCE: "Autobiographical Notes," in *The New Yorker*, Vol. XLVI, No. 31, September 19, 1970, pp. 40-99.

[An Argentine short story writer, poet, and essayist, Borges was one of the leading figures in modern literature. His writing is often used by critics to illustrate the contemporary view of literature as a highly sophisticated game. Justifying this interpretation of Borges's works are his admitted respect for stories that are artificial inventions of art rather than realistic representations of life, his use of philosophical conceptions as a means of achieving literary effects, and his frequent variations on the writings of other authors. In the following excerpt from an essay transcribed by di Giovanni, Borges recalls his work with Bioy Casares on their collaborative writings.]

One of the chief events of [my adulthood]—and of my life—was the beginning of my friendship with Adolfo Bioy Casares. We met in 1930 or 1931, when he was about seventeen and I was just past thirty. It is always taken for granted in these cases that the older man is the master and the younger his disciple. This may have been true at the outset, but several years later, when we began to work together, Bioy was really and secretly the master. He and I attempted many different literary ventures. We compiled anthologies of Argentine poetry, tales of the fantastic, and detective stories; we wrote articles and forewords; we annotated Sir Thomas Browne and Gracián; we translated short stories by writers like Beerbohm, Kipling, Wells, and Lord Dunsany; we founded a magazine, *Destiempo*, which lasted three issues; we wrote film scripts, which were invariably rejected. Opposing my taste for the pathetic, the sententious, and the baroque, Bioy made me feel that quietness and restraint are more desirable. If I may be allowed a sweeping statement, Bioy led me gradually toward classicism.

It was at some point in the early forties that we began writing in collaboration—a feat that up to that time I had thought impossible. I had invented what we thought was a quite good plot for a detective story. One rainy morning, he told me we ought to give it a try. I reluctantly agreed, and a little later that same morning the thing happened. A third man, Honorio Bustos Domecq, emerged and took over. In the long run, he ruled us with a rod of iron and to our amusement, and later to our dismay, he became utterly unlike ourselves, with his own whims, his own puns, and his own very elaborate style of writing. Domecq was the name of a great-grandfather of Bioy's and Bustos of a great-grandfather of mine from Córdoba. Bustos Domecq's first book was *Six Problems for don Isidro Parodi* (1942), and during the writing of that volume he never got out of hand. Max Carrados had attempted a blind detective; Bioy and I went one step further and confined our detective to a jail cell. The book was at the same time a satire on the Argentine. For many years, the dual identity of Bustos Domecq was never revealed. When finally it was, people thought that, as Bustos was a joke, his writing could hardly be taken seriously.

Our next collaboration was another detective novel, *A Model for Death.* This one was so personal and so full of private jokes that we published it only in an edition that was not for sale. The author of this book we named B. Suárez Lynch. The "B." stood, I think, for Bioy and Borges, "Suárez" for another great-grandfather of mine, and "Lynch" for another great-grandfather of Bioy's. Bustos Domecq reappeared in 1946 in another private edition, this time of two stories, entitled *Two Memorable Fantasies.* After a long eclipse, Bustos took up his pen again, and in 1967 brought out his *Chronicles.* These are articles written on imaginary, extravagantly modern artists—architects, sculptors, painters, chefs, poets, novelists, couturiers—by a devotedly modern critic. But both the author and his subjects are fools, and it is hard to tell who is taking in whom. The book is inscribed, "To those three forgotten greats—Picasso, Joyce, Le Corbusier." The style is itself a parody. Bustos writes a literary journalese, abounding in neologisms, a Latinate vocabulary, clichés, mixed metaphors, non sequiturs, and bombast.

I have often been asked how collaboration is possible. I think it requires a joint abandoning of the ego, of vanity, and maybe of common politeness. The collaborators should forget themselves and think only in terms of the work. In fact, when somebody wants to know whether such-and-such a joke or epithet came from my side of the table or Bioy's, I honestly cannot tell him. I have tried to collaborate with other friends—some of them very close ones—but their inability to be blunt on the one hand or thick-skinned on the other has made the scheme impossible. As to the *Chronicles of Bustos Domecq,* I think they are better than anything I have published under my own name and nearly as good as anything Bioy has written on his own.

Bioy Casares on an influential childhood impression:

When I was very young, my mother used to tell me stories of animals that dared to leave their burrows and run into dangers. The subject of havens and dangers still attracts me, as if I saw in it an image of man's destiny. I often wonder if one day I will be able to write civilized stories in which nothing ever happens and no violent episodes occur.

Adolfo Bioy Casares, translated by Emir Rodriguez Monegal from an interview in Spanish in Plural, *February, 1974.*

Alfred J. Mac Adam   (essay date 1973)

SOURCE: "The Mirror and the Lie: Two Stories by Jorge Luis Borges and Adolfo Bioy Casares," in *Modern Fiction Studies,* Vol. 19, No. 3, Autumn, 1973, pp. 353-62.

[*In the following essay, Mac Adam focuses on the use of language and narrative to demonstrate that two stories written jointly by Bioy Casares and Jorge Luis Borges, "El hijo de su amigo" and "La fiesta del Monstruo," satirize life in Buenos Aires during the first presidency of Juan Perón.*]

The literary collaborations of Jorge Luis Borges and Adolfo Bioy Casares are virtually unknown. This is understandable because Borges and Bioy (alias H. Bustos Domecq, B. Suárez Lynch, or B. Lynch Davis) have consistently regarded these texts as unimportant jokes. They have reprinted only a few and have guaranteed the others' consignment to oblivion by publishing them in newspapers or ephemeral journals. Another reason that the collaborations are not being read more widely, as widely as everything else with which Borges' name is associated (leaving aside the difficulty the uninformed reader would have in identifying Borges and Bioy with H. Bustos Domecq), is that many of the pieces are incomprehensible for today's readers because they are written in a baroque version of Buenos Aires slang. This linguistic barrier is compounded by the fact that many of the collaborations are filled with references to contemporary affairs, situations which were humorous only when the texts were written. They share the traditional fate of occasional literature, being committed to a specific historical moment. And yet, situated in a literary context which would include other manipulators of dialect and slang, such as Günter Grass and Carlo Emilio Gadda, they acquire an importance which even their creators may not have seen.

Two stories in particular, **"El hijo de su amigo"** and **"La fiesta del Monstruo,"** are such powerful satires of life in Buenos Aires during the Perón era that they constitute a major example of how artists respond to a particular social reality. Both stories were published in Montevideo: **"El hijo de su amigo"** (which is dated December 21, 1950) in 1952 and **"La fiesta del Monstruo"** (dated November 24, 1947) in 1955. Both texts circulated in manuscript form before being published, and neither has ever been published in Argentina.

"El hijo de su amigo," the better of the two stories, was originally published with a preface by Emir Rodrìguez-Monegal entitled "Sobre una mitología." This introduction locates the story in a particular Argentine tradition, the idealized vision of Buenos Aires, which, according to the critic, has passed through three stages: the first he sees symbolized by Macedonio Fernández, Borges' acknowledged master, the living presence of the nineteenth century in the twentieth, a mixture of "caudillos y tertulias literarias," which eclipsed the concept of Buenos Aires as a great metropolis. This vision was soon replaced by that of Buenos Aires as the world of the tango, the multileveled, cosmopolitan city. The third stage, that of Borges and Bioy, is ironic: it submits the values of the first two stages to an honest scrutiny which reveals all their injustices and defects. For Rodrìguez-Monegal, **"El hijo de su amigo"** is a caustic demonstration of the corrupt life of the Argentine capital. After pointing out that the plot of the story is trivial, he notes:

> Pero lo que importa es el tratamiento. A través del lenguaje se da todo: la miseria moral, la vileza, el ridículo, quedaban expresados en el giro que utiliza el relator, en su vocabulario, en sus preferencias sintácticas. Una comicidad explosiva, el ridículo abierto del asunto. Ella denuncia otra forma, más íntima, más necesaria del porteñismo.

From this perspective, the language of the story might seem to be a sign of realism, but it is precisely realism—taken either as an aesthetic goal or a particular style—which the story explodes. The only reality here is language; the action is a sham. Perhaps the language once belonged to an entire society, but here it becomes a self-parody, spoken by a mysterious narrator whose intentions are confusing. The problematic aspect of the story resides in the identity of this narrator. If his discourse is in fact a synecdoche for a spoken language, the relationship between him (the narrator-protagonist Urbistondo) and the society outside the text must also be a synecdoche. That is, Urbistondo must represent Argentine (particularly Buenos Aires) society, and the story must be a warped vision of real life. This is a difficult matter. Either the story is to be given a historical meaning by linking it to a world outside of it, or it is to be read as a bizarre tale whose "meaning" is aesthetic and not social. The two readings are not necessarily antithetic; they simply imply two ways of understanding the same text.

The story deals with Urbistondo's cinematic career, the maneuvers he follows in order to have one of his scripts accepted by the Sindicato de Operarios y Productores Argentinos (SOPA). His scheme, which he relates to a certain Ustáriz, who barely speaks, is a mass of contradictions and lies, beginning with his first words:

> Usted, Ustáriz, pensará de mí lo que quiera, pero soy más porfiado que el vasco de la carretilla. Para mí, el renglón libros es una cosa y el cinematógrafo es otra. Mis novelitas serán como el matete del mono con la máquina de escribir, pero la jerarquía de escritor la mantengo. Por eso la vez que me pidieron una comedia bufa para la SOPA (Sindicato de Operarios y Produc-

> tores Argentinos) les rogué por favor que se perdieran un poquito en el horizonte. Yo y el cinematógrafo . . . ¡salga de ahí! No ha nacido el hombre que me haga escribir para el celuloide.

In reality, no one asked Urbistondo to write a movie script. He found out that there was an open competition, and he wrote a script with the enchanting title "¡Terminaron casándose!" The description of how Urbistondo tries to convince one of the executives of the SOPA, Farfarello, that his is the best script and that there is no need to hold a competition is a *tour de force*. It is a perfect parody of the business lunch:

> Créame una vez en la vida, Ustáriz: soy todo un impulsivo, cuando conviene. Engolosinado, me lo apestillé a Farfarello: lo obsequié una gaseosa que consumimos *sotto* la vigilancia del cebú; le calcé un medio Toscanini en el morro y me lo llevé, en un placero, entre cuentos al caso y palmaditas, al Nuevo Parmesano de Godoy Cruz. Para preparar el estómago, embuchamos hasta sapo por barba; después tuvo su hora el minestrón; después nos dimos por entero al desgrase del caldo; después, con el Barbera, se nos vino el arroz alla Valenciana, que medio lo asentamos con un Moscato y así nos dispusimos a dar cuenta de la ternerita mechada, pero antes nos dejamos tentar por unos pastelones de albóndiga y la panzada concluyó con panqueques, fruta mezzo verdolaga, si usted me entiende, un queso tipo arena y otro baboso, y un cafferata-express con mucha espuma, que mandaba más gana de afeitarse que de cortarse el pelo. En ancas del espumoso cayó el señor Chissotti en persona en su forma de grappa, que nos puso la lengua de mazacote y yo la aproveché para dar una de esas noticias bomba, que hasta el camello de la joroba cae de espaldas. Sin gastarme en prólogos ni antesalas, me lo preparé suavito, suavito a Farfarello, para cortarle el hipo con la sorpresa que yo ya disponía de un argumento que sólo le faltaba el celuloide y un reparte de bufos que el día de pago de la SOPA entra en franca disolución. Aprovechando que uno de tantos caramelos pegote se le había incrustado en la cavidad, que ni tan siquiera el mozo de la panera se lo consiguió del todo extraer, principié a nenarrarle grosso modo, con lujo de detalles, el argumento.

This passage typifies both the entire story and Urbistondo as a narrator. His technique of simultaneous affirmation and negation: "soy todo un impulsivo, cuando conviene" or "principié a nenarrarle grosso modo, con lujo de detalles" characterizes his reliability as an orator; it demonstrates the factitiousness of his rhetoric. His fascination with food, his gluttony, and his nickname, Catanga Chica (Dung Beetle), add more details to what may be either a metaphoric portrait of life in Buenos Aires or a brilliant exercise in the grotesque. The digestive tract is the story's actual setting, and Urbistondo is its *genus loci*.

The meal, an Argentine version of Trimalchio's banquet, is merely a ruse whereby Urbistondo hopes to gain Farfarello's favor, but like most of his schemes, it fails. The SOPA rejects his script, but Urbistondo, after spying on the judging committee, discovers a love affair between two of its members, Mariana Ruiz Villalba de Anglada and

Julio Cárdenas, "el hijo de su amigo"—the son of the man who had once saved Urbistondo's life. First Urbistondo tries to blackmail Mariana, but when this fails, he turns to Cárdenas. Cárdenas tries to protect Mariana's nonexistent good name and pays Urbistondo what he wants by stealing money from the SOPA. When Urbistondo learns that Cárdenas is a thief, he demands even more money. Cárdenas refuses to pay, Urbistondo informs Farfarello, and Cárdenas commits suicide. To express its gratitude, the SOPA accepts "¡Terminaron casádose!" As Urbistondo says goodby to Ustáriz, he mentions that he has a date with "la señora Mariana."

The story's victim is its only honest man, Julio Cárdenas. But his honesty is useless in Urbistondo's world, and while Urbistondo knows the difference between good and evil, he submits all problems to the test of self-interest. His morality is based on a solipsistic interpretation of nineteenth-century utilitarianism which negates any possibility of community or even communication. He also assumes that his inverted sense of values is exclusively his and is sadly disillusioned when he finds that "la señora Mariana" is really like him:

> "Señora," le dije con la voz tembeleque, "yo seré un incorregible, un romántico, pero usted es una inmoral que no recompensa mi desvelo de observador. Estoy francamente desencantado y no le puedo prometer que me repondré de este golpe en un término prudencial."

He is shocked by her immorality; his own is above reproach.

Urbistondo's value system infects even his language, and it is here that we may see the thrust of the author's indictment of contemporary Argentina most clearly. Urbistondo's words, those of Argentine society, the representation of ideas and values, are merely masks. He uses them for purposes clear only for him and the reader, who is in the privileged, external position of reason. Urbistondo does not *mean* anything when he speaks, and his words stand only as gestures or ambiguous movements. Their semantic value drowns in his intentions which constitute a language beyond words. It is this misuse of language combined with the slang of a particular historical moment which makes the narrative impenetrable.

To retell **"El hijo de su amigo"** is to deform it because its most important element, the cosmos around Urbistondo and the SOPA, is not an actor in the plot. The drama of the tale is, therefore, of minor importance, whereas its actual subject, either Argentina during a dictatorship or any corrupt, meaningless world, is present without being named. The putrefaction of the world within (which may also be outside) the text is felt rather than defined. The result is that language becomes a mirror of life, a façade which reflects what it is simultaneously attempting to dissimulate. Borges and Bioy limit themselves to metaphor and present the reader with a world so far away from "reality" that its very exaggerations underline its similarities to the "real world" instead of its differences.

"La fiesta del Monstruo" is more obviously an attack on *peronismo*. Like **"El hijo de su amigo,"** it is a first-person narrative, a description of the events preceding a political rally. The narrator never describes the rally itself, the "fiesta" of the title, and this strange fact suggests that the story's focus is intended to be more than a portrait of the Perón era. The story's events are not presented in the documentary style of thesis literature, but in a way which suggests that they are the external manifestations of something whose identity is secret.

"La fiesta del Monstruo" is simultaneously comic and horrible, but the story's meaning is, again, not dependent on its plot. By the end of World War II, and certainly by 1955, no one could be shocked by reading about what he had seen during the 1930's and 1940's. The spectacle was also quite unlikely to amuse anyone. The lesson of **"La fiesta del Monstruo"** is transmitted by its language—taken as a sound, a cacophony—rather than by its drama or its semantic significance.

An expert on Quevedo who had lived in Buenos Aires during the Perón period would be the person best equipped to elucidate this tale because its syntax and imagery recall Quevedo's *conceptismo* and because it is impenetrable for someone unfamiliar with the linguistic peculiarities of the River Plate region. It is not simply the vocabulary of **"La fiesta del Monstruo"** or **"El hijo de su amigo"** which makes them difficult to read. *Lunfardo* (Buenos Aires underworld slang) has created an entire literature, both in Argentina and Uruguay, but in authors like Roberto Arlt, Juan Carlos Onetti, or Julio Cortázar, it is a slang used as a slang, and it never dominates a given work entirely. In Borges and Bioy, it makes up the stories' entire linguistic structure.

Language in these two stories is more important than the narrator who uses it because it exists independently of him rather than as an element of his personality. And yet, there is no way of separating the character from his language because he seems to emanate from it. Who is the narrator? With whom is he speaking? His identity is not important, just as the events which occur in the narrative are not important in themselves but as symbols or signs.

What matters in **"La fiesta del Monstruo"** is not the representation of one day in the life of a "cabecita negra." Although Perón is the "Monster" it is not only the dictatorship which the authors are trying to depict. The "Monster" is something more than a man, more than the dictator: it is a state in which humanity itself suffers violence, in which all values are subverted. It is a vision of the demonic world:

> the world of the nightmare and the scapegoat, of pain and confusion; the world as it is before the human imagination begins to work on it and before any image of human desire, such as the city or the garden, has been solidly established; the world also of perverted or wasted work, ruins and catacombs, instruments of torture and monuments of folly. [Northrop Frye, *Anatomy of Criticism*, 1957]

But **"La fiesta del Monstruo"** is not an apocalyptic vision: there is no indication that a cataclysm, a purifying disaster, is imminent. Its literary origin, seen through the eyes of German Expressionism, is Dante's *Inferno*, the city of unreason, and the names of its inhabitants are often those of Dante's devils: Graffiacane, Cagnazzo.

"La fiesta del Monstruo" depicts an unreal world from a perspective which reveals its inhabitants to be grotesque subhumans. The reader is in the position of the reasonable man with respect to any satire, and it is from his rational point of view that he can see the horror of this world of repression. The world which is generally believed to be internal and psychic in Kafka is external and palpable in Borges and Bioy, but, like Kafka, they dilute the horror with macabre humor.

The narrative technique of **"La fiesta del Monstruo"** is identical to that of **"El hijo de su amigo."** In both stories, a narrator addresses someone who is barely present. The reader finds himself involuntarily identified with that person because of the dramatic character of a unilateral dialogue as he does, for example, in "The Rime of the Ancient Mariner" or "My Last Duchess." This device simultaneously "locks" the reader into the story and transforms him into a denizen of the narrator's world: they both, if the reader works at it, "speak" the same debased language.

In both stories the narrator is a pathological liar, an ingenuous rogue. In **"El hijo de su amigo,"** as we have seen, the narrator is shocked when the lady he tries to blackmail laughs at his threats, and in **"La fiesta del Monstruo,"** the narrator expresses his desire, on three occasions, to sell the pistol entrusted to him by his beloved political party. His narrative techniques are identical to Urbistondo's. In the passage which follows, the protagonist describes the reception his group received as it passed through a Buenos Aires neighborhood:

> ¡Qué entusiasmo partidario te perdiste, Nelly! En cada foco de población muerto de hambre se nos quería colar una verdadera avalancha que la tenía emberretinada el más puro idealismo, pero el capo de nuestra carrada, Garfunkel, sabía repeler como corresponde a ese farabutaje sin abuela, máxime si te metés en el coco que entre tanto mascalzone patentado bien se podía emboscar una quintacolumna como luz, de esos que antes que usted da la vuelta del mundo en ochenta días me lo convencen que es un crosta y el Monstruo es un instrumento de la Compañía del Teléfono. No te digo niente de más de un cagastume que se acogía a esas purgas para darse de baja en el confucionismo y repatriarse a casita lo más liviano; pero embromate y confesá que de dos chichipíos el uno nace descalzo y el otro con patín de munición, porque vuelta que yo creía descolgarme del carro era patada del señor Garfunkel que me restituía al seno de los valientes.

The passage opens with an enthusiastic exclamation, and this tone seems to run through the entire first section of the passage. Nevertheless, not only does he call the neighborhood poor but also "muerto de hambre," an insult both in Spanish and in Italian. He describes the crowd as "ese farabutaje sin abuela," again using an Italianate expression as an insult. In the next section he describes the new adherents as "tanto mascalzone patentado," more macaronic Italian. He then notes that some timorous group

members tried to take advantage of the confusion ("el confucionismo") to run away. He seems to reproach them, but in the next clause he mentions that when he tried to jump off the truck, the group leader kicked him back "al seno de los valientes."

The essence of the narrative is a device which we may call the "flexible term." At any moment, the narrator's evaluation of a scene may reverse itself, but if the reader observes the discourse carefully, he sees that the inversion was suggested with the original idea. Thus, the enthusiastic crowd was from the beginning "muerto de hambre." This paradox slowly becomes a condemnation of the crowd, a condemnation which later dissipates. The narrator's attitude toward abandoning the group is also contradictory: he seems to say, "Some weaklings tried to get away in the confusion, but when I tried, I failed." When he says something he means nothing; that is, what is implied in one sentence is negated in the next.

Consistent with this linguistic relativism is the always fluctuating position of the narrator within his society. The narrator of **"La fiesta del Monstruo"** is, if anything, a supporter of the "Monster." He even seems to be a party member, with noble ideals, and yet the reader promptly learns that he is a short, fat man constantly picked on by his comrades. The party members do have one thing in common: they are all ignorant, mistreated men who tear up seats in buses and who attack a solitary Jew because they are many and he cannot possibly defend himself.

But with all of this sordidness there is humor. It is mixed with the language itself, which produces the same self-parodying effects as Yiddish. Perhaps all literary manifestations of *lunfardo* have something comic to them, something which may be seen in the burlesque rhetoric of the following passage. Here the narrator of **"La fiesta del Monstruo"** describes what happened when he tried to escape from his comrades on a bicycle:

> Tu chanchito te va hacer confidencial, Nelly; quien más quien menos ya pedaleaba con la comezón del Gran Spiantujen, pero como yo no dejo siempre de recalcar en las horas que el luchador viene enervado y se aglomeran los más negros pronósticos, despunta el delantero fenómeno que marca goal; para la patria el Monstruo para nuestra merza en franca descomposición, el camionero. Ese patriota que le saco el sombrero se corrió como patinada y paró en seco al más avivato del grupo en fuga. Le aplicó súbito un mensaje que al día siguiente, por los chichones todos me confundían con la yegua tubinana del panadero. Desde el suelo me mandé cada hurra que los vecinos se incrustaban el pulgar en el tímpano. De mientras, el camionero nos puso en fila india a los patriotas, que si alguno quería desapartarse, el de atrás tenía carta blanca para atribuirle cada patada en el culantro que todavía me duele sentarme.

The veil of flexible terms opens a bit here, and the reader can recognize that the narrator is admitting his (and his friends') fear. This confession disappears in the following sentences where he affirms that when a situation seems desperate someone always appears to turn defeat into victory: in the case of a soccer match, the player who scores the winning goal, in the case of the nation, the "Monster," and in the case of the group, the truckdriver. That "patriot" stopped the disintegration of the group by knocking down the one who had fled first and farthest: the narrator. After beating him up, the driver puts the men into single file, telling each man to kick the one in front if he tries to get away. When the narrator mentions "el culantro que todavía me duele sentarme," his implication is clear. The heroic vanguard of the "Monster's" party is nothing more than a group of cowards kept together by force. There is something of Chaplin's "The Great Dictator" in the churlishness of the fascists which is made doubly funny because of the narrator's slang.

The reasonable man as he reads this satire must laugh, just as he must become enraged because of its bizarre verisimilitude. This is the purpose of this particular tale, just as literary satire is the primary purpose behind some of the other collaborations, for example, the essays and false interviews of *Crónicas de Bustos Domecq.*

Today's reader of Borges and Bioy may see something in the collaborations of far greater importance than the parody of Argentine manners present in all of them. On one level, he may observe the fundamental humanity which led the authors to produce **"El hijo de su amigo"** and **"La fiesta del Monstruo,"** an impulse based on a desire to see reason prevail in human affairs rather than a desire to construct an ideologically compromised work of art. On another level, he may see the creation of a literary language, one which is in basic conflict with traditional literary language but which has its own historical origins.

To see the full significance of what Borges and Bioy have done with language, it would be necessary to reconsider the effects of Romanticism on literary language. In "Preface to Lyrical Ballads (1800)," Wordsworth says:

> The principal object, then, proposed in these poems was to choose incidents and situations from common life, and to relate or describe them, throughout, as far as was possible in a selection of language really used by men, and, at the same time, to throw over them a certain coloring of imagination, whereby ordinary things should be presented to the mind in an unusual aspect. . . . [*The Poetical Works of William Wordsworth* (1940-1949)]

Wordsworth wants to free poetry from the artificiality of what he calls "POETIC DICTION," the stylized phraseology and the overly refined level of language which had varied little since the Renaissance. He qualifies his idea of the "language really used by men" by saying that when it appears in his poetry it "has been adopted (purified indeed from what appear to be its real defects, from all rational causes of dislike and disgust). . . ." It is in Wordsworth's paradoxical attitude toward the "language really used by men" which he wants to use and yet must purify that we find the link between Romanticism and the past. Borges and Bioy or Carlo Emilio Gadda have made the literary language of the past and of Romanticism ironic by following Wordsworth's ideas to their logical conclusions.

From the moment in which Latin ceased to be a suitable vehicle for expression and writers turned to the vulgar tongues, communication was something desired by writers and their public. But the kind of vernacular used by writers was already a step away from the language spoken in the streets: Dante's Italian remains accessible to students of Italian literature today. Did he singlehandedly forge a literary language, or did there already exist a polished Italian in which the educated would speak to each other and which would differentiate them from peasants who would speak to each other in local dialects? The question may seem academic, but five centuries after Dante, Manzoni felt obliged to "purify" the language of his great novel by purging it of localisms and infusing it with the language of Tuscany.

Dialect became virtually synonymous with the grotesque in the bulk of European literary works after the Renaissance. In the nineteenth century, a novelist like Scott might introduce local language into some scenes for local color, but the linguistic norm for most writers would still be a neutral form of his national language. The literary public expected this, and there was little reason to destroy this link, based on communication, between artist and public. The nineteenth century may have exiled the artist, but it still continued to speak his language.

The reading public represented by the literary language of most novelistic works published before the Second World War would be in agreement with at least one aspect of the text before it, even if it disagreed with its description of society or its ideological tendency. The readers of Céline or Gadda or Borges and Bioy, on the other hand, find themselves in conflict with the very language of the text. For these men, localisms do not create verisimilitude; there is nothing picturesque in Céline's argot, nothing of the genre picture in the *lunfardo* used by Borges and Bioy. Nor should the reader assume that these authors are writing within Northrop Frye's "ironic mode": "A mode of literature in which the characters exhibit a power of action inferior to the one assumed to be normal in the reader or audience . . ." [*Anatomy of Criticism*]. They do not necessarily use a version of the spoken language—one as "purified" in the negative sense as Wordsworth's ordinary language—in order to depict a group of characters socially, economically, and politically below the level of the reader. The language of the lower classes and the underworld has acquired a stature which has liberated it from connotations of class (although these may be present) and has also widened the scope of literary irony.

There are antecedents: the Latin of the *Satyricon,* the argot literature of France, the language used by the poets of the *trobar clus.* But the relationship between an author like Teofilo Folengo, the creator of the macaronic epic the *Baldus,* and his readers and the relationship between the argot literature and its readers are exceptional cases. Literary language there, with the exception of Petronius, whose satiric intentions parallel those of modern authors, is a private language understood by initiates. The existence of a secret language understood by a special group of readers is not as important as the destruction of traditional links between reader and writer which is now taking place. The large scale appearance of argot in novels is an obstacle for those who are outside the area in which that argot is spoken. It is also true that the reader who comes from "outside" must work harder to read those texts than he did in the past and that this labor is not the same as that of the reader deciphering *Finnegans Wake*. The reader is alienated, and the importance of this alienation far exceeds that of the reader who becomes impatient as he reads the mixture of Latin and Italian in the *Baldus*.

An even more serious problem in the consideration of this new literary language is the need for the reader to divine the author's intentions. Contemporary aesthetics avoids this sort of speculation since the work of art is understood to be autonomous, free of the artist and his desires when he created it. And yet, the use of a language deliberately linked to a specific historical moment or a language, like that of Valle-Inclán in *Tirano Banderas,* which is a collage of the slang of an entire continent at a certain moment, demands that the critic examine the work in the light of extra-literary circumstances.

Only if this language is seen as metaphor, only if the situations described in the text are understood to be references to a hidden truth, will the verbal gesture implied by the argot or slang be understood. The mixture of argot and a deliberately baroque style by Borges and Bioy is a judgment about a specific historical situation seen from an ethical perspective. Their texts attempt to make the reader a temporary citizen of that world by making him learn its language, and from that experience he will emerge a changed person, one who has learned the value of the "language really used by men."

D. P. Gallagher   (essay date 1975)

SOURCE: "The Novels and Short Stories of Adolfo Bioy Casares," in *Bulletin of Hispanic Studies,* Vol. LII, No. 3, 1975, pp. 247-66.

[*In the following excerpt, Gallagher contends that "Bioy Casares's novels and short stories are comic masterpieces whose fundamental joke is the gap that separates what his characters know from what is going on."*]

On the one hand, there is a vast and inscrutable universe, manipulated by arcane and deliberate mystifiers; on the other hand a little man—a Venezuelan patriot [in *La invención de Morel*], a car mechanic [in *El sueño de los héroes*], a doddering *porteño* widower [in *Diario de la guerra del cerdo*]—who is painfully obliged to observe and suffer it. 'They' set the rules, 'they' know the answers. All that is left to our little man is frantically to guess, to deploy a hopeless but dogged 'furor conjetural' on the enigma. The enigma is always immeasurably vaster than the limited evidence he can ever have at his disposal for its elucidation. He can only judge by those few aspects of it that he experiences, and even they are perceived imperfectly by him. When the oddest and most difficult things to explain are occurring the chances are that he will be drunk, hungry, sleepy, feverish or in love. So his perception of the evidence is perpetually coloured by the condition of his emotions or of his body, and is therefore always in a state of unreliable transformation. And anyway, the most crucial clues are always missing.

Bioy Casares's novels and short stories are comic masterpieces whose fundamental joke is the gap that separates what his characters know from what is going on. The most notorious victim of that gap is the narrator of *La invención de Morel,* who frequently attempts to declare his love for one Faustine without realizing that she is a sort of holographic image who cannot therefore perceive his presence. Yet even the most trite situations that occur in Bioy's work contain the same fundamental dilemma. Thus his sex comedies in *Guirnalda con amores* or *El gran serafín* depict situations in which a man is convinced he has achieved a spectacular success only to discover that the girl's motives were notoriously less flattering than he imagined them to be. [In a footnote the critic directs: 'See for instance **"Encrucijada"** (*Guirnalda con amores*) or **"El don supremo"** and **"Confidencias de un lobo"** (*El gran serafín*).'] For not only the universe but every individual person is an enigma, and when one man confronts another, he can only work on the evidence the other chooses to project, and if the other is a woman his perception of that limited evidence will most likely be coloured anyway by his longing for her.

Bioy's little men are safe if they stick to their dingy rooms, or to their club or local café playing dominoes or talking horse-racing. They are in danger when they move out into the street—'Por no quedarse en su cuarto los hombres tropiezan con las desgracias' (*Diario*)—or, more seriously, when they travel. In other words disaster strikes when they move 'out of their element' into an area where their stock responses can no longer be applied, and it is there that the gap that separates what they know from what is going on begins to manifest itself. [In a footnote the critic adds: 'Bioy has furnished us with many cosmic comedies on that old standby, the Argentinian in Europe (see again **'Encrucijada'** and **'Confidencias de un lobo'**). Travel is prominent in his work, and his stories are very often set in hotels, lonely *estancias,* not to mention mysterious islands: places where characters are forced to react outside their normal habitat'.] Sometimes, the adventure is voluntary. Other times it is forced upon the characters by unforeseen circumstances: the presence of 'holographic images' indistinguishable from real people (*La invención de Morel*), the end of the world ('El gran serafín'), an unannounced yet speedily enacted decision to eliminate old men (*Diario*). In the latter cases *fantasy* is called upon to emphasize the perplexity in face of the unexpected of people who are unprepared for any but the most hackneyed conditions. In general, Bioy Casares imposes upon his characters an *adventure,* whether plausible or fantastic, in order to reveal their comic puniness.

Traditional adventure stories (those of say Stevenson, Defoe, Wells or Verne) have long been dear to Bioy as they have to Borges. Now what really are *Treasure Island, Robinson Crusoe* or *The Island of Dr Moreau* for instance but books in which a character has by choice or by necessity taken the inscrutable universe by the horns as it were, has left the bedsitter and risked going to find out what there is *over there*? Bioy Casares's novels, and in particular *La invención de Morel* and *Plan de evasión* (1945), are to a large extent *readings* of earlier, less sophisticated adventure stories. They are novels which reveal the extent to which the adventure story furnishes a dynamic dramatic form to express the gap that separates what a man knows from what there is. Of course Hawkins discovers what Long John Silver was up to and beats the pirates; Edward Prendick finds out all there is to know about Dr Moreau's menacing monsters and escapes them and Robinson Crusoe gets back to England. Yet what if the 'happy endings' were removed? What if the enigma remained an enigma?

In many adventure stories the cornerstone is often the hero's decision to enter a mysterious house, preferably on a windswept hill or in a dark forest. The rusty wrought iron gate creaks, there's a rustling noise (wind? a ghost? a hidden assassin crouching in wait?), he stumbles, there's a distant laugh: in short, a terrible suspense is created which reveals the hero's ignorance and fragility, even if in the end he solves everything. But what if he didn't? What if he were killed, like Borges's Lönnrot in the house through whose creaking gate he enters at Triste-le-Roy ['La muerte y la brújula', *Sur,* May 1942]? What if he discovers that the house is controlled by omnipotent seals who will never again allow him to leave it, as occurs in Bioy Casares's **'De los reyes futuros'** [in *La trama celeste*]? What if he discovers, like Joseph K, that he will somehow never *reach* the house, or castle, at all? Then we will have a story that devastatingly dramatizes the puniness of man. Or alternatively, is not the *end* of the conventional adventure story an exercise in wish-fulfilment, a fictive assertion (and in fiction there is no imaginable thing that cannot be asserted) that man can triumph over impossible odds and decipher enigmas? Bioy's adventure stories emphasize the suspense and mystery of the adventures without in the end resolving them. Sometimes, they *appear* to be resolved; the concluding 'explanation' seems to fit exactly. But usually the attentive reader will find that an alternative explanation fits equally well. Some, such as in *La invención de Morel,* are written in diary form: the man writing doesn't know, at the time of writing, what the next stage of the adventure has in store for him, so that we are immersed much more forcefully in the unpredictable contingencies of the present moment. Not only does he not know what is written on the last page: he will never reach it, and if he does, it will only be to write a final hurried note before the ultimate disaster. Others, such as *Plan de evasión,* are written in letter form: again, the present is immediate, the future unknown, the end an enigma to be conjectured by the reader after the narrator's correspondence briskly ceases. Always the effect is one of bringing to bear on the conventional adventure story a new perspective, a new reading, one in which we visualize what is implied, what is at stake in stories which we traditionally hurried through as a 'good read', unaware, perhaps, of how much our breathless longing to reach the explanatory end was telling us about our fundamental ignorance.

Now in two of Bioy's novels, in *La invención de Morel* and *Plan de evasión,* the adventure takes place on an island. The island is, I think, as important for Bioy as the labyrinth is for Borges. No doubt Bioy sees the universe as a labyrinth just as Borges does, but the island would seem to be significant for him because it is a *shut-off* and *isolated* component of the universe-labyrinth. For Bioy every human being would seem to be an island, the gulf between

one human being and another being as relentless as the sea that separates two islands. Local groups—*porteño* club-members, horse-racing enthusiasts, domino-players, football fans, patriots—also constitute islands, attempts to be shut off from the labyrinth or to settle for a convenient niche in it. And to leave the island is as dangerous as to embark on a stormy sea voyage.

The novel in which islands are most prominently significant is *Plan de evasión.* Enrique Nevers, after a family disgrace, is despatched from France on a mission to French Guiana. He discovers that the Governor, Castel, whom he must contact, is living on Devil's Island, and that for some reason access to Devil's Island has been prohibited by him. So he decides to instal himself on another island facing Devil's Island in order to discover what Castel, about whom the most peculiar rumours are circulating, is up to. For one, Devil's Island appears to be 'camouflaged', its buildings made almost indistinguishable from the vegetation. Is Castel mad? Has war been declared, the camouflage being designed to avert bombers? How much does Dreyfus (*sic*), the man who has been assigned to attend Nevers, know? Perhaps Castel's entire performance is 'una broma inescrutable, para confundirlo o distraerlo, con designios perversos?' At once, the gap that separates what Nevers knows from what is going on is established, and almost the entire novel consists of the 'furor conjetural' Nevers must bring to bear on the elusive and fragmented evidence at his disposal. On Devil's Island he can glimpse signs, goings on, yet all the time new evidence presents itself that forces him to discard a previous interpretation. All the time his central problem is that he cannot perceive the *design* behind what present themselves as purely gratuitous manifestations. In the end, he is forced to cross the channel and go and find out, risk the danger of *disembarking* on the prohibited island. When he does, he discovers a great deal, but he dies.

The island structure serves to dramatize the fact that man's perception of what there is is circumscribed by an *insular* perspective. That is to say, when examining the evidence of another island, he is fated to view it from the perspective of his own island. What he notices depends not only on what there is but also on what from his insular perspective he *expects* to find or is able to see, and his interpretation of what he happens to find depends not only on how it is but also on how he expects it to be, because he is fated to view it with *a priori* assumptions, because he examines it not on its merits, but in terms of whether or not it confirms an already adopted hypothesis. Finally, there is a *third* island, that which the reader inhabits, because the reader too in attempting to decipher the book, is also in the dark. He in turn must deploy a whole series of conjectures of his own: for instance, Nevers, in view of his somewhat frantic and disjointed prose style, may well be mad. He is certainly a most unreliable witness. May *he* not have an ulterior motive—'un designio perverso'—that he has not revealed? Is the reader too not a victim of 'una broma inescrutable'? How do we know that Castel's peculiar behaviour is not a figment of Nevers's imagination, or a lie of Nevers's obeying some arcane purpose? And like Nevers are we not too, as readers, doomed to an insular perspective? How much of the evidence are we missing, how subjective and partial is our interpretation of it? And finally how much of the evidence is withheld, how much of it is outside the field of vision open to us from our own island? Bioy Casares delights in his novels in playing with the impression that important evidence is missing (he is frequently cutting off conversations in mid-sentence or offering us *fragments* of revelatory letters), and that there is a great deal *he* knows which isn't in the text: for all we know there is an entire continent behind the island *we* perceive.

Now if islands are traps, prisons (Devil's Island doubly so, of course) the novel, as the title suggests, contains a *plan of escape*. This plan is Castel's mysterious design. Like Morel, Castel is a prodigious inventor, and he has devised a method of altering by surgery the sensory nerves so that there may occur a change in the interpretation of the stimuli they receive. 'Un cambio en el ajuste de mis sentidos haría, quizá, de los cuatro muros de esta celda la sombra del manzano del primer huerto'. Castel points out that our perception of the world depends on our sensory faculties. We can only perceive what they permit us to perceive. Change those faculties, and who knows what we would perceive? . . .

To be a man is to be an island as much as to be a *Nevers* or a football fan is to be one, for we are shut off from a whole series of unsuspected phenomena not only by our situation in life but also by the limitations of our senses themselves.

Now it is not accidental that Devil's Island is, indeed, a prison settlement, and Castel's *plan de evasión* consists of an attempt to alter the sensory nerves of three chosen prisoners in such a way that when locked in a cell they will interpret colour stimuli which he paints on its walls as the components of an altogether more liberating landscape. But what is this landscape to be? An island! . . .

[By] altering their sensory faculties he is able to liberate them from one island of limitations—their cell—in order to transport them to yet another *island,* less limited and more idyllic but nevertheless an island, limited by definition. Whatever combination of their sensory nerves he devises for them it will still be a combination, only one of a vast quantity of possible ones.

In **Plan de evasión** the island symbol is more explicit than in Bioy Casares's other books because the novel presents us so conspicuously with two main characters confronting each other from two respective islands. In **La invención de Morel** all the characters (insofar as there is more than one, since Morel and his friends turn out to be three-dimensional images of their deceased selves) are grouped together on one sole island. Yet **La invención de Morel** offers a formula that is not all that different from that of **Plan de evasión.**

Like Stephen Prendick in *The Island of Dr Moreau* (the transition from 'au' to 'l' acknowledges a tradition while pointing to its modification) the narrator is stranded on a very peculiar island indeed. At first sight deserted, it turns out to be occasionally populated by a group of nonchalant holidaymakers who appear to have arrived from nowhere and who occasionally disappear, not seeming moreover to

notice him at all, despite his frequently being in their company. Such is the enigma. Like Nevers and like Prendick, he attempts to bring to bear upon it a frenzy of conjecture. Are they involved in a complex conspiracy against him directed by the Caracas policeman from whom he has escaped? Their ignorance of the enigma that confronts them often drives Bioy's characters to paranoia. They come to believe that the peculiar manifestations which they cannot interpret are dictated by a complex conspiracy whose design it is to trap or mock them. Have loneliness, or the suspect roots he has been eating, prompted hallucinations? Has he for some reason become invisible, or has he died without realizing it? Are they 'Martians' living in another sphere of reality? They speak French, he observes. Maybe the French words they speak have a different meaning for them? The conjectures flow endlessly, and they are all wrong. For the 'people' he has been observing turn out, like the strange creatures on Dr Moreau's island, to be the victims of a scientific invention as astonishing as Castel's. The fact is that Morel, the inventor, has devised, a decade before Gabor, a spectacular method of three-dimensional filming. Morel's 'holographic images' are so perfect that they include their subjects' consciousness, and he can film all their five senses. Indeed there is no apparent difference in the end between the projected images and the persons filmed, except that the latter disintegrate after the film has been made, so that only the (identical) film version of them remains.

The peculiar phenomena of the island are thus 'explained'. And yet the explanation leaves much to be desired: as the narrator says, there are in it 'elementos para comprender *casi* todo'. It has internal inconsistencies, and also, very subtly, Bioy Casares leaves some of the more sensible of the original hypotheses very open. Is the narrator not in fact mad? His Carrolian logic is certainly very odd. Has *he* invented Morel, who speaks and thinks rather like him and who shares with him an obsession with immortality? The title is pointedly enigmatic—it could refer to the narrator's invention of Morel, or to his account of Morel's invention. Is he indeed having hallucinations? His visions rather pointedly remind him of people he knows. The reader of **La invención de Morel** is therefore forced into the same self-contradicting conjectures that the novel's narrator is forced into when 'reading' Morel's film: the same triple hierarchy of insular bafflement emerges that we found in **Plan de evasión,** involving the inventor (God? the writer?), the *voyeur* who attempts to interpret the inventor's manifestations (man? the critic?) and the reader who attempts to interpret the book.

In the manner of Wells, Bioy Casares has devised a splendid plot in **La invención de Morel** but, unlike Wells, he has furnished it with almost inexhaustible implications. Let us look at some of them.

In the first place the plot functions as a symbol of man's confrontation with an enigmatic universe, or with any more specific enigma. Needless to say Faustine, the member of Morel's party with whom the narrator falls in love, is one for the narrator. For the fact that Faustine is a sort of perfected holographic image means that though she has all the appearance of being a human being like any other, she cannot of course hear or see the narrator, because she can only perceive what she actually perceived when being filmed. Yet does any person really hear what another says to him? Are we not all living on different planes? Are we not all inscrutable *islands,* like the narrator and Faustine? The comedy rests of course on the gap that separates what the narrator knows about Faustine and the fact of what she is. The gap is a very spectacular one because Faustine is only an image, but it is merely a hyperbole of a gap that always separates Bioy Casares's characters when they confront each other. The enigmas that the narrator strains to solve are extreme versions of the enigmas that all Bioy Casares's lovers are faced with: like the lovers of **'Encrucijada', 'Confesiones de un lobo'** or **'Ad porcos'** he must resign himself to *interpret* the girl's *behaviour,* without ever being sure of its motives or causes.

Men are islands, a man's decision to make advances at a woman is comparable to an adventurer's decision to embark on a mysterious island. The advance is always comically magnified to almost epic proportions. . . .

The most normal activity—talking to a woman—is transformed into an epic *expedition,* full of the trappings of an adventure story: hiding in wait, spying before acting, putting a foot wrong . . . , losing consciousness, etc. You get the same atmosphere in a more conventional story like **'Ad porcos',** where an Argentinian is trying to decide whether or not to speak to a lady sitting beside him in a Montevideo theatre. His indecision is described over several pages. Are the people next to her with her? Might there not be a husband or fiancé sitting somewhere else in the theatre? She's smiled at him: but supposing she's a prostitute? In short, how much *danger* is he in? (**El gran serafín**). Such is the dilemma of the hypothesizing man in face of the unknown. In the end, the philosopher, the adventurer and the lover are all trapped in the same comic structure: that of the man whose knowledge of a situation falls disastrously short of its reality and who has not perceived a crucial clue: the banana skin on which he is fated to trip up.

For Bioy every human being would seem to be an island, the gulf between one human being and another being as relentless as the sea that separates two islands.

—D. P. Gallagher

At the end of **La invención de Morel,** the narrator decides to incorporate himself into the three-dimensional film of which Faustine is a part. After studying Faustine's gestures over the week that the film lasts, he deploys Morel's cameras and films himself next to Faustine, makes her words (which are generally spoken to Morel) sound as

though they were replies to *his* questions, and in short creates scenes that, to a potential outside observer, might suggest that Faustine was in love with him. Now **La invención de Morel** is said to have influenced the film *L'année dernière à Marienbad,* and certainly Robbe-Grillet has acknowledged a similarity between the two works. And there would indeed seem to be one thing that they have in common: the suggestion that when people (even lovers) talk to each other they don't really communicate. Someone's words may appear to be an answer to another's question, but are they really? Are we not all living (if one may borrow a perceptive expression that would have been relished by Castel) 'worlds (or islands!) apart' from each other?

There are further implications in Morel's invention. One could, for instance, read the narrator's dilemma as the dilemma of the ignorant layman with regard to the omnipotent, enigmatic and designing scientist. The layman can only witness the *behaviour* of a scientist's inventions; the causes of that behaviour are an enigma to him. And the scientist is moreover always many steps ahead of the layman. We noted that Bioy's characters frequently have an intimidated sense that 'others' are in control of things, and with respect to scientists perhaps we all do. The narrator's dilemma could also be that of the inhabitant of an underdeveloped country with respect to the developed world, where all the technology is and where the decisions are made. The narrator is deliberately set up as a somewhat absurd Venezuelan sage, humiliatingly aware that Morel might well be famous, but that he probably wouldn't have heard of him in Caracas. Finally, the narrator (and the reader) can be seen as a perplexed man witnessing the inscrutable machinations of God, or as a perplexed critic attempting to decipher a book. But whatever its specific detail, the pattern of confrontation is always the same one: that of a limited perspective brought to bear on a situation too vast for it to cope with.

Of course realist novels posit three-dimensional beings, and one can also infer from the novel a healthy joke about realist literature. Like Morel's 'holographic images' a character in a realist novel is posited as a real human being with five senses, a consciousness and, if necessary, a soul. And like Morel, realist novelists create 'immortal' people. Long after their creator or the real-life models on which they were inspired are dead, the characters of a novel come to life every time someone reads the novel they inhabit, just as Morel's images do every time they are projected (their functioning depends on energy derived from the island's tides). Morel's images could thus be read perhaps as the claims of realist fiction pressed to a logical conclusion. As such they expose the extent to which realist achievements fall short of realist aims, for whatever they are posited as, the characters of fiction are needless to say never quite as alive as Morel's images. But they also subversively demonstrate that, if those aims *were* fully realized, the characters of a book would be as disturbingly real as their creators, and further, they would be less fleeting, for they would not only possess all their author's attributes but would also be immortal. In other words, if a writer could, like God or a healthy womb, 'create' *real* characters, they would be as real as their authors and less ephemeral.

In a way of course it is true that a character in a book is less ephemeral than his author. We know more about Rastignac than we know about Balzac, because we know about Balzac only from what was written about him, words which only account for a fragment of his life, whereas Rastignac *is* merely what Balzac wrote about him. At best a dead man and a character of fiction are equals: both are inseparable from the words through which they are referred and from which we must infer them. So if we decide that Morel's images and Balzac's characters are fictive, we must reflect back on the status in reality of others whom we normally regard not to be. Who in the end is more fictive: Morel or his surviving image, Tolstoy's Napoleon or Napoleon himself, Marilyn Monroe or the images of her that survive on celluloid? What is the past but the words or images that remain of it? Why should the referents of these words or images be less fictive than the referents of novels or imaginative films? In the end we can only infer both.

In a famous essay called 'Kafka y sus precursores' [in his *Otras inquisiciones*, 1960], Borges wittily discovered 'Kafkaesque' scenes in such disparate places as Zeno's paradoxes, Kierkegaard and Lord Dunsany, and concluded (echoing Eliot) that 'cada escritor *crea* a sus precursores. Su labor modifica nuestra concepción del pasado, como ha de modificar el futuro'. A final level on which *La invención de Morel* functions is that of meditation upon disparate works of literature which has as a consequence their gentle modification. We have seen that Bioy makes Wells more profound by echoing his plots yet reading into them implications that Wells did not make explicit or was not conscious of. He does the same with other writers. For example a characteristically discreet clue—a reference to the chapel on Morel's island as having the shape of 'una caja oblonga'—leads one to examine Poe's story 'The Oblong Box', which describes the 'furor conjetural' a passenger on an ocean liner deploys in his effort to interpret the peculiar behaviour of some fellow-passengers in the cabin across the corridor from his. We soon realize that the narrator in that story is in fact in the same dilemma as the narrator of *La invención de Morel*. He too attempts to determine the design or cause behind an enigmatic (though not fantastic) effect, and he is doomed to view it from the *insular* perspective of his cabin. When we come to see how much of what can be said about Bioy's novel is applicable also to 'The Oblong Box', Poe's simple story is immeasurably enriched. The desperate ignorance, self-doubt, flimsiness of evidence and shifting hypotheses of the following passage are very much of the kind that Bioy's narrator engages in:

> After this there was a dead stillness, and I heard nothing more, upon either occasion, until nearly daybreak; unless, perhaps, I may mention a low sobbing, or murmuring sound, so very much suppressed as to be nearly inaudible—if, indeed, the whole of this latter noise were not rather produced by my own imagination. I say it seemed to *resemble* sobbing or sighing—but, of course, it could not have been either. I rather think it

was a ringing in my own ears. Mr Wyatt, no doubt, according to custom, was merely giving the rein to one of his hobbies—indulging in one of his fits of artistic enthusiasm. He had opened his oblong box in order to feast his eyes on the pictorial treasure within. There was nothing in this, however, to make him *sob*. I repeat, therefore, that it must have been simply a freak of my own fancy, distempered by good Captain Hardy's green tea. [Edgar Allan Poe, *Tales, Poems, and Essays*]

'Unless, perhaps', 'or', 'if indeed', 'it seemed', 'but', 'it could not have been', 'rather', 'no doubt', 'however', 'therefore', 'it must have been': the effect of reading *La invención de Morel* is to turn these innocent phrases into expressions of the problem of knowledge, and to convert Poe's narrator from a mere curious *voyeur* to a kind of tragic hero of epistemology.

It is noteworthy that *La invención de Morel* superficially resembles another tale of Poe's, 'MS Found in a Bottle', where a man finds himself stranded after shipwreck on a vessel whose crew do not see him, as though he had become invisible. As in Bioy's novel, the evidence for the tale is, moreover, an unfinished manuscript whose last sentence precedes the final catastrophe. Again, many passages of 'MS Found in a Bottle' could have been written by the narrator of *La invención de Morel*.

In a sense *La invención de Morel* would seem to be deliberately linking 'MS Found in a Bottle' to 'The Oblong Box', and thereby making an important point, that a fantastic story like the former is principally a hyperbole of the latter. Because of our insular perspective we can know nothing at the best of times. When a fantastic phenomenon such as invisibility presents itself, our ignorance is merely emphasized. And, as we have seen, in Bioy's own work, fantasy similarly *emphasizes* an epistemological gap that obtains even in his most realistic stories.

Bioy Casares's subsequent novels and short stories continue to explore the gap that separates what a man knows from what there is. Thus Gauna in *El sueño de los héroes* desperately endeavours to discover what occurred one carnival night when he was out drunk with his friends. He has an alarming impression that he died in a knife-duel yet cannot deny that he is still alive. Whenever he asks his friends to explain what happened they mysteriously change the subject. Like Morel, he alone appears to be in the dark with regard to something that seems to be known by *everyone*. The venerable Isidoro Vidal in *Diario de la guerra del cerdo* is in a similar dilemma, because for a time he is about the only old man in Buenos Aires who is not aware that an elaborate campaign is being conducted in that city to exterminate old men. Everyone's *behaviour* has changed (the *panadera* and the newspaper vendor are curiously short with him) but because of his ignorance he cannot perceive the *motives* or *design* behind the change. Even when he does become aware of the campaign, both he and his cronies are very hazy indeed about who ordered it and why.

Yet there is much more to these novels than a mere confrontation of limited men with an enigma deployed by 'others'. For instance, I think one could take *El sueño de los héroes* as Bioy Casares's contribution to that venerably ancient topic of Latin-American literature, the struggle between 'civilization' and 'barbarism'. Let us examine the novel more closely. Gauna, the mechanic who wakes up from a three-day drunken carnival jaunt with vague memories of having been killed by his friends the night before in a traditional Argentinian knife-duel then marries a girl, Clara, whose father attempts to educate him away from his *guapo* cronies. Indeed, the culture he proceeds to acquire leads him soon to despise his bragging circle. Yet three years after the carnival jaunt, to which he had invited his friends as a result of winning money at the races, he wins money at the races again. Compulsively, he is driven to invite his old friends once more for a repeat performance. They go to the same bars which they had visited previously, and on the third day he is killed by his friends in a knife-duel.

In short, the compulsive pull of *machista* barbarism is too strong for an ephemeral civilization artificially superimposed upon it: civilization is nothing but a hiatus separating two instances of the real thing, barbarism. [In a footnote the critic adds: 'Or *bar*-barism, in view of the fact that it is drink that brings it to light: *in vino veritas*. In an engaging story, **'Clave para un amor'** (*Historia prodigiosa*, 1961) we are told of a hotel in the Chilean Andes where there is a shrine to Bacchus. On September 17 (the hemispheric equivalent of March 17, the day of Bacchus's *liberalia*), a curious thing happens to the decorous clients of the hotel, who have notoriously been watching a film called *The Masked Ball*: they all start brutally to say what they think, and in general dangerously to *unmask* themselves. A man who is at heart a thief steals, another declares his love, etc'.]

The very structure of the novel is symbolical of how insubstantial that culture is, for if the end of a book is fundamentally a mirror-image of its beginning, it follows that the pages in between (those that describe Gauna's education) are transparent. One only has to visualize the book physically to grasp this point that the very structure makes.

Borges too has written about men whose whole lives turn out to have been insubstantial at the moment when, in a knife-fight which they cannot escape, they meet their violent 'American destiny'. For at the moment of its fulfilment, that violent American destiny makes nonsense of all that has preceded it. Destiny, or a force superior to his conscious will, certainly appears to be driving Gauna on. It is notable that he makes his fatal decision to embark on another carnival jaunt as a result of winning money at the races. The fruits of gambling, whether favourable or unfavourable, diminish freedom of choice by definition: to win a large sum of money is to have imposed upon one a change dictated by an *outside* agent (by a horse, a card, a number—the number 3 would appear to be Gauna's daemon). To gamble is to surrender one's freedom to forces outside one's control; to win as well as to lose at the races is to become a pawn of destiny. In the end no amount of control can save Gauna from succumbing to the ethos in which he has been reared and to which he has been des-

tined: that of gratuitous violence. And for him as for Borges's Laprida, the hero of 'Poema conjetural', one single act of violence overpowers and invalidates (or unmasks) all that has preceded it.

Bioy Casares's most recent novel, *Diario de la guerra del cerdo,* is, like *El sueño de los héroes,* deeply rooted in Argentina, and it too has many richnesses added to its already discussed basic structure—the confrontation of a perplexed man with decisions and manifestations deployed enigmatically by others. It tells the story of how suddenly, for no apparent reason, young people begin to kill old people in Buenos Aires, much to the authorities' indifference. Bioy Casares is not a trendy man, and it would be wrong to see the plot as a reflection of the current generation gap. The 'pig's war' designation is, I think, a coincidence topically speaking. The point is rather that Bioy has deliberately devised a somewhat abstract plot in order to show up certain archetypal mechanisms pertaining to persecution in general which would probably be disguised if the plot were more recognizably familiar, if the novel were about the persecution of the Jews for instance. If you make the object of a persecution in a novel a fantastic one, you are probably in a better position to investigate the nature of persecution in general. And indeed the novel parades all the structural mechanisms that perhaps all persecutions share. We witness the volatility of crowds, the persuasive power of demagogy, the problem of collaboration with the enemy (horizontal or otherwise), the problem of the divided family, the dilemma of those who believe they are not one of the victims (the old man who believes he is not yet old, like the Jew who believes he isn't a Jew), or of those who try to alter their appearance in order not to look conspicuous (the old man who dyes his hair, like the Jew who alters his nose). In general, the novel shows how easy it is to draw a dividing line anywhere between men, how easy it is to concoct an enemy.

In *The Go-Between,* L. P. Hartley introduced a game of cricket into his portrait of an aristocratic Edwardian family in order to show that all the forces at play in that family could be present too, in microcosm, in the most abstract of games. In the game of cricket those forces are present as bare structures, whereas in the family the same structures are disguised by the specific habits and specific characters of specific people. The batsman who didn't bat 'stylishly' (the plebeian farmer) was the most successful because he was not *inhibited* by style, and he was able to hit the *gentlemen* bowlers for six. Similarly, outside the game, the unstylish farmer was much more successful with the desired girl than her stylish, aristocratic fiancé was, again because he was not inhibited by repressive manners. But eventually, in the game, he is *caught out* on the *boundary* by the young go-between. Similarly, outside the game, the young go-between 'catches him out' copulating with the young lady of the house on a haystack, a sort of boundary too because it is the *limit* of behaviour: as a result he commits suicide, just as in the game he is forced to stop batting because he is *out*. I think that the plot of *Diario de la guerra del cerdo* is similarly an abstract game designed to expose the structure of persecution in an undisguised form, just as the plot of **La invención de Morel** is designed to expose the structure both of investigation and of communication. The more abstract the game, the more the padding which conceals the basic structure will be dismantled.

Much of what I have written so far about Bioy Casares's novels could be applied also to Borges's work. Borges too confronts limited hypothesizers with contingent reality, and Borges too forces his reader into a similarly intimidating hypothesizing enterprise with respect to the fiction he is reading. Yet Borges and Bioy Casares are very different writers. For instance, though both present characters whose most notorious characteristic it is to be limited, Borges would appear to be interested mainly in the mere fact that they *are* limited, whereas Bioy Casares is concerned to depict the specific forms their limitations take. Borges can of course offer a whole suggestive picture of the specific nature of a man's limitations in just one sentence. [In 'La muerte y la brújula' in *Ficciones*, he] can say of the editor of the *Yidische Zaitung* that he is 'miope, ateo y muy tìmido' and make us feel that there is nothing further to add. Yet Bioy Casares adds a great deal, and he may devote the best part of a novel to the investigation of what precise forms a man's timidity might take, of what precise effects his atheism and myopia might have on him. The difference in the two writers may be the difference between a novelist and a writer of lapidary short stories. Bioy Casares at any rate investigates the limitations of his characters in depth, and is as keen to depict the specific form their limitations take as he is to state the fact that they are limitations.

As far as the structure of the plot is concerned the fact that people devote their lives to playing dominoes or *truco,* or to talking football or horse-racing may be important merely because such activities are, interchangeably, restricted ones, safely yet ignorantly *insular.* Yet Bioy Casares is conspicuously concerned to depict the islands for their own sake. His descriptions of Gauna's cronies or of Vidal's cosy circle of *truco*-mad old men, of the local *confitería* or of the local bread-store, of the workshop in which Gauna works or of the drab lodgings in which Vidal lives, are notable for their meticulous specificity. The references are uncompromisingly local, and the local world is assumed momentarily to *be* the universe. But then an engaging authorial irony reveals that it is not and exposes its limitations by suggesting the possibility of another perspective from which its behaviour can be viewed. . . .

Bioy Casares has a Chekhovian skill in dissecting pathetic details in the behaviour of his characters: little quirks, mannerisms, or accidents of dress for instance, which again serve to circumscribe their limitations. The comedy and the pathos is of course enhanced when the ruthlessly dissected characters believe their absurd behaviour to be vastly important. The joke rests on the gap that separates what a character believes to be important from what is important, on the character's sublime confidence in his insular perspective. Thus doctor Valerga ('¿doctor en qué?' as El Brujo asks), the hero of Gauna's *guapo* circle, is an utterly idiotic man, yet he is incapable of speaking without the most portentous sententiousness. In **'El perjurio de la nieve'** a country doctor launches into a confident homily on the wonders of the radio as though he had invented it: 'le permitía oír el Colón y los discursos de una cantidad

de señores con puestos públicos' (**La trama celeste**). The narrator of **La invención de Morel** believes himself to be engaged on a devastatingly important study of Malthus.

Like Chekhov's schoolmasters, many of Bioy's local heroes deploy a vulgar, self-important banality which is at the same time touchingly pathetic. The spirit in which they live is summarized in the epigraph of the story **'Historia prodigiosa'**: '*Yo siempre digo: no hay nadie como Dios.* Una señora argentina.' Yet however self-important and confident, they are in the end grotesquely vulnerable: 'Los grandes ojos azules manaban lágrimas y un dedo experto corregía los deplorables efectos del *rimmel* corrido' (**El gran serafín**).

Their meticulously charted emotions, physique and class provenance are all measures of their limitations. Yet nowhere are their limitations more prominent than in their use of language. Language is the signature of Bioy Casares's characters. Their language tells us who they are, where they come from, what they are like—whether they are mad or in love or self-opinionated or timid and in particular what their values are. For Bioy Casares's characters are consistently attempting to impress each other, and his narrators to impress us, by imitating what they assume to be an impressive model of style. The language of each one is an unconscious parody of what they or the class or profession from which they come believe to be an impressive way of speaking or writing.

Let us look at some of the styles Bioy Casares's characters adopt in order to overwhelm us. Again, the joke lies in the gap that separates the self-importance of their endeavour from its limitations when viewed from a wider perspective.

Take in the first place the unforgettable provincial *escribano* in **'Las caras de la verdad'**, an amateur historian whose career is described to us by an admiring assistant:

> 'El escribano compone nuestra personalidad
> más ponderada, amén de nuestro historiador
> máximo y, a la verdad, único; desde muy niño,
> desde la remota mañana en que el manual de *Historia Argentina* de Aubin rodó en los faldones
> de su guardapolvo escolar, don Bernardo dedica
> los raros momentos de ocio a la investigación en
> los archivos locales y al acuse recibo de cartas de
> secretarios y tinterillos de las numerosas corporaciones a que pertenece en calidad de miembro correspondiente. En este campo de su actividad cosechó últimamente halagos publicitarios
> porque se mudó—según explicó un martillero de
> toda confianza—al bando revisionista. El mismo
> martillero me aseguró, eso sì, que don Bernardo
> no desplazó del pedestal de la gloria a ninguno
> de los viejos próceres, aunque encaramó también
> a fantasmones poco recomendables.' (**El gran
> serafín**)

One notes a sacred patriotic high style derived probably from school textbooks and the national anthem that is brutally undermined by colloquial lapses: 'eso sì', 'fantasmones'. The portentous tone of the *escribano*'s disciple is further undermined in the story by the fact that he has to use it to describe to us how his hero one day suddenly began to kill all his neighbours' animals because of his belief that the souls of these 'fantasmones' had been reincarnated in them. His quaint idea and the hallucinations that prompt it turn out to have been effected by some pills the doctor prescribed for him for a urinary complaint. . . .

The aggressive local word and the inelegant vulgar banality are . . . always there to subvert the pompous intentions of Bioy Casares's sages. In the end, they are trapped, in their use of language, in the same comic structure they are trapped in generally: when they are most sublimely confident in what they know, they fall flat on their face by uttering an inapposite expression and consequently give themselves away. In their use of language, as in every other activity they perform, a gap separates their aspirations from their execution of them, the comedy of the situation resting of course on the fact that we, from another perspective, recognize the gap whereas they do not.

Although *La invención de Morel* is not set in Argentina and Bioy Casares is at his best depicting Argentinian voices, it is impossible to appreciate that novel too without taking into account the language in which it is written. For nowhere does its narrator reveal himself more conspicuously than in his choice of words. Take the opening paragraph of the novel:

> Hoy, en esta isla, ha ocurrido un milagro. El verano se adelantó. Puse la cama cerca de la pileta de natación y estuve bañándome, hasta muy tarde. Era imposible dormir. Dos o tres minutos afuera bastaban para convertir en sudor el agua que debía protegerme de la espantosa calma. A la madrugada me despertó un fonógrafo. No pude volver al museo, a buscar las cosas. Huí por las barrancas. Estoy en los bajos del sur, entre plantas acuáticas, indignado por los mosquitos, con el mar o sucios arroyos hasta la cintura, viendo que anticipé absurdamente mi huida. Creo que esa gente no vino a buscarme; tal vez no me hayan visto.

The third sentence is structured in such a manner that it seems to imply that putting the bed next to the swimming pool was a precondition for bathing. [In a footnote the critic adds: 'It is not surprising that this novel was not much noticed when published in the United States. The American version of the sentence reads "I moved my bed out to the swimming pool, but then, because it was impossible to sleep, I stayed in the water for a long time". The American version confidently irons out all such revealing illogicalities. As a consequence, the book loses most of its charm'.] The references to the gramophone and to 'esa gente' render the assertion he makes on the following page that the island is deserted somewhat surprising. And one notes his somewhat frantic ('espantosa calma') or comically petulant ('indignado por los mosquitos') use of adjectives. His use of adjectives in general underlines the extent to which he is an engagingly but utterly absurd character: 'fue una operación *horripilante*', 'volví a encontrarme con uno de esos picaportes *inexorables*', 'Morel apareció con Alec (joven *oriental y verdinegro*)', 'hasta aquí un discurso repugnante'. So do his similes: 'Ya está el agua, en silencio, como una vaselina de bronce, forzándome las vías respiratorias'; or his sudden poetic outbursts: 'se apagaron (*sic*) los ruidos, como en un ambiente de nieve, como en las frías

alturas de Venezuela'. And it is on this dotty man that we must rely as our sole witness to the invention of Morel!

Bioy Casares's work has not, in my opinion, been given the prominence it deserves in Latin-American writing. Maybe he has suffered from his association with Borges, it having been assumed by some that Bioy was merely a glorified amanuensis, or in his own work a minor imitator of Borges, perhaps, who was not worth reading when one already had the superb original. And yet it is easy to demonstrate with relevant dates how open a question it is whether Borges has influenced Bioy Casares or whether it is Bioy who has influenced Borges. Borges was after all a poet and essayist when they first met in 1932, by which time Bioy was already a deployer of fictions. It is moreover a perhaps deliberate characteristic of Borges's prose that it is written in a style which, though subversively paradoxical, does not vary significantly from story to story. The Cretan Minotaur, the man who tells us about the lottery of Babylon, or the Scottish missionary Brodie all talk with much the same self-contradicting, oxymoronic Borgesian voice. In Bioy Casares's books, on the other hand, we have observed a use of language that is not only polysemantic in the Borgesian sense but also socially and psychologically polyphonous. And on the evidence of Bioy Casares's work, who could honestly deny that the books they have written together such as *Seis problemas para don Isidro Parodi* (1942) may well contain more of Bioy than of Borges? For only in Bioy's work is there anything comparable to that splendid gallery of parodied voices that Bioy and Borges have construed under the pseudonym of H. Bustos Domecq. Memories of Bioy's linguistic buffoons could be brought to bear on the following examples. First the pompous and absurd actor Gervasio Montenegro:

> 'Al día siguiente, ante el peligroso *capo lavoro* de algún *chef* calchaquí, pude examinar con bonhomía la fauna humana que poblaba ese angosto universo que es un tren en marcha'.

Second the poet Carlos Anglada:

> 'Usted me disculpará: yo hablo con la franqueza de una motocicleta . . . En mi escritorio, en mi usina de metáforas, para ser más claro . . . '

Finally Sarastano, the *compadrito*:

> 'le acepto que la Juana Musante tiene un cuerpo que a uno lo deja de cama, pero un tipo como yo que tuvo una historia con una señorita que ya es manícura, y después con una menor que iba a ser astro de la radio, no se perturba con ese corpachón atractivo, que puede suscitar la atención en Banderaló, pero que a la muchachada del centro la pone apática.'

And the Parodi stories all enact the formula that we have relentlessly discussed: that of the man who is blind to what is staring at him in the face, because he perceives the evidence from an excessively insular perspective, for instance because, as happens to Gervasio Montenegro, he is too vain to imagine that he was being duped. We noted that such a formula has characterized many of Borges's stories. The difference is that Bioy Casares and the authors of *Parodi* characterize the insularity so much more conspicuously for its own sake, and that characterization includes not only the detail of its behaviour but also the specific and revealing language with which it expresses itself.

It would be absurd to claim that Bioy Casares was a 'better' writer than Borges through being, in a sense, a more 'complete' writer, one more deeply rooted in a given historical reality. As Borges once said, 'La literatura no es un certamen'. It is anyway churlish to divide two great friends by comparing their value. But there do seem to be healthy signs that Bioy is now beginning to be identified as something apart from Borges, and that is a different matter.

He was first seriously noted as an important novelist in his own right in France in the early fifties. Robbe-Grillet reviewed *La invención de Morel* with some enthusiasm in *Critique* (No. 69, February 1953) and Blanchot devoted some pages on him in *Le livre à venir*. But neither writer did much more than summarize the plot of his most famous novel. Ofelia Kovacci's book of 1963 is a useful short introduction with a helpful bibliography, but it seldom ventures beyond paraphrase. For some reason it was the publication of *Diario de la guerra del cerdo* that gave Bioy a certain popular renown in Buenos Aires. He was suddenly interviewed in glossy magazines, suddenly partaking in the so-called 'boom' in Latin-American fiction, whose relentless creativeness his influence no doubt did much to mould. It may be that this man who through modesty has always shunned self-promotion is at last beginning to be appreciated despite himself. Serious appraisals that have recently emerged include Enrique Pezzoni's review of *Diario de la guerra del cerdo* in *Los Libros* (No. 7, Buenos Aires, January 1970), Jaime Rest's essay on 'Las invenciones de Bioy Casares', also in *Los Libros* (No. 2, August 1969) and Jacques Gounard's study 'Bioy Casares: entre Stevenson et Robbe-Grillet' in *Le Monde* of 9 August 1973. One hopes they are symptoms of greater things to come.

Robert M. Adams   (essay date 1975)

SOURCE: "No Escaping Evasion," in *Review,* No. 15, Fall, 1975, pp. 50-4.

[Adams is an American educator and author. In the essay below, he analyzes Bioy Casares's deliberate use of ambiguity and unresolved mystery in A Plan for Escape.*]*

Adolfo Bioy Casares has been known in this country chiefly as a friend and associate of Jorge Luis Borges; and while his independent reputation is increasing rapidly in South America (with the accrual of prizes, the adaptation of his books to film and other marks of reputation) in America the publication of *A Plan for Escape* seems likely to strengthen the impression of a Borges-affinity. So far as my limited bibliographical resources will serve, this is the third volume [as of Fall 1975] of Bioy to appear in English. The chief previous work was a novel, *Diary of the War of the Pig*; another volume goes under the title of the main novella, *The Invention of Morel.* This story was originally published in 1940; the volume was filled out with shorter fictions from *La Trama Celeste* (1948), the whole thing translated by Ruth Simms, and published by the University of Texas Press in 1964 as part of the Texas Pan-

American series. All this preliminary pedantry is simply a way of putting the new publication—more a novella than a novel—in the perspective of Bioy's work. In Spanish, where it includes at least six volumes in addition to those mentioned, the *oeuvre* of Bioy doubtless has a definable shape and direction; in English, it looks rather like a hopscotch. The volume under review was written in 1945, and is therefore earlier than anything else to appear in English, except *The Invention of Morel,* with which it has a good deal in common.

Both *Morel* and *Escape* center on that favorite figure of our cultural fantasies, the mad scientist. To make him omnipotent, the scientist must be isolated, and since H. G. Wells' *The Island of Doctor Moreau* (lurking in the background of both Bioy stories), desert islands have been much in vogue for this purpose. Bioy attempts no untoward novelties. In both his tales, the story is narrated by an outsider who comes to the island, is baffled by some baffling appearances, and finally penetrates to the heart of them: they turn out to involve a series of experiments in systematically deranged perception. The movement of both stories is thus from the outside inward. But there is another dimension to the present novel, a movement from the inside out, which surrounds the other motion without negating it, and which renders the latest book a good deal more intricate than the earlier one.

The narration of *A Plan for Escape* is beset with complexities and ambiguities which render practically everything said in the book subject to question. In theory, the basis of the story is the experience of Lieutenant Henri Nevers, who in March and April of 1913 was sent by his powerful uncle Pierre Brissac to serve as assistant warden on the Iles du Salut off the coast of French Guiana. The most famous of these islands is of course Ile du Diable, on which Captain Dreyfus was confined during the years 1894-1899. But though the narration is based on the letters of Lieutenant Nevers to his uncle Antoine in France, uncle Antoine actually quotes only a few scattered phrases from his nephew's letters, and tells the rest of the story in the third

Cover of a short story collection by Bioy Casares.

person. Though he is not consistently an omniscient narrator, he is often a preternaturally knowing one. Sometimes he writes as if he had been physically present at a
scene; on the other hand, he frequently professes to be limited to what his nephew has told him. He suggests several
times that his nephew is an unreliable witness, of "weak
character," perhaps a coward (though that possibility is
raised through the characteristically indirect device of denying the idea feebly) or maybe just a neurotic. We are
told the story of a scar which, as a young boy, Henri Nevers went out of his way to acquire undeservedly; the suggestion is of uncontrolled and indiscriminate guilt. Yet the
uncle himself gives every evidence of being a sly, evasive,
equivocal person; and the possibility must always be entertained that uncle Antoine is distorting or inventing the
story, or suppressing unknown portions of it, to serve ends
of his own. Certainly if the Lieutenant seems subject to
paranoid hallucinations, his uncle is afflicted with an extremely uneasy conscience and an impulse to hush things
up. For example, he never tells us, and we learn only late
in the book from a third witness, that Pierre and Antoine
are bitter and traditional enemies. Filtered through two
such crazed glasses, the events of the fable reach us in a
form the contradictory distortions of which we find it hard
to estimate. A third "outside" witness to events in the
penal colony appears only toward the end of the book. He
is just as equivocal, evasive, and suppressive as the first
two witnesses; his account clears up nothing. A "*plan de
evasión*" appears in some sense gratuitous; evasion comes
quite naturally to everyone in the book.

In brief, the structure of the world within which Lieutenant Nevers encounters his fantastic, but ultimately decipherable, enigma on Devil's Island is more enigmatic and
less decipherable than the enigma itself. The very texture
of unrelated life is absurd. As he enters to dine at the Frin-
giné's and is escorted by a servant to the drawing room,
Lieutenant Nevers passes through the "clandestine distill-
ery"—as if any such installation could be clandestine,
which any casual visitor to the house could not help seeing. The book works in two ways; as Nevers penetrates to
the heart of his problem, expounding its formal solution
in an extended lecture, confusion, blur, and overlay spread
outwards through the world surrounding the problem.
For instance, the first and most important figure that Nevers encounters on Devil's Island is a freedman named
Dreyfus: only after a while do we learn that he is called
Dreyfus merely because of his habit of talking about the
captain; his real name is Bordenave. He has a great passion for Victor Hugo, but it is not altogether clear that he
is not thinking of Victor Hugues, the buccaneer-patriot of
the French Revolution. "Dreyfus" is a craven, an abject
admirer of the prison commandant, Governor Castel; conditions in the camp are abominable, unspeakable, obscene.
But many of the camp's agents and functionaries are Jewish: Bernheim is a prisoner but a responsible prisoner,
Kahn is a warder. That sounds as if Henri Nevers were
a kind of Dreyfus, and so he is; but he is also
a shadow-Dreyfus on the straight. That is, he has been
condemned by his uncle Pierre to service in the penal colony on a charge of disloyalty, involving (or so we learn from
uncle Antoine) the family honor and the family salt works.
Some papers had been lost; there was talk of their having

been sold to foreigners; appearances compromised Nevers.
His "plan" (but we don't know when or where it was
formed, and none of his activities in the colony seem to
bear on it in any way) is said to have "consisted in presenting the salt mine affair, which had divided our family and
exiled him from France, as a public affair." The parallels
with Dreyfus are obvious here, and they are straight—that
is, he is the victim of a conspiracy carried out by an authoritarian establishment; his going to Devil's Island is the
result of a kind of blackmail, organized by his uncle
Pierre, who threatens to tell Henri's fiancée, Irene, of his
guilt. Its ultimate aim is to keep him on the island, not as
an official, but as a prisoner. When his cousin, Xavier Brissac, arrives, ostensibly as his replacement, Henri Nevers
is convinced he will be carrying orders for the detention
of the man he is apparently replacing. This suspicion,
however, is not confirmed by anyone or anything, anywhere else in the book.

Allegories, phantasms, doublings, and parallels abound in
the novel; they are not necessarily significant or insignificant. They may be the product of Nevers' peculiar mind;
a possibility is scouted that in some particular matter he
may be driven by a "diabolical need for symmetry." The
family seat of the Nevers-Brissac clan is the twin islands
of Oléron and Ré off La Rochelle in the Bay of Biscay. The
archipelago off the coast of South America and the archipelago off the coast of France form, throughout the book,
shimmering, mirage-like images of one another, before the
fevered eyes of Henri Nevers. Again, the date of the action
(spring of 1913, just a few months before the guns of August) seems somehow related to the shadowy figure of
Irene, who is engaged to Henri Nevers while he is in exile,
but then seems to be engaged to Xavier Brissac, who
comes either to replace him or to seal his permanent incarceration. Irene's name, of course, announces peace; for a
personage she is extremely intangible, but then for an allegory she is rather phantasmal too.

All conversations in the colony are equivocal and dream-
like: only the periphery of any subject ever gets discussed,
and then in innuendo and inconclusively. The same incident is repeated several times over in successive episodes.
Lurking at night in the underbrush on two separate occasions, Nevers sees two men carry two different bodies out
of two different huts on Devil's Island. He cannot see the
bearers' faces, cannot identify the bodies, cannot even
know if they are corpses or simply men temporarily inert,
and so can convey to Antoine and the reader neither the
cause nor the consequence nor very much about the nature of these events. Episode XXIX clearly intimates that
Henri Nevers fatally shot himself, probably on the night
of April 15; this, however, turns out to be a fantasy, for
we have further episodes, adventures, and discoveries,
dated as late as the 27th. The last unit of the book, a letter
from Xavier Brissac, also to his uncle Antoine, confirms
that there has been a convicts' revolt on the islands, that
Henri Nevers "showed courage" during the course of it,
but may actually have been sympathetic with it or even responsible for it. He may be dead by now, or may have escaped on a boat under pretext of pursuing the old warden's chief assistant, De Brinon. (But why was De Brinon
running away? And from whom? And with whom?) There

are mystifying hints all along that Castel, the prison commander, is trying to engineer an escape, perhaps for himself, perhaps for some of his charges, but these turn out to be exactly the opposite of the truth. The prospect of "liberation" fills him with horror. He is committed to imprisoning himself and a few of his favorite prisoners irrevocably in grotesquely designed cells, which, because of their deranged senses, they all take for delightful desert islands. The point, which is not very subtle in the first place, is underlined by the name of one of the boats plying between the penal colony and the mainland: it is the "Rimbaud," and at one point Henri Nevers thinks of his stay in the penal colony as a "season in hell." How much one chooses to make of these recurrent intimations of Rimbaud is of course very much one's private business as a reader.

At least the final lecture clears up the commandant's game, by identifying his particular "plan for escape." It is an escape inward, in which deranged senses are attuned to a deranged environment—rather like a drug-cultist's dream. But explaining this one mystery, central though it has been, leaves many others expanding, free-floating in the atmosphere. There is a great deal of business about the camp commandant accumulating dynamite on the island. Why? It is never used, never moved toward a possible use, and using it or accumulating it would be equally incompatible with the commandant's plan, as finally revealed to us. The parallel with 1913 Europe could be important or insignificant; we have no real way of guessing what the whole thing is about, beyond the macabre effect it produces at the moment. Less significant, perhaps, but no less tantalizing is a loose end that the author trails across his book at the beginning and again at the conclusion. Why does thirteen-year-old Charlotte Frinziné, with whom Nevers has scarcely exchanged a recorded word, present him with a golden mermaid? What is implied when this artifact, never mentioned in the interim, reappears among Nevers' surviving personal effects at the end of the book? The only bond between Nevers and Charlotte is a common reverence for René Ghill, the Poet of Harmony; and even that is more the work of the translator than the author.

[In a footnote, Adams adds: At the party given by the Frinzinés, early in the book, Nevers goes to the window, looks out, and recites some poems of Ghill; he sees a "girl" in the park making signs to him and laughing at him. Turning back to the party, he encounters Charlotte, who has a weakness for Ghill; she gives him a golden mermaid, and she too is described as a "girl." The implication is clear that she was the "girl" outside. But in the Spanish, the girl outside was a "mujer," and Charlotte is called a "niña." The English implies a relation—in fact an identity—that the Spanish rather distinctly avoids.]

The book thus strikes an unusual balance. By resolving an anomaly or ordering the fragments of a problem, the usual "mystery" book spreads the normal light of natural phenomena across an exceptional dark spot. Here, as the light of nature darkens, what seemed to be a mystery of iniquity turns out to be one area of life at least accessible to the mind, to explanation. The artificial paradise of Commandant Castel may be ghastly when seen from the outside—it

is a group of stoned, catatonic zombies wallowing slow-motion in the peristaltic waves of their own stunned nervous systems. But the outside from which it is seen is also ghastly, not so much physically, as in the painful, devious efforts of the characters to explain, to justify, to comprehend a reality that's as queasy and unpredictable as the English Channel on a choppy day. When he first comes to the Salvation Islands, Nevers travels *"entre señoras negras, pálidas, mareadas"*—and indeed the seasick texture of the physical world invoked by Bioy would turn a *"negra pálida,"* or vice versa. "Escape," then, must be defined, not as an escape from the island, but from the hallucinations, half-intentions, and tantalizing equivocations that surround it, and from which the fiction itself offers no escape. "Plan" must surely be ironic as well.

Stylistically, the book is sparse, dry, and flat, after the fashion of Borges; there is little heightening or rendering. Characterization is of the stick type, familiar from science fiction. Lieutenant Nevers, for example, has no father, no mother, no schooling, no profession, no friends, practically no memories, and, apart from the quite specific problem in which he is involved, very few experiences. The tropics of the South American landscape, within which he is set, could be extrapolated from an *Encyclopedia Britannica* description of Madagascar. Metaphors, imagery, and flights of highly colored fancy are non-existent. Bioy has written, less a novel than an extended parable—complicated, unlike those of Kafka which otherwise it resembles so much, by a few specific bearings of time, place, and history. The reverberations that the book contains are literary, philosophical, social; on the psychological side, they do not go much beyond the constant sense of unrelieved anxiety; stylistically, they are deliberately flat.

Translator Suzanne Jill Levine, after her pursuit of Sarduy's sinuous and sparkling *Cobra,* has enjoyed a relative holiday with Bioy's dry equivocations. Even at their most evasive, these equivocations define, with the clarity of strong sunlight on wrinkled sand, the things they are not saying; to render them, the quick, plain, unemphatic assertion which is the accepted style of modern translation, is exactly right. Here and there, though rarely on the whole, Ms. Levine falls into translaterese—that bastard dialect resulting from an original idiom which survives like one of Laocoon's snakes, to choke the English locution writhing to escape it. "The shine in his eyes was tearful" she manages to say on p. 39; that isn't English as spoke, nor any kind of kin to it. But such missteps are rare; the translation reads, on the whole, with the same crisp ease as the original. It's a deceptive ease, of course. In the phantom world of Bioy's Iles du Salut, slack and casual conversations generally have to be read for what they are artfully *not* saying, quite as much as for what they are. *Plan for Escape* is a cool, longheaded, understated entertainment; one is left wondering what an author of such resource has been up to in the thirty years since he wrote it.

Nathan Rosenstein   (essay date 1975)

SOURCE: "A Borges Disciple," in *The Village Voice,* Vol. XX, No. 44, November 3, 1975, pp. 53-4.

[*Rosenstein is a free-lance writer and critic. In the following review of* A Plan for Escape, *he praises the story's "inventiveness and audacity."*]

Adolfo Bioy-Casares, whose work is largely unheralded in this country, is an esteemed Argentine writer who has long been an important figure in Latin American literature. A disciple and frequent collaborator of Jorge Luis Borges, he is probably best known for *The Invention of Morel,* a story which was published more than three decades ago and which provided the basis for Alain Resnais's film, *Last Year at Marienbad.* Now, at a time when he is enjoying continued success at home with a bestseller called *Dormir al Sol,* Bioy-Casares is represented here by a newly translated version of another early '40s work, *A Plan for Escape.*

This short novel, firmly rooted in the Borges tradition, reminiscent of H. G. Wells, and thoroughly weird by conventional standards, is an exceptionally ambitious, intellectual mystery woven with horror and science fiction. From the outset its enigmatic nature is very much in evidence. In February, 1913, protagonist Henri Nevers, a French naval lieutenant, arrives in the penal colony consisting of three islands (including the infamous Devil's Island) off the coast of French Guiana. He is apparently there to help Pierre Castel, the colony's governor, run the prison; but the circumstances surrounding his separation from his family, his home, and his fiancee are not at all clear. The narrator, Nevers's uncle and correspondent, suggests that actually it was the head of their family who sent him away, but except for a few clues, he never quite states the exact nature of the domestic wrangle that discredited Nevers and led to his exile.

In any case, Nevers is revealed to be a rather vainglorious but weakhearted young man as he tries to suppress the terrible fears and sense of entrapment stirred within him by the penitentiary's distasteful atmosphere. He soon realizes that his unease is not only due to the pervasive filth and misery, but also to Castel, who is up to something out of the ordinary on Devil's Island. Nevers resigns himself to his sorry state of affairs and becomes obsessed with passing his stipulated year-long assignment on the island as painlessly as possible. "The mystery of Devil's Island does not concern me, even if it does exist. . . . Again I remembered that my stay in the Guianas was merely an episode in my life. Time would erase it, as it did other dreams."

Despite his resolve, within a couple of months Nevers's curiosity inexorably draws him into an investigation of Castel's covert operations. After witnessing a series of strange events and questioning a few of the prisoners, as well as the governor's aide Dreyfus (so nicknamed because he always talks about the famous ex-prisoner), he concludes that the governor is indeed making some potentially devastating plans and preparations. But of what sort, Nevers wonders. Is Castel planning a revolution? Is he planning to set himself up as the head of a Communist republic? Or is he an anarchist readying a prisoners rebellion? Perhaps he is merely a lunatic. The evidence is confusing and points in each of these directions. Suffice it to say that the denouement is an intricate, logically built-up tour de force exposing the author's concern with philo-

sophical concepts of time and space and how they might be related to the meaning of freedom.

If all of this sounds a mite preposterous, it is—but no discussion of the book's content can adequately capture the unusual kind of literary experience Bioy-Casares offers. The world evoked in this novel, despite its bizarreness, is made to seem real enough, which is all the more remarkable when it becomes apparent that it is a world in which ideas take on a greater importance than the characters themselves. Using stark prose, Bioy-Casares fashions a fictional maze abounding with subtle intimations, unanswered questions, strange symbols and correlatives. And in spite of its rewards, this is a style that can tax the patience of many readers, especially those with a low tolerance for obscurities and riddles. Yet, like the protagonist's own reaction to his plight, the overall effect is analogous to the experience of an uneasy, nonsensical dream: one is torn between the desire to leave behind its madness and the urge to find out more, to seek reassurance in unraveling its complexity.

The meaning of *A Plan for Escape* is ultimately a matter for endless speculation. In light of the translator's suggestion that the book may have been written as a response to the growth of fascism and nazism, it is tempting to interpret it almost as a kind of political morality play. In the last analysis, however, Bioy-Casares's interests may transcend such mundane concerns. Perhaps the most powerful theme at work here is the implicit and telling contrast of the intellect's great potential and the petty pursuits and intrigues of mankind. Heavy stuff, this, but served up with a blend of inventiveness and audacity that's hard to resist.

Love in *The Invention of Morel*:

In *The Invention of Morel,* what really mattered was not the fantastic machinery which could project three-dimensional images on the air, but the impossible love between the narrator and the woman he used to meet in his walks on the island: a woman made of film images. When the protagonist finds the machine that projects the images and learns how to make it work, he changes himself into an image that can be projected alongside her image. Thus, he is able to walk with her, to talk to her, to create the fiction that she is also looking and talking to him. That is what love is, Bioy Casares seems to say: a sustained fiction. The true invention of Morel is that one, and not the amusing but impossible "scientific" machinery. . . .

The protagonist of *The Invention of Morel* accepts the destruction of his body in order to be able to continue living next to the woman he loves: alive only as the images of movies are perpetually alive.

Emir Rodriguez Monegal, in "The Invention of Bioy Casares," Review, No. 15, Fall, 1975.

Margaret L. Snook   (essay date 1979)

SOURCE: "The Narrator as Creator and Critic in *The Invention of Morel,*" in *Latin American Literary Review,* Vol. VII, No. 14, Spring-Summer, 1979, pp. 45-51.

[*Snook is an American educator, author, and critic. In the following essay, she discusses aesthetic theory in* The Invention of Morel.]

Many of the first person narrators of Bioy Casares' fantastic fiction are writers, men whose literary interests vary from poetry to journalism. This literary background, often important in the characterization of the narrators, usually plays another vital role in the thematic development of the work. It provides the perfect opportunity, [according to Ofelia Kovacci in her biography, *Adolfo Bioy Casares* (1963)], for presenting theories related to creativity and writing, both recurrent themes in Bioy Casares' prose.

This use of the narrator-writer is especially significant in **The Invention of Morel,** which deals with substantially more than a scientist's attempts to gain immortality through a photographic device designed to capture the thoughts and sensations of its subjects. The novel is not only an ingenious adventure story set on an unchartered island in the Pacific, it is also a commentary on the relationship that exists between literature and other forms of artistic expression.

This theoretical dimension of the novel is revealed through careful consideration of the dual role played by the anonymous narrator as creator and critic. He is the author and commentator of the text in which he appears and makes frequent allusions to its tone and veracity. He is the editor and literary critic of the document written by the scientist Morel, which the narrator encloses within the body of his own text. The narrator is also the creator as well as critic of an unusual pictorial presentation, a floral image depicting the woman he loves. Each of these circumstances, the latter in particular, provides an opportunity for a literary discussion very relevant to the novel's interpretation.

However, like many of Bioy Casares' protagonists, the narrators seems inadequate for the task he undertakes. His creative ambitions and aspirations no doubt exceed his talent. The reader knows little about his background except that he is a writer: ". . . I am a writer who has always wanted to live on a lonely island. . . ." The gap that exists between the narrator's real accomplishments and his pretentions is perhaps indicated by his inability to complete two essays, "Defensa ante Sobrevivients" ["Apology for Survivors"] and "Elogio de Malthus" ["Tribute to Malthus"], both mentioned in the first entry of his diary. This failure is attributed to his involvement in the events that transpired on the island. In any case, an unoriginal apology of Thomas Malthus' ideas is included in his diary only to be removed by the fictitious editor before reaching the reader.

The narrator demonstrates a familiarity with a wide range of readings through references to such authors as Dante, Swedenborg, and Cicero, but the depth of his knowledge is questionable. Both the relative scarcity of these literary references and the inaccuracies demonstrated in his writings by the editor's corrections and clarifications cast a dubious light on the narrator's scholarship.

Nevertheless, it is through the limited perspective and often naïve statements of this narrator that the reader is given a glimpse of more profound truths. His simple, common sense language is a cloaking device meant to disguise the otherwise obvious theoretical discussions usually avoided in tales of adventure because they tend to slow the pace. This use of common sense language, constructed with clear and concise statements, to mask the self-reflecting discourse of the narrative is a familiar technique in Bioy Casares' works.

It is particularly effective in the description of the narrator's most important creative endeavor which is developed in five successive chapters. He creates a flower garden which in fact is a pictorial representation of himself adoring Faustine, the woman he has come to love while on the island. Later, he discovers that Faustine and her mysterious companions are images projected by Morel's invention. She had died as a result of the photographic process long before the narrator's arrival.

It is significant that the narrator, a writer according to his own words, should choose to communicate the story of his love to Faustine by means of a visual presentation as opposed to a written narration. He does this although he is aware of his personal limitations as a painter and acknowledges his lack of ability to the reader: "I have never worked with colors; I know nothing about art . . ."

The narrator also composes some verses as an inscription to be written with flowers directly beneath his floral images. After considering several possibilities, he decides in favor of the simple statement: "the humble tribute of my love."

His failure to achieve an illusion of depth in his portrait of Faustine and his inability to complete the project as he originally planned are attributed to the problems that arise in working with flowers: "But I was not able to create it as I had planned. In imagination it is no more difficult to make a woman standing than to make one seated with her hands clasped on one knee; but in reality it is almost impossible to create the latter out of flowers."

The deceptively simple language with which the narrator expresses his critical commentary on the garden conceals the deeper implications which lie beneath the surface of his words. His remarks allude first of all to the artist's need to consider the limitations imposed by the inherent characteristics of the medium he is using before determining the direction of his works. One cannot realistically tell a complete story in a drawing, nor can one paint a portrait with flowers or words. The writer cannot play the role of painter with any great degree of success nor can the painter achieve the same effects as the writer because each is dealing with essentially different art forms. Form in the plastic arts is basically spatial since the whole object can be presented and perceived in an instant of time. Literature, on the other hand, is composed of language "which is a succession of words proceeding through time" [Joseph Frank, "Spatial Form in Modern Literature," *Sewanee*

Review LIII (1945)]. The essential temporal and spatial properties of painting and prose place certain limitations on the artist. Consequently, although such projects as pictorial prose and narrative painting may be easy to conceive in theory, they are difficult to achieve in practice.

However, the implications of the garden episode are even broader in scope. They refer not only to past attempts at narrative painting but also to the modern writer's more recent efforts to create a work which lies in the direction of spatial form. In such works, the events are portrayed as occurring at the same moment in time thus breaking the pattern of gradual, sequential development characteristic of the traditional novel.

The narrator demonstrates a similar purpose when he chooses an art form that can be perceived in its entirety at one given moment in time in order to narrate the story of his love to the oblivious object of his affections. As such, it may be interpreted as an attempt to overcome the temporal restrictions of prose.

This concern with the traditional spatial and temporal definitions of art forms is not altogether unrelated to the general theoretical basis of the novel which deals precisely with the manner in which time and space define and limit man's existence.

The narrator's experiment with his unusual art form may have other closely related ramifications as well. His remarks reveal a concern with the manner in which his work is perceived both during and after the creative process. The individual components of his picture story, viewed separately from within the work itself, give no clear indication as to the form of the whole: "I had to concentrate on each part, on the difficult task of planting each flower and aligning it with the preceding one. As I worked, the garden appeared to be either a disorderly conglomeration of flowers or a woman." Only when the narrator removes himself from the work to gain a broader perspective can he view the project as a whole.

The narrator's message on the need for global perspective in comprehending his picture story may be applied to literature as well. In fact, it may be interpreted as a reference to the two types of reading activities that necessarily occur in the comprehension of any work of prose. The first reading is a temporal activity in which a succession of isolated phenomena unfold in the reader's mind. The second is a global reading or comprehension "which considers the work in its totality and contemplates the whole series of events in a simultaneous fashion, as in the plastic arts" [Marcello Pagnini, *Estructura literaria y metodo critico*, 1975].

Without applying this second global perspective, the reader will probably not appreciate the subtleties and irony of **The Invention of Morel,** to say nothing of its myriad of theoretical implications. Thus, statements made earlier in the novel cannot be understood until the final events have unfolded, until the scenes can be placed in proper perspective forming a complete picture.

A good case in point is the scene in which the narrator describes Faustine as she sits peacefully reading: "The sight of her: As if she were posing for an invisible photographer, she surpassed the calm of the sunset." The narrator is unaware at this time, and so is the reader, that Faustine had in fact posed unknowingly for an unseen camera and that it is this camera's image that both the narrator and the reader are contemplating. The irony becomes apparent only when the reader discovers the truth of the situation much later and is able to view the scene in relation to other events and as part of a comprehensible whole.

The narrator's reflections on the garden episode also explore the relationship between the artist and his work and the difficulties the artist experiences in maintaining proper perspective. This difficulty arises from the fact that the artist, like the anonymous narrator of our story, is often a critic of his own work. In order to play the dual role of critic and creator, he must detach himself from the work while at the same time he continues to identify with the work as its creator.

A task equally as difficult as that of maintaining a separation between his consciousness as author and his consciousness as critic is that of maintaining a separation between himself and the fictional character he creates, thus preserving the autonomy of the character. In short, the author must view the work from within and from without and must think like character and critic as well as creator. The difficulty in maintaining these different attitudes simultaneously is indicated in the narrator's remarks: "I was going to say that my experiment shows the dangers of creation, the difficulty in balancing more than one consciousness simultaneously."

The artist's and reader's perceptions of art forms in time and in space is not the only matter of consideration. The discussion centering around the garden episode also encompasses a comparison of the images created by literature, painting and science. The basic difference between the three lies in the degree of realistic detail they attempt to achieve and the amount of realism they are capable of producing. The verbal image is incapable of producing a three dimensional life-like object, and so the narrator resorts to a visual presentation in which he again fails to reproduce reality.

The narrator's brief and indirect reference to his garden images and his written descriptions of Faustine focus attention on this issue of realism in modern literature. He compares his pictorial and written images, created artistically with flowers and words, to the image produced scientifically by Morel. He concludes that his work is inferior because it lacks the realistic detail of Morel's image: "A recluse can make machines or invest his visions with reality only imperfectly, by writing about them or depicting them to others who are more fortunate than he."

His statement and what it seemingly implies give rise to some thought-provoking questions regarding the objectives of literary realism and the role of artistic creativity. It can be asked, for example, if creativity lies in duplicating reality with photographic precision, or if the artist should emulate the scientist's attitude and methods and evaluate the success of his attainments by comparing them to scientific achievements. Is the literary image mimetic in

nature or is it, according to Burke's conception, more reflective of inner reality? Such a concept would approxi-
mate the poetic image more to music than to painting.
Music also lacks the mimetic capacity of painting and is
a temporal art form, that is, one that is perceived as a succession of notes proceeding through time according to a
sequential pattern.

These questions, posed by the narrator's implied comparison of scientific and artistic images, are part of a broader
consideration of the type of literary realism advocated in
the nineteenth century. In fact, the entire plot of *The Invention of Morel* is interpreted by [D. P. Gallagher in
"The Novels and Short Stories of Adolfo Bioy Casares,"
in *Bulletin of Hispanic Studies,* LII (1975)] as a humorous
comment on the nature of nineteenth-century realism
which, like the scientist Morel, attempts to create three dimensional characters who think and feel.

The narrator's remarks concerning his diary also focus attention on the role of realism in the portrayal of language
and events in fantastic prose. He demonstrates an apparent awareness of modern theories regarding the advisibili-
ty of natural, everyday settings into which the fantastic
event is gradually introduced. The relationship between
verisimilitude and natural setting seems foremost in his
mind when he transcribes an important conversation between Morel and his guest:

> I tried to write down the above conversation ex-
> actly as it occurred. If it does not seem natural
> now, either art or my memory is to blame. It
> seemed natural enough then. Seeing those peo-
> ple, hearing them talk no one could expect the
> magical occurrence or the negation of reality
> that came afterward (although it happened near
> an illuminated aquarium, on top of long-tailed
> fish and lichens, in a forest of black pillars!).

Other literary allusions made by the narrator focus attention on fictional forms closely related to fantastic prose.
Their inclusion serves to highlight the difference in treatment that is accorded certain conventional devices in the
narrator's story. For example, various references to ghost
stories lead inevitably to a comparison of the narrator's
tale of strange appearances and disappearances to the traditional tale of phantoms, thus paving the way for the
ironic surprise that awaits the narrator and reader. The
ghosts of *The Invention of Morel* by no means resemble
the ghosts of supernatural stories. The phenomenon described by the narrator does not flagrantly contradict everyday reality. It bases its explanation on science, in which
modern man believes more readily than in the spiritual.

The narrator's comments on an accident that occurred
while working with Morel's equipment lead to yet another
comparison with tales of terror. The narrator carelessly allows his hand to be photographed. Later, the hand appears separately, engaged in the gestures it was performing
at the time it was photographed. Such a sight might create
suspense in the typical horror story, but it is treated by the
narrator as an insignificant event. However, its literary
possibilities do not go unobserved by the narrator:

> I am keeping the projector on so that the hand

> will not disappear. The sight of it is not unpleas-
> ant, but rather unusual.

> In a story, that hand would be a terrible threat
> to the protagonist. In reality—what harm can it
> do?

The fact that *The Invention of Morel* deals with questions
of literary criticism and issues related to fantastic prose
should come as no surprise in view of the ideas advanced
in the novel's prologue by Jorge Luis Borges. Borges introduces both topics in his discussion of Ortega y Gasset's
theories on the novel. Not only does he challenge the concepts set forth in *The Dehumanization of Art* but he also
raises the issue of realism and verisimilitude. Borges assigns a positive value to the term (artificial) concluding
that ". . . las obras de arte que tratan de ser realistas caen
en un error grave porque el arte no debe ser una imitación,
de la realidad sino una invención, una ficció." [. . . works
of art that try to be realistic fall into a grave error because
art should not be an imitation of reality but rather an invention, a fiction]. In addition to furthering our insight
into the novel's title, Borges' observations develop reader
awareness and receptivity for the aesthetic themes presented in the text through the narrator's commentaries.

M. E. Cossio   (essay date 1980-81)

SOURCE: "A Parody on Literariness: *Seis problemas
para Don Isidro Parodi,*" in *Dispositio,* Vols. V-VI, Nos.
15-16, Otoño-Invierno, 1980-81, pp. 143-53.

[*In the essay below, Cossio claims that* Six Problems for
Don Isidro Parodi *parodies literary convention through in-
versions on several levels including structure and liguistics.*]

In 1942, H. Bustos Domecq was born in Argentina and
immediately published his first book, ***Seis problemas para
don Isidro Parodi.*** Far from being supernatural, this
amazing happening was the natural result of the united effort of two well known writers already engaged in the discovery of a "brave new world": *Tlön.* In order to find it,
both Adolfo Bioy Casares and Jorge Luis Borges investi-
gated whether "*The Anglo-American Cyclopaedia*" had or
did not have the pages on "Uqbar." After such a detection
related by the latter in "Tlön, Uqbar, Orbis Tertius" they
collaborated in the "revelation" (creation?) of a fecund
"polymath" (cryptographer) called Honorio Bustos Domecq whose biography appears in the first two pages of his
own book, as the transcription of "la silueta de la educa-
dora, señorita Adelma Badoglio." Through it, the reader
becomes acquainted with Domecq and learns that he was
"in fact" born in Pujato (Province of Santa Fe) in 1893,
and that he had accomplished several literary deeds. One
of these, his reading in the "Centro Balear" of *his* "Oda
a la muerte de su padre" by Jorge Manrique, is worthy of
mention, since such a feat clearly shows the kind of author
the reader is dealing with: a writer who always tells the
truth, not his truth but the others', a plagiarist.

In an interview with Victoria Ocampo, Borges explained
where the name Bustos Domecq came from: "Creamos de
algún modo entre los dos un tercer personaje, Bustos Domecq—Domecq era el nombre de su bisabuelo, Bustos el

de un bisabuelo cordobés, mío—y lo que ocurrió después es que las obras de Bustos Domecq no se parecen ni a lo que Bioy escribe por su cuenta ni a lo que yo escribo por mi cuenta. Ese personaje existe, de algún modo. Pero sólo existe cuando estamos los dos conversando." Not only do these words elucidate the origin of the name and the intermittent existence of the character, but they also point out the dialogical structure of the text under study. It starts with the sentence "We transcribe. . . ." The use of the pronoun of the first person plural is ambiguous, since it can be understood as a merely rhetorical device used by the pseudo-author instead of the "I" or as a direct statement made, at this moment and only here, by the two actual authors united in the "we." Yet, the we is not a being but a written represented signifier, whose meaning lies in the writers and readers' discourse which keeps only the trace of their presence—their way of writing (of reading). On the other hand, "to transcribe" means to write down something that has already been written. This "already written" consists in Domecq's biography and bibliography given through the sketch of Miss Badoglio. Thus, from the very beginning, a dialogue of a dual nature is set up: it is carried on between the present text and that of the educator, and between writer(s) and reader(s). The latter will never know who is writing because there is not a subject or a "real" referent behind the text.

Bustos Domecq, the result of an act of talking (of a dialogue), is a chain of signifiers that, moving from one place (Bioy's) to another (Borges'), becomes the representation of speech in writing. As a signifier (sign-vehicle), this proper name stands for two real writers as well as for the fictional ones who appear in the text; as a signified (cultural-unit), it is the paradigm of the detective: Parod*i*/Parod*y* (in Spanish, Parod*i*/Parod*ia*). Thus the actual authors can no longer be identified as subjects (Selves?) but as the written signs which represent them in the mode of a signified absence—Bustos Domecq. This name is simultaneously a pseudonym (pen name), a pseudo-author (a parody of ownership), a character (narrator), a text ("a *bio-graphy*," "a writing without [actual] referent") and the first cipher (as both a concealment of meaning and a nonentity) of the riddle that *Seis problemas* poses to its reader(s). Such a riddle, however, cannot be solved till the questions it consists of are formulated. I attempt to deal with the problems of deciphering and interpreting that this formulation raises by analyzing the characters, the arrangement of each one of the stories, and the organization of the text as a whole.

The impersonal and omniscient narrator introduces the characters who go to Parodi's cell, records the dates of their visits, and reports Parodi's thoughts and attitude: "El 5 de septiembre, al atardecer, un visitante con brazal y paraguas entró en la celda 273. Habló en seguida; habló con funeraria vivacidad; pero don Isidro notó que estaba preocupado." Those characters who call on Parodi are oppressed by the problem of a crime. Whether innocent or guilty, they give the detective an account of the events in which they have been involved, acting as narrators for their own sake, their desire to be extricated; whereas Parodi, the imprisoned detective, tells his stories (the story of the crime) to them for the sake of truth. An exchange

of narratives and a transformation take place in each problem: the sender of the first narration becomes the receiver of the "real" story sent by Parodi, who is a born storyteller.

According to Walter Benjamin, the storyteller is either a man "who has come from afar" or one "who knows the local tales and traditions" ["The Storyteller," in *Illuminations*, translated by Harry Zohn, edited by Hannah Arendt, 1969]. Parodi is both. Having worked as a barber, he heard a lot; being outside of worldly time and space as a prisoner, he has been able to draw experience from his boredom ("the dream bird that hatches the egg of experience"). He is a good listener of tales and retells them showing "orientation toward practical interest," "having counsel for his listeners," and respecting the criminal when he is of a "sturdy nature." This is evidenced, in **"Las previsiones de Sangiácomo,"** by the following commendation: "A Sangiácomo viejo lo agrandó el odio. Se formó un plan que no se le ocurre ni a Mitre. Como trabajo fino y de aguante, hay que sacarle el sombrero." Like a traditional storyteller, the detective begins his stories with "a presentation of the circumstances in which he himself has learned what is to follow," interweaving his own experiences and insights with the events of the crimes: "Los de la policía, que son muy noveleros, no descubrieron nada . . . Pero yo, de tanto estar a galpón, me he puesto muy histórico y me gusta recordar esos tiempos cuando el hombre es joven y todavía no lo han mandado a la cárcel y no le faltan tres nacionales para darse un gusto."

Unlike Parodi, the visiting narrators report events that perplex them. Although they narrate what they have witnessed, still they do it from their own biased and peculiar standpoint. In their narrations, they themselves are the heroes, the protagonists, while the others are merely secondary figures. Another transformation follows when after having told their stories they listen to Parodi's. Just as their function changes from that of sender to that of receiver, so does their role shift from that of hero to that of dupe; and, conversely, the marginal figures become the leading characters—protagonists or antagonists—of the story of the crime as told by Parodi. Unmasking and fitting them all in the actual role they played in the criminal drama, the detective unfolds the "right" story, which is a summary of the "wrong" one, a reconstruction in the present of what "really" happened in the past. Hence most of the tales are constituted by two scenes: in the first one, the enigma is formulated (by the narrators) and, in the second, disclosed (by Parodi).

Two of the problems, however, are composed of more scenes and may, at first sight, seem to follow a different pattern. Textually divided into five parts, **"El dios de los toros"** formally consists of the presentation of a false enigma (snare in the first part and delay in the second), the formulation of the true enigma (narration of the crime in the third part and of the happenings surrounding it in the fourth), and the solution (disclosure in the fifth part). On the other hand, **"Las previsiones de Sangiácomo"** contains two enigmas instead of only one. Although it is textually split into six parts, it is formally composed of the formulation of the first enigma (narration of Pumita's death in the first part and of the events prior to her death in the second), the formulation of the second one (Ricardo's autobiography in the third part and, in the fourth, the narration of his suicide and the reading of the letter he left to his father, "Sangiácomo viejo"), and the revelation of the mystery one year after its decipherment was accomplished (the relationship between the two enigmas in the sixth part). Just as the other tales dramatize the pattern of formulation and disclosure in two scenes, so do these two make use of it in spite of their textual divisions.

Since the fifth part of **"Las previsiones de Sangiácomo"** is a delay set by the discourse for the reader and for Montenegro, the receiver of Parodi's revelation, I would like then to pause here for a moment and indicate that this is the only tale in which the (impersonal) narrator not only introduces the characters but appears also as the writer (author/narrator) of the stories. At the end of the second part he explains, in parentheses, how the conversation carried on in Villa Castellammare on the eve of Pumita's death was recounted to Parodi: "(Con bastante fidelidad, Carlos Anglada transmitió a Parodi esta conversación.)" Also, in the fifth part, the narrator briefly notifies the reader that the detective received the visits of the physician and the accountant of Sangiácomo and that their dialogues were long and confidential. This last adjective serves the narrator as a justification for not informing the reader about the content of those conversations—a justification reinforced at the end of the story by Montenegro's summary of what had happened in the year after the mystery was solved. The solution was not revealed because the criminologist, knowing from those conversations that Sangiácomo was on his deathbed, did not want to embitter his last months on earth with lawyers, judges, and policemen. Thus the vindication is not only textual, at the level of the sentence, but also ethical, at the level of semantics.

This way of writing (of reading) demands that the grouping of the characters be made on the basis of the specific action they perform in the narrative. The characters can then be set apart by their function into the following groups: (1) the *narrators* subdivided into the impersonal narrator (Domecq?), who "writes" the others' narrations, and the identified narrators (proper names), who "tell" the stories to Parodi; (2) the *protagonists* whose criminal plans and performances are not clear in the narrators' stories but become so together with their role (identity) in Parodi's; (3) the *antagonists* whose roles and schemes are stated for the first time in Parodi's recounting; (4) the *detective* whose role is as ambiguous as his name. Parodi, on the one hand, is the traditional detective, the one who puts in order the chronology of the happenings revealing the true identity of the characters; on the other hand, as his name metonymically indicates, he is a parody of the conventional sleuthhound—he is a prisoner. Accused of a crime he did not commit and unable to prove his innocence because of two adverse circumstances (to have owned a barbershop in "el barrio Sur" and to have rented a room to a police clerk who, not wanting to pay the rent he owed Parodi, testified against him), Parodi was then condemned to stay for twenty-one years in prison, living in "the proverbial cell 273." This phrase is repeated so many times that it calls for a special type of interpretation—a symbolic one.

In symbolism, the number 2 signifies conflict or ignorance which gives birth to wisdom; the number 7 indicates expression of conflict or judgment, dream voices, sound, and that which leads all things to their end; the number 3 means solution of conflict or judgment, man organizes the present, foresees the future, and benefits from the experience of the past. Furthermore, the three numbers add up to 12, which is symbolic of cosmic order and salvation. This figure corresponds to the signs of the Zodiac to which are linked the notions of space and time as well as the wheel or circle. Divided by 2, 12 gives 6, which corresponds to the cardinal directions and to the cessation of movement; hence 6 is associated with trial and effort. Curiously enough, *six* problems are brought to and solved by Parodi. The numerical composition has existed since antiquity, and this text (to some extent at least) follows it. Taking for granted and in its due worth this interpretation, each one of the numbers of his cell represents Parodi: 2 stands for his youth as a "compadrito," 7 stands for his maturation as an imprisoned detective, and 3 for his maturity as a "criollo viejo," as a storyteller. These numbers all together symbolize the mythical time and space, the wheel, in which he lives. In that paradigmatic cell 273, Parodi resides and solves the others' conflicts, not his own. His cell is the place where all the *texts* (characters and discourses) are united, interlaced or intercrossed. It is the *center* in which truth is found. But paradoxically, the place of truth is inhabited by a character who is there (and has to be there) because of a lie. Like a Lacanian (but laconic) psychoanalyst, Parodi discovers through the patient's words the true facts that have been repressed; like a semiotician, he decodes the meaning of the pseudocryptic messages (or lies) sent to him by the others, since "every time there is a lie there is signification." [Umberto Eco, *A Theory of Semiotics,* 1976]. Thus Parodi exemplifies the antithesis—truth and lie—that governs the whole text.

In the text, two different codes are at stake: the ironic code (the mixture of many discourses), the characters' farrago, and the historical code, Parodi's possible (though not verisimilar) stories. These codes share with the titles and the dedications of the stories (one of the invariants of this text) the form of a language articulated in denotation (titles) and connotation (dedications). While the titles are descriptive utterances, the dedications are modal utterances. Such a distinction presents two levels of the narrative; the combinatorial operation carried out by them articulates meaning, the possibility of transcoding. The dedications are signifiers, proper names which connote but do not describe, establishing connections outside the hindrance of time; they always refer to another code, to other texts, to the "already written," indicating that the meaning of the stories as discourse (message) has to be found outside the text itself. The titles, on the contrary, head the story which will be told in a logical (irreversible) order; they point up the chronological significance of the enigma—its disclosure is the closure of meaning—relating the beginning (of the story) to the end. Thus, on the one hand, there is an enigma, the narration of it, and the detection: the traditional form of the detective story; and on the other, there is the ennunciation of an enigma which is not narrated; it consists in a cultural reference. As such, this enigma calls for another kind of detection, that of literary research.

The first story, **"Las doce figuras del mundo,"** is dedicated to José S. Alvarez. Known chiefly as "Fray Mocho," Alvarez wrote many books portraying the "reality" of his time: Buenos Aires and the mores of its inhabitants circa 1890. Two of his books, *Memorias de un vigilante* and *Mundo lunfardo,* describe the habits and language of the national and foreign rogues. Certainly these descriptions have some bearing on Bustos Domecq's text. For one thing, it is not difficult to find in the narrator's characterization of Parodi the echo of Fray Mocho's description of the "compadrito" in *Mundo lunfardo.* For another, in the Spanish mixed with barbarisms that Domecq's characters use and his narrator writes, there seems to be no difficulty in finding vestiges of the forms of expression (the idiom of Buenos Aires during the immigration wave) that characterize Fray Mocho and his society as recorded in his books. Just as his texts elucidate Parodi's identity, the language (*parole*) of Domecq's characters, and the narrator's way of writing (style); so does his peculiar biography—a former police functionary turned into a writer who not only used many pseudonyms but also changed his own name from Ciriaco to Sixto for reasons of "euphony"—illuminate hidden levels of meaning in Domecq's act of dedication. For to dedicate the first problem to such an undefined personage is to connote the theme (understood as a question the text poses) all of the problems present, that of identity: where does identity lie?

"Las noches de Goliadkin" is dedicated to the "Buen Ladrón." Crucified with Christ on Calvary along with another, this "Good Thief" repented, like Goliadkin, of his misdeeds before dying. While Goliadkin is the *actant* of the story, the "Good Thief" is the *object* of the narrative; that is, the former, the thief in Montenegro's narration, acquires, at the end, the "value" of *good* through Parodi's recounting of the right story: "El joven, mareado por tanta suerte, tuvo una debilidad—cualquiera la tiene—y se alzó con el brillante . . . Resolvió dejarse matar y perder el brillante para salvarlo." The "Good Thief," a historical figure, is a subject who has already realized the performance that Goliadkin accomplishes here. Thus this character obtains with his death the quality of being good, the identity of the "Good Thief" whose story is a narrative structure prior to its manifestation: **"Las noches de Goliadkin."**

"El dios de los toros" is dedicated to Alexander Pope. This poet translated the *Iliad* and the *Odyssey*; also he wrote a mock-heroic banter on the foibles of fashionable society, *The Rape of the Lock,* and a mock-epic, *The Dunciad,* ridiculing pretentiousness and pedantry. Likewise Formento, the criminal of this story, writes mock-books, sneering at Anglada's, as Parodi explains to the latter: "Quien iba a decirle a uno que don Formento, mozo marica y fúnebre si los hay, supiera reirse tan bien de un zonzo. Todos sus libros son un titeo: usted se manda los *Himnos para millonarios,* y el mocito, que es respetuoso, las *Odas para gerentes.* . . ." Furthermore, Formento is trying to

reach the mass reader through a popular translation of *La soirée avec M. Teste,* entitling it *La serata con don Cacumen* (doubtlessly, a literal and very euphonical translation!). Thus Pope's works make understandable the personality of Formento, the narrator's irony, and the tone of Domecq's whole text—all of them done in Pope's manner.

"Las previsiones de Sangiácomo" is dedicated to "Mahoma." The prophet's life is a commentary on and exposition of the *Koran*; similarly, Sangiácomo's life is the explanation of the story of the crime. As Mohammed's hegira is the point of departure of the chronology of Islam and a turning point in his life, so Sangiácomo's migration from Italy to Argentina changes his social status and indicates the starting point of this story as Parodi explains: "Dios habla por la boca de los sonsos: en esa fecha y en ese lugar empieza realmente le historia." If the *Koran* sent to Mohammed supersedes the other prophets' messages, Sangiácomo's evil plan obliterates the highest one—destiny: "Planeó toda la vida de Ricardo: destinó los primeros veinte años a la felicidad, los veinte úlitimos a la ruina. Aunque parezca fábula, nada casual hubo en esa vida." Such a design, pertaining more to a prophet than to a criminal, makes Sangiácomo a forecaster comparable then to Mohammed.

"La víctima de Tadeo Limardo" is dedicated to Franz Kafka. Just as Kafka's life was guided by the desire for self-punishment, so was Limardo's. His inner wish to be hurt and humiliated evinces a parallelism with Kafka's character and characters: "Limardo logró al fin su propósito . . . Había venido de lejos; meses y meses había mendigado el deshonor y la afrenta, para darse valor para el suicidio, porque la muerte es lo que anhelaba."

The last problem, **"La prolongada busca de Tai An,"** is dedicated to Ernest Bramah. Ernest Bramah (Smith) wrote Max Carrado's serials, *The Wallet of Kai-Lung* and *Kai-Lung's Golden Hours* introducing a Chinese character with his peculiar way of talking "in the English tongue." Bramah's Chinese character is, like Domecq, an author/narrator. In one of *his* stories, Kai-Lung confesses to be guilty of unwished plagiarism in the following way:

> It was with a hopeless sense of illness of ease that this unhappy one reached the day on which the printed leaves already alluded to would make known their deliberate opinion of his writing, the extremity of his hope being that some would at least credit him with honourable motives, and perhaps acknowledge that if the inspired Lo Kuang Chang had never been born the entire matter might have been brought to a very different conclusion.

What Bramah's character, Kai-Lung, quoted above says is representative of the ontological problem of the parallel lives and works (unwished plagiarism) that Domecq's dedications bring about. These connections and correspondences are mysterious, since they point to a cyclical time or to magical correlations which are not clearly stated but only suggested through the literary allusions: the dedications. They hint that not only the criminal follows a pattern already accomplished by somebody else in another context, but also that *Seis problemas* is a pastiche, as it is ostensibly shown to be in the last story. Because of the deliberate imitation of or reference to previous works and writers, this text lends itself to establish paradigmatic associations between its own version of artistic design and other existent versions, between the identity of its fictional characters and the real writers alluded to. In so doing, the text erases time since the narration does not unfold historically but refers back to an original mystery—identity. Time is annulled. Parodi's recounting of the story does not exhaust its meaning because of the temporal gap between the tale-telling and the story-writing implied by the dedications. Then, again, there are two different narratives: the detective one, which needs no appeal to anything outside itself to be understood, and which ceases to have significance at the time when its outcome is known; and the narrative which is, paradoxically, not narrated but adverted, which cannot be explained by a logical sequence of the happenings but by a mythical (cyclical) time, and which does not stop the process of signification. Following the pattern of the detective story, Parodi's tales attribute identity; however, the concept itself is refuted by the other narrative that sends the narration back to a zone where there is not fixed time or space: mystery is always *there*. Thus *Seis problemas para don Isidro Parodi* is a paradigm of paradigmatic narratives, a text that joints together two opposite terms and maintains them in play: mystery and reason, eternity and historicism, identity and biography, individuality and likeness, originality and repetition.

In spite of its title, Domecq's text contains more than six problems and is *a* problem for its readers. It is composed of six stories, an introduction (transcription), and a prologue written by Gervasio Montenegro, one of Domecq's own characters. This means that the division between author and character is artificial. The threshold which separates the *writer* from the *written* may, therefore, be precarious, since it is here constituted by *a* writing. Writing is the (real?) stuff that composes both of them and, being an eternal process, sets up a circularity in which no one occupies a privileged position. Yet, in this art of writing, in this text, it is not so much a question of destroying privileges as of making fun of them. Everything and everybody are presented in such a humorous way that all anguish, whether metaphysical or ontological, disappears leaving its place to a rotund outburst of laughter. Thus this text is, first of all, a parody of the conventional detective stories, though, it follows the same pattern. In her book of detective fiction, [*The Development of the Detective Novel*, 1968] A. E. Murch describes it as follows:

> But many distinctive features that had originated in the nineteenth century still persisted—planning the clues and the solution before the rest of the story; giving the explanation in the form of a dialogue between a clever character and one who is less perceptive; presenting the story from the viewpoint of several different characters, of the victim himself, or even from that of the murderer; and particularly the convention of "fair play" between writer and reader.

All these features appear in Domecq's text. There, they are subject to mockery by means of the cracks, the obscenity of themes and language, the topical allusions, the frequent intrusion of the author (through the footnotes), and the exposure of the vices and nonsense of society. If this shows the satiric overtones of the text, the fact that its detective is a prisoner evinces its purpose: to make fun of the tradition, of the literary conventions, by a *reductio ad absurdum,* a "burla burlando" as Montenegro says in his prologue.

Secondly, this text parodies all sorts of discourse. In the narrative two languages are intertwined: the cultivated or bookish and the uncultivated or vernacular. The former is "spoken" by the characters who are highbrow *writers,* who, nonetheless, make continuous cultural mistakes such as attributing *Gil Blas* to Santillana instead of to its actual author Lesage, and who constantly drivel; for instance, they congratulate themselves for having found Parodi in, as if it could have been otherwise, or they compliment the imprisoned detective for having *chosen* to live in seclusion: "Usted, más sabio, ha elegido bien: la reclusión, la vida metódica, la falta de excitantes." The latter, the vernacular language, is "spoken" by the "compadrito" Savastano, who speaks in *lunfardo.* Parodi, a "compadrito" before his imprisonment and now an old criollo, knows both the vernacular and the bookish dialects; he mingles them when he wants to mock his distinguished visitors: "Pucha que la carne se vende bien en Avellaneda. Ese trabajo enflaquece a más de uno; a usted lo engorda," he says to Montenegro. Similarly, the narrator utilizes in his "writing" either one or the other according to the characters he introduces. By bringing them up through the description of the clothes they are wearing and using one of the words they usually utter, the narrator parodies the characters and their discourses beforehand; afterwards, they will do it all by themselves. For instance, he introduces Montenegro, a prig who always exercises his French, in this way: "Un caballero, de saco gris, pantalón de fantasía, guantes claros y bastón con empuñadura en cabeza de perro, descendió con una elegancia algo *suranée* y entró con paso firme, por los jardines." By consisting only of one sentence stuffed with many predicates, the narrator's description is a parody of any serious literary one.

Thirdly, *Seis problemas* parodies the world of the detective stories where the mystery is always unravelled. In the problems brought to Parodi, the solved mystery turns out to be a reference to another that cannot be brought to a conclusion (Parodi's own problem) or that cannot be elucidated—the strange and enigmatic parallelism between one's life and another's—so that the denouement of each problem is twofold: rational and ontological. Besides, the text begins with Montenegro's prologue in which he lays bare the principle of construction of Domecq's problems: "el planteo enigmático y la solución iluminadora." If we recall that Montenegro is the character who poses the second problem and who appears in the next ones (besides the fifth) as Parodi's helper or, according to his words, as the "true" detective, it is not difficult to realize that from the start the whole text is ironic and parodic through and through. Its cyclical organization supported by the appearance of the same characters not only in the stories but also in the prologue shows that the text is built on fictitiousness, spuriousness. Unlike the rational and truthful detective story, which sets itself to prove to the reader that mystery is an illusion, that there is always a rational, "real" explanation, Domecq's text, ending with the "true" magician's remark about the war ("Muchos hombres están muriendo ahora en el mundo para defender esa creencia"), sends the reader to the "reality" outside the text, to the world of chaos and regulated crime, when he has not yet left the world of order and reason, that of the detective story. The reader is then caught in between two realities, both of which are contrived and paradoxical.

Fourthly, this text is a parody of history. The footnotes that appear in the text are unrealistic; either they do not have a "real" referent (they are written by the pseudo-author or by his characters), or the referent is false insofar as having died in 1349 he could not have sent a note in 1942: "*Entia non sunt multiplicanad praeter necessitate* (Note remitida por el doctor Guillermo Occam)." The only thing that refers the text to reality is the dates at the end of the prologue and of the problems. The "real" is written there in italics: "*Pujato, 21 de Octubre de 1942.*" The dates insert fiction in space and time; read in context, they correspond to the chronology of the discourse. The first story was written in December 27, 1941; the prologue, in November 20, 1942; and the text was published in December 10, 1942. Accomplished in a year, the act of writing moved in a circular path, becoming a cyclical process whose first element follows the last. The end of the writing is, in fact, the beginning of the text. As such, the narrative inverts time. Just as writing is a logico-temporal process, so is reading. But the process is here reversed: we start reading what was written last.

Fifthly, Domecq's text parodies the reader's reality and role. He is not reading one text but three. The first text is the one that Montenegro addresses to the reader; this text represents the literal level of the work, its detective nature. The second text is the one that the author/narrator dedicates, addresses to other writers or historical figures (absent readers); this is the semantic text, the hidden argument. In the first text, the dedications precede the narration, subhead the story which will be narrated; while in the second, the same dedications, pertaining to elements that have to do with the whole text, are pervasive but somehow independent. These dedications are allegorical messages, since they have a concealed meaning that transcends the literal one of the stories. The third text is the transcription written by "we." Obviously, it is impossible to demonstrate who is its author and who is its reader. This third text is an assumed one made up of the copy of lineaments, a prelude based on a short motive: the fictitious author. These three texts form *Seis problemas para don Isidro Parodi* whose structure is dialogical: each sender is also a receiver. The *we*, who sends the first message, is the one who receives the last one: we, the readers. We ourselves, senders and receivers, are as fantastic and fictitious as Domecq because *we* have also been written. Since *we* started speaking without knowing the end of the utterance in which we had engaged, *we* have to accept the task of finishing it, of constructing a second code, a meaningful language, elaborated on the basis of the given one: the "already written." *We* have then to continue the dialogue by deciphering that first code. Thus the act of reading is pre-

ceded by an act of writing, and to write is nothing more than to transcribe, to copy—endless game, infinite tautology.

Sixth and last, by denying the possibility of any privileged position, of any original point of departure, Domecq's text posits itself as that which cannot be detected through rational means or explained through a logical discourse. Once the conveyance of identity has been denied to us, is it still possible to believe that we can possess meaning? Indeed *Seis problemas para don Isidro Parodi* no more parodies any critical (sleuthlike?) undertaking—let alone my own analysis—than it laughs at the countless repetition of the "already said."

V. S. Pritchett   (essay date 1981)

SOURCE: "Borges," in *The New Yorker*, Vol. LVII, No. 14, May 25, 1981, p. 137-40.

[*An English literary figure, Pritchett is considered a modern master of the short story and a preeminent literary critic. He writes in the conversational tone of the familiar essay, approaching literature from the viewpoint of a lettered but not overly scholarly reader. In the following excerpted review, Pritchett comments on the style of* Six Problems for Don Isidro Parodi, *identifying Jorge Luis Borges as the sole author of some distinctive passages and motifs.*]

[Jorge Luis] Borges and Adolfo Bioy Casares, the young disciple, decided to collaborate on a series of detective stories, *Six Problems for Don Isidro Parodi.* This sportive diversion looks like a "cure" for a writer who was feeling his way toward a durable and serious manner.

It is strange now to imagine a writer as distinctive as Borges working with anyone, yet the collaboration excited him. The result was indeed bizarre, and something like a boisterous lark or bout of wrestling with his friend. They were united by a pseudonym, H. Bustos Domecq—combining names of their great-grandfathers—and one can see how the lark was one of those holidays or accidents that stir a writer's latent powers. Part of Borges' intention was to create an Argentine literature for the Argentines, by satirizing the habits of a new society. About the collaboration, he has written in his "Autobiographical Essay":

> Bioy was really and secretly the master. He and I attempted many different literary ventures. We compiled anthologies of Argentine poetry, tales of the fantastic, and detective stories; we wrote articles and forewords; we annotated Sir Thomas Browne and Gracián; we translated short stories by writers like Beerbohm, Kipling, Wells, and Lord Dunsany; we founded a magazine called *Destiempo*, which lasted three issues; we wrote film scripts, which were invariably rejected. Opposing my taste for the pathetic, the sententious, and the baroque, Bioy made me feel that quietness and restraint are more desirable. If I may be allowed a sweeping statement, Bioy led me gradually toward classicism.

Their wild spoofing, punning, and parodying made them shout with laughter as they wrote, but no one laughed in Buenos Aires. The book was thought to be a bore. And the tangled plots of the tales do suggest headlong film scripts written to drive a director mad. The book certainly flopped. The earliest readers in a very self-satisfied establishment did not grasp that it parodied traditional Argentine illusions and the effects of the exposure of a new-rich society to the ideological turmoil of Europe in the thirties and forties. Alfonso Reyes, the Mexican critic, was one of the few who saw the hidden point of the tales. As for the classicism of Borges, one can now see many signs of the metaphysical writer who would soon after write masterpieces like "El Aleph" and "Tlön, Uqbar, Orbis Tertius." Many passages bring to mind the mingling strains of Poe, Chesterton, and the philosopher Berkeley, and suggest the strengthening hand of the Borges we know. Mere "mysteries" have no philosophical overtones. We cannot guess who had the ingenious idea of choosing for the infallible detective Don Isidro a man serving a twenty-one-year sentence for a murder committed by someone else. The police politely allow guilty, falsely accused, or self-accused persons to visit the master in his cell, where his role as a detective is entirely cerebral: he can never visit the scene of the crime; he has to decide on hearsay. Don Isidro is a sort of non-perambulatory Father Brown who does his psychological sums in his head. The authors even go to the impertinent length of introducing a criminal adroit enough to disguise himself as Chesterton's famous priest. Don Isidro soon sees through that.

Each tale begins with a misleading situation, which becomes sometimes so crammed with clues that the plot is hard to follow until we reach the acute, if improbable, solution. Part of the fun lies in the pompous introduction to the tales by a ponderous Academician, who also turns up occasionally as a character in the book. He is one of those Argentines of the period who scattered French clichés through their talk; he swears by his "*parole de gentilhomme,*" speaks of Don Isidro's "*trouvaille*" as an Argentine "achievement," and sneers at immigrants and at Jews. He inserts only one small criticism in his rhetorical praise of the book:

> But all is not flowers. The Attic censor in me condemns without appeal the tiring extravagance of colorful but episodic brush strokes—an overgrown thicket that clutters and obscures the Parthenon's sharp outline.

So they often do. The real strength of the authors lies in their power of gaudy caricature—and chiefly in the torrent of affected vernacular or self-dramatizing disclaimer which the visitors to Don Isidro pour out. The tales are told by a procession of loud talkers. "Ultraism" also plays its part in the metaphors. One Carlos Anglada says in Don Isidro's cell that he is inclined to "let myself drift on the ferry boat of my verbiage. A River Plate H. G. Wells, let me row upstream in time. I shall disembark on the possessive marriage bed." In the tale **"Tadeo Limardo's Victim,"** a swanking hoodlum is attacked by a man who "came at me like boiling milk." In the same story, the despised Limardo seems "like a loaf that nobody wants to buy," and yet slowly spreads over the place "like spilled oil." He is eventually killed and lies stretched on a bed "deader than a salami."

These phrases come from characters who are continually in voice. Some are from literary coteries, some are new-rich millionaires, some are giddy or loose women or shifty thieves. In the opening story—which is far too fantastic—the talker is a dull, obsequious fellow who seeks to join a peculiar secret society and has to recite the names of the governing constellations of astrology as if they were items in a card trick, but elsewhere all the theatrical voices of Buenos Aires are heard. Their language is flung about either like grotesque bouquets or like dirty linen. One cannot guess which collaborator contributed the lines, but Borges was certainly out to establish the real voice of the new Argentine. It would not be the voice of Madrid, for all his devotion to Cervantes and Quevedo, or that of the strange assortment of English writers he admired, from Sir Thomas Browne to Wells, Chesterton, and Conan Doyle.

Where we begin to detect the later Borges is in the serious concern for intellectual enigma, in the view of fiction as a game dignified by fateful, ancient overtones, and, of course, in the faked bibliographical footnotes with which, as a prisoner of his municipal library, he made the hours more bearable. If we take the case of Limardo, in his sleazy hotel, there is first the fact that he is a stranger who is despised. Suddenly, in an astonishingly dramatic scene, he preaches the sacredness of marriage vows to the astounded crooks. Why? Has he come to kill the lover of his faithless wife? How can such a coward, so easily put upon, bring himself to such an act? The excellence of this tale lies in its exposure of the minds of the evasive, watchful crooks, who are comically watching one another and diddling one another as they do so. Don Isidro sees that Limardo had come not to kill but to provoke his own death:

> It was true that he had brought a gun to kill someone, but that someone was himself. He had come a long way. For months and months, he had begged for abuse and insult in order to strengthen his nerve to kill himself, because death was what he longed for. I also think that before he died he wanted to see his wife.

That last sentence is devastating, for the reader has already seen that it is the wife who kills Limardo in defending, as she supposes, her lover. That extra turn of the psychological screw is surely pure Borges.

So also is the elaborate case of Ricardo in **"Free Will and the Commendatore."** This brainless polo-playing young dandy, a boasting womanizer, is the son of an Italian immigrant who has risen to great wealth and has assumed the rank. Don Isidro broods in his cell: the old Commendatore has known for years that Ricardo is really a bastard, the son of his faithless wife by another man. The father's vengeance lies in destroying the young man by covertly encouraging his vices, secretly buying mistresses for him—creating, in fact, a man who is a deceived fraud. The old man spends all his wealth so that this son will get nothing. Worse, he sees to it that the son hears the hollowness of his pretensions as a lover. Don Isidro ends the tale on a Borgesian note of ambiguity:

> The realisation that his whole life was a farce both bewildered and humiliated Ricardo. It was

as if suddenly you were told you were someone else. . . . He never said a thing against the Commendatore, whom he still loved. But he left a farewell letter that his father was sure to understand. That letter said, "Now everything has changed and will go on changing. . . . No other father in the world has done what my father has."

I think Father Brown-Borges wrote that suicide note.

The collaborators continued their parodying fit for a few years, until they found themselves getting wilder and more baroque, and then gave up. But they had exploited the fantasy life of the Buenos Aires of their time.

Nicholas Rankin   (essay date 1982)

SOURCE: "On the Inflationary Fringe," in *The Times Literary Supplement*, No. 4143, August 27, 1982, p. 920.

[*In the following review, Rankin provides a positive assessment of* Chronicles of Bustos Domecq, *describing the collection as "conservative satire."*]

In **"The Sartorial Revolution (I)"** [in *Chronicles of Bustos Domecq*] Eduardo S. Bradford, dandy of the Necochea seaside promenade from 1923 to 1931, is revealed as an impoverished fake. His millionaire's hat, horn-rimmed glasses, moustache, collar, necktie, watch chain, white suit with set of imported buttons, gloves, handkerchiefs and boots have been painted on to his body. Even the malacca cane. It is Argentina that parades its banality beneath the Emperor of Europe's cultural clothing in *Chronicles of Bustos Domecq,* twenty satirical sketches by Borges and his friend and collaborator Bioy Casares.

The two men met through Ocampo's *Sur* magazine around 1931; they shared the same passion for books. Their early collaborations included a commercial brochure for Bulgarian foodstuffs, written in a week at a Pardó *estancia,* and an anthology of Fantastic Literature, compiled while they were annotating Sir Thomas Browne. They wrote comic detective stories under *noms de plume*: H. Bustos Domecq penned *Six Problems for Don Isidro Parodi* (1942) and many of the characters from that book recur in the Chestertonian spoof *A Model for Death* (1946) by B. Suárez Lynch (not yet translated).

Originally written as pieces of journalism, the *Chronicles* were collected in 1967 into a book dedicated to Picasso, Joyce and Le Corbusier with an introduction by one Gervasio Montenegro, who recommends it as an "indispensable vademecum" to "the depths of the novel, the lyric, the essay, conceptualism, architecture, sculpture, the theater and the whole gamut of audio-visual media". An important index compiled by the "author" himself rounds the book off.

The *Chronicles* mark the apotheosis of H. Bustos Domecq from pseudonym to persona. The author of *Now I Can Read!* (City of Rosario School Board), once referred to in a Parodi mystery as "that man from Santa Fe who got a story published and then it turned out it had already been written by Villiers de L'Isle Adam", is now a champion hack on the pretentious fringes of Buenos Aires. Eight of

the *Chronicles* are literary jaunts through the cosmopolitan groves of Parnassus. Ramón Bonavena's *nouveau roman* "North-Northeast" features the northeastern quadrant of his table, where a 2B pencil is brilliantly described in "only twenty-nine pages". For F. J. C. Loomis, the title is the work: "The text of *Pallet,* for example, consists solely of the word 'pallet'." Words mean what Santia-

---

An excerpt from "The Nights of Goliadkin"

Tall, distinguished, bland, his profile romantic, his brush mustache tinted, Gervasio Montenegro stepped with blasé elegance into the police van and let himself be chauffeured to the penitentiary. He found himself in a paradoxical situation. The countless readers of evening papers throughout the fourteen Argentine provinces were outraged that such a famous actor should be accused of theft and murder; the countless readers of evening papers knew that Gervasio Montenegro was a famous actor because he was accused of theft and murder.

This priceless confusion was the exclusive doing of that alert reporter Achilles Molinari, who, in solving the mystery of Ibn Khaldun, had acquired so much prestige. It was also thanks to Molinari that the police allowed Gervasio Montenegro this highly unusual visit to the jail where in cell 273 the sedentary detective Isidro Parodi was serving time. (Molinari, with a generosity that fooled no one, attributed all his successes to Parodi.)

A skeptic at heart, Montenegro had his doubts about a detective who had formerly been a barber on Mexico Street, on the Southside of Buenos Aires, and was now a prison inmate. Montenegro's whole being, sensitive as a Stradivarius, shuddered at the prospect of this fateful visit. Still, he'd let himself be talked into it, well aware that he should avoid a falling out with Achilles Molinari, who, as Montenegro himself had put it, represented the fourth estate.

Parodi received the famous actor without looking up. In his slow, efficient way the detective was brewing maté in a small blue mug, which Montenegro was quite ready to sample. Parodi, however—no doubt owing to shyness—failed to offer him any. To put the detective at his ease, Montenegro patted him on the shoulder and lit a cigarette from a pack of Sublimes that lay on a stool.

"You've come early, don Montenegro. But I know what brings you. It's this business of the diamond."

"I see that these stout walls are no barrier to my fame," Montenegro hastened to remark.

"Correct. What better place than a jail cell to know what's going on all over the country—from the thieving in high places down to the cultural efforts of the lowliest radio actor."

Adolfo Bioy Casares and Jorge Luis Borges, in their Six Problems for Don Isidro Parodi, *translated by Norman Thomas di Giovanni, E. P. Dutton Publishing Co., 1981.*

---

go Ginsberg wants them to, but Tulio Herrera's art scrupulously eschews them—along with sentences, characters, scenes, etc. Review a book? Hilario Lambkin Formento reproduces the blurb on the jacket, and ends by copying whole volumes.

The sketches are not all whimsical ideas taken to grotesque extremes, for something of Argentina glares through them. There is more truth than humour in the rise of mediocrity being chronicled in a language rich in orotund bombast, from the land where inflation became part of the economy only long after it was a birthright, a state of mind. Ironies turn into prophecies, or perhaps it is just that a blind man's vision is less deceived by age. **"A Brand-New Approach"** is about historical revisionism; Bustos Domecq asks "Does a military defeat suit a nation of patriots?" and replies "Certainly not." So-called "pure" history has become an act of faith, or honest revenge. "Mexico has thus recovered, in print, the oil-wells of Texas, and we here in the Argentine . . . have recovered the South polar cap and its inalienable archipelago."

H. Bustos Domecq began in the timelessly dated world of whodunnits, and *Chronicles* has mysteries that cannot be revealed here. The reader must find alone the secret of G. A. Baralt's shoes (**"The Brotherhood Movement"**), the thing in Chubut sheep-rancher don Guillermo Blake's shed (**"The Immortals"**) and why the last game of soccer was played in Buenos Aires on June 24, 1937 (**"Esse est Percipi"**). . . .

Chronicles of Bustos Domecq is conservative satire, the *humor ingles* of funny names and the avant-garde rendered absurd. Characters such as the architect Hotchkiss de Estephano, *gastronome* Ishmael Querido and the sinister Dr Narbondo could almost appear in the newspaper columns of Beachcomber or Peter Simple. Potboiling, of course, but even the diversionary sketch-books of a master are interesting. "Addicts" of Borges's "jokes and puzzles" (the phrase is V. S. Naipaul's) will find irresistible fun in this book.

Thomas C. Meehan   (essay date 1982)

SOURCE: "Temporal Simultaneity and the Theme of Time Travel in a Fantastic Story by Adolfo Bioy Casares," in *Essays on Argentine Narrators,* Albatros Hispanofila, 1982, pp. 105-58.

[*Meehan is an American translator, critic, and professor of Spanish language and Spanish-American literature, specializing in Argentine fiction.*]

Adolfo Bioy Casares is probably best known as the author of *La invención de Morel* (1940) and as long-time friend and collaborator of his more famous compatriot, Jorge Luis Borges. However, over a period of forty years Bioy Casares has also created an impressive corpus of original prose fiction which includes eleven books of short stories and seven novels and novelettes. The bulk of Bioy's writings, largely overlooked by critics, may, like those of Borges, be broadly classified as fantastic literature.

The purpose of this essay is to examine the narrative struc-

ture and the fantastic themes of temporal simultaneity and time travel in **"El otro laberinto,"** one of six stories which make up an early collection of Bioy Casares' fantastic fiction titled *La trama celeste* (1948). **"El otro laberinto"** is an adventure story, but it is also a sort of literary mystery which challenges the reader to solve its enigma and perceive the intellectual underpinnings of its intricate organization before the narrator clarifies matters toward the end.

In a manner reminiscent of the cosmopolitan settings, events and characters, of Borges' writings, the action of the tale unfolds in Hungary in early 1904 against a background of Austrian political and social oppression of Magyar nationalist sentiment. Anthal Horvath, a prolific but unsuccessful novelist, reluctantly returns from an extended stay in Paris to his native Budapest only to be drawn irresistibly into a network of former university friends and conspirators plotting the murder of a despised Austrian police chief. István Banyay, Horvath's wealthy, lifelong friend and member of the Hungarian patriots, is a historian obsessed by an incident which had occurred exactly three centuries earlier. In 1604, a dead man was found in a sealed room of the Tunnel Inn of Budapest. The same ancient building now forms part of the Banyay family estate, and István occupies bachelor quarters in rooms contiguous to that in which the corpse had been found so long ago. Found on the dead body was a mysterious manuscript, apparently the biography of the deceased. This document had disappeared and subsequently became the object of a three-hundred year scholarly search. István Banyay, with more than a passing interest in seventeenth-century Hungarian history, finds the manuscript, but then he himself vanishes unexplainably. Anthal Horvath's investigation of his friend's disappearance leads to the astounding discovery that István, in possession of his manuscript, and in an attempt to escape the Austrian secret police, had entered the ancient room. In doing so, he magically stepped back (or "over") into the seventeenth century, whereupon he dropped dead of heart failure. Horvath subsequently offers his explanation of the facts in the case. He reveals his motive for, and the events which led up to, his forgery of the manuscript, which had brought about his friend's tragic death. Horvath's profound remorse over the senseless trick he had played on his friend seems to him ample justification for his contemplated suicide. The action comes full circle just preceding Horvath's entry into the fatal room where a glass of water and arsenic await him.

The foregoing schematic summary of **"El otro laberinto"** conveys only the barest idea of the story. It does not, however, communicate any notion of the rigorous plot structure or the richness of the fantastic themes and their metaphysical connotations which pose stimulating literary and intellectual challenges to the reader. The following comments will attempt to illuminate these facets of the tale. I will first examine the structure and then the themes.

"El otro laberinto" is organized into two large narrative configurations. Part I, subdivided into ten short, numbered chapters, is narrated in third person by an omniscient author. It is, however, told largely from the point of view of Anthal Horvath, who will later unmask himself as the great dissimulator and forger of the fateful manuscript. Part II combines Horvath's first person confession or "Comunicación a los amigos," conveniently printed in italics, with interspersed third person, omniscient author entries that comment and elaborate upon Horvath's confession. Although the time span of the action remains somewhat vague, it comprises a period of several months to, at most, a year. The narrative present is 1904, and the climax occurs at the end of the story, at dawn of March 17. Toward the end of the first part Bioy Casares introduces the mysterious disappearance of a main character, István Banyay, thus creating an enigma. The second part presents, again toward the end, the revelation of a fantastic explanation for that vanishing act. As Horvath announces, "*Intertaré la simple relación histórica de los hechos. . . .*"

Although the form of the story follows the pattern of the classic *relato fantástico,* Bioy has also drawn upon certain resources of detective fiction in shaping his material. The quotation just above, for example, reveals that certain events have happened prior to the main action and that information has been intentionally withheld from the reader in the manner of a mystery novel. The trajectory of the action, like that of the detective story (or gothic romance) moves from the "descripción de una situación ambigua o sobrenatural (mundo 'desconocido')" to an "explicacón *racional* o verosímil del fenómeno (mundo 'conocido')" [Jorge B. Rivera, "Lo arquetípico en la narrativa argentina del 40," in *Nueva Novela Latinoamericana 2,* edited by Jorge Laforgue, 1972]. (The difference here, of course, is that the "explanation" of the enigma, unlike that of the detective story, is neither rational nor verisimilar, but fantastic.) In addition, certain incidents appear, as in a mystery, in an apparently haphazard, somewhat bewildering manner, but they are later clarified. If the reader picks up the artist's system of cross-references, every detail eventually produces its resonance, and all is justified and explained. The puzzle is worked out.

Other features of mystery fiction are the use of the sealed room motif (here the magic room called the *museo*), the surprise ending, Horvath's investigation of four versions of István's disappearance, and the planting of several clues for the reader in the course of the story's first part. For example, in the first chapter of Part I, Horvath casually remarks that the day after his arrival in Budapest he had visited Professor Liptay in the library. Not finding Liptay, Horvath left him "un pequeño recuerdo que [a Liptay] le envió una muchacha francesa. . . ." Only in Part II will the reader discover that the "little souvenir" was the manuscript of the seventeenth-century dead man's biography forged by Horvath and his mistress, Madeleine, in Paris. Professor Liptay contends that only a man who expects little of life, a man without hope, would make the best assassin of the Austrian police chief. This constitutes a clue to what will happen to both István Banyay and Anthal Horvath. The former gives up all hope upon losing his beloved Erzsebet to Horvath, and the latter can expect little from a life of remorse after causing the death of his best friend.

Notwithstanding the above-mentioned elements of a mystery story, **"El otro laberinto"** is, in its most prominent structural contours, a model of the fantastic genre. In distinguishing between detective fiction and the *relato fantástico,* [Louis] Vax points out [in *Arte y literatura fantásticas,* translated by Juan Merino, 1965] that the former introduces the supernatural, usually at the outset, only to suppress it in the dénouement so that reason and logic may have the last word. "En el cuento fantástico, el planteamiento es inverso; lo sobrenatural, ausente al principio, domina el proceso que lleva al desenlace; es necesario que se insinúe poco a poco, que adormezca a la razón en lugar de escandalizarla." [In the "Prólogo" to *Antología de la literatura fantástica,* edited by Bioy Casares, Jorge Luis Borges, and Silvina Ocampo,] Bioy Casares himself has drawn a structural blueprint for the fantastic tale in similar terms. The author's ideas can be paraphrased as follows: into the midst of a realistic, credible atmosphere there intrudes a single incredible occurrence which surprises, bewilders, and causes fear and doubt. For the surprise to be most effective it should be carefully prepared, foreshadowed, and thus slightly attenuated.

It now becomes apparent that the basic components and narrative functions of the story's two main structural units coincide precisely with the above theories of both Bioy Casares and Vax with regard to the fantastic. The narrative strategy of Part I, and a characteristic of the author's style in general, is the deliberate creation of a believable atmosphere "full of localizing connotations" [according to Ofelia Kovacci in her *Adolfo Bioy Casares,* 1963], or what Jaime Rest has called "una densidad vital concreta" ["Las invenciones de Bioy Casares," *Los Libros,* No. 2 (agosto 1969)].

The impression of such a dense, specific reality is achieved by four technical means, the general lines of which can only be adumbrated here. First, there is the creation of a vivid impression of space, made up of a country (Hungary), its capital (Budapest), the previous existence of Horvath in another capital (Paris), and other Hungarian towns and places (Nyiregyhaza, Nagy-Banya, Tuszer). The fictional space is further filled by more specific references to the names of streets, parks, lakes, plazas, and fountains, a family estate, old buildings, coffeehouses, a tailor-shop, and a university library. In addition, this space is teeming not only with well-sketched secondary personages (Palma Szentgyörgyi, Erzsebet Loczy, Professor Liptay, Ferencz Remenyi), but also with other anonymous people (vendors, students, conspirators, police), as well as trolleys, horse-drawn coaches, trains, etc. Secondly, there is the creation of convincing human personalities and attention to character development (of the two protagonists, Horvath and Banyay, especially) which go well beyond those found in a *cuento* (normally briefer than an English short story) and the usually quite short fantastic tale of Borges, e.g., with whom the author is frequently compared.

Third is the presentation of a strong impression of human psychology: memories, faults and virtues (loyalty and disloyalty, courage and cowardliness), the interplay and conflict of emotions (anger, fear, loneliness, timidness, tenderness, indifference, arrogance, guilt and remorse). Principal factors here, as in most of Bioy's works, are the elements of friendship and love, which achieve the result of humanizing a style which tends toward being almost coldly cerebral at times, perhaps owing to the metaphysical abstract themes treated. Horvath and Banyay are depicted as lifelong friends, and the former's remorse upon discovering the awful truth about István's disappearance seems genuine. Illustrative of the amorous element is the fact that five man-woman relationships develop in **"El otro laberinto"**: Horvath-Madeleine; Horvath-Palma; Horvath-Erzsebet; István-Palma; István-Erzsebet. Indeed, love even emerges as a "magic" force in the strange, forged manuscript. Horvath writes: "*Y aquí debo señalar algo mágico en ese manuscrito fraguado, una anticipación que, en cierto modo, lo redime de su condición de impostura: hay una descripción del amor que inspira Erzsebet que es una pálida pero fiel descripción del amor, de la adoración, que ahora siento por ella*" (Bioy's italics). A fourth and final technique used to build a believable atmosphere is the careful elaboration of a realistic socio-political background. It is made up of elements such as the Magyar struggle against Austria for local national autonomy, economic class distinctions, academic politics, student unrest and violence, police brutality, etc.

The purpose of this elaborately constructed reality is to create a medium receptive to the entrance of the fantastic element, a "real" world which will bear the weight of a supernatural impact, contain and absorb it naturally. The reader's disbelief has now been willingly and sufficiently suspended. His reason has been adequately lulled so as to accept the intrusion of the fantastic without shock. Absent throughout Part I [with the exception, the critic adds in a footnote, of two references to István Banyay's supernatural powers of mental projection] and most of Part II, the fantastic emerges only toward the end of the second section and dominates the *desenlace* (as Vax indicated [in *Arte y literatura fantásticas,* translated by Juan Merino, 1965]). When the story's single fantastic incident makes its appearance, it is stated in an almost matter-of-fact manner, almost as an afterthought, as if to play down its importance: "*Por su parte, István sólo entró en el pasado. . . . Pero István no cayó muerto en el 'museo'; cayó en el cuarto de la posada del Túnel, en el siglo XVII.*" The reader is thus left wondering whether it might not have happened after all; he is in that state of uncertainty so essential to the fantastic genre, according to [Tzvetan Todorov, in his *The Fantastic: A Structural Approach to a Literary Genre,* translated by Richard Howard, 1975]. One even wonders whether Anthal Horvath is about to follow István into the past!

The main fantastic themes of **"El otro laberinto"** are the simultaneous existence of past and present and the ability of a man to travel from one of these dimensions to the other. At one point in his confession, Horvath provides the key in words that might well be applied to the story as a whole: "*La clave de este proceso es una cuestión de tiempo; si el tiempo es sucesivo, si el pasado se extingue, es inútil que yo busque una excusa. . . .*" (Bioy's italics). István's trip to the simultaneous past proves, as Horvath ultimately asserts, that "*el tiempo sucesivo es una mera ilusión*

de los hombres y que vivimos en una eternidad donde todo es simultáneo. . . ." (Bioy's italics).

However, as Bioy Casares stipulated, the reader discovers that the fantastic surprise ending can become all the more effective and esthetically rewarding when it is carefully prepared for. The writer's interweaving of the themes into the texture of his narrative bears witness to his craftsmanship as a storyteller. In numerous, subtle ways, the narrator is constantly pointing toward his fantastic dénouement with clues, symbols, motifs and foreshadowing. For example, often the opening lines of a fantastic tale are very significant, and the present story is no exception. Horvath's first thoughts of István are a hint at the temporal theme: "*Es como si detuviera el tiempo, o como si yo no hubiera estado en París; antes de irme, [István] hablaba de esto; ahora sigue hablando. Insiste en este episodio del pasado; olvida el presente.*"

Another important device used to prepare the terrain for the emergence of the fantastic is a technique frequently employed by Bioy Casares: he indirectly provides a key to his themes through literary references which have an integral function in the plot. Although **"El otro laberinto"** is replete with literary, philosophical and historical allusions, I will consider only those that directly bear upon the theme and form of the story. Each of the two large structural divisions is prefaced by an epigraph. That of Part I quotes a line from Ovid's *Tristia* [*Tristia Ex Ponto,* edited and translated by Arthur Leslie Wheeler (1965)]: "*dissimulare velis, te liquet esse meum.*" ["You wish to dissimulate, but clearly you are mine."] These words evidently allude to some form of deception, and the reader soon discovers that the author is about to lead him on a merry chase! The source is not III, iii, 18 of *Tristia,* as Bioy's quotation stipulates, but I, i, 62, which is the proem to the Latin poet's book. Writing from exile, Ovid apostrophizes his collection of poems in this line and sends it on its way to Rome as an emissary to plead for his pardon. Ovid goes on to say that, although his work still lacks a title, its style should enable readers to recognize him as its author. Bioy Casares is hinting at a secret author and a possibly spurious document. The epigraph of Part I thus becomes a clue to the fact that the manuscript found by István is a hoax, a document forged by Anthal Horvath as a joke to be played on his friend. The epigraph also suggests the form of the story, which is based upon a system of shifting perspectives: we observe an illusory dimension of reality in Part I, and only in Part II are we permitted to see the true face of that reality.

István later discovers that a different hand had interpolated another verse from Ovid in the manuscript: "*nulla venit sine te nox mihi, nulla dies*" ["no night comes to me without you, no day either"]. The *Tristia* verse number indicated (I, v, 7) is again incorrect. (Bioy's "game" with the reader continues!) Horvath will later confess to having added the beautiful, amorous verse as a "last countersign and as a greeting." He asserts that the "contraseña" was concealed in the intentionally wrong verse number (I, v, 7), which was addressed to István in the hope that his friend would discover the hoax of the apocryphal manuscript. The *Tristia* verse which does bear that number thus

Adolfo Bioy Casares (left) and his friend Jorge Luis Borges, with whom he has collaborated on a number of literary projects.

takes on significance also. It appears in a letter of Ovid *to a friend* (like Horvath to Banyay), and reads: "*scis bene, cui dicam, positis pro nomine signis*" ["you know well to whom I am speaking by means of these symbols substituted for your name"]. The love "greeting" was directed either to Madeleine or Erzsebet (in his bewilderment, Horvath is no longer sure for which woman he intended the verse). The correct number of the Ovidian verse "*nulla venit sine te. . .*" is III, iii, 18. The line is from one of the many poetic letters the Roman poet composed to his wife.

Two things are noteworthy here. First, Ovid's letter begins with words which, in the context of **"El otro laberinto,"** become another cryptic allusion to a "shadow writer": "*Haec mea si casu miraris epistula quare / alteris digitis scripta sit . . .*" ["If haply you wonder why this letter of mine is written by another's fingers . . ."] (*Tristia,* III, iii, 1-2). Secondly, the reader now discovers that the verse number given for "*nulla venit sine te. . .*" (III, iii, 18) corresponds, in a labyrinthine manner, to the reference which Bioy Casares had originally affixed to the epigraph of Part I, "*dissimulare velis, te liquet esse meum!*" All these dissimulations and deceptions point indirectly at the big deception perpetrated on mankind, namely that the traditional concept of linear time in a past-present-future continuum is a fraud. István Banyay's entry into the seventeenth century proves that all time is simultaneous. Eternity is now.

Two further allusions to writers of antiquity mirror the temporal theme. In the university library, Horvath observes a bust of Boethius (A.D. 470-525) and reads the inscription: "*HI OCULI VIDERVNT AETERNITATEM.*" ["These eyes saw eternity."] This Latin phrase obviously relates to the closing words of Horvath's confession, which are an overt statement of the theme of simultaneous times. On the basis of István's escape to the past, Anthal deduces that "*successive time is a mere illusion*" and that "*we live in an eternity where everything is simultaneous*" (Bioy's italics; my translation). The second reference reinforces these ideas. In a frieze around the ceiling of the library, Horvath reads "una cita del libro undécimo de las *Confesiones,* de San Agustín." Book Eleven of St. Augustine's *Confessions* contains (Chaps. XI-XXXI) his meditations on the problem of time. He demonstrates that "time and creation are cotemporal" and reaches conclusions that point to a completely subjective theory of time.

The epigraph to Part II of the story quotes a verse from a poem by Thomas Chatterton, "The Storie of William Canynge," which relates a dream vision of the past. The quotation appears in the original English but is deliberately incomplete: "*Straight was I carried. . . .*" Upon reading Chatterton, the reader will discover that the complete verse casts a spotlight upon the theme of time travel: "*Strayte was I carryd back to times of yore. . . .*" However, the implications of this literary reference are multiple since they further reinforce the motif of forgery and dissimulation alluded to in the epigraph to Part I of the story. It is significant that Bioy Casares should draw his epigraph from the writings of Thomas Chatterton, for the latter, like his contemporary, James Macpherson (1736-96), author of the controversial Ossian poems, was one of the notorious forgers of English literary history.

There are intriguing, thematic parallels between the plot of **"El otro laberinto"** and certain circumstances pertaining to Chatterton's "The Storie of William Canynge." In the latter work, the poet (supposedly Rowley), while resting beside a river, recollects the bellicose recent past of the now peaceful, scenic locale. The allegorical figure of Truth appears, puts the poet to sleep, and transports him back in time (like István's temporal journey) so that he may reconstruct the earlier life of his new friend, William Canynge, heroic lord mayor of nearby Bristol. Although Chatterton published the poem as if it were merely his own transcription of an authentic fifteenth-century manuscript by Rowley, literary historians are now certain that it is a hoax. Taking a leaf from Chatterton's book, Anthal Horvath, a struggling young writer like Chatterton, forges a three-hundred-year-old document to play a trick on his friend, István Banyay. While living in Paris, Horvath had been inspired by a performance of Alfred de Vigny's play, *Chatterton,* and, aided by Madeleine, his French mistress, he had created the fake biography later ("earlier!") found on the corpse in the seventeenth century. "*Después leí todo lo que pude hallar sobre el poeta que inventaba manuscritos y poetas*" (Bioy's italics). Bioy Casares hinted at such a development in Part I when he referred to Anthal's projected biography of Chatterton. Furthermore, again like the English poet, Horvath errs frequently in his attempt to duplicate the style of writing of an earlier period. Anthal's apocryphal manuscript is written mainly in modern Hungarian, but with occasional missing z's or diereses, many lexical archaisms, old orthographic forms, and even anachronisms. Since Madeleine, who was copying Horvath's rough draft to prevent István from identifying the handwriting, knew no Hungarian, misspellings abound in the document.

But the story of Chatterton informs **"El otro laberinto"** in even more subtle ways. If the reader consults Alfred de Vigny's play, he will discover that all the tragedy of the English poet's short existence, including poverty, literary forgery, futile struggle for recognition and, ultimately, suicide, is entirely mirrored in the life of Anthal Horvath. Throughout the story, Horvath's brooding and his somewhat melodramatic, even phony romantic posturing suggest that he views himself as a modern-day Chatterton, another unrecognized, misunderstood genius. The despondent tone of Horvath's "Comunicación a los amigos" is imbued with the melancholy spirit of Chatterton's final hours as they are presented in Alfred de Vigny's drama, *Chatterton,* which Anthal had seen in Paris. During the redaction of his confession, Horvath is so obsessed with the memory of the tragic, young English bard, with whom he obviously identifies, that he even inserts a line from another Chatterton poem, "Bristowe Tragedie," which expresses Horvath's own feelings at the moment of death: "Hay que morir, dijo el valiente Carlos. / Eso no temo."

Finally, by taking arsenic in water, Horvath imitates precisely the manner of Chatterton's suicide. Bioy Casares thus introduces another fantastic motif, the reversal of a traditional aesthetic principle, i.e., "life imitates art."

There is evidence pointing to the functional presence in the story of two other traditionally fantastic motifs which further buttress the theme of time travel. The first is that of the double or *Doppelgänger.* Upon the disappearance of István Banyay, Anthal Horvath immediately begins to assume his friend's identity and, in all probability, his destiny. Horvath is received "like a son" by István's parents, practically adopted into the wealthy family and invited to occupy their son's quarters next to the *museo.* As István's father reasons, "Horvath es la persona más cercana de István; faltando István, en cierto modo lo representa."

Anthal now proceeds to pursue István's activities. He continues the latter's work on the *Enciclopedia Húngara,* attends meetings of the Magyar patriots in István's place, takes up with Palma first and then transfers his love to Erzsebet, just as Banyay had. He even says he will write the biography of the seventeenth-century dead man who had so obsessed István. The similarities and repetitions of the twin protagonists accelerate at dawn of March 17. Horvath is seated at the same table in front of the window where Banyay was last seen by both Janós, the family coachman, and the Dollseller. Like István, Horvath also has now become a man without hope, as Professor Liptay had foreseen: upon reading in the newspaper of the student's assault on the office of the university rector, Anthal knows that police security will be increased, and that he will have no chance to kill Liptay, who has been branded as a traitor to the patriots. Horvath's own capture is imminent, and his heart pounds, "pesado y enorme," which recalls reiterated references to István's weak heart. When Janós leaves the study, Horvath writes furiously because he now realizes that things are repeating themselves and that he is about to follow István Banyay into the old room where death awaits. Toward the end, the image of a beckoning, open door to the *museo* strengthens the suggestion that Anthal, like István, will find the warp in time and escape into the past. When Anthal sees the same secret police agent dressed in gray whom István had seen approaching his apartment, he announces: "Ahora yo pasaré por la misma puerta. . . ." As he steps through that door, Horvath says he does not possess his friend's supernatural powers: "Yo tengo solamente un vaso de agua, un poco de arsénico y el ejemplo de Chatterton."

The fantastic motif of the double is related to the theme of time travel. Although Bioy Casares lets the reader draw his own conclusions, by the story's end the narrator has carefully prepared the suggestion that Anthal Horvath, as István Banyay's *Doppelgänger,* will repeat some form of the latter's temporal journey. Given the extent to which Horvath assumes the identity (and destiny?) of Banyay, there is every reason to believe that the former, upon entering the magic *museo,* will likewise be whisked away to another simultaneous past, perhaps to the time of his much admired Chatterton!

The *ámbito cerrado* is a second traditional motif of fantastic literature; it becomes a central image in **"El otro la-**

berinto." The *ámbito cerrado* is usually a secret space, an enchanted garden, for example, or some hermetically sealed room or recess where magic things happen. It is a place set off from reality, and it is always conducive to the fantastic. Such locations have been defined [by Kovacci in *Adolfo Bioy Casares*] as "lugares aptos para construir otra realidad, ámbitos físicos y metafísicos aislados por el mar separador de lo real y lo posible." Such a place is István Banyay's *museo* which is the same room in which the dead man was found three centuries earlier. The building containing it is significantly isolated, being located far from the manor house, "en los fondos del jardín." The stuffy, hermetic atmosphere of the *museo* is emphasized by the stagnant air found even in the adjoining rooms which serve as István's quarters.

The *museo* is appropriately named since a museum is a place where the past lives on in the present, thus reflecting the theme of simultaneous time dimensions. In Banyay's museum the past has, quite literally, "accumulated." The room once served as a kind of warehouse for a great uncle of István, who heaped up in the semi-darkness the countless objects bought to pamper his collector's whims. Here the past exists *in* the present, and here István Banyay, through an act of supernatural mental projection, finds a warp in the barrier dividing the simultaneous temporal dimensions and steps from present into past.

Careful scrutiny of the narrator's lengthy enumeration of objects and artefacts in the *museo* reveals that most are symbolically linked to various motifs and to thematic threads of the story. Each antique is invested with thematic resonance, or as Kovacci expresses it, "Cada objeto es al mismo tiempo unidad y manifestación de pluralidades como simbólicos laberintos." For example, the clocks designed like little villages with houses and figurines, as well as the astronomical instruments can be related to the general theme of time. The same can be said of the legend of the immortal Wandering Jew which decorates a Russian doll bearing the date 1785. Its presence in the collection proves, as the narrator states, that the origin of the legend is previous to the nineteenth century. A contrasting parallel to the Wandering Jew, who lives in successive incarnations *forward* in time, is the reference to Philip the Englishman, whose successive avatars apparently take place *backwards* in time. He was first "clockmaker to Hume" (XVIIIth century) and then, moving back in time, as István does, mimic ("mono") of Pope Sylvester II (Xth century) who is often credited, incidentally, with the invention of a mechanical clock (circa 996).

The elaborate chess set and billiard table are images related to the idea of "games" or "jokes," a motif repeated throughout the story. The big "joke," of course, was the innocent one that Anthal Horvath played on his friend. The forged manuscript was a game which got out of control and, unfortunately, turned into a grim joke for all them in the end: "Pero él [Horvath] no podía sospechar la terrible aventura que los esperaba." The many torture instruments collected in the *museo* may foreshadow the strongly intimated fact that Ferencz Remenyi, a member of the patriots, is tortured by the Austrian authorities before they play a cat-and-mouse game with him instead of just killing him outright (again the game and joke motif). He is given forty-eight hours to get across the border, a hopeless, illusory escape in space which parallels the "real" escape in time effected by István Banyay.

The optical instruments in the *museo* suggest the play of visual perspectives inherent in the structure of the narrative points of view employed in the story. Until the reader is given Anthal Horvath's first person perspective in Part II, our perception of the incidents in the tale is only partial. Our eyes, like those of István and Professor Liptay, have been closed or blinded to the deception practiced in the manuscript forgery. In Part I we are not permitted to see this hidden side of reality, although there are hints and clues scattered throughout.

Other objects in the *museo* are significant. The copies of the wooden dove and the bronze fly built by Regiomontanus are spurious ("ejemplares apócrifos") and as such relate directly to the motif of forgery and deception. Regiomontanus ("belonging to the royal mountain," i.e., to Königsberg, where he was born) was a German mathematician and astronomer (1436-76) whose real name was Johannes Müller. (Again the motif of concealment, dissimulation: note that Horvath also uses a pseudonym. He claims to be working on a "rigurosa novela de peripecias, que se publicará con mi seudónimo. . . .") Regiomontanus, one of those mysterious historical figures which fascinate Bioy Casares and Borges, was called to the court of Hungary (scene of the action of Bioy's tale) in 1468 to make a collection of Greek manuscripts. (A manuscript is a central image in the story.) He also assisted in reforming the calendar while at Rome in 1475 (theme of time).

Central in the development of the dual themes relating to time is the role of István Banyay who is soon revealed as a man who feels out of place in the twentieth century and more at home in the seventeenth: "Estoy acostumbrado a esa época; las demás se me figuran irreales. . . . Si no me vigilo creo que el siglo XVII es la época natural de la vida humana; más aún de mi propia vida. . . ." He is convinced that the century which so fascinates him actually exists in the room he calls the "museum": "Cuando trabajo en mis biografías para la Enciclopedia, imagino que el siglo XVII está en ese cuarto." Anthal Horvath attributes personality defects to his friend: István must attend to matters successively, one thing at a time; he is also unable to establish relationships and comparisons. Yet these same characteristics may be seen in a positive light. The first hints at István's great powers of concentration and his supernatural gift of mental projection which ultimately enable him to recreate "los objetos y los siglos," and thereby to seek refuge in the past. The second allows him to overlook certain inconsistencies in Anthal's forged manuscript, to intuit his own life in the false seventeenth-century biography, and to live out the life depicted therein: "Me pierdo en la vida que relata." It also enables him to overcome (or overlook) a "small matter" like the cause-and-effect relationship of reality by transporting that manuscript of the present into an apparently bygone time wherein it was lost and then eagerly sought by scholars for three centuries! The past is thus envisioned as vulnerable to the present, since the present can alter and affect the past.

István's supernatural powers of mental projection are suggested early in the story. They are later described in greater detail, but Banyay refers to a major difficulty he encounters in performing the feat: "Proyectar la forma, el color, la solidez, la temperatura . . . nunca me costó mucho. El peso da más trabajo." Supposedly, then, István managed to overcome this obstacle because he succeeded in lifting his bulky body and projecting it back three centuries! But the attentive reader may watch the author preparing even this small detail of the fantastic surprise ending. The description of the corpse found in the Tunnel Inn in the seventeenth century states: "Era corpulento, pero no obeso." However, the early descriptions of István emphasize his enormous size, his huge round head and his "ponderoso busto." The reader is thus tempted to hesitate, to doubt the intervention of the fantastic, i.e., to question whether the cadaver found in the inn was István Banyay. However, Horvath soon notices that his friend seems "algo más flaco." Professor Liptay later reports that Banyay is in an alarming condition: he is sick, has lost more weight, and Horvath finds him "casi flaco." István no longer has "excess baggage," and is now ready for his fantastic "flight through time!"

Anthal Horvath, as co-protagonist with István Banyay, plays a role no less important in the development of the temporal themes. Horvath also is convinced that the past is in the *museo*, but for him it is no consolation; it rather produces an unpleasant feeling: "Según Anthal Horvath, la visión de ese cuarto producía una desilusionada tristeza, como si allí estuviera todo el pasado, como si desde allí acecharan todas las esperanzas, todas las frustraciones y todas las modestas locuras de los hombres." Anthal has come home to Hungary seeking refuge in his time of troubles, economic and professional, but to him this return to his "provincial" homeland is humiliating and repugnant. He recalls verses by a Hungarian poet, Janos Aranyi, which should serve as a warning to him that he will find no external refuge. The reference to the Garden of Paradise is clearly a symbol of a place outside of time, in eternity: "*No busques el Jardín del Paraíso / el abismo arde ya en tu corazón / o florece la paz, que a tu alma educa.*" Longing for Paris, for Madeleine, and for wider cultural horizons than those afforded by Budapest, he angrily revises the last line: "*O florece París, que a tu alma educa.*" The sight of the familiar street scene outside his window and the recollection of a Hungarian folk song give him the impression that time has stood still here during his absence, that Budapest and the past represent, in the words of the song, his "montaña nativa, donde todo, hasta el pasado, nos ampara." Other lyrics of the same song proffer a second, unheeded warning and a premonition: Horvath looks at the street "por donde viene . . . el infortunio y la muerte." It is along this very street that he will later observe the approach of the thin man dressed in gray, an investigator for the Austrian secret police, the same person that István had seen before vanishing.

Nevertheless, Horvath feels safe in his well-known reality. Time has stood still here; all is as it was before. Despite the claims of the patriots that the city has changed, the evidence to the contrary seems to be everywhere before Anthal's eyes as he strolls through well-remembered streets. The enumeration of familiar things, which makes up the entirety of the brief second chapter of Part I, is intended to reinforce the thematic impression that the past lives on in the present. Anthal again flirts with the tailor's wife by whistling a German love song ("Wenn die Liebe in deinen blauen Augen"), and he feels now the same sentiments he had felt when younger "frente a esa misma puerta en muchas tardes de años anteriores." This impression that nothing has changed, that the past exists simultaneously in the present is intensified at the outset of Chapter III as Horvath drinks beer with his good friends at the familiar Turf café and listens to the music of traditional old czardas: "Horvath sintió con desagrado que los años de París se desvanecían de su vida, como si nunca hubieran existido, y que el repetido y pobre laberinto de sus costumbres en Budapest volvía a encerrarlo." Indeed, Anthal Horvath is entering a labyrinth, the "other labyrinth" of past time which will lead him to his death. In a sense, Horvath, like István, is returning to the past, his own past, as he gradually accepts and settles into the familiar ways of his previous life: "Reconoció que ninguna música le conmovía como las czardas, que le gustaba estar con sus amigos y que, en última instancia, él había nacido en Budapest."

No sooner, however, does Anthal accept his past reality when it begins to change. Since he has reentered the temporal flow, he naturally becomes more aware of the changes wrought by time. There are two reasons for this ambiguous, fluctuating reality. First, the tense political situation is turning the city into a prison for the Hungarian patriots. Second, and more importantly, Horvath knows something that the reader does not; he realizes that his little joke, the forged manuscript, is backfiring on him. István continues to believe in the authenticity of the document. Not yet a committed member of the patriots, a forger, doubly disloyal to his best friend, even unsure as yet of his love for Erzsebet, Horvath formulates a thought which is one of those frequently appearing sentences in fantastic literature which call the reader's attention to the real, "the most central aspects of our existence." Perhaps the most profound comment on life made by **"El otro laberinto"** is summed up in these words: "Debemos cuidarnos de que nuestras propias mentiras no nos engañen." Anthal later confesses: "*Estuve engañado sobre el alcance de mi obra*" (Bioy's italics).

After the discovery of Horvath's spurious manuscript and István's subsequent disappearance, the events involving Anthal begin to move so quickly that he loses all control of the situation. Helpless now to change political matters and seemingly paralyzed before the snowballing effects of his "joke," Anthal's safe, familiar world of reality gradually turns completely nightmarish, thus following the classic pattern of the fantastic story. Horvath emphasizes this at the beginning of his confession to his friends: "*Todo ba cambiado. . . . [Los amigos] participaron, día a día, en ese proceso de transformación; nunca sabrán cómo se apresuró el tiempo en Hungría, cuánto cambio trajo. Yo mismo, al regresar de París, no advertí inmediatamente que ya era otro mundo este mundo familiar. Ni siquiera lo advertí cuando Ist128n desapareció. De un modo gradual, sin revelaciones patéticas ni sobresaltos, penetré en esta pesadilla"* (Bioy's italics).

Two facts bring Horvath to a full realization of just exactly how nightmarish his secure world has become. With regard to the situation in Budapest, Anthal refers to his last meeting with Ferencz Remenyi as a "símbolo sobre la verdadera naturaleza de las cosas." The reader soon discovers the brutal truth that the real world of spies, police, dungeons and torture have reduced the once brave, happy, idealistic Ferencz to a sobbing, cringing, terrified animal. Their encounter took place in a grove of trees, and was enveloped, as Anthal states, in a "sombra de irrealidad." The real has thus become unreal and monstrous.

Second, what had seemed fantastic, unreal, has been realized. Aware of Banyay's supernatural powers, of the latter's obsession with the seventeenth century, and of descriptions of the manuscript found on the dead man, Horvath finally understands that what had begun as an innocent joke has ended in tragedy. His friend has entered the "other labyrinth," the endless labyrinth of time. He concludes, awestricken: 1) that the cadaver found in the Tunnel Inn of Budapest in 1604 was that of the young historian, István Banyay; 2) that the manuscript was István's photocopy of his (Horvath's) own counterfeit handiwork. Realizing that István was doubtlessly fleeing from the Austrian secret police, Anthal reconstructs what probably happened on the day of Banyay's disappearance:

> *István comprendió que era la policía secreta; pensó, con desesperada intensidad, en el cuarto que estaba más allá de la puerta de la izquierda, en el "museo." Siempre había imaginado que allí estaba el siglo XVII; ahora, su imaginación de aquel siglo se concentraba obsesivamente en una pieza de la posada del Túnel, de la posada que había entonces en el sitio donde sus abuelos edificaron el pabellón. Guardó el documento en el bolsillo de su capa, abrió la puerta y pasó . . . Tuvo tiempo de cerrar el pasador. Estaba muy agitado. Su corazón, que siempre había sido débil, falló. Pero István no cayó muerto en el "museo"; cayó en el cuarto de la posada del Túnel, en el siglo XVII.* (Bioy's italics)

When István informed Horvath that *in 1637* a French writer of travel books, Jean Baptiste Tavernier (1605-89), found an error in the manuscript concerning the source of a quote from Ovid's *Tristia,* Horvath had turned inexplicably pale and was unable to speak. We learn much later that Anthal had intentionally planted that error in his forged manuscript *of 1904* in order to assure that István would discover the hoax. Tavernier's discovery of Horvath's error, supposedly mentioned somewhere in the Frenchman's multivolumed *Six voyages . . . ,* makes Anthal aware that his reality has turned completely unreal and nightmarish, that forces beyond his comprehension are at work.

Horvath's fear and astonishment are brought on by his numbing realization of the fantastic reversal of the cause-and-effect relationship of things. In linear time, cause precedes effect; here the opposite prevails. Anthal's deliberate error in his fake manuscript written in *1904* takes place

"before" the *1637* discovery of that error by Tavernier! For this to happen, however, it was necessary for a twentieth-century man to travel to the seventeenth century with the forged manuscript containing the mistake. István's temporal journey to the past alters the subsequent three hundred years and influences the present actions of both protagonists. Since Anthal's fraudulent manuscript in a sense triggered that voyage in time, the reader must conclude that the future (i.e., 1904 seen from 1604) has determined the past (1604). Effect precedes cause, thereby negating the traditional concept of time. In the labyrinth of time, past, present and future become one. As the bewildered Anthal Horvath concludes: ". . . comprendí que yo había entrado en un mundo mágico."

In the foregoing analysis of **"El otro laberinto,"** we have seen how Adolfo Bioy Casares has skillfully woven the dual themes of temporal simultaneity and time travel into the entire creative fabric of his story. Plot, characters, setting, atmosphere, motifs, foreshadowing devices such as literary allusion, etc., and all other details are tightly bound into a well unified narrative structure. **"El otro laberinto"** is an esthetically pleasing example of the contemporary tale of fantastic fiction.

An excerpt from "Chronology"

1933. Tor, a publishing house, accepts my book of short stories, ***Diecisiete disparos contra lo porvenir* (*Seventeen Shots at the Future*).** The title betrays my conviction that I will regret having written those stories.

I give up reading Law and enroll in Philosophy and letters, where I feel even farther removed from literature. In a written examination, I compare poems of Baudelaire, Rimbaud, Marllarmé, and (God forgive me) Verlaine with the sentimental lyrics of tangos. Perhaps out of pity the professors pass me.

Readings: Russian novelists. Also, Berkeley, Hume, who were a sort of revelation for me.

1934. I meet Silvina Ocampo.

Readings: Valéry, Gide, Cocteau, Proust.

I publish a book of stories, ***Caos* (*Chaos*).** The Criticism is adverse; in one newspaper it is suggested that I ought to turn my talents to planting potatoes. I receive letters from people taking my part. Secretly I am in agreement with the critic, but I don't follow his advice.

Silvina tells me to give up my studies at the university to dedicate myself to writing. Borges tells me that if I want to be a writer, I can't be a lawyer, a professor, a publisher, or a magazine editor.

Readings: Wells, Conrad, Chesterton, Shaw, Kipling.

Bioy Casares, in his "Chronology," translated by Andrée Conrad, Review, *No. 15, Fall 1975.*

Thomas C. Meehan   (essay date 1985)

SOURCE: "The Motifs of the Homunculus and the Shrinking Man in Two Versions of a Short Story by Adolfo Bioy Casares," in *Hispanófila,* Vol. 28, No. 83, January, 1985, pp. 79-87.

Very little is known about the extensive literary production of Bioy Casares prior to the resounding success of his now almost classical fantastic novel, *La invención de Morel* (1940), because the author has consistently repudiated those early works and consigned them, perhaps justifiably, to oblivion. However, among the numerous stories he wrote from 1929 to 1937, Bioy apparently believed that two of them possessed some redeeming esthetic value, for he reworked and republished them much later under different titles. The purpose of the remainder of this study is to examine and compare briefly one of those narratives. The first rendition of the tale, titled **"Cómo perdí la vista,"** picks up the traditional motif of the homunculus or created human being, and Bioy Casares' revised version, bearing the title **"La sierva ajena,"** incorporates the perhaps slightly more modern motif of the shrunken man. Since my interest here is primarily in the "little man" motif, I will be able to include only the briefest of structural considerations, and then with exclusive attention to the story's second version where such matters take on more significance. The two renditions will be treated separately.

In **"Cómo perdí la vista,"** the anonymous narrator-protagonist, Argentine consul to Havana, Cuba in 1918, falls in love with and wins the heart of Elvira Montes, a woman given to unexplainable fits of hysteria and weeping. Elvira's unstable personality and tortured life are shrouded in mystery, but two incidents begin to reveal her secret to the narrator. One of his telephone calls to her home is answered by a shrill but masculine voice resembling that of a squealing rat. Elvira offers her beloved no explanation after their telephone conversation is abruptly cut off. On another occasion the lovers meet in a German bar in Havana, called the *Kiek in die Welt,* where the narrator comes upon Elvira from behind and overhears her apparently talking to herself, protesting her love for someone in frantic and desperate tones. A further clue is the fact that she is carrying a large purse at the time. The protagonist follows the distraught woman to her home and ultimately discovers that Elvira shares her affection for him with a tiny man ten centimeters tall who had been concealed in her purse at the bar. To retain his mistress' love, the narrator feigns friendship for the homunculus, but the latter, a fiendish imp, jealous of Elvira's love for the consul, blinds the sleeping man with a trident fashioned with upholstery needles. After nursing her sightless lover back ·to health, Elvira leads him on board a ship which will take them to Argentina. Once at sea, however, the blind and helpless narrator is horrified upon discovering that Elvira is nowhere on the vessel. She simply could not bring herself to abandon her darling "little man."

The three most interesting facets of the homunculus in this story relate to his appearance, personality and origin. He is described as a very black, wee, wizened creature with wrinkled, leathery skin. He is pampered, haughty, sneaky and totally lascivious. Apparently endowed with demonic power, he easily gains control of any feminine will. He has already driven Elvira's mother to insanity, he relentlessly chases after the female servants, and is clearly still in possession of Elvira at the end of the story. His wantonness also extends to include homosexuality, for he even pursues the narrator!

The identity and origin of the little man are unknown except to Elvira, who claims she found him hiding in the attic when she was eight years old, and he has been her "innocent love" and favorite "secret toy" ever since. However, a legend, rather awkwardly outlined by the narrator, reveals a more interesting beginning for the homunculus. Busily engaged in the creation, God heard a voice "in his nostrils [*sic*]" shouting slowly: "A-ta-na-pa!" Atanapa, the name of the homunculus, thus became God's first but unsuccessful attempt at fashioning a man. Although made of good materials, Atanapa turned out defective, evil and malicious. He gradually lost his memory, and now recalls only his earliest and his most recent years. After God gave him Eve, he simply continued his mischief in Eden causing floods and knocking boulders down upon the terrestrial paradise. When Adam appeared on the scene, Atanapa befriended him, and Eve frequently found herself alone! Angered, the Lord banished Atanapa, but granted him immortality. Since then he has sown discord and has been the bearer of nothing but misery and calamities. Persecuted by men, he took to hiding and "keeping an eye" on mankind, always "watching" for his chance to wreak havoc and get revenge. Hence, Atanapa's first appearance in the story takes place in a German bar called the *Kiek in die Welt,* that is, "A Peeper (or lookout) in the World." The name "Atanapa" is still under investigation, but I am informed that, in Aramaic, "Adam-aba" means "father of man"; that is, perhaps, "father of Adam?" However, that Atanapa is a satanic imp, there can be no doubt. His weapon, the trident, clearly identifies him as an evil harbinger from hell.

The general story line of the recast version, titled **"La sierva ajena,"** is essentially the same as that of **"Cómo perdí la vista."** A man falls in love with an unstable woman who is in the power of a tiny man, and the latter, out of rage and jealousy for his normal-sized rival, blinds him. Two very important differences are discernible in the second rendition, however: 1) the homunculus or created man motif is here replaced by the shrunken man motif; 2) the narrative structure of **"La sierva ajena"** is considerably more elaborate and artistic. Bioy Casares has learned much about the craft of fantastic fiction from 1937 to 1956, the respective dates of publication of his two treatments of the theme.

"La sierva ajena" employs the device of a framing tale which serves to mirror by contrast the story contained within it. The outer or frame story is presented in a context of quite realistic circumstances while the inner narrative is fantastic. An anonymous narrator humorously and satirically describes the "downfall," at one of her fashionable Buenos Aires cocktail parties, of a *grande dame* of *porteño* society named Tatá Laserna. Tatá melodramatically faints when a Belgian anthropologist shows her the shrunken head of her most recent lover, a world traveler-explorer who has been captured by Jíbaro Indians. Keller, an acquaintance of the first narrator, is reminded by this incident of the somewhat similar case of Rafael Urbina, Flora Larquier and Rudolf, who here play roles rather like those of the triple protagonists of the tale's earlier, less complicated version. At this point, Keller becomes a second narrator by recounting to a group of friends the story of the now blind Urbina, just as the latter had related it to him in France. Thus, long before introducing his one fantastic element, that of the tiny man, Bioy Casares first carefully creates a very believable, realistic background and setting into which the fantastic may intrude without undue damage to the verisimilitude of the tale. Some of the components which contribute to this realistic ambience are the following: a much larger cast of interesting, very human, primary and secondary characters; the detailing of their everyday lives and activities; a broader range of references to local realities of the bustling Argentine capital, a setting much more familiar to the author than Havana; and a more abundant use of dialogue and psychological probing of personages and their motivations. In addition, there is a generous dose of Bioy Casares' tongue-in-cheek humor and ironic satire of people, customs and literary tendencies. (e.g., Rafael Urbina, the blinded lover, is depicted throughout as a mediocre, presumptuous poet who writes *hai-kais.*)

The outstanding artistic achievement of this version, however, is the conception of Rudolf, the tiny creature in the tale. With the introduction of this diminutive being, a third narrator takes over the storytelling. Flora, the captive woman, relates to her normal-sized lover, Urbina, the identity and origin of her master, Rudolf. The latter was a German secret agent sent into Africa around 1900 to secure colonies for the imperialistic German government. Completely duped in Uganda by an Englishman named Sir Harry Johnston, Rudolf was captured by Pygmies and shrunken to a height of about eight inches. He was later rescued by the wife of an English explorer, Mary Thornicroft, and was subsequently and mysteriously acquired by Flora and her mother, who is now out of her mind. In the manner of true fantastic fiction, no attempt is made to explain how the magic of Rudolf's shrinking was accomplished.

However, although this one most important fact of his existence is left completely unclarified, Rudolf is made even more terrifyingly real than the imp in the first version of the story. Physically and psychologically, Rudolf is very similar to the Atanapa of the earlier story. Both are childish, cruel and lecherous; both are indestructible and are identified with satanic evil. (Rudolf has the face of a goat-like faun in addition to his trident; and both exercise hypnotic, almost absolute power over their *sierva* [hence the title]). Nevertheless, Atanapa remains somewhat vague, inhuman and unreal. In contrast, a whole human biography is created for Rudolf, thus making him much more convincing. His entire previous life is revealed in numerous, carefully described photographs of him taken during all stages of his earlier existence as a normal-sized man. These carefully described pictures are eloquent testimony to the "reality" of the fantastic shrunken man. There can be no doubt that this little man before the reader is the

same one who appears in the photographs. Indeed, the wizened tyrant even bears the exact dueling scars, present in every likeness of his furious face, which he acquired as a German university student. Things, past possessions such as sporting objects (tennis rackets, ice skates, dueling pistols and sabers), hunting trophies, garments, etc., surround the miniature creature and likewise proclaim loudly to the world the objectivity and truth of Rudolf!

Hence, while the divine and the supernatural played paramount roles in Atanapa's origin and history, the natural and the realistic predominate and triumph in the life of Rudolf. The reader is, therefore, practically obliged to believe in the marvelous reality of the shriveled little despot, Rudolf. This force of literary or artistic persuasion is implicitly related to Bioy Casares' aesthetics of the fantastic. *God* created Atanapa, the homunculus. *Man* (the Pygmies) produced Rudolf, the shrunken man. And Bioy Casares, the author-artist, has conceived both of them. As Borges and Bioy frequently and subtly remind their reader: perhaps a divinity was able to bring into being this labyrinthine, chaotic world and its strange denizens, but the intellect and artistic talent of man are equally capable of fashioning their own mazes and monsters. Sometimes the demons are minotaurs; at other times they are just the "little people."

John Updike (essay date 1986)

SOURCE: "The Great Paraguayan Novel and Other Hardships," in *The New Yorker,* Vol. LXII, No. 31, September 22, 1986, p. 104-16.

[*An extraordinary stylist, Updike is one of America's most distinguished men of letters. Considered a perceptive observer of the human condition, he is best known for such novels as* Rabbit Run *(1960),* Rabbit Redux *(1971), and* Rabbit Is Rich *(1981), which chronicle life in Protestant, middle-class America. In the following excerpted review of* The Invention of Morel, and Other Stories, *he notes the influences of Jorge Luis Borges on the fiction of Bioy Casares.*]

Adolfo Bioy Casares has been known in the English-speaking world primarily as a friend and collaborator of Borges, and the co-author of the ornate literary jokes of *The Chronicles of Bustos Domecq* (1967). Bioy Casares, however, is a prolific and successful writer on his own, and nearly a generation younger than Borges—he was born in 1914, and Borges in 1899. . . . *The Invention of Morel and Other Stories,* by Bioy Casares, arrives with a double Borgesian stamp: a preface by the master to the long title story, and pen-and-ink illustrations by Norah Borges de Torre, Borges's sister. The illustrations are clumsy and few and do little harm. The preface is a provocative and revealing critical document: like *The Invention of Morel,* it dates from 1940. It claims that this "Invention" is perfect ("To classify it as perfect is neither an imprecision nor a hyperbole") and represents a blow in the good fight against that deplorable nineteenth-century invention the plotless "psychological" novel, which includes Balzac, the Russians, and Proust. Borges was, we might say, the first self-consciously postmodern writer; his rebellion against

Proust and Joyce and Woolf and James took the form of preferring Shaw, Wilde, Wells, and Chesterton. His preface offers the detective story—at its peak in the thirties—as an example of what "works of reasoned imagination" might be. He and Bioy Casares collaborated on detective stories, as well as on film scripts, anthologies, and translations. In a sense, Bioy Casares—whom Borges called "really and secretly the master" in these collaborations—armed the Borgesian counter-revolution. He provided boyish bravado, a typewriter, and, in *The Invention of Morel,* a prime text; the little novel won a municipal literary award in Buenos Aires and impressed such rising literati as Octavio Paz and Julio Cortázar. Further, it came to the attention of another postmodern theorizer, Alain Robbe-Grillet, and influenced the betranced repetitions and overlaps of his film "Last Year at Marienbad." Robbe-Grillet's first novel, we need hardly add, was a variety of detective story, *Les Gommes.*

Read in 1986, *The Invention of Morel* entertains in the dated way of science fiction by Wells or Jules Verne. Technology betrays its own acolytes: Wells' Time Machine was a late-Victorian gewgaw, a "glittering metallic framework" with parts of nickel and ivory and crystal, a kind of idealized elevator cage, and Alfred Jarry went into futuristic raptures over the then newest thing, the bicycle. Bioy Casares, as of 1940, was understandably struck by the inventions of the motion-picture projector and the phonograph, which preserve reality as seen and heard; he imagines an island where an obsessed inventor, Morel, has constructed machines, tirelessly powered by the tides, that over and over project, in three palpable dimensions, the same recorded scenes of a week among friends. Thus he has created a kind of paradise, an eternity of reruns; the objects captured by his superphotography unfortunately wither and perish, but this seems a modest price to pay. Onto this island blunders our nameless narrator, who slowly comes to understand the illusion and, eventually, to enroll in it. Movies can't *do* that, we want to protest, just as elevators and bicycles can't become time machines. Nevertheless, there are ingenious technological plot twists: doors that normally open freeze shut when they are being projected, and broken walls implacably heal, sealing our hero in. And there are poignant moments: one of the projected beings, Faustine, becomes a love object for the castaway, and, as he disintegrates, his early life in Venezuela, from which he is a political exile, becomes another frozen paradise, projected in his head. But our interest in this rather too intricate fable, and in the six accompanying short stories from a 1948 volume, *La Trama Celeste,* tends to be magnetized by the elements that are, with a striking distinctness, Borgesian.

What could be more like Borges than this dream: "When I slept this afternoon, I had this dream, like a symbolic and premature commentary on my life: as I was playing a game of croquet, I learned that my part in the game was killing a man. Then, suddenly, I knew I was that man"? Or the lilt of these sentences, with their lifted eyebrow of complicated disclaimer: "He said that he waved his hand, and immediately afterward the gesture seemed false"; "After an extended stay in Paris, Horvath had returned

> I have discussed with the author the details of his plot [in *The Invention of Morel*]. I have reread it. To classify it as perfect is neither an imprecision nor a hyperbole.
>
> —*Jorge Luis Borges, in his "Prologue" to* The Invention of Morel, *1940.*

to his own country, almost famous and totally discredited"; "He treated love and women with a dispassionate scorn that was not devoid of courtesy"? Or these fey modifiers, so curiously vibrant: "I experienced an intimate heaviness in my arms and legs"; "She was wearing a dress that was extremely green"; "He had deep circles under his eyes and an expression of astonished fatigue"? The adjective "atrocious" recurs in Bioy Casares, and the image of a labyrinth, and that Borgesian device of the heterogeneous list, shorthand for the inventory of the maddeningly infinite universe. Abrupt islands of mathematical and topological distinctness imply the circumambient vague vastness, and the paradoxes of philosophical idealism are pursued to their monstrous conclusions. A dandified Gnosticism speaks in such an epigram as "To be alive is to flee, in an ephemeral and paradoxical way, from matter."

The imitation is startling; who was imitating whom? Borges came late to prose fiction; his first collection, *The Garden of Forking Paths,* was published in 1941, the year that Bioy Casares won a literary prize for *The Invention of Morel.* The older man may well have learned from the younger, or at least borrowed the courage of his own predilections. But to turn from even the best of Bioy Casares's short stories (**"The Celestial Plot,"** say, or **"The Perjury of the Snow"**) to those of Borges is to enter the realm of literature; there is greater conciseness and concreteness, a superior richness of mock-erudition and arch cross-reference, a jauntier and more challenging style. A poetic vision has entered in, and—we do not readily associate this quality with Borges—a warmth, a heat such as is generated deep in the geological strata, a spontaneous combustion of compacted learning and sublimated feeling. Even in those Borges short stories—"The Garden of Forking Paths," "Death and the Compass," "An Examination of the Work of Herbert Quain"—closest to the detective story there is an expansiveness of allusion, an amused intensity of tone that liberates us into something new, a fresh atmosphere, a frontier. These few dense and quirky short stories lifted the lid on Latin-American fantasy, as Gogol's "Overcoat" supposedly ignited the great days of Russian fiction. "Magic realism," then, can be seen to have a pedigree that reaches from Borges, through the fantasy of Chesterton and Stevenson—circumventing the triumphs of the realist-psychological novel—back to Poe. All seven of Bioy Casares's tales sound like Poe; they employ the

An essay from *The Chronicles of Bustos Domecq:*

"The Sartorial Revolution (II)"

If, as has been duly pointed out, the epithet *functional* is wholly out of fashion in the small world of architects, in sartorial circles it has attained prestigious and dizzying heights. Clearly, men's clothing presented a rather vulnerable flank to the onslaught of younger generations.

On the part of the hidebound there has been a signal failure to justify the beauty—or even the utility—of lapels, trouser cuffs, buttons that do not button, the knotted tie, and the hat band (or, as the poet has it, the "frieze of the fedora"). And so the scandalous arbitrariness of such useless embellishments has finally come under the public eye. In this respect, Poblet's [J. D. F. Poblet (or Pobblet), b. 1894—translator's note] condemnation is unanswerable.

It may be worthy of note that the new order springs from a passage by the Anglo-Saxon Samuel Butler. Butler remarked that the so-called human body is a material projection of the mind and that, when you come down to it, there is hardly any difference whatever between the microscope and the eye, inasmuch as the former is merely an improvement on the latter. The same, according to the trite riddle of the sphinx, might be said of the walking stick and the leg. The human body, in brief, is a machine: the hand no less than the Winchester, the buttocks than a wooden (or electric) chair, the skater than the skate. This is why the itch to flee from machinery is meaningless; man is but a working sketch to be supplemented, finally, by horn-rimmed glasses, by crutches, and by the wheelchair.

As is not infrequent these days, the great leap forward was born of the happy coupling of the dreamer (who operates in the dark) and the business tycoon. The former,

Professor Lucius Scaevola, was responsible for the general theory; the latter, the tycoon, was practical-minded Pablo Notaris, owner of the popular Red Monkey Hardware & Kitchenwares, Inc., now refurbished from basement to roof and universally known as Scaevola-Notaris Functional Tailoring, Ltd. We cordially invite the reader to pay a visit, without cost or obligation, to the modern establishment of the aforementioned firm of Messrs. Scaevola and Notaris, where he will be warmly welcomed and will receive the utmost in personal attention. A well-trained staff is on hand to see to the full satisfaction of the reader's every need, providing him—all at low, low prices—with the patented All-Round Glove, whose two components (matching, down to the last detail, the hands of the buyer) include every single one of the following finger extensions: *On the right hand*—The Thumb Drill, The Index Corkscrew, The Middle-Finger Fountainpen, The Ring-Finger Rubber Stamp, The Small-Finger Penknife; *on the left hand*—The Thumb Awl, The Index Hammer, The Middle-Finger Skeleton Key, The Ring-Finger Umbrella-Walkingstick, and finally, the Small-Finger Scissors. (No substitutions, please.) Other customers, perhaps, may wish to be shown the All-Purpose Highhat (second floor), which permits the easy conveyance of food products and valuables, to say nothing of a variety of things better left unmentioned. Not yet in stock but coming soon is the File-Suit, whose leading feature is the replacement of the old-fashioned pocket with the sliding drawer. The Trouser-Seat with built-in Double Steel Springs—at first opposed by the chairmaker trades—has so won the general approval of the buying public that its overwhelming success leaves us at liberty to omit it from this prepaid advertisement. Remember, readers, shop now and save later!

Adolfo Bioy Casares and Jorge Luis Borges, "Three Chronicles of Bustos Domecq," translated by Norman Thomas Giovanni in Tri-Quarterly, *No. 16, Fall 1969.*

first-person voice of detective stories (convenient because an omniscient narrator would give the mystery away) and of travellers' tales and journals—the voice of Robinson Crusoe and Arthur Gordon Pym, of European man in the menacing strangeness of the New World.

Wendy B. Faris (essay date 1987)

SOURCE: A review of *Historias desaforadas,* in *World Literature Today,* Vol. 61, No. 4, Autumn, 1987, p. 606.

[*Faris is an American educator, critic, and author. In the following review of* Historias desaforadas, *Faris comments on the collection's "melancholy tone of nostalgia and resignation."*]

The ten stories of **Historias desaforadas** provide a good introduction to the work of Bioy Casares, an early master of magical realism, better known to the world at large as the collaborator of Borges. Most of the stories inhabit that literary locus of magical realism, the domain of liminality, in which characters or states of being exist on the fringes of society or normality and thus lead us off the beaten track into unexplored or undiscovered countries of the

imagination. In order to do this convincingly, they often begin, as do the stories of Borges or Cortázar or Fuentes, in the casual midst of rigorously everyday reality. Events frequently dovetail as if by magic into one another: a translation job pays a narrator the exact sum he needs to buy a particular car; a house that another narrator comes upon in an alpine snowstorm contains just the man he has been looking for. They are all, in their different ways, in the title words of one story, "unexpected voyage[s]," filled with amazing coincidences. Appropriately enough, then, they concern strange and endearing characters, like a "despotic but upright" old colonel who doesn't believe in the statistics the narrator cites to him to prove Argentina's decline, claiming that the reason they all tell the same story is that they copy each other.

Within the eerie atmosphere and magical events, delicate psychological details lament and accept human frailties and disappointments: "Vanity is rather vulgar," for example, and "Every person is irreplaceable." A melancholy tone of nostalgia and resignation, but not despair, pervades many of the stories, a gentle, worldly, benevolent fatigue familiar to us from Borges's tales; and like the latter, they are almost always told in the first person.

I always wish collections of short stories would include the original dates of publication; *Historias desaforadas,* like most others, does not.

Margaret L. Snook   (essay date 1988)

SOURCE: "The Power Struggle: Gender and Voices in 'Moscas y arañas' by Bioy Casares," in *Monographic Review/Revista Mongrafica,* Vol. IV, 1988, pp. 268-277.

[*In the following essay, Snook examines the dynamics of the relationship between genders as well as narrative voices in "Moscas y arañas."*]

During an [unpublished 1987] interview, Bioy Casares once stated that he considered male/female the most interesting source of dramatic conflict for his works. Many of his fantastic stories, consequently, portray a male protagonist's attempts to be united or reunited with a woman. These attempts are met with all sorts of obstacles, including the intervention of powers beyond his comprehension or control, and are inevitably unsuccessful. The failed quest for union or reunion seems to be linked to the stories' underlying theme of duality that explores the separation or conflict between mind and body. The failed search for reintegration with the female counterpart mirrors the failed fantastic experiments at altering or influencing the relationship between physical and mental reality, for both seek an ideal, hence impossible, union of opposites.

The dualistic vision that underlies the fantastic hypothesis, and other aspects of the author's texts as well, is also evident in the depiction of the female whose role is usually defined by her relationship to men. Consequently, she is often cast in one of two stereotypical molds: the good, passive woman or the devious schemer. Bioy Casares sheds light on the role of the latter when he states [in "Entrevista con Adolfo Bioy Casares," *Prismal/Cabral,* 7/8 (Spring, 1982)] that, at times, he feels women are more intelligent than men or rather psychologically superior, and men, as a result, are reduced to the role of the fool or child at their sides. In such a situation, the woman is neither protective nor nurturing, but rather domineering and manipulative. The relationship between male and female is thus conceived in terms of a power struggle. Intelligence or psychological superiority is equated with a form of covert power which the female exercises, thereby symbolically castrating the male and annihilating his individuality. Moreover, this deceptive woman often resembles the Jungian concept [discussed in his *Symbols of Transformation,* translated by F. C. Hull (1956)] of the "Devouring Mother" who betrays the child or entraps him in her womb. She destroys the male, bringing about a figurative death, for his subsequent incapacitation or withdrawal from life results in a demise of authority and identity. The role of the schemer may thus be interpreted as a projection of the male's conflicting fear and desire of a return to the center or origins. It is interesting to note, in this respect, that the biological mother seldom appears in Bioy's works but that the traits usually attributed to the mother figure are subsumed in other female characters.

These patterns of male/female relationships are evident in a number of Bioy Casares' stories, for example **"El ídolo"** from *La trama celeste* (1945), **"Moscas y arañas,"** from

the volume *Guirnalda con amores* (1959), and **"Los afanes"** from *El lado de la sombra* (1962). This study will focus on the manner in which the power struggle paradigm is developed in **"Moscas y arañas"** through the relationships of the male protagonist Raúl Gigena, with his wife Andrea and with the mysterious boarder, Helene Jacoba Krig. In this particular story, the power play is heightened by the shifting narrative voice which underscores the conflict of authority in which the characters are engaged.

The text's title, **"Moscas y arañas,"** with its obvious reference to the concept of predator and prey, victim and victimizer, calls attention immediately to the story's central conflict. The title derives from a phrase uttered by Raúl Gigena in which he instructs his wife about the Darwinian concept of life: "Este mundo se divide en moscas y arañas. Tratemos de ser arañas que se comen las moscas." Raúl's allusion to the natural order reveals the manner in which the male bases many of his myths and patterns of behavior on events observed in the biological world. According to Simone de Beauvoir [in her *The Second Sex,* translated by H. M. Parshley, 1961] the myths that shape male/female relationships are also traceable to the male tendency to identify woman with Nature. Man entertains an ambivalent relationship with Nature; he exploits her but she crushes him; she is the womb that creates his being and the tomb to which he must return. She thus inspires conflicting feelings of admiration and fear. Moreover, the male myth of devouring femininity has crystallized around the image of certain predatory females, such as the spider and praying mantis, who consume their mates (Simone de Beauvoir). Such biological events lead to a conceptualization of life as battle between the sexes, a struggle between the powerful and the weak.

Raúl transposes the power struggle to the socio-economic plane and thus quickly establishes a successful business as a wine-broker upon his arrival in Buenos Aires. Subsequently, Raúl turns their large home into a boarding-house to efficiently utilize the unoccupied space and gain additional revenue. His business acumen and competency are contrasted against the sentimentality and domesticity of Andrea, who would have preferred the romantic coach house to the ugly "caserón" her husband bought. Even though the boarding-house eventually provides more than adequate financial income, Raúl refuses to relinquish the brokerage business which requires long hours away from home and which leaves him exhausted upon his return from work. This refusal can be interpreted as an expression of Raúl's need to assert his masculinity through his own economic power inasmuch as the boarding house is successful mainly through the industrious efforts of his wife Andrea. In their interpersonal relationship, it is clear that Raúl conceives of a dominant male role, the role of the "araña" once again, through the exercise of the power to make decisions. The passive role attributed to Andrea is evidenced, in turn, in her acquiescence to these decisions.

Shortly after the arrival of the Hertz couple to the boarding house, Raúl begins to experience disturbing dreams in which Andrea betrays him with the men in the boarding-house and with total strangers. During the daytime, his doubts about his wife's fidelity persist and drive a wedge between them. Raúl cannot decide if his wife is the devoted and loyal woman with whom he interacts daily or the wicked seductress revealed in his nightly fantasies. It is only after Andrea's suicide that Raúl discovers the source of these disruptive dreams and realizes that the reunion he now desires with Andrea is impossible. Shortly after learning of Andrea's death, Raúl discovers that he has been a pawn in a psychological power struggle waged by one of their boarders, the elderly and crippled Helene Jacoba Krig. Helene had telepathically transmitted thoughts to Raúl to separate him from Andrea and claim him for herself.

The association of Helene with the role of the spider or predator is first suggested by her physical attributes. Her depiction as a relatively motionless being, whose activities are confined to restricted spatial parameters, recall the inactivity of the patient spider within its web. The salient features of her physiognomy also invoke the image of the devouring spider: "La señorita tenía . . . la boca grande, los labios rojos, que descubrían dientes irregulares y mucha saliva. . . ." The words she utters on revealing her diabolical scheme to Raúl at the conclusion of the story also reiterate the roles of victimizer and victim into which they have been cast: "Hace mucho que tendí mis redes, que usted cayó. ¿Supone que revoltea por acá, por acullá? Desvaríos. Le juro que está en la red, por así decirlo, prácticamente. No proteste, no se altere. . . ." Raúl consequently, is thus reduced to the role of the subservient, obedient child trapped by the Jungian "Devouring Mother" who will feed on his youth and mobility. Helene's final words to Raúl, which repeat those used earlier to refer to her dog, whom she also controls through telepathy, underscore Raúl's humiliating and dehumanizing subjugation: "Al principio nadie me quiere. Poco a poco lo conquistaré. ¿Descubrirá algo, no es verdad, Raúl, en su Helene Jacoba?"

In the interaction between Helene and Raúl, two traditional binary operations which signify relationships of power or authority, master and pet, predator and prey, are metaphorically enacted and reduced to one: man and woman. Moreover, if one considers Raúl's ultimate circumstances as a surprise reversal from his customary role and as a dramatic shift within the binary opposition, one must also conclude that the position of victim or conquered he now occupies is ordinarily assigned to the other member of the dyad, the female. The role reversal, furthermore, suggests the unnatural and malevolent nature of the subversion of male authority, for Helene has resorted to covert, mysterious means to gain control. She has employed and abused a power which is not at the disposition of the average mortal male to rid herself of the wife and claim the husband/son. As such, she may be viewed as a relative of the witch who gains no societal approval for her victory, whose exercise of power is not sanctioned or condoned.

If the reader considers in broader terms, however, the na-

ture of the power struggle alluded to in the title of the text, some additional light can be shed on the concept of the victim. In a sense, both Helene and Andrea are also victims, trapped in the web of binary oppositions transmitted by language and culture, that allows for only winner or loser, saint or seductress, conqueror or conquered, predator or prey. Such a system contains no terms to mediate these extremes or provide gradations between them. Andrea is thus viewed by Raúl as alternately pure or deceitful; Helene is totally evil. Both are created to provide Raúl his complementary opposite, that is the suitable mate or the formidable enemy. In the case of Helene, the female may also represent a projection or extrication of the evil half or flaws within Raúl. Helene's remarks allude to this relationship between them when she states that she, in fact, is more compatible match for Raúl than Andrea since she shares his interest in power and his materialism: ". . . los dos no formaban lo que yo estimo un matrimonio harmónico. Andrea carecía, por ser una lírica, de mis condiciones para congeniar con su espíritu atento a la realidad, al dinero." The female is thus circumscribed by a binary linguistic and cultural code which defines her role in terms of her opposite, the male. Her ultimate domination by the masculine control of the word is reflected in the manner in which her story is inscribed within and dependent upon the male's story. Thus, **"Moscas y arañas"** concludes with the figurative death of Raúl, his loss of authority, when he is finally caught within the web.

Raúl's figurative movement toward the center of the web is mirrored in the text by allusions to other movements of characters from the periphery to the center. In the beginning of the story, Raúl and Andrea move from the province to Buenos Aires, the center of commerce. This is the only decision which Andrea makes, for she sees the need to be free of the influence of outsiders, presumably her in-laws. In terms of Andrea's aspirations, the movement would be termed centrifugal, directed away from the center. In terms of Raúl's materialistic ambitions, this movement is directed toward the center. Furthermore, and although somewhat paradoxical, Raúl's initial reluctance to detach himself from home is another indication of an attachment to center and provides an early indication of a child-like dependency. Once they have established their house in Buenos Aires, Raúl decides to take in boarders. The penetration of the outside world into the inner world of the boarding-house is further emphasized in the case of Helene by her foreign status. The penetration of Raúl's mind by Helene offers the culminating instance of this play on the binary opposition of inside/outside. This centripetal movement of the text is seen as negative in as much as as it leads to the ultimate downfall of Raúl.

The movement from outside to inside, implicit in the activities of the characters, is reflected in a similar shift in the positions of the narrative voices that relate the events of the tale. The first part of the story is recounted by a public, heterodiegetic narrator, that is, a person who apparently is not a character or participant in the fictional world. His comments are addressed to a public narratee, who also exists outside the fictional world and with whom the real reader or historical audience may identify. The narrator appears to possess privileged information about the characters' thoughts, feelings and their lives since he describes scenes and events he did not witness. Moreover, he does not provide any indications of secondary sources for his knowledge.

As the story progresses, the narrator departs from the convention of omniscience which characterizes the authorial stance of the preceeding section. He implies that his knowledge of events is based on memory and therefore subject to limitations and error: "Si no me equivoco, la aparición del matrimonio Hertz concidió con los primeros sueños de Raúl."

The unexpected departure from the conventions of unrestricted knowledge marks a new role and status for the narrator of the story. Until this point, no clear separation or distinction has been made between the heterodiegetic author and the narrating voice. Since the story begins in the third person mode and the narrating voice possesses an unlimited view of his characters, an identification between implied author and narrator might be assumed by the reader. According to Susan Snaider Lanser:

> Ordinarily, the unmarked case of narration for public narrator is that the narrating voice is equated with the textual author (the extrafictional voice or "implied" author) unless a different case is marked—signaled—by the text. In other words, in the absence of direct markings which separate the public narrator from the extrafictional voice, so long as it is possible to give meaning to the text within the equation author-narrator, readers will conventionally make this equation. [*The Narrative Act: Point of View in Prose Fiction,* 1981]

In **"Moscas y arañas,"** a definite textual signal of case differentiation is sent to the reader by the abrupt shift from the third person to first person mode, expressed by the pronoun *yo,* and not the conventional collective *nosotros* previously used to imply author and reader. Furthermore, by suggesting at this point in the text that the narrator has in some way learned of the story's events, his relationship to the narrative act and the fictional world is suddenly cast in a new light. The distance between him and the fictional personae is decreased while the distance between the extrafictional voice and the narrating voice is clearly established. Narration now appears to come from someone who, although not a participant in the events, is nonetheless related to the world of the characters. Thus, the discourse marks a movement of internalization into the fictional world.

Subsequent passages denote a further progression away from external mediation. The use of tagged direct discourse in the form of monologues and dialogues is extensive, thus allowing the characters to speak with minimal authorial intervention. The process of internalization of narrative voice reaches its culmination in the conclusion of the story, presented in the form of a dramatic monologue delivered by Helene Jacoba Krig. Minimal tag expressions, such as "she said," disappear from the text. Explanation of events is now given solely by a character or persona belonging to the fictional world who acts as a private narrator, that is, someone who has no direct access

to the extrafictional world. Her remarks are directed to Raúl, another fictional character, who serves as a private narratee in the communicative act. The process of internalization and reduction of authorial mediation is completed as narration now comes from the other side of the fictional act, from within the fictional world itself.

The character's power relationships with others are reflected in these shifts in narrative voice and in their inability to exercise control over discourse situations. During the first part of the story, the narrative is controlled by an anonymous third person narrator whose voice, as we have seen, is often identified by the reader with that of the implied author, which in this case is masculine. The absence of significant dialogue in this section between Andrea and Raúl not only reflects their status of authority or independence in relationship to the narrator, but to each other as well. It is clear that Raúl is reluctant to include Andrea in his activities and that Andrea is reticent to question or complain. The limitation of dialogue between Andrea and others may also denote her inability to participate effectively in discourse addressed outwardly and enunciated in the outside world. Her silence underscores her resignation, apparent in the narrator's descriptions: "Andrea se dejó persuadir por las razones de su marido" and "Andrea se resignó."

The occasional use of narrated monologues also alludes to the subordinated or dependent roles of the characters. Such statements, like those of indirect style, are narrated in the third person mode but usually transpose the future tense of direct discourse to the conditional, and the past to the pluperfect. Also notable is the use of grammatical forms (i.e., possessive adjectives and pronouns) which are characteristic of direct discourse and reflect the spatial, temporal and ideological perspective of the protagonists. Andrea's thoughts on the prospect of boarders in her home are conveyed through such a technique: "Ya no estarían solos, pero compartir la casa con los desconocidos que depara la suerte no es como compartirla con gente de la familia, que se creecon derecho a dirigir nuestras vidas y a opinar sobre todo." The narrated monologue fuses the authorial voice with that of the character, suggesting that it could issue from either source [suggests Dorrit Cohn in his "Narrated Monologue: Definition of a Fictional Style," *Comparative Literature* XVIII (1966)]. Thus, Andrea does not speak independently of the narrator nor is she seen as directly communicating with Raúl. The narrated monologue attributed to Raúl in the first part of the story, on the other hand, reveals a naiveté or child-like dependency on others. His ability to be manipulated by others is underscored by his use of words that are suggested or imposed by another. Specifically, his discourse discloses an influence of the advertisement media in adopting its phraseology while extolling the virtues of the ugly *caserón* he decides to buy instead of the carriage house preferred by Andrea. In both the case of Raúl and Andrea, the presence of the narrated monologue reflects the characters' limited authority or power status by underscoring the control or manipulation by the other of discourse situations.

The second part of the story is marked by the presence of two separate dialogues in which Raúl and Andrea verbalize their doubts about the other's fidelity. Each chooses an unreliable confidant as their interlocutor. The narrator thus exercises less control or less mediation, but the role that Andrea and Raúl play in these conversations still denotes their gradual loss of control over their existence or submission to superior authority. Each is placed in the position of asking questions of the corresponding male or female interlocutor, who is thus situated in the power position for they seemingly possess the knowledge or the answers that Raúl and Andrea do not.

The conclusion of the story is narrated in the form of a dramatic monologue delivered by Helene Krig in which she reveals that she is the true predator. The use of monologue in this instance allows Helene the opportunity to reveal her malevolent intentions without recourse to the narrator. She also assumes the task of disclosing the thoughts or reactions of other characters, a privilege originally exercised by the narrator. The monologue effectively portrays her control of Raúl by keeping her interlocutor, now her passive victim, silent and unheard. Her control of the situation is reiterated in her control of the narrative for in the conclusion her voice is the only one that is heard.

Although the voice with which the story concludes is feminine, the discourse still appears masculine. The lines Helene recites, and indeed her role, seemed predetermined by male-created stereotypes and myths of devouring femininity. She serves as a projection of the male's wishes and fears. Helene and her web may thus be interpreted as a metaphor of the dangers and undesirability present in a return to the center or origins. Moreover, although Helene traps Raúl within her web of conspiracy and domination, she also is trapped within and dependent upon Raúl's story because the narrative itself is centered on the male. In this respect, Helene occupies a position on the periphery. Ultimately, the reader may conclude that both Raúl and Helene are victims of a power struggle generated by a culturally and linguistically determined binary system of operations that can conceive of relationships only in terms of "insider" and "outsider," "winners" and "losers." In such a system, both male and female may suffer the loss of individual identity and become a complementary object constructed by and for the other.

Margaret L. Snook (essay date 1991)

SOURCE: "Boundaries of the Self: Autonomy versus Dependency in *La invención de Morel*," in *Chasqui*, Vol. XX, No. 2, November, 1991, pp. 108-15.

[*In the following essay, Snook examines the psychological boundaries that define the self as presented in* The Invention of Morel.]

In many of Bioy Casares' major novels and short stories, the author places his male protagonists in settings of physical confinement and situations of high anxiety from which they wish to flee. Thus many of his characters can be viewed as fugitives or "escape artists" who employ a variety of methods to elude their unpleasant circumstances. However, the characters' flight from the confines of prison, the island, the asylum, or the body, does not lead to personal freedom, as each protagonist ultimately suc-

cumbs to another form of subjugation or dependency. This basic pattern of flight from confinement, that culminates in some new form of mental or physical entrapment, reflects the texts' preoccupation with the material and psychological limitations that shape the individual's interaction with others.

Nowhere is this pattern more evident than in the author's first and most widely acclaimed novel, *La invencion de Morel.* In this 1940 work, the author bases his fantastic hypothesis on a type of metamorphosis of the human subject which results in the severing of mind from body. At the core of this scientific discovery, one discerns a preoccupation with the boundaries that paradoxically join and separate physical and psychological reality, the demarcations that define, shape, and limit the essence of human experience. This issue of body and ego boundaries, in turn, is closely linked in the novel to the concept of autonomy, a sense of self-containment and separateness from others.

According to the models provided by psychoanalytical theory, the infantile ego does not distinguish corporeal boundaries or separation between itself and the object world. Thus, the infantile subject cannot recognize the autonomy of others. The child identifies with and attempts to integrate into itself partial objects which give it pleasure, such as the mother's breast, gaze and voice. In order to overcome its narcissistic relationship to reality, the infantile subject must learn to differentiate between self and other. [In her *Feminism and Psychoanalytic Theory*, 1989, Nancy Chodorow] expounds upon this point, stating that an essential task of early childhood involves "the development of ego boundaries (a sense of personal psychological division from the rest of the world) and of a body ego (a sense of the permanence of one's physical separateness and the predictable boundedness of one's own body, of a distinction between inside and outside)." It is only through the absence of objects that the subject is able to establish this demarcation between itself and "other," between inside and outside, and develop an awareness of autonomy. Chodorow adds to these basic psychoanalytic conceptions of differentiation the view that adequate separation-individuation does not merely involve the perception of the otherness of the other. It involves the ability to experience "the object/other (the mother) in aspects apart from its sole relation to the ability to gratify the infant's/subject's needs and wants. . . ." True separation thus implies a recognition of the selfhood/subjectivity of the other.

Bioy's interest in these boundary issues and their existential ramifications is manifested in three major aspects of his novel. The nature of the relationships between men and women provides one revealing indication of the text's concern with psychological boundaries. Representations of attachment, separation, loss and absence highlight the description of these relationships throughout the narrative. However, the preoccupation with the definition of self is additionally manifested through the use of various linguistic constructs that characterize the narrator's discourse. For example, the binary opposition of inside/outside, which reflects these concerns with demarcation, is evident in the prevalence of emotionally charged terms that refer to the violation of spatial parameters. Moreover, the narrative strategy employed to relate the bizarre events of the tale also mirrors the text's concern with the issues of fragmentation and unity, dependency and autonomy. All three aspects of the text, male/female interaction, language and narrative form, reveal the subject's struggle and failed quest for independent selfhood, and thus bear significantly on the meaning of the novel.

The narrator of the tale, an escaped fugitive from Venezuela, seeks refuge on a mysterious island where he soon falls passionately in love with one of the island inhabitants, a woman named Faustine. The narrator much later discovers that Faustine and the other island inhabitants are not real people but holographic images produced by Morel's invention. This cinematic invention is capable of capturing not only the visual images but the thoughts and sensations of its subjects as well; their consciousness is thus severed and freed from the perishable nature of the body. Morel had photographed himself and his friends during their one week visit to his island, and their images will continue to reenact the same scenes indefinitely. Ironically, the photographic process which created the "immortal" images caused the rapid physical deterioration and demise of the subjects photographed. The dismemberment of the body that occurs as a result of the photographic process, consisting of the loss of hair, nails, skin and eventually limbs, is one of many textual references that allude to some form of fragmentation in the structuring of the lives and works of the characters.

Morel had used his scientific discovery to create his own private world in seven days in which all he desired was present, a reference which obviously parallels biblical accounts of creation. While Morel the inventor plays the role of a god-like figure, his actions also reveal the desire for omnipotence characteristic of the narcissistic infant. His island utopia provides him the eternal presence and control of Faustine, the woman he loves, and his invention serves, in the words of the inventor, to give perpetual reality to his "fantasia sentimental." The scientist's subsequent explanation of his invention further underscores its primary function in counteracting or negating absence and its use to summon forth the presence of the female. Morel sees his discovery as a logical advancement over earlier inventions, such as the telephone and television, which had performed in a limited way to counteract spatial and temporal absences. Through his discovery, Morel seeks to eradicate all boundaries and eliminate completely absence from the loved one. Morel thus ultimately seeks in his boundless union with Faustine that mythical oneness of being theoretically only possible in the Lacanian "absolute subject" or infant who has not yet made the discovery of difference or recognized the boundaries of the "other."

Morel's negation of Faustine's biological nature, together with his denunciation of procreation, underscore his rejection of differentiation. By denying the carnal nature of the body and the reproductive function, which accentuate the male/female difference, the signs of limitation or separateness are blurred or effaced and the subjects "denaturalized". In these circumstances, the female is also rendered in a non-threatening manner, since she cannot contradict

male control or the "image" he has created of her. In fact, Faustine now exists only as the "image" that Morel has created. Morel's world thus duplicates the biblical account of creation in yet another aspect; it depicts the construction of woman by and for man. As in the story of Adam and Eve, the male denies the female's power over life through procreation.

Morel's rejection of his own limited biological role of father, and his refusal to acknowledge any "father" figure of power and authority, God or Man, are symptomatic of his desire to assume the absolute role of the Omnipotent Father, the master of life and death, presence and absence. The empty chapel on the island and Morel's denunciations of his scientific peers are signs of this rejection of traditional, external authority. Moreover, Morel carries out his experiment without the knowledge or consent of those photographed. His desire to control their lives exhibits not only his god-like ambition but also the narcissism characteristic of the infantile subject who does not acknowledge the autonomous existence of the other. On his island, Morel recreates himself or provides for his rebirth into immortality. In a metaphorical sense, then, Morel becomes his own father. His island creation, like the heaven envisioned by patriarchal society, becomes the site for rebirth to a superior form, a transformation empowered for and by Morel.

The narrator of the tale duplicates many of the inventor's attitudes and activities. The narrator also denounces procreation, seeks immortality through a male created rebirth, and soon shares the inventor's desire for Faustine. In fact, Faustine's presence becomes equally essential to the narrator's existence.

Before discovering the holographic nature of Faustine, the narrator is tormented by Faustine's inexplicable behavior, the fact that she neither looks at him nor speaks to him. Her voice and her gaze become fundamental to his sense of being, as his statement clearly implies: "Sin embargo siento, quiza un poco en broma, que si pudiera ser mirado un instante, hablado un instante por ella, afluiria juntamente et socorro que tiene el hombre en los amigos, en las novias y en los que estan en su misma sangre."

Viewed within the perspective provided by psychoanalytical theory, the narrator's preoccupation with Faustine's gaze and voice would indicate an infantile, regressive mode of dealing with reality, an attempt to reclaim the lost partial objects and to restore primordial boundlessness. Thus the narrator assigns to these special attributes the power to complete his world, making any other form of social bonding unnecessary. Like the inventor Morel, the narrator fails in this instance to accept absence and separateness upon which a sense of autonomous being is predicated. At the same time, this infantile perception on the part of the narrator can also lead to a different interpretation of the large proportions attributed to Faustine, which at first seem the result of visual perspective. Her large dimensions may, in fact, be the result of the man looking through a child's eyes at an adult woman.

The gaze of the female, however, has additional significance when viewed in light of the narrator's previous erotic experiences and his fluctuation between the contrary pulls of autonomy and dependency. The narrator's desire to possess Faustine, a woman who cannot see him, parallels an earlier episode recounted by the narrator in his diary. While in Calcutta, the narrator had accompanied a friend to a brothel in which all the prostitutes were blind. The act of visual apprehension, also a symbolic act of appropriation, is thus denied in both instances to the female object of desire. Consequently, capture by the I/eye of the female other is averted. The threat to male autonomy is avoided by removing the power of appropriation from the female. In both instances, the narrator plays the role of voyeur, empowered by the fact that he can see without being seen.

However, Faustine's gaze is not the only perplexing circumstance which the narrator must confront. The narrator faces an equally distressing dilemma produced by his initial failure to understand or control Faustine's mysterious appearances and disappearances. Since the camera and projection equipment are controlled by the island tides, there are periodic disruptions in the transmission of the images. These separations cause extreme anxiety in the narrator. He is so preoccupied with a final disappearance, Faustine's departure from the island, that he dreams of a romantic scene in which they bid farewell amid passionate embraces. The physical union, of course, attempts to deny or negate any subsequent physical separation. The intensity of emotion the narrator expresses on this occasion is created precisely by the fear of separation, viewed as detachment from himself of that which constitutes a part of his being. His anxiety is an indication of his difficulty in accepting both his own and Faustine's separate ego and body boundaries. Separation is viewed consequently as a fragmentation, splitting or partial loss of the self.

Once the narrator has discovered the secret of Morel's invention, he then seeks and finds the means of superimposing his image on the original disk created by the inventor. After carefully studying the movements and conversations of Faustine and the others, the narrator inserts his own image with lines of discourse and gestures that create the illusion of interaction with the images. The meaning to be conveyed by these new scenes can be provided only from without by an imaginary "other" who is to play the role of observer or voyeur formally exercised by the narrator. It is for the benefit of this "other" that the narrator shifts his part from spectator to actor. His actions thus reveal his attempt to simultaneously negate or mask the boundaries between himself and Faustine while affirming his own boundaries in opposition to another that exists outside the filmic world.

Ironically, after having successfully eluded the judicial system, the narrator is "captured" by Morel's machine and more specifically by the image of the other, that of Faustine, which determines his ultimate destiny. The narrator consents to a form of imprisonment in his ultimate surrender of self to Faustine and the spatially limited confines of the disk. The narrator also accepts a total dependency on the other island images as well when he inserts his image among theirs. His simulated functions have no meaning without them. Moreover, he cannot remove or alter the original images without destroying the entire disk. The narrator therefore cannot exist without the presence of the others. Although at first disturbing, this dependency on Faustine and the other images ultimately pleases the narrator, as his words indicate: "Me alegra tambien depender—y esto es mas extrano, menos justificable—de Haynes, Dora, Alec, Stoever, Irene, etcetera (del propio Morel!)."

Viewed within the perspective provided by psychoanalytical theory, the narrator's attempt to efface the corporeal and ego boundaries between himself and Faustine represents symbolically an attempt at merging or fusion with the mother; it is a doomed and frustrated effort to recapture an original state of boundlessness and union with the other. The confines of the film disk then become both the enclosure of the tomb and the proverbial return to the womb. The narrator's desire to be joined with Faustine thus evokes the universal longing for reunion with the original love object.

Moreover, this association of Faustine with mother, womb, and tomb is supported by specific passages of the text. The references to the anachronic attire which Faustine wears, for example, clearly link her to a past time and a prior generation. The narrator's plea to the reader, at the conclusion of the text, to assist him by reintegrating the spatially dispersed atoms of Faustine, expresses his need to be united with the *original* woman. The narrator's desire cannot be totally satisfied with the replacement or symbolic substitution that the image represents. Like the son who defies societal laws and boundaries, he wishes to claim the original love object. However, the achievement of wholeness and the penetration of Faustine's ego boundaries are acts that depend on the intervention of another party, the reader of the narrator's text, who exists outside the parameters of Faustine's world and that of the narrator: "Al hombre que, basandose en este informe, invente una maquina capaz de reunir las presencias disgregadas, hare una suplica. Busquenos a Faustine y a mi, hagame entrar en el cielo de la conciencia de Faustine."

The narrator, while still under the illusion of finding the original Faustine, describes his quest as a difficult road leading toward "el necesario descanso de mi vida." The terms *necesario descanso* are highly suggestive, implying a required break or halt in movement, a final or eternal sleep. Faustine thus represents that sacred center of being, the womb or tomb, toward which the narrator flees. Once a subject has separated from the mother, this psychological merging or return to origins is experienced as psychic death. The narrator's endeavors to achieve fusion thus lead not only to his physical demise but to the annihilation of his individual, separate identity as well. His attempts to control his world and recapture his primordial state of being culminate in the surrender of that control and his autonomous selfhood.

The narrator's experiences projected upon the page or screen reveal the internal drama of the subject as it struggles with conflicting needs to both affirm and negate its own boundaries and those of the other. However, the nature of narrator's experiences with the island inhabitants is not the only aspect of the text through which the issue of boundaries is manifested. The narrator's fluctuation between boundedness and boundlessness, between union and separation, is also reflected in the language of the text, in the choice of words and grammatical forms that characterize the narrator's discourse. The narrator's concern with boundary issues is apparent, for example, in his use of details that establish the opposition inside/outside. Thus, the narrator's discourse abounds in references to walls, windows and doors that serve to establish the frontier or threshold between one space and another. This binary opposition, moreover, is manifested in the narrator's depiction of himself, his environment, and others as intruders. This term, and other emotionally charged expressions of physical transgression, denote the hostile crossing of boundaries and suggest the degradation of the subject as a result of this penetration. In his initial description of the island, the narrator states that the plants of the island *invade* each other's time and space. The sea *invades* the lowlands, forcing the narrator to seek shelter elsewhere. Throughout the first part of the novel, the narrator categorizes Morel and his guests as *intruders* in his world. Later, the narrator categorizes himself as an *intruder* in Morel's world of images. The narrator even describes his own person in terms of violated boundaries: "Ahora, invadido por suciedad y pelos que no puedo extirpar, crío la esperanza de la cercanía benigna de esta mujer indudablemente hermosa." At the same time, it should be noted that the narrator's tendency to shift between opposing roles or to simultaneously view himself as intruder and victim blurs the very boundaries between self and other, inside and outside, that he wishes to establish.

The narrator's concern with boundedness and boundlessness, with integration and separation, is also apparent in his descriptions of objects or people in terms of parts or fragments of the whole. Passages which depict the fragmentary nature of objects often utilize the same devices which serve to establish the opposition of inside and outside, (i.e., windows, doors, keyhole). However, while employing these terms as figures of demarcation, the narrator also underlines their function as framing devices that limit his visual perspective. They create marked spatial restrictions or boundaries cutting off or severing most of the scene from the narrator's field of vision. Consequently, what the narrator perceives and describes are fragments of the whole. It is this partialized view of the whole that he depicts, for example, when he tells the reader: "Pude ver, por la puerta abierta, parte de una silla y una pierna." This fragmented vision, in turn, represents an external counterpart of an internal process; it offers a fragmented version of the world as seen by an equally fragmented, divided self.

The narrator's discourse activities also reveal his awareness of the function of grammatical or linguistic logic in establishing the parameters of the self; specifically, he demonstrates an awareness of the function of subject pronouns in defining positionality and separateness between self and other. According to the linguistic theories advanced by [Émil Beneviste, according to Kaja Silverman in her *The Subject of Semiotics,* 1983], the signifier "I" acquires its meaning only within discourse and only through the opposition to the pronoun "you." Beneviste's model emphasizes the relational value of these pronouns, their mutual dependence in the production of significance. Moreover, this linguistic relationship of opposition and dependence implies a cognitive distinction between "me" and "not-me," between internality and externality. The subject's experience of differentiation thus shapes and is shaped by language. The narrator of Bioy's tale initially confronts a serious dilemma in defining his own boundaries and separateness in view of the absence of an oppositional "you." He resolves this dilemma by "inventing" a reader for his diary, a text ordinarily destined for the writer's eyes alone. This reader then occupies the position of the separate "you," and a dialogic situation is established. However, in this discourse situation the narrator again surrenders his autonomy by relinquishing the control over meaning to the editor and reader of the text. Furthermore, it should be observed that personal pronouns, such as "I" and "you," are less specific in identifying than a proper noun. The narrator never chooses to reveal his proper name, the one attribute that would firmly establish his individuality. [In a footnote the critic adds: "The narrator alludes ironically to this ambiguous function of 'I,' that is, its lack of inherent identifying properties, when he creates a floral representation of himself and Faustine. Through these visual means, he attempts to 'narrate' the story of his love to Faustine. Originally, the narrator plans to place the pronoun 'I' within parenthesis beneath the male figure. The use of a parenthetical construction produces irony since it is apparent to the reader that the content thus enclosed does not add any information that would actually assist in identifying the loosely configured male form. One might also speculate that the substantial representation of 'I' within parenthesis dramatizes the narrator's internal struggle to define his own spatial parameters and thus convey a sense of unity to a fragmented or split subject. Moreover, the narrator's critical comments on his garden scene evidence his conscious exploration of the temporal and spatial boundaries of various art forms through which subjectivity is expressed."]

The narrator's implicit and explicit references to boundaries or demarcations between self and "other" provide one device among many that serve to underscore the search for cohesion and the threat of separation and dispersement. The diary itself, consisting of separate entries whose omission of dates precludes any sense of temporal sequence and continuity, offers one more instance of the text's insistence on splitting and fragmentation. The partial recording of conversations and the pages of Morel's manuscript within the diary, together with the omission by the anonymous editor of the narrator's writings on Malthus, also allude to some linguistic form of dismemberment or incompleteness. In turn, these narrative devices reflect the subject's experiences of separation and its fragmented being in search of union. Moreover, the insertion or enclosure of one document within another, denoting each text's subjugation to or dependency on the other and its lack of autonomous existence, mirrors the ultimate fate of the narrator. Morel's manuscript is edited and inserted within the pages of the narrator's diary. In turn, the fictitious editor places the revised text of the narrator's diary within his edition. Although the boundaries of the individual texts are suggested through footnotes and quotation marks, none of the texts exists independent of the other.

In his novel, **La invencion de Morel,** Bioy Casares dramatizes the paradoxes of boundary, the contrary pulls of union and separation, thereby providing insight into the conflictive desires of his narrator for autonomy and dependency. Thus, his narrator flees imprisonment, survives the deprivations and hardships imposed by conditions on the island, and attempts to establish a sense of unified or self-contained being through his discursive activities with an "other" that he invents. At the same time, however, Bioy's subject cannot accept the pain of loss and separation, the perishability of life and the discontinuity of relationships, all attributes of the human condition. The aloneness of the free agent drives him to seek union with the "other," thus negating his own boundaries and those of the other. In the end, he surrenders his autonomy to escape individual freedom.

The text employs diverse metaphorical expressions of boundaries in its development of this issue and its existential ramifications. A sense of physical boundaries is conveyed by references to the prison which the narrator eludes, the sea which surrounds the island, the body which limits human experience, and the structure of enclosure which shapes the literary work. Temporal and psychological boundaries are revealed through the juxtaposition of the linear activities of the narrator with the repetitive movements of the islanders, and through the attachment and separation anxieties experienced by the narrator. Through its presentation of these boundary issues, the text explores the nature of autonomy and dependency. It becomes clear that the former is predicated on the recognition of demarcations and that their effacement leads to psychic and physical death.

None of the characters in Bioy's tale are whole, integral individuals, a fact dramatized by the scientific invention which creates a splitting or fissure in the subject and underscored by the text's recurrent allusions to various forms of fragmentation, separation, and incompleteness. In its exploration of these issues, the text implies that a sense of unified selfhood can be achieved only by transcending the losses and separations that the subject experiences. In order to do so, the subject must respect the integrity of individual boundaries, and it must recognize the other as independent subject or consciousness rather than as complementary object to be controlled or manipulated for pleasure. Ultimately, it is this ability to accept one's own boundedness and that of the other that determines the extent to which any subject will successfully operate as an autonomous, whole being. The failure of Bioy's anonymous narrator to achieve this transcendence and accept his own separateness, like many of the author's other male characters, inevitably leads to the annihilation of his individual identity.

Daniel Balderston (essay date 1992)

SOURCE: "Fantastic Voyages," in *The New York Times Book Review,* November 29, 1992, p. 15.

[*An American critic, Balderston is the author of* Out of

Context: Historical Reference and the Representation of Reality in Borges *(1993) and* The Latin American Short Story: An Annotated Guide to Anthologies and Criticism *(1992). In the following excerpt, he discusses Bioy Casares's approach to the fantastic in* A Russian Doll, and Other Stories, *and notes imitation of the work of his former collaborator Jorge Luis Borges and Argentine fiction writer Silvina Ocampo.*]

In "Tlön, Uqbar, Orbis Tertius," Jorge Luis Borges's great story of the creation of an encyclopedia about an imaginary planet, everything begins with a conversation between Borges and Adolfo Bioy Casares about the possibility of a work of fiction in which the presence of minute contradictions would permit a few readers to discover a disquieting plot quite different from the apparent one. The story was published in 1940, the year in which Mr. Bioy Casares published his first major novel, **The Invention of Morel,** with a plot pronounced "perfect" by Borges in his review of it, and also the year that Borges and Mr. Bioy Casares—together with Silvina Ocampo, Mr. Bioy Casares's wife and herself a major writer—published an anthology of fantastic literature (recently issued in English as *A Book of Fantasy*) that changed the course of Latin American literature.

A half century later, **The Invention of Morel** has inspired a disquieting parable of totalitarian power, Eliseo Subiela's film "Man Facing Southeast." Mr. Bioy Casares, by now the author of a number of other significant books including **A Plan for Escape,** The Dream of Heroes and The Diary of the Year of the Pig, has stayed faithful to the task of unsettling the reader with understated works of fiction in which some details don't quite fit, in which something is not quite right. His latest book, **A Russian Doll: And Other Stories,** continues his quest to present a contemporary reality distorted by elements of the fantastic and the grotesque.

Two stories in the collection, **"A Russian Doll"** and **"Underwater,"** invite the reader to take a look at what the interventions of modern science have done to life under water. In one, an Argentine visitor to Aix-les-Bains in France encounters an old acquaintance, Maceira, who (inspired by the movies) has come to the spa to look for an heiress to marry; the ensuing complications turn out to be more than the gold digger bargained for. The story resembles one of Kafka's in that the extraordinary happenings disrupt a dull and rather dreary reality; the fantastic events, however, grow out of an apocalyptic series of ecological catastrophes.

This contemporary flavor also informs **"Underwater,"** in which a story of unrequited love turns into a tale of horror, again because of scientific meddling with the natural environment.

One of the most impressive stories, **"The Navigator Returns to His Country,"** is also the briefest in the collection, and the least like Mr. Bioy Casares's other work. Here an employee at a South American embassy in Paris discovers an unexpected likeness between himself and a disheveled Cambodian student on the subway. The dream sequence in the story is brief and beautifully understated, serving to underscore the pain of both foreigners' waking reality.

This collection also contains some understated homages to two of the closest associates of Mr. Bioy Casares. "**A Meeting in Rauch**" is strongly reminiscent of the stories in Borges's 1975 collection, *The Book of Sand,* down to the bookish reference to Swedenborg's *Heaven and Hell,* a treatise on the world of spirits, that provides the idea for the metaphysical conceit in the story and even the name of the protagonist (Swerberg). More surprising, given the extreme differences in tone between their earlier writings, are Mr. Bioy Casares's quiet homages to Silvina Ocampo. "**Our Trip (A Diary)**" and the final "**Three Fantasies in Minor Key**" sound and feel like Ms. Ocampo, though perhaps the black humor and the violence are not so intense as in her own writing (a selection of her stories, *Leopoldina's Dream,* is available in English).

It is surprising to see Mr. Bioy Casares imitating Borges and Ms. Ocampo so late in his career. No doubt Mr. Bioy Casares began his career as a writer imitating Borges, but the imitation of Ms. Ocampo (considered by many a stronger writer than her husband) is new and unexpected. . . .

In the last two or three years Adolfo Bioy Casares has won a number of important awards, including Spain's coveted Cervantes Prize, and his work has been discovered by a new generation of readers across the Spanish-speaking world. His writing is not marked by the excess that many North American readers associate with Latin American writing; his brand of the fantastic is never disconnected from reality, and he is always attentive to the cadences—and the commonplaces—of everyday speech. One can only hope that the charms of this little collection will entice readers to discover—or rediscover—his earlier work, particularly *The Invention of Morel* and *The Dream of Heroes.*

Ana María Hernández   (essay date 1993)

SOURCE: A review of *El lado de la sombra,* in *World Literature Today,* Vol. 67, No. 1, Winter, 1993, pp. 154-55.

[Below, Hernández offers a positive assessment of the stories collected in El lado de la sombra.*]*

Originally published in 1962, *El lado de la sombra* heralded Adolfo Bioy Casares's partial return to fantastic fiction after *Guirnalda con amores* (1959). Of the ten stories in the collection, four deal with fantastic subjects; of these, "**El lado de la sombra**" is undoubtedly the best. In it a traveler to exotic lands encounters a former friend who has experienced a change in fortune. The story is told from the perspective of a first-person narrator—indeed, eight of the stories utilize first-person narration—whose descriptions of a Conrad-like Indonesian setting prepare the reader for the fateful encounter.

The story manifests some of Bioy's best traits. He elaborates a spellbinding plot, skillfully revealed in successive stages, and he creates an almost animistic atmosphere that foreshadows unfolding events: "Atribuí al trópico una irreprimible actividad envolvente contra presas marcadas,

entre las que fatalmente me encontraba yo." Veblen tells the narrator about his disastrous liaison with Leda, a femme fatale / ingenue who causes his ruin and later dies in a traffic accident. Leda and her cat Lavinia function as a set of doppelgänger. Lavinia is the stronger one: after she dies in a fire, Leda loses her power over Veblen, at least temporarily. Later, Veblen reencounters Leda in a local prostitute named Leto, who soon leaves him; it is Livinia, "returning" to life after a local fire, who triumphs in the end.

A psychological crime-thriller skillfully conceived and brilliantly executed, "**Cavar un foso**" deals with the inner mechanisms of ambition, guilt, and delusion. The story portrays a young couple who murder an elderly lady and steal from her in order to forestall bankruptcy. The couple must then confront two separate pursuers, who precipitate additional homicides. The narrative is structured to create a gradual intensification of suspense by the juxtaposition of a subjective element—the couple's guilt—and an objective one: the pursuers, whose motives we do not discover until the end.

"**Los afanes**," another jewel in the collection, chronicles the relationship between Eladio Heller—a hyperintellectual character with touches of the "mad scientist"—and his wife Milena, described as unabashedly original and unbearably snobbish: "Nunca habíamos encontrado una persona menos acomodaticia ni más agresiva." Both characters are portrayed in an ambiguous manner. Is he a genius or a sadist, or both? Is she a neglected wife or a possessive spider jealous of her husband's talent? Heller's ultimate invention is a device that captures the essence of a being and preserves it eternally. He first tries it on his dog Marconi, whom he had rescued from death years before; later, he transfers his own soul into the device. The use of a first-person narrator—a friend of Eladio's who loved Milena in secret—creates several levels of ambiguity, as we cannot be certain of his objectivity regarding either Heller or Milena.

Also notable is "**Un león en el bosque de Palermo**," wherein the author resorts to archetypal symbolism—the lion as passion, the forest as the unconscious—to reveal the disruption in the daily routines of local residents when a lion escapes from the zoo. The creation of a magical atmosphere is of paramount importance in this story; the piece has the cinematic quality that characterizes many of Bioy's stories and novels. (The author's interest in cinema is well known, and he has often collaborated on film ventures.)

Bioy, who often likes to cast writers and journalists as his protagonists, does so again in "**El calamar opta por su tinta**" and "**La obra**," the latter about a novelist who retires to an off-season resort to complete a work in progress. Here Bioy playfully refers to himself through his narrator when he declares that his works "me asegurarán un nicho . . . en la historia de la literatura argentina. Acaso no figure entre los exaltados ni entre los ínfimos; me conformo con un lugar secundario: en mi opinión, el más decoroso."

Certainly, *El lado de la sombra* reveals the best of the mature Bioy: rigorous, lucid, elegant, with an understated virtuosity that is dazzling to the discerning eye.

Evelio Echevarría   (essay date 1994)

SOURCE: A review of *A Russian Doll, and Other Stories,* in *Studies in Short Fiction,* Vol. 31, No. 1, Winter, 1994, p. 126.

[*In the following review of* A Russian Doll, and Other Stories, *Echevarría criticizes the collection's lack of "vital conflict" and thematic variation but praises Bioy Casares's elegant writing style.*]

Literary critics and Latin Americanists agree on classifying the Argentinean Bioy Casares as a fiction writer who, by dexterously combining the real and the fantastic, delves deep into the confused human mind. The present collection of short stories [*A Russian Doll, and Other Stories*] is his ninth. It is composed of six pieces averaging some 20 pages each, and three short glimpses. They have in common their topics, which confirm the opinion of the critics. The title of the book itself, taken from the first story, summarizes the contents: Russian dolls were manufactured having identical dolls one inside the other, so that if one broke, it was replaced by the next. This represents, among other things, interchangeability and duplicability in the human personality. These stories take place mostly during travels, since the author believes that traveling makes one's spirit freer. **"A Russian Doll"** shows the double standards in love of a man after a rich woman; when he loses her, he simply replaces her with another, not quite so rich. **"A Meeting in Rauch"** again deals with the impact of greed upon the human personality: it depicts a businessman so eager to make a deal that, in an encounter with God, he fails to recognize Him and treats Him rather rudely. Other stories cover male-female relationships, which, as usual for Bioy Casares, are pictured with obstacles that neither side is willing to overcome. **"Underwater"** is fantastic, fantasy being for Bioy Casares a form of surrealistic imagery that helps to explain a problem. The tale shows some lovers turned into salmons, so as to stay together and isolated from others. But others also invited to take such a way to happiness shrink and simply decide to stay dry.

As far as the argument is concerned, these stories are disappointing. Argentinean contemporary fiction writers have been repeating the same metaphysical topics for more than four decades. The great vital conflicts that characterize Spanish-American literature are not here. But these stories are not dull. Bioy Casares's elegant style . . . [helps] to make up for what arguments lack with something more vital.

Breaking the law of logic and reality, Bioy Casares continues to offer a succession of cases that impart a sense of isolation and helplessness, with nearly no hope or solution in sight. But his characters are resilient and even the symbol of the Russian doll seems to offer some comfort, for not everything is lost: "A gift from my father. . . . It had identical dolls inside, which are smaller. When one breaks, the others are left."

FURTHER READING

Criticism

Brown, Clarence. Review of *Chronicles of Bustos Domecq,* by Jorge Luis Borges and Adolfo Boy Casares. *The New Republic* (5 June 1976): 24-6.
  Attributes *The Chronicles of Bustos Domecq* almost solely to Jorge Luis Borges, describing it as "a hilarious send-up of Borges' better style." Brown carefully notes that the work represents deliberate self-parody, not unconscious self-parody.

Eco, Umberto. "Abduction in Uqbqar." In his *The Limits of Interpretation,* pp. 152-62. Bloomington: Indiana University Press, 1990.
  Analysis of deduction and conjecture as used by Don Isidro in *Six Problems for Don Isidro Parodi.* Eco maintains that the method of conjecture evident in the detective stories informs much of Jorge Luis Borges's own short fiction.

Frankel, Haskel. "Stories from Three." *The New York Times Book Review* (15 November 1964): 62-3.
  Comments on the style and technique of *The Invention of Morel, and Other Stories.*

Gray, Paul. "Bloodless Coup." *Time* 107, No. 13 (29 March 1976): 74.
  Offers a positive assessment of *Chronicles of Bustos Domecq,* which Gray perceives as a satire of modernism.

Levine, Suzanne Jill. "Science versus the Library in *The Island of Dr. Moreau, La invención de Morel* [*The Invention of Morel*], and *Plan de evasión* [*A Plan for Escape*]." *Latin American Literary Review* IX, No. 18 (Spring-Summer 1981): 17-26.
  Discusses *The Invention of Morel, A Plan for Escape,* and H. G. Wells's *The Island of Dr. Moreau* as literature revealing "the text's progressive awareness . . . of its own textuality." Levine contends that this self-reflexivity is most evident in the attitudes of Bioy Casares's and Wells's characters toward books and literature.

———. "Parody Island: Two Novels by Bioy Casares." *Hispanic Journal* 4, No. 2 (Spring 1983): 43-9.
  Asserts that *The Invention of Morel* and *A Plan for Escape* are self-reflexive works "because they reflect each other in [the] wider sense of parody as commentary on the nature of literature as a process of destruction and re-creation, but also because they synthesize a whole tradition of utopic works." Levine particularly stresses the novellas' ties to H. G. Wells's *The Island of Dr. Moreau.*

Mac Adam, Alfred J. "Satire and Self-Portrait" and "The Lying Compass." In his *Modern Latin American Narratives,* pp. 29-36; 37-43. Chicago: University of Chicago Press, 1977.
  "Satire and Self-Portrait" explores the metaphor of the "transformation of a man into an artist and, finally, the artist into art" in the novella *The Invention of Morel.* In "The Lying Compass," Mac Adam explicates *A Plan for Escape* as "a totally metaphoric text whose subject is metaphor."

Monegal, Emir Rodriguez. "The Invention of Bioy-Casares." *Review,* No. 15 (Fall 1975): 41-4.

Argues that Bioy Casares's novellas *The Invention of Morel* and *A Plan for Escape* and the novels *Asleep in the Sun, Diary of the War of the Pig,* and *The Dream of the Heroes* address limitations inherent in writing as well as in human physical existence, describing both writing and existence as prisons.

Spurling, John. "The Prison-Cell Detective." *The Times Literary Supplement*, No. 4080 (12 June 1981): 672.
    Negative review of *Six Problems for Don Isidro Parodi.*

Sturrock, John. "Argentine Detective and English Jockey." *The New York Times Book Review* (29 March 1981): 3, 29.
    Describes *Six Problems for Don Isidro Parodi* as an entertaining parody of detective fiction.

Tilles, Solomon. Review of *The Invention of Morel, and Other Stories (from "La trama celeste"),* by Adolfo Bioy Casares. *Hispania* XLVIII, No. 4 (December 1965): 944.
    Praises the collection's imaginative synthesis of human, occult, and scientific phenomena.

Weinberger, Deborah. "Problems in Perception." *Review*, No. 15 (Fall 1975): 45-9.
    Study of sensory and mental perception as presented in *A Plan for Escape.*

Additional coverage of Bioy Casares's life and career is contained in the following sources published by Gale Research: *Contemporary Authors,* **Vols. 29-32, rev. ed.;** *Contemporary Authors New Revision Series,* **Vol. 19;** *Contemporary Literary Criticism,* **Vols. 4, 8, 13;** *Dictionary of Literary Biography,* **Vol. 113;** *Hispanic Writers*; **and** *Major 20th-Century Writers.*

Charles Dickens

1812-1870

(Full name Charles John Huffam Dickens; also wrote under the pseudonym of Boz) English novelist, short story writer, dramatist, and essayist.

INTRODUCTION

Although Dickens is perhaps best known for his novels, he wrote short fiction throughout his career, from the early *Sketches by Boz* to the acclaimed Christmas stories and the journalistic *Uncommercial Traveller*. Dickens's short stories, like his longer works, mix humor with macabre imagery to create vivid illustrations of the lives of ordinary people. Designed to uncover social injustices and promote reform in his own time, the endearing characterizations and moving situations presented in Dickens's shorter pieces have appealed to audiences up to the present day; indeed, his short story *A Christmas Carol* is one of his most enduring works. For much of the English-speaking world, this tale has played an important role in defining the Yule spirit; according to May Lamberton Becker, "every year at Christmas time, thousands of families wherever the English language is known would scarcely think Christmas really Christmas without listening to this story read aloud."

Biographical Information

Dickens was the son of John Dickens, a minor government official who, because he continually lived beyond his means, was briefly imprisoned for debt. During his father's confinement, the twelve-year-old Dickens was forced to leave home and work in dreadful conditions in a blacking (shoe polish) warehouse. This experience left an indelible impression on Dickens, who portrayed the difficulties of the poor in most of his writings. Late in his teens, Dickens learned shorthand and worked as a reporter. In 1833 he began contributing sketches and short stories to various periodicals. These were eventually compiled into two volumes under the title *Sketches by Boz*. He continued to use serial publication for all of his works, including his novels, for he cherished the constant contact with his readers the method provided. Throughout his career, Dickens gave numerous public readings from his works in both England and America, an activity that left him exhausted. Many believe that increasing physical and mental strain led to the stroke Dickens suffered while working on the novel *The Mystery of Edwin Drood,* which he left unfinished at his death.

Major Works of Short Fiction

In his short fiction, Dickens variously combines humor, sentiment, autobiography, spirituality, and both Gothic and realistic elements. *Sketches by Boz,* provides comic

and closely observed characterizations drawn from Victorian London's lower and middle classes. Celebrated stories from this compilation include: "A Visit to Newgate," which details a criminal's final hours before his execution; "The Black Veil," a tale about a woman whose life is evaluated according to the worth of her husband; and "Mr. Minns and His Cousin," which shows that adherence to social conventions can cause misery. Continuing to focus on the lives of ordinary people, Dickens began writing Christmas stories, which include *A Christmas Carol, The Chimes, The Cricket on the Hearth,* and *The Haunted Man and the Ghost's Bargain.* His intention for these tales was, he wrote, "a whimsical kind of masque which the good humor of the season justified, to waken some loving and forbearing thoughts, never out of season in a Christian land." Generally, these books feature fallen protagonists who, through a chain of remarkable, even otherworldly, events, realize the mistakes they have made in life. For example, *A Christmas Carol* chronicles the transformation of Ebenezer Scrooge (Dickens's most famous character) from a miser to a generous being after he receives startling visits from the Ghosts of Christmas Past, Present, and Future. In *The Chimes* Toby Veck represents members of the lower class who have acceded to society's opinion that the

98

poor are inferior; his conversion involves restoring faith in himself and his class. *The Haunted Man and the Ghost's Bargain*—the most sophisticated version of the common theme in the estimation of many critics—portrays Mr. Redlaw's realization that his new-found ability to erase memories is harmful to others. After writing these holiday tales, Dickens, using material from his own life, penned the more journalistic *The Uncommercial Traveller*. One story in this collection, "Dullborough Town," describes the setting of Dickens's childhood, and another, "City of London Churches," recounts a love affair similar to the writer's first relationship.

Critical Reception

Hailed for his comic and journalistic abilities, powerful and provoking depictions of the poor, unforgettable characters, and the moral-filled Christmas stories, Dickens was one of the most successful writers of his time. Enormously popular in England, he was, before he turned thirty, honorably received in America as well. Dickens wrote of the reception: "There never was a king or emperor upon the earth so cheered and followed by crowds, and entertained in public at splendid halls and dinners, and waited on by public bodies and deputations of all kinds." Although some critics have asserted that *Sketches by Boz* focuses too heavily on the lower class and that the author's stories are at times too sentimental and laden with exaggeration, many have extolled them for their expressions of a fundamental faith in humanity and their unflagging censure of social injustice. A. Edward Newton perhaps best summarized the high esteem in which countless readers hold Dickens when he declared that "in the resplendent firmament of English literature there is only one name I would rank above his for sheer genius: Shakespeare."

PRINCIPAL WORKS

Short Fiction

Sketches by Boz [as Boz]   1836
A Christmas Carol   1843
The Chimes   1844
The Cricket on the Hearth   1845
The Haunted Man and the Ghost's Bargain   1848
Reprinted Pieces   1858
The Uncommercial Traveller   1861

*Other Major Works

The Posthumous Papers of the Pickwick Club [as Boz] (novel)   1837
Oliver Twist   (novel)   1838
The Life and Adventures of Nicholas Nickelby   (novel) 1839
Barnaby Rudge   (novel)   1841
The Old Curiosity Shop   (novel)   1841
American Notes for General Circulation   (travel essay) 1842

The Life and Adventures of Martin Chuzzlewit   (novel) 1844
Pictures from Italy   (travel essay)   1846
Dealings with the Firm of Dombey and Son   (novel) 1848
The Personal History of David Copperfield   (novel) 1850
Bleak House   (novel)   1853
Hard Times for These Times   (novel)   1854
Little Dorrit   (novel)   1857
A Tale of Two Cities   (novel)   1859
Great Expectations   (novel)   1861
Our Mutual Friend   (novel)   1865
No Thoroughfare [with Wilkie Collins]   (drama)   1867
The Mystery of Edwin Drood   (unfinished novel)   1870

*All of Dickens's novels were first published serially in magazines, usually over periods ranging from one to two years.

CRITICISM

The Edinburgh Review   (essay date 1845)

SOURCE: A review of *The Chimes,* in *The Edinburgh Review,* Vol. LXXXI, January, 1845, pp. 181-89.

[*In the excerpt below, the anonymous critic discusses Dickens's exposure of the plight of the poor in* The Chimes.]

'Pray, Mr Betterton,' asked the good Archbishop Sancroft of the celebrated actor, 'can you inform me what is the reason you actors on the stage, speaking of things imaginary, affect your audience as if they were real; while we in the church speak of things real, which our congregations receive only as if they were imaginary?' 'Why, really, my lord,' answered Betterton, 'I don't know; unless it is that we actors speak of things imaginary as if they were real, while you in the pulpit speak of things real as if they were imaginary.' It is a clever answer; and as applicable now as when the archbishop put the question. Indifference makes sorry work of Truth, in half of what is going on around us; and what truthful and serious work may be made of Fiction, Mr Dickens helps us to discern.

We do not know the earnestness to compare with his, for the power of its manifestation and its uses. It is delightful to see it in his hands, and observe by what tenure he secures the popularity it has given him. Generous sympathies and kindest thoughts, are the constant renewal of his fame; and in such wise fashion as the little book before us, he does homage for his title and his territory. A noble homage! Filling successive years with merciful charities; and giving to thousands of hearts new and just resolves.

This is the lesson of his ***Chimes,*** as of his delightful ***Carol***; but urged with more intense purpose and a wider scope of application. What was there the individual lapse, is here the social wrong. Questions were handled there, to be settled with happy decision. Questions are here brought to view, which cannot be dismissed when the book is laid aside. Condition of England questions; questions of starving labourer and struggling artizan; duties of the rich and pretences of the worldly; the cruelty of unequal laws; and the pressure of awful temptations on the unfriended, unassisted poor. Mighty theme for so slight an instrument! but the touch is exquisite, and the tone deeply true.

We write before the reception of the book is known; but the somewhat stern limitation of its sympathies will doubtless provoke remark. Viewed with what seems to be the writer's intention, we cannot object to it. Obtain, for the poor, the primary right of recognition. There cannot, for either rich or poor, be fair play till that is done. Let men be made to think, even day by day, and hour by hour, of the millions of starving wretches, heart-worn, isolated, unrelated, who are yet their fellow-travellers to eternity. We do not know that we should agree with Mr Dickens' system of Political Economy, if he has one; but he teaches what before all economies it is needful to know, and bring all systems to the proof of—the at once solemn and hearty lesson of human brotherhood. It is often talked about, and has lately been much the theme; but in its proper and full significance is little understood. If it were, it would possibly be discovered along with it that life might be made easier, and economies less heartless, than we make them. Such, at any rate, appears to be the notion of Mr Dickens, and, to test its worth, he would make the trial of beginning at the right end.

Begin, he would seem to say to us, with what the wretched have a right to claim as part of a lost possession. Acknowledge some spiritual needs, as well as many bodily ones, and let not your profession of raising the poor man be but another form of the cant that has kept him down. Pompous, purse-proud, pauper Charity will avail him little. Ground to the earth as he is, he may be even spared the further grinding of Justice, if, with a great, huge, dead, steam-engine indifference, it would but crush him to the shape of its own hard requirements. On the other hand, principles of the breed of *sans culottes* adjusted with the tie of a Brummell, Jack Cade progression in the West-end boots of Hoby, will make still scantier way in his behalf. And from that other extreme of sublimated sense in the city, which detects all kinds of sham but its own, and puts down distress and suicide as it would put down thieving, Heaven in its mercy help him!

Let us away, says Mr Dickens in effect, with all these cants. If we cannot have a higher human purpose, let us have fewer selfish projects. Better for the poor man, if we cannot yield him some rightful claim to nature's kindly gifts, he should be wholly set aside as an intruder at her table. But better far for us, that we know his claims, and take them to our hearts in time. That we understand how rich, in the common inheritance of man, even the poorest of the poor should be. That we clearly understand what Society has made, of what Nature meant to make. That we try in some sort to undo this, and begin by making our laws his security, which have been heretofore his enemy. That even in his guilt, with due regard to its temptations, we treat him as a brother rather than an outcast from brotherhood. For that, in the equal sight of the highest wisdom, the happiness of the worst of the species is as

much an integrant part of the whole of human happiness as is that of the best.

In this spirit the little story before us is concieved. There is bitter satirical exposure of the quackeries of *quasi*-benevolence. There is patient, honest, tender-hearted poverty, forgetting its weary wants, in the zeal with which it ministers to wants even wretcheder than its own. There is the awful lesson, too little thought of by the most thoughtful men, of how close the union is between wants of the body and an utter destitution and madness of the soul. There is profound intimation of the evil that lies lurking in wait for all the innocent and all the good over all the earth. There is the strength and succour of Guilt Resisted, and deepest pity for Innocence Betrayed. And all this, gently and strongly woven into a web of ordinary human life, as it lies within the common experiences; woven into that woof of tears and laughter, of which all our lives are day by day composed, with incomparable art and vigour, and the most compassionate touching tenderness.

Could we note a distinction in the tale, from the general character of its author's writings, it would be that the impression of sadness predominates, when all is done. The comedy as well as tragedy seems to subserve that end; yet it must be taken along with the purpose in view. We have a hearty liking for the cheerful side of philosophy, and so it is certain has Mr Dickens: but there are social scenes and experiences, through which only tragedy itself may work out its kinder opposite. Even the poet who named the most mournful and tragic composition in the world a Comedy, could possibly have justified himself by a better than technical reason. Name this little tale what we will, it is a tragedy in effect. Inextricably interwoven, of course, are both pleasure and pain, in all the conditions of life in this world: crossing with not more vivid contrasts the obscure struggle of the weak and lowly, than with fierce alternations of light and dark traversing that little rule, that little sway, which is all the great and mighty have between the cradle and the grave. But whereas, in the former stories of Mr Dickens, even in the death of his little Nell, pleasure won the victory over pain, we may not flatter ourselves that it is so here. There is a gloom in the mind as we shut the book, which the last few happy pages have not cleared away; an uneasy sense of depression and oppression; a pitiful consciousness of human sin and sorrow; a feeling of some frightful extent of wrong, which we should somehow try to stay; as strong, but apparently as helpless, as that of the poor Frenchman at the bar of the Convention, who demanded of Robespierres and Henriots an immediate arrestment of the knaves and dastards of the world!

But then, says the wise and cheerful novelist to this, there *are* knaves and dastards of our own world to be arrested by all of us, even by individual exertion of us all, Henriots and Robespierres notwithstanding. It was for this my story was written. It was written, purposely to discontent you with what is hourly going on around you. Things so terrible that they should exist but in dreams, are here presented *in a dream;* and it is for the good and active heart to contribute to a more cheerful reality, whatsoever and howsoever it can. For ourselves, we will hope that this challenge may be taken. Those things are to be held possible, Lord Bacon thought, which are to be done by some person, though not by every one; and which may be done by many, though not by any one; and which may be done in succession of efforts, though not within the hour-glass of one man's effort. And thus we will think it possible that something may at last be done, even by hearts this little book shall awaken to the sense of its necessity, in abatement of the long and dire conspiracy which has been carried on against poverty, by the world and the world's law.

In so far as there is the machinery of a dream, the plan of the *Carol* is repeated in the **Chimes.** But there is a different spiritual agency, very nicely and naturally derived from the simple, solitary, friendless life of the hero of the tale. He is a poor old ticket-porter of London; stands in his vocation by the corner of an old church; and has listened to the chiming of its Bells so constantly, that, with nothing else to talk to or befriend him, he has made out for himself a kind of human, friendly, fellow voice in theirs, and is glad to think they speak to him, pity him, sympathize with him, encourage and help him. Nor, truly, have wiser men than Toby Veck been wise enough to dispel like fancies. There has been secret human harmony in Church-Bells always; life and death have sounded in their matin and vesper chime; with every thing grave or glad they have to do, prayer and festivity, marriage and burial; and there has never been a thoughtful man that heard them, in the New-Year seasons, to whom their voice was not a warning of comfort or retrieval—telling him to date his time and count up what was left him, out of all he had done or suffered, neglected or performed. It is the New-Year season when they talk to Toby Veck; but poor Toby is not sufficiently thoughtful to avoid falling into some mistakes now and then respecting what they say.

He is a delightfully drawn character, this unrepining, patient, humble drudge—this honest, childish-hearted, shabby-coated, simple, kindly old man. There is not a touch of selfishness, even in the few complaints his hard lot wrings from him. Thus, when a pinching east wind has nigh wrenched off his miserable old nose at the opening of the story, he says he really couldn't blame it if it was to go. 'It has a precious hard service of it,' he remarks, 'in the bitter weather, and precious little to look forward to: *for I don't take snuff myself* '. But there is a wrong extreme even in unselfishness, and Toby is meant for its example. He has had such a hard life; has hope of so little to redeem the hardship; and has read in the newspaper so much about the crimes of people in his own condition—that it is gradually bringing him to the only conclusion his simple soul can understand, and he begins to think that, as the poor can neither go right nor do right, they must be born bad, and can have no business on the earth at all. But while he argues the point with himself, the bright eyes of his handsome little daughter look suddenly into his own, and he thinks again they *must* have business here, 'a little.' What follows lets us into their humble history; and we learn that this pretty, hard-working girl, has been three years courted by a young blacksmith; and that Richard has at last prevailed with Meg to run the risks of poverty against the happiness of love, and marry him on the morrow, New-Year's Day. So, for further celebration of this

coming joy, she has brought her father an unexpected dainty of a dinner of tripe; and as he eats it with infinite relish on the steps of an adjoining house, where they are joined by Meg's lover himself, the door opens and other personages step upon the scene.

Mr Alderman Cute and his friend Mr Filer. The Alderman, great in the city; shrewd, knowing, easy, affable; amazingly familiar with the working-classes; a plain practical dealer in things; up to all the nonsense talked about 'want,' all the cant in vogue about 'starvation,' and resolved to put it down. Mr Filer, a dolorous, dry, pepper-and-salt kind of man; great in calculations of human averages; and for filing away all excesses in food and population. Thus he falls at once on poor Toby's tripe, which he shows to be so expensive a commodity, with such a deal of waste in it, that Toby finds himself on a sudden robbing the widow and orphan, and starving a garrison of five hundred men with his own hand.' The Alderman laughs at this mightily, takes up the matter in his livelier way, and gives it quite a cheerful aspect. 'There is not the least mystery or difficulty in dealing with this sort of people if you only understand 'em, and can talk to 'em in their own manner.' In their own manner, accordingly, the good justice talks to them. He proves to Toby in a trice that he has always enough to eat, and of the best. He chucks Meg under the chin, and shows her how indelicate it is to think of getting married; because she will have shoeless and stockingless children, whom he as a justice will find it necessary to put down; or she will be left to starve, or practice the fraud of suicide, and suicide and starvation he *must* put down. He banters the young smith with increased urbanity as a dull dog and a milksop, to think of tying himself to one woman, a trim young fellow like him, with all the girls looking after him. And so the little party is broken up: poor Meg walking off in tears; Richard gloomy and down-looking; and the miserable Toby, in very depths of despair, receiving a sixpenny job of a letter from the alderman. He is now confirmed in his notion, that the poor have no business on the earth. The Bells chime as he goes off upon his errand, and there is nothing but the Cute and Filer cant in what they seem to say to him. 'Facts and figures; 'facts and figures!' 'Put 'em down; put 'em down!'

The letter is to a very great man, who flounders a little in the depth of his observations, but is a very wise man, Sir Joseph Bowley. It is about a discontented labourer of Sir Joseph's, one William Fern, whom the alderman has an idea of putting down; and Toby, in delivering it, has an opportunity of hearing *this* philosopher's views about the poor man, to whom he considers himself, by ordainment of Providence, a friend and father. The poor man is to provide entirely for himself, and depend entirely on Sir Joseph. The design of his creation is, not that he should associate his enjoyments, brutally, with food, but that he should feel the dignity of labour: 'go forth erect into the cheerful 'morning air, and—*and stop there!*' Toby is elevated by the friendly and fatherly sentiments, but as much depressed to hear they are repaid by black ingratitude. And his heart sinks lower as he listens to Sir Joseph's religious remarks on the necessity of balancing one's accounts at the beginning of a New-Year, and feels how impossible it is to square his own small score at Mrs Chickenstalker's.

He leaves the house of this great man, more than ever convinced that his order have no earthly business with a New-Year, and really are 'intruding.'

But on his way home, falling in with the very Will Fern whom the alderman and Sir Joseph are about to put down, he hears somewhat of the other side of the question. The destitute, weary countryman, jaded and soiled with travel, has come to London in search of a dead sister's friend; carries a little child in his arms, his sister's orphan Lilian; and sudden sympathy and fellowship start up between the two poor men. Fern denies none of the Bowley complaints of his ingratitude. 'When work won't maintain me like a human creetur; when my living is so bad, that I am Hungry out of doors and in; when I see a whole working life begin that way, go on that way, and end that way, without a chance or change; then I say to the gentle folks, *"Keep away from me. Let my cottage be. My doors is dark enough without your darkening of 'em more. Don't look for me to come up into the park to help the show when there's a birthday, or a fine speechmaking, or what not. Act your Plays and Games without me, and be welcome to 'em, and enjoy 'em. We've nought to do with one another. I'm best let alone!'"* Toby brings him to his sorry home; secretly expends the sixpence he has just earned, for his entertainment; and half loses his wits with delight as he sees his dear Meg (whom he had found in tears; her proposed wedding broken off as he imagines) bring back cheerful warmth and comfort to the poor little half-starved Lilian. There is not a more quiet, a more simply unaffected, or a more deeply touching picture, in the whole of Mr Dickens's writings; often as they have softened, in the light of a most tender genius, the rough and coarser edges of lowly life. His visitors gone to what indifferent rest he can provide for them, old Toby is again alone. He falls again into the thought of the morning; pulls out an old newspaper he had before been reading; and once more spelling out the crimes and offences of the poor, especially of those whom Alderman Cute is going to put down, gives way to his old misgiving that they are bad, irredeemably bad; which turns to frightful certainty when he reads about a miserable mother who had attempted the murder of herself and her child. But at this point his friends the Bells clash in upon him, and he fancies they call him to come instantly up to them. He staggers out of the house, gropes his way up the old church stairs into the Tower, falls in a kind of swoon among the Bells, and the DREAM has begun.

The third quarter of the little book opens with the goblin scenes; done with a fertile fancy, and high fantastic art, which tax even the pencil of Mr Maclise to follow them. The Bells are ringing; and innumerable spirits (the sound or vibration of the Bells) are flitting in and out the steeple, bearing missions and commissions, and reminders and reproaches, and punishments and comfortable recollections, to all conditions of people. It is the last night of the old year, and men are haunted as their deeds have been. Scourges and discord, music and flowers, mirrors with pleasant or with awful faces, gleam around. And the Bells themselves, with shadowy likeness to humanity in midst of their proper shapes, speak to Toby as these visions disappear, and sternly rebuke him for his momentary doubt of the right of the poor man to the inheritance which Time reserves for him. His ghost or shadow is then borne through the air to various scenes, attended by spirits of the Bells charged with this trust: That they show him how the poor and wretched, at the worst—yes, even in the crimes which aldermen put down, and he has thought so horrible—have yet some deformed and hunchbacked goodness clinging to them, which preserves to them still their right, and all their share in Time.

He sees his daughter after a supposed lapse of nine years, her hopes and beauty faded, working miserable work with Lilian by her side; and sees, too, that her own brave and innocent patience is but scantily shared by her younger and prettier companion. He sees the Richard that should have been his son-in-law, a slouching, moody, drunken sloven. He sees what the Bowley friends and fathers are; what grave accounts the punctual Sir Josephs leave unlooked at; and what crawling, servile, mean-souled mudworms of the earth, are the Aldermen who put down misery. He sees what their false systems have brought his poor Will Fern to, and hears his solemn warning. 'Give us, in mercy, better homes when we're a-lying in our cradles; give us better food when we're a-working for our lives; give us kinder laws to bring us back when we're a-going wrong; and don't set jail, jail, jail, afore us, every where we turn.'

More years pass, and his daughter is again before him; with the same sublime patience, in an even meaner garret, and with more exhausting labour. But there is no Lilian by her side. The worst temptation has availed, and those nineteen years of smiling radiant life have fallen withered into the ways of sin. We will not trust ourselves to say to what a height of delicate and lovely tenderness these sad passages are wrought, by the beauty of merciful thoughts. Most healthful are the tears that will be shed over them, and the considerate pity they will awaken for all human sin and sorrow. We see the fallen Richard, in sullen half-drunken dreams of the past, haunting Meg's miserable room; and there, at Meg's feet, we see poor Lilian die. Her earthly sin falls from her as she prays to be forgiven, and the pure spirit soars away. 'Oh, Youth and Beauty, happy as ye should be, look at this! Oh, Youth and Beauty, blest and blessing all within your reach, and working out ends of your beneficent Creator, look at this!'

But for the old man is reserved an even more desperate trial. After lapse of further years, his daughter Meg is presented in another aspect. As the last chance of saving Richard she has married him; on his death is left with an infant child; sinks to the lowest abyss of want; and at last into the clutches of despair. Seeing death not distant from herself, and fearing for her child the fate of Lilian, she has resolved, in Toby's sight, her father's, to drown herself and the child together. Hogarth never painted a scene of mingled farce and tragedy with more appalling strength, than one which precedes this terrible resolve. But before she goes down to the water, Toby sees and acknowledges the lesson taught him thus bitterly. He sees that no evil spirit may yet prompt an act of evil. He observes Meg cover her baby with a part of her own wretched dress, adjust its squalid rags to make it pretty in its sleep, hang over it, smooth its little limbs, and love it with the dearest love

Catherine (Kate) Dickens, drawn by Daniel Maclise shortly after her marriage to Dickens (Dickens Fellowship).

that God has given to mortal creatures. And he screams to the Chimes to save her, and she is saved. And the moral of it all is, that he, the simple half-starved ticket-porter, has his portion in the New-Year no less than any other man; that the poor require infinite beating out of shape before their human shape is gone; that, even in their frantic wickedness, there may be good in their hearts triumphantly asserting itself, though all the Aldermen alive say No; and that the truth of the feeling to be held towards them, is Trustfulness, not Doubt, nor Putting them Down, nor Filing them Away. 'I know,' cries the old man in an inspiration the Bells convey to him, 'that our inheritance is held in store for us by Time. I know there is a Sea of Time to rise one day, before which all who wrong us or oppress us will be swept away like leaves. I see it, on the flow!'

And as the imaginative reader fancies he sees it too; as he listens for the rush that shall sweep down quacks and pretenders, Cutes, Filers, and Bowleys; peradventure, as his lively fancy may even see old Toby clambering safely to the rock that shall protect him from the sweeping wave, and may watch him still hearkening to his friends the Bells, as, fading from his sight, they peal out final music on the waters . . . . Toby wakes up over his own fire. He finds the newspaper lying at his foot; sees Meg sitting at a table opposite, making up the ribands for her wedding the morrow; and hears the bells, in a noble peal, ringing the old year out and the new year in. And as he rushes to kiss Meg, Richard dashes in to get the first new-year's kiss before him—and gets it; and every body is happy; and neighbours press in with good wishes; and there is a small

band among them, Toby being acquainted with a drum in private, which strikes up gaily; and the sudden change, and the ringing of the Bells, and the lively music, so transport Toby, that he is, when last seen, leading off a country-dance in an entirely new step, consisting of that old familiar Trot in which he transacts the business of his calling.

May this wise little tale second the hearty wishes of its writer, and at the least contribute to the coming year that portion of happiness which waits always upon just intentions and kind thoughts.

Edward Wagenknecht   (essay date 1931)

SOURCE: "Dickens at Work: *The Chimes,*" in *Dickens and the Scandalmongers: Essays in Criticism,* University of Oklahoma Press, 1965, pp. 50-70.

[*Wagenknecht is an American biographer and critic. His works include critical surveys of the English and American novel and studies of Charles Dickens, Mark Twain, and Henry James, among many others. In the following excerpt, which was originally published in the 1931 edition of* The Chimes, *Wagenknecht asserts that this story is an important source for understanding Dickens's art and spirit.*]

The enormous vogue of **A Christmas Carol** has probably served, in a measure at least, to draw the attention of at least the casual reader away from the fact that Dickens wrote four other Christmas books on a similar plan. I do not claim that **The Chimes** is worthy to stand beside the incomparable **Carol.** I do not even think it attains the stature of **The Cricket on the Hearth.** But it does happen to afford an unusually interesting test case for the contemplation of Dickens as both artist and prophet: first, because we know more about the circumstances of its genesis and growth than we do of many of his works; and, second, because its social and moral teaching is not only daring but interestingly anticipative of some more recent attitudes.

The Chimes was written in Genoa in 1844. This time Dickens began not with a story or a situation, but with an idea, a character, and a purpose. Just as, in writing *A Child's History of England,* he found it impossible to write about the past without importing all the problems and prejudices of the present into it, so now, during his Italian journey, he found it impossible, as he gazed upon foreign scenes, to withdraw his mind from a constant preoccupation with the problems of the London poor. "Ah!" he cried to Forster upon his return, describing the glories of Venice, "When I saw those places, how I thought that to leave one's hand upon the time, lastingly upon the time, with one tender touch for the mass of toiling people that nothing could obliterate, would be to lift oneself above the dust of all the Doges in their graves, and stand upon a giant's staircase that Sampson [*sic!*] couldn't overthrow!" The purpose, then, here as in the **Carol,** was to strike a blow for the poor, and never was Dickens more passionately sincere, never did he give stronger evidence of his astonishing capacity for complete surrender to the emotional appeal of the creatures of his own fancy than when he was writing this book.

The method of **The Chimes** differs widely, however, from

that which he had used in the *Carol.* Here the protagonist, Scrooge, was an enemy of the poor, a man himself in comfortable circumstances, and the story, detailing his conversion, became in effect an appeal to the prosperous people of England, begging them to extend help and sympathy to those less fortunate than themselves. Implicitly, to be sure, this appeal inheres also in *The Chimes.* Indeed, at the very end it becomes explicit, in the author's direct appeal to the "listener," to "try to bear in mind the stern realities from which these shadows come; and in your sphere—none is too wide, and none too limited for such an end—endeavour to correct, improve, and soften them." But this is secondary. The principal character in *The Chimes* is the poverty-stricken ticket-porter, Toby Veck. He represents the poor themselves, not their oppressors, and it is as a symbol of the poor that he seems to Dickens to stand in need of conversion. Essentially the problem of *The Chimes* is a problem of faith—the individual's faith in himself and his ability to adjust to his world. Whatever else happens, Dickens seems to be saying, the poor must on no account be allowed to stop believing in themselves. Beauty and faithfulness and love are not incompatible with poverty; glee and merriment may even, on occasion, join hands with it. But once destroy the poor man's faith in himself and in the goodness of life, and there will be nothing left. Drunkenness, prostitution, arson, suicide, murder—all these must follow as the night the day.

In order to show that I have not misread his purpose, and to provide a basis for what is to follow, I must transcribe the following long sketch of how Dickens originally planned to develop *The Chimes.* It was sent, in a letter to his friend and future biographer John Forster, along with the First Quarter of the tale, in October, 1844:

> The general notion is this. That what happens to poor Trotty [nickname for Toby] in the first part, and what will happen to him in the second (when he takes the letter to a punctual and a great man of business, who is balancing his books and making up his accounts, and complacently expatiating on the necessity of clearing off every liability and obligation, and turning over a new leaf and starting fresh with the new year), so dispirits him, who can't do this, that he comes to the conclusion that his class and order have no business with a new year, and really are "intruding." And though he will pluck up for an hour or so, at the christening (I think) of a neighbour's child, that evening: still, when he goes home, Mr. Filer's precepts will come into his mind, and he will say to himself, "we are a long way past the proper average of children, and it has no business to be born": and will be wretched again. And going home, and sitting there alone, he will take that newspaper out of his pocket, and reading of the crimes and offences of the poor, especially of those whom Alderman Cute is going to put down, will be quite confirmed in his misgiving that they are bad; irredeemably bad. In this state of mind, he will fancy that the Chimes are calling to him; and saying to himself "God help me! Let me go up to 'em. I feel as if I were going to die in despair—of a broken heart; let me die among the bells that have been a comfort to me!"—will grope his way

up into the tower; and fall down in a kind of swoon among them. Then the third quarter, in other words the beginning of the second half of the book, will open with the Goblin part of the thing: the bells ringing, and innumerable spirits (the sound or vibration of them) flitting and tearing in and out of the church-steeple, and bearing all sorts of missions and commissions and reminders and reproaches, and comfortable recollections and what not, to all sorts of people and places. Some bearing scourges; and others flowers, and birds, and music; and others pleasant faces in mirrors, and others ugly ones; the bells haunting people in the night (especially the last of the old year) according to their deeds. And the bells themselves, who have a goblin likeness to humanity in the midst of their proper shapes, and who shine in a light of their own, will say (the Great Bell being the chief spokesman): "Who is he that being of the poor doubts the right of poor men to the inheritance which Time reserves for them, and echoes an unmeaning cry against his fellows?" Toby, all aghast, will tell him it is he, and why it is. Then the spirits of the bells will bear him through the air to various scenes, charged with this trust: That they show him how the poor and wretched, at the worst—yes, even in the crimes that aldermen put down, and he has thought so horrible—have some deformed and hunchbacked goodness clinging to them; and how they have their right and share in Time. Following out the history of Meg, the Bells will show her, that marriage broken off and all friends dead, with an infant child; reduced so low, and made so miserable, as to be brought at last to wander out at night. And in Toby's sight, her father's, she will resolve to drown herself and the child together. But before she goes down to the water, Toby will see how she covers it with a part of her own wretched dress, and adjusts its rags so as to make it pretty in its sleep, and hangs over it, and smooths its little limbs, and loves it with the dearest love that God ever gave to mortal creatures; and when she runs down to the water, Toby will cry "Oh spare her! Chimes, have mercy on her! Stop her!"—and the bells will say, "Why stop her? She is bad at heart—let the bad die." And Toby on his knees will beg and pray for mercy: and in the end the bells will stop her, by their voices, just in time. Toby will see, too, what great things the punctual man has left undone on the close of the old year, and what accounts he has left unsettled: punctual as he is. And he will see a great many things about Richard, once so near being his son-in-law, and about a great many people. And the moral of it all will be, that he has his portion in the new year no less than any other man, and that the poor require a deal of beating out of shape before their human shape is gone; that even in their frantic wickedness, there may be good in their hearts triumphantly asserting itself, though all the aldermen alive say "No," as he has learnt from the agony of his own child; and that the truth is Trustfulness in them, not doubt, nor putting down, nor filing them away. And when at last a great sea rises, and this sea of Time comes sweeping down, bearing the alderman and such mudworms of the earth away to nothing, dashing them to fragments in its fury—Toby will climb a rock and hear the bells (now faded from his sight) pealing out upon the waters. And as he hears them, and looks round for help, he will wake up and find himself with the newspaper lying at his foot; and Meg sitting opposite to him at the table, and making up the ribbons for her wedding to-morrow; and the window open, that the sound of the bells ringing the old year out and the new year in may enter. They will just have broken out, joyfully; and Richard will dash in to kiss Meg before Toby, and have the first kiss of the new year (he'll get it too); and the neighbours will crowd round with good wishes; and a band will strike up gaily (Toby knows a Drum in private); and the altered circumstances, and the ringing of the bells, and the jolly music, will so transport the old fellow that he will lead off a country dance forthwith in an entirely new step, consisting of his old familiar trot. Then quoth the inimitable [Dickens's whimsical name for himself]—Was it a dream of Toby's after all? Or is Toby but a dream? and Meg a dream? and all a dream! In reference to which, and the realities of which dreams are born, the inimitable will be wiser than he can be now, writing for dear life, with the post just going, and the brave C. booted. . . . Ah how I hate myself, my dear fellow, for this lame and halting outline of the Vision I have in mind. But it must go to you. . . . You will say what is best for the frontispiece.

Forster himself pointed out some of the principal differences between this first sketch and the story as it was written: "Fern the farm-labourer is not here, nor yet his niece the little Lilian (at first called Jessie), who is to give the tale its most tragical scene; and there are intimations of poetic fancy at the close of my sketch which the published story fell short of." Other differences remain to be noted. For example, the story as it now stands leaves no place for the christening of the neighbor's child which was first intended to occupy Toby's New Year's Eve; and the contemplated exposure of Sir Joseph Bowley has been omitted altogether. But the most striking and important change is that in the published version the Chimes do *not* intervene to save Meg from infanticide and self-destruction.

For all these changes the Ferns are directly responsible. When Toby unexpectedly took them into his house, it immediately became impossible for him to spend the evening with his neighbors. Dickens seems to have stumbled across them in the dark quite as suddenly as Toby himself did, and when they entered the story, they brought tragedy with them. The writer's mood seems now to have changed; he became more and more earnest, more and more relentless. He did not abandon his plan for the conversion of Toby, but in his most serious moments, he found himself thinking, more and more, of others. "You comfortable ones," one can almost hear him say, "you who regard the outcasts of the world as outcasts by choice, inferior creatures, evil to the heart's core. I will show you a child, an innocent, lovable child who will awaken all your sympathies. Then, virtually without preparation, I will plunge her, almost simultaneously, into girlhood and vice, and you who have loved her will not dare, as you read my pages, tell me that you would have done better in her

place." And if Lilian were to be destroyed, why not Meg also? He would employ no last-minute rescue, no jot of supernatural melodrama: he would let them go—Meg and her child—they must die. Those readers of his who had shuddered with horror over newspaper stories of women killing their children: for once he would show them why women kill their children. He would show a Dickens heroine doing it, not because she was bad but because she was good, because she wanted to save her child from something worse than death. And Richard? Richard should not be a good and happy husband. Instead he should become a disillusioned drunkard and a criminal. For once Dickens would eschew romance: he would study relentlessly the forces that doom the poor to the destruction of their bodies and their souls. Why not?—since the moral could be made all the more powerful that way. And so, calamity having thus been piled upon calamity, the contemplated return to the earlier mood of the story and the reintroduction of Sir Joseph Bowley were seen to be impossible, and the apocalyptic splendors originally planned for were dropped as unnecessary and ineffective.

I have not forgotten that it is Dickens whose mood I am here attempting to reconstruct, and I am not unaware that all this seems—for him—somewhat bitter. But not any more bitter, I believe, than the story itself, and we have his own explicit testimony that his experience in writing it was very unusual.

> This book . . . has made may face white in a foreign land. My cheeks, which were beginning to fill out, have sunk again; my eyes have grown immensely large; my hair is very lank; and the head inside the hair is hot and giddy. Read the scene at the end of the third part, twice. I wouldn't write it twice for something. . . . Since I conceived, at the beginning of the second part, what must happen in the third, I have undergone as much sorrow and agitation as if the thing were real; and have wakened up with it at night. I was obliged to lock myself in when I finished it yesterday, for my face was swollen for the time to twice its proper size, and was hugely ridiculous.

Again:

> Third of November, 1844. Half-past two, afternoon. Thank God! I have finished *The Chimes,* This moment. I take up my pen again to-day, to say only that much; and to add that I have had what women call "a real good cry!"

Concerning Forster's own suggestions toward the improvement of the tale, while it was yet in the manuscript stage, the biographer has, as usual, told us little, though what details he does give are in this instance rather clearer and more definite than usual. "The red-faced gentleman with the blue coat" who appears in the First Quarter with Alderman Cute and Mr. Filer, we owe indirectly to Forster: he replaces a "Young England gentleman" to whom the biographer objected. It seems clear also that Forster softened Mr. Filer on the ground that, as Dickens had originally drawn him, he would offend the political economists, which, for that matter, he did, even as he now stands. "File away at Filer, as you please; but bear in mind that the *Westminster Review* considered Scrooge's presentation of the turkey to Bob Cratchit as grossly incompatible with political economy."

In the Preface to the "First Cheap Edition" of his *Christmas Books,* Dickens explained of all of them that "the narrow space within which it was necessary to confine these Christmas Stories when they were originally published, rendered their construction a matter of some difficulty, and almost necessitated what is peculiar in their machinery. I never attempted great elaboration of detail in the working out of character within such limits, believing that it could not succeed." The effect on characterization here alluded to will be considered later. Here let us glance at the effect on construction. As we have already seen, the end of *The Chimes* was not in sight from the beginning, but it did appear at a comparatively early stage. By the beginning of the Second Quarter the general outline was fixed and the space to be devoted to each portion at least roughly determined. The advantage of this careful planning may be judged by its results: *The Chimes* is, in every way, an admirably constructed story.

Especially skillful is the way the story opens. The First Quarter begins with an introductory paragraph in which, after earnestly declaring that "a story-teller and a story-reader should establish a mutual understanding as soon as possible," Dickens runs off into his usual burlesque style, and issues a mock-challenge to his readers, offering to meet all doubters, individually if need be, and thus demonstrate the unquestionable truth of his initial statement that "there are not many people . . . who would care to sleep in a church." There follows, in the second paragraph, the famous personified description of the Night Wind, always likely to be the most fearsome and awe-inspiring element in the experience of anyone who should attempt such a rash experiment. The third paragraph takes reader and Night Wind together "high up in the steeple," inevitably the most ghostly part of the church. Now that we are in the steeple, we are ready, of course, for the introduction of the Chimes themselves, the description of which occupies the fourth and fifth paragraphs. And then the principal character, Toby Veck, enters the story also, quite casually and incidentally.

In paragraphs six to eleven Toby is described—his character, his occupation, his station in life. Then, in paragraph twelve, Toby and the Chimes are clearly connected. First we are told about the old man's love for the bells; then the author goes into a fanciful elucidation of the "points of resemblance between themselves and him." In the thirteenth paragraph there is more about Toby's love for the Chimes, and of how "he invested them with a strange and solemn character." Nevertheless, he "scouted with indignation a certain flying rumor that the Chimes were haunted." Hereupon the introduction ends; Meg enters with Toby's dinner; the dramatic method is now employed; and the story proper may be said to have begun.

Now what has been accomplished so far? More, I think, than may as yet be apparent. The tone of the story has been determined and its principal character introduced and described. The very first statement of all—idle as it seems and whimsically as it is maintained ("There are not

many people . . . who would care to sleep in a church")—has a certain suggestiveness in the way of foreshadowing, while the later insinuation of a "certain flying rumor that the Chimes were haunted" still further suggests the supernatural character of the tale. The air of weirdness may thus be said to predominate, but there are undertones which are quite as important. Thus, at the close of the second paragraph, we find this: "Ugh! Heaven preserve us, sitting round the fire!"—the appeal to the homing instinct and domestic comfort, always so characteristic of Dickens, the skillful suggestion that domestic comfort is to be an important part of the tale. A little later, the sympathetic quality of the Chimes is even more carefully suggested: they are "bent upon being heard on stormy nights, by some poor mother watching a sick child, or some lone wife whose husband was at sea." Then, the casual introduction of Toby Veck, as a kind of afterthought to the description of the Chimes themselves, suggests the curious way in which his life is to be bound up with them. Finally, this connection is made all the more inescapable by means of the comparison between Toby and the Chimes which has already been referred to.

It is not necessary to go through the entire story in such detail. But the element of careful preparation and foreshadowing is everywhere apparent. The first two quarters prepare carefully for the last two: all the elements which enter into Toby's waking life are given forth again, in new and hideous combinations, in his dream. Thus the dream is consistently presented to us *from Toby's own point of view.*

When he first appears before us, Toby is already a man whose faith in himself, in his class, and in life itself has been somewhat disturbed. There follows in quick succession a series of experiences all calculated to increase his doubts: Mr. Filer's demonstration that Toby himself is unpardonably past the average age, and that when he eats tripe he is stealing his food out of the mouths of widows and orphans; Alderman Cute's denunciation of Meg's desire to wed; Sir Joseph Bowley's horror that, unlike himself, Toby is not entering the New Year with a clean slate; finally, the hideous newspaper account of the poverty-stricken mother who has slain herself and her child. No one of these details is included idly. Each contributes to Toby's mood; each is to be used in working out the final resolution of the tale.

In the vision itself there are other careful bits of foreshadowing. Especially noteworthy for its delicate handling of a gross subject is the scene between Meg and Lilian in the Third Quarter, where we get the first hint that Lilian is to become a prostitute. Equally effective is Toby's repeated wondering, as he searches the throngs of his vision, concerning the whereabouts of Richard. In this way suspense is developed, and Richard's first appearance, dissipated and broken by hardship and disappointment, is made all the more impressive. The Chickenstalker episode, at the beginning of the Fourth Quarter, serves as legitimate comic relief, but it does more than that. It has a vital connection with the story, and the conversation between Mrs. Chickenstalker and Toby includes a careful summary of the various influences that have conspired to wreck Meg and Richard. Best of all is the use made of Meg's love for her child. " 'Thank God!' cried Trotty, holding up his folded hands. 'O God be thanked! She loves the child!' " But soon comes the warning voice: " 'Follow her!' was sounded through the house. 'Learn it from the creature dearest to your heart!' "

It would be interesting to know what were the original contents of the note which Toby carries to Sir Joseph Bowley. By the time this message is delivered, in the Second Quarter, Dickens has, as we have seen, made up his mind concerning the roles which Lilian and her uncle are to play in the working out of his story. But at the time the note is sent, this idea has not yet been developed. It is nevertheless entirely possible that the note may have been conceived originally just as it now stands—an expression of Alderman Cute's stern determination to put Will Fern down. Originally, we may suppose, the incident was intended simply to illustrate the characters of Cute and Bowley, and this before the idea had come to Dickens of introducing Will Ferm into the story as anything more than a name. As the thing stands, it does illustrate perfectly both the obsequiousness of Cute and the impotent grandiloquence of Bowley; what other purpose could any other note, in this contingency, have served? It is probable, then, that when the idea of Lilian came to Dickens, he picked up this thread, and made the incident, originally a very minor one, a bit of preparation for more important matters.

> The most startling thing about *The Chimes,* is that here, in 1844, we find Dickens asserting without compromise that prostitution, drunkenness, murder, arson, and revolution come into the world simply because, as our social order is constituted, some of its members never do get a fair chance for their share of the decencies of life.
>
> —*Edward Wagenknecht*

Dickens's own opinion with regard to characterization in his *Christmas Books* has already been cited. In *The Chimes,* Toby alone is anything more than the suggestion of a character. There is no character development even in Toby. but there is progressive revelation of character, and this extends clear through the first half of the tale. Here it is dropped, and our attention is centered upon the vision. Toby is individualized through description, soliloquy, and dramatic scene. The crowning revelation of his character comes in the Second Quarter, when he offers shelter to Lilian and Will Fern.

The other serious characters can hardly be said to be characterized at all. Lilian must have been real in Dickens's imagination, or he could not have been so moved as he was by her fall, but he can hardly be said to have communicat-

ed a sense of her reality to the reader. For this reason, the scene at the end of the Third Quarter seems to me artistically ineffective, though its social implications are suggestive indeed. Alderman Cute, Mr. Filer, and Sir Joseph Bowley—though we catch hardly more than a glimpse of each—are far more vivid, much more real than Lilian, Meg, or Richard. Next to Toby himself, Sir Joseph is certainly the best character. His passion for entering the new year with all the obligations of the old behind him is a convenient "tag" of the kind Dickens could always use skillfully, but better still is his highly characteristic speech—his curious hesitancy, his hovering on the edge of pious generalities only to lapse immediately again into the mundane.

So much for the art of *The Chimes;* what now of its spirit? First of all, it has a definite affinity with the teachings of Carlyle. After finishing the story in Genoa, Dickens made a special trip to England to read it to a group of friends. "Shall I confess to you," he writes to Forster, "that I particularly want Carlyle above all to see it before the rest of the world?" The tale has often been criticized on the ground of Dickens's alleged ignorance of the real causes of social misery. . . .

The most startling thing about *The Chimes,* however, is that here, in 1844, we find Dickens asserting without compromise that prostitution, drunkenness, murder, arson, and revolution come into the world, not because prostitutes, drunkards, revolutionists, and their kind are by nature viler than other human beings, and not because they love darkness better than light, but simply because, as our social order is constituted, some of its members never do get a fair chance for their share of the decencies of life. I do not pretend that Dickens would defend all his criminals thus; certainly no such plea could cover Fagin or Bill Sikes. But this is unmistakably his teaching in *The Chimes.* Lilian becomes a prostitute because her soul is crushed by unrewarded toil; Richard, frightened away from marriage and domestic happiness by his poverty, sinks lower and lower into drunkenness and sloth until at last he revenges himself upon society as a revolutionary firebrand; Meg slays her child to obviate the possibility that she may live to follow in Lilian's footsteps. And in every case, says Dickens, it is society, not these poor outcasts, that is to blame.

It must have been startling beyond belief in 1844, so startling that probably not many readers grasped all its implications. If they had, the matter could hardly have been permitted to pass off so quietly. For, on a broader scale, Dickens here lays down precisely the same principle which Bernard Shaw was to enunciate with reference to prostitution at the close of the century. Listen to Shaw's defense of *Mrs. Warren's Profession:*

> The play is, simply, a study in prostitution, and its aim is to show that prostitution is not the prostitute's fault, but the fault of a society which pays for a poor and pretty woman's prostitution in solid gold, and pays for her honesty with starvation, drudgery, and pious twaddle.

It is surely not necessary to enlarge here on the consternation with which *Mrs. Warren's Profession* was greeted well into the twentieth century. In some cases, the anxiety went to the length of expressing itself in police prosecution. William Winter, dean of American drama critics, saw in this play and others like it the overthrow of whatever was pure, lovely, and of good report in the theater.

The case of Richard has a definite bearing also on the much-mooted matter of Dickens's sentimentalism. In Toby's dream, Meg and Richard do finally marry, but they marry too late. As Mrs. Chickenstalker explains it to Toby: "He went on better for a short time; but his habits were too old and strong to be got rid of; he soon fell back a little; and was falling fast back, when his illness came so strong upon him." And even as she speaks, the word comes that Richard has passed away.

Now if there is anything characteristic of the sentimentalist, it is the belief that good resolutions can effect anything. It is notable, and it should be considered in the discussion of Dickens, that in this case good resolutions accomplish precisely nothing. As irrevocably as any determinist today, Dickens says: It is too late. The die is cast. Richard must perish.

But there is still another aspect of the story which we have not yet considered, and whose consideration may bring us closer to anything that has been said thus far to the secret of Dickens's art. It must be remembered that all the terrible things of which I have spoken take place in a dream. When Toby wakes up, it is to learn that Meg is going ahead with her wedding plans in spite of Alderman Cute, and the story ends in general festivity and merry-making. The enemy of Dickens points triumphantly to this circumstance as an example of the novelist's shallowness and cowardice. When he did face the realities of life, it was only in a dream! Dreams are realities in his world, and realities have become dreams. We close in a stifling atmosphere of bourgeois respectability. But let us see.

It must be admitted that out-and-out realism was not the fashion in Dickens's day, and great writers, as well as small ones, are conditioned by literary fashion. This is nowhere more evident than among those who object to Dickens's alleged optimism: they are simply following the pessimistic, naturalistic trend of *their* day! If they would really be independent and original, let them turn to romance. It would be far more audacious, in this year of grace, to write like Dickens (if they could!) than to write like Gorky. But a dream within a dream can hardly be considered, in any appreciable degree, more unreal than the dream itself. The whole story of *The Chimes* exists in the imagination: that which Toby dreams is quite as vividly presented as that which actually happens to him, and he who pretends that it would take a very brave man to present these things as having actually happened while any coward might present them as dreams, has surely forgotten that he is dealing, not with life, but with a work of fiction. Finally, it may be urged, the exigencies of his plan and purpose compelled Dickens to use the method he chose. The theme of the story was the restoration of Toby's faith in himself and his class. Following as it did in the wake of *A Christmas Carol,* supernatural machinery was absolutely necessary. Toby, like Scrooge, sees in a

dream the dark road whither he is tending: he wakens with relief and turns his feet in another direction.

Dickens may very well have believed that something like that actually could be effected in human experience. He was no wide-eyed innocent during his later years, and the atmosphere of some of the last novels is pretty somber. But he never became a futilitarian, and though he may have felt at times that he had lost the way, he always knew that there was a way. It is here, I think, that we touch the prime difference between Dickens and many contemporary writers. He saw evil quite as clearly as they do, and he was quite as courageous, but, unlike many of them, he had retained faith. And by this I do not mean faith in God merely (though that is involved in it) but faith in humanity and in the world's destiny. Consequently, where they deal in fears and despairs, he deals in hopes and promises. Consequently (though I assert no parity with Dante), his work is a great comedy, not a great tragedy.

G. K. Chesterton [in *Charles Dickens,* 1956] had much to say on this point in connection with his inquiry as to why it was that "this too easily contented Dickens, this man with cushions at his back and (it sometimes seems) cotton wool in his ears, this happy dreamer, this vulgar optimist . . . alone among modern writers did really destroy some of the wrongs he hated and bring about some of the reforms he desired." And he went on to answer his own question in words that are beautifully illustrated in *The Chimes:*

> And the reason of this is one that goes deep into Dickens's social reform, and, like every other real and desirable thing, involves a kind of mystical contradiction. If we are to save the oppressed, we must have two apparently antagonistic emotions in us at the same time. We must think the oppressed man immensely miserable, and, at the same time, intensely attractive and important. We must insist with violence upon his degradation; we must insist with the same violence upon his dignity. For if we relax by one inch the one assertion, men will say he does not need saving. And if we relax by one inch the other assertion, men will say he is not worth saving. . . .
>
> Out of this perennial contradiction arises the fact that there are always two types of the reformer. The first we may call for convenience the pessimistic, the second the optimistic reformer. One dwells upon the fact that souls are being lost; the other dwells upon the fact that they are worth saving. . . . The first describes how bad men are under bad conditions. The second describes how good men are under bad conditions.

There is much more to the same effect that I have not space to quote. Now turn, for illustration of the other method, to the suggestive analysis of Van Wyck Brooks (in *Emerson and Others* [1927]) of the reasons for what he considers Upton Sinclair's failure as a social reformer through fiction:

> But suppose now, that one wishes to see the dispossessed rise in their might and really, in the name of justice, take possession of the world.

Suppose one wishes to see the class-system abolished, along with all the other unhappy things that Mr. Sinclair writes about. This is Mr. Sinclair's own desire; and he honestly believes that in writing as he does he contributes to this happy consummation. I cannot agree with him. In so far as Mr. Sinclair's books show anything real they show us the utter helplessness, the benightedness, the naïveté of the American workers' movement. Jimmie Higgins does not exist as a character. He is a symbol, however, and one can read reality into him. He is the American worker incarnate. Well, was there ever a worker so little the master of his fate? That, in point of fact, is just the conclusion Mr. Sinclair wishes us to draw. But why is he so helpless? Because, for all his kindness and his courage, he is, from an intellectual and social point of view, unlike the English worker, the German, Italian, Russian, the merest infant; he knows nothing about life or human nature or economics or philosophy or even his enemies. How can he possibly set about advancing his own cause, how can he circumvent the wily patrioteers, how can he become anything but what he is, the mere football of everyone who knows more than he? Let us drop the "cultivated-class" standpoint and judge Mr. Sinclair's novels from the standpoint of the proletariat itself. They arouse the emotion of self-pity. Does that stimulate the worker or does it merely "console" him? They arouse the emotion of hatred. Does that teach him how to grapple with his oppressors or does it place him all the more at his oppressors' mercy? The most elementary knowledge of human nature tells us that there is only one answer to these questions.

With the justice or injustice of Brooks's evaluation of Upton Sinclair, I am not here concerned. The interesting thing is his substantial agreement with Chesterton that the pessimistic reformer is ineffective. Perhaps, after all, it was not mere cowardice and love of middle-class creature comfort that led Dickens to use humor and optimism in his pictures of the poor.

I began this study of *The Chimes* with the statement that it afforded a test case for the study of Dickens. The nineteenth century is not yet very far from us in point of time; it would not seem that any great feat of orientation must be performed in order to understand it. Yet if, as the advocates of the millennium assure us, we now move more rapidly in fifty years than we used to travel through the course of centuries, then it may well be necessary, now and then, to check up on our prepossessions to avoid the danger of judging nineteenth-century writers by their standards rather than our own. Many of the unfavorable judgments of Dickens that were in vogue some years ago, when he was less in fashion than he is at present, were, it seems to me, determined by failure to observe this caution, though I should hesitate to say that when we differ from him, the reason must be that we are right while he is wrong. Perhaps the most penetrating of all Chesterton's wise observations was that our time is a time, not the Day of Judgment.

Ganz on Dickens's underused talent as a humorist:

One cannot help thinking that Dickens never fully appreciated what *Sketches by Boz* revealed about the nature and extent of his talents; he indirectly minimized the originality of his humor by hankering to be a masterful weaver of plots, a moralist, and a serious critic of social conditions. Although such preoccupations are already perceptible in his earliest work, it is only in the later novels that we can gauge the extent to which they vitiate his humor. Surely the greater psychological complexity of these last works and the symbolic impact of their imagery but imperfectly atones for the decline of Dickens' most spontaneous gift, the humorist's alchemical power of transfiguring reality through the projection of his vision, the capacity to make us accept the vulnerabilities and uncertainties of the human condition in general and man's moral weaknesses in particular by provoking our own sympathy, imagination, and sense of incongruity in response to his own exercise of them. By liberating us momentarily from the restrictions of order and reason, by promoting that reconciliation between contrasting impulses, yearnings, viewpoints, even social positions which makes genuine love and tolerance possible, and finally by allowing us to perceive moral failings as often more absurd than harmful, indeed as tokens rather than denials of humanity, Dickens the humorist par excellence permits us, as *Sketches by Boz* clearly demonstrate, to achieve that momentary triumph over our limited human destinies which is the psychological equivalent of immortality.

Margaret Ganz, in "Humor's Alchemy: The Lesson of Sketches by Boz," *in* Genre, *1968.*

The Dickensian   (essay date 1935)

SOURCE: "The Reception of Dickens's First Book," in *The Dickensian,* Vol. XXXII, No. 237, December, 1935, pp. 43-50.

[*In the following essay, the critic presents extracts of original reviews of* Sketches by Boz.]

The Centenary of *Pickwick* is likely to overshadow another very important centenary in the life of Dickens, and we must not lose sight of the fact that Dickens's first book was published only about two months before the immortal *Pickwick* made his first bow to the public.

Sketches by Boz in two volumes at one guinea was published on or about 8th February, 1836; as we all know, it was a collection of short stories and sketches which had previously appeared in various publications. The publisher was John Macrone, and Dickens's correspondence with him was first published in *The Dickensian* in 1934. These letters threw many a side-light on the struggling young journalist, and showed the assistance given him by the editor of the *Morning Chronicle* in singing the praises of the new author.

Sketches by Boz was well advertised in the principal literary weeklies, of which there appear to have been quite as large a number then, as there are to-day.

The *Morning Chronicle* notice, the work of George Hogarth, Dickens's father-in-law-to-be, was as follows:

> We need hardly tell our readers that "BOZ" is a *nom de querre* assumed by a satirical essayist, whose lucubrations, during the past twelve months, have frequently appeared in our pages. The two volumes before us consist partly of a selection from the papers which this writer has contributed to various periodicals, and partly of matter hitherto unpublished; and he has been induced to publish the work (he says in his preface) by "the favourable reception which several of these Sketches met with on their original appearance." The new matter forms a considerable portion of the volumes, and includes some of the most remarkable and striking of the author's productions.
>
> These "Sketches" are evidently the work of a person of various and extraordinary intellectual gifts. He is a close and acute observer of character and manners, with a strong sense of the ridiculous and a graphic faculty of placing in the most whimsical and amusing lights the follies and absurdities of human nature. He has the power, too, of producing tears as well as laughter. His pictures of the vices and wretchedness which abound in this vast city are sufficient to strike to the heart of the most careless and insensible reader.
>
> His disposition, however, evidently leads him to look on the bright and sunny side of things; and a kindly and benevolent spirit tempers the severity of his ridicule of folly, and softens the gloom of his descriptions of vice. The same turn of mind makes him dwell with heartfelt satisfaction upon the pleasures, comforts, and innocent recreations of the middle classes of society, especially in London; witness his **"Christmas Dinner"** a charming paper, which might have been written by Washington Irving in one of his happiest hours.
>
> Our author possesses, too, a rich and fertile imagination.
>
> Many of these Sketches are in the form of tales, some of which are of considerable length. These tales are in general very interesting and entertaining; and several of them are so ingenious in their plot, so full of *ris comica*, and told in so dramatic a manner, that they want little more than a division into scenes to become excellent theatrical pieces. To one of them **"The Bloomsbury Christening,"** Mr. Buckstone is indebted for his very popular piece of "The Christening," and the admirable tales, **"The Great Winglebury Duel," "The Boarding House," "Horatio Sparkins,"** and the **"Passage in the life of Mr. Watkins Tottle,"** are equally rich in dramatic materials.
>
> The most remarkable paper in the book is that entitled **"A Visit to Newgate."** It contains a minute, and we believe, a very accurate description of this dismal abode, and of its guilty and miser-

able inmates. It is written throughout in a tone of high moral feeling, and with great eloquence, and must leave a deep and lasting impression on the mind of every reader. The concluding picture of a condemned criminal passing his last night on earth in his solitary cell is drawn with terrible power.

> The idea is similar to that of Victor Hugo, in his *"Dernier jour d'un condamne"* but there is a certain and artificial and exaggerated air—a sort of French *tournure*—in Victor Hugo's description, from which that of our countryman is free; and being equally eloquent and more simple, it is even more pathetic and impressive than the celebrated passage to which it may be compared.
>
> The book is richly illustrated by the modern Hogarth, George Cruikshank, who has evidently laboured *con amore,* and has equalled—indeed we may say surpassed—any of his previous efforts. The illustrations (of which there are a considerable number in each volume) are beautiful and highly finished etchings, admirable as pieces of art, and full of the truth, nature, grotesque humour, and irresistible drollery, which distinguish this unrivalled artist. Nothing can excel the ability with which he has embodied the conceptions of his coadjutor, and placed before the very eyes of the reader, the scenes and characters which "Boz" has presented to his imagination.

The earliest independent notice was that given in *The Literary Gazette* for 13th February where it had a prominent display:

> "The scenes of many coloured life he drew" may be fairly applied to the present essayist who displays not only humour and feeling, but a genuine acquaintance with his subjects in these numerous sketches of common life. The author has traced his characters, their occupations, their pursuits, and their pleasures with much talent and apparent fidelity; and those who wish to have a peep into pawnbrokers' shops, dancing academies, private theatres, ginshops, marine-stores, marine excursions, and similar resorts and occupations of the middling and lower orders, will find them cleverly and amazingly described in these pages. We would quote a specimen, but believe they are almost all already familiar to the readers of periodicals, being now only collected and improved in effect by the concordant pencil of George Cruikshank.

The Satirist which made a specialty of literary reviews gave the following notice during the same week, and Dickens must have felt proud indeed at so kind a reception:

> We have seldom read two more agreeable volumes than these. We have before had a laugh over some of the well-drawn sketches they contain, and which are in their way inimitable. The author is a man of unquestionable talent and of great and correct observation. George Cruikshank has ably executed his portion of the work, and entered fully into the spirit as well as the feeling of the writer.

In *The Sun* the book was advertised on the 15th February

and reviewed the same day at the top of a column in centre page, as follows:

> The majority of these "Sketches" have already appeared in the columns of an evening contemporary, and some few of them in the *Monthly, Magazine*; and as they were uniformly well received, the author has very properly consented to their republication. They evince great powers of observation, and fidelity of description combined with a humour, which though pushed occasionally to the very verge of caricature, is on the whole full of promise. But their principal merit is their matter of factness, and the strict literal way in which they adhere to nature. The characters are not idealities, but have all the "mark and likeliehood"—especially the admirable one of Long Dumps, the splenetic old bachelor—of set portraits. Two more amusing volumes in their way have not appeared this season, and we have little or no doubt that they will grow rapidly into favour with country readers, who must naturally feel a curiosity to read about the oddities which are to be met with, in such abundance, among the middle and lower classes of metropolitan society. The work is illustrated by George Cruikshank in his best manner. We subjoin a pleasing extract from an article entitled **"Hackney Coach Stands"** . . . .

The week following *The Athenæum* noticed the book in the following terms:

> Many of the papers in this collection have appeared before. They are well characterised by the writer, as illustrative of every-day life and every-day people. There are scenes and characters sketched with admirable truth; but a suspicion crossed our minds during the perusal, whether the subjects were always worthy of the artistic skill and power of the writer; some of the papers, however, are excellent.

An understanding review, certainly, yet the writer was not quite sure if the subject was sufficiently refined for the gifts of the writer; similar expressions will be found in some of the other notices which follow. The critics were not as yet accustomed to writers who could pen interesting sketches of "every-day life and every-day people."

The same week saw two other favourable notices in important weekly papers. The first here given is from *The Court Journal* of 20th February, 1836, where, first of all, Cruikshank takes all the honours.

> It is a bold thing to say, but we more than suspect that these illustrations comprise some of the very best things that Cruikshank ever executed; and we half suspect that they are, taken all together, his very best. They may not be so extravagantly droll as some, but they are more even and true to middle-life characters; there is more of slyness and quaintness of humour in them; and they are far more carefully executed. Even Cruikshank improves upon himself when he takes pains. Here, then, is one strong feature of recommendation; and the humour and variety of the sketches themselves, enable us to extend our favourable testimony still further. These vol-

umes are the merriest of the season. "Boz" is a kind of Boswell to society—and of the middle ranks especially. He is an old favourite of ours; we remember laughing at two or three of these sketches when they first appeared in a contemporary, and we roared at **"The Christening,"** as introduced by Mr. Buckstone at the Adelphi. Few of them are inferior even to that in broad humour—coarse, it is true, but very real. The subjects of "Boz" generally preclude refinement. Of these there are about thirty, all evincing a shrewd, quizzical insight into ordinary character, an apt knowledge of "every-day character." The keen, but not ill-natured spirit, and the truly whimsical humour of these sketches, will be displayed in a quotation or two. It hardly matters which chapters we select from.

There followed a generous selection from **"Shabby Genteel People."**

Sketches by Boz was advertised in the *News* and *Sunday Herald* in two separate places on the front page on 28th February. The previous week the following review had been given.

> These sketches have, if we mistake not, already appeared in the columns of *The Morning* and *Evening Chronicle*. They are replete with talent; and when we say that we are left in doubt whether we most admire the racy humour and irresistible wit of the "sketches" or of the "illustrations" in George Cruikshank's very best style, our readers will agree that we could not well give higher commendation. Some of the sketches display a feeling far deeper than the professed character of the work would prepare us to expect. In all, from grave to gay, the delineation of character displayed is inimitably accurate. So accurate are the characteristics of the Cockneys exhibited in these sketches, that they might have been aptly entitled "Idiosyncracies of Cockneydom." The broad humour with which the most pungent absurdities of each character are drawn forth, justify us in conscientiously prescribing these volumes as the best we have ever seen for a cure of the blue devils.

The same week *The Sunday Times,* where the book had been advertised the week before, said:

> The majority of these very pleasant sketches have already appeared in the columns of *The Evening Chronicle,* and the interest which they excited has, it seems, induced the author to publish them in their present form, with appropriate graphic illustrations of George Cruikshank, whose genius, like the purse of Fortunatus, is inexhaustible. If we mistake not, Boz whoever he is, will one day make Tom Hood look to his laurels.

Among the literary contents of *The Atlas* for 21st February, 1836, appeared the following review:

> Sketches by Boz, 2 Vols. A series of sketches, chiefly dedicated to the everyday life of London, which for the greater part, originally appeared in an evening paper. There is some raciness and whim in these essays, but they seem to have been

An illustration of a London pawnshop by George Cruikshank for
Sketches by Boz.

written in haste, and to want concentration and
design. The style is loose and rambling, and the
author sometimes falls into that manner of caricature and broad painting which is considered,
we believe, by those whose tastes are not very
delicate, to be clever of its kind, but which, we
confess, appears to us to be sheer vulgarity. The
difficulty of truly describing city life without reflecting its vulgarities, more or less, we admit;
but this writer has a *gout* for them which precludes him from the benefit of the argument of
necessity. Yet the work is, nevertheless, amusing, and some humorous wood-cuts by Cruikshank will help out its entertainment with the
multitude.

Before the month was out John Forster wrote the following review in *The Examiner*. At this time Forster had not
met Dickens; in fact a year elapsed before they first met
each other at the house of Harrison Ainsworth.

It appears in the most important part of the journal, in the
columns entitled "The Literary Examiner."

We were much struck by some of these sketches
when we first read them in the publication in
which they originally appeared, and a second perusal has strengthened the favourable impression. The author is a good observer; his perception of the ludicrous is quick, his humour is of
a rich vein, and his little touches of pathos scattered here and there, are of that kind which nature has placed in the closest neighbourhood to

humour. The style is unaffected, racy and agreeable.

The fault of the book is the caricature of Cock-
neyism, of which there is too much. This com-
mon-place sort of thing, is unworthy of the author, whose best powers are exercised obviously
with great facility on the less hacknied subjects.
He shows his strength in bringing out the meaning and interests of objects which would altogether escape the observation of ordinary mor-
tals.

We quote a short specimen of the author's manner.

(This was an extract from **"Omnibuses."**)

The Weekly Despatch was rather late in coming out with
its review; it did not appear until 28th February although
the book had been advertised in its columns with a very
bold headline "Boz's Sketches" three weeks before.

Here are two very agreeable volumes of sketches, and tales illustrative of every-day life and
every-day people. Some of the contents have appeared from time to time in various periodicals
and the author was justified by public approbation in collecting them, and reprinting them,
with additions, in their present shape. George
Cruikshank has enriched the work with numerous pictures in his peculiary characteristic style,
and the volumes will form a very pleasant and
handy addition to the library. They will amuse
all and instruct many. We trust the success of
this work will be such as to encourage the author
to future undertakings of a similar description.

This must have been not only very gratifying to "Boz,"
but helpful to the sales, for *The Weekly Despatch* had a
large and popular circulation. The concluding paragraph,
was no doubt well meant; yet it is interesting to note that
when, just over a month later, the first monthly part of
The Pickwick Papers appeared, this newspaper entirely ignored it, and subsequent issues.

The Morning Post on the March 12th, under the heading
"Literature," reviewed the book as follows:

Under the eccentric signature attached to the
above work, it may perhaps be recollected that
the columns of a contemporary have contained
a series of essays which have deservedly attracted much attention. They are now collected together, with sundry additional sketches, and it
must be admitted that they fully merit a more
lasting popularity than could have been afforded
by the ephemeral reputation of a newspaper. The
author is evidently a close and accurate observer
of events in "life's dull stream" and, he has infinite skill in giving importance to the complex
scenes of every-day occurrence. The varied aspects of society in the middle and lower classes
are touched off with admirable truth and veracity. The graphic descriptions of "Boz" invest all
he describes with amazing reality. This pleasing
vraisemblement is the great charm of these
"sketches" as they are modestly termed by the
author. Natural humour and striking fidelity
are, however, not the only praises to be be-

stowed. The pathetic powers of "Boz" are of a high order. We regret that our limits will not allow us to extract an inimitable specimen of the intense feeling he has displayed in the tale of the broker's man. These volumes ought to be read both in town and in country. The inhabitants of the great "Wen" will find correct and able pictures of metropolitan society, and provincial readers will have a good insight into the manners and customs of some extraordinary classes of people in the British capital. We should add that the "Sketches" are illustrated, and that the illustrator is George Cruikshank, the mention of whose name is sufficient to guarantee the perfection of the cuts.

The Metropolitan Magazine was one of the very first of the critical journals to recognise that "Boz" was an entirely new force in literature, one who was not traversing any of the old and well recognised paths.

In its issue for March, 1836, it said:

> We strongly recommend this facetious work to the Americans. It will save them the trouble of reading some hundred dull-written tomes on England, as it is a perfect picture of the morals, manners and habits of a great portion of English Society. It is hardly possible to conceive a more pleasantly reading book; delightful for the abundance of its sly humour, and instructive in every chapter. The succession of portraits does not reach higher than of the best of the middle classes, but descends with a startling fidelity to the lowest of the low. Where all are so good, it would be needless for us to particularise any one of these admirable sketches. . . .

There was a reference in this review to the suitability of many of the stories as admirable groundwork for light comedies and farces. Dickens had not overlooked this possibility as we know, and the notice in *The Metropolitan* must have been a commendable urge to him. It concluded:

> We do not know the author, but we should apprehend that he has, from the peculiar turn of his genius, been already successful as a dramatist; if he has not yet, we can safely opine that he may be if he will. Taken altogether, we have rarely met with a work that has pleased us more, and we know that our taste is always that of the public.

Chambers's Edinburgh Journal on April 9th reprinted **"The Boarding House"** with the following eulogistic note:

> The following tale is abridged from **Sketches by Boz,** illustrative of every-day life and every-day people. Two volumes, recently published by Mr. Macrone. This work appears to be an early—perhaps a first—attempt of some new writer; if so, we would recommend him to proceed, for, unless he fall off very miserably in his subsequent efforts, he can scarcely fail to become a successful and popular author. His chief object in the present publication had been to depict life and character, as exemplified in the ranks of the metropolis; and this he has accomplished in a style, which, bating a little caricature and exaggeration, strikes us as extremely happy. He has

much comic power, perceives traits which are not consciously noted by ordinary observers, and yet, when mentioned, remind everybody of the thing described. We warmly recommend these two volumes to the notice of our readers.

The Mirror of April 16th was somewhat supercilious. It remarked that the sketches were "descriptive of everyday life and every-day people and are certainly written with a considerable share of broad humour"; adding that they thought them "too every-dayish."

> They want relief and their incidents border too closely on the commonplace, so as to belong to the slightest magazine writing, which can only be said to amuse without any higher effect. This is to be regretted, because Sketches such as "Boz" can write may be pointed with a moral, and made the vehicle of some excellent instruction and improvement of the heart. Here is too much cockney vulgarity, and the incidents savour too strongly of low London life. We detach a few passages from Sketches free from these eccentricities.

Norman Berrow (essay date 1937)

SOURCE: "Some Candid Opinions on *A Christmas Carol,*" in *The Dickensian,* Vol. XXXIV, No. 245, December, 1937-38, pp. 20-4.

[*Here, in an essay that was originally presented as a lecture in May, 1937, Berrow reacts negatively to* A Christmas Carol.]

There has been much said this evening in praise, I might almost say in adulation, of Charles Dickens. Just by way of a change I want to offer a few words of criticism. In case some of you might consider these words as something of the nature of an attack, I should like to point out, though there is really no need to do so, that a man who stands in such an impregnable position as Dickens does not fear attack. But a little criticism may not be amiss.

I should like to give some honest opinions on *the* Christmas Book; and by *the* Christmas Book I mean A Christmas Carol, the best known of all the Christmas Books, the one that everybody knows—Dickens readers and others—the one on which young people so often cut their Dickens-teeth.

You will understand that these are my personal opinions. It is probable that a large number of you will disagree with me; if you do I hope you will get up and say so. Discussion is the life-blood of study, and we are a study-circle. Discussion is as good for the intellect as confession is for the soul.

Well, my candid opinion of *A Christmas Carol* is that it is the best of a rather poor lot of stories. In fact, when I consider that it was written by a giant and a genius like Charles Dickens, I think it is the poor best of an exceedingly poor lot.

To begin with, it is humourless. By that I do not mean that it isn't funny or witty—although it most decidedly isn't either—but I mean that it is, to my mind, devoid of that impalpable flavour that may permeate any book, grave or gay, serious or frivolous; that impalpable flavour that almost instantly puts the reader on good terms with himself and with the author. Humour is that quality in literature that gives content.

Humour has nothing to do with farce or wit. If you look up the word in any good dictionary you will find that it gives some such definition as this: "Disposition of mind or feeling; frame of mind;" and so forth. It is the quality in a book that gains your immediate sympathy with the author, the aims and objects of his writings, and all that he stands for as expressed in his work. In a word, humour, in a book, makes you good-humoured.

But *A Christmas Carol* does not give me content, and it does not make me good-humoured; I'm afraid it only irritates me. I have the queerest impression that, though Dickens set himself to write a happy story, he was not altogether a happy man when he wrote it.

My second grievance is that it is childish. The story may not be, but the style is. The opening paragraphs, for instance, give me the impression that Dickens was not writing for intelligent grown-ups, but for rather backward children. In the first page or two he seems to be hammering home a few points into the fickle and wandering mind of a backward child. By the time he has finished with the matter, it is quite clear to even a half-witted Troglodyte that, firstly, Marley was dead, and, secondly, that Scrooge was aware of the fact.

In this opening Dickens is, of course, making a bid for the reader's sympathetic attention to his tale; he is striving for that humour I have just spoken of. But honestly, he does not get my sympathetic attention. I think he fails lamentably.

This is very strange when we consider the glorious openings to some of his other books. Consider, for example, that brilliant discourse on the Chuzzlewit family tree; the account of that meeting that is our introduction to the Pickwick Club; the swing and the rhythm of the account of Veneering's first dinner-party. Veneering's dinner-parties were actually rather dreary affairs to attend; but to read about them is sheer delight, a delight which brings a smile to our lips and a sudden gush of warmth to our hearts whenever we come upon the name of Veneering. And that smile is not a smile of sympathy and affection for Veneering and Company, but a smile of sympathy and affection for Dickens and his handling of Veneering and Company. I have to admit that the name of Scrooge brings me no such joyous glow of recognition. I have no smile to summon up for his handling of the firm of Scrooge and Marley (deceased).

But my chief quarrel is with the story as a story. It has, of course, a moral, as I well know. But I hate morals hurled at my defenceless head with the vigour and mercilessness with which this one has been hurled. I prefer to extract the moral from a story for myself. And, having decided to write a moral story for Christmas, Dickens decided also to lay it on with a trowel. You don't gild lilies. You paint 'em. You gild refined gold—see Bible. He painted the lily.

A Christmas Carol is a story about Christmas and the awakening of the Christmas spirit in the stony breast of a miser and a skinflint through the medium of supernatural agencies. It is saturated with an exaggerated Christmas fervour; it is larded with soggy and indigestible lumps of sickly sentiment; and it is—or, rather, it is meant to be—made terrible and hair-raising by the introduction of three ghostly apparitions. Of these I say simply this: they may have raised the hair of our fathers and mothers, but I do not think they curdle the blood in our veins to any great extent. In these days we are, to use a colloquialism, more hard-boiled. And there is the inevitable impossible and sanctimonious infant in the person of Tiny Tim. I am sympathetic towards Tiny Tim because he was a cripple, but had he been a hale and hearty child I should have looked almost with kindness on any person who had made away with him.

Dickens, by the way, was never very happy with children. Look at Little Nell, with her graveyard complex; Paul Dombey, with his philosophical discourses on the subject of the wild waves' conversation; Kit Nubbles, with his unnatural conscientiousness; and others. To say the least of it, his child characters were more than a little smug They were angels. We all know very well that children are most decidedly not angels. I have not any children, but if I had and they started speaking and acting like Little Nell, or Little Paul, or Tiny Tim—even if they were cripples—I should have a doctor in right away, and suggest a good hearty blood-letting.

These harsh words are not directed against an author who struggled and fought and passed on to have his place taken by others who came after him. They are directed against the gigantic, irreplaceable figure of the greatest man in English literature, probably the greatest man in the literature of the world. Consequently they are spoken more in sorrow than anger, and without prejudice. They are the candid opinions of one who knows very well that there are those who will spring to the defence of a man, who, incidentally, does not need any defending.

Feeling as I do about the *Christmas Carol*, I rather wonder how Dickens ever came to write it. I have a theory about that, but first I should like to digress a little. I am, in my way, a very humble member of Charles Dickens's profession, and I have often been asked the question: Why does a man write books? Well, there are several answers. He may write a book for money. He has only to write two or three to see the fallacy of that particular answer. He may write a book to gain fame. But there again, apart from a few literary giants, the average author's literary fame—if any—is terribly evanescent and lost in the multitude.

As a matter of fact, the real reason why a man, or a woman, writes fiction is that there is a sort of poison in the blood that wells up and demands outlet in the form of literary expression. The man has to get rid of it or burst. That is a rather forceful way of putting it, but that is the idea. And if he is a born story-teller, no sooner does he get rid of one lot of poison than another wells up inside him. There are, of course, people who feel the urge to write but who never do write. In their case the poison is not so virulent. It wells up, simmers for a time, giving them a kind of mental indigestion, and then dies down again, and they go on with their jobs as usual. There are also pangs in mental creation . . .

But there are also pleasures. I personally get a lot of fun in concocting those slight, if blood-thirsty, yarns of mine. True, the mechanical process of typing three hundred or so pages is apt to grow rather wearisome, but the pleasure is there. A man writes what pleases him, and his writing gives him pleasure. That, of course, I need hardly point out, does not mean to say that it will necessarily please his readers. On the other hand, in my short experience, I have found out that there is a great deal of truth in Emerson's dictum: that a man who writes to please himself, pleases everybody; and a man who writes to please other people, pleases nobody.

Now, in the case of **A Christmas Carol**, I feel that Dickens set out to please other people, and not altogether to please himself. The writing of the **Carol** was not so much a pleasure to him as a task. Christmas had come round again, the next issue of his magazine was to be a Christmas number, therefore a Christmas story had to be written. And he wrote it, not because he wanted to write it, but because convention demanded that it should be written. And so he did not do himself justice.

I put forward another point to be considered at the same time. Dickens was in the hey-day of his production—I do not say powers, because his powers never waned—in the flood-tide of his popularity.

He was, I feel sure, an eminently modest man, as all truly great men are, but he was beginning to realise that he was a force in the land. The whole country was laughing uproariously at the antics of Pickwick and his disciples. It had wept over Oliver Twist, followed with breathless interest the adventures of Nicholas Nickleby, devoured *The Old Curiosity Shop* and *Barnaby Rudge,* and had plunged into *Martin Chuzzlewit.* Dickens had discovered that he could sway the nation, and so, when Christmas time of 1843 came round, he decided to sway the nation with a Christmas Moral Story. I can see him in his study, at the well-known desk with the sloping surface, driving a dogged pen and muttering:

"I'll make them feel good-will to all men; by Heaven, I will!"

He did the same the following Christmas, with **The Chimes**, and again I get that impression of dogged determination, of the accomplishment of a task. He begged for sympathy—not for himself, but for others—and at the same time, to give force to his message—I might almost say his lecture, his sermon—he made the flesh creep. Or he tried to.

And in placing this condition upon himself, in writing to order, as it were, the creating of a moral story containing nothing that would bring the semblance of a blush to the cheek of the young person and a vast amount of what was good for that same young person, I think we find something of the reason why these Christmas Books, again to my mind, fall far short of his usual brilliantly high standard.

There is not an atom of bitterness in what I have said. These books detract in no way from the huge enjoyment we all get in reading his other works. But I want to remind you, by way of conclusion, that we are Dickens students, and not just blind Dickens worshippers. We should never forget that, though he was a giant, a genius, a mob in revolt, as Chesterton once so aptly and pithily described him, he was also a very human man, subject to very human faults and frailties.

Ernest Boll　(essay date 1940)

SOURCE: "The Sketches by 'Boz'," in *The Dickensian,* Vol. XXXVI, No. 254, Spring, 1940, pp. 69-73.

[*In the essay below, American educator Boll examines how the stories in* Sketches by Boz *anticipate the themes and characters of Dickens's later novels.*]

We gain something worth while when, to our enjoyment of the individual writings of an author we add an understanding of his works as a comprehensive whole. We enjoy a person's sense of humour, or his good taste in clothes, or his power of quick sympathy, and dislike his bad temper, his penuriousness, or his accent; but we do not understand him until we make an effort to knit together the various threads of his nature into a complete pattern. The truth applies to a man's traits and to a man's books.

There are really many kinds of threads we can use to gather together an author's works: characters, situations, devices of craftsmanship, direct revelation, and many more. Some of the characters created by Dickens had an imaginative life in **Sketches by Boz** before they joined the novels. Naturally, we find more of them in the earlier novels than in the later. In three of them we see figures that were later to be called Nancy and Bill Sikes. They are a drunkard ruffian and the loyal, uncomplaining wife whom he neglects or beats. In the sketch, **"The Hospital Patient,"** the woman, before she dies of her husband's blows and kicks, protests to the police that she had hurt herself. The prostitute in the sketch, **"The Pawnbroker's Shop,"** whose eyes fill with tears at sight of a young woman and her mother pawning their last pieces of modest jewelry, might well have been Nancy. In the sketch, **"Meditations in Monmouth Street,"** there walks a stout broad-shouldered ruffian with a dog at his heels. It is Bill Sikes preparing for his life in *Oliver Twist.*

That amusing Mr. Dawkins, the Artful Dodger, who stars in the Bow Street Police Court in a burlesque drama of indignation over the blindness of English law, makes an anonymous appearance as a lad in Old Bailey, in the sketch, **"Criminal Courts."** The lad insists that fifteen gentlemen are waiting outside to vindicate his character. Like the Artful Dodger, he invites the court attendants to carry him off if they want him out, and he too relishes his little heroic scene before a kindred audience, the same kind of audience that still waits in a long queue in Newgate Street on mornings during Sessions.

The kill-joy was an impressive and very much loathed reality to Dickens. Gabriel Grub in *Pickwick Papers,* Scrooge in the **Carol,** Tackleton the toy manufacturer in

The Cricket on the Hearth, Mr. Dombey, and Gradgrind and M'Choakumchild in *Hard Times* are the main impersonations of the character of the kill-joy. We find him already in the sketch, **"The Bloomsbury Christening,"** under the truly depressing name of Nicodemus Dumps. Dumps enjoys only making everybody round him wretched. At the christening supper in honour of his nephew's first born he makes a doleful speech. He names all the evils the child might cause its parents to suffer, all of which misfortunes Dumps solemnly hopes the parents may be spared. He goes home pleased with the misery he leaves behind him. This kill-joy is not converted.

Dickens did not idealise his materials so much then as he was to idealise them later. One example of that contentment with the usual is the continued misanthropy of Dumps. Another is found in the story of **"The Drunkard's Death."** There we observe that the drunkard's daughter, who has kept house for him, ill as she was, deserts her father after he has in drunken carelessness turned informer against his son. The later Dickens would not have allowed this desertion to occur.

The majority of the characters in these youthful stories and sketches are, very naturally, young men of many kinds. Those two clerks, Thomas Potter and Robert Smithers realistic heroes of **"Making a Night of It,"** are very interesting for several reasons. The most important is that they are completely alive. The second is that Robert Smithers is a miniature self-portrait of Charles Dickens. Another is that they foreshadow those other gay young friends, Ben Allen and Bob Sawyer in *Pickwick*, Herbert Pocket and Pip in *Great Expectations*, Lightwood and Wrayburn in *Our Mutual Friend*. The gay young man is broadly comical as Dick Swiveller in *Old Curiosity Shop*, sinister as Steerforth in *David Copperfield*, pathetic as Richard Carstone in *Bleak House*, falsely glamourous as James Harthouse in *Hard Times*, despicably selfish as Tip Dorrit. He is irreclaimable and yet heroic as Sydney Carton. Sydney Carton died on the guillotine, but he was brought back to life again as Eugene Wrayburn, and reclaimed to virtue.

The agreeable young men, who are so happy when they are helping somewhere: Tupple in the sketch **"The New Year,"** and Percy Noakes, the manager of **"The Steam Excursion,"** and a "devilish good fellow"; continued to grow in the mind of Dickens. The composite figure grew in wisdom, in sense of humour, in power of sacrifice, until it took on the glorious personality of Mark Tapley, in *Martin Chuzzlewit*.

The elderly bachelors who are so lightheartedly discussed at the beginning of the story about Mr. John Dounce come to separate lives in the lovable persons of Pickwick, Grimwig in *Oliver Twist*, the Cheerybles in *Nickleby*, the Single Gentleman in *The Old Curiosity Shop*, and John Jarndyce in *Bleak House*.

The shabby-genteel who are described in **"Thoughts about People"** and in **"Shabby-Genteel People"** foretell a host of the pitiful and broken, among them the Chancery Prisoner in *Pickwick*, Newman Noggs in *Nickleby*, old Mr. Trent in *The Old Curiosity Shop*, Gridley in *Bleak House*,

and Frederick Dorrit, brother of the Father of the Marshalsea.

That mixture of rogue, comedian, and object of charity, Alfred Jingle, in *Pickwick*, has a younger brother in the **Sketches**; he is Horatio Sparkins, who, like Jingle, palms himself off as a gentleman, and talks exquisite nonsense as he tries to sustain the role. But Sparkins is exposed as a counter-jumper, the most junior of partners in a shabby Tottenham Court Road draper's shop.

But more than characters unite these early papers to the whole range of the novels. There are also situations that are returned to frequently enough to show that they represent a habit of mind, that they are the repeated expressions of the same personality. One of the most brilliantly impressive passages in *Oliver Twist* is that which creates the terror of Fagin during his last night in the condemned cell. The first version of the very same situation is found toward the end of the sketch, **"A Visit to Newgate,"** and it is as powerful as any of Dickens's masterpieces in that difficult art that I may call "subjective melodrama." The condemned prisoner dreams that he is walking with his wife; he begs her to forgive his unkindness toward her. He dreams his trial and his sentence. But in his dream he escapes from prison, and he runs with marvellous speed and ease out into the open countryside. But there he still feels anxious, oppressed . . . Then he wakes; it is the morning of his execution.

That dream race over the open fields at night is run again in the flight of Bill Sikes from Nancy's dead eyes, and in the escape of Smike from Squeers at the Dotheboys Hall.

The Christmas dinners and games that light up chapters of *Pickwick* and of the *Carol* with a heavenly humour we find already described in the sketch **"A Christmas Dinner."** We must in passing acknowledge that the gift of the Christmas story came to Dickens from Washington Irving. The huge feast, centering round a roast fowl, the baking of cakes and pies, the blazing fire, the filled glass, the Christmas pudding decorated with holly, the game of blind man's buff, the meeting of lips under mistletoe, the songs and speech-making, the bond of hearty affection, all these we find in this early sketch.

The situations describing tragedy and death also tie these sketches with scenes in novels. There are several death-bed scenes that anticipate deeply moving passages in the novels. They are an essential element in the art of Dickens.

The natural mistake that may occur in large inns whose corridors are labyrinthine, the mistake of guests entering the wrong room in search of their own, is mentioned in the story of **"The Great Winglebury Duel,"** and as such prepares us for Mr. Pickwick's surprise in the Great White Horse Inn in obtaining his first view, on embarrassing terms, of a lady brushing her hair before retiring for the night.

The spontaneous combustion that enables the rag and paper dealer, Krook, in *Bleak House*, to make his very dramatic final exit, was already thought of in the sketch, **"The Streets—Morning."** There, a general servant wishes, as she struggles through an early rising, that spontaneous combustion would ignite the kitchen fire for her.

In a third way do we find these early papers claiming an alliance with the whole pattern of Dickens, and that is in certain matters of style, and spirit, and form. To suggest his style, we have time for only one phase, an expression of his mental alertness and buoyant good humour, and that shall be his punning. In **"Private Theatres"** we hear this report about a complaint from the orchestra: "The flute says he'll be blowed if he plays any more." It's really an admirable little pun within a pun. There are also many puns set in a careful balance of phrasing. With reference to a delinquent tenant of a shop, in **"Shops and their Tenants,"** we learn that when he failed, he "locked the door and bolted himself."

And about the spirit of this early writing we shall notice again just one characteristic: the grand joy Dickens takes in a bustle. I don't mean the bustle that rustles; I mean the bustle that hustles: many actions, swiftly performed actions. We may even say that Dickens "spreads himself" on his bustles. Again and again, after whirling our imagination round with an account of activities in a crowded scene, Dickens stops to admire and comment on "the bustle and confusion" (**"The Boarding-House"** and **"The Steam Excursion"**); or the "life and bustle" (**"The Tuggses"**); or the "exhilarating bustle" (**"The Great Winglebury Duel"**). And there is no novel of Dickens that does not give us joy through its author's unique gusto in hustling life.

When we look for similarities in craftsmanship we notice that every kind of farce, humour, grotesquerie, satire, description, melodrama, burlesque, and sentimental mystery that was to be employed later is found represented in these early writings. The type of the sentimental mystery is of Dickens's own fashioning from earlier romance. We find it in the powerful story of **"The Black Veil,"** as fascinating a gem of the macabre as any that Poe wrote, and yet sane throughout, one of the great stories in English.

A deficiency in these stories that is not surprising to Dickensians is the absence of any normal sentimental romance, of sensible courtship. There is plenty of foolish and repented-of passion, there is coquetry and jealousy because of it, there is the loyalty of a brutally treated wife, there is young married love suffering persecution, but there is no scene of simple love-making. In only one story is there an adumbration of it. In the story of **"The Black Veil"** the young physician daydreams about his distant beloved, named Rose. The relative rareness with which Dickens throughout his novel-writing life could make convincing love-making that was not comical, or pathetic, or insanely passionate, is represented in this earliest collection of his writings by no attempt at all.

There is also, and this is my lastly, much of that direct confession that is a part of the many confidences Dickens makes to us throughout his novels and shorter papers. You will remember David Copperfield confessing his passion for imagining the lives of people he passed in London streets. In five of the sketches Dickens speaks about that love for creative speculation, and in all five he gives demonstrations of his marvellous genius in the art. Among these are the life-story of a youth, imagined from the observation of a number of suits hanging in a pawnbroker's shop, in **"Meditations in Monmouth Street,"** and that fine study of anxiety and terror in the last night of a condemned prisoner, in **"A Visit to Newgate."**

There are many more ties, of many kinds, between the *Sketches by Boz* and the novels. I have mentioned only a small proportion of the characters, situations, elements in style and form, and direct confidences of the author that claim for the *Sketches* the right of the closest organic membership with the whole body of Dickens's writing. And I have tried to show the benefit of understanding the connectedness of a writer's creative imagination from work to work. As a last point, much more important than any fact of ties between the early writings, and the novels, is the realisation that these early stories and sketches have an excellent merit in their own right, a high power of giving pleasure.

Edgar Johnson   (essay date 1951-52)

SOURCE: "The Christmas Carol and the Economic Man," in *The American Scholar,* Vol. 21, No. 1, Winter, 1951-52, pp. 91-8.

[*Johnson is a major Dickens scholar whose* Charles Dickens: His Tragedy and Triumph *(1952) is considered the definitive biography of the novelist. In the following essay adapted from that work, Johnson expounds on the social importance of* A Christmas Carol.]

Everyone knows Dickens' *Christmas Carol* for its colorful painting of a rosy fireside good cheer and warmth of feeling, made all the more vivid by the contrasting chill wintry darkness in which its radiant scenes are framed. Most readers realize too how characteristic of all Dickens' sentiments about the Christmas season are the laughter and tenderness and jollity he poured into the *Carol.* What is not so widely understood is that it was also consistently and deliberately created as a critical blast against the very rationale of industrialism and its assumptions about the organizing principles of society. It is an attack upon both the economic behavior of the nineteenth-century business man and the supporting theory of doctrinaire utilitarianism. As such it is a good deal more significant than the mere outburst of warmhearted sentimentality it is often taken to be.

Its sharper intent is, indeed, ingeniously disguised. Not even the festivities at Dingley Dell, in *Pickwick Papers,* seem to have a more genial innocence than the scenes of the *Christmas Carol.* It is full of the tang of snow and cold air and crisp green holly-leaves, and warm with the glow of crimson holly-berries, blazing hearths, and human hearts. Deeper than this, however, Dickens makes of the Christmas spirit a symbolic criticism of the relations that throughout almost all the rest of the year subsist among men. It is a touchstone, revealing and drawing forth the gold of generosity ordinarily crusted over with selfish habit, an earnest of the truth that our natures are not entirely or even essentially devoted to competitive struggle.

Dickens is certain that the enjoyment most men are able to feel in the happiness of others can play a larger part than it does in the tenor of their lives. The sense of brotherhood, he feels, can be broadened to a deeper and more active concern for the welfare of all mankind. It is in this light that Dickens sees the Spirit of Christmas. So understood, as the distinguished scholar Professor Louis Cazamian rightly points out, his "philosophie de Noël" becomes the very core of his social thinking.

> **For Dickens Christmas is primarily a human, not a supernatural, feast, with glowing emphasis on goose and gravy, plum-pudding and punch, mistletoe and kissing-games, dancing and frolic, as well as open-handedness, sympathy, and warmth of heart.**
>
> *—Edgar Johnson*

Not that Christmas has for Dickens more than the very smallest connection with Christian dogma or theology. It involves no conception of the virgin birth or transubstantiation or sacrificial atonement or redemption by faith. For Dickens Christmas is primarily a human, not a supernatural, feast, with glowing emphasis on goose and gravy, plum-pudding and punch, mistletoe and kissing-games, dancing and frolic, as well as open-handedness, sympathy, and warmth of heart. Dickens does not believe that love of others demands utter abnegation or mortification of the flesh; it is not sadness but joyful fellowship. The triumphal meaning of Christmas peals in the angel voices ringing through the sky: "On earth peace, good will to men." It is a sign that men do not live by bread alone, that they do not live for barter and sale alone. No way of life is either true or rewarding that leaves out men's need of loving and of being loved.

The theme of the *Christmas Carol* is thus closely linked with the theme of *Martin Chuzzlewit,* which was being written and published as a serial during the very time in which the shorter story appeared. The selfishness so variously manifested in the one is limited in the other to the selfishness of financial gain. For in an acquisitive society the form that selfishness predominantly takes is monetary greed. The purpose of such a society is the protection of property rights. Its rules are created by those who have money and power, and are designed, to the extent that they are consistent, for the perpetuation of money and power. With the growing importance of commerce in the eighteenth century, and of industry in the nineteenth, political economists—the "philosophers" Dickens detested—rationalized the spirit of ruthless greed into a system claiming authority throughout society.

Services as well as goods, they said, were subject only to the laws of profitable trade. There was no just price. One bought in the cheapest market and sold in the dearest. There was no just wage. The mill owner paid the mill hand what competition decreed under the determination of the "iron law of wage." If the poor, the insufficiently aggressive, and the mediocre in ability were unable to live on what they could get, they must starve—or put up with the treadmill and the workhouse—and even these institutions represented concessions to mere humanity that must be made as forbidding as possible. Ideally, no sentimental conceptions must be allowed to obstruct the workings of the law of supply and demand. "Cash-nexus" was the sole bond between man and man. The supreme embodiment of this social theory was the notion of the "economic man," that curiously fragmentary picture of human nature, who never performed any action except at the dictates of monetary gain. And Scrooge, in the *Christmas Carol,* is nothing other than a personification of economic man.

Scrooge's entire life is limited to cash-boxes, ledgers and bills of sale. He underpays and bullies and terrifies his clerk, and grudges him even enough coal in his office fire to keep warm. All sentiment, kindness, generosity, tenderness, he dismisses as humbug. All imagination he regards as a species of mental indigestion. He feels that he has discharged his full duty to society in contributing his share of the taxes that pay for the prison, the workhouse, the operation of the treadmill and the poor law, and he bitterly resents having his pocket picked to keep even them going. The out-of-work and the indigent sick are to him merely idle and useless; they had better die and decrease the surplus population. So entirely does Scrooge exemplify the economic man that, like that abstraction, his grasping rapacity has ceased to have any purpose beyond itself: when he closes up his office for the night he takes his pinched heart off to a solitary dinner at a tavern and then to his bleak chambers where he sits alone over his gruel.

Now from one angle, of course, *A Christmas Carol* indicts the economic philosophy represented by Scrooge for its unhappy influence on society. England's prosperity was not so uncertain—if, indeed, any nation's ever is—that she needed to be parsimonious and cruel to her waifs and strays, or even to the incompetents and casualties of life. To neglect the poor, to deny them education, to give them no protection from covetous employers, to let them be thrown out of work and fall ill and die in filthy surroundings that then engender spreading pestilence, to allow them to be harried by misery into crime—all these turn out in the long run to be the most disastrous shortsightedness.

That is what the Ghost of Christmas Present means in showing Scrooge the two ragged and wolfish children glaring from beneath its robes. "They are Man's," says the Spirit. "And they cling to me, appealing from their fathers. This boy is Ignorance. This girl is Want. Beware them both, and all of their degree, but most of all beware this boy, for on his brow I see that written which is Doom, unless the writing be erased." And when Scrooge asks if they have no refuge, the Spirit ironically echoes his own words: "Are there no prisons? Are there no workhouses?"

Scrooge's relation with his clerk Bob Cratchit is another illustration of the same point. To say, as some commentators have done, that Scrooge is paying Cratchit all he is worth on the open market (or he would get another job) is to assume the very conditions Dickens is attacking. It is not only that timid, uncompetitive people like Bob Cratchit may lack the courage to bargain for their rights. But, as Dickens knows well, there are many things other than the usefulness of a man's work that determine his wage—the existence, for example, of a large body of other men able to do the same job. And if Cratchit is getting the established remuneration for his work, that makes the situation worse, not better; for instead of an isolated one, his is a general case. What Dickens has at heart is not any economic conception like Marx's labor theory of value, but a feeling of the human value of human beings. Unless a man is a noxious danger to society, Dickens feels, a beast of prey to be segregated or destroyed; if he is able and willing to work, whatever the work may be—he is entitled at least to enough for him to live on, by the mere virtue of his humanity alone.

But the actual organization that Dickens saw in society callously disregarded all such humane principles. The hardened criminal was maintained in jail with more care than the helpless debtor who had broken no law. The pauper who owed nobody, but whom age, illness or industrial change might have thrown out of work, was treated more severely than many a debtor and jailbird. And the poor clerk or laborer, rendered powerless by his need or the number of others like him, could be held to a pittance barely sufficient to keep him and his family from starvation.

Against such inequities Dickens maintains that any work worth doing should be paid enough to maintain a man and his family without grinding worry. How are the Bob Cratchits and their helpless children to live? Or are we to let the crippled Tiny Tims die and decrease the surplus population? "Man," says the Ghost, "if man you be in heart, not adamant, forbear that wicked cant until you have discovered What the surplus is and Where it is. . . . It may be, that in the sight of Heaven, you are more worthless and less fit to live than millions like this poor man's child. Oh God! to hear the Insect on the leaf pronouncing on the too much life among his hungry brothers in the dust!"

Coldhearted arrogance and injustice storing up a dangerous heritage of poverty and ignorance—such is Dickens' judgment of the economic system that Scrooge exemplifies. But its consequences do not end with the cruelties it inflicts upon the masses of the people or the evils it works in society. It injures Scrooge as well. All the more generous impulses of humanity he has stifled and mutilated in himself. All natural affection he has crushed. The lonely boy he used to be, weeping in school, the tender brother, the eager youth, the young man who once fell disinterestedly in love with a dowerless girl—what has he done to them in making himself into a money-making machine, as hard and sharp as flint, and frozen with the internal ice that clutches his shriveled heart? That dismal cell, his office, and his gloomy rooms, are only a prison within which he dwells self-confined, barred and close-locked as he drags a chain of his own cash-boxes and dusty ledgers. Acting on a distortedly inadequate conception of self-

interest, Scrooge has deformed and crippled himself to bitter sterility.

And Scrooge's fallacy is the fallacy of organized society. Like his house, which Dickens fancifully imagines playing hide-and-seek with other houses when it was a young house, and losing its way in a blind alley it has forgotten how to get out of, Scrooge has lost his way between youth and maturity. Society too in the course of its development has gone astray and then hardened itself in obdurate error with a heartless economic theory. Scrooge's conversion is more than the transformation of a single human being. It is a plea for society itself to undergo a change of heart.

Dickens does not, it should be noticed, take the uncompromising position that the self-regarding emotions are to be eradicated altogether. He is not one of those austere theorists who hold that the individual must be subordinated to the state or immolate himself to the service of an abstract humanity. Concern for one's self and one's own welfare is necessary and right, but true self-love cannot be severed from love of others without growing barren and diseased. Only in the communion of brotherhood is it healthy and fruitful. When Scrooge has truly changed, and has dispatched the anonymous gift of the turkey to Bob Cratchit as an earnest of repentance, his next move is to go to his nephew's house and ask wistfully, "Will you let me in, Fred?" With love reanimated in his heart, he may hope for love.

There have been readers who objected to Scrooge's conversion as too sudden and radical to be psychologically convincing. But this is to mistake a semi-serious fantasy for a piece of prosaic realism. Even so, the emotions in Scrooge to which the Ghosts appeal are no unsound means to the intended end: the awakened memories of a past when he had known gentler and warmer ties than in any of his later years, the realization of his exclusion from all kindness and affection in others now, the fears of a future when he may be lonelier and more unloved still. And William James in *The Varieties of Religious Experience* provides scores of case-histories that parallel both the suddenness of Scrooge's conversion and the sense of radiant joy he feels in the world around him after it has taken place. It may be that what really gives the skeptics pause is that Scrooge is converted to a gospel of good cheer. They could probably believe easily enough if he espoused some gloomy doctrine of intolerance.

But it is doubtful whether such questions ever arise when one is actually reading the ***Christmas Carol.*** From the very beginning Dickens strikes a tone of playful exaggeration that warns us this is no exercise in naturalism. Scrooge carries "his own low temperature always about with him; he iced his office in the dog-days." Blind men's dogs, when they see him coming, tug their masters into doorways to avoid him. The entire world of the story is an animistic one: houses play hide-and-seek, door-knockers come to life as human heads, the tuning of a fiddle is "like fifty stomach aches," old Fezziwig's legs wink as he dances, potatoes bubbling in a saucepan knock loudly at the lid "to be let out and peeled." Scrooge's own language has a jocose hyperbole, even when he is supposed to be most ferocious or most terrified, that makes his very utterance seem half a masquerade. "If I could work my will," he snarls, "every idiot who goes about with 'Merry Christmas' on his lips should be boiled with his own pudding, and buried with a stake of holly through his heart. He should!" Is that the accent of a genuine curmudgeon or of a man trying to sound more violent than he feels? And to Marley's Ghost, despite his disquiet, he remarks, "You may be an undigested bit of beef, a blob of mustard, a crumb of cheese, a fragment of an under-done potato. There's more of gravy than of grave about you, whatever you are!"

All these things make it clear that Dickens—as always when he is most deeply moved and most profound—is speaking in terms of unavowed allegory. But the allegory of Dickens is in one way subtler than the allegory of writers like Kafka or Melville. Kafka is always hinting the existence of hidden meanings by making the experience of his characters so baffling and irrational on a merely realistic level that we are obliged to search for symbolic significances. And Melville, too, by a score of devices, from those rolling, darkly magnificent and extraordinary soliloquies to the mystery of Ahab's intense and impassioned pursuit of the White Whale, forces us to realize that this is a more metaphysical duel than one with a mere deep-sea beast.

Dickens, however, leaves his surface action so entirely clear and the behavior of his characters so plain that they do not puzzle us into groping for gnomic meanings. Scrooge is a miser, his nephew a warmhearted fellow, Bob Cratchit a poor clerk—what could be simpler? If there is a touch of oddity in the details, that is merely Dickens's well-known comic grotesquerie; if Scrooge's change of heart is sharp and antithetical, that is only Dickens' melodramatic sentimentality. Surely all the world knows that Dickens is never profound?

But the truth is that Dickens has so fused his abstract thought and its imaginative forming that one melts almost entirely into the other. Though our emotional perception of Dickens' meaning is immediate and spontaneous, nothing in his handling thrusts upon us an intellectual statement of that meaning. But more than a warm-hearted outpouring of holiday sentiment, the **Christmas Carol** is in essence a serio-comic parable of social redemption. Marley's Ghost is the symbol of divine grace, and the three Christmas Spirits are the working of that grace through the agencies of memory, example and fear. And Scrooge, although of course he is himself too, is not himself alone: he is the embodiment of all that concentration upon material power and callous indifference to the welfare of human beings that the economists had erected into a system, businessmen and industrialists pursued relentlessly, and society taken for granted as inevitable and proper. The conversion of Scrooge is an image of the conversion for which Dickens hopes among mankind.

Thea Holme   (essay date 1957)

SOURCE: An introduction to *Sketches by Boz* by Charles Dickens, Oxford University Press, London, 1957, pp. v-xi.

[*In the essay below, Holme praises Dickens's descriptive writing style in* Sketches by Boz.]

One evening in the autumn of 1832 the manuscript of a fictional sketch entitled **'A Sunday out of Town'** was dropped 'with fear and trembling into a dark letter-box in a dark office up a dark court in Fleet Street'. Its author, describing the event to a friend, gives a picture of the sequel. We see him in a Strand bookshop, hurriedly searching through a copy of *The Monthly Magazine.* He pauses, gazing at the page before him. His sketch—its name 'transmogrified' to **'A Dinner at Poplar Walk'**—is there, 'in all the glory of print'. Thrusting his way through the crowded Strand, the young Charles Dickens hurries blindly towards Westminster Hall where he may pace in solitude—'my eyes so dimmed with pride and joy, that they could not bear the street, and were not fit to be seen'.

The delight of seeing his work in print was the only reward offered by *The Monthly Magazine,* whose Editor presently sent a 'polite and flattering communication' asking for more. He was duly supplied with **'Horatio Sparkins'**, **'The Bloomsbury Christening'**, and **'The Boarding House'**. This last was the first sketch to bear the author's signature—'Boz'. The pseudonym was, as he afterwards put it, 'the nickname of a pet child, a younger brother whom I had dubbed Moses, in honour of The Vicar of Wakefield; which, being facetiously pronounced through the nose, became Boses, and, being shortened, became Boz'.

The following year, Dickens, who was now twenty-one and earning five guineas a week as a reporter on *The Morning Chronicle,* was sent to review a new farce at the Adelphi Theatre. He found that the author, J. B. Buckstone, had unashamedly used the plot and many of the jokes from his own sketch, **'The Bloomsbury Christening'**. Already he had been paid the doubtful compliment of plagiarism.

By now several influential men were becoming aware of young Boz, among them the successful author Harrison Ainsworth, who introduced him to his own publisher, Macrone. One night, after spending the evening at Ainsworth's house in Willesden, Dickens and Macrone walked back into the city together. The publisher declared that the **Sketches**, of which twenty or so had now appeared in *The Morning Chronicle* and other papers, were 'capital value'; and suggested their being collected into a volume for publication. Cruikshank the cartoonist, he added casually, might be the man to illustrate them. It is not difficult to imagine the enthusiasm with which this suggestion was received, or the eagerness with which Boz—in the spare time snatched from his travels as a parliamentary reporter in election time—was to fling himself into the production of a quantity of new sketches to complete the two volumes finally commissioned by Macrone. His mind was filled with ideas: he wrote with speed. In the end it was Cruikshank, not Dickens, who held up publication.

At last, on 7 February 1836, its author's twenty-fourth birthday, the First Series of **Sketches by Boz** was published. Its immediate success was almost immediately eclipsed; for some six weeks later the first number of *The Pickwick Papers* appeared. After a doubtful start this serial was to achieve, with the introduction of Sam Weller, a swift and enduring fame. By the time the Second Series of his *Sketches* appeared, Boz and *Pickwick* were household words.

'Perhaps', said *Cranford*'s Miss Jenkyns, 'the author is young. Let him persevere, and who knows what he may become if he will take the great Doctor for his model.' 'Doctor Johnson's style', she reiterated later—after listening 'with patient gravity' to a chapter of *Pickwick*— 'Doctor Johnson's style is a model for young beginners.'

It is true that Mrs. Gaskell, in introducing Boz as a bone of contention between two of her characters, was incidentally paying a witty compliment to the Editor who had commissioned her work. But the fictitious Miss Jenkyns's attitude may well have had its counterpart in reality. The impact of Dickens upon the more reactionary of his readers must have been startling. After the rolling phrases, the remote philosophizing characters of Johnson; the exotic phantasmagoria of Gothic romance; even after the fastidious realism of Jane Austen—'Let other pens dwell on guilt and misery. I quit such odious subjects as soon as I can'— the contrast is remarkable. Here was Boz, reflecting a completely new outlook, the outlook of the man in the street; setting down in his *Sketches* all the small events in the everyday life of common persons—bank clerks, shop assistants, omnibus drivers; laundresses, market women, and kidney-pie sellers: directing his powers of observation and description upon scenes and characters within the daily scope of any loiterer in London. 'I thought I knew something of the town', commented one of his fellow clerks in the law firm of Ellis and Blackmore; 'but after a little talk with Dickens I found that I knew nothing. He knew it all, from Bow to Brentford. . . . He could imitate, in a manner I never saw equalled, the low population of the streets of London in all their varieties.'

In these sketches we see a reflection of the tremendous social changes that were beginning to take place. On the one hand Dickens depicts in relentless detail the horrors of poverty, disease, and crime—legacy of eighteenth-century London; on the other the prosperous vulgarity of the rapidly rising middle class. The young Boz stood, as it were, between two worlds; and we are reminded that Dickens the Eminent Victorian was born in the reign of George the Third. Through his eyes we watch Hogarthian scenes of misery and despair, offset by brightly coloured pictures of mass jollification reminiscent of Frith's 'Derby Day'.

> The heat is intense this afternoon, and the people, of whom there are additional parties arriving every moment, look as warm as the tables which have been recently painted, and have the appearance of being red-hot. What a dust and noise! Men and women—boys and girls— sweethearts and married people. . . . Gentlemen in alarming waistcoats, and steel watchguards, promenading about, three abreast . . . ladies, with great, long, white pocket-handkerchiefs like small table-cloths in their hands, chasing one another on the grass in the most playful and interesting manner, with the view of attracting the attention of the aforesaid gentlemen—husbands in perspective ordering

> bottles of ginger-beer for the objects of their affections, with a lavish disregard of expense; and the said objects washing down huge quantities of shrimps and winkles, with an equal disregard of their own bodily health and subsequent discomfort—boys, with great silk hats just balanced on the top of their heads, smoking cigars, and trying to look as if they liked them—gentlemen in pink shirts and blue waistcoats, occasionally upsetting either themselves, or somebody else, with their own canes.

I suppose it is almost inevitable that one should consider these sketches in terms of painting, for their writer is already a master of pictorial description. He lays on his colours boldly, giving us sharp contrasts of light and darkness in his **'Visit to Newgate'**, and bringing to life with vivid touches his portraits such as **'The Last Cab Driver'** who is described as 'a brown-whiskered, white-hatted, no-coated cabman; his nose was generally red, and his bright blue eye not unfrequently stood out in bold relief against a black border of artificial workmanship'. His neck, we are told, 'was usually garnished with a bright yellow handkerchief. In summer he carried in his mouth a flower; in winter, a straw—slight, but, to a contemplative mind, certain indications of a love of nature, and a taste for botany.'

It is difficult to make a fair assessment of the literary value of these early sketches because, in doing so, one must temporarily forget the masterpieces of which they were the harbinger, and of which one is so frequently reminded by small inspired touches, or by the foreshadowing of characters as yet unborn. Dickens himself, years later, described his first book as 'often being extremely crude and ill-considered, and bearing obvious marks of haste and inexperience'. This may indeed be true of some of the 'Tales', such as **'Mr. Minns and His Cousin'** (the original **'A Sunday out of Town'**), which, after an amusing and carefully contrived start, ends with such suddenness that one wonders if the author had run out of paper; and also of the irritating humours of **'The Mudfog Association'** in which the comic genius of Boz seems to have lost its way.

But as an example of what is now called 'documentary' the *Sketches* deserve a unique place in literature. It has been pointed out elsewhere that more than half this volume's contents are facts: facts observed with an astonishing precision and wealth of detail. But Boz is no objective reporter: the facts he presents are invested with his own reaction to them, and in some cases are lifted by his imagination into tragedy or fantasy. An example of this is to be found in **'Meditations in Monmouth Street'**, where, speculating upon the contents of a second-hand clothes shop, he creates the life story of a wastrel from some of the garments displayed; and then, 'by way of restoring the naturally cheerful tone of our thoughts', begins to fit 'visionary feet and legs into a cellar-board full of boots and shoes'. With a swift stroke of invention he brings to life a whole cast of characters, imagines their relationships one with the other, and sets them before us in a sort of comic ballet.

It is interesting to note that at the time of their publication, the two *Sketches* singled out for praise were concerned with tragedy—**'The Black Veil'** and **'A Visit to Newgate'**. The former, which is included among the Tales, is a highly dramatic, not to say melodramatic, story, of which the theme is a recurrent one throughout the *Sketches*: the ruin of a woman's life by the worthlessness of the man to whom she has devoted it. In this case it is a mother whose fruitless efforts to save her son from the gallows have driven her insane. We are spared few of the horrors of this woeful tale; there are moments when the dialogue is worthy of the Radclyffian title.

> 'Who was he?' inquired the surgeon.

> *'My son'*, rejoined the woman; and fell senseless at his feet.

But in contrast we find masterly passages such as that describing 'the back part of Walworth'; and the 'corpulent round-headed boy' at the opening might be a rough sketch of the fat boy in *Pickwick*.

Dickens admitted that he found Newgate Prison 'a very difficult subject'. There is little doubt that he found it a heart-rending one. Reading this account one cannot fail to be aware of the pity with which his imagination works upon the mournful groups he describes: the women conversing through the bars of 'a kind of iron cage . . . through which the friends of the female prisoners communicate with them'; the three condemned murderers—one of them entertaining some hopes of reprieve, and holding aloof from his two companions, who, as the turnkey intimated in a confident undertone, 'were dead men'. After a pitiful description of fourteen infant pickpockets 'drawn up in line for our inspection' in the prison school, he writes, 'There was not one redeeming feature among them—not a glance of honesty—not a wink expressive of anything but the gallows and the hulks, in the whole collection'; and concludes, 'We have never looked upon a more disagreeable sight, because we never saw fourteen such hopeless creatures of neglect, before.' Here, surely, is something greater than pity and horror: the imaginative insight into the cause of crime which was later to inspire his relentless exposure of social evils. Already, it would seem, the foundations have been laid for *Oliver Twist*; and the images of Fagin and his gang have peered at their creator from out of the shadows of Newgate.

It is for the glimpses they afford us of their author that these sketches have a special fascination: not only in foreshadowings of future greatness but in those touches which reveal the young Boz himself. In **'Making a Night of It'** he gives us what is thought to be a self portrait. He is the romantic Smithers in his 'brown hat, very much turned up at the sides', who found his appreciation of a theatrical performance somewhat marred by the effects of Scotch whiskey and Havannah cigars. Young Boz must undoubtedly have met **'The Theatrical Young Gentleman'** who is the subject of another sketch, and who called Drury Lane the lane, and the Victoria the vic. His own interest in theatrical matters is unquestionable; and in **'Private Theatres'** it is clear that his knowledge of these places of entertainment extended backstage.

In the National Portrait Gallery there hangs a painting by Maclise, of which Thackeray declared, 'Here we have the real identical man, Dickens.' It shows a youthful figure seated in a crimson and gilt armchair before a writing desk, his left hand firmly placed upon a manuscript—an attitude which seems to suggest that he is playing, with enjoyment, the part of a famous writer. The pale smooth face is turned, like an actor's, full into the light. One observes the elegant folds of his black satin cravat, the neatness of his small well-polished boots. Then, drawing nearer, one becomes aware of the power and vitality in that face with its strong nose and sensuous, sensitive mouth—and the large brilliant eyes which, turned away from the artist, gaze thoughtfully out of the window. These are the eyes which observed the tragedy and comedy of life in such vivid detail; which saw and recorded brutality and pathos, courage and despair, and all the innumerable absurdities of human behaviour.

This portrait was painted three years after the publication of *Sketches by Boz,* when its subject was assured of fame; but it is not difficult to recognize the author of these early works. It is in company with this same youthful, energetic figure that, reading them, we walk the streets and visit the entertainments and institutions of the London of William the Fourth. There are many rewarding discoveries for the explorer among these pages; many opportunities to exclaim in echo of Thackeray, 'Here we have the real identical man, Dickens!'

Leslie C. Staples   (essay date 1958)

SOURCE: An introduction to *The Uncommercial Traveller and Reprinted Pieces, Etc.* by Charles Dickens, Oxford University Press, London, 1958, pp. v-x.

[*In the following essay, Staples centers on Dickens's use of autobiographical material in* The Uncommercial Traveller *and* Reprinted Pieces.]

The genius of Dickens needed space to attain its full stature. Twenty monthly 'parts' of thirty-two pages each were not too much for the telling of his tales. In the preface to the best known of his shorter works he complained of the difficulty of its construction within a 'narrow space'. He remarked that he 'never attempted great elaboration of detail in the working out of character within such limits, believing that it could not succeed'. And yet what memorable characters he did in fact create within the narrowest limits. In the novels one immediately recalls Trabb's boy and, within the narrowest limits imaginable, the nervous young man interposing in a conversation and getting no further than *Esker . . . ?* and then stopping dead. In the short articles we are to consider in this [essay], when space was indeed narrow, examples abound, perhaps less known but scarcely less remarkable.

It was as a journalist that Dickens first made his mark with the reading public, and a good case could be made out for the theory that if Dickens had never published a novel his collected journalistic pieces would have secured for him some small niche in the temple of fame. His earliest essays, collected under the title *Sketches by Boz,* make up a book which has been described as the Overture to the Opera of Dickens. Almost all the themes dealt with in the novels are foreshadowed here. They were the work of a high-spirited young man in his early twenties, and exhibit a gusto that is infectious and was to reach its fine flowering a year or two later in *Pickwick.*

The journalism [we shall consider] . . . is of a very different character, and is contemporary with his maturity, as is self-evident in much of *The Uncommercial Traveller.* There are no undisciplined high spirits here, but the polished prose of the established master. Yet for all their apparent effortlessness a world of pains had gone into their composition. One of the most revealing things to be seen at the Dickens House in London is a page of the manuscript of *Pickwick,* a masterpiece written at the age of twenty-four, which has no more than half a dozen words corrected, lying side by side with that of one of his later journalistic papers, which has hardly a line that was not scored out and rewritten.

Dickens's weekly journal *All the Year Round* had been running for two years, following its predecessor's eight, when he commenced the series he called *The Uncommercial Traveller.* Until then, all the contributions in these journals, with the exception of his own serialized novels, had been anonymous; but he was announced to be the author of these articles, among which are to be found the finest of his fugitive writings, and in which, as he explains in the prefatory paper, **"His General Line of Business,"** he proposed to travel, uncommercially, for the firm of Human Interest Brothers. In addition to recounting current experiences, he frequently drew upon his memories of the past, and not the least interesting feature of the papers is the autobiographical material that is to be found in many of them. Here is much that he probably originally intended for the autobiography that he never wrote, and much to supplement what we gather about his early life in *David Copperfield.*

The city of Rochester, 'the birthplace of his fancy', as it has been called, figures in many of his works, but in **"Dullborough Town"** we have his picture of it as the background of his own childhood, and not as a setting for his characters. His vivid memories of it should be read alongside the pictures painted of it in his first book, *Pickwick,* and again in his last, *Edwin Drood.* In every case the old city inspires him with the tenderest affection.

> Of course the town had shrunk fearfully since I was a child there. I had entertained the impression that the High Street was at least as wide as Regent Street, London, or the Italian Boulevard at Paris. I found it little better than a lane. There was a public clock in it, which I had supposed to be the finest clock in the world; whereas it now turned out to be as inexpressive, moonfaced, weak a clock as ever I saw. It belonged to a Town Hall . . . a mean little brick heap, like a demented chapel, with a few yawning persons in leather gaiters, in the last extremity for something to do, lounging at the door with their hands in their pockets, and calling themselves a Corn Exchange!

In **"Travelling Abroad"** there is the oft-quoted story of his being taken to Gad's Hill as 'a queer small boy' by his father, and shown the great house there. If he worked hard, he was told, he might one day come to live in a house like that. A parental prophecy that came true, for he did indeed come to live, and to die, there. More childhood memories are to be found in **"Nurse's Stories,"** in which Dickens makes yet another plea that a child's imagination should be treated with the most delicate care.

Memories of his early manhood are no less interesting. In **"City of London Churches"** we get a delightful glimpse of his first love affair. For Angelica, beside whom he writes of himself as sitting in an all but empty city church one Sunday morning, must surely have been Maria Beadnell, alias Dora Spenlow.

> I mind when I, turned of eighteen, went with my Angelica to a city church on account of a shower (by this special coincidence that it was in Huggin Lane), and when I said to my Angelica, 'Let the blessed event, Angelica occur at no altar but this!' and when my Angelica consented that it should occur at no other—which it certainly never did, for it never occurred anywhere, and oh Angelica, what has become of you, this present Sunday morning, when I can't attend to the sermon; and more difficult than that, what has become of Me, as I was when I sat by your side?

In **"Recollections of Mortality"** there is a humorous account of the purchase of his first horse, when he was living at Devonshire Terrace, and in the same paper the story of his serving on a coroner's jury empanelled to investigate the death of 'a very little mite of a child'. The story of his purchase of a performing goldfinch, and the little creature's refusal to perform without the personal attendance of its vendor, is to be found in **"Shy Neighbourhoods."**

Later recollections include those of his eccentric sculptor friend, Angus Fletcher, whose portrait as Mr. Kindheart in **"Medicine Men of Civilisation"** is not unworthy to stand beside many more elaborate portraits in the novels; and of his visit to the little house in Shadwell that was the seed of a great children's hospital, in **"A Small Star in the East."** And how delightful it is to meet again the little wooden midshipman of *Dombey and Son* in **"Wapping Workhouse."**

In addition to the autobiographical, the series has the widest of range, and embraces most of the author's extremely varied interests and styles; maritime rescue work in **"The Shipwreck,"** popular entertainment in **"Two Views of a Cheap Theatre,"** a very familiar subject such as the description of **"Titbull's Alms-houses,"** and characteristic imaginative writing such as **"Arcadian London,"** and **"Chambers,"** in which latter paper Dickens once again inveighs against Gray's Inn. Why, one wonders, did he so seldom miss an opportunity of doing so? Was he unhappy there, as a lawyer's clerk?

> I look upon Gray's Inn generally as one of the most depressing institutions in bricks and mortar known to the children of men. Can anything be more dreary than its arid Square, Sahara Desert of the law . . .

Despite the passage of a century, not to speak of the falling of high explosives, a great deal of the old London described in these chapters is still to be seen, and explorations in the author's footsteps are among the most rewarding experiences of the Dickensian in London. Many of the city churches so vividly characterized are still to be identified.

An interesting example occurs here of Dickens making amends for mistaken criticism. In **"A Small Star in the East"** he had something to say about the conditions under which people worked in East London lead mills. The passage coming to the notice of the gentlemen who ran the mills with which Dickens dealt, they got into touch with him and invited him to see how carefully they sought to protect their workers. Dickens made honourable amends in **"On an Amateur Beat,"** and his correspondence with the firm is now in the Dickens House in London.

Some attention has been paid in recent years to **"The Ruffian,"** but it is too controversial a matter to be usefully discussed in the limited space available here. The paper is long likely to remain fruitful material for assessing Dickens's social conscience.

Turning to **Reprinted Pieces,** we have a somewhat earlier collection, all the items of which appeared in *Household Words* between 1850 and 1856, and all anonymously. This selection of his contributions to that journal was made by Dickens himself for the Library Edition of his works. . . .

Here again, the autobiographical element is of great interest. Again we are taken back to his earlier days. **"Our School"** gives a vivid picture of his brief schooldays at Wellington House Academy in Hampstead Road: that part of it which was not sliced away by the construction of the London and Birmingham Railway, as described in the paper, remains to this day. Clearly it was not a remarkable school, but Dickens was glad to be at any kind of school after the misery of the blacking factory. Some of his recollections of it went into the creation of Creakle's school in *David Copperfield*. And then we have a delightful picture of Broadstairs, to which he regularly returned, summer after summer, from 1836 to 1851, in **"Our English Watering-Place."** Although considerably larger than in Dickens's day, the older part of the town has retained its character to a remarkable degree and the landmarks with which he deals are still to be seen. Readers of this chapter will also hail an old friend with a great deal of pleasure, Miss Julia Mills, from *David Copperfield*.

> Miss Julia Mills has read the whole collection of these books [in the circulating library]. She has left marginal notes on the pages, as 'Is not this truly touching? J. M.' 'How thrilling! J. M.' 'Entranced here by the Magician's potent spell. J. M.' She has italicized her favourite traits in the description of the hero, as 'his hair, which was *dark* and *wavy*, clustered in *rich profusion* around a *marble brow,* whose lofty paleness bespoke the intellect within.' It reminds her of another hero. She adds, 'How like B. L. Can this be mere coincidence? J. M.'

"Our French Watering-Place" is Boulogne, which almost replaced Broadstairs in Dickens's affection for a season or two. Apart from the autobiographical, the series deals with the widest range of subjects, from **"A Child's Dream of a Star,"** among the most sentimental of his writings, to **"A Mounment of French Folly,"** a fierce attack on what Dickens regarded as a great public scandal.

After presenting three miscellaneous items written at different periods of Dickens's life—**"The Lamplighter," "To be Read at Dusk,"** and **"Sunday under Three Heads"**—this volume concludes with three pieces commissioned for publication in America. The author received a thousand pounds for each of these; Forster comments on the unprecedented figure for writings of their length. Julius Slinkton in **"Hunted Down"** was founded upon Thomas Griffiths Wainewright, the poisoner and forger. Prominent in the contemporary world of letters, he was 'Janus Weathercock' of the *London Magazine.* We probably read more of him in Dickens's Jonas Chuzzlewit. **"Holiday Romance"** contains the favourite **"Magic Fishbone."** To one of its companion pieces, **"Captain Boldheart,"** its author was especially partial. **"George Silverman's Explanation"** has mystified most of the critics. It is possibly the least characteristic of Dickens's shorter writings. The key to it, in all probability, is psychological, as at least one commentator has demonstrated.

To know Dickns one must be familiar with a dozen major novels, but the knowledge is incomplete without some familiarity with his journalistic work. . . .

Butt cites a pivotal point in Dickens's writing career:

I believe [*A Christmas Carol*] to be important in Dickens's development as a story-teller, since it is the first time he had attempted to direct his fertile imagination within the limits of a carefully constructed and premeditated plot. There is indeed no external evidence, in the shape of letters or draft sketch, to show what were his initial intentions. But the book as it stands bears the marks of constructive care at the outset. The opening picture of the unregenerate Scrooge, surly towards his clerk and his nephew, is balanced by the closing picture of Scrooge transformed, his transformation evident in his treatment of clerk and nephew; and the process of transformation is nicely graded in the visitations of the three Spirits. This is the first occasion of Dickens discovering a plot sufficient to carry his message, and a plot coterminous with his message, a plot that is to say, the whole of which bears upon his message and does not overlap it. He had at last begun to keep a steadier eye upon the purpose and design of his work.

John Butt in "A Christmas Carol: *Its Origin and Design," in* The Dickensian, *1954.*

C. B. Cox   (essay date 1958)

SOURCE: "Comic Viewpoints in *Sketches by Boz,*" in *English,* Vol. XII, No. 69, Autumn, 1958, pp. 132-35.

[*In the essay below, English scholar and critic Cox traces the humor in* Sketches by Boz, *finding that the characters depicted represent for Dickens "the comic situation of man in the universe."*]

The scenes, characters, and tales included by Dickens in *Sketches by Boz* are of unequal merit. Many of the tales are simple and naïve in their treatment of character, and others, such as **"The Black Veil"** and **"The Drunkard's Death,"** are heavily melodramatic, but among these failures are other sketches which demonstrate why Dickens is one of the greatest of our humorists. His stories are not merely a series of fancies and jokes, but show through humour his attitudes towards man's position in society and in the universe. In *Sketches by Boz,* the comic viewpoints which are implied in his later works can be seen in the process of development.

Dickens's humour in his treatment of society operates on many levels. In these early sketches he often seems only to be laughing at oddities, at people who do not behave in conventional ways, but already his treatment of such characters implies much more than simple mockery of eccentrics. A good example of a more complex viewpoint is to be found in the description of the half-pay captain, one of the many portraits included under the heading "Our Parish." The captain is bluff and unceremonious, and invades the privacy of a quiet old lady, his next-door neighbour. Some ordinary jokes are included, such as the description of how the captain takes the lady's clock to pieces, and replaces the parts so that the large hand has done nothing but trip up the little one ever since; but one detail gives the sketch the true Dickens touch. The captain delights in making experiments with the old lady's property:

> 'One morning he got up early, and planted three or four roots of full-grown marigolds in every bed of her front garden, to the inconceivable astonishment of the old lady, who actually thought when she got up and looked out of the window, that it was some strange eruption which had come out in the night.

This passage shows that the captain is not just a curiosity to be laughed at because he is so unconventional. There is something beautiful in his fantastic idea of planting the marigolds. The scene suggests that even though man is a strange, comic figure, out of his peculiarities beauty is often created, coming, like the vision of marigolds to the old lady, with a shock of surprise. The same effects are given when Dickens describes the cabriolet-driver:

> In summer he carried in his mouth a flower; in winter, a straw—slight, but to a contemplative mind, certain indications of a love of nature, and a taste for botany.

The driver may be an oddity, but his habit of carrying a flower in his mouth shows a delightful response to beauty.

These simple examples point to important implications of Dickens's attitude towards society. Characters such as the half-pay captain and the cabriolet-driver are contrasted with people who have become the slaves of social conventions. There are many portraits of snobs such as Mr. and Mrs. Malderton and Flamwell in the story of Horatio Sparkins. Dickens suggests that the order and propriety which seem proper to civilized manners almost inevitably lead to a sense of dignity and pride which limit enjoyment of experience. His comic portraits underline the value of individuals who may seem odd to conventional eyes, but who succeed in finding a means of expression for their love of life. One of the purposes of civilized customs is to bol-

ster up man's faith in his own importance, to give our ordinary enjoyments, of eating and drinking, for example, a covering of pomp and ceremony, and to ensure that even our suffering is not without its proper dignity. Dickens prefers those who enjoy pleasure frankly and heartily, and who are not reticent in expressing their emotions. This is one of the reasons why both his gay pictures of Christmas exuberance and his emotional outbursts over human suffering have often found little favour with the sophisticated tastes of the twentieth century. He feels that civilized restraint can limit expression of affection and love, and withdraw the mind from sympathy with mankind. He admires men and women who commit themselves to life in all its fullness, and he suggests that such committal necessarily involves some sacrifice of what is normally considered as dignified behaviour.

A good example of these attitudes is to be seen in the story **"Mr. Minns and his Cousin."** Augustus Minns hates dogs and children:

> He was not unamiable, but he could at any time have viewed the execution of a dog, or the assassination of an infant, with the liveliest satisfaction. Their habits were at variance with his love of order; and his love of order was as powerful as his love of life.

The story is first of all a simple satire on Minns's ambition to impose order on all his actions. He is visited by a relative, Mr. Budden, whose large white dog puts its paws on the table, and begins to eat the bread and butter. He travels in a coach, and is joined by a child and its mother: 'The child was an affectionate and an amiable infant; the little dear mistook Minns for its other parent, and screamed to embrace him.' But the story is more than a series of jokes about man's inability to impose his sense of order and propriety on the raw material of life. Mr. Minns is contrasted with Mr. Budden, whose love of good eating and fellowship exposes the emptiness of the bachelor life of Mr. Minns. Mr. Budden is a jolly, lively man, who loves his wife and child, his brandy and water, and his country home. When he visits Minns for breakfast, he eats heartily with a fine disregard for conventional manners. Budden is comic in his excesses, but, like so many Dickens characters, his refusal to obey social conventions is the mark of his exuberant joy in life. In contrast, Mr. Minns's ordered existence is drab and cold.

Some of the most lively of *Sketches by Boz* represent this belief that we only enjoy ourselves to the full when we forget conventional standards of propriety. In his description of **"Greenwich Fair,"** Dickens gives a vivid account of *The Crown and Anchor,* a temporary ballroom:

> The dancing, itself, beggars description—every figure lasts about an hour, and the ladies bounce up and down the middle, with a degree of spirit which is quite indescribable. As to the gentlemen, they stamp their feet against the ground, every time 'hands four round' begins, go down the middle and up again, with cigars in their mouths, and silk handkerchiefs in their hands, and whirl their partners round, nothing loath, scrambling and falling, and embracing, and

knocking up against the other couples, until they are fairly tired out, and can move no longer.

Dickens pokes fun at the clerks and apprentices who finish the night of the dance with aching heads, empty pockets, and damaged hats; but the scene shows their energetic joy in life. All the feasts described in the sketches run to the same pattern. There is zest and animation, the best of food and drink, and exhilarated by the occasion, some gentleman always insists on giving a speech. His attempts at high-flown phrases sound ludicrous, and often his audience do not even understand him, but they applaud with great approval. These comic scenes show that we can never maintain a pose of dignity, and our attempts to do so will appear pompous; but as long as our desire to strut and stick our chests out does not stop us from enjoying ourselves, this does not matter. One of the reasons for Dickens's appeal to a wide popular audience is that he understood the value of committing onself to pleasure, whatever the loss of social dignity this may entail. He tells us to eat pickled onions with relish, to lie in the sun and allow our children to heap us over with sand, and, on all occasions, never to despise the pleasures of the ordinary man.

Although he admires the half-pay captain and the cabriolet-driver, Dickens is always aware that they are oddities. As such they represent for him the comic situation of man in the universe. Dickens sees that there is something peculiarly comic about the way man is tied to the body, and to one place on earth, and however seriously he takes his activities, they will soon be forgotten in the flow of time. We are all ignorant of the future, and our fate is often determined by forces over which we have no control. In *Sketches by Boz* Dickens's comic approach to the human predicament is reflected in simple form in the racy remarks of Mr. Bung, the beadle. Mr. Bung remarks that he is not 'one of those fortunate men who, if they were to dive under one side of a barge stark-naked, would come up on the other with a new suit of clothes on, and a ticket for soup in the waistcoat-pocket. . . . He is just one of the careless, good-for-nothing, happy fellows, who float, cork-like, on the surface, for the world to play at hockey with. . . .' These images show in comic form the haphazard way in which fate deals with man. Bung's vivid expressions make us laugh not only because they are a delightful freak of fancy, but because they suggest the crazy, unexpected quality of good fortune in this world. But the final effect of these images is not one of futility. The relish with which Bung describes his own fate, his delight in his own fancy, stand as a positive value, showing a vitality which fortune cannot overthrow. On one occasion Bung describes how he 'felt as lonesome as a kitten in a wash-house copper with the lid on'. He is a ludicrous figure, but not one to be sneered at, for he himself enjoys the oddity of his own misfortunes.

Many of the anecdotes in *Sketches by Boz* describe how man's energetic search after pleasure leads to comic misfortune, but also they show how the zest with which he performs these antics is a sign of vitality. Mr. Percy Noakes makes careful preparations for a party on a steamer up the Thames. There is singing and flirtation, cold boiled leg of mutton and hearty sirloin of beef, and the scene is one of colour and high-spirited frolic. Then come

wind and storm, no one can eat the food, and they return sick and dispirited. Whereas Mr. Bung's expressions suggest man's enslavement by fate, the party of Mr. Noakes shows man to be the sport of nature. These attitudes to misfortune are typical of the early work of Dickens. He is determined to be gay whatever may happen, to enjoy whole-heartedly the peculiarities of life. This is seen in an extreme form in the story of Mr. Watkins Tottle, where Dickens jokes about a shy, middle-aged bachelor whose misfortunes in money and in love end in suicide.

As Dickens developed, his view of misfortune and of evil grew more sombre, and he found it increasingly difficult to adopt the comic point of view. In *Sketches by Boz,* only occasionally do morbid anecdotes dispel the prevailing notes of joy and exhilaration, but already there are signs of a tragic awareness of life. Certain passages in *Sketches by Boz* are ambiguous in their effects because Dickens moves in one short passage from a comic to a tragic viewpoint. When describing gin shops, he begins with his usual delight in a scene of riot and confusion, but ends on a very different note:

> The knot of Irish labourers at the lower end of the place, who have been alternately shaking hands with, and threatening the life of, each other for the last hour, become furious in their disputes, and finding it impossible to silence one man, who is particularly anxious to adjust the difference, they resort to the infallible expedient of knocking him down and jumping on him afterwards . . . a scene of riot and confusion ensues . . . the landlord hits everybody, and everybody hits the landlord . . . the remainder slink home to beat their wives for complaining, and kick the children for daring to be hungry.

In this passage Dickens turns from laughter at inappropriate high spirits to a pathetic account of human cruelty. Yet even in his most vivid descriptions of suffering, he shows a faith in the power of love. In his story **"The Black Veil"** it is the love of the mother for the hanged felon which is the mainspring of the plot.

It is this faith in individual goodness which prevents Dickens's humour from ever becoming cynical. In his comic treatment of reality, he shows two very different approaches to the enigma of human existence. On the one hand, he sees man as a fool—like Mr. Percy Noakes or Mr. Watkins Tottle, a creature whose attempts to take himself seriously are worthy only of ridicule; yet, on the other hand, the vigour with which such characters pursue their activities redeems them from futility. Above all, Dickens's comic characters love people and love life. The comedy of Dickens suggests a fundamental paradox: man is a puny creature a few feet high whose pretensions are mocked by the vastness of time and space; he is also endowed with a capacity for love which makes the facts of time and space seem unimportant.

Harry Stone   (essay date 1962)

SOURCE: "Dickens' Artistry and *The Haunted Man,*" in *South Atlantic Quarterly,* Vol. LXI, No. 4, Autumn, 1962, pp. 492-505.

[*Stone is an American scholar and critic, whose works—many award-winning—include* Dickens and the Invisible World: Fairy Tales, Fantasy, and Novel-Making *(1979) and* The Night Side of Dickens: Cannibalism, Passion, Necessity *(1991). In the following excerpt, Stone examines the evolution of Dickens's writing style as evidenced by his skillful uniting of elements of fairy tale, allegory, autobiography, and psychology in* The Haunted Man.]

If one reads Dickens' novels chronologically, one is astonished upon beginning *Dombey and Son* (1847-48). The first half of *Dombey* is almost perfect in conception and execution; each scene connects with the next, each throws light on what has come before and what is yet to come. Dickens calls up intricate themes and images, develops them, sustains them, and finally merges them with one another. He introduces experimental techniques—the child's point of view, the microcosmic world as chorus—and does so with great assurance. But above all, he masters a new structural method, a method which fuses autobiography, psychology, symbolism, and fancy.

This transformation had hardly been hinted at in Dickens' earlier novels. His six previous novels blended the rich heritage of the eighteenth-century novel with an intermittent attention to new (or newly emphasized) Victorian concerns and techniques: serious attention to such elements as shabby-genteel life, reform, and symbolic plot structure. But such elements, especially the last, were not yet central to Dickens' conceptions and, despite occasional experiments and innovations, in the 1830's and early 1840's he was content to regard himself as continuing the tradition of the prose-fiction masters; characteristically, he replied to criticism of *Pickwick*'s desultory narrative method by invoking in his defense the methods of "some of the greatest novelists in the English language." Yet he was disturbed by the formlessness of *Pickwick*, and sought to give his subsequent novels a cohesiveness which would transcend their broken, month- by-month composition and publication. In part he succeeded. No other Dickens novel is quite so episodic and haphazard as *Pickwick*. But the machinery of lost wills, unknown relatives, and unbelievable coincidences which he used to integrate his novels prior to the Christmas books gave those novels only the appearance of unity; he had introduced no substantial change in his underlying method. *Martin Chuzzlewit,* the last of the early novels, was, it is true, designed to have a central theme, to exhibit selfishness in some of its many disguises, and the book was begun with the awareness that arrogant hypocrisy would be unmasked by the fairy-tale machinations of old Martin. But the unifying devices were still excrescences, the social criticism largely non-organic, and the milieu remote or exotic.

Yet even before the Christmas books Dickens had captivated the English-speaking world. His fame, however, was an acknowledgment of sheer creative exuberance. His preeminence resulted from a series of dazzling tours de force, from an ability to animate isolated characters and scenes with an eidetic reality. The contemporary reader adored Dickens not for his style, his criticism, his vision, or his architechtonics—all of which are undervalued even today—but because he invented Tony Weller, Little Nell, and Mrs. Gamp; or because he portrayed Bardell vs. Pickwick, Nancy being murdered, and Mr. Pecksniff drunk and amorous. Such set pieces are brilliant, and after the Christmas books there are multitudes of similar characters and scenes, but they do not tower above the rest of the work in the old manner; they are subordinated to the larger requirements of plot and theme, and must play their diminished roles on a stage crowded with new interests and new purposes.

This transformation was prompted by a variety of circumstances. The hiatus between *Martin Chuzzlewit* and *Dombey and Son* gave Dickens his first real chance for leisurely observation since he had begun to write. He found that both he and his age were in a state of transition. He was beginning to grow disenchanted with the fruits of success, and he had already begun to anatomize his mounting restlessness and unhappiness. At the same time he was gaining a new cosmopolitanism and objectivity. He could spend long periods away from England now. (He lived on the continent for almost half the four years between *Chuzzlewit* and the completion of *Dombey*.) The vantage point of Italy and Switzerland gave him a fresh perspective. He was able to view the new English society—the commercial-industrial society about which he would now write—with a critical detachment.

But above all, the years between *Chuzzlewit* and the completion of *Dombey* provided him with unique opportunities for literary experimentation. In the Christmas books he wrote during that interval (**A Christmas Carol** [1843], **The Chimes** [1845], **The Cricket on the Hearth** [1846], *The Battle of Life* [1847], and **The Haunted Man** [1848]—the last conceived and partly written in the interval, but not finished until *Dombey* was completed) he had five opportunities to experiment with structure, symbol, and subject matter, to manipulate in exceptionally fluid and foreshortened form old elements which had troubled him, and new elements he had not yet used or mastered. The Christmas books profoundly altered his artistic methods. In these works he set out self-consciously to blend autobiography, social criticism, storytelling, and fairy tales; as he put it, he was taking fairy tales and "giving them a higher form."

Dickens was using the term fairy tales in an idiosyncratic way; he was (to repeat what I have said elsewhere) giving a convenient label to his special blend of fairy story, fantasy, myth, magic, and folklore. That blend is all-important, for Dickens usually makes it subserve one of several purposes, and these purposes, plus the materials themselves, give his writings their characteristic fairy-tale quality. He likes, for instance, to create an atmosphere in which the supernatural seems plausible; or, conversely, he likes to take supernatural events and creatures and give them a factual underpinning. Or, yet again, by a species of double vision, he imposes an aura of fantasy on everyday places and persons: a real London house gradually metamorphoses into an enchanted castle, a veritable childhood nursemaid slowly emerges as a frightful witch. If Dickens has done his job well, such transformations build that extrarational resonance which causes the reader to suspend his disbelief. Dickens can now safely use non-realistic de-

Daniel Maclise's sketch of Dickens reading The Chimes *to his friends at best friend John Forster's house in London, December 1844 (Dickens Fellowship).*

vices and magical manipulations—spells, prophetic signs, reversals of fortune, blood relationships—to emphasize his thesis and enforce the demands of poetic justice. Such manipulations owe something to other traditions, to the Gothic novel, the ghost story, the melodrama, the pantomime, the "Ancient Mariner" genre, the Bunyanesque allegory, and the moral tract, for instance. But for Dickens such elements were primarily a reflex of his fairy-tale vision and purpose—significantly, he not only spoke of his Christmas books as fairy tales, he subtitled *The Cricket on the Hearth,* "A Fairy Tale of Home"—so that the term fairy tale may properly be used (and it will be so used in this essay) to designate this crucial confluence in his writings.

The method Dickens uses in his Christmas-book fairy tales for the times consists of taking a protagonist who displays false values and making him, through a series of extraordinary events, see his error. The fairy-tale machinery dominates the story, for the bulk of the action takes place in a dream or vision presided over by supernatural creatures who control what goes on. The resolution occurs when the happenings of the vision—a magically telescoped survey of the protagonist's life, and a masquelike representation of the consequences of his views—force him to reassess his life and undergo conversion. This structure was of immense value to Dickens. It gave him a framework that provided an aesthetic justification for the legerdemain which in his earlier works (especially in his finales) had always appeared, not as fairy-tale felicities, but as contradictory fairy-tale wrenchings which weakened the story. He could now show misery and horror and

yet do it in a context of joyful affirmation. He could depict evil flourishing to its ultimate flowering and still deny that flowering. He could introduce the most disparate scenes, events, and visions without losing the reader's confidence. He could manipulate time with no need to obey the ordinary laws of chronology. He could make his characters and events real when he wished them real, magical when he wished them magical. He could effect overnight conversions which could be justified aesthetically. He could teach by parable rather than exhortation. And he could deal with life in terms of a fairy-tale logic which underscored both the real and the ideal.

The Haunted Man epitomizes, in an especially complex and foreshortened form—a form which makes Dickens' artistry peculiarly amenable to analysis—techniques he would depend upon in all his subsequent writings.

—Harry Stone

These potentialities, fundamental ingredients in Dickens' mature narrative method, are exploited with varying degrees of success in all his Christmas books, but in none with such intricacy as in *The Haunted Man,* the last of his Christmas-book experiments. *The Haunted Man* epitomizes, therefore, in an especially complex and foreshort-ened form—a form which makes Dickens's artistry peculiarly amenable to analysis—techniques he would depend upon in all his subsequent writings.

The Haunted Man tells the story of Mr. Redlaw, a learned professor of chemistry who is appalled by the misery he sees about him. His own life has been filled with death, betrayal, and unfulfilled love, and he longs to blot out these memories which darken his daily existence. But his mind is divided. Although he yearns to escape from painful memories, he broods over the past. One Christmas Eve as he sits before his fire haunted by sad recollections, that part of his mind which desires to suppress memory takes on corporeal being as a phantom mirror image of himself. The phantom presses its arguments powerfully and wins Redlaw to its point of view. Redlaw will forget, he will have surcease from feeling, but he will retain his learning and acuteness. But the gift contains an additional feature: his forgetfulness will be transmitted to those he meets. Redlaw soon discovers his gift is a curse. For in forgetting past sorrow and feeling, he has destroyed all that is softening and human in life. Suffering and joy, loss and achievement are so intertwined that killing one kills the other. The unhappy multitudes whose misery he had hoped to relieve by his gift are not relieved. As he goes among them he produces discord; he destroys the knot of affection and forbearance which is the saving grace of their hard lives. Only two creatures take no infection from his approach. One, a street waif, remains unchanged because his bestial life has known no human feeling and so can know no loss. The other, Milly, the wife of one of Redlaw's servants, is love and goodness incarnate, and thus proof against his curse. His experiences teach him his error, and with the help of Milly, he redeems himself and removes the blight from those he has cursed.

Apart from *Dombey*, *The Haunted Man* was the most multi-leveled work Dickens had yet written. He had produced a story in which fancy, allegory, and psychological truth were balanced and coexistent. *The Haunted Man* can be read, really *must* be read, as fairy tale, symbolic exemplum, and psychological self-portrait. The very title of the first chapter, "The Gift Bestowed," recalls a typical fairy-tale situation in which a protagonist is given some special power which he is sure will be a blessing but which proves a curse. This fairy-tale situation is reinforced by the woodcut illustration (suggested and approved by Dickens) which appeared on the first page of the original edition and which depicts, among other things, scenes from the *Arabian Nights, The Tales of the Genii,* and *Cinderella*—all childhood favorites of Dickens and all mentioned in the story. But the characters and settings contribute most to the fairy-tale atmosphere. Redlaw's home is an enchanted castle, a group of mouldering medieval college buildings standing in the midst of the bustling city and wrapped in a symbolic atmosphere of murky shadows and muffled shapes. His home reminds one of a witch's castle. It was always "thundering with echoes when a distant voice was raised or a door was shut,—echoes, not confined to the many low passages and empty rooms, but rumbling and grumbling till they were stifled in the heavy air." With this and similar descriptions Dickens intensifies his mood,

until he creates an atmosphere in which the supernatural and the realistic mingle and then combine. Here, a few lines later, is Radlaw as he sits before the fire at the moment his Christmas Eve adventures begin:

> You should have seen him in his dwelling about twilight, in the dead of winter time.
>
> When the wind was blowing, shrill and shrewd, with the going down of the blurred sun. When it was just so dark, as that the forms of things were indistinct and big—but not wholly lost. When sitters by the fire began to see wild faces and figures, mountains and abysses, ambuscades, and armies, in the coals.

"You should have seen him in his dwelling about twilight, in the dead of winter time." The images and the associations they arouse are wonderfully appropriate, for Redlaw is another metamorphosis of Dickens' recurrent witch-godmother. Redlaw's witch-like appearance, his "hollow cheek . . . sunken brilliant eye . . . black attired figure . . . grizzled hair hanging, like tangled seaweed, about his face"; his witchlike traffic with phantoms and the secrets of nature (for he is a most learned chemist); and his witch-like ability to cast potent spells—all these mark him as the evil enchanter of fairy lore. Yet like many of Dickens' witch-godmothers, like old Martin and Scrooge, for example, he is not entirely evil; he is a good human being gone wrong, he can be redeemed. And Milly, like her prototype, Little Nell, in *The Old Curiosity Shop,* is the fairy princess, an embodiment of perfect goodness who will magically effect Redlaw's salvation. In *The Haunted Man* the Quilp-like character who is evil incarnate (to continue the parallel with *The Old Curiosity Shop*) has undergone the greatest change. The incarnation of evil is now combined with the abandoned waif, a portentous character whose origins go back to Dickens' own childhood, to his blacking-warehouse abandonment, and a character who reappears in his writings in countless permutations: as Oliver in *Oliver Twist,* Little Nell in *The Old Curiosity Shop,* the allegorical waifs in *A Christmas Carol,* Paul and Florence in *Dombey and Son,* David in *David Copperfield,* Jo in *Bleak House,* and Deputy in *Edwin Drood.* In *The Haunted Man* the very real waif—"a baby savage, a young monster, a child who . . . would live and perish a mere beast"—has become a symbol not merely of nascent evil but of society's guilt in producing evil. Continuing the process begun in the other Christmas books, Dickens' recurrent fairy-tale figures—the excrescential or allegorical waifs and ghosts and bell goblins of *A Christmas Carol* and *The Chimes*—are taking on an enlarged significance, and though retaining their fairy-tale or symbolic origins, are becoming more closely linked with contemporary life, realistic psychology, and thematic motifs.

In *The Haunted Man* Dickens uses many devices commonly found in fairy tales. He uses fairy-tale repetition, for instance, to enhance the tale's atmosphere of enchantment and to unify the story. The words of the phantom's gift-curse, words repeated throughout the story, intensify this unity and enchantment. Redlaw soon discovers that "blowing in the wind, falling with the snow, drifting with the clouds, shining in the moonlight, and heavily looming in the darkness, were the Phantom's words, 'The gift that

I have given, you shall give again, go where you will!' " The repetition of the curse becomes, in fairy-tale fashion, a magical refrain which gathers suspense until the climax and reversal when the curse-refrain is replaced by its opposite, a refrain which had been developed contrapuntally throughout the story: "Lord keep my memory green." But it is more than the curse, it is the imagery of Redlaw's loss associated with the curse—imagery connected with his new insensitivity to nature, time, and music—that is repeated. Furthermore, each time the curse is transmitted, the recipient signifies his infection by a telltale action: "the wandering hand upon the forehead." These and other repetitions (which are frequently joined with each other) become increasingly magical and ritualistic, as in the following pattern of reiterations: "Three times, in their progress, they [Redlaw and the waif] were side by side. Three times they stopped, being side by side. Three times the Chemist glanced down at his face, and shuddered as it forced upon him one reflection." The dovetailing of such incantations with their many analogues interconnects their meanings. For example, Dickens links the Redlaw-waif walk and its three pauses (labeling them "first," "second," and "third") with images of memory, night, moonlight, and music—images he had been reiterating throughout the story by means of the poetic leitmotif associated with Redlaw's fairy-tale curse. Once this leitmotif and its many associations are established, Dickens is able, by means of the leitmotif, to call up Redlaw's loss with great economy and centripetal effect. Fairy-tale repetition and incantation thus helped Dickens develop the unifying device of the symbolic leitmotif—a device he toyed with in his earlier novels, expanded in his first Christmas books, used effectively here and in *Dombey,* and then elaborated in many later works.

Paralleling the fairy-tale level of *The Haunted Man* is an allegorical level which underlines Dickens's message. Dickens was perfectly aware of the allegorical nature of what he had written. In the penultimate paragraph of *The Haunted Man* he points to the possibility of such an interpretation: "Some people," he wrote, "have said since, that he [Redlaw] only thought what has been herein set down; others, that the Ghost was but the representation of his own gloomy thoughts, and Milly the embodiment of his better wisdom. *I* say nothing." Dickens was suggesting various modes of interpreting his story but very properly endorsing no single mode. Yet any reader who failed to make use of each of his suggestions would miss part of what he was saying. To cite the most striking instance of this danger, the climactic scenes of *The Haunted Man*—the scenes in which Redlaw finds himself divorced from life, locked in his room with the beast-waif, and imprisoned by his mental state—these scenes, as we shall see in a moment, can only be appreciated in their full power in terms of the allegory.

The allegory of *The Haunted Man* is designed to enforce the message which the other levels develop—that good and evil are intertwined, that memories and feelings associate pain and joy, and that such associations can be dissolved only at the expense of that which makes one human. Redlaw, before he is given the gift, is man in his suffering but human condition; after the gift, he is man as

a mere analytical chemist, man in an emotionless, blighted, arid state. The phantom is that portion of Redlaw's mind which longs for surcease from feeling and tempts him to an attitude toward himself and his fellows which will produce such surcease. The gift is the symbolic result of Redlaw's assent to these promptings of his mind; it is the effect on himself and others of acquiescing in such a philosophy of life. Milly stands for love, and the softening, saving influence of love. The waif represents two things: first, human nature bereft of feeling and sympathy, that is human nature completely dehumanized, human nature which displays the end result of Redlaw's foolish yearnings; and second, the evil and guilt of a society which produces creatures such as the waif. Dickens uses the waif image in *The Haunted Man* to make the same point he had made with similar images in *A Christmas Carol* and *The Chimes,* but now the waif has become one of the central characters in his design; and the symbolism of the waif, lest any reader miss its sociological significance, is translated unmistakably toward the end of the story:

> "This," said the Phantom, pointing to the boy, "is the last, completest illustration of a human creature, utterly bereft of such remembrances as you have yielded up. No softening memory of sorrow, wrong, or trouble enters here, because this wretched mortal from his birth has been abandoned to a worse condition than the beasts. . . . All within this desolate creature is barren wilderness. All within the man bereft of what you have resigned, is the same barren wilderness. Woe to such a man! Woe, tenfold, to the nation that shall count its monsters such as this, lying here, by hundreds, and by thousands!"

The allegory of character is intensified by the allegory of setting. The worn-out leftovers of Mr. Tetterby's defunct business are ever-present tokens of his ineffectual personality; the tortuous slum Redlaw visits mirrors the twisted lives he finds within. But the chief backdrop for the action—Redlaw's college chambers—is the most revealing of the settings. The fortress in which he lives is a fitting representation of his mind. And when his mind changes, changes also occur in his frost-bound home. When he allows love to reenter his heart, his dungeon and heart reawaken alike: "Some blind groping of the morning made its way down into the forgotten crypt so cold and earthy . . . and stirred the dull deep sap in the lazy vegetation hanging to the walls, and quickened the slow principle of life within the little world of wonderful and delicate creation which existed there, with some faint knowledge that the sun was up."

In the first two chapters of *The Haunted Man*—comprising over 70 per cent of the text—allegory blends unobtrusively with fairy tale, psychology, and autobiography and adds force to what Dickens is saying. This force may be felt most powerfully in the climactic scenes already referred to, the scenes which end the second chapter. Those scenes commence with a journey. Redlaw needs someone who can guide him through the jumbled streets of the slums. He remembers that a waif has recently found his way from the slums into the college buildings, and he seeks the child out as a fitting conductor—a hell-babe guide for the streets of hell. Dickens does not make the connection with hell explicit, but his imagery makes the connection for him. Redlaw finds the waif "coiled asleep" on the floor before the fire, in a room where "the blaze was reddening" the "old beams in the ceiling and the dark walls." "The creature," says Dickens, "lay in such a fiery heat, that, as the Chemist stooped to rouse him, it scorched his head." The waif is so alarmed by Redlaw and so mistrustful of his proposition, that he snarls, "Let me be, or I'll heave some fire at you!" and instantly prepares "with his savage little hand, to pluck the burning coals out." Redlaw looks down at this "baby-monster" with "cold vague terror." "It chilled his blood to look on the immovable impenetrable thing, in the likeness of a child, with its sharp malignant face turned up to his, and its almost infant hand, ready at the bars." But the two make a compact, and the waif, running a few yards before or after Redlaw, and alternately burnishing the shillings Redlaw has given him or stuffing them into his mouth for safekeeping, takes Redlaw into the slum streets. By the time Redlaw has returned to his fortress chambers, he has gone through all the experiences necessary to teach him the significance of his error. He locks himself and the waif into his lonely rooms, throws the child a few shillings, and broods despairingly.

After an interval, Milly knocks on Redlaw's door. "Pray, sir, let me in!" she cries. Symbolically love is knocking at the locked chambers of Redlaw's heart and asking to be let in. "No! not for the world!" is his ironic answer. The waif, who has been fed and tended by Milly, cries out, "Let me go to her, will you?" (The evil which society has produced will respond to love, cries out for love.) Milly, not knowing Redlaw is the cause, tells him of the disasters his slum visit has brought. "Pray, sir, let me in," she repeats. Redlaw is horrified, contrite, anguished, but his heart is still frozen; he cannot really feel or remember, he is not yet ready to let love enter. "Pray, sir, let me in!" cries Milly, but Redlaw answers, "No! No! No!" and restrains the waif "who was half-mad to pass him, and let her in." Redlaw prays to his phantom alter ego for relief, vows not to taint Milly with his curse, and thus refusing to confront love, stands in an agony of guilt before the door he himself has locked. The phantom does not answer Redlaw's prayer. "The only reply still was, the boy struggling to get to her, while he held him back; and the cry, increasing in its energy . . . 'pray, pray, let me in!'"

With these words the second chapter ends. Dickens' method is effective and sophisticated. It reminds one of Hawthorne's technique, of those portions of *The Scarlet Letter* or "Rappaccini's Daughter" in which the central allegory shades into subtle and varied suggestiveness. For when Redlaw calls out to his fairy-tale phantom and hears Milly's allegorical plea, he is also acting out a psychological drama which, as Professor Edgar Johnson points out in his admirable biography [*Charles Dickens: His Tragedy and Triumph,* 1952] of Dickens, has parallels in Dickens' life. Dickens is an author who frequently, perhaps compulsively, freighted his work with cathartic autobiography. In his earlier writings, in the brilliantly satiric American scenes of *Martin Chuzzlewit,* for example, these autobiographical materials were usually forced upon the structure, disturbing and weakening it. The Christmas books

helped Dickens wed autobiography unobtrusively to the more universal levels of his writing; autobiography now usually increases the psychological richness of his work and strengthens his art.

The third concurrent level of Redlaw's story—the psychological and autobiographical—appears in *The Haunted Man* from the beginning. Dickens makes it easy for the reader to regard the phantom as the representation of Redlaw's "gloomy thoughts." The phantom materializes only after many directive signs, which can be explained as natural or supernatural, have heralded its appearance. These manifestations come in conjunction with Redlaw's internal debating and self-absorption. Consequently, when the signs coalesce and then develop into the full-fledged phantom, the reader is ready to accept the apparition as another part of the carefully developed fairy-tale atmosphere, and as an appropriate representation of one portion of Redlaw's mind. Once the latter notion is established, the story becomes a study of psychological strife. The conflict is depicted by utilizing the technique Tennyson used in "The Two Voices"; Redlaw's divided mind is engaged in a dialogue with itself:

> "If I could forget my sorrow and wrong, I would," the Ghost repeated. . . .
>
> "Evil spirit of myself," returned the haunted man . . . "my life is darkened by that incessant whisper."
>
> "It is an echo," said the Phantom.
>
> "If it be an echo of my thoughts . . . why should I, therefore, be tormented? . . . Who would not forget their sorrows and their wrongs?"
>
> "Who would not, truly, and be the happier and better for it?" said the Phantom. . . .
>
> "Tempter," answered Redlaw . . . "I hear again an echo of my own mind."

Dickens may well have been impelled to write this fairy tale of memory, love, and mental conflict because of the death a few months earlier of his sister Fanny. Her long deathbed talks with him had called up memories of their close childhood relationship (commemorated a few years later in **"A Child's Dream of a Star"**), other sadder childhood recollections, and later memories of more deaths and more separations. *The Haunted Man* is Dickens' attempt to come to terms with these memories, to find a philosophical justification for recollected sorrows. For as Professor Johnson demonstrates, Redlaw, even more than the young Scrooge, has much of Dickens in him. In many ways, Redlaw's occupation, mannerisms, and surroundings suggest Dickens himself. But the autobiographical parallels go deeper. Dickens openly attaches to Redlaw the emotional experiences which dominated his own life. Redlaw's early history is a mosaic of references to Dickens' blacking-warehouse days, neglectful parents, struggles with shorthand, British Museum studies, and affair with Maria Beadnell; to sisterly Mary Hogarth's coming to live with him, taking pride in his fame, and dying in his arms expressing her love for him; and to sister Fanny's closeness to him as a child and self-effacing deathbed conversations with him.

Dickens softened his own self-pity and resentment by creating the parable of Redlaw's rebellion and redemption. He was expressing in fictional fullness what later he said more succinctly in his own person. Speaking of his past suffering, and referring specifically to his mother and the blacking warehouse, he remarked "how all these things have worked together to make me what I am." The past, therefore, must be accepted not only as a humanizing influence, but as the *sine qua non* of his art.

But it is not the message or the autobiography, it is the technique which makes *The Haunted Man* significant. Professor Johnson, in concentrating on the former elements, neglects the crucial role that *The Haunted Man* and the other Christmas books played in Dickens' development. The characters, images, and actions which earlier had existed in disturbing isolation are now ordered and unified. The distance Dickens has traveled since his apprenticeship writings can be measured by comparing early fairy-tale characters—old Martin and Scrooge, say—with Redlaw. All three characters have the same attributes and purpose: they combine human and supernatural ingredients, and Dickens uses their special situations to twist or even reverse the plot and to teach lessons. Old Martin is a mere piece of machinery, Scrooge is a partially developed embodiment of social and autobiographical truth, but Redlaw is much more. His role in the story is so central and suggestive that his actions and words unite fairy tale, allegory, autobiography, and psychology. That this is so is largely the result of the fairy-tale conception which underlies the story. For the mood Dickens sets at the opening, the fairy-tale devices he used to unify his plot and emphasize his message, and the fabular quality he gives to what he is saying, prepare the reader for the apocalyptic truth he is trying to convey—a truth in which simple realism, ordinary events, and humdrum detail are less important than a heightened, extrareal vision of life which quickens one's perception of the very reality it transcends.

Yet *The Haunted Man* falls off sadly in its third and final chapter. There the various levels of the story come unstuck and produce the same artificial effects that weakened the *Carol, The Chimes,* and the apprenticeship novels. Dickens now reverses the tragic sequences he had set in motion earlier; he digs up lost relatives, rewards suffering finacées, and rehabilitates suicidal derelicts. Psychological truth, social seriousness, autobiographical analysis, aesthetic balance—all are sacrificed to a neat winding up in the old wrenching fairy-tale manner, and the violence done to everything but the fable destroys the effectiveness of the fable itself. The reader no longer suspends his disbelief. Fairy gold becomes ordinary lead, and the final effect is meretricious moral orderliness.

Dickens himself felt the Christmas books were deficient; perhaps this feeling was a major reason for his abandoning the form. "The narrow space," he wrote in 1852, "within which it was necessary to confine these Christmas Stories when they were originally published, rendered their construction a matter of some difficulty, and almost necessitated what is peculiar in their machinery." But even while planning *The Haunted Man* Dickens had begun *Dombey and Son,* his first full-length novel since his Christmas-

book experiments. Those experiments had served him well, for his later works are invariably enhanced with Christmas-book machinery. In the magical mansion and symbolic staircase motifs, the expressionistic ogress- and witch-figures of *Dombey and Son;* in the domesticated godmotherhood of Betsey Trotwood in *David Copperfield;* in the subtle fairy-tale portents and gifts, the over-all fairy-tale structure of *Great Expectations*—in these and a multitude of other ways he used Christmas-book techniques to superimpose meanings, universalize characters, probe psyches, heighten scenes, and tighten structures: to give his novels a deeper unity and a more inclusive richness.

Robert Browning   (essay date 1962)

SOURCE: "Sketches by Boz," in *Dickens and the Twentieth Century,* edited by John Gross and Gabriel Pearson, Routledge and Kegan Paul, 1962, pp. 19-34.

[*In the following essay, Browning depicts* Sketches by Boz *as a realistic account of early Victorian England.*]

Writing To John Forster from Lausanne in 1846, Dickens declared that he found it difficult to write fast when away from London:

> I suppose this is partly the effect of two years' ease, and partly of the absence of streets and numbers of figures. I can't express how much I want these. It seems as if they supplied something to my brain, which it cannot bear, when busy, to lose. For a week or fortnight I can write prodigiously in a retired place (as at Broadstairs), and a day in London sets me up again and starts me. But the toil and labour of writing, day after day, without that magic lantern, is IMMENSE!! [W. Dexter, *The Letters of Charles Dickens,* Vol. I, 1938.]

The *Sketches by Boz* is Dickens's first published work, and it is appropriate that it should record his intimacy with London and its citizens.

In 'Thoughts About People' (Characters, I), where Dickens describes a group of London apprentices on a Sunday jaunt, we can discern the stimulation the want of which he felt in Lausanne:

> We walked down the Strand, a Sunday or two ago, behind a little group; and they furnished food for our amusement the whole way. They had come out of some part of the city; it was between three and four o'clock in the afternoon; and they were on their way to the Park. There were four of them, all arm-in-arm, with white kid gloves like so many bridegrooms, light trousers of unprecedented patterns, and coats for which the English language has yet no name—a kind of cross between a great-coat and a surtout, with the collar of the one, the skirts of the other, and pockets peculiar to themselves.
>
> Each of the gentlemen carried a thick stick, with a large tassel at the top, which he occasionally twirled gracefully round; and the whole four, by way of looking easy and unconcerned, were walking with a paralytic swagger irresistibly ludicrous. One of the party had a watch about the

size and shape of a reasonable Ribstone pippin, jammed into his waistcoat-pocket, which he carefully compared with the clocks at St. Clement's and the New Church, the illuminated clock at Exeter 'Change, the clock of St. Martin's Church, and the clock of the Horse Guards. When they at last arrived in St. James's Park, the member of the party who had the best-made boots on, hired a second chair expressly for his feet, and flung himself on this two-pennyworth of sylvan luxury with an air which levelled all distinctions between Brookes's and Snooks's, Crockford's and Bagnigge Wells.

The stimulation was bred partly of familiarity and partly of the variety of spectacle, the sheer thickness of impressions. In different sketches, Dickens drops in at the bar of a large gin-shop and watches the washerwomen and Irish labourers taking their quarterns of gin, he calls at Bellamy's, the dining room of the Houses of Parliament, and marks a gourmet peer gloating over a Stilton, he joins the coal-heavers 'quaffing large draughts of Barclay's best' in the old pub in Scotland Yard, and he peers between the blue curtains of a West-end cigar shop to see the well-dressed malcontents relieving their boredom by flirting with the young lady 'in amber with large earrings' who sits behind the counter 'in a blaze of adoration and gas light'.

The London of the *Sketches* is not fictitious. Dickens's realism, unlike the superficial realism of Pierce Egan's *Life in London*, does not confer glamour on the sordid and squalid. And whereas Egan confines his regard to central London, St. James's to St. Giles, Dickens takes in the whole metropolis with its rapidly extending suburbs, such as Stamford Hill, Camberwell, Norbury, and Richmond. He chronicles much that is small in scale and dull-toned with such fidelity, that it is the distinction of the *Sketches*, as it is that of Joyce's *Dubliners*, that the reader senses the life of a whole city.

Just as the London of the *Sketches* is, despite changes, recognizably the London Hogarth drew, so it is recognizably the London we know today. Small eating-houses and taverns have not changed as much as might be thought. Their ambience is much the same. The chaffing humour of Dickens's cabmen and omnibus cads is still to be met with in their modern counterparts, taxi-drivers and bus conductors, when those are Cockneys. The British Museum still knows readers like the one described by Dickens in **'Shabby-Genteel People'** (Characters, X):

> He was in his chair every morning, just as the clock struck ten; he was always the last to leave the room in the afternoon; and when he did, he quitted it with the air of a man who knew not where else to go for warmth and quiet. There he used to sit all day, as close to the table as possible, in order to conceal the lack of buttons on his coat; with his old hat carefully deposited at his feet, where he evidently flattered himself it escaped observation.

> About two o'clock, you would see him munching a French roll or a penny loaf; not taking it out of his pocket at once, like a man who knew he was only making a lunch; but breaking off lit-

tle bits in his pocket, and eating them by stealth. He knew too well it was his dinner.

And the contents of junk-shops in the suburbs answer very well to the description in **'Brokers' And Marine-Store Shops'** (Scenes, XXI).

> On a board, at the side of the door, are placed about twenty books, all odd volumes; and as many wine-glasses—all different patterns; several locks, an old earthenware pan, full of rusty keys; two or three gaudy chimney-ornaments—cracked, of course; the remains of a lustre, without any drops; a round frame like a capital O, which has once held a mirror; a flute, complete with the exception of the middle joint; a pair of curling-irons; and a tinder-box. In front of the shop window are ranged some half-dozen high-backed chairs, with spinal complaints and wasted legs; a corner cupboard; two or three very dark mahogany tables with flaps like mathematical problems . . .

Of course, Dickens is more than a good observer, even in this his first book, but he was, in Henry James's phrase, 'one of the people on whom nothing is lost', and it is the first recommendation for this volume, that in it he gave such a lively account of what he saw and heard in London. At the time of writing most of the papers here collected, Dickens was a press reporter; and, whatever the deficiencies of his formal education, it is clear that he could hardly have had a better training for the craft of novel writing.

Modern reprints of *Sketches by Boz* follow the Chapman and Hall edition of 1839 in the disposition of material, most of which had previously appeared in journals and in the two issues by Macrone (First Series, 1836; Second Series, 1837). In 1839 the papers were distributed into four groups: 'Seven Sketches from our Parish', 'Scenes', 'Characters', and 'Tales'. This arrangement is perhaps regrettable inasmuch as the Parish sketches [in *Sketches by Boz,* 1836], with which a new reader is likely to begin, are too consciously droll for modern taste. The age was one of popular humorists, and the proliferating journals of the day were crammed with comicalities and *facetiae*. The Regency love of punning had not abated; both Theodore Hook and Thomas Hood were, at their worst, gravely funny. Dickens did not altogether escape the infection, and a few of the sketches are disfigured by tasteless drollery. The Parish sketches are not without merit, but they are much inferior to others in the collection.

Dickens owes not a little to the ephemeral publications of the eighteen-twenties and eighteen-thirties. Mr. Pickwick and (in the *Sketches*) Mr. Minns may be related to the literature of comic discomfort. But granting that, the differences are as remarkable as the affinities. It is instructive to compare John Poole's paper on 'Early Rising' [in *Sketches and Recollections*, 1835] with Dickens's **'Early Coaches'** (Scenes, XV). Poole exaggerates:

> Two towels, which had been left wet in the room, were standing on a chair, bolt upright, as stiff as the poker itself, which you might almost as easily have bent. The tooth-brushes were riveted to the glass in which I had left them, and of which (in my haste to disengage them from

their stronghold), they carried away a fragment; the soap was cemented to the dish; my shaving-brush was a mass of ice. In shape more appalling Discomfort had never appeared on earth.

Dickens is notably more restrained and more truthful, and leans not at all on tired figurative language:

> You proceed to dress yourself, with all possible dispatch. The flaring flat candle with the long snuff gives light enough to show that the things you want are not where they ought to be, and you undergo a trifling delay in consequence of having carefully packed up one of your boots in your over-anxiety of the preceding night. You soon complete your toilet, however, for you are not particular on such an occasion, and you shaved yesterday evening.

It says much for Dickens's taste that he eschewed the kind of extravanganza that Hook and Poole affected. If Dickens exaggerates, as he does in the 'Tales' and in later fictions, he does not do so pompously. The writing is brisk and nimble. The contemporary writer whose influence was strongest and most beneficent is Leigh Hunt. This is the third paragraph of Dickens's **'Greenwich Fair'** (Scenes, XII).

> The road to Greenwich during the whole of Easter Monday, is in a state of perpetual bustle and noise. Cabs, hackney-coaches, 'shay' carts, coal-waggons, stages, omnibuses, sociables, gigs, donkey-chaises—all crammed with people (for the question never is, what the horse can draw, but what the vehicle will hold), roll along at their utmost speed; the dust flies in clouds, ginger-beer corks go off in volleys, the balcony of every public-house is crowded with people, smoking and drinking, half the private houses are turned into tea-shops, fiddles are in great request, every little fruit-shop displays its stall of gilt gingerbread and penny toys; turnpike men are in despair; horses won't go on, and wheels will come off; ladies in 'carawans' scream with fright at every fresh concussion, and their admirers find it necessary to sit remarkably close to them, by way of encouragement; servants-of-all-work, who are not allowed to have followers, and have got a holiday for the day, make the most of their time with the faithful admirer who waits for a stolen interview at the corner of the street every night, when they go to fetch the beer—apprentices grow sentimental and straw bonnet makers kind.

With this we may compare Leigh Hunt's paper, 'A Now: Descriptive Of A Hot Day' [in *The Indicator*, June 28, 1820]:

> Now blinds are let down, and doors thrown open, and flannel waistcoats left off, and cold meat preferred to hot, and wonder expressed why tea continues so refreshing, and people delight to sliver lettuces into bowls, and apprentices water door-ways with tin-canisters that lay several atoms of dust.

I think that Dickens learnt from Hunt this technique of a congery of simple sentences (often in the passive). From Hunt, too, he may have acquired a feeling for the poetry of the urban scene. This influence, if influence it is, is completely digested in **'The Streets—Morning'** (Scenes, I). That sketch is written with a tact and delicacy that Dickens did not always command, and it called forth one of George Cruikshank's best designs in illustration, that of a street breakfast. A reader unacquainted with *Sketches by Boz* would do well to begin with it.

In **'Astley's'** (Scenes, XI), the sketch of a visit to the circus, a family party in the audience is described with a simplicity and economy that looks deceptively easy:

> The first five minutes were occupied in taking the shawls off the little girls, and adjusting the bows which ornamented their hair; then it was providentially discovered that one of the little boys was seated behind a pillar and could not see, so the governess was stuck behind the pillar, and the boy lifted into her place. Then pa drilled the boys, and directed the stowing away of their pocket-handkerchiefs, and ma having first nodded and winked to the governess to pull the girls' frocks a little more off their shoulders, stood up to review the little troop—an inspection which appeared to terminate much to her own satisfaction, for she looked with a complacent air at pa, who was standing up at the further end of the seat. Pa returned the glance, and blew his nose very emphatically; and the poor governess peeped out from behind the pillar, and timidly tried to catch ma's eye, with a look expressive of her high admiration of the whole family.

It is as fine a distillation of early Victorian England as any of the genre paintings it so much resembles. From the family group Dickens turns his regard to the clown, the riding-master, and the bare-back rider, with a digression on what such performers look like beyond the glamour of sawdust and flaring gas-jets. By this means Dickens neither ignores nor dispels the illusion. His viewpoint is neither naïve nor cynical:

> Nor can we quite divest ourself of our old feeling of reverence for the riding-master, who follows the clown with a long whip in his hand, and bows to the audience with graceful dignity. He is none of your second-rate riding-masters in nankeen dressing-gowns, with brown frogs, but the regular gentleman-attendant on the principal riders, who always wears a military uniform with a table-cloth inside the breast of the coat, in which costume he forcibly reminds one of a fowl trussed for roasting. He is—but why should we attempt to describe that of which no description can convey an adequate idea? Everybody knows the man, and everybody remembers his polished boots, his graceful demeanour, stiff, as some misjudging persons have in their jealousy considered it, and the splendid head of black hair, parted high on the forehead, to impart to the countenance an appearance of deep thought and poetic melancholy. His soft and pleasing voice, too, is in perfect unison with his noble bearing, as he humours the clown by indulging in a little badinage; and the striking recollection of his own dignity, with which he exclaims, 'Now, sir, if you please, inquire for Miss Woolford, sir', can never be forgotten. The graceful

air, too, with which he introduces Miss Wool-
ford into the arena, and, after assisting her to the
saddle, follows her fairy courser round the circle, can never fail to create a deep impression in
the bosom of every female servant present.

We must hesitate, even as Dickens does, to find the riding-
master ridiculous. The description of the man and his de-
portment, though ironical, is respectful. This man personates the idea of a circus riding-master to perfection. As
such he cannot be false, even though he owes his manly
chest to a table-cloth stuffed inside the jacket of his uniform.

Dickens is viewing the circus with evident nostalgia, as the
first paragraph of the sketch avows. The circus and its personnel were to the child the very enshrinement of beauty,
grace, and wit. For the grown man the enchantment has
fled, but not the affection. Such illusions and such impos-
tures are beneficent.

Dickens digresses, as he says, to describe the misery and
squalor of 'the class of people, who hang about the stage-
doors of our minor theatres in the daytime' hoping for employment:

> That young fellow in the faded brown coat, and
> very full light green trousers, pulls down the
> wristbands of his check shirt, as ostentatiously
> as if it were of the finest linen, and cocks the
> white hat of the summer-before-last as knowing-
> ly over his right eye, as if it were a purchase of
> yesterday. Look at the dirty white Berlin gloves,
> and the cheap silk handkerchief stuck in the
> bosom of his threadbare coat. Is it possible to see
> him for an instant, and not come to the conclu-
> sion that he is the walking gentleman who wears
> a blue surtout, clean collar, and white trousers,
> for half an hour, and then shrinks into his worn-
> out scanty clothes: who has to boast night after
> night of his splendid fortune, with the painful
> consciousness of a pound a week and his boots
> to find; to talk of his father's mansion in the
> country, with a dreary recollection of his own
> two-pair back, in the New Cut; and to be envied
> and flattered as the favoured lover of a rich heir-
> ess, remembering all the while that the ex-
> dancer at home is in the family way, and out of
> an engagement?

The poor player has an almost symbolic rôle. Many of
Dickens's fictional heroes are suspended between poverty
and riches, between comfort and squalor, between respectability and crime. The actor of bit parts in minor theatres
is, in a special way, of their number. He, and the circus
personnel who resemble him, acquire a moral significance
for Dickens: they act a lie, as (more subtly) Oliver Twist,
William Dorrit, and Pip act a lie. The riding-master who
personates a gentleman is a figure whom Dickens will not
ridicule, partly from sentimental regard, but partly, too,
from an unspoken, and probably unconscious, identification with the man. There are subtler and less amiable
frauds than a table-cloth thrust into a jacket.

'The Mistaken Milliner' (Characters, VIII) is not completely successful. The story is a little huddled. But it
opens brilliantly:

Miss Amelia Martin was pale, tallish, thin, and
two-and-thirty—what ill-natured people would
call plain, and police reports interesting. She was
a milliner and dressmaker, living on her business
and not above it. If you had been a young lady
in service, and had wanted Miss Martin, as a
great many young ladies in service did, you
would just have stepped up, in the evening, to
number forty-seven, Drummond Street, George
Street, Euston Square, and after casting your eye
on a brass door-plate, one foot ten by one and
a half, ornamented with a great brass knob at
each of the four corners, and bearing the inscription 'Miss Martin; millinery and dressmaking, in
all its branches'; you'd just have knocked two
loud knocks at the street-door; and down would
have come Miss Martin herself, in a merino
gown of the newest fashion, black velvet brace-
lets on the genteelest principle, and other little
elegancies of the most approved description.

If Miss Martin knew the young lady who called,
or if the young lady who called had been recommended by any other young lady whom Miss
Martin knew, Miss Martin would forthwith
show her upstairs into the two-pair front, and
chat she would—*so* kind, and *so* comfortable—it
really wasn't like a matter of business, she was
so friendly; and then Miss Martin, after contemplating the figure and general appearance of the
young lady in service with great apparent admiration, would say how well she would look, to
be sure, in a low dress with short sleeves; made
very full in the skirts, with four tucks in the bottom; to which the young lady in service would
reply in terms expressive of her entire concur-
rence in the notion, and of the virtuous indignation with which she reflected on the tyranny of
'Missis', who wouldn't allow a young girl to
wear a short sleeve of an afternoon—no, nor
nothing smart, not even a pair of ear-rings; let
alone hiding people's heads of hair under them
frightful caps. At the termination of this complaint, Miss Amelia Martin would distantly suggest certain dark suspicions that some people
were jealous on account of their own daughters,
and were obliged to keep their servants' charms
under, for fear they should get married first,
which was no uncommon circumstance—
leastways she had known two or three young ladies in service, who had married a great deal better than their missises, and *they* were not very
good-looking either; and then the young lady
would inform Miss Martin, in confidence, that
how one of their young ladies was engaged to a
young man and was a-going to be married, and
Missis was so proud about it there was no bearing of her; but how she needn't hold her head
quite so high neither, for, after all, he was only
a clerk. And, after expressing due contempt for
clerks in general, and the engaged clerk in particular, and the highest opinion possible of themselves and each other, Miss Martin and the
young lady in service would bid each other good
night, in a friendly but perfectly genteel manner:
and the one went back to her 'place', and the
other to her room on the second-floor front.

The first paragraph consists of three sentences. The first

two are statements made with almost epigrammatic incisiveness. The third is a long elastic sentence that interestingly develops a borrowed idiom, that of such a young lady in service: 'you would just have stepped up . . . you'd just have knocked . . . and down would have come Miss Martin herself '. Even in this mildly oblique way, the narration acquires actuality.

The second paragraph is made up of three long sentences. Here Dickens mingles third-person narration with *oratio obliqua* in the most fluent manner. The first sentence modulates into the serving-girl's speech 'and chat she would— *so* kind, and *so* comfortable'. From this mixed tissue there emerges an imagined colloquy eloquent of the lives and characters of Miss Martin and her customers. This is done without actually introducing any serving-girl, since none is needed for the story.

As so often in Dickens, the account is minutely particular. The handsome brass door-plate and Miss Martin's elegant costume are the tokens of her respectability, her gentility, and her professional skill. In feminine society the dressmaker may be a kind of leveller. A serving-girl, in her person and in her dress, may have the advantage, or may think she has the advantage, on her employers. And it is to this self-promotion, social and sexual, that Miss Martin ministers. Her understanding of her customers is perfect.

Again we may notice that Dickens is not ridiculing. There is no narrative condescension of the kind George Eliot might have shown.

'Thoughts About People' (Characters, I) is a good sketch, but one that may at first sight seem insipid. The style is restrained, the phrasing modestly telling. The sketch is largely occupied by two generic portraits: the unloved and the unloving. For the first, he takes an unmarried city clerk of middle age. By a judicious selection of glimpses— we see him arriving at the office, we see him at his books, at his eating-house, and at the home of his employer—the man is brought before us, and our sympathy secured. Dickens then turns for contrast to a class of men for whom he feels little sympathy. They are handled with considerable acerbity:

> These are generally old fellows with white heads and red faces, addicted to port wine and Hessian boots, who from some cause, real or imaginary—generally the former, the excellent reason being that they are rich, and their relations poor—grow suspicious of everybody, and do the misanthropical in chambers, taking great delight in thinking themselves unhappy, and making everybody they come near, miserable. You may see such men as these anywhere; you will know them at coffee-houses by their discontented exclamations and the luxury of their dinners; at theatres, by their always sitting in the same place and looking with a jaundiced eye on all the young people near them; at church, by the pomposity with which they enter, and the loud tone in which they repeat the responses; at parties, by their getting cross at whist and hating music. An old fellow of this kind will have his chambers splendidly furnished, and collect books, plate, and pictures about him in profusion; not so

much for his own gratification, as to be superior to those who have the desire, but not the means, to compete with him. He belongs to two or three clubs, and is envied, and flattered, and hated by the members of them all. Sometimes he will be appealed to by a poor relation—a married nephew perhaps—for some little assistance: and then he will declaim with honest indignation on the improvidence of young married people, the worthlessness of a wife, the insolence of having a family, the atrocity of getting into debt with a hundred and twenty-five pounds a year, and other unpardonable crimes; winding up his exhortations with a complacent review of his own conduct, and a delicate allusion to parochial relief. He dies, some day after dinner, of apoplexy, having bequeathed his property to a Public Society, and the Institution erects a tablet to his memory, expressive of their admiration of his Christian conduct in this world, and their comfortable conviction of his happiness in the next.

There Dickens stigmatizes what, morally, he recoils from. In Mr. Minns (Tales, II) and Mr. Dumps (Tales, XI) we see more of such life-haters. Mr. Minns is unfavourably shown in contrast to his vulgar, but genial relations. Scrooge is the best known of Dickens's life-haters.

Dickens spoke out against Victorian civility: a civility based on the pursuit of wealth and status, and riddled with snobberies and fetishes.

—Robert Browning

The sketch concludes with another generic portrait: that of the London apprentices. They are the 'anti-type'. Dickens remarks that 'they are usually on the best terms with themselves, and it follows almost as a matter of course, in good humour, with everyone about them'. For much the same reason Dickens likes hackney-coachmen, cabmen, and cads. He relishes, in especial, 'their cool impudence and perfect self-possession'.

The types are nicely brought into conflict in **'The Bloomsbury Christening'** (Tales, XI). The cold and irritable Nicodemus Dumps is chaffed by the omnibus cad:

> 'Don't bang the door so,' said Dumps to the conductor, as he shut it after letting out four of the passengers; 'I am very nervous—it destroys me.'
>
> 'Did any gen'lm'n say anythink?' replied the cad, thrusting in his head, and trying to look as if he didn't understand the request.
>
> 'I told you not to bang the door so!' repeated Dumps, with an expression of countenance like the knave of clubs, in convulsions.
>
> 'Oh! vy, it's rather a sing'ler circumstance about this here door, sir, that it von't shut without banging,' replied the conductor; and he opened

the door very wide, and shut it again with a terrific bang, in proof of the assertion.

In 'Omnibuses' (Scenes, XVI) Dickens enlarges on the
mischievous enterprise and ready wit of omnibus cads,
and in 'The Last Cab-Driver, And The First Omnibus
Cad' (Scenes, XVII) he introduces a notable individual,
Bill Barker ('Aggerawatin Bill'). Barker belongs to the
sub-criminal class, but Dickens can no more withhold admiration from him, than from the Artful Dodger.

At the end of the last-mentioned sketch, Dickens writes
regretfully, 'Slang will be forgotten when civility becomes
general'. As Pip's history shows, civility is, for Dickens,
a doubtful good. Characters like Bill Barker or Sam Weller are enviably uninhibited. They are like a gust of fresh
air in bourgeois society. They spoke out, as—on a very different level—Dickens himself spoke out in his writings.

What Dickens spoke out against was Victorian civility: a
civility based on the pursuit of wealth and status, and riddled with snobberies and fetishes.

In 'Horatio Sparkins' (Tales, V) the Malderton family
have the still-recognizable English weaknesses:

> Mr. Malderton was a man whose whole scope of
> ideas was limited to Lloyd's, the Exchange, the
> India House, and the Bank. A few successful
> speculations had raised him from a situation of
> obscurity and comparative poverty, to a state of
> affluence. As frequently happens in such cases,
> the ideas of himself and his family became ele-
> vated to an extraordinary pitch as their means
> increased; they affected fashion, taste, and many
> other fooleries, in imitation of their betters, and
> had a very decided and becoming horror of any-
> thing which could, by possibility, be considered
> *low*. He was hospitable from ostentation, illiber-
> al from ignorance, and prejudiced from conceit.
> Egotism and the love of display induced him to
> keep an excellent table: convenience, and a love
> of good things of this life, ensured him plenty of
> guests. He liked to have clever men, or what he
> considered such, at his table, because it was a
> great thing to talk about; but he never could en-
> dure what he called 'sharp fellows'. Probably he
> cherished this feeling out of compliment to his
> two sons, who gave their respected parent no un-
> easiness in that particular.

> The family were ambitious of forming acquaint-
> ances and connexions in some sphere of society
> superior to that in which they themselves
> moved; and one of the necessary consequences
> of this desire, added to their utter ignorance of
> the world beyond their own small circle, was,
> that any one who could lay claim to an acquain-
> tance with people of rank and title, had a sure
> passport to the table at Oak Lodge, Camberwell.

A young man with black whiskers, a white cravat, ingratiating manners, and poetical conversation has just 'come
out' at their local assembly, and it has been generally concluded from appearances that 'he must be *somebody*'. Mr.
Malderton is easily prevailed upon to invite him to Oak
Lodge, by Mrs. Malderton, who is looking for a husband
for her eldest daughter, twenty-eight and single. Mr.

Sparkins, the young man, accepts an invitation to Sunday
dinner, but the family's exultation at this *coup* is tempered
by regret when Mrs. Malderton's brother invites himself
for the same meal. This brother is one of those who speak
out:

> 'Upon my word, my dear, it's a most annoying
> thing that that vulgar brother of yours should
> have invited himself to dine here today,' said Mr.
> Malderton to his wife. 'On account of Mr.
> Sparkins's coming down, I purposely abstained
> from asking any one but Flamwell. [Flamwell is
> a small-time tuft-hunter.] And then to think of
> your brother—a tradesman—it's insufferable! I
> declare I wouldn't have him mention his shop,
> before our new guest—no, not for a thousand
> pounds! I wouldn't care if he had the good sense
> to conceal the disgrace he is to the family; but
> he's so fond of his horrible business, that he *will*
> let people know what he is.'

The dinner takes place. There is an exchange in which the
author makes his point with a pun:

> 'Talking of business,' interposed Mr. Barton [the
> vulgar brother], from the centre of the table. 'A
> gentleman whom you knew very well, Malder-
> ton, before you made that first lucky spec of
> yours, called at our shop the other day, and—'

> 'Barton, may I trouble you for a potato?' inter-
> rupted the wretched master of the house, hoping
> to nip the story in the bud.

> 'Certainly,' returned the grocer, quite insensible
> of his brother-in-law's object—'and he said in a
> very plain manner—'

> '*Floury*, if you please,' interrupted Malderton
> again.

The tale has a very simple peripety and discovery. Horatio
Sparkins who 'seemed like the embodied idea of the young
dukes and poetical exquisites' the Malderton girls
dreamed about, and who had a very flowery utterance ('he
talks just like an auctioneer' is the comment of the unen-
chanted younger Malderton son) is encountered unexpectedly by Mrs. Malderton and the girls, when they are on
a shopping expedition:

> At length, the vehicle stopped before a dirty-
> looking ticketed linen-draper's shop, with goods
> of all kinds, and labels of all sorts and sizes, in
> the window. There were dropsical figures of
> seven with a little three-farthings in the corner,
> 'perfectly invisible to the naked eye'; three hun-
> dred and fifty thousand ladies' boas, *from* one
> shilling and a penny halfpenny; real French kid
> shoes, at two and ninepence per pair; green para-
> sols, at an equally cheap rate; and 'every descrip-
> tion of goods', as the proprietors said—and they
> must know best—fifty per cent. under cost
> price'.

> 'Lor! ma, what a place you have brought us to!'
> said Miss Teresa; 'what *would* Mr. Sparkins say
> if he could see us!'

> 'Ah! what, indeed!' said Miss Marianne, horri-
> fied at the idea.

'Pray be seated, ladies. What is the first article?' inquired the obsequious master of the ceremonies of the establishment, who, in his large white neck-cloth and formal tie, looked like a bad 'portrait of a gentleman' in the Somerset House exhibition.

'I want to see some silks,' answered Mrs. Malcerton.

'Directly, ma'am.—Mr. Smith! Where *is* Mr. Smith?'

Mr. Horatio Sparkins answers the summons. English society being what it is, the Malderton family suffer the mortification of having sought the acquaintance of an assistant at a cut-price shop. Mr. Sparkins, like the chief salesman, is a bad portrait of a gentleman. As such, he is related to the riding-master of Astley's.

The same axiom, that snobbery is the comic flaw of the English, is illustrated by **'The Tuggses at Ramsgate'** (Tales, IV). Mr. Tuggs, who keeps a grocer's shop on 'the Surrey side of the water, within three minutes' walk of the old London Bridge', unexpectedly inherits twenty thousand pounds. His family all agree that to leave town is 'an indispensable preliminary to being genteel'. And they decide where to go, in this fashion:

> 'Gravesend?' mildly suggested Mr. Joseph Tuggs. The idea was unanimously scouted. Gravesend was *low*.
>
> 'Margate?' insinuated Mrs. Tuggs. Worse and worse—nobody there, but tradespeople.

Ramsgate is their choice, and there they fall in with a dashing couple, Captain and Mrs. Waters. They keep company, and go one day to the Pegwell Bay Hotel for lunch. Dickens's description of this middle-class idyll is beautifully ironic:

> Mr. and Mrs. Tuggs, and the captain, had ordered lunch in the little garden behind:—small saucers of large shrimps, dabs of butter, crusty loaves, and bottled ale. The sky was without a cloud; there were flower-pots and turf before them; the sea, from the foot of the cliff, stretching away as far as the eye could discern anything at all; vessels in the distance with sails as white, and as small, as nicely-got-up cambric handkerchiefs. The shrimps were delightful, the ale better, and the captain even more pleasant than either. Mrs. Captain Waters was in *such* spirits after lunch!—chasing, first the captain across the turf, and among the flower-pots; and then Mr. Cymon Tuggs; and then Miss Tuggs; and laughing, too, quite boisterously. But as the Captain said, it didn't matter; who knew what they were, there? For all the people of the house knew, they might be common people.

But Captain and Mrs. Waters are bad portraits of a gentleman and a lady, and they 'bounce' the Tuggses for a large part of their inheritance. The situations are unforcedly comic, and the life of a Victorian watering-place is brilliantly evoked.

The best of the Tales is probably **'A Passage In The Life Of Mr. Watkins Tottle'** (Tales, X). The characters are

well diversified: Watkins Tottle, timid and formal; Gabriel Parsons, rude and facetious; the wayward Fanny Parsons, the simpering Miss Lillerton, the smoothly ingratiating Reverend Charles Timson; Ikey and the denizens of the Cursitor Street sponging-house. The construction is artfully episodic, so that the first chapter includes the contrasting narration of Gabriel Parsons's wooing of Fanny, and the second chapter includes the story of the young couple hounded by vindictive parents (a story that anticipates that of 'The Queer Client' in *Pickwick Papers*). It has the kind of multiple texture that is a feature of Dickens's later work.

Dickens is commonly good at dinner-table scenes, but in the whole of his work there is none better than that where Parsons is endeavouring to tell a story:

> 'When I was in Suffolk—' said Mr. Gabriel Parsons.
>
> 'Take off the fowls first, Martha,' said Mrs. Parsons. 'I beg your pardon, my dear.'
>
> 'When I was in Suffolk,' resumed Mr. Parsons, with an impatient glance at his wife, who pretended not to observe it, 'which is now some years ago, business led me to the town of Bury St. Edmund's. I had to stop at the principal places in my way, and therefore, for the sake of convenience, I travelled in a gig. I left Sudbury one dark night—it was winter time—about nine o'clock; the rain poured in torrents, the wind howled among the trees that skirted the roadside, and I was obliged to proceed at a foot-pace, for I could hardly see my hand before me, it was so dark—'
>
> 'John,' interrupted Mrs. Parsons, in a low, hollow voice, 'don't spill that gravy.'
>
> 'Fanny,' said Parsons impatiently, 'I wish you'd defer these domestic reproofs to some more suitable time. Really, my dear, these constant interruptions are very annoying.'
>
> 'My dear, I didn't interrupt you,' said Mrs. Parsons.
>
> 'But, my dear, you *did* interrupt me,' remonstrated Mr. Parsons.
>
> 'How very absurd you are, my love; I must give directions to the servants; I am quite sure that if I sat here and allowed John to spill the gravy over the new carpet, you'd be the first to find fault when you saw the stain to-morrow morning.'
>
> 'Well,' continued Gabriel, with a resigned air, as if he knew there was no getting over the point about the carpet, 'I was just saying, it was so dark that I could hardly see my hand before me. The road was very lonely, and I assure you, Tottle (this was a device to arrest the wandering attention of that individual, which was distracted by a confidential communication between Mrs. Parsons and Martha, accompanied by the delivery of a large bunch of keys), I assure you, Tottle, I became somehow impressed with a sense of the loneliness of my situation—'

'Pie to your master,' interrupted Mrs. Parsons, again directing the servant.

'Now, pray, my dear,' remonstrated Parsons once more, very pettishly. Mrs. P. turned up her hands and eyebrows, and appealed in dumb show to Miss Lillerton. 'As I turned a corner of the road,' resumed Gabriel, 'the horse stopped short, and reared tremendously. I pulled up, jumped out, ran to his head, and found a man lying on his back in the middle of the road, with his eyes fixed on the sky. I thought he was dead; but no, he was alive, and there appeared to be nothing the matter with him. He jumped up, and putting his hand to his chest, and fixing upon me the most earnest gaze you can imagine, exclaimed—'

'Pudding here,' said Mrs. Parsons.

'Oh! it's no use,' exclaimed the host, now rendered desperate. 'Here, Tottle; a glass of wine. It's useless to attempt relating anything when Mrs. Parsons is present.'

This attack was received in the usual way. Mrs. Parsons talked *to* Miss Lillerton and *at* her better half; expatiated on the impatience of men generally; hinted that her husband was peculiarly vicious in this respect, and wound up by insinuating that she must be one of the best tempers that ever existed, or she never could put up with it. Really what she had to endure sometimes, was more than any one who saw her in every-day life could by possibility suppose.

That exchange does not forward the (very simple) plot, and it is only incidentally a presentment of character. But the story is about a bachelor who is to be coaxed into marriage, and it is the artist's concern to exhibit married life in more than one aspect. But one feels, in any case, that Dickens could not help it: the prompting to set down what he had so often heard was too strong.

No account of Dickens's fictions that concerns itself solely with the plot or with the moral scheme, important as those are, can do them justice. There is an unhappy boyhood and an unhappy manhood behind his life's writing, and the great novels are remarkable for the exploration of personality and the mechanism of society. But Dickens also felt the artist's primary need, to record. The ***Sketches by Boz*** give clear evidence of this. They are instinct with moral feeling, but they are, first and foremost, an artist's impressions of the life around him. For this reason, I suggest, he could not write for long in retirement.

William E. Morris　(essay date 1965)

SOURCE: "The Conversion of Scrooge: A Defense of That Good Man's Motivation," in *Studies in Short Fiction,* Vol. III, No. 1, Fall, 1965, pp. 46-55.

[*In the following essay, Morris examines Ebenezer Scrooge's "conversion" in* A Christmas Carol. *According to Morris, "Dickens does not intend Scrooge's awakening to be a promise for all covetous old sinners, but only a possibility to be individually hoped for."*]

As everyone knows, being called a "scrooge" is bad. When labeled like this, one is considered "a tight-fisted hand at the grindstone . . . Hard and sharp as flint, from which no steel had ever struck out generous fire; secret, and self-contained, and solitary as an oyster." In reality, and in short, one is a party-pooper, afflicted with general overtones of inhumanity.

This is the popular definition of the word *Scrooge,* and it is unfairly the usual description of Charles Dickens' Ebenezer Scrooge, of ***A Christmas Carol.*** Scrooge's conversion to a permanent goodness, which is every bit up to those impossible standards met by the totally admirable Cheerybles and Mr. Brownlow, seems to have been utterly forgotten, or ignored. Popularly lost is Dickens' last word on Scrooge: " . . . it was always said of him that he knew how to keep a Christmas well, if any man alive possessed the knowledge." By common consent Scrooge has been a villain at every Christmas season since 1843. Indeed, that reformed old gentleman might well answer, " 'It's not convenient, and it's not fair.' "

What "we" remember about ***A Christmas Carol*** is the flinty employer, the humbly simple (and sentimental) clerk, and sweet Tiny Tim. If the general reading public remembers Scrooge's conversion at all, it sees the alteration as a punishment brought about and maintained through fear. The conversion is seen as only a part of the story, when in fact it is what the story is *all* about. *A Christmas Carol* is not, as some readers seem to think, "The Little Lame Prince" or "The Confidential Clerk." It is the reawakening of a Christian soul, although (as Edgar Johnson makes clear [in *Charles Dickens, His Tragedy and Triumph,* 1952]) it is not a religious conversion. Religious or not, the story is a celebration of an important conversion, the sort of conversion on which Dickens pinned his hopes for social, moral, economic, and even political recovery in England. The carol sung here is a song of celebration for a Christmas birth that offers hope; it is not a song of thanks for revenge accomplished or for luck had by the poor. To be an "old Scrooge" is, in the final analysis, a good thing to be. And with careful rereading of the tale the clichés of a hasty public would surely disappear.

What is more damagingly unfair than the popular mistake is the critics' treatment of Scrooge's conversion, which ranges from Edgar Johnson's insistence that Scrooge is "nothing other than a personification of economic man" to Humphry House's assertion [in *The Dickens World,* 1941] that "his conversion, moreover, seems to be complete at a stroke, his actions after it uniform." At the critics' hands the enlightenment of Scrooge is not individual, believable, real, or even interesting. Perhaps the most surprising comment is this one by Chesterton [in *Chartes Dickens,* 1906]:

> Scrooge is not really inhuman at the beginning any more than he is at the end. There is a heartiness in his inhospitable sentiments that is akin to humour and therefore inhumanity; he is only a crusty old bachelor, and had (I strongly suspect) given away turkeys secretly all his life. The beauty and the real blessing of the story do not lie in the mechanical plot of it, the repentance of

Scrooge, probable or improbable; they lie in the great furnace of real unhappiness that glows through Scrooge and everything round him; that great furnace, the heart of Dickens. Whether the Christmas visions would or would not convert Scrooge, they convert us.

It is my contention that the story records the psychological—if overnight—change in Scrooge from a mechanical tool that has been manufactured by the economic institutions around him to the human being he was before business dehumanized him. His conversion is his alone, not that of "economic man"; Dickens does not intend Scrooge's awakening to be a promise for all covetous old sinners, but only a possibility to be individually hoped for. Further, if the visitations by Marley and the three spirits be accepted as dreams ("Marley was dead, to begin with. There is no doubt whatever about that."), their substance, as well as their messages and their effects, must have come from the recesses of Scrooge's own mind. And finally, if the conversion comes from within Scrooge, it could have been effected at a stroke, for surely it had been subconsciously fermenting for a long time. Of such things Christmas miracles, or epiphanies, may very well be made. Scrooge explains it: " 'I haven't missed it. The spirits have done it all in one night. They can do anything they like. Of course they can!' "

From the Marley-faced doorknocker to the third Phan-

tom's hood and dress shrinking, collapsing, and dwindling down to the bed post, Scrooge is dreaming, awake and asleep. The entire substance of the dreams has been all of Scrooge's own making; he has, in an agitated state, conjured up those things that he has until now hidden from himself but has not been unaware of: his own compounded sins, and Marley's; his happy and sad boyhood; his small sister and the memory of an unkind father; the gay times working under old Fezziwig on a Christmas long ago; Scrooge's denial of Belle, the girl he was to have married; the supposed or heard-of later happiness of the same girl (at Christmas, of course), married to another man; the eve of Marley's death; the Christmas gaiety of common people at the present Christmas season (which he had known, for he spoke harshly of it at his place of business only that afternoon); the happy Cratchit home this Christmas, with its touching sight of Tiny Tim and the blight of the subdued Cratchit opinion of Scrooge; Christmas present with miners, lighthouse keepers, and seamen—all more content than Scrooge despite their condition; the bright games at the Christmas home of his nephew, a place to which he was invited and angrily refused a few hours ago; the sight of the two tattered children under the Spirit's robes—the boy Ignorance, the girl Want; his own cheap funeral and the theft of his possessions; the scorn of him among business men; the death of Tiny Tim and the view of Scrooge's own tombstone. All these would have been known to him, through experience, imagination, or the public press or gossip.

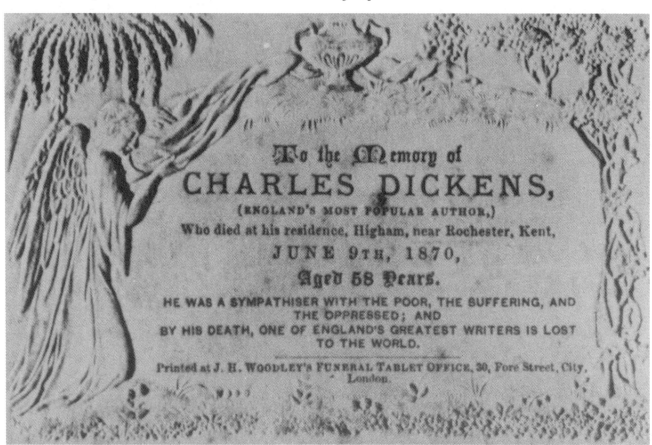

Memorial card reproducing the inscription on Dickens's gravestone in Poets' Corner, Westminster Abbey.

The dream visions are connected, as dreams, not only to what he knew or feared or imagined, but to each other through recurring scenes, motifs, verbal expressions, and physical props. They are believably motivated—that is, if dreams are ever believably motivated.

In Stave One, before Scrooge goes to sleep, Dickens presents several clues to what trouble his dreams; we can infer the other clues from the dreams themselves. First the reader learns that this afternoon is cold, foggy, and dark. And during the dreams cold, fog, and darkness persist and dominate until they are the atmosphere of the dreams. Cold, which dominates the day, runs through the dreams, relieved only by and for persons who share each other's company. It is not relieved for Scrooge, who in his dreams can no longer use the imagination which Dickens says he relied upon to defeat cold at his counting-house. Cold is the most persistent element in the story—more pervasive than even the fog and darkness. It is the temperature of the world that cannot be shed or blown away by anyone but must be lived with and among. It is triumphed over only by the philanthropy of fellowship (which might be more specifically called kindness, love, tolerance, and sympathy between individual persons), not by the misanthropy of solitaries or the collective bargaining of institutions (" 'I help to support the establishments I have mentioned—they cost enough: and those who are badly off must go there,' " explains Scrooge). Here is that assertion dramatized:

> The cold became intense. In the main street, at the corner of the court, some labourers were repairing the gas-pipes, and had lighted a great fire in a brazier, round which a party of ragged men and boys were gathered: warming their hands and winking their eyes before the blaze in rapture. The water-plug being left in solitude, its overflowing suddenly congealed, and turned to misanthropic ice.

The great fire in the brazier of the workmen is the exact opposite of Scrooge's "very small fire" and the one he allows his clerk ("it looked like one coal"); their rapture is not at all like Scrooge's grouchiness and gloom. In contrast to the laborers', Scrooge's overflowings are congealed and turned to misanthropic ice, like the water-plug left in solitude. It is the solitude of Scrooge that has congealed him so that no outside force of weather knows where to have him. It could not be less open to the warmth that in this story is equated to human companionship.

And yet Scrooge does feel the cold, in spite of what people thought. He has caught cold in the head; he does bundle up; he does sit close to the small fire in his chambers and brood over it. The denial of cold as an economic hindrance is part of a public role that he has taken on as he has slipped into isolation. Fuel costs money just as warmth costs human feeling; and human feeling leads into a world which he has come to foreswear. "What shall I put you down for?" asks one of the gentlemen who come in the spirit of charity to collect money for the needy on Christmas Eve. " 'Nothing!' Scrooge replied. 'You wish to be anonymous?' 'I wish to be left alone,' said Scrooge." What Scrooge comes to see (and thus the reason for his conversion) is that if one is left alone he does become anonymous.

Over and over in the dreams, this is Scrooge's fear: that he will be left and forgotten, that he will die and no one will care. This fear grows as the suggestion of anonymity recurs more frequently during the course of the dreams. Defense against cold is the first demand Scrooge makes of Bob Cratchit on the day after Christmas, for a fully awakened Scrooge says, " 'Make up the fires and buy another coal-scuttle before you dot another i, Bob Cratchit!' " At last Scrooge has determined to keep human warmth about him.

Fog and darkness become symbols for incommunication and isolation in the dreams; their opposites become symbols for communication and integration with mankind. Light and clarity of vision are subdued, except in flashes of Christmas past when Scrooge is a schoolboy at play, or a young man at old Fezziwig's party, or an onlooker at Belle's happy home. These flashes are only glimmers in a usually dark atmosphere. One of the few bright outdoor scenes is the one in which Scrooge is shown himself playing as a boy: "The city had entirely disappeared. Not a vestige of it was to be seen. The darkness and the mist had vanished with it, for it was a clear, cold, winter day, with snow upon the ground." But, as the Spirit of Christmas Past reminds him, "These are but shadows of the things that have been." Fog and darkness dominate until the last section of the story, when Scrooge awakes on Christmas morning and puts his head out the window to find, "No fog, no mist; clear, bright, jovial, stirring cold; cold piping for the blood to dance to; golden sunlight; heavenly day; sweet fresh air; merry bells. Oh, glorious! Glorious!" Throughout the dreams Scrooge's mind has kept the real weather of the day on which he retired.

Part of the darkness motif is figured in the games hide-and-seek and blindman's-buff. It may be paraphrased as "none are so blind as those that will not see." Apparently in the recent past Scrooge has noticed the blind men's dogs pulling their masters from his path, and then wagging their tails as though they said, " 'No eye at all is better than an evil eye, dark master!' " The observation must have been Scrooge's. Perhaps, too, was the plight of his house, "up a yard, where it had so little business to be, that one could scarcely help fancying it must have run there when it was a young house, playing at hide-and-seek with other houses, and forgotten the way out again." Even Scrooge on this evening is being buffeted like a blind man in trying to find his house amid the fog and dark. His flight of fancy about the house ("one could scarcely help fancying it") must surely reflect his unformulated yet subconscious worry about his own state, which the personification of the lost house parallels. Whether Scrooge knew that Cratchit hurried home to play blindman's-buff we do not know, though his dreams and his Christmas actions in behalf of the Cratchits indicate that he knew a great deal about his clerk's family. In any case, in his dreams Scrooge imagines a game of blindman's-buff at his nephew's home, and he also imagines Martha Cratchit playing a game of hide-and-seek with her father. The blind men are buffeted out of love; their awakenings are joyous—in Scrooge's dreams, in his yearnings. It must be the case with Scrooge that he is lost yet struggling to be found.

Cold, fog, and darkness afflict Scrooge's sight and feeling. The sound of bells also plagues him. It is significantly recurrent. At his counting-house it has long disturbed him: "The ancient tower of a church, whose gruff old bell was always peeping slyly down at Scrooge out of a Gothic window in the wall, became invisible, and struck the hours and quarters in the clouds, with tremendous vibrations afterward, as if its teeth were chattering in its frozen head up there." In his chambers, "his glance happened to rest upon a bell, a disused bell, that hung in the room, and communicated for some purpose now forgotten with a chamber in the highest story of the building." This is the bell that starts ringing mysteriously, then stops, and is followed by the clanking noise of Marley's ghost. This bell, as well as the others, symbolizes the mystery of what is lost to Scrooge—the proper use of time and service, of a call to human beings. Bells toll the coming of the spirits, though Scrooge's sense of time causes him to doubt their relevance ("The clock was wrong. An icicle must have got into the works.") Bells call happy people to church; they punctuate parties and other human assembly. At last Scrooge responds to bells without fear, but happily to "the lustiest peals he had ever heard." He has found the purpose for which the bell communicated with a chamber in the highest story of the building. He has had bells on his mind since the evening before, not merely because they marked time's passing but also because they connected people in warmth, worship, play, death, and love. This last would have a special tug upon Scrooge: the girl he was to have married long ago was named Belle.

The hardware of life haunts Scrooge, too—the forged metals which he has depended upon in place of human relations to secure, lock up, and insure what he will possess of existence. He has replaced with metal "solidity"; he has forged a chain, has relied on steel. But the hardware is unsubstantial. On Christmas Eve it melts into the hallucination of a doorknocker that comes alive in the likeness of Jacob Marley. And, though Scrooge doublelocks himself in, the hardware of Marley clanks to him, as does that of numerous other phantoms. Hardware reappears several times more as an undependable tool of life. The last of the Spirits takes Scrooge to a filthy den, a junk heap. "Upon the floor within, were piled up heaps of rusty keys, nails, chains, hinges, files, scales, weights, and refuse iron of all kinds. Secrets that few would like to scrutinise were bred and hidden in mountains of unseemly rags, masses of corrupted fat, and sepulchres of bones." It is here that the dreamed-of charwoman, laundress, and undertaker's man bring to sell for hard cash the only effects of dreamed-of dead Scrooge. And his imagined effects belong here, among the junk. For these, material possessions, Scrooge has traded human love. In the dreams his fear of losing them has emerged. Spirits from the outside world have come into Scrooge's counting-house this afternoon—his nephew, the charity gentlemen, the lad who sang through the keyhole:

> 'God bless you, merry gentleman!
> May nothing you dismay!'

They have asked for his money and love. Worse, they have threatened his only security: the belief in only material possession. In the dreams their invasion is reasserted by

magnification into phantoms who would take away his wealth.

Selling Scrooge's possessions in the dream, the women say, " 'Who's the worse for the loss of a few things like these? Not a dead man, I suppose?' 'No, indeed,' said Mrs. Dilber, laughing. 'If he wanted to keep 'em after he was dead, a wicked old screw,' pursued the woman, 'why wasn't he natural in his lifetime?' " Scrooge, like an old screw—a piece of hardware himself—has not been natural. This he has known subconsciously. He is struggling through metaphor to make himself aware of it; for he is not yet, in spite of appearances, inhuman. He is not yet as dead as a doornail, which, as Dickens observes at the outset, is considered "the deadest piece of ironmongery in the trade." It was what Marley was as dead as, but not Scrooge, thanks to his submerged conscience.

It is easy to see why several other motifs should run through Scrooge's dreams—the many references to death and burial, to the passage of time, to the poor, to persons unhappy alone and happy gathered together. They are life that Scrooge has tried not to live by.

One motif, marriage, needs exploration, however. The Christmas Eve of the dreams was not only the seventh anniversary of Jacob Marley's death—of Scrooge's last connection with a true fellow misanthropist—but it was also the afternoon he had replied to his nephew's invitation to dinner by saying he would see the nephew in hell first, then had blurted out as rationale: " 'Why did you get married?' " Love, to Scrooge, was the only symptom nearer insanity than the wish for a merry Christmas. Scrooge had built a wall of scorn against happy married life, and in the dreams we see his return to the problem, before and after the wall was built. In Stave Two, Belle sums up the problem: "You fear the world too much,' she answered, gently. 'All your hopes have merged into the hope of being beyond the chance of its sordid reproach. I have seen your nobler aspirations fall off one by one, until the master-passion, Gain, engrosses you.' "

But why does gain obsess him? Why has he given up Belle for gold? And why does marriage appall him? The answers may be revealed in the dreams. Taken back to his solitary and unhappy days as a schoolboy, Scrooge sees his old imagined friends of those days, characters from *The Arabian Nights,* and he cries: " 'And the Sultan's groom turned upside down by the Genii; there he is upon his head! Serve him right. I'm glad of it. What business had *he* to be married to the Princess!' " The groom is not good enough to marry the Princess, for he is poor. In the next scene of the dream Scrooge appears as a boy left at school while his classmates have gone home on holiday. He is discovered by his sister Fan (later to become mother of Scrooge's nephew), who announces her errand to take Scrooge home:

> 'To bring you home, home, home!'

> 'Home, little Fan?' returned the boy.
> 'Yes!' said the child, brimful of glee. 'Home, for good and all. Home for ever and ever. Father is so much kinder than he used to be, that home's like Heaven! He spoke so gently to me one dear

night when I was going to bed, that I was not afraid to ask him once more if you might come home; and he said Yes, you should; and sent me in a coach to bring you. And you're to be a man!' said the child, opening her eyes, 'and are never to come back here; but first, we're to be together all the Christmas long, and have the merriest time in all the world.'

We can conjecture the relationship between Scrooge and his father; surely the father had been a tyrant, and possibly he had shaped the ideal of marriage for his son. Or, if one guesses, perhaps the father's cruelty resulted from money worries so that Scrooge felt marriage was possible only if the husband were secure financially. This at least seems to have led to the rift between Scrooge and Belle, which could very well have stemmed from the example of Scrooge's father. The simple fictional childhood of *Arabian Nights* and *Robinson Crusoe* ("Poor Robinson Crusoe, where have you been, Robinson Crusoe?") has been lost, cut in upon by the harsh facts of economic life. Obsession with wealth for its own sake has begun as a desire to build a platform on which to base married life. The obsession has made love for anything but gold impossible. This is what ailed Scrooge—this and the submerged struggle against the master-passion, Gain at the expense of humanity and in the interest of dehumanization.

Scrooge has observed and evidently thought kindly upon the marriages of the Fezziwigs and Cratchits. But the former was overshadowed by fear of insecurity in marriage; Scrooge's youthful sympathy for the Fezziwigs' union was submerged. Similarly, Scrooge's reveling in the happy-and-threatened Cratchit family remained under his flinty consciousness until the dream conversion. Of his sister's marriage we learn only that it resulted in Fan's death; apparently Scrooge cannot think upon it further. He has believed the only safe road is the one to personal economic security. Travel along that road, as Scrooge takes it, necessitates avoidance of human love.

No change can come from without his mind. His emergence must originate in his mind, for that is where he has locked everything up. The dreams are remembrances and imaginings based on remembrance. They are subconscious fears. Moreover, they have been so tightly, inhumanly, pressed that they must burst forth, and Scrooge must either in his crisis reform totally or not at all. There is no degree of inhumanity. It is true that he overcompensates and becomes a ridiculous countercaricature. But then he has shocked himself severely. The understanding of self has been huge; so its early manifestations were bound to be foolish. If it is difficult to imagine such overnight conversion, it is even more difficult to imagine a gradual one. He is being smothered by his isolationist creed; so he must throw it off violently. Scrooge is either a human being and must understand it, or become a thing. On this fateful Christmas Eve he has denied all he has had of human life—family, friendship, love, charity—indeed, all fellow-feeling. He can no longer find life enough to breathe in isolation; he must break out into the world. The dreams—inner explosions of conscience—are the last resort.

They are not reform theory. They do not echo pamphlets, or legislation, or sermons from the public pulpit, but indi-

vidual human conscience. They come from the effects of a lifetime at last asserted. Thus they can, apparently at a stroke, overset the habits of many misled years.

Craig Buckwald   (essay date 1990)

SOURCE: "Stalking the Figurative Oyster: The Excursive Ideal in *A Christmas Carol*," in *Studies in Short Fiction*, Vol. 27, No. 1, Winter, 1990, pp. 1-14.

[*Here, Buckwald examines the theme of restriction and containment in* A Christmas Carol, *as exemplified by the description of Scrooge as "solitary as an oyster."*]

> Oh! but he was a tight-fisted hand at the grind-stone, Scrooge! a squeezing, wrenching, grasping, scraping, clutching, covetous old sinner! Hard and sharp as flint, from which no steel had ever struck out generous fire; secret, and self-contained, and solitary as an oyster.

If at the beginning of **A Christmas Carol** Ebenezer Scrooge apparently lacks a heart, he is at all times the undisputed heart of the story he inhabits. It is thus entirely fitting that this formal introduction to the miser's objectionable qualities, occurring in the piece's sixth paragraph, anticipates much in the narrative fabric that follows. We could, for example, profitably begin an interpretation of the tale with the first two figures in the description—the "tight-fisted hand" and the unproductive "flint"—for from them spring the images of closed and open and clasped and touching hands; feeble and potent fires; and brightness and darkness through which Dickens' Christmas message palpably appeals to the imaginations of its readers. And yet, the centrality of hand and flint notwithstanding, I want to focus on the culminating simile in which Scrooge is compared to an oyster. The oyster image, I argue, despite its unassuming character, is really a kind of master-trope for the story, one that casts new light not only on Scrooge but on imagery, structure, and meaning in the **Carol** as a whole.

To assess the oyster image's importance in the story, we need to begin with the simile's three-part characterization of Scrooge: "secret, and self-contained, and solitary." That the Scrooge of the first "stave" is "solitary as an oyster," isolated from his fellow creatures as an oyster's body is by its enclosing shell, needs only acknowledgment here. This fact is both generally evident in the story and specifically remarked by the narrator: "To edge his way along the crowded paths of life," we are told, "warning all human sympathy to keep its distance, was what the knowing ones call 'nuts' to Scrooge." By identifying reclusiveness and misanthropy with miserliness, the story characterizes Scrooge's habitual shunning of other people as the denial of the human commerce upon which a healthy society depends.

Unlike the accusation of reclusiveness, the charge that Scrooge is "secret . . . as an oyster" seems suspect. "Secret," if it is not to be confused with the other terms, implies in this context that there is not only something hidden inside of Scrooge but something *good*, some equivalent to an oyster's tasty flesh or cradled pearl. We might well be puzzled by such a notion because beneath the miser's outward chilliness, there seems to be, as the narrator says, more "cold within him." But true to the simile, Scrooge does have something better deep inside of him, though for the most part it is kept hidden even from us. Two earlier incarnations comprise the first part of his secret: once there was a Scrooge who, craving love, longed to leave school to join his family for Christmas just as later there was a Scrooge who gratefully, gleefully partook of the Fezziwigs' abundant and caring Christmas hospitality. Like the rooms in his present house that are now let out as offices, the younger Scrooge once belonged to a home; and like the house itself, which once "play[ed]" with other houses, the older Scrooge belonged to a festive community. The second part of Scrooge's secret is that, beneath his rough shell, something of his earlier incarnations still lives and can even on occasion be glimpsed, though by now, with respect to his daily life and outward behavior, it has been rendered as feeble as the small fire he allows his clerk; nearly as contained as fire within flint; and as incapable of issuing forth on its own as is his house, which, during its game of hide-and-seek, must have hidden itself "where it had so little business to be . . . and . . . forgotten the way out again." It is only granting this surviving inner warmth that Scrooge's feeling response to the ghostly visions, at first guarded but soon afterwards engaged-in openly, is at all probable.

It is the narrator's claim, however, that Scrooge is "self-contained . . . as an oyster" that proves the most fruitful, only partly because it addresses both the miser's solitariness and secrecy. If we take into account the way the adjective is colored by the oyster image—an image of a crusty shell "containing" an organism quite shut-off from the world around it—"self-contained" points to a condition best summarized thus: what there is inside a thing is kept under wraps, prevented from finding its way to the outside, and what might be larger is kept smaller. It is in this dual sense that the simile speaks expressively of Scrooge.

The narrator's first pointed words about Scrooge, "Oh! but he was a tight-fisted hand at the grindstone," prepare us for the extreme containment of his physical self. "The cold within him," we are told, "froze his old features, nipped his pointed nose, shrivelled his cheek, stiffened his gait"; we hear of his "thin lips" and "wiry chin." When, a few paragraphs later, we learn of Scrooge's predilection "to edge his way along the crowded paths of life, warning all human sympathy to keep its distance," it is impossible not to imagine him keeping to the edge of the sidewalk when he must venture out onto the London streets. In short, restriction defines, literally or imaginatively, not only Scrooge's physique and physiognomy but his stiff gait, the area trodden by that gait, and his bodily activity in general. In case we fail to notice these physical containments, we are given a foil in Bob Cratchit, who, when finally released from the dungeon-like counting-house for the holiday, emblematically celebrates his freedom in a burst of bodily kinesis. Cratchit, we are told, "went down a slide on Cornhill, at the end of a lane of boys, twenty times, in honour of its being Christmas-eve, and then ran home to Camden Town as hard as he could pelt, to play at blindman's-buff." The active expansiveness of the

clerk's physical presence, his body now vertical, now horizontal, his legs kicking out in front of him as he races home, is matched by the extravagance of his movement over land, twenty trips downhill when one would have been out of his way.

But later we are also given foils with an added dimension. When the Ghost of Christmas Past shows Scrooge the vision of Belle as a grown woman, she is at home with her daughter, and both are surrounded by activity personified—more children than Scrooge can count, and "every child . . . conducting itself like forty." The narrator, however, enviously sexualizes the "young brigands' " "ruthless" "pillag[ing]" of Belle's daughter. He confesses that though he longs to be "one of them," he could never take such liberties with the daughter's person:

> And yet I should have dearly liked, I own, to have touched her lips; to have questioned her, that she might have opened them; to have looked upon the lashes of her downcast eyes, and never raised a blush; to have let loose waves of hair, an inch of which would be a keepsake beyond price: in short, I should have liked, I do confess, to have had the lightest licence of a child, and yet been man enough to know its value.

Later, Scrooge witnesses a game of blindman's-buff played by the company at his nephew's house, during which the narrator disingenuously deplores the conduct of the young man called Topper, who somehow manages to pursue "that plump sister in the lace tucker" wherever she goes, and finally traps her in a corner where he engages in conduct "the most execrable." Whether in the horde of rampant children freely touching Belle's daughter, or in Topper's pursuit and braille identification of Scrooge's niece, the dimension of sexuality is admitted into the expansive physical activity which in the story counterpoints the unredeemed Scrooge's "stiff gait."

Scrooge's self-containment, of course, is more than physical. His obsession with business and wealth not only occupies his time and energy but constitutes the frame of reference by which he judges everything and everyone in his world: "can even I believe that you would choose a dowerless girl," says Belle to Scrooge in one of the first spirit's vision, "—you who, in your very confidence with her, weigh everything by Gain . . . ?" Proving Belle's appraisal, Scrooge earlier reacts harshly to his nephew's greeting of "merry Christmas":

> Merry Christmas! What right have you to be merry? what reason have you to be merry? You're poor enough.

> What's Christmas time to you but a time for paying bills without money; a time for finding yourself a year older, and not an hour richer; a time for balancing your books and having every item in 'em through a round dozen of months presented dead against you?

In addition to an idolization of wealth, Scrooge betrays in these lines a problem of *comprehension,* an inability to see beyond the containment of his own perspective and understand his nephew's opposing values: "what reason have you to be merry? You're poor enough," he cries in the second of his three questions. The fact that Scrooge concerns himself with his nephew's fortunes at all reveals that more than self-concern is at work here: he attempts to purge Fred of his Christmas spirit precisely because *it makes no sense to him* that Fred should keep it. In other words, Scrooge's anti-Christmas speech is, oddly enough, his least selfish moment in the first stave, for it is an attempt to disabuse Fred of unprofitable behavior for Fred's own good. The attempt is feeble, however, due to the very philosophy that Scrooge champions. As he says later to the "portly gentlemen" who urge him to know the conditions and suffering of the poor, "It's not my business. . . . It's enough for a man to understand his own business, and not to interfere with other people's. Mine occupies me constantly. Good afternoon, gentlemen!" Even Scrooge's unself-conscious use of the word "business" here for "responsibility" reveals that his perspective is contained by his miserly occupation, just as his lonely living quarters are surrounded by offices, or as an oyster's body is by its shell.

It is perhaps remarkable that Scrooge says as much as he does to Fred about the irrationality of the Christmas spirit, for speech is apparently another activity he prefers to curb. The scene with Fred is of great importance to the story because we witness in it the sparring of opposite philosophies of Christmas. Thus it is necessary that Scrooge, then Fred, each have his say, though Cratchit's applause from the next room after Fred's humane, eloquent utterance ensures that not even the most Scrooge-ish of readers will fail to recognize which philosophy the story sanctions. But once the positions are stated, little more is said, mostly because Scrooge closes his mind to any further discussion and shuts off his flow of words with a resounding "Good afternoon!"—an utterance that he repeats four times, until his nephew is convinced of the impasse and leaves the office. Scrooge also condescends to a brief and unpleasant exchange with the gentlemen who ask him for a Christmas contribution for the poor—an exchange also ended by an unambiguous "Good afternoon . . . !"—and two briefer ventings of spleen directed toward his clerk. We know of no other words he shares with anyone of flesh and blood until Christmas morning.

Marley's ghost clearly emblematizes an oyster-like containment of body and bodily activity when he laboriously drags up to Scrooge's sitting-room the heavy chain of "cash-boxes, keys, padlocks, ledgers, deeds, and heavy purses wrought in steel" which "wound about him like a tail." That his condition also represents containment of mental activity is revealed in the Ghost's declaration, "My spirit never walked beyond our counting-house—mark me!—in life my spirit never roved beyond the narrow limits of our money-changing hole." Leaving nothing to chance, the phantom makes the connection that hardly needs making: "would you know," he asks Scrooge, "the weight and length of the strong coil you bear yourself? It was full as heavy and as long as this, seven Christmas Eves ago. You have laboured on it, since. It is a ponderous chain!" Scrooge has, we might remember, just "double-locked" himself into his chambers for the night.

Which brings us to the message of the *Carol,* only part of

which, in accordance with Marley's appraisal of his own oyster-against-the-"ocean" life, has traditionally been grasped. Responding to the Ghost's lamentations, Scrooge says, "But you were always a good man of business, Jacob":

> "Business!" cried the Ghost, wringing its hands again. "Mankind was my business. The common welfare was my business; charity, mercy, forbearance, and benevolence, were, all, my business. The dealings of my trade were but a drop of water in the comprehensive ocean of my business!"

If Scrooge's notion of his life has been limited by too narrow a focus on financial gain, Marley's appraisal of his past life is similarly limited by too narrow a focus on social responsibility. While the story unequivocally prefers reformed Marleyism to unreformed Scroogism, it advocates the former philosophy as only part of a more inclusive program for existence.

A good life, the story tells us, is a vitally *excursive* one. Such a life requires, first, that the individual go beyond the containing limits of the merely self-concerned self to benevolent participation with one's proper society—that is, with humanity or, in Fred's words, with one's "fellow-passengers to the grave." Of course, this participation includes the guardianship of "the common welfare" that Marley outlines, and the love and festivity that he fails to mention, but also more-mundane behaviors such as walking full in the center of a busy sidewalk; frank and honest communication with members of one's family; spontaneous snow-sliding with neighborhood boys; knowledge and sympathetic understanding of other people, ideas, and things; friendly conversation with relatives, solicitors, and employees; even romance and physical sexuality. A "good man" or woman, according to the *Carol* if not to Marley, is social in a very wide sense of the word.

And yet, the story tells us, a properly excursive life also means that the individual, by engaging in the benignly expansive behavior that is all of our nature, realize *for his or her own benefit* the manifold possibilities of being, mental and physical. To put it another way: Scroogism not only damages society but the self that, through action and interaction, could be much more. It is this concern for the self's potential that accounts for the persistent and disturbing imagery of individual impairment and thwarted development in the story: the flint unproductive of fire to which Scrooge is compared; Scrooge's "shrivelled" cheek; the gold and coals in Scrooge's care that are not turned to the human comfort that is their purpose; Belle's daughter who figures to Scrooge the daughter he might have fathered; the Cratchits' threadbare and meager existence; and most pointedly, Tiny Tim, who is in the first scheme of things both lame and destined for a childhood grave. A concern for the self, independent of any concern with social justice, also accounts for the sympathy which the story encourages in us for Scrooge in his manifestly unhappy humbug existence and which is articulated by the *Carol*'s spokesperson for the Christmas spirit. As Fred says regarding his uncle's refusal to join him for Christmas dinner:

the consequence of his taking a dislike to us, and not making merry with us, is, as I think, that he loses some pleasant moments, which could do him no harm. I am sure he loses pleasanter companions than he can find in his own thoughts, either in his mouldy old office, or his dusty chambers. I mean to give him the same chance every year, whether he likes it or not, for I pity him.

The story, insisting again and again that self-interest and social good coincide, refuses either to choose or to distinguish between them. In the *Carol,* really one of the most optimistic of all possible worlds, self-interest (properly defined) and social good are quite simply the same thing. It is precisely this identity that is figured in the mutual pleasure-taking/pleasure-giving between Topper and the "plump sister" during blindman's-buff as well as in the nameless phantoms' misery over not being able to help others when Scrooge glimpses them from his own window; and it is precisely this identity that the miser Scrooge, setting his interest at odds with others', cannot see.

Appropriately, the final stave shows that Scrooge-the-oyster has opened his shell, or had it opened, or lost it altogether, as a condition of his redemptive humanization. Where initially he is unrelentingly "solitary," at the end he turns up at the door of his nephew and niece's where he is made to feel at "home" amid the Christmas company; in coming years, he becomes "a second father" to Tiny Tim and "as good a friend . . . as the good old city knew, or any other good old city, town, or borough, in the good old world." Similarly, where Scrooge initially keeps his surviving warmth of heart "secret" beneath a wintry exterior, fellow-feeling, sympathy, and joy cascade out of him when he wakes on Christmas morning.

To be sure, his gift to the Cratchits is anonymous. But rather than betraying a division between self and others, his anonymity demonstrates a selfless generosity apparently common enough in the world of the story that the collectors for charity readily assume Scrooge means this when he tells them to "put [him] down for" "Nothing!" But there is a further distinction to be drawn as well. The anonymity of Scrooge's gift, as well as similar instances of "secret" behavior in the story, socializes and thus redeems secrecy by making it a condition of festive surprises. We have seen such surprises when, on Christmas day, Martha is playfully hidden from, then revealed to, Bob Cratchit in the spirit of holiday merriment and when Topper seems to be blindfolded and disinterested, but inexplicably pursues the "plump sister" until he uncovers his matrimonial design with gifts of ring and necklace. In the final stave, playful surprise explains Scrooge's side-"splitting" glee that Bob Cratchit "shan't know who sends" his family the large prize Turkey, and is perhaps partly behind the miser's unannounced poking of his head into Fred's dining room when, for the first time ever, he has come to join the holiday celebration. And such surprise is triumphantly seen in Scrooge's reversal of manner, from "feign[ed]" surliness and displeasure to joyful fellow-feeling, when Bob arrives at the office late on the day after Christmas:

> "Now, I'll tell you what, my friend," said Scrooge, "I am not going to stand this sort of thing any longer. And therefore," he continued,

leaping from his stool, and giving Bob such a dig in the waistcoat that he staggered back into the Tank again: "and therefore I am about to raise your salary!"

Scrooge also escapes his various self-containments. Where the "old" Scrooge is contained in person and activity, the "new" Scrooge, like Bob Cratchit on Christmas Eve, explodes with joyful, expansive physical activity, flailing his arms as he wildly attempts to dress himself, "running to the window" and "put[ting] out his head," and then dancing while he shaves. When he gets out "into the streets," instead of keeping to the edge of the sidewalk, literally or figuratively, Scrooge meets passersby "with a delighted smile," heartily shakes hands with one of the "portly" men who visited his office the previous day, and "pat[s] children on the head." "He had never dreamed that any walk—that anything—could give him so much happiness." Scrooge never gets to engage in the sexual fondling that the narrator earlier envies, but he does show a decided, and joyful, inability to keep his hands to himself on the day after Christmas, playfully giving his clerk a powerful "dig in the waistcoat" as he offers him a raise and a clap on the back while he says—"with an earnestness that could not be mistaken"—"A merry Christmas, Bob!" In the same way, where the "old" Scrooge suffers from a containment of perspective, the "new" Scrooge clearly shows that he understands the importance of the Christmas spirit when, for instance, he unreflectingly chooses to enhance the Cratchits' meager celebration or decides to join the festivity at his nephew's home. Finally, where Scrooge at first seems intent on restricting his speech, he now exhibits a positive delight in it. Waking on Christmas morning, he spontaneously "Whoop[s]" and "Hallo[s]" to "all the world" his new-found Christmas spirit. He reveals a fondness for conversation when he shouts from his open window to a boy on the street below:

> "Do you know the Poulterer's, in the next street but one, at the corner?" Scrooge inquired.
>
> "I should hope I did," replied the lad.
>
> "An intelligent boy!" said Scrooge. "A remarkable boy! Do you know whether they've sold the prize Turkey that was hanging up there? Not the little prize Turkey: the big one?"
>
> "What, the one as big as me?" returned the boy.
>
> "What a delightful boy!" said Scrooge. "It's a pleasure to talk to him. Yes, my buck!"

Scrooge is so filled with Christmas spirit that even the boy's "smart" response is to him an "intelligent" one, and a simple question is "delightful"—so welcome is any conversation now to a man who has just found the joy of what lies beyond himself, that "everything could yield him pleasure." The identity of self-interest and social interest that the earlier staves so optimistically assert is also asserted in the final stave, most clearly in Scrooge's interaction with the poulterer's man and the boy when they return with the prize turkey: for every coin paid, there is at least one "chuckle" as Scrooge is giddy with the privilege of making expenditures that will bring the Cratchits happiness.

Scrooge, in short, finally passes beyond his shell. And yet, if we stopped here, we would be ignoring the peculiar resonance that the oyster image has for the larger structure of the story. To perceive it, we need to begin with a couple of facts about the *Carol.*

The first pertains to the "old" Scrooge. Though initially he is far from being another mobilely malignant Iago, neither is Scrooge the innocuous stay-at-home that a shut oyster is. If he were only this, people and dogs would not fear to meet him on the street as they do, nor would we be so sure in our disapproval of him. The truth is that Scrooge is a positive source of pain to others, though only if they have the misfortune of crossing his path, or in some other way rubbing against his immovable, "abrasive" character. When Fred wishes him, "A Merry Christmas, uncle! God save you!" Scrooge snaps back, "Bah! . . . Humbug!" Later, when an unlucky caroller stops at Scrooge's keyhole, the miser chases him away with a ruler. Of course, the best example is Bob Cratchit, who suffers in Scrooge's presence but whose spirits soar when he leaves the office. Interestingly, other characters can feel Scrooge's unpleasantness when his presence has merely been invoked. Bob's family feels it when, in the vision of Stave Three, he bids them toast his employer with their holiday concoction of gin and lemon, and, we are told, "the mention of his name cast a dark shadow on the party, which was not dispelled for full five minutes." Scrooge's niece, in another of the second spirit's visions, also finds the festivity of her evening disrupted by talk about her uncle. Scrooge's "abrasiveness," his power to cause discomfort through no special effort of his own, is surely one of the ways in which he is "hard and sharp as flint."

The second fact concerns nearly everybody in the story *except* Scrooge. The "old" Scrooge is unique in the sense that he lacks the Christmas spirit nearly all of the world of the *Carol* possesses so wholeheartedly. If Scrooge is "hard and sharp as flint," the other characters can be seen as "soft"—a word appropriate anyway to the human compassion and lack of severity comprising the Christmas spirit. Softness also inspires the words of the engagingly intrusive narrator. When, for example, the Ghost of Christmas Present reveals the power of his torch to placate angered dinner-carriers, the narrator enthusiastically explains, "For they said, it was a shame to quarrel upon Christmas Day. And so it was! God love it, so it was!" Even the narrator's active disapproval is expressed with appropriate softness—with lightness, even affection: "Oh! but he was a tight-fisted hand at the grindstone, Scrooge! a squeezing, wrenching, grasping, scraping, clutching, covetous old sinner!" The colloquial ring of the initial metaphor, and the participial *tour de force* that follows—both in charged exclamation—are simply too gleeful to allow us to feel the narrator is repulsed, alarmed, or even greatly disturbed by Scrooge's example. There is an amusement and relish in these lines reminiscent of the oral storyteller each time he or she introduces an eccentric character who has taken the polish of time and become a favorite. Perhaps nothing, however, so well articulates the dual attitude of the narrator toward Scrooge as the final "old sinner!"—a label expressing both disapproval and warm familiarity. To sum up, we can see how the story's fictional

world and the words of the narrator are consonant, enveloping the "hard," "sharp," "abrasive" Scrooge with concentric layers of "soft" matter.

My point, of course, is that Scrooge is lodged within his world, and his story, as an irritating grain of sand against the fleshy part of an oyster. A benefit of this analogy is that it not only describes the state of things in the first stave but also how the rest of the story works: Scrooge, undergoing a process of transformation through the visits of the three spirits, finally emerges as the story's "pearl."

There is some sense in regarding Scrooge's transformation as the result of a destructive process. If we see him as an oyster within a crusty shell, closed to the world, Marley's ghost and the three spirits force their way into his mind and heart just as they force their way into his locked apartments. They either pry open his shell bit by bit, or neutralize its hardness through the bombardment of pathetic visions: thus, sounds accompanying a childhood scene "fell upon the heart of Scrooge with a softening influence," and "he softened more and more" when his niece plays on the harp "a simple little air" once familiar to his sister. As a result of the visitations, Scrooge is able to pass through his containing shell as easily as he and the first spirit "passed through the wall" of his solitary dwelling en route to the place of his boyhood.

But the problem with this view of the transforming process is that it does an injustice to Scrooge. Is he defeated by the spirits who come to him for his benefit? Compared with his old humbug self, does the Scrooge of Christmas morning seem diminished in stature or completeness? The answer to both questions is clearly, no. The first spirit increases Scrooge by bringing into his everyday consciousness Christmas memories long-stored in some secret, lost place within him. The second and third spirits augment this consciousness with knowledge of the present and predictions of the future. Together, Marley's ghost and the spirits give Scrooge the wisdom of a new perspective, which then branches out in the qualities of love, compassion, altruism, and joyfulness that he previously lacked. Many of the visions, like that of the Fezziwigs' ball, are a pleasure to Scrooge, but even when he is most plagued by what the spirits show or say to him, he is only set back briefly, the pace of his travels allowing him little time for grief or self-reproach.

In fact, generally speaking, Scrooge's own spirit is unmistakably ascendent during the night. His curiosity, and desire to benefit from the unpreventable visitations, soon supply their own momentum. Vision after vision holds his attention and provokes his questions and comments; "the game of How, When, and Where" that is played at his nephew and niece's Christmas gathering even provokes guesses which none of the company can hear. By the time Scrooge meets the second spirit, it is clear that he accepts the entire supernatural enterprise as his own: " 'Spirit,' said Scrooge submissively, 'conduct me where you will. I went forth last night on compulsion, and I learnt a lesson which is working now. Tonight, if you have aught to teach me, let me profit by it'." With the appearance of the third spirit, whose "mysterious presence filled him with a solemn dread," Scrooge's determination and eagerness seem still greater: " 'Lead on!' said Scrooge. 'Lead on! The night is waning fast, and it is precious time to me, I know. Lead on, Spirit!' " Because he does possess this momentum, which aligns his will with that of the spirits, we see again how the story is both unequivocally critical of Scrooge's attitudes and behaviors, and merciful to Scrooge the man. Holding him up to rebuke and humiliation and blame is not the story's intent. Rather, the dissociation of the man from his sins allows Dickens to make his point doubly: Dickens condemns Scroogism while he exemplifies an un-Scrooge-like mentality by showing Scrooge authorial kindness.

If Scrooge may be considered ascendent during the night, he emerges positively triumphant on Christmas morning when, among other robust exuberances, he shouts from his window to the street below, adding his joyful noise to the general peals of church bells, "the lustiest peals he had ever heard." Scrooge's expansive vocalizing and bodily movements on Christmas morning are appropriate to a character who seems not to diminish but to grow stronger and more complete before our eyes.

A better way to regard the movement of the story is to discern the "abrasive" anti-Christmas Scrooge made compatible with the "soft" pro-Christmas company comprised of nearly all of the fictional world surrounding him and the narrator as well. Indeed, Scrooge finally joins the others in Christmas spirit and activities. And yet, we have to realize that Scrooge is not so much remade *in* the others' image as he is remade *according* to it. In no other character are Christmas qualities given such a dazzling embodiment as in Scrooge on Christmas morning: "I am as light as a feather, I am as happy as an angel, I am as merry as a school-boy. I am as giddy as a drunken man," he cries. Scrooge is so charged here with seasonal energy that he takes on multiple identities—another way in which he is "more" or greater at the end of the story than at the beginning. *Too* charged is more precise, for the "new" Scrooge ceases to be merely mortal: he is really the Christmas spirit personified, its pure essence, and an embodiment more important to the story's meaning than the allegorical and spooky Ghost of Christmas Present because he provides us with a human model of behavior, if also an exaggerated one. It is Scrooge's super-Christmas spirit which gives the story such a satisfactory climax (how less exciting if Scrooge awoke merely to become like Fred!) as well as dictates the brevity of the final stave—such dazzle cannot be prolonged without devaluation. Scrooge's dazzle is the appropriate end-product of the story, a treasured moment revealed only after the necessary processes of generation are complete. Dickens' story, it might be said, finally opens in the last stave to offer us this treasure, this "pearl." When Thackeray praised the *Carol* as "a national benefit, and to every man or woman who reads it a personal kindness," he implicitly paralleled its writing and publication with the giving of a gift [*Fraser's Magazine* 29 (February 1844)]. More Christmas present than mere gift, the story proceeds, even as it obeys the dynamic of a pearl-generating oyster, from the concealment of Scrooge's inner goodness to a climactic unwrapping of that goodness that involves each reader with Dickens in a personal enactment of a Christmas ritual. And so author and reader

participate in the excursive sociality that *A Christmas Carol* celebrates.

We can never know, of course, the extent to which Dickens conceived of the structure of his story according to the image of a pearl-generating oyster. But there is some reason to conclude that he would have welcomed such an interpretation as consonant with his own sense of how his story works and of the nature of his authorial role. The careful mothering of supernatural agents effects Scrooge's change, accreted wisdom making Scrooge both more than what he was and better. But behind these spirits is the narrator—certainly an alter-ego of Dickens himself—who really presides over the re-creation. Thus, we should not be surprised to hear the narrator's comment on Scrooge's Christmas laugh: "Really, for a man who had been out of practice for so many years, it was a splendid laugh, a most illustrious laugh. The father of a long, long line of brilliant laughs!" In Genesis we hear of another Creator who, once the work was done, looked down with approval on his Creation. Just what is created in *A Christmas Carol* is glimpsed in the newly awakened Scrooge's own words: "I don't know anything. I'm quite a baby. Never mind. I don't care. I'd rather be a baby. Hallo! Whoop! Hallo here!" In an oyster's experience, the nearest thing to a baby is a pearl.

FURTHER READING

Bibliography

Churchill, R. C., ed. *A Bibliography of Dickensian Criticism, 1836-1975*. Garland Reference Library of the Humanities, Vol. 12. New York: Garland Publishing, 1975, 314 p.
    Guide to writings about Dickens published between 1836 and 1975.

Cohn, Alan M., and Collins, K. K. *The Cumulated Dickens Checklist, 1970-1979*. Troy, N.Y.: Whitson Publishing Co., 1982, 391 p.
    Listing of 1970s publications on Dickens and his works.

Gold, Joseph. *The Stature of Dickens: A Centenary Bibliography*. Toronto: University of Toronto Press, 1971, 236 p.
    Catalogue of biographical and critical studies on Dickens.

Biography

Darton, F. J. Harvey. "Dickens the Beginner: 1833-1836." *The Quarterly Review* 262, No. 519 (January 1934): 52-69.
    Portrays Dickens's early years as a writer.

Dexter, Walter. "The Genesis of *Sketches by Boz*." *The Dickensian* XXX, No. 230 (Spring 1934): 105-11.
    Recounts the first periodical printings of Dickens's sketches and short stories later compiled in *Sketches by Boz*.

Forster, John. *Forster's Life of Dickens*. Abridged and revised by George Gissing. London: Chapman & Hall, 1907, 349 p.
    Standard biography for many years, written by Dickens's friend. Forster is often criticized for minimizing

Dickens's other friendships and omitting crucial facts, but this book contains valuable primary source material.

Johnson, Edgar. *Charles Dickens: His Tragedy and Triumph.* 2 vols. New York: Simon & Schuster, 1952.

Definitive modern biography. Johnson makes use of much previously unavailable material.

Criticism

Becker, May Lamberton. Introduction to *Christmas Stories: A Christmas Carol, The Chimes, The Cricket on the Hearth,* by Charles Dickens, pp. 7-10. Cleveland: The World Publishing Company, 1946.

Discusses the seasonal spirit in Dickens's Christmas stories.

Brown, John Mason. "Ghouls and Holly." In his *Seeing More Things,* pp. 161-67. New York: Whittlesey House, 1948.

Contemplates the tradition of reading *A Christmas Carol* during the Yuletide and examines Scrooge's conversion.

Butt, John. "*A Christmas Carol*: Its Origin and Design." *The Dickensian* LI, No. 313 (December 1954): 15-18.

Provides an analysis of Dickens's thoughts while writing *A Christmas Carol* and occurrences that may have influenced his composition.

Carlton, William J. "Portraits in 'A Parliamentary Sketch.' " *The Dickensian* L, No. 311 (June 1954): 100-09.

Surveys Dickens's depictions of Parliament members in *Sketches by Boz.*

Chesterton, Gilbert Keith. *Charles Dickens: A Critical Study.* New York: Dodd, Mead, & Co., 1906, 300 p.

Overview of Dickens's life and career. According to Chesterton: "*The Christmas Carol* is the conversion of an anti-Christmas character. *The Chimes* is a slaughter of anti-Christmas characters. *The Cricket,* perhaps, fails for lack of this crusading note."

Jaffe, Audrey. "Spectacular Sympathy: Visuality and Ideology in Dickens's *A Christmas Carol.*" *PMLA* 109, No. 2 (March 1994): 254-65.

Argues that *A Christmas Carol* casts Scrooge—and, by extension, the reader—as a "spectator" of society and links "visual representation to the production of individual sympathy and thus, ultimately, to social harmony."

Ley, J. W. T. " 'A Sledge-Hammer Blow': How 'The Chimes' Came to Be Written: The Source of Dickens's Inspiration." *The Dickensian* XIX, No. 2 (April 1923): 86-9.

Maintains that *The Chimes* was written to incite social reform in regards to the treatment of the poor.

Major, Gwen. "Scrooge's Chambers." *The Dickensian* XXIX, No. 225 (Winter 1932-33): 11-15.

Describes the probable site in London on which Dickens based Scrooge's residence.

McNulty, J. H. "Our Carol." *The Dickensian* XXXIV, No. 245 (December 1937-38): 15-19.

Ponders the realism in *A Christmas Carol* and describes the tale as the "one perfect short story Dickens wrote." McNulty also claims that "if every copy were destroyed to-day, it could be rewritten tomorrow, so many know the story by heart."

————. "A Double Centenary." *The Dickensian* XXXIX, No. 268 (September 1943): 163-65.

Marks the one-hundredth year since the publication of *A Christmas Carol* and *Martin Chuzzlewit.* McNulty identifies the similar uses in the two volumes of selfishness, conversion, fog, and snow.

Morley, Malcolm. "Ring Up *The Chimes.*" *The Dickensian* XLVII, No. 300 (September 1951): 202-06.

Chronicles various stage adaptations of *The Chimes.*

Newton, A. Edward. "The Greatest Little Book in the World." *The Atlantic Monthly* 132, No. 1 (December 1923): 732-38.

Proclaims *A Christmas Carol* "the greatest little book in the world," and adds that it "makes everyone want 'to make the world a little better'."

Additional coverage of Dickens's life and career is contained in the following sources published by Gale Research: *Concise Dictionary of British Literary Biography, 1832-1890*; *Dictionary of Literary Biography,* Vols. 21, 55, 70; *DISCovering Authors*; *Junior DISCovering Authors*; *Major Authors and Illustrators for Children and Young Adults*; *Nineteenth-Century Literature Criticism,* Vols. 3, 8, 18, 26, 37; *Something about the Author,* Vol. 15.

Nadine Gordimer

1923-

South African short story writer, novelist, critic, essayist, and editor.

INTRODUCTION

Gordimer has earned international acclaim as a writer who explores the effects of South Africa's apartheid system on both whites and blacks. Although the political conditions in her country are essential to the themes of her work, Gordimer focuses primarily on the complex human tensions generated by apartheid. Lauded for her authentic portrayals of black African culture, she is also praised for using precise detail to evoke both the physical landscape of South Africa and the human predicaments of a racially polarized society.

Biographical Information

Born in South Africa to Jewish immigrants from London, Gordimer published her first story at the age of fifteen. Her short fiction soon appeared in periodicals such as *Harper's* and the *New Yorker*. Except for several brief stays in England and the United States, she has remained in South Africa. Gordimer won the Nobel Prize in Literature in 1991.

Major Works of Short Fiction

Gordimer's first stories were published in various notable American periodicals and were subsequently collected in her first major volume, *The Soft Voice of the Serpent*. From her initial collection to her most recent, *Jump, and Other Stories*, Gordimer's short stories often portray individuals who struggle to avoid, confront, or change the conditions under which they live, in particular the repressive South African political system of apartheid. The short fiction included in *A Soldier's Embrace*, for example, offers an ironic historical overview of South African society. In *Something Out There* Gordimer examines the temperament of individuals who unwittingly support the mechanisms of racial separation. *Jump, and Other Stories* continues her exploration of how apartheid insulates the daily lives of blacks and whites in South Africa.

Critical Reception

Many critics have noted a connection between the tone of Gordimer's fiction and the deterioration of race relations and escalation of violence in her country during the late 1960s. Her work is viewed by many commentators as a social history of South Africa and its changing conditions; she is often praised for her delicate and insightful treatment of controversial issues. While some critics claim that her detached narrative voice lacks emotional immediacy,

many regard her fiction as compelling and powerful and commend her prose for its clarity and poetic elegance. Merle Rubin has summarized Gordimer's literary achievements as "a precise ear for spoken language that lent great authenticity to her dialogue; a sensitivity to the rhythms and texture of the written word that gave her prose the power of poetry; a keen eye that made her a tireless observer; an even keener sense of social satire based upon her ability to see through appearances to the heart of the matter, and a strong feeling of moral purpose, composed in equal parts of her indignation at the sheer injustice of South Africa's entrenched racial oppression and of her commitment to speak the truth as she saw it."

PRINCIPAL WORKS

Short Fiction

Face to Face 1949
The Soft Voice of the Serpent, and Other Stories 1952
Six Feet of the Country 1956

Other Major Works

CRITICISM

John Barkham (essay date 1952)

SOURCE: "African Smiles," in *The Saturday Review,*
New York, Vol. XXXV, No. 21, May 24, 1952, p. 22.

[*In the following review of* The Soft Voice of the Serpent,
*Barkham praises the subtlety and sensitivity of Gordimer's
narrative voice.*]

To the chorus of eloquent voices emerging from South Africa, add a new one, that of Nadine Gordimer. It is a fast
growing chorus. Paton, Lessing, Rooke, Van der Post, and
now Gordimer—until a few years ago none of these names
was known here; but they have begun to speak and their
voice is heard in the land. They will be heard from again,
especially Nadine Gordimer.

This flowering of talent in a remote outpost of civilization
is, of course, no accident. South African literature, both
English and Afrikaans, is reacting impressively to two tremendous stimuli. Afrikaans writing (unknown outside
South Africa) proudly and poetically reflects the Afrikaner's reconquest of his native land. And the English writ-

ers mirror their helpless compassion for the oppressed and
their anxiety over the strife which rends their beloved
country. To this latter group belongs Miss Gordimer.

Readers who seek in these score or so tales [in *The Soft
Voice of the Serpent*] any direct reflection of the headlines
will not find them there. Miss Gordimer is a subtle writer
who makes her points delicately and obliquely. A beach
interlude with an Indian fisherman, as in "The Catch,"
will indirectly tell you as much about the color bar in
South Africa as any editorial. A young couple (white, of
course) grow to admire an Indian fisherman who has land-
ed a big fish. Driving into the city later, they offer him a
lift. The presence of other white passengers suddenly
makes them conscious of his color—and therefore of his
"inferiority."

But most of these stories are not even remotely concerned
with headline types or affairs; rather with the happiness
and disappointments of daily living. Anyone who has lived
in South Africa, as this reviewer has done, will recognize
the accuracy of Miss Gordimer's types, the validity of her
situations, and the acuteness of her perception. This is
South Africa as it really is, not as it is painted for this purpose or that.

Easily the best story in the book is "A Watcher of the
Dead," an account of a family death and its attendant ceremony that is a marvel of selective detail and artistic sensibility. But each of these tales will strike its own chord of
significance. Some readers may see in the agonized penal
official of "Another Part of the Sky" a figure not unlike
that of Alan Paton, who, as head of the Diepkloof Refor-
matory, must in the past had found himself in situations
just like this. Others will undoubtedly admire the author's
apt use of symbolism, as in her juxtaposition of a legless
locust with a legless man. (The insect also had wings.)

Not all of Miss Gordimer's stories come off, but her batting average is high. "The Defeated" might have been a
poignant study of the unbridgeable gap between the first
two generations of immigrant Jews, but the point is
blunted by the over-coolness of the narrative style. Nor is
the author sufficiently emotional in handling the incipient
love affair that climaxes "The Hour and the Years."

But these are minor blemishes in what amounts to an unusually impressive debut. Miss Gordimer has elected to
make herself known to the American public through a medium at once demanding and ungrateful. She comes
through triumphantly. South Africa has a new and exciting interpreter.

William Peden (essay date 1952)

SOURCE: "Stories from Africa," in *The New York Times
Book Review,* June 15, 1952, p. 17.

[*William Peden is an American critic and educator who has
written extensively on the American short story and on
American historical figures such as Thomas Jefferson and
John Quincy Adams. In the following review, he applauds
Gordimer's debut volume of short fiction,* The Soft Voice
of the Serpent.]

A native of South Africa, where she still lives, Nadine Gordimer has published several of her stories in American magazines (*The New Yorker, Harper's, The Virginia Quarterly*). [*The Soft Voice of the Serpent*] is her first published volume, and her debut is an exciting one. Miss Gordimer is very young—in her early twenties, according to her publishers—and very talented.

All of these stories have South Africa as their setting. Miss Gordimer possesses a keen eye, a sharp ear and a devastating sense of smell. Place is an important element in her fiction; she is, however, no limited local colorist. Her primary concern is with specific individuals—an Indian fisherman, Johannesburg medical student, expatriated concession shopkeeper—who embody universal traits.

Most of Miss Gordimer's characters are faced with the problem of making dubious compromises between their rights as individuals and their responsibilities as members of society. The author sees life as a battle-ground for, on its most obvious level, the warfare of the classes. Some of her best work depicts the results of this warfare: **"The Catch,"** a story of a native fisherman and a city couple who at first admire him, later patronize him, and finally repudiate him; or **"Ah, Woe Is Me,"** an account of a serving woman's unsuccessful struggle to raise her children above the level of moral and social serfdom.

Gordimer's sympathetic treatment of human shortcomings and her belief in the dignity of simple people is refreshing and reassuring.

—*William Peden*

Many of Miss Gordimer's remaining stories mirror the hostility—unceasing, though seldom openly declared—between individuals: between man and woman, between parent and child, between intellectual and Philistine. She writes with discipline and moderation, unusual for so young an author; she avoids extremes of both subject-matter and method. Concerned with suggesting the essence of personality, she avoids the excesses of psychoanalytic writers. She possesses considerable social awareness, but only one or two of her stories become blatant social protests.

In her book her people are frightened, unsure of themselves, separated by individual, economic and social differences. They need understanding, not hatred or indifference. Many of them find it. The author's sympathetic treatment of human shortcomings and her belief in the dignity of simple people is refreshing and reassuring.

James Stern   (essay date 1956)

SOURCE: "Troubled Souls," in *The New York Times Book Review,* October 7, 1956, pp. 7, 34.

[*Stern is an Irish novelist, short story writer, translator, and critic. In the following review, he offers a positive assessment of Gordimer's* Six Feet of the Country.]

In this her second collection of stories [*Six Feet of the Country*] (eight of the fifteen have appeared in The New Yorker) Nadine Gordimer's range is far wider, the observation even keener, than that shown in her volume *The Soft Voice of the Serpent.* The quality of the prose, the authority and intelligence behind it, are surely unsurpassed by any other writer in South Africa today. What Miss Gordimer's admirers may miss here, however, is the abiding compassion of her novel, *The Lying Days.*

In *Six Feet of the Country* the author's primary concerns seem to be twofold: the behavior—usually malicious, occasionally shocking—of highly sophisticated white South African women toward members of their own sex; and the dilemma of serious, liberal-minded white South African women whose lives have been warped by the gulf separating them from the colored people. Not all these stories are about South Africans. There is one (**"Face From Atlantis"**) about some ex-Europeans who come from South Africa to New York, another of an American couple who went from New York to South Africa; and there are stories, it's true, about men, usually impoverished Central Europeans, who have emigrated to South Africa; yet almost all these stories are told from the female point of view—a view by no means complimentary to that sex, often less to the male.

The story that will interest those who have been waiting to hear how white Americans and Africans react to one another on African soil is **"Horn of Plenty,"** one of the two stories in the collection that have not been published before. Like many of Miss Gordimer's white women, Mrs. McCleary was a narcissist as well as "a beauty." In New York, where before her marriage she had been a popular hostess, Pat McCleary had employed a Negro woman who had been more to her than just a servant. It was at Mrs. Wilks that Pat had "yelled when she was irritable and on whose crooked shoulder she had wept when she wanted some man she couldn't have." It took Rebecca, an illiterate African who as a servant did everything perfectly but nothing whatever unless she was told, to make the American realize that a Mrs. Wilks "was necessary to free one to live."

Brilliant as the stories dealing with South Africa's colored problem are, there is in this collection one story which concerns only white people and which could have taken place in any civilized country at any time. Appearing originally in different form in *The New Yorker* under the title **"The Pretender,"** the story is now called **"My First Two Women."** In this reviewer's opinion it surpasses all Miss Gordimer's other stories in its simplicity and insight into human nature. The theme is the universal one of the child whose father has divorced his wife and married again. The pretender is the stepmother over whom the child, who tells the story in retrospect, realizes at the age of 5 that he possesses a power—"something of which I am convinced there is no innocence this side of the womb." What the boy does with this power and what the stepmother is unable to do for all her awareness, decency and love, is a story that can act as a lesson to "progressive" parents as well as to budding authors who may be under the illusion that the working of a child's mind is simple, and as simple to describe.

Sylvia Stallings   (essay date 1956)

SOURCE: "Stories of Love and Irony," in *New York Herald Tribune Book Review,* October 21, 1956, p. 3.

[*In the following review, Stallings provides a thematic analysis of the stories comprising* Six Feet of the Country.]

With each new book, Nadine Gordimer augments her status as a writer. *Six Feet of the Country,* a collection of short stories which have, with only two exceptions, already appeared in American magazines, establishes beyond any doubt that she is not merely a gifted regionalist but a writer of great sophistication who is aware of all the subtle innuendoes of human relationships. Her perception is intensely feminine, but she expresses herself with a fine unfeminine irony; compassionate, she rejects pathos.

Most of the fifteen stories here are concerned with one of two themes: the first, the baffling, tragic encounters of one race with another; the second, the no less complex and unsatisfactory meeting grounds of sex. Yet it is as if Miss Gordimer had taken care to prove that the banalities of love and sociology are misleading; that the human animal, whether it be white or black, old or young, man or woman, is capable of experiences outside the range of ordinary imaginative fiction. **"Which New Era Would That Be?"** and **"The Smell of Death and Flowers"** deal with attempts by well-meaning whites to protest against South Africa's racial injustice, but Miss Gordimer strips their humility away and shows the selfishness that lies behind even their best efforts.

> They thought they understood the humiliation of the pure-blooded black African walking the streets only by the permission of a pass written out by a white person. . . . There was no escaping their understanding. They even insisted on feeling the resentment *you* must feel at their identifying themselves with your feelings. . . .

Porcelain-skinned Joyce McCoy, at her first "mixed" party, cannot stop thinking about the fact that she dances no closer to, or farther from, a black man than her white beaux. The title story, in a quieter key, makes the same point that even the feudalism of the white man practicing paternalism toward his black workers means giving them what he wants to dispose of, rather than what they need.

When she writes of men and women, Miss Gordimer shows the same talent for nuance that characterizes Pamela Frankau's novels. With a strong feeling for the sensuous, she understands that it is nevertheless emotional and social overtones that make or break relationships; three or four of these stories are little master-places of psychology. **"A Wand'ring Minstrel, I"** gives a devastating glimpse of a marriage, revealed in the faces of the children sitting in rapt fascination around the man whom the adult members of the party have denounced as an irresponsible drunkard. A reverse denouement closes **"A Bit of Young Life,"**

where an entire resort hotel makes a pet of a young mother vacationing alone, only to be bitterly betrayed.

Love; the great motivator, is not the only one, and in **"Enemies"** Miss Gordimer gives us a brilliant portrait of an old woman clinging to a life of empty perfection. Sometimes these delicate motivations come from the world of childhood, as in **"Clowns in Clover,"** with its gradual revelation of madness. Terrifying and pitiable in another context is Carlitta of **"A Face From Atlantis,"** for the fate which overtakes a beautiful woman transplanted to an alien culture where her arrogance is misunderstood. The motif of the displaced European forever rootless in Africa or America turns up again, notably in **"The White Goddess and the Mealie Question,"** the only purely funny story in the book. It is one of the ways in which Miss Gordimer broadens our understanding that she reveals the immigrant and his way of life as South Africa's double-edged liability, just as it is America's.

Perhaps this element in the South African character has given Miss Gordimer her vivid grasp of contrasting worlds. Then it may also be true that even South Africa's appalling problems have done good work in making her young writers appreciate the value of the rare poetic vision.

Mary Ellen Chase   (essay date 1960)

SOURCE: "Miss Gordimer's Fine, True Art in Another Brilliant Collection," in *New York Herald Tribune Book Review,* January 10, 1960, p. 1.

[*Chase is an American novelist, children's author, educator, and critic. In the following review, she examines the style and scope of* Friday's Footprint.]

Whenever a careful reader makes the rare discovery that what is purposely *not* said on the pages before him is clearly far more important and filled with meaning than what *is* said, he reads yet again and with sharpened perception. Nadine Gordimer in these twelve short stories [in *Friday's Footprint*] and a longer one which she calls a novella often obscures or upon occasion omits occurrences, surroundings, dialogue, but only because by so doing she can more acutely and fully capture, or make, or at times restore a complete experience. The actual happenings which she deals with in these remarkably real and moving stories take place in various parts of her native Africa from Cairo to Johannesburg. They have to do with crocodile hunting at night, with the ironic and painful degradation of men and women, with a generous invitation which brings ruin and desolation in its wake, with a tropical river and its awful toll exacted both of the living and the dead, and with a wide variety of persons, Afrikaners and blacks, construction engineers and naturalists, small children, adolescents, and the old.

Yet the fact that all her characters and situations are engrossing as pure story material really means comparatively little in the face of their superb—shall we even say perfect?—presentation. They may and do "spread knowledge of things new," in Sainte-Beuve's words; but their real accomplishment through Miss Gordimer's gifted mind is, as the French critic adds, "to lend freshness to things known." Each story or incident probes mercilessly into human motives and human weaknesses, into guilt, fear, disillusionment, ambition, despair. Each reveals the universal human condition, whether in a Boer community or in Chicago, Paris, Hollywood, or the most isolated village anywhere at all. One knows all these people, for they are quite clearly oneself as seldom seen and less seldom honestly recognized and dealt with.

Perhaps every one of these brief narratives, for some of them are hardly stories in the accepted sense of the term, might be called a flash of insight or a moment of vision at a critical, often terrible, instant, whether in the life of a child, of a frightened, defeated woman, or of an unhappy, bewildered husband. Sometimes this piercing insight is realized by a chance, ill-timed remark, by a taste, a smell, a sound; at another time through a mass of blossoming cosmos by an African roadside. In each and every case it is revealing, often cruelly so, and not only to the hearer and the beholder, but to the reader as well. A great deal has been written about "the craft of fiction." Here it is wonderfully exemplified together with the *art* as well.

Anthologists who compile volumes of "the best stories" must not miss this book. College instructors whose task it is "to teach the short story" will find enough here to teach themselves as well as their students. And most of us who try to write fiction will find reason for despair, or, if we are generous enough, for hope in its larger sense as well as for unqualified admiration.

Mary Doyle Curran   (essay date 1960)

SOURCE: "Many Views from the Veld," in *The Saturday Review,* New York, Vol. XLIII, No. 3, January 16, 1960, p. 64.

[*Curran is an American novelist. In the following negative review of* Friday's Footprint, *she notes the uneven prose style and lack of psychological complexity in Gordimer's stories.*]

Nadine Gordimer's new collection of short stories (and a novella) is not the work of a novice. She has two other short story collections as well as two novels to her credit. Unfortunately, *Friday's Footprint,* the latest addition to her South African saga, betrays the enervation of the contemporary short story. The major flaw can be summed up in a quotation from one of the stories, **"The Last Kiss"**: "When people become characters, they cease to be regarded as human . . . ." There is a lack of warmth and compassion here that is typical of the "objective" short story. Casting a cold eye is the dominant attitude of the book. And when another approach is taken, as in the novella, **"An Image of Success,"** and in the story **"The Last Kiss,"** it degenerates into the falsity of undeserved pathos.

Miss Gordimer is trapped by the contemporary fad for the unresolved ending, leaving it to the reader to trek back through the veld to resolve the meaning. But the trek does not result in resolution. Stories such as **"Friday's Footprint," "A Thing of the Past,"** and **"Our Bovary"** do not have the linear complexity that in Joyce led so inevitably

and justifiably to the final revelation. The stories play on gratuitous shock. They suggest a psychological complexity that is, in fact, simply not there.

But, to repeat, the faults that appear in *Friday's Footprint* are those of the present-day short story: the lack of passion, the facile stance of wry irony, the tedium of protracted scenes where the author mistakes monotony for realism, types for people, and quantity of exposition for quality. Surely something vital and intense is going on in South Africa; most of these stories might have emerged from Darien, Connecticut.

The writing is uneven, wavering between rather boring and clumsy author interpolations and brilliant metaphorical remarks like: "She has a way of making my father confused, so that he finds his anger like a broken stick in his hands."

There is no question that Miss Gordimer has technical skill—as demonstrated by **"The Bridegroom."** But most of her stories echo with compromise and acceptance. The narrator of **"An Image of Success"** says, "I believe that early in one's life—often in childhood, long before the experience that might give the picture some accuracy—one forms images of various semi-abstract states, poverty, fame, wealth, and so on, past which one never really sees." It is past these images, these fantasies, that the good writer leaps. In this book Miss Gordimer fails to take that leap.

The great test, finally, of fiction, is how interesting it is, how long it stays in the memory, how often it recurs to the reader. Few of Miss Gordimer's stories will haunt one. **"The Path of the Moon's Dark Fortnight," "Little Willie," "The Bridegroom"** are the only selections in *Friday's Footprint* that speak with a memorable voice of their own.

Edward Hickman Brown   (essay date 1965)

SOURCE: "A Sudden Shaft of Light," in *The Saturday Review,* New York, Vol. XLVIII, No. 19, May 8, 1965, p. 33.

[*Brown is a South African critic. In the following review, he praises the maturity and emotional intensity of the stories of* Not for Publication.]

This superb collection of stories [*Not for Publication, and Other Stories*] most decidedly *is* for publication. And I believe it represents a giant step forward for Nadine Gordimer.

What has always puzzled me profoundly about her writing in the past was why so small a proportion of her deftly executed, perspicacious stories made a really deep impression upon me. Hers was clearly more than an exceedingly skillful technique allied to a perceptive eye and an acute ear. One was constantly aware that a sensitive and intelligent mind was at work behind the stories that generally depicted—with rare accuracy—people caught in varied postures of human frailty. I found them infinitely superior to her two earliest novels (I missed the last one); but, although I enjoyed and respected most of the stories at the time of reading, relatively few of them remained impaled upon my consciousness through the ultimate test of the passage of time.

My far from certain conclusion, when last I considered this matter several years ago, was that it might perhaps be a case of too much dispassion and detachment on Miss Gordimer's part, for one should surely not be so everlastingly conscious of the author's own cool intelligence hovering above her stories. But the entire issue now appears to be academic. For this collection confirms, quite dramatically, a new authority that I believed I had noticed in the odd story read in various periodicals over the past couple of years. Some indefinable additional ingredient has been added. For lack of a better term, we can only (and inaccurately) label it experience. And with it there seems to be less conscious striving after ever greater economy—nor any need of it.

It is a measure of Miss Gordimer's mastery over her subject that she moves one so easily and swiftly into the grip of each story, giving her art the illusion of effortlessness. Whatever the subtle extra element might be, the amalgam has magically jelled. This writer who has never been sufficiently honored in her native land can now surely rank with the finest exponents of the short story medium. Certainly, there are no inferior stories among the sixteen gathered together in this book. And, just as surely, each reader will come up with his own special favorite.

For myself, I particularly liked **"A Chip of Glass Ruby,"** a simple tale whose climax lies in the quiet but vivid moment of realization that comes to an uneducated Johannesburg Indian, a hawker of fruit and vegetables, when he suddenly knows what it was that made him marry an ugly widow with five children. The reader anticipates him in this knowledge; but, reading of this good woman—so natural and unpretentious and credible a spirit—who makes her protest against the injustice she sees around her just because she must, he learns many other things. Or perhaps he merely has his memory jogged.

It is a measure of Miss Gordimer's mastery over her subject that she moves one so easily and swiftly into the grip of each story, giving her art the illusion of effortlessness.

—*Edward Hickman Brown*

Miss Gordimer is a master at capturing a single electric moment of illumination. In **"A Company of Laughing Faces"** a sensitive girl of seventeen finds beauty and meaning in an initial confrontation with death that abruptly clarifies the confusion she had experienced during a seaside holiday while working so hard at the business of "having the time of her life" predicted by her mother. **"The Worst Thing of All"** ends in a different kind of moment, but with an equal dramatic force: here a husband stands revealed in all his shabby superficiality before the wife who

had previously clothed him in qualities of her own imagining.

"Tenants of the Last Tree-House" grasps the alternating clarity and vagueness of which a young girl's immediately pre-adolescent days consist. In **"Some Monday for Sure"** Miss Gordimer, writing in the first person from a man's viewpoint, sensitively evokes the feeling of alienation among black South African political refugees in Dar-es-Salaam, Tanganyika: the misery of the narrator's sister, unable to learn the language and painfully conscious of resentment on the part of her hospital coworkers; the brother's own homesickness in spite of his efforts to put a cheerful face on things.

I could go on and on. These excellent stories have the unmistakable ring of truth, and will not easily fade. Most should prove well worth rereading; half their number will in all likelihood become well-thumbed favorites of mine.

Miss Gordimer's regular readers would undoubtedly have bought the book regardless of anything I might have said. But this is a particularly fine opportunity for those who have not made her acquaintance to become familiar with a storyteller who seems to have matured into the equal of any about.

Honor Tracy (essay date 1965)

SOURCE: "A Bouquet from Nadine Gordimer," in *The New Republic*, Vol. 152, No. 2633, May 8, 1965, pp. 25-6.

[*Tracy is a English novelist and travel writer. In the following essay, she provides a mixed review of* Not for Publication.]

There is no living writer of short stories more interesting, varied and fertile than Miss Gordimer at her best. In this new collection, however, she does not always come up to her standard. The lyrical freshness is dulled, as so often in the works of maturity: now and again, humanity degenerates into motherliness; and several pieces are too long for their weight. This may be due to their being written in the first place for American magazines, for American editors love stories to be "extended," either from a simple respect for quantity as such or from the need to lure their readers through the jungle of advertisement. But whatever the reason for it, some of the work included here [in *Not For Publication*] would have a finer shape and a keener bite with the help of pruning.

The opening story, **"Not for Publication,"** is not merely too long but reads as if the writer were tired. There are too frequent lapses into what is death to any story, a bold, lazy summarizing where all should be illumined and made manifest. Much is admirable in this tale of a brilliant African beggar boy, discovered by a benevolent Englishwoman, educated by an Anglican priest, destined for great things by both, who then slips quietly back to his former life on the eve of a vital exam. Miss Gordimer understands the muddled emotions of the philanthropist, "the will to love pacing behind the bars of her glance," adopting her African tribe as another lonely woman might an orphan or a stray dog. She sees the egotism of the missionary spirit, even at its most apparently selfless, and she is alive to the hysteria of the African mind. But instead of weaving these strands artfully together, she raps out a series of brisk little messages, makes a number of informative little points. Her people are cases concerning whom she feels bound to instruct us.

With **"The African Magician,"** she is back to her own superb form. The story tells of a boatload of Belgian colonialists travelling up the Congo river a couple of months before the country's independence. They are a bunch of typical mediocrities, from the ship's Bore with his confidential growl and pally wink to the bright policeman's wife with her "They are just like monkeys, you know. We've taught them a few tricks." On each side is the vast mysterious African bush: natives flock to the landing-stages to sell ivory trinkets and bawl slogans. A shipboard entertainment is announced, with absurdly high rates of admission, and turns out to be a mere half-hour of stale, tedious conjuring-tricks. The next day—a beautifully true and engaging touch—there is a repeat performance: the travellers are to see the weary old turns all over again at the same ridiculous fee. But the canny Belgians protest, they want their money's worth, there has to be more. Two of the African crew argue with the conjuror, urge something on him, while the uncomprehending audience stares: he argues back, refuses, is adamant, then suddenly shrugs and proceeds to give a dazzling, terrifying display of African magic, mesmerizing and utterly dominating first a Congolese youth and then a Belgian girl.

Afterwards the narrator sees the wizard go ashore, looking like any young black clerk with his quiet clothes and attaché case, and brings her story to a perfect ending: "All Africa carries an attaché case now; and what I knew was in that one might not be more extraordinary than what might be in some of the others."

The story is memorable for the unity of feeling, the brilliant use of background in the heightening of mood and the honesty. The Belgians are dull and dreadful but they can and do run the Congo. The woman is mean to compare Africans to monkeys, but she is also right: the little conjuror trotting out his white man's tricks, bewildered and hurt by the white man's reaction, is the chimpanzee on the motor-bicycle. But then, dramatically, Miss Gordimer shows us that this is not all, that the African is monkeyish only when he apes the white man whom he cannot understand, and that he possesses a rich resource of his own, equally beyond the white man's power of comprehension; and in so doing demonstrates that artistic integrity packs a better punch than all the facile liberal clichés put together.

She succeeds again, beautifully, with **"A Company of Laughing Faces,"** where a young girl is taken by her jolly commonplace mother to a seaside resort full of similar people. "A wonderful place for youngsters . . . the kids really enjoy themselves there. . . ." For Kathy, being young is to be vulnerable, isolated, lost, often desperate, but she struggles to enjoy herself as her mother would wish. Mrs. Hack has not the least idea of what her daughter is like: a permanent gulf yawns between them. Kathy sees a little boy she has talked to on the beach lying drowned on the seabed, and begs to be taken home. Mrs.

Hack is loath to cut the holiday short but sees in this sensitivity something socially superior that they ought not to forego. In fact—and once again the ending is perfect—"the sight, there, was the one real happening of the holiday, the one truth and the one beauty," and the author's triumph is to make us realize that this was so.

I should mention **"Message In a Bottle,"** a tour de force concerned with the haphazard cruelty of life, told with apparent inconsequence and deeply moving; and **"Tenants of the Last Tree-House,"** dealing once more with the world of adolescence and the failure of communication between children and parents. "There was a math test on Thursday and I got 61 percent. . . ." In this vein Cavada writes her weekly letter home: but in a nursery cupboard among the outgrown clothes her mother finds a diary with an entry: "I love Peter—and adore him—and need him—for ever and ever," stands a little while thinking, then carefully hides the book away again. It is often in her simplest moments that Miss Gordimer is most poignant.

Pearl K. Bell (essay date 1971)

SOURCE: "Presuming in Africa," in *The Christian Science Monitor,* November 4, 1971, p. 11.

[*In the following mixed review, Bell examines Gordimer's treatment of South Africa's repressive political and social conditions in* Livingstone's Companions.]

In a recent review of a new novel by V. S. Naipaul, the Indian-Trinidadian writer, Nadine Gordimer remarked: "I have always believed that a writer writes one book all his life: whether consciously so or not, his work is of a piece."

In her own case this inescapable unity—more evident in some writers than in others, of course—has unfolded through a prolific career, now numbering five novels and five volumes of stories, and it has been shaped with particular insistence by the unique facts of her history. Almost all her attempts to refract the oddities and sameness of human experience through her nervously alert and probing sensibility have been stamped by her own place in time: she is South African and Jewish, and though both heritages are crucial to her work, it is the African presence that marks her special tone and resonance as a writer.

The life she has depicted under the gigantic burning sky of Africa is indissolubly part of a universally neurotic modern world in which men and women, often at a loose end, hang on by the skin of their teeth. Yet that same world is also peculiarly different because of the monolithic inequities and barbarities that have marked the past and present history of this primeval continent. A brooding, obsessive awareness of Africa in all its natural grandeur and social harshness is omni-present in most of Miss Gordimer's work, but her sophistication and intelligence lead to no simple judgments.

Although she is clearly appalled by the repressive division of black from white in the Union of South Africa, her voice is never shrill, for she is too ironically perceptive about the ambiguous varieties of outrage and passivity, all the strange faces of guilt, that everyone shows toward the black facts of life in her country.

Both the mystery and the horror of the marauding white presence in Africa are obliquely explored in **"Livingstone's Companions,"** the title story and the best of this new book of 16 stories.

As Miss Gordimer explains the title, "We all are [Livingstone's companions], we who live in or travel to Africa, because Livingstone, more than any other individual, was responsible for bringing Africa and Europe into confrontation, and that confrontation, in reality and in irony, is still being worked out today." A contemporary British journalist, assigned to retrace the steps of Livingstone's last journey, for an article on its centennial celebration, is trapped by heat, inertia, and boredom in a seedy hotel near the graves of the companions, those who accompanied Livingstone on this trek and died on the way.

In **"Open House,"** Miss Gordimer takes a shrewd look at visiting white liberals in Johannesburg. A South African woman, Frances Taver, who "was on the secret circuit for people who wanted to find out the truth," arranges a luncheon party with "representative" blacks for an eager American journalist. Knowing that he will return home in smug confidence that he now knows the black reality, though without discerning any of the nuances of hypocrisy and scorn beneath the party's banter, Frances tries to warn him that even those blacks "become what they are because things are the way they are. Being phony is being corrupted by the situation." But he cannot hear her meaning.

Yet the vast African severities do not dominate all these stories. Even there, most human crises rumble and explode within a predictably narrow domestic range, and Miss Gordimer can be marvelously exact, placing her details with insight and wit, in her portraits of modern-day Bovarys in whose lives boredom and indeterminate moralities and aspirations exact a fearful toll.

Inevitably, a gathering of stories has its weak and disappointing patches, and some of these stories aim at conventional effects in rather obvious ways; without her skillful imagery and meticulously rendered speech, a few of the stories would be banal. But most of *Livingstone's Companions* is a rich and passionate addition to the book Nadine Gordimer has been writing all her life.

Gordimer's writing, even in the least of these stories [in *Livingstone's Companions*], is like a Rolls-Royce driving through an uninteresting neighborhood. We can, if we choose, simply lean back in the flawless upholstery and enjoy the luxuriousness of the vehicle.

—*Anatole Broyard, in* The New York Times, *November 1, 1971.*

Thomas A. Gullason (essay date 1971)

SOURCE: A review of *Livingstone's Companions,* in *The Saturday Review,* New York, Vol. LIV, No. 49, December 4, 1971, pp. 50, 52.

[*Gullason is an American editor and critic. In the following essay, he offers a laudatory review of* Livingstone's Companions.]

One of the most stirring voices out of South Africa is the distinguished novelist, short-story writer, and essayist Nadine Gordimer. Along with Alan Paton, Dan Jacobson, and others, she has helped to expose the tragic oppression in her native land.

Livingstone's Companions is Miss Gordimer's fifth short-story collection. It continues her history of commitment to the human condition, which began in 1949 with her first volume, *Face to Face* (published here in 1952, with additional stories, as *The Soft Voice of the Serpent*).

A goodly number of the pieces in *Livingstone's Companions,* including the title story, **"Africa Emergent," "Open House," "Inkalamu's Place," "The Credibility Gap," "Abroad,"** and **"The Bride of Christ,"** make direct and indirect reference to the word that echoes throughout most of Miss Gordimer's writings—*apartheid.* And the tragedy of apartheid, as she demonstrates, affects both blacks and whites.

Often for ironic effect the author juxtaposes "progress" with "backwardness," mendacity with honesty, a sense of community with alienation and separation, domestic apathy with liberal activism, conscious realities with suddenly released unconscious realities. The well-meaning white narrator in **"Inkalamu's Place"** notes the "independence celebrations" and the modern "all-weather" road on which she is travelling. She visits the place of her youth to admire the grandeur of Inkalamu's estate, where she confronts Nonny, one of the native daughters of the deceased white Inkalamu. The narrator presumes too much: that Nonny is free, liberated from the past. But Nonny's only legacy—her father's estate—has deteriorated badly; and she is left behind in the march of civilization.

The white Manie Swemmer, in **"Abroad,"** has viewed many changes in the Africa he has helped to build. He sees blacks in white places, and shows that he is open-minded. But an Indian bolts the door to the hotel room he is to share with Manie. And when Manie himself is given a room with four beds, he bolts his door to make certain he will not have to share it with Africans.

In **"Africa Emergent"** a black messenger boy, Elias Nkomo, shows great talent as a sculptor. Offered a scholarship to study in America, he is provided with an exit permit, which means he can never go back to his homeland; a black friend, however, is given a passport, and can return home once he completes his drama training. Elias, who achieves in America a small vogue as a "real live African Negro," forsakes his creative work and finally commits suicide. His friend, the drama student, returns home Americanized; he wears a Liberace jacket and plastic boots. Only when the young man is arrested and imprisoned do his white friends (who are satirized) feel satisfied that he is not a spy.

Not all of the stories in *Livingstone's Companions* study the problems arising from apartheid. One of the best efforts, **"A Third Presence,"** is a taut drama of two sisters. Characteristically, Miss Gordimer opens her story right in the middle of things:

> When Rose and Naomi, daughters of poor Rasovsky the tailor, left school in the same year there was no discussion about what they should do, because there was no question about the necessity to do it. The old Rasovskys had got the naming of the daughters all wrong. Naomi was everything "Rose" suggested, Naomi was pretty and must marry the scrap metal dealer who would give a home to the old Rasovskys and the girls' brother; Rose, who cruelly bore her name along with the sad Jewish ugliness of her face, was clever and must get a job to help support the family.

And with her typical rush of impeccable details, Miss Gordimer surrounds the sisters with ironic and poignant situations. In the end, it is Rose's life which is fulfilling, Naomi's which is sterile. Not only has Rose inner beauty and strength, she even begins to acquire physical attributes which were Naomi's sole consolation.

"A Meeting in Space" studies, in part, the bankruptcy of American society. The American boy Matt is laden with the consumer riches of his country—cameras, tape recorder, a transistor radio—but he is without the love and attention of his busy parents. Clive, the boy from Africa, envies Matt's life style, but his parents raise the inevitable point: "What's there left for [children like Matt] to want when they grow up?" Set in an air terminal, **"No Place Like"** unmasks the frightening isolation of the modern age. The omnipresent plastic card is a passport to nowhere in this remarkable and frenetically paced impressionistic sketch. Other stories—**"Rain-Queen," "The Life of the Imagination,"** and **"An Intruder"**—dramatize the themes of sex and love.

The narrator of **"Inkalamu's Place"** says: "How secretly Africa is populated. . . ." Argus-eyed Nadine Gordimer exposes many secrets not only of contemporary Africa but of contemporary life at large.

Nadine Gordimer   (essay date 1976)

SOURCE: An introduction to *Selected Stories*, 1975. Reprint by The Viking Press, 1976, pp. 9-14.

[*In the following essay, Gordimer outlines her philosophy of short story writing.*]

> After I had selected and arranged these stories, the present publisher asked me to provide some kind of introduction to them. If they were now making their first appearance I might have recoiled from this invitation, but they have all been printed and some reprinted, and have therefore been through a period of probation. Whatever I may say about them now cannot alter what has been said by others, and can hardly increase or

lessen the likelihood of their being read—that must depend on the stories themselves.

The words are William Plomer's, but the attitude comes so close to my own that I do not hesitate to fly his declaration at the masthead of this book. William Plomer not only wrote some stories that have become classic, he also had a special interest in and fascination with the short story as a form used in widely diverse ways by others. His code holds good for me; for all of us. I take it further; if the story itself does not succeed in conveying all the writer meant it should, no matter when he wrote it, neither explication nor afterthought can change this. Conversely, if the story has been *achieved,* the patronizing backward glance its writer might cast upon it, as something he could now do with one hand tied behind his back but no longer would care to do at all, will not detract from it.

I wrote these stories [in *Selected Stories*] over thirty years. I have attempted now to influence any reader's judgment of or pleasure in them only to the extent implied by the fact that I have chosen some and excluded others. In this sense, I suppose, I have 'rewritten': imposed a certain form, shaped by retrospect, upon the collection as an entity. For everything one writes is part of the whole story, so far as any individual writer attempts to build the pattern of his own perception out of chaos. To make sense of life: that story, in which everything, novels, stories, the false starts, the half-completed, the abandoned, has its meaningful place, will be complete with the last sentence written before one dies or imagination atrophies. As for retrospect as a valid critique, I realize it has no fixed existence but represents my own constantly changing effort to teach myself how to make out of words a total form for whatever content I seize upon. This I understood only too clearly when I was obliged to read through my five existing collections of stories and saw how there are some stories I have gone on writing, again and again, all my life, not so much because the themes are obsessional but because I found other ways to take hold of them; because I hoped to make the revelation of new perceptions through the different techniques these demanded. I felt for the touch that would release the spring that shuts off appearance from reality. If I were to make a choice of my stories in five years' time, I might choose a different selection, in the light of what I might have learnt about these things by then. My 'retrospect' would be based upon which stories approached most nearly what I happened to have most recently taught myself. That is inevitable.

Why write short stories?

The question implies the larger one: what makes one write? Both have brought answers from experts who study writers as a psychological and social phenomenon. It is easier and more comforting to be explained than to try and explain oneself. Both have also brought answers of a kind from many writers; devious answers; as mine may be. (If one found out exactly how one walks the tightrope, would one fall immediately?) Some have lived—or died—to contradict their own theories; Ernest Hemingway said we write out our sicknesses in books, and shot himself. Of course I find I agree with those writers whose theories coincide at least in part with mine. What is experienced as solitude (and too quickly dubbed alienation) is pretty generally agreed to be a common condition conducive to becoming a writer. Octavio Paz speaks of the 'double solitude', as an intellectual and a woman, of the famous early Spanish-American writer, Sor Juana Inès de la Cruz. Growing up in a gold-mining town in South Africa as a member of a white minority, to begin with, my particular solitude as an intellectual-by-inclination was so complete I did not even know I was one: the concept 'intellectual', gathered from reading, belonged as categorically to the Northern Hemisphere as a snowy Christmas. Certainly there must have been other people who were intellectuals, but they no doubt accepted their isolation too philosophically to give a signal they scarcely hoped would be answered, let alone attract an acolyte. As for the specific solitude of the woman-as-intellectual, I must say truthfully that my femininity has never constituted any special kind of solitude, for me. Indeed, in that small town, walled up among the mine dumps, born exiled from the European world of ideas, ignorant that such a world existed among Africans, my only genuine and innocent connection with the social life of the town (in the sense that I was not pretending to be what I was not, forever hiding the activities of mind and imagination which must be suspect, must be concealed) was through my femaleness. As an adolescent, at least I felt and followed sexual attraction in common with others; that was a form of communion I could share. Rapunzel's hair is the right metaphor for this femininity: by means of it, I was able to let myself out and live in the body, with others, as well as—alone—in the mind. To be young and in the sun; my experience of this was similar to that of Camus, although I did not enter into it as fully as he did, I did not play football . . .

In any case, I question the existence of the specific solitude of woman-as-intellectual when that woman is a writer, because when it comes to their essential faculty as writers, all writers are androgynous beings.

The difference between alienation and solitude should be clear enough. Writers' needs in this respect are less clear, and certainly less well and honestly understood, even by themselves. Some form of solitude (there are writers who are said to find it in a crowded cafe, or less romantically among the cockroaches in a night-time family kitchen, others who must have a cabin in the woods) is the condition of creation. The less serious—shall we say professional?—form of alienation follows inevitably. It is very different from the kind of serious psychic rupture between the writer and his society that has occurred in the Soviet Union and in South Africa, for example, and that I shall not discuss here, since it requires a study in itself.

I believe—I *know* (there are not many things I should care to dogmatize about, on the subject of writing) that writers need solitude, and seek alienation of a kind every day of their working lives. (And remember, they are not even aware when and when not they are working . . .) Powers of observation heightened beyond the normal imply extraordinary disinvolvement; or rather the double process, excessive preoccupation and identification with the lives of others, and at the same time a monstrous detachment. For identification brings the superficial loyalties (that is,

to the self) of concealment and privacy, while detachment brings the harsher fidelities (to the truth about the self) of revealment and exposure. The tension between standing apart and being fully involved; that is what makes a writer. That is where we begin. The validity of this dialectic is the synthesis of revelation; our achievement of, or even attempt at this is the moral, the human justification for what we do.

Here I am referring to an accusation that every writer meets, that we 'use' people, or rather other people's lives. Of course we do. As unconscious eternal eavesdroppers and observers, snoopers, nothing that is human is alien to the imagination and the particular intuition to which it is a trance-like state of entry. I have written *from the starting-point* of other people's 'real' lives; what I have written represents alternatives to the development of a life as it was formed before I encountered it and as it will continue, out of my sight. A writer sees in your life what you do not. That is why people who think they recognize themselves as 'models' for this character or that in a story will protest triumphantly, 'it wasn't that way at all'. They think they know better; but perhaps it is the novelist or short story writer who does? Fiction is a way of exploring possibilities present but undreamt of in the living of a single life.

There is also the assumption, sometimes prurient or deliciously scandalized, that writers write only about themselves. I know that I have used my own life much the same way as I have that of others: events (emotions are events, too, of the spirit) mark exits and entrances in a warren where many burrows lead off into the same darkness but this one might debouch far distant from that. What emerges most often is an alternative fate, the predisposition to which exists in what 'actually' happened.

How can the eavesdropper, observer, snooper ever be the prototype? The stories in this book were written between the ages of twenty and fifty. Where am I, in them? I search for myself. At most, reading them over for the first time in many years, I see my own shadow dancing on a wall behind and over certain stories. I can make a guess at remembering what significatory event it was that casts it there. The story's 'truth' or lack of it is not attached to or dependent upon that lost event.

But part of these stories' 'truth' does depend upon faithfulness to another series of lost events—the shifts in social attitudes as evidenced in the characters and situations. I had wanted to arrange the selection in sequence from the earliest story collection to the latest simply because when reading story collections I myself enjoy following the development of a writer. Then I found that this order had another logic to which my first was complementary. The chronological order turns out to be an historical one. The change in social attitudes unconsciously reflected in the stories represents both that of the people in my society—that is to say, history—and my apprehension of it; in the writing, I am acting upon my society, and in the manner of my apprehension, all the time history is acting upon me.

The white girl in **'Is There Nowhere Else Where We Can Meet?'**, whose first *conscious* encounter with a black is that between victim and attacker—primary relationship indeed—is several years and a book away from the girl in **'The Smell of Death and Flowers'**, experiencing her generation's equivalent of religious ecstasy in the comradeship of passive resistance action in the company of blacks. Both white girls are twenty-five years and several books away from the whites in **'Open House'** and **'Africa Emergent'**, experiencing the collapse of white liberalism. The humble black servant bemoaning fatalistically in **'Ah, Woe Is Me'** (a very early story) could never have occurred in my writing by the time, again several books later, the young black political refugee is awaiting military training in exile and the **'Some Monday For Sure'** when he will return to a South Africa ruled by a black majority. Even the language changes from book to book: 'native' becomes first 'African' then 'Black', because these usages have been adopted, over three decades, by South Africans of various opinions, often at different stages. For example, the old Afrikaner in **'Abroad'** (a recent story) still speaks quite naturally of 'natives', whereas for English-speaking whites the use of the term 'African' is now general, no longer even indicating, as it would have ten years ago, that the speaker was showing his political colours as liberal if not leftist. The use of the blunt term 'Black' is now the reverse of pejorative or insulting: indeed it is the only one, of all generic words used to denote them, that has not been imposed upon but has been chosen by blacks themselves. (Though not all, in particular older and more conservative people, feel happy with it.) Its adoption by whites has a somewhat left-of-liberal tone, but much more significant is the fact that here whites are following black, not white usage.

What I am saying is that I see that many of these stories *could not have been written* later or earlier than they were. If I could have juggled them around in the contents list of this collection without that being evident, they would have been false in some way important to me as a writer.

What I am also saying, then, is that in a certain sense a writer is 'selected' by his subject—his subject being *the consciousness* of his own era. How he deals with this is, to me, the fundament of commitment, although 'commitment' is usually understood as the reverse process: a writer's selection of a subject in conformity with the rationalization of his own ideological and/or political beliefs.

My time and place have been twentieth-century Africa. Emerging from it, immersed in it, the first form in which I wrote was the short story. I write fewer and fewer stories, now, and more novels, but I don't think I shall ever stop writing stories. What makes a writer turn from one to the other? How do they differ?

Nobody has ever succeeded in defining a short story in a manner to satisfy all who write or read them, and I shall not, here. I sometimes wonder if one shouldn't simply state flatly: a short story is a piece of fiction short enough to be read at one sitting? No, that will satisfy no one, least myself. But for me certainly there is a clue, there, to the choice of the short story by writers, as a form: whether or not it has a narrative in the external or internal sense, whether it sprawls or neatly bites its own tail, a short story is a concept that the writer can 'hold', fully realized, in his imagination, at one time. A novel is, by comparison, staked out, and must be taken possession of stage by stage;

it is impossible to contain, all at once, the proliferation of concepts it ultimately may use. For this reason I cannot understand how people can suppose one makes a conscious choice, *after* knowing what one wants to write about, between writing a novel or a short story. A short story *occurs*, in the imaginative sense. To write one is to express from a situation in the exterior or interior world the life-giving drop—sweat, tear, semen, saliva—that will spread an intensity on the page; burn a hole in it.

Penelope Mortimer   (essay date 1976)

SOURCE: "Truth Teller in South Africa," in *The New York Times Book Review,* April 18, 1976, p. 7.

[*Mortimer is a Welsh novelist, short story writer, and critic. In the following review, she terms* Selected Stories *a social history of South Africa and praises Gordimer's use of the milieu in her stories.*]

South Africa, in the latter half of the 20th century, is an anomaly that incites more frustrated, personal indignation than any other political society.

There, on the tail of the vast black continent of Africa, sits the Union, authoritarian, racist, wealthy, implacably thickheaded, smugly disregarding every liberal principle and every concern for what we consider to be common humanity. We demonstrate, sign petitions, refuse to buy canned peaches; not altogether trusting the South African authorities to censor our work for us, we impose a cultural boycott, depriving the bastards of our tepid little intellectual plays until—presumably by means of other, more persuasive methods—they have seen the democratic light. South African writers consider it an honor not to be allowed back to their homeland. Secure in their exile, they talk a great deal and take up mysticism or feminism or Christian Science fiction—anything *real,* you understand, anything truly relevant to "the situation."

In the meanwhile, a very few extraordinary people (they must, one feels, be extraordinary people) continue to live and work in South Africa, stubbornly trying to tell us the truth. Of these, Nadine Gordimer is undoubtedly the most eminent. For over 30 years her novels and short stories have flowed steadily from the darkest tip of the dark continent, apparently fearless, her attitude, a unique blend of irony, compassion and disgust. The stories in this new collection were written between the ages of 20 and 50, and have been selected by Gordimer herself to show her development as a writer; but that is not all they show. A society, too, can age and sharpen and grow less amenable over 30 years.

. . . [*Selected Stories*] is, in its way, a work of social history: beginning with an elementary black and white encounter (the black is an ignoble, clumsy thief; the white, a woman full of the confusion and panic and aggression of the very young or very ignorant) and ending with the bitterness and disillusion of middle age ("We white friends can purge ourselves of the shame of rumors. We can be pure again. We are satisfied at last. He's in prison. He's proved himself, hasn't he?"), it spans a period of time in which nothing, except the fact of apartheid, has remained constant.

The 31 stories in the collection are taken from five books, and my own favorites are those that show Gordimer at her most receptive, wry and sunny, with a trained eye for the natural beauty of land, and water and an impartial ear for complaint, wherever it comes from—stories from the active, mature years, perhaps, in the middle of that 30-year marathon. During this time even her impatience with "do-gooders," white liberal benefactors, is tempered with affection.

In **"Which New Era Would That Be?,"** which seems to me the most successful of them all, we meet the young white social-rehabilitation worker, so sure of herself, with her "big, lively, handsome eyes, dramatically painted, that would look into yours with such intelligent, eager honesty." "It's hard to be punished," she says earnestly, "for not being black." Deranged by altruism, people do say such things.

> Even Jake, who had been sure that there could be no possible situation between white and black he could not find amusing, only looked quickly from the young woman to Maxie, in a hiatus between anger, which he had given up long ago, and laughter, which suddenly failed him. On his face was admiration more than anything else—sheer, grudging admiration. This one was the best yet. This one was the coolest ever.
>
> "Guilt, what-have-you . . ."

the poor girl mutters, trying to explain why she voluntarily lives in a black (at this point in history called "colored") slum—and Maxie, "the small, dainty-faced African in neat, businessman's dress . . . shrugged, as if at the mention of some expensive illness he had never been able to afford and whose symptoms he could not imagine." In relatively few pages this story crystalizes a vast, seemingly unmanageable conflict, reducing it in size if not in stature, to the insoluble problem of human inability to communicate. Because it seems insoluble, it still seems hopeless; but Gordimer's sympathies here are so alive, her reactions so sharp, her aim so accurate on every target, that one feels exhilarated by new and significant knowledge.

There are a number of other memorable stories in the collection, though none of them, to me, displays the dispassionate passion of this one. The isolation of one timid, sensitive woman at a rowdy philistine party in **"The Night the Favourite Came Home"**; the odd, perverse excitement of the crocodile hunt in **"The Gentle Art"**; the picture—a Happy Snap out of focus—of healthy middle-class kids having healthy middle-class fun in **"A Company of Laughing Faces"**; the puzzling heroism and beauty of Mrs. Bamjee, "the ugly widow with five children" in **"A Chip of Glass Ruby"**—in all these Gordimer has been inspired by her belief that "an imaginative writer must not allow a political bias to intrude in the creation of characters—because the whole value of writing should be its dispassionate view. The injustices will come through."

Not a didactic writer, like Solzhenitsyn or Doris Lessing, Gordimer stays at home and writes about what she sees

and hears and feels. The middle-class suburbs, the seaside resorts and vacations in the country, the teen-age mores, the conflicts of sex and background would be much the same as in any other WASP community if it weren't for the one thing that makes Gordimer stand out above her contemporaries—South Africa, her context and her content. Without this, she would probably belong in the ranks of those sensitive, perceptive writers of limited experience and no more than adequate talent. There is no point in trying to disassociate her work from the sorrow and the pity, the pain and the bitterness, that is her bonus for the life she has chosen to live and write about; there is no disguising the fact that one's admiration is greater for the act of writing than it is for the writing itself. Nevertheless, the plain, informative style—only very rarely touching the sublime, but only occasionally lapsing into the ridiculous—serves her material well. A more poetic or stylistically perfect prose might, against the enormity of her subject, seem almost indecent.

Without South Africa, Gordimer would probably belong in the ranks of those sensitive, perceptive writers of limited experience and no more than adequate talent.

—*Penelope Mortimer*

And the injustices do come through, loud and clear. We should be grateful; we should be troubled; and, somehow we should do something in return.

Eric Redman   (essay date 1976)

SOURCE: "Magician at Work," in *Book World—The Washington Post,* May 16, 1976, p. L1.

[*Redman is an American critic. In the following review, he lauds the scope of the stories included in* Selected Stories.]

Nadine Gordimer is a South African who writes critically about South Africa. This causes her trouble at home, of course, since the South African authorities tend to ban the works of dissidents. Yet Gordimer must consider foreign reviewers almost as irksome as Afrikaner censors. Like Solzhenitsyn, she too often finds herself hailed in England and America as a political rather than a literary figure—a form of praise, however laudatory, that inevitably demeans her art.

It ought to be possible to laud Gordimer's courage and still point out that she writes as well as anyone alive today. Americans most recently tasted her talents in *The Conservationist,* her sixth novel. The protagonist, a South African industrialist who buys a farm as a weekend retreat, discovers through his ownership of the land that the society itself, not just the soil, is breaking down and leaching away. The vision is one of decomposition, not apocalypse; the politics are ambivalent rather than polemical. The prose throughout is precise yet natural—flinty—with each word seemingly chosen for sound and texture as well as meaning.

The same high level of literary craft shows up in Gordimer's *Selected Stories,* a collection of 31 pieces gleaned from her earlier works. Many of the characters—lovelorn teenagers, adulterous wives—could be drawn from any country. But others, ranging from African guerrillas to Indian protesters to guilt-ridden "Europeans," are familiar to Americans for a different reason altogether: race has been our recurring nightmare for three centuries, too.

The short stories in this collection deal with many themes familiar to readers of *The Conservationist,* but their effect is more immediate and powerful. Like a good still photograph, the short story form is one that compresses and distills, reducing ideas and characters to their very essences. As Gordimer says in her introduction, "To write [a short story] is to express from a situation in the exterior or interior world the life-giving drop—sweat, tear, semen, saliva—that will spread an intensity on the page; burn a hole in it."

Gordimer burns many holes in these pages. Because the collection spans 30 years of her work, however, it's possible to observe how differently she burned the holes at age 20 than at age 50. The earlier stories often end suddenly, with a shock, like the suspense stories of Saki or O. Henry or Poe. The later ones progress more subtly, abandoning the quick jolt of irony for the gradual awakening of recognition, the private little epiphanies that come late at night, haunting an empty bed or a bush camp pitched lonely upon the veldt.

Africa, too, has changed during these 30 years. The earlier stories were written when most of the continent, not just its southern tip, lay under white rule, and when the Nationalist government had only recently come to power in Pretoria, bringing its apartheid legislation with it. Fittingly, relations between the races in these stories are primitive, often wordless. A native attacks a young girl in a field; a white matron hands out worn clothing to former servants who need much more; a vacationer coerces a native craftsman into selling a beautiful carving at a pathetic price.

The later stories show characters bound for a new era, yet laden with the heavy baggage of tradition. A white girl attends a clandestine interracial party and finds the trembling courage to demonstrate publicly and be arrested. Frightened Africans go underground, steal dynamite, and flee to foreign capitals to be trained as freedom fighters. A South African contractor takes a sentimental journey to Zambia, the Northern Rhodesia of his youth, and gamely buys drinks for black functionaries at a bar that was once "whites only." The struggles are personal, not just political, and none of the choices is easy.

As Gordimer's image of "sweat, tear, semen, saliva" suggests, these are also sensual stories, intimate and physical, suffused with a fascination for the body that neatly counterpoints South Africa's obsession with mere skin. Gordimer's characters yearn, and they yearn through their bodies. This urgent and earthy emptiness is probably

what makes even the most African of Gordimer's stories so universally appealing. A writer of greater delicacy might lose us at the first sight of a native hut.

My favorite among these stories is **"The African Magician,"** set in the first-class cabins of a river boat moving slowly through a black nation on the eve of independence. A native magician comes aboard to entertain the white passengers, and fails miserably in attempting to execute a few simple parlor tricks. The audience withholds its applause and demands something better; the magician had charged a "Western" price, and the audience will do him the "justice" of holding him to Western standards. Angered, the magician glares at a young bride in the audience, transfixes her, and to the acute discomfort of her peers—simply wills her forward to touch him in a gesture of complete submission. The symbolism is both erotic and political. But the true magician is Nadine Gordimer.

A. G. Mojtabai   (essay date 1980)

SOURCE: "Her Region Is Ours," in *The New York Times Book Review,* August 24, 1980, pp. 7, 18.

[*Mojtabai is an American novelist and critic. In the following review, she overviews the themes and plots of* A Soldier's Embrace.]

We paid attention when Nadine Gordimer's most recent novel, *Burger's Daughter,* was banned in her native South Africa. At once, this distinguished author of seven novels and eight volumes of short stories, whose work has sometimes been patronized as cool, quiet, regional, had a wide and receptive audience. Now that the ban and the attendant publicity have been lifted and Miss Gordimer resumes her work of scrupulously sifting the life around her, of discriminating, clarifying, connecting, I wonder—will we continue to listen?

I truly wonder, when so much of our current American entertainment (fiction included) seems a surfeit of unreality, given over to sensationalism or flights of escape—to commerce with dragons and trolls, or wallowing rapturously in blood. Of course, fantasy has its place, but how repetitive and thin dreams are! John Gardner's phrase "joyful terror" speaks volumes on the quality of our engagement with others, of our mounting estrangement from the world.

Miss Gordimer, in contrast, living in the thick of real trouble, is subdued, sober, very sober, indeed. She scarcely raises her voice, yet her voice reverberates over a full range of emotion. Her precision is very fine, her discriminations are reflective and subtle, her mind marvelously awake. She remains stubbornly in place, linked to the earth and to recognizable inhabitants and institutions of the earth. She is not a regionalist—or, if she is, her region includes ours, wherever we may be.

A Soldier's Embrace is her latest collection of stories. Only four out of the twelve have been previously published in the United States. Some are shapely, conventionally well-made tales; others have an air of, sometimes dazzling, improvisation; still others—the most interesting, I think—take long and calculated risks. All are set in Africa, yet their themes are universal: love and change, political transition, family, memory, madness, marriage and infidelity, to name a few.

The first story, **"A Soldier's Embrace,"** strikes me as one of the most memorable tales in the collection. It is risky in method, shuttling rapidly back and forth without transition, and the initial response of the reader may be blurred. We begin at a moment of celebration and return to the sensations of that moment as a counterpoint to the chronicle of subsequent disenchantment. The occasion is that of a cease-fire between the colonial army and the freedom fighters of an unnamed African country. The wife of a white liberal lawyer is in the crowd, caught up in the contagion, experiencing a moment of ecstatic shock, an unprecedented, overpowering sensation of human solidarity.

> They were grinning and laughing amazement. That it could be: there they were, bumping into each other's bodies in joy. . . . one side a white cheek, the other a black. The white one she kissed on the left cheek, the black one on the right cheek, as if these were two sides of one face. That vision, version, was like a poster; the sort of thing that was soon peeling off dirty shopfronts and bus shelters while the months of wrangling talks preliminary to the take-over by the black government went by.

The colonial soldier will soon return to his meager future:

> The fingernails she sometimes still saw clearly were bitten down. . . . Such hands had never been allowed to take possession. . . . He had not been killed, and now that [the] day of the cease-fire was over he would be delivered back across the sea to the docks, the stony farm, the scullery of the grand hotel.

And thus begins the inevitable falling-off, from the euphoria of pure possibility to the narrowing compromises and innumerable small corruptions of day-after-day. Guerrilla movement becomes Party, becomes Interim Council, will become Government, and there will be less and less work for the white liberal lawyer.

The tale that follows is not, in my reading of it, what the cover flap says it is—the story of a man unable to live with the fruition of his hopes. The *facts* are dispiriting:

> Shops were being looted by the unemployed and loafers (there had always been a lot of unemployed hanging around for the pickings of the town) who felt the new regime should entitle them to take what they dared not before. Radio and television shops were the most favoured objective for gangs who adopted the freedom fighters' slogans.

The lawyer's servant dreams of freedom as a rich merchant:

> . . . this was the only sort of freedom he understood, after so many years as a servant. But she also knew, and the lawyer . . . knew, that the shortages of the goods [he] could sell from his cart, the sugar and soap and matches and po-

made and sunglasses, would soon put him out of business.

The lawyer's black friends are increasingly inattentive. His great friend, Chipande, now confidential secretary to the future president, comes home from exile; he installs himself in the former colonial secretariat and fails to call. Eventually, he comes to the house but will not stay for supper, will not discuss what apparently can only be discussed by black men among themselves.

It is true that Chipande protests and even weeps "for a moment" when the lawyer and his wife finally decide to leave the country. And the lawyer gives this moment pause before dismissing it. Chipande's emotional outburst is doubtless genuine, and the lawyer's dismissal of it is not quite fair or accurate but, rather, one of those revisions of perception that signal and assist in the containment of hurt feelings. Still, it seems to me that the story is not best read as a catalogue of revised perceptions in the light of the lawyer's personal disappointment or unbending perfectionism. The incidents recounted speak for themselves; they are larger than the personal; they have a dismal plausibility down to the last detail: "She was deputed to engage the movers. . . . She had no choice but to grease a palm, although it went against her principles. . . ." A sad descent into the muddle of actual life in the actual world.

In the story **"Oral History,"** a chief's betrayal of his own village is rendered from a series of distant perspectives, some of which seem so remote as to be aerial reconnaissance views. This narrative detachment makes the tale all the more horrifying. The drama unfolding seems to belong to everyone, to no one, to the terrain itself.

We begin with a view of the chief's house:

> There's always been one house like a white man's house in the village of Dilole. Built of brick with a roof that bounced signals from the sun. . . . It was the chief's house. Some chiefs have a car as well but this was not an important chief. . . .

We are never intimate with the chief, never privy to his anguish, or to the thoughts that precipitate his moment of betrayal. Instead, we are given to see the normal compromised condition of his village: The chief exists on a government stipend; the Scottish missionaries have come and gone, leaving

> pretty pictures of white lambs and pink children at the knees of the golden-haired Christ. . . . The children were baptized with names chosen by portent in consultation between the mother and an old man who read immutable fate in the fall of small bones cast like dice from a horn cup.

Added to this is the fact that the village is close to a border and used as a shelter by those fighting against the army of the colonial government.

The chief seems simply a figure lost in the landscape, and when Miss Gordimer speaks of the "brittle fragmentation of the dead leaves" on the path to Dilolo, one thinks immediately of the fragmentation of the chief in his many scattered roles. We see him quarreling with one of the vil-

lage headmen, who was a member of the same circumci-
sion group in his boyhood; then we see "the middle-aged
man on whom the villagers depended"; then in the presence of his youngest wife, with whom he is at one moment
"a passionately shuddering lover," and at the next "one
of the important old with whom she did not count"; then
with his mother, where he becomes "a son—the ageless
category"; and finally with the white men at the army
post, where he "had to wait like a beggar rather than a
chief."

Given all these circumstances, a crisis of integrity really
needs no further explication, and the moment of decision
can be presented quite thoroughly in a seemingly offhand
manner:

> Towards midnight—his watch had its own
> glowing galaxy—he left his chair and did not
> come back from the shadows where the men
> went to urinate. . . .

"Town and Country Lovers"—the name given to two love
stories of white men and native black women—provides
a solid middle for the book, a ballast. They are rather symmetrical: Each begins in innocence (of a sort) and ends in
complicity with the system and a widening of the rift between the races. These two central stories are powerful in
their simplicity, in their bold oppositions of light and
shade, in the fierce moral indignation at their core, contained by the cool, iron restraint of the narration. Their
impact is immediate and clear. Other stories are slower to
make themselves felt, but take hold all the more profoundly when they do. I am thinking in particular of the rich
complexity, the fine shading, the lingering, troubling pre-
cariousness of the story **"A Soldier's Embrace,"** where we
are given, unforgettably, a glimpse of a social order only
just born—and already compromised by all that has gone
before.

But there seems little point in the listing of preferences.
The stories in this collection are varied in theme and method, and disparate perhaps in appeal. Yet all bear the signature of the author, Nadine Gordimer; all reveal a passionate intelligence at work.

**In Gordimer's work the extremes of South
Africa seem irreconcilable. She dramatizes
a people being drawn, along with their
homeland, toward a precipice. Although
she offers no answers as to what lies over
the edge, she is certainly not sanguine.**

—*Alice Digilio, in* Book World—The
Washington Post, *July 15, 1984.*

Vivian Gornick   (essay date 1980)

SOURCE: "Gordimer Confined," in *The Village Voice*,
Vol. XXV, No. 38, September 17-23, 1980, p. 40.

[*Gornick is an American nonfiction writer, editor, and critic. Below, she offers a negative assessment of* A Soldier's
Embrace, *describing the stories as "fragmentary" and the
collection "unsatisfying."*]

Nadine Gordimer's work—like that of a good doctor trying to find out where it hurts—applies steady pressure to
external circumstance until the live places beneath the surface stir with surprised feeling. Gordimer has written
seven novels and as many volumes of short stories, all set
in her native South Africa, mainly in and around middle-
class Johannesburg. Her knowledge of the politics of her
country is strong and her sense of the politicalness of life
profound, but her power resides in the force of sexual feeling that permeates her work and makes of racist South Africa a metaphor for the stunning sorrow of caged and harnessed lives.

It is interesting, in this sense at least, to compare
Gordimer with V. S. Naipaul, the Trinidad-born, British-
educated Indian writer whose work covers the same territory, so to speak—that is, colonized Africa, the decay of
empire, rising black fury—but whose sense of things is the
nether side of Gordimer's. In Naipaul there is neither sorrow nor pity, neither tenderness nor the curious calm of
deeply felt pain. Naipaul's Africa is all cold murderous
dread—sexual hysteria, depression, and terror. His sentences, each one spare and plain, add up to electricity on
the page; his books burn with an icy rage and a sometimes
contemptuous insistence on the void at the middle of
things. And always behind the words one can see the figure of the writer: the face twisted up in an agony of self-
disgust, the body held tightly as though in bondage, the
spirit clearly not at ease or at home anywhere in the world.

Gordimer's sentences are also spare and plain, but they accumulate slowly into a concentrate of thoughtful feeling
that is reserved and quiet, spread evenly rather than
packed densely. Her prose appears as a rather calm inspection of a world symbolically wide and flat, disproportion-
ately spacious and crowded, oddly silent and motionless.
In Gordimer's Africa there is tension and imminent violence, but it comes as in a dream, moving slowly through
mist into a country that is all stasis and puzzled, flickering
perception. This world is made of silent dusty sunlight.
People stand trapped in the sunny silence, dead-still, with
an ear cocked, straining to catch the meaning of it all.

Sex is the reminder of volatile life, and it comes up in
Gordimer as though traveling a vast distance from the
muffled center to a surprised moan as it hits the air. It is
the connective tissue between people whose skins are
black, or white, or black and white: the stirring memory
of the hot, live self, inside, unmoving . . . And one can
see the figure of this writer, too, behind the worlds. It is
that of a beautiful, intelligent, self-possessed woman un-
afraid of emotion, listening hard to make sense of this
awful human beauty all about her.

A Soldier's Embrace is Gordimer's eighth volume of short
stories, and while the collection contains many of her familiar settings and particular kinds of knowledge, it bears
only traces of her great artist's power. In two stories—**"A
Lion on the Freeway"** and **"Time Did"**—a man and a

woman are in bed. This man and this woman have been in Gordimer's bed a long time now, and the rumination their languorous lie-about gives rise to is often admirably associative, and always possessed of at least one memorable insight. Here, the insight comes in the second story. He's married, she's his mistress, they've been together years. As they lie together after making love, he says something that makes her realize it's over between them. The woman addresses the man silently in her mind:

> Many times you had thought: now. But the words had not come. A decision such as this could not be acted upon, once in my presence . . . in the end . . . your mouth opened of itself and told me something that *in the act of telling* could be told because it no longer concerned me. It was something that happened to you; the time has come when things can happen to you without happening to me.

Then there are the tales of black-white Africa. In **"A Hunting Accident"** a group of friends—political blacks in a newly independent country and a variety of white Europeans—go off for a day's hunting in the bush. An unexplained bullet zinging through the air brings them to a frightened halt. The following sentence speaks volumes: "The Swedish girl, already seated in the truck with the defensive smile of a terrified child, held to the hand, cold and tough as the feel of a tortoise's foot, of the old gun-bearer who had never before been touched by a white woman." And **"Town and Country Lovers,"** a pair of stories about the illegal coupling of blacks and whites, is penetrating in its ability to bring home the Nazi Germany quality of everyday life in South Africa.

Yet *A Soldier's Embrace* is unsatisfying. Rich and important as Gordimer's talent is, these stories are fragments; that is, they *feel* like fragments; even when they are fully articulated tales with point clearly aimed for and arrived at, they remain somehow unrealized, without the force or power to "remind" us deeply of the emotions they allude to. The skill with which Gordimer—like many great writers—tells a story by beginning in the interior middle gives pleasure; there is delight in the ingenuity with which the private vision is carefully made available. But it doesn't carry the conviction of a true unfolding; it's not as though you and Gordimer are slowly coming clear together; the interiority here is *too* interior; oddly stilted; self-conscious and image-making.

Perhaps it is impossible to tell stories now. Perhaps now it is only in novels that strength may accumulate; that the creative intelligence with a talent for the inner life has enough sentences to express fully an atmosphere uncontainable in a framed point; one that spills painfully over the edge and needs time of another shape to penetrate the thinking heart.

Ethel W. Githii   (essay date 1981)

SOURCE: "Nadine Gordimer's *Selected Stories*," in *Critique: Studies in Modern Fiction*, Vol. XXII, No. 3, 1981, pp. 45-54.

[*In the following essay, Githii compares several of* Gordimer's earlier and later stories in order to trace her thematic and stylistic maturation.*]

Nadine Gordimer's *Selected Stories* (1975) is a collection of short stories from an author whose eight novels and numerous articles and critical reviews form an impressive body of work extending over thirty years. Her precise observations and impressions of life in South Africa recorded in the stories have won for her a reputation that has grown through the years, while many of the stories have become classics both in literature of Africa and around the world. An examination of the stories will reveal the author's intellectual and moral development, as well as the artistic embodiment of that development. We shall also discover the extent to which the author's background and circumstances determine the shape and scope of her literary work—its content, themes, techniques, and levels of interpretation.

Although Gordimer began writing at the age of nine, partly in response to "a solitary" childhood during which "she read voraciously," at fifteen she published her first story, **"Come Again Tomorrow,"** in November of 1939 in *The Forum,* a Johannesburg magazine. Ten years later her first collection of stories, *Face to Face* (1949), was published in Johannesburg and signalled the beginning of a long and distinguished career. *Selected Stories* is drawn from five collections of stories, and her remarkable talent is immediately apparent in these stories that she selected herself. They show the full range of her imagination and understanding as well as her growth and subsequent development in quality over the years of her writing life. [In the *Times Literary Supplement,* July 7, 1966] a reviewer has written:

> When Nadine Gordimer's short stories first began to appear, she seemed to be the very best kind of New Yorker writer. . . . Although these stories tended to be constructed to a recognizable pattern, her sensibility and perception were already such that one was sure she would eventually burst the bonds. She did in fact achieve freedom and real stature with her first novel *A World of Strangers.* . . . Since then the stories as well as the novels have taken on new dimensions, though continuing to explore the same areas of experience. Those in *Friday's Footprint* are faultless in technique, sharper in irony than the earlier ones, but no less controlled . . . . Miss Gordimer improves steadily and excitingly from book to book.

Arranged in a chronological order that reveals both her personal and artistic development, *Selected Stories* shows as well Gordimer's awareness that Africa has also changed. The thirty-one stories were written between the ages of twenty and fifty, during a period in which the society itself has aged, sharpened, and grown less amenable. The perspective given to her readers is, therefore, historical—in the sense that the people, situations, relationships, and moments she describes are unique in the history of South Africa. Commenting on this point, Gordimer has said:

> I had wanted to arrange the selection in sequence from the earliest to the latest . . .

because . . . I myself enjoy following the development of a writer. Then I found that . . . the chronological order turns out to be an historical one. The change in social attitudes unconsciously reflected in the stories represents both that of the people in my society—that is to say, history—and my apprehension of it; in the writing, I am acting upon my society, and in the manner of my apprehension, all the time history is acting upon me.

In Gordimer's stories and, indeed, in all her work, politics, race relations, and the turmoil of blacks and whites trapped in South Africa operate as silent pressure and as subject matter. Against the silent backdrop of forest and veld with its geographic isolation and physical apartness, blacks and whites wait in alienation and despair, suffering patiently. [According to Martin Tucker, in his *Africa in Modern Literature,* 1967] Gordimer's work bears the air of "the compassionate observer rather than the passionate protestant, and it is filled with themes of understanding, forgiveness and adjustment." Although she never passes judgment and allows her characters to reveal their own motives and desires, her own attitude remains a unique blend of irony, compassion, and disgust. South Africa is undeniably present in all of her work: from the mining towns of Johannesburg with poor black townships, rich white suburbs, and Greek cafes—well documented in the novels—to the carefully chosen, unforgettable characters—bewildered whites, well intentioned liberals, disillusioned Africans, and determined colonialists—who spring to life from her stories. All is set against a magnificent African landscape—from the River Zaire to the Kalahari Desert, which becomes a dominant presence in the stories, emphasizing the wasted beauty of the occupied land.

Many great short-story writers have influenced Gordimer's work. In acknowledging her debt, she has noted [in *London Magazine,* May, 1963] that the stories of Pauline Smith and Katherine Mansfield "confirmed for me that my own 'colonial' background provided an experience that had scarcely been looked at let alone thought about, except as a source of adventure stories." Other influences include D. H. Lawrence, who changed her "way of looking at landscape and the natural world in general." Henry James made her aware of "form—a single sentence as much as an entire novel." From Hemingway she learned to leave things out, "or, rather, to hear the essential in dialogue." E. M. Forster influenced her handling of human relationships, "later came Conrad; and latest, Camus." Two South African writers, Uys Krige and William Plomer, have also greatly influenced her work. Krige encouraged her to publish in periodicals outside South Africa and provided an introduction to a literary agent in New York. In **"Leaving School"** she describes the effect of her first meeting with Krige: "that day I had a glimpse of—not some spurious 'artist's life,' but, through the poet's person the glint of his purpose—what we are all getting at." Plomer's short story, "The Child of Queen Victoria." made a deep impression on her, causing her to place it with Tolstoy's "The Death of Ivan Ilyich": "the whole idea of what a story could do, be, swept aside the satisfaction of producing something that found its validity in print."

Gordimer's early stories, when compared with the later ones, reveal some weaknesses which she later corrected: "Some of them were awful," she says of the stories in her first collection, adding that they were "concerned with catching the surface shimmer." The technique is particularly evident in **"The Soft Voice of the Serpent"** (1948), where a man who has lost a leg and is attempting to regain his faith in a garden identifies with a locust that also has a leg missing, until the locust flies off—he is bitter with the awareness of his own helplessness, for he had forgotten a locust could fly. The theme is a remarkable one, since the garden where he sits parallels the Garden of Eden. The voice of the serpent, the story implies, comes partly from the world of nature but is also an inner voice which whispers to man the condition of his mortality. The "surface shimmer" is evident in the analogies: the flowers shake "in vehement denial" of the man's hopes; a "first slight wind" lifts "in the slack, furled sail of himself"; the firs "part silkily as a child's fine straight hair in the wind"; and the locust's body is compared to "flimsy paper stretched over a frame of matchstick." In **"The Soft Voice of the Serpent"** Gordimer also uses another technique which she will dispense with later: the ending relies on the technique known as "the bitter bit," a reversal. Her later stories do not depend on surprise endings.

In fifteen of the twenty-one stories, the leading characters are not named, and many of the minor characters are also anonymous. In one story, **"The Catch",** she discusses the reason why several characters fail to learn each other's names: "So their you's and he's and I's took on the positiveness of names, and yet seemed to deepen their sense of communication by the fact that they introduced none of the objectivity that names must always bring." Five years later, however, names have come to represent closer personal relationships. In **"Horn of Plenty"** (1956), Mrs. McCleary, an American living in Johannesburg, is exasperated because her African maid, Rebecca, keeps calling her "Madam" instead of "Mrs. McCleary." She longs for the intimate relationship she had had with her Negro maid in New York. Ironically, Rebecca is confused and finds it difficult to understand Mrs. McCleary's insistence: after all, every white person wants to be called either "Madam" or "Master." Based on her previous experiences, Rebecca has learned to keep an enormous emotional distance between herself and her employers.

The early stories show Gordimer's potential development as a short-story writer. From the very beginning, she demonstrated her skill in the use of imagery; **"The Kindest Thing To Do"** (1945) is an excellent example, although critics agree that it is spoiled by overwriting. The story depends on images of lethargy in both humans and the setting to convey the atmosphere of a hot, lazy afternoon and to portray the dulling of the senses in the main character, a girl. The image of "drooping" is repeated and reinforces the mood of inertia: "Her head, drooping near the drooping, bee-heavy, crumpled paper chalices of the poppies, lifted half-protestingly, her lazy hand brushed the gray specks of insects which flecked the pages of Petrarch's 'Laura in Death.' " The long drawn-out sentences effectively describe the lazy afternoon and the soporific effect of the sun. Some of the later stories in the *The Soft Voice* *of the Serpent* (1952) show the extent of Gordimer's progress in making effective use of a *single* image. In many instances, she allows a single detail to make a revelation on its own, illuminating significant facets of character or emphasizing important points in the story. The recurrent image of the metronome in **"A Commonplace Story"** (1949), for example, tock-tocking even when it is not needed, emphasizes the monotonous existence of the music teacher. An empty box which once contained an expensive face powder in **"La Vie Boheme"** (1949) reveals to a younger sister the economic struggle her elder sister is facing. An African child in **"Ah, Woe Is Me"** (1949) responds to his mother's query as to why he caddies on the golf course instead of going to school by opening his hand to reveal two shining coins.

The first volume also reveals other things about Gordimer's technique. For one thing, it indicates a development in the handling of time. Most of the early stories are limited to a single episode or a very brief span of time. **"The Kindest Thing To Do"** covers a few minutes during which the girl neglects her dog and another few minutes during which she buries a bird that the dog has mutilated and that she herself has killed. The conclusion of the story shows still another few minutes when the girl is at a party, obviously forgetting what appeared to be a traumatic encounter with death. **"The Train from Rhodesia"** (1947) lasts only as long as the train makes the short stop during a long journey, while **"The Soft Voice of the Serpent"** is confined to the single episode described.

"A Present for a Good Girl" (1949) covers a much longer period than any of the previous stories, from September to just before Christmas, during which an old hag of a mother comes to pay installments on an expensive purse for her daughter. The jeweler's shop, the scene in each episode, remains the same as the old woman returns to it, thereby increasing our impression that her daughter must be deserving. When her daughter finally appears, she destroys all our illusions; that the time is Christmas makes for a kind of double irony. From here on, the stories cover longer periods, until they span twenty or thirty years, frequently without flashbacks. They also foreshadow other things to come in Gordimer's technique—the sharp focus at the end of the story and a heavy reliance on contrasts. **"The Train from Rhodesia"** is a good example of both. The train makes a stop on a long journey, and we are shown the rush of a crowd and venders around the train before focusing on a couple in one of the compartments. The technique is effective, for we are shown the overall picture of the Africans' struggle for existence and their reliance on the train for their livelihood. On the other hand, the sharp focus toward the end implies that the Africans are being exploited by the whites: the woman in the compartment is angry at the man for paying a paltry sum for a work of art, a lion carved in wood, showing a remarkable propensity for detail. Gordimer uses the sharp focus at the end increasingly in her later stories.

In discussing Gordimer's first volume of stories, a critic [Honor Tracy, in *New Statesman and Nation,* April 11, 1953] has said "her faults of occasional over-writing, of over-charging with emotion, of mild hysteria even, are the faults of immaturity while her splendid gifts are those of a born story-teller." In *Six Feet of the Country* (1956), her second volume of short stories, Gordimer shows an amazing mastery of the techniques and craft of short-story writing, and her development appears far beyond that of her first volume. Her eye and ear for the conversations and conventions of her surroundings are clearer, more sharply focused, and stylistically perfect; she maintains rigorous and unyielding control over her stories but allows the reader to discover the moral and social truths. Characters are named and more carefully drawn, while similes and metaphors replace other figures of speech and are fully used.

As an artist *within* but not *of* the society she writes about, Gordimer seems to have achieved "solitude" without "alienation": "I was able to let myself out and live in the body with others, as well as—alone—in the mind. . . . The tension between standing apart and being fully involved, that is what makes a writer. That is where we begin." Her heightened powers of observation, coupled with an excessive preoccupation and identification with the lives of others, imply an unusual disinvolvement and detachment which have resulted in lifelike characters. The style of writing is highly discursive. Gordimer takes the reader into confidence but excludes the reader from the action—presenting him with information he cannot adjust to suit his reactions. The approach is "more intellectual." The reader accepts the information in trust. Illumination, indignation, or compassion, which involve the reader in

Nadine Gordimer.

the action and make him understand the story, are left for the end, where a single episode pinpoints the meaning of the story: "Her technique is to present her characters for recognition, and then, by a shake of the kaleidoscope as it were, to reveal the different and truer pattern implicit in the behavior" [John Wakeman, in *New York Times Book Review,* January 10, 1960]. Gordimer's stories can be described as "plotless" because she is "preoccupied not so much with the how, but the why." The technique has proven most effective, despite the fact that she has not always succeeded in conveying the "why."

Of the several stories which exemplify this technique, two in particular are most effective. In **"A Bit of Young Life"** (1952) Mrs. Maisel vacations with her baby at a beach in Durban and becomes the darling of the hotel. Old ladies, young men—even Ed, a lady's man—all succumb to her charm. After she has returned to Johannesburg, they learn of her adulterous behavior which results in a scandalous divorce. Gordimer uses an omniscient viewpoint, which allows the reader to see Mrs. Maisel through the eyes of the other guests; therefore, the reader is beguiled also. At the end of the story Mrs. Maisel is alone in her flat in Johannesburg, having received the photographs of the baby taken by Ed. She finds the guilt of having duped the hotel guests a greater burden than her infidelity. The story is not about how first impressions are deceiving, as it appears. The final glimpse of Mrs. Maisel and an earlier one where she almost breaks down in tears because Ed insists that she cancel her plane reservation make a profound statement on society. Had Gordimer revealed the impending divorce sooner, the hotel's guests would have become a mob prepared to cast the first stones—they execrate her when they learn of the divorce. Mrs. Maisel is thus prevented from seeking out from among the guests the one person who could have helped her through the crisis she was silently undergoing. The ending implies that Ed would have been that person—which increases her guilt feelings.

A purse snatching by a native in **"Is There Nowhere Else Where We Can Meet?"** (1949) takes place on a lonely path across the veld. The incident might have become a melodrama of racial confrontation, but Gordimer chooses to show the hurt compassion of the bruised girl as she limps down the street and out of the story: "The poetic imagery of the girl's consciousness—the sky like gray silk, the platinum and black of the burned-over veld, the minute pleasure of the sticky pine frond—all invite us to share the girl's sense of wholeness. It is a sense of wholeness, symmetrical and balanced in design which includes the native when he first appears. . . . he completes the design, orderly and interesting in the girl's musings" [Robert Haugh, in *Nadine Gordimer,* 1974]. The assault, therefore, is as much a psychic bruise to the girl's sense of order as to her purse and person. The girl's awareness saves the story by sharing with the reader a truer, more universally human experience in a racial situation. The native is elevated above the condescension of the "victim" and shares the sadness of the human dilemma. He becomes "dignified by the girl's vision of his human potentiality," whereas "the role of 'victim,' in the polarized idiom of race conflict, offers no such dignity." It offers, instead, "pathos and sentiment." Although the story is simple, with few events,

"it rings like a carillon, true and right in its statement of sorrow and compassion. Among Miss Gordimer's many superb stories, it ranks first in my judgment for its beauty of conception, in lyric imagery, in its deft avoidance of tempting melodrama, in its total, profound achievement" [Haugh, *Nadine Gordimer*].

Friday's Footprints (1960) and *Not For Publication* (1965), Gordimer's third and fourth volumes of stories, place her in the ranks of the most distinguished modern writers. Her characters are incisively drawn from many strata of society, linked by their common loneliness and their inability to touch each others' lives except in very rare, fleeting moments. Many of Gordimer's stories portray the isolation of the individual, both black and white—in particular, the alienation among Europeans in her country. A character in her second novel, *A World of Strangers* (1958), describes it as: "Loneliness; of a special kind. Our loneliness. The lack of a common human identity. The loneliness of a powerful minority." This powerful minority is responsible for the circumstances of non-whites in their country and shares in a kind of collective guilt. They are made aware of their guilt when they travel to other countries: "That was the first time I encountered what I was soon to recognize as a familiar attitude among South Africans: an unexpected desire to dissociate themselves from their milieu, a wish to make it clear they were not taken in, even by themselves." The method of handling the loneliness, the guilt, and dissociating themselves from their milieu is described by Anna Louw, an Afrikaner persecuted by the government for fighting against apartheid: "you must understand that you are in a country where there are all sorts of different ways of talking about or rather dealing with this thing. One of the ways is not talk about it at all. Not to deal with it at all."

Livingstone's Companions (1971), Gordimer's fifth volume of stories, is made up of "twice-told" tales, for the stories have first appeared in various magazines. The title of the volume is more than just the title of the first story in the collection. Gordimer has commented that everyone who lives and travels in Africa is, in a real sense, a companion of Dr. Livingstone, the famous nineteenth-century explorer of the continent. He, more than anyone else, was responsible for bringing African and European cultures face to face in a confrontation; and as Gordimer says, the problems are still being solved "in reality and irony." These stories focus on character rather than events; they are about human relationships, the ways in which people see one another and see themselves. They involve chance encounters which bring people together in new, unforeseen ways. Several of the stories use relationships among members of families, showing how we reveal ourselves to one another in times of domestic crisis, whether the crisis is, on the surface, trivial or important. Gordimer is always sensitive to minority groups and their problems and has included in this collection stories about Jews, black Africans, and Asiatics living in Africa. In some instances she uses the perspective available to her as a woman; in others, her perspective as a liberal woman. These stories are varied, and they are sometimes ambiguous.

Nadine Gordimer's works do not yield simple themes or

interpretations. One can talk about "the loss of innocence, of growing up or of learning about death and the horror of loneliness" or "about love denied where love is most difficult but desperately needed . . . about the violations of love, about injury to one not loved enough . . . undeserved love, given from simple hearts." If her works have a single, predominant theme, it is that "men are not born brothers; they have to discover each other." In the concluding paragraphs of the introduction to *Selected Stories,* she says:

> My time and place have been twentieth-century Africa. Emerging from it, immersed in it, the first form in which I wrote was the short story. I write fewer and fewer stories, now, and more novels, but I don't think I shall ever stop writing stories. . . . A short story *occurs,* in the imaginative sense. To write one is to express from a situation in the exterior or interior world the life-giving drop—sweat, tear, semen, saliva—that will spread an intensity on the page; burn a hole in it.

[According to Haugh] Nadine Gordimer's stories "rank with the finest of their kind," "the best of Chekhov, Katherine Mansfield, Hemingway, James Joyce's *Dubliners."* Although they arise from the African scene, they are not about Africa; they reveal Gordimer's ability to plunge to the depths of human personality and to expose those hidden feelings which we dare not face. Consequently, they have universal appeal.

Christopher Lehmann-Haupt (essay date 1984)

SOURCE: A review of *Something Out There,* in *The New York Times,* July 9, 1984, p. C17.

[*Lehmann-Haupt is a Scottish-born American critic. In the following favorable review, he explores the varying narrative techniques employed in* Something Out There.]

Betrayal, crimes of conscience, the anguish of apartheid—the themes are familiar in this fine new collection of nine stories and a novella by Nadine Gordimer, most of them set in her native South Africa. What is surprising is the behavior of her characters. In one, a black woman you believe to be falling in love with a terrorist, whom she and her husband are hiding in their home, ends up going to the police and reporting the fugitive.

In another, a man who admits to his lover that he has been spying on her is answered by an embrace, we finish the story wondering who really has undermined whom. In **"Letter From His Father"** Hermann Kafka speaks from beyond the grave and answers the "Letter to His Father" that Franz Kafka wrote but never sent him: "You wake up as a bug, you give a lecture as an ape. Do any of these wonderful scholars think what this meant to me, having a son who didn't have enough self-respect to feel himself a man?" (Only Miss Gordimer could go so far in being sympathetic to the underdog's overdog, as it were, yet still be funny about it.)

These shorter stories establish a pattern of emotional response. Except in the Hermann Kafka letter, the author

does not depart radically from traditional narrative technique. Her stock-in-trade is her unerring eye for the physical and psychological detail, her laserlike concentration of the dramatic turning point—what Joyce's Dedalus would have called epiphany, or a Hollywood hack "the old switcheroo."

With swiftness and precision, she marshals our sympathies, sets the pace of her developments and narrows her options sufficiently to render her surprises plausible. We know that there will be a twist concerning the old letters that Beryl Fels discovers in **"Rags and Bones,"** just as we know that something will spoil the retirement plans of the couple in **"Sins of the Third Age."** But such is the subtlety of her stories' psychology that it is impossible to anticipate their outcome as a mere turning of their plots.

Then, having been trained like a Pavlov dog to expect the unexpected, we come to the title piece, a 90-odd-page story called **"Something Out There."** Again, as in the stories that precede it, the plot of the novella is thick with event. Some wild creature is marauding the plush suburbs of Johannesburg, stealing food, killing family poets, frightening people. No one can figure out what it is—a man, some sort of ape, perhaps a wildcat—but it makes "a nice change from the usual sort of news, these days."

"Nothing but strikes, exchanges of insults between factions of what used to be a power to be relied upon, disputes over boundaries that had been supposed to divide peace and prosperity between all," the passage continues.

Meanwhile, unnoticed by anyone, a young white couple and two black men take up residence in a framehouse outside Johannesburg and begin their preparations to blow up a nearby power station. As developments in the parallel plots unfold, we brace ourselves for their covergence—for the switcheroo or the moment of epiphany.

But there really isn't any. The twist is the difference in the story's technique. Not only does Miss Gordimer employ here the sudden shifts in point of view and the dialogue without quotation marks that she first introduced in her novel *Burger's Daughter* (1979), she also departs from the method of the collection's other stories by never tying up the package. We are left to contemplate the mystery of the wild creature, the provenance of a sacred work of art in the municipal art gallery and the deep history of a "mine-working" in which the terrorists at one point hide themselves.

"No one knows that with the brief occupation of Vusi and Eddie," the story concludes, "and the terrible tools that were all they had to work with a circle was closed; because before the gold-rush prospectors of the 1890s, centuries before time was measured, here, in such units, there was an ancient mine-working out there, and metals precious to men were discovered, dug and smelted, for themselves, by black men."

One appreciates the subtleties of this precisely crafted novella—the smug self-absorption of the Afrikaner real-estate couple who rent the farm to the terrorists, the despair of an old black retainer who loses his job when the farm changes hands, the irony that the white establishment seems more agitated by the rampaging beast than by the social revolution that is happening around it.

But is the story's final point really that the land belonged to "black men" before Europeans intruded? Is it supposed to be some kind of dig at the whites that they nickname the wild creature King Kong, or are we simply to accept him as a symbol of nature's corruption in the face of human disorder? I may be missing the real point, but I think I prefer Miss Gordimer in her less radical moods. I like the stories in this volume that show off what she's best at—the stories in which the complexity of human nature overwhelms ideology.

Salman Rushdie   (essay date 1984)

SOURCE: "No One Is Ever Safe," in *The New York Times Book Review,* July 29, 1984, pp. 7-8.

[*An Indian novelist, nonfiction writer, and critic, Rushdie is best known for his controversial treatment of Islam in his novel* The Satanic Verses *(1988). In the review below, he provides a thematic treatment of* Something Out There, *focusing on Gordimer's theme of betrayal.*]

Great white sharks, killer bees, werewolves, devils, alien horrors bursting from the chests of movie spacemen: The popular culture of our fearful times has provided us with so many variations on the ancient myth of the Beast, the "something" lurking out there that hunts us and is hunted by us, as to make it one of the defining metaphors of the age. In the jungle of the cities, we live among our accumulations of things behind doors garlanded with locks and chains, and find it all too easy to fear the unforeseeable, all-destroying coming of the Ogre—Charles Manson, the Ayatollah Khomeini, the Blob from Outer Space, Clearly, many of these forebodings are the product of affluence and of power. The haves and the powerful, fearing the uprising of the have-nots and the powerless, dream of them as monsters.

There is a wild animal roaming around the affluent white suburbs of Johannesburg in the long novella that gives its title to Nadine Gordimer's new collection [*Something Out There*]; but Miss Gordimer is the least lurid of writers, and her creature's worst offense is to bite a woman on the shoulder. Her prose is cool and meticulous, and the sightings of her Beast—probably a baboon, it is said—are for the most part low-key, even domestic; a leg of venison stolen from its hook in Mariella Chapman's kitchen; a photograph of thrashing treetops taken by the 13-year-old schoolboy Stanley Dobrow at his bar mitzvah; a shape, a pair of eyes seen in the vegetation at the edge of an exclusive golf course. And at the end of the piece the creature is quite matter-of-factly demystified; dead in a lane, it is no nightmare monster, but "only a baboon, after all; not an orangoutan, not a chimpanzee—just a native species." White South Africans have no need of dream ogres: it is reality that they fear, and the something out there is the future. The Naas Kloppers, the van Gelders and all the other rather stupid, somewhat caricatured bigots with whom Nadine Gordimer populates her tale go to some trouble to protect themselves, but the baboon shows them a most uncomfortable truth: "The Bokkie Scholtzs' house

is burglar-proofed, has fine wires on windows and doors which activate an alarm . . . They have a half-breed Rottweiler who was asleep, apparently, on the front stoop, when the attack came. It just shows you—whatever you do, you can't call yourself safe."

This quality of subversion, this deliberate use of banality in order to disturb, is what sets Miss Gordimer's version of the Beast myth apart. The pulp fiction and cinema that exploit this theme usually offer no more than an enjoyable scare, a sanitized *frisson*; they actually reassure us while pretending to terrify, ***Something Out There*** concentrates, by contrast, on the minutiae of the real world. The art lies in the refusal of all exaggeration, all hyperbole. From this refusal springs the story's authority, its unsettling menace. "Whatever you do, you can't call yourself safe."

A second narrative counterpoints that of the baboon. The other "something" out there beyond the white suburbs is a cell of four terrorists, two black men and a white couple, or rather, a white man and woman who are no longer lovers. Here again, Nadine Gordimer's purpose is to demystify a kind of 20th-century Beast. The four insurgents, listening to antiterrorist rhetoric on the radio, "were accustomed to smile as people will when they must realize that those being referred to as monsters are the human beings drinking a glass of water, cutting a hang-nail, writing a letter, in the same room; are themselves."

While the terrorists wait for the right time to blow up a power station, Miss Gordimer brings them expertly to life, not as beasts, not orangoutans or chimpanzees. Just a native species. She gives us, in effect, portraits of two rather differently odd couples—the white man and woman, Charles and Joy, awkward both with their black colleagues and with each other; and the black men: Eddie, the outgoing one, who jeopardizes their mission by hitching a ride into town for a night among the bright lights, and Vusi, the battle-hardened one, the still center of the group. The stilted, damaged humanity of this foursome is set against the bluff inhumanity of the inhabitants of the rich suburbs. Mr. and Mrs. Naas Klopper, the real-estate agent and his biscuit-making wife, with their split-level lounge and their arsenal of labor-saving devices and their impala-skin bar stools, are perhaps the story's real beasts.

The tone remains muted to the very end. The climax of the terrorist plot is made to happen, so to speak, offstage; the lives of Charles and Joy and Eddie and Vusi fade into hints, rumors, readings between the lines of the news. And the baboon, as we have seen, is simply shot. But then, in the last couple of pages, comes a brilliant stroke. Rising above its characters' essential unknowability ("Nobody really knows . . . whom they believed themselves to be"), and also their ignorance of their own histories and genealogies, the narrative, in a kind of rage against this excess of unknowing, places them all upon the map of history—puts them firmly in their context, or place. And just as Dr. Grahame Fraser-Smith, when he looked into the baboon's eyes on a golf course, fancied himself to be looking "back into a consciousness from which part of his own came," to be closing a circle, so the novella at its conclusion closes a circle, joining the far-off past to the approaching future;

and both of them (ominously for all the Kloppers caught within the circle's closing jaws) are black.

There are nine other stories in this collection, not all of them of the same distinction as the novella. One seems to me an unmitigated disaster. Miss Gordimer has taken upon herself the task of writing, on Hermann Kafka's behalf, a reply to his son's famous and never-sent "Letter to His Father." **"Letter From His Father"** is a 20-page, arch embarrassment, full of Homely Wisdom ("Well, we had to accept what God gave"), Literary Nudging ("Some say you were also some kind of prophet") and occasional fits of Thigh-Slapping ("Hah! I know I'm no intellectual, but I knew how to live!"). It may well be the case that Franz was unfair to Papa, but I am afraid Miss Gordimer has not done the old man any favors, either.

A second story, **"Rags and Bones,"** fails to escape the trap of inconsequentiality. It begins casually: "A woman named Beryl Fels recently picked up an old tin chest in a junk shop." And it remains desultory to the end. In the tin chest is a bundle of letters; they draw Beryl Fels into the story of an affair that took place in the 1940's between a distinguished male scientist and an equally distinguished woman writer. The lovers feel obliged to keep their secret, because "we are both people in the public eye; it's the price or the reward, God knows, of what we both happen to be." But when Beryl Fels looks into their lives, she can find no trace of either of them. The writer is unknown, not one of her books in print; the scientist has likewise vanished from the record. This is intended, I take it, as a cruel irony—the pain of their secrecy rendered absurd by the disintegration of their public status. But the story's casual tone, its reluctance to allow any heightening of feeling, prevents the irony from being felt by the reader.

Fortunately, the other seven stories are excellent. **"Blinder"** is about Rose, an old family retainer with a weakness for going on alcoholic binges, who suddenly has to cope with a different sort of befuddlement, a different "blinder"—that is, the death of her lover, Ephraim. This brief story is passionate, moving and beautiful. **"A Correspondence Course"** describes the friendship that grows between a young woman and a political prisoner, through the letters they write to each other. But the important character is Pat Haberman, the mother of the young woman, Harriet. While the man is safely in jail, she encourages the correspondence, even talks about it proudly to others, as proof of her liberalism. But then the man escapes, and comes to the house, and in an extraordinary final paragraph,

> Liquid flashes like the sweeps of heat that had gone through her blood at fifty took Pat to her bedroom. She locked that door, wanted to beat upon it, whimper. . . . To do something with her hands she filled a tooth-glass at the wash-hand basin and, a prisoner tending his one sprig of green, gave water to the pot of African violets for what she had done, done to her darling girl, *done for.*

The game has turned real, and, as we have seen, reality in Miss Gordimer's world is a thing of which to be afraid.

The remaining stories can be read as variations on the theme of betrayal. (And, of course, in the Kafka story, Miss Gordimer's Hermann is accusing Franz of betrayal, too, of betraying his family and his Judaism; and Pat Haberman in **"A Correspondence Course"** comes to feel she has betrayed her daughter.) In **"Sins of the Third Age,"** the treachery is sexual. The carefully-laid retirement plans of an elderly couple, Peter and Mania, are irrevocably altered when Peter has an affair; even when he chooses to put this affair behind him, the damage cannot be undone. Paradise has been lost. **"Terminal"** presents another version of the treason of lovers. A woman dying of an incurable disease makes a pact with her husband that he will not prevent her suicide. Her last act is to leave him a note: "Keep your promise. Don't have me revived." But he does; and when, after taking the pills, she has the "terror of feeling herself waking from it," the traitor is holding her hand.

And inevitably there are the betrayals of politics. In **"A City of the Dead, A City of the Living,"** in which Miss Gordimer magnificently describes life in the black ghetto, a poor woman, oppressed by the tension of having a wanted man hiding in her cramped home, squeals to the police. Her treason teaches her nothing; she longs to tell everyone, "I don't know why I did it," but nobody asks. Instead, people spit. In **"Crimes of Conscience,"** conversely, we see that betrayal can be a kind of education. The story is about a Government-paid infiltrator, Felterman, who seduces a radical woman in order to spy on her group. He senses a reserve in her, as if she were waiting for him to speak some password. Finally he discovers it: "I've been spying on you," he confesses, and she takes his head in her hands.

"At the Rendezvous of Victory" is a classic cameo portrait—of the guerrilla "general" for whom, after the success of his revolution, his old friend, now the Prime Minister of the newly-liberated nation, has less and less time. Miss Gordimer's portrait of Sinclair "General Giant" Zwedu, the discarded hero who will not toe the line and who becomes an embarrassment, is very deeply felt and imagined; and from Che Guevara, kept at a distance by Castro after their triumph, to the revolutionary fighters of present-day black Africa, it is a portrait with many echoes in real life. Like most of the stories in what is, in spite of a couple of false notes, a distinguished collection, it makes its point and creates its resonances not by any exaggeration or flashiness, but by the scrupulous depiction of what all Nadine Gordimer's readers will instantly recognize as the unvarnished truth.

Melvyn Hill (essay date 1984)

SOURCE: "The Politics of Good Intentions," in *VLS*, No. 28, September, 1984, pp. 6-8.

[In the following essay, Hill discusses defining characteristics of Gordimer's fiction, in particular the impact of South Africa's political and social landscape on her work.]

[Gordimer is] someone trapped in a world she cannot change. Her hope resides in a revolution others will have to bring about; her dream revolves in circles of betrayal, trust, and distrust. Gordimer is a master of the short story because she's compelled to be such a consummate ironist. Although she's best known for her novels, some of her finest writing and thinking occurs in the eight volumes of short stories she has published over the past 30 years. She's a virtuoso miniaturist, finding the precise form to represent an experience and the insight that attends it. But writing no more releases Gordimer from her impasse than it frees her readers (the pain in her stories makes them almost impossible to read all at once).

Despite recent invocations of revolution—in her most recent novel, *July's People,* and her novella **"Something Out There,"** the title story in her new collection—Gordimer's premises are not truly revolutionary. She shows the structure of apartheid but cannot offer a vision of the future. Revolutions reveal themselves only to those who make them. In **"Something Out There,"** Gordimer sets two black and two white saboteurs executing a plan to blow up a power station against suburbanites engaged by the romance of a monkey foraging in their backyards. The whites' fascination with wild animals merely distracts them from the pain and struggle imposed by apartheid. At the end of the story, Gordimer insists on the meaning of the revolutionary act she depicts: the blacks are returning to claim their land. (She was clearly inspired by the success of the African National Congress, whose saboteurs blew up the Koeberg nuclear power station, near Cape Town.) But an act of sabotage, even a brilliant and daring one, is a far cry from the revolving of power to blacks. Gordimer's politics are a matter of not being able to see the way to effective action, a matter of good intentions.

In her introduction to the *Selected Stories,* she confesses:

> There are some stories I have gone on writing, again and again, all my life, not so much because the themes are obsessional but because I found other ways to take hold of them. . . . I felt for the touch that would release the spring that shuts off appearance from reality.

A true passion is anything but an obsession; obsessions are traps that hold us back from experience, while passions seek a way to render eternally present an experience that seems true or beautiful or good. Gordimer is truly passionate in her loyalty to experience and dedication to craft. But she's also trapped. A dreamer who again and again repeats the same dream can be relieved of the repetition only by understanding its meaning. Gordimer repeats the same themes, unable to register their full meaning or to act on their imperative: the political transformation of a racist state. Her central theme—the one that defines her most passionate work and reveals her impasse at its most poignant—concerns whites and blacks, an African analogy to the theme of gentile and Jew in European writing. Gordimer is a Transvaal Jew, raised in Springs, on the gold-mining belt, and her husband is a refugee from Hitler's Final Solution. Widespread anti-Semitism among white South Africans, especially in the wake of the Third Reich, no doubt sharpened Gordimer's sensitivities for her vocation.

The conventional white South African thoughtlessly declares, "Ek is 'n Afrikaner" or "I am an African," but as soon as a black African enters the scene, these Afrikaners become European. They're terrified of being mistaken for black, and for the blacks they are nothing but the *witbaas* or *witnooi,* the white master or madam. Born into this world, Gordimer has taken on a Jewish hope of transcending the conflict between master and slave; that conflict, as Nietzsche pointed out, has dogged the Jewish relationship to Western society since Christianity began labeling the Jews as oppressors while subjecting them to constant oppression. Nietzsche claimed that the real oppression perpetrated by Jews was to have invented the religion to which the gentiles became bound. Gordimer's desire to be a white African, to forge an authentic white African consciousness, oppresses white South Africans who prefer to think of themselves as European. They resent her because she works on their conscience. She is the Jew who reminds Gentiles of the articles of Christian faith.

Gordimer opened her *Selected Stories* with **"Is There Nowhere Else We Can Meet,"** the account of a young white woman whose purse is snatched by a destitute and bedraggled black man on the veld—that vast, empty place outside society, the only place in South Africa where whites are unprotected by the trappings of their power. Because white South Africans are in thrall to the fear of violence, a petty theft by a starving man can take on the aura of murder and rape. **"The Life of the Imagination"** relocates this place where black meets white in the erotic fantasies of a suburban white woman who has cherished a dream of becoming "creative." Tired of dreaming, she starts a hot and hopeless affair with her children's doctor. Gordimer, writing with faultless grace, had me believing, almost to the end of the tale, that Barbara was about to come into her own as an artist. Even after Gordimer springs the affair on her unsuspecting readers—Barbara herself is taken by surprise—I kept waiting for the character to discover her work. The denouement comes late one night, after the couple has made love for the first time in the bed Barbara otherwise shares with her husband. The doctor has neglected to close the door through which he came and left. She listens to it bang in the wind, and imagines the following scene:

> They would come in unheard, with that wind, and approach through the house, black men with their knives in their hands. She, who has never submitted to this sort of fear ever in her life, could hear them coming, hear them breathe under their dirty rag masks and their *tsotsi* caps. . . . She was empty, unable to summon anything but this stale fantasy shared with the whole town, the whole white population. She lay there possessed by it, and she thought, she violently longed—they will come straight into the room and stick a knife in me. No time to cry out. Quick. Deep. Over.

Then, bringing us back to the quotidians Gordimer writes:

> The light came instead. Her sons began to play the noisy whispering games of children, about the house in the very early morning.

The innocence of first light, of children contrasts with the perversity of a world that transforms racial and sexual difference into the occasion for violence.

Though Gordimer, too, is trapped by South African reality, she lives outside the confines of white power to the extent that she can depict the world it has created. She stands, thinking, in a place where black and white seldom meet, a place where the truth of their relationship can emerge. Barbara's image of marauders, with "their dirty rag masks and their *tsotsi* caps," recalls the black robber on the veld who "had only a filthy rag—part of an old shirt? —without sleeves and frayed away into a great gap from underarm to waist." These ruined characters are the victims of white violation; ironically, they are as much the objects of white desire as of white terror. The *witsooi* and *witbaas* fear but crave violation by their victims, the source of their violent privilege. Without explicitly indicating the white bourgeoisie, Gordimer has exposed their decadence, the sole distinction they cart boast by way of an identity. And in her ironic, measured, and indirect way, she tells their story: that is her place in their world. For whites, the significance of Africa is what they have repressed, both politically and sexually. In **"Livingstone's Companions,"** an American reporter goes looking for the graves of those who died on the explorer's expedition. Gordimer leads Carl church through a complicated and tedious series of encounters that seem to be mere distraction from his assignment. He gets involved with a foursome—mother, absent stepfather, son, son's girlfriend, all white—who make a stab at running a shabby resort overlooking the explorers' graves. Gordimer delineates the neurotic sexual involvements of this foursome with rare skill, but to no apparent purpose: until the end of the story (she loves to bowl you over with her insight after convincing you she has nothing much to say), when Church suddenly remembers that he's supposed to visit the graves, those signifiers of the first whites in Africa, and relives the missionaries' moment of truth.

> It was difficult to breathe; it must have been hell
> to die here, in this unbearable weight of beauty
> not shared with the known world, licked in the
> face by the furred tongue of this heat.

Beauty unknown by the white world—repressed, you might say—returns in the form of heat that licks you with its furred tongue. This is enough to kill any respectable white explorer, or foursome. Gordimer's point, of course, is that poor Livingstone never found Africa. Those graves mark the place where the whites tried to bury a continent.

Repression often entails a betrayal of the original, whether a part of oneself or the truth of a situation. In **"The African Magician,"** Gordimer homes in on this betrayal. A congolese hypnotist has put a young white woman under his spell, only to have this act interrupted by white men in the audience. At the simplest level Gordimer seems to be saying that the whites could not abide this display of the black man's hypnotic sexuality. But the whites always project onto blacks their own repressed sex and violence, and then deplore them for it. Hypnosis, after all, works as a phenomenon of transference, in which the question of love is at stake. And it is love that the whites betray, because they cannot imagine blacks capable of love. Gordimer describes the young woman: "One of the disciples might have come before Christ like that. There was the peace of absolute trust in it." These whites have re-

pressed the Christian love that the missionaries preached in Africa. They betray themselves as much as they betray the magician's gentle and pious authority.

White South Africa—both English and Afrikaans—prides itself on its Christianity. And Gordimer often uses the Christian doctrine of love, or simply of charity, as a lens to focus on the way whites treat blacks. This leads to some of her most painful and hate-filled stories; the meanness and cruelty of these bible-thumping fundamentalists send shivers down the spine. In **"The Train from Rhodesia,"** a young man gives his sweetheart a toy lion he bought from an old black man, having beaten down the price from 35 cents to about 15 and then made the old man run after the train to get his money. The woman is mortified. "She sat there, sick. A weariness, a tastelessness, the discovery of a void made her hands slacken their grip, atrophy emptily, as if the hour was not worth their grasp."

Time and again Gordimer's stories have made me wonder whether I'm losing my grip. She evokes a brutality in the day-to-day details of like that throws me back to Dickens for a comparable sense of self-justifying cruelty, humiliation, and suffering. Gordimer ends **"The Train from Rhodesia"** with:

> The train had cast the station like a skin. It
> called out to the sky, I'm coming, I'm coming;
> and again, there was no answer.

The distancing quality of this image gives readers the chance to experience Gordimer's grief and fury without a hint of Dickensian sentimentality. Instead, the silence of the superintending sky offers a vision of an unutterably grim world. But these are all relatively early stories; the later work becomes increasingly straightforward about politics, and more desperate.

Daniel Mngoma in **"Something for the Time Being"** and Mrs. Bamjee in **"A Chip of Glass Ruby"** are heroes of the South African struggle. He gives up everything for the chance to fight apartheid, while his white sympathizers give only the little they believe they can without taking a risk. Daniel Mngoma says, "You think straight in prison because you've got nothing to lose. Nobody thinks straight, outside. They don't want to hear you." Mrs. Bamjee fights, as her daughter tells us, ". . . because she doesn't want anybody to be left out. It's because she always remembers; remembers everything—people without somewhere to live, hungry kids, boys who can't get educated—remembers all the time. That's how Ma is." Mngoma goes to jail for the sake of freedom and dignity; Bamjee goes out of the kindness of her heart. Both are silenced. So much for hope.

"A Correspondence Course," from *Something Out There,* is another recent story that explicitly confronts politics. Roland Carter, a white political prisoner, writes to a young white woman named Harriet Haberman, whose work he has admired in an academic journal. Harriet's mother, a liberal and humane woman, encourages the correspondence and takes pride in it:

> There were often appropriate turns in con-
> versation . . . for her to remark on how wonder-
> fully Roland Carter, already four years in pris-

on, kept his spirit unbroken, his mind lively, could still make jokes—her daughter Harriet exchanged letters with him. This remark would immediately "place" her and her daughter in respect. . . . Sometimes she added what a pity it was that more people who talked liberalism didn't make the effort to write to political prisoners, show them they were still regarded by some as part of the community. Did people realize that in South Africa common criminals, thieves and forgers, were better treated than prisoners of conscience?

But when Roland Carter escapes from prison and shows up to claim her daughter's hand, Mrs. Haberman is tortured with remorse about the way she has raised Harriet, now condemned to a life in exile, or to the underground. "To do something with her hands, she filled a tooth-glass at the wash-hand basin and, a prisoner tending his one sprig of green, gave water to the pot of African violets for what she had done, done to her darling girl, *done for.*" Decency is enough to get an ordinary citizen into serious trouble. An abyss underlies the most commonplace reality.

In **"Something Out There,"** a white security policeman says:

> There's something wrong with all these people who become enemies of their own country. . . . They're enemies because they can't enjoy their lives the way a normal white person in South Africa does.

The twist in Gordimer's new collection, the fateful note of despair, arises from a profound and pervasive sense of betrayal. Nobody in South Africa seems free of this sense, whether they know it or hide it from themselves. If Mrs. Haberman regrets "what she had done to her darling girl," imagine the pain of Alison Jane Ross, in **"Crimes of Conscience."** Alison, active in the political underground, falls in love with Felterman, who finally confesses he's a spy for the secret police. Gordimer once more traces the trouble back to the erotic. Spies depend on exploiting private sources of vulnerability, and sex is very private indeed. "Nobody knows how secret police recognize likely candidates; it is as mysterious as sexing chickens," she writes. Sex becomes a vehicle of betrayal: Felterman is Judas, the inverse of the black magician.

In **"Africa Emergent,"** the white friends of a black man decide they can trust him only after the secret police have put him in jail: "He's proved himself, hasn't he?" In **"A City of the Dead, A City of the Living,"** a black revolutionary seeks refuge with a respectable young black couple rather than take shelter in Ma Redebe's shebeen, or speakeasy, where the low-life characters hang out. Nanike Moreke, the housewife, turns out to be so desperate to protect the little she has that she betrays her guest, and Gordimer achieves one of her typical ironies:

> A week after the man was taken away that Sunday by the security police, Ma Redebe again met Moreke's wife in their street. The shebeenkeeper gazed at her for a moment, and spat.

Under the constant surveillance of security police, betray-

al becomes a way of life. Hannah Arendt once said about Nazi Germany, "If you go through a situation like totalitarianism, the first thing you know is the following: you *never* know how somebody will act." Gordimer's point is the same: you can never tell enemy from friend. With her emphasis on the theme of trust and betrayal, she gives us the story of Jesus from the pen of a Jew.

Although **"Something Out There"** ends on a revolutionary note, what is most convincing—and hopeful—in the story is not the act of sabotage, but the relationship that emerges between the two whites and two blacks. This "absolute trust," to use Gordimer's term from **"The African Magician,"** again evokes her Christian theme. Yet because that trust is premised on a shared, encompassing danger, it remains embedded in a paranoid structure. The difference is that the lines have been clearly drawn: by committing themselves to action, the saboteurs are confronting the issue of who is the enemy. And there it is, out in the open, begging the question. Gordimer has moved from a critique inspired by the Christian hope for love and trust between neighbors to the hope for future revolution.

For years now people have been expecting and predicting a black revolution in South Africa; Gordimer is one of the well-intentioned liberals who proclaim the justice and inevitability of that day. But her writing does not go beyond the impasse of her carefully cultivated white African consciousness. Gordimer's hope for revolution rests with others. Her writing exemplifies Hegel's concept of the "beautiful soul": being white, she cannot escape guilt, and does penance through her writing instead of acting.

The extent of Gordimer's hesitation to act came through dramatically during a lecture she gave a couple of years ago at the Institute for the Humanities; after a lengthy denunciation of the white regime in which she touched base with every left-wing theorist of note, she arrived at the subject of the draft in South Africa. Black revolutionaries, she said, were calling for the white boys to refuse their military service. She, however, objected, because this would force them into jail or exile. Last spring she told *People* magazine that she'd advised her own son to serve. This strikes me as an essential clue to Gordimer's politics, and the key to her impasse: she does not want liberal young whites to leave the country or become outlaws. She wants the system to change, but also wants her son to remain within the system.

Despite her acute portrait of the limits of decency in the case of Mrs. Haberman, the mother who loses her daughter to a white revolutionary, Gordimer takes the same stand. She believes it is still possible for decent people who remain within the law to have an effect. As a South African who had to grapple with whether to serve in the military, I find this position disturbing. To the extent that she supports the military, Gordimer shares the fundamental bad faith of white South Africa—that there is, in fact, a law. The omnipresence of the military and the police in South Africa reveals the truth of white-black relations: whites rule blacks by force, and the institutions they have modeled on the West merely camouflage the pervasive violence in their society.

The Botha government, which represents the so-called *verligte,* or enlightened, wing of the Nationalist Party, has lifted the ban on Gordimer's books. Having discarded those elements of the Party most closely tied to Hendrik Verwoerd's union of theology and race politics, this regime is less obsessed with the question of conscience in politics. It is less rigid in the ideology of apartheid—which has become a dirty word in South Africa—and readier to impose its will through blackmail, that fine art of combining violence with corruption. Botha's success can be measured by the result of the Nkomati accord he recently signed with Samora Machel. Already the African National Congress has been hounded out of Mozambique in return for Botha's agreement to halt South African support for the guerrillas fighting Machel's government. And similar pressure is being applied to Lesotho, Botswana, Swaziland, Zimbabwe, and Angola, as well as to the SWAPO leadership in Namibia. Inside South Africa, Botha is also trying to get nonwhites to comply. He has conceded limited power to people of mixed race and to the East Indians. Soon he will be offering a little something to the urbanized blacks. If his plan works, it is not inconceivable that one day all of these groups will advise their sons to serve in the draft.

In preparing this new phase of apartheid, he seems to have learned a lesson from Frantz Fanon, an unlikely teacher: with a little luck Botha may be able to cover enough black and brown skins with white masks to ensure that apartheid becomes a tyranny of the majority. There are no hints of this development in Gordimer's latest book. (Botha's impact has sneaked up on South Africa, like one of Gordimer's drawnout indirections that suddenly yields a surprise.) But there is an unrelenting and fateful twist to the variations on her constant themes, an ever deeper sense of despair—the dark side of the austere beauty she cultivates from her impasse. Gordimer is trapped in a state that coerces through fear of its army and secret police, and through the false hopes engendered by corruption. A tyranny that endures has to channel desire into the perversities of betrayal.

Gordimer's tortuous return to betrayal in erotic and political relations suggests that she is hesitating over a cup of truth too bitter even for her—perhaps because it would take away her fondest hope that, as a writer and a Jew, she can be exempt. Without recognizing the sin committed in the act of founding South Africa, one cannot understand that the society perpetuates apartheid to repress the guilt of its origins. Betrayal serves as a defense against recognizing the original sin—the one biblical theme Gordimer neglects. Unless there is a law that binds everyone to the same rules, violence and guilt will exact their toll down the generations.

Whites will continue to dominate in South Africa precisely because the system is so efficient in eliminating its opposition and corrupting the oppressed. As Daniel Mngoma says, too many people believe they have something to lose. The sad truth is that they are not prepared to lose it.

Leon Wieseltier   (essay date 1984)

SOURCE: "Afterword," in *Salmagundi,* No. 62, Winter, 1984, pp. 193-96.

[*Below, Wieseltier discusses the effects of apartheid on Gordimer's black and white characters in "Something Out There."*]

"Each torpid turn of the world has such disinherited children, / to whom no longer what's been, and not yet what's coming, belongs," Rilke wrote in 1922, in a castle. In 1930, in a prison, a similar inspiration about the inconclusiveness of the modern age came to Gramsci. "The crisis consists precisely in the fact that the old is dying and the new cannot be born," he wrote; and went on to add, in the manner of an intellectual, "in this interregnum a great variety of morbid symptoms appear." In 1981 Nadine Gordimer, whose work has married lyricism to criticism in a way that tempts you to talk of greatness, chose Gramsci's sentence for the epigraph of *July's People,* perhaps her most representative fiction; and in a lecture a year later, referring again to Gramsci (and casually to Rilke), she rigorously described the present period in South Africa, a country of a few castles constructed over many prisons, as an interregnum. It is a time, she said, in which white superiority has begun to crumble before "the black state that is coming." Into this gap this writer steps. Gordimer's work is classic in its debt to crisis and to change. From a decline in certainty comes a rise in clarity. (It did first in Isaiah 37:3 to whom all these moderns owe this metaphor of history's parturition.)

I have been asked to comment on **"Something Out There."** I have read some of Gordimer's novels and stories, but not nearly all. Like any situation in which evil is easy to spot, the South African situation is one I think I know; but I suspect that I don't. Enormity is not simple; it is merely large. It is hard for me to separate Gordimer, therefore, from the news that she brings. If I dwell more on her instruction than on her imagination, it is because evil has a way of embarrassing art, even the art that exposes it.

"Something Out There" is a rather simple story; a small band of terrorists, black and white, plan to destroy a power station, and destroy it, while the gentry all around live in terror of an escaped baboon, which is finally caught and killed. The protagonists are many, and there is not much effort expended to create their characters, though the terrorists are rather more fully drawn. This is in keeping, however, with the story's real subject, which is the tendency of things, not the tendency of men. You have the feeling about this story, as you do about the present history of South Africa, that its iterations are a matter of logic. There will be a climax, but there will be no release. If the work seems a bit too schematic, and the figures within it insufficiently made flesh, that is the price of its oppressive objectivity, of its air of a finality about which nothing can be done. The torture is in the structure—which may be said about South Africa as well.

In this novella, as in some of her other writings, Gordimer continues to describe the forms of corrupted consciousness that characterize the morally demented domain of apartheid. Her people may be divided into those that are aware of their corruption and those that are not; but all are corrupted. There are some things you cannot see and stay whole. Obviously this plays itself out differently in blacks and whites. About blacks, Gordimer is utterly unsentimental. There is nothing votive in her portraits of the victims, no sanctity about their suffering of the kind that would put an end to the activity of the analyzing mind. That hatred distorts the hater is commonly known; it must not be forgotten, however, that it distorts the hated, too. In the pathological relationship of power between blacks and whites, nobody is not crippled. There is no legal or political compensation for the experience of the loss of dignity; and it may be that the memory of that experience will doom the reconstruction of the country to an early era of destruction. Black terrorism in South Africa is growing more frequent, as it is in Gordimer's work, but even in South Africa, where terrorism would seem to make the most human sense, it makes no human sense. The fatuities of Fanon, for example, who made romance out of an earlier generation of African violence, and thought to settle the moral problem by calling healthy the innocently sick, are missing from Gordimer. She chronicles, instead, the steady inflamation of the blacks' inner lives, the full foul seething in their suffering souls. There emerges the impression of a class of victims that is obviously in the right, and turning to the wrong. Action is needed if evil is to go, but action sometimes costs; many of those who act will never forgive the agents of evil for leaving them no redress except the action that makes them guilty. The guilt of the innocent; that is the most profound plot of many liberation stories, slavery's last scar. Where there is logic, there are no heroes.

At which point I must hasten to distinguish Gordimer from Naipaul. Indeed, a large part of her achievement is to have refused the choice between the work of the mind and the work of the heart; to have banished sentimentality but not sentiment; to have detached herself from the scene for the purposes of understanding, but not removed herself from it completely. It is increasingly clear from Gordimer's recent work that this gifted writer is also a gifted intellectual. Ideas appear as the stuff of fiction—ideas are the most natural product of an interregnum and they are handled with rigor. Despite its sometimes showy surfaces, then, the fiction reveals a mind calmly at work, and aimed everywhere equally. The same may be said of Naipaul, of course. His, too, is a work of understanding; and he, too, is not deterred by the discovery that there are no heroes. But the similarity stops there. Naipaul is useless if you care about an outcome. Gordimer is quite useful. You can learn from her about the compatibility of the commitment to truth with the commitment to justice. You can learn that the activity of the mind does not always require you to live nowhere. In the reading of Naipaul there comes a point when you must accept his extraordinary distance or do without him. Never, in Gordimer. She sees that the fights for freedom have unanticipated consequences, but she does not become ironic. She sees that the story of masters and slaves is a great spectacle, but she does not become aesthetic. She plays it straight. And playing it straight is an old form of high seriousness, a method

of work which honors the magnitude of the subject more than it honors even the most exquisite sensibilities.

It is not the blacks that Gordimer writes with most authority about, however, but the whites. She is the supreme chronicler of their awakening, or of the failure of their awakening. The process itself consists in a competition between fear and knowledge. Their society, it turns out, is not so obvious. Life in South Africa is a vast system of common ceremonies and unarticulated arrangements by means of which its gross social division endures. As this system comes cracked, its privileged few learn for the first time about their real position, about the position of moral, historical, and social weakness in which minority tyrants always find themselves. They discover that in the depths of their dictatorship they were dependent; moreover, that they knew almost not at all the population whose docility they needed for their delusions. These are the unforgettable findings of Maureen Smales in *July's People,* whose slow illumination in a black village must be one of the great demolitions in fiction of the colonial consciousness, which often does not know that it is colonial.

The epistemological condition of South Africa's whites—and Gordimer's theme is nothing less—is rather plainly revealed in **"Something Out There."** The terrorists and the baboon are the true danger and the false danger, and it is no surprise that it is the false danger that the whites in the story choose to fear. Not that the terrorists, and by extension the explosive political climate of the country, are not also unknown. But they are not uncanny, as are the mysterious forays of the animal, and it is the notion that the danger is normal that must be avoided above all. **"Something Out There"** is about an illumination missed, about the lengths to which people will go to believe in the durability (never mind the justice; it is late for that) of their form of life. As the terrorists misdirect their anger, the suburbans misdirect their fear. The consequence is a restored feeling of coziness in the middle of the great South African mendacity, and another government crackdown.

A word about Gordimer's style. It is the perfect instrument of her intention. The style sticks to you, like unwanted information. It is precise, indeed it is too precise, as it must be if it is to deliver an environment that is estranged. It is poetic, but it is awkwardly poetic, as it must be to communicate the spiritual state of living in the aftermath of ancient assumptions. Sometimes it reminds you of Virginia Woolf—there is a passage in this novella about a woman in a bath that recalls Clarissa Dalloway's sober spell of self-knowledge in her attic bedroom—but tougher, more persuaded of things that last, of the full measure of moral and historical gravity that an ordinary perception may hold. Gordimer's people have outer agonies to go with their inner agonies. She is a master of impressions, and of interiority; but she is (to paraphrase Gautier) a woman for whom the outside world exists. Presumably not much proof of the outside world is needed in such a place.

"Something Out There" is a document of a universe that has been permanently disrupted. Like other writings of Gordimer, it asks how it is possible to know such disruption, and how it is possible not to. Even radical evil, it seems, has details that are difficult to grasp. Particularly here; the fact that Gordimer writes in English should not lull us into a feeling of familiarity. She may as well have been translated.

The influence of politics on Gordimer's fiction:

In my writing, politics comes through in a didactic fashion very rarely. The kind of conversations and polemical arguments you get in *Burger's Daughter* and in some of my other books—these really play a very minor part. For various reasons to do with the story, had to be there. But the real influence of politics on my writing is the influence of politics on people. Their lives, and I believe their very personalities, are changed by the extreme political circumstances one lives under in South Africa. I am dealing with people; here are people who are shaped and changed by politics. In that way my material is profoundly influenced by politics.

Nadine Gordimer with Jannika Hurwitt, in the Paris Review, *Summer, 1983.*

John Edgar Wideman (essay date 1991)

SOURCE: "So Much Is Always at Stake," in *The New York Times Book Review,* September 29, 1991, p. 7.

[*In the following favorable review* of Jump, and Other Stories, *Wideman commends Gordimer's eloquent, realistic portrayals of interpersonal relationships amidst the turbulent socio-political conditions in South Africa.*]

Nadine Gordimer's best writing keeps us aware it is being written, even when it fades to a kind of pulse or background music in the imagined world that absorbs us. What is described becomes real, but also more—and less—than real.

> Four shapes come forward along the beams; and stop. He stops. Motes of dust, scraps of leaf and bark knocked off the vegetation float blurring the beams surrounding four lionesses who stand, not ten yards away. Their eyes are wide, now, gem-yellow, expanded by the glare they face, and never blink. Their jaws hang open and their heads shake with panting, their bodies are bellows expanding and contracting between stiff-hipped haunches and heavy narrow shoulders that support the heads. Their tongues lie exposed, the edges rucked up on either side, like red cloth, by long white incisors.

Ms. Gordimer's South Africa is conveyed in passages of relentless sensual and emotional fidelity. Moments matter, deserve the painstaking eye for detail, the moral intelligence she devotes to rendering them, her determination to make each sentence count and her characters accountable. The lionesses encountered in **"Spoils,"** one of the strongest of the 16 stories in *Jump,* are described by the wife of the narrator as "unreal," a word identified as "one of the

catch-alls that have been emptied of dictionary meaning so that they may fit any experience the speaker won't take the trouble to define." The wife's casual failure to respect language teaches her a lesson. If we use language sloppily, we empty experience of meaning. And worse, by allowing language to use us, we become accomplices in the perversion of reality contained in the vocabulary of dehumanizing systems such as apartheid.

In **"Keeping Fit,"** a white, middle-aged South African accountant ventures forth on his morning jog, only to find himself swept up by a gang of black men, who chop another black man to pieces with pointed wires, cleavers and butcher knives. The accountant is rescued by the "butterscotch-coloured" arms of a matronly woman, who hides him in her squatter's shack in a black settlement until the explosion of violence subsides. When the jogger is finally on his way home again to his white suburb, he is filled with the need to recount the story of his fear, his shock, his discomfort in the "crowded deprivation" of the woman's hovel, his gratitude to her, his unease with her family, the horror of sudden, bloody murder. Confused, overwhelmed, he decides "he would never understand how to tell; how to get it all straight." He buries the urge to speak, and his silence is transformed into raw, inarticulate pain that precipitates a violent quarrel between the man and his wife.

Ms. Gordimer can be a merciless judge and jury. Her portraits obtain a Vermeer-like precision, accurate and remorseless, with no room for hope, for self-delusion, no room even for the small vanities of ego and self-regard that allow us to proceed sometimes as if at least our intentions are honorable.

—*John Edgar Wideman*

Ms. Gordimer takes upon herself this burden of getting it straight and telling it straight, which far too many of her compatriots have refused. Her eloquence breaks through the silence, parses it, shames it. She is a master of realistic narrative, the slow, patient accumulation of evidence. But she pushes beyond that mode in *Jump* to mythlike fable (**"Teraloyna"**), impressionistic prose poem (**"My Father Leaves Home"**), ironic fairy tale (**"Once Upon a Time"**) and an improvisation that might have been generated by an exercise in a creative writing class (**"A Journey"**).

Some of the stories are monologues: the voice of a black child relating his family's flight through the Kruger Park game preserve; the confessions of a traitor who "jumps" from the service of one regime to another. These examples of sustained ventriloquism are generally less convincing than other stories in which the point of view shifts, alternating among characters within the story and mediated by an external consciousness that powers all the voices. However, no story lacks those authentic details that seize the reader's attention. The turncoat in the story **"Jump"** is assailed by his recollection of young girls kidnapped and served up as sexual treats to mercenary soldiers. Though a new government has wrested control from the mercenaries and their handlers, young women (like the one driven by hunger to the turncoat's room) continue to be perks for those in power; "the thin buttermilk smell of her fluids and his semen comes to him as she bends to follow the ant's trail from the floor."

Readers of Ms. Gordimer's fiction (10 novels, 8 previous books of stories) know that the riveting details (often horrific, barbarous, corrosive), the epiphanies scattered through the narrative that shock and surprise, function within a larger vision. This expansive vision, its moral power and artistic integrity, are what elevate her fiction above that of most of her contemporaries. The tales in **Jump** are not committed to a specific political ideology but to the grand task of spiritual examination and social redemption.

Therein lie the considerable strengths of her writing and occasionally its weaknesses. Hard data, the tough-minded immediacy of concrete detail, always suggest that there is something more—an interface of current events with history, the ephemeral with the eternal. Perhaps that's the way it is daily in South Africa, a nation in the midst of profound transformation. Every gesture, each small act becomes charged, potent. Like being in love or at war, so much is always at stake. Things shimmer, rise, fall off the edges.

Ms. Gordimer can be a merciless judge and jury. Her portraits obtain a Vermeer-like precision, accurate and remorseless, with no room for hope, for self-delusion, no room even for the small vanities of ego and self-regard that allow us to proceed sometimes as if at least our intentions are honorable.

Her withering insights deflate us; they project a fine contempt for the human species. The author appears to grow weary, assaults us with what is despicable—not because she believes it can be ameliorated but because there is a fleeting relief, perhaps even pleasure, in finally, without apology, naming the mess, claiming it as our mess, our spoor. Stories that show or tell of man's inhumanity to man and simultaneously imply the possibility of a better world if the bad guys would lighten up, the good guys try harder, lack the unsettling energy of other stories that explain what is unchanging in the human condition. The shadowy, ambiguous muddle of **"Safe Houses"** or **"Some Are Born to Sweet Delight"** lingers long after **"The Ultimate Safari"** or the stark melodrama (reminiscent of Charles Chesnutt's 19th-century tragic-mulatto tales) of **"The Moment before the Gun Went Off."**

This pessimistic side of Nadine Gordimer raises sticky issues. If power corrupts all leaders, why celebrate the change from white power to black power? Might Ms. Gordimer's reservations about her fellow creatures be mistaken as reactionary, even anti-black? In the same context, are the betrayals of one partner by the other in racially mixed marriages (**"Some Are Born to Sweet Delight,"**

"Home") caused by individual choice or emblematic of racial difference, biological fate?

Each story in **Jump** stands on its own, but together they enhance and enlarge one another. A single truth is witnessed, a truth somehow missing in most fiction by white Americans that purports to examine our national life. No matter how removed one feels oneself from the fray, race and race relations lie at the heart of the intimate, perplexing questions we need to ask of ourselves: Where have I been? Where am I going? Who am I?

John Banville   (essay date 1991)

SOURCE: "Winners," in *The New York Review of Books,* Vol. XXXVIII, No. 19, November 21, 1991, pp. 27-9.

[*Banville is an Irish novelist and short story writer. In the following negative assessment of* Jump, and Other Stories, *he derides Gordimer's reportorial voice and contends that the short story medium is unsuited for her style of writing.*]

In the 1970s I had lunch one memorable day with the French novelist Nathalie Sarraute. It was a year or two after Samuel Beckett had been awarded the Nobel Prize. I knew that Mme. Sarraute had known Beckett since before the war, and I brought up his name in the not very honorable hope of hearing some gossip about the great man. When I mentioned the prize, Mme. Sarraute said, Yes, in Paris we say he deserved it. Though her English is fluent, I assumed this somewhat peculiar phrase was a Gallicism, and I merely nodded solemnly in agreement. What I did not know, however, was that there had been a serious falling out between the two writers. Immediately, this kindly and most gentle of women flashed at me a sour look and with what for her was almost harshness said, No, we say: *he deserved it.*

Is the Nobel laurel wreath a fitting recognition of a great artist, or merely the international establishment's way of turning a living writer into a monument? The prize committee has made some strange choices in the past, and there have been even stranger omissions: Joyce, Nabokov, Borges, Greene. . . . Of these four, Graham Greene would have seemed the most suitable candidate, since much of his work is set along that shifting boundary where literature and politics meet uneasily. The committee has always appeared distinctly chary of anything that smacks of art for art's sake, preferring its literature well salted with political or social concerns; in this it is at one with most Western liberal intellectuals, who tend to have a bad conscience when it comes to literature—fiction especially—confusing as they do the ethical with the moral, expecting not works of art but handbooks on how to live.

If Nadine Gordimer had not existed she would have had to be invented. She is the ideal Nobel laureate for these times: an Olympian yet totally "committed" writer with ten novels and countless short stories to her credit; a white South African who has spent a lifetime fighting apartheid; a member of the ANC; and, as an added bonus, a woman. That the gentlemen in Stockholm, as Beckett restrainedly called them, should have waited until this year to give her the prize is a testament less to their acuity than to their

caution. She should have had it years ago. She richly deserves it.

If there is a touch of Sarrauthian harshness here, it is because I have always had reservations about Nadine
Gordimer's work. There are some novels which are important but which have scant artistic value, and there are novels which are artistically successful and supremely unimportant, in the political sense. In the former category one
thinks of *1984,* in the latter, *Lolita.* Like all such distinctions, this one is clumsy, and much too dependent on personal taste to be of any real critical moment, and many
great books (Mann's *Doctor Faustus,* for instance) will
elude its categorizations. All the same, it is handy. Nadine
Gordimer's books are undeniably important; not all of
them are artistic successes.

Ms. Gordimer would probably dismiss such discriminations as quibbling. She has made the choice of commitment to a great cause, and this choice and this commitment constitute her artistic creed. Orwell himself observed
that his decision to be a political writer, far from hindering
him, brought him a sudden and almost blessed freedom:
his program was set, his way clear, no longer would he
spend his energies searching for the *bon mot* or the elegant
aperçu. Ms. Gordimer is not so brisk as this; she can write
with elegance and she makes fine discriminations, but at
the same time wishes to eat the cake of commitment. This
leads to some odd conjunctions. Here, for instance, from
one of her earlier (1966) novels, *The Late Bourgeois
World,* is a mother talking to her young son after she has
broken to him the news of the suicide of his father. The
boy ventures that "We've had a lot of trouble through politics, haven't we," and she replies:

> "Well, we can't really blame this on politics. I
> mean, Max suffered a lot for his political views,
> but I don't suppose this—what he did now—is
> a direct result of something political. I mean—
> Max was in a mess, he somehow couldn't deal
> with what happened to him, largely, yes, because
> of his political actions, but also because . . . in
> general, he wasn't equal to the demands he . . .
> took upon himself." I added lamely, "As if you
> insisted on playing in the first team when you
> were only good enough—strong enough for the
> third."

Even allowing that dialogue is not Ms. Gordimer's
strength as a novelist, this simply is bad writing. No mother would talk to a child like this; in life, perhaps, she
might, but not in fiction. This is something Ms. Gordimer
appears not to see, or at least to acknowledge: that truth
to life is not always truth to art.

Directly after that little speech, however, comes this:

> As he followed what I was saying his head
> moved slightly in the current from the adult
> world, the way I have sometimes noticed a plant
> do in a breath of air I couldn't see.

It is a splendid recovery, as the polemicist, the journalist,
steps back and allows the artist with her disinterested passion to take over.

There are moments, though, when even the artist's touch

fails. In **"Some Are Born to Sweet Delight,"** which is perhaps the weakest of the sixteen stories collected in *Jump,*
an English working-class girl is taking the first, tentative
steps toward an affair with her parents' lodger, a young
Arab:

> She set him to cut the gingerbread: —Go on, try
> it, it's my mother's homemade. —She watched
> with an anxious smile, curiosity, while his beau-
> tiful teeth broke into its crumbling softness. He
> nodded, granting grave approval with a full
> mouth. She mimicked him, nodding and smil-
> ing; and, like a doe approaching a leaf, she took
> from his hand the fragrant slice with the semicir-
> cle marked by his teeth, and took a bite out of
> it.

This is a magical little moment, beautifully observed and
rendered (despite the awkwardness of that "curiosity"); a
few pages later, however, when the couple make love for
the first time, the writer blunts the effect by repeating the
image: "Now she had the lips from which, like a doe, she
had taken a morsel touched with his saliva."

Is this quibbling on my part? Well, a writer has only words
out of which to make a world; the fiercest commitment,
to the grandest of grand themes, is no guarantee of artistic
success—and that is the kind of success Ms. Gordimer
seeks when she sits down to work in the unique solitude
of the writer. Too often in this collection she lets the words
go dead on the page; too often she is content merely to
state, as if what is stated (the grand theme?) will infuse the
material with energy and light. Things—people, artifacts,
ideas—are nothing in art until they are passed through the
transfiguring fire of the imagination. Nabokov remarked
that one of his difficulties in writing *Lolita* was that, after
having spent his time up to then inventing Europe, he now
had to invent America. Ms. Gordimer, in these stories at
least, is too much the reporter and not enough of an inventor.

The story quoted from above shows her at her weakest.
The girl falls in love with the young Arab, who makes her
pregnant, and sends her off to visit his family, first placing
in her handbag a bomb that will destroy the American air-
liner on which she is traveling, killing her and her unborn
child and all the others aboard. We know nothing of the
Arab, seeing him only through the girl's eyes.

> Then there was another disaster of the same na-
> ture, and a statement from a group with an apoc-
> alyptic name representing a faction of the
> world's wronged, claiming the destruction of
> both planes in some complication of vengeance
> for holy wars, land annexations, invasions, im-
> prisonment, cross-border raids, territorial dis-
> putes, bombings, sinkings, kidnappings no one
> outside the initiated could understand.

This is too easy. A piece of good, factual journalism on the
same subject—such an incident happened a couple of
years ago at Heathrow, though luckily the bomb was discovered before the young woman boarded the plane—tells
us more about the issues and even the people involved, and
probably would move us more, also.

There are three fine stories in *Jump,* and all three succeed precisely because the author insists on her authorial rights, as it were, and concentrates on the personal, on the predicament of human beings caught in a bad place at a bad time. **"The Ultimate Safari,"** in which a black girl describes a terrible journey from war to relative peace, fairly quivers with angry polemic, yet achieves an almost biblical force through the simplicity and specificity of the narrative voice.

> We were tired, so tired. My firstborn brother and the man had to lift our grandfather from stone to stone where we found places to cross the rivers. Our grandmother is strong but her feet were bleeding. We could not carry the basket on our heads any longer, we couldn't carry anything except my little brother. We left our things under a bush. As long as our bodies get there, our grandmother said.

"Home" is a frightening study of the way in which a marriage between a Swedish scientist and the South African daughter of a politically active family is poisoned by the woman's commitment to her mother and brothers when they are detained by the police. The husband, unable fully to identify with the fierce loyalties of the family, wonders if his wife has taken a lover; in the end, however, he recognizes the truth.

> Perhaps there was no lover? He saw it was true that she had left him, but it was for them, that house, the dark family of which he was not a member, her country to which he did not belong.

The finest story here is **"A Journey."** The narrator, a writer whom we are invited to identify as Ms. Gordimer herself, flying home to Africa from Europe, sits across the aisle from "a beautiful woman with a very small baby and a son of about thirteen" and makes up a life for them, involving love, infidelity, and the son's first step across the threshold of adulthood; it is a superb little piece, which could have been set anywhere, at any time: it is, in other words, universal. Here, as she does too seldom elsewhere in the collection, the author trusts her artistic energy, and makes up a plausible world. We can see the writer sitting in her plane seat, engaging in that pure and extraordinary form of play which is art. First the boy speaks:

> I'm thirteen. I'd had my birthday when I went away with my mother to have the baby in Europe. There isn't a good hospital in the country where my father is posted—he's Economic Attaché—so we went back where my parents come from, the country he represents wherever we live.

The father, meanwhile, has come to the end of a love affair (it is a masterly piece of artistic fact that no details of this affair are given), and arrives at the airport buoyed up by the prospect of starting afresh the old life.

> Through a glass screen he sees them near the baggage conveyer belt. . . . They are apart from the rest of the people, she is sitting on that huge overnight bag, he sees the angle of her knees, sideways, under the fall of a wide blue skirt. And the boy is kneeling in front of her, actually kneeling. His head is bent, they are gazing at something. Someone. On her lap, in the encir-

cling curve of her bare arm. The baby. The baby's at her breast. The baby's there . . . . He doesn't know how to deal with it. And in that moment the boy turns his face, his too beautiful face, and their gaze links.

> Standing there, he throws his head back and gasps or laughs, and then pauses again before he will rush towards them, his wife, the baby, claim them. . . . But the boy is looking at him with the face of a man, and turns back to the woman as if she is his woman, and the baby his begetting.

It is an affecting, slightly eerie, and above all lifelike moment; it is all the more strong because there are so few such moments in this collection.

Ms. Gordimer has written a large number of short stories, but I think it is not really her medium. The form constricts her, she is not willing to obey its rules; she is inclined to be offhand, to present us with bits of "life" like so many picked-up pieces. She needs the broader expanses of the novel, which afford sufficient room for her talent for leisured scrutiny of motive and action. Whatever her flaws as a writer, she has produced much powerful and moving work, especially in her more recent novels such as *Burger's Daughter* and, her latest, *My Son's Story.* Toward the close of the latter her narrator states for her the program which, as an activist and as a writer, she has followed since the start of her career, which is to make plain for the rest of us "what it really was like to live a life determined by the struggle to be free, as desert dwellers' days are determined by the struggle against thirst and those of dwellers amid snow and ice by the struggle against the numbing of cold."

Karen Lazar   (essay date 1992)

SOURCE: *"Jump and Other Stories:* Gordimer's Leap into the 1990s: Gender and Politics in Her Latest Short Fiction," in *Journal of Southern African Studies,* Vol. 18, No. 4, December, 1992, pp. 783-802.

[*In the following essay, Lazar examines Gordimer's attitude toward Feminism as evidenced in her short fiction collection.*]

There is something of a critical lacuna in relation to Nadine Gordimer's short fiction when compared with the extensive and scholarly criticism available on her novels. My aim is to go some way towards filling this gap, focusing on the anthology which came out more or less simultaneously with Gordimer's winning of the Nobel Prize and which has arguably received more readerly attention than her other anthologies. I examine *Jump And Other Stories* (hereafter *Jump*) in relation to its historical moment and in relation to the short fiction which precedes it in her oeuvre. Gordimer's trajectory on questions of race and class is well-known: she has moved from a position of 'uneasy liberalism to a recognition of the marginality of liberalism and of its inherent hypocrisies, and finally into a "revolutionary" attitude' [Dorothy Driver, in *English in Africa* 10, No. 2, 1983]. The continuation of this trajectory in *Jump* is clear, although it may be complicated by the paradox of Gordimer's overt political partisanship in her public utterances as against her continuing insistence that she is not an 'ideological' writer, that her main aim is to 'write well'.

My method in establishing the place of *Jump* in her trajectory, and in its moment of history, is to observe cross-themes and topoi within the anthology. The primary topoi concerned are the jump, the hunt, the habit of self-enclosure, and the sex/politics nexus. Each story can be read as a text speaking to other texts within the anthology, as well as to numerous intertexts within her earlier work. [In the introduction to her *Selected Stories*] Gordimer herself has said 'There are some stories I have gone on writing, again and again, all my life, not so much because the themes are obsessional but because I found other ways to take hold of them'. Some of the stories in *Jump* can be read as 'rewritings' of earlier concerns, now imbued with the hindsight and the substance of the 1990s. The entire anthology *Jump* may also be read as *one* text, the most recent Gordimer text, written in the years spanning the repressive last years of the 1980s and the *perestroika* years leading up to and succeeding February 1990 (Mandela's release). Following Clingman's characterisation of Gordimer's work as 'history from the inside', *Jump* can be read as an albeit mediated and partial version of the subjective and inter-subjective political history/histories that the author has recently witnessed.

One can readily see a path in Gordimer's political attitudes and their manifestations in her fiction. However, there is another aspect to her thinking that is less easy to document in anything approaching a linear fashion: her fictional representations of women and her attitudes to feminism. Elsewhere, I have attempted to show that Gordimer's politicisation around issues concerning women is not in synchrony with her (more conventionally defined) 'political' radicalisation. Her treatment of women in her fiction and her utterances on gender reveal an uneven and ambivalent relationship with feminism. She has been known to dismiss feminism as 'piffling', and has fervently declared (even recently) that she is 'not a feminist'. In part her dismissal of feminism in the early 1980s had to do with how she perceived it: as a unitary phenomenon with bourgeois ends and bourgeois means. She has more recently conceded that there is a 'harder, more thinking' feminism that understands the necessary connection between culture, class and gender and the relative urgencies of various political projects. And yet, one cannot help noting that in her enormous reservoir of works read (the Nobel speech alone mentioned Gramsci, Sartre, Brecht, Kazantzakis, Rushdie, Mann, Camus, Dostoyevsky, Achebe and others) there is seldom evidence of works by women or feminist theorists.

A disarming non-synchrony does seem to exist between her radical attitudes to 'politics' (and everything that goes into their making) and her attitudes to feminism. The reasons for this are not clear. Perhaps Gordimer needs to be seen within her generation. Her formative intellectual schooling occurred at a time when feminist ideas would have been largely peripheral. Perhaps, too, the belief (still prevalent) in some quarters of South Africa's liberation movements—that feminism is a 'Western' concept and

that gender is a secondary (tertiary?) site of struggle—might have confirmed Gordimer in her impatience with feminism. South Africa does not in fact have much of a women's movement to boast of (the reasons for this are manifold) and again, she might have been thus confirmed in her perception of gender struggle as irrelevant. It appears that she herself has never met with much discrimination in the publishing world, or in other realms of her public life for that matter, and this may also explain her disengagement from feminist discourses.

This is not to say that Gordimer's work does not on occasion offer sympathetic and transgressive readings of female subjectivity. Stories such as **'A Chip of Glass Ruby'** (*Not For Publication*) and **'The Termitary'** (*A Soldier's Embrace*) offer appreciative portraits of the resourcefulness and strength of women. Stories such as **'Good Climate, Friendly Inhabitants'** (*Not for Publication*) and **'The Intruder'** (*Livingstone's Companions*) offer a grasp of the abusive, entrapping situations that women find themselves in. Driver suggests that these sympathetic and politicised portraits of women become more marked and frequent in Gordimer's work in more recent years. By my reading, however, such portraits invariably exist alongside denigratory or ironical portrayals of women, even in her recent work. The overall impression one gains of her representations of women is of variability, as opposed to the more straightforward and linear route of her political depictions. This anomaly persists in *Jump.* The latter part of this essay deals with Gordimer's sometimes puzzling representations of women and the interactions between politics and sex in this text.

Gordimer always chooses the order of the stories within each anthology (she does not leave this to editors), and the title of the anthology. Her habit is to place the titular story at the start of each collection. The first story often sets the tone and establishes the salient questions and scenarios of each anthology. Thus it is to the story **'Jump'** that we must first look. Its main character is a turned ex-soldier for an anti-revolutionary group, now a supporter of the revolutionary movement. The man is holed up in a hotel after his public coming out, and waits for the revolutionaries (now in government) to provide him with house and job. Gordimer has long been interested in betrayals and changes in allegiance: it is a theme that has traversed her work for decades. Some of her fictive betrayals are political, some sexual, some an interweaving of the two, some to do with existential or metaphysical choices and failures.

'Jump' testifies to Gordimer's curiosity in the phenomenon of high-profile political 'turnings' that the late 1980s have seen in Southern Africa. Examples are the case of Dirk Coetzee, the ex-police killer who gave himself up to the ANC and then became a member (and spent a long while waiting in Lusaka while the ANC decided what to do with him); or the case of the various 'askaris' (turned ANC guerrillas) who have turned up in South Africa to testify against their erstwhile comrades. Gordimer's story probes the question: why do such turnabouts occur? What makes a person shun the ideology that previously held him/her in such a strong grip? The answer she offers for her protagonist in this story (perhaps wishfully) is not a cynical one, not to do with mercenariness. Her protagonist gives himself up because he has seen too much: ' . . . the murderous horde that burns down hospitals, cuts off the ears of villagers, rapes children' (*Jump*).

The story is, in a sense, about different kinds of knowledge. Against the mass of disinformation and military euphemism Gordimer sets the onset of individual knowledge: 'Can't be explained how someone begins really to know. Instead of having intelligence by fax and satellite'. The impact of the destabilising civil wars in post-independence southern Africa is brought home in the narrative through the unlikely person of an ex-perpetrator. The man's solitude is almost surreal, heightened time and again by his playing of a tape of grandiose music from an American Vietnam movie to no audience but himself. Those who 'turn' may find themselves sleeping slightly more easily, but also without a political or emotional home.

The titular motif in **'Jump'** is a crucial and polyvalent means of signification. The protagonist's initiation into parachute-jumping in late adolescence is a metonym for his rite of passage into manhood—a passage into violence and killing. The story's end brings back the jump motif. Making a rare trip to the window, the man sees what he cannot bear to see, the mutilation he once fostered: 'the orphaned children running in packs round the rubbish dumps, the men without ears and women with a stump where there was an arm . . . Jump . . . Not now; not yet'. Manhood-as-courage, resonant in the word 'jump' throughout the story, has given way to the will to suicide—as expiation. Gordimer's stories almost always involve a radical shift in power relations of some kind: between antagonists, sexual or political, or between what those antagonists stand for more broadly. The trajectory of a mere word in a story may often be enough to signal such a shift: as in the case of *jump* which signifies domination yielding to self-disgust.

As the collection's first story, the questions **'Jump'** raises must have significance for the text as a whole. Surely its significance lies in its grasp of the twists and turns, the oddities and complications, the 'jumps' that characterise the current conjuncture in South Africa? Gordimer seems to see the 1990s as a time for, if not infinite possibilities then certainly numerous ones as regards moral, political and sexual scenarios. Since the early 1980s she has been attentive to the 'morbid symptoms' that characterise South Africa's interregnum and which show no signs of letting up as the 1990s proceed. Two other stories in the anthology establish a 'post-February 1990' mood and both contain irony and morbidity. In **'Safe Houses'** a returned exile finds himself still living the life of an exile as he goes about underground politics (of the kind suggested by Operation Vula in 1991) in Johannesburg. In **'Amnesty'** a young rural black woman cannot fully celebrate the amnesty that has freed her lover from Robben Island, for her life is changed not at all: it is still a life of waiting and destitution while her man grows more and more absent.

Gordimer's concern with political promises that get broken and with the onset of political disenchantment is not new. Scepticism about politics has always, in some way or another, been a mark of her fiction, dating from her early discomfort with liberalism in the 1950s and 1960s, through to her critique of neo-colonialism from the 1970s onwards (as shown, for instance, in *A Guest of Honour*), to her most recent novel where she casts a loyal but stern eye over the internal machinations of South Africa's (Congress) Movement (*My Son's Story*). Perhaps what typifies her stand over the past decade is a series of paradoxes. While her reticence about the ultimate reliability of political promises (of all shades) seems to have deepened, so too has her commitment to groups such as the ANC: 'I am a member of the African National Congress, I would call that a fundamental position. It is surely committing oneself to the future' [Interview with Mike Nicol, *The Weekly Mail,* February 22-28, 1991]. She seldom fails to show her partisanship on public platforms, and 'committed' themes are closer to the surface of her work than ever before. And yet she insists (as she has for decades) that she does not write from an ideological position: 'Just think of the range of different characters. It is quite clear that I do not write from an ideological position. I am a writer, not a propagandist'. She stresses that, as a writer, her first commitment is to her craft. Her choices as a 'citizen' or a 'human being' are a different story:

> I think my purpose in life has never changed, it has been set simply on trying to write well, on trying to become a writer. But at the same time I am also a human being . . . Writing is what I can do and I have put everything into it, whereas the things outside the writing, well, there are calculations there, those things are not done unreservedly. In other words, although I have given a lot of myself—and certainly all my conviction- to the struggle I have never given the whole of myself. There are many who may say that's my value, but perhaps on the contrary it's my limitation.

Whatever critics or readers of her latest work may make of it, one cannot ignore Gordimer's insistence that her writing is not 'ideological' in intention. Her avowed intention continues to be a predominantly aesthetic one: 'to write well'.

Gordimer has often insisted that part of 'writing well' is the ability to adapt one's forms—not for the sake of mere experimentalism, but so as to suit the demands of one's ideas. In keeping with the ever more demanding and fluctuating political content of the late 1980s and early 1990s—where virtually every discourse is up for grabs, where erstwhile enemies of democracy are now using its language—Gordimer has chosen to extend and diversify her use of the short story form. There are several notable formal movements in *Jump* which build on the developments present in her earlier work. First, shifts in tense and temporal dislocations are more frequent in this batch of stories than in earlier ones, where a linear chronology in time was the pattern of most of her narratives. Such temporal dislocations (interspersals of present with past) have been done before, in *July's People* and *My Son's Story* most notably, but never so extensively in her short fiction. Examples in this anthology of stories where various time-schemes alternate with one another are **'Jump', 'Amnesty'** and **'My Father Leaves Home'**, to name but a few. The effect of intermingling narrative present with narrative past in all these stories is to suggest the intimate interconnectedness of history with contemporaneity, as well as the impossibility of shedding one's past in any idle fashion.

Complementing the comprehensiveness of her treatment of time is a marked tendency in the anthology to refuse singularity of narrative viewpoint within individual stories. Numerous stories (a much higher proportion than in previous anthologies) incorporate perspectival shifts in the course of their unfolding: from first-person to third-person narration, or from one first-person voice to another. This 'roving microphone' technique insists upon the relativity and multiplicity of 'truth' and vision, an insistence that is highly appropriate to the ever more complex substance of the 1990s. Stories in which various viewpoints and perceptions are juxtaposed against each other to striking effect are **'Journey', 'Spoils', 'What Were You Dreaming', 'Teraloyna', 'Once Upon A Time'** and **'My Father Leaves Home'**. In all of these tales, figures viewed as he/she/they through the more distant lens of history/someone else/the author, are then given the intimate chance of speaking as an 'I'—a fact which at once lends complexity and contingency to each narrative. Harsher critics of Gordimer might suggest that for all the attempted multivocality, what comes across is sometimes merely a variation of one voice—Gordimer's voice (especially if one takes 'voice' in the Bakhtinian sense of meaning, not so much speech/viewpoint as different language registers from different parts of a social context. In that case, such critics might say that Gordimer is more bound to her own particular class-located and culture-located register than she would care to admit).

In keeping with what is nonetheless an increased acknowledgement of multivocality, Gordimer also begins to acknowledge (in a more thoroughgoing way than in any previous work) her own storytelling presence in the text. This is in opposition to her technique of controlled, detached 'omniscient' narration used frequently (though by no means exclusively) in earlier work. Several times she points to the fabricated nature of what she puts in front of us, so as to highlight the numerous other fabrications that could have occurred, as in **'A Journey'**: 'I don't know where they had been, why they had gone. . . . I only know this was [the baby's] first journey. I continued mine; they have disappeared. They exist only in *the alternate lives I invent*' (emphasis mine). In the same story she even invents herself as a peripheral character in the narrative, seen through the eyes of a thirteen-year-old boy: 'The seat across the aisle was vacant, only a lady with grey hair in the window seat. We didn't speak to her'. (It is also tempting to read the 'lady with grey hair' who mediates between the Coloured hitchhiker and the British do-gooder in **'What Were You Dreaming'** as Gordimer herself—why else does she offer us this famed signifier of her appearance, and in the same language as in the other story?).

So Gordimer partially dethrones herself, removes herself from the text as the central or authoritative source of knowledge (a position that some of her earlier realism, with its linear, cohesive narratives, permitted her). This dethroning, this enunciating of fictional practice, suggest

an endeavour on Gordimer's part to newly acknowledge the difficulties and partialities of representation. In her Nobel Lecture in 1991, which considers the relationship between writing and being, Gordimer comments:

> . . . from what is regarded as old-hat psychological analysis to modernism and postmodernism, structuralism and post-structuralism, all literary studies are aimed at the same end: to pin down a consistency . . . to make definitive through methodology the writer's grasp at the forces of being. But life is aleatory in itself, being is constantly pulled and shaped this way and that by circumstances and different levels of consciousness. There is no pure state of being, and it follows that there is no pure text, 'real' text, totally incorporating the aleatory. It surely cannot be reached by any critical methodology, however interesting the attempt. To deconstruct a text is in a way a contradiction, since to deconstruct is to make another construction out of the pieces . . . So the literary scholars end up being some kind of storyteller, too.

This foregrounding of the 'aleatory' and her recognition of the constitutive nature of interpretation, throw light not only upon the nature of literary criticism but also on the process of writing itself. For Gordimer, at least at this point in her thinking, there is no 'pure text' (whether she held to such a concept earlier in her career is beyond the scope of this discussion). The stories in *Jump* demonstrate precisely the inevitable limits of seeing and telling with a thoroughness unprecedented in her short fiction.

What is not new in this anthology is the fact that Gordimer frequently uses a first-person voice to signify a black speaker. Her first such attempt (that I know of) at depicting black experience 'from the inside' was in the story **'Some Monday for Sure'** from *Not For Publication,* where the speaking 'I' is a young black exile waiting to receive military training in an unnamed African country. Since that point, various critics have disputed her right to depict black experience, claiming that it is presumptuous of her to attempt representations of that which she cannot possibly know, and that such depictions bear the mark of inauthenticity. Gordimer has consistently defended herself against such statements, claiming that a writer's imaginative empathy, and her years of living in the same country with blacks, give her the right to write about whatever interests her:

> We have been not merely rubbing shoulders but truly in contact with one another; there is a whole area of life where we know each other, despite the laws, despite everything that has kept us apart . . . I have gone through the bit of falling over backwards and apologising because I am white . . . If I write about blacks I feel I have the right to do so. I know enough to do so. I accept the limitations of what I know.

In *Jump* Gordimer steps up the number of stories with a black first-person narrator and takes a further leap into speaking of/for the Other by making some of these narrators children. Her method of attempting to depict the viewpoint of such figures is to keep her language consistently simple. At times this leads to a stark and moving effect and is appropriate to the solemnity of the subject matter, as in **'The Ultimate Safari'**, where the aftermath of a Renamo raid is described: 'Our grandfather, walking a little behind some young men, went to look for our mother but didn't find her. Our grandmother cried with other women and I sang the hymns with them. They brought a little food—some beans—but after two days there was nothing again'.

But at times this method makes for an effect of not so much simplicity as simplism, as if Gordimer has forgotten to put energy, viability or interiority into the voice which speaks. There are several instances where her language is flat and unconvincing, as in **'Amnesty'** where the black rural woman waits for her absent man: 'I am up with the clouds. The sun behind me is changing the colours of the sky and the clouds are changing themselves . . . There's a huge grey rat moving across the sky, eating the sky. I'm watching the rat . . . eating the sky, and I'm waiting. Waiting for him to come back'. Naming, describing, speaking for illiterate black figures is always likely to be a challenging task for Gordimer. Perhaps her construction of voice in moments such as that just cited could benefit from a deeper and more cautious consideration of the problematic posed here by Gayatri Spivak [in her *In other Words: Essays in Cultural Politics,* 1988]: 'I see no way to avoid insisting that there has to be a simultaneous other focus: not merely who am I? but who is the other woman? *How am I naming her?* how does she name me? Is this part of the problematic I discuss?'

If one of Gordimer's current concerns is the ironical and multivalent potential of this historical moment and its discourses, another is the predatoriness still present in South African society. Various critics have pointed to the striking lack of levity or humour in Gordimer's work, its weightiness. Her repeated use of the idea of the hunt in this anthology suggests that moods of rapacity and ugliness in South African society may eclipse lighter moods (at least for this writer), even in the current era of apparent will-to-change. The topos of the hunt functions—sometimes allegorically, sometimes literally—as a way of investigating social relations and ways of being. Gordimer has gone along on several hunting trips over the years, and if her fictional recreations are anything to go by, her response to such trips is uneasy. During the 1960s several of her stories showed a love for the land and a strong awareness of being on the African continent. At this point Gordimer is strongly self-identifying as an African, and her identification has a striking sensory/existential component. In **'The Gentle Art'** (*Friday's Footprint*) the narrative descriptions suggest awe at the sheer space, light and colour around her: 'The enormous trees of Africa, ant-eaten and ancient, hung still, over the hut; down on the margin of the river in the sun the black-and-lemon chequered skin of a crocodile made a bladder of air in the water . . . At night there was nothing—no river, no hut, no crocodile, no trees; only a vast soft moonless darkness' (*Selected Stories*). This story's main figure is a crocodile hunter described in very ambivalent terms: killer and profiteer he certainly is, but the reader is struck by his strength, knowledge of the landscape and affection for the creatures he hunts.

In a responding story in **Jump,** namely **'Spoils'**, the main character is not so much a hunter as a 'conservationist' (a word replete with ironies—conserver of what?—since Gordimer's text of that name). Unlike the crocodile hunter, this (now less romantic) figure is made uncomfortable by the sheer 'otherness' of the beasts he watches: 'They have no beauty except in the almighty purpose of their stance . . . the stasis, the existence without time . . . there in the eyes of the lionesses. Between the beasts and the human load, the void'. The 'human load' can be read as the load of intellect, fragmentation, politics, killing. In this story Gordimer suggests a continuum of hunting, strung together by a litany of hunting words—'spoils', 'carrion', 'kill'. The unselfconscious drives of the lions are somehow less shocking than the killing of innocents in war, a subject that gets interspersed in the conversation over drinks, or than the subterranean sexual hunt, the 'chemistry', that occurs between the main character and the 'hard, slender' young woman at the lodge. It is only Siza, the black man who leads them to the lion's kill, who seems to fall outside the circle of hostility, alienation and conquest that the white visitors occupy—a fact metonymically suggested by his attitude to the slain zebra. Whereas the other figures in the text are either morbidly fascinated or repulsed by this untrammelled version of 'meat', Siza sees it for what it is, and cuts a segment off the carcass for his hungry family: 'The black man has thrust, made his incision . . . It is not a chunk or a hunk, but neatly butchered, prime—a portion'. The final impression surrounding the white company, and most especially the 'wit' who is its centre, is one of squeamishness yet rapacity, an unappealing mix.

Elsewhere in the anthology politics-as-hunt and sex-as-hunt are again explored. In **'Safe Houses'** an activist establishes his own peripatetic trail around Johannesburg, aware that he needs to cover his scent by constantly changing his trail. Eventually his hunters catch him anyway. In **'My Father Leaves Home'** the analogy between the hunting of animals and the hunting of Jews is made explicitly clear in near stream-of-consciousness prose: 'I hear the rustle of fear among creatures. Their feathers swish against stalks and leaves . . . the men with their thrashing sticks drive the prey racing on . . . there was nowhere to run to from the village to the fields as they came on and on, the kick of a cossack's mount ready to strike creeping heads, the thrust of a bayonet lifting a man by the heart like a piece of meat on a fork'. The narrator's sudden grasp of her father's experience of a pogrom is triggered by the blind rustles of a birdchase. The sensory acuteness of the writing itself acts to concretise what was previously beyond narratorial/authorial cognisance. At the story's end Gordimer globalises her insights: 'I did not know that I would find, here in the woods, the beaters advancing, advancing across the world'. This final phrase—'across the world'—asserts racism's tenacity over time and space. The hunted often become hunters when the tide of power turns, an irony of which the elderly father seems unaware (but the narrator lucidly not) when he says 'You speak to me as if I was a kaffir'.

A story dealing with the sexual hunt is **'The Find'**. A twice-married, now single man finds a sapphire ring at a holiday resort. He advertises his find and then interviews the women who come to claim it. Finally, he gives it to the woman whom he is most struck by (and who is clearly not the ring's owner) and marries her. All parties in this story come off unflatteringly. The hordes of women who claim ownership of the 'find' all seem calculating and voracious. The man at the centre of it all sizes up the claimants as if they were applying for a job whose nature is secret, and then the job turns out to be wifedom. Gordimer's tone in this story is more than usually inscrutable. Her meaning seems to lie most squarely in the title, as usual dual in dimension: the 'find' in the story is not so much the ring as the woman who gets given it. The fact that appraisals of the latter come to the reader through the man's eyes and that her sexuality and beauty are paramount in this appraisal, suggest that he practises the ancient patriarchal habit of valuing women as objects of the gaze. It is apparent that on this occasion Gordimer withholds sanction from such a practice (although her own attitudes to loss of female beauty through ageing are highly ambivalent, as I shall discuss later).

The story which explodes all the other hunting stories in the anthology is **'The Ultimate Safari'**. The irony of its title interrogates the luxuriousness of game lodge lifestyles and of subtle sexual courtships. The story recounts the escape of a depleted family from bandit attacks in Mozambique, their imperilled traipse across the Kruger Game Park and their time at a refugee tent camp in South Africa. The dismal details of the story, offered in the unselfpitying voice of a black child, suggest why this safari is an 'ultimate' safari: few journeys could compete with the sheer human annihilation entailed in this one. It is also an 'ultimate' safari in that it is likely to be the girl's last: there is no home to journey back to. The story exists on an intimate continuum with **'Jump'**: the limbless, destitute people whom the ex-parachuter cannot face outside his shaded window could have been the girl's parents. The fact that **'The Ultimate Safari'** ends within a South African setting points to the radical contiguity, the interconnectedness of South Africa's politics with that of its neighbours. The 'borders' that the refugees cross seem porous and arbitrary in the extreme, suggesting that the idea of a sovereign nation-state with inviolable borders is farcical in the light of South African incursions into and support for rogue fighters in Mozambique.

The foregrounded 'veracity' of the last story, its documentary and naturalistic register, contrast sharply with the strange story **'Teraloyna'** which can be read as an exercise in allegorical meaning-construction. The story is also about a hunt. The site is an (imaginary) island which has been depopulated of its 'natives'. They have been absorbed into the culture and economy of the nearby mainland (a not much disguised South Africa), but differentially so, since some are lighter in colouring than others: 'The raw-faced, blue-eyed ones, of course, disappeared among the whites . . . The islanders who were absorbed into the darker-skinned communities became the Khans and Abramses and Kuzwayos'. The island has been turned into a weather station and is now overrun by cats. Unbeknown to most on the mainland the cat crisis reaches emergency proportions, and South African conscripts are

called to the island to shoot them *en masse*. Among these conscripts is 'the young fellow who could have lost a blue eye by means of a stone thrown by a black, but was merely grazed to ooze a little of his Teraloyna blood-line'.

What is Gordimer getting at in this story? The tale invites reading as an allegory of imperialism. The island's name, Teraloyna, is a bastardised version of the French 'loin terre'—faraway land. The metropole's will to use and strip 'far lands' goes a long way to explaining the plight of the Third World in the past few centuries. The story also points to the ludicrousness of racial classifications: a set of blue eyes make all the difference to where one enters the social hierarchy in hegemonic South Africa, or anywhere for that matter. Finally, Gordimer seems at pains to depict the way historical cycles turn against previous ones: the boy with the urge to kill and with Teraloyna blood in him is an instance of victim turned victimiser, much like the pogrom-fleeing South African racist in **'My Father Leaves Home'**. In this case the victims are cats. The fact that there is a whole colony of them and that they are no longer functional (as pets to the weathermen) but annoying, suggests that their mass killing is a kind of metaphoric genocide, a fictional 'Final Solution'. Imperialism and genocide are thus placed alongside each other as ideas in a single text, speaking much for Gordimer's opinion of the imperial habit.

The obverse of the will to conquer is self-enclosure, fear of the Other. I have elsewhere discussed Gordimer's parodic rendering of stereotypes of the Other in her 1984 novella **'Something Out There'** and her satire of whites' obsession with arming and walling themselves against marauders. In *Jump* the theme of self-enclosure returns, again parodically. In **'Once Upon A Time'** Gordimer borrows and subverts the genre of the bed-time story, making full use of the hyperbole inbuilt in this genre. In singsong, go-to-sleep-now language, the narrator recounts how a mother and a father spent time choosing how to make their house secure from a catalogue of safety bars, alarms and panic buttons: 'Both came out with the conclusion that only one was worth considering. It was the ugliest but the most honest in its suggestion of pure concentration-camp style . . . Placed the length of walls, it consisted of a continuous coil of shining and stiff metal serrated into jagged blades'.

Gordimer's fairy tale possesses a particularly ghoulish South African ending: 'Next day [the little boy] pretended to be the prince who braves the terrible thicket of thorns to enter the palace . . . the shining coiled tunnel was just wide enough for his little body to creep in, and with the first fixing of its razor-teeth in his knees and hands and head he screamed and struggled deeper into its tangle'. If one of the codes of the typical fairy story is to include the nemesis of the damned, in Gordimer's sardonic code the nemesis for whites comes at the cost of a white child maimed from the *inside* of the fortress. An obsession with danger breeds more danger. Gordimer has a sharp eye for home-grown semiotics. The barbed wire in this story, the red headbands worn by the violent gang of men in **'Keeping Fit'**, the 'tiger-streaked hair' of the bored, monied housewife in **'Safe Houses'**, all testify to her close observation of the signifiers of South African living.

The creation of domestic fortresses in South Africa's affluent suburbs has its uses: for revolutionaries. To return to **'Safe Houses'**—the underground white activist of this story finds sanctuary, and time off the job, in the house and eventually the bed of a politically callow, well-preserved white woman. She is unconscious of who he really is and easily relates to him as 'Harry', his false persona. The fact that he can be so persuasively taken for 'Harry' suggests that he could have been *like* Harry, could have opted for a life of safety and 'safe houses'. The disjuncture between the two characters' codes foregrounds the transgressiveness and dedication of his choice. For decades Gordimer has written about leftists who have to make do with lives on the run or 'safe houses' as places of abode. What is a new dynamic in this story is that 'Harry' sleeps with his unwitting host. In **'Something Out There'** (1984) the feared and demonised Other/beast is not far away from the heart of white culture (the errant monkey, shadowy harbinger of the other guerrillas encamped outside the city, makes rushed forays into white kitchens and steals legs-of-lamb). In the more recent story the penetration of the subversive into the 'safe' is as intimate as it can get. The story suggests that the woman's 'safety'—her blitheness, her privilege—stands to be undermined by the very movement that her lover represents: and she would never dream how close it is.

'Safe Houses' is also a rejoinder to a much earlier story: **'Open House'** from *Livingstone's Companions.* In that story a black underground activist is not amused by his white friend's self-conscious and meaningless display of 'multiracialism'. She puts together a racially mixed luncheon party for some breathless American visitors, and the blacks she invites are all urbane, co-opted and highly bourgeois—and offensive to the revolutionary who glimpses the party from the margins of the garden. Like 'Harry' in the recent story, the black activist lives a life of dodging and moving, but is much more strictly confined to peripheries. The title of this story is, as usual, bivalent and ironical: a truly open house was not a possibility in South Africa during the time when the story was written. The black figures who come into Frances' house and move around freely in public do so precisely because they are no threat to the system that keeps others out. Many of Gordimer's stories contain a centre and a periphery: house and backyard, suburb and township, interior and exterior. The dichotomisation of space invariably stands for the gulf between different zones of consciousness and being. Comparing the 1970s story to the 1990s story, and marking the extent to which 'Harry' has come out of the garden and into the house, so to speak, it is obvious that Gordimer is seeing subversion as less ex-centric and more centric, more possible, imminent in the current decade.

'Comrades' in *Jump* is also a story that deals with different zones of being, separate realities. A well-meaning white activist brings home a group of young black 'comrades' from a conference and feeds them in her dining room. (They in turn call her 'comrade' in acknowledgement of her departure from white codes—a benevolent act of nam-

ing typical of an alternative discourse well-known to Gordimer). For all her attempts at sharing her reality with them, and getting to know theirs, the protagonist realises that 'this room, the space, the expensive antique chandelier, the consciously simple choice of reed blinds, the carved lion: all are on the same level of impact, phenomena undifferentiated, indecipherable. Only the food that fed their hunger was real'. Outside her house what is 'real' to them are the AK-47's and bombs they sing about. It is a challenge for a single consciousness simultaneously to hold the reality of the youths and that of their host in mind, or to grasp what might constitute a truly substantial 'comradeship' between them. The narrative tone approaches awe, perhaps even defeat, in the face of the enormity of the gulf that this story sets up.

Turning now to a topos present in much of Gordimer's work: the interweaving of politics and sex. Gordimer has frequently said that politics and sex are the two abiding drives of human existence. In this anthology a spectrum of interactions between the two imperatives is depicted, and most of them inscribe shifts in power, betrayals or twists. Gordimer sometimes uses sexuality as an analogue for politics, for example, in *The Conservationist* (1974) where Mehring's political rapacity is also expressed in his degrading treatment of women. Sex is also sometimes inscribed as a catalyst for political discovery, as in **'The Train From Rhodesia'** (*The Soft Voice of the Serpent*) where the young female protagonist is simultaneously alerted to her own distaste for racial exploitation and the estrangement at the heart of her marriage. In *Jump* sex is not so much used as an analogue or a catalyst for politics as an adjacent vehicle of expression. Five different types of sex/politics nexus are to be found in the following five stories.

'Home' is a story which deals with life outside detention for a young Coloured woman whose close family members have been imprisoned. Her anxiety, her preoccupied state, her sense of impotence dominate the story. Her husband, a Swedish scientist, cannot do anything to help her. As silence and distance grow between them, he becomes convinced that she is having an affair. It is only after she has made contact with her detained family and some of her anguish has lifted, that he begins to see 'perhaps there was no lover'. In this story, sexual paranoia is a displaced means of experiencing exclusion from political being. The Swede, being foreign, cannot enter the state (of absorption into politics) that his wife occupies. He can only conceive of her cut-off state in sexual terms, terms that he knows. Gordimer highlights the woman's solitary, frenzied state—the state of being unhappily, powerlessly 'home' while others are in prison—by having her viewed, *wrongly,* through another character's perspective.

'Some are Born to Sweet Delight' is a particularly striking story in the sex/politics nexus it constructs. Gordimer describes an unnamed non-South African setting which turns out to be England. A young working-class English girl, Vera, falls in love with the foreign lodger, Rad, who lives in her parents' house. His nationality is also left unnamed, but his physique and eating habits denote Arab origins. (Why Gordimer is so coy about naming her setting or her characters' national origins is unclear). The lodger seduces Vera and, when she falls pregnant, pacifies her shocked and bigoted parents by promising to marry her, and arranging for her to make a plane trip to his country (without him) to meet 'his people'. He plants a bomb in Vera's baggage and she and a planeful of people explode over the sea. Gordimer has obviously been prompted by tragedies such as the Lockerbie disaster to probe the nature of extreme political violence and cynicism. The rampant destructiveness of such 'apocalyptic' politics is accompanied by conscienceless exploitation of young female sexuality. Perhaps the plot mechanisms in the story are a little cumbersome; but Gordimer's careful juxtaposing of annihilation and innocence, politics and sexuality, is not.

'The Moment Before the Gun Went Off' brings together two (disparate) situations which frequently appear in South African news: the shooting of black labourers on conservative white farms, and the discovery that a leading Afrikaner figurehead has 'illegitimate' black offspring. In this story Marais van der Vyfer is grief-stricken when he accidentally shoots dead his trusted black 'friend' and servant, Lucas, on a hunting jaunt. But Lucas also turns out to be Marais' son. Gordimer sketches in a furtive family triad in the following words: 'The dead man's mother and he stare at the grave in communication like that between the black man outside and the white man inside the cab the moment before the gun went off'. Here, the conservative politics that Marais subscribes to forbid the interracial sex that he himself has practised. Sex and politics in this case are completely at odds with one another: politics is public and legitimate, sex is secret and damnable (the more so for being accompanied by affection).

The two other stories in the anthology which involve a prominent sex/politics interaction have already been mentioned: **'Amnesty'** and **'Safe Houses'**. In the former, the sexual dimension of a love relationship is completely subjugated to the urgencies and pressures of political struggle. The young black rural woman waits, and waits, while her activist lover throws his energies into ending the hardships of the nation. Gordimer has long been interested in the nature of political sacrifice, and has expressed a 'fascination with the strength of political commitment, and how it changes people, takes them out of themselves, beyond themselves, transcends their personal emotions'. In **'Amnesty'** she looks at the intimate and negative effect of such sacrifice on others. In **'Safe Houses'**, Harry finds himself erotically involved with his unknowing hostess. Sexuality is depicted as 'time out', as an apolitical space away from subversion. Sex itself is a 'safe house'.

So here is the array of sex/politics nexi in the five stories just discussed: sexuality as paranoia in the face of political absence; sexuality as means-towards-an-end, the end being large-scale political assassination; sexuality as illegitimate when racially 'other'; sexuality as subjugated to politics; sexuality as time out from politics. All of these situations exhibit an uncomfortable relationship between sex and politics. They are seen as competing sites, used or eclipsed by each other, but not really as properly interactive. What I mean by this is that sex is rarely seen by Gordimer as a *politics in itself,* as a site of being that merits a political

critique. Although she recognises that politics and sex share a crucial ingredient, namely the operation of power, this does not mean that she sees sexuality as (at least in part) politically constituted. Her sexual scenarios are always more atomised in their construction, less inclusive of social being than her political scenarios. She does insist that politics may intrude into the personal, but this is not the same thing as seeing that 'the personal is political', namely that the most intimate of human encounters are fundamentally shaped by socially constructed habits of control and abuse. Her treatment of sexuality in this anthology, although subtle and varied, suggests a way of seeing sex that sometimes borders on the essentialist: namely, that sex is a drive with its own rules and imperatives that politics may or may not interfere with (that fact being incidental). This way of seeing sexuality is also sometimes reflected in her representations of women in the anthology, and it is to these that I now turn.

Looking at *Jump* as an anthology, one sees some patterns emerge in the way women are represented. There are clusters or types of female figure that exist across the text. There are the sheltered, shallow white suburban wives whose main concerns are the preservation of appearances, the pursuit of the commodity and the quest for the perfect burglar bar. This cluster's most damning trait is perhaps their failure of imagination—their inability to imagine the reality of any other lifestyle but their own. Gordimer spares no sarcasm on this group. Examples can be found in **'Once Upon A time'**, **'Keeping Fit'** and **'Spoils'**. Connected with this cluster but slightly more kindly treated are characters such as those in **'A Journey'** and **'A Find'**: women on the wrong side of forty but, crucially, still beautiful. In earlier stories such as **'Out Of Season'** and **'Enemies'** (*Six Feet of the Country*), Gordimer's tone suggests an anxiety (even annoyance) at the female ageing process. Loss of desirability seems to imply, for the characters in these stories, loss of social viability and importance. Gordimer has said: 'A woman cannot forgive herself for ageing'. In *Jump* the close-to-menopausal beauties seem to have acquired their men in the nick of time, as suggested by phrases like 'She was certainly forty . . . There was no sign of a fold where her breasts met' and 'well-used but beautiful hand'. Women who manage to defy the ageing process or ward it off, women who preserve the body-beautiful, again seem to come in for veiled but discernible authorial sanction.

Another category of women in the text whose representation is predominantly via the body are the young pretty figures who appear (fleetingly) as lovers or potential lovers of the male protagonists in stories such as **'Jump'** and **'Spoils'**. In the latter story, this figure is set up as a sexual rival to an ageing, nagging suburban wife (from the first character cluster). The young woman's youth and desirability declare the contest won virtually before it starts. Here, sexuality is all-determining in the definition of character. A further cluster of young female figures in the anthology are those whose sexuality is also a crucial defining feature in their representation, but cast as impressionable and vulnerable to male abuse. Moreover, that sexuality is accompanied by themes of 'love' and related subjective processes, rather than simply being an objective signifier of the woman's status. Stories in which these fecund, awakened and manipulated young women occur are **'Some Are Born To Sweet Delight'** and **'Amnesty'**.

Moving now to the more 'political' types of female figure in the anthology. We have the cluster of stoical black matriarchs, who lead their families to relative safety or who offer refuge to terrified whites, as in **'The Ultimate Safari'** or **'Keeping Fit'**. Destined to inspire admiration as these figures are, both of them are quite sketchily, even stereotypically presented: as big-bosomed, uncomplaining and sagacious. We also have the activist's girlfriend in **'Spoils'** who clearly belongs in a category of female figures we have seen before—the unattractive radical: 'The prisoner holds the hand of his pale girl with her big, nervously-exposed teeth; no beauty, all love'. Elsewhere I have discussed various denigrating portraits of left-wing women in Gordimer's work, and have shown how she may use a mechanism of devaluing a figure's sexuality when she wishes to question her political worth (as in the case of Clare Terreblanche in *Burger's Daughter*) and conversely of ensuring a figure's desirability when she wishes to boost her political worth (as in the case of Rosa Burger, and Hillela in *A Sport of Nature*). In *Jump*, yet another left-wing woman comes across as disregardable, due to the negatively suggestive physique Gordimer allots her. Again, the body determines the status of the woman in the text, this time so as to efface her from the realm of political and social seriousness.

Looking now to activist figures in the anthology who are slightly more endorsed by Gordimer. In **'Home'** we see the young Coloured woman being eaten up by anguish while her family is in prison. Although she is a political figure, Gordimer suggests that her politics is somewhat passive, even ineffectual, when compared with the more daring actions of her imprisoned brother. There are also the older, white activist figures, as in **'Comrades'** and **'What Were You Dreaming'**, who are represented as benevolent, intelligent—but not very subversive! Their political seriousness in each case is undermined by the fact that the black youths alongside them in the text view them as wholly 'other', as too far in the realm of the comfortable for real significance in the political scheme of things. And this cluster of older women comes across as asexual, lacking in body, benign and motherly in type but somehow peripheral to the potency of revolution.

So what does *Jump*'s panoply of women consist of? Spoilt and smug wives; gracious but ageing beauties; young and sexy lovers; manipulable girls new to sex; ugly and adoring left-wing women; anguished but slightly pathetic activists; well-meaning, elderly activists; stereotypical black matriarchs. Where, in this anthology, are there women who are imbued with a power or agency that is multidimensional, neither stemming just from the body nor from political benevolence? The representations of women throughout the anthology tend more towards the uni-dimensional than the accompanying representations of men. Arguably, the compactness of the short story does not permit Gordimer to elaborate on the possible facets of her representations, but nonetheless, her men are permitted a greater combination of human functions and are less susceptible to eclips-

ing by other figures than her women. For instance, the extremist figure who blows up the plane in **'Some Are Born to Sweet Delight'** is clearly not endorsed by Gordimer and yet she confers on him a subtlety of personality—eating habits, reading habits, sexual language—that make the accompanying female figure (his victim) seem like a stock type by comparison. In **'Spoils'** the most prominent male figure is an amalgam of (not always pleasant) shrewdness, thoughtfulness, solitude, sociality, sexuality. The other male figures, although more thinly presented, all possess opinions, know about money and politics, have a private life. The women in this story seem to exist in the outermost sphere of representation, as diffuse figures that dampen or arouse desire in the men. The baseline in Gordimer's representations of women is invariably sexuality (as a lack or as a presence), whereas in her representations of men no such baseline exists, allowing her a much greater range of exploration in relation to male figures.

One story not yet discussed, **'A Journey'**, perhaps symptomatises the position of women in *Jump* most clearly. The woman in this story is on her way home to an African country in which her husband is a diplomat, with a newborn baby and a thirteen-year-old son. The narrator, across the aisle from them in the plane, notices the peculiar and devoted intimacy between the boy and the mother and starts to build on it in her mind, arriving at the idea that the father had had an affair; his wife's pregnancy had been ambivalently received; she had returned to Europe to have the baby; and, in the father's absence, the boy's Oedipal/incestuous love for his mother had grown. This is an unusual (overblown?) reworking of an old theme: that of the sexual triangle, in which two rivals for an object's attention struggle for power and conquest. Here the man's rival is his own son. The narrative splits into two: the woman is viewed through the perspectives of both her son and her husband, but *nowhere* is her own perspective given. She is at once central to the story and decentered.

In Gordimer's previous stories some female figures are constructed in subtle, multifarious terms and empowered as agents and subjects, while others are constructed in denigratory or objectifying ways. In this anthology, various aspects of South African womanhood are split off, dichotomised and assigned to individual figures, such that the representations of women tend to be truncated, reduced and static, giving women a marginal and decentered status relative to the more lively and layered status of men. The problematic treatment of women persists in *Jump*, in spite of the broader political acuity concerning the nature of current South Africa evident in many of the stories. Such a non-synchrony of treatment and attitude is puzzling in so lucid an author.

Does Gordimer 'jump' into the 1990s with this latest anthology? To be sure, various features do suggest a confident step forward into this decade, building on the growths and shifts present in her earlier work. These features include the perspectival and temporal complexities of her narratives, which indicate an attempt to grapple with forms appropriate to the fragmentary nature of the 1990s. Also striking is the marked political understanding she displays in relation to the moods of the current historical moment, as conveyed in the topoi of the jump, the hunt and the enclosure. However, her sometimes static and truncated representations of women are a continuing concern to this feminist critic: perhaps one leg still lags behind the other in her jump.

Jeanne Colleran   (essay date 1993)

SOURCE: "Archive of Apartheid: Nadine Gordimer's Short Fiction at the End of the Interregnum," in *The Later Fiction of Nadine Gordimer,* edited by Bruce King, St. Martin's Press, 1993, pp. 237-45.

[*In the following essay, Colleran discusses the ways in which socio-political conditions in South Africa inform Gordimer's work.*]

> It is obvious that the archive of a society . . . cannot be described exhaustively . . . on the other hand it is not possible for us to describe our own archive, since it is from these rules that we speak . . . it emerges in fragments.
>
> Michel Foucault, *Archeology of Knowledge*

All of Nadine Gordimer's fictional projects could be described as working to construct an archive of apartheid, a record which as an artist she is bound to keep, transcribing the 'consciousness of her era' (*Selected Stories*), however much that consciousness is inevitably limited by the machinery of apartheid itself. Now after ten novels and eight collections of short stories, much can and has been said about this archive: its emphasis, primarily, on the strained sensibilities of white South Africans, its appropriation of real historical figures and events, its growing, now committed alignment with identifiable political movements, its attempt to serve instrumentally as an agent for social change. The problems confronting this archival effort have been articulated most eloquently by Gordimer herself, but whatever from these obstacles have taken— whether bannings, censorship, political disenfranchisement, or the 'split' historical position from which Gordimer must account for her word—they have been met, and therefore the archive exists: a monumental task of monument-making for all those who have suffered under apartheid, struggled against it and work toward its demise.

The latest entry in the archive is a collection of short stories, *Jump,* published just as it was announced that Gordimer had received the Nobel Prize for Literature. When the announcement was made, Gordimer was out of South Africa in New York on a promotional tour for her new book. Such seems fitting, for these stories, like her earliest ones and the some two hundred in between, have appeared first before the eyes of an overseas readership; all of the pieces in *Jump,* in fact, were published previously in American magazines. With their tell-tale tags of social explanation (such as the side comment in **'The Moment Before the Gun Went Off'** that the Immorality Act had been repealed or the history lesson about the Cape Coloured squeezed into **'What Were You Dreaming?'**), the stories take up again the 'professional responsibility' for 'the transformation of society' that Gordimer sees as the

fundament of commitment for a South African writer (*The Essential Gesture*). Like Frances Taver, her own character from the 1971 collection, ***Livingstone's Companions,*** Nadine Gordimer, as both writer and critic, is on the 'circuit for people who wanted to find out the truth about South Africa' (*Selected Stories*).

'The truth about South Africa' is not the same thing as the truth about apartheid. The former, bound to history, noosed to the individual, can only be, as Foucault tells us, a fragmentary truth, part of and partial to, the times and the teller. But about apartheid, the truth is not fragmentary: it is diamond-hard, rock-solid as any nugget unearthed from a Transvaal mine. Unvarnished, it is the 'unconscious will to genocide . . . in some whites' ('Letter'); polished, it is the 'belief in the old biblical justification for apartheid' ('Letter') or in the 'South African government's vocabulary of racist euphemisms' (*The Essential Gesture*).

'Teraloyna', the centrepiece of the collection, tells the truth about apartheid. It unmines the history of a mythic island which was once inhabited by people 'coloured neither very dark nor very light' but which is now overrun by hundreds of wild cats. The story's ending relies on a metonymic slide of meaning, a technique which Gordimer frequently employs in her short fiction, particularly as a means of closure. Elliptical, sparse, economic, the metonomy operates by virtue of contiguous positions and by slippage between these positions: non-causal events are aligned next to each other; public, social realities are placed alongside private, psychic obsessions. The emotional configuration underlying the one spreads to the other. The trope of metonomy thus mimics linguistically the psychological process by which events cannot be excised from their angle of refraction or stripped of their emotional overlay. In **'Teraloyna',** the young white men who have 'under command and sometimes out of panic' shot schoolchildren and mourners as well as rioters, without bothering to distinguish between them, have been recruited to clear the island of the cats. This time, 'game for it', the young men need not concern themselves about making distinctions; they'll have 'abundant targets', of all colours, and they will be free to 'kill, kill them all'. Though told as fable, seemingly disqualifying itself as an historical document, the story nonetheless lays tacit claim to that power of moral authority most associated with a fable's axiomatic ending. In **'Teraloyna'** the implied adage asserts that blocked desire—the desire for blood, the will to genocide—will reappear elsewhere. It will look other than what it is, this blood-thirst, perhaps take on the appearance of an environmentalist rightening the balance of the ecosystem or a young man called to respond to the 'emergency within the Emergency', but it will reappear and pursue its prey.

The rest of the stories in *Jump* tell the truth about South Africa. For Gordimer this task, a task similar to what Jacques Derrida has described as the 'properly reversible structure' of holding the mirror up to the law ('Laws'), is one more fraught and more fragmentary than telling the truth about apartheid. As she attempts to describe from within and as exhaustively as she can her own archive, giving at least fictional names to the 'archival record of the unnameable' (Derrida, 'Racism'), Gordimer is consummately aware of the duality of her mediating role, one which is as compromised as it is critical. In **'A Journey'**, Gordimer offers a story which interrogates its own presumptions as well as its subject. Through the voice of the story's first narrator, a 'lady with gray hair' in the window seat of an aeroplane, who observes another woman across the way travelling with her newborn child and older son, Gordimer accedes that the trio exists 'only in the alternate lives I invent, the unknown of what happened to them preceding the journey and the unknown of what was going to happen at its end'. As the narrative yields to other points of view, first the son's and then the absent father's, it signals its own partiality, and in doing so, Gordimer establishes the vocal extremes of this collection. Against the firm pitch of **'Teraloyna'**, the ferocious sound of moral authority, is set the tremulous uttering of the self-reflexive, self-questioning narrative of **'A Journey'**. Between these, the sure voice of political commitment and the qualified voice of a narrative conscious of its own narrativity, the rest of the stories fall.

Gordimer has stated that the short story, with its 'art of the present moment' is, in important ways, more able than the novel 'to convey the quality of human life' ('Symposium',). 'Fragmented' and 'restless' in form, but absolved both of the onerous convention of the 'prolonged coherence of tone' that defines the novel and of the burden of 'cumulative' meaning, the short story is less 'false to the nature of whatever can be grasped of human reality'. For these and other reasons, a *collection* of short stories may be the vehicle most conducive to telling whatever truths can be told about South Africa. Some of the reasons are obvious: the range and variety of voices it is possible to include within the boundaries of the collection are suggestive of the even greater multiplicity of voices, attitudes, and constituencies that comprise South African society and compete—or co-labour—to determine its future. Implicit in this multiplicity is the relentless insistence on the end of cultural monopoly, an insistence whose tacit political power derives, in this instance, from the *form* itself of the story collection. Also, the brevity of the stories allows for an unsustained representation of the Other of Gordimer's South Africa. The voice of the white bourgeoisie does not fill the space of this collection in the same way that it reverberates throughout Gordimer's novels, and while the clearings opened for other voices are necessarily narrow ones, the concision actually authenticates these voices, making them at once more credible and less usurped. Given that the unknowability of the Other is in South Africa the palpable result of all the legislation erected to maintain the colour bar, and not simply part of the problematics of the postmodern critique of representation *per se,* the strictures imposed by brevity seem, in fact, to be virtues. The replacement of an intensely focused penetration into one or more consciousnesses—be it that of a conservationist, an activist's daughter, or the son of a coloured schoolteacher—with an assemblage of fragmented, partial, non-cumulative narratives, invites the reader to participate in a very differently-mediated discursive journey. Rather than *critically* following those few traces inscribed to track the fluctuating sensibilities of one or two primary consciousnesses, the reader is asked to read

diacritically, across the silences between stories, around the tacit significance of their placements or alignments, and through the implied priorities of tales told first or last or middle.

The activity of reading diacritically, at the edges of certain social sites, in the centre of others, is a corollary to the kind of political education that Gordimer deems necessary for white South Africans who must move—conceptually, physically—outside of their protected enclaves and, like Bam and Maureen Smales of *July's People,* into the homes occupied by the rest, the majority of South Africans. It is this kind of education that the white jogger of **'Keeping Fit'** unwittingly acquires when, in the course of his morning run, he mistakenly crosses over past the 'outward limit' of his route, past the 'industrial buffer' between suburb and township and finds himself in the 'squatter camp which had spread to the boundary'. The movement of the text, from a centre of hegemonic power to the edges of disenfranchisement and back again, mimics the larger epistemological excursion required both to initiate and to sustain any kind of valid critique, be it motivated by a postmodern scepticism about cultural authority and its representation or by the sheer polarities of South African society. Thus the jogger crosses boundaries that are more intellectual than physical, though it is the encounter with an unknown physical reality that initially overcomes him. The stern respectability of the black woman who pulls him out of the pathway of a mob engrossed in murderous, angry pursuit; the meagre shanty where he cowers; the gratuitousness of his recreational run; the gravity of the racing mob: these are the events and the lives which, now exposed, require radical reformulations to be made. But when he is back on the 'right side', wanting somehow to tell what has happened during his extraordinary journey between safe points—the security-system of his own home, and the temporary security he was still somehow able to claim in the black woman's shanty—the jogger knows he will never 'understand how to tell' it; he will 'never get it all straight'.

Gordimer's stories, like the jogger in **'Keeping Fit'**, often end up in a place of wordlessness. The silences which settle at the end of pieces like **'The Moment Before the Gun Went Off '**, **'Home'**, and **'Some Are Born to Sweet Delight'** are, however, differently sounded. For Marais Van der Vyver, the Afrikaner farmer who had accidentally shot one of his farm-hands dead, the silence is born of bewilderment and sorrow. For this labourer, whose mother was one of the black women on the farm, was not just 'the farmer's boy; he was his son'. His conception, an illegal engendering, has been decriminalized, but the change in statute neither legitimized the boy's status nor the father's grief. And so the Afrikaner must mourn mutely, suppressing again what had once been suppressed in his name, allowing again, only, a deadly silence.

In other stories, wordlessness is the only response possible to the devastating sense that life has outstripped any ability to account for it, and so the counter-counter-revolutionary of **'Jump'** wordlessly considers suicide, and the husband and wife of the allegorical **'Once Upon a Time'** say nothing, though the housemaid is hysterical and the gardener weeps, as they retrieve the bleeding, shredded body of their own son, caught in the razor-thorn serrations of the barbed wire fence they had themselves erected. Some of the stories in the collection suggest events intellectually or emotionally inaccessible, either because they are horrifically inexplicable—like the young woman in **'Some Are Born to Sweet Delight'** who, with her unborn child, is the victim of her terrorist/lover's aeroplane bombing—or because they recount lives lived outside a particular, impenetrable circumference. Such is the case in **'Home'**, where a foreigner, a Swedish ichthyologist, is married to an Indian woman. He has access to her lovely body (though this too fades) but none to those recesses of familial identification and loyalty which claim her when her mother is taken into detention. Suspecting betrayal, wondering if his wife has taken a lover during the hours she labours for her mother's release, the husband senses only that his wife has left him for 'the dark family of which he was not a member, her country to which he did not belong'. Like many other of Gordimer's stories and novels, **'Home'** is a place where intimacy and unknowability, like a couple caught in embrace, must co-habit.

Gordimer does not always score the tone of her stories in the direction of silence, though perhaps she agrees with Wittgenstein that 'in art it is hard to say anything as good as: saying nothing'. *Saying* nothing does not of course mean that nothing is shown, and in this sense the *collection* of stories operates in a manner which, like collage or montage, 'mounts a process in order to intervene in the world, not to reflect but to change reality'. As a kind of 'intellectual montage' where real elements operate as part of the discourse, and signifiers, selected and charged, are 'remotivated within the system' of new frames, the stories in *Jump* appropriate figurally—that most obsessive image of recent South African history the dead child. Dead children—or tortured or damaged children—haunt the collection; they are found in nearly half of the stories, and appear in each of the collection's first three pieces as, first, the child offered up as sexual reward in **'Jump'**; then as the shredded little boy of **'Once Upon a Time'**, and next as the malnourished baby brother, soon surely to die, of **'The Ultimate Safari'**. Their near-presence wordlessly, repeatedly insists: this is the cost, this is the cost, this is the cost.

Significantly, the stories sunk into silence are most often those about white South Africans, caught at the end of the Interregnum without an expressible sense of future or commitment. Not so the stories about black South Africans, particularly **'The Ultimate Safari'** and **'Amnesty'**, and, as 'interventions' in the world, they speak to the last stages of apartheid's dismantling. For the small girl of **'The Ultimate Safari'**, a refugee from Mozambique, the future is mostly illusive—she plans to return home where she imagines her missing mother and grandfather wait for her—but it is never elusive nor hopeless. So, too, for the black woman narrator of the collection's last story, **'Amnesty'**, who has waited through her lover's imprisonment on Robben Island for him to return and marry her. Released, return he has, not to marry but to keep on working for the revolution. Now it is for this she waits: the revolution not of his homecoming, but of their homegoing. On this scene of waiting, waiting for home and, significantly,

the birth of her child, the collection ends though the process it has begun does not: one amnesty has been given, another is still needed.

Alan R. Lomberg (essay date 1993)

SOURCE: "Once More into the Burrows: Nadine Gordimer's Later Short Fiction," in *The Later Fiction of Nadine Gordimer,* edited by Bruce King, St. Martin's Press, 1993, pp. 228-36.

[*In the essay below, Lomberg traces Gordimer's changing attitudes towards life and love in her short fiction.*]

In the introduction to her *Selected Stories,* Nadine Gordimer suggests that the process of composition is, for her, like burrowing into a warren 'where many burrows lead off into the same darkness but this one may debouch far distant from that'. An instance of that is provided by the development of two stories in *A Soldier's Embrace* into the novella which is the title story of *Something Out There.*

One of the stories which provides intimations of the subsequent 'exploration' in *Something Out There* is **'Oral History'**. In that, a chief, trying to protect his village from attack by reporting 'guerrillas' in it, finds that the 'arrests' that were to be made become instead an army attack which devastates the village. There is the cruel irony that he had taken his bicycle with him when he went to make his report, and that it 'would have been lost if it had been safe in the kitchen when the raids came'. Gordimer dryly reveals the chief's suicide through the remark 'No one knows where the chief found a rope, in the ruins of his village.' There is a notable intimation of perseverance and endurance, though, in the concluding report of the return of the surviving villagers and their gradual rebuilding of the village.

In terms of style and foreshadowing, **'A Lion on the Freeway'** is a more interesting preparation for *Something Out There.* It has an aura of dreaminess, reflecting the half-sleep in which thoughts and reminiscences run through the narrator's mind. The development proceeds by association and accretion. The 'Open up!' develops threateningly into 'Open your legs' which leads to a recollection of love-making 'once . . . near the Baltic' thence to love-making 'heard . . . once through a hotel wall'. Parallel to that progression, and interspersed with it, is a progression related to the lion and its roar, a progression which culminates in the fusion of the sound of the lion—'that groan straining, the rut of freedom bending the bars of the cage'—with that of a group of black strikers, 'A thick prancing black centipede with thousands of wavy legs advancing'. There is a further intimation, through a device used more than once in the story—'(no spears anymore, no guns yet)'—that the strikers, like the lion, are waiting to reclaim their country.

Those earlier explorations develop into the stories in *Something Out There* which deal with the socio-political and socio-economic situation of apartheid South Africa. In **'A City of the Dead, A City of the Living'**, one of the protagonists (Moreke's wife) reflects on the young man they are sheltering: 'You only count the days if you are waiting to have a baby or you are in prison.' That curious combination is indicative of the circumstances by which the man has come into their lives. Were he a relative, even a distant one, they would have been obliged to give him shelter; but 'This one is in trouble', and his claims on them are only justifiable in that 'If you are not white, you are the same blood here'.

While providing a detailed picture of township life with its privations and its special sense of community in the midst of poverty, together with a high rate of infant mortality (indicated by the otherwise unnecessary qualification that this is the woman's fifth 'living' baby), and the unhygienic conditions and multiple uncertainties, Gordimer traces the progress of events in parallel with the woman's private thoughts and feelings about the man who is 'in trouble'. The woman's ambivalence is shown to be moving towards self-protection in a manner similar to that of the chief in **'Oral History'**. The wish not to be involved is reflected in her thoughts: 'how long does it take for a beard to grow, how long. How long before he goes away'. In the end, it is fear of being punished for complicity, an unuttered tendency towards self-preservation, that drives her to report the man's presence to the police. Even then, she has mixed feelings: 'I don't know why I did it. I get ready to say that to anyone who is going to ask me, but nobody in this house asks'. Judgement of her action is, however, clearly provided by Ma Radebe, the shebeen-keeper, who, when she next saw the woman in the street, 'gazed at her for a moment, and spat'. That terse conclusion emphasizes the fact that, however much may go unspoken, there is no question where loyalties should lie.

The ambivalence of Moreke's wife parallels the uncertainty of the chief in **'Oral History'**. He had worried that his report to the army 'was not coming out as he had meant nor being understood as he had expected'. Moreover, the villagers *'never saw'* but only 'heard the government say on the radio' that the strangers the chief was reporting committed atrocities to force people to connive with them. More importantly, various aspects of these stories build towards the novella, **'Something Out There'**, in which there is a much fuller treatment of a general anxiety about something numinous about which people hazard an identity only so that fear might be made manageable.

The 'beast' in the novella is more menacing than the 'lion' on the freeway because it is not just a threatening, misunderstood sound in the night; it has attacked, and continues to do so. The city's inhabitants have a range of suppositions about the nature of the 'beast', and there is the predictable 'embroidering' which takes place when opinion needs to be bolstered by details which will make supposition convincing. Encounters (and purported encounters) with the 'something' outline that process by which a creature or event moves from the real to the surreal, and thence into legend. While tracing that progression, Gordimer also provides cameo portraits of various social groups—from the correspondents of a Sunday newspaper who use the opportunity to air their own gripes, to a group of medical specialists out playing golf, there of whom decide the mystery creature is 'one of the black out-of-

works'. In all these instances Gordimer uses the sightings as a basis for some cutting social criticism, implicit in some cases, more direct in others. Mrs Naas Klopper (whose husband has rented a farm to the two white members of a four-person guerrilla group) equates accounts of the predator with 'good old stories of giant pumpkins'. Important things happening in the world are considered an irritation at best, compared to the incidents of 'normal' life. For the four medical specialists, their Thursday afternoon golf game is more important than their patients. A more general selfishness is reflected in the lack of concern of people in one neighbourhood when the creature no longer appears to be active there: 'So long as it attacked other people's cats and dogs, frightened other people's maids— that was other people's business'. The most absurd response is that the animal 'wouldn't have had to live the life of an outlaw' if it had stuck to 'its proper station in life'. That remark has obviously been transferred from its application to people who, under the apartheid system, are expected to do just that.

The remark may also be seen as applicable to the four guerrillas. In a pattern akin to that of **'A Lion on the Freeway'**, their story, beginning with Charles' and Joy's renting of the farm from Naas Klopper, is carefully interwoven with the reports of, and reactions to, the various attacks of the animal. An interesting reaction (and one that is typical of Gordimer's style) comes after the creature has ripped the flesh from a leg of meat hung in the window of his house by a sergeant who interrogates political detainees. The sergeant's superior says that the man's wife ought to learn to handle a gun because 'Next time it might be more than a monkey out there in the yard'. That casual, reasonable remark is one of a kind that Gordimer adroitly deploys; its dramatic irony subsists in the fact that we know that there are four people out there who are planning an attack on a power plant. After the attack, there is irony as well in Mrs Klopper's providing a degree of anonymity while trying, conversely, to identify the black man she had seen at the farm: 'Just like any other black— young, wearing jeans that were a bit smart, yes, for a farm boy'. There is irony of a slightly different sort in one of those small details that are inimitably part of Gordimer's style: in a police photograph of various captured weapons (some of them thrown in 'for added effect, as a piece of greenery gives the final touch to a floral arrangement'), Mrs Klopper sees 'her own biscuit tin, in which she had made the offering of rusks' to Charles and Joy.

While the stories discussed so far show an interplay of ideas and style and reflect one of Gordimer's persistent concerns—chronicling life in her country and the changes that evolve over the years—other stories reveal more strikingly her experimentation with new structures and approaches. In **'For Dear Life'**, the normal transitional and/or signalling phrases have been stripped away. The point of perception switches from one narrator to another so that only the form of expression and the nature of the concerns expressed are left to indicate to the reader that this is the independent narrator, the pregnant woman previously observed in the story, the father of that woman, and so on, down to the child itself ('Behind me, the torn membranes of my moorings') emerging from the womb.

As Gordimer has herself observed, there are some stories she has 'gone on writing, again and again'. Prominent among those must be Gordimer's repeated treatment of love affairs. While the primacy of the body is something she has spoken of as applying particularly to adolescence and early adulthood, she treats love relationships at many stages of life, and her heroes and heroines are usually engaged in extra-marital affairs. As with Bray in *A Guest of Honour* or Liz in *The Late Bourgeois World,* a change of partner seems to be an inevitable concomitant of developing changes in attitudes and beliefs. As in her other work, Gordimer is constantly in search of the truth about things; not, however, in an abstract manner, but as it emerges in real situations, with all their distinctive colour and flavour and (often) incongruity, paradox and irony as well. The truths that emerge in her fiction are more accurate and significant than *'the* truth' that can supposedly only emerge from non-fiction.

Truths about love relationships in these two collections range over a span from adolescence to middle-age, and arise from reminiscences as well as from more immediate events. The narrator of **'A Need for Something Sweet'** looks back at an affair of his youth with an older woman who represented an adolescent fantasy lover. He harks back to it from the position of a settled middle-aged man who has just had 'a few words with the wife'. It is an instance of sloughing off something considered to have been a minor aberration of one's 'salad days': 'Who would believe a clean youngster could get mixed up with a woman who would end up like that'. That sort of *ex post facto* rejection takes different forms in the two parts of **'Town and Country Lovers'**, but reflects an important aspect of Gordimer's thinking about the way our lives develop, whether in terms of our love affairs in particular or our values and beliefs in general.

Another good pointer to Gordimer's view of love comes in **'Time Did'** when the narrator speaks of the 'great confessional of our early intimacy . . . that, paradoxically, real life familiarity (in marriage, for example) seals off'. She also remarks of her lover: 'your delight in the variety of my sex delighted me, too. How many men really love women?' There is a certain familiarity about this narrator which, combined with the structure of the piece, reveals Gordimer reworking aspects of a previous work. With her assertiveness, occasional hesitation, and petulant defensiveness, she reminds one of Liz in *The Late Bourgeois World.* This new venture into the 'burrows', however, has several distinct qualities. The opening, without even a 'whistle' of introduction, is cryptic: we have no idea who the narrator is, nor the person being quoted. More than with Liz, the focus here is on a dying relationship. The narrator notes that her lover is seeing in her 'the final softening of the flesh that is coming to you as a man one day, your death as a lover of women'. Moreover, as 'Time' has its way, 'the schema of cosmetics . . . chalks a face that no longer exists'. This 'truth' is a variation on the more general one of the various changes that take place over the course of our lives, and which everyone who is honest must acknowledge.

'A Hunting Accident' also provides a variation on the theme of love affairs. In the midst of the actual hunt—finely described by Gordimer—we become aware that Christine is engaged in her own 'hunt'; the reference to 'her' photographer in the opening line making her possessive attitude clear, a point reinforced in subsequent lines. She is later concerned that the photographer's behaving as if he were 'incredibly staid' would 'give other people the wrong impression of the kind of man she chose'. The quietly affectionate quality of that relationship bears certain resemblances to that of **'Sins of the Third Age'**, in which the subdued tone reflects the mostly muted, nervous quality of the protagonists' responses to each other and to their situation. The only indication of their identity and why they had eventually decided to settle in a 'fifth country' (Italy) is revealed in the simple statement that he had 'a number branded on his wrist', just as the harrowing ordeals they must have experienced are intimated by the statement that her hands 'retained no mark of the grubbing—frost-cracked and bleeding—for turnips, that had once kept her alive'. Like their existence, which was that of 'a well-made life' which 'did not happen; was carefully planned', **'Sins of the Third Age'** is neatly arranged and subdued in tone, culminating in the toneless 'there had never been a sign of what had been found, and lost again'. He had had an affair, a fact he conveyed to her by simply saying, 'I've met somebody', which remark made them 'two new people' who 'didn't know what subject they had in common'. In the same matter-of-fact way, he subsequently announces the end of the affair by saying, 'I gave up that person'.

Gordimer takes a very different approach in **'Crimes of Conscience'**, where the relationship, which seems to develop naturally from a casual acquaintance, is misunderstood. There is an echo of the effect that the man's announcement of his affair in **'Sins of the Third Age'** had on his relationship with his wife when the narrator of **'Crimes of Conscience'** likens one development to that of a situation in which an 'old friend suddenly becomes something else . . . as if a face is turned to another angle.' In this case, however, on the 'next day . . . nothing's changed'. Unknown to her, this new friend has not become 'something else' but has been so all along. Like Harriet in **'A Correspondence Course'**, this narrator appears to be one of those young whites who have been 'dumped by their elders with the deadly task of defending a life they haven't chosen for themselves'. Thus, she feels she has been giving her lover 'a course in the politics of culture', whereas her attempts to reveal aspects of her earlier life (such as her time in prison) have simply been feeding him with the information he is meant to get out of her, his purpose becoming clear when he reveals, 'I've been spying on you'. While the relationship is similar to others Gordimer presents—she had, for example, lived for three years 'with someone who, in the end, went back to his wife'—the difference—relative guilelessness encountering the deception of an agent of the secret police—is a reflection of the developing social and political situation in South Africa between the time of the earlier and later stories in the two collections.

'**Blinder**' provides an interesting contrast to relationships in other stories since the principal relationship here is between an employer and a servant. Although there is never any question of the difference in status—the usual social distance reinforced by the fact that the employer is white and the employee black—there is an aura of mutual affection and symbiosis to the relationship. The focus on the maid produces some of the acute observations that are typical of Gordimer: the human body is like the sea, 'into which no abuse could be thrown away' since it would be certain to be 'cast up again'; and the maid, who regularly goes on a binge (the 'blinder' of the title) has a face 'ennobled with the bottle's mimesis of the lines and shadings of worldly wisdom'. Gordimer also comments on two important aspects of the South African situation, one applicable anywhere, the other peculiar to that place: the poor are people 'to whom things happen but who don't have the resources to make things happen, don't have the means, either, to extricate themselves from what has happened'— 'black' and 'poor' being largely synonymous in this situation. The other point is that there is no resentment between Ephraim's wife and his lover, Rose, the maid; instead, there is acceptance of the fact that the socio-economic circumstances of apartheid have made it necessary for a man, far from home, to take a temporary partner.

Gordimer's persistent concern to capture in words the truths of love and life involves a process of re-exploration, and of attempts to find new structures by which she can best reflect the ideas that emerge from her own examination of life.

—*Alan R. Lomberg*

Those circumstances are also important in the two stories which contain the fullest treatment of the development and termination of love affairs, the two parts of '**Town and Country Lovers**'. The title, sounding almost like a fictional relative of *Home and Garden Magazine,* belies the outcomes of the relationships. In both cases the couple end up in court, but not because they have done anything that, in almost any other country, would have led to legal action. In the second of the two stories, the relationship between Paulus (the farmer's son) and Thebedi (the daughter of one of the black farm workers) is lovingly developed from the early exchange of gifts between them to the sexual relationship that seems as inevitable as it is natural, and—unnaturally—illegal. Gordimer chronicles the early white lies they tell to cover up the growing relationship,

and Paulus' adolescent exaggerations about his life at boarding school. Part of the *dénouement* is prepared for early on when 'a boy in the Kraal called Njabulo . . . said he wished he could have bought her a belt and earrings'— gifts Thebedi had received from Paulus. When Paulus eventually discovers that he is obviously the father of the baby Thebedi has borne, there is uncertainty about what Thebedi heard when Paulus went alone into the hut where the baby was. When she is first questioned, an apparent confusion of feelings leads her to claim that 'she saw the accused pouring liquid into the baby's mouth' and that he had 'threatened to shoot her'. Her testimony is different when the case eventually comes to trial, and she has had another baby, by Najabulo, by then her husband. Clearly recovered from her early dumbstruck horror, Thebedi dismisses the affair as 'a thing of our childhood'. The male protagonist of the first part of '**Town and Country**' lovers had dismissed his affair by saying that even in his own country it was 'difficult for a person from a higher class to marry one from a lower class'. The ironies here are obvious.

Thebedi's dismissive remark is important because it relates to an important aspect of Gordimer's philosophy. The remark is echoed at the conclusion of '**You Name It**' when the narrator reflects on the situation of the illegitimate child she bore and which her husband still supposes is his. She observes that there must be other children 'whose real identity could be resuscitated only if their mother's youth could be brought back to life again'. These remarks, together with that of the narrator in '**A Need for Something Sweet**', clearly reflect Gordimer's belief that, as we grow, we change, even to the extent that we come, in later life, to regard our youthful personalities as those of different people.

Gordimer's persistent concern to capture in words the truths of love and life involves a process of re-exploration, and of attempts to find new structures by which she can best reflect the ideas that emerge from her own examination of life. Her development as an artist, then, runs parallel with the development of her views on love and life. Common to both is that fidelity to experience results in changes without which there can be no true growth. We are not products of some form of Freudian determinism, whereby what we become in later life always has a referent in childhood experience. Instead, if we are honest, we must acknowledge that we keep changing as we grow older, and our responses to life, our attitudes and values, alter as we affirm the changes wrought by experience. Moreover, life is full of irony, paradox and incongruity, not something neat and seamless, unless we choose to ignore deliberately the details which keep disturbing the pattern and which lead to changes such as those reflected in the eventual estrangement of Thebedi and Paulus, from which point their lives will diverge and reflect little of that 'thing of [their] childhood'.

The narrator of *A Sport of Nature* puts Gordimer's position clearly: 'Only those who never grow up take childhood events unchanged and definitive, through their lives'.

FURTHER READING

Criticism

Beauman, Sally. Review of *Livingstone's Companions*, by Nadine Gordimer. *The New York Times Book Review* (31 October 1971): 6, 22.
Favorable review.

Broyard, Anatole. "The New African Landscape." *The New York Times* (1 November 1971): 39.
Stylistic and thematic analysis of *Livingstone's Companions*.

Enright, D. J. "Which New Era?" *The Times Literary Supplement* (30 March 1984): 328.
Positive review of *Something Out There*. Enright comments: "Nadine Gordimer survives as a writer of distinction by virtue less of her themes than of her distinction as a writer."

Hardwick, Elizabeth. Review of *Something Out There*, by Nadine Gordimer. *The New York Review of Books* XXXI, No. 13 (16 August 1984): 3-4, 6-7.
Positive assessment.

Haugh, Robert F. *Nadine Gordimer*. New York: Twayne Publishers, 1974, 174 p.
Full-length critical volume examining Gordimer's work.

Hayes, Richard. "The Moment of Illumination." *The Commonweal* LVI, No. 8 (30 May 1952): 204.
Commends the stories in *The Soft Voice of the Serpent*, asserting that "Gordimer is, indeed, so much a mistress of this time and place, so verbally dexterous, so mercilessly accurate in her sensory responses, that one anticipates the performance of a potentially major writer."

Jones, D. A. N. "Limited by the Law." *The Times Literary Supplement* (9 January 1976): 25.
Review of *Selected Stories*. Jones discusses the defining characteristics of Gordimer's short fiction.

Kanga, Firdaus. "A Question of Black and White." *The Times Literary Supplement* (11 October 1991): 14.
Thematic and stylistic examination of *Jump, and Other Stories*.

Lazar, Karen. "Feminism as 'Piffling'? Ambiguities in Nadine Gordimer's Short Stories." In *The Later Fiction of Nadine Gordimer*, edited by Bruce King, pp. 213-27. New York: St. Martin's Press, 1993.
Analyzes Gordimer's short stories "in the light of her multi-faceted, uneven and changing attitudes to women's oppression and feminism." Earlier version of this essay appears in the entry above.

Mathabane, Mark. "Tales of the White Tribe." *The Washington Post Book World* XXI, No. 36 (8 September 1991): 9.
Mixed review of *Jump, and Other Stories*.

Mazurek, Raymond A. "Gordimer's 'Something Out There' and Ndebele's 'Fools' and Other Stories: The Politics of Literary Form." *Studies in Short Fiction* 26, No. 1 (Winter 1989): 71-9.
Explores how Gordimer and Njabulo Ndebele "embody similar political ideas through divergent fictional forms."

Nordell, Rod. "Miss Gordimer and Africa." *The Christian Science Monitor* (11 October 1956): 10.
Favorable review of *Six Feet of the Country*, contending that the stories "go beyond provincial applications to make a statement, however bleak, however limited, on the ways of mankind."

O'Grady, Desmond. "South Africa and the Storyteller." *The Washington Post Book World* XIV, No. 29 (15 July 1984): 4-5.
Mixed review of *Something Out There*.

Peden, William. "Eternal Foreigners." *The Saturday Review*, New York, XXXIX, No. 43 (27 October 1956): 16-17, 25.
Contends that "with *Six Feet of the Country* Nadine Gordimer emerges from the category of gifted beginner and assumes the stature of one of the most distinguished younger contemporary writers."

Phelps, Lyon. "Humane Comedy." *The Christian Science Monitor* (22 June 1965): 9.
Positive assessment of *Not for Publication, and Other Stories*.

Rubin, Merle. "Gordimer's Stories: A Stark, Harsh View of South African Life." *The Christian Science Monitor* (9 August 1984): 24.
Provides a thematic overview of *Something Out There*, asserting that "more strongly than ever before, Gordimer not only expresses a pessimism about political and social conditions in South Africa, but she also gives voice to a far more universal sadness about life in general."

Schwartz, Lynne Sharon. "Figures in a Landscape of Sun and Shadow." *The Washington Post Book World* X, No. 36 (7 September 1980): 1, 4.
Examines narrative techniques in *A Soldier's Embrace*. Schwartz contends: "The notion of duality—the definitive fact about Gordimer's South Africa—permeates these dozen stories, all of them about impossible combinations producing discord, imbalance and functional failure, whether of a society, a family, or a pair of lovers."

Theroux, Paul. "The Presence of Africa." *Book World—The Chicago Tribune* V, No. 48 (28 November 1971): 19.
Thematic analysis of the stories comprising *Livingstone's Companions*.

Tuohy, Frank. "Breaths of Change." *The Times Literary Supplement* (25 April 1980): 462.
Discusses the main themes of *A Soldier's Embrace*.

Interviews

Bazin, Nancy Topping, and Seymour, Marilyn Dallman, eds. *Conversations with Nadine Gordimer*. Jackson: University Press of Mississippi, 1990, 321 p.
Collection of interviews with Gordimer over several years.

Additional coverage of Gordimer's life and career is contained in the following sources published by Gale Research: *Contemporary Authors,* Vols. 5-8, rev. ed.; *Contemporary Authors New Revision Series,* Vols. 3, 28; *Contemporary Literary Criticism,* Vols. 3, 5, 7, 10, 18, 33, 51, 70; *Discovering Authors*; and *Major 20th-Century Writers.*

Dashiell Hammett

1894-1961

(Full name Samuel Dashiell Hammett) American novelist and short story writer.

INTRODUCTION

A celebrated author of American crime fiction, Hammett is widely considered the originator of the "hard-boiled" detective story. Writing in a terse prose style frequently compared to that of Ernest Hemingway, Hammett featured callous, cynical private detectives who became the archetype for scores of similar protagonists in American television, popular literature, and film. The style Hammett pioneered beginning in the early 1920s was a radical departure from that of the traditional English mystery story, replacing genteel sleuths such as Sherlock Holmes with workmanlike detectives who operate in the violent and seedy world of urban crime. Generally recognized as an important contribution to American literature—a status rarely achieved by the works of popular genre writers—Hammett's best fiction features stylized prose, intricate plotting, and an original type of hero who confronts the lawless nature of American society in the 1920s and 1930s.

Biographical Information

Hammett was born in St. Mary's County, Maryland, and attended school in Baltimore until the age of thirteen. Beginning in 1915, he was employed by the Pinkerton National Detective Agency, but his career as a private detective was interrupted by service in World War I. Hammett never saw action in Europe during the war but contracted tuberculosis while stationed in the United States. He returned to the Pinkerton Agency in 1919, but additional hospitalization for the disease ensued, and he eventually left the detective firm around 1921 to concentrate on writing. Success as a fiction writer made Hammett a hot property for Hollywood producers in the 1930s; many of his novels were adapted into films, and he continued to work on screenplays when his prolific output of fiction diminished after 1934. In the latter part of the 1930s, Hammett became increasingly involved with leftist causes, and it is believed by some scholars that he became a member of the Communist Party of the United States at that time. Following service in World War II, Hammett's political activities drew the attention of anti-communist politicians; he served a six month sentence for refusing to divulge information about suspected revolutionaries, and after he was released from prison all royalties from his writings were seized for back taxes. The final years of his life were spent in poverty and ill health. He lived often with friends, including the playwright Lillian Hellman, his longtime companion, until his death from lung cancer in 1961.

Major Works

The majority of Hammett's short stories feature the nameless Continental Op, a detective for the Continental Detective Agency. The Op stories date from early in Hammett's writing career and continued to be written until he made the transition to long fiction several years later—though the character of the Op was also featured in Hammett's first two novels. Most of the Continental Op stories first appeared in *Black Mask,* a pulp fiction periodical that fostered the growth of hard-boiled detective fiction. From 1923 to 1927, over thirty of Hammett's stories appeared in *Black Mask,* fitting well with the magazine's emphasis on action-oriented plots and realistic detail. Hammett's innovations began with the character of the Op, a slightly overweight detective who is most often depicted as middle-aged and prone to the ailments and routines of many men in mid-life. The character was initially based on Hammett's boss at the Pinkerton Agency, and the author likewise made use of his own detective experience to create the stories. As a result, violent underworld criminals populate his fiction. The story "The Whosis Kid," for example, features a team of greedy jewel thieves who turn against one another in a bloody free-for-all that results in four murders. The Op, in turn, does not shy away from violence, and killing foes is frequently a part of his job. He will also break the law when it stands in the way of his goals, but his actions are guided by a personal code of conduct that he does not violate. Other characters are not so virtuous; "$106,000 Blood Money" reveals one of the Op's fellow detectives in league with criminals, and Hammett frequently depicts high society figures associating with wrongdoers. The greatest threat to the Op's code comes from women. A favorite Hammett situation involves a seductive female criminal who attempts to use her allure to elude the detective or entice him to join her side. The Op often confesses his attraction for these women, but his response to Princess Zhukovski in "The Gutting of Couffignal" is a typical rebuff: "You think I'm a man and you're a woman. That's wrong. I'm a man-hunter and you're something that's been running in front of me. There's nothing human about it." Setting the precedent for other hard-boiled detectives, the Op is far removed from emotion of all kinds. His cool demeanor is portrayed in large part through the first-person narration employed in all of the stories. The Op relays events in an objective tone, reporting only what he sees and hears, placing emphasis on surface details rather than underlying feelings. This approach, along with the short declarative sentences used in the stories, have led to the frequent comparisons between Hammett and Hemingway. The unemotional aspects of Hammett's writing are offset, some critics note, by more sensitive characteristics, such as the detective's stubbornly defended code of honor. The Op's tenacious pursuit of solutions to crimes has also been viewed as the behavior of a romantic hero and is often compared to a knight's quest for the Holy Grail in medieval literature.

Critical Reception

While Hammett's novels such as *The Maltese Falcon* and *The Glass Key* are recognized as notable literary accomplishments, his short fiction has received a more moderate reaction. Critics generally concede that Hammett surpassed other crime fiction writers of his time; as Edward Margolies writes in *Which Way Did He Go?*, Hammett "wrote better than most, his narratives were more inventive, and he possessed a sense of humor." Noting weaknesses in his stories, some commentators have charged that Hammett's characterization in these works often relies on clichés—racial, sexual, and otherwise—resulting in one-dimensional figures, especially among the criminals that face the Continental Op. Other critics have objected to the extreme violence and implausible plots of the stories. Leonard Michaels, writing in the *New York Times Book Review*, sounded this complaint, declaring that events in the short works "tend to be absurd—unintentionally absurd." Hammett's intentions have become a frequent concern with contemporary reviewers. Several critics have noted that the Op frequently reaches conclusions that are hard to believe, but they offer different reasons for this. Some accuse Hammett of flawed story writing, of creating improbable resolutions without laying the necessary groundwork within the narrative. Others, such as Steven Marcus, declare that Hammett intentionally created the Op's improbable deductions. In this analy-

sis, Hammett intended the Op to be a character who constructs his own fictions within the story much as an author creates a fictitious narrative. In this fashion, some critics reason, Hammett used his work to comment on and draw attention to the storytelling process, an approach that would later become important to many experimental writers, especially in the 1960s and 1970s. Despite differing interpretations, the bulk of critical commentary is largely agreed on two points regarding the author's short fiction: as Hammett's earliest work, it is the stories that first illustrated his important innovations in the crime fiction genre, and served as a training ground where Hammett worked out many of the techniques that he later refined in his novels.

PRINCIPAL WORKS

Short Fiction

$106,000 Blood Money   1943
The Adventures of Sam Spade, and Other Stories   1944
*The Continental Op   1945
A Man Called Spade, and Other Stories   1945
The Return of the Continental Op   1945
Hammett Homicides   1946
Dead Yellow Women   1947
Nightmare Town   1948
The Creeping Siamese   1950
†*Woman in the Dark: More Adventures of the Continental Op*   1951
A Man Named Thin, and Other Stories   1962
The Big Knockover: Selected Stories and Short Novels   1966
*The Continental Op: More Stories from "The Big Knockover"   1967
*The Continental Op   1974

Other Major Works

The Dain Curse   (novel)   1929
‡*Red Harvest*   (novel)   1929
The Maltese Falcon   (novel)   1930
The Glass Key   (novel)   1931
Secret Agent X-9   (comic strip)   1934
The Thin Man   (novel)   1934
Watch on the Rhine   (screenplay)   [adapted from the play by Lillian Hellman]   1943

---

*The three books entitled *The Continental Op* are different story collections.

†The novella *Woman in the Dark* was first published serially in *Liberty Magazine* in 1933.

‡An earlier, serial version of *Red Harvest* entitled *The Cleansing of Poisonville* was published in *Black Mask* beginning in 1927.

CRITICISM

Ross Macdonald   (essay date 1964)

SOURCE: "Homage to Dashiell Hammett," in *Mystery Writers' Annual,* April, 1964, pp. 8, 24.

[*Macdonald, a highly regarded author in the crime fiction genre, was the author of numerous books, including a series of novels featuring private investigator Lew Archer. In the following excerpt, he notes some minor shortcomings of Hammett's fiction, but praises him as an effective and innovative writer.*]

I have been given some space to speak for the hard-boiled school of mystery writing. Let me use it to dwell for a bit on the work of Dashiell Hammett. He was the great innovator who invented the hard-boiled detective novel and used it to express and master the undercurrent of inchoate violence that runs through so much of American life.

In certain ways, it must be admitted, Hammett's heroes are reminiscent of unreconstructed Darwinian man; *McTeague* and *The Sea Wolf* stand directly behind them. But no matter how rough and appetent they may be, true representatives of a rough and appetent society, they are never allowed to run unbridled. Hammett's irony controls them. In fact he criticized them far more astringently and basically than similar men were criticized by Hemingway. In his later and less romantic moments Hammett was a close and disillusioned critic of the two-fisted hard-drinking woman-chasing American male that he derived partly from tradition and partly from observation, including self-observation.

Even in one of his very early stories, first published by [H. L.] Mencken in *Smart Set,* Hammett presents a character who might have been a parody of the Hemingway hero, except that he was pre-Hemingway. This huge brute is much attached to his beard. To make a short story shorter, the loss of his beard reveals that he used it to hide a receding chin and make him a public laughingstock. This isn't much more than an anecdote, but it suggests Hammett's attitude towards the half-evolved frontier male of our not too distant past. Shorn and urbanized, he became in Hammett's best novels a near-tragic figure, a lonely and suspicious alien who pits a hopeless but obstinate animal courage against the metropolitan jungle, a not very moral man who clings with a skeptic's desperation to a code of behavior empirically arrived at in a twilight world between chivalry and gangsterism.

Like the relationship of Charles Dickens and Wilkie Collins, the Hemingway-Hammett influence ran two ways. Hammett achieved some things that Hemingway never attempted. He placed his characters in situations as complex as those of life, in great cities like San Francisco and New York and Baltimore, and let them work out their dubious salvations under social and economic and political pressures. The subject of his novels, you might say, was the frontier male thrust suddenly, as the frontier disappeared, into the modern megalopolis; as Hemingway's was a similar man meeting war and women, and listening to the silence of his own soul.

Hammett's prose is not quite a prose that can say anything, as Chandler overenthusiastically claimed it could. But it is a clean useful prose, with remarkable range and force. It has pace and point, strong tactile values, the rhythms and colors of speech, all in the colloquial tradition that stretches from Mark Twain through Stephen Crane to Lardner and Mencken, the Dr. Johnson of our vernacular. Still it is a deadpan and rather external prose, artificial-seeming compared with Huck Finn's earthy rhetoric, flat in comparison with Fitzgerald's more subtly colloquial instrument. Hammett's ear for the current and the colloquial was a little too sardonically literal, and this is already tending to date his writing, though not seriously.

Analysis of any kind is alien to this prose. Moulding the surface of things, it lends itself to the vivid narration of rapid, startling action. Perhaps it tends to set too great a premium on action, as if the mind behind it were hurrying away from its own questions and deliberately restricting itself to the manipulation of appearances. It is in part the expression of that universally-met-with American type who avoids sensibility and introspection because they make you vulnerable in the world. At its worst such prose can be an unnecessary writing-down to the lowest common denominator of the democracy. But at its best it has great litotic power, as in some of Hemingway's earlier stories. . . .

Philip Durham   (essay date 1965)

SOURCE: "Hammett: Profiler of Hard-Boiled Yeggs," in *Los Angeles Times,* November 21, 1965, "Calendar" section, p. 1.

[*In the following review of* The Novels of Dashiell Hammett, *Durham notes the importance of Hammett's short stories and their influence on his novels.*]

What can one say about the novels of Dashiell Hammett except that they are as superbly written as one remembers them from more than 30 years ago? Here are five novels, all familiar to my generation: *Red Harvest, The Dain Curse, The Maltese Falcon, The Glass Key* and *The Thin Man.* But for the present generation—whose only contact with Hammett may be through a television rerun of "The Maltese Falcon"—Knopf [the publisher of *The Novels of Dashiell Hammett*] could have provided a preface. A short one might have gone like this:

What is now known in America and England as the *Black Mask* school of writing began in the early spring of 1920 in a pulp magazine called *Black Mask,* founded by Henry L. Mencken and George Jean Nathan. After six months Mencken and Nathan sold their pulp magazine for a nice profit. Under the subsequent editorship of such capable men as Phil Cody and Harry North, *Black Mask* took on a specific character. Within two or three years the heroic man of violence emerged. The private investigator was poised and indestructibly ready to take over as the protector of American ideals.

The "golden decade" of *Black Mask* began in November, 1926, under the editorship of Capt. Joseph T. Shaw. The new editor had a vision—that through *Black Mask* he could make a unique contribution to American literature. In the pages of his magazine Shaw singled out the stories of Dashiell Hammett as approximating what he had in mind: "simplicity for the sake of clarity, plausibility and belief." Shaw wanted action, but he held that "action is meaningless unless it involves recognizable human character in three-dimensional form."

With Shaw as the editor and Hammett as the leader, the *Black Mask* school flourished for 10 years. The editor insisted that his writers observe a cardinal principle. They were to create the illusion of reality by allowing their characters to act and talk tough rather than by making them do it. Instead of telling the reader how infallible the actors were, the authors permitted their heroes to demonstrate their abilities.

Perhaps the best known hero of the *Black Mask* school was the Continental Op (the private operator from the San Francisco office of the Continental Detective Agency). Dashiell Hammett, the creator of the Op, had had a varied career, including service in World War I and several years as a Pinkerton detective. Hammett—who knew a man who once stole a Ferris-wheel—began to turn his experiences into stories.

Dashiell Hammett, as the leader of the hard-boiled school of detective fiction, began to experiment with writing techniques. In his *Black Mask* stories he worked with plot, trying to keep it from becoming too obviously stereotyped. He created a protagonist in his short stories who would later stand up in longer works of fiction. He used the theme of the rugged individualist righting social wrongs. He concentrated on the objective, hard-boiled style, trying to make it as action-packed as possible.

During the 32 months from November 1927 to June 1930, Dashiell Hammett's four important novels were published serially in *Black Mask*. . . . They were clearly his best fiction, but they were successful only because he had previously worked out everything in them in his short stories.

—*Philip Durham*

In his *Black Mask* short stories from 1923 to 1927, Hammett developed his style. According to Raymond Chandler, Hammett "was spare, frugal, hard-boiled, but he did over and over again what only the best writers can ever do at all. He wrote scenes that seemed never to have been written before."

The clipped prose, the Hammett trade-mark, appeared in the early stories. Action abounded, but the economy of expression implied even more action than was visible. "**The Golden Horseshoe**" provided an example of violence in tempo.

A character named Gooseneck fired at one called Kewpie at the moment she threw a knife at him. Kewpie was "spun back across the room—hammered back by bullets that tore through her chest. Her back hit the wall. She pitched forward to the floor." The knife caught Gooseneck in the throat, and he "couldn't get his words past the blade."

In "**Women, Politics and Murder**" the style rattled like machine-gun fire: "My bullet cut the gullet out of him."

The hero of the short stories developed with the style. Although he played the traditional knightly role, he did not look the part. He was nameless, fat and 40.

In "**Zigzags of Treachery**" he did not like eloquence because "if it isn't effective enough to pierce your hide, it's tiresome; and if it's effective enough then it muddles your thoughts." He was not "a brilliant thinker," yet he had "flashes of intelligence." He was a man of action who liked his jobs to be "simply jobs—emotions are nuisances during business hours."

By 1927 Hammett was ready for more sustained fiction. His hero, style and setting had developed beyond the limits of the short story. In February and May of 1927 *Black Mask* carried two of Hammett's long stories—"**The Big Knock-Over**" and "**$106,000 Blood Money**"—which were published together as his first novel. One hundred and fifty of the country's finest crooks gathered in San Francisco where they simultaneously knocked over the Seaman's National and the Golden State Trust. During the noisy affair 16 cops were killed and three times that many were wounded; 12 bystanders and bank clerks were killed; and the bandits lost seven dead and had 31 of their number taken as bleeding prisoners. After the shooting died down, the Op and two assistants took over the job. They took care of the crooks who were left and then tidied up the town.

If there is such a thing as the poetry of violence, Hammett clearly achieved it in his first novel, "**$106,000 Blood Money.**" The Continental Op got with the rhythmical spirit of the occasion: "It was a swell bag of nails. Swing right, swing left, kick, swing right, swing left, kick. Don't hesitate, don't look for targets. God will see that there's always a mug there for your gun or black-jack to sock, a belly for your foot."

During the 32 months from November 1927 to June 1930, Dashiell Hammett's four important novels were published serially in *Black Mask—Red Harvest The Dain Curse, The Maltese Falcon* and *The Glass Key.* They were clearly his best fiction, but they were successful only because he had previously worked out everything in them in his short stories. The first two continued the Op as the first person narrator, although he changed character somewhat in the second. The third developed the swaggering Sam Spade. And the fourth created a variation on the character in Ned Beaumont and also used the third person viewpoint.

Red Harvest (dedicated to Joseph Shaw) was originally a group of separate stories referred to under the general title "The Cleansing of Poisonville." They revolved around the Op at his hard-boiled best. The Op set out to clean up a crime-ridden city by playing everyone off against the middle. By his own count one and a half dozen criminals were murdered. He admitted that he could "swing the play legally," but he decided that it was "easier to have them killed off, easier and surer."

The Op did not allow himself any sexual diversion, but he did go in for some very heavy drinking.

Dashiell Hammett's last major effort, *The Thin Man,* was obviously written under excessive Hollywood influence. The original version of the novel had been planned and begun in 1930, in the style of that period. Only 65 pages were completed. The setting was San Francisco and its environs, the viewpoint the third person, the detective a kind of modified Op.

The most interesting aspect of the fragment was the unreal quality that Hammett insisted on attaching to the hero. He was referred to as untouchable, as not even a corpse but a ghost, as one with whom it was impossible to come into contact—like trying to hold a handful of smoke.

It was three years, one of which was spent in Hollywood, before Hammett returned to his fragment. Unable or unwilling to continue it, he wrote a different novel by the same name.

The Thin Man, dedicated to Lillian Hellman, was not published in *Black Mask.* It is a good novel in the older tradition of detective fiction but it does not belong in the *Black Mask* school.

For some, Dashiell Hammett wrote beyond the tradition of detective fiction by specifically expressing the giddiness of the 1920s—the period when violence and brutality were accepted as simply a part of the times. For many, Hammett's hero spoke for men who had lost faith in the values of their society.

Newsweek (essay date 1966)

SOURCE: "Continental Op," in *Newsweek,* Vol. XVIII, No. 4, July 25, 1966, p. 93.

[*In the following review of* The Big Knockover, *the critic discusses characterization in the Continental Op stories.*]

Like his literary contemporaries—Hemingway, Fitzgerald, Faulkner, Nathanael West—Dashiell Hammett was a kaleidoscope of the contradictions of the American character, contradictions that were marshaled into great writing only rarely even by the greatest of that generation. Hemingway had his stoic Hemingway heroes, Fitzgerald his ravaged idealists and Hammett had his detectives, the super-professional private cops who turned the human quest into a manhunt and bulldozed their way through desperation with (literally) a gun in one fist and a blackjack in the other.

The hero of all but one of these stories, which have been put together in hard covers for the first time [in a collection entitled ***The Big Knockover***] by Hammett's great friend of 30 years, playwright Lillian Hellman, is not Sam Spade or Nick Charles but that prince of private eyes, the nameless Continental Op. Like Hemingway's Jake Barnes,

like Fitzgerald's Gatsby, the Op is a hard-headed realist wrapped around a tender-souled idealist. The stories are short-order caldrons of corruption, duplicity, violence and cynicism, but somehow, not far from the surface, the scent of a once and future paradise comes through, where toughness and tenderness lie down unashamedly together.

"She was neither tall nor short, thin nor plump. She wore a black Russian tunic affair, green-trimmed and hung with silver dinguses . . . She was probably 20. Her eyes were blue, her mouth red, her teeth white, the hair-ends showing under her black-green-and-silver turban were brown and she had a nose. Without getting steamed up over the details, she was nice." Here is tough-tender Hammett in a nutshell, trying to steer a safe course between seeing sharply and feeling softly, and drawing a picture like a cross between Aubrey Beardsley and John Held Jr.

The stories are full of fascinating females, most of them mixtures of sugar and cyanide, ranging from the runaway hellions of the Op's many "missing-daughter jobs" to the inscrutable Lillian Shan, to Angel Grace Cardigan, the honorable con girl, to the epic figure of Big Flora, the "handsome, brutal . . . fight-bred animal." But there is almost no sensuality—the fat, fortyish Op ("who had forgotten what it was like to believe in fairies") simply ricochets from girl to girl with the efficiency of a bullet, doing what he has to do, saying what he has to say, killing whom he has to kill and only rarely feeling what he has no time to feel. "I know other words," he says, "but we'll stick to this one . . . nice."

The girls, even the lethal ones, are flowers in a jungle of poisonous weeds—Bluepoint Vance, Snohomish Shitey, the Dis-and-Dat Kid, Donkey Marr, last of the bowlegged Marrs, Toby the Lugs "who used to brag about picking President Wilson's pocket in a Washington vaudeville theater," and Toots Salda, "the strongest man in crookdom, who had once picked up and run away with two Savannah coppers to whom he was handcuffed." The Op doesn't believe in fairies, but his adventures are twentieth-century fairy stories in which crushing the most unconscionable rat bastards becomes a kind of reverse utopia, the lost paradise which is re-won by cool thinking, tight-lipped palaver and grim homicidal efficiency—Galahad with a gat.

The collection is uneven, but the amazing and wonderfully American thing is that pulp fiction (most of the stories were written for *Black Mask*) can be so brilliantly conceived and beautifully welded. There are at least two Hammettian masterpieces—**"Dead Yellow Women,"** a labyrinthine, humorous, careening Chinese-box construction of shocks and surprises, and **"The Big Knockover,"** in which Hammett's penchant for the supersonic triplecross reaches almost epic proportions.

Hammett is the tragedy of the American between-wars writers writ small—but sharp and intense. That tragedy surfaces in **"Tulip,"** an unfinished "novel" of the 1950s in which Hammett makes a belated and poignantly disastrous attempt to construct a philosophical work out of the outer and inner life which he was never able to get into his fables of violence and chicanery. In the end, it is the Fatima-smoking, poker-playing Continental Op, that paterfamilias of private eyes, who speaks for Hammett and the lost paradise of his tabloid terrors. "I've got horny skin," says the Op, "over what's left of my soul."

Frederick H. Gardner   (essay date 1966)

SOURCE: "Return of the Continental Op," in *The Nation,* New York, Vol. 203, No. 14, October 31, 1966, pp. 454-56.

[*In this excerpt from a review of* The Big Knockover, *Gardner comments on Hammett's literary style and imaginative use of the detective fiction genre.*]

Fitzgerald said he was haunted by the conviction that Ring Lardner "got less percentage of himself on paper than any other American author of the first flight." Hammett got even less on paper, so much less that his rank is uncertain. His use of language is, certainly, "first flight." He did for American slang—the argots of hobos, cowboys, seamen, boxers, longshoremen, miners, Wobblies, and, of course, cops and robbers—what Mark Twain had previously done for the American vernacular: used it on the level of art. Hammett never merely played lexicographer to the underworld. He selected the witty, colorful elements of the jargon and used them naturally, knowledgeably, without dazzling or digressing for the sake of innovation but always to advance his story. In **"Fly Paper,"** for example, as the Op tries to figure out where a criminal has fled, he reasons:

> The big man was a yegg. San Francisco was on fire for him. The yegg instinct would be to use a rattler to get away from trouble. The freight yards were in this end of town. Maybe he would be shifty enough to lie low instead of trying to powder. In that case, he probably hadn't crossed Market Street at all. If he stuck, there would still be a chance of picking him up tomorrow. If he was hightailing, it was catch him now or not at all.

As for commonplace profanities, Hammett would skirt them with a graceful précis such as: "He called her four unlovely names, the mildest of which was, 'a dumb twist,' " Occasionally he would slip in a newly coined obscenity to test his editor's conversance with the ever-changing language. One editor failed to blue-pencil the word "gunsel." He took it to mean a gunman's young assistant; it actually meant a homosexual hanger-on. Other writers of detective stories, emulators of Hammett, repeated the editor's mistake and began using "gunsel" in the inaccurate sense. Their errors stuck and the word, when it is used nowadays, is usually used incorrectly.

The imitators proliferated and Hammett soon became typecast as "the founder of the hard-boiled school of detective fiction." It might be useful to consider his work in terms of what had come before. Twain had made the literary break with Europe, but those in the first flush of freedom always look back to make sure the bonds are really broken, and that's what Twain did in *The Innocents Abroad.* Hammett was second-generation free of the genteel tradition; to him "abroad" meant across the Pacific, not the Atlantic.

Hammett shared with Twain, and perhaps derived from him, a narrative style based on the most American of all forms of humor: understatement. Consider the way Twain begins *The Mysterious Stranger*:

> It was in 1590—winter. Austria was far away from the world, and asleep; it was still the Middle Ages in Austria, and promised to remain so forever. Some even set it away back centuries upon centuries and said that by the mental and spiritual clock it was still the age of Belief in Austria. But they meant it as a compliment, not a slur, and so it was taken and we were all proud of it.

And the way Hammett gets into *Red Harvest*:

> I first heard Personville called Poisonville by a red haired mucker named Hickey Dewey in the Big Ship in Butte. He also called a shirt a shoit. I didn't think anything of what he had done to the city's name. Later I heard men who could manage their r's give it the same pronunciation. I still didn't see anything in it but the meaningless sort of humor that used to make richardsnary the thieves' word for dictionary. A few years later I went to Personville and learned better.

Since he conceives of murder and mayhem as proper subjects for matter-of-fact humor, Hammett's stories never become gruesome even though the situations are inherently gruesome. In **"The Big Knockover"** (a tale I thought was part of **"Blood Money,"** but which is run separately in [*The Big Knockover*]) the Op comes into a house containing fourteen dead men, eleven poisoned, three shot. Instead of describing the gore, Hammett provides a roster:

> There was the Dis-and-Dat Kid, who had crashed out of Leavenworth only two months before; Sheeny Holmes; Snohomish Shitey, supposed to have died a hero in France in 1919; L. A. Slim, from Denver, sockless and underwearless as usual, with a thousand-dollar bill sewed in each shoulder of his coat; Spider Girrucci wearing a steel-mesh vest under his shirt and a scar from crown to chin where his brother had carved him years ago; Old Pete Best, once a congressman; Nigger Vojan, who once won $175,000 in a Chicago crap game—*Abracadabra* tattooed on him in three places; Alphabet Shorty McCoy; Tom Brooks, Alphabet Shorty's brother-in-law, who invented the Richmond razzle-dazzle and bought three hotels with the profits; Red Cudahy, who stuck up a Union Pacific train in 1924; Denny Burke; Bull McGonickle, still pale from fifteen years in Joliet; Toby the Lugs, Bull's running-mate, who used to brag about picking President Wilson's pocket in a Washington vaudeville theatre; and Paddy the Mex.

Understatement, coolness if you will, enables Hammett to keep some distance from his characters. He needs the distance because, shades of Twain, he is torn between fondness for human beings and disgust over their depravity. Hammett's Op is frequently turning in women whom he would not turn down. Sam Spade does so in *The Maltese Falcon.* The Op, in **"Blood Money,"** shoots a young colleague whom he particularly likes when the colleague turns to crime (because *he* cannot resist a girl). In *The Dain Curse,* a man whom the Op was once "chummy with" turns out to be the villain. Thus the style based on understatement lends itself to an understatement of theme, freeing Hammett from the sentimentality and good-against-evil framework of the traditional mystery. To the Op each case is just a job, not a moral crusade.

Hammett's use of understatement is often mistaken for terseness. He could narrate in what seems like the rhythm of spoken words, and his stories move fast; but he also has a great penchant for elaboration, which he indulges with every character, no matter how minor, who comes onto the scene. You can go through the tale called **"The Scorched Face,"** count the number of people (and even buildings) that figure in it and the number of descriptions, physical or otherwise, given for them. The numbers are equal. A maid, interviewed briefly, goes undescribed, but we learn that a lawyer who doesn't figure in the tale at all is "a pink faced, white-haired old boy named Norwall, who had the reputation of knowing more about corporations than all the Morgans, but who hadn't the least idea as to what police procedures was all about." Upon inspection, Hammett's style is the opposite of terse. His settings are exotic, and his inclination as a plotter is toward the more intricate and inclusive.

Why he allowed himself to be confined so strictly by his subject matter, why he relied on the mystery situation to bring a story to life is a mystery more profound than any the Continental Op ever tackled. Hammett himself tries to solve it in **"Tulip."** Tulip is the name of a retired lieuten-

ant colonel under whom Pop (as Hammett was known in the Aleutians) served in World War II. When they first met Pop "had a feeling that he might come to represent a side of me." Now Tulip is visiting Pop at the country place where he resides—reading, tinkering with gadgets, scrutinizing the natural world, but not writing—after his release from prison. An egotist, Tulip wants his life story written up by Pop. This starts Pop to thinking about his own life:

> I've been in a couple of wars—or at least in the Army while they were going on—and in federal prisons and I had t. b. for seven years and have been married as often as I chose and have had children and grandchildren and except for one fairly nice but pointless brief short story about a lunger going to Tijuana for an afternoon and evening holiday from his hospital near San Diego I've never written a word about any of these things. Why? All I can say is they're not for me. Maybe not yet, maybe not ever. I used to try now and then—and I suppose I tried hard, the way I tried a lot of things—but they never came out meaning very much to me.

Fitzgerald wrote that Lardner's topic, baseball, was "a boy's game with no more possibilities in it than a boy could master, a game bounded by walls. . . . However deeply Ring cut into it, his cake had exactly the diameter of Frank Chance's diamond." The Pinkertons did for Hammett what the Cubs did for Lardner; they provided material but walled him in. Eventually this man who deplored violence must have developed a deep ambivalence toward writing about it. Fitzgerald says that when Lardner became ambivalent toward his work he fell into "a habit of silence." Hammett did, too. He tried "to start a new literary life" with **"Tulip,"** Hellman writes in the introduction. But the novel is sad and truncated, like Pete Rieser's career:

> "When you write," Pop tells Tulip, "you want fame, fortune and personal satisfaction. You want to write what you want to write and to feel that it's good and to sell millions of copies of it and have everybody whose opinion you value think it's good, and you want this to go on for hundreds of years."

His writing brought Hammett fame and fortune. If it did not bring him personal satisfaction in fullest measure, I like to think that the difference was made up by the pride he took in Hellman's work. It was he who got her going as a serious writer by suggesting that she use an actual event as the basis of a play; that advice led to *The Children's Hour.* Through the years, Hellman acknowledges, his encouragement and criticism, his physical presence, helped her develop as a playwright. Evidently her progress meant a great deal to him. When he expressed his disappointment over an early draft of *The Autumn Garden* he told Hellman: "You started as a serious writer. That's what I liked, that's what I worked for." On another, quite different occasion, he spoke of her as "my left arm."

I think Hammett is due for a renaissance and I hope *The Big Knockover* hastens it. Crime on the scale Hammett described is less significant in America now that the gang-

Hammett at work, January 1934.

sters belong to country clubs and sit on the boards of directors. But significance, literary or otherwise, is not this book's selling point; the cult of nostalgia is. Dashiell Hammett, after all, created the character Humphrey Bogart merely portrayed. One of his smaller accomplishments, I think, but it would be good to see Hammett in vogue no matter how ironic the reason.

Walter Blair   (essay date 1967)

SOURCE: "Dashiell Hammett: Themes and Techniques," in *Essays on American Literature in Honor of Jay B. Hubbell,* edited by Clarence Gohdes, Duke University Press, 1967, pp. 295-306.

[*In the following excerpt, Blair offers an overview of Hammett's career, noting many similarities between the works of Hammett and Ernest Hemingway.*]

The influence of subliterary works (sentimental fiction and poetry, popular humor, melodrama, and the like) on literary works, or the ways literary works shape subliterature often are fascinating. Without Gothic fiction Poe and Hawthorne would have been impossible; without Scott and Dickens nineteenth-century American humor, with all its vulgarity, could not have been written. An instance is the career of Dashiell Hammett (1894-1961), writer of detective fiction. Two uncertainties furnish difficulties but add interest to a consideration of him: (1) the possibility that Hammett's writings, despite their genre, are good enough to classify not as subliterature but as literature, and (2) the impossibility of one's being sure about the precise direction of the influence—about who influenced whom. Regardless, affiliations between the detective story fictionist and some of his more reputable contemporaries, particularly Ernest Hemingway, have great interest, and in his best novel, Hammett brilliantly, and I think uniquely, adapted current techniques to his genre.

Hammett's lasting popularity and repute suggest that his work may be of more than ephemeral value. Having crowded practically all his writing into a decade, he published practically nothing after January, 1934. But between that date and his death twenty-seven years later, his novels and collected short stories sold four million copies in paperback editions; three of his novels (*Red Harvest,* 1929; *The Dain Curse,* 1929; and *The Maltese Falcon,* 1930) were collected in an *Omnibus* in 1935; and *The Complete Novels* (the three above plus *The Glass Key,* 1931, and *The Thin Man,* 1934) appeared in 1942. A few months after Hammett's death, a million copies in paperback of his various works were issued; in October, 1965, *The Novels of Dashiell Hammett* was reset and printed from new plates; in June, 1966, his **The Big Knockover: Selected Stories and Short Novels** appeared; and, the following month, three of his novels (*Glass Key, Falcon, Thin Man*) were reissued in paperback editions.

The nature of the critical acclaim that accompanied such successes raises the strong possibility that something more than sensational appeals was responsible. Granted, a share of these sales may well have been stimulated by portrayals of Hammett's characters in popular movies, in radio and television series, even in comic strips. But surely a good share was stimulated by Hammett's remarkable—perhaps unique—reputation.

Indicative of the nature of this is the fact that *The Maltese Falcon* went through at least fifteen printings as part of a prestigious collection, the Modern Library. Indicative, too, is the esteem in which the author was held by enthusiastic readers who belonged to a rather unusual group. Detective stories for about five decades (since World War I) were read, liked, and discussed by many professional men, political leaders, pundits, and professors. As a result, a genre of subliterature was assessed and in some instances praised by highly influential—as well as perceptive and articulate—readers. The admiration of these readers for Hammett's writings has been consistently strong and widespread. In addition, leading reviewers of mystery novels and informed historians of the genre such as Howard Haycraft and Ellery Queen, and famous practitioners such as Raymond Chandler and Erle Stanley Gardner habitually and casually—as if there were no possible question about the matter—referred to him as the greatest writer in his field, perhaps even "a genius." Finally, respected literary men not as a rule much interested in mystery fiction manifested warm admiration for Hammett—Somerset Maugham, Peter Quennell, and Robert Graves of England; André Malraux and André Gide of France; and a trio of American Nobel prize winners—Sinclair Lewis, William Faulkner, and Ernest Hemingway. Quennell in 1934 correctly remarked that Hammett was almost alone among mystery writers "in being praised by writers as a serious writer and by good novelists as a master of their business."

Available details about Hammett's life before he began to write indicate that it provided unusual and exploitable experiences but scant training for a writing career. Born in 1894 in St. Mary's County on the eastern shore of Maryland, he attended a technical school, Baltimore Polytechnic Institute, and was a dropout from its nonliterary program at thirteen. During the next several years he had a number of quite unliterary jobs—messenger, newsboy, freight clerk, timekeeper, stevedore, yardman, and machine operator. After that for eight years he was an operative for the Pinkerton Detective Agency, his chief literary exercises presumably being the writing of reports on his cases. He then served during World War I as a sergeant in the ambulance corps. After emerging from the war with damaged lungs and after a period of hospitalization and a brief return to detective work, he began to make use of remembrances of his sleuthing in articles and stories.

His writings were first published early in the 1920's, some in *Pearson's Magazine,* some, unpredictably, in H. L. Mencken's *Smart Set,* most of them in a pulp mystery magazine, *Black Mask.* At first the writings attracted little attention, in part it may be because one Carroll John Daly had briefly preceded Hammett in writing what would in time be dubbed hard-boiled detective stories, in part because the importance of originating this genre was not recognized or at least discussed at the time, in part because before long other writers (Gardner, for instance) began to publish similar stories. Then an editor, Joseph T. Shaw, decided that since Hammett was "the leader in the thought that finally brought the magazine [*Black Mask*] its distinctive form," he should be featured and the featuring, coupled with Hammett's outstanding talent, gave his stories pre-eminence. And when between 1929 and 1934, Hammett's five novels were published by Alfred A. Knopf and individually and collectively were enthusiastically praised far and wide, justifiably or no, he came to be known as the founder of the school.

The short stories as well as the more famous novels in time were appreciated for their innovations. For, drawing upon memories of his Pinkerton career, Hammett pictured crime and the work of a private operative (so everybody said) in a much more "real" fashion than they had been pictured before; and since the first-person narrator in many stories was a detective and since in all the stories the dialogue was largely that of dicks and criminals he used an economical vernacular style which seemed unusually lifelike.

Especially when compared with that of earlier mystery stories, Hammett's subject matter was revolutionary. From the time of their most venerable ancestor, Poe's C. Auguste Dupin, leading fictional detectives had been gentlemen and they had been erudite. In 1927, in a review of a book [*The Benson Murder Case,* in *Saturday Review of Literature,* Jan. 15, 1927] about one of the most exquisite and purportedly learned of such sleuths, Hammett himself scoffs at the type and at the ignorance of its portrayers about crime:

> This Philo Vance is in the Sherlock Holmes tradition. . . . He is a bore when he discusses art and philosophy, but when he switches to criminal psychology he is delightful. There is a theory that anyone who talks enough on any subject must, if only by chance, finally say something not altogether incorrect. Vance disproves this theory: he manages always, and usually ridiculously, to be wrong. His exposition of the technique employed by a gentleman shooting another gentleman who sits six feet in front of him deserves a place in a *How to be a detective by mail* course.

Raymond Chandler praised Hammett for doing away with the unrealities here attacked:

> Hammett gave murder back to the kind of people that commit it for reasons, not just to provide a corpse; and with the means at hand, not with hand-wrought duelling pistols, curare, and tropical fish. He put them down on paper as they are, and made them talk and think in the language they customarily used for these purposes.

The linking of matter that is "real" ("put them down on paper *as they are*") with a style that is "real" occurs in much of the praise of the detective story writer. Chandler further remarks that at its best the style "is the American language."

Anyone familiar with discussions of developments in presumably more serious American fiction during the 1920's will recognize oft-repeated concerns—with the increased "reality" of the matter and with the "Americanization" of the style. Edmund Wilson saw both in Ernest Heming-

way's earliest fiction and mentioned them in a *Dial* review of it in October, 1924. "Too proud an artist to simplify in the interest of conventional pretenses," went one sentence, "he [Hemingway] is showing you what life is like." Elsewhere:

> . . . Miss Stein, Mr. Anderson, and Mr. Hemingway may now be said to form a school by themselves. The characteristic of this school is a naïveté of language, often passing into the colloquialism of the character dealt with. . . . It is a distinctively American development in prose—as opposed to more or less successful American achievements in the traditional style of English prose. . . .

After *Red Harvest* appeared in 1929, critics of Hammett frequently compared him to Hemingway. "It is doubtful," wrote Herbert Asbury in a review of that first novel, "if even Hemingway has ever written more effective dialogue. . . . The author displays a style of amazing clarity and compactness, devoid of literary frills and furbelows, and his characters speak the crisp, hard-boiled language of the underworld . . . truly, without a single false or jarring note." Gide asserted that the author's dialogues "can be compared [among American writers] only with the best in Hemingway." Peter Quennell held that the last of the novels, *The Thin Man* of 1934, provides interior evidence that Hammett admired Hemingway, since it "contains portraits, snatches of dialogue written in a terse colloquial vein—and lurid glimpses of New York drinking society, that Hemingway himself could not have improved upon."

Quennell was not alone in believing that Hemingway influenced Hammett, but a few critics wondered whether Hammett might not have influenced Hemingway. Gide said that some of Hammett's dialogues could "give pointers to Hemingway or even Faulkner." However, since both authors began to write and to publish obscurely almost simultaneously, the likelihood appears to be that neither shaped the earlier writings of the other. And by the time each had mastered his craft, the possibility of either shaping the work of the other was very small. Resemblances arose more probably because of similarities in temperament, in experiences, and in background.

Not only were the two alike in picturing a world that met the post-World War I demand for "more reality" and in using a style that was "more laconic" and "more colloquial"; they were alike in other important ways. Wounded by the war and unhappy in the postwar world, both were battered by disillusionment and cynicism, and both created worlds and characters justifying their attitude. Their protagonists are forced to cope with such worlds and their inhabitants. "Hemingway's favorite characters," André Maurois has noticed, "are men who deal with death and accept its risk": the same remark of course could be made about Hammett's favorite characters. Moreover, as Joseph Haas recently remarked [in the Chicago *Daily News,* June 18, 1966], "Their similarities don't end there, either. Their heroes were much alike, and we find it easy to put Sam Spade in Jake Barnes' place, or to imagine that Robert Jordan and the Continental Op[erator] could have become good friends. They all lived by that simple, sentimental code of loyalty, courage and cynicism in a world of betrayal." Many discussions of Hemingway's morality indicate that his code was a rather more complex one than Haas suggests; and so, I venture to say, was Hammett's. Interestingly, both men were accused from time to time of having no standards—probably because they both were contemptuous of many pre-World War I standards and because they both admiringly portrayed heroes who were. Oscar Handlin has said of Hammett's heroes: "Their virtues were distinctly personal—courage, dignity, and patience; and to them the hero clung for their own sake, not because the client for whom he fought had any worth. Honor to Sam Spade was conformity to a code of rules which he himself invented, a means of demonstrating his own worth against the world." The same, or something very like it, could be said of the codes of Hemingway's heroes.

Both men's lives were shaped by similar personal codes. That Hemingway's life was has been clearly demonstrated. Hammett's code compelled him at the age of forty-eight to enlist in the United States army for service in World War II and to carry out a dull assignment in the Aleutians not only with meticulous care but with gusto. Lillian Hellman tells of another instance in 1951:

> He had made up honor early in his life and stuck with his rules, fierce in his protection of them. In 1951 he went to jail because he and two other trustees of the bail bond fund of the Civil Rights Congress refused to reveal the names of the contributors to the fund. The truth was that Hammett had never been in the office of the Committee and did not know the name of a single contributor. The night before he was to appear in court, I said, "Why don't you say that you don't know the names?" "No," he said, "I can't say that. . . . I guess it has something to do with keeping my word . . . but . . . if it were my life, I would give it for what I think democracy is and I don't let cops or judges tell me what I think democracy is."

He served a term of six months in a federal prison.

The codes of both Hemingway and Hammett related not only to their lives but also to their writing. "The great thing," remarked the former in 1932, "is to last and get your work done and see and learn and understand; and write when there is something that you know." In a late uncompleted story, **"Tulip"** [published in **The Big Knockover** in 1966], a character obviously voicing Hammett's opinions states a similar belief that an author must write only about matters that have real significance for him. The speaker, a professional fictionist, has never written a word about some of his experiences: "Why? All I can say is that they're not for me. Maybe not yet, maybe not ever. I used to try now and then . . . but they never came out meaning very much to me."

Both authors believed strongly that harsh self-discipline was an essential to good writing. Hemingway did not go to Stockholm to receive the Nobel prize in 1954 because he refused to interrupt his writing of a novel that was going well. His manuscripts attest to the fact that, word by word, he wrote with infinite care. Lillian Hellman testifies that, when writing a novel (*The Thin Man*), Hammett similarly let the task of composition possess him: "Life changed: the drinking stopped, the parties were over. The locking-in time had come and nothing was allowed to disturb it until the book was finished. I had never seen anybody work that way: the care for every word, the pride in the neatness of the typed page itself, the refusal for ten days or two weeks to go out even for a walk for fear something would be lost."

During the last few decades probably no other aspect of the technique of fiction has loomed as large in the concerns of critics and the conscious procedures of authors as the fictional point of view. Fictionists as different—and as influential—as Mark Twain and a bit later Henry James independently noticed the tremendous significance the choice of this had in shaping their fiction. James, and after James many leading critics, have discussed exhaustively the authors' or the narrators' insights into characters' thoughts and feelings, and the authors' or the narrators' biases and attitudes, as the narratives reveal them. Often the discussions have been very illuminating.

In about twenty-five short stories and in the first two of Hammett's novels, *Red Harvest* and *The Dain Curse,* the first-person narrator and the solver of the puzzle is an operative employed by the Continental Detective Agency. Unlike the exquisites of chiefly ratiocinative mystery stories this man (whose name is never revealed) is short, plump, and middle-aged, thus in his very ordinary appearance contrasting with a Dupin or a Sherlock Holmes. In an early story, **"The Gutting of Couffignal,"** he explains that for him his enthusiasm about his job is a strong motive:

> . . . I like being a detective, like the work. And liking work makes you want to do it as well as you can. Otherwise there'd be no sense to it. . . . I don't know anything else, don't enjoy anything else, don't want to know or enjoy anything else. You can't weigh that against any sum of money. Money is good stuff. I haven't anything against it. But in the past eighteen years I've been getting my fun out of chasing crooks and solving riddles. . . . I can't imagine a pleasanter future than twenty-some years more of it.

As Leonard Marsh has noticed, the Op's methods were accordingly different:

> The conventional tale focused on the investigator's mental prowess; the later variety stressed the detective's physical engagement with the criminal. . . . in [Hammett's] stories he saw crime not as a completed history to be attacked with the mind, but as a dynamic activity to be conducted with force as well as cunning. . . . the Op adapts venerable investigative concepts to modern police methods. He painstakingly collects facts. He goes to the street, not to the study or the laboratory, fortified by familiarity with criminal behavior, by his wit, courage, endurance, luck. . . . He obtains information by surveillance and by questioning anyone remotely associated with crime. Finally, he often seeks help from other private operatives, from hotel and police detectives, from hired informants, from taxi drivers and railroad employees.

These techniques would be worthless, however, without the Op's ability to deduce the relevance of information and to exploit errors or weaknesses while in direct contact with his adversaries. . . .

Since action plays so large a part in the process, and since the detective's ratiocination is detailed at intervals and briefly, the narrator can (like a Twain, a Conrad, or a Hemingway) tell much of his story very concretely. Erle Stanley Gardner notices that the Continental Op stories in *Black Mask* "were told in terms of action . . . told objectively, and there was about them that peculiar attitude of aloofness and detachment which is so characteristic of the Hammett style." The same might be said of the novels in which the Continental Op appeared. And the operative's frequent concentration on the action and withholding of statements about his own reactions added mystery and suspense. Gide noticed this in *Red Harvest,* which he called "a remarkable achievement, the last word in atrocity, cynicism, and horror": "Dashiell Hammett's dialogues, in which every character is trying to deceive all the others and in which the truth slowly becomes visible through the haze of deception, can be compared only with the best in Hemingway."

Even the first-person narrator's feelings and thoughts are often withheld. An outstanding instance is in Chapter XXVI of *Red Harvest,* wherein, after a drugged sleep on Dinah Brand's living room Chesterfield, the Op awakens to find himself in the dining room, his right hand holding an ice pick, the sharp blade of which is buried in Dinah's left breast. "She was lying on her back, dead," he goes on. Then he tells of his actions—his examining the body, the room, the adjacent rooms, and of his departing—all without a word detailing his emotional reactions or his thoughts about the woman's death.

The Continental Op disappears after *The Dain Curse,* and the next two novels, *The Maltese Falcon* and *The Glass Key,* are told in the third person. . . . [In] both books the author abjures insight into any of the characters' thoughts or feelings. What Walter R. Books says about *The Glass Key* is true of both: "Mr. Hammett does not show you [the characters'] thoughts, only their actions. . . ." Because not one but practically all the characters are either tight-lipped stoics or superb liars, the reader's attempts to discover what makes characters tick, what they are trying to do and how, are baffled, and the mystery is greatly augmented.

In *The Thin Man,* Hammett returns to the first-person narrator, here a former detective, Nick Charles, who is persuaded to make use of his detecting skills again. Nick is very different from the Continental Op: he is attractive, sophisticated and witty. He resembles the earlier narrator in being cynical and worldly and in being unrevealing about his emotional and intellectual responses to most people and events. In the final novel as in the first, the author therefore utilizes a fictional point of view that is well adapted to the genre which he is writing—one productive of mystery and suspense.

Raymond Chandler on Hammett:

Hammett gave murder back to the kind of people that commit it for reasons, not just to provide a corpse; and with the means at hand, not hand-wrought dueling pistols, curare and tropical fish. He put these people down on paper as they were, and he made them talk and think in the language they customarily used for these purposes. . . . Hammett's style at its worst was as formalized as a page of *Marius the Epicurean*; at its best it could say almost anything.

Raymond Chandler, in his The Simple Art of Murder, *1972.*

Steven Marcus   (essay date 1974)

SOURCE: An introduction to *The Continental Op* by Dashiell Hammett, edited by Steven Marcus, Random House, 1974, pp. ix-xxix.

[*In this excerpt Marcus discusses the philosophical underpinnings of Hammett's work; he also finds that Hammett's protagonists are often involved in a "fiction-making" activity that establishes them as unique figures in the crime fiction genre. For a rebuttal to Marcus's assertions, see Roger Sale's essay dated 1975.*]

I was first introduced to Dashiell Hammett by Humphrey Bogart. I was twelve years old at the time, and mention the occasion because I take it to be exemplary, that I share this experience with countless others. (Earlier than this, at the very dawn of consciousness, I can recall William Powell and Myrna Loy and a small dog on a leash and an audience full of adults laughing; but that had nothing to do with Hammett or anything else as far as I was concerned.) What was striking about the event was that it was one of the first encounters I can consciously recall with the experience of moral ambiguity. Here was this detective you were supposed to like—and did like—behaving and speaking in peculiar and unexpected ways. He acted up to the cops, partly for real, partly as a ruse. He connived with crooks, for his own ends and perhaps even for some of theirs. He slept with his partner's wife, fell in love with a lady crook and then refused to save her from the police, even though he could have. Which side was he on? Was he on any side apart from his own? And which or what side was that? The experience was not only morally ambiguous; it was morally complex and enigmatic as well. The impression it made was a lasting one.

Years later, after having read *The Maltese Falcon* and seen the movie again and then reread the novel, I could begin to understand why the impact of the film had been so memorable, much more so than that of most other movies. The director, John Huston, had had the wit to recognize the power, sharpness, integrity, and bite of Hammett's prose—particularly the dialogue—and the film script consists almost entirely of speech taken directly and without modification from the written novel. Moreover, this unusual situation is complicated still further. In selecting with notable intelligence the relevant scenes and passages from the novel, Huston had to make certain omissions. Paradoxically, however, one of the things that he chose to omit was the most important or central moment in the entire novel. It is also one of the central moments in all of Hammett's writing. I think we can make use of this oddly "lost" passage as a means of entry into Hammett's vision or imagination of the world.

It occurs as Spade is becoming involved with Brigid O'Shaughnessy in her struggle with the other thieves, and it is his way of communicating to her his sense of how the world and life go. His way is to tell her a story from his own experience. The form this story takes is that of a parable. It is a parable about a man named Flitcraft. Flitcraft was a successful, happily married, stable, and utterly respectable real-estate dealer in Tacoma. One day he went out to lunch and never returned. No reason could be found for his disappearance, and no account of it could be made. " 'He went like that,' Spade said, 'like a fist when you open your hand.' "

Five years later Mrs. Flitcraft came to the agency at which Spade was working and told them that " 'she had seen a man in Spokane who looked a lot like her husband.' " Spade went off to investigate and found that it was indeed Flitcraft. He had been living in Spokane for a couple of years under the name of Charles Pierce. He had a successful automobile business, a wife, a baby son, a suburban home, and usually played golf after four in the afternoon, just as he had in Tacoma. Spade and he sat down to talk the matter over. Flitcraft, Spade recounts, "had no feeling of guilt. He had left his family well provided for, and what he had done seemed to him perfectly reasonable. The only thing that bothered him was a doubt that he could make that reasonableness clear" to his interlocutor. When Flitcraft went out to lunch that day five years before in Tacoma, " 'he passed an office-building that was being put up. . . . A beam or something fell eight or ten stories down and smacked the sidewalk alongside him.' " A chip of smashed sidewalk flew up and took a piece of skin off his cheek. He was otherwise unharmed. He stood there " 'scared stiff,' " he told Spade, " 'but he was more shocked than really frightened. He felt like somebody had taken the lid off life and let him look at the works.' "

Until that very moment Flitcraft had been " 'a good citizen and a good husband and father, not by any outer compulsion, but simply because he was a man who was most comfortable in step with his surroundings. . . . The life he knew was a clean orderly sane responsible affair. Now a falling beam had shown him that life was fundamentally none of these things. . . . What disturbed him was the discovery that in sensibly ordering his affairs he had got out of step, and not into step, with life.' " By the time he had finished lunch, he had reached the decision " 'that he would change his life at random by simply going away.' " He went off that afternoon, wandered around for a couple of years, then drifted back to the Northwest, " 'settled in Spokane and got married. His second wife didn't look like the first, but they were more alike than they were different.' " And the same held true of his second life. Spade then moves on to his conclusion: " 'He wasn't sorry for

what he had done. It seemed reasonable enough to him. I don't think he even knew he had settled back into the same groove that he had jumped out of in Tacoma. But that's the part of it I always liked. He adjusted himself to beams falling, and then no more of them fell, and he adjusted himself to their not falling.' " End of parable. Brigid of course understands nothing of this, as Spade doubtless knew beforehand. Yet what he had been telling her has to do with the forces and beliefs and contingencies that guide his conduct and supply a structure to his apparently enigmatic behavior.

To begin with, we may note that such a sustained passage is not the kind of thing we ordinarily expect in a detective story or novel about crime. That it is there, and that comparable passages occur in all of Hammett's best work, clearly suggests the kind of transformation that Hammett was performing on this popular genre of writing. The transformation was in the direction of literature. And what the passage in question is about among other things is the ethical irrationality of existence, the ethical unintelligibility of the world. For Flitcraft the falling beam "had taken the lid off life and let him look at the works." The works are that life is inscrutable, opaque, irresponsible, and arbitrary—that human existence does not correspond in its actuality to the way we live it. For most of us live as if existence itself were ordered, ethical, and rational. As a direct result of his realization in experience that it is not, Flitcraft leaves his wife and children and goes off. He acts irrationally and at random, in accordance with the nature of existence. When after a couple of years of wandering aimlessly about he decides to establish a new life, he simply reproduces the old one he had supposedly repudiated and abandoned; that is to say, he behaves again as if life were orderly, meaningful, and rational, and "adjusts" to it. And this, with fine irony, is the part of it, Spade says, that he " 'always liked,' " which means the part that he liked best. For here we come upon the unfathomable and most mysteriously irrational part of it all—how despite everything we have learned and everything we know, men will persist in behaving and trying to behave sanely, rationally, sensibly, and responsibly. And we will continue to persist even when we know that there is no logical or metaphysical, no discoverable or demonstrable reason for doing so. [In a footnote the critic observes: "It can hardly be an accident that the new name that Hammett gives to Flitcraft is that of an American philosopher—with two vowels reversed—who was deeply involved in just such speculations."] It is this sense of sustained contradiction that is close to the center—or to one of the centers—of Hammett's work. The contradiction is not ethical alone; it is metaphysical as well. And it is not merely sustained; it is sustained with pleasure. For Hammett and Spade and the Op, the sustainment in consciousness of such contradictions is an indispensable part of their existence and of their pleasure in that existence.

That this pleasure is itself complex, ambiguous, and problematic becomes apparent as one simply describes the conditions under which it exists. And the complexity, ambiguity, and sense of the problematical are not confined to such moments of "revelation"—or set pieces—as the parable of Flitcraft. They permeate Hammett's work and act as formative elements in its structure, including its deep structure. Hammett's work went through considerable and interesting development in the course of his career for twelve years as a writer. He also wrote in a considerable variety of forms and worked out a variety of narrative devices and strategies. At the same time, his work considered as a whole reveals a remarkable kind of coherence. In order to further the understanding of that coherence, we can propose for the purposes of the present analysis to construct a kind of "ideal type" of a Hammett or Op story. Which is not to say or to imply in the least that he wrote according to a formula, but that an authentic imaginative vision lay beneath and informed the structure of his work.

Such an ideal-typical description runs as follows. The Op is called in or sent out on a case. Something has been stolen, someone is missing, some dire circumstance is impending, someone has been murdered—it doesn't matter. The Op interviews the person or persons most immediately accessible. They may be innocent or guilty—it doesn't matter; it is an indifferent circumstance. Guilty or innocent, they provide the Op with an account of what they know, of what they assert really happened. The Op begins to investigate; he compares these accounts with others that he gathers; he snoops about; he does research; he shadows people, arranges confrontations between those who want to avoid one another, and so on. What he soon discovers is that the "reality" that anyone involved will swear to is in fact itself a construction, a fabrication, a fiction, a faked and alternate reality—and that it has been gotten together before he ever arrived on the scene. And the Op's work therefore is to deconstruct, decompose, deplot and defictionalize that "reality" and to construct or reconstruct out of it a true fiction, i. e., an account of what "really" happened.

It should be quite evident that there is a reflective and coordinate relation between the activities of the Op and the activities of Hammett, the writer. Yet the depth and problematic character of this self-reflexive process begin to be revealed when we observe that the reconstruction or true fiction created and arrived at by the Op at the end of the story is no more plausible—nor is it meant to be—than the stories that have been told to him by all parties, guilty or innocent, in the course of his work. The Op may catch the real thief or collar the actual crook—that is not entirely to the point. What is to the point is that the story, account, or chain of events that the Op winds up with as "reality" is no more plausible and no less ambiguous than the stories that he meets with at the outset and later. What Hammett has done—unlike most writers of detective or crime stories before him or since—is to include as part of the contingent and dramatic consciousness of his narrative the circumstance that the work of the detective is itself a fiction-making activity, a discovery or creation by fabrication of something new in the world, or hidden, latent, potential, or as yet undeveloped within it. The typical "classical" detective story—unlike Hammett's—can be described as a formal game with certain specified rules of transformation. What ordinarily happens is that the detective is faced with a situation of inadequate, false, misleading, and ambiguous information. And the story as a whole is an exercise in disambiguation—with the final scenes

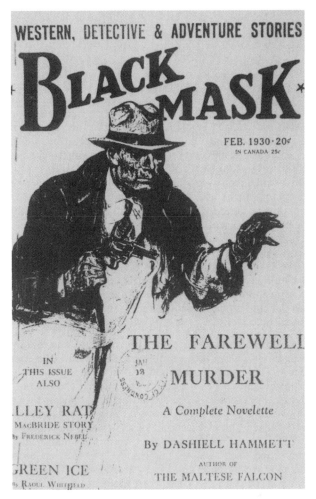

Cover from a 1930 edition of Black Mask *that featured one of Hammett's stories.*

being a ratiocinative demonstration that the butler did it (or not); these scenes achieve a conclusive, reassuring clarity of explanation, wherein everything is set straight, and the game we have been party to is brought to its appropriate end. But this, as we have already seen, is not what ordinarily happens in Hammett or with the Op.

What happens is that the Op almost invariably walks into a situation that has already been elaborately fabricated or framed. And his characteristic response to his sense that he is dealing with a series of deceptions or fictions is—to use the words that he uses himself repeatedly—"to stir things up." This corresponds integrally, both as metaphor and in logical structure, to what happened in the parable of Flitcraft. When the falling beam just misses Flitcraft, "he felt like somebody had taken the lid off life." The Op lives with the uninterrupted awareness that for him the lid has been taken off life. When the lid has been lifted, the logical thing to do is to "stir things up"—which is what he does. He actively undertakes to deconstruct, decompose, and thus demystify the fictional—and therefore false—reality created by the characters, crooks or not, with whom he is involved. More often than not he tries to substitute his own fictional-hypothetical representation for theirs—and this representation may also be "true" or mistaken, or both at once. In any event, his major effort is to make the fictions of others visible as fictions, inventions, concealments, falsehoods, and mystifications. When a fiction becomes visible as such, it begins to dissolve and disappear, and presumably should reveal behind it the "real" reality that was there all the time and that it was masking. Yet what happens in Hammett is that what is revealed as "reality" is a still further fiction-making activity—in the first place the Op's, and behind that yet another, the consciousness present in many of the Op stories and all the novels that Dashiell Hammett, the writer, is continually doing the same thing as the Op and all the other characters in the fiction he is creating. That is to say, he is making a fiction (in writing) in the real world; and this fiction, like the real world itself, is coherent but not necessarily rational. What one both begins and ends with, then, is a story, a narrative, a coherent yet questionable account of the world. This problematic penetrates to the bottom of Hammett's narrative imagination and shapes a number of its deeper processes—in *The Dain Curse,* for example, it is the chief topic of explicit debate that runs throughout the entire novel.

Yet Hammett's writing is still more complex and integral than this. For the unresolvable paradoxes and dilemmas that we have just been describing in terms of narrative structure and consciousness are reproduced once again in Hammett's vision and representation of society, of the social world in which the Op lives. At this point we must recall that Hammett is a writer of the 1920's and that this was the era of Prohibition. American society had in effect committed itself to a vast collective fiction. Even more, this fiction was false not merely in the sense that it was made up or did not in fact correspond to reality; it was false in the sense that it was corrupt and corrupting as well.

During this period every time an American took a drink he was helping to undermine the law, and American society had covertly committed itself to what was in practice collaborative illegality. There is a kind of epiphany of these circumstances in **"The Golden Horseshoe."** The Op is on a case that takes him to Tijuana. In a bar there, he reads a sign:

ONLY GENUINE PRE-WAR AMERICAN AND

BRITISH WHISKEYS SERVED HERE

He responds by remarking that "I was trying to count how many lies could be found in those nine words, and had reached four, with promise of more," when he is interrupted by some call to action. That sign and the Op's response to it describe part of the existential character of the social world represented by Hammett.

Another part of that representation is expressed in another kind of story or idea that Hammett returned to repeatedly. The twenties were also the great period of organized crime and organized criminal gangs in America, and one of Hammett's obsessive imaginations was the notion of organized crime or gangs taking over an entire society and running it as if it were an ordinary society doing business as usual. In other words, society itself would become a fic-

tion, concealing and belying the actuality of what was controlling it and perverting it from within. One can thus make out quite early in this native American writer a proto-Marxist critical representation of how a certain kind of society works. Actually, the point of view is pre-rather than proto-Marxist, and the social world as it is dramatized in many of these stories is Hobbesian rather than Marxist. It is a world of universal warfare, the war of each against all, and of all against all. The only thing that prevents the criminal ascendancy from turning into permanent tyranny is that the crooks who take over society cannot cooperate with one another, repeatedly fall out with each other, and return to the Hobbesian anarchy out of which they have momentarily arisen. The social world as imagined by Hammett runs on a principle that is the direct opposite of that postulated by Erik Erikson as the fundamental and enabling condition for human existence. In Hammett, society and social relations are dominated by the principle of basic mistrust. As one of his detectives remarks, speaking for himself and for virtually every other character in Hammett's writing, "I trust no one."

When Hammett turns to the respectable world, the world of respectable society, of affluence and influence, of open personal and political power, he finds only more of the same. The respectability of respectable American society is as much a fiction and a fraud as the phony respectable society fabricated by the criminals. Indeed, he unwaveringly represents the world of crime as a reproduction in both structure and detail of the modern capitalist society that it depends on, preys off, and is part of. But Hammett does something even more radical than this. He not only continually juxtaposes and connects the ambiguously fictional worlds of art and of writing with the fraudulently fictional worlds of society; he connects them, juxtaposes them, and sees them in dizzying and baffling interaction. He does this in many ways and on many occasions. One of them, for example, is the Maltese Falcon itself, which turns out to be and contains within itself the history of capitalism. It is originally a piece of plunder, part of what Marx called the "primitive accumulation"; when its gold encrusted with gems is painted over, it becomes a mystified object, a commodity itself; it is a piece of property that belongs to no one—whoever possesses it does not really own it. At the same time it is another fiction, a representation or work of art—which turns out itself to be a fake, since it is made of lead. It is a *rara avis* indeed. As is the fiction in which it is created and contained, the novel by Hammett.

It is into this bottomlessly equivocal, endlessly fraudulent, and brutally acquisitive world that Hammett precipitates the Op. There is nothing glamorous about him. Short, thick-set, balding, between thirty-five and forty, he has no name, no home, no personal existence apart from his work. He is, and he regards himself as, "the hired man" of official and respectable society, who is paid so much per day to clean it up and rescue it from the crooks and thieves who are perpetually threatening to take it over. Yet what he—and the reader—just as perpetually learn is that the respectable society that employs him is itself inveterately vicious, deceitful, culpable, crooked, and degraded. How then is the Op to be preserved, to preserve himself, from being contaminated by both the world he works against and the world he is hired to work for?

To begin with, the Op lives by a code. This code consists in the first instance of the rules laid down by the Continental Agency, and they are "rather strict." The most important of them by far is that no operative in the employ of the Agency is ever allowed to take or collect part of a reward that may be attached to the solution of a case. Since he cannot directly enrich himself through his professional skills, he is saved from at least the characteristic corruption of modern society—the corruption that is connected with its fundamental acquisitive structure. At the same time, the Op is a special case of the Protestant ethic, for his entire existence is bound up in and expressed by his work, his vocation. He likes his work, and it is honest work, done as much for enjoyment and the exercise of his skills and abilities as it is for personal gain and self-sustainment. The work is something of an end in itself, and this circumstance also serves to protect him, as does his deliberate refusal to use high-class and fancy moral language about anything. The work is an end in itself and is therefore something more than work alone. As Spade says, in a passage that is the culmination of many such passages in Hammett:

> I'm a detective and expecting me to run criminals down and then let them go free is like asking a dog to catch a rabbit and let it go. It can be done, all right, and sometimes it is done, but it's not the natural thing.

Being a detective, then, entails more than fulfilling a social function or performing a social role. Being a detective is the realization of an identity, for there are components in it which are beyond or beneath society—and cannot be touched by it—and beyond and beneath reason. There is something "natural" about it. Yet if we recall that the nature thus being expressed is that of a man-hunter, and Hammett's apt metaphor compels us to do so, and that the state of society as it is represented in Hammett's writing reminds us of the state of nature in Hobbes, we see that even here Hammett does not release his sense of the complex and the contradictory, and is making no simple-minded appeal to some benign idea of the "natural."

And indeed the Op is not finally or fully protected by his work, his job, his vocation. (We have all had to relearn with bitterness what multitudes of wickedness "doing one's job" can cover.) Max Weber has memorably remarked that "the decisive means for politics is violence." In Hammett's depiction of modern American society, violence is the decisive means indeed, along with fraud, deceit, treachery, betrayal, and general, endemic unscrupulousness. Such means are in no sense alien to Hammett's detective. As the Op says, " 'detecting is a hard business, and you use whatever tools come to hand.' " In other words, there is a paradoxical tension and unceasing interplay in Hammett's stories between means and ends; relations between the two are never secure or stable. And as Max Weber further remarked, in his great essay "Politics as a Vocation": "the world is governed by demons, and he who lets himself in for . . . power and force as means, contracts with diabolic powers, and for his action it is *not*

true that good can follow only from good and evil only from evil, but that often the opposite is true. Anyone who fails to see this is, indeed, a political infant." Neither Hammett nor the Op is an infant; yet no one can be so grown up and inured to experience that he can escape the consequences that attach to the deliberate use of violent and dubious means.

These consequences are of various orders. "Good" ends themselves can be transformed and perverted by the use of vicious or indiscriminate means. (I am leaving to one side those even more perplexing instances in Hammett in which the ends pursued by the Op correspond with ends desired by a corrupted yet respectable official society.) The consequences are also visible inwardly, on the inner being of the agent of such means, the Op himself. The violence begins to get to him:

> I began to throw my right fist into him.
>
> I liked that. His belly was flabby, and it got softer every time I hit it. I hit it often.

Another side of this set of irresolvable moral predicaments is revealed when we see that the Op's toughness is not merely a carapace within which feelings of tenderness and humanity can be nourished and preserved. The toughness is toughness through and through, and as the Op continues his career, and continues to live by the means he does, he tends to become more callous and less and less able to feel. At the very end, awaiting him, he knows, is the prospect of becoming like his boss, the head of the Agency, the Old Man, "with his gentle eyes behind gold spectacles and his mild smile, hiding the fact that fifty years of sleuthing had left him without any feelings at all on any subject." This is the price exacted by the use of such means in such a world; these are the consequences of living fully in a society moved by the principle of basic mistrust. "Whoever fights monsters," writes Nietzsche, "should see to it that in the process he does not become a monster. And when you look long into an abyss, the abyss also looks into you." The abyss looks into Hammett, the Old Man, and the Op.

It is through such complex devices as I have merely sketched here that Hammett was able to raise the crime story into literature. He did it over a period of ten years. Yet the strain was finally too much to bear—that shifting, entangled, and equilibrated state of contradictions out of which his creativity arose and which it expressed could no longer be sustained. His creative career ends when he is no longer able to handle the literary, social, and moral opacities, instabilities, and contradictions that characterize all his best work. His life then splits apart and goes in the two opposite directions that were implicit in his earlier, creative phase, but that the creativity held suspended and in poised yet fluid tension. His politics go in one direction; the way he made his living went in another—he became a hack writer, and then finally no writer at all. That is another story. Yet for ten years he was able to do what almost no other writer in this genre has ever done so well—he was able to really write, to construct a vision of a world in words, to know that the writing was about the real world and referred to it and was part of it; and at the same time he was able to be self-consciously aware that the whole thing was problematical and about itself and "only" writing as well. For ten years, in other words, he was a true creator of fiction.

Roger Sale (essay date 1975)

SOURCE: "The Hammett Case," in *New York Review of Books,* Vol. XXII, No. 1, February 6, 1975, pp. 20-2.

[*Sale is an American educator and the author of several books, including* Discussions of the Novel *(1960) and* Literary Inheritance *(1984). The following review provides a response to Steven Marcus's introduction to* The Continental Op *(see excerpt dated 1974), debating Marcus's assertions about the "fiction-making" activities of the Continental Op. Sale also finds the stories in the collection to be inferior examples of Hammett's talent.*]

In the early Fifties, when I first read Dashiell Hammett, he seemed to fit perfectly an image my friends and I had then of a writer who had made being a writer into a romantic occupation. He had lived in "the real world," he had suffered years of obscurity and poverty as he learned to write a clean, honest prose, he had written books that were out of print and hard to find, he had gone to Hollywood and drunk too much and stopped writing, he had chosen to go to jail rather than talk at a communist conspiracy trial, he had some undetailed beautiful relation with Lillian Hellman. Compared to that, Fitzgerald and Hemingway were too gaudy, available for anyone's romancing.

About Hammett's writing, I now see, we held an ambivalent attitude that bespoke an uneasiness we could not recognize. On the one hand we pointed to the battered paperbacks we had struggled to find and said: "There, with Op and Spade and Nick Charles, is the real thing, serious writing about crime and detection." On the other hand we implicitly diminished that achievement by dreaming that in the intervening years Hammett had been struggling to write a great, a "mature" novel that would show the world he was as good as we wanted to claim he was. When pressed, I would admit to preferring Raymond Chandler, even to hankering after new young toughs like John D. MacDonald and John Ross Macdonald. But Hammett was the first, and the years of writing stories for *Black Mask* had to be honored somehow. Our conversations would dwindle into asking which was Hammett's best book, and, since claims could be made for many of them, it was easier to talk that way than to ask if any was very good.

By 1961, when Hammett died, it no longer seemed as important to sustain romantic images of writers, though the battered paperbacks had been carefully packed away with each move, and one could hardly fail to be moved by Hellman's eulogy: "He believed in the salvation of intelligence, and he tried to live it out . . . and never, in all the years, did he play anybody's game but his own. He never lied, he never faked, he never stooped." And her 1965 memoir, which may well be the best thing either of them ever wrote, did much to make Hammett into the heroic figure we had all vaguely created years earlier; it was then published as the introduction to ten Continental Op pieces called *The Big Knockover,* and that volume, plus *The Nov-*

els of Dashiell Hammett, which had been published a year earlier, gave his best work the permanence it deserved.

Both collections were well received, but not given the rather lavish attention that has recently been paid to *The Continental Op,* a new book of seven stories selected and introduced by Steven Marcus. I note, for instance, that local libraries that don't have one or both of the earlier hardcover collections have been quick to acquire this one. And Marcus's introduction takes a much loftier tone than any other I've heard in discussions of Hammett. It's all a shame. The stories are inferior work—Marcus might well have done better by rescuing the few minor tales that have never been reprinted from *Black Mask*—and those who come to Hammett for the first time via this volume will get only snatches that show why anyone should read him. With a writer who is very limited at his best, this kind of exposure is especially unwelcome.

Yet one can see what Marcus has in mind, perverse though it seems to be. He wants to take those stories which have almost no interest either as conventional fiction or as conventional detective fiction and to claim that this is where you find Hammett pure. The Op, he says, "undertakes to deconstruct, decompose, and thus demystify the fictional—and therefore false—reality created by the characters, crooks or not, with whom he is involved." True enough, though that is a fancy way to say something pretty obvious. Then:

> It should be quite evident that there is a reflective and coordinate relation between the activities of the Op and the activities of Hammett, the writer. Yet the depth and problematic character of this self-reflexive process begin to be revealed when we observe that the reconstruction or true fiction created and arrived at by the Op at the end of the story is no more plausible—nor is it meant to be—than the stories that have been told to him by all parties, guilty or innocent, in the course of his work. The Op may catch the real thief or collar the actual crook—that is not entirely to the point. What is to the point is that the story, account, or chain of events that the Op winds up with as "reality" is no more plausible and no less ambiguous than the stories that he meets with at the outset and later.

Thus Hammett becomes a candidate for existential sainthood. What makes Marcus's point useless is that in so far as it is true it is mostly a sign of the mediocrity of the stories. We assume, and the Op assumes, that in each case his job is like that of the classic detective: winnow true from false, fact from fiction. We do not assume that a nameless and faceless figure, operating out of a named but equally faceless San Francisco, will act like Philo Vance or Ellery Queen. Nor does Hammett offer his characters in such a way that anyone can care who did what to whom. But if the Op's account of events isn't plausible, it's meant to be, even if it isn't tidy or illuminating. If it isn't to the point that he catch the real thief, then his whole demeanor as an operative—who seeks no reward for himself, who is never violent wantonly—is a fraud. When it doesn't matter what the Op or anyone else does, and that is certainly true in many pages here if not true of whole stories, it makes for very dull reading.

Take **"The Main Death,"** for example, Hammett's forty-fourth published story, so he was no beginner. The Op is asked by a collector named Gungen to find out who killed his employee, Jeffrey Main, and to recover the $20,000 that was stolen from him and that belongs to Gungen. Mrs. Main's story is that she was awakened by a scuffle, found her husband fighting two masked figures, one of whom shot Main. His empty wallet and a woman's handkerchief are found on the roof of a nearby apartment. The Op sees Gungen and discovers the handkerchief is owned by his wife. As he leaves he spots a woman leaving too, and he has her tailed to the apartment of two local con men, Coughing Ben Weel and Bunky Dahl. From Mrs. Gungen Op learns that Main had been her lover and that on the afternoon he died they had been together and he had been robbed by two men who fit Weel's and Dahl's description. Op finds them, shakes them down for the twenty grand, masking himself as a thief and not as a cop so he can then let them go and keep them from implicating Mrs. Gungen in her affair with Main. All this means that Mrs. Main's original story was a lie, so Op confronts her and learns Main had committed suicide and Mrs. Main had covered up to gain his insurance.

It just isn't true to say of a story like this, as Marcus does:

> What Hammett has done—unlike most writers of detective or crime stories before him or since—is to include as part of the contingent and dramatic consciousness of his narrative the circumstance that the work of the detective is itself a fiction-making activity, a discovery or creation by fabrication of something new in the world, or hidden, latent, potential, or as yet undeveloped within it.

The Op uncovers the fabrications woven by Main, Mrs Main, and Mrs. Gungen; he himself does not fabricate, nor is his consciousness contingent or dramatic except as the uncoverer of "real" truths. He does not, to be sure, chortle or offer lengthy accounts of his methods of deduction, or act as though the world after the uncovering is significantly different from the way it was in the beginning. If his account of Main's death isn't plausible, it at least fits all available facts, as in any detective fiction. The Op is like the queen in chess, able to move both straight and diagonally, as it were, in a world of pawns, bishops, and rooks. But he is a piece, more truly within his world than are most detectives.

This is precisely what's wrong. When the cast is cardboard, when the relations among the characters are devoid of interest, when the Op succeeds by allowing for no human motive except the most simply conceived greed and lust, when the plot moves these figures around like wind—up dolls, there is nothing to make any of it matter. No theory, furthermore, true or false, that Marcus can supply can create an interest by saying "But that's the point" and by going on about contingencies and fiction-making detectives. Hammett was not a hero to himself, but he took himself seriously, and Marcus's way of making him pretentious has the effect of making him trivial.

Perhaps most of Hammett's admirers would not, however, take a line like Marcus's; when he is praised, it is almost always for his writing. In these stories it is mostly drearily literary. The most frequent event here, outside of conversation, is gunfighting, and Hammett could never do anything with guns except pile up elegant variations: "From behind the roadster, a pistol snapped at me, three times"; "An orange streak from the car ahead cut off my wonderment"; "A flash from somewhere near the roadster's heels"; "The girl's pistol barked at the empty touring car"; "Darkness—streaked with orange and blue—filled with noise"; "A gun thundered"; "Gunpowder burned at my face"; "Two points of light near the floor gave out fire and thunder"; "Twin flames struck at me again." Get the Op in a room with a couple of toughs, put him in a car chasing another, and these stiff, self-conscious phrases pile up ludicrously.

Or take a single passage:

> The Kid jumped close.
>
> He knew knives. None of your clumsy downward strokes with the blade sticking out the bottom of his fist.
>
> Thumb and crooked forefinger guided blade. He struck upward. Under Billie's shoulder. Once. Deep.
>
> Billie pitched forward, smashing the woman to the floor under him. He rolled off her and was dead on his back among the furniture stuffing. Dead, he seemed larger than ever, seemed to fill the room.
>
> The Whosis Kid wiped his knife clean on a piece of carpet, snapped it shut, and dropped it back in his pocket. He did this with his left hand. His right was close to his hip. He did not look at the knife. His eyes were on Maurois.

Perelman, or just ripe for Perelman? In "The Simple Art of Murder," Raymond Chandler says, "Hammett's style at its worst was almost as formalized as a page of *Marius the Epicurean*," and every story in **The Continental Op** shows it: "He looked dead, and he had enough bullet holes in him to make death a good guess"; "Even if I hadn't known Rringo was looking at me I could have felt his eyes on me."

Nor is it hard to say how such bad writing came to be. Among *Black Mask* readers Hammett was very popular, and he thus learned what made stories sell and kept putting the Op through his predictable paces. He was pretty thoroughly committed, from habit or design, to the idea that human beings were not very interesting, so no character he could invent could hold his interest. Now and again he came up with a good plot which could give his writing some purpose, but since he had to keep writing, good plot or no, there was little for him to attend to most of the time but the prose itself. When that happens, the prose becomes stylized almost immediately, words are pieces in a jigsaw.

Hammett himself must have realized some of this by the late Twenties, after he had been writing for seven or eight years. He began to write what the pulps liked to call novelettes; two put together became **Blood Money,** groups of four became *Red Harvest* and *The Dain Curse.* It is still the Op, still cross, double-cross, and triple-cross, but Hammett begins to blow up his writing, to crack wise, to be self-confessedly ornate—not all at once, but you don't find sentences like "The room was black as an honest politician's prospects" or "It was an even mile in the darkness to the head of the stairs we had come up" very often in the stories in the Marcus collection. As can be seen, most such sentences aren't much good, but they allow the Op and Hammett to have a sense of style, rather than force them, as the earlier stories tend to do, into self-defeating stylization. Of course this sense of self as style is not at all what Marcus wants to praise Hammett for, but it was not only what could keep Hammett interested—he stopped writing stories for *Black Mask* in 1930—but what allowed him to do his best work.

To do that he needed someone besides the Op, whose anonymous integrity had worn pretty thin, and he assayed three different characters with three different styles in his last three novels: Sam Spade in *The Maltese Falcon,* Ned Beaumont in *The Glass Key,* and Nick Charles in *The Thin Man.* It is at this point that we can turn to the otherwise deflecting question of which is the best book.

Hammett himself preferred *The Glass Key,* and so, to judge by what he later did with the private eye form, did Chandler; there is much to be said for the preference. *The Maltese Falcon* isn't all that much different from the Op novels, and if Spade is a clearer figure it is mostly because he is more openly selfish and nasty, and there isn't much Hammett can do except let him bark away. *The Thin Man* is silly fun, warmed by the relation of Nick to Nora, warmed as Hammett himself was by his new relation with Lillian Hellman, but otherwise an inconsequential effort to make a casual virtue out of casual plotting. Yet *The Glass Key* is the best because Hammett here tries to make the style of his hero matter; Ned Beaumont's poses are poses, capable of costing something. It is a fumbling book because Hammett wouldn't commit himself enough to what he was doing, wouldn't try to assess how much Beaumont dummies up because of his feeling for a friend, or how much it matters to him that he seem more a gentleman than a thug.

The code always said that one doesn't talk about such things, and the success or failure of *The Glass Key*—and all Hammett, all Chandler, all Ross Macdonald, too—depends on how well the hero's relation to this code is handled. Hold to it completely, act as if there were no prices for so doing, and you have the boring Op; begin to act as if there were prices to be paid and inevitably self-pity begins to creep in: I kept my word, and I took my beating, etc. can lead to some dreary and immoral posing. What Hellman has shown us, however, is that Hammett himself believed in the code, and suffered because he did; the dignity with which he was willing to do so tinged his life with greatness. Better, then, to let the self-pity come in if it must, better to deal with it openly as best one can. Better to say life matters, especially if you really think it does.

Hammett cannot handle all this in *The Glass Key,* but he

tries. Beaumont can cry, and attempt suicide after his beating, he can lash out at others because he is unhappy with himself, he can stand paralyzed at the end after he tells his friend Madvig he is going away with the woman Madvig loves and Beaumont does not. The writing in this book is on the edge of all Hammett himself could not write about, but that is not a bad place for his writing to be.

Given this, if Marcus wanted to reprint some currently unavailable Hammett stories he would have been better off, I think, calling his collection "The Early Dashiell Hammett" or some such title. That would give the Op the historical importance he had for Hammett, *Black Mask,* and the hard-boiled story in general. After all, being a Pinkerton agent had given Hammett some material and a way to look at life, but neither plots nor style. The plots he borrowed—not literally, but in the sense that he wasn't going to try to do without them or invent a new kind—and the style had to be invented and evolved even as he had to keep churning out stories in order to live. No need to complain that these stories are crude, primitive, effortful; no need, either, to elevate these very qualities into high art. He did quite a bit in his ten years of writing, and he was a real pioneer. If the best of Chandler and MacDonald and Macdonald is better than his best, if the middling stuff of quite a few writers is better than his middling stuff, there isn't one who doesn't know how much he made them possible.

H. H. Morris   (essay date 1978)

SOURCE: "Dashiell Hammett in the Wasteland," in *The Midwest Quarterly,* Vol. XIX, No. 2, Winter, 1978, pp. 196-202.

[*In the following essay, Morris notes similarities between the works of Hammett and those of several other writers who have depicted corruption in society.*]

Critics of the subgenre long ago recognized Dashiell Hammett's impact upon crime and detective fiction. Along with Raymond Chandler, who, coincidentally, wrote one of the first essays discussing this impact, Hammett was one of the giants who established an American voice and style that stood in opposition to the British-dominated country-house school. His criminals were habitual wrongdoers, not insane spinsters, vicars, or retired colonels. His detectives were hardworking professionals, not gentlemen amateurs solving murders for lack of a more edifying hobby. He wrote about killings committed with the weapons men routinely use for murder, not exotic poisons or knives made of ice. Most importantly, Hammett set his crimes in a believable and recognizable environment.

This use of environment makes Hammett worthy of discussion as a serious American novelist and short story writer. His achievements in crime fiction have tended to obscure his genuine literary talents, just as his rugged dignity before a Congressional inquisition has turned him into a hero cast in the hard-boiled mold of his own characters. Because he chose prison over "squealing," to use a term a Hammett character would choose, the integrity of the man overshadows the accomplishments of the artist. It is easy to forget that his defiance of a congressional committee was not his first attempt to expose moral bankrupt-cy among the powerful.

Hammett's vision of America was that of a man staring at a vast wasteland. He shared with Sinclair Lewis the be-lief that the nation's traditional leaders lacked integrity, that the balance sheet had replaced ethical codes of con-duct. Like F. Scott Fitzgerald, Hammett saw the children of the rich as spoiled seekers after illicit thrills. With Faulkner, he wrote of society's dregs, the misfits con-demned to live out a nightmare existence with no hope of escape. Hammett was one more writer of the 1920's and 1930's who took the naturalism of Dreiser and Norris as a received fiction technique and applied it to life around him.

None of these comparisons should suggest that Dashiell Hammett belongs among the giants, that in leaving him out of standard American literature anthologies editors have overlooked a great novelist. His writing is flawed. He fit too well into the *Black Mask* ambience. His strained metaphors and thieves' argot come across as stylized and artificial, and in the future readers will need the cumber-some network of explanatory footnotes found in most edi-tions of John Gay's *The Beggar's Opera*. Hammett's char-acters are often flat, distinguished from one another only by colorful nicknames, physical descriptions, and police records. Because pulp fiction demanded lots of action, his plots dominate all other story elements.

There are many points for comparison between Gay and Hammett. They lived in different centuries and different cultures; one wrote for the stage, while the other wrote mass fiction, yet both found incontrovertible proof that the seamy underbelly of society is an honest reflection of the dishonest upper stratum. Hammett's leftward leaning political notions can tempt the critic into sweeping gener-alizations about class warfare, the material dialectic, and basic proletarian virtues. Gay is a good antidote. He lived and wrote long before Marx, saying the same things that Hammett said. So did Mark Twain, who called the Grant Administration "The Great Barbecue"; so did Geoffrey Chaucer, who wrote about crooked summoners and par-doners; so did Dante, who populated hell with the crooked leaders of the Italy of his time. Hammett's attack on his corrupt society was part of an honorable literary tradition.

Nonetheless, Hammett was unique to his time and place. In choosing to write hard-boiled crime stories and novels, he committed himself to producing works that would please a mass audience unwilling—or unable—to search for subtleties. As a crime writer he had but two choices: to create a milieu that matched the conventions surround-ing certain romanticized characters (Robin Hood, A. J. Raffles, Sherlock Holmes), or to set his stories in an envi-ronment that readers connected with reality. Drawing upon the knowledge he had gained as a Pinkerton employ-ee, Hammett chose recognizable reality.

He could have stopped with genuine criminals pursued by hardworking cops who considered the third degree a rou-tine investigative method. This alone would have sufficed to make him important in crime and detective fiction, for his literary abilities were far above the standards demand-ed of the subgenre's practitioners. Hammett went far be-yond this safe point, however. He saw—and wrote about—a culture in which petty criminals went to jail while the truly big crooks ran for Congress. When he wrote about this phenomenon, his readers recognized it as the story behind the headlines in their local newspapers.

The Glass Key revolves around an election in a small town somewhere near New York City. Ned Beaumont, the pro-tagonist, works for Paul Madvig, the local political boss. Bootlegging and bank robbery, illegal gambling debts col-lected by a man with a badge issued by the D.A., police who are careful to arrest only those criminals not protect-ed by the incumbent political machine, a newspaper editor paid off by criminal elements—these are the action ele-ments that keep the novel moving. The central problem is the murder of Taylor Henry, wastrel son of the power-ful, patrician Senator Henry, with whom Paul wishes to ally himself through marriage with the lawmaker's daugh-ter. Paul is suspected of the murder, so loyal Ned sets out to clear his boss. Ultimately, Ned proves that the rich sen-ator has sunk to murdering his own son—and that the sen-ator is quite willing to let Paul take the blame for the crime.

Red Harvest is set in the western mining town of Person-ville, better known as Poisonville. The usual assortment of crooks and grifters creates a lot of problems for the anonymous Continental Op, but the real source of the evil that gives Poisonville its name is the mine owner who dab-bles in politics. Elihu Wilsson is so compromised by his own crimes that he is afraid to let the Op investigate the murder of his own son.

Even detectives can be tainted by wealth. Nick Charles drinks too much, having retired from detecting after mar-rying the rich Nora. Circumstances force him out of re-tirement to solve the case of *The Thin Man* because this crime involves many of the wealthy people with whom he now socializes. He is soon moving through New York's speakeasies and renewing old acquaintances among the criminal set. The rich, especially the younger ones search-ing for thrills, are eager patrons of the speakeasies and friends of the crooks.

This same concept, that the children of the rich are wast-rels, underlies many of Hammett's shorter works. "Fly Paper" is "a wandering daughter job" in which the wealthy Sue Hambleton consorts with criminals for thrills. Ann Newhall, alias Nancy Regan, of "The Big Knockover" and "$106,000 Blood Money" is a wealthy young heiress involved with some of the 150 criminals who rob a bank and start a gang war in the subsequent double-cross. Demonstrating all the instances where the criminal environment and the world of the wealthy and powerful interact in Hammett's work would require a major study.

The importance of his attitude lies less in his influence on subsequent crime writers than in his success in a mass au-dience subgenre. A writer who aims his work at the uned-ucated or unsophisticated must reflect their perceptions and beliefs. Hammett succeeded by assuming that his readers perceived the wasteland as clearly as did the literary and intellectual elites. Furthermore, the made this assumption several years before The Great Depression ended the presumed age of optimism that followed World War I.

He wrote always about greed. Both wealth and power corrupted his characters. Dishonest cops and politicians were the norm. Nick Charles and Sam Spade, the two detectives whom the moviemakers turned into pallid, posturing imitations of Hammett's harsh originals, found the desire for easy wealth a temptation too great to overcome. None of his protagonists, not even the nameless Op, is so bound by ethics that he reflexively refuses to break the law. Hammett created such characters in the sure belief that his readers held a puritan view of tainted man that would have met with Michael Wigglesworth's dour approval.

In Hammett's environment, the law itself was often at fault. This, too, came from reality. Prohibition had turned previously upright citizens into defiant law-breakers. Only outlaws operated gambling emporiums, yet gambling was a gentleman's traditional pastime. Society's strictures had become absurd, and a free man could only resist them. If there is any Romantic element in Hammett's worldview, it is the glorification of every individual, the passionate commitment to personal freedom that underlies the American myth of the frontier. Reformers who tell another man how to live are useless busybodies, which is why the Op refuses to deal with them in **"Corkscrew."**

At the same time, Hammett avoided the trap of romanticizing the underworld. Dinah Brand, in *Red Harvest,* is not the whore with the heart of gold; she is instead a greedy bitch destroyed by her lust for money. Babe McCloor, in **"Fly Paper,"** honestly loves Sue Hambleton, but that love in no way ennobles him. He remains a violent criminal, and no one mourns when he is hanged for the murder that avenges Sue's death. Senator Henry's evil, his willingness to let Paul Madvig suffer for a murder Paul didn't commit, in no way excuses the crimes that *The Glass Key*'s political boss routinely commits or authorizes in order to maintain his machine's power and his own position of leadership.

This view of a corrupt universe is what makes the comparison of Hammett to Lewis and Fitzgerald so accurate. All three wrote in a conservative style. All three assumed that their readers comprehended the impulse to gain material wealth—and that these same readers recognized the impulse's potential for destroying those who followed it. None of them posited an America where the people fully believed in the pious public virtue so ostentatiously professed by politicians and preachers. Hammett, however, carried the idea of public despair over and disenchantment with American life much further than did the other two. Lewis strove for outrage. By exposing corruption and hypocrisy he hoped to anger his readers into action. Fitzgerald wanted a bittersweet sadness. He made his sad, rich young men suffer from their sins, so that readers could feel sorry for them. Hammett gave his readers credit for more intelligence. He assumed that they would suffer the full numbness of helpless recognition.

Recognition began with real criminals and detectives who

couldn't spell nobility, let alone practice it. The reader who had met a real cop recently could quickly place the typical Hammett detective. Equally real were the crooked politicians, the wastrel rich, the popularity of cocaine, the openly operated speakeasies, the human greed permeating every level of society, the corrupting influence of power, and the helplessness and concomitant apathy of the average citizen. The sum of Hammett's work is a powerful jeremiad indicting virtually all of American society.

His world was as much the wasteland as London/Limbo, the "Unreal City / Under the brown fog of a winter noon." His lost youth are as numb to genuine human feeling as the small house agent's clerk and the typist copulating lovelessly on a couch. His bootleggers, dope runners, and political wheeler-dealers offer the same false dreams as Madame Sosostris. The good men and women, those who want the decent society promised in the civics textbooks that extol the American dream, are as impotent as the Fisher King. But while Eliot holds out the hope of the impending rescue by Parsifal, Hammett never suggests that any man can enter the ruined tower and find the Holy Grail. The rain will never come. Hammett's Wasteland will remain parched and sterile, a place where human evil and corrupt leaders will reach out to blight every level of society.

. . . your private detective does not—or did not ten years ago when he was my colleague—want to be an erudite solver of riddles in the Sherlock Holmes manner; he wants to be a hard and shifty fellow, able to take care of himself in any situation, able to get the best of anybody he comes in contact with, whether criminal, innocent bystander, or client.

—Dashiell Hammett, in his introduction to the Modern Library edition of The Maltese Falcon, *1934.*

William Marling   (essay date 1983)

SOURCE: "The Short Stories," in his *Dashiell Hammett,* Twayne Publishers, 1983, pp. 19-46.

[*Marling is an American educator and poet whose books include* William Carlos Williams and the Painters *(1982) and* Raymond Chandler *(1986). In the following excerpt, Marling presents a detailed analysis of the author's short fiction, emphasizing the allegorical aspects of the stories.*]

Hammett's Early Short Stories

Hammett's stories rise above the efforts of his fellow *Black Mask* writers because they are framed by Hammett's own almost insupportable tensions. On the one hand, writing afforded him a way of maintaining his aloofness and pride, of identifying and rejecting the inauthenticities he had seen. Working for the Pinkertons, he found most people false, most emotion to be tactical fabrication. The inauthenticity extended, in Hammett's view, to innocent parties, such as Fatty Arbuckle, whom Hammett found guilty on other counts. These other counts are deviations from an ideal character, of which James Wright or Natty Bumppo stand as examples. Hammett's inner duty was to turn up the lie, to speak for the little man.

On the other hand, Hammett, the writer, dealt in the inauthenticities of fiction. Better than most, he could mislead his readers, or suddenly reverse field; under this cloak he remade a world that had not treated him kindly. At the end of a Hammett story, the reality the hero uncovers is no more plausible than the alibi of his suspect. "What happens in Hammett," writes Steven Marcus [in the introduction to *The Continental Op*, 1974; see excerpt dated 1974], "is that what is revealed as 'reality' is a still further fiction-making activity . . . the consciousness present in many of the Op stories and all the novels is that Dashiell Hammett, the writer, is continually doing the same thing as the Op." This consciousness that the process of discovery is a fiction—that the hero's ability to find hidden, latent, and unseen clues in the fictional world gives him superhuman powers—endows Hammett's best work with the external appearance of realism and the internal tensions of the quest or the allegory.

That part of the Hammett hero that puzzles readers, because it is so closely guarded, is the heart of Hammett, at once proud and disengaged yet moved by an unquenchable sense of injustice. Like Jack London and other realists, Hammett in his earliest stories uses an unseen ballast of social concern to mitigate the apparently ruthless or uncouth action of the hero. Hammett began, in fact, with an extraordinary insight into the lives of the office worker, the laborer, the underdog, and the misfit. These first uncollected stories are not detective stories at all.

The narrator of **"Nelson Redline"** condones his fellow office workers' laziness: "each day's task equalled each other day's task, with no allowance for our becoming more expert with practice, so that toward the end of our term, by carefully concealing our increased proficiency, we had rather an easy time of it." But sympathy never becomes sentiment. This narrator notes, when a co-worker breaks the office code, how the clerks "nurse that momentary speechlessness into deliberate ostracism." When the shunned character flees, the narrator adds, "there was the undeniable fact that all philosophic justification is with him who runs. So, in justice, I couldn't condemn him."

The story **"An Inch and a Half of Glory"** explores the rise and demise of an office worker whose rescue of a child from a burning building leads him to believe that "desk jobs were well enough for a man who could not rise above them. But nowadays there was a scarcity of—hence there must be a demand for—men whose ancestral courage had not been distilled out of their veins."

Hammett's understanding of the emotions of these working class characters, who were to be his readers, was exceptional. One of his narrators told the audience: "I don't know exactly why I went to his room with him. I knew it was going to be an uncomfortable, even a painful, hour—that he was going to say things that having to listen to would embarrass me. But I went with him to give him an opportunity to explain, to defend himself. My former casual liking for him had, I think, nothing to do with it. That was gone now. I felt sorry for him, in a vague way that made me try to conceal from him my present repugnance." This embarrassment at and aloofness from personal emotion limits Hammett's development in the proletarian direction, and is clearly Hammett's own feeling, as acquaintances have testified. It is also the deep uneasiness from which both his rejection of the unauthentic and his fictionalizing arise. Hammett felt uncertain about emotions; as he remarked when he incarnated them in one unpredictable character [in the story **"Faith"**], "you don't know approximately what they will do under any given set of circumstances, and so they are sources of uneasiness and confusion. You can't count on them. They make you uncomfortable."

Some of the early stories, such as **"The Breech"** and **"Nelson Redline,"** have this dis-ease at their thematic centers. Hammett's narrators prefer to be several steps removed, where they may observe the laws of social organization: "Without conventions any sort of group life is impossible, and no division of society is without its canons. The laws of the jungle are not the laws of the drawing room, but they are as certainly existent, and as important to their subjects" [**"Faith"**]. It was this interest in the larger social mechanism, in its codes and real functions, that prompted Hammett to read Spencer, Darwin, and later Marx. This "ballast" of social concern is never visible as emotional empathy, but always manifest in a concern for social process.

Hammett tried at first to reveal his detective's emotional life, but the experiment reinforced his decision to remain distant and to employ an objective point of view. In **"The Hunter,"** the ruthless culling of the authentic from the inauthentic holds a personal emotional danger for the detective. It is the problem of means and ends, as Vitt, the detective, simulates moods that he thinks will be of use:

> "That's tough." He put into the word and feature all the callousness for which he was fumbling inside. "But the way it stands is that if you're going to fight me on this check business, I'm going to make the going as tough as I can for the pair of you."
>
> Vitt seized the irritation that the idiocy of this reiteration aroused in him, built it up, made a small anger out of it, and his discomfort under the gazes of the woman and child grew less.
>
> A suspicion that all of this was ridiculous came to the detective, but he put it out of his mind. After he got a confession out of his man he could remember things and laugh. Meanwhile, what had to be done to get that confession needed an altogether different mood. If he could achieve some sort of rage. . . .

This simulation makes Vitt merely an actor, and frees him—as is necessary for an allegoric hero—from the personal cost of his actions. But what Vitt does is beat up, arrest, and imprison a penny-ante forger, whose motive is a desire to feed and clothe a widow and her children. Hammett saw the problem, and in the final sentence, after booking the criminal, his Vitt "hastened up to the shopping district. The department stores closed at half past five, and his wife had asked him to bring home three spools of No. 60 black thread." Hammett intended to frame Vitt in a domesticity comparable to his victim's—to show that they were both job-doers, that the impersonal commercial operations of capitalism rolled over both. As he remarked earlier in the story, "A detective is a man employed to do certain defined things: he is not a judge, a god. Every thief has his justification, to hear him tell it." But what the story shows is that a realistic detective, set in a real world, inevitably becomes a hollow man, because the inauthentic that he seeks to destroy, arrest, or remove is inextricably entwined with the authentic, the real, and the emotional. He is as culpable as those he arrests.

The alternative is to make the detective a judge and a god, but to do it covertly. He must be the one who hears the thieves, appraises their justifications, and pursues destruction of the inauthentic while sparing the real. He must not deal with emotions except as falsehoods that ravel the plots he is commissioned to unravel. If he moves on this level, an enormous power comes into his hands, of which the reader is initially ignorant; it is the detective who decides what alibi will be valid, what clue to follow, and, to borrow Robert Champigny's phrase, "what will have happened" at the story's end. In Hammett's work this power is most evident when the detective is drawn taut between world-weary realist and knight in pursuit of the grail.

It took Hammett some time to settle on the move away from emotional intimacy with his characters; at first, in such published stories as **"The Sardonic Star of Tom Dooley"** and **"The Joke on Eloise Morey,"** he took refuge in heavy irony. But in late 1923, when he wrote **"The Second-Story Angel"** and **"Itchy,"** his touch lightened. In the second piece Hammett sketched a crook who believed what he read about himself in the newspaper and was captured as a consequence: "Fiction, Itchy knew, meant stories, books. He had never thought of stories as having any connection with actuality, any relation to it. But it seemed they did, and not only with life but with him personally. Books had been written about men like him; that was what the newspapers were getting at." The cavalier manner in which Hammett moves Itchy toward his demise marks his acceptance of the fictional tools at his command.

The Continental Op

The result of Hammett's early work was a detective whom he called, simply, the Continental Op. The Op began as an idealized character. Hammett himself told Frederick Danney that he was modeled on James Wright, his Pinkerton boss in Baltimore. But the Op soon moves in semi-allegoric ways. Much of a reader's appreciation of him rests on an understanding of social code and how Hammett manipulates it to make allegoric gestures. Having grown up with genres like the detective and the western, Americans are not highly conscious of how the cues are manipulated. Because the Op delivers these details objectively, the reader assumes the Op is fair. The reader is thus

allowed to be suspicious and to believe himself objective at once, and he assumes that the Op shares his state of mind.

The epitome and chief cause of this effect is Hammett's use of a first-person narrator who purports to be objective. Like a camera eye, the Op only tells what he is seeing; he is never omnipresent, except in the resolutions of stories, and, being nameless, he invites the reader to share his experience. Hammett afflicts the Op with the problems and habits customary to office-workers: back trouble, insomnia, thinning hair and thickening belly. The Op plays cards, gripes about paperwork and complains when the company does not deem Oakland "out of town" for expense account purposes. Details that might forestall complete identification—a wife, bills, politics—are eliminated. Realistic detail and social code screen allegoric structures from the reader's view.

The most obvious of these structures derives from Hammett's understanding that the core of the American detective story, a fascination with death, was also an old topic of allegory. For the reader a good yardstick on this is the Op's changing attitude toward death. Obviously he cannot die, but in the earlier stories Hammett brought him to the edge of death frequently; it was a good way to bare the Op's soul, to elicit reader sympathy. Later the Op's brushes with death became rude gestures at fate, and he succumbed eventually, not to death, but to world-weariness. William Ruehlman calls him a "saint with a gun" and places him in the tradition of James Fenimore Cooper's frontier romances. John Cawelti, another critic, calls him a "traditional man of virtue in an amoral and corrupt world," forced to "take over the basic moral functions of exposure, protection, judgment and execution." But as the following section will show, the Op's code is blurry, if not cynical, when he reaches full development. More to the point is Angus Fletcher's comment that such a semi-allegoric figure stands "part way between the human and the divine spheres," and can "act free of the usual moral restraints, even when he is acting morally, since he is moral only in the interests of his power over other men."

The fascination with death is evident even in the earliest stories. In **"The Tenth Clew"** the Op is blackjacked and believes he is dying when his attackers dump him in San Francisco Bay.

> Weariness settled upon me, and a sense of futility. The water was no longer cold. I was warm with a comfortable, soothing numbness. My head stopped throbbing; there was no feeling at all in it now. No lights, now, but the sound of fog-horns . . . fog-horns . . . fog-horns ahead of me, behind me, to either side, annoying me, irritating me.

Hold off, Charon—the Op rouses himself. Life is valuable for the Op yet, as it is in **"The House in Turk Street"** when he overhears the inscrutable Tai vetoing his execution: "My gratitude went out to the British voice! Somebody was in favor, at least to the extent of letting me live. I hadn't been very cheerful these last few minutes." But this same story, slightly later, shows a more cautious Op: "I might have stalked my enemies through the dark house,

Hammett in the dust jacket photo for The Thin Man, *1934.*

and possibly have nabbed them; but most likely I would simply have succeeded in getting myself shot. And I don't like to be shot."

After this story and its sequel, **"The Girl with the Silver Eyes,"** the Op never puts himself deliberately in the path of danger. This heightens the implicit fear of death, or the fear of what death will reveal.

Only a year later, in **"The Golden Horseshoe,"** the Op is no longer "a young sprout of twenty or so, newly attached to the Continental Detective Agency." Instead, he says, "the fifteen years that had slid by since then had dulled my appetite for rough stuff." This story and **"The Whosis Kid"** (March 1925) mark the maturation of the Op's career. Emphatically a working stiff, he suffers for the drinking bouts he initiates in the first story, and makes sure that he gets his "three square" a day in the second.

The Op's dehumanization by his work coincides with the rise of his "god-like" powers. In **"The Golden Horseshoe,"** his ends—the necessity of success—have begun to corrupt his means. Much of the story's impact owes to the violence done the reader's sense of justice by the suggestion that God isn't fair. In **"The Whosis Kid"** Hammett reveals the Op as calculating:

> For myself I counted on coming through all in one piece. Few men *get* killed. Most of those who meet sudden ends *get themselves* killed. I've had twenty years of experience at dodging that. I can count on being one of the survivors of whatever blow-up there is. And I hope to take most of the other survivors for a ride.

The Op's explanation is really an assurance that he is immortal, since the great unstated condition is death.

In **"The Scorched Face"** (May 1925) the Op exercises any means at his disposal. He invades the privacy of Mr. Correll, whose wife committed suicide. When Correll objects, the Op thinks: "That was silly. I felt sorry for this young man whose wife had killed herself. Apart from that, I had work to do. I tightened the screws." A few lines later the Op threatens to "advertise" her suicide in the newspapers. The Op's obvious use of immoral powers in the name of morality, is increasingly displaced on his boss, the Old Man "with his gentle eyes behind gold spectacles and his mild smile, hiding the fact that fifty years of sleuthing had left him without any feelings at all on any subject."

In **"The Big Knockover"** and **"$106,000 Blood Money,"** the Op's use of immoral means for moral ends succeeds only because Hammett makes him exceptionally empathetic. "I was no fire-haired young rowdy," he says. "I was pushing forty, and I was twenty pounds overweight. I had the liking for ease that goes with that age and weight." He no longer does any spadework; he merely judges the guilty at the right time. He tells readers he is an organization man "settled down to cigarettes, guesses on who'd be the next heavyweight champion and where to get good gin," but he is headed for the same dehumanization that characterizes his boss.

> Fifty years of crook-hunting for the Continental had emptied him of everything except brains and a soft-spoken shell of politeness that was the

same whether things went good or bad—and meant as little at one time as another. We who worked under him were proud of his cold-bloodedness. We used to boast that he could spit icicles in July, and we called him Pontius Pilate among ourselves, because he smiled politely when he sent us out to be crucified on suicidal jobs.

The Op of **"The Tenth Clew"** is gone. It is no mystery that after **"$106,000 Blood Money,"** the Op says, "I'm going to take a couple of weeks off," but never returns.

Classical Formulas in the Op Stories

Hammett wrote the first widely anthologized Op story, **"The Tenth Clew,"** in late 1923. In style and plot this story marks a new level of accomplishment. The first part of it concerns nine clues, some plausible, most preposterous, that seem to link the murder of Leopold Gantvoort to a vengeful Frenchman, Emil Bonfils. But the clues prove contradictory: Hammett is employing one of Poe's classic formulas—the trail of false clues laid down by the murderer. Finally the Op, and his police colleague Sergeant O'Gar, discover the tenth clue, which is that the first nine are false. They decide that the mystery rests with old Gantvoort's girl friend, Creda Dexter. Judging from her beauty, the Op infers a romantic triangle. He breaks the case by confronting her "brother" Madden, who, with an accomplice, blackjacks and dumps the Op into San Francisco Bay. But the Op revives in time to nab the pair with Sergeant O'Gar. The crime is pinned to Madden, who adopts an Iago-like silence, but his "sister" Creda confesses for him, providing the denouement and making her professed innocence and genuine love for old Gantvoort more credible. The interesting use of the classic "false trail" is not well carried out; Madden's purpose in setting out the misleading clues and in telephoning the Op are unexplained. Also left rough is the Op's comment at the end: "I don't believe her [Creda's] enjoyment of her three-quarters of a million dollars is spoiled a bit by any qualms over what she did to Madden." The facts set out earlier clearly make young Gantvoort the heir. Despite the loose ends, **"The Tenth Clew"** shows the hand of a confident stylist: every word is in a chosen place. There is more rapidity of pace and consistency of characterization than Hammett had yet been able to attain.

The classic formulas also appear in **"The Gatewood Caper"** (October 1923), a less satisfying story in which the central enigma is a variant of the "sealed room" problem. When millionaire Harvey Gatewood's daughter is "kidnapped," the Op and Sergeant O'Gar advise him to pay the ransom, so they may find, follow, and arrest the criminal. He does, but they do not; the "kidnapper" vanishes into an alley with no apparent egress. As customary, there is an unexpected "means." The criminal has rented an apartment on the alley, and "vanished" by locking the back door to his building behind him, then exiting through the front door.

Hammett returned to the sealed room problem seven years later in **"The Farewell Murder,"** another middling story. The problem here is how Karalov, who hires the Op, could be killed by Sherry, whom the Op is certain was

at the time on a train to Los Angeles—a suspect in a locked room, in other words. The answer is that Sherry did not do it; Karalov's apparent friend Rringo did it. Hammett does not play fairly with the reader, however, since at the time of the murder he portrays Rringo as suffering a disabling injury.

The classic problems were not Hammett's strength, nor the chief interest of his editors at *Black Mask,* but he did pay homage to them again in an exceptional later story, **"Fly Paper."** The Op calls this search for runaway Sue Hambleton "a wandering daughter job." Before he can find her, she is poisoned, which causes the other principals to kill each other. When the Op investigates the deaths, he finds a copy of *The Count of Monte Cristo* wrapped in flypaper behind a refrigerator. "Ah, the arsenical fly paper, the Maybrick-Seddons trick," exclaims his boss. But the sequence and motive for the murders remain unclear until the Old Man remembers a passage in the novel that explains the mechanics and psychology of slow poisoning. Though both the logic and resolution of **"Fly Paper"** come from *The Count of Monte Cristo,* the homage is a graceful close to an excellent story.

Hammett's early investigation of the classic formulae turned up no impelling material, however; the formulas were not adaptable to a Natty Bumppo readership. They emphasized foiling the reader and astonishing him with witty resolutions. Hammett preferred, and saw that his audience required, strong plotting and vivid characterization in an intensely physical world.

Thus **"The House in Turk Street,"** published in the spring of 1924, adds a detailed foreground and a "romantic interest" to achieve its complexity. While inquiring after a runaway, the Op meets the elderly Mr. and Mrs. Quarre, who invite him in for tea and cookies. Shortly afterward, an ugly con named Hook puts a gun to the surprised detective's head: he foolishly reveals to the Op that the Quarres are a front for a bond-heist involving himself, an English-educated Chinese named Tai, and a beautiful woman with grey eyes named Elvira. The Op has stumbled on their hide-out. They bind and gag him and prepare to leave; the Op is entirely the bystander in a plot that develops through the misapprehended meaning of his appearance.

Then Elvira, who has seduced Hook, decides to use the confusion as a cover to steal the bonds. She appeals to Hook to kill Tai. He tries and fails, but Elvira hides the bonds during the tussle. Only the Op sees, which establishes a link between the two of them: "her eyes twinkled with a flash of mirth as they met mine," he reports. After the gang departs, the Op escapes with Tai's aid, and kills Hook when the latter returns. Then he hides the bonds in a new place, waiting for Tai and Elvira to return and interrogate him. They do, leading Hammett to discover one of his best stock situations—the "apartment drama" with a central female character—and one of his best themes: that greed divides the crooks and makes possible their capture.

When Elvira finds the Op, "her eyes snap scornfully." When Tai finds them both, he offers to "give her" to the Op, though he loves her. The scene in the apartment is a tense three-cornered stand-off. For the first time in any

Hammett story, events turn on a woman who is both criminal and attractive. In the gunplay that follows, initiated when the disgruntled Quarres return and Tai kills them, Elvira escapes. Only Tai is left alive to hear the Op explain ironically that he "was trying to find a young fellow named Fisher who left his Tacoma home in anger a week or two ago." The resolution unfolds more promising material than the story's development contained. Besides the ironic ending, the sketch of "Tai Choon Tau . . . the brains of the mob" anticipates the later Chang Li Ching and a legion of Fu Manchu bad-guys after him.

Hammett recognized that the crooks divided among themselves in the claustrophobic confines of an apartment offered a potent dramatic situation. It placed the treacherous face to face, heightened tension by reducing movement, and by joining constriction and violence, offered a metaphor for modern life. Introduced to such a locale, the characters need only be left to work out their fates.

Hammett tried it again in **"The Whosis Kid"** a bit later. Hunting the character of the title, the Op incidentally rescues Inés Almad, a dark foreign siren. He accompanies her home, and in her apartment meets the Kid and Edouard Maurois, who have come to divide with Inés the loot from a robbery. Since crooks never share in Hammett's stories, a stand-off and violence ensue. The resolution is neither as tidy nor as ironic as in **"The House in Turk Street,"** but many of the details—Inés is threatened with a strip-search, the mastermind is an oily foreigner—will appear in *The Maltese Falcon*. What could animate **"The Whosis Kid"** but does not is the relation between the Op and the principal female character. Inés, like Elvira, is a femme fatale, but neither the Op nor his creator have clarified the degree to which the detective is vulnerable.

Hammett addressed that material in a sequel to **"The House in Turk Street"** involving Elvira. **"The Girl with the Silver Eyes"** was published in the *Black Mask* in June 1924. In this story Elvira changes her name to Jeanne Delano. The poet Burke Pangburn thinks her the most beautiful woman in the world. She wins Pangburn by praising his poetry, convinces him to forge a check on his rich brother-in-law for $20,000, and then disappears. The Op thinks the case suspicious; at first he declines it out of regard for his agency's reputation. "I am only a hired man and have to go by the rules," he says. When the Continental Agency takes the case, he proceeds in a methodical, realistic manner. He goes to banks; he compares checks and signatures; he traces baggage tickets and transfers; he checks weather reports and prevails on clerks at taxi companies to search their log-books. These days of work he condenses into one paragraph when he gives an update to the Old Man.

When Delano and Pangburn are seen together at a roadhouse of larcenous repute, the Op deploys one of his informants. In Porky Grout—"a liar . . . a thief . . . a hophead"—Hammett portrays the marginal type nakedly. The trick is "keeping him under my heel," notes the Op. While Grout stakes out the roadhouse, the Op meticulously tracks down more leads. Someone in Baltimore has mailed Pangburn letters from Delano, someone else taxied between her abandoned apartment and the Marquis

Hotel. The Op sweet-talks telephone operators to learn more, and then dispatches Dick Foley, one of the most extraordinary minor characters in the Hammett opus, to tail the suspect: " 'Damnedest!' The little Canadian talks like a telegram when his peace of mind is disturbed, and just now he was decidedly peevish. 'Took me two blocks. Shook me. Only taxi in sight'." The appearance of Foley underlines the increasing complexity of Hammett's code. Communication in the most objective manner possible is now an implicit yardstick of character for the Op, as well as the form of Hammett's narrative. Immediately after Foley, loudmouthed Porky Grout appears, boasting to the Op, "I knocked it over for you, kid!"

The shoot-out, car chase, and confrontation that follow on the Op's reconnaissance of the roadhouse constitute an exceptional passage in Hammett's work. Watching Jeanne Delano the Op notices "a mocking smile that bared the edges of razor-sharp little animal-teeth. And with the smile I knew her!" This detail of physiognomy will typify most of Hammett's later femme fatales, and tells that his interest has shifted. Burke Pangburn and his brother-in-law fade. "This is the idea," announces the Op, as he bursts into the room, "I want the girl for a murder a couple of months back." The lights go out and they fight; the change in pace is prose adrenalin. Footwork and preparation so methodical that they seem to be ritual purification lead to pure action, which is given its sanctity by emerging allegoric relationships. Not Burke, not the forgery, not the gunplay but the Op's quest for Jeanne is what counts. Can he withstand her allure? Burke is dead by this point. Tai is dead. Porky Grout dies defending Jeanne from the Op. She flees. But the detective has a huge, powerful car at his disposal. He overtakes Jeanne and Fag Kilcourse. Kilcourse dies. It is Jeanne and Everyman.

"She was a thing to start crazy thoughts even in the head of an unimaginative middle-aged thief catcher," says the Op. "She looked at me with a gaze that I couldn't fathom. . . . I was uncomfortable along the spine." All manner of thrust and parry between the sexes follows, the Op adopting the role of gallant, Jeanne that of damsel. They stop along the roadside. Jeanne attempts his seduction:

> If you were to take me in your arms and hold me close to the chest that I am already leaning against, and if you were to tell me that there is no jail ahead for me just now, I would be glad of course. But, though for a while you might hold me, you would be only one of the men with which I am familiar: men who love and are used and are succeeded by other men. But because you do none of these things, because you are a wooden block of a man, I find myself wanting you. Would I tell you this, little fat detective, if I were playing a game?

After several minutes, the Op comes to his limit. "You're beautiful as all hell!" he shouts, and flings her against the door. He remembers Porky Grout and the other dead; only the Op's quest sets him above them. He can resist Jeanne because once she paints his fate allegorically, his code sanctions any action that preserves the quest. Hammett attended to strictly realistic interpretations as well: Jeanne has said a few pages earlier that "everyone in the world is either a fellow crook or a prospective victim." The twin detailing of his decision makes the reader forget that the Op is really "a judge and a god."

When he somewhat uncertainly turns Jeanne in, she "put her mouth close to my ear so that her breath was warm again on my cheek, as it had been in the car, and whispered the vilest epithet of which the English language is capable," says the Op. End of story—a tour de force of plot and characterization, but also a discovery for Hammett of the depth and potency of archetypes.

When he returned to the theme eighteen months later, in **"The Gutting of Couffignal,"** Hammett made more explicit the danger posed by the femme fatale and the Op's proper response. Princess Zhukovski offers her body. "You think I'm a man and you're a woman. That's wrong," the Op responds, "I'm a man-hunter and you're something that's been running in front of me. There's nothing human about it."

The Op in Adventure Stories

In 1924 Hammett wrote the first in a series of stories that beckoned to the "adventure" readership. **"The Golden Horseshoe"** takes place in Tijuana; it was followed the next year by **"Corkscrew,"** a detective Western set in Arizona; by **"Ber-Bulu,"** in the Philippines; by **"Dead Yellow Women,"** in Chinatown; and eventually by the Balkan intrigue of **"The King Business."**

"The Golden Horseshoe" is an average piece of plotting and detection, but it is important for the development of the Op's character and for its stunning conclusion, which rests on the Op's willingness to falsify evidence. Initially the story concerns Norman Ashcraft, a missing architect whose wife wants him back. Ashcraft cannot decide whether to return and commits suicide (he will be reincarnated as the character Flitcraft in *The Maltese Falcon*). When he dies, Ashcraft's identity is assumed by a hotel burglar named Ed Bohannon, who finds Mrs. Ashcraft willing to send him generous amounts of money in exchange for vague promises that he will return.

The Op is called in to determine the whereabouts of "Ashcraft" and the likelihood of his return—nothing exciting, but the Op, to whom Hammett adds paunch and years, is slightly weary anyway. He stakes out the post office, first intimidating and then jailing an accomplice of Ashcraft in order to get his address. It is the "Golden Horseshoe Cafe" in Tijuana. Hammett sketches the scene of "dirty side streets taking care of the dives that couldn't find room on the main street" with great fidelity.

He finds Ashcraft easily, and engages him in a three-day drinking contest. The rivalry works toward Hammett's central insight into the underworld: universal greed leads to universal mistrust. "Ashcraft and I were as thick as thieves, on the surface, but neither of us ever lost his distrust of the other, no matter how drunk we got." When the binge ends, the Op returns to San Francisco, where he finds Mrs. Ashcraft and her two servants dead. He suspects Bohannon as the mastermind and returns to Tijuana to see if he can discover an accomplice. He settles on the bar's bouncer, a "tall, skinny man with a long yellow

neck" named Gooseneck Flinn. The Op hires four men to enter the bar and identify Flinn, and when they do Flinn panics. The Op wants the same from Bohannon and his girl friend, but Flinn and the girl kill each other. After an auto chase and a foot race, complete with arroyo shootout, the Op captures Bohannon, who explains how he hid in a closet during the real Ashcraft's suicide. But he declines to state that he arranged Mrs. Ashcraft's murder. When the Op asks him to pick up the nearer of two cigarettes if he "did a certain thing," however, Bohannon reveals his complicity. Both know this is inadmissible in court. Satisfied that Bohannon is responsible for the deaths, the Op administers justice:

> "I can't put you up for the murders you engineered in San Francisco; but I can sock you with the one you didn't do in Seattle—so justice won't be cheated. You're going to Seattle, Ed, to hang for Ashcraft's suicide."
>
> And he did.

The unfortunate Bohannon set himself up for the ironic ending by destroying a suicide note that Ashcraft left; the Op's sentence seems immediately appropriate because it implies a causal relationship linking past and present, but a rereading shows that the Op has made a simple subjective evaluation of character. Hammett developed this ending earlier, in **"The Joke on Eloise Morey,"** and pressed the appeal of biblical vengeance under the guise of impartial justice again in other stories.

The reverse side of this "justice" is shown in **"The Scorched Face,"** published in *Black Mask* in May 1925. Myra and Ruth Banbrock are missing, another "wandering daughter case" (like **"Fly Paper," "$106,000 Blood Money,"** and **"The Gatewood Caper"**). The Op is unable to learn much, until Mrs. Stuart Correll, one of the girls' friends, commits suicide after interrogation. A difference in the testimonies of Mrs. Correll and the Banbrocks give the Op his first lead, but it goes nowhere.

Then Hammett introduces Pat Reddy, "a big blond Irishman who went in for the spectacular in his lazy way." Reddy's absolute sense of justice once led him to arrest, and later to marry, the daughter of a wealthy coffee-importer. But he "kept on working," notes an approving Op; "I don't know what his wife did with her money, but . . . there was no difference in him. . . ." The only favorable portrait of the rich in the Hammett opus, Reddy plays Chingachgook to the Op's Natty Bumppo. Their case is becalmed until an up-country grape grower discovers a charred photograph that he recognizes from the newspapers. The Op and a deputy stalk through the woods, the Op admitting "I'm a shine Indian." They find Ruth Banbrock: "At the base of a tree, on her side, her knees drawn up close to her body, a girl was dead. She wasn't nice to see. Birds had been at her."

But the leads go nowhere. The Op resorts to basic detective work; he makes lists of all of those who have committed suicide recently and he interviews their relatives. He discovers that many of them knew Raymond Elwood, a sleek young real estate agent. Dick Foley, by now a regular supporting actor, tails Elwood, discovering that he spends afternoons with various wealthy women in a yellow house on Telegraph Hill.

The case breaks when Myra appears at the house. Rephrasing one of Poe's maxims, the Op notes that "The crazier the people you are sleuthing act, as a rule, the nearer you are to an ending of your troubles." Deciding that his policeman friend can get the necessary papers "fixed up afterward," the Op persuades Reddy to break into the house. They find "a small room packed and tangled with bodies. Live bodies, seething, writhing. The room was a funnel into which men and women had been poured. . . . Some had no clothes."

Several people are killed, including Raymond Elwood and his corps of burly black servants, before the Op finds a photography darkroom and a safe in the basement. There too is Myra, smoking gun in hand. She has killed Hador, the mastermind of the extortion ring, a "queer little man" who dressed in "black velvet blouse and breeches, black silk stockings and skull cap, black patent leather pumps. His face was small and old and bony but smooth as stone, without line or wrinkle." Everything but cloven feet.

"Hador was a devil," explains Myra; "He told you things and you believed them. You couldn't help it." This exculpation prepares Pat Reddy, the only one accountable to the law, for a rationale that will cover up Myra's crime. The Op points out that two women have committed suicide rather than admit to the orgies. How many more will try when the news of Hador's death leaks out? The Op constructs an alternate version, in which Reddy shoots Hador. He wins Reddy's assent, but the policeman is reluctant when the Op proposes to destroy all the evidence: "They're photographs of people, Pat, mostly women and girls, and some of them are pretty rotten." But most of them are rich. And though the Op eventually wins Reddy to his notion of the greater common good, the Op is simply protecting his client for her rich father. Reddy is the only standard-bearer of justice in the story; the Op is a hired man of the rich. Lest a reader ponder this too deeply, Hammett adds a twist, as in **"The Golden Horseshoe."** Here, though, he makes the Op the benefactor of the unwitting Reddy: "The sixth photograph in the stack," notes the Op at the end, "had been of his wife—the coffee-importer's reckless hot-eyed daughter."

"The Scorched Face," viewed objectively, shows that the rich escape justice. Hammett invites the reader to think that justice is done because the essentially innocent are protected; but in fact Myra has murdered Hador. Codes begin to bend as Hammett discovers the Op's entrancing power to create alternate realities. The rich are sympathetic only through Reddy, but his principal characteristic is that he has not changed—he acts poor, and could not be further from the adventurism of the rich. A cynicism about wealth, born of his reading, begins to tint Hammett's work.

"Dead Yellow Women"

"Dead Yellow Women" is one of the best stories Hammett ever wrote. He set this long, 20,000 word piece (*Black Mask,* November 1925) in San Francisco's Chinatown, and the place has hardly had a rest in detective fiction since. The plot turns on the collaboration of Lillian Shan, a severely beautiful Chinese-American woman, with Chang Li Ching, the feudal lord of Chinatown. Unknown to the Op, whom Miss Shan hires to investigate two murders at her seafront mansion, Shan and Ching run guns to the anti-Japanese forces of Sun-yat-sen. Shan's mansion is the debarkation point, but the murders do not figure in.

The Op penetrates Chang Li Ching's circle through two informers, a Filipino boy called Cipriano and a career con named Dummy Uhl. Like Porky Grout, Uhl proves untrustworthy, so the Op arranges for his informer to shoot him with blanks, then has Dick Foley tail Uhl when he flees. Foley makes one of his best cameo appearances:

> "Good pickings!" he said when he came in. The little Canadian talks like a thrifty man's telegram. "Beat it for phone. Called Hotel Irvington. Booth—couldn't get anything but number. Ought to be enough. Then Chinatown. Dived in cellar west side Waverly Place. Couldn't stick close enough to spot place. Afraid to take chance hanging around. How do you like it?"

The quarry is a con called the Whistler; in the Continental files the Op finds a picture of him, wearing a Japanese war medal as he bilks Japanese immigrants of their money, and he puts the photo in his pocket.

All leads converge on Chinatown, which becomes a microcosm of the inscrutability and hostility of a larger world. But the Op is reduced to sitting on the doorstep of Chang Li Ching, his idealized foe ("my idea of a man worth working against," says the Op). To find him the Op must run a maze, with a Chinese guide. This passage echoes grail motifs so closely that, when the Op engages Ching on his own terms, which are wordplay, the unexpected levity surprises the reader: it suggests that verbal play is the core of the quest. Ching addresses the Op: "If the Terror of Evildoers will honor one of my deplorable chairs by resting his divine body on it, I can assure him the chair shall be burned afterward, so no lesser being may use it. Or will the Prince of Thief-catchers permit me to send a servant to his palace for a chair worthy of him?" The Op decides to play: " 'It's only because I'm weak-kneed with awe of the mighty Chang Li Ching that I dare to sit down,' I explained."

The interview produces no leads. The case cracks when Dick Foley, shadowing the Whistler, seizes on the bootlegging activities of Lillian Shan's boy friend Jack Garthorne, who says that the Whistler runs illegal immigrants and liquor into the country and only a few guns out. Garthorne's role is to romance Shan away from the scene.

When the Op returns to converse with Chang Li Ching, he finds Garthorne, a "slavey" girl, and then Lillian Shan dressed as a Mongolian queen—"come back to her people," she explains. The Op tells how the Whistler has duped her.

They confront Ching and the Whistler in another part of the labyrinth. To avoid verbal gymnastics, the Op gives Ching the "photograph of The Whistler standing in a group of Japs, the medal of the Order of the Rising Sun on his chest." When the Op next looks, the Whistler is "slumped down in an attitude of defeat," killed by mysterious means. The rest of the story's principals go free; justice is served when Ching gives seven of the Whistler's men to the police. Hammett ends the story with a bad joke about Chinese restaurants and a note from Ching alluding in flowery language to the fact that he has discovered the Op's means of solving the case.

Except for a few racist overtones (Hammett's repeated references to "the smell of unwashed Chinese"), the story is told from a sustained distance. The Op rarely drops his irony and detachment, which reinforces the effect of the hyperbolic conversations and distracts the reader from the quest motifs. The solution to the quest lies at the end of labyrinths and mazes; not only are these actual blind alleys in Chinatown, but figurative ones, such as Lillian Shan's research into "old cabalistic manuscripts." The solution to the quest turns out to be a facsimile of reality adroitly manipulated by the Op: the "real" but false photo of the Whistler. This fools even Ching, whose final note expresses his resolve to "not again ever place his feeble wits in opposition to the *irresistible will* and dazzling intellect" of the Op (my italics). The irony grows when the reader realizes that the note is a compliment, paid by one of his finest creations, to the author, who points to his own "irresistible will" in planning and executing the plot that lead on Ching and the reader.

Like **"Dead Yellow Women," "The Gutting of Couffignal"** (December 1925) is an attempt to find a usable, exotic locale near San Francisco. An example of Hammett's style at its smoothest, this story is organized on the scale of war rather than on that of private detection. Both stories intend to paint broad canvases, for Hammett was training for longer work. In **"Couffignal"** he hoped to sustain a long narrative drive, but got bogged down in unexplained details. He returned to a manageable scale in his two notable efforts of 1926, **"The Nails in Mr. Caterer"** and **"The Creeping Siamese,"** the latter attempting to exploit the Chinese theme again, but with mixed results. Then Hammett's work tailed off a bit. . . .

Toward Longer Works

It was eleven months before another short story appeared, but when it did Hammett showed that his eye was on longer, more profitable work. **"The Big Knockover"** (February 1927) and its sequel **"$106,000 Blood Money"** are test canvases for the landscape of clashing armies in *Red Harvest.*

They are also excellent stories in themselves. As **"The Big Knockover"** opens, the Op passes information to a known con in a speakeasy. He enjoys the trust of criminals now, moving as easily among them as among the police. In fact, though he is tipped off to a huge bank robbery, the Op waits until the next day to inform his clients. As he approaches these banks the next morning, the Op sees a massive robbery in progress. Hammett introduces here a new and important motif—criminal gangs more powerful than the police, with leaders as rationally agile as the best detectives. After thirty-six dead bodies litter the initial pages, the possibility of society as leviathan emerges.

The female interest in the story is Angel Grace Cardigan,

who appeared in the earlier **"Second-Story Angel,"** a 1923 satire on pulp writers. Angel Grace is a crook with a code, a new kind of character; she believes in dealing fairly, but she "can't go over." Not nearly so honorable, the Op sets her up for a tail by Dick Foley. Meanwhile he and Counihan, a later version of Pat Reddy, trail Red O'Leary, the visible ringleader of the heist. He goes to a speakeasy, where they extricate him and his girl friend from a brawl. The way out is a peril of passages and halls; Hammett clearly liked the effect he had achieved in **"Dead Yellow Women,"** for two men and a woman again achieve a crumbling moment of peace, a "promise of emptiness."

Outside the speakeasy, the Op finds it necessary to shoot O'Leary in the back surreptitiously to prevent him from fleeing. Then the Op accompanies him to a central hideout, the retreat of ringleaders Big Flora and Papadopoulos. The latter, a "shabby little old man" who follows Flora's orders, is the first in a series of sympathetic "rheumatic" or tubercular characters. Big Flora ties up the Op and puts him under the trembling gun of Papadopoulos. Convinced that the heist has been foiled, the old man arranges for the Op to capture O'Leary, then Pogey and Big Flora, in exchange for his freedom and Nancy Regan, O'Leary's girlfriend. Only after his departure does the Op learn that the innocuous old man is Papadopoulos, the mind behind the crime.

"The Big Knockover" is important because it is a long piece of writing, over 20,000 words, in which Hammett stretched Poe's boundary of the "tale" by linking a large number of crooks in one plot. To make the plot move, however, he had to kill off characters wholesale—at the end, there are fifty-eight known dead. This continued to be the problem with such plots, though Hammett was able to extend this one into a less bloody, equally effective sequel, **"$106,000 Blood Money."**

"$106,000 Blood Money" derives its narrative power from a series of betrayals, a theme of more interest than simple, benumbing murders. The story commences when Tom-Tom Carey announces to the Op that he intends to collect the $106,000 reward offered for Papadopoulos's capture. His ostensible motive is the murder of his brother, Paddy the Mex, in the bank robbery. But since he admits to betraying his brother, the theme of duplicity is established, and no character's motive is beyond suspicion. The Op strikes a deal with Tom-Tom: "If you turn in Papadopoulos I'll see that you get every nickel you're entitled to. . . . And I'll give you a clear field—I won't handicap you with too much of an attempt to keep my eyes on your actions." This is the first time Hammett perceived that he could enlist reader sympathy in a deal between the Op and a crook; usually he opened with an account of the crime by one of the aggrieved.

The Op ties Tom-Tom almost immediately to the murder of millionaire Taylor Newhall, whose estate hires the Op to investigate. He pursues a number of false leads while Hammett introduces the cast required for the finale. Angel Grace Cardigan, Paddy the Mex's girl friend, tracks down Big Flora Brace, his killer, and befriends her. Jack Counihan, the dashing young operative of **"The Big Knockover,"** leads the Op into a suspicious gunfight. Angel

Grace and Big Flora break out of prison; Tom-Tom tracks them to Papadopoulos's hiding place, and alerts the Op that he is moving in.

Sending an operative to protect the nearby heiress of Taylor Newhall, the Op goes with Counihan and Tom-Tom to make the arrest. Linehan and Foley follow. When they approach the hideout they discover that Nancy Regan, Papadopoulos's co-escapee, is really Ann Newhall, the heiress. Sequestering her, they close in on the house. Counihan climbs a second story window to make the arrest, apparently without gunplay. When the Op, Tom-Tom, and the reserves arrive, Papadopoulos makes a break and Tom-Tom kills him.

The Op calls Counihan outside, and reveals to all—including the surprised reader—Jack's complicity with the crooks. His is the folly of having fallen in love with Nancy Regan/Ann Newhall. In a grilling as merciless as any he gives criminals, the Op reduces Counihan to ashes before the others. "The prospect of all that money completely devastated my morals," confesses Jack. But the Op will not settle for commonplaces. "You met the girl and were too soft to turn her in," he accuses. "But your vanity—your pride in looking at yourself as a pretty cold proposition—wouldn't let you admit it even to yourself. You had to have a hard-boiled front." With Counihan reduced, the Op "stood up straight and got rid of the last trace of my hypocritical sympathy."

He demands Counihan's gun, but the latter seems ready to shoot. Tom-Tom shoots first. Linehan, in turn, kills Tom-Tom. Then the Op reveals his unsuspected allegiance: "I stepped over Jack's body, went into the room, knelt down beside the swarthy man. He squirmed, tried to say something, died before he could get it out. I waited until my face was straight before I stood up." After a moment's reflection, it becomes clear that the Op regards Tom-Tom more highly than his fellow detective, that he has arranged the humiliation leading to Jack's death, and that he regards anyone who leaves himself open to sentiment or love as foolish. These are lessons that clarify Sam Spade's later decision about Brigid in *The Maltese Falcon.*

For the Op, however, the incident signals an end, because his superhuman ability to say what happens next has moved beyond self-mocking irony to an attack on his fellow questers that is only a step from self-destruction. In the story's last lines the Op says, "I felt tired, washed out." When he talks over the events with that superannuated office deity, the Old Man, the Op realizes that "for the first time in the years I had known him I knew what he was thinking. . . . 'It happened that way,' I said deliberately. 'I played the cards so that we could get the benefit of the breaks—but it just happened that way.'" But of course the Op arranges it that way, and the fact that he does vitiates the allegoric level so much that, if he continues in this direction, Hammett will have to take up the problems of existentialism and absurdism. The Op will end here, because he has gotten too serious for popular culture.

Hammett's Style

The prose that Hammett discovered in the Op stories was at once deft and muscular, a style "that, at its best, was capable of saying anything," wrote Raymond Chandler. It has drawn praise from numerous critics because this prose practices, in few words, devices of tone, transition, and plot long thought to require more space. Many readers assume that Hammett's prose is simply the "tough talk" typical of American fiction in the 1920s. It is, but it goes beyond what previously existed. Tough writing has been dissected with insight by Walker Gibson [in his *Tough, Sweet and Stuffy,* 1975], who writes that the tough narrator is in fact more concerned with "feelings than he is with the outward scenes he presents, or with cultivating the good wishes of the reader to whom he is introducing himself. He can ignore these traditional services to the reader because he assumes in advance much intimacy and common knowledge."

Gibson sets up a number of tests, and Hammett—like Hemingway or O'Farrell—meets all of them. His diction is characterized by short, simple, largely Anglo-Saxon words. In a typical story his vocabulary is 77 percent monosyllabic, and only 2 percent of his words are not Anglo-Saxon. Hammett's stress on clarity is manifest in Dick Foley, who satirizes euphemisms such as "in conference," and "a victim of foul play."

Hammett's prose aligns with other "tough talk" criteria: it features the first-person pronoun, eschews the passive voice, and employs short clauses. Hammett's average sentence, in his early work, is thirteen words long. Highly descriptive passages run into flab at fifteen words. Fight scenes are built of sentences averaging eight words each, some only three or four words long.

> My arms had Maurois. We crashed down on dead Billie. I twisted around, kicking the Frenchman's face. Loosened one arm. Caught one of his. His other hand gouged at my face. That told me the bag was in the one I held. Clawing fingers tore at my mouth. I put my teeth in them and kept them there. One of my knees was on his face. I put my weight on it. My teeth still held his hand. Both of my hands were free to get the bag.

These sentences were not only easy to read, but formed their own tiny paragraphs in the narrow columns of the pulp format. The resulting white spaces indicated a quickened pace of action. Later on Hammett wrote fight scenes of remarkable rhythm, a sort of fistic poetry: "It was a swell bag of nails. Swing right, swing left, kick, swing right, swing left, kick. Don't hesitate, don't look for targets."

The speed of this prose resides in its verbs. In a sample section of **"The Scorched Face,"** 20 percent of the words are verbs. They tend to be simple and active, especially when the Op speaks or describes his actions, and only compound or passive when Hammett characterizes the rich or fills in a case history.

Hammett also gives the impression of eliding his story for his reader. Time and space are compressed as the reader moves from scene to scene. If the Op seeks information from someone windy or inarticulate, he summarizes the content: "I finally got it, but it cost me more words than I like to waste on incidentals." In **"The Golden Horse-**

shoe" the Op dashes to his "rooms for a bagful of clean clothes and went to sleep riding south again," thus spanning the distance between San Francisco and Mexico in a sentence. No time is wasted on travel; essential detail after essential detail creates a sense of necessity in what comes next.

This speed allowed Hammett to write economical transitions. He often delays the revelation of a new scene until late in the transitional sentence, forcing the reader to absorb other information first. In **"The Tenth Clew,"** for instance, "Half a dozen police detectives were waiting for us when we reached the detective bureau." When he is rescued from death in the Bay: "Half an hour later, shivering and shaking in my wet clothes, . . . I climbed into a taxi at the Ferry Building and went to my flat." Periodic sentences are a staple of good writing, but rarely has a writer used them so successfully to engage the reader in a new scene when he is expecting explication of the preceding one.

Equally deft are Hammett's creations of minor characters, an indispensable stock of detective fiction. At the beginning of **"The Tenth Clew,"** he created and dismissed a butler in the same sentence, then passed two hours in twenty words. More celebrated, perhaps, are his descriptions of San Francisco. In reality these are spare and functional, setting important scenes, such as the Op's approach to Chinatown in **"Dead Yellow Women"**:

> Grant Avenue, the main street and spine of this strip, is for most of its length a street of gaudy shops and flashy chop-suey houses catering to the tourist trade, where the racket of American jazz orchestras drowns the occasional squeak of a Chinese flute. Farther out, there isn't so much paint and gilt, and you can catch the proper Chinese smell of spices and vinegar and dried things. If you leave the main thoroughfares and showplaces and start poking around in alleys and dark corners and nothing happens to you, the chances are you'll find some interesting things— though you won't like some of them.

Hammett could achieve the effects appropriate to those "alleys and dark corners." The feeling of directionlessness in the Op's first trip to see Chang Li Ching's house is achieved by the sudden prevalence of the first-person pronoun without the usual emphatic verbs: "I was confused enough now, so far as the directions were concerned. I hadn't the least idea where I might be." When he required the reader to remember the topography of a locale for later action Hammett laid out the scene with scientific precision:

> The White Shack is a large building, square-built of imitation stone. It is set away from the road, and is approached by two curving driveways, which, together, make a semi-circle whose diameter is the public road. The center of this semi-circle is occupied by sheds under which Joplin's patrons stow their cars, and here and there around the sheds are flower-beds and clumps of shrubbery. We were still going at a fair clip when we turned into one end of this semi-circular driveway.

Such stylistic facility did not come automatically. An early draft of **"The Sign of the Potent Pills"** shows that the young Hammett was susceptible to editorializing and overwriting. He improved by rewriting and editing his old work. . . .

It was a made, not a found, style. Some of its hallmarks seem dated—"I encouraged my brain with two Fatimas"—but it is a style that spoke to and for a large audience. "Hammett gave murder back to the kind of people that commit it for reasons, not just to provide a corpse; and with the means at hand, not hand-wrought dueling pistols, curare and tropical fish," wrote Raymond Chandler [in *The Simple Art of Murder,* 1972]. "He put these people down on paper as they were, and he made them talk and think in the language they customarily used for these purposes. . . . Hammett's style at its worst was as formalized as a page of *Marius the Epicurean*; at its best it could say almost anything."

Hammett responding to the rejection of two Continental Op stories by *Black Mask*:

The trouble is that this sleuth of mine has degenerated into a meal-ticket. I liked him at first and used to enjoy putting him through his tricks; but recently I've fallen into the habit of bringing him out and running him around whenever the landlord, or the butcher, or the grocer shows signs of nervousness.

There are men who can write like that, but I am not one of them. If I stick to the stuff that I want to write—the stuff I enjoy writing—I can make a go of it, but when I try to grind out a yarn because I think there is a market for it, then I flop.

Whenever, from now on, I get hold of a story that fits my sleuth, I shall put him to work, but I'm through with trying to run him on a schedule. . . .

I want to thank both you and Mr. Cody for jolting me into wakefulness. There's no telling how much good this will do me. And you may be sure that whenever you get a story from me hereafter—frequently, I hope—it will be one that I enjoyed writing.

Dashiell Hammett, in a letter to the editors, Black Mask, *No. 7, 1924.*

James Naremore   (essay date 1983)

SOURCE: "Dashiell Hammett and the Poetics of Hard-Boiled Detection," in *Art in Crime Writing: Essays on Detective Fiction,* edited by Bernard Benstock, St. Martin's, 1983, pp. 49-72.

[*Naremore is an American educator and the author of several books, including* The World without Self: Virginia Woolf and the Novel *(1973) and* The Magic World of Orson Welles *(1979). Here he comments on several facets of Hammett's work, including the author's ability to imbue pulp magazine stories with artistic literary qualities.*]

Dashiell Hammett is a profoundly romantic figure, and the most important writer of detective fiction in America after Edgar Allan Poe. During the years when he was doing his best work—chiefly the late 1920s—he managed to reconcile some of the deepest contradictions in his culture. He was a man of action and a man of sensibility, an ex-private-eye who looked like an aristocrat; he wrote five novels and a few dozen stories which provided material for scores of film, radio and television adaptations, but at the same time he evolved one of the most subtle and influential prose styles of his generation. Unfortunately Hammett was an alcoholic in an era when alcoholic authors were glamorous, and this helped cut his work short. In other ways, too, he was a deeply symptomatic writer of the twenties, and his career seems to have ended with the historical conditions that had sustained it. Afterwards, according to Stephen Marcus [in his introduction to *The Continental Op*; see essay dated 1974], 'His politics go in one direction; the way he made his living went in another—he became a hack writer, and then finally no writer at all.'

There is, however, an admirable integrity about Hammett's behaviour in those later years. He worked in Hollywood for a while, but he did not neurotically dramatise himself in the manner of Fitzgerald, nor did he try to write a Hollywood novel. He was not suicidal like Hemingway (whom he resembles in so many other ways), and when a doctor told him he would have to quit drinking or die, he quit. In the fifties he was imprisoned and then blacklisted for his Marxist political sympathies, but unlike many others he did not complain publicly and refused to make himself a martyr. **"Tulip,"** the unfinished autobiographical novel he worked on when he left prison, is touchingly pastoral and a fascinating account of his attitude towards his work: 'When you write,' his protagonist says at one point,

> you want fame, fortune and personal satisfaction. You want to write what you want to write and to feel it's good, and you want this to go on for hundreds of years. You're not likely ever to get all these things, and you're not likely to give up writing and commit suicide if you don't, but that is—and should be—your goal. Anything else is kind of piddling.

Such behaviour indicates that Hammett was probably as strong as any of his heroes, who are all to some extent like him. The Continental Op has a job similar to the one Hammett once had with the Pinkerton Detective Agency; Sam Spade has Hammett's first name (Samuel Dashiell Hammett); Ned Beaumont resembles Hammett physically; and Nick Charles's life with Nora is based on the one Hammett shared with Lillian Hellman in the early thirties. More importantly, all these characters speak with what might be called the Hammett voice, which can be heard in the passage quoted above. Its diction is homely; its syntax mainly declarative statements strung together with conjunctions. It has a fine rhythm which depends on the rather calculated run-on syntax, the driving repetition of certain words and the variation between long and short periods; nevertheless, this rhythm is meant to seem more

instinctive than eloquent. It is a transparent language, of the sort that wants to cut through the crap and get down to truths so basic to the culture that they seem like natural laws. It sometimes makes an appeal to commonplace notions of behaviour, trying to sweep away lies and rationalisations. For example, here is Ned Beaumont speaking to Janet Henry in *The Glass Key* (1931), when she tells him about one of her dreams: 'I think you made that up. It starts out to be a nightmare and ends up something else and all the dreams I ever had about food ended before I ever got a chance to do any actual eating.' And here is Nick Charles telling Nora what will happen to all the characters in *The Thin Man* (1938) after the murder has been solved: 'Nothing new. They'll go on being Mimi and Dorothy and Gilbert just as you and I will go on being us and the Quinns will go on being the Quinns. Murder doesn't round out anybody's life except the murdered's and sometimes the murderer's.

This less deceived language is always placed in the dialogue of the detective or in his first-person narration, rather than in the neutral, third-person descriptions, where Hammett's prose is much more ambiguous and stylised. It is a dramatised voice, taking the form of a virile man talking to women, children or mendacious crooks. It isn't quite the voice of Reason, as with Dupin or Holmes, because it has less to do with solving puzzles than with exposing various kinds of falsehood or naïveté. Nor is it quite the voice of Metaphysics or Morality, as with Father Brown (even though in a general sense any fictional detective becomes the story's omniscient narrator and hence a type of God), because Hammett is sceptical of absolutes and his heroes are not virtuous. It is more like the voice of Male Experience, and it usually speaks with brutal frankness after a period of reticence or silent knowingness. In *Red Harvest* (1929), when the ageing capitalist tells the Continental Op that he wants a 'man' to 'clean this pigsty of a Poisonville for me, and to smoke out the rats, little and big', the Op replies, 'What's the use of getting poetic about it? If you've got a fairly honest piece of work to be done in my line, and you want to pay a decent price, maybe I'll take it on. In *The Maltese Falcon* (1929), when Brigid argues that Spade can't turn her over to the police because he loves her, he comments, 'But I don't know what that amounts to. Does anyone ever? But suppose I do? What of it? Maybe next month I won't. . . . Then I'll think I played the sap.' Clearly it is a voice which cannot be taken in by abstract appeals to morality or even love, and while it situates itself on the right side of the law, it is too honest to give the usual reasons for being there. As Ned Beaumont says, 'I don't believe in anything.'

The sceptical, unpretentious honesty of Hammett's various spokesmen is one of the things that marks him as a writer with serious aspirations. But because he is a writer of detective stories, and because he is such a classic instance of the literary tough guy, he presents special problems for the critic who wants to take him seriously. His fiction is a rare combination of light entertainment and radical intelligence. He challenges the easy distinctions between popular and high art, and the critical language that normally sustains those divisions; any critical approach to him is likely to go awry if it becomes too serious, too sociological or too frivolous. A much greater problem is that the toughness of his characteristic voice is sexualised, linked to fantasies of male power, and nowadays especially it invites an easy clinical interpretation. Even Neil Simon has been able to joke about Sam Spade, in *Murder by Death,* where the private eye is revealed as a closet gay. Hence the sexual case against Hammett needs to be acknowledged at the outset, in order to get at the complexities beyond it.

The pen may not always be a substitute penis, but with Hammett it often seems to be. His best prose has a Parnassian hardness, a lack of 'feminine' adornment, and many of his titles have a phallic quality. He writes about strong, silent men who have an acute sense of discipline, and about predatory women who have to be sent off to prison. His detectives are usually bachelors, but unlike their nineteenth-century predecessors they are loners, eating meals in various restaurants or hotel rooms, living as far from domesticity as a frontier scout. They are somewhat homophobic—see, for example, the Continental Op's reaction to Burke Pangburn in **'The Girl with the Silver Eyes'**, or Sam Spade's reaction to Cairo and Wilmer in *The Maltese Falcon*—and although they are attracted to the sexy females they encounter, the only women they trust are the ones who behave like boy scouts. Thus Nora Charles is de-

scribed by a veteran cop as a lady with 'hair on her chest', and Sam Spade compliments Effie Perine, his 'boyish' secretary, by saying 'You're a demned good man, sister.' Of course Hammett wrote charmingly about married life in *The Thin Man* but Nick and Nora Charles are only buddies compared to Ned Beaumont and Paul Madvig, the male couple of *The Glass Key,* who have an intense, passionate, sometimes violent relationship that feels more like love.

Hammett was fond of blood sports and military camaraderie, and he wrote fiction in which women are always 'other' to a central male consciousness. It would be meaningless to call him a latent homosexual because everyone is always potentially another sex; nevertheless his work speaks a masculine ideology, generally portraying women as naïve students of male wisdom or as dangerously amoral creatures. What redeems Hammett is that his protagonists never become proto-fascist superman of the James Bond variety. His novels are written in an impersonal, detached style that sometimes allows the male ethos to undermine itself, and his readers are not allowed to settle into a comfortable identification with characters like Sam Spade. The sparse autobiographical evidence indicates that Hammett *was* tough, in a way that goes far deeper than braggadocio or sportsmanship. His temperament was

Hammett testifying before the Senate Committee on Government Operations chaired by Senator Joseph McCarthy, March 1954.

egalitarian, and his later work, no doubt tempered by his relationship with Lillian Hellman, shows that he was somewhat dissatisfied with the figure of the phallic detective; the autobiographical protagonist of **"Tulip"** even jokes about homophobic 'he-men'. In any case, a properly useful analysis of Hammett's sexual politics should avoid glib ego-psychology; it should focus on Hammett's language rather than his 'personality', partly because he was always deeply concerned with problems of literary form, and partly because his style was an historical phenomenon.

American literature of the twenties was generally hard-boiled, and if Hammett had not become the 'father' of the tough detective, someone else probably would have. Actually his attraction to the detective story is as much a sign of his aestheticism as of his love of male action. Like Chandler, he began by writing verse, and like the other aesthetes of his period he found his true vocation by reacting against the genteel, prettified, vaguely homosexual tone of the nineties. (Dupin and Holmes were of course nineteenth-century aesthetic types.) In the teens the manner of Pater and Wilde had given way to the manner of T. E. Hulme, and metaphors of sculpture began to replace metaphors of music in poetic theory. Pound, Yeats and the early Imagists had tried to purge poetic language of 'rhetoric' and beauty, a project later supported by the writers who experienced the first world war. The 'little magazine' became a vehicle for most of these authors, but Hammett's distinction is that he applied the new literary sensibility to the pulps, attacking bourgeois values from below rather than from above. In fact, *Black Mask*, where his hard-boiled stories first appeared, was begun by H. L. Mencken as a way of supporting *The Smart Set*, a little magazine which published some of the early modernists. Hammett was therefore very much a part of the literary atmosphere of his period, and it is no accident that he and Hemingway became popular at virtually the same moment.

Hammett's writing, like Hemingway's, is an especially clear instance of the irony and suspicion of noble language which can be found everywhere in post-war literature, a phenomenon admirably documented by Paul Fussell in *The Great War and Modern Memory* [1975]. Indeed Hammett was a veteran of the war, which left him with a serious respiratory ailment, and all his life he was fascinated with combat. Among the other extra-literary influences on his work, his experience as a Pinkerton agent in the years before and after the war is obviously of major importance. San Francisco, where he worked in the early twenties, was the most aesthetically pleasing of American cities, but it was also the home of the Hearst Press, the Barbary Coast and the most famous of Chinatowns. It had some of the feel of the wild west, and Hammett lived there during one of the most brutal phases of the national history—a period of unrestrained capitalism and vicious labour struggles, of official corruption in the White House and of legal hypocrisies spawned by Prohibition. In America in those days, as Sam Spade says, you could 'take the lid off life,' in much the same way as the war had taken the lid off European civilisation. Nevertheless, the Depression had not yet arrived, and it was still possible to view it all in terms of rath-

er detached, cynical adventure stories. Hammett was in a good position to become the Flaubert of detective fiction.

The reputation Hammett ultimately achieved is succinctly stated by his current paperback publishers, who describe him as the 'creator of the modern, realistic crime novel'. We should remember, however, that the origin of any literary form is impossible to establish, and as Hammett's protagonist in **"Tulip"** says, 'Realistic is one of those words when it comes up in conversation sensible people put on their hats and go home.' Hammett's work seems real in the sense that it constructs a relevant model of his society, but also in the sense that it never departs truly from the realist conventions of the nineteenth century. He was a key practitioner of what was immediately named a 'modern' style, but much of his early work was geared to the demands of pulp fantasy. Before examining some of the more unusual aspects of his fiction, therefore, it may be useful to emphasise the typical fantasies he offers his readers.

One of his stories, **'The Gutting of Couffignal'**, has an amusing self-reflexive moment which alludes to his function as an entertainer. The Continental Op has been hired to guard some expensive wedding presents at a reception on the island of Couffignal, just off the California coast. After the guests have left and the owners of the house have gone up to bed, he pulls up a chair beside the mound of gifts and decides to pass the time by burning a few Fatimas and reading a book:

> The book was called *The Lord of the Sea,* and it had to do with a strong, tough, and violent fellow named Hogarth, whose modest plan was to hold the world in one hand. There were plots and counterplots, kidnappings, murders, prison-breakings, forgeries and burglaries, diamonds large as hats and floating forts larger than Couffignal. It sounds dizzy here, but in the book it was as real as a dime.

With a few qualifications, this is a good description of the story Hammett is writing, which suddenly turns into a tale of bombings, burglaries and conspiracies, peopled with Russian emigré crooks, a femme fatale, and assorted thugs who plan to loot the entire island. Like all of Hammett's work, the story contains elements of mystery, including an ending in which the detective uncovers a killer we had not expected. Nevertheless, Hammett is writing adventures as much as puzzles, so he keeps his detective in physical danger, transforming the intellectual quest into an actual chase, with bullets flying through the air. The audience for *Black Mask* seems to have expected such plots, and Hammett gave them true thrillers, stories that are still interesting for the way they subordinate everything to flat, paratactic statements of action.

But if, as Graham Greene once suggested, the key to the modern thriller lies in the formula, 'adventure happening to unadventurous men', then Hammett's work is more modern than *The Lord of the Sea*. Certainly his hero is no Hogarth. All his early fiction concerns a short, fat, forty-ish man with no name and no life beyond his job with the San Francisco branch of the Continental Detective Agency. He is an unglamorous and hence 'realistic' creation who, in terms of his general social status, probably resembles the majority of Hammett's first readers. There is in fact a potentially Walter-Mittyesque comedy (which Hammett takes care not to exploit) in the disparity between the Op's appearance and his physical powers. For example, in a quasi-Western story called 'Corkscrew', involving murder in an Arizona mining town, the Op rides a bucking bronco which tosses him four times; on the last try he punches out a cowboy who wants to restrain him from remounting. A bit later in the same story, the Op has a street fight with an ex-boxer, who breaks his fist on the Op's jaw.

In *Red Harvest* he spends all night drinking gin with a blonde, takes a cold bath, and has a fight with a killer, whom he overpowers and hauls to the police; he then takes another cold bath and has another battle with *two* killers, knocking one out and beating the other to the draw; finally, having been grazed on the wrist with a stray bullet, and without even the benefit of another cold bath, he captures an escaped convict in a dark alley and solves a murder mystery that has had the local police fooled for years.

True, during all this the Op complains about being old and out of shape, and after the events in *Red Harvest* he needs a good twelve hours of sleep. Nevertheless, to borrow one of Hammett's similes, he is as tough as a bag of nails. He resembles the other great detective heroes in being improbably heroic and a bit eccentric—outwardly the quintessential company man, he seems to love his rough life for its own sake. He is an effective instrument of fantasy precisely because he does not encourage readers to imagine that they are handsomer, younger or richer (W. H. Auden's test for 'escapist' literature); instead he encourages the notion that such things do not matter, given courage, stamina and a certain hard-edged view of life.

The Op needs these last qualities because he inhabits a world of almost cataclysmic violence; some of his longer adventures have as much action as a Keystone cops film and more corpses than an Elizabethan revenge tragedy. It is difficult to keep count of the dead in 'The Big Knockover', '$106,000 Blood Money', 'Corkscrew', *Red Harvest* and *The Dain Curse* (1929), all of which have plots that leap from one killing to another and scenes of pitched battle that portray a society literally at war. Hammett published this longer fiction serially in *Black Mask,* making each instalment build to a violent climax or to the solution of a mystery, then having the story continue because the ultimate resolution was not at hand. Even granting the demands of their form, however, the Op stories contain an extraordinary amount of death and destruction. In 'The Big Knockover', an army of crooks invades the San Francisco financial district, loots the two largest banks and has a shoot-out with the entire police department; they escape with the bank money, but their greed makes them begin killing one another, so that the Op's pursuit of them leads to whole rooms full of dead bodies. A comment the Op makes during one of the brawls in the story is an apt description of Hammett's work as a whole during this period:

> Swing right, swing left, kick, swing right, swing left, kick. Don't hesitate, don't look for targets.

> God will see that there's always a mug there for your gun or blackjack to sock, a belly for your foot.

Sometimes this delirious violence freezes into a tableau, as if Hammett were providing material for the pulp illustrations. In *Red Harvest* a prize-fighter wins a match, and as his hand is raised in victory a knife comes whistling out of the audience, its 'silvery streak' ending as the blade plunges into the fighter's neck. In *The Dain Curse* the crazed leader of a religious cult attempts ritual murder on a crystal altar illuminated by a beam of blue light, his carving knife poised over the body of a semi-nude woman who is bound head and foot. In 'The Girl with the Silver Eyes', a crook named Porky Grout stands in the middle of a roadway, 'the dull metal of an automatic in each hand', and blasts away at an automobile which is rushing towards him like a 'metal comet'. In 'Dead Yellow Women' the Op is trapped on a stairway in the secret passageway of a house in Chinatown; below him is a beautiful girl with a 'red flower of a mouth' and four Tong-warriors reaching for their automatics; above him is a big Chinese wrestler with a 'foot of thin steel in his paw'.

It is difficult to tell how much burlesque is intended in these over-heated visions—although Hammett seems to me to have a greater sense of humour in the Op stories than is usually recognised. The Op recounts everything in deadpan fashion, as if he were making raw reports under pressure. The style gives him a plausible character, and it suggests that Hammett himself has the same values as his protagonist, doing a quick professional job in a relatively disreputable but adventurous trade, with a minimum of fuss and a single-minded determination to get the story told. In a sense, the plainness of the language contributes to the illusion of realism and honesty, especially when Hammett combines the spectacular events with documentary detail or accounts of the more quotidian aspects of the Op's job. He fills the stories with precise, almost city-map-style references to San Francisco street and place names, and he likes to include bits of information about the 'inside' of professional detective work. In this regard it is worth noting that the self-reflexive passage quoted earlier from 'The Gutting of Couffignal' has a double function: at the same time that it declares an affinity between Hammett and the traditional romancers, it also contrasts the Op's workaday world with that of literature. Hammett may have been writing melodramas, but he knew how to make them as real as a dime.

Hammett soon abandoned the Op and began to write more subtle, complex fictions, but even at the first it was clear that his work was as much about language as about toughness and mystery. Although much of his early prose seems to have been hastily composed, it inevitably contains moments of wordplay and lapidary stylisation. Sometimes the clipped, stark language seems pushed toward a kind of self-parody. Here, for example, is an excerpt from the opening of a piece called 'The Farewell Murder':

> I was the only one who left the train at Farewell.

> A man came through the rain from the passenger shed. He was a small man. His face was dark

and flat. He wore a gray waterproof cap and a gray coat cut in military style.

He didn't look at me. He looked at the valise and gladstone bag in my hands. He came forward quickly, walking with short, choppy steps.

He didn't say anything when he took the bags from me. I asked:

'Karalov's?'

He had already turned his back to me and was carrying my bags towards a tan Stutz coach that stood in the roadway beside the gravel station platform. In answer to my question he bowed twice at the Stutz without looking around or checking his jerky half-trot.

I followed him to the car.

Three minutes of riding carried us through the village. We took a road that climbed westward into the hills. The road looked like a seal's back in the rain. . . .

Presently we left the shiny black road for a paler one curving south to run along a hill's wooded crest. Now and then this road, for a hundred feet or more at a stretch, was turned into a tunnel by tall trees' heavily leafed boughs interlocking overhead. . . .

The flat-faced man switched on the lights, and increased our speed.

He sat rigidly erect at the wheel. I sat behind him. Above his military collar, among the hairs that were clipped short on the nape of his neck, globules of moisture made tiny shining points. The moisture could have been rain. It could have been sweat.

We were in the middle of one of the tunnels.

The flat-faced man's head jerked to the left, and he screamed.

In terms of 'content' this is nothing more than the ordinary paraphernalia of Gothic melodrama. The language, however, is more interesting. There is first the play on the name 'Farewell', which suggests that Hammett is interested in something more than pure representation. Then there is the narrator's style, which is so curt that it vaguely resembles free verse, given a kind of significance by all the empty white space around the lines. The language is radically simple, but it can't be described as telegraphic because it contains several deliberate repetitions, little jerking points of emphasis which create a nervous rhythm in keeping with the chauffeur's 'short, choppy' steps: 'A man came through the rain from the passenger shed. He was a small man'; 'He didn't look at me. He looked at the valise and gladstone bag.' Everything has been reduced to a series of bald, brief statements, so that even the simplest figures of speech or variations of syntax are foregrounded. For example, once the car speeds away from the station and into the woods, a complex, alliterative cadence asserts itself: the road 'was turned into a tunnel by tall trees' heavily leafed boughs interlocking overhead'. The imagery works along similar lines, confining itself to a few notes of

colour or references to the chauffeur's 'flat face', until a single, vivid simile appears: 'The road looked like a seal's back in the rain.'

In keeping with the demands of a journal like *Black Mask,* the opening of **'The Farewell Murder'** is designed to get the story underway as quickly as possible, without windy exposition or authorial promises of dangers to come, offering what the pulp writers used to call narrative 'hooks' to keep the reader turning pages. Hammett conveys everything in dramatic form, but even though he tells everything from the Op's point of view, he has been selective about how much subjectivity he allows us to see. The Op is a sort of *camera obscura*; if he is fatigued by his journey, baffled by his reception, fearful of the speed of the car or the sudden scream, he does not say so. This was a style much admired by the French existentialists in the forties and fifties, who gave it a sort of philosophic interpretation; to them it was a 'zero degree' prose suggesting a mind living completely in the present, in touch with an imminent reality. The cerebral French in those days had a tendency to romanticise the physical Americans, but there is some truth to what they believed. One of the deepest pleasures of reading Hammett may come from the illusion he creates of a mind which never seems alienated, uncertain or even seriously troubled. It isn't a primitive consciousness because it registers things with a certain aesthetic grace; if the world it describes is violent, it responds to that violence by simply attending to the business at hand.

FURTHER READING

Bibliography

Layman, Richard. *Dashiell Hammett: A Descriptive Bibliography.* Pittsburgh: University of Pittsburgh Press, 1979, 200 p.

> Bibliography of Hammett's work with reproductions of first edition dust jackets.

Biography

Hellman, Lillian. Introduction to *The Big Knockover: Selected Stories and Short Novels of Dashiell Hammett,* edited by Lillian Hellman, pp. vii-xxi. New York: Random House, 1966.

> Memoir of Hellman's life with Hammett.

Layman, Richard. *Shadow Man: The Life of Dashiell Hammett.* New York: Harcourt Brace Jovanovich, 1981, 312 p.

> Frequently cited as the definitive biography of Hammett.

Nolan, William F. *Dashiell Hammett: A Casebook.* Santa Barbara: McNally & Loftin, 1969, 189 p.

> Biographical study of Hammett's career and literary impact. An extensive bibliography and a list of motion pictures created from Hammett's fiction and screenplays are included in the volume.

Criticism

Day, Gary. "Investigating the Investigator: Hammett's Continental Op." In *American Crime Fiction: Studies in the*

Genre, edited by Brian Docherty, pp. 39-53. New York: St. Martin's Press, 1988.

> Examines the Op's method of investigation, concluding that the detective "explains by disproving story, yet his explanations are themselves stories which conceal another story."

Margolies, Edward. "Dashiell Hammett: Success as Failure." In his *Which Way Did He Go?: The Private Eye in Dashiell Hammett, Raymond Chandler, Chester Himes, and Ross Macdonald,* pp. 17-31. New York: Holmes & Meier Publishers, Inc., 1982.

> Biographical study of Hammett's work. Margolies suggests that "Hammett's Marxism in the 1930s may have . . . contributed to his creative paralysis."

Michaels, Leonard. A review of *The Continental Op. New York Times Book Review* (8 December 1974): 1, 10, 12, 14.

> Partially negative assessment that criticizes the characterization and organization of Hammett's stories.

Yasunari Kawabata

1899-1972

Japanese novelist, short story and novella writer, critic, and essayist.

INTRODUCTION

Kawabata was an internationally acclaimed fiction writer who was the first Japanese to win the Nobel Prize in literature. His works are noted for their blending of a modern sensibility with an allusive, highly nuanced style derived from traditional literature. Kawabata strove, in both his short and long fiction, to create exquisitely detailed images that resonate with meanings that remain unexpressed. Describing the effect of reading Kawabata's work, Thom Palmer observed that his stories "comprise a variety of levels and potentials. There are gradations of meaning, innumerable approaches at interpretation, a sophisticated array of doors and windows through which one can access the text. With Kawabata, one may locate, or perhaps even experience, a subtle epiphany, feel a little throb of excitement from the tale or its telling, but it's a highly subjective, intuitive occurrence."

Biographical Information

Born in Osaka in 1899, Kawabata was orphaned at an early age; his father died when he was two, and his mother died the following year. Biographers point out that the young Kawabata suffered several other losses and earned the sobriquet "Master of Funerals" for the number of ceremonies he attended in his youth, including those of his grandparents, with whom he lived after his parents died, and that of his only sister. Kawabata began his literary activities while still in his teens. In 1914 he wrote his earliest known story, "Jūrokusai no Nikki" ("Diary of a Sixteen-Year Old"), recording his impressions at the time of his grandfather's death. He attended Tokyo Imperial University and obtained a degree in Japanese literature in 1924. As a young man Kawabata was interested in Western literature and artistic movements. Proficient in English, he read James Joyce's *Ulysses* in its original language and was strongly influenced for a time by stream-of-consciousness techniques. In 1924 Kawabata joined with Riichi Yokomitsu and other young writers to found the literary journal *Bungei Jidai* (*The Age of Literary Arts*), the mouthpiece of the Shinkankaku-ha (The Neo-Sensualist or New Perceptionist) movement. Kawabata and other members of this short-lived but influential movement experimented with cubism, dadaism, futurism, and surrealism in an effort to capture the pure feelings and sensations of life. Although Kawabata's active participation in such movements is generally regarded as exploratory and temporary, he maintained an interest in modern literary currents throughout his life. During his career Kawabata won a number of Japanese literary awards and honors, as well

as the German Goethe Medal (1959), the French Prix du Meilleur Livre Etranger (1961), and the Nobel Prize (1968). He also served as author-in-residence at the University of Hawaii in 1969. Kawabata took his own life in 1972; he left no note, and the reasons for his suicide are unknown.

Major Works of Short Fiction

Best known as a novelist, Kawabata nevertheless wrote short stories throughout his career, and he himself suggested that the essence of his art lay in his short pieces. In English, his short fiction is principally represented by two collections: *House of the Sleeping Beauties and Other Stories* (translated by Edward Seidensticker in 1969) and *Palm-of-the-Hand Stories* (translated by Lane Dunlop and J. Martin Holman in 1988). The former contains, in addition to the title work "Nemureru Bijo," the stories "Kata Ude" ("One Arm") and "Kinjū" ("Of Birds and Beasts"). The latter features just over half of the estimated 146 very brief pieces that Kawabata called *tanagokoro no shōsetsu* ("stories that fit into the palm of the hand"). Sometimes little more than a page in length, these highly condensed, allusive stories range in tone from the humorous to the poignant. In form, they may consist of the evocation of a single image or mood, or may possess more complex structures. His last, "Gleanings from Snow Mountain," written just prior to his death, distills his full-length novel *Yukiguni* (*Snow Country*) into a story of some nine pages. "Izu no Odoriko" ("The Izu Dancer"), one of Kawabata's first literary successes, was also published in an English translation by Seidensticker in the anthology of Japanese fiction *The Izu Dancer and Other Stories* (1964).

Critical Reception

Although novels make up the largest part of Kawabata's output, critics generally consider the economy and precision of his short fiction more reflective of his artistry. Many have pointed out that Kawabata's longer works are often structured as a series of brief suggestive scenes of the sort that typically constitute his stories. As Holman observed in his introduction to *Palm-of-the-Hand Stories*, the very short story "appears to have been Kawabata's basic unit of composition from which his longer works were built, after the manner of linked-verse poetry, in which discrete verses are joined to form a longer poem." Masao Miyoshi also detected a similarity between Kawabata's method and the writing of poetry when he compared the author's technique in "The Izu Dancer" to that of haiku poems: Kawabata, he noted, "instead of explaining the characters' thoughts and feelings, merely suggests them by mentioning objects which . . . are certain to reverberate with tangible, if not identifiable emotions." Critics commonly praise Kawabata's images for their vivid clarity and their power to evoke universal human fears of loneliness, loss of love, and death. Yukio Mishima, for example, likened the intensity Kawabata creates in "House of the Sleeping Beauties" to being trapped on an airless submarine: "While in the grip of this story," he stated, "the reader sweats and grows dizzy, and knows with the greatest immediacy the terror of lust urged on by the approach of death." Gwenn Boardman Petersen found sadness and longing recurring concerns for the author, and Arthur G. Kimball judged Kawabata's treatment of such themes the source of the timeless quality of his works.

PRINCIPAL WORKS

Short Fiction

"Izu no Odoriko" [*"The Izu Dancer"*] 1926
House of the Sleeping Beauties and Other Stories 1969
Palm-of-the-Hand Stories 1988

Other Major Works

Yukiguni [*Snow Country*] (novel) 1937
Sembazuru [*Thousand Cranes*] (novel) 1952
Yama no oto [*The Sound of the Mountain*] (novel) 1954
Go sei-gen kidan [*The Master of Go*] (novel) 1954
Mizuumi [*The Lake*] (novel) 1955
Onna de aru koto [*To Be a Woman*] (novel) 1956-58

Utsukushisa to kanashimi to [*Beauty and Sadness*] (novel) 1965
Utsukushii nihon no watakushi [*Japan the Beautiful and Myself*] (Nobel Prize lecture) 1969
Kawabata Yasunari Zenshu. 35 vols. (collected works) 1980-83

CRITICISM

Thomas Fitzsimmons (essay date 1969)

SOURCE: A review of *House of the Sleeping Beauties*, in *The Saturday Review*, New York, Vol. 52, No. 24, June 14, 1969, pp. 34-5.

[*Fitzsimmons is an American poet, educator, and critic with a special interest in Japanese culture. In the following highly favorable assessment of* House of the Sleeping Beauties, *he perceives a theme unifying the three stories in the volume: the "lasting and lucid vision of one aspect of human fear."*]

Are you afraid of people? Of individuals in all their howling singularity? Do you carry somewhere deep inside you a primitive awareness that other human beings are the most baffling, complex, unpredictable phenomena you will ever have to cope with on this earth?

This is the theme of the three stories contained in 1968 Nobel Laureate Yasunari Kawabata's ***House of the Sleeping Beauties***, in which the author explores the fear that compels a man to try to reduce other persons to things, or to replace them with less threatening creatures.

There is an astonishing honesty of vision in the title story about an old man who both needs and dreads to have other people close to him. Unlike the regular customers of the House of the Sleeping Beauties, Eguchi retains a touch of sexual potency. The house was designed to enable old men near death to pass the night with lovely young girls, so heavily drugged they would not waken no matter what was done to them. Although their virginity was considered safe, the other ways in which they might be used while asleep were not overlooked; the proprietress warns Eguchi that he must not "put his finger in the mouth of the sleeping girl, or try anything else of that sort."

Old Eguchi is the only real character in this story. The girls are mere presences, but intensely physical ones, and Eguchi dwells long on the details of their flesh, hair, nails, color and, especially, odor. Somewhat aroused by his inspections, Eguchi moves to take one of the girls in her sleep, whatever the consequences. He is, however, startled and frightened off by the actuality of her virginity.

In much of Kawabata's work virginity is a powerful and mysterious force, almost a focus of worship. In this story it emerges clearly as an aspect of his fascination with the effort to keep human relations as neat—*i.e.,* inhuman—as possible. Virginity is "clean," an adjective Kawabata's characters apply to a landscape, a woman's genitals, or the entire quality of a human relationship.

Eguchi's experiences in the House trigger a series of memories and nightmares about his lovers, wife, daughters, and a fourteen-year-old prostitute, revealing finally how barren all these relationships were and leading to a fierce determination to reach somehow, anyhow, these sleeping girls who are only the latest manifestation of the unreachable other. But their evasion is complete—and completely ironic, since they are wholly available as flesh. The result is that old Eguchi has an ever stronger desire to hurt, even to kill one of them. Thus he is led to consider the next step in minimizing a human relationship. He asks for the same potent drug that is given to the girls. Then the step beyond that: death and the utter "neatness" of two corpses lying side by side through the night, growing cold together.

In the short **"One Arm,"** a fantasy dating from the 1930s, a young man spends the night with the arm of a young girl, which she removes and lends to him. He passes the hours rehearsing his fears, and when he tries, as she has suggested, to replace one of his arms with hers, he is seized with panic. He tears her arm from his shoulder and flings it away, unable to unite with even this small portion of another.

In the longer and more recent **"Of Birds and Beasts"** the narrator is a middle-aged man who has abandoned as far as possible relations with humans, preferring animals and birds. This is some gain: fear-based actions that might earn him mockery or retaliation from people now lead only to the suffering and destruction of pets, and to some small mourning. Again Kawabata uses external events to unwind the narrator's memories—in this case, the details of a long but sterile affair with a dancer.

The focus and strategy of these three stories, though written over a span of years, is essentially the same. They reveal a lasting and lucid vision of one aspect of human fear. The honesty with which that vision is allowed to appear in the pages of this book has finally clarified for me Kawabata's preoccupations with the relationship between persons and non-persons and with metaphors clustering around virginity and "cleanness," which have puzzled me again and again as I have read him over the years. Someone, I think, chose these stories very carefully, someone deeply sensitive to Kawabata's whole life work, probably the only man sensitive enough to Kawabata's style to have come near to rendering it successfully into English—the translator, Edward G. Seidensticker.

Years ago in Japan a friend casually referred to Kawabata as the inventor of the *haiku* novel. In those days I shared more fully than I knew my culture's tendency to reduce mystery by carefully describing its peripheral aspects in mechanical terms. Thinking that *haiku* was a matter of syllable count, sound agreement, seasonal reference, etc., I was puzzled—as puzzled as you might be by the phrase "sonnet novel," if you think the technicians' formula concerning meter, rhyme scheme, number of lines, etc., says something important about sonnets. In time I came to understand that the term *haiku* refers to a certain quality of vision that is adequately named only by the works of art

it has shaped. As an attempt at defining that quality I offer: reduction to essence, the power of suggestiveness, restraint from discursive comment, the drama inherent in *seeing*, freshness, boldness, simplicity.

Like the sonnet vision, which focuses on the resolution of conflict, the *haiku* vision can produce strong or weak experience. The strong experiences provided by any art preserve our dreams, safeguard our mysteries, offer illumination. Since prose fiction is the artistic strategy most successfully employed by the technicians who would turn every art form into just one more means of manipulating people and minimizing any possibility of illumination, the term "*haiku* novel" says something important about just what it is Yasunari Kawabata does with words. He does it well.

Yukio Mishima (essay date 1969)

SOURCE: An introduction to *House of the Sleeping Beauties and Other Stories* by Yasunari Kawabata, translated by Edward G. Seidensticker, Kodansha International, 1969, pp. 7-10.

[*Mishima is considered one of the most important modern Japanese writers. Both prolific and versatile, he wrote dozens of novels, dramas, short stories, essays and screenplays. His works often reflect his adherence to traditional Japanese values, a dedication which was ultimately demonstrated in his ritual suicide in 1970. In the essay below, he extols the interwoven themes and precise scenic detail in the title story of the collection* House of the Sleeping Beauties.]

There would seem to be, among the works of great writers, those that might be called of the obverse or the exterior, their meaning on the surface, and those of the reverse or interior, the meaning hidden behind; or we might liken them to exoteric and esoteric Buddhism. In the case of Mr. Kawabata, *Snow Country* falls in the former category, while **"House of the Sleeping Beauties"** is most certainly an esoteric masterpiece.

In an esoteric masterpiece, a writer's most secret, deeply hidden themes make their appearance. Such a work is dominated not by openness and clarity but by a strangling tightness. In place of limpidness and purity we have density; rather than the broad, open world we have a closed room. The spirit of the author, flinging away all inhibitions, shows itself in its boldest form. I have elsewhere likened **"House of the Sleeping Beauties"** to a submarine in which people are trapped and the air is gradually disappearing. While in the grip of this story, the reader sweats and grows dizzy, and knows with the greatest immediacy the terror of lust urged on by the approach of death. Or, given a certain reading, the work might be likened to a film negative. A print made from it would no doubt show the whole of the daylight world in which we live, reveal the last detail of its bright, plastic hypocrisy.

"House of the Sleeping Beauties" is unusual among Mr. Kawabata's works for its formal perfection. At the end the dark girl dies, and "the woman of the house" says: "There is the other girl." With this last cruel remark, she brings down the house of lust, until then so carefully and minutely fabricated, in a collapse inhuman beyond description. It may appear to be accidental, but it is not. At a stroke it reveals the inhuman essence in a structure apparently built with solidity and care—an essence shared by "the woman of the house" with old Eguchi himself.

And that is why old Eguchi "had never been more sharply struck by a remark."

Eroticism has not, for Mr. Kawabata, pointed to totality, for eroticism as totality carries within itself humanity. Lust inevitably attaches itself to fragments, and, quite without subjectivity, the sleeping beauties themselves are fragments of human beings, urging lust to its highest intensity. And, paradoxically, a beautiful corpse, from which the last traces of spirit have gone, gives rise to the strongest feelings of life. From the reflection of these violent feelings of the one who loves, the corpse sends forth the strongest radiance of life.

At a deeper level, this theme is related to another of importance in Mr. Kawabata's writing, his worship of virgins. This is the source of his clean lyricism, but below the surface it has something in common with the themes of death and impossibility. Because a virgin ceases to be a virgin once she is assaulted, impossibility of attainment is a necessary premise for putting virginity beyond agnosticism. And does not impossibility of attainment put eroticism and death forever at that same point? And if we novelists do not belong on the side of "life" (if we are confined to an abstraction of a kind of perpetual neutrality), then the "radiance of life" can only appear in the realm where death and eroticism are together.

"House of the Sleeping Beauties" begins with old Eguchi's visit to a secret house ruled over by "a small woman in her mid-forties." Since the reason for her presence is to make that extremely important remark at the conclusion, she is drawn with ominous detail, down to the large bird on her obi and the fact that she is left-handed.

One is struck with admiration at the precision, the extraordinary fineness of detail, with which Mr. Kawabata describes the first of the "sleeping beauties" the sixty-seven-year-old Eguchi spends the night with—as if she were being caressed by words alone. Of course it hints at a certain inhuman objectivity in the visual quality of male lust.

> Her right hand and wrist were at the edge of the quilt. Her left arm seemed to stretch diagonally under the quilt. Her right thumb was half hidden under her cheek. The fingers on the pillow beside her face were slightly curved in the softness of sleep, though not enough to erase the delicate hollows where they joined the hand. The warm redness was gradually richer from the palm to the fingertips. It was a smooth, glowing white hand.
>
> Her knee was slightly forward, leaving his legs in an awkward position. It took no inspection to tell him that she was not on the defensive, that she did not have her right knee resting on her left. The right knee was pulled back, the leg stretched out.

Thus the girl who has become a "living doll" is for the old man "life that can be touched with confidence."

And what a splendidly erotic technique we have when old Kiga sees the *aoki* berries in the garden. "Numbers of them lay on the ground. Kiga picked one up. Toying with it, he told Eguchi of the secret house." From this passage or near it, the feeling of confinement and suffocation begins to come over the reader. The usual techniques of dialogue and character description are of no use in **"House of the Sleeping Beauties,"** for the girls are asleep. It must be very rare for literature to give so vividly a sense of individual life through descriptions of sleeping figures.

Arthur G. Kimball   (essay date 1970)

SOURCE: "Last Extremity: Kawabata's *House of the Sleeping Beauties,*" in *Critique: Studies in Modern Fiction,* Vol. XIII, No. 1, 1970, pp. 19-30.

[*In the essay below, Kimball closely scrutinizes the imagery in "House of the Sleeping Beauties," detecting numerous pairs of opposing or contradictory images in the story.*]

In his Nobel Prize acceptance speech, Yasunari Kawabata refers to his essay, "Eyes in Their Last Extremity." The title comes from the suicide note of the famous short story writer, Akutagawa Ryunosuke (1892-1927). As his remarks show, Kawabata has pondered the question of suicide and rejects it as an unenlightened act. But the phrase which so struck him, "eyes in their last extremity," is incarnate in the person of old Eguchi, protagonist of **"House of the Sleeping Beauties."** In this novel, Kawabata poignantly explores the intimate thoughts of an old man searching for the meaning of his existence. In his sensual yearnings, erotic fancies, and subtle attempts at self-deception Eguchi probes back to the source of life. But the quest is a failure; he ends a lonely old man, chilled with the knowledge of his aloneness.

The novel is at once traditional, from one called the "most Japanese" of writers, and modern—as modern as geriatrics, senior citizens, and "Sunset Villages." The traditional side is apt to puzzle Western readers, who may well wonder what sort of guide-rails one can grasp hold of when crossing this "spiritual bridge spanning between East and West," as the Nobel prize citation described the novelist. The something "Japanese" about Kawabata is a meditative, sympathetic, sometimes wistful, and highly evocative understanding of nature, or rather, of the subtle interplay between nature and human existence. It has deep roots in the heritage of Japan's past, both religious and literary, from Buddhist reflection and Shinto mystique as well as their artistic calling card, the haiku poem. Thus, in **"House of the Sleeping Beauties,"** the wrist of one of the sleeping girls brushes over old Eguchi's eye and the scent brings "rich new fantasies." The old man's thoughts are like a poem; "just at this time of year, two or three winter peonies blooming in the warm sun, under the high stone fence of an old temple in Yamato." The flowers in turn suggest old Eguchi's daughters. This passage, and others like it, illustrate what one critic has described as the "painfully delicate nuances and almost immeasurable subtlety peculiar to Japanese art and literature" [George Saito, *The Oriental Economist,* October 1962].

But even for Japanese readers the Nobel prize winner's works sometimes appear strange and even uninviting. Is it because Kawabata's sad, fragmented world is also a world of resignation, of quiescent Buddhism? Is the voice of this most Japanese of Japanese authors the voice of the past? And if so, is his famous Nobel speech the swan-song of an age? Kawabata's translator, Edward Seidensticker, raised these and other questions in an address given in Tokyo in April, 1969. Commenting that Kawabata's great theme was loneliness, the impossibility of love—in short, alienation—Professor Seidensticker asked: why then is Kawabata neglected by a generation of young people that so visibly demonstrates its feeling of alienation? The answers are not easy to obtain. Nor is it entirely clear that the current generation does in fact neglect its Nobel winner. In any case, however "traditionally Japanese," however much "of the past," and however puzzling, Kawabata's artistry has much which declares its timeliness and relevance for the present.

What indeed could be more relevant—to any age—than loneliness, the hopelessness of love, alienation? From the frustrated lovers of *Snow Country* to the dreamily desiring man in **"One Arm,"** Kawabata brilliantly evokes the poignancy of thwarted love. His other major themes too are universally appealing. The "darkness and wasted beauty" which "run like a ground bass through his major work," represent an integral part of the heritage of both East and West [quotation from Seidensticker's Introduction to *Snow Country*]. Again, old age and death too preoccupy Kawabata. He said after World War II that he could write only elegies, and in keeping with this resolve wrote such works as *The Sound of the Mountain* and *Thousand Cranes.* **"House of the Sleeping Beauties"** can be added. Puzzling then, he may be, in great part no doubt due to his poetic, elliptical style, but Kawabata is very much relevant, "contemporary" in the sense that universal themes are always contemporary. And his major themes are all presented in **"House of the Sleeping Beauties."**

Like Tanizaki's *Diary of a Mad Old Man,* Kawabata's works reveal the inner workings of an old man's mind, recording his efforts to make the erotic most of his last days. But Kawabata's novel has a sinister note, and the crimson velvet curtains of the sleeping beauties' room create a setting which might have come from one of the macabre works of Edgar Allan Poe. The sinister note is sustained, for death suffuses the narrative; from the opening pages where one reads that "the wind carried the sound of approaching winter" to the final lines where the dark girl's body is dragged downstairs, the reader suspects death. And death comes, as inevitably as it must soon come to old Eguchi. Kawabata's artistry manifests itself in the way he combines the suggestions of death with bits of setting, builds up suspense, and uses indirection to achieve a unified tone. The result would satisfy Poe's criterion for the ideal short story, one which has a "unique or single effect." The effect in this case is a feeling of inevitability, a gloomy sense that something is coming to an end, and that at the end death waits.

Thus Yukio Mishima [in his introduction to the volume] speaks of **"House of the Sleeping Beauties"** as a work dominated by "strangling tightness" and likens it to "a submarine in which people are trapped and the air is gradually disappearing." The reader, he says, "knows with the greatest immediacy the terror of lust urged on by the approach of death." Kawabata carefully cultivates this feeling of "tightness." The opening words of his story are a warning which at once suggests danger and a strange eroticism. Old Eguchi is "not to put his finger into the mouth of the sleeping girl, or try anything else of that sort." Kawabata quickly adds the sinister note. The house has a "secret," and a locked gate, and when Eguchi arrives, all is silent. The woman who admits him has a strange and "disquieting" bird design on her obi (kimono waist band). Images of death soon accumulate. The secret house is near the sea, and the sound of the waves is violent. "It was as if they were beating against a high cliff, and as if this little house were at its very edge. The wind carried the sound of approaching winter, perhaps because of something in old Eguchi." The winter season and the nearby sea, both archetypal symbols of death, suggest the mood. Eguchi, before entering the room of the sleeping girl, recalls lines from a poetess who died young: "the night offers toads and black dogs and corpses of the drowned." He wonders if the sleeping girl will resemble a drowned corpse.

Small wonder that old Eguchi begins this first visit to the secret house with "apprehension" and an "unpleasant emptiness." As the reader first suspects, then gradually realizes with deepening awareness, that "emptiness" is Eguchi's own. For the old man's series of visits to the House of the Sleeping Beauties is a series of confrontations with himself, a set of experiments in self-analysis in which his identity is very much at issue. What could force one to be more intensely introspective than a meeting where the other person is only a presence, a body, and where one's musings, questions, charges are met only with silence or the slight movement of a hand? At such time any "dialogue" is self-generated, self-sustained, and ultimately self-directed. And what, for an old man, could more intensify the confrontation than to have that other person a kind of polarizing opposite, a soft, beautiful, and silent young woman? Such a meeting would heighten memories, call forth old sensations, and force a measurement of oneself in relation to their presence and the present moment. Thus Eguchi begins his quest.

Nearing seventy years of age, Eguchi is like the secret house seems to be when the waves roar, perched on the edge of the cliff above the sea. Yet still clear of mind, and still virile to some extent, he grows irritable at any suggestion that he might be senile or helpless like other old men who visit the house. "I'm all right," he growls at the woman of the house when she cautions him to be careful of the wet stones and tries to help him, "I'm not so old yet that I need to be led by the hand." But his vision is that of one in his last extremity. "An old man lives next door to death," he says in the final chapter. And what is it to be an old man, in one's last extremity? People in their thirties sometimes experience the first traumatic shudder in realization of time's fleetness. By the forties, horizons have constricted, doors have closed, the vocational crisis is reached. At fifty, the backward look begins, the crisis of identity becomes acute, depression sets in. And what of the old man, nearing the end? What hopes and pleasures remain? What self-deceptions lure him on? What does he hope to gain from the house of the sleeping beauties?

Kawabata divides his narrative rather formally, into five chapters. Unlike the familiar dramatic form, however, the final section is not a denouement; rather, the story builds to a climax which comes only in the last pages. In each of the first four chapters, Eguchi visits the secret house and spends the night, each time sleeping by the side of a different girl. In the fifth chapter, Eguchi's fifth visit, the old man finds that he has been allotted two girls. Before this last visit, Eguchi learns that one of the old men has died while staying in the secret house. For both Eguchi and the reader, this fact, together with the discovery that there are to be two girls instead of one, heightens the suspense. In the night one of the girls dies, and at the end of the novel old Eguchi, shocked, stands gazing at the remaining beauty and wonders where they have taken the body of the other.

On his first visit the apprehensive Eguchi experiences a number of sensations and finds himself probing his past. As an older person often remembers, recreates, and sometimes writes "the story of his life" to forestall death and define his existence, so Eguchi relives from earlier days. The imagined smell of baby's milk starts a series of associations. He first remembers a geisha lover's jealous anger over the baby milk she smelled on his coat. This in turn calls up the memory of a lover he had before he married. He remembers a particular meeting when her breast had become lightly stained with blood. He next recalls the middle-aged woman who counseled him to count potential lovers as a means of getting to sleep. Soon his thoughts turn again to the girl "whose breast had been wet with blood," and he remembers especially the cleanness of her secret parts and of seeing her in Kyoto in the midst of flowers and bamboo. When he takes one of the two sleeping pills provided, he dreams, first of embracing a woman with four legs, and next, that one of his daughters has borne a deformed child. The child is hacked to pieces in preparation for disposal. Horrified, Eguchi awakens to the four crimson walls. He takes the second pill and sleeps till morning. On this first visit, a number of images filter through Eguchi's mind and blend together; dreams and memories mingle, erotic fancies and nostalgic reflections produce babies, blood, women's breasts and secret parts, thoughts of sleep, and the women of Eguchi's life. On subsequent visits they reappear, sometimes in altered form.

On his second visit two weeks later, Eguchi, somewhat more nervous than before, finds an even more beautiful girl awaiting him. Aroused by caressing her and by her "witch-like" beauty, he decides to violate the rules, discovers the girl is a virgin, and, surprised, resists the temptation. The girl's warm scent brings visions of flowers, and flowers recall memories of his three daughters. He especially remembers his youngest and how, when she had lost her virginity to a suitor, he had taken her on a trip to "revive her spirits," and they had seen a famous 400-year-old camellia tree. In the camellia-like richness of the body

next to him he feels "the current of life, the melody of life, the lure of life." This time Eguchi takes both sleeping tablets at once. His second visit has produced a melange of sensations akin to the first; the deep red of the girl's lipstick and the reflection of the crimson curtains on the girl's skin mingle with visions of the camellia and thoughts of virginity, women's breasts, mother, and sleep.

Eight days later, Eguchi makes his third visit to the secret house. Whereas the second girl was "experienced," the third is "still in training," the woman of the house informs him. The sight of the young girl and the two usual sleeping tablets causes Eguchi to ponder what it would be like to "sleep a sleep as of the dead." He then remembers a young married woman he had met at a night-club and taken to his hotel three years before. "I slept as if I were dead," she had told him in the morning. His pleasure in hearing this "stayed with him like youthful music." Next, the sleeping beauty's open mouth and tongue recall a young prostitute Eguchi had disliked and dismissed on carnival night. He begins to ponder the problem of evil, recalls past sexual pleasures, and finally, embracing the sleeping girl, dozes and dreams of golden arrows and flowers. He awakens and rings in vain for the woman of the house; he wants to take some of the drug and sleep that deep, death-like sleep. The old man's thoughts have drifted from erotic fancies—the rounded shoulders, open mouth, and tongue—to thoughts of pregnancy, flowers, and especially, sleep.

Before retiring on his fourth visit, Eguchi and the woman banter about death and "promiscuity," and, when he asks about "the worst one can get by with" in the house, the remarks turn to suicide and murder. When he lies beside the girl he feels that his successive visits have each brought "a new numbness" inside him. The girl's strong scent reminds him again of the milky smell of a baby. He imagines a wild bird skimming the sea's waves, "something in its mouth dripping blood." Eguchi amuses himself with erotic play around the girl's face: "Taking the lower lip at its center, he opened it slightly. Though not small in proportion to the size of her lips, her teeth were small all the same, and regularly ranged. He took away his hand. Her lips remained open. He could still see the tips of her teeth. He rubbed off some of the lipstick at his fingertips on the full earlobe, and the rest on the round neck. The scarcely visible smear of red was pleasant against the remarkably white skin." Eguchi closes his eyes, envisions a swarm of butterflies, and wonders if the bosom of the girl evoked the image. He leaves on her breasts "several marks the color of blood." In the morning he asks for, and is refused, extra sleeping medicine.

One can see in the structure of the narrative both progression and thematic unity. Eguchi's visits to the secret house follow the deepening season; autumn turns to winter and the fall rains become sleet and snow. The final visit is made in "dead winter." The suspense too deepens, as Eguchi's thoughts become increasingly serious and macabre. Part of the subtle build-up is the old man's gradually increasing desire for stronger medicine and the growing urge to join the sleeping beauties in their death-like sleep. Unity is achieved by the concentration on character—primarily old Eguchi—and on place, by the continual piling up of sensuous imagery. Eguchi is in turn aroused, soothed, stimulated, troubled, and calmed by the touch, smell, and sight of the soft flesh beside him in the red room. Again, unity is heightened by the recurrence of like or similar images; virginity, sexual experience, pregnancy, and babies vie or blend with the thoughts of flowers, parts of a woman's body, blood, and the sleep of death. Like Nathaniel Hawthorne, Kawabata is especially deft in his use of color. The house of sleeping beauties is a house of whites, reds, and blacks: the whiteness of skin and milk, the redness of velvet curtains and blood, the blackness of night, death, and the dark sea.

Like Hawthorne too, Kawabata symbolically probes the human heart. Indeed the crimson-curtained room is both heart and womb. It is heart, where an old man living a death-in-life confronts his paradoxical opposite, a young woman who is life-in-death; here he relives his past loves and puzzles over his existence. Eguchi probes deeper and deeper into his consciousness or "heart" as he returns repeatedly to the secret house. And it is womb; in its warm comfort, Eguchi's thoughts turn to baby's milk, pregnancy, sex, blood, and death. It is a feminine world, where the women of Eguchi's life parade through his dreams and reveries. Maternal in its appeal, the crimson room lures him ever deeper in thought and farther back in time, inevitably, to the first woman of his life, his mother, in whom the notions of babies and breasts, his hopes, fears, and anxieties, the sensations of blood and death have their source.

On a cold night in the dead of winter Eguchi makes his fifth visit to the secret house. An old man has died while sleeping beside one of the beauties, and references to that death dominate Eguchi's conversation with the woman of the house. Eguchi is startled to learn that this time there are two girls. In another Hawthorne-like touch, Kawabata makes one dark, the other fair. Eguchi turns to the dark girl first. Her lips remind him of a girl he had kissed forty years before, who had insistently denied having lipstick, despite the evidence produced by Eguchi's handkerchief. He next turns to the light girl and then, sandwiched between the two, takes one of the sleeping pills. As drowsiness overcomes him, his thoughts turn to the first woman of his life; "Now at sixty-seven, as he lay between two naked girls a new truth came from deep inside him. Was it blasphemy, was it yearning? He opened his eyes and blinked, as if to drive away a nightmare. But the drug was working. He had a dull headache. Drowsily, he pursued the image of his mother; and then he sighed, and took two breasts, one of each of the girls, in the palms of his hands. A smooth one and an oily one. He closed his eyes." His mother had died when Eguchi was only seventeen. He recalls the grief and terror of that scene. " 'Yoshio. Yoshio.' His mother called out in little gasps. Eguchi understood, and stroked her tormented bosom. As he did so she vomited a large quantity of blood. It came bubbling from her nose. She stopped breathing. . . . 'Ah!' The curtains that walled the secret room seemed the color of blood. He closed his eyes tight, but that red would not disappear."

Thus Eguchi, an old man standing on the brink of senility/death, yearns to return to the source from which he first gained reason and life. In his "last extremity" he lies

symbolically cradled with the protective covering of the two girls, and, clinging to their breasts, journeys in thought to a time of security and warmth. In the blood-red room the dark and light girls, their feet intertwined ("One of her feet was between the feet of the fair-skinned girl") encircle the old man like the yin and yang of totality, and he longs with incestuous longing to penetrate again that comforting oneness, that matrix which is a mixture of life, hope, escape, and death. But his memory of mother is primarily a memory of suffering and death; the breasts that haunt his memory are withered, and no fresh milk will come from them. And so Eguchi dreams a succession of nightmares, erotic dreams of his honeymoon, of coming home to mother, and of blood-red flowers. He awakens to find the magic circle broken: the dark girl, of whom he had first murmured, "Life itself," is dead. Eguchi emerges from the warm, dreamy, illusory sleep to feel the cold press upon him for the first time. It is as if part of himself has died. He hears the callous remarks of the woman telling him, "Go back to sleep. There is the other girl," and as the car takes the dark girl's body away, Eguchi stands shivering with extra sleeping medicine in his hand, gazing at the remaining fair beauty.

The reader who has come to identify with Eguchi will share something of the chilled numbness which characterizes the old man in the final scene. One has a sense of near paralysis, of having been reduced by events to a state of catatonic immobility. Perhaps it is this which prompts Mishima's submarine analogy. The suffocating or numbing effect again illustrates Kawabata's narrative skill. He achieves it by filling his short work with countless examples of paradoxical or contradictory thoughts and appearance/reality opposites. They emerge, sometimes several to a page, throughout the novel. The result is tension, and for the reader, the feeling that he is pulled in different directions, none of them clear, or, as in Mishima's analogy, the feeling that he is trapped, immobilized by the certainty that death is inevitably approaching but that he can only remain fixed and gasp for air.

The contraries are apparent first in the nature of the story itself. Ugly old men sleep beside beautiful young girls; the young girls are alive, yet death-like in sleep. They are real persons, but the situation is artificial. The opposites of life/death, old-age/youth, ugliness/beauty, and reality/illusion continue throughout. Eguchi's thoughts expand these themes. On his first visit he recalls that he has passed ugly nights with women. "The ugliness had to do not with the appearance of the women but with their tragedies, their warped lives." But he wonders if there is anything "uglier" than an old man lying beside a drugged girl. The woman's repeated admonitions about "rules" add further tension. Impotent old men might wish to, but cannot violate the restrictions on behavior except in limited ways. Eguchi, however, can, but is caught between his own sense of integrity and the hopelessness of the situation even if he should "break the rules." Feeling the paradoxical strangeness of his visit, Eguchi complains inwardly that "not the smallest part of his existence" reaches the girl.

The tension of opposites increases on subsequent visits. Eguchi thinks he will not return to the secret house, but does. He feels guilty about his first visit, but acknowledges that "he had not in all his sixty-seven years spent another night so clean." Eguchi expects the same girl, but gets another, one whom the woman describes ironically as "more experienced." To his protestations about "promiscuity," the woman mockingly refers to gentlemen she can "trust"—but then adds laughingly, "And what's wrong with being promiscuous." Eguchi has thought that sleeping girls represent "ageless freedom" for old men; he now wonders if the secret house conceals the "longing of sad old men for the unfinished dream, the regret for days lost without ever being had." When the girl talks in her sleep, Eguchi has a conversation which is not a conversation; he wonders if the guilt he feels is painful or if the secret feelings actually add to his pleasure. The ambiguity of his second visit is summed up as he muses upon how the girl can be "experienced"; his oxymoronic conclusion is that she is a "virgin prostitute."

On his third visit Eguchi hears that the girl, though sleeping, is somehow supposed to be "in training." The sight of the young girl's body saddens him and evokes a death wish; he longs for "a sleep like death," but hovers between this desire and the desire to stay awake for enjoyment. Aroused by the presence of the girl, he contemplates an "evil" deed, then stops to consider what evil might really be, and what evil he might have done in his life. The girl, he imagines, might even be a kind of Buddha. His thoughts thus lead ironically to another contradiction: she is temptation to evil, yet her "young skin and scent might be forgiveness" for sad old men. The contradictions continue through Eguchi's last visit which begins with steaming tea to counteract the freezing cold. But now death dominates the atmosphere and the crimson curtains seem like blood. What has begun as a curious search for new pleasure and vitality has ended in death; the girl Eguchi calls "life" is dragged lifeless down the stairs of the secret house.

Thus Eguchi learns—for even an old man must learn—the brittleness of his existence, the subtlety of self-deceit. The young flesh beside him is real enough: real to the hand, the nose, the eye, the ear, the mouth; it is the illusion of youth that deceives. The thin-lipped woman of the house, like some ancient hag-guardian of the hell of self-delusion, mocks those who enter her domain. Her callous remarks and actions, like the artificial light which must remain on throughout Eguchi's nights in the crimson room, reveal the cold secrets of the house of the sleeping beauties. For Eguchi, the safe warmth of the womb is no escape; the only "escape" is death itself. The comfortable oneness of things has been broken. In his last extremity he stands, a chilly old man asking questions of himself.

Mervyn Brock (essay date 1971)

SOURCE: A review of *House of the Sleeping Beauties*, in *Japan Quarterly*, Vol. XVIII, No. 3, July-September, 1971, pp. 351-54.

[*In the following excerpt, Brock is harshly critical of the pieces in* House of the Sleeping Beauties; *he finds the title story, for example, "so dull that it requires positive effort to struggle through its sargasso sea of lifeless anatomical detail, to read page after page of its repetitive variations on a basically obnoxious theme."*]

Kawabata Yasunari was born in Osaka on June 11th 1899. He lost both parents in his second year, his grandmother in his eighth and his grandfather in his sixteenth: losses from which he has, perhaps, never fully recovered. At Tokyo University he studied first English literature and then Japanese literature. While still a student he published *Shōkonsai Ikkei* (Scenes from Memorial Services for the War Dead) in 1921 and *Kaisō no Meijin* (An Expert at Attending Funerals) in 1923; so that, when he graduated in 1924, he was already fairly well known as a rising young writer associated with the *Shinkankakuha* (Neo-Sensualist) Group led by Yokomitsu Riichi. Though that Group originated in an attempt, under basically French influence, to break away from conventional Dickensian, Balzacian and even Zolaesque concepts of the plot and structure of the novel, its stress upon traditional Japanese lyrical beauty and the "language of the heart" brought it into close sympathy with that general reaction then taking place against the early schools of socio-proletarian writing. The main importance of Kawabata's association with this Group is that, though he is now generally regarded as an essentially Japanese writer, the strongest influences upon him during his most formative period were not Japanese; and one may observe throughout all his subsequent work the influence of Proust and, behind Proust, of Ruskin. Kawabata made his real mark with the publication during 1925 of **"Izu no Odoriko"** (**"The Izu Dancing Girl"**) in the magazine *Bungei Jidai* (Age of Literary Art) of which he had been a co-founder. This book displayed all the main characteristics of his best subsequent work: a deep sense of the world's sadness, a melancholy eroticism and a gentle, almost wistful, nihilism. Already, too, the book contained the beginnings of that technique of understatement, superficially disjointed incident and a subtly hinted analysis of character for which he has been rightly praised. The best of these later works are *Yukiguni* (*The Snow Country*), begun in 1935 but not finished until 1947, *Yama no Oto* (*The Sound of the Mountain*) of 1949, *Sembazuru* (*Thousand Cranes*), published in 1950 but still unfinished, *Mizuumi* (*Lake*) of 1954 and *Koto* (*The Ancient Capital*) of 1962. He, of course, also published a considerable number of other literary works, especially short stories, but, since little of this other work had been translated into English by the time he won the Nobel Prize for Literature in 1968, it is fair to assume that the award was made on the basis of a comparatively small handful of his longer novels. . . .

The book now under review [*House of the Sleeping Beauties*], though doubtless it was somewhat hurriedly put together to exploit Kawabata's award, does give the reader a better over-all picture of Kawabata's writing than that conveyed by the handful of books cited by the Swedish Academy. The book contains three stories: **"Of Birds and Beasts"** (**"Kinjū"**) first published in July 1933, **"House of the Sleeping Beauties"** (**"Nemureru Bijo"**) first published in 1960-61 and **"One Arm"** (**"Kata Ude"**) first published in 1963-64. The first story is a typically drifting reminiscence about the deaths of birds and animals by an aging man on his way to see a dance-recital by an aging mistress, the meanness of whose nature was her chief attraction. "He remembered the Chikako of ten years before. Her face when she had sold herself to him had been like a dog's." It is an unpleasant story, though beautifully written, and one finishes it with the feeling that the owl which so disliked the main character (for which reason, of course, the main character admired the owl) was a very sound judge of character. The second story, the best of the three, is fascinating but erotically sickly fantasy about a woman's arm. " 'I can let you have one of my arms for the night,' said the girl. She took off her right arm at the shoulder and, with her left hand, laid it on my knee." It is perhaps worth mentioning that the English translation of this story, though the present book contains no acknowledgment of the fact, was first published in the January 1967 issue of the *Japan Quarterly.*

The third and longest story in this book has been widely praised as one of the finest studies ever written about senile lust, and the introduction by the late Mishima Yukio describes it as an esoteric masterpiece. I find this praise a gross exaggeration and the general pretentiousness of the introduction helps to explain why Mishima, widely rumored to have been himself a candidate for the Nobel Prize, did not win it. The story tells of an unusual establishment where impotent men, if sufficiently wealthy, may spend the night with a drugged young girl: indeed, if so desired, with more than one drugged young girl. As the narrator himself remarks, "Could there be anything uglier than an old man lying the night through beside a girl put to sleep, unwaking? Had he not come to this house seeking the ultimate in the ugliness of old age?" This justified reflection is repeated again and again in the course of the narrator's five visits to the house of the sleeping beauties. The tale is bodied (one might say corpsed) out with a series of similarly sick considerations. "He was tempted. He peered into the open mouth. If he were to throttle her, would there be spasms along the small tongue?" "But the misdeed did not take clear shape in Eguchi's mind as cruelty and terror. What was the very worst thing a man could do to a woman?" "If he were to strangle her, what sort of scent would she give off." Kawabata also manages to include an account of the death of an elderly client and an account of the death and disposal of one of two girls with whom the narrator has passed the night. It is a thoroughly nasty story and, though beauty can be wrung from the most unlikely subjects, Kawabata seems unable to resist the temptation to make nastiness yet more twistedly nasty. Thus, though this story could be defended as an artist's appreciation of the terrors of impotence, it is typical of Kawabata's approach that the narrator of the story obtains access to the house under false pretenses: for it is made abundantly clear that he is not, in fact, impotent. The gentle, melancholy eroticism which characterizes Kawabata's best work has become in this story a sour and warped lubricity. These criticisms may, of course, make the tale sound interesting but it is, in fact, so dull that it requires positive effort to struggle through its sargasso sea of lifeless anatomical detail, to read page after page of its repetitive variations on a basically obnoxious theme.

Kawabata's acknowledgment, immediately his Nobel

Prize had been announced, of his debt to his translators, typical of the man's warm generosity, is equally typical of his perceptiveness. With one exception, all previous winners of the Nobel Prize for Literature were representatives of the Western literary tradition and it is no reflection on the solitary exception, Sir Rabindranath Tagore who won it in 1913, to suggest that, had he written only in Bengali and never in English, he would not have gained the recognition which he so thoroughly deserved. Since 1901, when the Nobel Prizes were established, Japan has produced several writers (notably Natsumi Sōseki) eminently qualified to win the prize for literature. But it was not until after 1945 that translations of Japanese literature became available in sufficient and continuing quantity to make a genuine impact on the Western world. Such a flow of translations depends, of course, upon the existence of an adequate body of translators: and one may reasonably wonder to what extent current world interest in Japanese literature, even Kawabata's award, reflect the fact that during the late Pacific War it was just as necessary that some Americans should learn Japanese as that others should land on Iwo Jima. Though already by 1957 some of Kawabata's work had been translated into Dutch, English, Finnish, French, German, Italian, Swedish and Yugoslavian, it is to the Americans that the West really owes the new generality of its appreciation of Japanese literature.

Masao Miyoshi   (essay date 1974)

SOURCE: "The Margins of Life," in *Accomplices of Silence: The Modern Japanese Novel,* University of California Press, 1974, pp. 95-121.

[*In the excerpt below, Masao examines Kawabata's early experimentation with European avant-garde aesthetics in several short stories. The critic finds "The Izu Dancer," however, a tradition-based piece that provides an "alternative to the eccentric internationalism of [Kawabata's] 'modernist' stories."*]

Early in his career Kawabata Yasunari (1899-1972) was a member of the Neo-Perceptionist school (Shin Kankaku Ha). The existence of this group, as a part of Japanese literary history, is not so interesting or important in itself: its creed, like those of the Naturalists, the Anti-Naturalists, and other groups, derives from imported avant-garde European manifestoes, and, like most, suffers from poor digestion of same. Thrown into their modernist mélanges are bits and dollops of Paul Morand, Andreyev, Croce, Bergson, futurism, cubism, expressionism, dadaism, symbolism, structuralism, realism, Strindberg, Swinburne, Hauptmann, Romain Rolland, Schnitzler, Lord Dunsany, Wilde, Lady Gregory, and a lot else—all assembled, presumably, to spice the domestic literary staples, but in fact to preserve a conservative aesthetic against the encroaching Marxists. Most of its members are now forgotten (with the exception of Yokomitsu Riichi, who, however, became a very different sort of writer later on), and Kawabata's position in the group was not a dominant one. Nonetheless, when looked at as a serious attempt at enlarging the novelistic possibilities of the Japanese language, the modernist practices of the group must be recognized as vital in the formation of Kawabata's style.

Kawabata's main contribution to the group's platform, "The New Tendency of the Avant-Garde Writers" (*Shin-shin Sakka no Shinkeikō Kaisetsu*), published in 1925, makes a plea for the new—new perception, new expression, and new style—and strongly emphasizes the importance of sense perception for the novelist. While not being very precise in his "epistemology of expressionism," and dodging most of the hard problems of his theme, Kawabata does spell out the need for a new language to replace the existing "lifeless, objective narrative language." "Dadaist," "Freudian," "free associative," "subjective, intuitive, and sensuous" expression—all such terms are left undefined, but in the context of his discussion they do suggest a coherent feeling for a certain style. He would have a language for the novel that would reflect immediately the inchoate state of a man's thoughts, feelings, and sensory experience. Instead of syntactically complete sentences, the characters (or the narrator) ought to be allowed to speak sometimes in fragments, which will not only suggest more accurately the author's view of the particular situation but will give the reader a fuller picture of the characters and their surroundings. In such a language, the seer is not yet separated from the seen, the speaker from the spoken. To illustrate his point, Kawabata provides a sample sentence or two ("My eyes were red roses" as preferable to "My eyes saw red roses"), but unfortunately this tends to muddle the discussion more than clarify it. . . .

The imprint of Neo-Perceptionism on Kawabata continues strong in those works written over the ten years following this "modernist" manifesto. Stories and longer works like **"The Ghost of the Rose"** (**"Bara no Yūrei,"** 1927), *The Red Gang of Asakusa* (*Asakusa Kurenai-Dan*, 1929-30), **"Needle and Glass and Fog"** (**"Hari to Garasu to Kiri,"** 1930), and **"The Crystal Fantasy"** (**"Suishō Gensō,"** 1931), to mention only a few, are all marked by boldly experimental features. The deformation of idioms, such as in the sentence "an illness entered the core of the body" in **"Needle and Glass and Fog"**; a long interior monologue, very much after Molly Bloom's, in **"The Crystal Fantasy"**; the predominantly nominal and asyntactic construction of *The Red Gang of Asakusa*; the hundred miniature "novels" later collected into one volume as *The Palm-Sized Stories* (*Tanagokoro no Shōsetsu*, 1922-50)—these are the most conspicuous examples. Determinedly "modern" too are their themes and settings. The characters are typically urban "new types," whose life style is self-consciously "Western." The wife in **"The Crystal Fantasy,"** for example, living in a "Western" room with "Western" furniture, sits at her dressing table polishing her nails and looking out on her greenhouse. Her stream of consciousness could be that of a European woman, since, with the exception of one mention each of Tokyo, a Japanese writer, and a Japanese swimmer in the strange catalogue of items several pages long, the story is quite cosmopolitan in its references.

I do not mean, of course, that in these experiments Kawabata succeeds in creating anything like the cosmopolitan as a type of person recognizable across all linguistic and cultural borders. The notion of a cosmopolitan is itself quite specific to modern Western culture. The fact is, in the complexion of their feelings and emotions his charac-

ters are unmistakably Japanese. **"The Crystal Fantasy,"** for instance, puts the cosmopolitan wife in the context of a tension between her medical and scientific interests and her sexual fantasies—in itself an unlikely situation for a Japanese woman of the time—and yet her relationship to her husband at once defines her as Japanese. There is a very uncomfortable gap in the work between its intellectual intention and its actualization by a sensibility formed out of the traditional expectation and response. Whatever stylistic feat Neo-Perceptionism may have achieved here, one realizes, it is not so much surrealistic in effect as *haiku*-like, still imbued as it is with the age-old associations and conventions despite its being set in a modern frame of reference. Natsume Sōseki undoubtedly knew this a generation before, and Kawabata, too, came to know it as he matured. For all its youthful wrongheaded theorizing, Neo-Perceptionism taught Kawabata a great deal about the possibilities of Japanese for prose fiction. . . .

One of Kawabata's earliest and least experimental stories, **"The Izu Dancer"** (**"Izu no Odoriko,"** 1926), stands up better than his modernist attempts. Like *Pillow of Grass,* **"The Izu Dancer"** is a first-person story of a trip to the country. Unlike the Sōseki story, however, the voice here is lyrical throughout, and not mediated either by irony or by manipulation of time between the events and the telling. The student-narrator's experience is set in the fresh provincial scene by means of an evocative, slightly nostalgic language which is neither elaborate nor learned. While *Pillow of Grass* is a complex experiment in the narrative sequence, **"The Izu Dancer"** has the forthright appearance of a single unadorned episode. There is more quiet understatement and less surprise. And, finally, as against Sōseki's hero who moves from uninvolvement toward greater involvement, Kawabata's moves in the other direction, toward less involvement.

The student is attracted to a girl in a traveling family of dancer-entertainers whom he meets while on vacation, but he does not exactly know what he wants from the encounter. Right away, he realizes he is tormented with the thought of her "entertaining" her clients. Next morning, however, as a fierce storm clears, he sees her nude in the outdoor bath:

> One small figure ran out into the sunlight and stood for a moment at the edge of the platform calling something to us, arms raised as though for a plunge into the river. It was the little dancer. I looked at her, at the young legs, at the sculptured white body, and suddenly a draught of fresh water seemed to wash over my heart. I laughed happily. She was a child, a mere child, a child who could run out naked into the sun and stand there on her tiptoes in her delight at seeing a friend. I laughed on, a soft, happy laugh. It was as though a layer of dust had been cleared from my head. And I laughed on and on. It was because of her too-rich hair that she had seemed older, and because she was dressed like a girl of fifteen or sixteen. I had made an extraordinary mistake indeed.

No longer threatened by the need to discover and test his

sexuality, the "I" really comes to love the girl as they roam from one mountain village to another in the company of her family. She responds to his affection, and they discover very gentle and tender feelings for each other. The story ends as they part and the young man returns to school.

There are several episodes which are seemingly unrelated to the main line of the story. One is toward the end where another boy, bound for Tokyo to take his high school entrance exams, consoles the narrator for his loss. The hero's initiation is effectively postponed and in a sense universalized as he goes to sleep "warmed by the boy beside [him]," who of course faces his own initiation into school life away from his family.

The avoidance of direct total involvement in heterosexual love is not unique to this story, since most of Kawabata's central man-woman relationships do not build upon the mutual full engagement of two people. Frequently, his women are remote and virginal—"pure" as he sometimes calls them—and, whatever the author's psychological determinants for this may be, there is a kind of aching persistent eroticism permeating his later novels which is inseparable from the wistful and often intense longing that typically marks Kawabata's male characters.

The atmosphere of freshness and innocence enveloping **"The Izu Dancer"** comes, I think, from Kawabata's utterly simple language which sets the experience down among the trees and clean air and wet grass of a country resort. In contrast to the urban environments of his Neo-Perceptionist works, the setting of this story recalls the province of the traditional *haiku*. There is also the circumstance that Kawabata, instead of explaining the characters' thoughts and feelings, merely suggests them by mentioning objects which, in a country setting, are certain to reverberate with tangible, if not identifiable, emotions.

> It was after midnight when I left their inn. The girls saw me to the door, and the little dancer turned my sandals so that I could step into them without twisting. She leaned out and gazed up at the clear sky. "Ah, the moon is up."

Here Kawabata, as he chisels this plain, clear prose reaching back to the old tradition, appears determined to find some alternative to the eccentric internationalism of his "modernist" stories.

Gwenn Boardman Petersen   (essay date 1979)

SOURCE: "Kawabata Yasunari," in *The Moon in the Water: Understanding Tanizaki, Kawabata, and Mishima,* The University Press of Hawaii, 1979, pp. 121-200.

[In the excerpt below, Petersen details the imagery and allusive language of "House of the Sleeping Beauties."]

Dancing figures—expressions of loneliness or focusing a sense of loss—move through *Onsen-yado* (*A Hotspring Inn,* 1929) as through *Snow Country,* through *Niji* (*The Rainbow,* 1934), through *Hana no Warutsu* (*Flower Waltz,* 1936), and even through *Funa Yūjo* (*Boat Prostitute*), a play that had its premier at Tokyo's Kabuki-za in October 1970. Written originally for dance master

Nishikawa Koisaburō and adapted for the Osaka stage as *Biwa Monogatari* (*Tale of the Biwa* [or *Tale of the Lute*]), this is in some ways reminiscent of **"Izu no Odoriko"** in its interweaving of journey, longing, and loss.

Its source is in the tales of Heike warrior Kagekiyo (subject of Nō and Kabuki dramas, too). After the Heike defeat, instructed in the dance by her dying mother (Kuretake), the girl Murasaki travels the country seeking her father. But she does not recognize him in the blind old man with a lute. He hears that a girl has been singing of a lost child—words he had taught his wife Kuretake—but by the time he looks for Murasaki, she has left. In the final scene, though father and daughter do meet and Murasaki hears the old man sing her mother's song, she is now a prostitute (the result of her poverty in the aftermath of the Heike-Genji wars). Their recognition is both unspoken and deeply moving, and it ends with parting.

Whether or not this recurrent, lonely dancing figure is related to the Michiko of Kawabata's 1921 diary entries is a question similar to the problems of his early experiences with death. Again, whatever the experience was, it has clearly been transmuted into poetic and sensitive perceptions of feelings that must not be reduced to a clinical statement of Kawabata's "longing" for virgins (Mishima's suggestion). Michiko and Kawabata were engaged for a few weeks in 1921, and Kawabata has recorded his plans for living with her in Kikuchi Kan's house. (They were not yet planning to be married, and in any case the house was not vacated, and the episode ended). Later entries in the *Literary Autobiography* show how he saw this figure on trains, on theater posters, in front of a café. And the figure of a young girl much like the Izu dancer can be found in *Kagaribi* (*Fishing Fire,* 1924), in *Hijō* (*Emergency,* 1924), in *Arare* (*Hail Storm,* 1928; but first entitled *Bōryokudan no Ichiya*), and in *Nanpō no Hi* (*Fire in the South,* 1923). In *Nanpō no Hi* the 23-year-old man thinks 16-year-old Yumiko will, as his bride, bring back his own "boy nature," a childhood happiness he had never known.

Loneliness, death, and figures moving through the "floating world" (whether read as the Gay or Pleasure Quarters, or in the philosophical sense of transience) come to rest in **"Nemureru Bijo"** (Sleeping Beauty or Beauties; unfortunately translated as **"House of the Sleeping Beauties,"** although Kawabata is concerned not with the house but with the richly poetic implications of beauty and with fresh explorations of the traditional linking of beauty and sorrow). As already noted, there is an ambiguity in his title—"beauty" is written with the two ideograms for beautiful (*bi*) and woman (*jo*). Since the Japanese language does not distinguish number, the title simultaneously suggests several women, a woman, or even Woman.

More than one woman is involved, and the sleep itself is neither natural nor the enchantment of fairy tale. The familiar Sleeping Beauty wakened by her Prince is far indeed from the beauties who lie in this strange house. It is an establishment maintained for elderly gentlemen: they can spend the night with young girls who are most conveniently drugged. But it should be noted that for all of them the physical pleasures of sex are now replaced by dream and reverie.

The protagonist, Eguchi, comes again and again: his memories (rather than the sleeping beauty) are awakened. His experiences in the present are linked through sights, scents, and sounds with memories of the past. At one point, envying the girls' deep sleep, he asks the woman who manages the establishment for some of the "medicine" for himself: she tells him that it is too potent for old men. (Ironically, he alone of the visitors still has the capacity for full enjoyment of the girls, although that would break the house rules.) At the end, he lies between two young girls. But he wakes one morning to find one of them already dead and cold. When he rings for the madam, she calmly has the girl carried off, after telling Eguchi he might as well go back to bed with the second girl—it is too early in the morning for him to leave.

Once again, however, this bare outline gives little idea of the real nature of Kawabata's novel. Again there are flashes of light and dark, repeated sounds, changed patterns, symbolic hints given through season and setting or through phrases of dialogue that take on meaning with each repetition. Once again details are linked in delicate associations of barely perceived images. For instance, the opening scene is of an unmarked inn, a room decorated with an autumn scene, but offering Eguchi no clue to its hidden nature. Only the woman in charge suggests a concealed horror: a hint of death in the whitish color of her obi and a feeling of disquiet that comes to Eguchi from the qualities of the eyes and feet of the bird decorating her obi.

Eguchi is told to listen to the waves and the wind. And these are the sounds that mark his strange progress from the first girl—lovely in her setting of crimson curtains, representing "life itself," and emanating the milky scent of a nursing baby—to the unvoiced horrors of the conclusion. Like Eguchi, we hear the wash of the waves, sometimes loud, sometimes receding, their rhythm linked with the music of his feelings. The reader finds in the lyrical rendering of Eguchi's heart going out to the girl something quite different from Tanizaki's boy seeking his stepmother's milky breast in "Bridge of Dreams"; we are reminded of an entry in Kawabata's diary for 1924: "Love is my only lifeline." The milky scent brings to Eguchi other memories—so that once more we move back in time from the sounds and scents of *this* moment to moments in the past (sometimes unpleasant, sometimes matching the beauty of his perceptions of this girl).

In this scene, Kawabata's technique of composite images and linked memories is beautifully demonstrated as the roar of waves sounds against the cliff. The ocean echoes in the girl's body: it is the rhythm of life pulsing at her wrist. With his eyelids closed, Eguchi sees the image of a butterfly, its movements simultaneously set to the music of the waves and of life. But its color is white. This whiteness dissolves to the white cap worn by the baby of another girl, bringing recollections of the time when Eguchi ran off to Kyoto with that girl (a girl who said that the baby was not his).

Other stories, too, present dreams or reveries in which memories of past experience offer hints of present meaning (especially *Sound of the Mountain*). But we must remember that actions in real life, as in dreams, are often incom-

plete, although Kawabata may fill in details at least partially during later episodes. In the second episode, thinking of various flowers, Eguchi remembers his daughters, especially the girl who had lost her virginity to one suitor but married the other. He remembers her through a 400-year-old camellia tree they had seen together, and its various qualities suggest the girl, her troubles, and his own feelings. (The camellia symbolizes bad luck in the manner of the flowers' falling "like severed heads"—a more precise clue than in *Snow Country,* where a meeting between Shimamura and Komako in the Camellia Room was no more than a subliminal hint of coming misfortune.) As Eguchi remembers the tree, he hears a sound like a faint roar: the faint roar inside that remembered tree (perhaps a swarm of bees) hints at the sound of the waves that are now outside the window of the room where Eguchi lies with a sleeping girl.

But the reverie or dream of the tree was set in motion by Eguchi's response to this second girl's "rich" scent. The hints of enchantment accompany an overflowing sensuousness—and here Kawabata displays his customary subtlety in conveying sexuality. Flower images become more erotic and more sensual than any of Tanizaki's accounts of warm flesh and seductive toes. Kawabata is using the familiar Japanese *hana* (flower), a synonym for girl and feminine beauty and found in countless "flower" phrases. In other stories, the scent of a white peony, the golden and feminine petals of a flower, the quality of magnolia petals, simultaneously suggest the deep attraction of Woman and the aroused passions of the narrative's particular man.

This richly seductive quality in Eguchi's second girl is linked with a mystery—hinted in signs that she is dreaming and also suffering nightmares during their hours together. In contrast, the third girl is inexperienced and small. She is also frightened and had wanted a companion to share her night of sleep: Eguchi's comment that "two would not be so bad" foreshadows his final visit. The first girl suggested life, the second in various ways hinted of qualities not human, the third is wild and undeveloped. Yet again the novel's ending is foreshadowed in hints that we only begin to understand after the final episode is over: Eguchi's wish for a drugged (deathlike) sleep beside the girl who lies as though dead, associated with memories of a satisfied woman in the past, one who also slept soundly (as though dead). He has a sense of fleeting happiness; but he also has a momentary impulse to strangle this girl.

Simultaneously, Eguchi has a sense of something wrong—as his own conduct progressively breaks the rules of the house. This third girl's tongue protruding from her mouth reminds him of a young prostitute long ago; at the same time it stimulates him to an act more exciting than simply putting his finger to her tongue. Yet he also thinks of her in terms that recall earlier allusions, as he remembers stories in which prostitutes and courtesans were Buddhas incarnate. The sense of touch and barely perceived scents here bring *visual* memories. With eyes again closed, Eguchi sees golden arrows and deep purple hyacinths, while waves can be heard sounding gently against the cliff.

With the final episodes, symbols again crowd too thickly for annotation. The autumn scroll of maples has been changed at his fourth visit: the scene is of winter snow. Again in the use of *shi* there are hints of four and of death, although the fourth girl is warm and the sweet scent of Woman is stronger than before. Her skin is white, and the warmth that envelops Eguchi is reminiscent of scenes with Komako in *Snow Country*. The white butterfly of Eguchi's first "sleeping beauty" now becomes two butterflies seen by his closed eyes, these two becoming two pairs, then five, and finally a swarm (a link with the swarm of bees sounding in the camellia tree and thus an unvoiced memory of his youngest daughter, while we also remember that the sound of the bees was likened to the sound of the waves and is therefore doubly linked with that rhythmical accompaniment to Eguchi's visits and his memories). Behind Eguchi's closed eyelids this swarm of butterflies becomes a field of white flowers: once more, white carries hints of death, while the flowers give subliminal clues that a girl will be dead at the novel's end.

The final episode is the fifth: two girls—one dark and cold and the other of shining beauty in the tradition of Kawabata's complementary pairs, with hints of *in'yō* contrasts of dark and light and the number five of mystic harmony. To the continuing rhythm of the ocean's sounds, with subtle changes in that rhythm, Eguchi's memories and his present actions merge, separate, flow gently far back in time, and return to now. He remembers the man who died at this inn, but he finds "life itself" in the dark girl (who is modern and slightly foreign in size and figure); there is an oily quality to her flesh that is wild and pungent. He then turns to the small-boned and sweetly scented second girl. But it is impossible to render in English the delicacy with which Kawabata shows Eguchi lying between the dark and light girls, gently clasping one breast of each.

Now Eguchi's thoughts glide back to memories of his mother's death and forward to contemplation of his own. At the same time, the skin of the dark girl takes on a strangely unpleasant quality. In his nightmare of flowers—looking like great red dahlias that seem to bury the house to which he had brought his bride—there are links with earlier fancies of blood and a preparation for his forthcoming waking nightmare: the discovery that the dark girl is dead. The woman of the house comes in response to Eguchi's call. There are hints recalling the earlier moment when Eguchi thought of strangling one of the sleeping girls: but Eguchi assures the woman that he has done nothing wrong (and in any case, she keeps denying that the girl *is* dead). Told to go back to sleep, Eguchi hears the woman dragging the dark girl downstairs; and he turns back to the form of the fair girl "in shining beauty."

But as he does so, there are sounds to provoke more memories: a car drives away, recalling the elderly client who died at this house and whose body was tactfully taken to a nearby inn. The girls in their deathlike sleep, however, were a dream of life for the men who came to lie with them. Eguchi's own clinging to life is suggested in each episode, as in the first, where the girl's pulse was linked with the rhythm of life, the waves of the ocean (perhaps linked with "wave of woman" in *Thousand Cranes*), and Kawabata's own references to the "lifeline of love."

Whether he is dealing overtly with death or with life, Kawabata uses both symbolism and allusive language in ways that should delight admirers of Henry James. Yet the commentator who spoke of the affinity of James and Kawabata neglected several important differences—especially the ways in which Kawabata *hints* of emotion (rather than James's verbal dissections of feelings and relationships). The economy of words in Kawabata, moreover, is very far from the convoluted Jamesian syntax and narrative. Even to speak of narrative in the Kawabata context is to miss the point, and the reader of translations must continually be alert to the fact that relative pronouns, definite verbs, and statements of intention are generally the translator's interpretation of suggestions that are beautiful in Japanese but chaotic if forced into literal English "equivalents."

Katsuhiko Takeda   (essay date 1983)

SOURCE: "Biblical Influence upon Yasunari Kawabata," in *Neohelicon*, Vol. X, No. 1, 1983, pp. 95-103.

[*In the essay below, Takeda identifies Western literary influences on numerous Kawabata short stories.*]

Yasunari Kawabata, who died in 1972, was a towering figure in the Japanese literary world. But the number of his readers in the West was always rather limited and his literary fame there alternated between eminence and eclipse until after he received the Nobel Prize for literature in 1968.

His literary works are often considered to be genuinely traditional, but if we read them carefully, we come to the realization that they contain modern elements. It is a fact that Yasunari Kawabata used the traditional Japanese technique of association in his novels. But it would be a mistake to view his literature as nothing more than a continuation of the Japanese tradition. Throughout his life Kawabata had a deep interest in Western literature, particularly 19th and 20th century literature.

Kawabata often used the Bible in his works. He considered the Old and New Testaments as the most important literary classics in Western literature. Direct quotations from the Bible are found in his literary works—novels, short stories, and essays. The quotations are from seven books of the Old Testament and nine books of the New Testament. We can surmise that his knowledge of the Bible was very broad. His interpretations of the scriptural passages are profound. I am intrigued by the following coincidence. When Kawabata wrote in 1936, the short story **"Father and Mother"**, in Japanese **"Chichi Haha"**, he quoted a passage from *Song of Solomon*, chapter 2, verse 7.

> I adjure you, O daughters of Jerusalem,
> by the gazelles or the hinds of the field,
> that you stir not up nor awaken love
> until it please.

The shepherd maiden sings this verse in order to plead with the women of the King's court not to cajole her, but to allow her free choice to express her love for anyone her heart chooses. Quoting this verse Kawabata alludes to the protagonist's decision not to stir up nor awaken love in a young girl whom he encounters at a summer resort.

There is an interesting parallel to this quotation from *The Song of Solomon* in J. D. Salinger's "A Young Girl of 1941 With No Waist At All". In this short story, Barbara, who is enjoying a voyage with her fiance's mother, is proposed to by another man. Barbara is so upset that Mrs. Woodruff, one of the other passengers, takes notice. In remarking to her husband that she wishes Barbara would not be tempted by the proposal, she quotes this same refrain from *The Song of Solomon.*

It is, of course, merely a coincidence that Kawabata and Salinger quote the same scriptural passage in the same type of situation. But it does show how well Kawabata understood *The Song of Solomon.* Kawabata's use of other quotations from the Bible plays an important role, for example, in explaining a character's psychology, a protagonist's destiny or a human weakness.

One more example will reveal how precisely Kawabata interpreted Biblical passages. That example is the short story **"The Tree of Life"**, in Japanese **"Inochi no Ki"**, in which he quotes Walt Whitman's poem, "To A Common Prostitute". Even the title of Kawabata's story will remind Western readers of the Bible. "The Tree of Life" is repeatedly found in the Old and New Testaments. He undoubtedly chose this title from *The Revelation to John,* because in the final scene he quotes from 22: 1 and 2 as follows:

> Then he showed me the river of the water of life, bright as crystal, flowing from the throne of God and of the Lamb through the middle of the street of the city; also, on either side of the river, the tree of life with its twelve kinds of fruit, yielding its fruit each month; and the leaves of the tree were for the healing of the nations.

When Kawabata wrote **"The Tree of Life"**, the Japanese were in the midst of despair and chaos because of enduring hunger and fearful anxiety of the effects of the atomic bombs. They were groping blindly for a way to reconstruct their nation. Works written just after World War II are very dark, lacking in a hope for life. Kawabata symbolizes his hope for Japan's rebirth in his use of this quote. But if we read the whole story we come to understand this passage also symbolizes how a young man and a young woman, both caught up in the turmoil of war, are bound together by love.

This story is tinged both by the darkness of wartime and the emerging light, however dim, of postwar Japan. The contrast is well described and emphasized with quotations from the Bible. In the story, the despair of approaching death drives almost all young officers to the brothels. Military authorities allow this one last pursuit of pleasure. One night three young officers go to a brothel and one of them asks his girl friend to come with him without mentioning where they are going. At the brothel another officer recites to the prostitutes the first line of the first stanza of Walt Whitman's "To A Common Prostitute".

> Be composed—be at ease with me—I am Walt Whitman, liberated and lusty as nature

Kawabata uses this quote skillfully to contrast with the biblical quotations. In a footnote on "To A Common Prostitute" in their 1973 edition of *Leaves of Grass,* Bradley and Blodgett write, "The poet may have thought of this poem as a variation upon the Biblical account of the woman taken in adultery," that is, *John* 8: [4-7],

> They say unto him, Master, this woman was taken in adultery, in the very act. Now Moses in the law commanded us, that such should be stoned: but what sayest thou? This they said, tempting him, that they might have to accuse him. But Jesus stooped down; and with his finger wrote on the ground, as though he heard them not. So when they continued asking him, he lifted up himself, and said unto them. He that is without sin among you, let him first cast a stone at her.

These passages are known as "An incident in the temple." As I will explain below, Kawabata quotes *John* 8: 7.

> "Let him who is without sin among you be the first to throw a stone at her."

The young girl, who accompanied young officers to the brothel, quotes this passage to him when she is asked what she thinks about the prostitutes. This quotation reveals that she feels that she is as sinful as the prostitutes. Although strictly speaking, she is still a virgin, she feels guilt because she has already decided in her heart to have a physical relationship with the young officer.

Kawabata links Whitman's poem with the Biblical quotation very skillfully. On the surface a short quotation from Whitman's poem and one verse from the *Book of John* do not seem to be closely related, but a careful reading of the story brings out this interrelationship. Throughout Kawabata's novels we find how adroitly he uses this technique of association.

One of Kawabata's surrealistic short stories has the same title **"One Arm"**, in Japanese **"Kataude"**, as that of Tennessee Williams. This is beautifully translated by Professor Edward G. Seidensticker in the recently published collection ***The House of Sleeping Beauties.*** There are some quotations from the Bible in **"One Arm"**, one of which comes from *Ecclesiastes.* Kawabata describes the anguish a young girl feels when she loses her virginity.

> Her anguish was not common to all women in the act of surrender. And it was with her only the one time. The silver thread was cut, the golden bowl destroyed.

This is Prof. Seidensticker's translation. The last sentence is reminiscent of *Ecclesiastes* 12: 6. The original Japanese is quite the same as the colloquial translation of the Old Testament.

> . . . the silver cord be snapped, or the golden vial be cracked . . .

Ecclesiastes has its melancholy refrain, "vanity of vanities, all is vanity". Such thought is prevalent in Japanese literature, so Kawabata likes to read this book. The author of this book exalts the beauty of life while he expresses dejection at the sham, hypocrisy, injustice and vanity prevailing everywhere. This contradictory mood of faith and futility is often found in Kawabata's works.

In **"One Arm"** Kawabata uses scriptural verse very literally to symbolize the loss of virginity, but if we read between the lines, we come to this conclusion: Kawabata wants to lay stress on what he believes man's basic attitude towards woman to be. A man's first feelings of love for a woman are for her purity. He wishes her to remain a virgin forever, yet at the same time he wishes for union. This is the contradiction in man's ego. Impressed with the contradictory mood of *Ecclesiastes,* Kawabata has used the images 'silver cord' and 'golden vial' to refer to virginity. The weaving of this quote into the narrative is so natural that critics have never noticed it.

Now I would like to discuss why Kawabata was interested in religion and how he acquired his deep knowledge of the Bible. This is closely connected with his biography.

Kawabata was born in 1899 in Osaka, the first son of a medical doctor, but lost his parents very young. He had a single sister four years older, who died when he was ten. Since they had to live separately after his mother's death, he saw her infrequently. Brought up as an orphan, he could not help being obsessed with the thought of death. It is natural that such a child would be interested in religion earlier than other children. While still in high school, he began reading religious books, both the teachings of Buddha and the Christian Old and New Testaments. This interest is reflected in his biographical novel, *A Boy,* in Japanese *Shonen,* written in 1948. In his college days his interest in religion compelled him to read even more obscure tracts such as *The Egyptian Book of the Dead.* Kawabata sometimes went to Protestant churches and read further in the Bible. In his unfinished novel, *Life's Brevity,* in Japanese *Tamayura,* written in 1965, the protagonist explains how he came to read the Bible. It can safely be said that this is a reflection of Kawabata's own experiences. A brief quotation from this novel will illustrate this point.

> Naoki had frequented a nearby Christian Youth Association while a student at Tokyo University. Of course he had often read the Bible. And he had come across numerous quotations from the Bible while studying English and German. He had also read the Old Testament because of his interest in comparative mythology and folklore. Such a holy scripture as the Bible is always a fresh source wherever and by whomever it is read. Now that Japan has surrendered and he was middle-aged, he thought that his feelings toward the Bible greatly differed from the feelings he had had as a student.

This passage suggests to us that Kawabata pursued his interest in the Bible and that he was deeply impressed by his reading.

When we investigate his earlier works we are impressed with numerous quotations from both Buddhist scriptures and the Bible. He wrote many tiny vignettes. One is entitled **"The Weaker Sex"**, in Japanese **"Yowaki Utsuwa"**, in 1924 and another **"The Book of the Dead"**, in Japanese **"Shisha no Sho"**, in 1928. There can be no doubt that the

former is based on *1 Peter* 3:7—"Likewise you husbands, live considerately with your wives, bestowing honour on the woman as the weaker sex . . ."—and the latter is based on *The Egyptian Book of the Dead,* because he quotes Chapter 83 and Plate 27.

Finally, I would like to give several examples to show the scope of Kawabata's interest in Western literature. During college, he translated into Japanese John Galsworthy's "The Road", Lord Dunsany's "The Oases of Death" and Anton Chekhov's "After the Theater". His undergraduate thesis shows us that he owes his theoretical method mainly to C. T. Winchester's *Some Principles of Literary Criticism.* He also quotes Marie-Jean Guyau's *L'art au point de vue sociologique* and Charles-Augustin de Sainte-Beuve's *Causeries Lundi.* Reflections of his interest in Western literature are not confined to his earlier works. He even read James Joyce's *Ulysses* in the original in his 30's.

From his encounters with such writers as Joyce and Faulkner, Kawabata became interested in the technique of "stream of consciousness", which he introduced to Japanese readers in his works. He also employed the traditional Japanese literary technique of association which is the essential element of linked verse (in Japanese "renga"). Although they might seem different, these two techniques, one Western and the other Japanese, have common elements, and come together in Kawabata's literary works.

The most important of those elements is the idea of progression and association in feelings, ideas, and language. Perhaps the best examples of Kawabata's use of progression and association can be found in several of his well-known novels. For example, *The Sound of the Mountain,* in Japanese "Yama no Oto," and *The Ancient Capital: Kyoto,* in Japanese "Koto", both of which have been translated into several Western languages.

In conclusion, it is necessary to state that the study of Kawabata's literary works is still in its infancy, even in Japan. More research into Kawabata's literary sources, techniques, and characters is needed if we are to adequately understand his literature. What we must avoid is the simple judgement that Kawabata's literature is "traditional" (dentoteki) or Japanese (nihonteki). As I have tried to show in this paper, Western literature, particularly the Bible, is an integral key to opening the doors to Kawabata's works.

Donald Keene (essay date 1984)

SOURCE: "Kawabata Yasunari," in *Dawn to the West, Japanese Literature of the Modern Era: Fiction, Vol. 1,* Holt, Rinehart and Winston, 1984, pp. 786-845.

[Keene is an American scholar and critic who has produced a number of translations and studies of Japanese literature. The following excerpt is taken from his discussion of Kawabata in the fiction volume of his acclaimed two-part literary history of contemporary Japanese letters. Here he surveys Kawabata's early short fiction, particularly "The Izu Dancer," placing it in the context of the author's life and artistic development.]

Kawabata in traditional dress.

Kawabata's first work was probably **"Jūrokusai no Nikki" ("Diary of a Sixteen-Year-Old")**. According to the afterword Kawabata wrote in 1925, this work was composed in 1914 and only slightly changed when he published it eleven years later. He described finding the manuscript in an uncle's storehouse, written on the kind of composition paper used by middle-school students. The diary covers twelve days in May of 1914 and breaks off a week before his grandfather died. Kawabata commented, "The strangest thing was that I had not the least recollection of the events described in the diary. . . . I confronted the honest emotions of a forgotten past. But the grandfather I had described was uglier than the grandfather of my memory. For ten years my mind had been constantly cleansing my grandfather's image."

Kawabata would return again and again to memories of the last days of his grandfather, but never more effectively than in this early work. Some scholars, after careful stylistic examination of the diary, have concluded that, despite Kawabata's insistence on its authenticity, it was probably composed in 1925. Perhaps the most convincing evidence to support this conclusion is that the style of the diary, unlike that of other examples of Kawabata's juvenilia, is free from literary language and conventional flourishes. But regardless of the date of composition, it is an extraordinary evocation of the relations between the boy and the dying old man. The love—and the disgust—the helpless

invalid arouses in the boy is superbly conveyed by an unerring choice of details and by the strikingly modern style, which is closer to that of the New Sensationalists than to the models Kawabata usually followed in his boyhood compositions.

Perhaps the most famous passage is the one that occurs when the boy returns home to find that his grandfather, now blind and almost unable to move, has been waiting impatiently for his return. The grandfather asks the boy to bring the urine glass and put his penis into it.

> I had no choice but to expose him and do what was asked, though it went against the grain.
>
> "Is it in? Is it all right? I'm starting now. All right?" Couldn't he feel his own body?
>
> "Ahh, ahh, it hurts. Ohh. It hurts something terrible." It caused him pain to urinate. To the accompaniment of breathing so labored it sounded it might stop any minute, there rose from the depths of the urine glass the sound of pure water of a valley stream.
>
> "Ohh. It hurts." The pain seemed more than he could bear. As I listened to his voice I felt the tears come to my eyes.
>
> The water had boiled so I gave him some tea to drink. Coarse tea. I had to prop him up for each sip he drank. The bony face, the white hair ravaged by baldness. The quivering hands of bones and skin. The Adam's apple of his scrawny neck, bobbing up and down with each gulp. Three cups of tea.

The ironic comparison of the sound of the old man urinating and the murmur of a pure stream flowing in the valley explicitly underlined the intensity of the experience. The conversations between the old man and the boy given elsewhere in the story are fragmentary, as if they knew each other so well that a few words sufficed to convey their thoughts. The use of the Osaka dialect also made these snatches of conversation seem especially authentic.

It is hard to believe that a boy, especially a boy who was much under the influence of old-fashioned literature, could have written so simply about the death of his only blood relative; but some details, such as the hope the boy expresses that if he keeps writing the diary until he reaches one hundred pages his grandfather will recover, ring true as utterances from the world of childhood. Quite possibly Kawabata changed more than he admitted when he published the work; in another afterword, written in 1948, he stated that the afterword of 1925 was "fiction" (*shōsetsu*). He insisted, however, that the text itself was written as he sat by his grandfather's bed. **"Diary of a Sixteen-Year-Old,"** in any case, has earned a place in most selections of Kawabata's important works.

Kawabata's first published story, **"Shōkonsai Ikkei" ("A View of the Yasukuni Festival,"** 1921), was, however, in a totally dissimilar mood. It describes a circus equestrienne and her friends in an unmistakably Modernist manner. The conversations are fragmentary and sometimes cryptic and Kawabata has deliberately made it difficult to distinguish between dream and reality in the narration. **"A**

View of the Yasukuni Festival" attracted considerable attention when first published, and demonstrates why Kawabata was at first considered so advanced a Modernist. As a story, it is immature, but the style—the jagged skips that would be a hallmark of the New Sensationalists, though this was well before the movement was launched—and the "objectivity," especially the author's noninvolvement with his characters, were fresh and attracted favorable attention. Kikuchi Kan, a figure of enormous importance in the literary world, was so impressed that when Kawabata visited him, hoping to secure from Kikuchi an introduction to publishers who wanted translations of English literature, Kikuchi astonished the young man by treating him like a person of great consequence. Kawabata revealed to Kikuchi that he needed money because he was planning to marry a girl of sixteen (fifteen by Western reckoning); Kikuchi, far from attempting to dissuade him from making such an early marriage, offered the couple the use of his house while he was abroad, and promised to send him an allowance of fifty yen a month. He said he would ask Akutagawa to help get Kawabata's stories published in magazines.

Kikuchi's interest marked an auspicious beginning for Kawabata's career. Kikuchi also introduced him to Yokomitsu Riichi, urging the two to become friends. The friendship that developed affected most of Kawabata's writings during the next decade and was the most valued of his life. However, Kikuchi's generous offer of a house during Kawabata's first year of wedded life never materialized, in part because Kikuchi did not go abroad, but mainly because the girl Kawabata had intended to marry wrote him saying she could not go through with the marriage. The shock of this betrayal, as he considered it, lingered in Kawabata's memory for years and was given direct and indirect expression in many works.

The most important literary product of this disappointment was Kawabata's story **"Izu no Odoriko"** (**"The Izu Dancer,"** 1926), the work that not only brought him fame but, even more than his longer novels, remains the one many people remember him for. In order to shake off the depression after having been jilted, Kawabata went on a walking tour of the Izu Peninsula in the autumn of 1918. He fell in with a group of traveling entertainers, and was touched by the readiness with which they accepted him. Such performers were considered hardly more than beggars; indeed, there were signs at the entrances to some villages warning "Beggars and Itinerant Performers Stay Away." Kawabata was attracted to the young dancer of the troupe, but he was especially gratified to overhear several of the performers agree when discussing him that he was "nice"; he had earlier convinced himself that no one could ever really like him.

Four years earlier, in 1922, Kawabata had written an autobiographical account of his journey to Izu called **"Yugashima no Omoide"** (**"Memories of Yugashima"**). This work was never published, but Kawabata used some of the material when writing **"The Izu Dancer,"** and the rest went into the novella *Shōnen* (*Boys*), written in 1948-1949. He stated on completing the latter work that he had now destroyed the original manuscript of **"Memories of Yu-**gashima."** Only about a third of the manuscript was devoted to the dancer; the rest described his love for a middle-school classmate. This love was of the utmost importance to Kawabata, as he recalled thirty years later. A letter he wrote to his beloved friend (but never sent) contained such phrases as, "I feel that you are the god who will redeem me. . . . You are the fresh shock of my life." Kawabata in later years explained this attraction to another boy in terms of having grown up in a household without women. Some of the revelations of his love for his classmate, called Kiyono in *Boys*, were submitted as a high school essay (as he recalled to his astonishment), but there were parts that he never dared show the other boy. Kawabata did not forget this experience, the first he had of being loved, and when as a man of fifty he wrote *Boys* he stated that he had felt much deeper love for Kiyono than for the Izu dancer. Yet his manuscript about Kiyono remained unpublished, perhaps because he judged that readers would not accept so unconventional a theme. He chose instead to write a story about the performers he had casually encountered in Izu, recognizing that it would have more general appeal. The wisdom of this decision was confirmed by the popularity of **"The Izu Dancer."**

Kawabata quoted in *Boys* a few tantalizing fragments of his meeting the Izu dancer as originally related in **"Memories of Yugashima."** This is how the unpublished story had opened:

> Every year the number of itinerant players who make their way from one hot spring resort to the next, performing where they can, seems to be decreasing. My memories of Yugashima start with some traveling players. That first trip to Izu glitters in my memory with the light from the comet that was a beautiful dancer and with the sights along the way from Shuzenji to Shimoda that were like the comet's tail. It was in the middle of autumn, just after I was promoted to second year at high school, and this was the first journey worthy of the name I had taken since coming to Tokyo. I spent one night at Shuzenji. While walking along the Shimoda Highway to Yugashima, just after passing the Yukawa Bridge, I ran into three girls, traveling performers, on their way to Shuzenji. The dancer who carried the drum stood out among them, even at a distance. I turned back again and again to stare at them, and I thought that at last I had really experienced the joy of travel.

Compare the foregoing with the opening of **"The Izu Dancer"**:

> The road ahead began to twist. Just as I was thinking that I must be getting close to Amagi Pass, a shower swept by me with incredible velocity, whitening the dense cedar forest as it passed.

> I was twenty. I was wearing the regulation high-school cap, a dark blue and white kimono with a *hakama,* and I had a student bookbag slung over my shoulder. It was on my fourth day out since I began my travels in Izu. I had spent one night at Shuzenji Hot Springs and two at Yugashima Hot Springs, and now I was climbing

Amagi in my high wooden clogs. I was enchanted by the mountains that rose in layers one
above the other, by the virgin forests, and by the
suggestion of autumn in the deep valleys, but at
the same time a kind of expectation kept agitat-
ing my heart as I hurried along the road. Before
long heavy drops of rain began to fall. I quickened my pace up the steeply twisting road, and
breathed a sigh of relief when I at last managed
to reach an inn at the northern end of the pass,
only to halt in my tracks at the entrance. My expectations had been almost too perfectly answered: a troupe of itinerant players was stopping there. . . .

I had seen the dancer and the others twice before. The first time was when I was on my way
to Yugashima. I had run into them near the Yu-
kawa Bridge as they were heading for Shuzenji.
There were three young women, and the dancer
had carried a big drum. I turned back again and
again to stare at them, and I thought that at last
I had really experienced the joy of travel.

Although the later version borrowed phrases and even one
sentence from **"Memories of Yugashima,"** the effect is unmistakably different. The earlier version is more personal,
rather in the manner of the "I novel"; in the later version
the "I" is hardly more than a nameless high school student
who observes the scenery and the people he encounters.
Nakamura Mitsuo suggested that the "I" of **"The Izu
Dancer"** corresponds to the waki of a Nō play, an itinerant priest or anonymous traveler whose function is to introduce the spectators to the shite, the central character
of the play. This is true of the men in other works by
Kawabata, who serve mainly to set off the women; though
sometimes they appear to resemble the author, they are
not the vehicles for his reflections and emotions as in an
"I novel" but hardly more than the waki who induces the
shite to appear before us.

Kawabata himself dismissed his Izu stories (including
"The Izu Dancer") as being mere "traveler's impressions." This statement, made in 1934, reflected the extreme diffidence he always showed with respect to his
works, but perhaps this was also his conviction. At the
time that he wrote **"The Izu Dancer"** he was deeply involved with the New Sensationalist school. He insisted in
articles he wrote on behalf of the movement that "newness" was all, and expressed boredom with established
patterns of expression:

> Our eyes burn with desire to know the unknown.
> Our mutual greetings are expressions of our de-
> light at being able to discuss together whatever
> is new. If one man says, "Good morning," and
> another replies, "Good morning," it is boring.
> We have become quite weary of literature that
> is as unchanging as the sun that comes up from
> the east today exactly as it did yesterday. It is
> more interesting if one man says, "The baby
> monkey walks along suspended from its moth-
> er's belly," and the other replies, "White herons
> really have long talons, don't they?"

"The Izu Dancer" was clearly not new in the manner advocated by the New Sensationalists. There is nothing re-

motely startling in the expression. The reader is charmed
by the story, impressed by Kawabata's skill in capturing
the atmosphere of Izu and portraying the figures he encountered, but if one finds newness it will be in the emergence of a new and important writer, not in stylistic mannerisms. Other works of the period, notably the scenario
Kawabata wrote for the New Sensationalist film *Kurutta
Ichipēji* (*A Page out of Order,* 1926), demonstrate that he
was quite capable of creating works that followed the
Modernist principles. **"The Izu Dancer"** seems unrelated
to Modernism, and that may be why Kawabata dismissed
it so casually.

The story of **"The Izu Dancer"** is quickly told. The narrator is attracted to a dancer, the youngest of a troupe of
itinerant performers he meets in Izu. He thinks of asking
her to spend the night in his room, but when by accident
he sees her emerge naked from the steam of an outdoor
hot spring, he discovers she is still a child, despite her
grownup clothes and way of arranging her hair. This discovery, far from disappointing him, frees him of con-
straint, and he happily accompanies the troupe to Shimo-
da, where they part. Aboard the ship on which he returns
to Tokyo he weeps, but not out of sadness.

The popularity of **"The Izu Dancer"** probably owes much
to the film versions, the oldest the one directed by Gosho
Heinosuke in 1933. The story has been interpreted, perhaps also because of the films, as a rare example in modern
Japanese literature of the pure love of adolescents. If this
is true, **"The Izu Dancer"** is a distinctly unfamiliar variety
of love story. Although the student hopes for a while to
lie with the dancer, he never addresses to her anything resembling a lover's endearments, and he is relieved, even
purified, when he realizes that she is too young for love-
making. She represents for the student the romance of
travel, rather than romance itself, and for this reason it is
preferable that the ideal not be tarnished by physical involvement. Kawabata throughout his career was attracted
especially by virginal, inviolable young women. These
were by no means the only women he wrote about, and
they are not necessarily his most successfully achieved
portraits, but for Kawabata they seem to have represented
the essence of beauty. Perhaps, as Mishima Yukio suggested, Kawabata was fascinated by virginity because it is impossible to take it without losing it.

Kawabata's insistence on the mystic beauty of virginity
was traced by another critic to Kawabata's first experience
of love for the girl who betrayed him. This critic believed
that Kawabata's painful disappointment in real life indeli-
bly affected his treatment of women in his works of fiction.
The pure maidens do not gradually develop into mature
women, but the two remain forever apart and distinct. Indeed, Kawabata generally found ugliness rather than
beauty in mature women, and that may be why they are
more effectively characterized in his novels than the beautiful virgins. Kawabata was at pains to deny this critic's
"discovery" of the source of his Izu dancer, but ended by
wondering if there might not be something to the theory,
though he himself was unaware of ever having thought of
his fiancée when describing the dancer.

Douglas Seibold (essay date 1988)

SOURCE: "A World Distilled: The Short Fiction of Japan's Nobel Laureate," in *Chicago Tribune—Books,* August 21, 1988, p. 7.

[*In the laudatory review below, Seibold admires the polish and precision of the pieces in* Palm-of-the-Hand Stories.]

Born in 1899, the same year as Hemingway and Borges, Yasunari Kawabata was venerated in his native Japan, and his writing attracted as much attention from the West as that of any of his compatriots since Lady Murasaki. His career climaxed in 1968 with his being awarded the Nobel Prize, and to this date he is the only Far Eastern writer to be so honored.

The translators and publishers of *Palm-of-the-Hand Stories* take their title from a volume Kawabata published in the 1920s, at the beginning of his career, though this collection includes stories of similar scope that he wrote throughout his life; the final piece here is dated 1972, the year of his suicide.

Better than half the stories date from the '20s and all of them are extremely brief, few running over three pages in length. The longest is the last, entitled "Gleanings from Snow Country," a nine-page distillation of one of Kawabata's best-known novels.

As would be expected, these stories are distinguished by their remarkable compression and poem-like intensity of imagery and symbolism. Yet for all their brevity they are resonant with meaning and import, exhibiting how Kawabata was able "to endow a small space with spaciousness," as translator Lane Dunlop notes in his share of the introduction. Kawabata himself said of them, "Many writers, in their youth, write poetry; I, in my youth, wrote *The Palm-of-the-Hand Stories*. The other translator, J. Martin Holman, suggests that these short pieces may have been Kawabata's most natural form of expression and that—like renga, the traditional Japanese form of linked verses—his longer works are constructed of these basic units.

During his lifetime Kawabata was considered something of a traditionalist, and much of his work seems concerned with perpetuating familiar Japanese themes and modes of expression, while still faithfully capturing his vision of contemporary Japanese life. That vision is not a particularly sunny one, and it grew darker with time—especially after Japan's defeat in World War II and subsequent westernization extinguished or perverted ever more of its traditional culture.

These stories are not limited to any particular subject matter, but all except one are set in Japan, and certain settings and images recur, such as the hot-spring inn (which, as another translator, Edward Seidensticker, has said, often offers "special delights for the unaccompanied gentleman"), the harbor town, women's hairdos and, particularly, pairs of lovers and spouses.

If Kawabata has a favorite subject here, it is probably love and its vicissitudes. About marriage he sometimes reads like a Japanese John Cheever, and nowhere more so than in "The Rainy Station," wherein two wives and old rivals, awaiting their husbands at a suburban train station, try to one-up each other upon meeting for the first time in years.

In another story, "The White Flower," a young girl is advised by an older woman to "Take care in marriage. It wouldn't do to have someone too strong. A man who looks weak, with no diseases and a pale complexion, would be all right . . . someone who always sits properly, doesn't drink, and smiles a lot." This poor girl keeps finding herself about to succumb to the charms of various suitors, only to lose interest as they take an inevitable wrong step in their pursuit of her. One, a writer, asks her to "put your soul in the palm of my hand for me to look at, like a crystal jewel. I'll sketch it in words. . . ."

Where that writer failed in his courtship, Kawabata has succeeded. These stories are jewels, indeed, each one a soul, a life, or a whole world distilled to palm-sized proportions.

Marian Ury (essay date 1988)

SOURCE: "A Man and the Idea of a Woman," in *The New York Times Book Review,* August 21, 1988, p. 11.

[*In the following favorable evaluation of* Palm-of-the-Hand Stories, *Ury notes that each of the pieces in the volume is "less a story in the usual sense than a node of storytelling, where sounds, textures, tastes, colors, trajectories and intimations are gathered, ready to expand over an invisible canvas."*]

A woman, breaking with her married lover, gives him a pair of canaries as a memento of their affair. The birds, which initially had been placed in the same cage by the bird seller through chance and are now unable to survive without each other, come to symbolize for the lover his relationship with his wife, who had cared for the birds and averted her eyes from his affair. Now that she is dead, the husband writes to his former mistress asking her permission to kill the birds and bury them with his wife. In another story [in *Palm-of-the-Hand Stories*], a man who has taken an aversion to his wife and left her sends a series of letters from ever more distant post offices enjoining her and their daughter to make no sound. Mother and daughter cease "eternally to make even the faintest sound. In other words," Yasunari Kawabata says, they die. "And, strangely enough, the woman's husband lay down beside them and died, too."

In yet another of Kawabata's "palm-of-the-hand stories," a little girl carrying a branch of crimson berries with green leaves gives it to a woman in a new silk kimono who is seated on the veranda of a shabby inn. The girl's father is a charcoal burner, and he is sick; the woman has been receiving unstamped love letters from her postman. The season is autumn. This is less a story in the usual sense than a node of storytelling, where sounds, textures, tastes, colors, trajectories and intimations are gathered, ready to expand over an invisible canvas. Inevitably, the stories, like Kawabata's longer fiction, are compared with haiku; but another comparison might be with the work of Virginia Woolf, especially the autobiographical fragments of *Mo-*

ments of Being and *Mrs. Dalloway,* with its deceptive appearance of fragmented time and movement, its moments of illumination and its flashes of an immanent, inexplicable reality. Insistently Japanese, Kawabata was also well acquainted with European modernist literature.

Kawabata's stories are difficult to summarize—many of the finest elude even the attempt. In one of my favorites, **"The Wife of the Autumn Wind"** (the translation of the title seems not quite right; "The Wife in the Autumn Wind" might be better, or perhaps "The Autumn-Wind Wife"), the event narrated is the shadowy encounter between the protagonist and the devoted wife of a dying man, his neighbors at a hotel—or rather, between the protagonist and the idea of the woman, for what we are made to see is his discovery of some strands of her hair after she has left the hotel on a brief errand. What the story is *about* is sweetness, drabness (and its sensuous appeal), cold, the nearness of death, the coming of an autumn typhoon, the varieties of love and tenderness and the unbridgeable gap between the protagonist and the woman. It is just over two pages. There is not a word in it that could be dispensed with.

The longest of these palm-of-the-hand stories are perhaps a half-dozen pages; the shortest are less than a page. There are 70 in this volume, about half of an output that spanned their author's writing career. He is said to have considered these very short stories his finest work.

Yasunari Kawabata was born in 1899. He received the Nobel Prize in Literature in 1968—the only Japanese writer thus honored so far and a somewhat controversial choice, since not every Japanese critic likes him. He died in a gas-filled room in 1972, a probable suicide. He is well known in the West for *The Master of Go,* a minimalist novelization of a newspaper account of a competition at go, a distant cousin of chess, in which an aging master was defeated, and for *Snow Country,* an enigmatic novel of unreciprocated love set in what is, for Kawabata, a region of voluptuous white and cold. As a child, he was repeatedly orphaned. His father died when he was 2 years old, his mother when he was 3, his only sister when he was 9 and his grandfather—his last surviving close relative—when he was 16. According to the instructive chapter on Kawabata in Donald Keene's history of modern Japanese literature, *Dawn to the West,* the boy came to be known as a "master of funerals" from his authoritative demeanor at funeral services.

Intense sorrow often brings with it a heightened esthetic perception: to the sufferer, shabby tenements seem to glow with color, and past and present time to collapse into one and become almost tangible. Not only death but deafness and blindness appear repeatedly in these stories—the latter depicted as a special, ecstatic kind of seeing. Death itself is a metamorphosis, one of many kinds in these stories. An older sister gives herself to the lover of her younger sister who is ill, and imagines herself also marrying the sister's husband after the sister's death. A woman recognizes the face of her mother in her daughter. A meek young woman, loving her husband to distraction, cuts her hair, wears thick spectacles and tries to grow a mustache and join the army so as to be exactly like him; ultimately, God

transforms her into a lily. Kawabata's characters, incapable of ordinary human intimacy, dream of the merging and dissolution of the self.

Frederick Smock   (essay date 1989)

SOURCE: "Small Lanterns," in *The American Book Review,* Vol. 10, No. 6, January, 1989, p. 15.

[*In the following review, Smock praises the concision and the highly evocative quality of the pieces in* Palm-of-the-Hand Stories.]

Somewhere in my future is a small, simple apartment, maybe a couple of rooms near the sea somewhere, with high windows and a fireplace. On the mantel over the fireplace is a small stack of books, the only books in the place, those dozen or so volumes necessary to life. One of those books is Yasunari Kawabata's **Palm-of-the-Hand Stories.**

These very short stories, which span his writing life, are the distillation of a beautiful talent. Kawabata won the Nobel Prize for Literature in 1968 for his [longer works], **"The Izu Dancer,"** *Thousand Cranes, Snow Country,* and the others, which were so important to Japan's modern literature. But Kawabata believed that the very short story—the story that fits into the palm of one's hand—holds the essence of the writing art. It is to fiction what the haiku is to poetry. (His last work was a miniaturized version of *Snow Country,* shortly before he committed suicide in 1972.)

The grand themes are all here—love, loneliness, our capacity for disillusionment, the tensions between old and new—under the lens of Kawabata's microscope. The short form is suited to his love of detail, his preference for the finite gesture whose meaning reverberates through time.

In **"A Sunny Place,"** the oldest story in the collection, a young man meets a woman at a seaside inn—it is the beginning of love—but the woman is painfully disconcerted by his habit of staring, and turns her head away. Embarrassed, he averts his own gaze, to a sunny spot on the beach, and thus discovers the origin of his bad habit. "After my parents died," he tells us, "I had lived alone with my grandfather for almost ten years in a house in the country. My grandfather was blind. For years he sat in the same room, in the same spot, facing the east with a long charcoal brazier in front of him. Occasionally he would turn his head toward the south, but he never faced the north. . . . Sometimes I would sit for a long time in front of my grandfather staring into his face, wondering if he would turn to the north. . . . I wondered if the south felt ever so slightly lighter even to a blind person." As a happy result, this memory heightens the intimacy the young man feels toward the woman.

A further testament to the power of Kawabata's economical stories: a movie was once made of **"Thank You,"** a four-page story whose dialogue consists chiefly of *thank-yous.* It tells of a bus driver who takes a mother and daughter from their harbor town to the city, where the daughter is to be sold into a wealthy man's harem; but the driver's politeness to the cartmen they pass on the way so touches the daughter that her mother implores him to allow her one night of genuine affection before her enslavement.

I have returned many times to this story, looking for the source of its power—their (ambiguous) night together, the enigmatic figure of the bus driver, the journey's dreaded end? And I cannot be sure that I have located it. But I have felt it.

His better stories work this way. Swiftly. Mysteriously.

Kawabata wrote nearly 150 "palm" stories, of which 70 are published here, including **"Gleanings from Snow Country,"** his last. The translators have rendered the stories in faultlessly simple language, as befits them.

For these stories are like small lanterns whose colored lights can be seen from very far away—little truths, nestled in a valley, the valley of the palm.

Thom Palmer   (essay date 1989)

SOURCE: "The Asymmetrical Garden: Discovering Yasunari Kawabata," in *Southwest Review,* Vol. 74, No. 3, Summer, 1989, pp. 390-402.

[*In the following essay, Palmer examines Kawabata's* Palm-of-the-Hand Stories *in an attempt to demonstrate that the form the author employed in these pieces was much more congenial to his talents than the novel form.*]

In 1968, Yasunari Kawabata became the first Japanese writer to receive the Nobel Prize for Literature. Concerning this unprecedented citation, Professor Donald Keene, in his gargantuan work of scholarship (*Dawn To The West,* 1984), writes: "The Japanese public was naturally delighted to learn of the award, though surprise was expressed that a writer who was difficult to understand even for Japanese should have been so appreciated abroad."

While it seems an odd instance of refreshing insight that the Swedish Academy (emphatically Occidental in literary sensibility, at least until 1968), chose Kawabata, one of the most scrupulously traditional of modern Japanese writers, the greater likelihood is that the selection was influenced more by timing than by appreciation. One story maintains that, regardless of the nominees for that year—Lawrence Durrell, Albert Moravia, Gunter Grass, Robert Graves, and Mao Zedong, among others—the Academy's decision to recognize a writer from Japan was predetermined (another typically belated gesture at geographical equilibrium). Sweden dispatched an agent to reconnoiter the literary situation in The Land of the Rising Sun. By this point in the century, Japan's principal literary voices had entered, or were nearing, eclipse. Jun'ichiro Tanazaki had died just three years before. Kawabata's "disciple," the volatile and prolific Yukio Mishima, was a mere forty-three years old, and still in the midst of his *chef d'oeuvre,* the tetralogy, *Hojo no Umi* (The Sea of Fertility). Even if Mishima's spectacular public *sepukka* in 1970, upon completion of his multi-volume novel, could have been anticipated, the militant nationalism of his last years was the kind of extremist persona that makes Stockholm quail. The somewhat esoteric Kawabata, then, was in the right place at the right time. This is not to begrudge him the

honor. On the contrary, the 1968 Nobel Prize for Literature was one of those rare, extremely rare occasions, when merit and circumstance coincided.

In awarding their prize, the Nobel Committee cited three of Kawabata's novel-length works: the enigmatic masterpieces, *Snow Country* (1937), *Thousand Cranes* (1952), and the rather less accomplished *The Old Capital* (1962). His novel *The Sound of the Mountain* (published in tandem with *Thousand Cranes* and awarded the literary prize of the Japanese Academy in 1952), was unmentioned. This is curious because there is some consensus that *The Sound of the Mountain* is Kawabata's most successful, fully realized work in the long form, a form that was not at all congenial to his style, his writing habits, or the traditional aesthetics that dominated the essence of his fiction.

The fundamentals of this aesthetic, and of Kawabata's fictive vision, evolved from some of Japan's earliest literary texts, the touchstones of Japanese literature, for which Kawabata had a deep, enduring reverence, particularly Lady Murasaki's eleventh-century work, *The Tale of Genji,* Buddhist canonical texts, and Basho's seventeenth-century *haiku.* Kawabata provides the edifying analogy for this vision, this aesthetic, in his Nobel acceptance speech, *Japan, the Beautiful, and Myself* (tr. by Edward Seidensticker, 1969): "The Western garden tends to be symmetrical, the Japanese garden asymmetrical, and this is because the asymmetrical has the greater power to symbolize multiplicity and vastness. The asymmetry, of course, rests upon a balance imposed by delicate sensibilities."

Just as the architectonic symmetry of Western literature can be traced as far back as Homer's meticulously symmetrical *Iliad,* so can the asymmetry of the "Japanese garden," this delicately imposed balance symbolizing multiplicity and vastness, be evidenced in Lady Murasaki's *Genji,* a work that served as a crucible for almost an entire literature. In his intelligent, concise book, *Modern Japanese Fiction and Its Traditions,* J. Thomas Rimer explains that the Western reader, "surrounded by the rich emotional universe [Murasaki] has provided for him, may have some initial difficulties in persuading himself precisely what the narrowly defined purposes of [*Genji*] might be. There seem so many possibilities. The text... is obviously planned on an enormous scale, and its structure is organic. Themes and characters appear and disappear, swept along by movements of time, which moves all before it. *Genji* . . . was not planned in such a way that every detail of its structure and design can be referred back to some central, tightly organized conception in the mind of the author. In fact, time in Lady Murasaki's novel flows precisely like a river, occasionally picking up bits of extraneous, even irrelevant, information, which the author was not always at great pains to remove."

This essence of organic structure, the flowing, streaming movements of time, was ultimately the pervasive force that shaped, or formed the character of, Kawabata's fiction. He was bound to it, artistically and intellectually— the suggestive power of the asymmetrical text, spreading ever outward.

This is not to say that Kawabata was dismissive toward the aesthetics of Western literature. Much of his early work was deemed Modernist in a fundamentally Western sense of that word, and one detects the influences of Proust, Freud, and—most explicitly—Joyce, in Kawabata's story, **"Needles, Glass, and Fog,"** and his 1931 novel, *Crystal Fantasies,* works in which Kawabata experiments with stream-of-consciousness.

But Joyce's *Ulysses,* that masterwork of Modernism, despite its ostensibly free-flowing "streams" of thought and other apparent caprice, nevertheless follows a rigorous design and "tightly organized conception." It's a work of ingenious, intricate symmetry. Kawabata's "Modernism" was chiefly technical; he never attempted to import the essence of the Western novel, but he trafficked in its innovations to perhaps expand and enrich his own literary inheritance.

His success was uneven, and only obliquely discernible. His forays into stylized territories were brief, abortive. What Western literature contributed to Kawabata's artistic growth was perhaps a deepened appreciation for the beauty and traditional virtues of Japanese art and cultural sensibility, and the unique efficacy they brought to fiction writing.

There, in part, lies much of the difficulty of his work to Japanese and especially Western readers. As an artist profoundly conscious of his Japan and its indigenous literary texts, Kawabata seemed constitutionally unable to produce a novel in the patented notion of that form—a notion by then assimilated by modern Japanese letters—a self-contained and ultimately self-referential structure, an object of art existing independently and completely. Kawabata's "novels" are not really novels at all; the term is an anomaly. (*Shosetsu,* the Japanese approximation for the word *novel,* literally means "brief account," and was only in usage one hundred years when Kawabata won his Nobel.) Much of his long fiction fits the criteria for the Post-Modern "anti-novel": plotless, amorphous strings of text holding the frail beads of character, recurrent images, abstruse "themes," carefully constructed tableaus. Works like *Snow Country* and *Thousand Cranes* are best described as extended narratives. They are, after Lady Murasaki's *Genji,* meandering rivers of sensation, organic structures, suggesting vastness and enormity without necessarily growing to such proportions. Their purposes and component parts are elusive, unstressed, and nebulous, and the works, as a whole, seem unfinished.

In *Snow Country,* the conflict and tensions that form the plot dynamics are so restrained and impalpable that they must almost be intuited. What seem to function as the climactic events of the novel—a conversation of delicate nuances between the dilettante Shimamura and the geisha Komako, followed by a fire that kills the other significant female, Yoko—are subtle to the point of obscurity. In *Thousand Cranes,* Kawabata eschews subtlety altogether, opting for out-and-out omission; before we are given any explanation, or even sufficient information to speculate on the possible signification of the thousand-crane-pattern kerchief that furnishes the title, the book stops.

That is the way of Kawabata's extended narratives. They don't end, they stop. This mystifying abruptness was intensified by the standard practice of serialization. In twentieth-century Japan, Kawabata and his contemporaries composed novels in the fashion of nineteenth-century British and American writers, by periodical installment. While this arrangement of producing for deadline furnished Kawabata with a welcomed discipline, it was certainly ill-suited to his literary temperament. He wrote for a number of magazines, some of which catered to the literati, others geared toward less discerning tastes. Chapters of a work-in-progress would appear in a variety of publications, until Kawabata discontinued a particular narrative to turn his attention to another project. Other works might run on interminably (*Tokyo People,* 1955, reached 505 installments before its publication in four volumes), before stopping with characteristic inconclusiveness. When a "completed" narrative appeared in book form, Kawabata sometimes appended or elided chapters, or sometimes did not, leaving it flawed by the repetitions endemic to serialization. Writing novels was an arduous task. The aesthetic fulfillment they provided Kawabata is indistinct. He was trying to find harmony with an artistic form essentially antithetical to his genuine, singular strengths. Speaking specifically of *Thousand Cranes* and *The Sound of the Mountain,* he addressed this dilemma:

> Each should have been a short story that concluded in one episode. All I did was to keep sounding the overtones of what I had written. For that reason, I should have ended both works after the first chapter; such is the brutal truth. The rest was probably mere self-indulgence. The same holds true of *Snow Country.* I console myself with the hope that one day I shall write a novel that will be provided from the start with the framework for a long novel and with a theme, and not be a mere prolongation of the first chapter in my usual way.

> (tr. Donald Keene)

Still, the idea that these works might be "mere self-indulgence" is probably mere self-deprecation. Like his fiction, Kawabata was quiet, modest, a helpful and sedulous writer who deferred to the natural lyricism he perceived in life, and the possibilities for transcendence that this lyricism offered the spirit and the intellect. Despite the ambiguity and irresolution of his narratives, their resonating overtones, like richly colored glazes, form works of elegant, textured beauty. That he persevered in so untenable a form and managed to produce contemporary works of timelessness and grace is a testament to his recondite genius.

And like so many of our Occidental geniuses—Joyce, Picasso, Stravinsky, Pound, and Kafka, to name a few from this century—Kawabata's art evolved under the specific conditions exerted by his vision. An insistent, idiosyncratic perception, if forceful enough, ultimately develops its own form, or retools ancient and existing forms to accommodate its character, its tonality, and its intent. For more than fifty years, Kawabata composed small pieces of fiction that he called *tanagokoro no shosetsu* (stories that fit in the palm of one's hand). These are artistic cells, microfictions. Broadly, they displayed Kawabata's traditional Eastern affinity for the efficiency and beauty of the miniature. Beyond a matter of taste, however, the pieces demonstrate Kawabata's literary gifts in their most potent, purified forms. The "palm-sized" stories constitute the marrow of his artistic essence, and this essence is a constant refinement and exploration of the East's prototypical aesthetics and philosophical thought. They are stylized, intuitive studies of the tension, mystery, melancholy, and beauty of being alive in an ephemeral, unfathomable universe.

Unless one could read Japanese, however, these short, short works, which Kawabata sometimes referred to as the essence of his art, lay long untranslated. Finally, seventeen years after Kawabata's death, a selection of over seventy palm-sized stories are available in English (*Palm-of-the-Hand Stories,* 1988), perhaps occasioned by the West's invigorated interest in things Japanese. Whatever the inspiration, the availability of these works is significant, and an opportunity (for those of us not scholars of Japanese literature), not necessarily to reevaluate Kawabata, but to approach an understanding of a major twentieth-century literary figure for the first time.

Kawabata wrote 146 palm-of-the-hand stories. Their dates show that Kawabata produced them in clusters; he composed them in abundance in the 1920s, the significant first decade of his literary career. The number dwindles in the first half of the 1930s, then stops. Near the end of World War II, however, he resumed writing palm-sized stories (during the war years, Kawabata spent a great deal of time rereading Lady Murasaki's *The Tale of Genji* and other early Japanese texts), and there follows another gap of more than a decade. His final piece of fiction, **"Gleanings from Snow Country,"** was composed three months before his suicide in 1972, and is a particularly telling, palm-sized version of the novel written thirty-five years before. It is obvious from these groupings that as his reputation grew, so did his obligations to other projects, leaving him less time for work that he perhaps found preferable. But the fact that these stories span almost his entire literary life reveals his profound affection for the form, and his need to return to it, dispelling any idea that it, like his excursions into Modernism (or Surrealism, "New Sensationalism," "New Psychologism"—other schools to which he matriculated) was simply affectation or experimentalism.

The appellation, "stories that fit in the palm of one's hand," like the fiction it describes, is both simple and intricate, luminous with suggestive subtleties. If Kawabata intended it strictly as an image conveying the physical brevity of the pieces, its incongruity—a story we can cup in our palm like an insect, a bit of water, a stone—would seem merely quaint. But this incongruity invites us to consider the correctness of the image; it has the expansive, unfolding potential of *haiku.* What one can hold in the palm of one's hand can be an object of simple, possessable beauty, yet with a suggestion of vastness beyond the immediacy of the object, like a diamond, with its complex arrangement of light, and inner planes, wrought by eons of pressure, a miner's physical labor, a cutter's steely precision;

or, more in keeping with Kawabata's environment, the beauty of an ancient tea bowl, with its lacquerings of personal, social and artistic suggestion.

The uncanny aptness of Kawabata's image, at once succinct and spacious, is easier to grasp after reading these small works. They adhere to no formula. Besides those that function as actual stories, some are merely descriptions of dreams, others are autobiographical sketches. There are stories that read like folk tales, fables, parables, and Zen koans. So much is implicit, so many of the tensions, paradoxes, and harmonies are reliant on one's sometimes uncooperative facility for sudden comprehension that the tales often seem impenetrable, elliptical, or porous. For the most part, Kawabata sounds no overtones, just tones; he provides a construct of events, objects, relationships, and natural settings, and it is up to a reader's individual understanding of some element or nuance in the text to give a palm-sized story its completeness.

The stories don't function as humor, however, in which one must possess a certain level of knowledge in order to feel the shock of intended irony. They comprise a variety of levels and potentials. There are gradations of meaning, innumerable approaches at interpretation, a sophisticated array of doors and windows through which one can access the text. With Kawabata, one may locate, or perhaps even experience, a subtle epiphany, feel a little throb of excitement from the tale or its telling, but it's a highly subjective, intuitive occurrence. Intended or otherwise, this is the corollary of all literature: that exclusive intimacy a writer shares with his each individual reader. Only, in Kawabata, this exclusivity is intensified by his balancing of what he includes and what he omits, resulting in—as in the asymmetrical garden—a symbolic vastness. Even his grace notes and apparently decorative images offer a palate of possible shadings. Abstract and synesthetic, they often change the texture of a story, turning the real into the surreal, the conscious into the hallucinatory: "The smell of the surf was like a green light"; "A child walked by, rolling a metal hoop that made the sound of autumn"; "The spring snickered yellowly."

Palm-sized stories don't necessarily defy definitive critical interpretation. On the contrary, they encourage it while at the same time rendering it pointless. Borges wrote: "Since we can no longer see through a text to its origins, in intention or ascertainable meaning, we must either reject interpretation, or allow every possible reading as a valid addition to the omnilogue of texts." I imagine that Kawabata would be well satisfied if one approached his fiction with the intellectual innocence of the latter (along with Wittgenstein's plea: "Don't think, look!").

To a twentieth-century reader, Eastern or Western, it's difficult to abandon this divining rod that trembles for significance, for indisputable meaning. Even Lane Dunlop—who shared translating duties with J. Martin Holman for the new North Point edition—in his first experience with palm-sized stories in the late seventies, admits he "mistook their subtlety for slightness, their lack of emphasis for pointlessness." Exegesis and interpretation are adjunct to the mental process of reading. A palm-of-the-hand story requires the kind of synthetic appraisal we give to paintings, photographs, sculpture, or architecture: one first *sees* a work, perceives it, assimilates it. It requires a reader to read, as per Nabokov's instruction to his Cornell students, "not with his heart, not so much with his brain, but with his spine." And brevity of Kawabata's stories wonderfully facilitates this kind of reading. They flit by us, like something we think we've seen in the corner of our eye. Many of them are short enough to be taken in in one breath and, like the following piece titled **"The Ring"** [1924], quoted in their entirety:

> An impecunious law student, taking some translation work with him, went to a mountain hot-spring inn.
>
> Three geishas from the city, holding their round fans to their faces, were napping in the little pavilion in the forest.
>
> He descended the stone stairs at the edge of the forest to the mountain stream. A great boulder divided the current of the stream; swarms of dragonflies hovered and darted there.
>
> A girl was standing naked by the bathtub that had been carved out of the boulder.
>
> Thinking she was eleven or twelve, he ignored her as he shed his bathrobe on the beach and lowered himself into the tub at the girl's feet.
>
> The girl, who seemed to have nothing else to do, smiled at him, showing herself off, as if to attract him to her rosy pink body. A split-second glance at her told him that she was the child of a geisha. Hers was an abnormal, precocious beauty, in which one could sense her future purpose of giving sensual pleasure to men. His eyes, surprised, widened like a fan in their appreciation of her.
>
> Suddenly, the girl, holding up her left hand, gave a small scream.
>
> "Ah! I forgot to take it off. I went in with it on."
>
> Allured despite himself, he looked up at her hand.
>
> "Little brat!" Instead of being irritated at having been taken in by the girl, he suddenly felt a violent dislike for her.
>
> She'd wanted to show off her ring. He didn't know whether one took off one's ring or not when one entered a hot-spring bath, but it was clear that he'd been caught by the child's stratagem.
>
> Evidently, he had shown his displeasure in his face more strongly then he'd thought. The girl, turning red, fiddled with her ring. Hiding his own childishness with a wry smile, he said casually, "That's a nice ring. Let's have a look at it."
>
> "It's an opal."
>
> Sure enough, as if very happy to show it to him, the girl squatted at the edge of the tub. Losing her balance as she held out the hand with the ring on it, she put her other hand on his shoulder.
>
> "An opal?" Receiving an intense impression of her precocity from her pronunciation of the word, he tried repeating it.
>
> "Yes. My finger's still too small. I had the ring made specially of gold. But now people say the stone's too big."
>
> He toyed with the girl's little hand. The stone, a gentle, luminous, warm egg-yolk color suffused with violet, seemed extraordinarily beautiful. The girl, bringing her body straight forward, closer and closer, and gazing into his face, seemed beside herself with satisfaction.
>
> This girl, in order to show him the ring better, might not be surprised even if he took her, all naked as she was, onto his lap.

"The Ring" is relatively straightforward, as palm stories go, but, like a painting, it can be enjoyed immediately, unconditionally, for its choice of colors, the arrangements of its elements, the ending tableau. Curiously enough, it also has something of the circumstantial ambiguity of a painting. Off in the background of the hot-spring setting, Kawabata has placed "Three geishas from the city, holding their round fans to their faces . . . napping in the little pavilion in the forest." He never explicitly establishes any relationship between them and the naked girl, even after the student culls her past, present, and future from his "split-second glance." The geishas are simply there. It's up to the reader to embrace the obvious (if it is obvious), or succumb to uncertainty, or just to accept them as pictorial detail and visual balance.

But the story is complete, elegant, and satisfying, on a purely artistic, sensory level. Kawabata's structural precision and stylistic beauty mitigate a feeling of compression. Instead, it has a fullness, a density, and this is achieved, upon closer examination, by a subtle system of assonance and harmony between character and action, character and color: the geishas with their "fans to their faces," and the student, later, with "his eyes, surprised, widened like a fan"; the naked girl, young—"her rosy pink body"—but with a lurid future of sensual pleasure, and her opal, "a gentle, luminous, warm egg-yolk color," but suffused with a far more livid color, violet. Kawabata suggests that her intelligence is too big for her years, just as her gem is too big for her hand. She exposes her immaturity by turning red, while the student conceals his childishness "with a wry smile," —a coincidental reversal that alludes, again, to the napping geishas.

These vertices of association, and the delicate ambiguity and suggestiveness adumbrating almost all of the story's elements, give **"The Ring"** a fullness of tone and texture that often eluded Kawabata in many of his extended narratives. The palm-sized stories gave his diaphanous touches room to expand. One wonders how resolute was his "hope that one day I shall write a novel that will be provided from the start with the framework for a long novel and with a theme." In his 1934 work, *Lyric Poem*, Kawabata wrote, "Compared to the vision of the Buddhas and their life in the world beyond as depicted in the Buddhist scriptures, how very realistic is the Westerner's vision of the other world! And how puny and vulgar. This is true even of Dante and Swedenborg . . ." Of himself he wrote that same year: "I believe that the classics of the East, especially the Buddhist scriptures, are the supreme works of literature in the world. I revere the sutras not for their religious teachings but as literary visions . . . I have received the baptism of modern Western literature and I have myself imitated it, but basically I am an oriental, and . . . I have never lost sight of my bearings" (tr. Donald Keene).

Perhaps his nagging infatuation with Western literature's notion of size and self-containment was the residual effect of this baptism. But the "hope" of creating a universe was never quite as compelling as the desire to emulate and celebrate one. The profundity of this orientalism and the allure of its vision, in both literary (*The Tale of Genji*) and Buddhist canonical texts, provided Kawabata with his greatest inspiration, and palm-of-the-hand stories were the most pliant medium for this inspiration.

J. Thomas Rimer, in the work cited earlier, furnishes a valuable gloss on the traditional virtues of Japanese literature. One of these virtues, *yugen,* "sometimes defined as 'mystery and depth' . . . is an elusive one, yet of central importance in the history of Japanese aesthetics. Shotetsu, a medieval poet and critic, defined *yugen* as 'feelings that cannot be put into words, for example the effect of the moon veiled by a wisp of cloud or of scarlet mountain foliage enshrouded in autumnal haze.' Such a definition might suggest the beauty of overtones, but the meaning of *yugen* goes deeper still . . . the term suggests a transcendental beauty behind the surface that exists on another plane of reality to which the work of art may help to lead the reader."

The concept of *yugen* is unmistakable in all of Kawabata's work, but it flowers most lavishly in the atmosphere of the palm-of-the-hand story.

In January 1972, Kawabata put his 1937 book *Snow Country* through the alembic of *yugen,* and produced **"Gleanings from Snow Country,"** distilling an exquisite novel into a palm-sized story of astonishing, concentrated beauty. The dilettante Shimamura, in the train that is returning him to the mountain hot-spring inn and the geisha, called Komako in the novel but simply "the woman" in the palm-sized rewriting, is sharing a compartment with "the girl," (here again, Yoko in the original). The sun has set, and the darkness outside has made Shimamura's adjacent window into a transparent mirror. He gazes at the reflection of the girl.

> The evening scene flowed in the depths of the mirror. The mirror itself and the objects reflected in it moved like a double-exposed motion picture, with no connection between the actors and the scene. Morover, as the actor, with mutable transparency, and the scene, with its misty flow—as the two fused together, they depicted an unearthly world of symbols. Especially when the lights in the fields and mountains shined in the middle of the girl's face, his heart fluttered with the inexpressible beauty . . .
>
> Then a light burned in the middle of her face; the reflected image was not strong enough to eliminate the light from outside, and the light did not

obliterate the reflection. So the light drifted across the girl's face, but it did nothing to illuminate or brighten her. It was a cold, distant light. As it shined about her pupil—in other words, in the instant when the light and the girl's eye were superimposed—her eye was transformed into a beautiful, bewitching, glowing insect that floated on the waves of the night darkness.

The balance of the tale, about eight pages, observes several episodes between Shimamura and "the woman," which Kawabata condensed and isolated, and which are busy with darkness, cold, and reflections, until finally, at story's end:

> Shimamura looked toward [the woman], then shrank back. The depths of the mirror reflected the white snow. And the woman's red cheeks floated amid the snow. The pure, clean beauty was inexpressible.
>
> Was the sun about to rise? The brilliance of the snow in the mirror increased as if it were burning cold. And with it the purple-black luster of the woman's hair in the mirror grew deeper.

The story brings not only *Snow Country* but all of his art into sharpest focus, and is a near-perfect rendering of *yugen.* Possibly even Kawabata understood, with **"Gleanings from Snow Country,"** that he had epitomized his life in art. Three months later, after a day of working over a manuscript, Kawabata retired to an apartment where he often wrote, that overlooked the sea, and asphyxiated himself. He was 72. There was no reason, no explanation, and no note, from this artist who, as Donald Keene writes, "said that he neither admired nor could sympathize with suicide." What remained were simply articles of *yugen*: a hose for inhaling gas, the body of Japan's Nobel laureate, and an *oeuvre* of exquisite prose. Perhaps this transcendence, as concise and ambiguous as a palm-of-the-hand story, was simply part of Kawabata's ongoing exploration of the vastness of the asymmetrical garden.

Martin Lebowitz   (essay date 1991)

SOURCE: "The Mysterious East," in *The Virginia Quarterly Review,* Vol. 67, No. 4, Autumn, 1991, pp. 778-79.

[*In the essay below, Lebowitz maintains that the compression of detail in the stories in* Palm-of-the-Hand Stories *is reflective of aspects of both primitivism and sophistication in Japanese culture.*]

If, as historians have noted, giantism is an aspect of decadence, miniaturization—emblematic of love, tenacity, and control—expresses the mystique or teleology of a humane society. These stories [in **Palm-of-the-Hand Stories**] are rarely more than four pages in length. The particularity and concreteness of the Japanese mentality reflect a sort of primitive vitalism or vitality. Still, it is correct to say of all liberal, humane, and progressive societies that they embody, along with pristine elements of energy, formal prototypes that are civilizing in their implications and effect. So far as miniaturization partakes of the primeval energy of things, it reflects elements at once of primitivism and sophistication. One is tempted to say that the combination of these two factors defines civilization, as opposed, for one thing, to decadence.

In one of these stories, a character remarks that the girl he loves is remembered well, but only by his finger (!). Human association—"love"—particularly in our time, contains something so casual that it is nothing as much as physical or material contact. It is not simply violence or sex that accounts for such events but the random character of modern experience in which the immanence and imminence of disorder impart a physical ascendency to romanticism itself. Romantic materialism as an aspect of modernity is a notable subject, quite relevant here.

In the same story, snow is symbolic of repression. The woman in this story has "cold hair," and the hero is psychologically cold. This "coldness" reflects something essential to an advanced or cultivated association—the creative dialectic of passion and repression—plus that formal principle essential to functional progress. The elusive question is what here to define as primitive.

Kawabata died in April 1972, a suicide. A Nobel laureate (1968), his controlling themes are loneliness, love, time as something concrete both for the mystic and the rationalist, and perhaps above all death. Death for the Japanese mentality, as mystical as it is rationalistic, becomes a sort obsession for Kawabata, in respect to the tone of his writings and its pervasive overtones. Its overtones become a subject matter, and death is a controlling theme.

The publisher prints one of the stories on the dust jacket, called **"Love Suicides."** The protagonist takes a dislike to his wife and deserts her. Two years later, a letter comes from a distant land, saying, "Don't let the child bounce a rubber ball. It strikes at my heart." The wife complies. More and more letters come making similar requests. The wife continues to comply. Finally a letter from a different land insists, "don't make any sound at all, the two of you, not even the ticking of a clock!" Thus they cease eternally to make even the faintest sound. The husband lies down, curiously, beside them and dies, too.

On a prosaic level the theme is that husband and wife never parted, overcome rather by a fatal disenchantment or spell. The true theme is that the incongruity or ambivalence of so-called interpersonal relations is itself a type of suicide.

An old lady planning to sell her daughter to a strange man, possibly brutal and oppressive, confronts the bus driver who is to take them to their destination. The bus driver is the incarnation of courtesy and graciousness, and the lady remarks, "So it's your turn today . . . If she has you to take her there, Mr. Thankyou, she is likely to meet with good fortune. It's a sign that something good will happen." Is the view expressed here based on psychology, metaphysics, superstition, or mysticism? Or is it based on naturalism? Naturalism, too, is an effort to integrate moral and existential considerations. It is the philosophy of the Orient, particularly Japan and China, that suggests that the cultivated personality has it all over intellectualism as such.

The culture of the Orient, based on formalism, repression,

and teleology, is highly cultivated but not lacking in primitive overtones. This is a combination of attributes that may define the quality of humanistic society in any age. Yet again, it is not easy to define what, if anything, in this context is truly primitive.

Primitivism is a static relation to the past, an incarceration in the past. Primitivism may be defined as the opposite of moral development, which may be synonymous with development itself. Thus the question whether the culture of Japan is primitive or not—or in what degree—is not that easy. One might note that the alterations introduced by science are existential rather than moral, although they sometimes have more effects.

No doubt the cultures of Japan and China defy the conventional categories of primitive or retrograde as against progressive and enlightened. The essence of Japanese culture is sufficiently "advanced" without being decidedly humane to be better than much in the West. Without being truly liberal or "forward-looking," some cultures may be superior to others that are.

FURTHER READING

Criticism

Anderer, Paul. Review of *Palm-of-the-Hand Stories. The Journal of Asian Studies* 48, No. 4 (November 1989): 865-66.
    Admires the "sense of warmth and fragility" that "offsets the cool formalism of Kawabata's spare and rigorous method" in the stories in this volume.

Brown, Sidney DeVere. "Yasunari Kawabata (1899-1972): Tradition versus Modernity." *World Literature Today* 62, No. 3 (Summer 1988): 375-79.
    Retrospective survey that attempts to "put Kawabata in the context of his times and reconstruct those times . . . from the fragments about the world around the writers and artists, the dilettantes and lovely traditional Japanese women who inhabit his stories."

———. Review of *Palm-of-the-Hand Stories. World Literature Today* 64, No. 1 (Winter 1990): 197.
    Favorable assessment of the juxtaposition of images, the "spare, elliptical style," and the suggestiveness of the short pieces in this collection.

Dunlop, Lane. "Three Thumbprint Novels from the Japanese of Yasunari Kawabata." *Prairie Schooner* 53, No. 1 (Spring 1979): 1-10.
    Translations of three stories: "The Grasshopper and the Bell Cricket," "The Silverberry Thief," and "The Young Lady of Suruga."

Grigson, Geoffrey. "Stories by Kawabata." In his *The Contrary View: Glimpses of Fudge and Gold*, pp. 200-03. London: The Macmillan Press, 1974.
    Praises the "maximal artistry" evident in the stories in *House of the Sleeping Beauties.*

Jordan, Clive. "Sleeping and Waking." *New Statesman* 78, No. 2003 (1 August 1969): 153-54.
    Review of *House of the Sleeping Beauties* that extols the

way in which Kawabata "creates an elegiac sadness which comes from balancing life's rich potential against lost and limited opportunities" in the title story.

Makoto Ueda. "Kawabata Yasunari." In *Modern Japanese Writers and the Nature of Literature*, pp. 173-218. Stanford, Calif.: Stanford University Press, 1976.
    Broad-ranging interpretation of Kawabata's long and short fiction in relation to major literary theories and the views expressed in the author's own expository essays and criticism.

Stuewe, Paul. Review of *House of the Sleeping Beauties*. *Books in Canada* 12, No. 3 (26 March 1983): 26.
    Offers high praise for Kawabata's writing, which "confronts the most basic contradictions of human life with poise and serenity, and makes high art of the existential ebb and flow that will ultimately lay us low."

Additional coverage of Kawabata's life and career is contained in the following sources published by Gale Research: *Contemporary Authors*, Vols. 93-96, 33-36 (rev. ed.); and *Contemporary Literary Criticism*, Vols. 2, 5, 9, 18.

Stephen King

1947-

(Full name Stephen Edwin King; has also written under the pseudonyms Richard Bachman and John Swithen) American novelist, short story and novella writer, scriptwriter, director, critic, and nonfiction writer.

INTRODUCTION

King is a prolific author of best-selling horror and suspense fiction. In his novels and stories, he blends elements of the traditional gothic tale with those of the detective story, the modern psychological thriller, and science fiction. His works feature colloquial language, clinical attention to settings, and an emphasis on contemporary problems, including marital infidelity and peer group acceptance, all of which lend credibility to the bizarre, often supernatural incidents that dominate his narratives.

Biographical Information

King was born in Portland, Maine. His father, a merchant sailor, left the family when King was a year old, leaving King's mother to support him and his older brother. King began writing short stories as a child, and while a student at Lisbon Falls high school in Maine he won an essay contest sponsored by a scholastic magazine. King published short stories in various magazines and completed manuscripts for many of his later novels while attending the University of Maine at Orono, earning a B. A. in English in 1970. After graduating, King took a position as an English instructor at the Hampden Academy in Hampden, Maine, where he stayed for two years. From 1978 to 1979, King served as a writer-in-residence at the University of Maine, and was granted the university's Career Alumni Award in 1981.

Major Works of Short Fiction

King has published several collections of short fiction, including *Night Shift* and *Skeleton Crew*, which are comprised of detective stories, science fiction, and horror tales, and other collections, such as *Different Seasons* and *Four Past Midnight*, which focus primarily on the terrors of everyday existence. In "Gray Matter," which appeared in *Night Shift*, Richie Grenadine, "a big fat man with jowls like pork butts and ham-hock arms," gradually mutates into a glob of gray protoplasm after a work-related injury forces him to stay at home, where he drinks a case of beer nightly. *The Body*, a novella that appeared in *Different Seasons*, is narrated by Gordie Lachance, a thirty-four-year-old writer modeled after King, and traces the narrator's coming-of-age experience when, as a ten year old, he and three friends set out to find the body of a young boy who had been hit by a train. *The Body* was adapted as a screenplay and was produced as the film *Stand By Me* in

1986. *The Library Policeman*, which appeared in *Four Past Midnight*, expands on the childhood myth of policemen who are sent by the library to arrest children whose books are overdue. In "The Ten O'Clock People," collected in *Nightmares and Dreamscapes*, smokers who limit themselves to a few cigarettes a day are the only people who can see the hideous aliens intent upon taking over the planet because these smokers belong to a personality type that is not susceptible to the psychological disguise worn by the aliens.

Critical Reception

Many critics fault King for unwieldy and lengthy narratives, one-dimensional characters, hackneyed subjects and use of cliches, excessively vulgar language, and frequent digressions, but credit King's ability to create scenarios in which eerie, supernatural events occur in everyday settings and involve ordinary characters, a combination that makes the situations more plausible and realistic, and consequently more frightening and compelling to the reader. Although some critics agree with Paul Gray, who referred to King as the "master of post-literate prose," many commentators have praised King's talent for writing stories that appeal to a broad audience and affect his readers on many levels. Robert Cormier has commented: "King still writes like one possessed, with all the nervous energy of a young writer seeking his first big break. He never cheats the reader, always gives full measure. . . . He is often brilliant, and makes marvelous music, dark and sinister."

PRINCIPAL WORKS

Short Fiction

Night Shift   1978
Different Seasons   1982
Skeleton Crew   1985
Four Past Midnight   1990
Nightmares and Dreamscapes   1993

Other Major Works

Carrie   (novel)   1974
Salem's Lot   (novel)   1975
*Rage [as Richard Bachman]   (novel)   1977
The Shining   (novel)   1977
The Stand   (novel)   1978
The Dead Zone   (novel)   1979
*The Long Walk [as Richard Bachman]   (novel)   1979
Firestarter   (novel)   1980
Cujo   (novel)   1981
*Roadwork [as Richard Bachman]   (novel)   1981
Stephen King's Danse Macabre   (nonfiction)   1981
The Dark Tower: The Gunslinger   (novel)   1982
*The Running Man [as Richard Bachman]   (novel)   1982
Christine   (novel)   1983
Cycle of the Werewolf   (novel)   1983; also published as *Silver Bullet*, 1985
Pet Sematary   (novel)   1983
The Talisman [with Peter Straub]   (novel)   1984
*Thinner [as Richard Bachman]   (novel)   1984
IT   (novel)   1986
The Dark Tower: The Drawing of the Three   (novel)   1987
Misery   (novel)   1987
The Tommyknockers   (novel)   1987
The Dark Half   (novel)   1989
The Dark Tower: The Waste Lands   (novel)   1991
Needful Things   (novel)   1991
Gerald's Game   (novel)   1992
Dolores Claiborne   (novel)   1993

*These five novels were collected in 1984 as *The Bachman Books.*

CRITICISM

Michael Mewshaw   (essay date 1978)

SOURCE: A review of *Night Shift*, in *The New York Times Book Review,* March 26, 1978, pp. 13, 23.

[*Mewshaw is an American novelist, short story writer, non-fiction writer, and critic. In the following review, he provides a negative assessment of* Night Shift.]

Still in his early 30's, Stephen King has already produced three novels—*Carrie, Salem's Lot* and *The Shining*—which, by a process as eerie and unfathomable as their spooky plots, mutated into "packages." (A "package," for anyone not familiar with lit-biz argot, is a thin envelope of words, flexible enough to contain huge volumes of money and hot air. Once floated in book form, it is likely to become a best seller, then a "major motion picture" or a short television series.) Having signed a multibook contract for more than $1 million, Mr. King has now published a collection of his short stories, most of which first appeared in *Cavalier* magazine, and there seems little likelihood that ***Night Shift*** won't be commercially successful.

Yet for all this, Mr. King remains disarmingly modest. In a foreword he concedes that much horror fiction is formulaic and that he is "not a great artist." He is simply obsessed by the subject of fear, wants to convey this obsession as palpably as possible, and believes he can best do so by emphasizing "story value." "Characterization, theme, mood, none of these things is anything if the story is dull."

Some of his plots are indeed imaginative, even ingenious. In **"Gray Matter"** a beer-swilling slob metastasizes into a loathsome, oozing monster that reproduces like an amoeba. In **"Battleground"** a professional hit man is attacked by toy soldiers—an amusing variation on Gulliver among the Lilliputians. In **"Trucks"** motorized vehicles declare war on man.

But it seems not to have occurred to Mr. King that style is crucial to story, as are characterization and theme. His own characters seldom serve any purpose save as ballast for his bizarre plots, and because he has no greater ambition than to shock, his best stories have about as much thematic content as Gahan Wilson's macabre cartoons. His worst stories strain mightily to generate one last *frisson*, using twist endings that should have died with O. Henry, the hoariest cliches of the horror-tale subgenre ("I was shaking in my shoes") and lines that provoke smiles rather than terror ("Warwick was . . . eating a cold hamburger with great relish"). It's baffling to think that anybody might find these stories fascinating or frightening, but as Stephen King writes, "there's still strange things in the world."

Bill Crider   (essay date 1978)

SOURCE: A review of *Night Shift*, in *Best Sellers*, Vol. 38, No. 1, April, 1978, pp. 6-7.

[*Crider is an American novelist, educator, and critic. In the following review, he praises the realism of King's stories in* Night Shift.]

[The stories in Stephen King's *Night Shift*] all begin in our normal world, where everything is safe and warm. But in almost every instance, something slips, and we find ourselves in the nightmare world of the not-quite-real, where vampires walk, where there are demons to be summoned or exorcised, where innocent people suffer and die for reasons neither they nor we can quite understand, where there are (just as we had always feared) *things* in the cellar.

Such stories require a willing suspension of disbelief, of course, but they also require an author who is an expert manipulator, one who can make horror seem not only plausible but almost logical. King is an expert, and many of these stories will not be easily forgotten. Every smoker who has ever wanted to stop should read **"Quitters, Inc."** School teachers will get a chill from **"Sometimes They Come Back."** Afraid of rats? Read **"Graveyard Shift."** Hate machinery? Try **"Trucks"** or **"The Mangler."** Perhaps the latter is the best example of King's skill at what he does. The idea of a steam ironer possessed by a demon seems laughable, but no one who reads **"The Mangler"** is going to laugh for very long.

The narrator of **"Gray Matter"** says, "I am saying that there's things in the corners of the world that would drive a man insane to look 'em right in the face." Stephen King writes about the things in the corners, and he forces us to look into their faces.

Thomas Gifford   (essay date 1982)

SOURCE: "Stephen's Quartet," in *Book World—The Washington Post,* August 22, 1982, pp. 1-2.

[*Gifford is an American novelist and critic. In the following review, he lauds King's conversational writing style in* Different Seasons.]

It's not often that a single individual puts you in mind of both J. B. Priestley and Yogi Berra, but when someone does you might as well pay attention. An extraordinary occurrence. But then Stephen King, who managed this paradoxical feat, is not an ordinary writer. Though, to further confuse the issue, it is precisely King's remarkable ordinariness that makes him what he is, one of the world's best-selling authors—and one who pretty well dwarfs the meager talents with whom he customarily shares the tops of the lists. Before I further complicate my observations on King and his new collection of novellas, *Different Seasons,* let me get back to Priestley for a moment.

Priestley, in his working prime, which spanned 40-odd years, seemed all but unable to stop the flow of words from his pen. Most of the words were particularly well chosen, and as the cataract poured forth he built remarkably detailed, realistic worlds, novel after novel, play after play, however fanciful the themes. We were chatting about this enormous output one snowy spring day in his comfortable study and he fixed me with what must always have been intended by the expression "a gimlet eye" and said: "Gifford, the important thing is to do the work, keep writing,

whether you feel like it or not. Just keep it coming, let nothing get in your way."

I was reminded of this stricture recently as I regarded the apparently bottomless well of Stephen King's word supply. Like clockwork they come, *The Stand, The Shining, Cujo,* on and on, richly observed, full of the particular ordinariness of our lives and times—and worlds are built within each work, built and then dismantled in spasms of horror which have become his trademark. A Lovecraft for our times. Ozzie and Harriet and Beaver and Wally with brain tumors, and things that eat people held back by fraying ropes in damp cellars.

Now with *Different Seasons,* works written at different times following the completion of one novel or another, he's doing a king of Yogi Berra, showing he can hit the off-speed curve, the change-up well off the plate, and still drive a fastball to the opposite field. Let me explain. Berra used to say he could hit it if he could reach it. King has done some reaching—not to be confused with stretching, as in "stretching" his talent—and drilled some liners off the green monster of his own particular muse.

Each of the novellas herein reflects a slightly different tone, thus the "seasons" of the title, but the devoted will not be disappointed: each has a decidedly macabre quality. The first, and best *Rita Hayworth and Shawshank Redemption,* has some really lovely things in it—the story of two men in prison for a very long time, one unjustly convicted of murder and the other who has long ago paid for the murder he committed. How they deal with their lives, their friendship, and the quirky fate life has chosen for them makes for the kind of story that sticks in your mind.

The second story, *Apt Pupil,* is the most overtly startling of the four: a nightmare in which a teen-aged all-American lad discovers a Nazi relic, a war criminal, living in his idyllic California village. The symbiosis which develops between them is not subtle, not psychologically sophisticated, but utterly pathological. And it does make a hell of a story. The other two stories don't require description; they are more King. Which is sort of dumb sounding, but there is a crucial point about King.

He is obsessed by the piling up of words, incident, a cliché locked in time, values which represent a year unlike the years on each side of it, the rubbing of personalities upon one another—all the values of the traditional storyteller. His art lies in his artlessness. His prose style is utterly conversational: he is literally telling you the story. The constant references to pop culture, which might irritate in another writer, don't irritate here because King *is* pop culture, an artifact himself. He speaks the vernacular, the patois, and it informs his thought.

What can I say to make this point clearly? Try this: he is the storyteller his readers would want to be if they were indeed storytellers. In *A Man's a Man,* Bertolt Brecht says of Jeriah Jip, his Everyman hero, "He is one of us!" which explains everything, all the appeal. The important thing to acknowledge in King's immense popularity, and in the Niagara of words he produces is the simple fact that he can write. He can write without cheapening or trivializing himself or his audience. You may or may not enjoy these

stories but you won't feel cheated or demeaned by them.
They will entertain; they may disturb you only slightly, superficially. You will feel as if you've just stepped into a
time warp and seen a new episode of TV's *Alfred Hitchcock Presents* or *The Twilight Zone* or *The Outer Limits.*
I am convinced that King is aiming roughly at that response.

Wait. Let me try again. I think I've got it. Think of Stephen King and Steven Spielberg; work on that simple
equation. One with words, the other with images. Elemental story values, broad strokes. You begin to grasp an explanation of both phenomena. *E.T., Poltergeist, Close Encounters, Jaws, Carrie, The Shining, Firestarter, Cujo . . .
Raiders of the Lost Ark,* **Different Seasons.**

Such popular phenomena represent accomplishments and
impulses our culture has no need to be ashamed of. And
these days that is cause for rejoicing.

Kenneth Atchity   (essay date 1982)

SOURCE: "Stephen King: Making Burgers with the
Best," in *Los Angeles Times Book Review,* August 29,
1982, p. 7.

[*Atchity is an American poet, editor, educator, and critic.
In the following review, he offers a positive assessment of*
Different Seasons.]

In the afterword to [**Different Seasons**], Stephen King
calls his "stuff " "fairly plain, not very literary, and sometimes (although it hurts like hell to admit it) downright
clumsy." He summarizes a career of horror novels as
"plain fiction for plain folks, the literary equivalent of a
Big Mac and a large fries from McDonald's."

To find the secret of his success, you have to compare
King to Twain, Poe—with a generous dash of Philip Roth
and Will Rogers thrown in for added popular measure.
King's stories tap the roots of myth buried in all our
minds. No wonder he's popular: He understands people.

King's visionary flights in these four novellas show us the
natural shape of the human soul—a shape even more horrifying, for its protean masks, than the ghouls he has conjured up in the novels. His productivity is based on his
awareness that audience psychology responds to the simple elements of fiction, presented directly: "The tale, not
the teller."

In **Rita Hayworth and Shawshank Redemption,** he hooks
us blatantly with the narrator's predicted triumph. Within
a page or so, he can admit the falseness of the hook—and
we don't care. For King, the art is to reveal the art. We
adore the special effects.

The story shows men painting out of the darkest corners:
" . . . It was as if Tommy had produced a key which fit
a cage in the back of his mind, a cage like his own cell.
Only instead of holding a man, that cage held a tiger, and
that tiger's name was Hope. Williams had produced the
key that unlocked the cage and the tiger was out, willy-
nilly, to roam his brain."

In **The Body,** King shows his skill at assuming a young-

ster's character, at the same time expressing how Americans sound not at their best but in their everyday voices:

> Different strokes for different folks, they say
> now, and that's cool. So if I say summer to you,
> you get one set of private, personal images that
> are all the way different from mine. That's cool.
> But for me, summer is always going to mean
> running down the road to the Florida Market
> with change jingling in my pockets, the tempera-
> ture in the gay nineties, my feet dressed in
> Keds . . . the GS&WM railroad tracks running
> into a perspective-point in the distance, bur-
> nished so white under the sun that when you
> closed your eyes you could still see them there
> in the dark, only blue instead of white.

The narrator tells us why he joined his friends on their expedition into self-terrorizing: "I went because of the shadows that are always somewhere behind our eyes . . . the
darkness on the edge of town . . . and at one time or another I think everyone wants to dare that darkness in spite
of the jalopy bodies that some joker of a God gave us
human beings. No . . . not in spite of our jalopy bodies
but because of them."

Moments of confession sneak into this story, without de-
tracting from its momentum. The narrator is, like King,
a writer:

> My wife, my kids, my friends—they all think
> that having an imagination like mine must be
> quite nice; aside from making all this dough, I
> can have a little mind-movie whenever things get
> dull. Mostly they're right. But every now and
> then it turns around and bites . . . you with
> these long teeth, teeth that have been filed to
> points like the teeth of a cannibal. You see things
> you'd just as soon not see, things that keep you
> awake until first light.

The most chilling story in the collection, perhaps the most
horrifying King has published to date, is **Apt Pupil,** subtitled "Summer of Corruption."

" 'Great!' Todd said. 'I want to hear all about it.'

"Dussander's eyes squeezed closed, and then opened slowly. 'You don't understand. I do not wish to speak of it.'

" 'You will, though. If you don't, I'll tell everyone who
you are. . . . Today I want to hear about the gas ovens,'
Todd said. 'How you baked the Jews.' His smile beamed
out, rich and radiant. . . . "

The repulsion of the all-American newsboy extorting from
the dying Nazi the chilling details of his role in the war
is bad enough, but what evokes the infernal depths of
human nature is the transfer of evil and inhumanity from
one to the other by story's end. The boy is innocent no longer, and the reader recognizes his own face in King's mirror:

"Todd smiled at him. And incredibly—certainly not because he wanted to—Dussander found himself smiling
back."

King's afterword describes his conversations with editor
Bill Thompson concerning his career. Thompson was

afraid King might be typed as a horror writer—just as Alan Rinsler, his present editor, later expressed his fear that King might stop publishing horror. King allowed that things could be worse: "I could, for example, be an 'important' writer like Joseph Heller and publish a novel every seven years or so, or a 'brilliant' writer like John Gardner and write obscure books for bright academics who eat macrobiotic foods and drive old Saabs with faded but still legible GENE MCCARTHY FOR PRESIDENT stickers on the rear bumpers."

Whatever King and his editors decide about his image, our appetite for his McDonald's shows no signs of abating.

Alan Cheuse   (essay date 1982)

SOURCE: "Horror Writer's Holiday," in *The New York Times Book Review,* August 29, 1982, pp. 10, 17.

[*Cheuse is an American novelist, short story writer, autobiographer, and critic. In the following review of* Different Seasons, *he articulates King's strong points and shortcomings as a fiction writer.*]

"The most important things lie close to wherever your secret heart is buried, like landmarks to a treasure your enemies would love to steal away. And you may make revelations that cost you dearly only to have people look at you in a funny way, not understanding what you've said at all, or why you thought it was so important that you almost cried while you were saying it. That's the worst, I think. When the secret stays locked within not for want of a teller but for want of an understanding ear."

Thus speaks Gordie Lachance, millionaire horror-writer and narrator of *The Body,* one of four short novels bound together within the covers of *Different Seasons,* horror-writer Stephen King's ninth work of fiction. Over the last decade Mr. King has certainly not wanted for ears; he is one of the most popular writers of our era. But unlike other vulgar—in the root sense of speaking in the voice of and to the average person—best-selling authors, Mr. King seems to have remained unsatisfied by mere popularity. As the speech of his fictional counterpart seems to suggest, the author of some of the best horror stories since those of Ambrose Bierce and H. P. Lovecraft may want more than acceptance. And it's precisely this quest for understanding, the drive to make his vision not only well known but deeply felt, that appears to have led him to publish this uneven, though often surprising, volume.

The first surprise comes early: The opening prison narrative titled *Rita Hayworth and Shawshank Redemption* shows us that the creator of such studies of the criminal mind as *The Shining* and *The Dead Zone* can effectively treat innocence as well as guilt. Set in a fictional state penitentiary in the author's home state of Maine, the tale is told in the first person by Red, a prisoner and entrepreneur who has as one of his best customers a former banker and convicted murderer, Andy Dufresne. Dufresne stands out among the lifers in the yard long before Red discovers his real story; the man is a cultivated type who, even as he's fighting off the brutal sexual advances of Shawshank's population of "sisters," apparently spends his time alone

shaping and polishing pieces of quartz from the yard. This dedication to an art form of sorts impresses Red, who thought he had seen it all:

> First the chipping and shaping, and then the almost endless polishing and finishing with those rock-blankets. Looking at them [a pair of cuff links Dufresne has given him in exchange for a favor], I felt the warmth that any man or woman feels when he or she is looking at something pretty, something that has been *worked* and *made*—that's the thing that really separates us from the animals, I think—and I felt something else, too. A sense of awe for the man's brute persistence.

It's difficult to imagine any reader feeling a sense of awe at the way Mr. King bullies his way through this tough-guy novella about Dufresne's struggle to establish his innocence and free himself by any means possible, but the piece does give off a certain warmth. And if it's not "pretty," it is still an admirable departure from the genre that made the author famous.

Apt Pupil, the second and longest narrative in the volume, also stands as the most disappointing. It is a psychological study of the tandem corruption of Todd Bowden, a Southern California high-school student, and Kurt Dussander, the Nazi war criminal he discovers in his own hometown. The story links the sunny present of America with the nightmare past of death camps and all of what Todd calls their "gooshy" atrocities. Big theme here—but in execution the piece comes off as somewhat silly, with the tone wavering between that of cartoon images from horror comic books and the worst variety of pulp fiction: "He tasted life on his tongue like a draught of wine straight from the bottle." When Dussander cremates his cat in the kitchen oven, the novella begins to reek of more than baking feline flesh. And later, when each of this unlikely pair begins a series of murders, the stench may prove overpowering.

But if Mr. King stumbles in *Apt Pupil,* he picks himself up again and continues at a fast clip with *The Body,* which is narrated by his doppelgänger, Gordie Lachance. In this supposed memoir we return to the scene of a number of crimes from Mr. King's earlier fiction—Castle Rock, Me., the setting of *The Dead Zone* and *Cujo*—but the style here is once again in the psychological rather than the supernatural mode. Narrator Lachance takes us back to the initiation rite that may have formed him as a successful writer—the overnight trek into the Maine woods he took with three other working-class friends in search of another teenager's rotting corpse. He sees the story as one of those revelations that exact a high price emotionally but help a writer to understand his past and "get ready for some future mortality." There's some pretentiousness to Lachance's tale, especially in the inclusion of two stories that he published in little magazines early in his career, some swipes at writers such as John Gardner (who, ironically, professes to be one of Mr. King's greatest fans), praise of Ralph Ellison, and some Mailerlike conceit ("And although no one is ever going to call me the Thomas Wolfe of my generation, I rarely feel like a cheat. . . ."). But there's a lot to admire in this recollection of dead and dead-end kids—and a scene in which the boys attempt to cross a railroad trestle as the tracks begin to hum may induce a permanent fear of hiking.

Readers who fear that Mr. King may have hiked permanently out of the territory in which they love to see him travel will be reassured to learn that in *The Breathing Method,* the final novella in this collection, he returns to the horror story as a conquering hero. Tipping his hat to, among others, Jorge Luis Borges and Peter Straub, he invents a New York City men's club whose members gather for an annual pre-Christmas terror-telling session. Here other voices whisper in other rooms, and a genteel physician turns something as contemporary as the Lamaze Method into a vehicle for a frightening fiction about old New York. The natural narrative force that previously has helped Mr. King overcome his often clumsy prose and sophomoric philosophizing churns through these pages stronger than ever before; and yet he's never written anything that seems so polished and finished.

As a collection *Different Seasons* is flawed and out of balance, but that shouldn't deter anyone with a taste for interesting popular fiction. Each of the first three novellas has its hypnotic moments, and the last one is a horrifying little gem.

David Morrell, Alan Ryan, and Charles L. Grant (essay date 1982)

SOURCE: "Different Writers on *Different Seasons,*" in *Shadowings: The Reader's Guide to Horror Fiction: 1981-1982,* edited by Douglas E. Winter, Starmont House, 1983, pp. 38-43.

[*Morrell, Ryan, and Grant are all noted authors of horror and suspense fiction. In the following forum, which originally appeared in the journal* Fantasy Newsletter *in 1982, they each provide an analysis of one of the four novellas in the collection* Different Seasons.]

[David Morrell on *Rita Hayworth and Shawshank Redemption*:]

Writers can be loosely separated into two groups—those who put in and those who take out. So F. Scott Fitzgerald believed. By this standard, anyone familiar with the work of Stephen King knows which category he belongs in. He's a putter-inner. He develops, amplifies, elaborates. His prose is packed with evocative descriptive details; his plots are crammed with twists and turns. We find exceptions, of course: his first novel, *Carrie,* is fairly short and lean, as is *The Mist.* A few of his short stories (**"Strawberry Spring,"** for example) move along briefly and simply. For the most part, though, he tends toward bigness and fullness. A recently completed novel, *IT,* runs to almost 1300 manuscript pages. *The Gunslinger,* one of his many publications this year, is a part of an epic, *The Dark Tower,* that he estimates will eventually reach 3000 manuscript pages. Putter-inner indeed.

The impressive scope and density of his work is matched by the variety of forms he has turned to: short stories, novels, screenplays, essays, a non-fiction book about horror, and a comic book adaptation of his movie *Creepshow.*

What was left for him to do? His latest book, *Different Seasons,* provides the answer. Somewhere between the short story and the novel lies a literary twilight zone called the novella. Roughly 30,000 words, it can't be called short, but it's not exactly long either — a half-breed, if you will. In an afterword, King explains that following *Salem's Lot, The Shining, The Dead Zone* and *Firestarter* he had "just enough gas left in the tank to throw off" one of these. Now all four are collected here.

Their subject seems as new to him as their format. Only one of the pieces belongs to the horror genre with which King's readers associate him, though some horrific passages do appear in two others. Alan Ryan . . . and Charles Grant will discuss them in the . . . reviews that follow. My own responsibility is the first novella, *Rita Hayworth and Shawshank Redemption,* which isn't horrific at all. Not to worry, though. I bring good news—it's wonderful, moving, entertaining. King is a master story-teller, no matter what kind of subject he writes about. Assuming you've read it (or plan to), I'll avoid discussing the plot, except to note that it's set in a prison and deals with the friendship between two convicts serving life terms. There's action, mystery, sentiment, an uplifting theme, a surprise conclusion. I read it at forty-thousand feet and never once remembered to grip the arms of my seat to hold the plane up. The reason I began this brief review by discussing King as a putter-inner is that I can't get over the amount of story King stuffs into this novella's 100 pages. Another writer might have taken three times the space and still not achieved the density King does. Lots of vivid description, plenty of interesting background, plot complications galore, and all this texture is combined with speed. I attribute this amazing effect to King's understanding of the novella format. Too long to be short, too short to be long. The paradox results in characteristics normally associated with either the short story or the novel but not with both. In choosing this format, King gets the best of both extremes. Of course, the format alone can't account for the success of *Rita Hayworth and Shawshank Redemption* (the title, by the way, is cleverly related to the plot). In an epigraph, King warns us to trust the tale, not its teller. Frankly, I'd just as soon trust the teller, and in this case, my trust paid off.

. . . . .

[Alan Ryan on *Apt Pupil*:]

Like many writers, I spend a lot of time standing around in bookstores. Very often, the remarks one overhears are at least as interesting as the latest titles just appearing on the shelves. For a writer, listening to random, unsolicited comments in front of the "Bestseller" or "New Releases" shelves can be a very instructive and revealing exercise.

I heard a great deal of comment on *Cujo* when it was first published in hardcover. I heard more comments on it when, a year later, the paperback arrived. I heard people talking about it with friends and with clerks and cashiers. They hated it.

In the Barnes & Noble Bookstore on New York's Eighth Street, an outlet with an unusually high percentage of sophisticated, experienced readers, one asked a friend if she had read it. "Oh, I hated it," the friend replied. "I read all his other books and liked them, but this one was too much. It's just savage and cruel. The way he tortures everybody . . ."

Much could be said in response to this, of course, but I think the woman's meaning is clear. She simply does not wish to believe that the world is such a difficult, demanding, and often cruel place in which to live, that reality can be so damned harsh. If that woman presses on and continues to read Stephen King's work—and I'm satisfied that she will—she is going to be one very disturbed lady when she finishes *Apt Pupil.*

King's story-telling rests on a solid bedrock of reality and, to a very large extent, it is this casual realism that makes his everyday horrors so unnerving. Todd Bowden, the "apt pupil" of the second story in *Different Seasons,* is thirteen years old and, King tells us in the very first sentence, "the total all-American kid." When we first see him, he is delivering newspapers, riding "his twenty-six-inch Schwinn," and wearing "Nike running shoes."

On that first page, Todd is blond, blue-eyed, and "smiling a summer vacation smile." Much later in the story, when he smiles again, it looks very different indeed. "Todd smiled: a weird upward corkscrewing of the lips. A strange sardonic light danced and fluttered in his eyes." And on the last page: "He was smiling excitedly, his eyes dancing . . . the excited smile of tow-headed boys going off to war."

> King manages in *Apt Pupil* to make the story both realistically particular and universally applicable, creating a kind of double-whammy of horror for the reader. He gets us involved with the actual characters and at the same time lets us know, through their very realism, the quality that makes them so much like us, that they could, with little more than a name transplant, actually be us.
>
> —*Alan Ryan*

Much, of course, has happened along the way. Todd has met and become inextricably tied—both circumstantially and psychologically—to Kurt Dussander, an ex-commandant of a Nazi concentration camp, now living out his last years under an alias in the California sunshine. Under the unwilling but detailed tutelage of Dussander, Todd is drawn more and more into a fatally entangling web constructed of Dussander's recollections and his own dark taste for horror. He especially likes, as we all do sometimes, the "gooshy" parts, something to keep in mind the next time you hear the traffic reporter on the radio warning about rubber-necking delays at the site of an auto accident.

It may just be, King leads us to suspect in *Apt Pupil,* that there is nothing about smiling Todd Bowden in *particular,* as an individual, that leads him down the same path Kurt Dussander has followed, a path of random violence and bloodshed, crimes directed not at individuals but at anyone who happens to come along the road. Rather, when we view the story on an allegorical level (or simply react to it on an allegorical level, as that lady in the bookstore unconsciously does), we suspect that, as with the events in *Cujo,* the story could just as readily take place next door . . . or, worse still, just down the hall or around the corner or even in the mirror. If "the things that live in the catacombs" ever get out, King suggests, "most of them would look like ordinary accountants. . . . And some of them might look like Todd Bowden."

King manages in *Apt Pupil* to make the story both realistically particular and universally applicable, creating a kind of double-whammy of horror for the reader. He gets us involved with the actual characters and at the same time lets us know, through their very realism, the quality that makes them so much like us, that they could, with little more than a name transplant, actually be us.

I don't think the unhappy lady in the bookstore is going to like *Apt Pupil* any more than she liked *Cujo.*

. . . . .

[Charles L. Grant on *The Breathing Method*:]

Literary critics are perhaps too fond on occasion of proclaiming certain narrative frameworks outdated. Stories told in the form of letters and/or journals are supposedly passé, as are those whose narrator is sitting at a campfire or in a train compartment or in a club room. Style (the manner in which an author puts his words together) does, of course, change with the times when we are speaking of so-called popular literature.

There are styles which, by virtue of the author's power with words, transcend the contemporary. And no critic who has ever lived has yet been able to travel into the future in order to see just which style has that particular transcendence.

By the same token, it is sheer folly to deny an author a literary framework simply because it has been used before, no matter how often, no matter how popular it once was.

A true storyteller uses whatever works for the story being told; and there are few better frameworks than a narrator sitting down with an audience (both within and beyond the fiction itself) and saying: "I am going to tell you a story. You can believe it or not as you will, but it happened."

Stephen King, perhaps the time's premier storyteller, isn't afraid to resurrect "old" frameworks. One of these is the club setting. He has used it twice—in **"The Man Who Could Not Shake Hands"** and now in *The Breathing Method.* And in both instances he has also exhibited the understanding that, in the best of these types, there is always more than one story being told—the main story, which is ended by the last page, and peripheral ones dealing with the club members, which may or may not end before the narrator is finished.

What is marvelous about the club at 249B East 35th Street is its uniqueness. It is at the same time Kiplingesque and King—not an ordinary club, not an ordinary building, its staff very far from ordinary indeed. One does not go to 249B and listen to a story; one goes, listens and experiences rather odd things. The narrator of *The Breathing Method,* David, is at once telling the story he heard and the story he has lived over the years he has been going to the club—"if it is a club."

The Breathing Method itself (that tale told by member Emlyn McCarran) is King speaking with a different voice, less colloquial and less emotional than usual; in that respect, perhaps less powerful than it might have been. But it succeeds in spite of this because of the setting—where the emotion and the power come from those listening rather than the speaker.

In this case, the club motto—"It is the tale, not he who tells it"—is more than accurate, because the tale of a doctor and his young female patient gains depth not from its particulars, but from eliciting reactions, especially from David.

There will be calls, I would imagine, for more stories to come from 249B—and I am certainly doing the same. Yet there is one I don't want to know—how how the club was created, who "Stevens" really is and what is really upstairs—because it is not always what you say, but what you don't say, that brings the chill in spite of the fire on the grate.

Algis Budrys (essay date 1983)

SOURCE: A review of *Different Seasons,* in *Fantasy & Science Fiction,* Vol. 64, No. 2, February, 1983, pp. 61-9.

[*Budrys is a Russian-born novelist, short story writer, editor, and critic. In the following review, he lauds King's storytelling method in* Different Seasons, *comparing King's style to that of Roald Dahl and John Steinbeck.*]

Different Seasons, a collection of four novellas by Stephen King, is an excellent piece of reading. Although one of the stories is little more than a set-piece in imitation of Roald Dahl, and another is most interesting as a gritty documentary on life in a state penitentiary, garnished by a slight and anti-climactic tale of romanticized escape, the other two stories are towering achievements.

One of these is in many ways conventional King horror-fantasy; that is, it gains its effects by concretizing a fantasy so horrible none of us will openly admit we all have it. But Todd Bowen—one of King's patented big-eyed All-American teenagers—does not shrink from the possibilities. When he uncovers the hidden Nazi concentration camp commander and makes him his prisoner, his object is to hear, to his heart's salivating content, what it felt like to have that species of absolute power.

But there are traces in that story of something even deeper, and certainly less cheap. The growing contention be-

tween the psychotic golden boy and the utterly rational Nazi reveals tensions and uncovers complexities in the human condition that you will not find in *Cujo, Firestarter,* or most other King blockbusters. Soon enough, the story degenerates into bang, bang, slash slash, but for a moment—a moment that might cause actual discomfort to readers who take to King as a horse takes to a nosebag—it has trembled on the brink of being painted in something besides primary colors.

[*The Body*] threw me and continues to throw me, and here is how and why:

In a little Maine town, four boys trembling on the verge of pubescence are living their last summer before they turn into the kinds of shits their older brothers are; before they set foot on the pathways that lead inevitably to being as drunken, shiftless and contemptible as their fathers are. Having learned the location of another boy's body—he was an outsider, wandering alone in the woods, and was killed by a train—they set out to "find" it and claim its discovery.

The actual discovery is made by one of the older boys; shiftless, dissolute, and going where he had no business to be, that boy is constrained from announcing the find. He does discuss it where his younger brother overhears him. So, when the four young boys set out on a journey of many miles overnight along the railroad track, having carefully provisioned themselves, concocted a cover story, and systematically heartened themselves, what they are affirming is not only their superior energy and ingenuity but the power of purity. They are saying that it is not inevitable to succumb to the shot-and-beer joint and the laborer's job; that the despair of their elders is not justified.

Now, I submit to you, folks, that this story, set, incidentally, in the same town as *Cujo,* and beset by the same love/ignorance for cars—King speaks of a "Hearst" shifter, and makes several other trivial but astonishing errors in an area where he flatly claims knowledgeability—I submit to you, folks, that this story is not only literature but major literature, at least in first draft. Furthermore, although it has its flat spots and other problems typical of first drafts, it essentially sustains its pitch throughout. Stephen King is—and obviously long has been—the peer of John Steinbeck and several other guys. I mention Nobelist Steinbeck because he is the one whose work King's *The Body* most resembles, and in some respects—its astonishing ability to depict real adolescents, for one—excels.

These four stories all came about in a curious manner. They are spurts of leftover energy. Each was written immediately after one of King's big novels, and, presumably, was written purely because King wanted to, and hardly cared where, when, and if it would sell. I think there is a major datum—and a cheap shot—in pointing out that the slick, essentially empty fantasy of *Breathing Method* is the latest, while *The Body* is the earliest.

There is another datum, and another shot, in pointing out that the narrator of *The Body*—one of the exploring boys—is a storyteller, proto-writer, and, in later years, the author of a couple of collegiate literary short stories. These are reproduced within the text of *The Body.* The narrator—who turns out to be a rather older man, remembering the events of his boyhood—professes to see them as essentially trivial. Personally, I found the one rather promising and the other funnier than hell, but they're his stories and I suppose he's entitled to judge them. The thing is, you see, this older narrator looking back both on boyhood and on his naive collegiate literary aspirations, has now grown up to be Gordon LaChance, world-famous author of blockbuster horror novels for the mass market, a condition in which he says he is content.

Douglas E. Winter   (essay date 1984)

SOURCE: "The Mist" and "Different Seasons," in *Stephen King: The Art of Darkness,* New American Library, 1984, pp. 86-94, 104-11.

[*Winter is an American fiction writer and critic. In the following essays, he examines* The Mist *and* Different Seasons.]

In *The Mist*, Stephen King conjures the quintessential faceless horror: a white opaque mist that enshrouds the northeastern United States (if not the world) as the apparent result of an accident at a secret government facility. This short novel is a paradigm of the complicated metaphors of Faustian experimentation and technological horror consistently woven into the fiction of Stephen King. Those who read *The Mist* will not likely forget the haunting inability of its characters to comprehend, let alone explain, what is happening to them. It has been claimed that the central fantasy of horror fiction is "that the unknowable can be known and related to in some meaningful fashion" [John Cawelti, *Adventure, Mystery and Romance,* 1976]. *The Mist* completely belies that view, presenting a chilling dislocation in which horror and mystery are no less adequate than science, religion, or materialism to explain the human condition. As in Kafka's *The Metamorphosis* (1937), the whys and wherefores are secondary, even tertiary, as King unveils a reality that cannot be solved and, indeed, that cannot even be understood. In so doing, he demolishes the artifices through which we perceive reality, noting how much science, religion, and materialism shape our thinking and our lives, and questioning whether these shapes are desirable.

The technological horror theme is an obvious exploitation of the subversive tendencies of horror fiction. The common interpretation of the massive interest in supernatural fiction in the late 1800s, when many classic ghost stories were published, is that these stories represented the "swan song" of an earlier, pre-technological way of life. That view is put forward often to explain the current upsurge of interest in macabre fiction and film. Charles L. Grant has noted that horror fiction serves as "the dark side of Romanticism," not simply a medium of escape but a rejection of the real horror and skepticism generated by our technological civilization in favor of a sentimental vision that confirms the possibility of the unknown. It thus seems quite logical that the contemporary horror story often utilizes an exaggeration or extrapolation of modern technology as its surrogate for the unknown, operating as a cautionary tale that simultaneously rejects technology while

reassuring the reader that things could nevertheless be worse.

The halcyon years of "technohorror" were the 1950s, when fear of the ultimate possibilities of mankind's technology, omened by the nuclear devastation of Hiroshima and Nagasaki, was exposed at the visceral and readily dismissed level of the grade B science fiction movie. As the 1960s and 1970s progressed, celluloid unrealities called *Them* (1954) and *The Beginning of the End* (1957) were hauntingly evoked in grim realities with equally colorful names like Agent Orange, Three Mile Island, and Love Canal. Our belated awareness of the negative implications of technology, coupled with growing doubts about the ability of technology to solve the complex problems of modern society, has rendered "technohorror" a theme of undeniable currency, requiring the horror writer to take but a simple step beyond front-page news.

As a child of the fifties whose anxieties were fed by B movies and whose "fall from the cradle" occurred with the sublime intersection of *Earth vs. the Flying Saucers* and the launching of the Soviet Sputnik satellite, it seems only natural that Stephen King has written about "technohorror" since his earliest efforts at fiction. His high school story **"I Was a Teenage Grave Robber"** concerned the monstrous results of secret experiments with corpses, while his first serious attempt at a novel, *The Aftermath*—also written during high school—depicted a postholocaust world molded by the directives of a computer that scientists could no longer control. Although *Carrie* included a suggestion of genetic mutation, *The Stand* was King's first published novel to probe in depth the fears generated by technological civilization. Both *The Stand* and *Firestarter* linked science and authority in an amoral tryst, yet concluded with an optimistic hope for new beginnings. In *The Mist*, King posits only the end.

David Drayton, the narrator of *The Mist*, is a commercial artist—a person whose career is devoted to creating artificial representations of human life. With his wife, Stephanie, and five-year-old son, Billy, Drayton leads an almost idyllic existence at a lakefront home near Bridgton, Maine—a replica of the home where King and his family lived from the summer of 1975 to the summer of 1977. Their life is shattered by a freakish summer storm that sends the Draytons to their cellar, where David has a remarkable precognitive dream—the very same dream, in fact, that caused Stephen King, after weathering such a storm, to write the story:

> I had a dream that I saw God walking across Harrison on the far side of the lake, a God so gigantic that above the waist He was lost in a clear blue sky. In the dream I could hear the rending crack and splinter of breaking trees as God stamped the woods into the shape of His footsteps. He was circling the lake, coming toward the Bridgton side, toward us, and behind Him everything that had been green turned a bad gray and all the houses and cottages and summer places were bursting into purple-white flame like lightning, and soon the smoke covered everything. The smoke covered everything like a mist.

In the morning, a peculiar mist brews over the lake. It is

moving across the water toward Bridgton—moving against the wind. When Drayton's wife asks what it is, Drayton thinks: " . . . the word that nearly jumped first from my mouth was *God.*"

Drayton drives his son and a neighbor into town to report downed electrical lines and to obtain grocery supplies. They find the Federal Foods Supermarket jammed with people. Speculation is rampant that something has gone wrong at the government's secret "Arrowhead Project" across the lake. As Drayton waits in the checkout line, he is distracted by an intangible concern. Billy interrupts his reverie, and Drayton observes: " . . . suddenly, briefly, the mist of disquiet that had settled over me rifted, and something terrible peered through from the other side— the bright and metallic face of pure terror."

The mist settles over the supermarket, and although many people rush out to view the peculiar phenomenon, none returns. Gradually, with fever-dream intensity, the "pure terror" infecting Drayton is animated as the monstrous inhabitants of the mist are divulged. Tentacles writhe out of the mist to snatch away a bag-boy; bug-things stretching four feet in length flop along the store windows, only to be gobbled up by pterodactyl-like monstrosities that plummet out of the mist. Huge spidery creepy-crawlers spin corrosive webs, and segmented parodies of lobsters crawl across the parking lot. The spawn of the mist seem endless in horrifying variety; but the mist, and what it signifies, is more important than its monsters: "It wasn't so much the monstrous creatures that lurked in the mist. . . . It was the mist itself that sapped the strength and robbed the will." The mist takes on a symbolic significance—it is the unknown, not only in a physical sense but as the realm of experimentation.

Conspicuous by its absence from *The Mist* is a stock character of the "technohorror" nightmare—the scientist. We are offered only straw men: two young soldiers trapped within the supermarket who commit gruesome suicide in confirmation of the feared source of the disaster. The culprits of the Arrowhead Project remain as faceless and opaque as the mist itself. And this only increases our unease; there is no patent lunatic or misguided zealot on which to foist our responsibility.

The Mist takes the form of a nightmarish, surreal disaster film. The besieged occupants of the supermarket are a representative sample of humanity, put to the test of the external threat of the mist and the internal claustrophobia— and madness—of the supermarket. They undergo hysteria and fragmentation, and acts of courage and of stupidity result only in bloodshed while the inevitable leadership struggles take place.

King deftly creates the tension between illogic, religion, and materialism that is his forte. Drayton's neighbor, a vacationing New York City attorney, proves not to be a pillar of objectivity or calm; rather, he heads a group of people—wryly described by Drayton as the "Flat Earth Society"—which simply refuses to believe in the disaster despite quite tangible evidence. They walk into the mist, to their deaths. Another group, which grows in number as time passes, believes perhaps too strongly in the disaster,

interpreting it as God's punishment. They are headed by Mrs. Carmody, an otherwise innocuous old lady given to folk tales and remedies, who seemingly thrives on the disaster. This group soon demands a human sacrifice in appeasement of the mist. A third group, including Drayton, attempts a rational, pragmatic solution to the horror. They construct defenses, fight off the intrusions of monsters, and ultimately undertake an ill-fated expedition to a neighboring pharmacy. Their failure gives credence to the increasing zealotry of Mrs. Carmody and leads Drayton to organize an escape effort.

Readily apparent in *The Mist* is the influence of George A. Romero, virtuoso director of the classic low-budget horror film *Night of the Living Dead* (1968) and its powerful sequel, *Dawn of the Dead* (1979). On one level, Romero's films plunder our dire unease with death and decay, hypothesizing that the dead will return to life with a singular hunger for human flesh. On another level, however, these films consider, in an intelligent and ironic sense, the horrific siege of reality. Romero terms his masterwork "an allegory meant to draw a parallel between what people are becoming and the idea that people are operating on many levels of insanity that are only clear to themselves." [*Filmmakers Newsletter,* quoted in Danny Peary, *Cult Movies,* 1981.]

In *Night of the Living Dead,* Romero's zombies trap a group of strangers within a deserted farmhouse. Romero inverts the commercially successful disaster film, supplanting melodrama with nihilistic abandon: the young, attractive lovers are killed in an escape attempt; the older businessman becomes a raving coward rather than a calculating, take-charge leader; the little girl turns on her mother, butchering her with a garden tool and then devouring her; the "token" black becomes the leader—and only survivor—of the defense, only to emerge the next morning so shattered by the experience that he is mistakenly shot as a zombie. The theme is replayed to an almost absurdist premise in *Dawn of the Dead* (which was produced after *The Mist* had been written, but before it was published), in which a similar band of survivors barricades itself within a suburban shopping mall.

The thematic parallels between *The Mist* and Romero's "Living Dead" films are numerous; perhaps more striking is the manner in which the imagery of *The Mist* evokes the intensely visual and visceral quality of film. "You're supposed to visualize the story in grainy black and white," notes King. Unlike any of King's earlier fiction of length, it is written entirely in first-person singular and structured on a scene-by-scene basis. And its narrator consistently repeats, as if in self-assurance, that the creatures of the mist are the stuff of grade B horror movies. Not only does King thereby reinforce the several levels of perspective; he presents an irony equal to that of the "just the flu" epitaph of his short story **"Night Surf "**—that the end of the world, when it comes, should indeed resemble a grade B horror movie.

The defense of the Federal Foods Supermarket takes on surreal aspects that intermingle shock and sardonic humor, paralleling the shopping mall confrontations of *Dawn of the Dead.* One of the pterodactyl-like creatures breaches the defenses, savaging a bystander before being set aflame. King recounts the incident with delightful imagery and an obvious send-up of the gravely serious narrator of traditional Gothic fiction:

> I think that nothing in the entire business stands in my memory so strongly as that bird-thing from hell blazing a zigzagging course above the aisles of the Federal Supermarket, dropping charred and smoking bits of itself here and there. It finally crashed into the spaghetti sauces, splattering Ragu and Prince and Prima Salsa everywhere like gouts of blood.

A bug-thing immediately clambers through the broken window, but before the male defenders can act, a sixty-year-old school teacher, Mrs. Reppler, charges with a can of Raid in each hand and sprays it to death.

Although clearly self-conscious, *The Mist* is not parody. Like George Romero, King attempts—and succeeds—in balancing a pandemonium seesaw whose ends are occupied by pure horror and outrageous black humor. We are disturbed by *The Mist* because, like its narrator, we do not know exactly what to do when confronted by its horrors: "I was making some sound. Laughing. Crying. Screaming. I don't know."

The typical disaster film produces a fascist answer—strong leadership will persevere, while the weak are dispensable. In *The Mist,* Stephen King, again like George Romero, holds differently: horror produces not the best but the worst in people, and when it does produce a semblance of good, that good is usually unrecognizable to the world outside. Drayton is less than a heroic figure; uncertain of the fate of his wife, he nevertheless feels compelled to have sex with another of the survivors, and he is drawn into the doomed expedition to the drugstore. Finally, under the compulsion of the growing religious mania of Mrs. Carmody and her followers—and of the simple urge to see the sun again—Drayton leads a tiny group to his Land Rover, again suffering the loss of two companions. By the novel's close, Drayton and his comrades are barricaded within a Howard Johnson's; only then does he ponder the difficulty of refueling—and only then does he face the possibility that the mist may go on forever.

The flight from the supermarket is Stephen King's most literal and most Lovecraftian night journey. Drayton's narrative has no ending in the traditional sense. His group is heading south, hoping for refuge from the dark and seemingly endless tunnel of the mist, but they find only a surreal landscape of desolation and monstrosity. Yet the ultimate horror is nearly unseen, and it is all the more horrible given Drayton's dream on the night before the coming of the mist:

> Something came; again, that is all I can say for sure. It may have been the fact that the mist only allowed us to glimpse things briefly, but I think it just as likely that there are certain things that your brain simply disallows. There are things of such darkness and horror—just, I suppose, as there are things of such great beauty—that they will not fit through the puny doors of human perception. . . .

> I don't know how big it actually was, but it passed directly over us. . . . Mrs. Reppler said later she could not see the underside of its body, although she craned her neck up to look. She saw only two Cyclopean legs going up and up into the mist like living towers until they were lost to sight.

This numinous vision, a nonrational confrontation with the apparently divine, omens the impossibility of escape. The growing sense of a mysterious profanity, latent in the religious hysteria of Mrs. Carmody, is manifest in this dark mirror-image of the God of Drayton's dream. Like *The Stand, The Mist* explicitly evokes Biblical stories of plagues embodying the wrath of God—and, of course, the archetypal story of the great flood. Although *The Stand* confirms the power of faith, *The Mist* refuses to offer a rainbow signaling man's triumph over adversity and the promise of a new day. As if animating Novalis's aphorism—"Where there are no gods, demons will hold sway"—King offers a universe without salvation, imbued with the feeling of one's own submergence—of being ant-like, trivial, before the footsteps of an unseeable God-thing.

For many readers, horror fiction is meaningful because its acceptance of the existence of evil implies the existence of good. Indeed, Russell Kirk contends [in *The Surly Suller Bell,* 1962] that supernatural fiction confirms "hierarchical" Christian values. *The Mist* is particularly terrifying because it proposes a transcendence of notions of good and evil, right and wrong; King moves his characters and readers through an ever-darkening universe of chaos and hostility. The line separating civilization from chaos—and indeed, life from extinction—has parted like the mist, and only "pure terror" remains.

The fiction of Stephen King offers no theological polemic, although—the aesthetics of *The Mist* notwithstanding—it does not embrace entirely the "cosmic pessimism" of H. P. Lovecraft. King's stories typically celebrate the existence of good, while graphically demonstrating its cost. In *Carrie, The Stand,* and *The Dead Zone,* King offers the intervention of God as a potential—and indeed, persuasive—explanation of events. His version of God harkens less to modern Christian values and their source, the New Testament, than to those of the Old Testament, and particularly the Book of Job. On the other hand, King's most optimistic and pessimistic novels, *Firestarter* and *Cujo,* ironically lack any explicit religious elements.

In *The Mist,* King uses religion as well as materialism not as a dramatic foil to horror, but as its counterpoint. Just as he pushes the aesthetics of horror to the limit, so too are the aesthetics of religion and materialism tested in the extreme. In *The Mist,* as in several of his novels—*Carrie, The Dead Zone,* and *The Talisman*—religious fanaticism is an artifice of control, the means by which its proponents impose the illusion of order upon a situation virulent with chaos. Similarly, the seeming obsession of David Drayton in *The Mist* with brand names and products—from an opening comparison of power saws to the final resting place at Howard Johnson's—reflects materialism as an artifice of control. The numinous vision climaxing *The Mist* profoundly disintegrates any remaining illusions of order—and indeed, suggests horribly that order may lie at the heart of chaos. King's lesson seems clear: that order—or at least release from chaos—cannot be imposed; if it exists, and to the degree that it exists, it will be discovered.

Writing about the horror story [in his "Introduction" to *The Arbor House Treasury of Horror and the Supernatural,* 1981], King has noted:

> The best tales in the genre make one point over and over again—that the rational world both within us and without us is small, that our understanding is smaller yet, and that much of the universe in which we exist is, so far as we are able to tell, chaotic. So the horror story makes us appreciate our own well-lighted corner of that chaotic universe, and perhaps allows a moment of warm and grateful wonder that we should be allowed to exist in that fragile space of light at all.

Although the dark, apocalyptic quality of *The Mist* suggests that our "fragile space of light" may be dwindling, David Drayton's night journey through the mist has not yet reached its end. The novel's final word is "hope," even if this hope is clouded by ambiguity and despair. And unlike Drayton, the reader has the protection of perspective. The setting of *The Mist,* so reminiscent of the grade B horror film, is one of total security; we can leave at any moment, the lights will flicker on, and we can step safely into a more familiar world.

. . . . .

At 249B East Thirty-fifth Street in New York, we are told, there stands a nondescript brownstone house to which only certain people are invited. Inside meets a curious, informal club whose common thread is a penchant for the telling of tales. Toward the close of an evening the club members will gather their chairs in a semicircle before the massive fireplace in the library. A story will be told; then a toast will be raised, echoing the words engraved upon the keystone of the fireplace mantel: "*It is the tale, not he who tells it.*"

You will not find that brownstone in New York City, but it stands at the heart of Stephen King's collection of four short novels, *Different Seasons*. The members of the club at 249B East Thirty-fifth Street have a special fondness for the tale of the uncanny, but "[m]any tales have been spun out in the main room . . . tales of every sort, from the comic to the tragic to the ironic to the sentimental." In *Different Seasons*, King moves beyond the horror fiction on which his fame is securely based to present those "tales of every sort," told through an array of fictional storytellers, all of whom ask the reader to judge the tale, not he who tells it.

The four novellas of *Different Seasons* were written between 1974 and 1980, each immediately after King completed a book-length novel, but they were offered for publication for the first time in this collection. Their different tones and textures reflect the "different seasons" of the title, yet beneath each lurks a decidedly macabre quality. "Sooner or later," King notes, "my mind always seems to turn back in that direction. . . ."

The opening novella, *Rita Hayworth and Shawshank Redemption*, finds King working the theme of innocence as effectively as he considered the theme of guilt in *The Shining*. Set in the fictional Shawshank state penitentiary in southwestern Maine, it is the first-person narrative of an inmate identified only by the nickname Red. Serving triple life sentences for murders, Red has become the prison's entrepreneur—"I'm the guy who can get it for you"—but his story is less about himself than another lifer whom he meets and befriends in the prison yard. Andy Dufresne is a former banker, convicted of the murder of his wife, and he makes curious purchases from Red's black market enterprise: a rock hammer and a poster of Rita Hayworth. Dufresne insists upon his innocence, and Red's story tells of how the irresistible force of that innocence succeeds against the seemingly immovable object of Shawshank. In challenging the constricting, dehumanizing environment of the prison—from the sexual brutality of the "sisters" to the corrupt prison overseers to the ever-present walls of stone—Dufresne displays a quality that is symbolized for Red in his seeming dedication to a form of art, the shaping and polishing of stones taken from the yard:

> First the chipping and shaping, and then the almost endless polishing and finishing with those rock-blankets. Looking at them, I felt the warmth that any man or woman feels when he or she is looking at something pretty, something that has been *worked* and *made*—that's the thing that really separates us from the animals, I think—and I felt something else, too. A sense of awe for the man's brute persistence.

"Hope Springs Eternal" is the subtitle of the novella, and in it, King extols the power of hope: "[H]ope is good thing . . . , maybe the best of things, and no good thing ever dies." But hope, we learn, is nothing without persistence—and in the end, Dufresne's persistence is the only vindication of his innocence, as his years of chipping a hole through the wall of his cell, hidden by the poster of Rita Hayworth and her pin-up queen successors, provide the only avenue to freedom.

Apt Pupil, the second and longest installment of the volume, is subtitled "Summer of Corruption," and it is a tale of demons by daylight: the corruption of "the total all-American kid," Todd Bowden, through his fascination with an aging Nazi war criminal Kurt Dussander. On the novella's first page, we meet thirteen-year-old Todd—blond, blue-eyed, and "smiling a summer vacation smile." Ever the perfect student, Todd discovers Dussander living out his final, impoverished days hidden in Todd's idyllic California hometown. He is not shocked by Dussander's role as death-camp commandant, but intrigued; he blackmails Dussander, promising not to reveal Dussander's identity if the former S.S. officer will tell him stories of the camps: "I want to hear about it. . . . Everything. All the gooshy stuff."

The telling of tales of the past horrors produces a nightmare symbiosis, in which Todd becomes the "apt pupil" to Dussander's reluctant tutelage. The placid, plastic modernity of sunny California—captured wryly through snapshot glimpses of suburban life—crumbles before dark memories of the Holocaust. The partnership inexorably takes on a pathological bent as Dussander, haunted by the specters of his past, embraces again his murderous ways, while Todd sets out upon the painfully familiar path of American violence. His smile has changed; on the story's last page, it has become "the excited smile of tow-headed boys going off to war."

King's message is simple and chilling; in the words of his Nazi-hunter, Weiskopf (who himself is identified as a storyteller):

> "[M]aybe there is something about what the germans did that exercises a deadly fascination over us—something that opens the catacombs of the imagination. Maybe part of our dread and horror comes from a secret knowledge that under the right—or wrong—set of circumstances, we ourselves would be willing to build such places and staff them. Black serendipity. Maybe we know that under the right set of circumstances the things that live in the catacombs would be glad to crawl out. And what do you think they would look like: Like mad Fuehrers with forelocks and shoe-polish moustaches, *heil*-ing all over the place? Like red devils, or demons, or the dragon that floats on its stinking reptile wings?"
> "I don't know," Richler said.
> "I think most of them would look like ordinary accountants. . . . And some of them might look like Todd Bowden."

The centerpiece of *Different Seasons* is its third novella, *The Body*. It is patently autobiographical, told by a narrator, Gordon Lachance, who is a *doppelgänger* for Stephen King—a bestselling writer of horror fiction "who is more apt to have his paperback contracts reviewed than his books." Subtitled "Fall from Innocence," it is the story of Lachance's first, childhood view of a dead human being.

Stephen King's first confrontation with death occurred at age four, according to his mother, when one of his playmates was killed by a passing train. In *The Body*, Lachance tells of an adventure that he had at age twelve, to which he attributes his evolution as a writer: an overnight quest with three friends through the woods outside Castle Rock, Maine, in search of the body of a boy purportedly killed by a train. The story unfolds through stories—indeed, two of Lachance's early short stories are reprinted in the text (**"Stud City"** and **"The Revenge of Lard Ass Hogan,"** both which, in fact, are early King short stories originally published in college magazines.

"The only reason anyone writes stories," King tells us here, "is so they can understand the past and get ready for some future mortality." A recurrent theme of King's fiction is the completion of the wheel whose turn begins in childhood. "The idea," he has said, "is to go back and confront your childhood, in a sense relive it if you can, so that you can be whole." We are haunted by our childhoods, by the important things we lost on the long walk to adulthood: the intensity of loves and fears, the talismanic rituals and objects of affection, and the moments of certain comprehension of our place in the scheme of things. To tell of these things now, as adults, exacts a high price:

> The most important things lie too close to wherever your secret heart is buried, like landmarks

to a treasure your enemies would love to steal away. And you may make revelations that cost you dearly only to have people look at you in a funny way, not understanding what you've said at all, or why you thought it was so important that you almost cried while you were saying it. That's the worst, I think. When the secret stays locked within not for the want of a teller but for want of an understanding ear.

Unlocking that secret is difficult, as King laments: "The most important things are the hardest to say, because words diminish them." In *The Body*, he reaches out to his past more directly than in any other story—crossing a bridge of time not unlike the railroad trestle that is the setting for the novella's most frightening scene. What he finds are memories of childhood friendships, of laughter and bravado, of tears and pain, all tinged with a wistful nostalgia. When he returns to the present, that bridge (again like the trestle) is gone, but the storyteller—and his story—endure.

The final novella of *Different Seasons* is set in that mysterious brownstone at 249B East Thirty-fifth Street. "A Winter's Tale" for the collection, *The Breathing Method* answers the question "Who will bring us a tale for Christmas then?" Christmas, the traditional time for the telling of ghostly tales, offers the visitants to 249B East Thirty-fifth Street (and the readers of *Different Seasons*) the horror tale expected of Stephen King, written in a framework evocative of both Jorge Luis Borges and Peter Straub (to whom the story is dedicated).

The narrator of *The Breathing Method* is a middle-aged, unambitious attorney whose foremost love is books. He tells the story of his introduction to the club at 249B East Thirty-fifth Street and, in turn, of the Christmas tale that is told there one night. This story within the story is the reminiscence of an elderly, genteel doctor whose experiments in the 1930s with a predecessor of the Lamaze "breathing method" of childbirth produce a frightening result when the mother dies in labor.

As these levels upon levels of narration suggest, *The Breathing Method* serves as a fitting conclusion for King's collection of stories about storytelling. That imaginary brownstone at 249B East Thirty-fifth Street encompasses the jail cell where Red begins his tale of Andy Dufresne, the small bungalow where Kurt Dussander recalls the crimes of an uneasily buried past, and the room where Gordon Lachance taps out his sentimental retrospective on an IBM keyboard. The stories all flow from that brownstone—a metaphor for the storyteller's mind—whose keeper, appropriately enough, is named "Stevens":

> [T]he question that came out was: "Are there many more rooms upstairs?"
>
> "Oh, yes, sir," [Stevens] said, his eyes never leaving mine. "A great many. A man could become lost. In fact, men *have* become lost. Sometimes it seems to me that they go on for miles. Rooms and corridors. . . . Entrances and exits.". . .
> "There will be more tales?"
> "Here, sir, there are *always* more tales."

Sandra Stansfield—the doomed, husbandless mother of

The Breathing Method—completes the cycle of King's seasonal protagonists. Each faces the rite of passage—from childhood to adulthood, innocence to experience, life to death—as inevitable as the change of seasons. When Gordon Lachance describes the railroad tracks that defined his journey, he pinpoints King's obsession with the theme:

> There's a high ritual to all fundamental events, the rites of passage, the magic corridor where the change happens. Buying the condoms. Standing before the minister. Raising your hand and taking the oath. Or, if you please, walking down the railroad tracks to meet a fellow your own age halfway . . . It seemed right to do it this way, because the rite of passage *is* a magic corridor and so we always provide an aisle—it's what you walk down when you get married, what they carry you down when you get buried.

In the night journeys of *Different Seasons*, we find a "brute persistence" as relentless as the rite of passage, the change of seasons—and in that persistence, the dilemma and a final horror. When Sandra Stansfield refuses to allow even her own death to prevent her from giving birth, King offers a parting image of a stone statue as timeless as the stone walls of Shawshank in which the collection of stories began:

> [T]he statue . . . stood, looking stonily away . . . , as if nothing of particular note had happened, as if such determination in a world as hard as senseless as this one meant nothing . . . or worse still, that it was perhaps the only thing which meant *anything*, the only thing that made any difference at all.

The four short novels of *Different Seasons* [confirm] . . . that the deepest horrors are those that are real. Indeed, the very reality of *Apt Pupil* caused some concern at King's paperback publishing company, New American Library, which initially asked that the novella not be used. As King recalls:

> They were very disturbed by the piece. Extremely disturbed. It was too *real*. If the same story had been set in outer space, it would have been okay, because then you would have had that comforting layer of "Well, this is just make-believe, so we can dismiss it."

> And I thought to myself, "Gee, I've done it again. I've written something that has really gotten under someone's skin." And I do like that. I like the feeling that I reached between somebody's leg like that. There has always been that primitive impulse as part of my writing.

> I don't really care for psychoanalyzing myself. All I care about is when I find out what it is that scares me. That way, I can discover a theme, and then I can magnify that effect and make the reader even more frightened than I am.

> I think I can really scare people, to the point where they will say, "I'm really sorry I bought this." It's as if I'm the dentist, and I'm uncovering a nerve not to fix it, but to drill on it.

As these comments suggest, in answering the questions of whether Stephen King can write more than horror fiction, *Different Seasons* did not presage a change in the direction of King's writing. John D. MacDonald's prediction in the "Introduction" to *Night Shift*—"Stephen King is not going to restrict himself to his present field of intense interest"—has proved correct, but only to a point—a point on which King is highly vocal:

> [T]here are a lot of people who are convinced that, as soon as I have made enough money, I will just leave this silly bullshit behind and go on to write *Brideshead Revisited* and spy novels and things like that. I don't know *why* people think that. This is all I've ever wanted to write; and if I go out and I write a novel about baseball or about a plumber who's having an affair with some other guy's wife—which I have written, by the way—that is just because it occurred to me at the time to write that story. And I don't think anybody would want me deliberately to reject an idea that really excited me.

As if to make his point certain, the projects that followed *Different Seasons* have proved decidedly horrific. Close on the heels of its publication came the release of *Creepshow*, the first motion picture created specifically for the screen by Stephen King, and two flat-out horror novels, *Christine* and *Pet Sematary*.

Susan Bolotin (essay date 1985)

SOURCE: "Don't Turn Your Back on This Book," in *The New York Times Book Review,* June 9, 1985, p. 11.

[*In the following review, Bolotin provides a mixed assessment of* Skeleton Crew.]

Stephen King's fiction, at its best, is equivalent to the post-Expressionist art found in the tiny galleries of Manhattan's East Village, where painters, sculptors and collagists often turn to the aggressive headlines of tabloid newspapers for inspiration. What erupts in their work is an apocalyptic world, at once magnetic and repulsive, in which good howls at evil, nature runs headlong into technology, humor provides life's one grand escape and "control" is a word with little meaning.

At its worst, Mr. King's writing resembles generic campfire stories.

Skeleton Crew, a fat collection of short fiction and two forgettable poems, as indiscriminate in its assemblage as its author can be with words, shows off Mr. King's virtues and failings. He makes mistakes, sentences such as this one: "There was a bit of pain, but not much; losing her maidenhead had been worse." He pokes fun at himself, by confessing to "literary elephantiasis" and saying, in his introduction, that he writes "like fat ladies diet." But unfortunate images and bloat aside, Mr. King is a real talent: his scary tales are fun to read and, I would argue, accurate gauges of our deepest nightmares.

The book's opener, *The Mist,* a story so long that less prolific souls might call it a novel, proves you can't fool Mother Nature. When the Army pursues an ominous top-secret project, all hell literally breaks loose. Mr. King escalates our worst anxieties into a hyperbolic fairy tale. In his world, the evil creatures that attack the classic sleepy village, the deaths of loved ones and the tests that the narrator-prince undergoes do not dissolve into a last, happy-ever-after sunset. The story is, however, written in typically cinematic King style; the first sentence starts a reader's internal movie projector humming.

In the 11 years since he published *Carrie,* Stephen King's reliance on the symbols of popular culture—not just movies, but rock-and-roll, advertising jingles, hot cars—has become legendary and spoofable, perhaps because he understands these symbols better than some more upscale writers who likewise sprinkle their stories with brand names. His uncensored and uncensoring subconscious allows him to absorb the world around him and in him, and to spit it out almost undigested, as if he were walking around in a constant hypnagogic state.

This condition is in some ways (or at least to some people) enviable. He conjures up the forgotten artifacts of childhood—talismans such as the fortune-telling Magic Eight-Ball—more easily than someone 10 years on the couch. And how many of us could bear living with such a rampant imagination? Mr. King provides a clue to what it might be like in his slightly ingenuous "Notes" section. He is telling how he came to write **"Survivor Type,"** a silly but effective story from the gross-me-out school of literature. (A doctor, stranded on an island after a shipwreck, progressively amputates parts of his body and eats himself. After he dines on his left foot, he writes in his journal, "I kept telling myself: Cold roast beef. Cold roast beef. Cold roast beef.") Anyway, Mr. King explains: "I got to thinking about cannibalism one day . . . and my muse once more evacuated its magic bowels on my head. I know how gross that sounds, but it's the best metaphor I know." Freud would have gone crazy—and so would Mr. King's readers, if he did not distance himself from his material through humor, self-awareness and irony.

Take, for instance, **"The Raft,"** a wonderfully gruesome story about four innocent kids marooned in the middle of a lake by a human-eating water slick that looks like "dark, lithe Naugahyde." One of the boys, so terrified that he punches himself in the nose to feel the vitality of his own blood, keeps his cool long enough to tell the creature to "go to California and find a Roger Corman movie to audition for."

But, again, what saves Mr. King's stories from genre purgatory is his moral vision. He is in love with his readers, as someone in his income tax bracket might well be, and he wants to share his world view with them. He believes that primal, mythological beings and rites have extraordinary power; that we should stand in awe of nature; that good does not always beget good; that death is not necessarily dreadful; that violence is an expression of powerlessness; that creativity demands listening to inner voices; that madness attracts all of us; that true love never dies.

Sometimes, as in **"Cain Rose Up,"** in which an anal-retentive type turns into a mass murderer, or in **"Nona,"** a failed attempt at Bergmanesque ghostliness, his visions

run amok. Sometimes, as in **"The Monkey,"** a story about an evil toy, or in **"Uncle Otto's Truck,"** about a machine that avenges murder, the vision is predictable. But as a character in *The Mist* says, conveniently explaining the popularity of books about the supernatural: "When the machines fail . . . when the technologies fail, when the conventional religious systems fail, people have got to have something. Even a zombie lurching through the night can seem pretty cheerful compared to the existential comedy/horror of the ozone layer dissolving under the combined assault of a million fluorocarbon spray cans of deodorant." The felicitous phrase is not always Mr. King's strong suit, but our very own Brother Grimm almost always speaks the truth.

Peter Nicholls (essay date 1985)

SOURCE: A review of *Skeleton Crew,* in *Book World—The Washington Post,* June 16, 1985, pp. 1, 13.

[*Nicholls is an Australian critic. In the following review of* Skeleton Crew, *he lauds King's use of colloquial images and dialect, while asserting that occasionally King's use of vulgar language or imagery is detrimental to his narratives' effectiveness as well as his characters' appeal.*]

Stephen King could no doubt make a megabuck deal for a paraphrase of the telephone directory, so a simple short-story collection (his third) may seem unsurprising. When you think about it though, it reveals a commendable absence of greed. Even for Stephen King (and especially for anybody else) short stories are not great money spinners. If he writes them, it must be because he enjoys writing them.

Skeleton Crew makes it obvious that King is not worried now, if he ever was, about his pulp-magazine past. There are stories here from 1968 onwards. As his first collection, *Night Shift*, did not appear until 1978, there seems no reason why some of these stories should not have been published then rather than now; presumably he was more self-conscious then. These days he can afford to be amused by his own juvenilia (some from the University of Maine magazine *Ubris*) and rightly so. The early stories are pretty good, but the real winners are recent.

There are two poems (better than some of you might have expected) and 20 stories. Four stories are classics. The other 16 are, without exception, highly readable; eight definitely above average and none of them contemptible. Other critics might call the score a little differently, but overall there can be no argument: the big guy from Bangor, Maine, has made another touchdown. No question, King is the most successful good ol' boy in the book business, though he continues to give the impression (can it be true?) of being unspoiled by success.

King is, of course, well known as an excellent contriver of laid-back New England dialect (Ayuh, those old fellers sitting on a bench and yarning), and also of a generalized downmarket prose, either straight-from-the-shoulder or filtered-through-the-beercan. But it would be a mistake for King to become over-confident about his mastery of the common touch. In his afterword he tells an anecdote about the difficulty he had in selling a story (**"Mrs. Todd's Shortcut"**) to women's magazines. It seems that two of them turned it down "because of that line about how a woman will pee down her own leg if she doesn't squat." Well, Steve, I don't want to be difficult, but the same line made me wince too, and it didn't do a bit of good to the story; it makes a likeable narrator seem momentarily insensitive, even vulgar. I suspect that a lot of us plain folks who admire King's work do so in spite of, and not because of, this sort of thing. My granny, herself plain folks, would have said "That Stephen King should wash his mouth out with soap."

But one's adverse judgments are really quite mild. Several of the stories, as with too many genre short stories, are of the kind which one describes to friends in sentences that begin "Did you ever read the story about . . . ?" For example, in more than one interview, when asked to define the term "gross-out," Stephen King has referred to his own story **"Survivor Type,"** which appears here. This is well told, but once you have heard someone say, "Did you ever read the story about the man on the desert island who got so hungry he ate himself?," there is not a lot of point in reading the actual story. As gross-outs go, I preferred the scene in **"The Raft"** where a teen-age couple, menaced by a floating and carnivorous blob, make desperate love. Unfortunately, the young man notices too late that "HER HAIR IS IN THE OH GOD IN THE WATER HER HAIR . . . Randy screamed. He screamed. And then, for variety, he screamed some more."

The short story is not, on the face of it, a form to which King's undoubted talents are suited. Polished gemstones of precision are not his line, and mandarins and collectors of lapidary delights should seek their pleasures elsewhere. One joins King for more leisurely, outdoor pursuits: a ramble through the graveyard perhaps, with the chill of fall in the air.

Even in the short story, however, King's refusal to be hurried can pay dividends, especially in **"Mrs. Todd's Shortcut,"** a vibrant, memorable tale about a young woman obsessed with the possibility of finding ever shorter automobile routes between her home village and Bangor, 79 miles as the crow flies. As the shortcuts become more elaborate, the back roads wilder and the distance shorter, it is no longer certain through what dimension these tracks are cutting, but some nasty little animals get caught up in the radiator grille. Part of the story's strength lies in the ironical, moving contrast between the relaxed telling of the tale and the mad hurry it encapsulates.

The other three classics vary in tone. **"The Monkey,"** perhaps, cuts closest to the white dead bone in its tale of a children's toy which laughs and bangs its cymbals when death is due. Here King's well known sore spot (highly visible in *Pet Sematary*), which has to do with parental love and fear and mortal threats to children, is hectically picked at yet again. On a much more expansive and amusing note, *The Mist* (almost a short novel) is by far the best supermarket-menaced-by-horrible-monsters story ever likely to be written, and some of the nastiest monsters are human. (Some, on the other hand, have tentacles, enor-

mous claws, and leave footprints in the blacktop deep enough to hide a car in.)

Finally, something out of the way for King: a piece of true-blue surrealism, beautifully judged and paced, **"Big Wheels: A Tale of the Laundry Game (Milkman ✔ 2)."** The horror in this one bubbles up through the beercans that are central to its imagery, and the reader discovers more about the soft white underbelly of blue-collar life than he could conceivably want to know.

Skeleton Crew is probably better than the first collection, *Night Shift*, and as good in its very different way as the second, *Different Seasons.* King does not have too much to worry about, though he has one failing, perhaps because he likes to be liked. In a few too many stories (including the last, **"The Reach"**) he sacrifices the hard edge of his vision for something that can only be called cute.

James C. Dolan   (essay date 1985)

SOURCE: A review of *Skeleton Crew,* in *Best Sellers,* Vol. 45, No. 5, August, 1985, p. 168.

[*Dolan is an American educator and critic. In the following review of* Skeleton Crew, *he suggests that King's stories are powerful because of the "realization by the reader that the line between his own life and that of the horror tale is very fine."*]

You need only cable TV to know how much this country during the last few years has been in the throes of a horror film epidemic, the "Halloween Syndrome." If you have the stomach for it, you may have been able to see enough to sort the artistic from the trash. I suspect that *Night of the Living Dead* would be near the top of your horror hierarchy, and Stephen King on your elite list of chiller creators. Remember *Carrie, Cujo,* and *The Shining*? King wrote them all.

What is it that makes a story "horrible"? Reading *Skeleton Crew* might help us to decide. Most of the twenty stories and two poems really make your flesh crawl. This is not a book to read in huge gobbets, but a collection to savor one at a time. The selections that make up the "crew" of "skeletons" are of several different types of the story horrible: the lost in space fantasy, the gory exploits of the psychopathic killer, a twist on the cannibalism motif, the classic mirror story—to name a few. But it's not gory details alone that create horror though they do add that gut-wrenching element so many readers eagerly anticipate. Even that takes—in prose, at least—the kind of imagination and verbal dexterity that enables the reader to re-create the scene and the action vividly enough for him to feel the twinge of terror that thrills and entertains.

The events, in addition to being believable, must happen to characters we can accept and identify with as fully human. No one outside the *Wizard of Oz* gets gooseflesh at the chilling adventures of a straw man. King's people are palpable, usually ordinary, individuals, and we are led to accept their reactions to the strange things that befall them as recognizably human. Many of King's narrators, as you might expect, are telling their own stories; they, too, speak with individual voices that place us in the action.

The essence of horror, however, I would think is the realization by the reader that the line between his own life and that of the horror tale is very fine. How do we know that some small alteration in the mind's patterns won't make us into killers or eaters of men? The image in the mirror has always asked men to question the validity of their perceptions. We all harbor childhood fantasies of the eerie-looking person, or place, or object that seemed to us to bear a threat. King's stories, along with their obvious entertainment value, offer the thoughtful reader a look at his life from new angles. Not all of them are finally frightening; there is comedy here, as in **"The Word Processor of the Gods,"** tragedy in *The Mist,* satire in **"The Jaunt."**

Skeleton Crew is an excellent book to keep by your chair for a short read in the evening. I promise you that you'll never look at a sandy beach or a Delete key the same way again.

Leonard G. Heldreth   (essay date 1987)

SOURCE: "Viewing 'The Body': King's Portrait of the Artist as Survivor," in *The Gothic World of Stephen King: Landscape of Nightmares,* edited by Gary Hoppenstand and Ray B. Browne, Bowling Green State University Popular Press, 1987, pp. 64-74.

[*Heldreth is an American educator and critic. In the following essay, he provides a thematic analysis of* The Body, *discussing King's treatment of maturation and use of narrative writing to "[shape] important experiences into a form to be communicated."*]

Steven King begins *The Body* with *"The most important things are the hardest things to say. . . .* Words shrink things that seem limitless when they were in your head to no more than living size when they're brought out. . . .*"* Shaping important experiences into a form to be communicated is one of the major themes of the novella, and into it King incorporates several levels of archetypal experience. He cites the "high ritual to all fundamental events, the rites of passage, the magic corridor where the change happens"; and even at the beginning of the walk down the railroad tracks, "bright and heliographing in the sun," Gordon Lachance knows he will never "forget that moment, no matter how old I get"; as the adventure progresses, the hike turns "into what we had suspected it was all along: serious business." The journey the four boys take to find Ray Brower's body is more than just a walk along railroad tracks; extending through time as well as space, it integrates diverse rites of passage into one intensely concentrated experience.

In the introduction to *Night Shift*, King asserts, "All our fears add up to one great fear. . . . We're afraid of the body under the sheet. It's our body." Consciousness of the physical body—its sensations, vulnerability and ultimate termination—is the focus of horror literature; and while *The Body* is not a horror story, bodily sensations, the physical self, and the dangers that beset it are emphasized and analyzed. Starting over the GS&WM trestle high above Castle River, Gordon Lachance becomes "acutely aware of all the noises" inside him: "The steady thump of my heart, the bloodbeat in my ears like a drum being played with brushes, the creak of sinews like the strings of a violin." Halfway across, when he hears the approaching train, he describes for over a page how "all sensory input became intensified." Other descriptions of intense physical sensations appear in passages describing the leech pond, the episode with the doe, and the beating Gordon receives from Ace Merrill and Fuzzy Bracowicz.

Beyond an awareness of the human body, a growing realization of its physical vulnerability draws the boys on the journey. The narrator's concern for such vulnerability appears in his comparison of Brower's body to "a ripped-open laundry bag," in his description of the dead boy's eyes filling with hail, and in his concern for the boy "so alone and so defenseless in the dark. . . . If something wanted to eat on him, it would." Lachance went on the hike because of mortality, "the shadows that are always somewhere behind our eyes . . . what Bruce Springsteen calls the darkness on the edge of town." Going to view Brower's body is one way of acknowledging and defying death: "everyone wants to dare that darkness in spite of the jalopy bodies that some joker of a God gave us . . . not in *spite* of our jalopy bodies but *because* of them."

This desire to confront the darkness inherent in the body pulls the boys forward on what is, at the literal level, a journey to see death. The subtitle, "Fall from Innocence," refers not only to their loss of innocence but also to the fall of Man and the punishment of that fall by death. The boys' language indicates their awareness that this trip is more than just an overnight adventure. When Vern Tessio first announces the trip in the clubhouse and considers the consequences, he states, "This is worth it," and later he emphasizes, "we *hafta* see him . . . we *hafta* . . . but maybe it shouldn't be no good time." Gordon, speaking for the others, acknowledges, "the fascination of the thing drew us on. . . . We were all crazy to see that kid's body . . . we had come to believe we *deserved* to see it." What fascinates the boys at a level below their conscious thought is the archetype of the journey, whose significance they sense: "Unspoken—maybe it was too fundamental to be spoken—was the idea that this was a *big* thing." They never really question their "decision to walk down the tracks," for such a journey forward, in time and growth as well as in space, is as inevitable as boys growing into men.

This journey begins by moving them away from home and boyhood toward the world and adolescence. "Home . . . is a metaphysical principle and an ontological condition embodied in a place: the location which affirms who I am, projects what I may be, and vindicates whatever I have had to do to get there" [Langdon Elsbree, *The Rituals of Life: Patterns in Narratives,* 1982]. Abused or neglected by parents, each of the boys has been forced into a social identity which he despises; for each of the boys, home has become a limitation. Teddy fights against being labeled the son of a "looney" by Milo Pressman, Vern rejects being treated like a juvenile delinquent because of his brothers, Chris rejects his brothers and his father, and Gordon withdraws from his family that ignores him. Their small town environment has forced them into being "clearly defined contestants with titles, insignia, and traditional sexual or social roles," but they reject these roles, and part of their initial momentum, as they set out, "is the need to break away, or find a new home, identity, or commitment" [Elsbree]. When they are alone, Chris lectures Gordon on the need to go to college and escape: "I know what people think of my family in this town. I know what they think of me and what they expect. . . . I want to go someplace where nobody knows me and I don't have any black marks against me before I start." In the excerpts from Lachance's writings, Chico rejects his family and its lifestyle to head for Stud City while Lard Ass Hogan takes his revenge on his parents and small town society.

The movement of the journey to escape is contrasted with inertia, stagnation, and images of drowning. Chris warns Gordon to leave friends who will "drag you down. . . . They're like drowning guys that are holding onto your legs. You can't save them. You can only drown with them." Gordon equates this image of drowning with a life unrealized in two later instances: he dreams of the corpses of Vern and Teddy pulling down first Chris and then himself, and he comments about Chris, "I could not just leave him to sink or swim on his own. If he had drowned, that [best] part of me would have drowned with him, I think." Yet three of the boys do die without realizing their potentials.

The journey in contemporary literature tends to include "only the temporary lovers, friends, associates; more rarely the hard-won intimacy with a single companion, or two" [Elsbree], and Gordon acknowledges that "Friends come in and out of your life like busboys in a restaurant . . . when I think of that dream, the corpses under the water pulling implacably at my legs, it seems right that it should be that way." In such a psychic journey, "the self is grateful to find it has the strength to escape the predation of others and to travel on alone" [Elsbree].

In addition to breaking out of a confining existence, Gordon tries to escape the domination of his dead brother together with the guilt he feels about Denny's death. Gordon has always been ignored by his parents and most of the town while they doted on his brother. Even George Dusset extols Denny's virtues and has "a beautiful vision" of the dead boy while he cheats Gordon at the scales. At Denny's graduation Gordon had rebelled and drunk too much cheap wine, but after the older brother's death the guilt returns, and Denny's ghost announces in dreams, "*It should have been you, Gordon.*" The same guilt appears in Lachance's story when the corpse of Chico's brother Johnny returns with similar words. Brower's death, like Denny's, was accidental, and by walking to confront that illogical death—and thus his own and his brother's mortality—Lachance moves away from blind acceptance of the guilt and inferiority imposed on him by his parents and the town toward an acceptance of himself and the nature of existence: "Some people drown, that's all. It's not fair, but it happens."

Thus, while this expedition moves toward death in that the goal is a corpse, it also moves toward death in the sense of a journey forward in time toward the demise of the boys' own bodies. Dylan Thomas in the poem, "Twenty-Four Years," describes "a journey / By the light of the meat-eating sun" whose "final direction" is toward "the elementary town," and the boys are embarked on that same mortal trip. Brower's journey is over, as are those of the athletes who were crippled or killed, proving to Gordon they "were as much flesh and blood as I was." Dennis Lachance has also entered the "elementary town," as has his literary equivalent, Johnny May; and the beavers seen alongside the tracks will soon join them: "They'll shoot them some beavers and scare off the rest and then knock out their dam. . . . Who cares about beavers?" Foreshadowings of the boys' own mortality appear all about them, e.g., in their flipping a "goocher" at the town dump and in Gosset's quoting the Bible to Gordon, " 'In the midst of life, we are in death.' Did you know that?" Teddy flirts with death in his truck-and-train-dodging and nearly finds it when he falls from the top of the tree. Chico thinks, *"Nothing happened to Johnny that isn't going to happen to you, too, sooner or later,"* and the adult Gordon finally recounts the later deaths of Teddy, Vern, and Chris.

Complementing these foreshadowings are images that confuse the quick and the dead to highlight the boys' inevitable deaths. After Chris falls down in the same position as Brower's body, Gordon looks "wildly at Chris's feet to make sure his sneakers were still on," and when Gordon tells the LeDio story, he sees the dead hero's face replaced by the imagined face of Ray Brower. But Gordon's chief confusion is between himself and the corpse, for in confronting Ray Brower's death, he is facing his own. His dream of Denny concludes with the corpse's accusation, "It should have been you," but, so far as his parents are concerned, Gordon feels he is already dead. The "old reliable standby, 'Did your mother ever have any kids that lived?' " loses its humor when compared to Gordon's earlier remark about his mother's feelings after Denny's death: "Her only kid was dead and she had to do something to take her mind off it." The adult Lachance, looking back on his experiences at twelve, thinks "That boy was *me.* . . . And the thought which follows, chilling me like a dash of cold water, is: *Which boy do you mean?*" The confusion is natural, for, like Margaret in Gerard Manley Hopkins' poem, "Spring and Fall: to a young child," it is himself he mourns for.

Any realistic account of boys at the edge of adolescence inevitably involves sexual imagery, and *The Body* incorporates as one of its thematic strands the sexual preoccupations, ambiguities, and uncertainties of its pubescent heroes. The boys, all "close to being thirteen," reveal their sexual preoccupation in their language, whose most common expletive is "balls." For example, to describe fear, Vern says, " 'My balls crawled up so high I thought they was trine [sic] to get back home,' " and Gordon describes fear as a pole-vaulter who "dug his pole all the way into my balls, it felt like, and ended up sitting astride my heart." Chris refuses to take a drink "even to show he had, you know, big balls."

Sexual fears and insecurity are evident in the many references to injured testicles. When Gordon pulls Teddy off the fence around the town dump and they fall, the narrator complains, "He squashed my balls pretty good. . . . Nothing hurts like having your balls squashed." In the later fight with Ace Merrill and Fuzzy Bracowicz, Gordon receives a knee in the crotch and protects his "wounded balls," which Aunt Evvie Chalmers warns him "are going to swell up to the size of Mason jars." Worse than injured testicles are lost testicles, a threat personified by Pressman's dog, Chopper: "every kid in Castle Rock squeezed his balls between his legs when Chopper's name was mentioned." According to rumor, Chopper has been taught to attack certain parts of the body, and an intruder into the town dump "would hear the dread cry: 'Chopper! Sic! Balls!' And that kid would be a soprano the rest of his life."

The climax of this expedition is a test of masculinity in which a pistol that belongs to Chris's father decides the victory between younger boys trying to prove their masculinity and older ones trying to assert their power. A contest "where the testing and defense of self is central" [Elsbree] is a common activity in adolescence, and such contests appear throughout *The Body*: it opens with card games, climaxes with the fight over the body, and concludes with the boys trying to survive the game of life. The story also incorporates elements of the contest in other ways. Gordon's surname, Lachance, carries the connotation of a game, and his best memories of Denny, who was an All-Conference halfback, involve watching him play ball. In the embedded story, Lard Ass Hogan enrolls in the pie eating contest and, in his own way, wins.

The major contest, the fight over Ray Brower's body, sets older and younger brothers against each other. Both Chris and Vern are facing their actual brothers across the battle line, and it is Ace's mention of Denny that triggers Gordon's response: in insulting Ace he is striking back at all the people who have praised Denny and expected Gordon to be like him.

The contest in which the younger boys achieve a qualified victory echoes, perhaps ironically, epic engagements in the structure of its action and in its battle prize. The corpse has no value except as an object with which to achieve honor or fame, and, as the story concludes, even that value is denied the participants. The two groups stand on opposite sides of a water-logged bog with Brower's body between them like the Greeks and Trojans on opposite sides of the river Scamander. First, insults and dares are exchanged; then minor warriors, Charlie Hogan and Billy Tessio, start forward, but are called back by Ace Merrill, their leader; Ace offers to negotiate with the other leader, Gordon Lachance; Gordon returns an insult and both sides prepare for battle. Then Chris, exhibiting his version of the armor of Achilles, fires the revolver and changes the odds. The phallic gun is particularly appropriate, as are the insults ("Bite my bag," "Suck my fat one"), for the conflict is one of masculine pride, and "Apart from words, the male often fights with the usual phallic extensions of self and/or weapons of power." Although Jackie Mudgett pulls out a knife, the more potent, adult weapon of the younger boys decides the battle, a victory anticipated by Gordon's earlier firing of the gun (sexual maturation) in

the alley behind the Blue Point Diner: " 'You did it, you did it! *Gordie did it!*' "

When the boys return home, Gordon, like the Greek heroes after battle, ritually cleans himself—"face, neck, pits, belly . . . crotch—my testicles in particular"—and throws the rag away. But the epic echoes and the masculine pride ("Biggest one in four counties") are all illusions; after the excitement of battle cools, Gordon acknowledges that Ray Brower's body is "a tatty prize to be fought over by two bunches of stupid hick kids." Such heroics have little merit beyond schoolboy conflicts, Lachance implies, because the outcome of any contest depends more on chance than ability, and the odds are against the individual: "they tell you to step right up and spin the Wheel of Fortune, and it spins so pretty and the guy steps on a pedal and it comes up double zeros, house number, everybody loses."

A similar nonheroic attitude manifests itself in Lachance's ambiguous attitude toward sexuality. In the **"Stud City"** excerpt, Chico is a sensitive but typical car-crazy teenager with his libido in overdrive; the section opens with his deflowering a virgin and ends with his "rolling" on Route 41. But this early writing also describes sex as "Bozo the Clown bouncing around on a spring. How could a woman look at an erect penis without going off into mad gales of laughter?" The older Lachance describes the excerpt as "an extremely sexual story written by an extremely inexperienced young man" and as "the work of a young man every bit as insecure as he was inexperienced." The insecurity remains, however, in the comments of the older Lachance. It manifests itself in his feelings toward Chris, in his remarks about masturbation, in the leech episode, and in his literary allusions. When they separate after the hike, the twelve-year-old Gordon feels self-conscious about his love for Chris, acknowledging that "Speech destroys the functions of love"; later, as they study together every night through high school, he wonders if his former friends will think he went "faggot," but defends himself by saying, "it was only survival. We were clinging to each other in deep water." When he hears of Chris's death, he drives out of town and cries "for damn near half an hour," yet he cannot share his feelings, even with his wife, for such action would be considered feminine. Sexuality can be seen as hilarious but the rest of the macho creed remains locked in place: strong feelings must be expressed only in isolation or in a joking fashion.

Masturbation, another subject usually treated with humor, also has a serious side in the story. Jokes about it run through the story from Vern's "Fuck your hand, man," through the initial verdict on the swim and the parting speech of Gordon and Chris, to the last comment on the treehouse which "smelled like a shootoff in a haymow." But masturbation is also a part of the nostalgia for childhood innocence: for the boy "masturbation is freedom and omnipotence." The adult Lachance associates the pleasure of his early writing with masturbation: "The act of writing itself is done in secret, like masturbation. . . . For me, it always wants to be sex and always falls short—it's always that adolescent handjob in the bathroom with the door locked." Using masturbation as a metaphor for writing conveys the boy's and the adult's real attitudes better than the comments which the boys self-consciously swap among themselves.

The most disturbing sexual image in the story is the leech which attaches itself to Gordon's scrotum while he is swimming. When he discovers it, the leech is "a bruised purplish-red" and has "swelled to four times its normal size." When he pulls the leech loose, it bursts and "My own blood ran across my palm and inner wrist in a warm flood." As they leave, he looks back at the leech, "deflated . . . but still ominous." The image is of self-castration (pulling the leech loose) during tumescence and is more than a young man on the edge of adolescence can handle: he faints. The leech, a clinging third testicle, is swollen with blood like an erect penis (the opposite side of the image of Bozo the clown cited in **"Stud City"**), and both Chris and Gordon understand the inherent symbolism of the act. The deflation and the sexual significance, even for later years, are underlined by the adult Lachance's equating "the burst leech: dead, deflated . . . but still ominous" with the "used condoms" floating off Staten Island. When his wife asks about the crescent-shaped scar left by the leech, he automatically lies, for even symbolic castration experiences are not subjects to be shared with wives.

This castration image, raised earlier in the Chopper rumors, is underscored by Lachance's references to Ralph Ellison's novel, *Invisible Man*. He equates himself with the protagonist for he is as invisible to his parents as Jack the Bear is to society. Gordon's dreams in the novella are negative—dreams of people pulling him down or of his dead brother's return—and *Invisible Man* concludes with a dream in which the narrator is castrated by Bledso and the others who have been running his life. They ask him, "How does it feel to be free of illusion?" and he replies, "Painful and empty." Gordon also has been freeing himself of illusion: at the sound of the train's horn, his illusions fly apart letting him "know what both the heroes and cowards really heard when death flew at them"; he finds he cannot trust George Dusset's arithmetic; and in the meeting with Chopper, he gets his "first lesson in the vast difference between myth and reality"; he has few illusions about teachers after Chris's account of the stolen milk money; and he loses his illusions about death when he smells the decay and sees the beetle come out of Brower's mouth. The leeches lurking beneath the smooth surface of the pond complete the lesson about appearances: "The harder lesson to be learned is essentially paradoxical: how to live without illusion . . . and yet remain committed to some meaningful and coherent picture of things." For Lachance, the commitment is to writing: *"The only reason anyone writes stories is so they can understand the past and get ready for some future mortality . . . "* This statement echoes Ellison's statement at the end of *Invisible Man:* "So why do I write, torturing myself to put it down? Because in spite of myself I've learned some things."

Understanding the self requires understanding the past, and the story's final journey is Gordon Lachance's archetypal "return to a remembered place after years of absence" [Elsbree]. He returns in memory to the boys' journey down the railroad tracks, he fantasizes returning as an adult for the berry pail, and he describes an actual return to Castle Rock. Since the original events, he had "thought remarkably little about those two days in September, at least consciously. The associations the memories bring to the surface are as unpleasant as week-old river-corpses brought to the surface by cannonfire." But in recounting the associations he offers his "inner life, its genesis, changes, restlessness, and moods . . . a journey . . . through the growth of consciousness and self . . . and its interplay with the external world" [Elsbree]. At times he feels "like the pre-adolescent Gordon Lachance that once strode the earth, walking and talking and occasionally crawling on his belly like a reptile." He also identifies with the young man who wrote **"Stud City,"** "a Gordon Lachance younger than the one living and writing now . . . but not so young as the one who went with his friends that day." The narrator, trying "to look through an IBM keyboard and see that time," can "almost feel the skinny, scabbed boy still buried in this advancing body," for these and other stages in his development form a graph of personal identity, the self as "a construct or a series of constructs of subjective time which is inadequate to resist the march of chronological and historic time" [Elsbree]. In an interview, Ralph Ellison argues that the search for identity "is *the* American theme. The nature of our society is such that we are prevented from knowing who we are," and that the search for and unification of his identity should be a major theme of a writer as American as Stephen King is not surprising. The final (or current) identity achieved is defined in the last pages of the work: "I'm a writer now . . . and most of the time I'm happy," although in an interview with Douglas E. Winter, King reserves his right to switch identities: "I'm just trying on all of these hats."

Writing enables Lachance to come to terms with the emotions engendered by the adventure. The narrative exists in three reflexive forms—the basic story, the reprints of **"Stud City,"** and **"The Revenge of Lard Ass Hogan"**—the latter two being set in a different typeface. Within these forms are various narrators, from the twelve-year-old boy to the "best-selling novelist who is more apt to have his paper back contracts reviewed than his books." The parts of the narrative comment on each other. For example, the older Lachance evaluates the writing of his younger self, while the Hogan story begins as an oral account told by a twelve-year-old, switches to a published version written by the successful novelist, and then returns to the twelve-year-old's point of view. Later Chris warns Gordon that the pie story may "never get written down" after the reader has already read it printed, and he suggests that "Maybe you'll even write about us guys," the account of which the reader is holding.

Writing succeeds for Gordon because it offers control over experience. In writing **"Stud City"** he found "a kind of dreadful exhilaration in seeing things that had troubled me for years come out in a new form, *a form over which I had imposed control.*" Writing and religion, *"The only two useful artforms,"* permit a pattern to be imposed on the chaos of life: at the end of *Invisible Man* Ellison states, "the mind that has conceived a plan of living must never lose sight of the chaos against which that pattern was conceived." Writing permits a systematic formulation of the plan or world view and provides the means for keeping it before not only the author but all of his readers. As the narrator of *Invisible Man* asks at the end, "Who knows but that, on the lower frequencies, I speak for you?"

Most of the other themes of the work are incorporated through metaphors with writing. The body examined is not only Brower's but also the body of experience Gordon has shaped into the work and the body of works he has produced; the contest is the writer's attempt to decipher and communicate order out of raw experience; and sex appears in his analogy of writing to masturbation and artificial insemination. Writing, most of all, defines experience in relation to the narrator, a function he embodies in the metaphor of the blueberry pail which Ray Brower lost and which Lachance dreams of retrieving. He wants to "pull it out of time" and to read his own life in its rusty shine—"where I was, what I was doing, who I was loving, how I was getting along, where I was." Yet the act of writing has given him the blueberry bucket: through *The Body* he has retrieved the past, looked in its mirror, and found his "own face in whatever reflection might be left." The words whose power he denies at the beginning of the narrative have enabled him to capture and communicate the experiences of his life.

To see Gordon Lachance as Stephen King is tempting. Many of the details match: the wife, three children, the million dollars from horror stories, the books made into movies, the youngest son who might be hydrocephalic, even the luck (LaChance) which King acknowledges. Ray Brower's death by train and Gordon's close brush with it reflect the story King tells of an incident when he was four in which another child was killed by a train, although he states, "I have no memory of the incident at all; only of having been told about it some years after the fact."

Concluding that Lachance is King would be tempting but unnecessary, for whether the writer is Lachance or King, an examination of a story or any cultural artifact returns us "to both the culture and the maker as individualized expressions of certain universal human capacities and experiences, of which the living through stories is paramount. It is this perspective which is so valuable—one which sees the human symbolizing process of story making as fundamental to culture, to our creation of an inhabitable world" [Elsbree].

Stevens, King's namesake in *The Breathing Method*, the next story in the collection which contains *The Body*, says "Here, sir, there are *always* more tales"; and indeed, as long as there are more lives, there *are* always more tales, for although each individual repeats basic archetypal patterns in his journey from life to death, his variations, like Kings' brand names, root him in his time and mark him of his place. By translating these experiences into fiction, by sharing both the universalities and the particularities of existence, King and other writers help to break down the loneliness of life and even of death.

> King . . . yanks his reader in by the collar of his or her common sense and then flings him/her out blabbering and terrified by the unexpected twists of the comfortably mundane.

> —*Sue Martin, in* Los Angeles Times Book Review, *August 25, 1985.*

Michael A. Morrison   (essay date 1990)

SOURCE: "Stephen King: Time Out of Joint," in *Book World—The Washington Post,* August 26, 1990, p. 9.

[*In the following review, Morrison offers praise for* Four Past Midnight.]

Regular visitors to the world of Stephen King know that its horrors burst forth from the least likely places—the four novellas in [*Four Past Midnight*] find horror in a transcontinental night flight, a camera, a small-town library, and a quiet Maine summer town during the off-season. Some of the environs and themes in these stories are familiar; others are not. One is the penultimate Castle Rock story, a prequel to the forthcoming *Needful Things.* Another, King tells us, is the last of his tales "about writers and writing and the strange no man's land which exists between what's real and what's make-believe." Still another takes us to the midwestern American town of Junction City, Iowa, where King proves that his talents as a regionalist extend beyond Maine into Sherwood Anderson country.

King is above all a master storyteller, and these stories grab hold and will not let go. And, being tales of horror, they have their share of suspense, violence, monsters and eye-popping special effects. But what makes them special—in the way the best of King's work and so little of the rest of modern horror fiction is special—is the believable, often moving ways his characters react when confronted with the unknown.

When, for example, Sam Peebles loses two books that he borrowed from the Junction City Public Library and sweet-faced, white-haired librarian Ardelia Lortz dispatches the Library Police to get them back, the ensuing events shatter the bedrock of pragmatism and rationality on which Sam has built his life. His search for the missing books turns into a quest of selfhood that takes him into the soul of small-town America and ends in a battle royal with a protean creature akin to the monster in *It,* King's mega-novel of small-town evil.

And when, in *The Langoliers*, a handful of passengers on an American Pride airlines "red-eye" flight from Los Angeles to Boston awaken half an hour after takeoff to find that somewhere between the Mojave Desert and the Great Divide their L1011 has taken a detour into the Twilight

Zone, they must each cope with the shock of the inexplicable and then join in a community of sharing and sacrifice if they are to survive.

Not all of King's people are as well-equipped as Sam Peebles or the passengers on Flight 29 to deal with an incursion of the monstrous. In *Secret Window, Secret Garden*, writer Morton Rainey comes to Tashmore Glen, Maine, to recuperate from his "eerily quick and quiet no-fault divorce" only to find himself face to face with every writer's nightmare: a charge of plagiarism. Weakened by depression, a severe writer's block and barely suppressed rage at his adulterous wife, Rainey is in no condition to deal with his accuser, let alone with the amazing strings of events that occur when he sets out to prove his innocence. In this story King interweaves character, theme and stunning plot reversals with far greater control than in his earlier, less successful novels about writers, *Misery* and *The Dark Half*.

Often King's most memorable characters are larger-than-life recreants whose lack of decency and compassion makes them sitting ducks for the supernatural. Reginald "Pop" Merrill, sole proprietor of the Emporium Galorium and featured player in the last of these novellas, stands out as the most irresistible of King's Dickensian grotesques. Sporting a twinkle in his eye, rimless spectacles, a vest and a corncob pipe, Pop seems just a crusty blend of "cracker-barrel philosopher and hometown Mr. Fixit." But behind this facade is a mean-spirited, duplicitous soul whose allegiance to the technological debris that fills his junk store is far stronger than to the Maine community where he lives. Pop represents the sick undersoul of Castle Rock and a thousand like towns and is a fitting companion for the Sun Dog that gives this story its title.

With the exception of this story, which suffers from the digressions and repetitions that have marred King's last few novels, the tales in *Four Past Midnight* are exceptionally well crafted. King shapes his material with the sure hand of a master woodworker, tossing off unexpected similes, deftly using dreams to reveal character, subtly planting clues to coming revelations, and skillfully managing the coincidences on which his stories often hinge. If, like me, you have loved King's work for years but were pretty disappointed in his last several novels, then you'll be delighted with *Four Past Midnight*, his best work since *Pet Sematary*.

As King notes in his ingratiating introduction, these stories share a preoccupation with time "and the corrosive effects it can have on the human heart." But they share with the rest of his work a deeper concern for basic values such as selflessness, honesty and friendship. Now, as the blood and chaos of their spectacular finales begin to fade from memory, what I am left with is the warmth of King's abiding faith in "that stubborn, intangible spark which carries life on in the face of the most dreadful reversals and ludicrous turns of fate."

King often seeks inspiration in graveyards, condemned buildings, and other isolated locations.

Andy Solomon (essay date 1990)

SOURCE: "Scared but Safe," in *The New York Times Book Review,* September 2, 1990, p. 21.

[*In the following review, Solomon asserts that while* Four Past Midnight *contains many of King's weaknesses as a fiction writer—including awkward prose—the collection is successful in providing readers with a way to escape the frightening aspects of modern life.*]

A decade ago, in *Danse Macabre,* Stephen King made his literary esthetic clear: "I try to terrorize the reader. But if . . . I cannot terrify . . . I will try to horrify; and if I find I cannot horrify, I'll go for the gross-out. I'm not proud." The figures on his royalty checks suggest this strategy works, and he sticks to it closely in *Four Past Midnight*. Unlike Mr. King's adventurous novel *The Eyes of the Dragon,* this quartet of short novels risks few departures from earlier form.

By now, everyone knows Stephen King's flaws: tone-deaf narration, papier-mâché characters, clichés, gratuitous vulgarity, self-indulgent digressions. Each is amply present in these pages ringing with echoes of earlier King. Most tales revisit the old Maine setting. The characters are types rather than individuals. Even the taste for the crude looks familiar—five pages rendered with more detail than we care for to describe a man's getting interrupted in the bathroom by a phone call.

Not proud at all, Mr. King rehashes plot devices as well. Like an earlier work, *The Stand,* one of these novellas, *The Langoliers*, eliminates all humanity but for a few survivors, this time on a plane that has passed through a "time rip." This ploy of minimizing his cast serves Mr. King's purpose; he constantly relies on there being no one around with the common sense his characters invariably lack—until the last moment when, miraculously, they realize exactly how to avert catastrophe.

However, we don't read Stephen King for common sense, originality or insight into the adult world. Many who wouldn't want the fact broadcast read this master of suspense to escape their helpless fear of the headlines and to re-experience the more innocent terrors of childhood, to be once again a preschooler whose heart pounds from a nightmare.

In this collection, only *Secret Window, Secret Garden*, because it is about an adult's psychological disintegration, fails to achieve that effect. *The Langoliers* exploits the primal infant's fear of abandonment, even of ceasing to exist. *The Library Policeman* reawakens the most haunting dimensions of childhood admonitions. In *The Sun Dog*, the terrifying agent is a boy's Polaroid camera. Mr. King's recurring tactic of making the ordinary function in a bizarre way always hooks the child in us. Significantly, this "simplified" Polaroid is too complex inside to fix. We had hoped, growing up, for comforting knowledge of how the world works, but the technology opening onto the 21st century has out-raced us.

Also abundant here is another source of Mr. King's mass appeal, springing ironically from his clichéd diction, what Paul Gray in *Time* magazine once called "postliterate prose." Admittedly lazy, —he says "I'm a lazy researcher"—Mr. King often avoids laboring at description by summoning pre-existing images from cartoons, old movies, television shows and commercials. Here, sinister men wear "white *Andromeda Strain* suits." People wind up in a "dreary version of Fantasyland." A ruffled adulterer, when caught, looks, "like Alfalfa in the old Little Rascals." Men wish for guns "like the one Dirty Harry wore." Slacks are "the color of Bazooka bubble gum."

As the poet laureate of pop, Mr. King is read by many who might otherwise never read fiction at all. He creates an immediate and familiar landscape and could form the ideal bridge from the Road Runner to Dostoyevsky's Raskolnikov.

There is little here Mr. King has not done before, but once again he proves difficult to lay aside.

Edward Bryant (essay date 1990)

SOURCE: A review of *Four Past Midnight,* in *Locus,* Vol. 25, No. 4, October, 1990, pp. 23-4.

[*Bryant is an American science fiction novelist, short story writer, playwright, and critic. In the following review, he finds the novellas in* Four Past Midnight *highly entertaining.*]

At least for us outsiders, there seems to be a lesson in Stephen King's new collection, *Four Past Midnight*. Just as happened in the similarly structured four-novella set, *Different Seasons*, the master story-spinner of the American century demonstrates what he can do when he writes comparatively short and direct, punching right to the heart and brain, cutting to the bone, tapping tear ducts and adrenal glands as though they were sugar maples. I say "comparatively" because King's novellas in this book are about as long as other people's entire paperback originals back in the dear, dead days before literary gigantism became both a menace to North American forests and an inflated, greedy-guts pass to popular marketability.

In baseball terms, *Four Past Midnight* bats about .850, not too shabby in any league. The four novellas each have distinctly individual personalities. They each provide entertainment commensurate with the reader's investment of time in reading them, and all have something legitimate to say about the author-as-craftsman. A lot of the charm of the book is in what it says about writing and the writer himself, as well as treating the primary thing, the fiction.

Like the proverbial one-ton gorilla, Stephen King can do anydamnthing he wants, and he uses that power wisely and well in *Four Past Midnight*. At least half the book is the author rethinking and reworking old materials—not rewriting as such, but still making some considered and thoughtful decisions about previous stories and themes he's tackled. Most of the rest of us never get a second chance, so it's a pleasure to see a colleague handle that challenge and, for the most part, make it work.

The binding energy of this large book is provided by the author's introduction and story notes. There's a little autobiographical material here, some astute observation, and some useful literary footnoting. The tone is fascinating, and to me not nearly so extroverted as most of King's previous, similar notetaking. I may be 'way off as an observer, but the auctorial feeling seems a little bemused, rather sober, a whole lot wry. It's concise, useful, and highly readable, connoting a writer who's been through a lot over the past fifteen or twenty years. Give him enough time to fill out his first quarter century as a creative artist, and King will probably write one killer of a literary autobiography.

Ah, but how's the fiction? It's a four-course banquet.

Four Past Midnight leads from strength with *The Langoliers*, a rather more satisfying and successful version of the survival themes in *The Mist*. But while *The Mist*, in both its incarnations, never really felt complete in terms of plot sequence and closure, *The Langoliers* does most everything right, setting up intriguing characters, a decent plot, challenging problems for the folks in the story, and a genuinely horrendous set of antagonists to deal with.

I read the story on a flight from Denver to Philadelphia, which turned out to be a highly appropriate venue. A dozen airline passengers on a redeye from L.A. to Boston wake up from bad dreams to find everyone else on the flight missing, and the widebody L1011 droning along on autopilot. Fortunately, one of the survivors is a deadheading commercial pilot returning home to deal with the accidental death of his ex-wife. The other passengers include a little blind girl, a British secret agent, and a businessman who demonstrates by his nastily swinish ways the need for eugenics when it comes to breeding yuppies. Once the pilot takes control of the plane and everyone has a chance to look around, it becomes clear that something is dreadfully wrong at ground-level America, 36,000 feet down. There are no lights, no signs of city. There's no signal on the airwaves when the survivors use the plane's radio. If this sounds vaguely like an old *Twilight Zone* episode, don't worry. The truth turns out to be much more like Jerry (*Costigan's Needle*) Sohl than Rod Serling. At a loss for a better plan, the survivors fly east, avoid Boston because of heavy cloud cover, and land in Bangor, Maine. The airport's still there, all right, but it's deserted. And there's something seriously wrong with little things like sound, and the air itself, and well . . . *everything*. The psychic little girl detects the ominous approach of something terrible from the east.

The Langoliers is not supernatural horror. If one is looking for a neat label, the novella is indeed horror, but of a rigorously science fictional nature. It poses a series of problems that the characters have to solve. King covers his rear well when it comes to keeping the plot complicated, yet plays fair with common sense and logic. Every time you think the writer has forgotten something, *bingo,* the cast catches on to what's happening and does something ingenious but reasonable. Menace comes both internally and externally, and it's suitably scary. No character, no matter how sympathetic, is safe. And when the final menaces, phildickian Odor Eater sorts of agents of entropy, come on the scene, all ready to devour whatever cast-off obsolete reality the humans now inhabit, well, it's a real party.

At 239 pages, this novella could easily have been expanded into a behemoth. But it wasn't, and we should be grateful. No cereal extenders here. In terms of evoked characters, a complete plot, and some nice imaginative imagery, *The Langoliers* works just fine.

The second novella, *Secret Window, Secret Garden*, takes another angle of approach to *The Dark Half,* but without a lot of feinting, flinching, or extraneous running around. This is a 146-page portrait of a writer in deep trouble. Morton Rainey is a best-selling novelist living by himself up in the Northeast after separating from his wife. One afternoon he's confronted by a redneck cracker from Mississippi who claims Rainey stole one of the man's stories. Plagiarism, whether deliberate or unconscious, blatant or subtle ("Well . . . gee, friends, I thought it was just good research . . .") is always a matter of some interest to writers. If we haven't committed that deadly sin ourselves, we've perhaps been the victim, or, more likely, we've watched the whole sordid mess enfold friends or acquaintances.

At any rate, poor Mort Rainey's immediate assumption is that he's the innocent victim of a complete loon. After all, he's got *proof* of his blamelessness. But then the fissures start to develop in the sturdy walls of his comparatively safe life.

When you start to suspect that everything you know is wrong, that's when fear begins. *Secret Window, Secret Garden* is full of fear. It's a writerly story that I hope will mean something to the readers whose only conscious connection with writing was filling out the reservation coupon for this book at their local mall chain bookstore.

And if there's a problem with the story, it's probably the sort of thing writers can debate at bleary literary parties. The author makes a conscious decision at the end, when he determines whether *Secret Window, Secret Garden* is a supernatural fantasy, a weird version of ugly realism, or an ambiguous fictive mugwump. I think maybe the total effect is diminished by the choice that's nailed down. That quibble aside, the rest of the story hums. Well . . . like teeth grinding.

The Library Policeman is one of those great childhood images that Stephen King has turned into nearly 200 pages of midwestern nightmare. Did *your* parents or teachers ever tell you that carelessly overdue books would be reclaimed by the Library Cop? He's one of the great archetypes, along with the gum collector, that original recycler who scrapes up the stale Beeman's and Wrigley's from the undersides of cafe booths and movie house seats.

Anyhow, smalltown Iowa realtor Sam Peebles finds himself in serious trouble with the Library Policeman after he checks a couple reference books out of the local library. Sam has never before visited his town library, nor has he visited *any* library in quite a long time. He doesn't consciously realize it, but he has his reasons.

In this one, King does a terrific job of setting up a bucolic, Jimmy Stewart sort of landscape, and then sets Wes Craven in charge to direct it to destruction. Like the first story in *Four Past Midnight*, *The Library Policeman* is satisfyingly complete in itself. Everything's here. It doesn't need to be any longer than it is. The sympathetic characters are nicely drawn. Themes of abuse, whether child or substance, run through the story, and they're handled effectively and with candor.

There is an inhuman monster, however, and when the thing appears in its true form, all snotty, mucoid, and basically disgusting, it's simply not as menacing as when it was passing for human in the shadows. Again, it's an artist's choice: show the critter with the potential for diminishing its effect because of the zipper in the back of the suit? Or try to let it continue playing off the fertile imagination of the reader's worst fantasies?

At any rate, **The Library Policeman** is a good, satisfying tale, and it's also, just like **The Langoliers**, got the potential for translating to a very effective movie.

Four Past Midnight winds up with **The Sun Dog**, marginally the shortest piece in the book, and possibly the least effective. Not that it's bad, mind you, just less satisfying in its incompleteness.

The author, in his story note, cops to **The Sun Dog** being a sort of transitional piece between *The Dark Half* and *Needful Things,* the novel King says will be his last statement on Castle Rock, Maine. The story's about all the sinister things that happen when Kevin Delevan receives a Polaroid Sun 660 instant camera for his 15th birthday.

Something strange goes wrong immediately. Regardless of what the viewfinder shows, every picture taken with the camera depicts a genuinely mean-looking dog on a sidewalk. More, there's a sequence of movement to the dog from print to print. And as the dog starts to react to the photographer and move closer to the camera, it appears to be readying a spring and, worse, changing into some sort of demonic creature that looks like it just might be powerful enough, somehow, to break through from its world to ours. Naturally, this realization puts a damper on Kevin's amateur photography, but only encourages Pop Merrill, the local junk store dealer who, upon learning of the camera's magic quality, figures he can unload the Polaroid for big bucks to some New Age mystical-types.

The idea of an instant camera from hell (cursed? haunted?) is a perfectly fine EC Comics sort of image. The problem is all the questions that are raised and never addressed. Where does the camera come from? Why does Kevin get it? Just what is the relationship between the other world of the instant photos and this one? It may well be that *Needful Things* will answer these and other queries. But for now, **The Sun Dog** is all the reader has to work with. And there's no sense of closure, physical or psychological, to leave the reader with a reasonable sense of completion, satisfaction. The characters are flesh and blood, the horror conceit is good, but the story, *as* story, is frustrating.

And that's why I can't say the collection bats a thousand. But pretty damned close. Just as did **Different Seasons,** **Four Past Midnight** shows off the author to advantage. Stephen King has the talent to do well at whatever length

of fiction he chooses to address, but it seems that the novella form is particularly hospitable. It's long enough to allow most of the benefits of the long form, yet short enough to require tight writing.

Good job.

Arthur W. Biddle (essay date 1992)

SOURCE: "The Mythic Journey in 'The Body'," in *The Dark Descent: Essays Defining Stephen King's Horrorscope,* edited by Tony Magistrale, Greenwood Press, 1992, pp. 83-97.

[*Biddle is an American educator and critic. In the following essay, he examines* The Body *as a narrative that follows the traditional pattern of the "mythic journey."*]

> There's a high ritual to all fundamental events,
> the rites of passage, the magic corridor where
> the change happens. [King, *The Body*]

"The magic corridor where the change happens" is the special territory of Stephen King. This zone of extraordinary power takes many shapes. In *It* Ben Hanscom maintains a connection to his own adolescent past by returning again and again in memory to the glassed-in corridor that connects the children's wing to the adult section of his hometown library. Finally, at the end of the novel, this conduit is fully realized when Ben and the Losers' Club merge past and present in their return to Derry. In *The Talisman* the Oatley Tunnel is the symbolic passageway for Jack Sawyer from the protected world of his mother to the depraved town of Oatley. In **The Body** the "magic corridor" for Gordie Lachance and his friends is the railroad tracks they follow in their search for the dead Ray Brower.

The fundamental event in **The Body** is the coming into identity of the young hero, Gordon Lachance. From Friday afternoon until Sunday morning at the end of August 1960, Gordie undergoes a series of trials that bring him to selfhood, to identity both as a young man and as a writer. The narrative pattern that King employs is the archetypal rite of passage that marks the transition from one life stage to another.

In a recent interview, Stephen King acknowledged the influence on his work of mythologist Joseph Campbell: "I was particularly taken by the book *The Hero with a Thousand Faces*" [Magistrale, *Stephen King,* 1992]. That influence shapes the structure and major themes of King's tale of the journey of four boys on the brink of adolescence. Their adventure, especially that of the central hero Gordie, recapitulates the timeless rites of passage that order human experience. In his *The Hero with a Thousand Faces,* Campbell summarizes the pattern:

> The standard path of the mythological adventure of the hero is a magnification of the formula represented in the rites of passage: *separation—initiation—return:* which might be named the nuclear monomyth. A hero ventures forth from the world of common day into a region of supernatural wonder: fabulous forces are there encountered and a decisive victory is won: the hero

comes back from this mysterious adventure with the power to bestow boons on his fellow man.

The modern reader has become accustomed to viewing the journeys of Jason or Ulysses [both Homer's and Joyce's versions] or even Jesus in these terms. But it may seem a bit pretentious to apply the mythic pattern to the experiences of four twelve-year-olds in the Maine of 1960. Critic Northrop Frye recognizes the modern author's difficulty in incorporating "a mythical structure into realistic fiction." The solution is what Frye calls "displacement," essentially deemphasizing and disguising the mythic elements in order to achieve plausibility. King accomplishes this displacement with great skill: the story of *The Body* works for the contemporary reader as a nice bit of adventure that seldom strains credulity. Yet, the underlying structure is clearly that of Campbell's monomyth: "a separation from the world, a penetration to some source of power, and a life-enhancing return."

The "kingdom" of Castle Rock is a drought-stricken, heat-beaten wasteland. The soil is barren; no garden has produced a crop in this the driest and hottest summer since 1907. The metaphoric ruler of this land—King of Castle Rock—is Gordie's father, a figure of abject futility as he stands amidst the dust of his ruined garden, "making useless rainbows in the air" with his watering hose. He looks "sad and tired and used. He was sixty-three years old, old enough to be my grandfather," Gordie observes. His powers have deserted him, and as a result his entire realm suffers a corresponding loss of vitality. The older Lachance is a modern version of an ancient figure—the Fisher King. Jessie L. Weston remarks, "the intimate relation at one time was held to exist between the ruler and his land; a relation mainly dependent upon the identification of the [Fisher] King with the Divine principle of Life and Fertility" [*From Ritual to Romance,* 1957]. Mr. Lachance and Castle Rock are in death's grip.

Reinforcing this theme of sterility in the Kingdom is Gordie's mother, who has suffered alternating periods of fertility and barrenness. After three miscarriages she was told she would never have a child; five years later she became pregnant with Dennis. Ten years after that at age forty-two she conceived Gordie, whose birth is unusual: "the doctor had to use forceps to yank me out." His parents have told him this story many times: "They wanted me to think I was a special delivery from God."

Special delivery from God or not, Gordie was always ignored in favor of his older, more talented brother Dennis. When Denny was alive, Gordie felt like Ralph Ellison's Invisible Man: "Nobody ever notices him at all unless he fucks up. People look right through him." With Denny's death in a jeep accident, his parents behave as if they have nothing to live for. The senior Lachance is a king without an heir: "He'd lost a son in April and a garden in August." When his father notices Gordie at all, it is only to attack his friends as "a thief and two feebs," and by implication to put Gordie into the category of social misfit. Gordie accounts for his mother's distracted behavior by flatly pointing out that "her only kid was dead." He sees himself as the true target of the ultimate putdown, "Did your mother ever have any kids that lived?"

One result of this treatment at the hands of his parents is his fear of his brother's ghost, which he is sure lurks in Denny's closet. In his dreams Denny's battered and bloody corpse emerges from his closet and confronts him: "It should have been you, Gordon. It should have been you." These dreams are the product of the guilt Gordie feels for being alive. Subconsciously he feels that his survival somehow makes him responsible for Denny's death as well as for his parents' grief. Gordie dreads that "it" might yet become him, accounting in part for the power that Vern's tale of the discovery of Ray Brower's body exerts over him. These fears move out of his dreams and into his writing—**"Stud City," "The Revenge of Lard Ass Hogan,"** and the Le Dio stories—a literature of guilt and death.

Joseph Campbell provides some insight into the role Gordie is to play in the ensuing adventure. The hero of the monomyth "and/or the world in which he finds himself suffers from a symbolical deficiency" (Campbell). In *The Body* that deficiency is two-fold: both personal and societal. Gordie experiences a grave crisis of identity, not so much an uncertainty about *who* he is, but *that* he is. If no one acknowledges your presence, do you really exist? Gordie's very being is called into question. Thus as soon as Vern tells about his brother's discovery of the body, Gordie empathizes with the dead boy: "I felt a little sick, imagining that kid so far away from home, scared to death." His ego is so undeveloped that he needs to view the body of young Ray Brower to be sure it is not he himself who has died. He also needs to acknowledge the existence of death in life, something he was unable to do at Denny's funeral. Ray Brower's body offers a concretization of Gordie's many fears. Only through this quest can Gordie begin to deal with the shadow that hangs over all our lives.

The second symbolical deficiency inheres in the world in which he lives, a parched and infertile wasteland, like the land of the Fisher King. On the surface, the sterility of Castle Rock is a result of the prolonged drought and extraordinary heat of the summer of 1960. But at a deeper level, it is the aridity of a community that cannot love. Castle Rock is a place where parents maim their children by burning their ears, bruising their faces, or destroying their spirits. Where teachers steal and shift the blame to their students by lying. Where shopkeepers cheat their innocent customers. And where public employees train their dogs to attack children. The destructive machine appetites of Castle Rock are shown throughout the book—from Milo's junkyard of American waste to the pollution of the Castle River to the life-threatening train itself bearing down on the boys from the direction of the town. The true purpose of Gordie's journey, then, is to remedy these two deficiencies of self-identity and sterility of the kingdom, although he is aware of only the first and that but inchoately.

Twelve-year-old Gordon Lachance is, admittedly, an unlikely candidate for hero. But that shouldn't be a total surprise. The archetypal hero of the monomyth always fulfills a pattern according to the nature and the requirements of the particular narrative. Campbell describes two variations on the type of the hero and the fruit of his adventure:

Typically the hero of the fairy tale achieves a domestic, microcosmic triumph, and the hero of myth a world-historical, macrocosmic triumph. Whereas the former—the youngest or despised child who becomes the master of extraordinary powers—prevails over his personal oppressors, the latter brings back from his adventure the means for the regeneration of his society as a whole.

Like the hero of the fairy tale, Gordie is the youngest and the despised child who confronts a variety of personal oppressors: his parents, the storekeeper, the dumpkeeper and his dog, the older boys. Only by mastering these trials will Gordie be able to achieve identity. But as the son of the King, he is also called upon to redeem the realm; through his tests he will develop the extraordinary powers required to regenerate his society. By tracing the course of his quest, we may come to understand the achievement of these prizes.

"You guys want to go see a dead body?" Vern Tessio sounds the call to adventure by bringing news of the discovery of the body of a boy missing for three days. By announcing the challenge to find the dead Ray Brower, twelve-year-old Vern acts as herald who calls the hero to the adventure. Chris Chambers supports the call and embellishes it: "We can find the body and report it! We'll be on the news!" Gordie's three friends—Chris Chambers, Vern Tessio, and Teddy Duchamp—have also been scarred by the adult world and denied its love. The boys see this as an opportunity to achieve attention and perhaps even affection.

Campbell explains that the call "signifies that destiny has summoned the hero and transferred his spiritual center of gravity from within the pale of his society to a zone unknown." As we shall see, Gordie is challenged to an adventure which promises a spiritual transformation through a dying and a re-birth. Jungian analyst Erich Neumann supports the psychological import of this type of archetypal experience: "The dragon fight of the first period [onset of puberty] begins with the encounter with the unconscious and ends with the heroic birth of the ego." In accepting the call, Gordie (accompanied by Chris, Vern, and Teddy) enters on a quest that, unlike their existence in Castle Rock, is life-confirming and morally unambiguous. "We knew exactly who we were and exactly where we were going."

Although their preparations are scant (mainly concocting stories to cover their absence), they sense intuitively the significance of the journey ahead. It is high noon when they set off. The older Gordie, sitting at his computer twenty years later, reflects: "I'll never forget that moment, no matter how old I get."

Leaving behind the security of home, the boys walk through the afternoon heat until they come to the dump, that repository of "all the American things that get empty, wear out, or just don't work any more." Situated on the edge of town and populated by a vaguely demonic assortment of rats, woodchucks, seagulls, and stray dogs, it marks the limits of their known world. The dump functions as what Campbell calls the threshold, representing

"regions of the unknown" that are "free fields for the projection of unconscious content." Poised on the brink of puberty, the boys have outgrown their old haunts and pastimes. To develop, they must move forward. But first they must penetrate the threshold to the source of power.

Barring the way are the threshold guardians, Milo Pressman, the dumpkeeper, and his dog, Chopper. Campbell points out that the watchman functions as the guardian of established bounds of consciousness: "And yet—it is only by advancing beyond those bounds, provoking the destructive other aspects of the same power, that the individual passes, either alive or in death, into a new zone of experience." Reminiscent of Cerberus, the three-headed watchdog of the underworld encountered by Aeneas, Chopper is "the most feared and least seen dog in Castle Rock." Legends abound. Chopper, it was said, had been trained not only to attack, but to attack specific parts of the body on command from Milo. The command every boy dreaded to hear was "Chopper! Sic! Balls!"

As in the subsequent episode with the leeches, the boy's paramount fear is emasculation. The pubescent boy, unconfirmed in his sexuality, is sensitive to every threat, real or imagined. Their town and families have symbolically emasculated them. And the boys' frequent teasing about being a "pussy" or being "queer" and the boasting of penile size impress the centrality of this concern to all of them. Gordie doesn't even see Chopper as he races for the fence and safety, but he feels him gaining. Like Cerberus, that other threshold guardian, Chopper is perceived as a hound from Hell: "shaking the earth, blurting fire out of one distended nostril and ice out of the other, dripping sulphur from his jaws." It is only when Gordie has scaled the fence and looks back through its mesh from a place of safety that he actually sees that Chopper is a rather ordinary mongrel of medium size: "My first lesson in the vast difference between myth and reality." Paradoxically, though, King's narrative (as well as Jung's and Campbell's world views) shows that myth and reality are not poles apart. Indeed reality recapitulates myth. So that even though Chopper may not be truly a hound of Hell, he fulfills the function of threshold guardian perfectly well. And as both the reader and Gordie will soon discover, the journey to see the body emphasizes the similarities, rather than the differences, "between myth and reality."

Gordie's experience at the dump allows him passage beyond the realm of ordinary existence in Castle Rock, through trial, to new possibilities. With his friends he leaves the dump/threshold much as Ulysses departed from the Cyclops, hurling imprecations. The threshold gained, the adventurers move into unfamiliar territory and new tests of their will.

Gordie and his friends have now completed the first phase of the rite of passage: separation from the known world. As they seek to penetrate to a source of power thus far denied them, they, and especially Gordie, will have to pass even more severe tests. Although Gordie is accompanied by three friends, they play distinctly supporting roles as far as the mythic quest is concerned. They are reminiscent of J. R. R. Tolkien's merry band of Hobbits who support Frodo on his adventures in Middle Earth. Chris Chambers, of course, does stand out as Gordie's special friend and guide, more like Tolkien's Sam or Dante's Virgil than Don Quixote's Sancho Panza. (Their relationship and the special kind of love they share is too rich a theme to explore here.) But though Chris and the others participate in the communal tests, only Gordie is tested alone. He is the singular hero challenged to relieve the symbolical deficiencies of self and society through an act of initiation.

The mature narrator characterizes the rites of passage as "the magic corridor where change happens." "Our corridor," he continues, "was those twin rails, and we walked between them, just hopping along toward whatever this was supposed to mean." Those twin rails pose a more-than-symbolic threat, though, when the boys must cross a railroad trestle over the Castle River. Its height—fifty feet above the river—is dizzying. Its length—well over a hundred yards—is terrifying because the time of the next train remains unknown. The will to face the danger is perceived as a test of masculinity: "Any pussies here?" Chris asks. Gordie accepts the dare "and as I said it some guy pole-vaulted in my stomach. He dug his pole all the way into my balls, it felt like, and ended up sitting astride my heart." To Gordie, the fear of death is perceived largely as a sexual threat. Chris and Teddy lead the way, followed by Vern and then Gordie far behind.

Gordie is halfway across when he has to stop to calm his jitters and overcome his dizziness: "that was when I had my first and last psychic flash." He realizes that the train is coming and that he will surely be killed if he is caught on the trestle. Fear grips him, he urinates involuntarily, time stops. Transcendent terror causes mind and body to disconnect. He is unable to move. "An image of Ray Brower, dreadfully mangled and thrown into a ditch somewhere like a ripped-open laundry bag, reeled before my eyes." The gut-wrenching fear that Gordie felt when he first heard of the boy's death was premonitory. In his mind's eye he is reliving Ray Brower's fate, he is *becoming* Ray Brower. That thought breaks the spell, freeing Gordie to rise from the railbed like "a boy in underwater slow motion."

Gordie never saw the train, just as he never saw Chopper during his pursuit. The train, Chopper, the mills of Castle Rock, the fate that took Dennis away—all seem larger than life, like Ace and his gang of bigger boys. One purpose of Gordie's journey is to humanize these mythic enemies by obtaining control over them.

When the four find a cool, shady spot where they can rest and recover, Gordie admits his fear, "I was fuckin *petrified*." But in facing that fear Gordie gains a new-found strength. "My body felt warm, exercised, at peace with itself. Nothing in it was working crossgrain to anything else. I was alive and glad to be." Through his brush with death he has discovered a new sense of wholeness and well-being. Twice he has been pursued, once by a creature of nature, Chopper, and once by a creature of technology, the train. Twice he has confronted the worst fears of his subconscious and the threat to his emerging ego and survived. In the next test he is actually touched by death.

The group walk only a mile beyond the trestle before mak-

ing camp for the night. After an improvised supper and a manly cigaret, they lie in their bedrolls talking about things twelve-year-olds talk about: cars, baseball, teachers. Gordie thinks about how different nightfall is in the woods with no lights and "no mothers' voices" calling their children to the safety of home. Teddy tells about witnessing a near-drowning at White's Beach. What they don't talk about is Ray Brower, but Gordie thinks about him, "so alone and defenseless. . . . If something wanted to eat on him, it would. His mother wasn't there to stop that from happening." A necessity of every boy's journey to adulthood is leaving forever the comforting bosom of the mother. Gordie feels the pain of that separation and the danger to which it exposes him; he does not yet understand the potential gains of the break: freedom and power.

When Gordie finally falls asleep, he has the first of two swimming dreams: he and Denny are bodysurfing at Harrison State Park. The dream is interrupted as he awakens, confused and disoriented, unsure of where he is or what woke him. Then he hears a drawn-out unearthly scream. Everyone is awake now and speculating on the source: a bird? a wildcat? Ray's ghost?

Again Gordie dreams of swimming, this time with Chris at White's Beach, the scene of the near-drowning Teddy had told of earlier in the evening. As the boys swim out over their heads, one of their teachers floats over on an inflatable raft and orders Chris to give Robert Frost's "Mending Wall" by rote. In despair he begins to recite, then his head goes under water. He rises again, pleads with Gordie to help him, and sinks beneath the surface once more.

> Looking into the clear water I could see two bloated, naked corpses holding his ankles. One was Vern and the other was Teddy, and their open eyes were as blank and pupilless as the eyes of Greek statues. Their small pre-pubescent penises floated limply up from their distended bellies like albino strands of kelp. Chris's head broke water again. He held one hand up limply to me and voiced a screaming, womanish cry that rose and rose, ululating in the hot summer air. I looked wildly toward the beach but nobody had heard. The lifeguard . . . just went on smiling down at a girl in a red bathing suit.

As Chris is dragged under a last time, his eyes and hands implore Gordie's help. "But instead of diving down and trying to save him, I stroked madly for the shore." Before he can reach safety, though, he feels the grip of "a soft, rotted, implacable hand" pulling him down. The dream ends when he is shaken into wakefulness by Teddy's grip on his leg.

Every element of this dream either derives from Gordie's recent experiences and present fears or presages events yet to come. The dream again links Gordie with Ray Brower, the child as helpless victim cornered by forces larger than himself. The corpses of Vern and Teddy grow from Chris's earlier observation that "your friends drag you down. . . . They're like drowning guys that are holding onto your legs. You can't save them. You can only drown with them." Their small limp penises reflect both their physical immaturity and Gordie's fears about his sexual adequacy. Their corpses also foreshadow their deaths at an early age, although Gordie couldn't have foreseen that. And Chris will be murdered when he is only twenty-four years old. His imploring figure reflects his reliance on Gordie, as an understanding friend in the present and as a mentor in the college prep courses in high school. His thin womanish scream is the unexplained cry they heard earlier in the night. Fearful for his own life, Gordie does not dive down to save Chris. Instead, he looks to the adult world on the beach for help. In the person of the lifeguard charged with protecting swimmers, that world ignores Gordie's pleas, just as the adult world of Castle Rock has failed to heed the cries of its children. As Gordie himself is being dragged under water by "a soft, rotted, implacable hand," he is awakened by Teddy; it is time to stand his tour of guard duty.

This dream represents the first stage of Gordie's night sea journey, an archetypal pattern symbolic of rebirth. Briefly, the archetype as employed by Virgil, Dante, and the author of the Book of Jonah among others, sees the hero making a perilous journey, usually by night, into the depths of the sea or a dark cavern. He may be swallowed by a sea monster. Joseph Campbell characterizes the hero's perilous journey as a descent "into the crooked lanes of his own spiritual labyrinth." Entering a cavern, the belly of a whale, or the depths of the sea, the hero leaves behind the upper world of light and life to confront his own death. Jungian analyst Erich Neumann explains that puberty is a time

> of rebirth, and its symbolism is that of the hero who regenerates himself through fighting the dragon. All the rites characteristic of this period have the purpose of renewing the personality through a night sea journey, when the spiritual or conscious principle conquers the mother dragon, and the tie to the mother and to childhood, and also to the unconscious, is severed.

The second part of the archetypal pattern, the dragon fight, will take place the next day.

During the rest of the night Gordie passes in and out of consciousness. Finally, he awakens from a light sleep to discover that dawn has broken. He is savoring his solitude when he notices a deer standing less than thirty feet away, looking at him. The impact of the sight nearly overwhelms him: "My heart went up into my throat. . . . I couldn't have moved if I had wanted to." When he perceives the deer to be looking at him "serenely," Gordie projects into her being, "seeing a kid with his hair in a sleep-scarecrow of whirls and many-tined cowlicks." It is as if "he" (some part of him) has moved out of his body and looks at that twelve-year-old standing there. The doe emphasizes her trust of Gordie by confidently crossing the tracks and beginning to feed. "She didn't look back at me and didn't need to." They coexist in a state of perfect trust and harmony. The deer remains until an approaching train frightens her off.

"What I was looking at was some sort of gift, something given with a carelessness that was appalling." For the psychic meaning of this remarkable gift, we look to the symbolic values of the deer. The opening lines of the Jerusalem Bible version of Psalm 42 equate the deer with the human spirit: "As a doe longs for running streams, so longs my soul for you, my God." Cirlot's *A Dictionary of Symbols* doesn't treat *doe,* but identifies an analogous animal, the gazelle, as "an emblem of the soul" and of "the persecution of the passions and the aggressive, self-destructive aspect of the unconscious." Another related animal, the stag, is said to represent "the way of solitude and purity." Interestingly, the same source notes that the stag is "the secular enemy of the serpent," a variation on which will figure prominently a little later in the adventure. What this gift seems to signify is the awakening of Gordie's spiritual nature. The deer is his soul, which he had not known before. Although the boy doesn't understand all this, he does intuit the deer's import: "for me it was the best part of the trip, the cleanest part, and it was the moment I found myself returning to, almost helplessly, when there was trouble in my life." We realize that this state of grace is not carelessly given at all, but earned by Gordie's inner readiness. An awakened soul is essential for the tests that are yet to come. When Gordie returns to the camp and the other boys, he doesn't tell them about the deer. This is his secret.

A final obstacle stands between the boys and the object of their quest, between Gordie and the development of his ego. That obstacle is the dragon who guards the treasure, denying access to all comers. In his discussion of the child archetype, Carl Jung asserts that "the threat to one's inmost self from dragons and serpents points to the danger of the newly acquired consciousness being swallowed up again by the instinctive psyche, the unconscious" [*The Archetypes and the Collective Unconscious,* 1969]. Gordie's recent experiences of individuation—crossing the threshold, escaping the train, seeing the deer—have strengthened and developed his conscious ego and his spiritual dimension. But he is not yet secure. As Neumann pointed out earlier, the dragon must be slain in order to sever the tie "to the mother and to childhood, and also to the unconscious." As dragons are scarce in Maine, the leeches infesting the beaver pond must function as a displaced dragon, just as the pond itself is a continuation of Gordie's sea journey into the unconscious.

Gordie's dreams have anticipated this swim and warned of the threat that the unconscious poses to the developing consciousness. When the four boys emerge from the pond after their swim, they discover their bodies covered with bloodsuckers. Gordie and Chris take turns plucking the repulsive creatures off the other's body. Then Gordie sees "the granddaddy of all of them clinging to my testicles, its body swelled to four times its normal size."

Jung relates a patient's dream that is remarkably like Gordie's situation. In the dream "a snake shot out of a cave and bit him [Jung's patient] in the genital region. This dream occurred at the moment when the patient was convinced of the truth of analysis and was beginning to free himself from the bonds of his mother-complex" [Campbell]. The snake-dragon-leech, by threatening Gordie's sexuality, is attempting to prevent maturation and the subsequent ego independence it represents.

Terror-stricken, Gordie can't bring himself to touch the

leech and appeals to Chris to remove it. But Chris cannot help. Gordie must confront the dragon himself. "I reached down again and picked it off and it burst between my fingers. My own blood ran across my palm and inner wrist in a warm flood. I began to cry." Although Gordie has killed the leech, he himself is wounded. The leech, the chthonic symbol of the subterranean world of the unconscious, appears to have achieved mastery even in the moment of its own death. Gordie faints, that is, he loses his consciousness, and falls to the ground as if dead. Symbolically the wound is fatal. This is as it must be: Gordie has to die in order to be reborn. The sacrificial blood that he sheds is in the cause of his own growth and of the redemption of his society. Neumann explains that "the transformation of the hero through the dragon fight is a transfiguration, a glorification, indeed an apotheosis, the central feature of which is the birth of a higher mode of personality."

That transfiguration marks for Gordie a significant step in his passage from childhood to maturity, establishing an ego consciousness independent of his parents. This development is both a fruit of his quest and a precondition for the successful completion of his journey which he resumes when he regains consciousness.

As the four boys approach their destination, the weather begins to change. The arrival of storm clouds signals the end of three months of bright clear skies. The boy's shadows grow "fuzzy and ill-defined." Then the sun is blotted out: "I looked down and saw that my shadow had disappeared entirely." To Jung the shadow is the primitive, instinctive part of the psyche. Gordie stands poised on the brink of discovery. Elemental forces are gathering to punctuate the climax of the adventure. A cosmic blue-white fireball races along the track, passes the boys, and then disappears without a trace.

When Vern, the herald who called the adventure, spots Ray Brower's pale white hand sticking out of the underbrush, the skies open, loosing a downpour. "It was as if we were being rebuked for our discovery, and it was frightening." Rebuked perhaps, but the rain marks the end of the drought that has oppressed the land for months. The consequences for the life of the community of Gordie's long journey have already begun.

In death Brower is defenseless against the chthonic forces: black ants crawl over his hand and face, a beetle creeps out of his mouth and stalks across his cheek. Gordie is sickened, but what makes a stronger impression still is that Ray's feet are bare. His sneakers are caught in some brambles several feet away. The realization hits Gordie hard: "The train had knocked him out of his Keds just as it had knocked the life out of his body." The Keds are a powerful symbol for Gordie—of youth, of life, of the physical journey itself. He reflects on what death means for a twelve year old, what he wouldn't get to do, ordinary things like pulling a girl's braid in homeroom or wearing out the eraser on his pencil. Through the agency of a pair of filthy tennis shoes, Gordie finally is able to transmute death from an abstraction to a concretion and to understand it as a denial of life.

When Ace Merrill, Eyeball Chambers, and their gang arrive to claim the body as their prize, Chris and Gordie warn them off. Gordie senses the unfairness of it: "as if their easy way was the right way, the only way. They had come in cars." The older boys are disqualified from victory, from achieving the goal, not only because they took the easy way but also because they have broken the law in stealing the car. They represent negative forces that would usurp the treasure.

Ace Merrill orders Gordie to be sensible and relinquish the treasure and credit to his gang. Gordie's scorn is as great as his courage: "Suck my fat one, you cheap dime-store hood." His assertion of masculine dominance enrages Ace, who starts toward him intending to break both his arms. Only through Chris's introduction of a weapon, his father's pistol, is Gordie spared an immediate beating. Firing the gun first into the air and then at Ace's feet, Chris drives off the usurpers. That Chris, not Gordie, uses the gun is striking, but is in accord with Chris's status as the leader of the gang, war chief of the tribe. Gordie's role has always been that of the shaman, the story-telling medicine man in touch with the spirit world.

The big boys driven off, Chris and Gordie discuss what to do with the body. The strength of Chris's desire to carry it out of the woods suggests the depth of his need for approval and acceptance by his parents and the entire adult world. Finally, he is persuaded by his friend not to risk potential trouble if the big boys somehow implicated them in Brower's death.

As they leave, Gordie reflects on Ray Brower and mortality: "He was a boy our age, he was dead, and I rejected the idea that anything about it could be natural." Why? Probably because he felt he could guard against extra-natural causes; it was the natural ones that sneak up on you. The berry pail haunts him, though. Throughout his adventure Gordie has projected onto the missing boy. His own sense of self was so fragile that he had to see the body to be sure it wasn't himself. This confusion is evident in the mature writer's reflection: "That boy was *me*, I think. And the thought which follows, chilling me like a dash of cold water, is: *Which boy do you mean?*" The matter is still not entirely settled. We see the twenty-two-year-old Gordie exploring similar themes in **"Stud City."** Even the thirty-four-year-old writer is troubled from time to time. He remembers the berry pail and thinks about finding it: "it's mostly just the idea of holding that pail in my two hands, I guess—as much a symbol of my living as his dying, proof that I really do know which boy it was—which boy of the five of us."

Unlike the journey to the body, the return is uneventful. Retracing their steps, the boys cross the trestle and pass through the dump without incident. The town is still asleep when they arrive at five o'clock on Sunday morning, a propitious time for a return or a rebirth. Chris needs confirmation of their adventure: "We did it, didn't we? It was worth it, wasn't it?" "Sure it was," Gordie assures him. The parting from Vern and Teddy is routine, but between Chris and Gordie there is an undercurrent of things left unsaid: "I wanted to say something more to Chris but didn't know how to. . . . Speech destroys the functions of love, I think."

After the two boys part, there remains for Gordie one final act to conclude the adventure: the ritual cleansing and dressing of wounds. Standing at the kitchen sink, he scrubs his body all over with especial attention to his crotch. The mark left by the leech is fading, but a tiny scar will always serve as a reminder of his struggle.

What has Gordie's *agon* accomplished? At the onset of the journey two kinds of deficiencies required remedy. The first was Gordie's own psychic need to defeat his personal oppressors and to grow beyond the bounds of childhood. As he recapitulated the archetypal rites of passage, he prevailed over Milo and Chopper, the leeches, and the older boys. He achieved his goal of discovering the body and helped prevent the negative forces represented by the older boys from claiming it. He confronted the loss of his brother and his own worst fears of death and emasculation. He forged bonds of affection and mutual support with Chris. He moved beyond childhood and mother in the discovery of his spirit and the development of his own ego.

The second deficiency that Gordie was called upon to remedy was the sterility and lack of love in the kingdom of Castle Rock. Here, the fruit of his journey would appear less than "a world-historical, macrocosmic triumph" [Campbell]. His actions have not created a revolution of fertility and love. Yet Gordie's initiation does have results that impact on the larger community. When Gordie and his companions arrive at Ray Brower's body, the skies open and rain pours down for the first time in three months, ending the devastating drought that has plagued the land. When Gordie and Chris stand up to Ace Merrill's gang, they reestablish a rule of justice that had been lost in Castle Rock. And Gordie's actions testify to a truth forgotten by the adult world—the truth of love and caring. His concern for the lost body of Ray Brower initiates his quest. His love for Chris closes it and enables the one-time loser to succeed in a college prep course in high school and go on to college and graduate school.

But it is as writer that Gordie can have the greatest influence on his world. In a 1989 interview [published in *Stephen King, The Second Decade*] Tony Magistrale asked about the use of writers as protagonists in several of King's recent books.

> [Magistrale]: *But it also seems to me that in the many books which feature writers and writing you have endowed these characters with certain powers. . . .*
>
> [King]: Well, we do have powers. The guy in *The Dark Half* says that writers, actors, and actresses are the only recognized mediums of our society.

The storyteller is shaman, then, the one in touch with the world of spirit. His function is to reveal that world to his people.

The early stories (**"Stud City"** and **"The Revenge of Lard Ass Hogan"**) show the suffering and the guilt and the need

for retribution experienced by the young Gordon Lachance. The final story, told by the mature narrator, of four twelve-year-olds venturing along the railroad tracks to see a dead body—that story demonstrates the power of honesty, courage, and love. The great boon that Gordie Lachance brings back from his quest are those values that offer redemption for his society.

Gene Doty   (essay date 1992)

SOURCE: "A Clockwork Evil: Guilt and Coincidence in 'The Monkey,'" in *The Dark Descent: Essays Defining Stephen King's Horrorscope,* edited by Tony Magistrale, Greenwood Press, 1992, pp. 129-36.

[*Doty is an American educator and critic. In the following essay, he explores themes and narrative technique in "The Monkey."*]

In **"The Monkey,"** Stephen King has used an extremely unlikely object to arouse terror in his readers, a toy that is "nothing but cogs and clockwork" [*Skeleton Crew*]. This [essay] will explore the means by which King makes the monkey's association with the deaths in the story convincing and answer William F. Nolan's charge that, while powerfully written, **"The Monkey"** "lacks interior logic" [*Kingdom of Fear: The World of Stephen King,* 1987].

Douglas Winter, who calls **"The Monkey"** "one of King's best short stories," sees the monkey as representing a random, or fated, evil, "without apparent logic or motivation." Tony Magistrale takes an opposite view when he says that the monkey represents Hal's "dark recollections" of "childhood . . . guilt and anxiety." The tension between these two possible understandings of the monkey creates much of the effect of the story.

The question of the story's "interior logic" centers on the relationship between Hal and the monkey. There is an alternative to Winter's view that the monkey is an external, irrational evil, and Magistrale's view that the monkey is an objective correlative for Hal's guilt. In explaining this third possibility, I will also show the interior logic, which Nolan says the story lacks.

In the story, Hal Shelburn returns to his boyhood home after his aunt's death, bringing with him his sons, Dennis (aged 12) and Petey (aged 10), and his wife, Terry. His sons discover the monkey in the attic, and its discovery brings back the fear and guilt that Hal felt after discovering the monkey as a young child. After perceiving its association with several deaths, including his mother's, Hal attempts to destroy it by throwing it down a dry well. The story narrates the "present" when Hal as an adult has to deal with the monkey again, but the narration is interwoven with extensive flashbacks to Hal's childhood experiences with the monkey.

Hal first finds the monkey in his mother's attic when he is four years old. The monkey holds two cymbals, which it is supposed to clash together when wound up. Hal quickly discovers, to his disappointment, that the monkey does not work when he winds it up, but it does sometimes spontaneously clash its cymbals together. The horrible thing is that when it does so, someone dies. Its first victim is a child who falls from a tree. Other victims include Hal's and his brother's babysitter, a dog, yet another child, and the boy's mother.

The deaths associated with the monkey are not narrated in chronological order, but in an order of increasing emotional intensity. The effect of the interweaving of Hal's childhood and adult experiences is to identify Hal the adult with Hal the child, and also to create a strong link between Hal and Petey, his younger son. The interweaving also establishes a strong but ambiguous link between Hal and the monkey.

King describes the monkey both as a mindless mechanism and as taking malicious pleasure in the deaths it causes. Being a mere mechanism, it lacks conscious purpose; nor does it act directly to cause the deaths with which it is associated. Hal, as the viewpoint character, connects the monkey with the deaths. No one but Hal, and at the end Petey, perceives the connection between the monkey and the deaths. Through Hal, the reader is convinced of the connection between the monkey's cymbals and the deaths.

On one level the monkey embodies our dread of the accident that can befall any of us at any time. As much as we would like to pretend otherwise, none of our lives are secure. Heart embolisms, enraged lovers, drunken drivers, bizarre accidents: all of these and more are possible every moment of our lives, and all of them bring death in **"The Monkey."** Hal's life seems to have a large share of such dreadful accidents, beginning with the disappearance of his father, who may have been a victim of the monkey also, although neither Hal nor the reader is ever sure of this.

In connecting the monkey with the deaths, Hal has found a cause for these irrational accidents. Tragically, the monkey is beyond Hal's control and understanding. William F. Nolan asks the obvious question; why doesn't Hal "simply *destroy* the monkey?" Part of the answer is that the monkey exerts a will of its own, returning from the junk dealer whose truck Hal has thrown it on, reappearing in the same carton he originally found it in, and even appearing again twenty years after Hal had thrown it into a dry well. Terrified of the monkey, the child Hal is powerless to destroy it, disable it, or throw it away. Hal's inability to rid himself of the monkey suggests that the connection between them is complex.

When Hal takes the monkey to the well to dispose of it, he almost falls through the rotten boards covering the well, and becomes badly scratched by the thorns growing around it. This scene clearly suggests that the monkey has the power to destroy Hal, that Hal endangers himself when he threatens the monkey. In an earlier incident, when he is seven, after kicking the monkey violently, Hal "hears" the monkey telling him that Hal can kick as much as he wants, the monkey is "not real, just a funny clockwork monkey," implying that Hal really cannot injure or deter it; the monkey is both intimately linked to Hal and independent of his conscious control.

On this occasion, which results in the death of another child, Hal attacks the monkey, determined "to stomp it, smash it, jump on it"; but as Hal rushes the monkey, it sounds its cymbals again, quietly, "and a sliver of ice seem[s] to whisper its way through the walls of [Hal's] heart, impaling it, stilling his fury and leaving him sick with terror again." The monkey has the power to act on its own, even though it is "merely" a toy. Furthermore, the terror that the monkey instills in Hal keeps him from being able to destroy it.

On the day his mother dies, Hal comes home from school to find the monkey on a shelf in his room, after he thought he had hidden it in the attic where he originally found it. So far in the story, Hal's father has disappeared, Beulah the babysitter has been shot, and Bill's friend, Charlie Silverman, has been run over by a drunk. Hal connects the monkey's sounding its cymbals to the deaths and suspects that the monkey is connected to his father's disappearance. Now, home from school, Hal approaches the monkey "as if from outside himself—as if his own body had been turned into a windup toy at the sight of the monkey." Hal watches himself take down the monkey and turn the key, and he hears its mechanism begin to work. The nightmarish quality of this experience is due to Hal's awareness of the significance of what he is doing, and his inability to stop himself from winding up the monkey.

When his mother dies (of a brain embolism—there is always a natural cause for deaths associated with the monkey), Hal and the monkey exchange conditions. Hal becomes an automaton, doing the monkey's will, and the monkey becomes alive: "it *was* alive . . . and the vibration he felt through its balding brown fur was not that of turning cogs but the beating of its heart." In addition to the loss of his mother, Hal feels "guilt: the certain deadly knowledge that he had killed his mother by winding up the monkey on that sunny after-school afternoon." Neither Hal nor the monkey is the physical cause of his mother's death, but Hal feels guilty because he associates the monkey's action with her death—and he wound up the monkey.

Hal's relationship to the monkey is complex. When Hal first finds the monkey, it startles him because he thinks it is alive. Then, realizing it is a toy, he is delighted: "Its funny grin pleased him." Remembering the incident as an adult, Hal wonders if there was not another element in his initial response to the monkey: "Hadn't there been something else? An almost instinctive feeling of disgust?" As this passage shows, when Hal remembers his initial, childhood response to the monkey, he is unsure of exactly what that response was. But what King records in the narrative of Hal's discovery is delight. This delight expresses an immediate bond between Hal and the monkey, a bond that leads to his obsession with it. Because of this bond, Hal believes that the monkey has somehow caused the deaths of several people, a dog, and even a fly.

Hal is not simply the witness and indirect victim of the monkey's malevolence. Instead, several details indicate a close relationship between Hal and the monkey. When Hal returns to his childhood home at the beginning of the story, he looks into the well where he had thrown the monkey twenty years before. At the bottom of the well, Hal sees a reflected face, which he at first thinks is the monkey's. However, as Hal quickly realize, the reflected face is his own. Throughout the story, Hal "hears" the monkey's voice speaking to him personally and directly. The monkey also influences Hal's consciousness and his actions; for instance, the monkey tries to get Hal to wind it up. After Hal has tried to get rid of the monkey by putting it on a rag-man's truck, it returns, and "speaks" to him: "Thought you got rid of me, didn't you? But I'm not that easy to get rid of, Hal. I *like* you. We were made for each other, just a boy and his pet monkey, a couple of good old buddies."

The story is not really about a spooky toy monkey; it is about Hal, his fears and shames, and his desperate efforts to deal with them. Hal, like any normal child, must experience resentments toward the other people in his life, and, consequently, must also fantasize about their deaths. Abandoned by his father, orphaned by his mother's death, Hal has more than the usual reasons for resentment and fantasies of what his life might have been. Such resentments and fantasies create guilt in the normal person, and in Hal's case, they bind him to the deadly monkey. This guilt, violence, and anxiety link Hal and the monkey at a deep level but also make them antagonists. Hal struggles with the monkey, seeking to resist the attraction it exerts on him, and to cleanse himself of the negative qualities it expresses.

Hal's childhood guilt and rage have carried over into his adulthood. The monkey expresses a destructive urge in Hal as a father and husband. Hal feels an "uncontrollable hostility toward Dennis [his older son] more and more often." In this scene, Hal slams Dennis against the door several times; the monkey grins,"as if approbation." The monkey's malevolent grin expresses a facet of Hal himself. As a man and a father, Hal is unpredictable and violent. He fears the growing disaffection of his older son, Dennis, and is inwardly terrified that something awful will happen to his younger son, Petey. He feels alienated from his wife, who is taking "a lot of Valium." These anxieties and frustrations lead Hal to unintended violence against his son. They also repeat the fears of his childhood, providing the emotional context for the monkey's return; Hal is bonded to the monkey by his fear and guilt.

Petey, the favored son, shares Hal's sensitivity to the monkey. Having touched the monkey, he tells Hal that he both hates and likes the way the monkey feels. Then he informs Hal, "Daddy, I don't like that monkey" and also recognizes that the monkey is "bad." Like Hal, Petey has heard the monkey's voice, urging him to wind it up: "Wind me up, Petey, we'll play, your father isn't going to wake up, he's never going to wake up at all." The monkey has displaced Hal's father, and now seeks to displace Hal as Petey's father. The monkey's power of initiative and malevolent will are shown clearly as it seeks Hal's death.

When Hal rows out on the lake to sink the monkey, it appears to him that Petey regresses from nine years old to four. Significantly, Hal was four when he first found the monkey. Even though Petey does not go out in the boat with Hal, he definitely plays a part in sending the monkey to the bottom of the lake. From his position on the shore, Petey encourages and exhorts Hal, and warns him of the cloud that blows up with the storm. The love between fa-

ther and son makes it possible for Petey to help Hal reexperience his original contact with the monkey, and rid his life of its maliciousness by banishing the fear and guilt rooted in his own childhood.

Even though it appears to be an ordinary toy, there are several indications that the monkey is unnatural. These include the monkey's apparent delight in the deaths it causes, as well as the anxieties it produces in Hal. King's repeated descriptions of the monkey's teeth and grin imply that the monkey consciously relishes its role in bringing death and suffering to human beings. In these descriptions, King clearly suggests that the monkey is more than a toy, but the descriptions do not in themselves suffice to make the monkey an objective agent of evil.

The reader is partly convinced of the monkey's malice by the credibility of Hal's experience. Hal is believable largely because, like many of Kings's characters, he is one of us. One might see him in line at Radio Shack or at a PTA meeting. He experiences the same family difficulties that many middle-class fathers face. The reader can easily recognize and identify with these experiences and emotions.

Thus, the reader is prepared to accept Hal's memories of his childhood, as well as the new terrors he experiences after returning to his childhood home and rediscovering the instrument of his earlier terrors. Many readers will find their own childhood fears and anxieties intensified in the unusual ones that Hal experiences.

The story has a subtler dimension that gives the monkey its air of dread: even though nothing shows it directly causing the deaths, it is clearly connected with them. In fact, all of the deaths are "accidental," with natural causes to explain them. The closest thing to an act directly caused by the monkey is the death of the fly toward the end of the story. Petey drops the bag with the monkey in it; the monkey's cymbal strikes a rock and clangs. At that moment, a fly drops dead. But the only connection between the sounding of the cymbal and the death of the fly is that they happen in immediate succession. No direct causal link between the two is apparent.

There is a suggestion in the story that the monkey is more than a clockwork toy. When Hal rows out onto the lake to sink the monkey into the deepest part, a monkey-shaped cloud appears in the sky, associated with a storm that arises suddenly: "The sun was behind the cloud, turning it into a hunched, working shape with two gold-edged crescents held apart." King makes the nature of the monkey more complex by giving the earthly monkey a "celestial" counterpart, a cloud-spirit that manifests when the monkey is in great danger, almost bringing about Hal's death through the storm.

Just before Hal drops the monkey in the lake at the end of the story, he talks to Petey about its origins. Hal recognizes that while the monkey must have originally been one of many identical toys, subsequently "something bad" had happened to it. Hal then speculates that perhaps "most bad things" are not conscious of their badness, "that most evil might be very much like a monkey full of clockwork." The monkey combines the horror of a mindless evil with that of a deliberately malicious evil, as it seems both a (broken) mechanical toy and a living force that Hal cannot throw away or destroy. And, as stated before, the only connection between the monkey and the deaths is Hal's consciousness of the coincidence of its clanging its cymbals as each death occurs.

Throughout the story, the pattern of simple coincidence is the same: the monkey sounds its cymbals, and then someone dies. The question remains, What is the link between the cymbals and the deaths? Or, in William F. Nolan's phrase, What is the "interior logic" of the story? The monkey's role in the deaths is established through Hal's interpretation of events. Just because one event precedes or accompanies another does not mean it causes the other event. However, from an emotional and symbolic perspective, Hal's connecting the cymbals with the deaths is quite convincing.

The sound of the cymbals often initiates Hal's hearing the monkey's voice. In terms of sound-associations and resonances, when Hal (at seven years old) throws the monkey down the well, he hears the cymbals' *jang-jang* after it has hit the bottom, and flees, "his ears still *jangling*" (my emphasis). In several sentences that climax this section, King uses notable alliteration, establishing a cluster of sounds associated with the monkey's deadly action:

> If the monkey wanted to c*l*ap its he*ll*ish cymba*l*s now, *l*et it. It could c*l*ap and c*r*ash them for the c*r*aw*l*ing *b*ugs and *b*eet*l*es, the *d*ark things that *m*a*d*e their home in the we*ll*'s *st*one gu*ll*et. It would *r*ot *d*own there. Its *l*oathsome *c*ogs and whee*l*s and *spr*ings would *r*u*st d*own there. It would *d*ie *d*own there. In the *m*ud and *d*ark*n*ess. *Sp*iders would *sp*in it a *shr*oud. (emphases mine)

The sounds in these sentences are woven together so closely and subtly that there are more repetitions and partial alliterations than I have emphasized. The syntactical repetitions also contribute to the effect of this passage, which is an emotional and imagistic climax, effectively expressing the dreadfulness of the monkey.

Closely associated with the sound of the cymbals is the clicking sound the key makes when it is turned. In the scene narrating Hal's original discovery of the monkey (at age four), King describes the sleet "ticking" off the windows "sporadically," and off the roof "hypnotically." Both adverbs are significant: the monkey only works "sporadically," and it affects Hal "hypnotically." Further, the resemblance between the "ticking" of the sleet and the various "clicks" that the monkey's key makes is an example of the way sounds cluster around meaning, and, in the process, become expressive of the irrational qualities of experience. And, of course, the wintry chill of the sleet is congruent with the tone of the whole story.

The coincidence between the monkey and the deaths has an overwhelming and dreadful meaning for Hal because of his guilt over his part in its action, his fear of the monkey's apparent independence, and the emotional impact of the deaths themselves. The reader, in so far as he or she identifies with Hal's experiences, shares in the uncanny dread aroused by the monkey's association with the deaths and the apparent impossibility of getting rid of it.

"The Monkey" presents a world in which evil constantly threatens human beings, who do not even have the comfort of being afflicted by a personal evil, which they might at least be able to understand. The clockwork monkey's maliciousness embodies the accidental, irrational evil and suffering that constantly threaten all of us. In a world in which parents are absent (Hal's father), violent (Hal himself), or drugged (Hal's wife), the child must survive by his own resources. The return of the monkey puts Hal back in a child's state of terror and powerlessness. Paradoxically, by returning to a child-like state, Hal is able to relive his link with the monkey, and to untie the bonds of guilt and fear that connect him to it. His love for Petey gives him additional access to the innocence and directness of childhood. Through their shared love and courage, Hal and Petey are able to defeat the evil represented by the monkey, an evil that lies both outside them and inside them. Working together, Hal and Petey integrate the child and the adult.

Douglas Winter and Tony Magistrale posit two opposite interpretations of Hal's relationship to the monkey, Winter suggesting that the monkey is an objective evil, external to Hal, and Magistrale suggesting that it is a subjective evil, expressive only of Hal's personal fears and guilts. I have shown that the monkey's relationship to Hal is both objective and subjective—that the monkey is an evil beyond Hal's understanding and control, while at the same time, it is an evil intimate to Hal, a vehicle of his fears and guilts. One could say that the monkey embodies a more universal Evil, while Hal simply embodies a more personal evil.

The open-ended conclusion of "The Monkey" shows the subtle relationship between Hal and the evil toy. After Hal has sunk the monkey in the lake, he imagines a boy, fishing with his father, hooking the stuffed animal and reeling it in, "weeds draggling from its cymbals, grinning its terrible, welcoming grin." Then the story ends with a newspaper column describing "hundreds of dead fish" found in the lake. King suggests that, while Hal may finally have rid his life of the monkey, it is not finished and is biding its time.

Ray Olson (essay date 1993)

SOURCE: A review of *Nightmares and Dreamscapes,* in *Booklist,* Vol. 89, No. 21, July, 1993, p. 1918.

[*In the following brief review, Olson responds favorably to* Nightmares and Dreamscapes, *noting King's successful imitations of such writers as Conan Doyle and Raymond Chandler, as well as such television shows as "The Twilight Zone" and "Alfred Hitchcock Presents."*]

When you're reading him, you can think that Stephen King is the best writer in America. [**Nightmares and Dreamscapes,** his] first collection of shorter stuff in eight years, includes plenty of reasons for harboring that litcritically heretical thought. Mind you, nothing in it suggests King's about to go toe to toe with Updike, Mailer, Bellow, et al. But which of them has, all at once, his color and vitality, his sheer joy in words and the power of the imagination? Okay, he's a "genre writer," but one who's brilliantly revivified the visceral poetry and allure of the fantastic, emblematic romance tradition that, traceable back to the Bible and Greek mythology, flowers in America most famously in Hawthorne. Yet it is Dickens and Kipling whom King's verve and dynamism most powerfully bring to mind, even if, when he decides to flat-out imitate an old master, he chooses—as he does here, in fact—Conan Doyle and Raymond Chandler. (For the record, the Doyle pastiche is a delightful Holmes case that Dr. Watson solves first, and the Chandler *hommage* propels the whole hard-boiled milieu into the empyrean of metaphysics while managing to be funny.) In less direct imitations, King pens a hard-boiled vampire story that's both amusing and thoroughly chilling, sets up "Twilight Zone" and "Alfred Hitchcock Presents" situations and works them out better than those excellent TV series would have, and creates striking variations upon themes by Shirley Jackson. But star of this volume, and a nonfiction piece, is "Head Down," which traces the winning season of a little league team that included King's son. This may be the most suspenseful and moving writing he's ever done, a sports story that everyone who cares about American prose should read.

Publishers Weekly   (essay date 1993)

SOURCE: A review of *Nightmares and Dreamscapes,* in *Publishers Weekly,* Vol. 240, No. 31, August 2, 1993, p. 62.

[*The following is a laudatory review of* Nightmares and Dreamscapes.]

[*Nightmares and Dreamscapes*] is a wonderful cornucopia of 23 Stephen King moments (including a teleplay featuring Sherlock Holmes and Dr. Watson, a poem about Ebbet's Field and a brilliant *New Yorker* piece on Little League baseball) that even the author, in his introduction, acknowledges make up "an uneven Aladdin's cave of a book." There are no stories fans will want to skip, and some are superb, particularly **"You Know They Got a Hell of a Band,"** in which a husband and wife drive through a town that may literally be rock-and-roll heaven; **"The Ten O'Clock People,"** about unredeemable smokers; and **"The Moving Finger,"** which chronicles a digit's appearance in a drain. Together with *Night Shift* and *Skeleton Crew,* this volume accounts for all the stories King has written that he wishes to preserve. The introduction and illuminating notes about the derivation of each piece are invaluable autobiographical essays on his craft and his place in the literary landscape. An illusionist extraordinaire, King peoples all his fiction, long and short, with believable characters. The power of this collection lies in the amazing richness of his fevered imagination—he just can't be stopped from coming up with haunting plots.

Edward Bryant   (essay date 1993)

SOURCE: A review of *Nightmares and Dreamscapes,* in *Locus,* Vol. 31, No. 4, October, 1993, pp. 29, 31.

[*In the following review, Bryant praises* Nightmares and Dreamscapes *for its wide range of subjects, tones, and*

moods, and commends King's revisions of his previously published stories.]

In the introduction to his new story collection, *Nightmares and Dreamscapes*, Stephen King refers to the volume as "an uneven Aladdin's cave of a book." That's a good analysis, an apt potential blurb that will never be used, and is a bit harsher on the book than it deserves. King notes that he publishes a reprint collection about once every seven years (the first two were *Night Shift* in 1978 and *Skeleton Crew* in 1985). So far as the author's concerned, all the short stuff worth reprinting is now in print, and we can maybe expect another collection in a year starting with a "2."

Nightmares and Dreamscapes is one hefty tree-mugger. At 810 pages, it's only a dozen pages shorter than the first published version of *The Stand.* The first printing will issue 1.5 million copies, so you needn't squirrel away first editions as though they were *The Shining* or *Carrie.* Besides King's intro and an entertaining section of story notes, the collection contains 20 pieces of fiction (some original to this volume), a teleplay, a poem, a long essay, and a fable. So much for the stats. What about the behemoth (carefully neglecting to specify whether I'm referencing the book or the author)? Is this collection going to offer more ammo to such goofball grudge-bearers as the *Time* critic who, some years ago, labeled King "the master of postliterate prose"?

I don't think so. If you're a reader, you'd have to possess a heart of stone and a brain of cauliflower not to warm to this genial giant. Reading *Nightmares and Dreamscapes* is something like I'd imagine the menu to be if one were to spend a long weekend's slumber party at the King manse in Bangor. Many, many hours listening to Uncle Steve telling askew epigrams, gross anecdotes, broadly funny bits, dramatically scary stories; hamming it up, doing all the voices and the effects; in short, doing what storytellers do best. Entertaining, thrilling, and diverting the audience.

To wit:

"Dolan's Cadillac" previously existed only as a luxury item, a finely produced chapbook from Lord John Press. This is a nice tough Jim Thompson sort of revenge play about a school-teacher patiently and implacably out to get the mobster who ordered his wife murdered. Another former luxury item is **"My Pretty Pony"**, a genuinely affecting tale of wisdom passing between the generations. The origin of the story is unbelievably complicated—that's why the end-notes are fascinating. **"My Pretty Pony"** was originally published by the Whitney Museum for something like $2,300, clock and batteries included. Later it appeared as a disastrously designed $50 trade hardback from Knopf.

One of King's salient characteristics is his evolution through the swamps of popular culture. We share similar steepings in music, reading, and pop phenomena. Hence I nod my head in vehement empathy when he mentions the Ripley's Believe It or Not illustration of a guy wearing a lit candle in a hole drilled in his cranium. Some of the stories in this collection ring faint chords, suggesting near or distant influences. A good example is **"The House on Maple Street"**, one of the volume's originals. King mentions that this one's based on the final illustration in Chris Van Allsburg's magnificent kids' book, *The Mysteries of Harris Burdick.* True enough. But a part of this tale of rebellious children and an unsympathetic stepfather also seems to go back to the '50s. In an evident *hommage,* the children are named Bradbury. They could, with equal appropriateness, have been called the Matheson kids. Remember "Shipshape Home"? **"The House on Maple Street"** has its own identity, but it also has resonances.

> **King answers his critics through demonstration. His range of concerns is broad. While his experiments don't always work, he's always willing to try something new, something that does not carbon-copy his past work. He fiddles, tinkers, tweaks, and outright revises work until he believes it's right.**
>
> —*Edward Bryant*

Another of the new pieces is **"The Ten O'Clock People"**, a nice novella about an innocent guy in the banking business who discovers that aliens are running the world. It's a paranoids' delight in which only a certain level of active smokers are capable of penetrating the hideous aliens' psychic disguise. Episodic, this account of human rebellion and betrayal offers some good observations about addictive personalities—as well as paralleling some of the tone of John Carpenter's *They Live.*

I'd forgotten how many recent original anthologies King's contributed to until I started reading the collection. **"You Know They Got a Hell of a Band"** is a good devil's advocate's jaundiced take on rock'n'roll by an acknowledged rock devotee. This account of a yuppie couple trapped in the sargasso of lost rock stars somewhere deep in the Oregon wilderness has its moments. King allows as how sometimes Bad Things really *do* happen to Good People for no real reason other than random circumstance, a dramatic structure that can be debated. The story also tries to skate on a few gross-out details when the real horror lies a lot deeper. First published in *Shock Rock,* the story's grown on me a bit. So has **"Home Delivery"**, King's contribution to Skipp and Spector's zombie anthology, *Book of the Dead.* When I first read it, I thought this account of a Maine island woman's coming to terms with the loss of her husband and the collapse of the entire world came across too much as the beginning of a novel. Now it seems much more self-contained and emotionally satisfying. I must be mellowing.

You want vampire stories? There are a couple of back-to-back bloodsuckers. **"The Night Flier"** is a nastily accurate portrait of a tabloid reporter in search of a possible vampiric aviator. **"Popsy"** may well feature the same vampire

in a satisfying revenge fantasy of a very bad man stealing a small child from a shopping mall.

A taste for the gruesome? **"Chattery Teeth"** puts a travelling label salesman and a pair of wind-up novelty dentures into a collision course with a young psychopath. **"Crouch End"** is a beautifully atmospheric Cthulhu Mythos story about an American tourist woman losing her husband in a very peculiar—eldritch, even—London neighborhood. **"Rainy Season"** skirts the edge of ridiculousness, but still manages to evoke some chilly moments as an every-seven-years rain of toads descends upon a Maine village.

Don't like toads? There's plenty more on the agenda. **"Sorry, Right Number"** is a *Tales From the Darkside* script about prescient knowledge and doom. No happy ending here. **"The Doctor's Case"** is a Sherlock Holmes piece in which Watson gets, for once, center stage. Inspector Lestrade has an unusual role as well. Nicely done. **"Umney's Last Case"** is a piece of Chandleresque metafiction about a tough detective doing his best to puzzle out and survive a complete reality crunch. **"The Fifth Quarter"** is a hard-edged crime tale. All show some of the breadth of King's interests and abilities.

Ditto for **"Sneakers"** (an unusual haunting in the record trade), **"Dedication"** (an impressive handling of race relations, voodoo, and love), **"It Grows on You"** (a solid and keenly observational treatment of community secrets), and **"Suffer the Little Children"** (a vintage King tale about the worst fears of a teacher). There are plenty more I haven't mentioned. This is a *long* book.

As well, it is a satisfying one. King answers his critics through demonstration. His range of concerns is broad. While his experiments don't always work, he's always willing to try something new, something that does not carbon-copy his past work. He fiddles, tinkers, tweaks, and outright revises work until he believes it's right. First time out doesn't make it sacred.

Oh, and let me mention the really great stuff at the end. "Head Down" is a *New Yorker* essay about a year in the life of a competitive Little League team from Bangor. I read it just before I watched the televised 1993 Little League championship game between Long Beach and Panama. Timing couldn't have been better. "Brooklyn August", a baseball poem, and **"The Beggar and the Diamond"**, a retelling of a Hindu parable, make for perfectly appropriate codas.

What a feast! In *The Stand,* King dedicates the novel to his wife and refers to the novel as "This dark chest of wonders." The phrase could not be better tailored to describe *Nightmares and Dreamscapes* as well.

Richard E. Nicholls   (essay date 1993)

SOURCE: A review of *Nightmares and Dreamscapes,* in *The New York Times Book Review,* October 24, 1993, p. 22.

[*In the following review of* Nightmares and Dreamscapes, *Nicholls declares that while critics may not be impressed by*

King's "baggy—if exuberant—tales," fans will find the collection entertaining and satisfying.]

Pay no heed, Stephen King says in the introduction to **Nightmares and Dreamscapes,** to the critics, their voices "the ill-tempered yappings of men and women who have accepted the literary anorexia of the last 30 years with a puzzling (to me, at least) lack of discussion and dissent." There's certainly nothing skimpy about this collection of large, leisurely short stories packed with dozens of gaudy, baffled characters reluctant to believe the varied but uniformly outrageous threats that confront them, forever trying to talk or think themselves out of some unpleasant situation until, inevitably, they're trapped. Even the horrors here are oversized: a resilient vampire with a particularly gross sense of humor; an invading army of hungry, meat-eating toads; and, most marvelous, batlike beings who are passing quite successfully as humans and can be seen as they truly, hideously are only by smokers—and *only* by those smokers who ration themselves to a few cigarettes a day. Fans of Mr. King's work will find here his usual menu: wild conspiracies; repellent, zestful monsters; scenes speckled and splashed with gore. Critics, that yipping chorus that seems to unsettle Mr. King more than all the ghouls in his stories, are unlikely to be converted by these baggy—if exuberant—tales.

FURTHER READING

Bibliography

Collings, Michael R. *The Annotated Guide to Stephen King: A Primary and Secondary Bibliography of the Works of America's Premier Horror Writer.* Mercer Island, Wash.: Starmont House, 1986, 176 p.

> Book-length bibliography of King's works through 1986.

Collings, Michael R., and Engebretson, David A. *The Shorter Works of Stephen King.* Mercer Island, Wash.: Starmont House, 1985, 202 p.

> Annotated bibliography of King's short fiction through 1985.

Criticism

Collings, Michael R. *The Many Facets of Stephen King.* Mercer Island, Wash.: Starmont House, 1985, 190 p.

> Organizes and studies King's works according to common themes, subjects, and styles. Includes a primary and secondary bibliography.

———. *The Stephen King Phenomenon.* Mercer Island, Wash.: Starmont House, Inc., 1987, 144 p.

> Examines various aspects of King and his works to identify the author's status as a figure in mass culture.

Egan, James. "Apocalypticism in the Fiction of Stephen King." *Extrapolation* 25, No. 3 (Fall 1984): 214-27.

> Analysis of King's treatment of world destruction in his horror fiction.

———. " 'A Single Powerful Spectacle': Stephen King's Gothic Melodrama." *Extrapolation* 27, No. 1 (Spring 1986): 62-75.

> Examination of King's blend of Gothic elements and melodrama.

———. "Technohorror: The Dystopian Vision of Stephen King." *Extrapolation* 29, No. 2 (Summer 1988): 140-52.

> Analysis of anti-technological aspects of King's fiction.

Gray, Paul. "Master of Postliterate Prose." *Time* 120, No. 9 (30 August 1982): 87.

> Comments on King's use of popular culture in *Different Seasons*.

Magistrale, Tony. *Landscape of Fear: Stephen King's American Gothic.* Bowling Green, Oh.: Bowling Green State University Popular Press, 1988, 132 p.

> Collection of new and previously published essays on such subjects as King's treatment of technology and social phenomena.

Schweitzer, Darrell, ed. *Discovering Stephen King.* Mercer Island, Wash.: Starmont House, 1985, 219 p.

> Includes essays on general themes by Ben P. Indick, Michael R. Collings, and other commentators, as well as a bibliography.

Underwood, Tim, and Miller, Chuck, eds. *Fear Itself: The Horror Fiction of Stephen King.* New York: New American Library/Signet, 1982, 286 p.

> Collection of general essays and observations by such critics and practitioners of the horror genre as Peter Straub, Fritz Leiber, Charles L. Grant, and George A. Romero.

———. *Kingdom of Fear: The World of Stephen King.* New York: New American Library/Signet, 1987, 270 p.

> Contains seventeen essays on King's fiction by various critics, including Leslie Fiedler, Ben P. Indick, and Chuck Miller.

———. *Bare Bones: Conversations on Terror with Stephen King.* New York: McGraw-Hill Book Company, 1988, 211 p.

> Collection of interviews previously published in such periodicals as *Playboy* and *Heavy Metal*.

Additional coverage of King's life and career is contained in the following sources published by Gale Research: *Authors and Artists for Young Adults,* Vol. 1; *Bestsellers* 1990, No. 1; *Contemporary Authors,* Vols. 61-64; *Contemporary Authors New Revision Series,* Vols. 1, 30; *Contemporary Literary Criticism,* Vols. 12, 26, 37, 61; *Dictionary of Literary Biography Yearbook,* 1980; *Major 20th-Century Writers*; and *Something about the Author,* Vols. 9, 55.

John McGahern

1934–

Irish short story writer, novelist, playwright, and script-writer.

INTRODUCTION

A controversial and provocative Irish literary figure, Mc-Gahern writes traditionally structured fiction in which he challenges many of his homeland's conventional social, sexual, and religious values. Focusing on protagonists for whom life in modern Ireland has become restrictive and repressive, he examines such themes as the failure of love, the erosion of marital compatibility, the difficulty of maintaining hope, and the burden of Irish parochialism and religious conservatism. Often employing religious diction, imagery, and motifs, McGahern presents a vision of contemporary Ireland characterized by symbols of death, darkness, infertility, and impotency.

Biographical Information

McGahern was born in Dublin and raised in County Roscommon in the west of Ireland. After completing his studies at University College in Dublin, he taught for seven years at a National Boys School in Clontarf. In 1963 McGahern published his novel *The Barracks* to critical acclaim. His next novel, *The Dark*, was banned by the Irish Censorship Board in 1965, and when all legal action appealing the ban of the novel failed, McGahern left Ireland temporarily, visiting various cities and universities in continental Europe, England, and the United States. He currently lives on a farm in Leister, Ireland.

Major Works of Short Fiction

McGahern has published four volumes of short fiction. His stories are often populated with characters unable to find respite from the unrelenting demands of everyday life. In his first collection, *Nightlines*, the recurring cycle of birth, love, and death is portrayed as a disappointing pattern. The stories in *Getting Through* display guarded optimism in the human spirit, although the dominant mood remains bleak. *High Ground* denotes McGahern's concern with father and son relationships, the banality of conformity and compromise, and sexual and religious conflicts. McGahern's thematic and stylistic development as a short fiction writer is evident in *Collected Stories*, which was published in 1993.

Critical Reception

Although McGahern has been faulted by those who consider his portrayal of characters dominated by rural values a misrepresentation of contemporary Ireland's more cosmopolitan identity, critics generally commend his incisive

delineation of Irish parochialism and his commentary on the vacuousness of much of modern life. McGahern is often compared with a broad range of other writers, especially James Joyce, Samuel Beckett, and Anton Chekhov; yet, he is consistently praised by commentators for the singularity of his narrative voice and vision. As Patricia Boyle Haberstroh maintains: "McGahern's position as not only one of Ireland's most important novelists but also as one of the best contemporary writers of English prose derives ultimately from the originality and uniqueness of his fiction."

PRINCIPAL WORKS

Short Fiction

Nightlines 1970
Getting Through 1978
High Ground 1985
Collected Stories 1993

Other Major Works

The Barracks (novel) 1963
The Dark (novel) 1965
The Leavetaking (novel) 1974
The Pornographer (novel) 1979
Amongst Women (novel) 1990

CRITICISM

David Pryce-Jones (essay date 1971)

SOURCE: "Country of the Aged and the Sad," in *The New York Times Book Review*, February 7, 1971, p. 30.

[*Pryce-Jones is an Austrian-born English novelist, biographer, and critic. In the following review, he discusses the bleak vision presented in the short fiction of* Nightlines.]

The Ireland of John McGahern's stories is not the country other Irish writers describe. Here, to be sure, are the Shannon and Oakport and the hill of Howth—but only as accidents of geography, as parts of a setting into which people have blundered and where they no longer belong, if they ever did. Mr. McGahern is free from the emerald sentiments that have been invested in his native land. He is his own master, and his stories owe nothing to anybody.

If this is an Ireland virtually without a past, it is without a future too. The opening story in *Nightlines* has a young man returning from London to come to terms with his old father, who has remarried. All he can do is to go away again from this country of the aged and the sad.

In their unwisdom and smallness, those who are left behind in Mr. McGahern's Ireland cannot be awakened from themselves, since there is nothing to awaken them to. Their very occupations (like farming and fishing) are coming to an end. Some who persist, such as a country policeman, lose their reason. A carpenter like Lavin, in a poignant story of that title, goes crazy with unfulfilled sexuality before he is taken off to the poorhouse. For his characters, the author uses a narrow range of names. One of them is Moran—repeated, one feels, because it sounds so close to moron.

The present, then, is existing in the middle of nothing and its standstill very much interests Mr. McGahern. One of the finest stories in this collection is **"Korea,"** in which a boy is about to leave home, to break the immobilization of his life. For the last time, he is helping his father to fish the nightlines that give this book its title—on the stretch of river from which the family makes a precarious living. The father wants him to emigrate to America, in the knowledge that the boy will be drafted into the Army there. If his son is then killed on active service, the father will receive from the Army more life insurance money than fishing can ever produce. The boy has his would-be murder under consideration as he baits the hooks for his father—and the image of a hook pulling its unknown catch to disturb some dark, still water is a suitable one to apply to Mr. McGahern's work.

In **"Korea"** the relation of father and son is framed by the box of worms they use as bait. On another occasion, a dead marriage is similarly framed by the smell of a shark rotting on a nearby beach. It is the author's technique, his whole style, to take something from the external world—the wheels of a train, an umbrella, the sea, rain—and to merge into it the components of his story.

Success depends upon picking external symbols apt enough to bear the weight put upon them. In **"Christmas,"** for instance, an orphan is given a present of an unwanted toy airplane: he destroys it, and we are made aware that he cannot fly away from where he is. Such moments of banality are more than compensated by the way Mr. McGahern usually brings together the contrasting elements of his stories. In an irregular but calculated prose he achieves a mood all his own, which is shabby and hurtful and lyrical—"refining our ignorance" in the phrase he puts into the mouth of one of his characters.

Two stories make a particular impact. In **"Hearts of Oak and Bellies of Brass,"** laborers on a building site are waiting for one of their number, Jocko, to turn up to be paid for work he has not done. Jocko is a methylated-spirits drinker; his co-workers have been out to get him and their chance has come. Eight or nine years ago a good many English writers were trying to see the violence of primitive men as something akin to ritual, which was a halfway effort to beautify it. That fashion has passed, but its cruelty is recorded here, as part of what is elsewhere called "the stupidity of human wishes."

"Peaches," the story in which the above-mentioned shark is featured, is the length of a novella. A writer, discontented in his rented house in Spain, works too little and drinks too much and has a protracted, neurotic quarrel with his wife. They leave for England the moment a local magistrate (who is also the local fruit-grower and the archetypal Fascist) makes a pass at the wife—but movement will resolve nothing. **"Peaches"** might have been any writer's summer vacation story. Mr. McGahern, using a foreign setting for the first time, shows how well he can extend anywhere he pleases the themes of desolation he has already found at home.

Michael Irwin (essay date 1978)

SOURCE: "Sorrowful Pipings," in *The Times Literary Supplement*, No. 3976, June 16, 1978, p. 663.

[*Below, Irwin explores the somber tone that permeates the short stories of* Getting Through.]

Most of these graceful, melancholy tales are set in Ireland. They deal in love, frustrated or misplaced, and in intimations of mortality. A lonely aging man advertises for a wife, but panics and runs away when the chosen woman suffers a heart attack. A priest, reminded by a trick of the sunlight of a funeral he attended thirty years before, confronts the prospect of his own end. In two of the stories the main character is James Sharkey, a schoolteacher, who appeared briefly in John McGahern's novel *The Leavetaking*. Here, as there, he is a sorrowful man, crossed in love, who sees his premature baldness as a first hint of death, and so wears a hat continually, outdoors, indoors, and even in church. In **"Faith, Hope and Charity"** he has to tell the family of one of his former pupils that the young man has been killed in an accident. In **"All Sorts of Impossible Things"**, perhaps the best-balanced and most moving story in the collection, he is desolated by the death of an old friend.

John McGahern writes with unobtrusive concision. So much of his skill lies in selection, or rather in omission, that his terse narrative seems free and full. He has the Irish gift of being able to move fluently and unselfconsciously between a simple and a heightened style. There are ten stories in this narrow volume, but in each of them he finds scope to create both a situation and an atmosphere. Pace and proportion seem effortlessly adjusted: there is no sense of expository strain. **"Swallows"**, for example, begins like this:

> The wind blew the stinging rain from the Gut, where earlier in the bright weather of the summer the Sergeant had sat in the tarred boat, anchored by a rope to an old Ford radiator that clung to the weeds outside the rushes, and watched taut line after taut line cut like cheesewire through the water as hooked roach after hooked roach made a last surge towards the freedom of the open lake before landing slapping on the floorboards.

The succession of sharp details, the growth and the encroaching rhythm of the long sentence draw the reader immediately into the story.

Mr McGahern's economy is the more remarkable in that he is characteristically concerned not with a single event or mood but with a series of such events or moods. The happening that provides his ostensible subject takes its significance from a previous history that is skilfully implied. The immediacy of the narrative is delusive: the present merges with the past or with the future, "story" dissolves into theme. This habit of imagination is so marked as to become a habit of style. In the passage quoted above only the first nine words are directly relevant to the tale that is to be told. The description lapses bewilderingly from a particular moment in the present to a still more vivid frequentative past. Within a sentence the reader knows that the meaning of the story will extend well beyond its anecdotal content.

All this is to say that Mr McGahern has his own way of solving one of the obvious problems facing writers of the short story: that of giving imaginative extension to a single episode. Repeatedly he will lead a character towards a moment of stereoscopic vision in which experiences widely separated in time are suddenly juxtaposed by memory and seem to be significantly connected. A colourless life, or a group of colourless lives, can come to display a pattern of pain and loss. Sometimes, as in **"Doorways"**, the point is made a little too insistently:

> And suddenly the dead man climbing on the bus, the living girl asking me not to go to Sligo in the rain outside the hotel, I on the bus to Sligo to collect some letters, Barnaby and Bartleby, even now in their Dublin doorways patiently

watching the day fade, seemed to be equally awash in time and indistinguishable, the same mute human presence beneath the unchanging sky . . .

The kind of relationship between disparate scenes and sights made explicit in this passage is implicit in virtually all Mr McGahern's stories. Even the shortest of them has resonance: some slight incident is made to disclose a mode of living and an attitude to experience.

But I must admit to having read this accomplished collection with rather more admiration than pleasure. The tune that is piped is so unfailingly sorrowful that the stories come to seem confined. It is plain that this author will never be surprised out of his own sadness. The end of one of his narratives is often implicit in its very beginning. **"Stoat"** starts with a rabbit squealing in death. The fate of the animal, like that of the roach mentioned in **"Swallows"**, is already a comment on the human predicament as Mr McGahern sees it. For all its many merits *Getting Through* is a depressing work.

> The mood of *Getting Through* is a down one, and I think we can legitimately complain that Mr. McGahern sometimes puts his thumb on the scales to heighten moroseness and weigh his characters with more woe than they have earned or deserve.
>
> —*Julian Moynahan, in* The New York Times Book Review, *July 13, 1980.*

Terence Brown (essay date 1979)

SOURCE: "John McGahern's *Nightlines*: Tone, Technique and Symbol," in *The Irish Short Story*, edited by Patrick Rafroidi and Terence Brown, Colin Smythe Ltd., 1979, pp. 289-301.

Thomas Kilroy, playwright and novelist, provided the critic of Irish fiction with one of those clarifying and organising generalizations which illumine much that one has almost unconsciously accepted, when he wrote [in the *Times Literary Supplement,* March 17, 1972]:

> At the centre of Irish fiction is the anecdote. The distinctive characteristic of our "first novel", *Castle Rackrent*, that which makes it what it is, is not so much its idea, revolutionary as that may be, as its imitation of a speaking voice engaged in the telling of a tale. The model will be exemplary for the reader who has read widely in Irish fiction: it is a voice heard over and over again, whatever its accent, a voice with a supreme confidence in its own histrionics, one that assumes with its audience a shared ownership of the told tale and all that it implies: a taste for anecdote, an unshakeable belief in the value of human actions, a belief that life may be adequately encap-

sulated into stories that require no reference, no qualification, beyond their own selves.

This tone of voice, a voice redolent, despite many momentary doubts, of basic social certainties is a tone that sounds recognizably in the anecdotal fiction of William Carleton, in the tales of Somerville and Ross, later in the episodic sequences of Kavanagh's *The Green Fool*. This is a fiction that has roots in an enclosed oral culture, in the countryman's regard for the tale, for "experience passed on from mouth to mouth and intelligence that comes from afar". It is a fiction that, delighting in objectivity, is undisturbed by the subjective or the psychologically complex, unless they can be embodied in concrete actions.

This Irish tone, unselfconsciously rejoicing in linguistic afflatus, survived the shift in the early twentieth century from the tale of countryside and farm, to the story set in shop, convent, school and presbytery, set in the *petit bourgeois* world of post-revolutionary Ireland. It survives as the dominant tone of the Irish school of short story writers, in O'Faolain, in O'Connor, in Mary Lavin. So the following opening, from an O'Faolain story, "The Old Master", is entirely characteristic of the mode:

> When I was younger, and so, I suppose, in the nature of things, a little more cruel, I once tried to express John Aloysius Gonzaga O'Sullivan geometrically: a parabola of pomposity in a rectangle of gaslight. The quip pleased everybody who knew the reference—it was to his favourite stand, under the portico of the courthouse, his huge bulk wedged into the very tall and slender doorway.
>
> I said *gaslight* because John Aloysius rarely came to work before the afternoon, when they lit the gas in the dim entrance hall, and its greenish, wateryish light began to hiss high up in the dome. There he would stand, ten times in the afternoon, smoking, or watching the traffic, or gossiping with some idling clerk. He had a sinecure in the fusty-musty little law library, a room no bigger than a box. He used to say, in his facetious way, that he left it often because he exhausted the air every half hour.

In this we note the slightly garrulous pleasure in the act of telling the tale; the rhythms and syntax ("smoking, or watching the traffic, or gossiping with some idling clerk") are those of a voice preparing for a protracted discourse, welcoming digression and expansion, proffering intimacy. This is a world that has time for anecdote, for the kind of tales in which landscape and milieu can be rendered, almost gratuitously, in passages of sustained rhythmic ease, where they are as much aspects of how the world is, in its timeless permanency, as the narrative events are the objective revelations of the unchanging vagaries of human nature. So, the Irish school of short-story writing, that an unwary critic might too readily assume to be a school of provincial realism, seems to me to have its sources in an oral culture's delight in tale-telling, in anecdote.

But while the Irish short story may have its roots in an oral culture (many of the stories seem written as much for performance as for silent reading in the arm-chair) it also begins to move away from the objectivity of tale, touched

as it almost invariably is by romantic subjectivism. So, in O'Connor and O'Faolain we often encounter a central character who is a sensitive outsider in society, or he is an adolescent experiencing anguished dissatisfaction in a provincial environment. And in Mary Lavin, at her best, strangeness of incident suggests a romantic intensification of feeling amidst the small-town banalities, while in her less successful works grotesquerie of character or event hints at gothic moods.

For the young Irish writer beginning to write in the 1960's, especially the writer who chose the Irish provincial world as setting for his work, this narrative tone for an Irish fiction must have seemed inevitable as must a technique of realism tinged with romanticism. As Kilroy further reminds us:

> I am attempting here to discuss the experience of writing fiction in modern Ireland. . . . The contemporary Irish writer of fiction must surely be aware that his local heritage differs in kind from that of an English or a French writer. Its difference has to do with the emergence of Irish fiction, both novel and short-story, from a culture which already had its native, long-standing, oral tradition of fictionalizing experience, a mode that has continued to challenge the composition of literary fiction even to the present day.

The case of John McGahern is exemplary. His first published novel *The Barracks* (1963) manages its fiction in a narrative tone recognisably within the tradition I have been identifying. The prose is reflective, expansive, open syntactically and rhythmically to accumulation of event, deed, detail of milieu and to narrative comment. It is a prose untroubled by doubts as to the value of its own movements and procedures as it confidently renders the way things are in the provincial milieu that is so intimately known. So *The Barracks* opens:

> Mrs Regan darned an old woollen sock as the February night came on, her head bent, catching the threads on the needle by the light of the fire, the daylight gone without her noticing. A boy of twelve and two dark-haired girls were close about her at the fire. They'd grown uneasy, in the way children can indoors in the failing light. The bright golds and scarlets of the religious pictures on the wall had faded, their glass glittered now in the sudden flashes of firelight, and as it deepened the dusk turned reddish from the Sacred Heart lamp that burned before the small wickerwork crib of Bethlehem on the mantelpiece.

Tone and strategy here are not so distant from the idioms and rhythms of story-telling. One notes in particular the conversationally-managed movement away from particulars to sociable generality ("They'd grown uneasy, in the way children can") establishing an audience that is allowed to contribute its knowledge to the narration before the narrator returns with ease to the details of a specific world.

Some of McGahern's best writing is in this assured conventional mode. The implicit, uncomplicated belief in the value of recounting allows for extended passages in which the novelist possesses his world, characters in their settings, landscapes and actions, with the unselfconscious confidence of a story-teller absorbed with his material. In passage after passage in his three novels McGahern concentrates on the particularities of the Leitrim, Roscommon border-country (passages which, extracted from their context, read remarkably like the openings of Irish short-stories).

> It started to rain as he gulped his meal, the first drops loud on the pane, and it was raining steadily by the time they were on their way to the field.

> Between the lone ash trees, their stripped branches pale as human limbs in the rain, Mahoney worked. The long rows of the potatoes stretched to the stone wall, the rows washed on the top by the rain, gleaming white and pink and candle-yellow against the black acres of clay; and they had set to work without any hope of picking them all. Their clothes started to grow heavy with rain. The wind numbed the side of their faces, great lumps of clay held together by dead stalks gathered about their boots.

As with the conventional Irish short stories, those of O'Connor and O'Faolain, this objectivity in McGahern is somewhat disturbed by romanticism, for in his three novels the central character is a sensitive adolescent or young man whose feelings in the midst of a constricted provincial environment are the central points of interest. But the traditional temper, tones and techniques in McGahern's fictions are disturbed in a further much more important way; McGahern is aware of an urban and fragmented culture encroaching upon the stable, provincial, rural world upon which in Ireland the anecdotal, orally-based tale ultimately depends. When the earlier writers took account, as they did occasionally, of the modern urban world it was without any real sense that the encounter with novel experience might require significant aesthetic innovations. They continued indeed to write as if literary modernism had nothing to teach them. McGahern does not.

It is evident even in his most conservative novel *The Barracks* that McGahern, while confident and skilled in portraying the provincial world he knows, recognises a need for modern Irish fiction to meet more stringent demands. It must be attentive to the recent major social changes in the country, in an art that more appropriately reflects the complex psychological currents that stir in its turbulent waters. So McGahern is consciously experimental in his work, welcoming the resonance of image and symbol to the enclosed worlds of rural and small-town Ireland, taking his protagonists away from their childhood farms and fields to the confused cultural settings of modern Dublin and London.

McGahern, as symbolist, is absorbed by the potency of ritual, particularly by the Catholic rituals associated with death, with burial and with Holy Week. In his three novels, imagery drawn from these various rites is employed to ground his fiction in a deeper sense of the way things are, than was the case in traditional Irish short stories and novels. The imagery serves to imply a metaphysical di-

mension to experience, unknowable except in the mysterious patterns that ritual reveals in life itself, inducing in the participants of ritual an emotional awareness of metaphysical depth. Memory and meaning, myth and mystery, passion and pattern, seem controllable for the protagonists of the novels and for the author himself only through the mediation of rite and symbol.

> Before the post-office the people knelt in the dry dust of the road for Benediction. The humeral veil was laid on the priest's shoulders, the tiny bell tinkled in the open day, the host was raised and all heads bowed, utter silence except for the bell and some donkey braying in the distance. Kneeling in the dust among the huddled crowd it was hard to fight back tears. This was the way your life was, you belonged to these people as they to you, you were linked together. One day that Sacred Host would be your burden to uphold for them while the bell rang, but it was still impossible to join in the singing as the procession resumed its way, only listen to the shuffle of boots through the dust. Wash me ye waters, streaming from His side, it was strange, all strange and the candles burning against the yew trees in the day.

Such moments, however, run grave tonal risks, dependent as they usually are in the novels on the imagery of a specific church and tradition. For the novelist, writing out of a culture where these images are almost unconsciously understood, must uneasily recognise that in the wider world, where he will most probably find his readers, these familiar properties will suggest not the mystery of ultimate things but the curiosity of the primitive, the exotic. So at times in McGahern's works one senses that the descriptions of rite and custom operate less as symbols than as passages of local colour. There is a note of explanatory insecurity in these passages, a tendency to tonal uncertainty.

It is in his collection of short-stories, *Nightlines* (1970), that we see McGahern attempting to resolve this problem. In this volume McGahern seeks to write short-stories exploiting symbolist possibilities without depending on the traditional metaphors of church and religion. He seeks symbols within the physical properties of his fictional environments, in event and deed. So the symbolism is unobtrusive, tonally contained within the movements of narration, without any sense of the insecurity occasioned when, as in the novels, more explicit symbolism is attempted.

McGahern's short-stories, like his novels, occupy a middle ground between the conservative traditionalist mode and modernist experiment. Where O'Connor and O'Faolain wrote their tales of enclosed provincial worlds, McGahern also senses that a short-story must in part depend on such hermetic self-sufficiency. But the social conditions that allowed the earlier writers to explore a stable, self-confident Irish world no longer obtain. So McGahern writes of artificially self-contained worlds. He sets a story in a railway carriage, in a school, on a London-Irish building site, in a guest-house, in a police-station, on a boat in the middle of a lake, in an isolated house on the Mediterranean. In most of them a sensitive central character, so familiar from Irish fiction in general and from McGahern's novels in particular, suffers in an unpleasing milieu. In **"Wheels"** an adult returns to the pain of his provincial origins. In **"Coming into his Kingdom"** a child experiences the discomforts of sexual awakening. In **"Hearts of Oak and Bellies of Brass"** the narrator struggles to anaesthetise his cultural and emotional awareness with back-breaking labour; in **"Strandhill, the Sea"** the narrator is a troubled kleptomaniac; in **"Lavin"** he is an adolescent discovering homosexual feelings and sexual disgust; in **"My Love, My Umbrella"** he is a young Dubliner enduring the agonies of an unrequited passion, in **"The Recruiting Officer"** an alcoholic, failed Christian brother, eccentric and tired rebel.

In *Nightlines* the tone of traditional Irish short-story-telling is not entirely forsaken either. At moments, in fact, one suspects the author's nerves fail him in his literary experimentalism and he falls back on familiar, proved techniques. So in **"Wheels"**, at the opening of the collection, we encounter a very curious blend of prose-impressionism with a structure reminiscent of a much more direct and anecdotal kind of short story.

> Grey concrete and steel and glass in the slow raindrip of the morning station, three porters pushing an empty trolley up the platform to a stack of grey mail-bags, the loose wheels rattling, and nothing but wait and watch and listen, and *I listened to the story they were telling.* (my italics)

Elsewhere the anecdotal Irish speaking voice is heard quite clearly, as in so many discursive Irish tales.

> There was no reason this life shouldn't have gone on for long but a stupid wish on my part, which set off an even more stupid wish in Mrs Grey, and what happened has struck me ever since as usual when people look to each other for their happiness or whatever it is called. Mrs Grey was Moran's best customer. She'd come from America and built the huge house on top of Mounteagle after her son had been killed in aerial combat over Italy. (**"Christmas"**)

McGahern's short-stories are most interesting when these tones and techniques are avoided, when the processes of his prose combine an unsentimental apprehension of the physical world with symbolist resonance and where he manages to generate the symbolic charge of his tales without dependence on the dynamism of a traditional religious or cultural symbol system. In his novels the rituals of the Church provided that charge; in *Nightlines* McGahern turns to imagery of wheel, river, sea. The wheels of the first tale are the wheels of a train bearing a man back through his past across the Shannon and also the "ritual wheel", the repetition of a life in the shape of a story that had as much reason to go on as stop. And the collection ends with a character, who has recognised that life "is all a wheel", contemplating the Shannon as it flows to the sea. [In *Two Decades of Irish Writing*, 1975] Roger Garfitt has suggested that "McGahern sometimes seems more Buddhist than Catholic" and sees the imagery of the Wheel as possibly owing something to that tradition. But, if this is so it functions in a much less obtrusive way than does the Catholic imagery of the novels.

It is in the detailed interrelationship of the facts of McGahern's stories, the blend of event, physical milieu and meaning that McGahern's symbolism is least obtrusive and, I think, most effective. Each story employs one or two central images which, as Henri D. Paratte remarks [in *The Irish Novel in Our Time*, edited by M. Harmon and P. Rafroidi, 1976], "offer a symbolic frame to his vision of reality". That vision is austerely metaphysical but reductively so as the human world of desire and meaning is set against images which suggest iron physical law, machine-like inevitability, cruelty, decay, the ritual wheel which breaks all backs as it turns. The world of these stories is a world of chainsaws, hooks, chains, ice, flame, shovels, metal, shot, coffin-wood, bait, mallets, chisels, rusting tools, iron-bolts, whips with metal tips, glass inseminating plungers, knives, pumps, concrete lavatories, ticking clocks.

The framing images of each McGahern story contain within them accumulations of detail and fact which further serve to symbolise the writer's ambiguous, metaphysically bleak vision of reality, though they do so without any suggestion of overt symbolist technique. It is only on a close examination of these works that a reader realizes how far he is here from the direct, unselfconscious discourse of the traditional tale-teller, how much he is in the hands of a skilled, very self-conscious imagist. For in McGahern the moments of traditional tone distract from the modernist techniques.

"Hearts of Oak and Bellies of Brass" is a sketch of life on a building site in a London summer. The workers are Irish and the central character is a countryman who has sold his sensitivity for the dulled, unfeeling security of life as a wage-slave, which anaesthetises pain and fear of death:

> I love to count out in money the hours of my one and precious *life*. I sell the hours and I get money. The money allows me to sell more hours. If I saved money I could buy the hours of some similar bastard and live like a royal incubus, which would suit me much better than as I am now, though apparently even as I am now suits me well enough, since I do not want to die.

His ambition is, as he puts it, "to annul all the votes in myself". This he does in accommodating himself to the regular, monotonous violence of the building site, its gratuitously violent language, the sexual animality, the sudden eruptions of physical force. Through the story, imagery of machines plays a crucial role in establishing a sense of monotonous dehumanization. A steel hopper, metal buckets, a brass medal bearing a worker's number, the "back of the hopper bright as beaten silver in the sun" and, centrally, the sharp, silver blade of a shovel, serve as metaphors of a dangerous physical violence, a dehumanised instinctual energy in the story. The movements of the shovels further suggest the sexual drives that find release only in violence of tongue and in prostitution.

> The familiar tirade would continue, predictable as the drive and throw of their shovels . . .

> The hooter went. The offered breasts withdrew.

A window slammed. "The last round", someone said.

The mixer started. The shovels drove and threw: gravel, sand, gravel; gravel, sand, gravel, cement.

The wheel of labour turns in this tale. It is sensitivity and human hope that are broken by its mechanical, grinding revolutions.

As the hopper came down again he shouted in the same time, "Shovel or shite; shite or burst", and the shovels mechanically drove and threw . . . It'd go on as this all day.

The longest piece in the collection is **"Peaches"**. It is also the story where the texture of the narrative is most dense with symbolic intimations of the kind I have been identifying. The plot is fairly straightforward. A moderately successful novelist is living in a rented Spanish villa with his Northern European wife. The relationship is in crisis. Creativity is at low-ebb. Neurosis and tension dominate the conversational exchanges, while the smell of a decaying shark on the beach, referred to at various points in the work, suggests the decay of marital compatibility. But there are many other details which embody the story's meanings. The relationship is as infertile as the man's (throughout they are "He", "She") imaginative powers. So there are frequent functionally ironic images of containers being filled to overflowing with liquid. A swimming pool is filled by a pump—"the three started to watch in the simple fascination of water filling the empty pool", water is poured into clay jars, a wine glass is filled "to the brim from the Soberano bottle", peaches in an orchard are sprayed by a "machine on metal wheels". This latter image resonates with another important image complex in the tale—that of machines as artificial and uncreative. The pool is filled by a pump; the woman is obsessed with the possibility of machines replacing people, electric light seems a poor substitute for the religious-sexual mystery of candle-flame, a Vespa scooter is dangerous, risky. The movement of the story in this world of significant patterns of detail can be readily studied in the passage where the couple make love. Section VIII of the piece begins with the image of the decomposing shark; the couple take a swim and in the sea they move to sexual union. But afterwards their lovemaking on the clinical "white sheet of the bed" is crude, acquisitive. Instead of the imagery of sea where they "let the waves loll over them" the man postpones his orgasm by "trying to make up what each gallon cost of the load of water that had been put in the pool that morning". Then he "held her close for her to pump him until she came". The fraught tension of their infertile, uncreative sexual coupling is then suggested in the tense dialogue with its syntactic bluntness:

"Why do you want?"

"Our relationship would get much better. But how would it do you good".

The conversation and the section end with the machines, the reductive images of sterility, danger, of cold metaphysical austerity, that are the frightening equivalents of the rotting shark, the ripe peaches proffered as tokens of lust at the story's climax.

"We'll be happy", the man said.

Later, as he got the Vespa out of the garage, he heard the clean taps of her typewriter come from the upstairs room.

The economical skill of passages such as this in **Nightlines,** with their subtle blend of image, dialogue and action suggest the degree to which McGahern has moved away from the expansive, anecdotal mode of much Irish fiction to tautly economical stories as metaphysically resonant as his novels, but without their overt traditional symbolism and techniques.

McGahern's stories are lean, taut, and lacerating; perhaps no one writing today can command idiomatic Irish with such savage effect.

—Robert Emmet Long, in the Saturday Review, *New York, May 1, 1971.*

Anatole Broyard (essay date 1980)

SOURCE: A review of *Getting Through,* in *The New York Times,* July 12, 1980, p. 15.

[*Broyard is an American essayist and critic. In the following mixed review, he provides a thematic analysis of the short stories in* Getting Through.]

In the first story in John McGahern's **Getting Through** collection, a young woman who wants to write is obsessed by a Chekhov story called "Oysters." She keeps reconstructing it in her mind, altering it to her taste. As she sees it, an 8-year-old boy and his father are starving in the streets of Moscow, too refined to beg. The boy sees a sign in front of a restaurant that says, "oysters."

He asks his father what an oyster is. He has never heard of one. His father explains, and the boy imagines a frog sitting in a shell, starting out with great glittering eyes, its yellow throat moving. It squeals and bites at your lips as you eat it alive.

The boy is horrified by the idea of an oyster. Yet, in his hunger, his delirium, he cries, stretching out his hands in the street: "Oysters! Give me some oysters!"

Beautiful in itself, the image is also interesting for the way it establishes a pattern for some of the other stories in **Getting Through.** In these stories, the men are like that boy crying out for oysters, only they cry out for love. Love, too, lives in a shell and has great glittering eyes. It squeals and bites at your lips as you eat it alive.

The boy in the Chekhov story is given some oysters as a joke by two strange men. In his desperation, he even tries to eat the shell. In several of Mr. McGahern's stories, his characters try to eat the shell of love, too. They can't tell what is food and what is not.

When they are denied love, they are relieved. Not to have to taste the strangeness, to swallow the ambiguousness. Isn't the best part, they ask themselves, the crying out, the stretching of the arms, the hunger and the delirium? Hunger is energy, and lovelessness is freedom, "the very day in its suspension," as one character puts it.

In a story called **"All Sorts of Impossible Things,"** a man proposes to a woman he has known for a long time because his hair is beginning to fall out. When she refuses him, he vows to wear a hat for the rest of his life. He will never bare his head again to love, to the sky, the sun or the wind.

Once in a while in *Getting Through,* love wins out against all odds. When it does, Mr. McGahern, writing about his native Ireland, knows exactly how to describe it. Here is a man looking at a woman who makes him happy for the moment:

> She was not garlanded by farms or orchards, by a house by the sea, by neither judges nor philosophers. She stood as she was, belonging to the morning, as they both hoped to belong to the evening.

In **"The Wine Breath,"** the lover is a priest, and so the love takes different forms. The priest loves a man who died 30 years ago. It is not a sexual love, but a love for what the man represented, for the world he moved through, a world of familiar sentiments and open fields and the mass still in Latin.

"It was as if the world of the dead," the priest thinks, "was as available to him as the world of the living." He reflects that "he would be glad of a ghost tonight," to relieve his haunting of himself. In a fine image, he expresses his sense of dislocation:

> Sometimes he saw himself as an old man that boys were helping down to the shore, restraining the tension of their need to laugh as they pointed out a rock in the cast he seemed about to stumble over, and then they had to lift their eyes and smile apologetically to the passersby while he stood starting out to sea.

In **"Swallows,"** a young state surveyor drives out in the rain to examine the scene of an accident with a police sergeant. They go back for a bite to eat at the sergeant's cottage, and noticing a violin in the surveyor's car, the sergeant asks him to play. The surveyor plays a theme from Paganini. When he drives out into the rain again, the sergeant is left in his shabby, isolated cottage with the sound of Paganini, the idea of Paganini, the remoteness and the nearness of him.

In **"The Gold Watch,"** a young man gives his father a watch in a complex gesture of ambivalence. He knows that his father hates being given things: he never wanted to be given a son. The young man looks on with grim satisfaction as his father breaks rocks with a sledge, trying to destroy the watch on his wrist, and then plunges his arm into a barrel of water. The father wishes to destroy not only the

gift, but the idea of time as well, time which has made him old, which has made him a father.

Some of the stories in *Getting Through* don't quite get through. They wander to a stop in inscrutable epiphanies, like a wandering into a cul-de-sac. Mr. McGahern's cul-de-sacs, though, tend to have gardens. It is also possible that the meaning of some of these stories lies in the search for meaning, a puzzled staring all around. The condition of perplexity may be our most attractive aspect.

Patricia Craig   (essay date 1985)

SOURCE: "Everyday Ecstasies," in *The Times Literary Supplement,* No. 4302, September 13, 1985, p. 1001.

[*Craig is an Irish editor and critic. In the following review of* High Ground, *she surveys the characters and settings of McGahern's short fiction and praises his realism and attention to detail.*]

In **"Oldfashioned"**, perhaps the most highly-charged and accomplished of the stories in his new collection [*High Ground*], John McGahern allows himself a loaded observation about the works of an Irish documentary filmmaker:

> they won him a sort of fame: some thought they were serious, well-made, and compulsive viewing, bringing things to light that were in bad need of light; but others maintained that they were humourless, morbid, and restricted to a narrow view that was more revealing of private obsessions than any truths about life or Irish life in general.

Change the medium, and you have a summary of McGahern's own experience, especially with regard to his novel *The Dark* (1965), against which a lot of affronted voices were raised. Some of these voices were choleric and Catholic; others belonged to people who resented being disheartened by McGahern's joyless view. *The Dark*—a very seedy evocation of adolescent suffering and anxiety—does seem to have been written out of a profound *malaise*; it's good to note a raising of spirits in subsequent fiction by this author. Not that he is ever exactly ebullient; his strengths instead would seem to lie in a steady approach, an encompassing sense of time passing, and a feeling for things like the everyday ecstasies which typically occur in a room in Rathmines, or near Stephen's Green.

High Ground, in fact, opens with a broken relationship and ends with a flourishing one, a positive note thereby being struck. In between are some instances of dignified behaviour, and some tests of loyalty—the latter concerning country schoolmasters young and old, and the choices that confront them. In the title story, to take that example, a boy with a new degree is invited to oust the old master whom drink has impaired. He himself was once the master's star pupil. The prospect of sudden advancement is held out to him by an upstart. Out of these few facts, McGahern makes a poised and resonant tale. As for the need to conduct yourself with decorum—it may be especially pressing if you are an unassertive girl, a maidservant, seduced and let down by the local lady-killer. Eddie Mac, in the story of that title, spectacularly abandons, along with his herdsman's post, the woman he has impregnated. This story, like its sequel (**"The Conversion of William Kirkwood"**) opposes two qualities, Irish wildness and Anglo-Irish mildness. Or, if you like, Irish unease and Anglo-Irish self-possession.

McGahern isn't after anything so crass as local colour, but locality is important, whether it's a Dublin dance-hall he's envisaging or a Georgian country parsonage complete with walled orchard, lawn and garden. In the first of the Dublin stories, a man is left by his girlfriend and goes adrift for a while in the company of some drunkards. There is another story in which we are asked to accept the peculiarity of an intending nun, in her last days of freedom, accompanying a man to a hotel room (to compound the pattern, he's an ex-seminarist). In fact, McGahern doesn't seem to have a wide range of female characters at his disposal; and this one, typically a nurse, is also typical in being clear-headed, guileless, nerveless and unironic.

A common masculine figure in McGahern's work is the warped Irish father: one or two of these get into *High Ground,* blusterers, grudge-bearers, graceless and glum. They don't loom especially large, however; that's a hell confined to childhood. More agreeable in disposition is the type of old man who ruefully compares himself to Oisin in the wake of the Fenians, the ethnic simile persisting in the face of modern innovations, church bingo, colour television and the like. McGahern, charting social change, notes the disappearance from Irish country roads of bicycles, horses, carts, traps and sidecars. He notes the modernization of the Mass and the advent of the minibus. The newer Irish ways are offered without comment, unless a comment is implicit in McGahern's faintly elegiac tone. He writes, as always, with authority and gravity, and with an instinct for the most appropriate detail.

McGahern wastes no words. His spare, terse and sometimes elliptical prose seduces with its lyricism, shocks with its electric dialogue, jolts sometimes with unexpected humour.

—*Lesley Glaister, in* **The Spectator,** *October 17, 1992.*

Joel Conarroe   (essay date 1987)

SOURCE: "Strong Women, Dreamy Men," in *The New York Times Book Review,* February 8, 1987, p. 9.

[*Conarroe is an American critic and educator. In the following favorable review of* High Ground, *he compares McGahern's short stories to the work of several highly accomplished modern authors.*]

John McGahern, the author of such highly regarded novels as *The Pornographer* and *The Leavetaking,* has been

called an Irish Chekhov, and one does find in his understated prose a fusion of high seriousness and low comedy, of heartbreak and heartburn, reminiscent of the Russian master. Other writers are brought to mind too by his fine new book, *High Ground,* a collection of stories. When his characters engage in hostile wordplay, the potential violence barely held in check, they sound like Pinter people. The dreamy men and practical women are cousins to Sean O'Casey's strong Junos and inept paycocks. Many of the characters, moreover, paralyzed by convention and habit, are unable to escape their parochial fates; their powerlessness suggests a central motif in James Joyce. (Mr. McGahern's men are also sometimes paralyzed by strong drink; these are hearty fellows who prepare for a night of serious imbibing by inhaling three quick whiskies.)

The one explicit literary allusion in the book, curiously, is not from O'Casey or Joyce but from A. E. Housman. The title character in **"Eddie Mac"** is a soccer hero who is chaired "shoulder high" from the field following some glorious exploits, and the reader remembers "To an Athlete Dying Young":

> The time you won your town the race
> We chaired you through the market-place;
> Man and boy stood cheering by,
> And home we brought you shoulder-high.

In a later stanza Housman describes the nature of disenchantment:

> Smart lad, to slip betimes away
> From fields where glory does not stay
> And early though the laurel grows
> It withers quicker than the rose.

Eddie Mac does indeed slip away, literally, stealing some valuable property from his employer and leaving his pregnant sweetheart to fend for herself, his former heroics long since turned to ashes.

Loss and betrayal are Mr. McGahern's great themes, and several of the stories are calculated to discomfit an attentive reader. (The compressed prose, every rift loaded with ore, must be read as deliberately as lyric poetry.) In **"The Conversion of William Kirkwood,"** one of two especially impressive tales, the man who has taken in Annie May, Eddie Mac's abandoned lover, and raised her daughter to young womanhood is engaged to a woman who suddenly announces that "Annie May will have to be given notice." This prospect sets up the realization that the marriage cannot take place "without bringing suffering on two people who had been a great part of his life, who had done nothing themselves to deserve being driven out into a world they were hardly prepared for." If stories can break hearts, this one will.

A second moving story, **"Oldfashioned,"** treats another of the author's obsessive themes, the conflict between fathers and sons. The tale, rich in characters and plot development, would have emerged, from a less laconic writer, as a novella or even as a full-blown novel. A sensitive working-class lad becomes a kind of adopted son to a wealthy couple who want to sponsor him to Sandhurst, the famous military academy, so he can prepare for a career in the British Army. The boy's real father quickly and violently deflates the dream: "Well, then. I have news for you. You're going to no Sandhurst whether they'd have you or not, and I even doubt if the Empire is that hard up." Much later the son makes a series of documentary films "about the darker aspects of Irish life," even though the people that really interest him are "all dead." It is tempting to find an autobiographical source in this narrative, but if works like Philip Roth's brilliant novel *The Counterlife* haven't taught us not to confuse fictional characters with their creators, then we are beyond hope of education.

In addition to the struggle between rigid fathers and their rebellious sons, these stories invoke other passionate conflicts—between men and women, union members and those who "cross the line," Roman Catholic and Protestant, the older and younger generations, and even between poets and more prosaic folk ("They say the standing army of poets never falls below ten thousand in this unfortunate country"). Only two of the stories strike false notes. In one, **"High Ground,"** a young man who is urged to supplant the benign, hard-drinking principal of his school days—a particularly awful act of betrayal—overhears the old man, at the end of the story, praising his former students. Given the usual credibility of Mr. McGahern's plots, this neat juxtaposition seems contrived. The other unconvincing narrative, **"Bank Holiday,"** treats an idealized affair between a middle-aged Dubliner and a young visitor from America. Unlike the author's plausible depictions of love gone awry, this is not a compelling picture of contemporary life, in Dublin or anywhere else; Mr. McGahern is more persuasive in evoking the moon's dark side than in describing moonlight and roses.

If two stories fail to convince, however, the other eight not only succeed, but even invite second and third close readings. It strikes me, in fact, that with this book, his seventh, Mr. McGahern joins a charmed circle of contemporary Irish writers that includes Edna O'Brien, Seamus Heaney and Thomas Kinsella, not bad company by any standard. His work surely merits a wider audience than it has so far enjoyed.

Antoinette Quinn   (essay date 1989)

SOURCE: "Varieties of Disenchantment: Narrative Technique in John McGahern's Short Stories," in *Journal of the Short Story in English*, No. 13, Autumn, 1989, pp. 77-89.

Nightlines, the title of John McGahern's first collection of stories, (1970), promises a series of sombre narratives; *Getting Through,* the title of his second, (1978), connects communication with strategies of survival; *High Ground,* (1986), his most recent collection, hints at elevations of theme or perspective, but a perusal of the title-story reveals the ironies of eminence. John McGahern's short fictions are studies in disillusionment and its apathetic aftermath, in alienated authenticity and the sad stoicism of the undeceived.

At first glance his fictional terrain may seem familiarly uncomfortable to readers of James Joyce, Frank O'Connor and Sean O'Faolain. Stories set in dreary, Irish provincial towns and villages or in the bars, dingy interiors and wet streets of Dublin. Unheroic white-collar heroes—teachers, police sergeants, civil servants, translators, failed writers, a priest. However, where his predecessors were actually or avowedly concerned with the representation of Irish life, writing chapters of moral history, diagnosing urban paralysis, forging an uncreated racial conscience, revealing Catholic Ireland to itself in an unflattering looking glass, McGahern's focus is on the ostensibly unrepresentative, on characters estranged from their families, professional milieux, social contexts, on solitaries, celibates, farmers' sons who have disinherited themselves, dropouts, bachelors who have not summoned enough sustained enthusiasm to marry. Neither self-deluded nor capable of overcoming their limitations, they are condemned characters, trapped in a world from which death is the only exit. Yet McGahern's heroes are neither freaks nor grotesques, denizens of stables, caves, dustbins, sandheaps. They lead lives of covert desperation, usually contriving to conform outwardly to social mores or rôle-expectations to the extent that their alienation or despair escapes public notice.

When I claim that these low-pulsed, phlegmatic, dispirited heroes may be only ostensibly unrepresentative, it is because their nihilism, their insistent consciousness of the pointlessness and purposelessness of their lives, their obsession with death, seem to me to derive less from Heideggerian existentialism than from a belated post-Christian reflectiveness pursued, for the most part, in the context of a casual, untroubled Irish Catholicism. Accustomed to living *sub specie aeternitatis* they now 'get through' each day in the certain knowledge of ultimate extinction. An idealist sensibility and a *contemptus mundi* have outlived the religious belief that engendered them. ('Faith, Hope and Charity', in the story of this title, are three hard-up musicians who provide cheap entertainment.) McGahern's undeceived heroes are ill-adjusted to the finite; theirs is the peculiar hopelessness of former Catholics recently deprived of a teleological metaphysic. They are disappointed men, discontented with the quotidian, grudging and aggrieved, haunted by a phantom promise. Their dilemma is 'what to make of a diminished thing' and they confront it listlessly or with grim humour. *Carpe diem* has no place in their philosophy. They endure but seldom enjoy. They are usually unsuccessful in love because distrustful of consolation. Woman offers them only a temporary respite from despair. McGahern's bachelors are celibates in retreat from life, or men who, failing to resolve a dichotomy between the real and the ideal, pursue love with intermittent ardour and waver about marrying. The motherlessness of so many of his characters may help to account for the joylessness of their disaffection; they lack a primal emotional bonding. Expecting little happiness in the here and none in the hereafter these disillusioned antiheroes devote themselves to developing their defences against present or future disappointment, protecting themselves against passion or commitment and 'the stupidity of human wishes'. They disengage from prevailing social and cultural pieties through withdrawal rather than conflict or debate. Their resistance is passive: they simply 'prefer not to'. One even chooses a Bartleby as rôle-model.

McGahern engages the reader's sympathy for his morose

heroes by mediating his fictions through a central consciousness or first person narrator. This is a peculiarly appropriate technique for representing the alienated consciousness, defining the hero's own sense of his isolation from his world. McGahern's heroes are often anonymous and are rarely portrayed externally but they are always self-aware and self-analytic. The narrative, presented from their point of view, dwells on the discrepancy between their public personae and their private attitudes or on the philosophical divide between their anguished nihilism and the nonchalant Catholicism conventional in the society. A reflectively disaffected central consciousness is the vehicle for much of the jaundiced humour of these stories. McGahern's heroes are sometimes sardonically amused at their own despondent singularity, sometimes derisively contemptuous of cheerful, successful, but deluded acquaintances. Through the intimacy of the point of view technique the reader is encouraged to compassionate with these malcontents' strategies for 'getting through' life. In many instances we are led to respect their dedicated pursuit of alienated authenticity; their unwaveringly honest confrontation with the misery of their existence; they appear nobly ignoble.

McGahern's short fictions modulate from realism into lyricism. The realist mode enables him to focus on the humdrum drabness and routine banality of his characters' lives and contexts. It is also secular and finite, firmly excluding transcendental comfort. Realism laced with lyricism is the mode best adapted to the portrayal of disenchantment. McGahern's narrators are at their most lyrical in evoking lost Edens and, more particularly, lost Eves. Failure in love is a recurrent theme; childhood disillusionment is treated only in *Nightlines.* These are timebound stories and their central preoccupation is with representations of human life in time: clockwatching, pastimes, repetition and predictability, recollection or oblivion, the fugitiveness of the present, apprehension as to the future, beginnings and, especially, endings, the mind's capacity to disregard time and place, and chronological time's measured indifference to the human story.

Where postmodernist fiction amazes the reader with its labyrinthine structures of forking paths and teases him out of escapist identification with a dizzying array of narrative choices McGahern employs realism to portray his characters' indifference to alternatives or to close off their options. Any change of course is pointless or illusory since life is a story in which all plots are unhappy and all narratives conduct towards ultimate closure. In *Nightlines* the narrator of **'Hearts of Oak, Bellies of Brass'** attempts to 'annul all the votes' in himself through the choice of a brutalizing life on a London building site. A blackly comic story within a story in **'Wheels'**, which tells of a Sergeant who in attempting to hang himself almost drowned by mistake and roared for help, is regarded by the narrator as an analogue to his own life, a story about having neither the will to live nor the courage to die unpredictably. This narrator's sense of the absurdity of his life's 'journey to nowhere' is syntactically conflated with his indifference towards the continuation or cessation of his autobiographical narrative: 'the repetition of a life in the shape of a story that had as much reason to go on as stop'. The theme of

indecisive passivity, inertia in the face of alternatives, is resumed in the concluding story of *Nightlines.* A teacher's tale of his exit from the Christian Brothers, which closely approximates the shape of his own life, is, like the sergeant's failed suicide, an instance of McGahern's technique of deploying anecdote as image. Lacking 'the resolution to stay or the courage to leave' he lay in bed until his religious superiors finally made his decision for him. He is afflicted with what he diagnoses as 'a total paralysis of the will, and a feeling that any one thing in this life is almost as worth doing as any other'. In the narrative present he manages to survive by escaping from his rôle into alcoholic anaesthesia every evening. His pupils who appear to choose a clerical career as Chistian Brothers are really pressganged into God's service as the story's title, **'The Recruiting Officer'** implies, their reward, an education they couldn't otherwise afford. To the one who got away these would-be 'fishers of men' are really fish who have risen to the bait.

Like *Nightlines, Getting Through* also concludes with a story which questions voluntary change, **'Sierra Leone'**. Here the narrator, gazing at the corpse of his apparently unhappily married stepmother, ironically prevaricates on the subject of her now closed alternatives:

> Would she have been happier with another? Who knows the person another will find their happiness or unhappiness with? Enough to say that weighed in this scale it makes little difference or all difference.

His ex-girlfriend's departure to Sierra Leone to seek a happy future with her older married lover prompts this underwhelmed reflection on wish-fulfilment:

> All things begin in dreams and it must be wonderful to have your mind full of a whole country like Sierra Leone before you go there and risk discovering that it might be your life.

Such a guarded and qualified hypothesis might appear a rhetorical technique for rendering the psychic timidity that inhibits adventure. However, the narrator's dubiety as to the heroine's future happiness in **'Sierra Leone'** is endorsed through the narrative device of having it conclude a collection which began with a story about a woman who travelled hopefully to fulfil her dream and ended up disillusioned and destroyed.

In this opening story, reflexively entitled **'The Beginning of an Idea'**, a successful theatre producer abandons her familiar world to pursue a career as a novelist in Spain. Having failed as a writer and been doubly raped she returns feeling like a corpse, icy and coffined. Within the imagery of the story she is also an oyster who has slid out of her protective shell and been devoured. Inspired by Chekhov's story, 'Oysters', and by two sentences she herself had composed on the dead Chekhov's last journey to Moscow in an oyster wagon, she had embarked on a fictional recreation of his life. Through the somewhat irritating device of reiterating her two sentences McGahern traces her course from obsession to writer's block. The fictional ending that had seemed to her a beginning was really only an ending, after all. Her imaginative obsession with Chekhov's final journey culminates ironically in her inarticulate reenactment of it in her own person. Is a heroine who has committed the existentialist crime of attempting to spend her life imagining another's life being punished by final absorption into her own text? Or is McGahern demonstrating that there is no better alternative, that changing one's career or circumstances is pointless? Why bother to live somewhere else 'when you can be just as badly off at home'?

McGahern's heroes in *Getting Through* are more cynical about their options than his heroines. A teacher recognizes that winning the girl or the silver cup are among the 'sorts of impossible things' and the spurned narrator of **'Doorways'**, footloose and fancy free on a Sligo morning, knows that his apparent choices are merely 'all sorts of wonderful impossibilities'. In **'Swallows'** where 'getting through' is lugubriously translated as 'killing time', a Sergeant and his housekeeper both while away their time unprofitably, he fishing and giving away his catch, she knitting socks mechanically for a few pence. The alternative proposed by the narrative of a visitor is cruelly inapposite, a story about how Paganini overcame his humble circumstances and lived life creatively to the last. For the sergeant, who could once manage a few Irish dance tunes on the fiddle, Paganini's career falls into the category of 'wonderful impossibilities' and the visitor's story only serves to arouse his latent discontent with the limitations of small town life. His housekeeper is better off, deaf to alternatives and contentedly absorbed in her limited progress from the heel to the toe of a sock. As one character remarks on the subject of greyhounds:

> They say there's only two kinds to have—a proper dud, or a champion—the in-between are the very worst.

The tragedy of McGahern's heroes is that they are neither duds, nor champions, but in-between people, intelligent and sensitive enough to savour the full bitterness of their disappointed lives.

McGahern exploits the narrative strategy of the flashforward to convey not choice, but predictability. The Sergeant of **'Swallows'** can script the evening's conversation in advance. The courting narrator of the comic romance, **'My Love, My Umbrella'**, foresuffers wet Sunday outings as a married man down to the excruciating detail of the condensation on the windshield as he stares out to sea from his car and quells 'the quarrels and cries of the bored children in the back seat'. In **'Parachutes'** the narrator foresees a young couple's inevitable future on a suburban housing estate:

> the child in the feeding chair could be seen already, the next child, and the next, the postman, the milkman, the van with fresh eggs and vegetables from the country, the tired clasp over the back of the hand to show tenderness as real as the lump in the throat, the lawnmowers in summer, the thickening waists. It hardly seemed necessary to live it.

Irish garrulity in McGahern's short fictions is a pragmatic evasion of existential reflection. Marooned together in **'Strandhill, The Sea'** his holidaymakers swap 'informa-

tions' all day, every day, ironically escaping from any confrontation with reality through 'the despotism of fact':

> Conversations always the same: height of the Enfield rifle, summer of the long dresses, miles to the gallon—from morning to the last glows of the cigarettes on the benches at night, always informations, informations about everythings, having come out of darkness now blinking with informations at all the things about them, before the soon when they'll have to leave.

Comic realist summary modulates into discursive moral censure almost imperceptibly here as daytime becomes synchronous with lifetime and departure with death. A recent story, **'Oldfashioned'**, deploys a similar comic technique of mimetic summary to illustrate the Irish country person's insatiable appetite for 'news', any news, however trivial, from local gossip to minor wonders farther afield.

McGahern's undeceived heroes tend to be more taciturn or reticent than their voluble neighbours. They have perfected a rhetoric of covert disengagement. Cliched politeness, the 'guaranteed responses' that impede any genuine conversational exchange, these are their most common forms of self-insulation against empathy or involvement. The narrator of **'Wheels'** prefers music to 'talk' in the office but when compelled to converse colludes in 'the lies that give us room' and parries his father's emotional appeals with a hollow semblance of common sense and consolation. He is practised in the art of self-effacing and non-provocative obsequiousness:

> As I grow older I use hardly anything other than these formal nothings, a conciliatory waiter bowing backwards out of the room.

The hero of **'Hearts of Oak, Bellies of Brass'** who is endeavouring to reduce himself from a state of *pour-soi* to *en-soi*, learns the minimal language of his fellow-workers on a London building-site. Like the prostitutes who inhabit the condemned houses on the site they trade their times and their bodies for money and the password to acceptance in their society is 'fukken':

> the repetitious use of fukken with every simple phrase came harsh at first and now a habit, its omission here would cause as much unease as its use where 'Very kind. Thank you, Mr. Jones' was demanded.

'Yes', that most positive of responses, with which Joyce had concluded *Ulysses*, becomes a bored mimicry of assent for McGahern's schoolteacher during the routine annual seaside holiday with his mother:

> and I walk by her side on the sand saying, 'Yes and yes and yes'. . .

McGahern's realist art strains towards the condition of vision, seeking out a single image that will define the narrative's central preoccupation and reinforce or transcend the principal character's cheerless brooding. Its central image is often foregrounded in the story's title. The title-image of **'Wheels'**, the first story in *Nightlines*, rotates throughout this opening narrative and on into the concluding story, suggesting life's predictable circularities, the pointlessness of its onward motion. The narrator of **'Wheels'**, whose story begins and ends with a train journey, is obsessed with life's aimlessness, the body's 'journey to nowhere', the cycle of the generations from nurturing to dependency, the equal tedium of progress or regress along life's groove. He is the first of McGahern's cheated characters, embittered by memories of his own youthful optimism, when the wheel seemed to be revolving towards a welcome future. The closure of his narrative is appropriately anticlimactic:

> all the vivid sections of the wheel we watched so
> slowly turn, impatient for the rich whole that
> never came but that all the preparations promised.

McGahern's 'wheel' represents what Hardy allegorized as 'Time's mindless rote'. In *Nightlines* life's meaningless monotony is sometimes suggested through rhyme, rhythm and repetition. Irish school children in their 'infant prison house' learn by rote, reciting the nonsense rhyme: *Eena, meena, mina moo, capall, asal agus bo.* The 'rise and fall' of their voices are echoed in the repetitive routines and work shanties of the adult Irish on the London building site of **'Hearts of Oak, Bellies of Brass'**: the rhythmic drive and throw of the shovels, the filling and rise of the hopper and Murphy's chant, 'shovel or shite; shite or burst'. The narration of these actions and phrases is itself repeated within the narrative, a simultaneous mimesis and metaphorizing of monotonous recurrence. Mimesis is almost indistinguishable from metaphor in **'My Love, My Umbrella'**, a comic romance in which love-making is humorously inseparable from the phallic erection of a black umbrella. In **'Peaches'** a dead shark is deployed as an objective correlative of the effect of writer's block, an intolerable stench of 'decomposition' which pollutes his environs. Narrative imagery is deployed excitingly throughout **'Peaches'** but the story is uncomfortably Hemingwayesque.

In *Getting Through,* where McGahern is obsessed with death, from the image of Chekhov's coffin in the opening lines to the narrator's stepmother's death in the final story, there is often more disjunction between mimesis and metaphor than in *Nightlines.* The image of death as a stoat relentlessly stalking his prey is well realized but its integration into the story, **'A Stoat'**, is too obviously contrived. A bald teacher's continual wearing of a hat to signify *timor mortis* in **'All Sorts of Impossible Things'** is naively allegorical. Perhaps the bleakest and most realistically unaccommodating of all McGahern's narrative images in *Getting Through* occurs in **'Doorway'**, where the slight realist tale of a failed love-affair proves too insubstantial a context for the powerful title-symbol. The occupants of the doorways, two almost interchangeable figures with two similar-sounding names, Barnaby and Bartleby, pass their days silently in close proximity but apart, each in his separate frame. Doorways, which function as images of entrance, exit and the threshold between, are visual analogues of the volume's title, *Getting Through.* At one point they are compared to 'coffins stood on end', a terminally punning reminder that life is lived in a context of death. The two isolated Beckettian figures, who scavenge for their food, occupy a minimal amount of space and shelter and live by an unvarying routine, represent human life at its most basic, 'getting through' as survival. Barnaby and Bartleby are solipsists who ignore each other and are indifferent to the attentions of passersby. They never communicate in words. Yet to the disappointed narrator of this story they are exemplary human images: in their strict observance of a disciplined aimlessness, their rigid adherence to absurd routines, their isolation and complete disengagement from their context, their passivity, they embody strategies for survival.

A sardonic perspective on human finiteness, on evasion of or confrontation with existential despair, is frequently expressed in narrative terms through ironies of closure. Time is often alluded to in McGahern's finales. **'The Recruiting Officer'** concludes with its teacher looking forward to an evening's alcoholic anaesthesia before 'the morning's dislocation'. **'A Slip Up'** finishes with the would-be farmer's public(house) procrastination, a postponement of routine:

> trying to put off the time, when he'd have to go
> up to the counter for their next round.

'Where do we go from here', asks the newly widowed father as **'Sierra Leone'** draws to its close. 'Not anyhow to Sierra Leone', is his son's mental response, though aloud he contrives a soothing form of noncommittal procrastination:

> I suppose we might as well try and stay put for
> a time . . . that is, until things settle a bit, and
> we can find our feet, and think.

When the dying priest in **'The Wine Breath'** conjures up an alternative narrative to his own concluding autobiography he imagines a young man who feels himself 'immersed in time without end', thereby permitting McGahern the terminal irony of ending his story with the phrase 'without end'. **'Faith, Hope and Charity'** closes with the opening bars of a tune and the start of a discourse, enabling the author to end on the word 'began'. The topic that launches the final disgruntled discourse is young people's early sexual initiation:

> Earlier and earlier they seem to start at it these
> days . . .

'Gold Watch' from *High Ground,* a narrative meditation on human life in time, is in many respects the quintessential McGahern story. It is the most ambitious and among the most achieved of his short fictions, a story whose mimetic and metaphoric concerns are intricately interrelated. Here he returns to one of his most obsessive themes, the failed father/son relationship, first announced in **'Wheels'**, the opening story of *Nightlines.* The concomitant theme of disinheritance is also reintroduced through the titular gold watch, a family heirloom which for the narrator son symbolizes a compensatory alternative to the family farm he has rejected. This wary, defensive narrator is one of McGahern's few successful heroes: he has a rewarding career, marries the golden girl, acquires the coveted gold watch and seems assured of a gilded future. Refusing public acknowledgement of the familial and patriarchal symbolism of the gold watch and always self-righteous in his dealings with his father, he buys a literal replacement for the family heirloom, a modern watch, expensive, ugly and, of course, 'duty-free'. This the father sets about destroying to signify the severance of their relationship, when all else fails steeping it in a barrel of crop spray. Since the son's rejection of the family farm is the origin of their poisonous quarrel, the corrosion of the substitute watch with farm chemicals is symbolically appropriate. The conclusion of the narrative universalizes the watch image, making it symbolize chronological time. All the temporal tropes on which the story draws—seasonal cycles, the progression from childhood to parenthood, the procession of the generations—and its final religious or Romantic expectation of revelation, 'some word or truth', are undermined by the realist recognition that chronological time is merely successive. An anti-epiphanic epiphany! **'Gold Watch'** is the work of a meticulous, old-fashioned craftsman, every cog precisely positioned in relation to its balance wheel and mainspring. McGahern is here consciously telling the time. The narrative ends by separating the gold watch as artifact from the concept of chronological time. It concludes with the phrase 'time that did not have to run to any conclusion'. Time is mindless, purposeless and interminable; narrators and narratives both seek a meaningful progression and terminate.

For my part I shall conclude by discussing my favourite story from *High Ground*, **'Parachutes'**. Like so many of McGahern's stories this is an anti-romance, but one that does not strain to achieve universality. McGahern's narrative strategy in **'Parachutes'** is to begin with an unhappy ending and to end with a happy beginning. Such reversal of chronology in a love story enables him to achieve an anticlimactic structure. This is the story of a fall from 'a pure dream of Paradise' to unendurable 'hell' in the real world, hell being a city much like Dublin. The objective correlatives of empirical reality are for the first person narrator a dishevelled lilac bush, blue railings, three milk bottles with silver caps, granite steps, the phenomena that surround him in the clear, disillusioned perspective of the morning after his fall. The dramatis personae of this real world are the Mulveys, a shiftless, bickering, Bohemian couple and their friend, Eamonn Kelly, impoverished acquaintances whom he plies with drink, purchasing their company to stave off the tortures of solitude. The Mulveys are impatiently awaiting a payment cheque from an editor, Halloran, and the externalized narrative of their expectancy and suspense ironically counterpoints the internalized narrative which encompasses it, a story of aftermath punctuated with, and ultimately overwhelmed by, retrospection. Irritated by Halloran's delay in paying them the Mulveys break open the suitcase he had left with them as surety and disclose his secret sexual perversity but they fail to probe the narrator's secret sexual suffering. A 'move in the right direction' in the realist dimension of the story, a cash advance from Halloran, serves as the prelude to a contrary narrative movement from realism into dream, imagery and rhythmic lyricism.

Narrative focus shifts from the pub interior outdoors, to reveal a vision of fragile beauty hovering briefly by the portals of the disenchanted, ordinary world:

> The state was so close to dreaming that I stared
> in disbelief when I saw the first thistledown, its
> thin, pale parachute drifting so slowly across the

open doorway that it seemed to move more in water than in air. A second came soon after the first had crossed out of sight, moving in the same unhurried way. A third. A fourth. There were three of the delicate parachutes moving together at the same dreamlike pace across the doorway.

The Mulveys speculate on the squalid origins of this transitory, gossamer beauty, an ironic counterpointing of sordid realism and metaphoric imagining which serves the narrative function of providing a solid, empirical basis for, while also deferring, the story's final flight into symbolic lyricism. Ultimately, the wafting thistledowns are associated through imaginative choreography with the dance that started the narrator on his love-affair, the take-off from realism into dream:

> 'Do you like waltzes?' were the first words she
> spoke as we began to dance.
>
> She did not speak again. As we kept turning to
> the music, we moved through the circle where
> the glass dome was still letting in daylight, and
> kept on after we'd passed the last of the pillars
> hung with the wire baskets of flowers, out beyond the draped curtains, until we seemed to be
> turning in nothing but air beneath the sky, a sky
> that was neither agate nor blue, just the anonymous sky of any and every day above our lives
> as we set out.

In this, the concluding paragraph of his story, the narrator twirls his partner rhythmically, phrase by phrase, into an

Caricature drawing of McGahern by David Levine. Reprinted with permission from The New York Review of Books. *Copyright (c) 1993 Nyrev, Inc.*

aerial dance, floating them into their future together. A story which opens with the parting of the ways, with the woman's entreaty to stay behind and not leave with her, concludes with the start of their shared journey, an apparently open ending structurally blocked by the narrative technique of beginning with closure.

The title-image, overtly assigned a metaphoric role only in the final section, is a pervasive symbolic presence throughout the story. It is the imagistic correlative of its anticlimactic structure, a visual analogue to the narrative of a fall from heaven. Notions of risky adventure, of brief, unsustainable flight, of the inevitability of a return to earth, are implicit in McGahern's choice of the parachute metaphor. The title-image also serves as a visual comment on the narrative's intersecting plots since the reader is made aware that the narrator was exploited by the woman as a saving support in her depressed descent from the dizzy heights of her previous love-affair just as he, in turn, clings to the frail support of the Mulvey's company in his own emotional downward dive. Other allusions within the text subtly recall the title-image. The narrator wishes for a radar screen on which to plot the movements of his departed lover; Claire Mulvey says that her frequent rows with her husband help to 'clear the air'.

McGahern's brief meditation, 'The Image', (*The Honest Ulsterman,* December 1968) reveals the poetics underlying his aesthetic achievement in **'Parachutes'.** For him, 'the image' is inseparable from 'the rhythm and the vision':

> The vision, that still and private universe which each of us possess but which others cannot see, is brought to life in rhythm, and by rhythm I think of the dynamic quality of the vision, its instinctive, its individual movements . . .

Characteristically, he associates art and 'the image' with transitoriness and failure, and, in particular, with the failure of love, again anticipating **'Parachutes'.** The image is a 'grave . . . of dead passions and their days' and 'the need of permanence' creates 'the need for shape or form'. **'Parachutes',** a fiction in which suspense is subordinate to suspension and realism is subverted by the precarious magic of a doomed lyricism, seems to me the finest justification of McGahern's disenchanted art.

High ground, for this anti-romantic writer, is less a place to aspire towards than to descend or fall from. Despite its title, however, there are some signs in this last volume that he is contemplating the move to a different fictional terrain, a middle ground between the nadir of despair and the unattainable or unsustainable altitudes of ecstasy. In the concluding story, **'Bank Holiday',** he is in a rare holiday mood. Even Dublin's climate has improved: 'the rain, the constant weather of this city', gives way to 'unusual weather, hot for weeks'. The hero, who in late middle age is given a third time lucky chance of finding happiness, recognizes the importance of celebrating life's ordinary, everyday drama rather than judging by criteria of aspiration and failed achievement. Patrick Kavanagh, for all his personal rebarbativeness, is this hero's exemplary poet. 'To realize sympathetically the natural process of living' would now seem to be the older, mellower McGahern's

fictional aim. *High Ground* appears to conclude with the traditional romantic promise of happiness ever after, but disenchantment dies hard. McGahern cannot succumb entirely to fairytale convention, so love and good fortune are still somewhat qualified by inertia and hypothesis:

> They were so tired and happy that it was as if they were already in possession of endless quantities of time and money.

Nicola Bradbury   (essay date 1989)

SOURCE: "High Ground," in *Re-reading the Short Story,* edited by Clare Hanson, Macmillan Press, 1989, pp. 86-97.

[*Below, Bradbury provides a thematic and stylistic overview of* High Ground.]

'High Ground' is the title story of the contemporary Irish writer John McGahern's third collection—he has also written four novels. It is not the leading story of the volume, however: that one (the first) is called 'Parachutes'. These stories, and these titles, fascinate me, because they are at once (as their altitude suggests) aloof, distinct, cool and yet (as the ambiguities of the titles hint) prepared to enter into a relationship, to establish a stance or line between reader and text: prepared by the writer, as I take it, who creates the taste by which he is to be enjoyed, first by designating the space within which this process is to take place.

It is the relationship between the sense of process and that of design in the short story—specifically, here, in these two stories and in the relationship between them—that I want to explore.

Perhaps I had better confess at the outset that you may feel this question is compromised by the writer and the works I have chosen. Though I shall not assume that you have read *High Ground* I expect you will recognise its characteristic preoccupations and procedures: the fascination with personal crises of disappointment and loss, particularly within the family, which seem obscurely to point beyond the personal. These belong not only to this collection and to McGahern's work, but familiarly to the Irish short story, which exploits the capacity to move, as in McGahern's work it quietly does, from the personal to the national, and the emotional to the political, if not overtly, then by implication—though it is occasionally explicit, as in the story here called **'Oldfashioned',** where the local Sergeant's son is befriended by the English Colonel and his lady. In **'Parachutes'** and **'High Ground'** the sorrow of the abandoned lover wandering in the dislocation of Dublin streets, trapped between obsessive memories and the importunities of his drunken friends, or the unease of the young man whose choice between personal loyalty and advancement shifts into the public sphere of politics and job: these constitute intimate crises, but are also felt to be symptomatic of an encroaching national confusion of romantic and historic loyalties and political pragmatism: an identity compromised on the one hand by outdated affiliations and on the other by self-abnegation in a dislocated modernity.

The question arises, whether in this context it is possible to sustain my opening claim that the writer creates the taste by which he is to be enjoyed, first by designating the space within which this process is to take place. Is the space in fact a given: the space of Ireland, and of Irish history (a space in time)? Is the writer bound simply to move within this area? The consistency of tone and the interrelationship of stories within the *High Ground* volume, and McGahern's work as a whole, might be judged either to support or to refute this idea. Figures are recalled, and situations developed; a world is constituted, polarised between the cold alienation of Dublin, and the different chill of a lost country (not named, but thought to be McGahern's own Co. Leitrim). Is this a matter of text or context, within the writer's control, or governing his procedures?

I shall return to these questions and to the Irish tradition later, but for the moment I want to focus on that aspect of consistency which might be regarded as thematic or stylistic, or both together, but which we might all agree seems characteristic both of the author and of the chosen form: that is the predominant quality of self-containment in these stories, which challenges us to approach each one individually. It is this independence of stance, together of course with the wry, exact recognition of everything which qualifies it, all the trammels of circumstance, personal, social, historical, literary even, to which Irish writers from Yeats and Joyce onwards have exhibited such an ambivalent exasperation and reverence: this embattled independence is what allows, and even challenges us to take these stories on analytically, and not primarily as subjectively bound descriptions of the conditions of their generation. This is what makes the stories readable to an audience outside those specific conditions, which makes them literary texts.

It is the conjunction of this embattled independence with the short story form that I want to explore. What is it within the work that tells us, formally, what to expect, and hence determines readerly satisfaction and disappointment; and how is this formal strain related to the matter of the text?

Henry James wrote of the novel form that its distinguishing characteristic is elasticity, the capacity to grow more true to its character in proportion as it strains, or tends to burst, with a latent extravagance, its mould. It is not, in other words, a formal property, but a formal propensity, a capacity, which James sees as the thing which makes the novel what it is: its genetic inheritance, if you like. Given this critical coup with the notoriously anarchic novel form, it is remarkable how resistant to definition the short story has proved: how hard it has been to do more than find two main concerns, with plot and atmosphere, each apparently requiring quite different formal properties: the story and the sketch. Why should the short story be harder than the novel to define? Perhaps because James's technique has not been followed: we have expected to find outlines; but we should perhaps look rather for directions, an inherent determination rather than achieved definition. The notion of determination against definition may even indicate what the link is between matter and form, since

we could also interpret this in psychological, or indeed in political terms.

The titles of our stories give us a starting point: or perhaps I should say, a direction. The sense of movement develops between their various available meanings, and in the space between the two titles, and between the titles and us. '**High Ground**', for instance, could be geographical or moral; we could think of painterly ground, and bas relief; we can not escape an inherent tension between the verticality of 'high' and the horizontal of 'ground'. Both '**High Ground**' and '**Parachutes**' work in naturalistic and in symbolic ways, and this is characteristic of the stories too: it may indeed prove to be their determining characteristic. From the volume title *High Ground* to the opening '**Parachutes**' we are precipitated into movement, a fall; and we are prevented, too, from moving too fast: it is an impeded movement—so that a sense is developed not merely of space but also of time: together with verticality, there is velocity. If the elasticity of the story form stretches between naturalism and symbolism, it could also be held taut by the space/time rhythmic interchange, and the balance of being and knowing, state and process. What I hope to show is how these stories are held by these two possibilities, between being and knowing, and how this is reflected in the text by the prose rhythms (I do not mean just the stylistic traits, though in this short paper I will concentrate on prose style as it is so immediate to our experience as readers)—the rhythms of statement which are caught between rhythms of discovery and rhythms of recovery: one, if you like, proper to the High Ground of Ireland, and the other to the space which the text creates for itself.

The prose rhythms seem to correspond to the title of '**Parachutes**' in their arrested development; and the opening interchange, which I shall quote in a moment, also asserts this tendency through its obliquity. Both rhythms and obliquity could be seen as mimetic of emotional distress; but they also function as the necessary and enabling condition of the narrative: thus answering to both the suggestions of '**Parachutes**'—the fall and the salvation—and in this the opening movement anticipates the eventual gently ironic twist by which the 'parachutes' which appear in the last pages of the tale are no machines of prevention at all, but organisms of propagation: the drifting seed-heads of thistledown, which rise before they fall, and disperse to create new growth, though at the cost of much waste. They look like the skirts of the dancing girl, and they figure the failed affair: brief, extravagant, but not quite wasted, since it gives the germ of this tale. And if we move, as I suggested we might, from the personal to the political, there is another irony in the translation of military equipment to natural forms, and there is salvation implicit in the undetermined but irrepressible fecundity of the Dublin waste ground where the thistles, and the stories, grow.

That political dimension is immanent though never explicit in the imagery from the first.

'I want to ask you one very small last favour.'

'What is it?'

'Will you stay behind for five minutes after I
leave?'

It was the offer of a blindfold, to accept the darkness for a few minutes before it finally fell.

The opening announcement of foreclosure, the determined, simple cadences, the inversion for the reader of
ending and beginning, of darkness and light, the powerful,
threatening image of the blindfold, are brilliantly compressed and oblique. This obliquity is made to take the formal mimetic stress of emotional expression: into the deadpan, we read anguish. The direct first person is discreetly
harnessed by the deictic construction introducing an emo-
tive metaphor: '*It was* the offer of a blindfold . . .' There
is a sequence of short, declarative sentences, stripped of
most modifiers and qualifiers, which acts like a stylistic
tuning fork to our readerly ear, so that elaboration when
it comes reaches its full effect: and the effect is both one
of recovery, the recreation of the moment, and of discovery, bringing out the acute sensation of loss. Between these
the statement is polarised as achievement *and* failure:
being and knowing are set at odds, though vitally interdependent: only in this parting is the quality of relationship
between them laid open to our view.

She turned and walked away. I was powerless to
follow. She did not once look back. The door
swung in the emptiness after she had gone. I saw
the barman looking at me strangely but I did not
care. The long hand of the clock stood at two
minutes to eight. It did not seem to move at all.
She was gone, slipping further out of reach with
every leaden second, and I was powerless to follow.

The story follows the circular rhythms of recall; as it
began with 'one very small last favour', it ends (Milton-
ically) 'as we set out'; and implicit in this rondo is the disruption of the parting: a disruption which finds its stylistic
counterpart in the narrative decorum of the first person
mode (that is, a singleness laid open to view). My argument is that McGahern uses these devices of style—and
larger motifs: narrative circularity, repetition and the interplay of space and time—all introduced easily without
violence to the illusion of naturalism, but with an ulterior
purpose: not to displace naturalism, but within its conventions to express, or explore, or simply activate a different
level of significance, which is the one we respond to not
just as readers but specifically as short story readers. In
promoting the distinct interests of process and of design,
he instructs us how to read.

This argument not only supports the double force of a
style which is both mimetic and self-conscious, engaging
and cool, which we might perhaps expect in an unhappy
love story, but it also makes critical room for those occurrences in the text which I think might otherwise be hard
to explain or justify. The devices I have in mind range
from a series of references to books—the pages of a book,
another slim volume, a Roman missal—to the kind of literary discussion which quotes Burns and Hazlitt, or the
conversational dissection of the words 'comprehension'
and 'apprehension'—terms which we can scarcely suppose

to be merely accidental or merely plausible in a naturalistic sense.

These literary joggings of the elbow are reminiscent (perhaps again designedly so) of Joyce—not only in *Dubliners*
but in *Portrait* and *Ulysses* too—where issues of language
and text serve not only for personal characterisation but
also to raise the historical matter of Ireland, colonialism,
and domination in religious, economic, and even family
and sexual politics.

In '**Parachutes**' these textual signals crop up intermittently, and not, I think, simply at random: what happens is
that the text oscillates between an inner and an outer space
and time, and these shifts are marked by the intrusion of
the textual prompts. So the opening movement shows the
speaker waiting in a bar for his lover to leave, rushing out
to look for her, then coming on a group of friends in another bar: and his private world clashes with their social
existence; but we feel the awkwardness through this curious signal:

Paddy Mulvey was reading a book, his eyes constantly flickering from the page to the door, but
as soon as he heard my name called his eyes returned fixedly to the page.

The friends are guarding a brown leather suitcase for Halloran: another cache of secrecy, which will eventually be
forced open—to reveal women's underwear and a missal—illustrating, as I take it, both the indecorum and the
inutility of such inquisitiveness, and so indirectly endorsing the value of mystery. The pages, the suitcase, the slim
volume, do not prompt curiosity in the protagonist: they
are the signal for recoil to his own secrets:

I tried to listen but found the arid, mocking
words unbearable. Nothing lived. Then I found
myself turning towards a worse torture, to all I
wanted not to think about.

The inner space and the pocketed time of memory are
given a specific narrative location and duration: dinner a
few days before Christmas at her sister's home. McGahern's feeling for locality allows a close match of naturalistic specificity and symbolism here. The claustrophobia is
insistently detailed:

The house her sister lived in was a small semi-
detached in a new estate: a double gate, a garage,
a piece of lawn hemmed in with concrete, a light
above the door. The rooms were small, carpeted.
A coal fire burned in the tiled fireplace of the
front room.

From this fireplace the cosy prospect of a predictable future is disturbing; but the 'vague unease' is finely slanted
through a postmortem on the way home. It is not the polite sidestepping nor the open expostulation of conversation that designates the emotional cramp of the design, but
the shifts and returns of mood and tense amongst the verbs
in this account. The transposition of conflict to the level
of syntax is strangely decent, yet unyielding. This is the
precise rhythm of history and future, the circumscription
of possibility:

'What did you think of them?' she'd asked as she took my arm in the road outside.

'I thought they were very nice. They went to a great deal of trouble.'

'What did you think of the house?'

'It's not my kind of house. It's the sort of house that would drive me crackers.'

'What sort of house would you like?'

'Something bigger than that. Something with a bit more space. An older house. Nearer the city.'

'Excuse me,' she said with pointed sarcasm as she withdrew her arm.

I should have said, 'It's a lovely house. Any house with you would be a lovely house,' and caught and kissed her in the wind and rain. And it was true. Any house with her would have been a lovely house. I had been the fool to think that I could stand outside life. I would agree to anything now. I would not even ask for love. If she stayed, love might come in its own time, I reasoned blindly.

And this is where a hiatus, a shift towards the story's present, confronts us—unlike the romantic escapist Yeats' echo of 'the wind and the rain'—with the inexorable consistency of its experience. The sequence may look superficially inconsequential; but at another level, the following casual remark articulates a continuing theme and links the 'then' and 'now' worlds through their concern with what is and what might have been.

> 'Do you realise how rich the English language is, that it should have two words, for instance, such as "comprehension" and "apprehension", so subtly different in shading and yet so subtly alike? Has anything of that ever occurred to you?'

This was Mulvey now.

'No, I hadn't realised.'

The pluperfect is exactly right: I hadn't realised, but now I have: that is what the story is about.

'**Parachutes**' moves in two ways: random, like the drifting seedheads, and determined, like the falling aviator; and the relation between the two could be described as suspension, which is the office of the parachute and the condition of the short story. It is at once provocatively self-referential and engagingly inexplicit. A paragraph ostensibly relating the last moments in the bar, for instance, is also an epitome of the whole tale: but it does not claim to be that, and so the effect is not one of closure, but the statement in which recovery and discovery are exactly poised, where the space has been made for what had to be said. Vocal and balletic rhythms here distance and objectify the feeling which informs the last sentence of this extract, at once coolly controlled and extraordinarily passive and impersonal: 'A whole world had been cut from under me.' This blind fall is carefully prepared:

> They started to quarrel. I bought a last round. It was getting close to closing time. Eamonn

Kelly had begun an energetic conversation with himself, accompanied by equally vigorous gestures, a dumbshow of removing hat and gloves, handshakes, movements forward and back, a great muttering of some complicated sentence, replacing of hat and gloves. The Mulveys had retreated into stewing silences. I was bewildered as to what I was doing here but was even blinder still about possible alternatives. A whole world had been cut from under me.

'**High Ground**' is like '**Parachutes**' in several ways: the Irish setting; the first person mode; the negotiation of time through memory; the apprehension of an unstatable future against which the story's present is played out. But it is different too. Less urbane (the setting is rural, the speaker a younger man), less literary, less provocative towards the reader, and stronger in its affirmations. It looks more naturalistic, but the effect is a more direct confrontation with conditions of being; less concern with ways of knowing. Whatever perspective we have on '**High Ground**' stresses design more heavily than process. In '**Parachutes**' prose and narrative rhythms engage our attention; in '**High Ground**' it is contours which require our notice: place is foregrounded, and even time has a solid, almost tactile quality: so the busy man 'won't beat around the bush', while the old Master's walls are hung with ancient calendars that have faded into the paper.

> **McGahern is writing out of an Irish tradition, a specific short story tradition, working within these conditions, which provide not only obsessive themes, but also an attitude, a literary tone, poised between dispassionate control and deep engagement.**
>
> —*Nicola Bradbury*

A sense of place is economically and even sardonically sketched in a series of small details approaching visual/verbal puns. Here worldly advance is signalled by a sequence of houses built on each others' insurance money in a sort of domestic cannibalism. Not yet engaged in that world, the young protagonist lets his boat drift, sits with his lover in a borrowed Prefect, goes home to help reroof his father's house: he lives amidst drifting and making do, amidst continuities and reciprocity. The arrivist Senator, however, appears in a different relation to the land:

> He had bulldozed the hazel and briar from the hills above the lake, and as I turned to see how close the boat had come to the wall, I could see behind him the white and black of his Friesians grazing between the electric fences on the far side of the reseeded hill.

He sits on the wall and comes 'to the point'. What he offers young Moran is a 'position'. The issue, through another pun, is one of 'principle': the headship of his old school, where his Master would be turned 'out on the road'. Which way to turn? Where to stand?

This is not answered. The conclusion is low-key and determinedly naturalistic, couched in the Master's conversation from the high stool in the bar ('The downward slope from the high stool is longer and steeper than from the top of Everest.'), where he speaks of high things. He extols the high values of home, of staying still, 'practically at the source of the Shannon'. He claims, 'There are people in this part of the country digging ditches who could have been engineers or doctors or judges or philosophers had they been given the opportunity.' But we hear him through the listener outside, and this perspective complicates the security of place, and suggests the non-naturalistic significance of the moment too. The tale is rounded to a close which holds all the possibilities—the ways of advance, retreat and of evasion—in careful balance: process is captured in design, and the mutual compromise of knowing and being are presented through the narrative contentions of youth and age, and the dimensions of time and space. Perhaps it is worth noting that while **'Parachutes'**, the disappointed love story which opens the collection, is followed by **'A Ballad'**, **'High Ground'** comes near the middle of the volume, and is held between **'Crossing the Line'** and **'Gold Watch'**. Between space and time.

In approaching these tales as examples of the short story form I have tried to work within the confines of the individual text and then the collection, taking the line any reader might follow, and exploring how the author has laid down directions, and created both parameters and volume, made the space of the story: in this process, the dimensions of space and time are material for his art. But they are also, of course, the conditions within which he works: there is a context for these texts, both geographical and historical, in literature and in life, and this certainly also conditions our reading and must be taken into account as we look for what I began by calling the 'inherent determination' of the form.

John McGahern, who lives near the border, is writing out of contemporary Ireland, out of an embattled, impoverished and fiercely self-conscious land: one with a peculiar sensitivity to geography and to history. He is also writing out of an Irish tradition, a specific short story tradition, working within these conditions, which provide not only obsessive themes, but also an attitude, a literary tone, poised between dispassionate control and deep engagement. The name I am sure you have been waiting for me to acknowledge is Joyce, and *Dubliners,* like Dublin, is certainly a presence in McGahern's world: not simply (if it can be called simple) through the sense of place, but also through the techniques of oblique progression through a sequence of tales at once separate and interlinked, and through the exposed solipsism of stream-of-consciousness poised against direct speech. But there is also another precursor, whom McGahern himself acknowledges. This is George Moore. His collection of stories, *The Untilled Field,* has a relationship to McGahern's country stories which balances *Dubliners* and the city; both, of course, are subsumed in a larger category of Irish stories, for in both

the presence of the other Ireland is felt beneath the surface. Moore, like Joyce, and later McGahern, writes of an Ireland bound in by bigotry and poverty, but also by beauty and pride; an Ireland which cannot be borne but can never wholly be left behind, even though the young emigrés, the 'wild geese', have flocked since the famine to America, while Irish intellectuals have turned to Europe, and particularly to Paris, for a freedom compromised at home by the hold of the church and the irreconcilable demands of political confusion. What Moore calls the 'depopulation question' lies behind every coming-of-age, every romance, every new job or old home, every struggle and betrayal: life is lived, or endured, in the knowledge of a possible exile, possible renunciation, or betrayal, which is both personal and national. George Moore's fine story 'The Wild Goose' ends with a paragraph which **High Ground** could accommodate with ease:

> He left early next morning before she was awake in order to save her the pain of farewells, and all that day in Dublin he walked about, possessed by the great joyful yearning of the wild goose when it rises one bright morning from the warm marshes, scenting the harsh north through leagues of air, and goes away on steady wing-beats. But he did not feel he was a free soul until the outlines of Howth began to melt into the grey drift of evening. There was a little mist on the water, and he stood watching the waves tossing in the mist thinking that it were well that he had left home—if he had stayed he would have come to accept all the base moral coinage in circulation; and he stood watching the green waves tossing in the mist, at one moment ashamed of what he had done, at the next overjoyed that he had done it.

It is not just the emotional and moral territory that we recognise here, but, as I should like to argue, the way we come to know them: the directions implicit in the phrasing itself: the prose rhythms, the balance of literal and figurative language, the nervous accuracy of tense, mood and voice in the verbs, which tell us where the boundaries lie that this tale strains against, and urges the need to overstep. May I give the last sentence again, with this in mind, as a fitting conclusion?

> There was a little mist on the water, and he stood watching the waves tossing in the mist thinking that it were well that he had left home—if he had stayed he would have come to accept all the base moral coinage in circulation; and he stood watching the green waves tossing in the mist, at one moment ashamed of what he had done, at the next overjoyed that he had done it.

D. J. Enright   (essay date 1992)

SOURCE: "Stuck in the Slot," in *London Review of Books,* Vol. 14, No. 19, October 8, 1992, pp. 9-10.

[Enright is an English man of letters who has spent most of his career abroad, teaching English literature at universities in Egypt, Japan, Berlin, Thailand, and Singapore. The author of critically respected works in a variety of genres, he is best known for his poetry, which is conversational in

style and often reflects his humanistic values through por-
traits of Far Eastern life. According to William Walsh,
"Enright is a poet with a bias toward light and intelligibili-
ty," and his critical essays are frequently marked by sar-
donic treatment of what he considers the culturally preten-
tious in literature. Below, he offers a stylistic and thematic
analysis of the short fiction in McGahern's The Collected
Stories.]

One of John McGahern's stories begins thus: 'There are
times when we see the small events we look forward to—a
visit, a wedding, a new day—as having no existence but
in the expectation. They are to be, they will happen, and
before they do they almost are not: minute replicas of the
expectation that we call the rest of our life.' The story
ends: 'I was free in the Sligo morning. I could do as I
pleased. There were all sorts of wonderful impossibilities
in sight. The real difficulty was that the day was fast falling
into its own night.' In between, nothing happens (the girl
doesn't want the narrator 'the way some people cannot eat
shellfish or certain meats'), albeit the opening sentence is,
not wholly unexpectedly, borne out.

**Mary Lavin once remarked that her two
novels should probably have been broken
up into short stories. McGahern's stories
often look like chapters of potential
novels.**

**—*Michael L. Storey, in* Studies in Short
Fiction, *Winter, 1994.***

A sentence in McGahern's most recent novel, *Amongst
Women* (1990), is similar; it concerns Moran, the farmer,
on the occasion of his second wedding: 'During the entire
day he felt a violent, dissatisfied feeling that his whole life
was taking place in front of his eyes without anything at
all taking place.' The lives McGahern customarily describes are narrow—by the standards of fiction, narrow in
the extreme; what discontent is felt is far from divine;
thoughts of what might have been, though painful, are not
trusted far and hence not unduly wept over. These stories
might be termed tragedies, but inaccurately, since whatever expectations arise and collapse are small and contained
by a sense of impossibility closely akin to stoical resignation. 'If everything was right, we'd appreciate nothing.'
But we read on in fear, not of any vulgar, stock sexuality
or physical violence, but in fear of further unhappiness.
We hope for small mercies for McGahern's characters.

He is something of a Samuel Beckett writing in relative
longhand, less emblematically and, I would say, more humanly. One of his ostensibly more enterprising characters,
who has escaped to work in the oilfields of Saudi Arabia,
comes home on leave with habitual expectations, with the
intention of standing rounds of drinks and distributing
presents; after a few days the excitement dims into a recognition of 'the poor fact that it is not generally light but
shadow that we cast.' The great event of his leave turns

out to be organising an uncle's funeral: one of those pieties
which, someone in another story says, 'are sometimes substitutes for life in this country—or life itself'.

Sexual passion is extramarital and short-lived, or for
young fellows feeling their oats, in whom repression largely accounts for its fierceness. Otherwise love—or some
sort of drive that serves in its place—means marriage and
children, wanted or not: 'an old con trick of nature' which,
one man reflects, never fails. (Although the widower who
advertises in the papers for companionship 'view marriage', and meets a decent gentle soul, slings his hook
when he finds she has a dicky heart.) The narrator of Mc-
Gahern's novel of 1979, *The Pornographer,* ponders that
when he had loved, it was uncertainty that gave an edge,
the 'immanence of No that raised the love to fever'; when
Yes is spoken love prepares to fly out of the window. This
truistic view is much reiterated by the narrator of Proust's
novel, whose experience has it that painful anxiety alone
keeps love in existence: 'We love only what we do not
wholly possess'; a state of affairs which, looked at with
eyes less jaundiced, ought to ensure love a reasonable lease
of life. And the editor in *The Pornographer* touches coarse-
ly on a Proustian theme when he proposes, with a rueful
glance at the sexual athletics displayed in the fiction he
prints, that one reason for art's supremacy is 'just because
of the very limitations of life'. (Such philosophical gener-
alisations are in keeping with the characters who utter
them: to wit, never stunningly original, lofty or amplified.)
In McGahern's **'Sierra Leone'**—a deceptively exotic
title—a character muses that the rich dream of life he enjoyed during the Cuban crisis, 'the last quiet evening of the
world before it was all consumed by fire', had dissolved the
next morning when the world was safe again. There is a
close parallel in Proust's *La Prisonnière*: as a man prepares
to fight a duel, life suddenly acquires a higher value in his
eyes, there are pleasures to enjoy, important work to do.
He escapes without a scratch, and at once finds the same
old obstacles standing between himself and life's pleasures
and labours.

Little though there is to be said for a solitary life, family
life seems harder to endure; it is something to be run away
from, often into another form of family life: which admittedly can be richer or easier at times, as Moran's daughters
in *Amongst Women* testify. One of the grimmest trials suffered by those of McGahern's people who have broken
away is 'going home'. Moran's daughters, who do love
their father, that unstable mixture of tyranny and charm,
brave it collectively; his son Luke firmly refuses to go
home. 'Unfortunately the best part of these visits is always
the leaving,' says a young woman in one of the stories, a
law graduate working in Dublin: 'After a while away
you're lured into thinking that the next time will somehow
be different, but it never is.' Parents expect you to live in
their present, your past: a bullying no more acceptable in
being to some extent superfluous, for you've never altogether broken free. But the children, no longer children,
still go home; even the obdurate Luke, safe in London, at
least meets his father half-way, at the wedding in Dublin
of one of his sisters; family ties, begrudged loyalties, must
be another of nature's old con tricks.

Another writer McGahern brings to mind is the poet Patrick Kavanagh. McGahern's story **'Bank Holiday'**, despite its curious but endearing earnestness ('I find myself falling increasingly into an unattractive puzzlement,' the chief character says, 'mulling over that old, useless chestnut, What *is* life?'), is a notably happy one, even—given the prevalently low temperature—heart-warming. All the same, Kavanagh's lines in 'One Wet Summer', 'As it is I praise the rain / For washing out the bank holiday with its moral risks,' does chime with much in McGahern's world. It was noted of Moran that 'Anything easy and pleasant aroused deep suspicion.' The succeeding lines in Kavanagh's poem admit, 'It is not a nice attitude but it is conditioned by circumstances / And by a childhood perverted by Christian moralists.' It's hard to be sure, in McGahern, whether religion is a burden or a blessing. Probably both; the Lord takes away with one hand and gives with the other. If those pieties were abandoned, what would replace them? The woman's question in Kavanagh's 'The Great Hunger'—'Who bent the coin of my destiny / That it stuck in the slot?'—echoes throughout the stories, and while there are partial or contributory answers, there is no convincing one. Bent coins are just another old con trick, which no one is grandiose or presumptuous or priestly enough to refer to original sin. One visionary gleam is manifest, to a glum, listless priest: the evening light on snow, renewed (Proustianly again) thirty years later by another evening's watery light falling on white chips of sawn beechwood. The priest would rather have his dead mother back. The priesthood attracted him not for any spiritual exaltation it might bring but as 'a way of vanquishing death and avoiding birth'. Possibly—the prose is so tentative or indeterminate here—the image of light and his thoughts of his mother leave traces of reconcilement and a muted joy.

If we are to speak in such terms it is sex, rather, that is the opium of the people, of the male section; though not a very potent drug. Sex and work, or work instead of sex. In **'Faith, Hope and Charity'** it is observed of two men that they slave away all year as labourers in England in order to squander their earnings during one summer month back in Ireland. 'As men obsessed with the idea that all knowledge lies within a woman's body, but having entered it find themselves as ignorant as before, they are driven towards all women again and again, in childish hope that somehow the next time they will find the root of all knowledge, and the equally childish desire for revenge since it cannot be found.' McGahern's women are customarily and distinctly the superior sex, more direct, more simply affectionate, open and resilient, actually made of sterner stuff and yet more sensitive to others; and certainly free from any obsession with ideas about where knowledge is to be found. They stand up to the men as bravely as they may, bowing before the storm but not breaking, while the men bluster, bemoan, strike out, or sulk.

It is not that they are shallow, nor that they are sweetened or sentimentalised; they know the depths, they are more modest in assessing the attainable heights and nimbler in rising to them. Rose, Moran's second (and barely deserved) wife, receives an oddly phrased but powerful tribute: her 'tact was so masterful that she resembled certain people who are so deeply read that they can play with all ideas without ever listing books.' The story **'A Ballad'** begins squalidly enough, and then a forced marriage turns into a successful one, another tribute to a patient, strong-minded woman. Elsewhere a nurse spends a night, one night only, with a young man, then announces that she is about to enter an Order, the Medical Missionaries. Enlightened though he is, a teacher of Latin and History, this startles him: surely an incongruous preparation for her new life? She argues that women have been known to spend the night before marriage with another man: 'We were free. That's the way it fell.' Now she is not free, and he still is. He has no beliefs, only preferences—for decency, affection, pleasure, good steak; she believes in one thing.

The occasional lyrical passages that have been noted in McGahern, seemingly extraneous, as if he is going to turn poetic on us, are transient and more often than not add to the melancholy, the sense of loss. The woman whose hipbones 'gave promise of a rich seedbed' remains a virgin, technically. A barman watches his wife's face, 'beautiful in its concentration, reflecting each move or noise she made as clearly as water will the drifting clouds', only to make sure she won't spot him helping himself to the whiskey. While there is nothing in the stories, or elsewhere in the novels, as broadly comic as the moment in *The Pornographer* when the porn-fictional Colonel asks the boatman if he fancies an aphrodisiac, and the boatman replies, 'To tell you the truth, I never sooner one drink more than another,' there is a scattering of quiet jokes, or ambiguous ones. Such as the second-hand tractor described as 'not fit to pull you out of bed'. Or the schoolboys from the Christian Brothers walking out in threes because there is less risk of buggery than if they walked in pairs. (These are boys who cross themselves before jumping into the sea.) More elaborately, and wryly, the retired man in **'A Slip-Up'** waits for his wife as usual outside Tesco's in London, but this time she has forgotten him, and he stands there for hours, in his fantasy back in Ireland on the farm they gave up, working there, getting on with what had been his real life. And, a simpler brand of humour, the trendy young priest mentioned in passing in **'Oldfashioned'**, who instructs his congregation that God wants them to want children, a bungalow, a car, and colour television; he plays the guitar in hotels, and to show how little the Roman collar means to him, he pulls it off and drops it into the soup: when fished out, it is found to be plastic and made in Japan.

Rarely can anyone have depicted a small and constricted world in such detail and with such unfussy cogency, a world moreover which is at once remote, for many readers, and yet strangely familiar. Familiar at any rate to people of my generation, of a time before expectations were formally established as a right presumably given by a non-existent God. Interconnections abound. Mahoney, the hated and loved father of *The Dark* (1965), looks like a preliminary sketch for Moran of *Amongst Women*. The same or very similar characters recur. **'Sierra Leone'** has a stepmother called Rose, a querulous father, and an inconvenient visit home. **'Gold Watch'** features a tyrannical

> The short story is exactly the right form for McGahern's 'documentaries'; the assiduous reader is surprisingly unaffected by the sameness, the overlapping of theme, feeling and figures, the pinched circumscription, the almost dogged, almost perverse embracing of disenchantment, the quiet desolation.
>
> —*D. J. Enright*

father, another stepmother Rose, a son going home for the summer, another tense confrontation. In 'Wheels' a son visits his alienated father and his uneasy stepmother, Rose. One might wonder whether McGahern didn't have himself in mind when he told in that first-rate story, **'Old-fashioned'**, how the Garda's son went on to make a series of television documentaries about 'the darker aspects of Irish life', which some viewers thought a serious and valuable exposé while others considered them 'humourless, morbid, and restricted to a narrow view that was more revealing of private obsessions than any truths about life or Irish life in general'.

The short story is exactly the right form for McGahern's 'documentaries'; the assiduous reader is surprisingly unaffected by the sameness, the overlapping of theme, feeling and figures, the pinched circumscription, the almost dogged, almost perverse embracing of disenchantment, the quiet desolation. In fact—much to the reader's, or this reader's, disbelief—one story gives an appetite for the next. There must be some truth in what someone says in *The Barracks,* his first and most purely tragic novel: 'All real lives are profoundly different and profoundly the same.' To which, in the corrective tone characteristic of the author, the speaker adds: 'Sweet Jesus, *profoundly* is an awful balls of a word, isn't it?'

Josephine Humphreys   (essay date 1993)

SOURCE: "A Lifetime of Tales from the Land of Broken Hearts," in *The New York Times Book Review,* February 28, 1993, pp. 1, 27.

[*Humphreys is an American novelist and essayist. In the following positive assessment of* The Collected Stories, *she provides an overview of McGahern's plots and characters.*]

One way to approach a story is to think of it as the writer's response to the most important question he can ask. The response is often complex, ambiguous and changeable, but the question is simple and almost always the same. The bigger the question, the riskier the fiction. In the story **"Bank Holiday"** in John McGahern's *Collected Stories,* a 50-year-old man tells the woman he loves, "I find myself falling increasingly into an unattractive puzzlement, mulling over that old, useless chestnut, What *is* life?"

That's Mr. McGahern's chestnut—the biggest. Old in-

deed, but useless only to those who are stupid or happy or both. Asking about it is hazardous. Later in **"Bank Holiday,"** the woman calls to her lover from the bedroom, teasing. "I hope you're not puzzling over something like 'life' again," she says. But Mr. McGahern, one of Ireland's most distinguished writers, has been doing just that through five novels (from *The Barracks* in 1964 to *Amongst Women* in 1990) and these 34 stories (some of which have appeared in his three previous collections). The life he puzzles over is Irish, rural, hard. Despair drains away the usual human consolations; family and church and romantic love are all infected in some way, and "What *is* life?" is a very difficult question indeed.

Mr. McGahern's response to it is usually made through pure narrative—that is, through event and dialogue alone, without interpretation. His characters may struggle to discover meaning in their circumstances, but the reader's sense, increasing with each story, is that logical answers are going to be elusive, solutions impossible. Mr. McGahern is drawn again and again to certain specific scenes, and doesn't hesitate to rework the basic situation of an earlier story in order to circle back around it, to get at it again. More than one story involves a stepmother named Rose, who deflects as best she can the brutal cruelty of her husband; but she is not always exactly the same Rose, and the father is sometimes a policeman and sometimes not. More than once a young man falls in love, and the love goes bad; or he escapes from the church; or he goes home to visit, for the last time, his aging father. The similar stories don't indicate continuity or sequence; instead, they're retakes, as if the author were a film director and had decided to shift the details and reshoot from a different angle—this time with the young man as a lawyer or a teacher, and next maybe with the young woman on the rebound or about to become a nun or pregnant.

In the story called **"Oldfashioned,"** the young man is a director, and his films are about "the darker aspects of Irish life." Critics find them "more revealing of private obsessions than any truths about life or Irish life in general." A critic who would say the same of Mr. McGahern's work would have failed to understand the wellspring of fiction. Private obsessions can be the surest path toward the truth of life in general. It appears that Mr. McGahern's obsessions have led, over time, from a vision of despair (life as a "journey to nowhere," as the son in the first story, **"Wheels,"** calls it) to something more mysterious.

People long to escape in the early stories, maybe to Dublin or London or America, where they think there might be something more to life than "scratching our arses, refining our ignorance." Some allow themselves to hope only for a less literal escape. In **"Strandhill, the Sea,"** a boy can no longer bear the killing tedium of a small coastal town: "The need to escape to some other world grew fiercer, but there was no money." The only place he can go is into fiction, the stolen comic books to which he turns for his heroes and gods. Love, in stories like **"My Love, My Umbrella"** and **"Doorways,"** can sometimes look like the great escape, a "dream of paradise," says the narrator in **"Parachutes"**; but paradise is actually on the verge of collapse just at the moment when it seems most attainable. Marriage, as in **"Peaches,"** can be a nightmare.

In some of the stories, a source of compensation is offered (but usually goes unnoticed); it is "the solid world," often delivered in a few simple words, as in **"The Wine Breath"**: "There was the lake, the road, the evening." The apprehended physical world, Ireland itself, in sky and sound, plants, creatures—specific, colored and textured—is a hope. Not because it is beautiful, but because it exists and can be seen and can be recalled.

Mr. McGahern, a master of the clean, plain, powerful description, is able to convey the strange phenomenon of immanence, the presence in material things of nonmaterial significance. "I saw the white tinsel of the sea thistle," the young man of **"Doorways"** says, "the old church, the slopes of Knocknarea, the endless pounding of the ocean mingled with bird and distant child cries, the sun hot on the old stones, the very day in its suspension, and thought if there was not this tension between us, if only we could touch or kiss we could have all this and more, the whole day and sea and sky and far beyond."

That vision, of love not as end but as means of gaining the world, is made more explicit in **"Along the Edges,"** a two-part story about the kind of love that fails and the kind that works: "They would have to know that they could know nothing to go through the low door of love, the door that was the same doorway between the self and the other everywhere."

"The Country Funeral," the final entry in the collection, represents as full a recovery from despair as one would want from the writer of these brilliant stories—that is, a recovery that's tentative and still grounded in puzzlement rather than a conversion to happiness. Three grown brothers, disaffected in various ways, attend the funeral of an uncle they never loved. By processes that none of them can explain—simply by gathering with the dead man's friends, hearing and telling stories, witnessing the funeral ritual, watching a rabbit hop out of the briers on a hill, drinking themselves into a stupor—they are reconciled not only with one another but also with their history and their land. (And the place to which desperation once drove Ireland's youth is mentioned only in a joke about some good-for-nothing neighbors: "The Whelans were never liked. They are all in America now.")

When one of the brothers says, "Gloria is far from over," he means the small, isolated town of Gloria Bog, where the uncle has been buried. But there is another *gloria,* a radiance to be discovered beyond the self; and he may mean that, too.

John Banville   (essay date 1993)

SOURCE: "Big News from Small Worlds," in *The New York Review of Books,* Vol. XL, No. 7, April 8, 1993, pp. 22-4.

[*Banville is an Irish novelist and critic. Below, he discusses the defining characteristics of McGahern's short fiction.*]

As they were controversial, they won him a sort of fame: some thought they were serious, well made, and compulsive . . . bringing things to light that were in bad need of light; but others maintained that they were humourless, morbid, and restricted to a narrow view that was more revealing of private obsessions than any truths about life or Irish life in general.

Thus is described the work of the documentary film maker who is the central character of one of John McGahern's stories: it is also, whether consciously or unconsciously on the author's part, an accurate account of popular and critical attitudes toward McGahern's own work. Throughout his career, beginning thirty years ago with his novel *The Barracks,* one of his best, to *Amongst Women,* which was nominated for a Booker Prize in 1990 and brought him the broad recognition that should have been his from the start, he has also produced a steady stream of short stories. These he has now collected into a single, substantial volume, adding two new tales, one of them surely a masterpiece.

McGahern is, at fifty-eight, one of the last Irish writers to have suffered directly at the hands of a Church-dominated state. In 1965 his novel *The Dark* was banned by the Irish Censorship Board for its sexually explicit language—essentially, the use of a few four-letter words—and as a result he was dismissed from his job as a teacher in a Dublin school. For the next decade or so he lived and worked abroad, returning in the 1970s to Ireland, where he now lives on a small farm in County Leitrim, in the northern part of the Republic near where he was born, one of the poorest and most mournfully beautiful parts of the country.

It is this muted little corner of the world that provides the setting for McGahern's most convincing fictions; the best of his novels and the best of his stories are set there, on the fringes of Gloria Bog, with the Iron Mountains in the distance and the River Shannon flowing past on its long journey south. He writes of the lives of small farmers, agricultural technicians (there is in this volume a wonderful, grotesquely funny story about a drunken group of artificial inseminators attending a formal dance), country schoolteachers, priests. Yet McGahern is not a fond pastoral writer casting a sentimental eye over a nest of simple folk; his is a dark, relentless vision: he is far closer to Samuel Beckett and James Joyce than to Frank O'Connor or Sean O'Faolain. Here is the embittered spurned lover of **"Parachutes"**:

> I came to a quiet side street where I sat on the steps of one of the houses. There were five steps up to each house. The stone was granite. Many of the iron railings were painted blue. Across the street was a dishevelled lilac bush. They'd taught us to notice such things when young. They said it was the world.

Earlier in the same story, the narrator describes a grim luncheon at his girlfriend's newly married sister's house.

> It was as if we were looking down a long institutional corridor; the child in the feeding chair could be seen already, the next child, and the next, the postman, the milkman, the van with

fresh eggs and vegetables from the country, the tired clasp over the back of the hand to show tenderness as real as the lump in the throat, the lawnmowers in summer, the thickening waists. It hardly seemed necessary to live it.

No dates are attached to the stories; the convention is unnecessary here. McGahern is one of those rare artists (Philip Larkin is another) who do not "develop." His style and his vision seem to have been already formed when he started to write. An early story such as **"Strandhill, the Sea,"** from his first collection, *Nightlines* (1970), has the same decorous authority, sly humor, and oddly stilted grace as the final, extended tale here, **"The Country Funeral,"** written after *Amongst Women*.

A characteristic of McGahern's work, criticized by some reviewers over the years, is that it is set in no clearly identifiable period. The emotional atmosphere of his novels and stories is an unending 1950s, even when internal evidence indicates a later decade. He seems to operate within a Proustian conception of time: the work is set in a stylized childhood landscape through which the adult narrator wanders as in a vivid dream, and just as in *A la recherche du temps perdu* we never quite know what Marcel's age is at any stage of the action, so in McGahern's fiction we cannot say exactly what period of the past forty years we are in.

This floating quality can be very effective in the stories with a rural setting, but in those that take place in Dublin, or Spain, or Finland, it sometimes creates an undermining sense of dislocation, a fuzziness around the edges which detracts from the force of the narrative. In one story, however, **"Oldfashioned,"** he performs a small miracle of chronology; the story should not work, but it does. It begins with a marvelous portrait of a kindly Protestant couple who "take up" the son of the local police sergeant and offer to arrange a career for him in the British army. The plan is thwarted by the intransigence of the father, a former Republican guerrilla fighter. Any other writer would have stopped there and been satisfied with a small, well-wrought vignette of Irish life. McGahern, however, extends the story over another few pages, drifting with deceptive ease through three decades of change and disillusion, until the sergeant's son, now a film maker, returns home (or "home") to shoot a program called *My Own Place*.

> The camera panned slowly away from the narrator to the house, and continued along the railings that had long lost their second whiteness, whirring steadily in the silence as it took in only what was in front of it, despite the cunning hand of the cameraman: lingering on the bright rain of cherries on the tramped grass beneath the trees, the flaked white paint of the paddock railing, the Iron Mountains smoky and blue as they stretched into the North against the rim of the sky.

In its quiet force and melancholy acknowledgment of what life will and will not offer, this story can stand beside the best of Chekhov or Turgenev.

McGahern avoids stylistic showiness, a weakness of many

Irish writers past and present, eschewing the florid metaphor and the stately cadence in favor of a plain, in places awkward, direct prose. He sticks with confidence and tenacity to a handful of themes and situations: life's opportunities lost, love sought and rarely found, the evanescence of passion, moments of glimpsed beauty, the bitter passions that hold families together and apart.

This last is a constant in all his work. The oedipal urge is especially strong, and surfaces in story after story. Behind almost everything McGahern has written stands the lowering figure of the father, who achieved his most convincing and powerful incarnation in the character of Moran, the monstrous, iron-willed, much-loved, and much-feared old IRA man who dominated the novel *Amongst Women*. In the stories he appears most memorably and most chillingly as the old farmer in **"Gold Watch,"** who regards kindness as a sign of weakness and whose son's marriage "might even make him happy for a time if he could call it my betrayal."

Read in sequence as they are arranged here, the stories follow what seems an autobiographical trajectory; yet if they are recounting the story of a life they do so in the only legitimate way, by a heightened detachment. The best of these tales manage a magical blend of the specific and the general, and the result looks eerily like life itself, not in the drab sense of social realism, but in the distillation of moments of stillness and insight that are like those moments, rare and precious, when we seem to ourselves most acutely and receptively alive. When he makes an occasional lurch into clumsy philosophizing ("But all of life turns away from its own eventual hopelessness, leaving insomnia and night to lovers and the dying"), what in a lesser writer would be no more than a wrong note sounds like a whole chord gone out of tune. Such discordances are the more startling for being so rare.

> **McGahern sticks with confidence and tenacity to a handful of themes and situations: life's opportunities lost, love sought and rarely found, the evanescence of passion, moments of glimpsed beauty, the bitter passions that hold families together and apart.**
>
> —*John Banville*

This collection of half a life's work in the short-story form would be a very considerable achievement even without the addition of the two new stories. **"The Creamery Manager"** and **"The Country Funeral"**; with them the book mysteriously takes on a shape and a unity that transform it from a mere collection into a satisfying whole. In the **"Country Funeral,"** which runs to more than thirty pages and is the longest story in the book, as well as the most recent, he achieves a further refinement of the spareness that is the hallmark of his talent. The tensions and barely

contained extremes of anger and sorrow that will modulate throughout the story are introduced with a sureness
of touch in the opening paragraphs.

> After Fonsie Ryan called his brother he sat in his
> wheelchair and waited with growing impatience
> for him to appear on the small stairs and then,
> as soon as Philly came down and sat at the table,
> Fonsie moved his wheelchair to the far wall to
> wait for him to finish. This silent pressure exas-
> perated Philly as he ate.
>
> "Did Mother get up yet?" he asked abruptly.
>
> "She didn't feel like getting up. She went back
> to sleep after I brought her tea."
>
> Philly let his level stare rest on his brother but
> all Fonsie did was to move his wheelchair a few
> inches out from the wall and then, in the same
> leaning rocking movement, let it the same few
> inches back, his huge hands all the time gripping
> the wheels. With his large head and trunk, he
> sometimes looked like a circus dwarf. The leg-
> less trousers were sewn up below the hips.

With the force and surface simplicity of a folk ballad the
story recounts a trip to the country—yet again, Gloria
Bog and environs—by three brothers to attend the funeral
of their Uncle Peter, their mother's brother, in whose forbidding house on the edge of the bog they had spent the
summers of their youth: "They were coming into country
that they knew. They had suffered here." The characters
of the brothers are sketched with skill and cunning, and
the portrait of rural life and its enduring ceremonials of
birth and death has great emotional power. As Uncle
Peter's wake begins:

> Maggie Cullen made sandwiches with the ham
> and turkey and tomatoes and sliced loaves. Her
> daughter-in-law cut the sandwiches into small
> squares and handed them around on a large oval
> plate with blue flowers around the rim. Tea was
> made in a big kettle. There were not many glass-
> es in the house but few had to drink wine or
> whiskey from cups. Those that drank beer or
> stout refused all offers of cup or glass and drank
> from the bottles. Some who smoked had a curi-
> ous, studious habit of dropping their cigarette
> butts carefully down the narrow necks of the
> bottles. Some held up the bottles like children to
> listen to the smouldering ash hiss in the beer
> dregs. By morning, butts could be seen floating
> in the bottoms of several of the bottles like
> trapped wasps.

With honesty and directness, John McGahern has fashioned a world as unmistakable as Beckett's or Proust's or
Faulkner's. In stories such as **"The Country Funeral"** he
shows an unsentimental respect for the people whom he
has made his subject. He has held to hard-won truths and
made a great thing out of simple components. Patrick
Kavanagh, a poet whom McGahern admires, might be
speaking for both of them when he says in his poem **"Innocence"**:

> They said
> That I was bounded by the
>   whitethorn hedges

> Of the little farm and did not
>   know the world.
> But I knew that love's doorway to
>   life
> Is the same doorway every
>   where. . . .
> I cannot die
> Unless I walk outside these white
>   thorn hedges. . . .

Eamon Grennan   (essay date 1993)

SOURCE: A review of *The Collected Stories,* in *America,*
Vol. 169, No. 3, July 31-August 7, 1993, pp. 20-2.

[*Grennan is an Irish poet and critic. In the following review,
he examines McGahern's fiction, terming it "essential reading for anyone interested in the interior life of modern Ireland, in modern fiction, in the short story, in good writing."*]

The voice that tells these splendid stories—and in so many
of them it seems to be the same slightly mournful but unflinching voice—wells up out of modern Irish consciousness itself, carrying with it such central issues as displacement (often from country to city), social and spiritual rupture and chronic loss. To deal with issues of such weight,
McGahern has forged a style of extraordinary fidelity to
the facts, both the external facts of the phenomenal world
and the internal facts of a painfully alert consciousness. In
many of his stories, the experience of the narrator or central character boils down to watching and listening, his
emotional life in part a consequence of how the world of
phenomena impinges on him.

In McGahern's way of doing things, the hard facts of the
actual are always registered first, insisting on the tangible
here and now of the world in which human action takes
place and in which the extensions of memory and feeling
and thought can happen. Within this world, McGahern
sets small dramas of troubled sexuality, loneliness, familial
aches and pains (the father-son struggle most bitterly
prominent among them), of bodies and spirits at doleful
odds with one another, their circumstances and themselves.

The fact of death is omnipresent; no other short story collection I know contains as many funerals as this one does,
culminating in the long and masterly last piece in the
book, **"The Country Funeral."** And death is present, too,
as a metaphor for the quality of many of these lives lived
in emotional, psychic and spiritual backwaters. Life in a
McGahern story is mostly a sorrowful mystery. Sexual
love, however, is also a constant, providing a possible
counterforce to the melancholic pressure of time, decay
and the more general inability of human beings to make
each other happy. McGahern's ability to dramatize love
through particular affairs of the heart and loins (in stories
like **"Doorways," "Gold Watch," "Sierra Leone," "Like
All Other Men"** and **"Bank Holiday"**) is both serious and
authentic, reminding me, at times, of the troubled erotic
poems of John Montague.

Like Montague, McGahern can provide a wonderfully
rich account of the ordinary pleasures and difficulties of

the love affair, with its contained and precious sense of lovers' time, the way everything takes the mark of excitement, the mortal shades falling over all that sweetness. And although the point of view is invariably male, the women in these stories have their own substance and intelligent independence, qualities that make them stronger than the men.

Unsparingly melancholic as his conclusions often are—bathed in the unflinching realism he levels at the love between men and women, at its vulnerability, its illusions and disillusions, its speechless chasms—McGahern's account of sexual love, of the actual texture and tone of it, is entirely convincing. By setting love and desire inside the ring of time, he insures that his vision of them is both philosophical and moral. But their actual groundedness in time and place, in the recognizable idioms of feeling and the palpable world, saves his investigation from being abstract. In contrast to William Trevor, who tells his stories from a different perspective and vantage point entirely, often from a distance, McGahern is in rapt close-up to the action, in the midst of its pain and enchantment. No other male Irish writer deals so truly and disturbingly with the depredations of love, with its "sadly mystical" pleasures and its sometimes "extraordinary breathing space."

Love in these stories can generate vitality and positive feeling, becoming (as it does at the end of one story) an image of fortitude, of making do. " 'Well, anyhow we have to face the day,' she said, dispelling it in one movement; and they took one another's hands as they went to meet the day, the day already following them, and all about them." Sexual love resists the grip death otherwise seems to have on the world. And at certain moments, such love can even provide a glimpse of something like a spiritual center: "When they rose and washed in the flat in all its daylight, it seemed as if it was not only a new day but the beginning of a new life. The pictures, the plates, the table in its stolidity seem to have been set askew by the accidental night, to want new shapes, to look comical in their old places." While it may at times offer intimations of mystery, sexual love is not "the Mystery" in its purest form. That exists in moments when an awareness of some transcendental possibility cuts through the local bric-a-brac.

From this point of view, the story at the core of McGahern's work is **"The Wine Breath."** It concerns an unnamed priest intensely conscious of "the solid world . . . everywhere around him," but who experiences a couple of moments of radiance, when he knows a kind of soul in things. In one of these moments, seeing evening light fall on wood-chips, he "felt himself (bathed in a dream) in an incredible sweetness of light." This sensation, in turn, takes him back 30 years to a funeral, to its swaying line of mourners and the experience of "a blinding white light"—only a moment of it—"in that lost day." Through the priest, McGahern gives free rein to something central to his own imagination—something sacred, the loss of which (like the critical loss of the mother or mother-figure that haunts myriad short stories and novels) shadows and determines his "sense of the world." In **"The Wine Breath,"** the purest relationship between the actual and the transcendent is established, the two brought together

in an unforgettable recognition of *immanence,* of some sacral presence guaranteeing the secular world. While setting the two (or three?) worlds together, however, this story also allows for their difference, accommodates a skepticism that insists on their separation, refusing to resolve the perplexed and perplexing gap between.

In another story, the author seems to reflect on his own art and achievement by describing a television director who has made some documentary films about the darker aspects of Irish life. "As they were controversial, they won him a sort of fame: some thought they were serious, well made and compulsive viewing, bringing things to light that were in bad need of light; but others maintained that they were humorless, morbid and restricting to a narrow view that was more revealing of private obsessions than any truths about life or Irish life in general."

Such style, finally, enables McGahern's **Collected Stories** to create one of the most complete and coherent worlds in Irish fiction since Joyce. These stories are essential reading for anyone interested in the interior life of modern Ireland, in modern fiction, in the short story, in good writing. The book shows just how faithful McGahern has been to his obsessions, engaging them again and again in order to get exactly the reality they wrestle with. The book should be read as a necessary part of any account of the way we have been, and the way—given the enduring humanity of the stories—we are.

For me, **The Collected Stories** are "serious, well made and compulsive." Certainly they echo private obsessions, but this makes them all the more painfully revealing of "life" and "Irish life in general." Their publication, like the recent appearance of the collected stories of William Trevor, means that the map of Ireland, humanly speaking, is now drawn in finer and more telling detail than ever before.

Denis Sampson   (essay date 1993)

SOURCE: A review of *The Collected Stories,* in *Irish Literary Supplement,* Vol. 12, No. 2, Fall, 1993, pp. 11-12.

[*In the following review, Sampson traces the development of McGahern's short fiction.*]

Nightlines. Getting Through. High Ground. In retrospect, the titles of John McGahern's three volumes of stories seem to light up the stages of his development as an artist—images which evoke the atmosphere of each book and at the same time suggest the energy and movement of a talent discovering itself and then growing towards maturity. These three volumes are reprinted with little change in **The Collected Stories,** and to them is added a brief, late story, **"The Creamery Manager,"** and a novella, **"The Country Funeral"**—34 stories in all. This novella is a tour de force written in the afterglow of *Amongst Women* and occupies a place in this world of the stories much like that occupied by "The Dead" in the collection which was McGahern's first inspiration.

In *Nightlines* (1970), early stories like **"Coming into his Kingdom"** or **"Korea"** or **"Lavin"** are disturbing revelations of male disillusionment and violence. Stories of boyhood in the country with an abusive father, of frustrated lovers away from home, of teachers, laborers and farmers in their paralyzing routines are fragments of a world which is unrelentingly dark.

As the images associated with the title suggest, these fictions represent a grim sense of cruelty and of the absurd; this is a world in which pleasure and joy have been blasted by violence, and the rules of personal and social life are strictly survival of the fittest. Technically, these stories owe much to *Dubliners,* not simply in the taut atmosphere, the formal conciseness or the style of "scrupulous meanness," but in the use of epiphany: revelation is at once shocking and exhilarating.

The subtlety and brevity of these early fictions signals McGahern's distance from the acknowledged Irish masters of the time, O'Connor and O'Faolain. As in *The Dark,* the representation of Irish country life is stripped of all traces of romantic realism and western pastoral. While the drama of character and scene remain, these fictions are close to Beckett in the intensity of their understatement. The controlled impersonality of style reflects a repression of nostalgia and of pain but it is also a way of exploring repression, silence, and the inadequacy of traditional forms of storytelling for capturing the truth of this world.

The opening and closing stories, **"Wheels"** and **"The Recruiting Officer,"** are masterpieces which extend the technical accomplishment of earlier work: the style is now more complex and varied in capturing layers of comic and satiric ironies with broad social reference to authoritarian personalities and systems, especially the Catholic Church and the schools. The psychological war which the ex-Christian Brother/teacher in **"The Recruiting Officer"** has been fighting for his own survival has left him going around in circles in "a total paralysis of the will . . . a feeling that any one thing in this life is almost as worthwhile doing as any other."

The claustrophobic world of the victimized self, imaged first in childhood and adolescence, is given adult dimensions, and it becomes evident that McGahern is not simply writing traditional stories of growing up or loneliness but is conducting a philosophical investigation of paralysis through stylistic experiment. The reader is called on to respond to a type of fiction which is increasingly experimental and conscious of its own patterns as fiction. These stories anticipate the experimental styles of *The Leavetaking* and *The Pornographer.*

But as McGahern became increasingly his own master in technique, it became evident in *Getting Through* (1978) and then *High Ground* (1985) that his vision was constantly changing. He calls on the reader to recognize that change by introducing each collection with a striking story on the nature of art and the character of the artist: **"The Beginning of an Idea"** and **"Parachutes."** These stories are urbane and satirical explorations of failure in love and failure in writing, and, implicitly, they instruct the reader on how to read the symbolic parables which follow.

The countryside and the family situation in the fiction of the 1960s remain recognizable as the reference point for all of McGahern's later work. The atmosphere of abuse and despair changes, however, so that already in the 1970s

the handful of stories which present a cast of country characters adds up to a more comic view of that world, and in *High Ground* McGahern achieves a kind of anthropological perspective on the life of groups and communities. This sense of a social and historical overview of the circumstances of Irish country life gradually deepens, and stories like **"Oldfashioned"** and **"The Conversion of William Kirkwood"** prepare the way for *Amongst Women.*

At the same time, McGahern explores city life in a series of stories of lovers, teachers and artists. The depiction of Dublin which began in **"My Love, My Umbrella"** is extended throughout the next two collections. The city is seen with Joycean attention, a place of pubs and frustration and tentative love affairs. It is a world which is an enlargement in some ways of the country world, a place where young men can go for freedom and adventure. There is room here for experiment, for happy accidents, for the growth of love. Characters travel. A European dimension is introduced, also, in continental settings and, especially, in literary and symbolic motifs. A lighter touch allows for the inclusion of various tones, romantic, comic, satirical, and this variety evokes a sympathy and compassion for the bewildering complexity of ordinary experience.

These changes in distance and perspective mirror a vision which is simultaneously freed from the static and dark world of the early fictions and also aware that what appears to be linear development is, in another perspective, circular. While the contrast between the provincial and the metropolitan modes of life is marked, in many stories the two are interwoven. It becomes evident in the stories, as in the novels, that a drama of opposites—an unending drama of yearning and loss, desire and defeat, beginnings and endings, departures and returns—is central to McGahern's work. The ritualized movement from city to country, first introduced in **"Wheels"** and reintroduced in **"Sierra Leone"** and **"Gold Watch,"** reappears in many forms—of home holidays, of emigrants returning, of going back in memory, of going back to die—and these processes are central also to the *The Leavetaking, The Pornographer,* and *Amongst Women.*

The work of the early 1980s, collected in *High Ground,* brings all of the familiar situations and themes to a new point of clarity. Stories of the country and of the city, of lovers and farmers and teachers, of ordinary people in ordinary circumstances, map a world which is now accepted in its mysterious processes of change. Time and place become the dominant characters in this world. Individual lives, marked by pain or love, despair or hope, are woven into a tapestry with other lives, all mirroring each other, meeting and parting in a kind of dance. **"Parachutes,"** which opens with the parting of lovers ends with a memory of a waltz, the moment when they met, "we kept turning to the music . . . until we seemed to be turning in nothing but air beneath the sky . . . the anonymous sky of any and every day above our lives as we set out."

McGahern writes of this heartbreaking immediacy, the overwhelming significance of the moment in the natural—and unnatural—process of change: the life-or-death choices of youth as in stories like **"Crossing the Line"** or

"High Ground" or the flash of sudden recognition of the wrong word said, the fatal turning point in a love affair. Actions become rituals; symbols and myth resonate behind a surface texture which remains close to the coarse grain of everyday circumstances. The tones of the visceral and the hilarious, the anguished and the detached, the compassionate and the satirical, mingle from sentence to sentence so that Ardcarne and Cootehall and the streets of Dublin become the site of a sense of life which finally yields nothing to formula or dogma: "I stood in the moonlit silence as if waiting for some word or truth, but none came, none ever came; and I grew amused at that part of myself that still expected something, standing like a fool out there in all the moonlit silence, when only what *was* increased or diminished as it changed, became only what is, becoming again what *was* even faster than the small second hand endlessly circling in the poison." This is from **"Gold Watch,"** and while the disillusioned residues of Irish Catholicism may inform this sensibility, McGahern's accomplishment is to infuse each object and each moment of a life with a luminous sense of anxious and frail significance. The precision of style is suffused with immense compassion and openness to hard-won joy.

Such consistency and concentration are the signs of an intimately known world, the artist's growth a matter of going not out but in deep, and McGahern's world (in which person, place and memory are miraculously fused) is recalled to us in story after story. While McGahern has touches of the provincial realist, his sense of character, nature and story separate him from the writers of the 1930s; the speaking voice here is not a translated *seanachai* although McGahern is just as close to the voices and textures of his world as any Irish storyteller. Nor is there any masquerade of charm or wonders although the local place is rich in the distinctive traces of individual lives and reveals its own amazing and fragmentary narratives. Internal references to places, characters and events in other stories remind the reader that all the stories are interweaving; as the narrator in **"Wheels"** put it, "repetition of a life in the shape of a story that had as much reason to go on as stop." Lives take on shapes; the shapes change; time passes; the present and the past assume mysterious circling patterns; an individual life is absorbed by the flow.

As we read forward in this volume, we realize that it is not simply McGahern's material which is observed or presented in this way: we are participating in the evolving consciousness of McGahern as artist. His organic development is shared with the reader through the double retrospective impulses of experiences re-imagined and the self-conscious patterns of repetition and variation. Nowhere is this more strikingly evident than in the new novella which rounds out the collection, **"The Country Funeral."**

The "rich whole" of life, which in **"Wheels"** seems to be an innocent vision inevitably destroyed by an incremental disillusioned adolescence and adulthood, now seems to be apprehended by three brothers who travel to the west of Ireland for the funeral of an uncle. The suffering and the absurdities of adult life are not denied, and the decision of one brother to return from working in the Middle East to live on the small farm next to Gloria bog is muted; but there is an implicit sense of eternal rightness in the accommodation to death which the story enacts through the funeral rites and through the symbolic position of the cemetery in the landscape. This novella recapitulates many situations, themes and motifs in earlier stories, but most strikingly of all it mirrors and reverses the vision and meaning of the opening story. It is as if the artist himself has traveled in a great circle of experience and perception. This collection is made to be the "rich whole" of the artist, all the fragments finally put into a satisfying order.

FURTHER READING

Criticism

Fitzgerald, Penelope. "The Great Importance of Small Things." *The Times Literary Supplement*, No. 4671 (9 October 1992): 21.

    Discusses the imagery and characters in the short fiction of *The Collected Stories*.

Glaister, Lesley. "Seizing the Moment." *The Spectator* 269, No. 8571 (17 October 1992): 31-2.

    Thematic and stylistic analysis of *The Collected Stories*.

Jamal, Zahir. "The Rub." *New Statesman* 95, No. 2465 (16 June 1978): 822-23.

    Favorable review of *Getting Through*.

Koenig, Rhoda. "Pluck of the Irish." *New York* 26, No. 4 (25 January 1993): 60.

    Examines stylistic aspects of the short fiction in *The Collected Stories*.

Long, Robert Emmet. Review of *Nightlines*, by John McGahern. *Saturday Review* 54 (1 May 1971): 41-3.

    Laudatory assessment. Long maintains: "McGahern's stories are lean, taut, and lacerating; perhaps no one writing today can command idiomatic Irish with such savage effect."

Moynahan, Julian. "Deeper into the Bog." *The New York Times Book Review* (13 July 1980): 14, 29.

    Mixed review of *Getting Through*.

O'Rourke, William. "Among the Lonely Souls of Ireland." *Tribune Books* (14 February 1993): 1, 6.

    Asserts that the tales in *The Collected Stories* "are utterly convincing, poignant and moving, and the writing is unflinching and spare, but I would not recommend reading more than a handful at one sitting. They are bitter pills, and you do not want to swallow too many at once. . . ."

Paulin, Tom. Review of *Getting Through*, by John McGahern. *Encounter* L, No. 6 (June 1978): 70.

    Positive assessment.

Storey, Michael L. Review of *The Collected Stories*, by John McGahern. *Studies in Short Fiction* 31, No. 1 (Winter 1994): 118-20.

    Discusses the defining characteristics of McGahern's short stories.

"Ireland Intensified." *The Times Literary Supplement,* No.
3587 (27 November 1970): 1378.
    Mixed review of *Nightlines.*

Additional coverage of McGahern's life and career is contained in the following sources
published by Gale Research: *Contemporary Authors,* Vols. 17-20, rev. ed.; *Contemporary
Authors New Revision Series,* Vol. 29; *Contemporary Literary Criticism,* Vols. 5, 9, 48;
Dictionary Literary Biography, Vol. 14; and *Major 20th-Century Authors.*

"Bartleby, the Scrivener"

Herman Melville

American novelist and short story writer.

The following entry presents criticism of Melville's short story "Bartleby, the Scrivener: A Story of Wall Street," first published in two installments on November 1 and December 1, 1853, in *Putnam's Monthly Magazine*. For an overview of Melville's short fiction, see *SSC*, Volume 1.

INTRODUCTION

The account of a young man's inability to conform to life on Wall Street in the mid-nineteenth century, "Bartleby, the Scrivener" is hailed by some scholars as the first modern American short story for its break with the moralizing, overt allegorizing, romantic characters, form, and other traits of earlier, traditional tales. More critical attention has been devoted to "Bartleby, the Scrivener" than any other short story by Melville, and the work's symbolic suggestiveness, thematic depth, and narrative ambiguity ensure its continuing appeal. Lea Bertani Vozar Newman has observed: "Whatever other chords 'Bartleby' may touch in the reader, the alienation that links this story to works by Dostoevsky, Kafka, and Camus attests to its modernity."

Plot and Major Characters

"Bartleby, the Scrivener" is narrated by a Wall Street lawyer who deals in investment opportunities for wealthy clients. A recent hire, Bartleby, works diligently at first copying legal documents but gradually begins to decline his responsibilities with the statement "I would prefer not to." Eventually Bartleby refrains from all copying and stares at the wall immediately outside of a window in the law office. Only when clients become affected by Bartleby's idiosyncratic and unnerving behavior does the lawyer take significant action, choosing to move his place of business to another building rather than fire Bartleby, who "would prefer not to" quit the lawyer's service; Bartleby refuses to vacate the building and is consequently jailed for vagrancy. The narrator, feeling somehow responsible for Bartleby's condition and incarceration, visits Bartleby, whom he finds dead from self-imposed starvation. At the conclusion of the story, the narrator relates a rumor about Bartleby's occupation prior to becoming a scrivener: Bartleby worked in the postal service's dead-letter office, where all lost, improperly addressed, or otherwise undeliverable mail ends.

Major Themes

Of "Bartleby, the Scrivener," Lewis Leary has stated: "Its charm resides in what Melville preferred not to reveal, so that no one key opens it to simple, or single, or precise meaning." Much of the story's complexity originates in the limited narrative perspective of the lawyer, who unin-

tentionally reveals more about himself than he intends while relating the few facts known about Bartleby. As a result, differing and sometimes conflicting themes have been attributed to the story. Some interpretations focus on the lawyer, variously characterizing him as self-serving or well-meaning; Bartleby has been perceived as psychotic, comical, nihilistic, Christ-like, or devoid of a social persona. As well, Bartleby is commonly identified as the portrait of a writer alienated by society for his refusal to "copy" the formula established by popular writers. Other commentators, focusing on the bleak mood and conclusion of the story, describe "Bartleby, the Scrivener" as a condemnation of capitalist society, a statement on the absurdity of life, or a disheartening existentialist commentary. Further intepretations present the story as a satire of specific historical individuals, a parable about failed Christian charity, a critique of contemporary philosophies, or a metaphor for the divided psyche of an individual; still another set of essays explicate "Bartleby, the Scrivener" in terms of Melville's other works.

Critical Reception

Written in the wake of *Moby-Dick* (1851) and *Pierre*

(1852), which were regarded as critical and popular failures during his lifetime, "Bartleby, the Scrivener" is Melville's first published short story. Financially strapped by the poor reception of his earlier efforts, Melville began contributing stories and sketches through the mid-1850s to popular magazines as a source of steady income. His short fiction was on the whole favorably received but Melville died generally unknown and unappreciated. The novella *Billy Budd*, left in manuscript at his death, was not published until 1924. Its appearance, along with Raymond M. Weaver's 1921 biography *Herman Melville: Mariner and Mystic* and other critical attention, led to a revival of interest in the Melville canon. Most commentators at this time emphasized the autobiographical element of "Bartleby, the Scrivener," contending that the author intended to depict an artist misunderstood by society. Another early and influential school of critics applied a psychological approach, diagnosing Bartleby as schizophrenic, manic depressive, autistic, or mad. The complex and subtle critical history of "Bartleby, the Scrivener" is best encapsulated in essays by Lea Bertani Vozar Newman and Milton R. Stern.

CRITICISM

Leo Marx (essay date 1953)

SOURCE: "Melville's Parable of the Walls," in *The Sewanee Review*, Vol. LXI, No. 4, Autumn, 1953, pp. 602-27.

[*Marx is an American educator and critic. In the following seminal essay, he examines the autobiographical aspect of "Bartleby, the Scrivener," focusing on the symbol of the walls and the depiction of the artist's situation in society.*]

> Dead,
>
> 25. Of a wall . . . : Unbroken, unrelieved by breaks or interruptions; absolutely uniform and continuous.
>
>   *—New English Dictionary*

In the spring of 1851, while still at work on *Moby Dick*, Herman Melville wrote his celebrated "dollars damn me" letter to Hawthorne:

> In a week or so, I go to New York, to bury myself in a third-story room, and work and slave on my "Whale" while it is driving through the press. *That* is the only way I can finish it now—I am so pulled hither and thither by circumstances. The calm, the coolness, the silent grass-growing mood in which a man *ought* always to compose, —that, I fear, can seldom be mine. Dollars damn me. . . . My dear Sir, a presentiment is on me, —I shall at last be worn out and perish. . . . What I feel most moved to write,

that is banned, —it will not pay. Yet, altogether, write the *other* way I cannot.

He went on and wrote the "Whale" as he felt moved to write it; the public was apathetic and most critics were cool. Nevertheless Melville stubbornly refused to return to the *other* way, to his more successful earlier modes, the South Sea romance and the travel narrative. In 1852 he published *Pierre*, a novel even more certain not to be popular. And this time the critics were vehemently hostile. Then, the following year, Melville turned to shorter fiction. **"Bartleby the Scrivener,"** the first of his stories, dealt with a problem unmistakably like the one Melville had described to Hawthorne.

There are excellent reasons for reading **"Bartleby"** as a parable having to do with Melville's own fate as a writer. To begin with, the story *is* about a kind of writer, a "copyist" in a Wall Street lawyer's office. Furthermore, the copyist is a man who obstinately refuses to go on doing the sort of writing demanded of him. Under the circumstances there can be little doubt about the connection between Bartleby's dilemma and Melville's own. Although some critics have noted the autobiographical relevance of this facet of the story, a close examination of the parable reveals a more detailed parallel with Melville's situation than has been suggested. In fact the theme itself can be described in a way which at once establishes a more precise relation. **"Bartleby"** is not only about a writer who refuses to conform to the demands of society, but it is, more relevantly, about a writer who foresakes conventional modes because of an irresistible preoccupation with the most baffling philosophical questions. This shift of Bartleby's attention is the symbolic equivalent of Melville's own shift of interest between *Typee* and *Moby Dick*. And it is significant that Melville's story, read in this light, does not by any means proclaim the desirability of the change. It was written in a time of deep hopelessness, and as I shall attempt to show, it reflects Melville's doubts about the value of his recent work.

Indeed, if I am correct about what this parable means, it has immense importance, for it provides the most explicit and mercilessly self-critical statement of his own dilemma that Melville has left us. Perhaps it is because **"Bartleby"** reveals so much of his situation that Melville took such extraordinary pains to mask its meaning. This may explain why he chose to rely upon symbols which derive from his earlier work, and to handle them with so light a touch that only the reader who comes to the story after an immersion in the other novels can be expected to see how much is being said here. Whatever Melville's motive may have been, I believe it may legitimately be accounted a grave defect of the parable that we must go back to *Typee* and *Moby Dick* and *Pierre* for the clues to its meaning. It is as if Melville had decided that the only adequate test of a reader's qualifications for sharing so damaging a self-revelation was a thorough reading of his own work.

"Bartleby the Scrivener" is a parable about a particular kind of writer's relations to a particular kind of society. The subtitle, "A Story of Wall Street," provides the first clue about the nature of the society. It is a commercial society, dominated by a concern with property and finance.

Most of the action takes place in Wall Street. But the designation has a further meaning: as Melville describes the street it literally becomes a walled street. The walls are the controlling symbols of the story, and in fact it may be said that this is a parable of walls, the walls which hem in the meditative artist and for that matter every reflective man. Melville also explicitly tells us that certain prosaic facts are "indispensable" to an understanding of the story. These facts fall into two categories: first, details concerning the personality and profession of the narrator, the center of consciousness in this tale, and more important, the actual floor-plan of his chambers.

The narrator is a Wall Street lawyer. One can easily surmise that at this unhappy turning point in his life Melville was fascinated by the problem of seeing what his sort of writer looked like to a representative American. For his narrator he therefore chose, as he did in **"Benito Cereno,"** which belongs to the same period, a man of middling status with a propensity for getting along with people, but a man of distinctly limited perception. Speaking in lucid, matter-of-fact language, this observer of Bartleby's strange behavior describes himself as comfortable, methodical and prudent. He has prospered; he unabashedly tells of the praise with which John Jacob Astor has spoken of him. Naturally, he is a conservative, or as he says, an "eminently *safe*" man, proud of his snug traffic in rich men's bonds, mortgages and deeds. As he tells the story we are made to feel his mildness, his good humor, his satisfaction with himself and his way of life. He is the sort who prefers the remunerative though avowedly obsolete sinecure of the Mastership of Chancery, which has just been bestowed upon him when the action starts, to the exciting notoriety of the courtroom. He wants only to be left alone; nothing disturbs his complacency until Bartleby appears. As a spokesman for the society he is well chosen; he stands at its center and performs a critical role, unravelling and retying the invisible cords of property and equity which intertwine in Wall Street and bind the social system.

The lawyer describes his chambers with great care, and only when the plan of the office is clearly in mind can we find the key to the parable. Although the chambers are on the second floor, the surrounding buildings rise above them, and as a result only very limited vistas are presented to those inside the office. At each end the windows look out upon a wall. One of the walls, which is part of a skylight shaft, is *white*. It provides the best light available, but even from the windows which open upon the white wall the sky is invisible. No direct rays of the sun penetrate the legal sanctum. The wall at the other end gives us what seems at first to be a sharply contrasting view of the outside world. It is a lofty brick structure within ten feet of the lawyer's window. It stands in an everlasting shade and is *black* with age; the space it encloses reminds the lawyer of a huge black cistern. But we are not encouraged to take this extreme black and white, earthward and skyward contrast at face value (readers of *Moby Dick* will recall how illusory colors can be), for the lawyer tells us that the two "views," in spite of their colors, have something very important in common: they are equally "deficient in what landscape painters call 'life'." The difference in color is

less important than the fact that what we see through each window is only a wall.

This is all we are told about the arrangement of the chambers until Bartleby is hired. When the lawyer is appointed Master in Chancery he requires the services of another copyist. He places an advertisement, Bartleby appears, and the lawyer hastily checks his qualifications and hires him. Clearly the lawyer cares little about Bartleby's previous experience; the kind of writer wanted in Wall Street need merely be one of the great interchangeable white-collar labor force. It is true that Bartleby seems to him peculiarly pitiable and forlorn, but on the other hand the lawyer is favorably impressed by his neat, respectable appearance. So sedate does he seem that the boss decides to place Bartleby's desk close to his own. This is his first mistake; he thinks it will be useful to have so quiet and apparently tractable a man within easy call. He does not understand Bartleby then or at any point until their difficult relationship ends.

When Bartleby arrives we discover that there is also a kind of wall inside the office. It consists of the ground-glass folding-doors which separate the lawyer's desk, and now Bartleby's, from the desks of the other employees, the copyists and the office boy. Unlike the walls outside the windows, however, this is a social barrier men can cross, and the lawyer makes a point of telling us that he opens and shuts these doors according to *his* humor. Even when they are shut, it should be noted, the ground glass provides at least an illusion of penetrability quite different from the opaqueness of the walls outside.

So far we have been told of only two possible views of the external world which are to be had from the office, one black and the other white. It is fitting that the coming of a writer like Bartleby is what makes us aware of another view, one neither black nor white, but a quite distinct third view which is now added to the topography of the Wall Street microcosm.

> I placed his desk close up to a small side-window in that part of the room [a corner near the folding-doors]—a window which originally had afforded a lateral view of certain grimy back yards and bricks, but which, owing to subsequent erections, commanded at present no view at all, though it gave some light. Within three feet of the panes was a wall, and the light came down from far above, between two lofty buildings, as from a very small opening in a dome. Still further to a satisfactory arrangement, I procured a high green folding screen, which might entirely isolate Bartleby from my sight, though not remove him from my voice. And thus, in a manner, privacy and society were conjoined.

Notice that of all the people in the office Bartleby is to be in the best possible position to make a close scrutiny of a wall. His is only three feet away. And although the narrator mentions that the new writer's window offers "no view at all," we recall that he has, paradoxically, used the word "view" a moment before to describe the walled vista to be had through the other windows. Actually every window in the office looks out upon some sort of wall; the important difference between Bartleby and the others is that he is closest to a wall. Another notable difference is implied by the lawyer's failure to specify the color of Bartleby's wall. Apparently it is almost colorless, or blank. This also enhances the new man's ability to scrutinize and know the wall which limits his vision; he does not have to contend with the illusion of blackness or whiteness. Only Bartleby faces the stark problem of perception presented by the walls. For him external reality thus takes on some of the character it had for Ishmael, who knew that color did not reside in objects, and therefore saw beyond the deceptive whiteness of the whale to "a colorless, all-color of atheism." As we shall see, only the nature of the wall with which the enigmatic Bartleby is confronted can account for his strange behavior later.

What follows (and it is necessary to remember that all the impressions we receive are the lawyer's) takes place in three consecutive movements: Bartleby's gradually stiffening resistance to the Wall Street routine, then a series of attempts by the lawyer to enforce the scrivener's conformity, and finally, society's punishment of the recalcitrant writer.

During the first movement Bartleby holds the initiative. After he is hired he seems content to remain in the quasi-isolation provided by the "protective" *green* screen and to work silently and industriously. This screen, too, is a kind of wall, and its color, as will become apparent, means a great deal. Although Bartleby seems pleased with it and places great reliance upon it, the screen is an extremely ineffectual wall. It is the flimsiest of all the walls in and out of the office; it has most in common with the ground glass door—both are "folding," that is, susceptible to human manipulation.

Bartleby likes his job, and in fact at first seems the exemplar of the writer wanted by Wall Street. Like Melville himself in the years between *Typee* and *Pierre,* he is an ardent and indefatigable worker; Bartleby impresses the lawyer with probably having "been long famished for something to copy." He copies by sun-light and candle-light, and his employer, although he does detect a curiously silent and mechanical quality in Bartleby's behavior, is well satisfied.

The first sign of trouble is Bartleby's refusal to "check copy." It is customary for the scriveners to help each other in this dull task, but when Bartleby is first asked to do it, to everyone's astonishment, he simply says that he prefers not to. From the lawyer's point of view "to verify the accuracy of his copy" is an indispensable part of the writer's job. But evidently Bartleby is the sort of writer who is little concerned with the detailed accuracy of his work, or in any case he does not share the lawyer's standards of accuracy. This passage is troublesome because the words "verify accuracy" seem to suggest a latter-day conception of "realism." For Melville to imply that what the public wanted of him in 1853 was a kind of "realism" is not plausible on historical grounds. But if we recall the nature of the "originals" which the lawyer wants impeccably copied the incident makes sense. These documents are mortgages and title-deeds, and they incorporate the official version of social (property) relations as they exist at the time. It occurs to the lawyer that "the mettlesome poet, Byron"

would not have acceded to such a demand either. And like the revolutionary poet, Bartleby apparently cares nothing for "common usage" or "common sense"—a lawyer's way of saying that this writer does not want his work to embody a faithful copy of human relations as they are conceived in the Street.

After this we hear over and over again the reiterated refrain of Bartleby's nay-saying. To every request that he do something other than copy he replies with his deceptively mild, "I would prefer not to." He adamantly refuses to verify the accuracy of copy, or to run errands, or to do anything but write. But it is not until much later that the good-natured lawyer begins to grasp the seriousness of his employee's passive resistance. A number of things hinder his perception. For one thing he admits that he is put off by the writer's impassive mask (he expresses himself only in his work); this and the fact that there seems nothing "ordinarily human" about him saves Bartleby from being fired on the spot. Then, too, his business preoccupations constantly "hurry" the lawyer away from considering what to do about Bartleby. He has more important things to think about; and since the scrivener unobtrusively goes on working in his green hermitage, the lawyer continues to regard him as a "valuable acquisition."

On this typically pragmatic basis the narrator has become reconciled to Bartleby until, one Sunday, when most people are in church, he decides to stop at his office. Beforehand he tells us that there are several keys to this Wall Street world, four in fact, and that he himself has one, one of the other copyists has another, and the scrub woman has the third. (Apparently the representative of each social stratum has its own key.) But there is a fourth key he cannot account for. When he arrives at the office, expecting it to be deserted, he finds to his amazement that Bartleby is there. (If this suggests, however, that Bartleby holds the missing key, it is merely an intimation, for we are never actually provided with explicit evidence that he does, a detail which serves to underline Melville's misgivings about Bartleby's conduct throughout the story.) After waiting until Bartleby has a chance to leave, the lawyer enters and soon discovers that the scrivener has become a permanent resident of his Wall Street chambers, that he sleeps and eats as well as works there.

At this strange discovery the narrator feels mixed emotions. On the one hand the effrontery, the vaguely felt sense that his rights are being subverted, angers him. He thinks his actual identity, manifestly inseparable from his property rights, is threatened. "For I consider that one . . . is somehow unmanned when he tranquilly permits his hired clerk to dictate to him, and order him away from his own premises." But at the same time the lawyer feels pity at the thought of this man inhabiting the silent desert that is Wall Street on Sunday. Such abject friendlessness and loneliness draws him, by the bond of common humanity, to sympathize with the horrible solitude of the writer. So horrible is this solitude that it provokes in his mind a premonitory image of the scrivener's "pale form . . . laid out, among uncaring strangers, in its shivering winding sheet." He is reminded of the many "quiet mysteries" of the man, and of the "long periods he would stand looking out, at his pale window behind the screen, upon the *dead brick wall.*" The lawyer now is aware that death is somehow an important constituent of that no-color wall which comprises Bartleby's view of reality. After this we hear several times of the forlorn writer immobilized in a "*dead*-wall revery." He is obsessed by the wall of death which stands between him and a more ample reality than he finds in Wall Street.

The puzzled lawyer now concludes that Bartleby is the victim of an "innate" or "incurable" disorder; he decides to question him, and if that reveals nothing useful, to dismiss him. But his efforts to make Bartleby talk about himself fail. Communication between the writer and the rest of Wall Street society has almost completely broken down. The next day the lawyer notices that Bartleby now remains permanently fixed in a "dead-wall revery." He questions the writer, who calmly announces that he has given up all writing. "And what is the reason?" asks the lawyer. "Do you not see the reason for yourself?" Bartleby enigmatically replies. The lawyer looks, and the only clue he finds is the dull and glazed look of Bartleby's eyes. It occurs to him that the writer's "unexampled diligence" in copying may have had this effect upon his eyes, particularly since he has been working near the dim window. (The light surely is very bad, since the wall is only three feet away.) If the lawyer is correct in assuming that the scrivener's vision has been "temporarily impaired" (Bartleby never admits it himself) then it is the proximity of the colorless dead-wall which has incapacitated him. As a writer he has become paralyzed by trying to work in the shadow of the philosophic problems represented by the wall. From now on Bartleby does nothing but stand and gaze at the impenetrable wall.

Here Melville might seem to be abandoning the equivalence he has established between Bartleby's history and his own. Until he chooses to have Bartleby stop writing and stare at the wall the parallel between his career as a writer and Bartleby's is transparently close. The period immediately following the scrivener's arrival at the office, when he works with such exemplary diligence and apparent satisfaction, clearly corresponds to the years after Melville's return to America, when he so industriously devoted himself to his first novels. And Bartleby's intransigence ("I prefer not to") corresponds to Melville's refusal ("Yet . . . write the *other* way I cannot.") to write another *Omoo,* or, in his own words, another "beggarly *Redburn.*" Bartleby's switch from copying what he is told to copy to staring at the wall is therefore, presumably, the emblematic counterpart to that stage in Melville's career when he shifted from writing best-selling romances to a preoccupation with the philosophic themes which dominate *Mardi, Moby Dick* and *Pierre.* But the question is, can we accept Bartleby's merely passive staring at the blank wall as in any sense a parallel to the state of mind in which Melville wrote the later novels?

The answer, if we recall who is telling the story, is Yes. This is the lawyer's story, and in his eyes, as in the eyes of Melville's critics and the public, this stage of his career *is* artistically barren; his turn to metaphysical themes *is* in fact the equivalent of ceasing to write. In the judgment of his contemporaries Melville's later novels are no more meaningful than Bartleby's absurd habit of staring at the dead-wall. Writing from the point of view of the Wall Street lawyer, Melville accepts the popular estimate of his work and of his life. [In a footnote the critic adds: "It is not unreasonable to speculate that Melville's capacity for entertaining this negative view of his work is in fact a symptom of his own doubts about it. Was there some truth to the view that he was merely talking to himself? He may have asked himself this question at the time, and it must be admitted that this fear, at least in the case of *Pierre* and *Mardi,* is not without basis in fact."] The scrivener's trance-like stare is the surrealistic device with which Melville leads us into the nightmare world where he sees himself as his countrymen do. It is a world evoked by terror, and particularly the fear that he may have allowed himself to get disastrously out of touch with actuality. Here the writer's refusal to produce what the public wants is a ludicrous mystery. He loses all capacity to convey ideas. He becomes a prisoner of his own consciousness. **"Bartleby the Scrivener"** is an imaginative projection of that premonition of exhaustion and death which Melville had described to Hawthorne.

To return to the story. With his decision to stop copying the first, or "Bartleby," movement ends. For him writing is the only conceivable kind of action, and during the rest of his life he is therefore incapable of action or, for that matter, of making any choice except that of utter passivity. When he ceases to write he begins to die. He remains a fixture in the lawyer's chamber, and it is the lawyer who now must take the initiative. Although the lawyer is touched by the miserable spectacle of the inert writer, he is a practical man, and he soon takes steps to rid himself of the useless fellow.

He threatens Bartleby, but the writer cannot be frightened. He tries to bribe him, but money holds no appeal for Bartleby. Finally he conceives what he thinks to be a "masterly" plan; he will simply convey to the idle writer that he "assumes" Bartleby, now that he has ceased to be productive, will vacate the premises. But when he returns to the office after having communicated this assumption, which he characteristically thinks is universally acceptable, he finds Bartleby still at his window. This "doctrine of assumptions", as he calls it, fails because he and the writer patently share no assumptions whatsoever about either human behavior or the nature of reality. However, if Bartleby refuses to accept the premises upon which the Wall Street world operates, he also refuses to leave. We later see that the only escape available to Bartleby is by way of prison or death.

Bartleby stays on, and then an extraordinary thing happens. After yet another abortive attempt to communicate with the inarticulate scrivener the narrator finds himself in such a state of nervous indignation that he is suddenly afraid he may murder Bartleby. The fear recalls to his mind the Christian doctrine of charity, though he still tends, as Melville's Confidence Man does later, to interpret the doctrine according to self-interest: it pays to be charitable. However, this partial return to a Christian view leads him on toward metaphysical speculation, and it is here that he finds the help he needs. After reading Jonathan Edwards on the will and Joseph Priestley on necessity, both Christian determinists (though one is a Calvinist and the other on the road to Unitarianism), he becomes completely reconciled to his relationship with Bartleby. He infers from these theologians that it is his fate to furnish Bartleby with the means of subsistence. This excursion in Protestant theology teaches him a kind of resignation; he decides to accept the inexplicable situation without further effort to understand or alleviate the poor scrivener's suffering.

At this point we have reached a stasis and the second, or "lawyer's" movement ends. He accepts his relation to Bartleby as "some purpose of an allwise Providence." As a Christian he can tolerate the obstinate writer although he cannot help him. And it is an ironic commentary upon this fatalistic explanation of what has happened that the lawyer's own activities from now on are to be explicitly directed not, insofar as the evidence of the story can be taken as complete, by any supernatural force, but rather by the Wall Street society itself. Now it seems that it is the nature of the social order which determines Bartleby's fate. (The subtitle should be recalled; it is after all Wall Street's story too.) For the lawyer admits that were it not for his professional friends and clients he would have condoned Bartleby's presence indefinitely. But the sepulchral figure of the scrivener hovering in the background of business conferences causes understandable uneasiness among the men of the Street. Businessmen are perplexed and disturbed by writers, particularly writers who don't write. When they ask Bartleby to fetch a paper and he silently declines, they are offended. Recognizing that his reputation must suffer, the lawyer again decides that the situation is intolerable. He now sees that the mere presence of a writer who does not accept Wall Street assumptions has a dangerously inhibiting effect upon business. Bartleby seems to cast a gloom over the office, and more disturbing, his attitude implies a denial of all authority. Now, more clearly than before, the lawyer is aware that Bartleby jeopardizes the sacred right of private property itself, for the insubordinate writer in the end may "outlive" him and so "claim possession . . . [of his office] by right of perpetual occupancy" (a wonderful touch!). If this happens, of course, Bartleby's unorthodox assumptions rather than the lawyer's will eventually dominate the world of Wall Street. The lawyer's friends, by "relentless remarks," bring great pressure to bear upon him, and henceforth the lawyer is in effect an instrument of the great power of social custom, which forces him to take action against the nonconforming writer.

When persuasion fails another time, the only new stratagem which the lawyer can conceive is to change offices. This he does, and in the process removes the portable green screen which has provided what little defense Bartleby has had against his environment. The inanimate writer is left "the motionless occupant of a naked room." However, it soon becomes clear to the lawyer that it is not so easy to abdicate his responsibility. Soon he receives a visit from a stranger who reports that the scrivener still inhabits the old building. The lawyer refuses to do anything further. But a few days later several excited persons, including his former landlord, confront him with the news that Bartleby not only continues to haunt the building, but that the whole structure of Wall Street society is in danger of being undermined. By this time Bartleby's rebellion has taken on an explicitly revolutionary character: "Everyone is concerned," the landlord tells the lawyer, "clients are leaving the offices; some fears are entertained of a mob. . . ."

Fear of exposure in the public press now moves the lawyer to seek a final interview with the squatter. This time he offers Bartleby a series of new jobs. To each offer the scrivener says no, although in every case he asserts that he is "not particular" about what he does; that is, all the jobs are equally distasteful to him. Desperate because of his inability to frighten Bartleby's "immobility into compliance," the lawyer is driven to make a truly charitable offer: he asks the abject copyist to come home with him. (The problem of dealing with the writer gradually brings out the best in this complacent American.) But Bartleby does not want charity; he prefers to stay where he is.

Then the narrator actually escapes. He leaves the city, and when he returns there is word that the police have removed Bartleby to the Tombs as a vagrant. (He learns that even physical compulsion was unable to shake the writer's impressive composure, and that he had silently obeyed the orders of the police.) There is an official request for the lawyer to appear and make a statement of the facts. He feels a mixture of indignation and approval at the news. At the prison he finds Bartleby standing alone in the "inclosed grass-platted yards" silently facing a high wall. Renewing his efforts to get through to the writer, all the lawyer can elicit is a cryptic "I know where I am." A moment later Bartleby turns away and again takes up a position "fronting the dead-wall." The wall, with its deathlike character, completely engages Bartleby. Whether "free" or imprisoned he has no concern for anything but the omnipresent and impenetrable wall. Taking the last resort of the "normal" man, the lawyer concludes that Bartleby is out of his mind.

A few days pass and the lawyer returns to the Tombs only to find that they have become, for Bartleby, literally a tomb. He discovers the wasted figure of the writer huddled up at the base of a wall, dead, but with his dim eyes open.

In a brief epilogue the lawyer gives us a final clue to Bartleby's story. He hears a vague report which he asserts has a "certain suggestive interest"; it is that Bartleby had been a subordinate clerk in the Dead Letter Office at Washington. There is some reason to believe, in other words, that Bartleby's destiny, his appointed vocation in this society, had been that of a writer who handled communications for which there were no recipients—PERSON UNKNOWN AT THIS ADDRESS. The story ends with the lawyer's heartfelt exclamation of pity for Bartleby and humankind.

> The unique quality of "Bartleby the
> Scrivener" resides in its ability to say
> almost nothing on its placid and
> inscrutable surface, and yet so powerfully
> to suggest that a great deal is being said.
>
> —*Leo Marx*

What did Melville think of Bartleby? The lawyer's notion that Bartleby was insane is of course not to be taken at face value. For when the scrivener says that he knows where he is we can only believe that he does, and the central irony is that there was scarcely a difference, so far as the writer's freedom was concerned, between the prison and Wall Street. In Wall Street Bartleby did not read or write or talk or go anywhere or eat any dinners (he refuses to eat them in prison too) or, for that matter, do anything which normally would distinguish the free man from the prisoner in solitary confinement. And, of course, the office in which he had worked was enclosed by walls. How was this to be distinguished from the place where he died?

> The yard was entirely quiet. It was not accessible
> to the common prisoners. The surrounding
> walls, of amazing thickness, kept off all sounds
> behind them. The Egyptian character of the ma-
> sonry weighed upon me with its gloom. But a
> soft imprisoned turf grew under foot. The heart
> of the eternal pyramids, it seemed, wherein, by
> some strange magic, through the clefts, grass-
> seed, dropped by the birds, had sprung.

At first glance the most striking difference between the Wall Street office and the prison is that here in prison there are four walls, while only three had been visible from the lawyer's windows. On reflection, however, we recall that the side of the office containing the door, which offered a kind of freedom to the others, was in effect a fourth wall for Bartleby. He had refused to walk through it. The plain inference is that he acknowledged no distinction between the lawyer's chambers and the world outside; his problem was not to be solved by leaving the office, or by leaving Wall Street; indeed, from Bartleby's point of view, Wall Street *was* America. The difference between Wall Street and the Tombs was an illusion of the lawyer's, not Bartleby's. In the prison yard, for example, the lawyer is disturbed because he thinks he sees, through the slits of the jail windows, the "eyes of murderers and thieves" peering at the dying Bartleby. (He has all along been persuaded of the writer's incorruptible honesty.) But the writer knows where he is, and he offers no objection to being among thieves. Such minor distinctions do not interest him. For him the important thing is that he still fronts the same dead-wall which has always impinged upon his consciousness, and upon the mind of man since the beginning of time. (Notice the archaic Egyptian character of the prison wall.) Bartleby has come as close to the wall as any man can hope to do. He finds that it is absolutely impassable, and that it is not, as the Ahabs of the world would like to

think, merely a pasteboard mask through which man can strike. The masonry is of "amazing thickness."

Then why has Bartleby allowed the wall to paralyze him? The others in the office are not disturbed by the walls; in spite of the poor light they are able to do their work. Is it possible that Bartleby's suffering is, to some extent, self-inflicted? that it is symptomatic of the perhaps morbid fear of annihilation manifested in his preoccupation with the dead-wall? Melville gives us reason to suspect as much. For Bartleby has come to regard the walls as permanent, immovable parts of the structure of things, comparable to man's inability to surmount the limitations of his sense perceptions, or comparable to death itself. He has forgotten to take account of the fact that these particular walls which surround the office are, after all, man-made. They are products of society, but he has imputed eternality to them. In his disturbed mind metaphysical problems which seem to be timeless concomitants of the condition of man and problems created by the social order are inextricably joined, joined in the symbol of the wall.

And yet, even if we grant that Bartleby's tortured imagination has had a part in creating his dead-wall, Melville has not ignored society's share of responsibility for the writer's fate. There is a sense in which Bartleby's state of mind may be understood as a response to the hostile world of Wall Street. Melville has given us a fact of the utmost importance: the window through which Bartleby had stared at the wall had "originally . . . afforded a lateral view of certain grimy backyards and bricks, but . . . owing to subsequent erections, commanded at present no view at all, though it gave some light." Melville's insinuation is that the wall, whatever its symbolic significance for Bartleby, actually served as an impediment to (or substitute for?) the writer's vision of the world around him. This is perhaps the most awesome moment in Melville's cold self-examination. The whole fable consists of a surgical probing of Bartleby's motives, and here he questions the value, for a novelist, of those metaphysical themes which dominate his later work. What made Bartleby turn to the wall? There is the unmistakable hint that such themes (fixing his attention on "subsequent erections") had had the effect of shielding from view the sordid social scene ("grimy backyards and bricks") with which Melville, for example, had been more directly concerned in earlier novels such as *Redburn* or *White Jacket*. At this point we are apparently being asked to consider whether Bartleby's obsession was perhaps a palliative, a defense against social experience which had become more than he could stand. To this extent the nature of the Wall Street society has contributed to Bartleby's fate. What is important here, however, is that Melville does not exonerate the writer by placing all the onus upon society. Bartleby has made a fatal mistake.

Melville's analysis of Bartleby's predicament may be appallingly detached, but it is by no means unsympathetic. When he develops the contrast between a man like Bartleby and the typical American writers of his age there is no doubt where his sympathies lie. The other copyists in the office accept their status as wage earners. The relations between them are tinged by competitiveness—even their names, "Nippers" and "Turkey," suggest "nip and tuck." Nevertheless they are not completely satisfactory employees; they are "useful" to the lawyer only half of the time. During half of each day each writer is industrious and respectful and compliant; during the other half he tends to be recalcitrant and even mildly rebellious. But fortunately for their employer these half-men are never aggressive at the same time, and so he easily dominates them, he compels them to do the sort of writing he wants, and has them "verify the accuracy" of their work according to his standards. When Bartleby's resistance begins they characteristically waver between him and the lawyer. Half the time, in their "submissive" moods ("submission" is their favorite word as "prefer" is Bartleby's), they stand with the employer and are incensed against Bartleby, particularly when his resistance inconveniences *them*; the rest of the time they mildly approve of his behavior, since it expresses their own ineffectual impulses toward independence. Such are the writers the society selects and, though not too lavishly, rewards.

One of Melville's finest touches is the way he has these compliant and representative scriveners, though they never actually enlist in Bartleby's cause, begin to echo his "prefer" without being aware of its source. So does the lawyer. "Prefer" is the nucleus of Bartleby's refrain, "I prefer not to," and it embodies the very essence of his power. It simply means "choice," but it is backed up, as it clearly is not in the case of the other copyists, by will. And it is in the strength of his will that the crucial difference between Bartleby and other writers lies. When Nippers and Turkey use the word "prefer" it is only because they are unconsciously imitating the manner, the surface vocabulary of the truly independent writer; they say "prefer," but in the course of the parable they never make any real choices. In their mouths "prefer" actually is indistinguishable from "submission"; only in Bartleby's does it stand for a genuine act of will. In fact writers like Nippers and Turkey are incapable of action, a trait carefully reserved for Bartleby, the lawyer, and the social system itself (acting through various agencies, the lawyers' clients, the landlord, and the police). Bartleby represents the only real, if ultimately ineffective, threat to society; his experience gives some support to Henry Thoreau's view that one lone intransigent man can shake the foundations of our institutions.

But he can only shake them, and in the end the practical consequence of Bartleby's rebellion is that society has eliminated an enemy. The lawyer's premonition was true; he finally sees Bartleby in death. Again the story insinuates the most severe self-criticism. For the nearly lifeless Bartleby, attracted neither by the skyward tending white wall, nor the cistern-like black wall, had fixed his eyes on the "dead" wall. This wall of death which surrounds us, and which Melville's heroes so desperately needed to pierce, has much in common with the deadly White Whale. Even Ahab, who first spoke of the whale as a "pasteboard mask" through which man might strike, sensed this, and he significantly shifted images in the middle of his celebrated quarter-deck reply to Starbuck:

> All visible objects, man, are but as pasteboard
> masks. . . . If man will strike, strike through the

mask! How can the prisoner reach outside except by thrusting through the wall? To me, the white whale is that wall, shoved near to me.

Like the whale, the wall will destroy the man who tries too obstinately to penetrate it. Bartleby had become so obsessed by the problem of the dead-wall that his removal to prison hardly changed his condition, or, for that matter, the state of his being; even in the walled street he had allowed his life to become suffused by death.

The detachment with which Melville views Bartleby's situation is perhaps the most striking thing about the fable. He gives us a powerful and unequivocal case against Wall Street society for its treatment of the writer, yet he avoids the temptation of finding in social evil a sentimental sanction for everything his hero thinks and does. True, the society has been indifferent to Bartleby's needs and aspirations; it has demanded of him a kind of writing he prefers not to do; and, most serious of all, it has impaired his vision by forcing him to work in the shadow of its walls. Certainly society shares the responsibility for Bartleby's fate. But Melville will not go all the way with those who find in the guilt of society an excuse for the writer's every hallucination. To understand what led to Bartleby's behavior is not to condone it. Melville refuses to ignore the painful fact that even if society shares the blame for Bartleby's delusion, it was nevertheless a delusion. What ultimately killed this writer was not the walls themselves, but the fact that he confused the walls built by men with the wall of human mortality.

The eerie story of Bartleby is a compassionate rebuke to the self-absorption of the artist, and so a plea that he devote himself to keeping strong his bonds with the rest of mankind.

— Leo Marx

Is this, then, as F. O. Matthiessen has written, "a tragedy of utter negation"? If it is not it is because there is a clear if muted note of affirmation here which must not be ignored. In the end, in prison, we are made to feel that the action has somehow taken us closer to the mysterious source of positive values in Melville's universe. "And see," says the lawyer to Bartleby in the prison yard, "it is not so sad a place as one might think. Look, there is the sky, and here is the grass." To the lawyer the presence of the grass in the Tombs is as wonderful as its presence in the heart of eternal pyramids where "by some strange magic through the clefts, grass-seed, dropped by birds, had sprung." The saving power attributed to the green grass is the clue to Melville's affirmation. [In a footnote the critic adds: "Recall that two years before, in the letter to Hawthorne which I quoted at the beginning of this essay, Melville had contrasted the unhappy circumstances under which he wrote *Moby Dick* to 'the silent grass-growing mood in which a man *ought* always to compose.' Later in the same letter he described his own development in the identical image which comes to the mind of the lawyer in **'Bartleby'**:

> I am like one of those seeds taken out of the Egyptian Pyramids, which, after being three thousand years a seed and nothing but a seed, being planted in English soil, it developed itself, grew to greenness, and then fell to the mould.

The fact that this same constellation of images reappears in **'Bartleby'** in conjunction with the same theme (the contrast between two kinds of writing) seems to me conclusive evidence of the relation between the parable and the 'dollars damn me' letter."]

The green of the grass signifies everything that the walls, whether black or white or blank, do not. Most men who inhabit Wall Street merely accept the walls for what they are—man-made structures which compartmentalize experience. To Bartleby, however, they are abstract emblems of all the impediments to man's realization of his place in the universe. Only the lawyer sees that the outstanding characteristic of the walls, whether regarded as material objects or as symbols, is that they are "deficient in . . . 'life'." Green, on the other hand, *is* life. The color green is the key to a cluster of images of fecundity which recurs in Melville's work beginning with *Typee*. It is the color which dominates that tropical primitive isle. It is the color of growth and of all pastoral experience. Indeed the imminent disappearance of our agrarian society is an important motive for Ishmael's signing on the Pequod. "Are the green fields gone?" he asks as *Moby Dick* begins. And later he says, in describing the ecstacy of squeezing sperm: "I declare to you that for the time I lived as in a musky meadow." So he gives a green tint to his redeeming vision of "attainable felicity," a felicity which he says resides in the country, the wife, the heart, the bed—wherever, that is, men may know the magical life-giving force in the world. And *Pierre*, published the year before **"Bartleby,"** also begins with a vision of a green paradise. There Melville makes his meaning explicit. He compares a certain green paint made of verdigris with the "democratic element [which] operates as subtle acid among us, forever producing new things by corroding the old. . . ."

> Now in general nothing can be more significant of decay than the idea of corrosion; yet on the other hand, nothing can more vividly suggest luxurance of life than the idea of green as a color; for green is the peculiar signet of all-fertile Nature herself.

By some curious quirk of the human situation, Bartleby's uncompromising resistance, which takes him to prison, also takes him a step closer to the green of animal faith. Melville deftly introduces this note of hope by having the lawyer compare the grass in the prison yard to the mystery of the grass within the pyramids. In time greenness, the lawyer suggests, may penetrate the most massive of walls. Indeed green seems virtually inherent in time itself, a somehow eternal property of man's universe. And in a Wall Street society it is (paradoxically) most accessible to the scrivener when he finds himself in prison and at the verge of death. Why? If Bartleby's suicidal obsession has

taken him closer to grass and sky, are we to understand that it has had consequences both heartening and meaningful? Is Melville implying, in spite of all the reasons he has given us for being skeptical of Bartleby's motives, that an understanding of his fate may show us the way to a genuine affirmation? Before attempting to answer these questions, it is appropriate to note here how remarkable a fusion of manner and content Melville has achieved. While the questions are never explicitly asked, they are most carefully insinuated. The unique quality of this tale, in fact, resides in its ability to say almost nothing on its placid and inscrutable surface, and yet so powerfully to suggest that a great deal is being said. This quality of style is a perfect embodiment of the theme itself: concealed beneath the apparently meaningless if not mad behavior of Bartleby is a message of utmost significance to all men.

While the presence of the grass at Bartleby's death scene is the clue to Melville's affirmation, the affirmation can only exist outside of the scrivener's mind. Green now means nothing to him. In the Wall Street world he had known, the green fields *were* gone; he was able to see neither nor sky from the walled-in windows. The only green that remained was the artificial green painted upon his flimsy screen, the screen behind which he did his diligent early work. But the screen proved a chimerical means of protection. Again Melville seems to be pointing the most accusing questions at himself. Had not his early novels contained a strong ingredient of primitivism? Had he not in effect relied upon the values implicit in the *Typee* experience (values which reappeared in the image of the inaccessible "insular Tahiti" in *Moby Dick*) as his shelter from the new America? Was this pastoral commitment of any real worth as a defense against a Wall Street society? The story of Bartleby and his green screen, like the letter to Hawthorne (dollars damn me!), denies that it was. In this fable, artificial or man-made green, used as a shield in a Wall Street office, merely abets self-delusion. As for the other green, the natural green of the grass in the prison yard, it is clear that Bartleby never apprehended its meaning. For one thing, a color could hardly have meant anything to him at that stage. His skepticism had taken him beyond any trust in the evidence of his senses; there is no reason to believe that green was for him any less illusory a color than the black or white of the walls. We know, moreover, that when he died Bartleby was still searching: he died with his eyes open.

It is not the writer but the lawyer, the complacent representative American, who is aware of the grass and to whom, therefore, the meaning is finally granted. If there is any hope indicated, it is hope for his, not Bartleby's, salvation. Recall that everything we understand of the scrivener's fate has come to us by way of the lawyer's consciousness. From the first the situation of the writer has been working upon the narrator's latent sensibility, gradually drawing upon his capacity for sympathy, his recognition of the bond between his desperate employee and the rest of mankind. And Bartleby's death elicits a cry of compassion from this man who had once grasped so little of the writer's problem. "Ah, Bartleby! Ah, humanity!" are his (and Melville's) last words. They contain the final revelation. Such deeply felt and spontaneous sympathy is the nearest equivalent to the green of the grass within reach of man. It is an expression of human brotherhood as persistent, as magical as the leaves of grass. Charity is the force which may enable men to meet the challenge of death, whose many manifestations, real and imagined, annihilated the valiant Bartleby.

The final words of the fable are of a piece with Melville's undeviating aloofness from his hero: they at once acknowledge Bartleby's courage and repudiate his delusion. If such a man as the lawyer is ultimately capable of this discernment, then how wrong Bartleby was in permitting the wall to become the exclusive object of his concern! The lawyer can be saved. But the scrivener, like Ahab, or one of Hawthorne's geniuses, has made the fatal error of turning his back on mankind. He has failed to see that there were in fact no impenetrable walls between the lawyer and himself. The only walls which had separated them were the folding (manipulatable) glass doors, and the green screen. Bartleby is wrong, but wrong or not, he is a hero; much as Ahab's mad quest was the necessary occasion for Ishmael's salvation, this writer's annihilation is the necessary occasion for Everyman's perception.

Among the countless imaginative statements of the artist's problems in modern literature, **"Bartleby"** is exceptional in its sympathy and hope for the average man, and in the severity of its treatment of the artist. This is particularly remarkable when we consider the seriousness of the rebuffs Melville had so recently been given by his contemporaries. But nothing, he is saying, may be allowed to relieve the writer of his obligations to mankind. If he forgets humanity, as Bartleby did, his art will die, and so will he. The lawyer, realizing this, at the last moment couples Bartleby's name with that of humanity itself. The fate of the artist is inseparable from that of all men. The eerie story of Bartleby is a compassionate rebuke to the self-absorption of the artist, and so a plea that he devote himself to keeping strong his bonds with the rest of mankind. Today, exactly a century after it was written, **"Bartleby the Scrivener"** is a counter-statement to the large and ever-growing canon of "ordealist" interpretations of the situation of the modern writer.

H. Bruce Franklin   (essay date 1963)

SOURCE: "Worldly Safety and Other-worldly Saviors," in *The Wake of the Gods: Melville's Mythology,* Stanford University Press, 1963, pp. 126-52.

[*Franklin is an American critic with a special interest in the work of Herman Melville. In the following excerpt, he interprets "Bartleby, the Scrivener" as a religious allegory, particularly emphasizing Christian and Hindu motifs in the story.*]

There are essentially three ethics available to man—action in and of the world, action in the world for other-worldly reasons, and nonaction, that is, withdrawal from the world. We might call the extreme of the first the ethic of Wall Street, the extreme of the second the ethic of Christ, and the extreme of the third the ethic of the Eastern monk. Wall Street's ethic seeks the world as an end; Christ's ethic prescribes certain behavior in this world to get to a better

world; the Eastern monk's ethic seeks to escape all worlds. **"Bartleby"** is a world in which these three ethics directly confront one another.

To read **"Bartleby"** well, we must first realize that we can never know who or what Bartleby is, but that we are continually asked to guess who or what he might be. We must see that he may be anything from a mere bit of human flotsam to a conscious and forceful rejecter of the world to an incarnation of God. When we see the first possibility we realize the full pathos of the story; when we see the last possibility we realize that the story is a grotesque joke and a parabolic tragedy.

But of course the possibility that Bartleby may be the very least of men does not necessarily contradict the possibility that Bartleby may be an embodiment of God. For as Christ explains in Matthew 25, the least of men (particularly when he appears as a stranger) is the physical representative and representation of Christ. Upon this identification depend the Christian ethic, the next world to which Christ sends every man, and the central meanings of **"Bartleby"**:

> 34 Then shall the King say unto them on his right hand, Come, ye blessed of my Father, inherit the kingdom prepared for you from the foundation of the world:
>
> 35 For I was ahungered, and ye gave me meat: I was thirsty, and ye gave me drink: I was a stranger, and ye took me in:
>
> 36 Naked, and ye clothed me: I was sick, and ye visited me: I was in prison, and ye came unto me.
>
> 37 Then shall the righteous answer him, saying, Lord, when saw we thee ahungered, and fed thee? or thirsty, and gave thee drink?
>
> 38 When saw we thee a stranger, and took thee in? or naked, and clothed thee?
>
> 39 Or when saw we thee sick, or in prison, and came unto thee?
>
> 40 And the King shall answer and say unto them, Verily I say unto you, Inasmuch as ye have done it unto one of the least of these my brethren, ye have done it unto me.
>
> 41 Then shall he say also unto them on the left hand, Depart from me, ye cursed, into everlasting fire, prepared for the devil and his angels:
>
> 42 For I was ahungered, and ye gave me no meat: I was thirsty, and ye gave me no drink:
>
> 43 I was a stranger, and ye took me not in: naked, and ye clothed me not: sick, and in prison, and ye visited me not.
>
> 44 Then shall they also answer him, saying, Lord, when saw we thee ahungered, or athirst, or a stranger, or naked, or sick, or in prison, and did not minister unto thee?
>
> 45 Then shall he answer them, saying, Verily I say unto you, Inasmuch as ye did it not to one of the least of these, ye did it not to me.

Christ is here saying that the individual comes to God and attains his salvation when he shows complete charity to a stranger, and he rejects God and calls for his damnation whenever he refuses complete charity to *one* stranger, even "the least of these." As the story of Bartleby unfolds, it becomes increasingly apparent that it is in part a testing of this message of Christ. The narrator's soul depends from his actions toward Bartleby, a mysterious, poor, lonely, sick stranger who ends his life in prison. Can the narrator, the man of our world, act in terms of Christ's ethics? The answer is yes and no. The narrator fulfills the letter of Christ's injunction point by point: he offers money to the stranger so that he may eat and drink; he takes him in, finally offering him not only his office but also his home; when he sees that he is sick, he attempts to minister to him; he, alone of all mankind, visits and befriends the stranger in prison. But he hardly fulfills the spirit of Christ's message: his money is carefully doled out; he tries to evict the stranger, offers his home only after betraying him, and then immediately flees from him in the time of his greatest need; it is his demands on the stranger which have made him sick; he visits the stranger in prison only once while he is alive, thus leaving him alone for several days before and after his visit, thus leaving him to die entirely alone. At the heart of both the tragedy and the comedy lies the narrator's view of the drama, a view which sees all but all in the wrong terms: "To befriend Bartleby; to humor him in his strange wilfulness, will cost me little or nothing, while I lay up in my soul what will eventually prove a sweet morsel for my conscience."

According to Christ's words in Matthew 25, it would make no difference to the narrator's salvation whether Bartleby is the Saviour incarnate or merely the least of his brethren. And certainly reading **"Bartleby"** with Matthew 25 in mind defines the central issues, no matter who Bartleby is. But the story repeatedly suggests that Bartleby may not be merely the least of Christ's brethren but may in fact be the Saviour himself. Again I wish to emphasize that we are certainly not justified in simply taking Bartleby to be an incarnation or reincarnation of Christ (except in the terms of Matthew 25). But if we do not entertain the possibility that Bartleby is Christ, although we still see most of the tragedy, we miss a great deal of the comedy. Bartleby's story is the story of the advent, the betrayal, and torment of a mysterious and innocent being; this is a tragic story no matter who the being is. These events carefully and pointedly re-enact the story of Christ, and there is nothing funny about this. Nor is there anything inherently funny about the fact that for all we know Bartleby may be God incarnate. The central joke of the story is that although the narrator comes close to seeing this possibility without ever seeing what he sees, his language continually recognizes and defines the possibility that Bartleby may be Christ. The narrator's own words define his own tragedy as cosmic and comic.

The narrator tells us that he is an "eminently *safe* man," an "unambitious" lawyer who, "in the cool tranquillity of a snug retreat," does "a snug business among rich men's bonds and mortgages and title-deeds." He tells of receiving the "good old office" of "Master in Chancery," which greatly enlarges his business. This is the time which he sig-

nificantly labels "the period just preceding the advent of Bartleby." After mentioning this office only once, he digresses for several pages. When he next mentions it, he calls it simply—and significantly—"the master's office." This joke introduces the pointedly ambiguous description of the advent of Bartleby:

> Now my original business . . . was considerably increased by receiving the master's office. There was now great work for scriveners. Not only must I push the clerks already with me, but I must have additional help.

> In answer to my advertisement, a motionless young man one morning stood upon my office threshold, the door being open, for it was summer. I can see that figure now—pallidly neat, pitiably respectable, incurably forlorn! It was Bartleby.

So Bartleby is a being who answers the narrator's call for "additional help" at a time of "great work for scriveners." The narrator responds by placing "this quiet man within easy call, in case any trifling thing was to be done."

Bartleby at first does an "extraordinary" amount of work, but, "on the third day," begins to answer "I would prefer not to" to the narrator's petty orders. Who is this being? The narrator can only tell us that "Bartleby was one of those beings of whom nothing is ascertainable, except from the original sources, and, in his case, those are very small."

As Bartleby, by merely standing, sitting, and lying still, step by step withdraws from the world, the narrator follows him, leaving behind, bit by bit, his worldly values. Slowly the narrator's compassion for Bartleby and his sense of brotherhood with him emerge, and as they emerge we see more and more clearly that the drama involves the salvation of both Bartleby—the poor, lonely stranger—and the narrator—the "safe" man who in many ways represents our world. As this drama becomes clear, the narrator's language becomes more and more grotesquely ironic.

At the beginning of his withdrawal, Bartleby is only saved from being "violently dismissed" because the narrator cannot find "anything ordinarily human about him." In the next stage of his withdrawal, Bartleby stands at the entrance of his "hermitage" and "mildly" asks "What is wanted?" when the narrator "hurriedly" demands that he proofread the copies, Bartleby answers that he "would prefer not to," and the narrator tells us that "for a few moments I was turned into a pillar of salt."

The narrator, as boss of the office, plays god. What he does not realize, but what his language makes clear, is that he may be playing this role with God himself. The narrator tells us that he "again advanced towards Bartleby" because "I felt additional incentives tempting me to my fate." "Sometimes, to be sure, I could not, for the very soul of me," he ironically admits, "avoid falling into sudden spasmodic passions with him."

The narrator even discovers "something superstitious knocking at my heart, and forbidding me to carry out my purpose . . . if I dared to breathe one bitter word against this forlornest of mankind." At this point we need hardly remember Matthew 25 or that Melville referred to Christ as the Man of Sorrows to see why the narrator should look to his salvation instead of his safety. But when the narrator surmises that Bartleby has "nothing else earthly to do," he blandly asks him to carry some letters to the post office.

The narrator then realizes that Bartleby is "absolutely alone in the universe," but his response to this cosmic loneliness is to tell Bartleby that "in six days' time he must unconditionally leave the office." On the appointed day, the narrator tries to dismiss Bartleby with words that become grotesquely ludicrous if they are seen as an inversion of the true roles of these two beings: "If, hereafter, in your new place of abode, I can be of any service to you, do not fail to advise me by letter." Perhaps the narrator has already received in very clear letters all the advice he needs, a description of what service Bartleby might be to him in his new place of abode, and what his own place of abode will be if he rejects the advice and denies the man. (But perhaps, as the last few paragraphs of the story hint, Matthew 25 and its entire context is now the Dead Letter Office.)

Shortly after saying these words, the narrator discovers that this very day is "an election day." Still, "a sudden passion"—the very thing which the narrator's words had recognized as endangering his "very soul"—makes him demand that Bartleby leave him. The scrivener gently replies, "I would prefer *not* to quit you." The narrator reminds Bartleby ironically that he has no "earthly right" to stay; Bartleby "answered nothing" and "silently retired into his hermitage."

This infuriates the narrator; as he says, the "old Adam of resentment rose in me and tempted me concerning Bartleby." But on this election day the narrator saves himself for the time being "simply by recalling the divine injunction: 'A new commandment give I unto you, that ye love one another.'" "Yes," he says, "this it was that saved me." But the narrator fails to grasp what he has seen; he defines this love "as a vastly wise and prudent principle"; "mere self-interest" becomes his most clearly perceived motive to "charity."

After some day pass in which he has had a chance to consult "Edwards on the Will" and "Priestley on Necessity," the narrator has his most complete revelation of his own drama:

> Gradually I slid into the persuasion that these troubles of mine, touching the scrivener, had been all predestinated from eternity, and Bartleby was billeted upon me for some mysterious purpose of an all-wise Providence, which it was not for a mere mortal like me to fathom. Yes, Bartleby, stay there behind your screen, thought I; I shall persecute you no more; you are harmless and noiseless as any of these old chairs; in short, I never feel so private as when I know you are here. At last I see it, I feel it; I penetrate to the predestinated purpose of my life. I am content. Others may have 'loftier parts to enact; but my mission in this world, Bartleby, is to furnish you with office-room for such period as you may see fit to remain.

According to Christ's own words in Matthew 25, the narrator is absolutely right; he has finally seen his mission in the world.

But the narrator's resolution of his dilemma is short-lived. It withers quickly under the "uncharitable remarks obtruded upon" him by his "professional friends." He confesses that the whispers of his professional acquaintance "worried me very much." When he then thinks of the possibility of Bartleby's "denying my authority," outliving him, and claiming "possession of my office by right of his perpetual occupancy," the narrator resolves to "forever rid me of this intolerable incubus." Even then, after he informs Bartleby that he must leave, and after Bartleby takes "three days to meditate upon it," he learns that Bartleby "still preferred to abide with" him, that "he prefers to cling to" him. This sets the stage for the narrator's denial of Bartleby, for he decides that "since he will not quit me, I must quit him."

To hear the full significance of his three denials of Bartleby, we must hear the loud echoes of Peter's three denials of Christ. Matthew 26:

> 70 But he denied before them all, saying, I know not what thou sayest.
>
> 72 And again he denied with an oath, I do not know the man.
>
> 74 Then began he to curse and to swear, saying, I know not the man.

Even closer are Peter's words in Mark 14:71: "I know not this man of whom ye speak."

The first denial:

> "Then, sir," said the stranger, who proved a lawyer, "you are responsible for the man you left there." . . .
>
> "I am very sorry, sir," said I, with assumed tranquillity, but an inward tremor, "but, really, the man you allude to is nothing to me."

The second denial:

> "In mercy's name, who is he?"
>
> "I certainly cannot inform you. I know nothing about him."

The third denial:

> In vain I persisted that Bartleby was nothing to me—no more than to any one else.

After the narrator's three denials of Bartleby, he belatedly makes his most charitable gesture toward him, offering, "in the kindest tone I could assume under such exciting circumstances," to permit him to come to his home. But Bartleby answers, "No: at present I would prefer not to make any change at all." The narrator leaves; the new landlord has the police remove Bartleby to the Tombs. The narrator then learns of Bartleby's procession to his Golgotha:

> As I afterwards learned, the poor scrivener, when told that he must be conducted to the

Tombs, offered not the slightest obstacle, but, in his pale, unmoving way, silently acquiesced.

Some of the compassionate and curious bystanders joined the party; and headed by one of the constables arm in arm with Bartleby, the silent procession filed its way through all the noise, and heat, and joy of the roaring thoroughfares at noon.

"Quite serene and harmless in all his ways," Bartleby is, like Christ, "numbered with the transgressors" (Mark 15:28). The world places him in prison where, amidst "murderers and thieves," he completes his withdrawal from the world.

When the narrator more or less meets the last condition laid down in Matthew 25—visiting the stranger in prison—all his charity is shown to be too little and too late. Before Bartleby leaves the world he says to the narrator, "I know you," and adds, without looking at him, "and I want nothing to say to you." At this point we can hear new ironies in the narrator's attempt to dismiss Bartleby: "If, hereafter, in your new place of abode, I can be of any service to you, do not fail to advise me by letter." Thus, when the narrator retells the rumor of Bartleby's having worked in the Dead Letter Office, he describes in part himself, in part Bartleby, and in part the scriptural letters which spell the hope of salvation. "The master's office" has become the Dead Letter Office.

> Dead letters! does it not sound like dead men? . . . pardon for those who died despairing; hope for those who died unhoping; good tidings for those who died stifled by unrelieved calamities. On errands of life, these letters speed to death.
>
> Ah, Bartleby! Ah, humanity!

But all this is only half the story. For if the narrator is weighed and found wanting, what then of Bartleby himself? At least the narrator at times can show compassion, sympathy, and charity. Indeed, he at times much more than transcends the worldly ethics with which he starts and to which he tends to backslide. (One must bear in mind while evaluating the narrator's behavior that he is continually defending himself from two possible accusations—that he is too hard-hearted and that he is too soft-hearted.) Although he begins by strictly following horological time, he conforms more and more closely to chronometrical time. And he is after all certainly the most charitable character in the story. What time does Bartleby follow, and, finally, how charitable is he? Or is it possible to account for the actions of a being who is almost by definition enigmatic?

Because "Bartleby was one of those beings of whom nothing is ascertainable, except from the original sources, and, in his case, those are very small," he is almost as difficult to judge as to identify. But whether he is finally a god incarnate as a man or only a man playing the role of a crucified god, his behavior fits a pattern which implies an ethic.

If, as the Plotinus Plinlimmon pamphlet asserts in *Pierre*, chronometrical time is an impossibility for man, if man is left with the choice in the world between following chronometrical time and being destroyed or following horological time and being contemptible, if, then, no action in the world can be at the same time safe and worthy of salvation, what is there left for man to do? One answer is that man can try to live out of the world, can withdraw from the world altogether. This is the answer which forms the counterpoint with worldly ethics in both **"Bartleby"** and **"Benito Cereno,"** each of which dramatizes a particular and different kind of monasticism.

Bartleby's monkish withdrawal from the world has been described by Saburo Yamaya [in *Studies in English Literature* XXXIV, 1957] and Walter Sutton [in *Prairie Schooner* XXXIV, 1960] as essentially Buddhistic in nature. Yamaya shows the connections between Buddhist Quietism and the stone imagery of both *Pierre* and **"Bartleby,"** citing as one of Melville's sources this passage from Bayle's *Dictionary*:

> The great lords and the most illustrious persons suffered themselves to be so infatuated with the [Buddhist] Quietism, that they believed insensibility to be the way to perfection and beatitude and that the nearer a man came to the nature of a block or *a stone,* the greater progress he made, the more he was like the first principle, into which he was to return.

Sutton quite accurately perceives (apparently without reference to Yamaya) that Bartleby, in achieving "the complete withdrawal of the hunger artist," has attained what "in Buddhist terms . . . is Nirvana, extinction, or nothingness," and he suggests that at this point in his life Melville was unconsciously approaching Buddhism. But Melville was probably quite aware that Bartleby's behavior conforms very closely to a kind of Oriental asceticism which Thomas Maurice had spent about fifty pages describing.

The Oriental ascetic who most closely resembles Bartleby is the Saniassi, a Hindu rather than a Buddhist. It seems probable that once again Maurice's *Indian Antiquities* served as a direct source for Melville's fiction. Maurice describes in detail the systematic withdrawal from the world practiced by the Saniassi, and many details have a surprising—and grotesquely humorous—correspondence to the systematic withdrawal from the world practiced by Bartleby. For instance, in the fifth stage the Saniassi "eats only one particular kind of food during the day and night, but as often as he pleases." Bartleby "lives, then, on ginger-nuts . . . never eats a dinner, properly speaking; he must be a vegetarian, then, but no; he never eats even vegetables, he eats nothing but ginger-nuts." "During the last three days," the Saniassi "neither eats nor drinks." During Bartleby's last few days, he prefers not to eat.

The fact that external details of Bartleby's withdrawal closely parallel some of the external details of the Saniassi's withdrawal is not nearly so significant as this fact: Bartleby's behavior seems to be the very essence of Maurice's description of the Saniassi's behavior. In fact, Maurice's general description and judgment of the Saniassi often seems to be a precise description and judgment of Bartleby.

Most striking are the very things which Maurice claims

are peculiar to the Saniassi. He observes that one of the principal ways in which the Saniassi is distinguished from the Yogi is "by the calm, the silent, dignity with which he suffers the series of complicated evils through which he is ordained to toil." The Saniassi "can only be fed by the charity of others"; "he must himself make no exertion, nor feel any solicitude for existence upon this contaminated orb." The Saniassis' design "is to detach their thoughts from all concern about sublunary objects; to be indifferent to hunger and thirst; to be insensible to shame and reproach."

Perhaps most important to the judgment of Bartleby is the Saniassis' "incessant efforts . . . to stifle every ebullition of human passion, and live upon earth as if they were already, and in reality, disembodied." This may at once help account for Bartleby's appearing as a "ghost" or as "cadaverous" to the narrator and explain what ethical time he follows, for "it is the boast of the Saniassi to sacrifice every human feeling and passion at the shrine of devotion." Like Bartleby, the Saniassi "is no more to be soothed by the suggestions of *adulation* in its most pleasing form, than he is to be terrified by the loudest clamours of *reproach* . . . By long habits of indifference, he becomes inanimate as a piece of wood or stone; and, though he mechanically respires the vital air, he is to all the purposes of active life *defunct*."

"Bartleby" is, then, in part the story of a man of the world who receives "the master's office"; who advertises for help; who is thereupon visited by a stranger being who in an "extraordinary" way at first does all that is asked of him; who treats this strange being with contempt; who nevertheless receives from this being what seems to be his purpose in life; who betrays this being; and who watches and describes the systematic withdrawal of this being. It is also in part the story of this strange being, who replays much of the role of Christ while behaving like an Hindu ascetic, and who ends by extinguishing himself and making dead letters of the scripture which describes his prototype.

John Gardner   (essay date 1964)

SOURCE: " 'Bartleby': Art and Social Commitment," in *Philological Quarterly,* Vol. XLIII, No. 1, January, 1964, pp. 87-98.

[*Gardner was an American novelist, educator, and critic with a special interest in medieval literature. As a critic, he championed the moral function of literature. In the following essay, he analyzes the relationship of the individual to society as portrayed in "Bartleby, the Scrivener."*]

In **"Bartleby,"** man looks at man, artist looks at artist, and God looks at God. To understand that the narrator is at least as right as Bartleby, both on the surface and on symbolic levels, is to understand the remarkable interpenetration of form and content in the story. Most Melville readers have noticed that on one level, Bartleby can represent the honest artist: he is a "scrivener" who refuses to "copy," as Melville himself refused to copy—that is, as he refused to knock out more saleable South Seas romances. But if Bartleby is the artist, he is the artist manqué: his is

a vision not of life but of death; "the man of silence," he creates nothing. A better kind of artist is the lawyer, who, having seen reality through Bartleby's eyes, has turned to literature. Nor is he the slick writer: "If I pleased," he says, "[I] could relate divers histories, at which good-natured gentlemen might smile, and sentimental souls might weep." That is, popular fiction. The phrase "If I pleased" is significant: "please" is the narrator's substitution, later, for Bartleby's infectious "prefer." Like Bartleby, the narrator does what he prefers to do—but within certain reasonable limits. The reader may smile or weep at Bartleby's story, but the narrator's chief reason for choosing it is that he is seriously concerned with "literature." Close reading reveals that the story he tells is indeed a highly organized literary work, a story that is as much the narrator's as it is Bartleby's, ending with the narrator's achievement of that depth of understanding necessary to the telling of the story.

An important part of what the narrator at last understands is the conflict between the individual and society. The individual feels certain preferences which, taken together, establish his personal identity; society makes simultaneously necessary and unreasonable demands which modify individual identity. Thus the individual's view of himself and the view others have of him can become two quite different things separated by a substantial wall (communication is difficult); thus, too, the socialized man's identity and his view of his identity can be walled apart (self-knowledge is difficult). And man's dilemma cannot be resolved, for if one insists on one's own preferences and thereby affirms one's identity, one finds oneself, like Bartleby, walled off from society and communion with other men; and on the other hand, if one gives in to the necessary laws of social action, one finds oneself, like Bartleby's employer, walled off from active obedience to the higher laws of self and, in a sense, reality. Wall Street is the prison in which all men live.

The conflict between the rule of individual preference and the necessary laws of social action takes various forms in **"Bartleby."** Conflicts arise between individual and social impulses within each of the first three scriveners, Turkey, Nippers, and Ginger Nut, and also between individual traits in the scriveners and the necessary requirements of their employer, whose commitment is perforce social, for he must do his job well to survive. But for the action of the story, the most important conflicts are those rooted in the relationship of the lawyer and Bartleby, that is, the conflicts between employer and employee, between the lawyer's kindly nature and his recognition of the reasonableness of society's harsh demands, and between Bartleby and the world.

In many ways the lawyer and Bartleby differ. The lawyer is a successful, essentially practical man with highly developed feelings for social position (he mentions coyly that he was "not unemployed" by John Jacob Astor), the value of money (the office of Master in Chancery is "pleasantly remunerative"), "common usage and common sense," and above all, as he tells us John Jacob Astor has observed, "prudence" and "method." Bartleby, on the other hand, is merely a clerk with an obscure past, a man little concerned with practicality in the ordinary sense, and apparently quite uninterested in social position, money, or usage and sense. He is totally lacking in prudence—he courts dismissal at every turn—and for method he relies upon "preference," often preference "at present." The narrator at first cannot understand Bartleby, for good reason, and Bartleby prefers not to understand the narrator or the society the narrator represents. At the same time, the two characters are in some respects similar. Early in the story the narrator tells us, "I am a man who, from his youth upwards, has been filled with a profound conviction that the easiest way of life is the best"; and Bartleby shares the narrator's profound conviction: what he cannot share is the narrator's opinion that the easiest way must be socially acceptable, or even "reasonable." The narrator is also like Bartleby in that he does not seek "public applause"; but Bartleby goes further, he does not avoid public censure. Finally, the narrator is decorous and "eminently *safe*"; so is Bartleby: the narrator is positive that Bartleby would not copy in shirtsleeves or on Sunday, and the narrator has "singular confidence in his honesty."

Perhaps partly because the narrator and Bartleby are both different and similar, the conflict between them triggers a conflict within the narrator's mind. He knows that as employer he has the authority to make demands of a scrivener, whatever the scrivener's preference, for if employers cannot function as employers, society cannot work; but despite his knowledge, the narrator cannot bring himself to force Bartleby to obey or get out. When Bartleby first refuses to comply with a request, the narrator merely thinks, "This is very strange. . . . What had one best do?" and, being pressed by business, goes on with his work. When Bartleby refuses to comply with another request, the narrator is shaken and for a moment doubts the assumption behind employer-employee relations. When Bartleby uses it as a *modus operandi,* the narrator's opinion that "the easiest way of life is the best" conflicts with his equally firm opinion that the laws of social action are of necessity right; and in his momentary uncertainty the narrator turns to his office, a miniature society, for a ruling. Even their ruling is not much help, however, for to act on it would be to become involved in unpleasantness, and this the narrator would prefer to avoid in favor of some easier way—if any is to be found. Once again he avoids the issue, in the socially approved way, by turning his mind to his work.

---

the most important conflicts in "Bartleby" are those rooted in the relationship of the lawyer and Bartleby, that is, the conflicts between employer and employee, between the lawyer's kindly nature and his recognition of the reasonableness of society's harsh demands, and between Bartleby and the world.

— *John Gardner*

Bartleby's unconventional insistence on his preferences, and his indifference to the demands of his social setting, the office, leads the narrator to wonder about him, that is, to want to understand him. He watches Bartleby narrowly and finds him more enigmatic than before. Bartleby never seems to leave, he exists on ginger nuts, and in the miniature society of the office his corner remains a "hermitage." Judgment cannot account for the man, and though imagination provides "delicious self-approval," it too fails to provide understanding. The conflict in the narrator's mind between acceptance of Bartleby as enigmatic eccentric, on one hand, and insistence on Bartleby's position as employee, on the other, leads to no action while the narrator is in a charitable mood; but when he is not, he feels a need to force Bartleby into revealing himself actively, not just passively—that is, to make himself vulnerable by showing "some angry spark answerable to my own." The narrator's goading excites the other scriveners, but it cannot reach Bartleby. At last, for the sake of keeping peace in the office, and also because some of Bartleby's preferences coincide with the preferences of society ("his steadiness, his freedom from all dissipation, his incessant industry"), the narrator comes to accept Bartleby, and the narrator's internal conflict is temporarily resolved.

When the narrator learns that Bartleby lives at the office, the internal conflict reawakens. As he looks through Bartleby's things, the narrator's judgment hurls him onto the truth: Bartleby is "the victim of innate and incurable disorder," in a word, he is mad. Common sense demands that he be gotten rid of, for, as the narrator sees, the practical fact is that "pity is not seldom pain," and one cannot work well (as one must in this world) when one is suffering. The narrator gives his scrivener one last chance: he asks Bartleby to tell him about his past; if Bartleby will answer like a sensible man, the narrator will keep him on. As he asks it, the narrator insists, sincerely enough, "I feel friendly towards you." And the effect is interesting: Bartleby hesitates "a considerable time" before answering, and for the first time his composure breaks—his lips tremble. *"At present,"* he says (and he is using the phrase "at present" for the first time), "I prefer to give no answer." It seems that the narrator has cracked the wall between them; but if so, he does not know it at the time. The narrator's common sense goes deep and now, when he is on the threshold of his scrivener's secret self, self-delusion saves the narrator from what, as he rightly sees, cannot help Bartleby and can only hurt himself. Misinterpreting what has happened, he feels "nettled" and says, "Not only did there seem to lurk in [Bartleby's manner] a certain calm disdain, but his perverseness seemed ungrateful, considering the undeniable good usage and indulgence he had received from me." Even so, common sense is not quite triumphant: "I strangely felt something superstitious knocking at my heart, and forbidding me to carry out my purpose [of firing Bartleby], and denouncing me for a villain if I dared to breathe one bitter word against this forlornest of mankind." Instead of sensibly dismissing the mad scrivener, the narrator chooses mercy, not justice, and humbly begs Bartleby to promise to be a little reasonable "in a day or two." Bartleby's answer, of course, is as delightfully mad as the request: "At present I would prefer not to be a little reasonable." And Bartleby, or the will of the individual, wins. Indeed, individualism is doing very well: Everyone in the office is saying "prefer" these days. Social dicta become polite suggestions waiting upon the individual's taste ("If [Bartleby] would but prefer to take a quart of good ale every day . . ."); legal etiquette becomes a matter of individual choice (the narrator is asked what color paper he prefers for a certain document). Bartleby's success is complete when, preferring to do no more copying, and preferring to remain in the office, he gets the narrator to prefer to put up with him.

In voluntarily choosing to accept Bartleby as "the predestined purpose of my life," the narrator makes a choice which, unfortunately, he is not free to make. From the point of view of society, the choice is odd, unacceptable (like Colt's choice to murder Adams—a choice Colt would not have made, the narrator says, if the two of them had not been alone). Bartleby is such an oddity in the office that at last the narrator must choose between Bartleby and his own professional reputation. As the sane man must, the narrator chooses society and denies Bartleby: he moves out of the office. When moving out proves insufficient—for society holds him accountable—the narrator reluctantly goes the whole route: he would not have acted with the cruel common sense of the landlord, but preferring to choose the inevitable, he gives the testimony requested in the landlord's note. The betrayed Bartleby pronounces the judgment: "I know you." Even now the narrator feels friendly towards Bartleby, and certainly he cannot be blamed for his action; nevertheless, betrayal is betrayal, and both of them know it.

The sequel provides us with an insight into the background of Bartleby's derangement and provides the narrator with belated understanding of his scrivener. As the narrator understands the matter, and we have no reason to doubt his interpretation, Bartleby's former occupation as dead-letter clerk heightened the natural pallid hopelessness of Bartleby's character by giving him a queer and terrible vision of life. The narrator thinks, as Bartleby must have thought before him, "Dead letters! does it not sound like dead men?" Letters sent on missions of pardon, hope, good tidings—errands of life—end in pointless flames; and the dead-letter clerk sees no other kind of mail (if, in fact, there is any other kind). What he knows about letters he comes to know of man. The bustle of activity, scrivening, clerking, bar-tending, bill-collecting, traveling—all tumble at last against the solid wall, death. Bartleby prefers not to share the delusions of society. For him, the easiest way of life is the best because whether one spends one's time "not unemployed" by John Jacob Astor or spends it "sitting upon a banister," one dies. He is not "luny," as Ginger-Nut thinks, but mad. Estranged from the ordinary view of life (he does not even read the papers), Bartleby perceives reality; thus whereas the narrator, when he looks out his windows, sees at one end a wall "deficient in what

Wall Street, New York City—the setting of "Bartleby, the Scrivener"—as it appeared shortly before the story's publication in 1853.

landscape painters call 'life" and at the other end "a huge, square cistern" Bartleby sees, respectively, death and the grave.

Except at the moment when he is tempted to feel affection for the man who feels friendly towards him, there is within Bartleby no conflict at all. He is dead already, as the narrator's recurring adjective, "cadaverous," suggests. Whatever the exigencies of the moment, he cannot be made to forget the walls enclosing life. He has walked for some time in the yard "not accessible to common prisoners," for the yard in the Tombs is life itself: "The surrounding walls, of amazing thickness, kept off all sounds behind them. The Egyptian character of the masonry weighted upon me with its gloom. But a soft imprisoned turf grew under foot. The heart of the eternal pyramids, it seemed, wherein, by some strange magic, through the clefts, grass-seed, dropped by birds, had sprung." But though Bartleby suffers no conflict within, he is engaged in a conflict more basic than that in which the narrator is involved. The narrator wishes to avoid unpleasantness—and if possible, to do so without loss of self-respect. Bartleby wishes to shape his own destiny, at least within the little space between the walls of birth and death. The narrator, when he has "looked a little into 'Edwards on the Will,' and 'Priestley on Necessity,' " slides into the persuasion that his troubles have been predestined from eternity, and he chooses to accept them, voluntarily relinquishing his will to "an allwise Providence." But Bartleby insists on freedom. When the narrator suggests that he take a clerkship in a dry-goods store, he answers, "There is too much confinement about that." The narrator's reaction: "why, you keep yourself confined all the time!" misses the point, for confinement, if one chooses confinement, is free agency, and circling the world, if required of one, is not. Melville makes the point dramatically. When Bartleby will neither tour Europe with some young man nor live in the narrator's home, the narrator flees from Bartleby, the landlord and the tenants who may again besiege the law office. He runs from the building, up Wall Street toward Broadway, catches a bus, surrenders his business to Nippers, and turns to still wilder flight, driving about in his rockaway for days. In his restless flight he is less free than the man on the banister.

But in the end, no individual, not even Bartleby, can be free. The freedom of each individual curtails the freedom of some other, as poor Colt's freedom curtails the freedom of Adams (murdered men have no preferences), and as Bartleby's freedom curtails that of the narrator. Thus the limits imposed upon freedom by the laws of Nature are narrowed by the laws of society: Bartleby must be jailed. Inside the prison, "individuals"; outside, "functionaries." Betrayed by the narrator and the society he represents, confined in a smaller prison and, as he says, knowing where he is, Bartleby has only one freedom left: he may prefer not to live. And he does.

Melville suggests in various ways that the conflict between Bartleby and the world (and the conflict within the narrator's mind) is one between imagination and judgment, or reason. Judgment supports society: ethical law is the law of reason: imagination, on the other hand, supports higher values, those central to poetry and religion: moral law is

the law of imagination. Ethical law, always prohibitive, guarantees equal rights to all members of the group, but moral law, always affirmative, points to the absolute, without respect to the needs of the group. Thus ethical law demands that scriveners proofread their copy; but the narrator says, "I cannot credit that the mettlesome poet, Byron, would have contentedly sat down with Bartleby to examine a law document of, say five hundred pages. . . ." And when the narrator sees that Bartleby is mad and must be dismissed, that is, when common sense bids the narrator's soul be rid of the man, the narrator cannot bring himself to go to Trinity Church. Reason and imagination also divide the narrator's mind: each time Bartleby's stubborn preferences force the narrator into thought, the narrator thinks in two ways, by imagination (when he sees in poetic or religious terms) and by reason (when he works out logical deductions after studying facts); and the results of the two ways of thinking differ sharply. Reason tells the narrator that Bartleby exists on ginger-nuts but somehow does not become hot and spicy; "imagination," explaining "what proves impossible to be solved by . . . judgment," tells the narrator that Bartleby is a "poor fellow" who "means no mischief " and "intends no insolence." When the narrator examines Bartleby's belongings, imagination leads him close to an understanding of Bartleby the individual: as he detects, through empathy, the loneliness of Bartleby, he sees that he and Bartleby are "both sons of Adam," and he begins to suffer "sad fancyings—the chimeras, doubtless, of a sick and silly brain." He adds, "Presentiments of strange discoveries hovered round me. The scrivener's pale form appeared to me laid out, among uncaring strangers, in its shivering winding sheet." Reason, however, leads the narrator in a different direction. He sees that the man is mad (a social judgment) and that, after giving Bartleby a fair chance to prove himself sane, he must fire him. Throughout the story, the narrator's generous impulses, as well as his attempts at self-justification when common sense fails to drive out the sense of guilt, take religious form: by leaps of faith, or imagination, he understands Bartleby, and when he is considering doing harm to Bartleby for the sake of his own reputation, he consoles himself with words like "charity" and "love," allowing himself to believe that what he plans is after all for Bartleby's good, not his own. (The narrator is self-deluded, not hypocritical, for as he tells the story now he understands and, usually, acknowledges the mistakes he made at the time of his Bartleby troubles. Mistakes he does not acknowledge openly he treats in comic terms, as he treats his ethical perversion of the moral injunction "that ye love one another.")

If the narrator's interpretation of Bartleby's madness is correct, imagination, presenting a metaphor which relates dead letters and men, is the basis of Bartleby's plight. In other words, he is a man who has seen a vision and, holding true to his vision, can no longer operate in the ordinary world. In a sense, he is a queer sort of fanatic, operating on the basis of a religion of his own.

Obviously the conflicts in **"Bartleby,"** together with the germs of symbolic extension of meaning, are rooted in character; and the legitimacy of the conflicts, whether they are seen as conflicts between the individual and society or between will and necessity, is equally clear. Thus the story is not a melodrama (between, say, the stupid reviewer of *Pierre* and the pure, heroic author) but an honest fictional representation of a dilemma which, in ordinary life, cannot be resolved. In the end the narrator understands. Learning that Bartleby was a dead-letter clerk, he achieves Bartleby's vision: he sees by a leap of imagination exactly what Bartleby must have seen—dead letters, dead men, limited human freedom. This vision is the terrible outcome foreshadowed earlier: "And I trembled to think that my contact with the scrivener had already and seriously affected me in a mental way. And what further and deeper aberration might it not yet produce?" From the beginning the narrator has been imaginative—in fact, like Bartleby, has been given to "fancyings" and "chimeras"; but unlike Bartleby, he also possesses judgment. When he needs to, he can control his fancies. Unlike Bartleby, he creates: he originally created his practice, he has created "recondite documents," and he is now creating a work of art. Reason must impose order upon the chaos of imagination.

Symbolism in **"Bartleby"** supports this view of scrivener as visionary and narrator as creator. The religion of ordinary scriveners is the routine of the law office or the will of the lawyer: the narrator speaks of Turkey as the "most reverential of men," values his "morning services," and cannot get him to give up his afternoon "devotions"; and the narrator tells us that Turkey eats ginger-nuts as though they were "wafers." Bartleby is another matter: his arrival is an "advent," there is nothing "ordinarily human about him," he is full of "quiet mysteries," and when the narrator leaves Bartleby alone in the office Bartleby stands "like the last pillar of a ruined temple." He dies at last among "murderers and thieves." And whereas Bartleby is Christ-like, the narrator is Jehovah-like: the voice behind the story, like the voice behind *The Confidence Man,* is mythical, for the speaker here is God, the story that of his reluctant change from the legalistic, tribal deity of the Old Testament to the God of Love and Justice in the New Testament. As Melville treats the material, Christ is not a son of God but (as the Old Testament Jehovah sees him) an "incubus," thus not a revelation sent by God to man but rather a nightmare creature who drives God into self-knowledge (as, on the literal level, Bartleby drives the lawyer to self-knowledge).

The narrator and Jehovah are linked in numerous ways. The narrator is officially "Master" in Chancery. Like Jehovah, he keeps out of the public eye and works "in the cool tranquillity of a snug retreat." The narrator's first scrivener, Turkey, is the militant archangel Michael. His nickname is possibly meant to suggest not only the red-necked, irascible fowl emblematic of thanksgiving but also the terrible Turk. He has a face which "beams," "blazes," and "flames" like the sun, and he considers himself, rather insolently, the narrator's "right hand man." He uses his ruler as a sword and is in charge of the narrator's forces, marshalling and deploying "columns" (the narrator speaks later of his "column of clerks"), and charging "the foe." His "inflamed" ways are always "worse on Saturdays" (the Sabbath). The second scrivener, Nippers (pincers), is symbolically linked with Lucifer. He is a "whisk-

ered, sallow, and, upon the whole, piratical-looking young man" who suffers from "ambition" as well as indigestion. He is impatient with the duties of a mere copyist, and his ambition is evinced by "an unwarrantable usurpation of strictly professional affairs, such as the original drawing up of legal documents." (The Devil is famous for making pacts: consider poor Faust.) His indigestion (spleen) is "betokened in an occasional nervous testiness and grinning irritability, causing the teeth to audibly grind together . . . , unnecessary maledictions, hissed, rather than spoken, in the heat [inferno] of business. . . ." He has his own kingdom, for the narrator says, "Among the manifestations of his diseased ambition was a fondness he had for receiving visits from certain ambiguous-looking fellows in seedy coats, whom he called his clients." He is "considerable of a ward-politician," occasionally does "a little business at the Justices' courts," and is "not unknown on the steps of the Tombs." As gods and would-be gods control willful men, so Nippers jerks his desk about as if it were "a perverse voluntary agent and vexing him." The third scrivener, Ginger Nut (Raphael, perhaps)—for Milton the messenger and sociable angel is official cake (or "wafer") and apple (forbidden fruit?) purveyor for the establishment.

Much of the humor in Bartleby depends upon the reader's perceiving the symbolic level, for comic effect arises out of the tendency of surface and symbolic levels to infect one another: the narrator, an ordinary man, is comic when he behaves like God, and God is comic when he behaves like man; and other tensions between surface and symbol (Turkey—Michael, Nippers—Lucifer) work in the same way. Ground glass folding doors (through which, presumably, we see darkly) divide the narrator's premises into two parts. "According to my humor," the narrator says, rather pleased with himself, "I threw open these doors, or closed them." He also takes pleasure in his clever disposition of Bartleby: Bartleby sits inside the doors (all others are outside) but sits behind a screen "which might entirely isolate Bartleby from my sight, though not remove him from my voice." Puns frequently contribute to this humor. The words "original" and "genius" work as they do in *The Confidence Man.* And when the narrator becomes resigned to Bartleby he says, "One prime thing was this—*he was always there . . .*" (Melville's italics). When the scrivener's being "always there" proves a not unmixed blessing, the narrator says:

> And as the idea came upon me of his possibly turning out a long lived man, and keep occupying my chambers, and denying my authority; and perplexing my visitors; and scandalizing my professional reputation; and casting a general gloom over the premises; keeping soul and body together to the last upon his savings (for doubtless he spent but half a dime a day), and in the end perhaps outlive me, and claim possession of my office by right of his perpetual occupancy . . . I resolved to gather all my faculties together, and forever rid me of this intolerable incubus.

Ere revolving any complicated project, however, adapted to this end, I first simply suggested to Bartleby the propriety of his permanent departure. . . . But having taken three days to meditate upon it, he apprised me, that his original determination remained the same; in short, that he still preferred to abide with me.

(The funniest barrage of puns in the story is *keeping soul and body together to the last upon his savings.*) But the effect of the symbolic level is not always—and is never entirely—comic. When the narrator abandons his office to Nippers at the time of Bartleby's arrest, one is more distressed than amused. One is moved, too, by the rich final line of the story: "Ah, Bartleby! Ah, humanity!" A man who behaves like God may be queerly admirable. The narrator puffs up his chest like God, but he is also capable of infinite compassion, he is dedicated to the spirit of the law (he will not get rid of Bartleby by laying an essentially false charge on him), and he can survive.

The lawyer-turned-artist is creative, like God, because he has judgment. He has imagination like "the mettlesome poet Byron," but unlike Byron (Melville seems to suggest) the lawyer has the judgment to see that the commitment of art is to man. One reason for the social commitment of art, as we have seen, is that society cannot operate without voluntary or involuntary diminution of the individual will. But Melville offers, in **"Bartleby,"** another reason as well. The final line of the story is both an equation and an opposition: "Ah, Bartleby! Ah, humanity!" Man lives on a walled-up street where the practice of law flourishes and justice is operative only in the mind. If justice is to be introduced into the ordinary world, if man is to receive recompense for being stopped in mid-action by dry lightning (like the narrator's man from Virginia), justice must come either as a Christian afterlife or as a transmutation of purely conceptual experience—that is, as art. The first seems no longer certain: the office of Master in Chancery is now defunct, "a [damned] premature act." We must find some other pleasant remuneration. The betrayed Bartleby gets justice and mercy at last, though; for Bartleby, whose freedom was limited in life by the inescapability of death, is now transmogrified to eternal life in art. Before Bartleby, the office was governed by law; but the recondite document at hand is a New Testament of sorts, at once ethical and moral. It insists upon law in this world, but it also provides justice. Though life must of necessity be characterized by limited freedom, voluntary self-diminution, there will be, after life, art. The artist rolls the stone away—that is the narrator's creative act—and man escapes from the Tombs.

Lionel Trilling   (essay date 1967)

SOURCE: "Bartleby the Scrivener: A Story of Wall Street," in *Prefaces to The Experience of Literature*, Harcourt Brace Jovanovich, 1979, pp. 74-8.

[*A respected American critic and literary historian, Trilling was also an essayist, editor, novelist, and short story writer. His exploration of liberal arts theory and its implications for the conduct of life led Trilling to function not only as a literary critic, but also as a social commentator. In the following essay, which originally appeared in* The Experience of Literature *(1967), he describes Bartleby as an individual alienated by the capitalist spirit.*]

In a letter he wrote to Hawthorne in 1851, Melville, speaking of his friend in the third person, offered him this praise: "There is the grand truth about Nathaniel Hawthorne. He says NO! in thunder; but the Devil himself cannot make him say *yes*. For all men who say *yes*, lie. . . ." Melville was referring to Hawthorne's relation to the moral order of the universe as it is conventionally imagined, but his statement, which has become famous, is often read as Melville's own call to resist the conformity that society seeks to impose. It was taken in this way by one of the notable students of Melville, Richard Chase, who quotes it at the beginning of an account of Melville's attitude toward the American life of his time and goes on to say that "although Melville was not exclusively a nay-sayer, his experiences and his reflections upon the quality of American civilization had taught him to utter the powerful 'no' he attributes to Hawthorne. He learned to say 'no' to the boundlessly optimistic commercialized creed of most Americans, with its superficial and mean conception of the possibilities of human life, its denial of all the genuinely creative or heroic capacities of man, and its fear and dislike of any but the mildest truths. Melville's 'no' finds expression in the tragic-comic tale of **'Bartleby the Scrivener'**" ["Herman Melville" in *Major Writers of America*, edited by Perry Miller, Vol. I].

But although this great story tells of a nay-saying of a quite ultimate kind, perhaps the first thing we notice about Bartleby's "no" is how far it is from being uttered "in thunder." And exactly its distance from thunder makes the negation as momentous as it is; the contrast between the extent of Bartleby's refusal and the minimal way in which he expresses it accounts for the story's strange force, its mythic impressiveness. Whether he is being asked to accommodate himself to the routine of his job in the law office or to the simplest requirements of life itself, Bartleby makes the same answer, "I prefer not to"—the phrase is prism, genteel, rather finicking; the negative volition it expresses seems to be of a very low intensity. Melville is at pains to point up the odd inadequacy of that word *prefer* by the passage in which he tells how it was unconsciously adopted into the speech of the narrator and his office staff, and with what comic effect.

Actually, of course, the small, muted phrase that Bartleby chooses for his negation is the measure of his intransigence. A "NO! in thunder" implies that the person who utters it is involved with and has strong feelings about whatever it is that he rejects or opposes. The louder his thunder, the greater is his (and our) belief in the power, the interest, the real existence of what he negates. Bartleby's colorless formula of refusal has the opposite effect—in refusing to display articulate anger against the social order he rejects, our poor taciturn nay-sayer denies its interest and any claim it may have on his attention and reason. "I prefer not to" implies that reason is not in point; the choice that is being made does not need the substantiation of reason: it is, as it were, a matter of "taste," even of whim, an act of pure volition, having reference to nothing but the nature of the agent. Or the muted minimal phrase might be read as an expression of the extremest possible arrogance—this Bartleby detaches himself from all human need or desire and acts at no behest other than that of his own unconditioned will.

It is possible that Melville never heard of Karl Marx, although the two men were contemporaries, but Melville's "story of Wall Street" exemplifies in a very striking way the concept of human alienation which plays an important part in Marx's early philosophical writings and has had considerable influence on later sociological thought. Alienation is the condition in which one acts as if at the behest not of one's own will but of some will other (Latin: *alius*) than one's own. For Marx its most important manifestation is in what he called "alienated labor," although he suggested that the phrase was redundant, since all labor is an alienated activity. In Latin *labor* has the meaning of pain and weariness as well as of work that causes pain and weariness, and we use the word to denote work that is in some degree enforced and that goes against the grain of human nature: a culprit is sentenced to a term of "hard labor," not of "hard work." By the same token, not all work is alienated; Marx cites the work of the artist as an example of free activity, happily willed, gratifying and dignifying those who perform it.

In undertaking to explain the reason for the alienated condition of man, Marx refused to accept the idea that it is brought about by the necessities of survival. Man, he said, can meet these necessities with the consciousness of free will, with the sense that he is at one with himself; it is society that alienates man from himself. And Marx held that alienation is at its extreme in those societies which are governed by money-values. In a spirited passage, he describes the process of accumulating capital in terms of the sacrifice of the free human activities that it entails: "The less you eat, drink, and read books; the less you go to the theatre, the dance hall, the public-house; the less you think, love, theorize, sing, paint, fence, etc., and the more you *save*—the greater becomes your treasure which neither moth nor dust will devour—your *capital*. The less you *are*, the more you *have*; the less you express your own life, the greater is your *externalized* life—the greater is the store of your alienated being." This describes the program for success in a money society; it was followed, we may note, in his early days by John Jacob Astor, who commands the ironized respect of the narrator of **"Bartleby the Scrivener,"** and no doubt to some extent by the narrator himself. Those members of a money society who do not consent to submit to the program are, of course, no less alienated, and they do not have the comforting illusion of freedom that the power of money can give.

> **It is possible that Melville never heard of Karl Marx, although the two men were contemporaries, but Melville's "story of Wall Street" exemplifies in a very striking way the concept of human alienation which plays an important part in Marx's early philosophical writings and has had considerable influence on later sociological thought.**
>
> — *Lionel Trilling*

It can be said of Bartleby that he behaves quite as if he were devoting himself to capitalist accumulation. He withdraws from one free human activity after another. If "the theatre, the dance hall, the public-house" had ever been within his ken, they are now far beyond it. If there had ever been a time when he delighted to "think, love, theorize, sing, paint, fence, etc.," it has long gone by. He never drinks. He eats less and less, eventually not at all. But of course nothing is further from his intention than accumulation—the self-denial he practices has been instituted in the interests of his freedom, a sad, abstract, metaphysical freedom but the only one he can aspire to. In the degree that he diminishes his self, he is the less an alienated self: his will is free, he cannot be compelled. A theory of suicide advanced by Sigmund Freud is in point here. It proposes the idea that the suicide's chief although unconscious purpose is to destroy not himself but some other person whom he has incorporated into his psychic fabric and whom he conceives to have great malign authority over him. Bartleby, by his gradual self-annihilation, annihilates the social order as it exists within himself.

An important complication is added to the story of Bartleby's fate by the character and the plight of the nameless narrator. No one could have behaved in a more forbearing and compassionate way than this good-tempered gentleman. He suffers long and is kind; he finds it hard, almost impossible, to do what common sense has long dictated he should do—have Bartleby expelled from the office by force—and he goes so far in charity as to offer to take Bartleby into his own home. Yet he feels that he has incurred guilt by eventually separating himself from Bartleby, and we think it appropriate that he should feel so, even while we sympathize with him; and in making this judgment we share his guilt. It is to him that Bartleby's only moment of anger is directed: " 'I know you,' " says Bartleby in the prison yard, " 'and I want nothing to say to you.' " The narrator is "keenly pained at his implied suspicion" that it was through his agency that Bartleby had been imprisoned, and we are pained for him, knowing the suspicion to be unfounded and unjust. Yet we know why it was uttered.

Bartleby's "I prefer not to" is spoken always in response to an order or request having to do with business utility. We may speculate about what would have happened if the narrator or one of Bartleby's fellow-copyists, alone with him in the office, had had occasion to say, "Bartleby, I feel sick and faint. Would you help me to the couch and fetch me a glass of water?" Perhaps the answer would have been given: " 'I prefer not to.' " But perhaps not.

Peter E. Firchow   (essay date 1968)

SOURCE: "Bartleby: Man and Metaphor," in *Studies in Short Fiction,* Vol. V, 1968, pp. 342-48.

[*Firchow is an American critic. In the following essay, he examines the meaning and significance of the final paragraph of "Bartleby, the Scrivener."*]

"Bartleby," as the anonymous narrator informs us at the very outset of Melville's story, is a brief account of that portion of the life of this strangest of all scriveners that the narrator has been privileged to see with his "own astonished eyes." Of other, more ordinary scriveners, he almost apologetically explains, he might have related "divers histories," or written even "the complete life." But not for Bartleby: for him "no materials exist" to compile a "full and satisfactory biography." The narrator terms this lack of information "an irreparable loss to literature," and the reader who has pored long over this enigmatic story is tempted to share his sentiments. For want of anything more definite, he must, however, accept the narrator's would-be explanation that Bartleby is simply "one of those beings" about whom very little can be known "except from original sources." He must content himself with viewing Bartleby through the eyes of the narrator alone, and reconcile himself to all the narrator's possible limitations, since "that" is, finally, all there is to be known about the mysterious copyist—with one exception, "one vague report" that the narrator promises will appear in the sequel.

This vague report, as it turns out at the end of the story, is identical with the "one little item of rumor" that comes to the narrator's attention "a few months after the scrivener's decease." The narrator, prudent as usual, hastens to assure the reader that he cannot vouch for the "basis" of this rumor and that he is therefore reluctant to assert its truth. Nevertheless, observing that this news "has not been without a certain suggestive interest" to him, he communicates it to "some others" who might be similarly interested. Bartleby, so the rumor runs, had once been employed as a subordinate clerk in the dead letter office in Washington and had lost his job when there was a change in the political administration.

That is all there is to this little item of rumor—very little indeed, one is tempted to add. And yet the whole story leads up to it. At the beginning, Melville drops the hint that it will possibly illuminate the mystery of Bartleby: it is the only detail of Bartleby's earlier life that Melville gives us, the only thing, therefore, we can use as an external reference point to explain Bartleby's enigmatic behavior. And at the end of the story the narrator explicitly tells us that it has "a certain suggestive interest." Suggestive of what? If we look at past interpretations of the story, not suggestive of very much; by and large the critics have not shared the narrator's interest in this additional information about Bartleby. Yet the narrator seems to insist upon

its importance to the story as a whole. Why? Is this simply an aesthetic blunder on Melville's part, an inartistic excrescence, a tasteless red herring that Melville serves up to conclude an already richly ambiguous repast?

Such, at any rate, has been the conclusion of at least two critics who have paid something more than the most rudimentary attention to it. [In *College English,* February, 1962] Mordecai Marcus condemns it as "an artificial conclusion tacked on as a concession to popular taste," and Charles G. Hoffman goes even further in asserting that it is "the flaw that mars the perfection of the whole. Melville did not leave well enough alone. The ending is anticlimactic." [*South Atlantic Quarterly,* 1953].

Nevertheless, despite these condemnations, the ending is relevant and important to the story. The narrator himself sees that, though of doubtful veracity, this information is of great help in understanding Bartleby and Bartleby's behavior. So, almost immediately after communicating it, he asks the reader to conceive of Bartleby as someone inherently and environmentally ("by nature and misfortune") given to a "pallid hopelessness" even before taking on his clerkship in the dead letter office. The duties of this position, the narrator goes on to speculate, only serve to increase Bartleby's propensity toward melancholy, since he must continually handle and consign to the flames letters that bear irrefutable testimony to the futility of man's attempts to help man:

> Sometimes from out the folded paper the pale clerk takes a ring—the finger it was meant for, perhaps, moulders in the grave; a banknote sent in swiftest charity—he whom it would relieve, nor eats nor hungers any more; pardon for those who died despairing; hope for those who died unhoping; good tidings for those who died stifled by unrelieved calamities.

Surrounded by the tangible proofs of man's unhappiness, Bartleby succumbs completely to his already partially existent despair and resolves to take no active part in a life that absurdly rewards all hope with frustration. In the narrator's view, then, the period of Bartleby's life with which the story as such is concerned represents only the inevitable and final working out of a process of retreat from life—or flight into death—that had already begun and had been fully determined by Bartleby's earlier experiences in the dead letter office.

The narrator's analysis of Bartleby's basic "problem" in the light of his previous position is unquestionably one possible interpretation of the story, all the more "possible" since it is the one suggested by the teller of the story himself. Though, to be sure, one should remember here that it might also simply be a further instance of the narrator's habit of rationalizing Bartleby, either of rationalizing him away in a moral sense, or of attempting to fit him into a rational, *i. e.,* rationally explicable, pattern. I shall deal with this possibility somewhat more fully later in this essay. For the moment let us examine the narrator's interpretation as a valid one.

On the surface, this semi-environmental, rational explanation of Bartleby's eccentric behavior seems compelling. It is difficult to quarrel with except on the grounds that it does in fact remain pretty much on the surface. Bartleby is reduced to very little, if anything, more than a kind of stock, sensitive soul, someone who is pushed into extreme depression and eventual madness through a lamentable, if perhaps admirable, hyper-awareness of the wretchedness of the human condition. But Bartleby seems to be more than merely that, and for that reason the narrator's conventional explanation seems unsatisfying.

Moreover, his explanation, though superficially valid, does not really take into account all that happens, explicitly and implicitly, in the story. It does not, for example, really explain the behavior of the narrator himself when confronted by the mysterious scrivener: why he is so fascinated by Bartleby, why he so persistently attempts to analyse and identify Bartleby. But this confrontation of the narrator and Bartleby is certainly at the heart of Melville's story, and it is this heart that the narrator's own interpretation does not even attempt to reach.

Does this mean that the narrator's explanation is to be rejected? Yes and no, I think. Yes, because ultimately it is a superficial and inadequate explanation; no, because the "suggestive interest" of the new biographical data presented by the narrator at the end of the story is not exhausted by the explanation he himself presents. Much more is implied by it than he explicitly derives from it.

If we look more closely at the passage in which the narrator presents his analysis of the new information about Bartleby, another possible interpretation "suggests" itself, not so much through the information itself (though that, too) as through the narrator's emotional response to it. Immediately after recounting Bartleby's previous activity, the narrator pauses to describe his emotional state: "When I think over this rumor, hardly can I express the emotions which seize me." And in the next sentence he asks himself: "Dead letters! does it not sound like dead men?" When the narrator makes this analogy, he can hardly mean that dead letters *sound* like dead men either *in verbo* or *in re*. He cannot mean here *sound* in the normal sense of something that is heard, for unquestionably the two phrases, except for the repeated first word, do not sound the same. What the narrator means by *sound* must consequently be something else, something more like *evoke* or *suggest*. To look at the word in this sense, however, is to uncover one of the most fundamental and fundamentally important metaphors in the story: namely that Bartleby is a dead letter.

The identification of Bartleby with a letter illuminates the central situation of the story. We can then see Bartleby as a letter sent to the narrator and apparently containing a message of importance for him, though the narrator is not entirely sure that this human letter is in fact addressed to him or that it does contain a message for him. Seen in the light of this metaphor, the central situation of the story is transformed into the attempt of the narrator to decipher the address and the message of a letter that has somehow fallen into his hands. The central situation, then, is one of an attempt to communicate and a failure to do so.

An examination of the story reveals much in support of such a view. The narrator, for example, is professionally

a "conveyancer and title hunter, and drawer up of recondite documents of all sorts," and his additional position of Master of Chancery shows him as particularly well qualified to read and understand difficult and obscure "documents" of all kinds. He is also, in the words of his own description of himself, a "*safe*" and "prudent" man. Unlike his employees, Turkey and Nippers, he is an eminently rational man: he is never guilty of the unreasonable behavior of Nippers in the forenoon or Turkey in the afternoon. He is a reasonable man *all of the time*; and he shows this rationality most strikingly in his treatment of Bartleby, so much so, indeed, that the narrator almost becomes a symbol of the rational attitude and Bartleby of the irrational. For example, in dealing with the inscrutable scrivener, the narrator at times operates on something he calls the "doctrine of assumptions": that is, he assumes that if he acts in a certain rational fashion, then Bartleby must respond in logically foreseeable ways. Bartleby of course does not respond in these ways; and on the irrational, immovable rock of Bartleby, the rational doctrine of assumptions founders. Even more obviously, when the narrator asks Bartleby to promise in future to be "a little more reasonable," Bartleby characteristically replies that he would "prefer not to be a little reasonable." It is because Bartleby and Bartleby's behavior will simply not fit into the narrator's habitually rational pattern of thought that the narrator is at such a loss in dealing with him. Transposed into the terms of the metaphor, this situation can be seen as one in which the narrator attempts to read the human letter that Bartleby is, without seeing that it is written in a "language" he does not know and therefore cannot understand.

The narrator, however, gradually comes to understand that any attempt to interpret Bartleby's significance in a rational manner must be futile and that he must accept the irrational Bartleby for what he is. Significantly, this realization comes to the narrator in terms that explicitly contain the idea of Bartleby as something *sent* to him: "Gradually I slid into the persuasion that these troubles of mine, touching the scrivener, had been all predestined from eternity, and Bartleby was billeted upon me for some mysterious purpose of an allwise Providence, which it was not for a mere mortal like me to fathom." To be sure, the narrator soon undergoes another change of heart when he sees that an acceptance of Bartleby on Bartleby's own terms will necessarily entail great embarrassment for him in his profession. Not possessing enough courage to rid himself of Bartleby by evicting him forcibly, he leaves himself. In doing so the narrator is, as it were, attempting to avoid accepting the human letter that Providence has sent him; he refuses it by changing his address and successfully resisting all subsequent attempts to have Bartleby "forwarded" to him.

This refusal leads directly to Bartleby's removal to the Tombs—a prison, as the name clearly indicates, that is the metaphoric equivalent of the dead letter office. And like the dead letters that must inevitably be destroyed, Bartleby, too, must die. Still, there may be a final difference, for, as the narrator piously notes as he closes the scrivener's eyes, Bartleby has gone to join " 'kings and counselors' ";

unable to reach his earthly destination, perhaps he has finally arrived at his heavenly one.

There are also certain other elements of the story that can perhaps be better understood through a perception of the letter metaphor. The stress on the fact that Bartleby's appearance is "cadaverous," that he is "pallid," or the narrator's vision of Bartleby's corpse "laid out, among uncaring strangers, in its shivering winding sheet," all these seem to point in hindsight to an equation of Bartleby with a *dead* letter. Furthermore, the oft-noted fact that all the characters in the story, except Bartleby, are either anonymous (the narrator) or pseudonymous (Turkey, Nippers, and Ginger Nut) gains new significance in the light of the epistolary metaphor. Because of their anonymity or pseudonymity, none of them is compelled to accept Bartleby-the-letter as addressed to them personally. They are therefore able to disclaim responsibility for what finally happens to him.

> **A recognition of the function of the final paragraph and of the letter metaphor that is embedded in it reveals that there are no loose ends in this story, but that "Bartleby" is a carefully and fully integrated work of art.**
>
> **— Peter E. Firchow**

Also, the narrator's inability to "read" Bartleby emphasizes more strongly the already sharp division between them, a division not merely between the rational and the irrational, but also between the active and the passive. The narrator's activity is evident in his attempts to understand and aid Bartleby; Bartleby's passivity is made obvious by the images of death that accompany him throughout the story, though it emerges, too, in his use of his favorite word, *prefer*. This word seems to imply the existence of an active will in Bartleby, a will that has and makes a conscious choice. However, it should be noted that this word is usually qualified by a preceding *would* and is *invariably* followed by a *not*. Thought Bartleby has a choice, at least theoretically, he never exercises it; his response is automatically and inexorably negative. In Carlyle's terms, he is essentially a "nay-sayer" and the narrator essentially a "yea-sayer." Despite this, however, the narrator is in a curious fashion in the same position *vis-à-vis* Bartleby as the scrivener was *vis-à-vis* his letters: that is, after seeing all his attempts to succor Bartleby fail, the narrator, like Bartleby in his dead letter office, cannot avoid coming to certain conclusions about the human condition. In arriving at these conclusions, however, the narrator, unlike Bartleby, still keeps his head. As he himself recognizes, he is saved because he is "safe" and "prudent," in a word (also his word) because he has common sense: whereas Bartleby is destroyed because he lacks these qualities. This recognition comes to the narrator immediately after he has been made aware of the full extent of Bartleby's solitude and

misery, and after his first rush of heartfelt pity has subsided into fear:

> My first emotions had been those of pure melancholy and sincerest pity; but just in proportion as the forlornness of Bartleby grew and grew to my imagination, did that same melancholy merge into fear, that pity into repulsion. So true it is, and so terrible, too, that up to a certain point the thought or sight of misery enlists our best affections; but, in certain special cases, beyond that point it does not. They err who would assert that invariably this is owing to the inherent selfishness of the human heart. It rather proceeds from a certain hopelessness of remedying excessive and organic ill. To a sensitive being, pity is not seldom pain. And when at last it is perceived that such pity cannot lead to effectual succor, *common sense bids the soul be rid of it.* (Italics mine.)

According to the rumor at the end of the story and the narrator's inferences from it, Bartleby encounters much the same problem during his service in the dead letter office; but Bartleby, it would seem, lacked the "common sense" to bid his soul be rid of the pity he felt. One is reminded in this connection of one of Ishmael's concluding statements in the "Try-Works" chapter of *Moby Dick*: "There is a wisdom that is woe; but there is a woe that is madness."

The final long paragraph of the story indicates then—and the epistolary metaphor serves to emphasize—that **"Bartleby"** is basically a story about the human and not the social condition, that it is less a social indictment and more a symbolic account of the isolation of man, of the impossibility of real communication between men. And a recognition of the function of the final paragraph and of the letter metaphor that is embedded in it reveals that there are no loose ends in this story, but that **"Bartleby"** is a carefully and fully integrated work of art.

Gordon E. Bigelow   (essay date 1970)

SOURCE: "The Problem of Symbolist Form in Melville's 'Bartleby the Scrivener'," in *Modern Language Quarterly*, Vol. 31, 1970, pp. 345-58.

[*Bigelow is an American critic and educator. In the following essay, he proposes that the symbolism in "Bartleby, the Scrivener" is too rich to be reduced to a single, definitive meaning.*]

One proffers another critique of Melville's **"Bartleby"** with some diffidence, feeling overawed by a recent bibliography of criticism of the story which contains 117 items and includes the names of the most formidable Melville scholars [Donald M. Fiene, "A Bibliography of Criticism of 'Bartleby the Scrivener,'" in *Melville Annual 1965. A Symposium: "Bartleby the Scrivener,"* edited by Howard P. Vincent, 1966]. The diversity of critical reaction to the story is striking. Some critics focus upon Bartleby, some upon the unnamed lawyer-narrator, some upon both. Some read the story as a parable of the thwarted artist, as Melville's *non serviam* to a hostile Philistine society; some read it as a study in abnormal psychology in which Bartleby, or the narrator, or both, are schizophrenic; some read it as a social satire, a bitter attack upon a society too much devoted to heartless commercialism; some read it theologically, as a parable of free will, moral responsibility, and judgment; some read it existentially, stressing Bartleby's Kafkaesque alienation in an absurd universe. Some see Bartleby as a projection of the narrator's own death wish (or Melville's), or as the narrator's alter ego, or as his conscience; some see him as a Christ figure, or as Christ himself incarnated in a nineteenth-century Wall Street law office. Some discuss "symbols" in the story: the whiteness, the dead walls, the living green of the grass in the courtyard of the prison where Bartleby dies.

In an attempt to illuminate some aspect of the story or other, critics have cited parallels or sources or influences in the Bible, Hawthorne, Poe, Emerson, Thoreau, Dostoevski, Gogol, Chekhov, Camus, Kafka, Kierkegaard, Buber, Pascal, Montaigne, and Shakespeare. The lawyer-narrator has been related in some fashion to Melville's brother Allen, his uncle Peter Gansevoort, his father-in-law Chief Justice Lemuel Shaw of Massachusetts, Evert Duyckinck, Everyman, the Prophet Jonah, Captain "Starry" Vere, Captain Amasa Delano, and the Lord God Jehovah. Bartleby himself has been related to Christ, to one of the least of Christ's brethren, to Everyman, Benito Cereno, Billy Budd, the Confidence Man, Ishmael, Ahab, Pierre, Plotinus Plinlimmon, Israel Potter, Pip, Hunilla, a tragic white-faced clown, a Buddhist monk, a sannyasi Hindu monk, Natty Bumppo, Mahatma Ghandi, Job, Teufelsdröckh, Holmes's Elsie Venner, Thoreau, Poe's William Wilson, Walter Mitty, and Melville himself.

With this great multiplicity of readings we encounter not simply variety but out-and-out contradiction. Can Bartleby be like a sannyasi, practicing a systematic resignation which eventually sublimes away his life, and at the same time be like Christ, whose function is to redeem life? Can the narrator be a cynical hedonist and, at the same time, a compassionate Good Samaritan? Can such disparate readings of the story all be valid? I think the answer is *yes.* Not that all readings seem equally satisfying or that any reading will do; but most, including those that are mutually contradictory, seem to have some validity. All seem partial, able to account for some aspects of the story but not for others. Virtually all seem written in answer to the same compelling question: what does the story *mean?* I do not propose here another reading of this sort, though I believe others are possible. I would like to shift the question to read: what kind of thing is this story? Perhaps by asking questions about form it will be possible to "explain" the other critiques, at least to the extent of explaining why there are so many of them. It will soon become apparent that my problem here, and my purpose, is as much to grope toward a critical method for dealing with fiction of this sort as to produce an interpretation of this particular story.

I begin with an assumption which serious readers of Melville have made for some time—that he is a symbolist writer and **"Bartleby"** a symbolist story. By symbolist, I mean a story that is intentionally symbolic in mode, not simply symbolic in the organ-tone sense that would apply to all literature. More specifics of what I take symbolic to mean will emerge in subsequent discussion. Although I will discuss symbolism in the story, this will be no safari into deep reading of particular symbols. It is not symbols like raisins in a cake, but symbolism as a way of seeing, as a literary form productive of meaning, which is my topic. It will be convenient to discuss the various aspects of symbolist form as if they were discrete factors which could be examined separately. Actually, each one involves all the others, since all originate in a single mysterious center of which each is but one vector.

(1) *Symbolic pregnance; implied metaphor*

One hallmark of symbolist writing is its ability to arouse in the reader a haunting sense that he is in the presence of deep meaning which he *feels* but cannot quite articulate. Poe records the experience in "Ligeia," where the narrator, peering deep into Ligeia's eyes, feels always on the verge of penetrating the mystery they contain, like a man on the verge of remembering something he has forgotten and cannot quite bring to mind. "What was it?" [he asked himself]. "I was possessed with a passion to know. . . . How frequently, in my intense scrutiny of Ligeia's eyes, have I felt approaching the full knowledge of their expression—felt it approaching—yet not quite be mine—and so at length entirely depart!" This is the first part of the experience with a symbolist writing, the engrossing, compelling sense of engagement, the continuous question: what does it mean? Then the recurring sense of approaching enlightenment, as if the mind were about to enclose the meaning in full knowledge, only to have this illumination fade away before the climactic revelation. From the sheer number of readings, it seems clear that **"Bartleby"** has this ability to engage and to arouse the question of meaning. From the great variety of readings, it seems clear that no one has arrived at a definitive version of its meaning, and one suspects that probably no one ever will.

All readers sense that the characters, the events, the elements of setting in this story imply meaning beyond themselves. Nothing remains what it seems. This is what Coleridge meant by the "translucence" of the symbol, whereby a larger meaning than is contained in an object is seen through the object. Ernst Cassirer's suggestive phrase for this is "symbolic pregnance." W. Y. Tindall calls it "embodied or immanent analogy" and finds it to be the chief differentia of the symbolist mode in literature. He suggests that in fiction of this kind most story elements seem to be one-half of an analogy whose other half is unstated. In the present story, the words "wall" or "dead-wall" or "Wall Street" will not remain at rest as simple elements of realistic description. One feels continuously compelled to search for the other thing they belong to. One stands, as it were, on one foot, urgently looking for the place to put the other foot down so that one can stand at ease; and for "wall" this may be any of a number of different places—"death," "alienation," "wasteland"—because the author does not specify. But it is important to note that the first element of symbolist form is not a thing but a force, a pulling or urgency, a compulsion to find "meaning," and this is why so much of the criticism of the story takes the form of exegesis.

Implied or unstated metaphor also exists in **"Bartleby"** at other more generalized levels usually subsumed under the word "myth" in current criticism; this sometimes involves principles other than analogy. One such principle is the *principle of juxtaposition,* whereby two things are simply placed together without comment so that each becomes involved in the other's ambience, thus producing a tensive area of meaning somewhere between the two which partakes of both but has its own distinct character. Along with this often goes a second principle which might be called the *principle of cumulation or resonance,* which simply means the device of repeating juxtapositions of a similar kind until a definite tone or "resonance" is established. Melville does not say that Bartleby is Christ or even that he is like Christ; he simply assigns to him phrase after phrase and action after action which accumulate an unmistakable resonance of particular meaning: "man of sorrow," "forlornest of mankind," "He answered nothing," "his wonderful mildness," "He was always there," "Having taken three days to meditate . . . he still preferred to abide with me." In the context of Western culture, such phrases inevitably configure to form one possible version of the unstated half of an implied metaphor. A similar cumulation conjures into hovering presence over the story the passage from Matthew 25 where Christ as judge separates the goats from the sheep. Nothing explicit in the story certifies the implication of judgment, and some elements of the story stand opposed to it; but it is hard to escape the strong suggestion that Bartleby is Christ or one of Christ's poor, and that the lawyer-narrator and the other persons in the Wall Street law office, that is, Wall Street itself and the civilization it represents, are under judgment in accordance with the way they react to the silent scrivener.

(2) *Meaning as process or flow*

In a well-known passage from the preface to *The Scarlet Letter,* Hawthorne tells of finding an embroidered piece of ragged red cloth rolled up in parchment. As he contemplated this object, he felt that deep meaning streamed forth from it, subtly communicating itself to his sensibilities, but evading the analysis of his mind. But he also felt that this meaning was "most worthy of interpretation," that is, of reduction to concept or idea or moral principle. Most critics have approached **"Bartleby"** in this fashion, looking upon it as if it had a single fixed, topical meaning, or as if it were a sign pointing to a meaning outside of itself in a realm of ideas, and the critic's job were to paraphrase that meaning, or to decipher a somewhat blurred inscription on that sign so he could tell us what it pointed to. The trouble is that the story points in a number of different directions at the same time, as the multiplicity of readings suggests. In one of these directions might lie a realm of eternal order and unchanging ideas, but in another lies an absurd universe without rational order, and in still another direction the existential world of the 1850's, and perhaps beyond all of these an ineffable realm of the Absolute. To deal with the story, we are at last driven back to the story, which we discover points mainly to itself; and we learn that we must grant the story its own mode of existence, which may overlap other modes but does not correspond to any other in a one-to-one relationship. The story

as a whole would appear to be a "symbol" in Cassirer's sense of an intellectual or spiritual form "which produces and posits a world of its own" [*Language and Myth,* translated by Susanne K. Langer]. He notes that "symbolic forms are not imitations, but *organs* of reality." "We must see in each of these spiritual forms," he writes, "a spontaneous law of generation; an original way and tendency of expression which is more than a mere record of something initially given in fixed categories of real existence."

Much of our problem with **"Bartleby"** dissolves if we cease to expect it to have a single meaning, but instead look upon it as a generator of a continuous flow of meaning, which means kinetically, organically, as it is *experienced* by a particular reader. If the flow is stopped, analytical reason will simply burn a hole through this kind of literary fabric. In Lewis Carroll's *Through the Looking Glass,* Alice made this discovery when she found herself at one point in a quaint little shop:

> The shop seemed to be full of all manner of curious things—but the oddest part of it was, that whenever she looked hard at any shelf, to make out exactly what it had on it, that particular shelf was quite empty; though the others round it were crowded full as they could hold. "Things flow about here so!" she said at last.

Alice also discovered that one aspect of this flow was a metamorphic change of forms. A few moments earlier the quaint little shop had been a forest; the long-nosed white sheep knitting behind the counter had been the white queen. Change in **"Bartleby"** is not so startling, but change there certainly is.

(3) *Metamorphosis; ambiguity*

Not delineation, with its stable, clearly realized forms, but chiaroscuro, with its shadows and areas of meaning defined by contrasting highlights, is the technique employed in this story—chiaroscuro and a continuous shifting of forms. In spite of a relatively straightforward plot and a certain realism in the Wall Street setting, very little remains stable. The story is polarized along an axis between the narrator and Bartleby, but both poles of this axis change continuously and even, as we shall see, merge into one another.

Bartleby may be simply a pale, silent scrivener, a human derelict; or he may be a schizophrenic in a catatonic trance, or another incarnation of Christ, or a petulant, stubborn nonconformist, refusing to be "reasonable." One's reading of the story depends upon which of these one takes him to be, and equally important, which of a number of contradictory possibilities one takes the narrator to be, for he is equally unstable. He tells us that he is an "eminently safe" man, esteemed by his rich clients for his prudence; he openly admits that he lives by the hedonistic principle that "the easiest way of life is the best." On Sunday mornings he attends a fashionable church, but he also equates the Christian law of love with self-interest. He is a kindly employer, but speaks with bemused callousness of the poverty of his employees and of the withering boredom and frustration of their work. During most of the story he is "the boss," who benefits from and wields the power of an oppressive and ruthless society. But he fits no single stereotype or category; he is no Scrooge; he is too indecisive and too humane.

He is further defined and further blurred by his relationship to Bartleby. If we heed the massive evidence suggesting that Bartleby is Christ or one of Christ's poor, then the narrator should be defined by how he answers the divine command given in Matthew 25 to feed such poor, to clothe him, and to visit him when sick or in prison. The lawyer-narrator does indeed respond to Bartleby in most definite fashion, but his response runs a bewildering spectrum. He is at first indifferent to him, no more aware of him than of the office furniture. But as Bartleby progressively refuses to do his work or to leave, the narrator tries to reason with him, to bribe him, to intimidate him, to evict him; and when the stranger will not forsake him, he moves out and leaves him alone on the premises. He appears on all counts to violate the divine command, yet paradoxically he also fulfills it. When Bartleby is sick and in prison, he visits him and gives money to feed him. He offers to find him another kind of work, he offers him his office, and finally he offers to care for him in his own home. So that in the end his reactions to Bartleby vary from detachment, to ironic amusement, to anger, to bewilderment, and at last to deep and genuine compassion. The story suggests that he is like Pilate in questioning the stranger, like Judas in betraying him to the law, like St. Peter in thrice denying him, but also like the Good Samaritan in caring for him.

In coming to terms with the narrator, or with Bartleby, which handle does one grasp? Melville has made it impossible to fix upon one to the exclusion of the others. As in so many of Hawthorne's stories, the reader is presented with multiple choices, but with no indication as to which choice he should make. One can produce a stable thematic reading of this story only by accepting certain facets of character to the exclusion of others; otherwise, like Alice we must accept the fact that "things flow about here so." This means that at last we must accept in a fiction of this kind the principle of metamorphic change and a degree of paradox and ambiguity which no effort of mind can compel into focus; we must settle for *indefiniteness* as the basic condition of the symbolist writing, for Wallace Stevens' "ever-never-changing same."

(4) *Perspectivism*

When Alice was talking to Humpty Dumpty, she could not decide whether to compliment him on his belt or his cravat. " 'If I only knew,' she said, 'which was waist and which was neck' "—that is, which frame of reference or perspective to adopt. This same quandary constitutes another part of our problem with **"Bartleby."**

Point of view in this story is usually understood to be established by the lawyer-narrator, who tells the reader directly about his experience with the pale scrivener. No one could quarrel that the story comes to us from the mouth of the lawyer, but since he and the person he chiefly contemplates are in a continuous process of metamorphic change, it is difficult to say what perspective, except a floating one, is established. We start out assuming that we

are to be told a story about a scrivener named Bartleby, but before long we suspect that this may be a story about the narrator himself, or perhaps it is really about ourselves, about all men.

We encounter the same difficulty in our attempt to adopt some stance toward Bartleby. Like the narrator, we are not sure whether we ought to hate him or to love him. We do not know whether we have common cause with him or with the narrator, or with both, or with neither, or something of all of these. Which perspectives are available to us will depend, not only on the story, but also radically upon our own subjectivity. Meanings stream forth from the story, but one sees only those meanings caught by one's own lens or filter. In part one sees a version of oneself reflected back from the story, and this is a symbolist principle with which Melville himself was thoroughly familiar. Everyone recalls the chapter from *Moby Dick* where the doubloon has been nailed to the mast and Captain Ahab and each of his mates in turn stand before the symbolic object and ruminate in Shakespearean soliloquy about its meaning. We recognize at once that the remarks of each reveal the man as much as the coin, and we recall the words of Pip the wise fool: "I look, you look, he looks; we look, ye look, they look."

The critiques of **"Bartleby"** clearly reveal this same pattern: the psychologist sees schizophrenia; the reader interested in archetypes sees a father-son myth; the reader oriented to biography and history sees a Melville family allegory; the reader oriented to theology sees a reenactment of the Passion and a parable of Judgment. This same kind of perspectivism would of course hold true in some measure for any art work, as the innumerable readings of *Hamlet* bear witness, but it is especially relevant to a symbolist writing where so much is deliberately left problematic. It is through this opening that the symbol-chaser breaks through to gambol about with freest abandon. With so few elements of the story certifiable or even specifiable, the field is open for the most extravagant intrusion of the reader's subjectivity. This whole matter of subject and object, of the inner and outer worlds and their relationship, is particularly interesting in literature of the symbolist mode, and it constitutes one major aspect of our next rubric.

(5) *Presence and coalescence*

Most of us who inherit Western culture still live by the dualism of Descartes which separates mind from matter, thinking subject from the objects of thought. And most of us are also positivists, tending to accept as "real" chiefly those aspects of reality which can be dealt with using the methods of physical science. We habitually view reality in visual, spatial terms; we convert sensory experience into solid, fixed objects which we locate *out there* in space. We allow these objects to have the measurable properties of mass, extension, and motion, and a life which is an invisible dance of atoms, but we reserve their other qualities such as color and smell to our own subjectivity.

These attitudes tend to suppress another kind of life which might be called the "felt presence" of some aspect of the real world. This can manifest itself in a person, a tree, a stone, a mountain, a cloud, an animal, or a river. Primitive peoples commonly have a strong awareness of such presence or mana, which they often conceive as spiritual beings like nymphs or dryads which inhabit various parts of the phenomenal world. This is not personification or the projection of the ego upon the natural realm as in Ruskin's pathetic fallacy. It involves a flow of spiritual force the other way—from out there in—which is met by a flow from in here out. Wordsworth was keenly aware of such presence from boyhood, and many modern poets allude to it. Hopkins' "inscape" and "instress" are related to it, as are Joyce's *quidditas* and epiphany, D. H. Lawrence's "divine otherness," Wallace Stevens' "vital, arrogant, fatal, dominant X," and William Carlos Williams' way of viewing the red wheelbarrow in the rain.

In Martin Buber's well-known formulation, the *I*, by becoming bound up *in relation with* some part of the world, begins to see it as a *Thou*. I-It of Cartesian dualism becomes I-Thou of co-presence. In such case a tree ceases to be simply a thing, but is accepted as having a kind of personhood. "The tree is no impression," writes Buber, "no play of my imagination, no value depending upon my mood; but it is bodied over against me and has to do with me, as I with it. . . ."

Presence of this sort figures in this story chiefly in two ways—in Bartleby and in the Wall Street setting. One way of defining the action of the story is to describe it as the modulation of the narrator's attitude toward Bartleby from I-It to I-Thou. We watch the narrator's gradual renunciation of his own sovereign will (his "doctrine of assumptions") and his ego-centered universe in which Bartleby exists only as object; and we see his gradual acknowledgment of Bartleby's unique presence (Bartleby's "preferences"). Bartleby's silent presence gradually infiltrates the entire office and all the people in it, as is made plain by the spread of his word "prefer."

The Wall Street setting must also be seen here as presence. Continuous symbolic notation of dead walls, cisterns, bricks and mortar, stones, whiteness, the Tombs, and pyramids creates a dark entity which makes itself felt as a sinister, engulfing, deathlike force. Wall Street is a place, but it is also people, and we come here to one phase of "coalescence." The place is permeated by particular facets of human character, which it expresses: acquisitiveness, selfish hedonism, callous exploitation of the weak, ruthless suppression of nonconformity. As in William Carlos Williams' *Paterson,* the city is the people, the people are the city. There is an "interpenetration both ways." All the characters in the story express the Wall Street presence in some fashion; all *are* Wall Street, ironical master and suffering victim alike. This is particularly apparent in Bartleby's fellow scriveners, Turkey and Nippers, who are usually admired for their grotesque Dickensian vividness. These two function almost more as part of setting than as agents, expressing the crushing presence of the place quite as well as do the dead walls.

"Coalescence," that meeting of I and Thou in a binding relation, or that interpenetration of subject and object in a realm of co-presence, occurs in the story in other ways. Suppose we restrict our view for the moment to the "world" created by the story itself. In this case, the lawyer-narrator would appear as subject; and Bartleby, the other characters, and all aspects of setting would assume the nature of objects. But as several critics have noted, Bartleby and the narrator overlap in so many respects that Bartleby has been called the narrator's alter ego. Bartleby strikes most readers as an Everyman, but so does the narrator. Both are described as sons of Adam; both epitomize Wall Street. And as we have just noted, the main course of events in the story shows the narrator ending his own exclusiveness step by step to enter at last the circle of Bartleby's existence. There is, in a word, a progressive coalescence of subject and object at this level.

If we enlarge our circle of consideration so that the reader becomes subject and the story as a whole becomes object, we find the same tendency toward coalescence. Just as the narrator contemplates Bartleby, so do we over his shoulder, his dilemma of what to do about him becoming our dilemma, his question of meaning our question. We cannot help identifying with Everyman-narrator—or, paradoxically, with Everyman-Bartleby. As readers, we merge with both master and victim, and recognize that from either perspective their world is also our world.

We should not fail to connect what we have said about presence and coalescence to earlier comments about meaning as process or flow. Presence usually makes itself felt in fleeting moments of impact upon the senses, often upon senses other than sight. It comes, is vividly apprehensible for a moment, and is gone, like Emily Dickinson's hummingbird or Wallace Stevens' pheasant disappearing into the brush. Melville's story, it seems to me, works upon us in exactly this fashion, producing strong but passing moments of awareness, which are the despair of criticism because, as Hawthorne said, they evade the analysis of our mind. Closely related to the evanescent movement of presence in symbolist fiction is a shifting polarity which becomes our next major topic.

(6) *"Field," or tensive context, and synecdoche*

In a striking passage from E. E. Cummings' experimental play *Him*, the main character reads from his notebook the following reflections about the nature of the real world:

> These solidities and silences which we call "things" are not separate units of experience, but are poises, self-organising collections. There are no entities, no isolations, no abstractions; but there are departures, voyages, arrivals, contagions. I have seen an instant of consciousness as a heap of jackstraws. This heap is not inert; it is a kinesis fatally composed of countless mutually dependent stresses, a product-and-quotient of innumerable perfectly interrelated tensions. Tensions (by which any portion flowing through every other portion becomes the whole) are the technique and essence of Being.

This passage nicely summarizes much of the modern symbolist view of reality, but we are particularly interested at this point in two parts of it: the idea of kinetic tension as the essence of reality, and the idea of one portion of a kinesis somehow becoming the whole.

Cummings' words run parallel to statements by the philosophers of symbolism: "Every actual thing," writes Alfred North Whitehead, "is something by reason of its activity; whereby its nature consists in its relevance to other things, and its individuality consists in its synthesis of other things so far as they are relevant to it." Susanne Langer makes a similar statement when she describes meaning as a function of a term: "A function is a *pattern* viewed with reference to one special term round which it centers; this pattern emerges when we look at a given term *in its total relation to the other terms about it.*" Charles Olson and others have made familiar the concept of a poem as a high-energy construct, analogous to a force field in physics, and Olson insists that poetry should be "composition by field."

I propose that Melville's story should be regarded as such a field and that it has meaning according to the tensive relationships which it sets up. The elements of the field we have already sufficiently noted—the Wall Street law office, the various characters, the events—but we should take a longer look at the power of tensive context to *create* meaning, and understand how one portion of such a field can in a real sense become the whole. Bartleby's often-repeated statement, "I would prefer not to," will provide a good illustration. Taken by itself, this is simply an innocuous refusal, a "no" couched in genteel language. Within the context of this story it becomes charged with multiple meanings of unusual poignance. It is an epitome of Bartleby's heroic (or petulant) refusal to co-operate with the establishment. It is tragic because expressive of Bartleby's estrangement and death by inanition. It is comic according to the principle of repetition described by Bergson. It represents the noble ethic of Christian passive resistance, or the principle of resignation and fatalistic despair, or the principle of existential free will, or the oppressive spirit of capitalist exploitation, and so on. Most of the currents of meaning within this complex story can be seen to flow through this simple sentence. *Within its context* it invokes all the other elements of that context.

Here we can see operating one of the fundamental principles of symbolism—the flow of the many in the one, the one in the many. For lack of a better term we can call this the *principle of synecdoche,* though the limitations of the old rhetorical definition are apparent. This is no simple substitution of a part for the whole. There is no substitution at all. The part retains its own integrity as part while at the same time belonging to and invoking the whole. The principle is easiest to observe, perhaps, when the part is a person rather than so abstract a thing as a sentence. Bartleby himself could serve admirably as a synecdoche for the entire story, but so could the narrator, and so, with more effort of imagination, could Turkey or Nippers. At still another level, the principle of synecdoche functions with great power if one takes the whole story as a microcosm of the modern world.

It should be noted, as we conclude, that Melville makes no use in this story of the incantatory and musical techniques so important to symbolist poets like Poe and Mallarmé. But even though it is heretical these days to speak of an author's intentions, one wonders if part of Melville's intention with **"Bartleby"** was not like Poe's openly avowed intention in his poems—to be *affective,* to modify the consciousness of the reader. Poe wanted his poems to have an effect like that of music, to produce an "elevation of the soul." John Senior has argued convincingly that some symbolist poems, like those of Mallarmé, seem to be intended to act like *yantras,* those symbolic designs used by oriental occultists to assist the process of meditation by unhinging the mind from its customary anchors to physical reality and freeing it to penetrate to visionary realms. It is tempting to suggest that something like this was part of Melville's intention with **"Bartleby,"** though "proof" is hard to come by.

In our attempt to identify the elements of symbolist form in this story, we have returned again and again to the great inclusive principle of process or flow. The story seems to be a piece struck from Whitman's "float forever held in solution," implicit with the same ambiguity and mystery as life itself, with that inscrutability which fascinated and appalled Melville during his whole career. Most of us feel uneasy in the presence of something which resists the grasp of our minds. We have that little corner of Ahab in us which hates the inscrutable thing. Perhaps that is because, as Blake prayed to be, we need to be delivered "from single vision and Newton's sleep"—from the limited vision of empirical science. We may need at least what Blake described as the "two-fold vision," the ability to perceive analogically, in images, in order to come to terms with **"Bartleby."** Until we have this kind of vision, which I suspect was Melville's own when he wrote the story, we must remain like the baffled narrator in Poe, peering deep into Ligeia's eyes, always on the verge of knowing the secret contained in their depths, but fated to exclaim at last: "What was it? I was possessed with a passion to know. . . ."

Sanford Pinsker (essay date 1975)

SOURCE: " 'Bartleby the Scrivener': Language as Wall," in *College Literature,* Vol. II, No. 1, Winter 1975, pp. 17-27.

[*Pinsker is an American scholar and poet, and the author of several books on contemporary American literature. He has a particular interest in American humor and is known for his own witty critical style. In the following essay, he interprets "Bartleby, the Scrivener" as a statement on the inability of language to fully circumscribe human experience.*]

Melville's puzzling story **"Bartleby the Scrivener"** threatens to make scriveners of us all, endlessly writing those dead letters called literary criticism. Scholars with a biographical bent have pointed out the parallels between the disaffected Bartleby and his equally disaffected author. Both were professional scriveners; both "preferred" to withdraw. For others, the story is a study in the application of passive resistance, one a Gandhi might have read for aid and comfort. More recently attention has shifted from Bartleby to the lawyer who narrates Bartleby's tale and, in the process, attempts to understand him. I am convinced that looking an enigmatic figure like Bartleby in the eye is something akin to staring into a blank wall. And whatever else critics might be, they are not Supermen. One must come at a Bartleby from a safely oblique angle—by focusing on that "eminently *safe* man," the lawyer-narrator, whose sensibilities are crucial to an understanding of Melville's story.

As epigraph for that impressionistic study in human guilt, *Lord Jim,* Joseph Conrad chose the following maxim from Novalis: "It is certain my conviction gains infinitely, the moment another soul will believe in it." Granted, willing believers are never found in large supply, *Lord Jim* is an account of the complications that arise when one heart opens to another. Initially, it is Jim who needs a sympathetic Marlow; later, it is Marlow who is haunted by Jim's memory, as he tries to convince an "audience" (and himself?) about the meaning of such a life. The novel's "title" may refer to Jim, but the *novel* itself is Marlow's. For the ambivalent Marlow, to become Jim's secret-sharer is as dangerous and slippery an enterprise as it ultimately is a humanizing one. Thus, Conrad tests out the complexities which lurk just beneath our clearly defined notions about right and wrong, as well as the isolation which results from even the best attempts at empathy. Melville's **"Bartleby the Scrivener,"** on the other hand, is less concerned with the possibilities of *opening* oneself to another "conviction" than it is in demonstrating the barriers which impede the process. Significantly enough, Melville's sub-title is "A Story of Wall Street." Unlike Marlow, Melville's narrator discovers that language only makes the haunting Bartleby more perplexing and less definable. "Walls" are the central motif of Melville's story, extending from the Wall Street locale suggested by the sub-title, through a maze of physical walls which separate one man from another and, finally, to those walls of language which make human understanding impossible.

According to the late John Jacob Astor, the lawyer-narrator is a man whose first grand point is "prudence" and his second, "method." Such commendations mean much, especially to one who loves repeating Astor's name because "it hath a rounded and orbicular sound to it, and rings like bullion." The symmetry here—circular, rounded images, as if an emblem of completeness itself—suggests a man with a taste for the classics, exactly the sort of person who would keep a bust of Cicero on his shelf. To be sure, ironies always lurk around the dark corners of such a walled-in, safe world. By *safe,* what the narrator really means is unthreatened, secure, pompously smug in his assurance that God is in His heaven, Cicero is on his shelf, and all is right on Wall Street.

"Walls" are the central motif of Melville's story, extending from the Wall Street locale suggested by the sub-title, through a maze of physical walls which separate one man from another and, finally, to those walls of language which make human understanding impossible.

— *Sanford Pinsker*

In short, the lawyer is a man out to control a tiny universe with an inflated and self-serving rhetoric. Melville's tone, on the other hand, makes it clear that the lawyer is no exception to the rule which operates daily in, say, angry letters-to-the-editor: given enough space, most people betray themselves in print. For example, the lawyer-narrator proudly claims that he seldom loses his temper. And yet Melville juxtaposes this quietism with a revealing burst of indignation:

> . . . but I must be permitted to be rash here and declare that I consider the sudden and violent abrogation of the office of Master of Chancery, by the new Constitution, as a ———— premature act; inasmuch as I had counted upon a life-lease of the profits, whereas I only received those of a few short years. But this is by the way.

Whatever else the deleted expletive and unbridled passion might signify, it is hardly "by the way." The lawyer's sensibility is revealed by the widening distances between rhetoric and existential reality. In this sense descriptions given to Turkey and Nippers are necessary pre-conditions of a world in which Bartleby will become an unsettling intruder.

Turkey is characterized as:

> . . . a short, pursy Englishman of about my age, that is, somewhere not far from sixty. In the morning, one might say, his face was of a fine florid hue, but after twelve o'clock meridian—his dinner hour—it blazed like a grate full of Christmas coals; and continued blazing—but, as it were, with a gradual wane—till 6 o'clock P.M. or thereabouts, after which I saw no more the proprietor of the face, which gaining its meridian with the sun, seemed to set with it, to rise, culminate, and decline the following day, with the like regularity and undiminished glory.

The result may be an eccentric, volatile personality, but one with clock-like regularity: during the morning hours he is "the quickest, steadiest creature, too, accomplishing a great deal of work in a style not easy to be matched," while, in the afternoon, he is "incautious in dipping his pen into his inkstand." Blots, a noisy chair, spilled sand boxes, split pens and a generally "indecorous manner" follow lunch like the night the day. An older notion of psychology might write Turkey down as a Humour character, most probably phlegmatic. To modern ears the lawyer's description sounds like a textbook definition for the manic-depressive—albeit, one regularized until he emerges as tolerable.

This is especially true if one sees Turkey and Nippers as complementary units in a scenario of absurdity. Nippers is a neurotic, one who brings his anal temperament to the scrivener's table; as compulsion would have it, he "could never get this table to suit him":

> He put chips under it, blocks of various sorts, bits of pasteboard, and at last went so far as to attempt an exquisite adjustment by final pieces of folded blotting-paper. But no invention would answer. If, for the sake of easing his back, he brought the table lid at a sharp angle well up toward his chin, and wrote there like a man using

the steep roof of a Dutch house for his desk—then he declared that it stopped the circulation in his arms. If now he lowered the table to his waistbands and stooped over it in writing, then there was a sore aching in his back. In short, Nippers knew not what he wanted.

To the beleaguered lawyer, there is a "logical" explanation and/or convenient rationale for the apparent craziness which surrounds him. Turkey claims that "we are *both* getting old" and the remark strikes home. Prudence demands that he restrict the sort of work given to the afternoon (and, therefore, accident-prone) Turkey, but "humanity" requires that he keep him. With Nippers, "Ambition and indigestion" explain the neurotic quirks. In short, there are *words*—names, labels, etc. —which help to bring the erratic behavior within the bounds of what could be called "tolerable irritations." Besides,

> It was fortunate for me, that owing to its peculiar cause—indigestion—the irritability and subsequent nervousness of Nippers, were mainly observable in the morning, while in the afternoon he was comparatively mild. So that Turkey's paroxysms only coming on about twelve o'clock, I never had to do with their eccentricities at one time. Their fits relieved each other like guards. When Nippers's was on, Turkey's was off; and vice versa. This was a good natural arrangement under the circumstances.

In short, there is a fearful symmetry here which the lawyer can depend upon. Such is the stuff of which his "good natural arrangement" is made.

Bartleby calls the consensus reality into question by refusing to be rhetorically understood. The physical walls which separate employer and scrivener operate at one level of reality; the walls of language operate, more insidiously, at a deeper one. According to the lawyer, compromise is what makes life both safe and comfortably satisfying. His description of the office provides a model of the bureaucratic mind at its most functional:

> I should have stated before that ground glass folding-doors divided my premises into two parts, one of which was occupied by my scriveners, the other by myself. According to my humour I threw open these doors, or closed them. I resolved to assign Bartleby a corner by the folding-doors, but on my side of them, so as to have this quiet man within easy call, in case any trifling matter was to be done. I placed his desk close up to a small side-window in that part of the room, a window which originally had afforded a lateral view of certain grimy back-yards and bricks, but which, owing to subsequent erections, commanded at present no view at all, though it gave some light . . . Still further to a satisfactory arrangement, I procured a high green folding screen, which might entirely isolate Bartleby from my sight, though not remove him from my voice. And thus, in a manner, privacy and society were conjoined.

The "high green folding screen" suggests an ironic garden in much the same way that the lawyer's notion of a "privacy and society" conjoined is an ironic comment on the

facts of the situation. Removed from sight—the purpose, after all, of *walls*—Bartleby is, nonetheless, within easy range of verbal commands. His is a "green world," albeit one made from barriers of convenience. It is here that the nuances suggest ironic parallels to the biblical Garden. Like Adam, the lawyer gains dominion over the "others" of his world by *naming* them. Language is, then, a medium of control, of that which simultaneously creates a reality and imposes it. To be sure, if the green screen is an ironic touch, so too are the identifications between an Adamic use of language and that found in the postlapsarian world of Wall Street. Which is to say, the law office is emblematic of the human tragedy writ small; if the timid lawyer is no Cicero (on principle he "never addresses a jury," much less a Cataline), he is also no Faust, no Hamlet. In his insistence that language can pluck the heart out of human mysteries he is more akin to meddlers like Rosencranz and Guildenstern.

Bartleby's recurrent "I would prefer not to" is as effective a ploy as his "choice" of this particular lawyer-narrator is fortunate. What is essential, of course, is not so much the battle cry of passive resistance (*anybody* can learn to regurgitate "I would prefer no to") but a certain *style* on the part of the speaker and a certain *vulnerability* in the audience. The alternating current thus established completes the necessary relationship between victimizer and victim. In Melville's story, the special (albeit, acceptable) tyranny of the lawyer is obvious; he manipulates office personnel in much the same way he rearranges furniture, balancing a Turkey with a Nippers, the tedious work of copying against his own best advantage. If eccentricity of the Turkey/Nippers stripe betrays a human touch which can be controlled, Bartleby's very passivity calls the prevailing ground rules into question:

> Not a wrinkle of agitation rippled him. Had there been the least uneasiness, anger, impatience or impertinence in his manner; in other words, had there been anything ordinarily human about him, doubtless I should have violently dismissed him from the premises.

This is what I mean by the force of personal *style*. Bartleby is the enigmatic personality *par excellence,* the mystery always incarnate. His haunting presence brings the lawyer's half-ridden vulnerabilities into bold relief. In a recent psychoanalytic treatment of the story Morton Kaplan quotes this line—"But there was something about Bartleby that not only strangely disarmed me, but in a wonderful manner, touched and disconcerted me"; and then adds this commentary:

> We note that he still imagines violence, which he refers to now as a "dreadful passion," as his only alternative to inaction. There is, in his repeated association to violence, the suggestion that he is passive with Bartleby because, for him, *any* action implies getting violent. . . . Perhaps, we can begin to infer, the overridding motive of his life has been a struggle to contain violence latent within him, violence needing only the smallest conflict to set it off. [Morton Kaplan and Robert Kloss, *The Unspoken Motive,* 1973]

Later Kaplan provides a psychoanalysis of Bartleby himself, suggesting that he suffers from a psychosis "so complete that he breaks with reality." However, such confusions of a character's function and an analysand's problem reduce literature to mere formula, and criticism to Viennese jargon. This is especially true of Melville's disturbing story. That Bartleby may—or may not—be a psychotic is simply beside the point. In any event, the textual evidence is scanty, and it is Bartleby's impact on the lawyer which remains the crucial matter. As Kaplan would have it, the lawyer's vulnerability results from overcompensating for a latently violent personality. As a man of *law,* intimations of the "criminal hidden within" can indeed have unsettling consequences. *That* story, however, is Joseph Conrad's "The Secret Sharer," not, I would submit, Herman Melville's **"Bartleby the Scrivener."**

Rather it is the *silence* in Bartleby's posture, his Sphinx-like refusal to elaborate, which is so distressing. In the crucial scene when Bartleby first utters the choral refrain about "preferring not to," sound business practice, pragmatism and all the lawyer has lived by would demand that he simply chuck the insolent fellow out. Instead, he hesitates, betraying himself in a highly significant bit of rationalization: "But as it was, I should have as soon thought of turning my pale plaster-of-Paris bust of Cicero out of doors." Later it is Bartleby who will keep "his glance fixed upon my [i. e. the lawyer's] bust of Cicero, which, as I then sat, was directly behind me, some six inches above my head." The plaster-of-Paris bust not only represents that blankness associated with the story's motif of "walls," but the efficacy of language as well. As I have mentioned, rhetoric is the means by which understanding is achieved and necessary accommodations are made. The tight-lipped Bartleby signals that final breakdown of communication which is one form of the apocalypse. The lawyer's deepest fears are not those of latent violence made manifest, but fears of having to confront the isolation and loneliness which result when language itself disintegrates.

The remainder of the story, then, is a carefully paced account of the lawyer's reluctant initiation into these dark realities. It begins with an appeal to consensus reality, one the lawyer describes as "some reinforcement for his own faltering mind." Ironically enough, to ward off the absurdity which Bartleby represents, the lawyer confides in Turkey and Nippers:

> "Turkey," said I, "what do you think of this? [i.e. Bartleby's refusal to proof-read copy] Am I not right?"

> "With submission, sir," said Turkey, with his blandest tone, "I think that you are."

> "Nippers," said I, "what do *you* think of it?"

> "I think I should kick him out of the office."

Certainly their moods shift with the stylized grace of a Morris dance—on this occasion [i. e. morning] Turkey is as tranquil as Nippers is frenetic. Subsequent confrontations about the reluctant Bartleby reverse the poles. Only Ginger Nut, the office errand boy, has a view which does not change: "I think, sir, he's a little *luny.*"

Naturally the lawyer cannot accept such a simplistic

(however accurate) view of Bartleby, despite his need for even Ginger Nut's assurance. "*Luny*" is, after all, hardly a sophisticated and/or ingenious way of accounting for the pale scrivener's psychology. But to deduce a theory of vegetarian/ginger-nut psychodynamics—ah, that is a Bartleby (and a causation) of quite another stripe:

> He lives, then, on ginger-nuts, thought I; never eats a dinner, properly speaking; he must be a vegetarian then; but no; he never eats even vegetables, he eats nothing but ginger-nuts. My mind then ran on in reveries concerning the probable effects upon the human constitution of living entirely on ginger-nuts. Ginger-nuts are so called because they contain ginger as one of their peculiar constituents, and the final flavouring one. Now what was ginger? A hot spicy thing. Was Bartleby hot and spicy? Not at all. Ginger, then, had no effect upon Bartleby. Probably he preferred it should have none.

Such "logic" betrays a sensibility bent on reducing the enigmatic to the managable. Language can only function as a *cul de sac* where a phenomenon like Bartleby is concerned; once again, Melville's comic tone tells us more about the lawyer's limited sensibilities than it does about the object of his scrutiny. And, yet, the lawyer persists. No

Caricature drawing of Melville by David Levine. Reprinted with permission from The New York Review of Books. *Copyright (c) 1993 Nyrev, Inc.*

matter how much a Bartleby might "prefer not" being defined, Melville's narrator is obsessed with *definition*.

The Sophoclean ironies that result from such crossed purposes are foreshadowed early: "To befriend Bartleby; to humour him in his strange wilfulness, will cost me little or nothing, while I lay up in soul what will eventually prove a sweet morsel for my conscience." Befriending a Bartleby, is, of course, a dangerous and very costly business. As the innocent lawyer soon discovers, it requires more than merely carrying a skittish employee on the payroll or disrupting an already tenuous office routine. Rather, it is to risk daily exposure to a nihilism so complete that normal life—with its normal illusions and vanities—is no longer possible.

For example, one Sunday morning the lawyer happens to stop into his Wall Street office, only to discover that Bartleby has assumed squatter's rights. The desolate scene inspires the following gush of purple prose, suitably sprinkled with classical sound and fury:

> His poverty is great; but his solitude, how horrible! Think of it. Of a Sunday, Wall Street is deserted as Petra; and every night of every day is an emptiness . . . And here Bartleby makes his home; sole spectator of a solitude which he has seen all populous—a sort of innocent and transformed Marius brooding among the ruins of Carthage!

What the bombast leaves out, of course, is that this is a loneliness both Bartleby and the narrator share. After all, the narrator, too, spends his Sundays alone. In something like the unconscious motivation associated with primal scene fantasies, the lawyer "accidently" discovers his lonely alter-ego. The difference, however, is that the lawyer resists what such an initiation might teach. Language serves as a means to both falsify (sentimentalize?) the experience and reinforce the barriers between Bartleby and himself.

Granted, the seeds of curiosity have been sown. But while the narrator might escalate the *degree* of his concern, it remains depressingly similar in *kind*. By this I mean, the lawyer continues to believe that human behavior is rational, that, with the right information, he can understand Bartleby at last:

> "Will you tell me, Bartleby, where you were born?"
>
> "I would prefer not to."
>
> "Will you tell me *anything* about yourself?"
>
> "I would prefer not to."

Unlike the lawyer, Bartleby appreciates the power of silence. His rule—like that of the Delphic oracle—is a simple one: Never too much.

But if Bartleby lingers on as a noncooperative mystery, his impact—i. e., on the lawyer-narrator and the law firm—is all too clear. "Prefer," for example, gets picked up as a grim office joke:

> "*Prefer not,* eh?" gritted Nippers—"I'd *prefer* him, if I were you, sir," addressing me—"I'd *prefer* him; I'd give him his preferences, the stub-

born mule! What is it, sir, pray, that he prefers not to do now?"

> Bartleby moved not a limb.
>
> "Mr. Nippers," I said, "I'd prefer that you would withdraw for the present."

Worse, people *outside* the office begin talking—or, at least, that is what the obsessed lawyer imagines. In short, the consensus reality about Bartleby also has a "preference."

Appropriate action must be taken—Bartleby must be dismissed. But as the lawyer soon discovers: "The great point was, not whether I had assumed that he would quit me, but whether he would prefer so to do. He was more a man of preferences than assumptions." *Assumptions*, of course, depend upon a world where causes lead to predictable effects; you fire an employee—he then leaves your office. Bartleby's "preferences" destroy that fragile fabric by substituting a highly personal reality for the one others live within:

> "Will you, or will you not, quit me?" I now demanded in a sudden passion, advancing close to him.
>
> "I would prefer *not* to quit you," he replied, gently emphasizing the *not*.
>
> "What earthly right have you to stay here? Do you pay rent? Do you pay my taxes? Or is this property yours?"
>
> He answered nothing.

Even selected readings in predestination ("Edwards on the Will"; "Priestly on Necessity") are to no avail. In something like a direct proportion, the lawyer's obsession to *know* about Bartleby (i. e., to label his bizarre behavior) increases as the whispered rumors about this curious employee spread along Wall Street. The impossible situation reaches its crescendo when the lawyer decides that moving his office (rather than Bartleby) is the better part of valor.

One is hardly surprised when this frantic escape to a newer, larger office does not work. The psychological cords which bind the lawyer to Bartleby may have been woven from interlocking strands of attraction/repulsion, but they retain a potency mere distance cannot remove. The lawyer feels a responsibility nearly as insidious as their relationship has been. One side of the coin speaks to his self-styled humanism, his sense of charity and fair play, while the other is bent upon bringing Bartleby into that circle of human beings defined by pragmatism and the preservation of the status quo. The result is a last-ditch effort at saving the self-destructive Bartleby; its form is that of desperate catechism:

> "Now one of two things must take place. Either you must do something, or something must be done to you. Now what sort of business would you like to engage in? Would you like to reengage in copying for some one?"
>
> "I would prefer not to take a clerkship," he replied, as if to settle that little item at once.
>
> "How would a bartender's business suit you? There is no trying of the eyesight in that."

"I would not like it at all; though, as I said before, I am not particular."

His unwonted wordiness inspired me. I returned to the charge.

"Well then, would you like to travel through the country collecting bills for the merchants? That would improve your health."

"No, I would prefer to be doing something else."

"How then would going as a companion to Europe to entertain some young gentleman with your conversation, —how would that suit you?"

"Not at all. It does strike me that there is anything definite about that. I like to be stationary. But I am not particular . . ."

"Bartleby," said I, in the kindest tone I could assume under such exciting circumstances, "will you go home with me now—not to my office, but my dwelling—and remain there till we can conclude some convenient arrangement for you at our leisure Come, let us start now, right away."

I have quoted this negative catechism at some length because the rhythm of practical solution and nihilistic refusal is crucial to an understanding of the story. Some human complexities cannot be radically reduced, however well-intentioned the advice. At a certain point Melville's comic tone intrudes upon the confrontation. Bartleby, for example, insists too much about not being "particular," while the lawyer suggests, in all seriousness, that a Bartleby "entertain" some young gentleman with his "conversation."

Moreover, the contrapuntal rhythms cited above have a Modernist parallel in Ernest Hemingway's "The Killers." Like Melville's lawyer, Nick Adams is a believer in practical solutions to existential problems. Ole Andreson's recurrent "no" in the face of imminent death provides that stark initiation which seems every American protagonist's fate. Adams's Innocence is, of course, suggested by his highly emblematic name. The anonymous lawyer of Melville's tale puts the matter more obliquely:

> For the first time in my life a feeling of overpowering stinging melancholy seized me. Before I had never experienced aught but a not-unpleasing sadness. The bond of common humanity now drew me irresistibly to gloom. A fraternal melancholy! For both I and Bartleby were sons of Adam.

Confronted by Ole's utter resignation, Nick suggests alternatives which include "taking a powder," calling in the cops, fighting back and, finally, making a "deal." When his illusions are systematically destroyed—and Ole's death promises to become a brutal fact—Nick takes refuge in a final emotional summation: "It's too damned awful!"

Melville's lawyer, on the other hand, takes his solace in extravagant and falsifying rhetoric. Which is to say, if Bartleby steadfastly refuses to be reasonable in life, the lawyer can provide a missing rationale posthumously:

> . . . Bartleby had been a subordinate clerk in the Dead Letter Office in Washington, from which he had been suddenly removed by a change in administration. When I think over this rumour I cannot adequately express the emotions which seize me. Dead letters! does it not sound like dead men . . . ? For by the carload they are annually burned. Sometimes from out the folded paper the pale clerk takes a ring: —the finger it was meant for, perhaps, moulders in the grave; a bank-note sent in swiftest charity: —he whom it would relieve, nor eats nor hungers any more; pardon for those who died despairing; hope for those who died unhoping; good tidings for those who died stifled by unrelieved calamities. On errands of life, these letters speed to death.

Ah Bartleby! Ah humanity!

Like his ingenious theory about the effects of eating ginger-nuts, *rumors* about the Dead Letter Office provide the lawyer with a convenient platform on which to replace enigmatic silence with inflated language. But this time, of course, Bartleby cannot interfere, cannot "prefer" some other, more complicated, explanation of his life. Death may well be the final barrier which human understanding cannot cross. And yet, as Bartleby puts it at the Tombs, "I know where I am." It is the lawyer whose rhetoric falsifies not only the strange compulsions which drive a Bartleby, but those which continue to affect him as well. Melville's vision is split into two voices—one incorporated in the exclamatory phrase "Ah Bartleby! Ah humanity!" and the other which whispers about a darker humanity we cannot know in words.

R. Bruce Bickley, Jr.   (essay date 1975)

SOURCE: " 'Bartleby' as Paradigm," in *The Method of Melville's Short Fiction*, Duke University Press, 1975, pp. 26-44.

[Bickley is an American educator and critic with a special interest in the work of Herman Melville and Joel Chandler Harris. In the following excerpt, he provides an overview of "Bartleby, the Scrivener," noting the influence of Washington Irving and Nathaniel Hawthorne on the story's style, structure, and themes.]

Technique and biography cannot be kept entirely separate in examining **"Bartleby, the Scrivener. A Story of Wall-Street"** (*Putnam's*, Nov., Dec. 1853); Melville's shift to magazine-writing, however his earlier work may have prepared him for it, was largely precipitated by circumstances. *Moby-Dick* and *Pierre* had not done well, and Melville seemed to lack the psychic and aesthetic energy to write another novel. . . . In October [1852] he was invited to contribute to Putnam's new magazine, and the possibility of earning income by the page seemed especially attractive. Then, in November, he visited Hawthorne and [the tentative plans for a story entitled "Agatha" came up in discussion]. Additionally, and this fact has not been given special attention, Melville acquired two volumes of Irving's works in June, 1853, just before he began writing **"Bartleby."**

Of these several circumstances, the most significant for my study is that two accomplished writers of short fiction were present at the birth of Melville's first magazine story. . . . Melville had had several years of preparation for his new art form and would always bring his own literary predispositions to bear on it. Yet he was ever dependent upon his sources, too, from Ellis's *Polynesian Researches* to Shakespeare, in the novels; in writing his short stories he consulted Irving and Hawthorne, and with some frequency. Irving's presence is chiefly felt in the narrative technique of **"Bartleby"** and Hawthorne's in the story's metaphysical dimensions. Also, both writers appear to have contributed considerably to Melville's method of characterization. These influences came together in a rather complex way.

The story seems to have owed its initial form and narrative design to the example of Irving. Melville had consciously or unconsciously been under Irving's influence for several years (Evert Duyckinck once felt that Melville began his career by modeling his writing on Irving's), even though he had, for rhetorical purposes, undercut Irving's significance as a writer in his review of the *Mosses* and in a complimentary letter on Hawthorne. No New York man of letters could avoid breathing in a little of Irving with the atmosphere, and [Melville's characters] Tommo, Omoo, Redburn, and White-Jacket were all to some degree Crayonesque "sketchers" on tour. In addition, as William Hedges notes [in *Washington Irving: An American Study, 1802-1832,* 1965], Irving influenced *Mardi,* and there are strains of "gothic risibility" and Knickerbockerism in the "conceited" prose of Ishmael.

Melville acquired the two volumes of Irving's works in the summer of 1853, and it seems likely that he was rereading Irving during the next three years. The rhetorical design and narrative strategy of several of Melville's tales parallel Irving's, and Crayon and his storytelling acquaintances are, it would appear, models for at least five of Melville's short story protagonists. It seems that Irving's example reinforced Melville's own best tendencies in first-person narration, and the new magazinist would have had reason to look to the older writer for short story ideas and form. The basic similarities between Irving's and Melville's tales are in matters of narrative perspective. Essentially, the "bachelor" is the controlling consciousness in Irving, as he was in Melville's novels and would continue to be, with some interesting variations, in his tales. As storyteller within the framing devices of *Bracebridge Hall* and *Tales of a Traveller* (where, characteristically, a dinner-table acquaintance of Crayon's reads a manuscript or recounts an adventure first- or secondhand), or as Crayon himself in *The Sketch Book,* the bachelor-observer senses his estrangement from the world and lingers as a nonparticipant on the fringes of life. Prone to sentiment, both real and affected, and even to mild neurosis, Irving's sketchers often ironically reveal more about themselves than about the external reality they pretend to describe.

Melville, following up his instincts and earlier narrative strategies, modifies and expands the Crayonesque prototype in his magazine works. The first-person narrator acquires the rhetorical stature of an authentic protagonist who enters into the action of the sketch-become-tale rather than remaining outside, as observer or as teller of a story involving someone else. In other words, Melville deemphasizes Irving's often cumbersome framing devices and allows his narrators to tell their own stories. Compared to Irving's, his method is at once more dramatic and rhetorically demanding of the reader: it multiplies the possibilities for irony, making the narrator's moods and attitudes an emotional and intellectual grid through or around which the reader must, in Jamesian terms, "see."

These patterns are at work in **"Bartleby."** The lawyer-narrator is a Crayonesque sketcher who enjoys storytelling and could, if he pleased, "relate divers histories, at which good-natured gentlemen might smile, and sentimental souls might weep." Conservative, and himself a sentimentalist, the lawyer anticipates the narrative personae in several stories, **"I and My Chimney," "Jimmy Rose,"** and **"The Paradise of Bachelors."** He insists on telling his reader about Bartleby, who was the "strangest" scrivener he ever saw. However, in acknowledging at the outset the difficulty of the task he has set for himself, for "no materials exist, for a full and satisfactory biography of this man," the narrator hints at one of the central ironies of the story: he will never succeed in "characterizing" Bartleby. The scrivener's personality, inner drives, and sensibilities will remain relatively unknown quantities to the narrator. The lawyer's character sketch is, in effect, a series of attempts to align or harmonize his clerk with something he himself knows or can respond to, and these attempts continually fail. Although the lawyer never realizes it, the "chief character . . . to be presented" will not be Bartleby, but himself.

Aside from its general method, **"Bartleby"** may also owe its particular generic form to Irving. As an extended anecdote about an idiosyncratic law clerk, the story bears a resemblance to the eighteenth- and early nineteenth-century sketches of character published in the periodicals. More particularly, John Seelye suggests [in "The Contemporary 'Bartleby,'" *American Transcendental Quarterly* 7, Summer, 1970], Melville responded to Putnam's invitation to write magazine pieces by turning to the popular tradition of the "mysterious stranger" tale, which originated in America with Irving's "The Little Man in Black" (*Salmagundi*). Although Hawthorne and Poe also contributed to the genre prior to 1853 ("Wakefield," 1834, and "The Man of the Crowd," 1840), Seelye contends that the delineation of the various responses by villagers to Irving's silent stranger and the "tag-end" explanation of the Little Man's origins were patterns imitated in **"Bartleby."**

There are, however, even more substantial similarities between Melville's tale and another story which Seelye ascribes, in passing, to the genre: "The Adventure of the Mysterious Stranger" in *Tales of a Traveller.* Irving's tale is related to Crayon in the first person by an Englishman, who had met the subject of his story in Venice. He was a young Italian, physically similar to Bartleby in his pallor, emaciation, and haggardness of brow, who kept to himself yet who for an unknown reason needed to be near people. To the narrator the young man appears "tormented by some strange fancy or apprehension" and was afflicted with a "devouring melancholy." Inexplicably, the morose Italian chooses the narrator as a companion, as Bartleby does the lawyer, but remains uncommunicative about his troubles, commenting only that he needs sympathy but cannot talk with his befriender.

The Englishman tries to reason the Italian out of his melancholia, but to no avail: he "seemed content to carry his load of misery in silence, and only sought to carry it by my side. There was a mute beseeching manner about him, as if he craved companionship as a charitable boon." As the story progresses, the silent sufferer begins to have the same kind of effect upon Irving's indulgent narrator that the withdrawn scrivener would have upon Melville's "charitable" lawyer, yet neither man is capable of turning away the afflicted creature who seems to need his companionship. Observes Irving's narrator: "I felt this melancholy to be infectious. It stole over my spirits; interfered with all my gay pursuits, and gradually saddened my life; yet I could not prevail upon myself to shake off a being who seemed to hang upon me for support." Melville's lawyer responds similarly when he discovers that Bartleby had been sleeping in the office at night: "For the first time in my life a feeling of overpowering stinging melancholy seized me. . . . The bond of a common humanity now drew me irresistibly to gloom. A fraternal melancholy!"

Irving's mysterious stranger eventually disappears. Characteristic of Mr. Knickerbocker's reliance on the story-within-a-story, however, he leaves his benefactor a manuscript which (in the next tale of a traveler) explains his history: he had murdered an unprincipled rival suitor and was fleeing the authorities. For reasons that will be discussed below, Melville leaves Bartleby's story essentially untold, although he does throw an Irvingesque sop to the common reader in the form of a "sequel." Irving had helped Melville find a structure for his first magazine tale and had offered him a compelling narrative strategy to build upon. Melville saw that he could multiply the thematic and rhetorical possibilities of his tale by involving the reader psychologically in the narrator's repeated experiences with a "mysterious" stranger. As in Irving's tale, no single encounter of lawyer and clerk is sufficient to explain the enigmas of Bartleby's character, and if the narrator's vision remains incomplete, so, Melville implies, may the reader's.

While "The Adventure of the Mysterious Stranger" seems to have provided a pattern for Melville to follow, Bartleby is a more intense and suggestive character than Irving's romantically melancholic figure; there seem to be stronger influences from another quarter. Melville claims in *The Confidence-Man* that "original" characters are usually observable "in town," and there is considerable evidence to suggest that Melville turned to that skeptical and taciturn friend from nearby Lenox, with whom he had just shared the Agatha story, as he composed the portrait of Bartleby. If Melville's first short story is his most compelling tale, perhaps it is because when he wrote it he was haunted by the image of Nathaniel Hawthorne and by one of Hawthorne's most powerful themes, withdrawal and isolation.

As a nay-sayer, Bartleby is philosophically reminiscent of, and perhaps to some extent based upon, those protagonists in Hawthorne's gloomier short fiction whom critics have viewed as portraits of the artist, and in whose alien-

ation is symbolized Hawthorne's own skeptical retreat. Goodman Brown's capitulation to pessimism and despair over the human condition, Parson Hooper's incommunicative withdrawal behind his mask, and Wakefield's more impish perversity synthesize in Bartleby, another alienated hero. Philosophically, in **"Bartleby"** and, with varying emphases, in later stories as well, Melville seems to have confronted anew the implications of Hawthorne's perception of "blackness." In this first story, however, he defined the ultimate extension of a Hawthornean world-view: a self-willed death. Bartleby, unlike Agatha, finally capitulates to the suffering he has experienced and to his skepticism about the possibilities for human understanding and love.

In commenting upon *The House of the Seven Gables* in a letter to Hawthorne in April 1851, Melville creates an image of both the novel and its author. He writes that the book is like a "fine old chamber" in one corner of which there is "a dark little black-letter volume in golden clasps, entitled 'Hawthorne: A Problem.' " Bartleby, a symbol of that "certain tragic phase of humanity" that Melville saw embodied in Hawthorne and in his fiction as well, is also "A Problem" and a black-letter study. Hawthorne said "No! in thunder," and, Melville adds, "all men who say *yes*, lie"; to the same effect Bartleby states "I would prefer not to." The scrivener declines to adopt the distorted values and dehumanizing strictures of the outside world, and his soft-spoken refusal to join the ordinary course of life carries a strength of conviction equal to Hawthorne's emphatic "No!" Bartleby may speak for Hawthorne but he also speaks for mankind, and, true to his problematical nature, he whispers two different messages. Representing those who would "prefer not" to commit themselves to a meaningless way of life, he is a stoical study in what Melville terms in his story "passive resistance"; but through him Melville also warns humanity against a self-destructive surrender to a vision of blackness.

Melville may have begun his tale as a parable of his own encounters with Hawthorne and his writings, but he used with brilliant effect a sentimental "sketcher" of somewhat limited perception to broaden the psychological and symbolical dimensions of his story. For the unnamed narrator comes to represent any man who, forced at last to question the assumptions and values he has always lived by, hesitates to admit to himself and to his readers that he faces a crisis at all; who, pushed beyond the limits of his own understanding and humanity, rationalizes his failings.

The first of Melville's short fiction "bachelors," the lawyer begins his story with an Irvingesque "author's account of himself." This opening sketch serves two rhetorical functions. It reveals the lawyer to be something of a sentimentalist, interested in conveying to his reader what he believes will be poignant impressions of his own personal "involvement" in his strange scrivener's life. Secondly, and more important, the self-portrait discloses how inextricably bound up the lawyer is in the material world.

The ethic that informs the narrator's life style, and too often his judgment as well, is that of free-enterprise capitalism. However, the narrator is not an ambitious lawyer; a man of "peace," he is content to do a "snug" business among rich men's bonds and mortgages, in the "cool tranquillity" of his "snug retreat" on Wall Street. His hero, and former client, is the late John Jacob Astor, a name that, he admits with a flourish, "I love to repeat; for it hath a rounded and orbicular sound to it, and rings like unto bullion." Astor had once commended him for his "prudence" and "method," yet in bragging that his associates consider him "an eminently *safe* man," the lawyer unwittingly suggests that inside knowledge about even financially shady deals would be secure with him.

The narrator comes to represent any man who, forced at last to question the assumptions and values he has always lived by, hesitates to admit to himself and to his readers that he faces a crisis at all; who, pushed beyond the limits of his own understanding and humanity, rationalizes his failings.

— *R. Bruce Bickley, Jr.*

A telling sign of his prudent but always utilitarian approach to his world is the office routine itself. He is willing to indulge the idiosyncrasies of Turkey and Nippers so long as they are, at least during half of each working day, "useful" to him. Thus, while Bartleby continues with his copying, although he may "prefer not" to follow certain orders, his employer keeps him on as a "useful" servant (the narrator will employ the word again when he introduces Bartleby to the "useful" grub-man in the prison). When the scrivener gives up copying, however, and his uselessness begins to interfere with the "method" of the lawyer's office, Bartleby constitutes a threat.

The rhythmic pattern of events prior to Bartleby's inevitable dismissal makes up the story's essential form: from the introductory self-portrait to the page-long "sequel" concerning the scrivener's earlier work in the Dead Letter Office occur approximately a dozen confrontations between the employer and his clerk. Melville's structure is rhetorically quite effective. It enables him to exhibit several distinctive responses to the enigma of Bartleby, none of which succeeds in revealing his character. Thus the levels of available meaning are multiplied, and the reader is left free to identify with any, or none, of the lawyer's emotional and mental reactions to his scrivener. Melville would find this method useful later, in the encounters of narrators and "original" characters in **"The Fiddler," "The Lightning-Rod Man,"** and **"Benito Cereno,"** for example. Melville's rhetorical strategy dictates that no interpretation of Bartleby offered by the lawyer could ever be complete, for the scrivener is a phenomenon totally alien to the narrator's experience and sensibilities. Yet the story raises an even larger rhetorical question. The lawyer may have his limitations, but does not Melville also suggest that Bartleby is incapable of giving enough of his own self to deserve even that charity which his employer extends?

Where does the moral or ethical emphasis of the tale rest, finally? In the best Ishmaelian tradition, Melville offers no neat answers.

Among his dozen or so confrontations with the scrivener, six of the lawyer's encounters are crucial in terms of method and meaning. Melville seeks at the initial stage of employer-employee interaction to identify the reader with the lawyer's perspective, for purposes of immediacy and verisimilitude; quickly, however, Melville tests the reader-narrator relationship by skewing the lawyer's angle of perception.

Thus, at Bartleby's first preference not to perform some routine clerical tasks, the narrator is portrayed as baffled and stunned, as almost anyone would be. With the second round of Bartleby's preference-stating, however, a measurable amount of separation takes place between lawyer and reader. The lawyer decides, with a certain logic but with a recognizable degree of self-congratulation, that because Bartleby is "useful" to him he should befriend his clerk; in so doing he could "purchase a delicious self-approval" for his conscience. The lawyer's studied self-righteousness gives way to what he claims to be a disturbing if not a painful awareness of Bartleby's spiritual condition, in the third phase of the encounters. He is surprised to find one Sunday that Bartleby has been sleeping in the office at night, solitary and companionless; but how authentic or sincere is the narrator's recounting of his discovery?

> Immediately then the thought came sweeping across me, what miserable friendlessness and loneliness are here revealed! His poverty is great; but his solitude, how horrible! Think of it. Of a Sunday, Wall Street is deserted as Petra; and every night of every day it is an emptiness. This building, too, which of week-days hums with industry and life, at nightfall echoes with sheer vacancy, and all through Sunday is forlorn. And here Bartleby makes his home; sole spectator of a solitude which he has seen all populous—a sort of innocent and transformed Marius brooding among the ruins of Carthage!

The lawyer has a felicitous turn of phrase, but his effusiveness is over-elegant and melodramatic—more appropriate to a romantic sketcher of "fine sentiments," trying to appeal to his audience, than to a sensitive perceiver of human need.

"A fraternal melancholy!" exclaims the lawyer as he contemplates Bartleby's loneliness. "For both I and Bartleby were sons of Adam." Just as the reader is beginning to ask how much real communion there is in a fit of sympathetic melancholia, the narrator's mood passes. When he recalls forlorn Bartleby's "pallid haughtiness" and his habit of staring incommunicatively upon the dead brick wall outside his window, the lawyer feels "melancholy merge into fear" and "pity into repulsion." In attempting to account for this shift the protagonist says, defensively, "They err who would assert that invariably this is owing to the inherent selfishness of the human heart." After all, "it was his soul that suffered, and his soul I could not reach." Of course this is precisely the point; the lawyer seeks on the next morning to "reach" Bartleby's soul in a common-sense fashion—by asking him questions about himself—failing to understand that an uncommon Bartleby who prefers to say nothing about himself cannot be so easily plumbed.

In the fourth confrontation, the lawyer's rational analysis of his clerk's behavior and its effects reinforces what his emotional responses had told him. He realizes that both he and his other assistants have, unconsciously, got in the habit of using the word "prefer," and he knows now that he must surely dismiss this "demented man" who is affecting them all in a "mental way." The scrivener's decision to do no more copying provides the lawyer his excuse, and he gives Bartleby six days to leave.

Up to this point Melville has portrayed his enigmatic scrivener from a narrative perspective that has undergone several reorientations. Initially, the lawyer is simply perplexed by Bartleby's behavior, nothing more; then he looks at his clerk from the standpoint of self-righteousness, again as would a self-styled victim of melancholia, and yet again as a utilitarian rationalist. These four stances do not assist in revealing the "true" Bartleby to the lawyer, nor are they meant to; Bartleby is simply not going to make himself available for revelation.

In the fifth confrontation the scrivener undergoes metaphysical analysis, although the metaphysics is only rhetorical tomfoolery on Melville's part. From behind the persona of his narrator he toys with the reader for two full pages using a very large pun on the Doctrine of the Assumption, the Catholic belief that the Virgin Mary ascended into Heaven on August 15. Having given Bartleby severance pay, the lawyer assumes that he would now leave. "I *assumed* the ground that depart he must," recollects the lawyer, "and upon that assumption built all I had to say." But the narrator is "thunderstruck" six days later to find Bartleby still there. Characteristically, his response is melodramatic and exaggerated: ". . . I stood like the man who, pipe in mouth, was killed one cloudless afternoon long ago in Virginia, by summer lightning; at his own warm open window he was killed, and remained leaning out there upon the dreamy afternoon, till some one touched him, when he fell." Melville's punning on the Assumption grows explicit:

> What was to be done? or, if nothing could be done, was there anything further that I could *assume* in the matter? Yes, as before I had prospectively assumed that Bartleby would depart, so now I might retrospectively assume that departed he was. . . . I might enter my office in a great hurry, and pretending not to see Bartleby at all, walk straight against him as if he were air. . . . It was hardly possible that Bartleby could withstand such an application of the doctrine of assumptions. But upon second thoughts the success of the plan seemed rather dubious.

Dubious indeed, for Bartleby is Bartleby, not the risen Virgin Mary. Further along, Melville makes one last punning reference to the metaphysical question of Bartleby's power to transcend this mortal sphere. Still baffled by the clerk's continuing presence in the office, the lawyer demands: "What earthly right have you to stay here?"

Melville's pun on the Assumption is but one of several *jeux-de-mots* and witty asides in **"Bartleby."** The humorous dimensions of the story are an essential part of its surprising fullness and complexity of texture; the reader enjoys the Dickensian idiosyncrasies of Turkey and Nippers and laughs at the narrator for his sentimentality and propensity to over-dramatize his own plight, but the humor ceases when Bartleby's fate begins to close in on him.

The last important confrontation between lawyer and clerk raises the moral and theological questions that Melville was most concerned with in his story. Angry that the scrivener has achieved a "cadaverous triumph" over him, the lawyer is just barely able to contain what he now finds to be almost murderous thoughts about Bartleby. Luckily, he acts in accordance with his previously advertised virtue of prudence, and he recalls the charitable commandment "that ye love one another." Comforting himself during the next few days by reading "Edwards on the Will" and "Priestley on Necessity," he is nearly convinced that "Bartleby was billeted upon me for some mysterious purpose of an all-wise Providence, which it was not for a mere mortal like me to fathom." But the narrator's Christian charity and faith capitulate to human pride and a slightly paranoid imbalance. His professional acquaintances criticize him for retaining in his chambers an odd vagrant who does absolutely no work, and the lawyer's imagination—more neurotic than melodramatic now—projects a lurid scene:

> And as the idea came upon me of [Bartleby's] possibly turning out a long-lived man, and keep occupying my chambers, and denying my authority; and perplexing my visitors; and scandalizing my professional reputation; and casting a general gloom over the premises; keeping soul and body together to the last upon his savings (for doubtless he spent but half a dime a day), and in the end perhaps outlive me, and claim possession of my office by right of his perpetual occupancy: as all these dark anticipations crowded upon me more and more . . . a great change was wrought in me. I resolved to gather all my faculties together, and forever rid me of this intolerable incubus.

Yet his mood would shift again. The dismayed narrator is still essentially a "man of peace," incapable of physically ejecting Bartleby and hesitant to summon the police. Instead, he moves his entire office elsewhere, and, "strange to say—I tore myself from him whom I had so longed to be rid of."

The lawyer is baffled by his scrivener because he is conditioned by the method of his profession and his life. Although one faults the protagonist for his blindness, Bartleby might, after all, have affected anyone as he did the narrator. [In "Melville's Comedy of Faith," *ELH* 27, December, 1960, William Bysshe Stein] contends that the lawyer cannot "involve himself emotionally" in the isolation of Bartleby, because the effort would entail "too great a strain upon his capacity for love and pity." And so, perhaps, with the reader. However, the lawyer's post-separation guilt and uncertainty about his lack of meaningful involvement only reinforce our image of his ineffectuality. Able to put up with occasional troublesome quirks in his office workers so long as they perform their duties, the lawyer fails when the humane indulgences that Bartleby seemed to seek grow too taxing. When his former landlord sends word that he must do something about the man he abandoned, the frustrated lawyer literally denies his scrivener thrice—in effect betraying him into the hands of the authorities. His denials make him feel guilty, but his eleventh-hour efforts at the prison to provide for his clerk, his offers of lodging and a job and his paying for meals that Bartleby prefers not to eat, come too late. In his three most emphatic and resolute statements Bartleby tells his one-time employer, "I know you," "I want nothing to say to you," and "I know where I am."

As a "reward" for his puzzled readers and as a gesture by which he hopes to clear himself of any accusations of irresponsibility and uncharitableness towards Bartleby, the lawyer passes along "one little item of rumor" as a possible explanation of his scrivener's strange personality. Bartleby's experiences in the Washington Dead Letter Office had apparently convinced him that all life held was deprivation and despair—thus his pitiable forlornness.

Yet Melville would not so easily explain away the scrivener, nor so readily pardon the narrator. Surely there are more significant meanings latent in Bartleby's insistent use of the word "prefer" and in the walls he seems to identify with. During one of their encounters the narrator tested the extent of his scrivener's perversity by asking him to run an errand to the Post Office (probably the last place, if the rumor is correct, that Bartleby would ever want to go). The scrivener gives his standard reply, "I would prefer not to." "You *will* not?" demands the lawyer; "I *prefer* not," answers Bartleby (italics Melville's). The lawyer, characteristically, offers no meaningful interpretive commentary on this crucial distinction, but for the modern reader the sequence is an intriguing prefiguration of the existential dilemma. In **"Bartleby"** Melville portrays not only an obsessive Hawthornean vision of blackness, but also an image of one man's confrontation with what he feels to be the meaninglessness of the universe. Ahab had spoken of an "unreasoning force," inexorably in control of all nature, that denies man both identity and power. There is no possibility of meaningful action, Bartleby seems to say, and it is certain that man cannot successfully will anything. Perhaps the only tenable stance is merely to *prefer* to do something; this gives one at least a temporary hedge against fate, and somehow it is not quite so painful if one's "preferences" are denied. Bartleby never says "I *will* not," and the lawyer, habitually an avoider of conflicts and a postponer of decisions until his "leisure," never pushes his clerk beyond his preferences. At one point in the story the lawyer explains how difficult it was for him to put up with all those "peculiarities, privileges, and unheard-of exemptions" of Bartleby's, failing to realize that the "exemptions" Bartleby enjoyed were not of the clerk's making, but of his own.

Melville suggests that all man can choose to do is to endure and to state his wishes, although there are always hazards in making an obsession out of preferring. For if the lawyer errs in judgment, so does Bartleby in preferring

to attach himself to one whom he, for some reason, has chosen to be his companion in his isolation ("I would prefer *not* to quit you," the scrivener tells his employer late in the story). Does Bartleby, the almost catatonic isolato who seems deathly afraid of even being brushed against by a fellow clerk, have the right to expect comfort or companionship from a person with whom he is incapable of sharing even the smallest modicum of his inner self? Unlike Ahab, Bartleby has neither strength nor will to aggress through the walls which hedge him in, a prisoner, and the lawyer's desertion is for the clerk like the final turning of the key in the lock. Indeed, Bartleby seems voluntarily to have made himself a prisoner of the walls he sees, perhaps because they, alone, do not make any demands on his privacy.

The scrivener, suggests Henry Murray, used silence and immobility to defend his integrity, but in the process he became alienated and a misanthrope ["Bartleby and I," in *Melville Annual 1965, a Symposium: "Bartleby the Scrivener,"* edited by Howard P. Vincent, 1966]. Thus, he dies alone and in a manner appropriate to his fundamental preference to remain separate: he prefers, finally, not to eat and dies with his head resting on the cold prison stones, rather than on humanity's pillow.

As Melville experimented with aesthetic distance and narrative form in his magazine fiction he returned frequently to two basic narrative personae: that of the genial, sentimental anecdotist who enjoys painting sketches of character or social settings, or writing familiar essays about himself, and that of the ironic protagonist who, in a sense, becomes the victim of his own story. Works in the first category include **"Jimmy Rose"** and **"I and My Chimney,"** while **"The Fiddler"** and **"Cock-A-Doodle-Doo!"** feature the second type of narrative pose. **"Bartleby"** is paradigmatically significant because it illustrates both basic narrative postures: the lawyer is genial and an engaging anecdotist, but he is at the same time an ironic figure of incomplete perceptions. None of Melville's stories is free of rhetorical irony, and hence, as **"Bartleby"** would suggest, one should not force distinctions between "sentimental" narrative and "ironic" narrative too far.

Thomas P. Joswick (essay date 1978)

SOURCE: "The 'Incurable Disorder' in 'Bartleby the Scrivener'," in *Delta,* England, Vol. 6, May, 1978, pp. 79-93.

[*In the essay below, Joswick compares thematic aspects of "Bartleby the Scrivener" to those of Melville's controversial novel* Pierre.]

"Pray leave me; who was ever cured by talk?"

Herman Melville, *The Confidence-Man*

"Bartleby the Scrivener: A Story of Wall Street" was Melville's first publication following what the majority of contemporary reviewers considered his most disastrous and blasphemous novel. Because of that scathing critical condemnation of *Pierre,* which included suggestions of insanity about its author, many twentieth-century readers have tried to resolve the enigmas of **"Bartleby"** by finding in this remarkable story a bitter commentary on Melville's fate as a writer in America. Such readings usually seek to identify Melville's career, or his estimate of it, with Bartleby's, arguing that Bartleby's occupation, and the rewards he received from it, are a sarcastic parody of the literary trials and compensations Melville endured and received for *Pierre.* While these interpretations do acknowledge that **"Bartleby"** is a response to *Pierre,* even a response directed toward a literary situation, their biographical bias nonetheless tends to obscure what interesting correlations the two share as adjacent works in Melville's canon. The connections between *Pierre* and **"Bartleby"** are more compelling than any biographical reading can indicate, for there is a certain, if yet inadequately defined, thematic and temporal development in Melville's fiction, one that Melville himself frequently indicated in his letters. He suggested at one time, for example, that his writing was like the continuous unfolding of a plant toward a blighted center, and we might do well to follow that analogy and read **"Bartleby"** as a sort of fruitless blossoming in Melville's fiction—not a fulfillment or a replenishing repetition of the promising seed, but a peeling away to expose a disease at the center. If in *Pierre* Melville strikes—in the words of one reviewer—"with an impious [. . .] hand at the very foundations of society," he continues that unmasking of origins in **"Bartleby,"** revealing through the unassuming prose of the narrator the inherent disorder at the center of man's social, as well as literary, purpose.

The images of disease to situate **"Bartleby"** in Melville's canon are particularly apt, for the story itself centers on what is assumed to be Bartleby's "innate and incurable disorder." Moreover, the plot unfolds around the repeated failures of the narrator to accommodate that disorder in his own life, let alone to "cure" it by any of his rationalistic means. The lawyer has been comically tolerant of the stomach ailments and alcoholic intemperance of Nippers and Turkey, and for a short time, because he believes his new scrivener's "eccentricities are [also] involuntary," he is able to make use of the "incurably forlorn" Bartleby. Even in refusals, his new employee is deferential, and so the lawyer can pronounce him "a valuable acquisition." Yet because his initial assumption about Bartleby's "strange peculiarities" persist, the lawyer soon can no longer accommodate what he thinks must be Bartleby's "excessive and organic ill," and in a comic scene that I will discuss at the end of this paper, he begins to fear that Bartleby's "demented mind" is contagious—a sure sign of which is the lawyer's own "involuntary" use of the word "prefer." Never questioning then his assumptions about Bartleby's "disorder," nor ever quite understanding the severe limitations of his own attempts to manage or "cure" it, the narrator, at the end of the story, sadly repeats to the grub-man at the Tombs his belief that Bartleby is "a little deranged."

And so he might be. But any speculation along that line, interesting as it might become, would remain in collusion with the protective assumptions of the narrator, the most important of which, and the least recognized, concerns the nature of literature itself. The intentions indicated at the beginning and the sentimental sigh exhaled at the end make it clear that the story is the lawyer's final attempt,

after his economic and Christian "self-interest" have failed, to make of Bartleby something "ordinarily human." In other words, the story anticipates an audience that will share an assumption about the curative power of literature, that by its ordering and faithful truthtelling, literary language might shield us from the disorder that threatens our certainties of self and society. And so it does, at least on the one level of reading—more penetrating than the narrator's own understanding of the case—that would accept Bartleby's presumed madness to be the extremity by which we measure our own humanity. According to this reading, Bartleby might be a kind of diminished and wasted Ahab, a tragic and diseased measure of humanity, from whom the reader is protected, however, by a fictive world where the sharks glide by "as if with padlocks on their mouths." Yet the comparison to *Moby-Dick* is inadequate, for in both *Pierre* and **"Bartleby"** the shielding power of fiction is less certain than it is for Ishmael. In fact, in *Pierre* the literary act becomes as contaminated as the hero's, the narrator forced to become a "canting showman," a tortured member in the "guild of self-imposters." And while **"Bartleby"** lacks the painful self-consciousness of *Pierre,* it too is another case in which the literary act not only fails to cure or cover the disorder that grounds human experience, but in itself it reenacts the disorder or disease we would pretend to be shielded from.

Because he has little of the self-reflection of *Pierre*'s narrator, the lawyer himself does not glimpse the complicity his writing creates in the disorder his story-telling is intended to cure, just as he is morally blind to the complicity his Christian virtues of "self-interest" have in his three times denial of a Christ-like Bartleby. As a writer his method is simply to render faithfully what his own "astonished eyes saw of Bartleby," and to describe the environment of walls that eventually paralyze Bartleby, without ever, in either case, accurately interpreting what is there. Marred as it is by his obtuseness, the lawyer's declared method of truthtelling nonetheless shares the intentions of many Melvillean narrators, that "an anxious desire to speak the unvarnished truth will gain for him the confidence of his readers." More happens, however, to those apparently honest intentions in **"Bartleby"** than in Melville's first fiction, where those intentions were initially examined. As I have tried to show elsewhere, the narrator's desires in *Typee* are subverted by the hero's undermining the foundations of self and society during his quest for origins in the exotic South Sea islands. In **"Bartleby,"** the writer's intentions to gain the confidence of his readers lead to a literary bond that joins writer and reader in the very disorder that establishes human experience.

The connection between literature and origins may be found in the first paragraph of the story. After a slightly self-congratulatory note on the originality of his story, the lawyer introduces the subject of his tale by lamenting two significant losses. While of other scriveners he might write the complete life, no materials exist for a "full and satisfactory biography" of Bartleby. "It is," the lawyer says, "an irreparable loss to literature." That loss is explained by a prior one—a loss of origins. "Bartleby was one of those beings of whom nothing is ascertainable, except from the original sources, and, in his case, those are very small." Indeed, all we know from the "original sources" is Bartleby's own enigmatic preference not to. The initial situation of the story, consequently, is such that lacking certain knowledge of origin, or finding only a deferential refusal and negation of origin, the lawyer cannot provide a totalizing history, one that assures us of origin and purpose, for the simulacrum of such a history—the literary biography—has been pre-empted. In other words, the "irreparable loss to literature" that the lawyer laments implies the loss of a teleological form to literature—a loss so poorly supplemented in this story by the sequel with which it ends. Instead of satisfactorily completing the lawyer's history, the sequel only renews our questions about those "original sources" that might authenticate a providential or purposeful design for our tragically wayward humanity.

Different though it is from Melville's earlier fiction, the lawyer's literary situation is not new, for by virtue of the losses I have mentioned, he shares a writer's dilemma with Pierre and *Pierre*'s narrator. One example must be sufficient for my argument here. After his first interview with Isabel, Pierre's sense of his own history is challenged enough that he comes to reject "all the speculative lies" that gave form to those novels which he had initially imitated to create a "providential" heritage and destiny. "Like all youths, Pierre had conned his novel-lessons; [. . .] but their false, inverted attempts at systematizing eternally unsystemizable elements; their audacious, intermeddling impotency, in trying to unravel, and spread out, and classify, the more thin than gossamer threads which make up the complex web of life; these things over Pierre had no power now." The loss to literature of an imitated teleology derives for Pierre from a loss of an ascertainable origin, and that double loss makes his own history irredeemably confused. More importantly for my purpose, however, the double loss also engenders a new form for literature:

> He saw that human life doth truly come from that, which all men are agreed to call by the name of *God*; and that it partakes of the unravelable inscrutableness of God. By infallible presentiment he saw, that not always doth life's beginning gloom conclude in gladness; [. . .] that while countless tribes of common novels laboriously spin vails of mystery, only to complacently clear them up at last; . . . yet the profounder emanations of the human mind, intended to illustrate all that can be humanly known of human life; these never unravel their own intricacies, and have no proper endings; but in imperfect, unanticipated, and disappointing sequels (as mutilated stumps), hurry to abrupt intermergings with the eternal tides of time and fate.

Though the lawyer's mind is by no means profound, his story is a fitting example of the literature Pierre describes: formally considered, its "disappointing sequel" is no "proper ending"; philosophically considered, the inability of the literary form to systematize the disorder of "eternally unsystemizable elements" derives from a loss of origin.

The lawyer's situation appears different from Pierre's, to

be certain, for in the story the "inscrutableness" of origin concerns only Bartleby directly, not God. Yet by his contradiction of social and epistemological forms, the "motionless" scrivener casts into doubt as well the "all-wise Providence" whose natural or transcendent causation might explain a "predestinated purpose" of history. The lawyer's appeal to Jonathan Edwards and Joseph Priestly for their interpretations of divine agency is essentially no different than his appeal to other explanations about Bartleby. In all cases, appearances and assumptions, which also provide the rationale for the narrative itself, are hypostatized into "doctrines," and in all cases, Bartleby's preference not to dismisses belief in those "doctrines," not so much by pointing to a fuller truth underlying the surface, as by indicating an irrational disorder within the seeming certainties of the orderly human institutions. "Do you not see the reason for yourself ?" Bartleby at one time challenges, for the explanation of his preference not to lies in what is apparent, not in what is mysterious. Bartleby's preference, in other words, does not indicate the impulse of a Dionysian will rejecting the apparent orders of life for a hidden, albeit negative, Truth underlying phenomena; what his preference does indicate is the disorder present in all the structures, literature included, by which man defines himself and his world.

Much of the ironic humor of the story depends on recognizing that disorder, especially at those times when the lawyer tries to define Bartleby by the institutional forms he is accustomed to. What he discovers is that Bartleby cannot be so defined, for he defies the logic of those forms. The lawyer tries, for example, to classify Bartleby by a legal logic, accounting Bartleby by all appearances to be a vagrant. But what kind of vagrant or wanderer is he, the lawyer asks himself, "who refuses to budge? It is because he will *not* be a vagrant, then, that you seek to count him *as* a vagrant. That is too absurd." And yet it is precisely on the charge of vagrancy, despite the absurdity of the legal and etymological definitions of the word applied to him, that Bartleby is imprisoned in the Tombs. It is important to remember, however, that the legal definition of Bartleby is only one of many contradictions or absurdities by which he is characterized, defined, and even figuratively imprisoned at times throughout the story. The lawyer is aware, for example, that Bartleby contradicts his expectations of physical responses, for Bartleby eats only "hot, spicy" ginger-nuts, but is himself neither hot nor spicy. Yet with unintentional irony, the lawyer also imagines that Bartleby initially "gorges himself on [his] documents," only, of course, to die of starvation at the end. The lawyer is also aware of Bartleby's reticence, yet compares him to Cicero, and later even suggests he become a traveling companion "to entertain some young gentleman with [his] conversation." In another interesting play of contraries, the lawyer frequently declares that he wishes Bartleby close to him only so he can feel more private. Yet when the lawyer identifies psychologically with his scrivener, he finds that Bartleby confuses the certainties of emotional responses, for he arouses pity and a sense of fraternal melancholy in the lawyer, only to have "melancholy merge into fear, that pity into repulsion." And finally and most significantly, the lawyer's suggestion of a religious affirmation of Bartleby at the end of the story is presented by a contradiction parallel to all the others in the story: dead, Bartleby now "lives without dining."

That final contradiction is essentially no different than others in the story, and it would be a mistake to radicalize it as the source and explanation, appealing to the Truth of a senseless organic unity might keep the form of a religious paradox, invert its content, and say: Bartleby, by a kind of negative mysticism, sees the hidden Truth by which this world is condemned to superficialities and lies; the Truth is mysterious and negative, while man's world is fashioned by appearances and ungrounded optimism. Such a solution, however, implies a metaphysics that proves inadequate for the story, if only because Melville had already examined and rejected a similar metaphysics in *Pierre.* In the novel, Isabel initially proposes such an explanation, appealing to the Truth of a senseless organic unity beneath the world's "superinduced superficies." Isabel prefers the "far sweeter mysteries" of that hidden reality over any "surmises" or "assumptions" about reality, because "though the mystery be unfathomable," she says, "it is still the unfathomableness of fullness; but the surmise, that is but shallow and unmeaning emptiness." Her metaphysical dichotomies of mystery/surmise, fullness/emptiness, organic/artificial, and substance/shadow parallel those that appear later in Plinlimmon's pamphlet, which argues that the world's self-interested ethics derive from a contradictorily coherent metaphysics—a "meridianal correspondence" between a true world and "an artificial world like ours." "Greenwich wisdom," Plinlimmon's ethical argument runs, may appear folly "in this remote Chinese world of ours," yet "it follows not from this, that God's truth is one thing and man's truth another; but [. . .] by their very contradiction they are made to correspond." In both cases there is an appealing metaphysical consolation—that our true life flows unimpaired beneath the artificial surface, or that the ethical and social contradictions of the human realm are defined and ultimately dissolved by the Truth of Providence. In both cases the artificial nature of human institutions rests on a fundamental and certain ground, either natural or transcendent, that is not contaminated by the artificial.

Isabel's and Plinlimmon's consolations of a grounding for human life are rejected by Pierre, however, and for him they become other layers of the illusions and artificiality to which man is condemned. On the one hand, Pierre discovers that Isabel's "mystery" lies in "her history itself," not in some essence hidden beneath the surface. In other words, the mystery exists as a particular structure or particular narrative. It does not exist beyond time, but within time; or, more precisely, the mystery exists as human time. On the other hand, once turned to the confusions of human time, Pierre comes to reject Plinlimmon's contradictorily coherent metaphysics by concluding that in time self is "a nothing" compelled to enter wholly groundless and "fictitious alliances" with others. Why this compulsion toward disorder? "It is the law," Pierre says, "That a nothing should torment a nothing." Similar to Plinlimmon's metaphysics, this law is inscribed, as it were, in the very structure of man's temporal existence. But differing from Plinlimmon's, this law does not resolve an order out of the disorder. Moreover, this law is neither transcendent

nor natural; it is simply what is repeated in the artificial structures of human existence.

I do not believe that Melville retreats in **"Bartleby"** from *Pierre*'s rejection of the metaphysics of substance and origin. In the story as well as in the novel, such a metaphysical thinking is replaced by examining the structures of history and the law of disorder inscribed in those structures. In *Pierre,* however, those structures are more readily apparent, since Isabel is willing to narrate her personal history, and Pierre himself likens his life to a mythical narrative about patricide and incest—ultimate forms of the disorder that grounds human history. Bartleby, on the other hand, declines to inform the lawyer about anything in his past, particularly about his genealogical ties to the past. Moreover, he eventually severs as well all ties to the present by declining to do anything "ordinarily human," and as a consequence, he seems "absolutely alone in the universe. A bit of wreck in the mid-Atlantic." Yet it is precisely this tatters of personal history, the severed ties to time and humanity, that the lawyer tries to repair throughout his story and especially in the sequel. The rumor of Bartleby's service in the Dead Letter Office suggests to the lawyer that Bartleby's history, far from being isolated, is representative, for it includes all sorts of tales about the cruelties of chance and error that man is subject to. This speculation of the lawyer's certainly challenges any "doctrine of assumption" about the nature of a purposeful history, for it supposes that chance is, paradoxically, the law of man's temporality. And yet such a speculation seems another way to avoid Bartleby's challenge to see the reason for ourselves in what is before our eyes. The law of human history is more determined in the repetition of events than the elements of chance, mutability, or human error can account for. In fact, rather than admitting the freedom for novelty and redemption that the occasions of hazard, chance or free will would provide, Melvillean time tends to be static, like the figure of the maelstrom—a fixity created by the whirling of its elements. Or, in **"Bartleby,"** time is static like a wall or a pyramid, in which we see "the parts of the past as parts of the future reversed."

It is in fact with his eyes fixed on the wall that Bartleby challenges the lawyer to see the reason for himself, and it is because the lawyer fails to see the reason in the wall that he also fails to understand Bartleby. (In the specific occasion, the lawyer thinks that Bartleby is complaining of poor eyesight.) Because of the lawyer's lack of comprehension, however, as well as Bartleby's own silence, the reader too is often at a loss of what the significance of the wall might be. Any critical speculation about it is tentative, and must rely solely on textual connections within the story or within other of Melville's works. Two patterns in these textual connections have been frequently examined, but neither has led to a discussion about the historical significance of the wall. The first begins with the ready-made pun Melville had in writing about Wall Street, the economic/political capital of his society. This interpretation proceeds to show how the trade of stocks and bonds engenders a dehumanizing social structure, the physical emblems for which are the walls that paralyze and imprison Bartleby. A second interpretation bases itself on intertextual connections, and usually refers back to *Moby-Dick,* particularly to the passage in which Ahab compares the whale to a wall pushed up close to him. In this argument, Bartleby's wall becomes an emblem of the brute materiality of existence, behind which there is either a malicious design, an unreasoning power, or simply an emptiness. These two patterns do not exhaust the possibilities, however, and I wish to suggest two others that will lead to an examination of the disorder within human history.

The intra-textual evidence I will propose is certainly less interesting by itself than that which connects the wall to the debilitating economic structures of Wall Street. I wish simply to note, however, that within the story the wall has certain historical and mythical associations. First, the wall Bartleby stares at from the lawyer's office, while "black by age and everlasting shade," is a "subsequent erection," now blocking what at one time afforded "a lateral view of certain grimy backyards and bricks." These details make the wall seem at once ancient and modern, timeless and fashioned, static like a thing of nature and derivative like the things of man. Such a suggestion is reinforced later in the story when the lawyer is impressed by the "Egyptian character" of another wall that Bartleby stares at. The yard in the Tombs where Bartleby dies seems like "the heart of the eternal pyramids" to the narrator, and the character of its masonry weighs upon him with its gloom. This second association is more than an historical allusion, however, since the (empty) pyramid for Melville is the physical emblem of a primal myth. Charles Olson, in one of his many brilliant insights into Melville's fiction [*Call Me Ishmael: A Study of Melville,* 1947], argues that the pyramid is the archetypical wall, for it embodies both the sense of static time and the myth of man's vain assault on the heavens. Melvillean time, Olson says, "was not a line drawn straight ahead toward future, a logic of good and evil. Time returned on itself. It had density, as space had, and events were objects accumulated within it. [. . .] The acts of men as a group stood, put down in time, as a pyramid was, to be reexamined, reenacted." Moreover, as Olson continues, "whether it is the appropriation of space involved, or the implied defiance of time or the enceladic assault on the heavens, MASONRY is especially associated with MYTH in man."

The myths associated with masonry are all ones of disorder and conflict; they are narratives of the law that is inherent in human temporality. The myth of Enceladus, as it is interpreted and presented in *Pierre,* is certainly Melville's most extended and detailed narrative of the law in his later fiction. In the novel, the stone that occasions Pierre's visionary dream of Enceladus may be either "a demoniac freak of nature or some stern thing of antediluvian art," just as the walls in **"Bartleby"** seem neither wholly natural nor simply made. The law represented by the stone and the walls is likewise neither the order of nature nor the pattern that man's free and arbitrary will has fashioned. The law is like the pyramid for Melville: "Man seems to have had as little to do with it as Nature." Nonetheless, the law governs the structure of man's temporal existence by condemning him to repeat a beginning disorder, which, in turn, has derived from man's irreparable loss of origin and his demoniac desire to confront the absent origin. The Enceladus myth is perhaps the best ac-

count of the law, since in it the beginning disorder is represented by patricide, and man's desire for the lost origin is represented by the "accumulatively incestuous match" of creation itself. Yet for the purposes of analyzing **"Bartleby,"** we can avoid for once the complexities of *Pierre* by turning to Melville's letters for a briefer description of the myth associated with masonry.

In one of his letters to Evert Duyckinck, Melville humorously chides his friend for returning to New York City to live "among the bricks & cobblestone *boulders.*" While most of the passage about stones and mortar consists in Melville's hyperbolic joking about the evils of city life, he does at one time turn semi-serious, and, as an indication of the constancy of his thinking about masonry, he says, "There is one thing certain, that, chemically speaking, mortar was the *precipitate* of the Fall; & with a brickbat, or cobblestone *boulder,* Cain killed Abel." Once again, masonry is defined by myth: mortar is what is left after an Edenic origin is forfeited, and bricks are the instrument of a beginning disorder, one that is repeated when Cain goes off to build the first city.

If I have been right to follow these mythical associations with walls in Melville's thinking, the question remains, how does the law of disorder, which establishes and condemns human history, function in **"Bartleby"**? One answer may be found in the drama of betrayal that gives form to the plot of the story. While Bartleby challenges all the lawyer's accustomed forms and world usages, the latter, with a logic similar to Plinlimmon's, often interprets his scrivener's contradictions as a radical grounding for his faith in those very forms and usages. With his typical mixture of Christian and economic doctrines, for example, the lawyer is able to make use of his contrary employee, concluding that "to humor him in his strange willfulness, will cost me little or nothing, while I lay up in my soul what will eventually prove a sweet morsel for my conscience." Later in the story, the lawyer once again finds that his actions toward Bartleby, despite Bartleby's obstinate preference not to abide by accustomed forms, confirm a doctrine that combines Christian charity with worldly prudence. "Aside from higher considerations," the lawyer rationalizes, "charity often operates as a vastly wise and prudent principle—a great safeguard to its possessor." And finally, after consulting Edwards and Priestly, the lawyer concludes that to furnish the indifferent Bartleby with office-room is "the predestinated purpose of [his] life." But if the lawyer decides that Bartleby is the ultimate test of his Christian and economic principles, his beliefs cannot stand the strain of their inherent contradictions, and he ends by betraying and denying what he has argued is the "predestinated purpose" (the origin and end) of his religious and social forms—a betrayal Bartleby acknowledges when in the Tombs he tells the lawyer, "I know you [. . .] and I want nothing to say to you." In short, by acting with Christian self-interest, the lawyer ends by repeating the beginning acts of human disorder, denying, like Cain, that he is his brother's keeper.

The lawyer's literary intention to tell the truth does not absolve his complicity in the drama of betrayal that I have briefly sketched; in fact, his story-telling is a different form of the betrayal or disorder that structures human history. As I have argued earlier, the lawyer's literary situation begins with the biographical form pre-empted for a want of "original sources." To employ Melville's chemical analogy, we might say that the story is the *precipitate* of the double loss of origin and teleological form. Despite these losses, however, the lawyer, prompted by some "evil impulse" or burning temptation, desires to confront the absence of origin and make of it in the story something "ordinarily human." It is indeed a demonic desire to preserve and validate the illusions upon which his religious and social forms rest. Bartleby is like "an intolerable incubus" to the lawyer, for his preference not to abide by accustomed forms challenges the lawyer's most essential notions of self, without which any action or purpose in the world is reduced to an empty masquerade. The lawyer's writing is based on the intention to preserve human subjectivity as an essentialist center, and for this reason he attempts various explanations of Bartleby's strange preference. He tries, for example, to attribute the preference to either an organic or a mental disorder, and when that fails, he would have Bartleby admit that his refusals are acts of a free and arbitrary will, a confession which Bartleby, of course, rejects. Bartleby's preference is neither naturally determined by explicable causes nor willfully imposed upon the world with a calculated design. It is instead a kind of zero degree of intentionality, a blankness to which the lawyer must give a "coloring" in order to protect his own vanity against the suggestion that self is a nothing, a transitory appearance in a repeated disorder.

One way that might shield the lawyer from the emptiness of self is to turn the "colorings" of self into a literal language or a socially useful language, but to be successful that strategy depends on forgetting or denying that the literal or social language of self is in fact a fictive gesture, a way of continually failing to supplement the absence of origin and purpose for human activity. This is the lawyer's narrative strategy with his readers, I believe, that would allow the language of self to become the reconstituted center protecting man's vanity of an essential self. But once tainted with Bartleby's blankness, the language of self is forever suspect or contaminated. The language becomes unhinged from its empirical referents or its social functions. Regarded from this view, the lawyer's fears that Bartleby's "demented mind" is contagious are partially well founded. It is not necessarily true that Bartleby is deranged; however, when the language he has disrupted from its empirical and social designations is once again appropriated for those uses, confusion and disorder result. In that comic scene when the lawyer and other scriveners begin to use the word "prefer," the lawyer becomes very much aware that the word is employed "involuntarily [. . .] upon all sorts of not exactly suitable occasions." The word no longer designates the choices of a free and essential self, nor does it function appropriately within the social code of human conduct. Inserted as it is in the minds and conversations of the characters, the word disrupts the lawyer's assumed continuities of self and society and points to their fragile instability. What the humorous scene implies is that neither self nor action is the center of language. The word "prefer," like the words "vagrant," "copier," and "forger," is an empty sign by itself, and may

be explained only by a play of contradictions that can never be resolved.

The lawyer's story-telling cannot bring a halt to the disorder Bartleby confronts him with, for his intention to tell the truth depends on forgetting the fictive and artificial nature of the truth to be told. The lawyer's pact with his readers is to confirm the certainties of self and society by declaring that the disorder within human existence is the property of an individual self. This declaration is the reverse of what Bartleby leads to, that self is the property of a repeated disorder. The cure of a "self-interested" literature fails because the language it must employ is already tinged with the emptiness and confusion it desires to deny. "As soon as you say *Me,* a *God,* a *Nature,*" Melville once wrote to Hawthorne, "so soon you jump off from your stool and hang from the beam. Yes, that word is the hangman." To speak or to write is to be already a part of the empty masquerade of western metaphysics that would assure us of origin, purpose, and end for our history. To prefer not to as Bartleby does, however, is to acknowledge the disorder directly, avoiding all the splendid indirections of the fictions that perpetuate the same disorder. Bartleby's preference not to abide by the fictive forms of human life stems not from an insight into a Truth hidden beneath them, but from a recognition of the "incurable disorder" and vanity that establishes them.

The true appeal and significance of "Bartleby":

We can only wonder at the smugness of people who spend their days ironing out every last jot and tittle in Melville's text but to whom his most despairing tales are merely satires directed against someone else. . . . I do not know who Bartleby was. I have always thought he was the stranger in the city, in an extreme condition of loneliness, and the story a fable of how we detach ourselves from others to gain a deeper liberty and then find ourselves so walled up by our own pride that we can no longer accept the love that is offered us. While there is "irony" in the story, it is directed not against Bartleby but against the good-hearted, mediocre, ineffectual narrator, Bartleby's employer, who admits, "I might give alms to his body; but his body did not pain him; it was his soul that suffered, and his soul I could not reach." **"Bartleby"** is a story of the ultimate difficulty human beings have in reaching each other, and I do not think Melville was writing about anyone, except as he drew (How could he help it? Where else would he have learned it?) on his own situation and his bitter understanding of himself. Surely a little less bookish source-hunting, a little more awareness of what attracts us to Melville, would make it impossible for us to be so "scientific" about his intentions, when they can still be found in the life around us.

Alfred Kazin, in The New Yorker, *February 12, 1949.*

Morris Beja   (essay date 1978)

SOURCE: "Bartleby & Schizophrenia," in *The Massachusetts Review,* Vol XIX, No. 3, Autumn, 1978, pp. 555-68.

> *History and Development of Symptoms.* The patient, a young apprentice in Chartered Accountancy, was admitted to hospital in January 1958, at the age of 23 years. . . . On leaving school at 17 he embarked on a career of his own choosing, that of chartered accountancy with a City firm. For the first five years his performance was beyond reproach. . . .
>
> . . . The initial change was a general slowing up and impairment in efficiency in carrying out all his usual activities, both at work in the office and at home. . . .
>
> . . . When setting out for work . . . he began to stop and stand still at street corners, aimlessly looking about for 5-10 min. A few weeks later, he stopped going to work altogether, and thereafter, for a period of one year, he remained at home and did not leave the house except on one occasion for a few hours only. . . .
>
> He preferred to stay up very late at nights. . . . In general he preferred to remain upright and would each day stand rigidly in the same spot for periods varying from 1 to 3 hours. . . .
>
> . . . Movement by the patient was associated with visual perceptual distortion of the environment which he described at various times as "a flatness," "a flat streak of colour," "a painting," "a wall". . . .
>
> . . . "I can do something about what I see. For example I could turn round and look at this blank wall. But I can't do anything about sounds. . . ." [James Chapman, et al., "Clinical Research in Schizophrenia—The Psychotherapeutic Approach," *British Journal of Medical Psychology* 32, 1959]

Although we are twice told what the patient described in this case history "preferred" to do, readers familiar with Herman Melville's **"Bartleby the Scrivener: A Story of Wall Street"** will probably be most struck by all that he would prefer not to. Yet while few readers would deny the similarities—some of them, indeed, almost uncanny— between Bartleby and the schizophrenic described above, many critics nevertheless resist any application of "clinical" terms to Bartleby. Sometimes they do so out of a general distaste for treating imaginative artifacts as "people." But even readers who do not recognize the legitimacy of such an absolute restriction will remember the admonition by the lawyer (who tells us all we know about Bartleby) that "no materials exist, for a full and satisfactory biography of this man." And they will realize, in any case, that too easy an application of clinical terms can be reductive; if Bartlebys are much more common in the world than we usually acknowledge, it is not merely because people with schizophrenic symptoms are so common. Yet if we refrain from the assumption that the victim of schizophrenia is Other, an awareness of psychological contexts should help rather than impair us. The mistake is to take an either/or

approach: either **"Bartleby"** is a psychological study, or it is a socio-economic one, or a metaphysical one, or an existential one, or an autobiographical one, and so on.

A clinical analysis of Bartleby would probably identify him as at least schizoid, probably schizophrenic. "Schizoid" refers to a non-psychotic personality disorder in which key traits are withdrawal, introversion, aloofness, difficulty in recognizing or relating to "reality," and an acute over-sensitivity coupled with an inability to express ordinary hostility or aggressive feelings. But we may feel that even the term schizoid does not do justice to the depths of Bartleby's disturbance. "I think, sir, he's a little *luny,*" says Ginger Nut with the brutality of innocence; his comment comes fairly early in the story; by the end it would probably seem to most people to err on the side of understatement.

We learn little about Bartleby's "case history"—though enough to feel that his parallels with the patient described in the passages quoted at the start of this essay are not gratuitous. If there is any doubt, let me indulge in a citation of another case study, that of "A. J.":

> After leaving school . . . the patient obtained many odd jobs. . . . He did not hold any one job longer than several weeks; neither was he regular in performing his duties in the several occupations. He finally became altogether unemployable and stayed home.
>
> His behavior became more seclusive and he gradually withdrew from community life. When people visited the house he would run out of the room and hide under the bed. He would sit with his head bowed most of the time. Sometimes he would refuse to dine with the rest of the family and would wait until they were through. . . . On some occasions he made rather strange remarks to his mother; e. g., "I am automatic". . . .
>
> A visiting social worker finally persuaded the mother to bring A. to the local mental hygiene clinic for an examination. It took some time to get him out of the worker's car and persuade him to enter the clinic building. He seated himself under the stairs near the waiting room, facing the wall. . . . [Albert I. Rabin, "Schizophrenia, Simple Form," in Arthur Burton and Robert E. Harris, eds., *Case Histories in Clinical and Abnormal Psychology,* 1947]
>
> And so I found him there, standing all alone in the quietest of the yards, his face towards a high wall . . . (**"Bartleby"**).

If Bartleby is indeed psychotic, his disorder is probably the most common of all psychoses: schizophrenia. More specifically, I believe, he displays the symptoms and behavior patterns of "schizophrenia, catatonic type, withdrawn." [The critic adds in a footnote: "Although a number of commentators have applied the term 'schizophrenic' to Bartleby, few have been much more specific than that or have pursued the implications of the term in its clinical sense."] He is detached, withdrawn, immobile, excessively silent, yet given to remarks or associations that do not make sense to others, depressed, at least outwardly apathetic and refraining from all display of ordinary emotion, possibly autistic, and compulsively prone to repetitive acts or phrases ("I would prefer not to").

The trait that leads one to specify "catatonic type" is of course one of Bartleby's most notable characteristics: "his great stillness," his "long-continued motionlessness." Of Bartleby's first appearance the lawyer says: "In answer to my advertisement, a motionless young man one morning stood upon my office threshold, the door being open, for it was summer." Melville has carefully arranged this appearance so that we are not told that Bartleby walked into, or even entered, the lawyer's office: he is there, immobile. We see this feature develop, but even our first glimpse of him shows that he has been immobile at the best of times. On the first occasion of Bartleby's use of his enigmatic phrase, "without moving from his privacy, Bartleby, in singularly mild, firm voice, replied, 'I would prefer not to'," his mildness and immobility conveying the fact that what he is doing is not so much an act as a form of inaction. From that point on "he never went to dinner; indeed . . . he never went anywhere." Eventually the lawyer is forced to move, since Bartleby will not: as the scrivener says in a rare burst of volubility, "I like to be stationary." Finally, told that he must be taken to the Tombs, Bartleby "offered not the slightest obstacle, but, in his pale, unmoving way, silently acquiesced."

Such quotations can perhaps help to recall for the reader the emotional experience of reading **"Bartleby"**—an experience which reading such case histories as those I have cited (moving as they may be in themselves) cannot begin to match. We are concerned here with truly powerful work of art, and the psychological terms which seem "applicable" to Bartleby *in themselves* clarify very little. Indeed, when their purposes are distorted in order to provide us with handy labels they end by perverting our response to the story—and may even become aids in developing relatively painless ways of dealing with (that is, dismissing) Bartleby's painful case. Clearly, terms like "schizophrenia, catatonic type, withdrawn," however accurate, do little more than identify symptoms. To understand Bartleby in any real way—to "come to terms" with him in any but a superficial sense—we would have to go beyond them and attempt to get at what a therapist, again, would call the *etiology* of Bartleby's . . . "incurable disorder." That is not easy, of course: "it was his soul that suffered, and his soul I could not reach."

Recent psychological thought may help; specifically, I would like to explore Bartleby's plight in light of the work of R. D. Laing. Probably the most forceful aspect of Laing's approach has been his refusal to regard schizophrenics, for example, as "them," and the rest of us as "us." In our context, resisting the temptation to distinguish in any facile manner between the normal lawyer and the schizophrenic Bartleby reinforces the critical interpretations which see the two men as "doubles" of one another. But although those interpretations have sometimes been enlightening, they have strongly stressed what the scrivener and his behavior reveal to us about the lawyer, not what we learn about Bartleby. Of course, many critics (nowadays, perhaps most) do in fact claim that the story

is the lawyer's more than it is Bartleby's, and many others implicitly assume it. But that does not tie in with my own experience of Melville's story; for me and—as far as I have been able to tell from my conversations with friends, colleagues, and students—for most people, the center of interest remains Bartleby. And if that is so, then we want to know how he may have come to his present pass—and indeed where he is. We want to know what is "wrong" with him, and not just what his being the lawyer's double reveals about the lawyer.

In Laing's terms—indeed his most famous ones—both the lawyer and Bartleby are men with divided selves: cut off from others and from the world, but also self-divided, dissociated. Laing believes (and is of course far from alone in doing so) that "no one can begin to think, feel or act now except from the starting point of his or her own alienation" [*The Politics of Experience*, 1967]. In their different ways both Bartleby and the lawyer try to avoid the necessity to "begin to think, feel or act." Bartleby's mode of avoidance leads the world to call him "luny"; the lawyer's mode—he is, after all, an "eminently *safe* man"—leads the world to give him the title of Master in Chancery. Clearly, then, there are vast differences in the outward success of their two situations, but it is nevertheless essential to recognize some basic similarities in their modes of being-in-the-world. For "what we call 'normal' is a product of repression, denial, splitting, projection, introjection and other forms of destructive action on experience. . . . It is radically estranged from the structure of being."

Insofar as we may sense a fundamental accuracy in that view, we may come to look upon Bartleby's mode of adaptation as a pathetic attempt to make himself *truly* "sane." As Laing puts it, "the madness that we encounter in 'patients' is a gross travesty, a mockery, a grotesque caricature of what the natural healing of that estranged integration we call sanity might be." These remarks, though general, are surely suggestive in regard to Bartleby; more specific is a passage reminiscent of Plato's Allegory of the Cave. Laing is discussing the degree to which we—those of us who are "normal"—are "out of touch" with "the inner space and time of consciousness":

> The situation I am suggesting is precisely as though we all had almost total lack of any knowledge whatever of what we call the outer world. What would happen if some of us then started to see, hear, touch, smell, taste things? We would hardly be more confused than the person who first has vague intimations of, and then moves into, inner space and time. This is where the person labeled catatonic has often gone. He is not at all here: he is all there.

The essential point to recognize about Bartleby's behavior is that from his perspective it is not silly, or inappropriate, or "absurd," but relevant, rational, proper, and "preferable"—indeed inevitable. For him, what we call schizophrenia becomes a refuge—the awful result of a desperate attempt to avoid insanity. In other words, it is a *tactic.* According to Laing, *"without exception"* the "behavior that gets labeled schizophrenic is *a special strategy that a person invents in order to live in an unlivable situation.* " Of course, words like "tactic" and "strategy" should not be confused with the pejorative sense in which a cynic might use them to refer to malingering, gold-bricking patients who are seen as simply "trying to get attention": the devices of people like Bartleby are desperate ones, resorted to at great cost.

The fact that such behavior seems the only *rational* choice to people in Bartleby's sort of plight is too often unrecognized, even by professional therapists. Of the patient described at the start of this essay, the writers of the case study remark that "he had no insight," as shown by his persistence "in the view that his behaviour was justifiable and could be logically explained." To a layman, such terminology seems to lend support to Laing's attacks on the myopia of so many psychiatrists in their relationship to their patients. *Of course* this patient views his behavior as justifiable, and to be sure that behavior *could* "be logically explained"; in effect he asks, like Bartleby, "Do you not see the reason for yourself?" —a question we might expect from a therapist as much as from a patient. The patient described as having "no insight" is quoted: "Although you are one integral thing, there are certain things you can do without. For example an amputated leg. You can remove some part of you and you still remain yourself. My body is not quite separate but not quite integral either." Laing, in discussing the anxieties of dissociation from one's own body—the fears of the "unembodied self"—also recognizes that "there is a sense of course, in which such an attitude could be the height of wisdom": "when, for example, Socrates maintains that no harm can possibly be done to a good man. In this case, 'he' and his 'body' were dissociated" [*The Divided Self: An Existential Study in Sanity and Madness*, 1959].

At one point in Melville's story, the lawyer begs Bartleby to "begin to be a little reasonable": " 'At present I would prefer not to be a little reasonable,' was his mildly cadaverous reply." Such a remark makes him seem somehow simultaneously inside himself and outside himself, as if he were both a patient and a therapist calling attention to the patient's behavior. And, as always, Bartleby's words suggest that his behavior is a volitional response to his situation, consciously—even provocatively—made. To Bartleby, moreover, it is the preferable, appropriate response, whether "reasonable" or not. The lawyer of course cannot comprehend "such perverseness—such unreasonableness." When he demands of Bartleby, "What earthly right have you to stay here? Do you pay any rent? Do you pay my taxes? Or is this property yours?" the scrivener is silent: "He answered nothing." Inevitably—for the questions are irrelevant. From Bartleby's perspective, his right to remain is not earthly. It lies not in taxes and property, but in something other, or something internal: in mind, or in soul.

I hope my comments do not make it seem as if I am embracing some sort of sentimental or excessively "romantic" view of either Bartleby or schizophrenic patients. I am especially wary of this danger because I am not certain that it is one that Laing himself always avoids, in his desire to convey the ways in which what we call mental disease may be health, and the ways in which "breakdowns" may in fact be or become "breakthroughs." As Robert Coles

put it during a panel discussion on Laing, it is misleading to overlook the "terror . . . that some people on this earth feel": "I suspect there is a difference between us and the mad patients and I suspect that we don't know it quite as well as the mad patients do." Or as Bartleby replies to the lawyer's attempts to comfort him in the Tombs, "I know where I am." We may be tempted to romanticize Bartleby as an existential hero (certainly many critics are), a prophet better off in his sane madness than the rest of us in our mad sanity; but Bartleby knows where he is.

Still, if Bartleby's refrain of "I would prefer not to" is a sign of anguished mental illness, it is also his forceful psychic response to existence on this earth. As Laing (like of course other psychologists before him) has been wise enough to perceive, the enigmatic statements of patients "are psychotic, not because they may not be 'true' but because they are cryptic: they are often quite impossible to fathom without the patient decoding them for us." But Bartleby would prefer not to. So when we ask, with the perplexed lawyer, "what is the reason" for Bartleby's behavior, and the scrivener replies, as we have seen, "Do you not see the reason for yourself?" few of us will confidently respond that yes, to be sure we do, certainly.

Nevertheless, out of an urge to dive rather than be eminently safe, I would like to suggest that Bartleby is a victim of what Laing calls [in *Self and Others*, 1969] "ontological insecurity"—which in its "preliminary form" entails "partial loss of the synthetic unity of self, concurrently with partial loss of relatedness with the other," while in its "ultimate form" we have "the hypothetical end-state of *chaotic nonentity*, total loss of relatedness with self and other." We are always "between being and non-being," and faced with the fear of the latter—or, for that matter, of the former—we may resort to whatever measures of security we can find. Laing quotes a patient, not his own: "The only thing I was sure of was being a 'catatonic, paranoid and schizophrenic.' I had seen that written on my chart. That at least had substance and gave me an identity and personality" [*Divided Self*]. That remark is reminiscent of Dostoevsky's study in existential paranoia, the underground man: "Question: What is he? Answer: A sluggard; how very pleasant it would have been to hear that of oneself! It would mean that I was positively defined, it would mean that there was something to say about me." A patient closer to Bartleby, however, is one described in both *The Divided Self* and *Self and Others*—Peter, "a young man who was preoccupied with guilt *because* he occupied a place in the world, even in a physical sense":

> A peculiar aspect of his childhood was that his presence in the world was largely ignored. . . . He had been physically cared for in that he had been well fed and kept warm, and underwent no physical separation from his parents during his earlier years. Yet he had been consistently treated as though he did not 'really' exist. . . . He believed that to make his presence felt he would have to go to such extremes that no one would want to have anything to do with him, and thus he came to make the central enterprise of his life to be nobody. (*Self and Others*.)

Such a "solution" is no help at all—though perfectly reasonable from the perspectives of a Peter and a Bartleby, who seem to share an awareness of what is happening to (of what they are doing to) themselves. Laing quotes Tillich: "Neurosis is the way of avoiding non-being by avoiding being." Just as schizophrenia can be the result of a desperate attempt to avoid insanity, so Bartleby's retreat from being may result from an attempt to escape from non-being.

It seems to me that Bartleby is especially relevant to the last of Laing's "three forms of anxiety encountered by the ontologically insecure person: engulfment, implosion, petrification" [*Divided Self*]. *Petrification* entails a retreat into stasis or even catatonia which is one of those modes of self-preservation by which we are accomplices in our self-destruction. One may so dread being "petrified," "turning, or being turned, from a live person into a dead thing, into a stone," that the terror brings about what is feared. Laing tells of a young woman who dreamed that her parents had turned into stone, and who afterward herself fell "into a state which was remarkably similar to the physical petrification of her family that she had dreamt about"; and then he makes an important observation which strikes me as extremely suggestive in regard to Bartleby:

> It seems to be a general law that at some point those very dangers most dreaded can themselves be encompassed to forestall their actual occurrence. Thus, to forgo one's autonomy becomes the means of secretly safeguarding it; to play possum, to feign death, becomes a means of preserving one's aliveness. . . . To turn oneself into a stone becomes a way of not being turned into a stone by someone else.

When one is turned into a stone by someone who ignores one's identity or autonomy, or who regards one as a "thing," "an *it*," one is "depersonalized"—and, as Laing observes, "depersonalization is a technique that is universally used as a means of dealing with the other when he becomes too tiresome or disturbing."

Certainly it is easy enough to show that Bartleby is regarded and treated as an inorganic object, a thing, even by the fundamentally kind and impressively patient lawyer:

> Had there been the least uneasiness, anger, impatience or impertinence in his manner; in other words, had there been anything ordinarily human about him, doubtless I should have violently dismissed him from the premises. But as it was, I should have as soon thought of turning my pale plaster-of-paris bust of Cicero out of doors.

He also compares Bartleby to "a bit of Windsor soap," or "the last column of some ruined temple," and describes him as "a fixture in my chamber." Even at one of his most sympathetic moments, when he recognizes the "predestinated purpose" of his life to be that of providing Bartleby with "office-room," the lawyer expresses himself in similar imagery: "I shall persecute you no more; you are harmless and noiseless as any of these old chairs." Surely at least one of the sources for Bartleby's having become a "thing" is that he has been looked upon and treated as one.

But Laing provides still further hints indicating the sources behind Bartleby's petrification. We have already touched upon the paradoxical possibility that Bartleby has adopted petrification as a form of self-protection. Unfortunately, like so many psychological defenses, petrification is not merely futile but more destructive than what it is supposed to provide a defense against—notably, the world: "If the whole of the individual's being cannot be defended, the individual retracts his lines of defence until he withdraws within a central citadel. He is prepared to write off everything he is, except his 'self.' But the tragic paradox is that the more the self is defended in this way, the more it is destroyed."

Alternatively, the self may be protected or defended by means of its denial: this will be seen, however, as a repudiation of the "false self." The "false self" is the "personality" that one has in the outer world, which relates with that world and is observed by others, but which is divorced from one's "true," "inner," "unembodied" self. In Laing's observations on the development of "the false-self system" [in *Divided Self*], we may trace as well Bartleby's development as Melville's story proceeds: "The observable behaviour that is the expression of the false self is often perfectly normal. We see a model child, an ideal husband, an industrious clerk. This façade, however, usually becomes more and more stereotyped, and in the stereotype bizarre characteristics develop." Finally, "if the individual delegates all transactions between himself and the other to a system within his being which is not 'him,' then the world is experienced as unreal, and all that belongs to this system is felt to be false, futile, and meaningless." While the false-self system becomes more "extensive" and "autonomous," it also "becomes 'harassed' by compulsive behaviour fragments," and "all that belongs to it becomes more and more dead, unreal, false, mechanical." In the meantime, the inner self remains "transcendent, unembodied, and thus never to be grasped, pinpointed, trapped, possessed." Given such distinctions, when the false self is repudiated, there may be nothing left.

Moreover, dividing the self in such a way not only entails dissociation from and within oneself, but inevitably leads as well to dissociation from others. In repudiating the false self—the self after all that relates to others, however "falsely"—one repudiates all contact with other people. Bartleby obviously does that, yet even as he does so his dissociation from others takes a form that surely reveals an appeal to the lawyer for some mode of contact.

But the lawyer, however sincerely he tries, cannot seem sufficiently to help Bartleby, whose increasingly disconcerting behavior seems to be a way of getting back at him in some awful manner. Indeed, this attack apparently takes the form, as it often does in mental patients, of imitation of the person seen as the persecutor or aggressor. At the start of Melville's story we are introduced to the lawyer as "a man who, from his youth upwards, has been filled with a profound conviction that the easiest way of life is the best. Hence, though I belong to a profession proverbially energetic and nervous, even to turbulence, at times, yet nothing of that sort have I ever suffered to invade my peace." He tells us that he is "one of those unam-

New York Review of Books *sketch that accompanied an essay entitled "Bartleby and Manhattan." The illustration depicts an early twentieth-century urban dweller seemingly subdued by life in the city, which is represented by the background skyline.*

bitious lawyers who never address a jury," preferring "the cool tranquillity of a snug retreat." In other words, he is a person who would prefer not to do anything very active. Even his later attempts to get rid of Bartleby can hardly be taken seriously, and perhaps they more than anything else display his deep tendency toward inaction and passivity.

> There is a tendency for the false self to assume *more and more of the characteristics of the person upon whom its compliance is based.* . . .
>
> The *hatred of the impersonation* becomes evident when the impersonation begins to turn into a *caricature.*
>
> The impersonation of the other by the false self is not entirely the same as its compliance with the will of the other, for it may be directly counter to the other's will. (*Divided Self*)

This "concealed indictment" of the impersonated other "reaches its most extreme form" in such manifestations as the "echolalia [repetition of words or phrases], and flexibilitas cerea [inert flexibility] of the catatonic." The indict-

ment is less concealed in Bartleby's case when, in the Tombs near the end of the story, he says to the lawyer, "I know you . . . and I want nothing to say to you."

Although it has become commonplace to be condescending toward or even contemptuous of the lawyer, Bartleby's quiet indictment becomes all the more devastating in its effect upon us when we realize that the lawyer is more patient, more generous, and more self-aware than most of us would be. (Or than we are: if, say, we are teachers—as I am—how many of us have responded so admirably and so personally to the students who appear in our offices and reveal in obscure ways that they are, or potentially are, Bartlebys?) Yet even the lawyer fails.

An indictment of the lawyer is a mode of accusation against the world he represents, just as withdrawing from others entails withdrawing from that world. People trapped in a "double bind" or an otherwise impossible, unlivable situation may—as in the notable instance of prisoners in concentration camps—abandon the world and the aspects of one's supposed self that are most "in" the world. In the brutal parlance of everyday life, Bartleby dissociates himself from the outer world because he can no longer take it.

The ultimate form of withdrawal from the world is death. Bartleby seems all along to desire death—in existential terms, to be choosing nonbeing over being—even as, in a paradoxical but relentlessly logical way, his retreat into a death-like state of immobility may also reflect his *fear* of death: we have seen Laing quote Tillich on neurosis as "the way of avoiding non-being by avoiding being" (*Divided Self*). Of Peter—whom he quotes as having once said, "I've been sort of dead in a way. I cut myself off from other people and became shut up in myself. And I can see that you become dead in a way when you do this"—Laing writes that he had "set about trying to reduce his whole being to non-being; he set about as systematically as he could to become nothing. Under the conviction that he was nobody, that he was nothing, he was driven by a terrible sense of honesty to *be* nothing." If Bartleby shares that terrible honesty, its most pressing manifestation is probably his refrain of "I would prefer not to." At first to be sure it refers merely to proofreading, but as time goes on its reference becomes more and more encompassing until in the end it becomes all-inclusive—until, indeed, it refers to all of life and living. For poor Bartleby would prefer not to.

Discussing the dilemma of the person "in an alienated untenable position," Laing says that as soon as he "realizes that he is in a box, he can try to get out of it. But since to *them* [others] the box is *the whole world,* to get out of the box is tantamount to stepping off the end of the world, a thing that no one who loves him could sit by and let happen" (*Self and Others*). Good intentions can be murderous, or simply ineffective: when on the second occasion of Bartleby's refusal to read copy and his statement that he "would prefer not to," the lawyer finds himself "not only strangely disarmed" but "in a wonderful manner, touched and disconcerted," he tells us: "I began to reason with him."

That is all well and good, but not likely to work. Later, the lawyer is wiser, and he recognizes that it is Bartleby's "soul that suffered, and his soul I could not reach." Indeed, the first task in helping a person with Bartleby's problems is no doubt to *reach* that person. The *"sense of identity requires the existence of another by whom one is known"* (*Divided Self*). Even that, however, is not enough, as the lawyer realizes still later, "recalling the divine injunction: 'A new commandment give I unto you, that ye love one another.'" Obeying that call involves a complete breakdown in the normal relationship between employer and employee, just as Laing calls for the complete breakdown in the traditional relationship between psychotherapist and patient: "The main agent in uniting the patient, in allowing the pieces to come together and cohere, is the physician's love, a love that recognizes the patient's total being, and accepts it, with no strings attached."

Only an inordinately cynical reading of Melville's story will fail to recognize that the lawyer does come to experience genuine love for the scrivener. "Ah, Bartleby! Ah, humanity!" ends his narration: this from the man who, as we have seen, has earlier felt the absence of "anything ordinarily human" in his employee. But his love never attains—perhaps it rarely if ever can attain—the absolute totality apparently demanded or needed by Bartleby. As a result, the lawyer does not succeed in thrusting through the wall that Bartleby has set up—the wall that Bartleby has become. As Bartleby lives and ends his life facing walls we may keep in mind Laing's quotation—in the context of a warning in regard to the danger of the "tendency to *become what one perceives*"—of a patient, Julie: "That chair . . . that wall. I could be that wall. It's a terrible thing for a girl to be a wall." Or for a young man, too.

Milton R. Stern   (essay date 1979)

SOURCE: "Towards 'Bartleby the Scrivener'," in *The Stoic Strain in American Literature,* edited by Duane J. MacMillan, University of Toronto Press, 1979, pp. 19-41.

[*Stern is an American critic. In the following excerpt, he assesses critical perspectives on "Bartleby, the Scrivener."*]

When Ishmael asserted that the changefulness of life 'requires a strong decoction of Seneca and the Stoics to enable you to grin and bear it,' he was offering a jocular way to handle the shock and horror that accompany the discovery of our human oneness in our common, mortal victimization by the conditions of life. **'Bartleby the Scrivener'** is a tale of that discovery, not by seafarers in the vastness of natural force and space, but by landlubbers in claustral immurement.

Some critics are tempted to find stoic heroism in the pallid law-office clerk and to dismiss the lawyer-narrator as merely a wicked victimizer. Other critics more wisely sense a more complex connection between the two men. When I follow the lead offered by a view of Bartleby as stoic hero, I find that treating the tale as an example of Bartleby's stoicism results in oversimplifications and dead ends that do not account for tone and imagery. The insistence on stoicism is negatively useful because it leads to the conclusion that Melville was playing with other, deeper aspects of victimization than grinning and bearing it. Attempts to heroize Bartleby with ideological particularity diminish the dimensions of this perennially fascinating tale, so central among Melville's works. All such attempts seem to arise from the readers' desires to identify and secure Melville within their own rather than his contexts. A review of **'Bartleby'** criticism is a useful approach to critical caveats which define the directions that future readings might usefully take.

Melville made mirrors. No other writer in English since Shakespeare has assumed so many protean shapes, and so invitingly, for his readers. **'Bartleby'** especially is one of the weird pieces in which readers find whatever they came to seek. The ideological possibilities of **'Bartleby'** are enormous: the seer of psychiatric, political, literary, metaphysical, or religious positions is sure to find in the tale a paradigm for his own advocacy. So, a critic reading critics becomes like Ishmael contemplating water as the mirror of the self: 'And still deeper the meaning of that story of Narcissus, who because he could not grasp the tormenting, mild image he saw in the fountain, plunged into it and was drowned. But that same image, we ourselves see in all rivers and oceans. It is the image of the ungraspable phantom of life; and this is the key to it all.' What image could be more tormenting and mild than that of the tormenting, mild Bartleby? The critical literature concerning **'Bartleby'** exposes the process of interpretative criticism as very often a narcissistic operation in which each reader sees the tale as a mirror of the Gestalt within his own mind.

But the story itself is a fixed thing; it undergoes no more revision by Melville. Though each reader shifts it, unlike water it does not shift itself. Gestalts fix more of the story's details than do others. If much criticism is foolish, not all criticism is useless. And each critic knows that although he too will find the key to it all in a version of his own vision, there are priorities of value to be found in a criticism of the criticism; some visions are better than others.

The political Gestalt of Leo Marx's 'Melville's Parable of the Walls' [*Sewanee Review* 61, 1953], for instance, remains a valuable mirroring because it illuminates more details within the story than does a set of literary parallels like Egbert S. Oliver's 'A Second Look at "Bartleby" ' [*College English* 6, 1945], which sees the pallid scrivener as a type of Thoreau. When we move beyond the story to the references the criticism furnishes, Marx provides a more usably wide focus: his Gestalt expands rather than contracts the area within which the story exists. For all its gratuitous contumaciousness, an essay like Kingsley Widmer's 'Bartleby and Nihilistic Resistance' [in *The Ways of Nihilism: Herman Melville's Short Novels,* 1970], fixes many more details in a brilliantly suggestive and useful mirror than does the pedantically narrow angle of vision of works like Mario L. D'Avanzo's 'Melville's "Bartleby" and Carlyle' [in *Bartleby the Scrivener, Melville Annual 1965 Symposium,* edited by Howard P. Vincent, 1966], which, in effect, makes Carlyle the ghostwriter of **'Bartleby.'**

When George Bluestone commented on the making of his film out of the tale, he provided pertinent caveats for critics precisely because he had to specify details in order to recreate them in another medium, and therefore had to examine closely the components of his own Gestalt. His activities led him quickly to a concentration on what was usable for translation, and this process led him, in turn, to an important conclusion about the puzzling scrivener: one cannot specify in event, in historical or literary parallel, or in psycho-biography, exactly what made Bartleby the way he was. Bluestone realized that his film would lose power if it attempted to show the cause of Bartleby's depression precisely because in this area Melville provided no usable details. The film would have to centre on what Melville did provide, which was the effect of whatever it was that turned Bartleby into Bartleby: 'To explain the malaise is to explain it away' ['Bartleby: The Tale, the Film' in *Bartleby the Scrivener, Melville Annual 1965 Symposium*]. In accounting for the criticism available to him in 1962, when he made the film, Bluestone summed up his findings as follows: 'Critics have seen . . . ["Bartleby"] as a tale (1) of exorcism, in which Bartleby figures as a surrogate for Melville, the artist protesting the killing demands of hack work; (2) of psychosis, a classic case of depression, or catatonic schizophrenia, with overtones of homosexuality; (3) of the alter ego, Bartleby as a projec-

tion of the death-urge in the Lawyer, a kind of early 'Secret Sharer'; (4) of social criticism, a critique of industrial America symbolized by an implacable Wall Street. Certainly there are overtones of all these.' There is, however, another category at least as important as any that Bluestone has listed, and that is the Gestalt in which the tale is seen as a metaphysical treatise in which man is a homeless wanderer in a universe of indifference, meaninglessness, and absence of moral point or purpose. This last critical vision often merges with Bluestone's first and fourth categories, and provides one of the few general areas of critical agreement.

> Melville made mirrors. No other writer in English since Shakespeare has assumed so many protean shapes, and so invitingly, for his readers. 'Bartleby' especially is one of the weird pieces in which readers find whatever they came to seek.
>
> —*Milton R. Stern*

When we look at the criticism that appeared up to the time of Donald M. Fiene's bibliography [of **'Bartleby the Scrivener'** commentary, in *Bartleby the Scrivener, Melville Annual 1965 Symposium*], which includes work published through 1965, and add to it a few pieces published later, we become aware that the **'Bartleby'** mirror attracts and reflects more water-gazers in certain areas than in others. When many disparate individuals begin to fix the tale into one or two dominant shapes, and especially when those shapes encompass and account for the greatest number of details in the tale, the cumulative effect is to make criticism a useful act as it incrementally defines areas of agreement and, more important, the areas that are problematical and require more and new attention. Accumulated criticism spotlights the points at which we must try to shift our own Gestalts and begin anew with a basic experience of the details in question.

Those who see Bartleby as a type of the writer living in but alienated by a heartless bourgeois society join at many points with those who see the tale as a metaphysical and psychological examination of the terrible loneliness that results from a vision of the universe as empty of meaning: Bartleby becomes the typal figure who repudiates established society, its shallow vision of human experience, and its concomitant easy beliefs. For both groups of readers the lawyer and Bartleby represent conflicting opposites: the lawyer represents the establishment, the unexamined life, the surface vision with its facile hopes; and Bartleby is his rebellious, stoic victim. Depending upon the critic's Gestalt, the lawyer represents (1) the selfish capitalist society; (2) the repressive world of law and order; (3) the world of rationality, (3a) the world of self-deceiving rationalization, (3b) the world of genteel consciousness; (4) the world of orthodoxy; (5) the world of surfaces; (6) all of the above. Bartleby represents (1) the man who will no longer conform to the standards of the capitalist world; (2) Christianity, or Christliness, or—sometimes—Christ; (3) the unconscious, (3a) the hidden recognition of the world as meaningless chaos, as the absurd, (3b) the lawyer's conscience, (3c) the world of preferences, will, and revolution; (4) the stoic tragic view; (5) the defeated stoic writer-artist-rebel; (6) the heroic stoic writer-artist-rebel; (7) the defeat of the stoic human will; (8) the stoic triumph of human will; and (9) any of the above that are not too obviously mutually contradictory.

Many of those who see Bartleby as a redemptive challenger of the lawyer see him as a type of Christ, while those who see him as a passive or defeated challenger may make him a type of the absurd itself. The view of him as Christ is as much a catch-all as any other category, ranging from a rather rigid and silly assertion that the lawyer is Jehovah, Bartleby is Christ, Turkey is Michael, Nippers is Lucifer, and Ginger Nut—the poor little kid—is Raphael, to Bruce Franklin's much more useful and suggestive considerations of the mythic possibilities within the tale [*The Wake of the Gods*, 1963]. It is also possible to see Bartleby as Christ, even though passive and defeated, if one sees him as an 'emasculated' Christ. But whether he is seen as active or passive, almost all critics agree that he typifies the principle of *non serviam* in whatever world he is said to inhabit. The line of logic leads critics from the *non serviam* relationship Bartleby maintains with his employer to a speculation about Bartleby as a kind of *doppelgänger* or, at least, a conscience for the lawyer. Here too there is a range of opinion, from Bartleby as the embodiment of the principle of the English Court of Chancery, 'the Keeper of the King's Conscience,' to Bartleby as the lawyer's hidden death-wish.

Three firm agreements emerge from the welter of hermeneutics, propaedeutics, and ephemera. One is that Bartleby becomes the repudiator of the civilization and vision that the lawyer stands for. The second is that Bartleby cannot be defined except through a definition of the lawyer. The third is that the lawyer, at least at the beginning of the story, is the bad guy. I delay discussion of the first until I look at Bartleby a bit later in this essay. The second should be obvious, by virtue of the narrative method, without any critical aids. The third is fixed through a series of self-revelations that every critic who has examined the lawyer has noted.

The revelations always cited are the lawyer's conviction that 'the easiest way of life is the best'; that he never suffers any real involvement in his law cases to invade his peace; that he loves the 'cool tranquillity' of his 'snug retreat' as he does 'a snug business among rich men's bonds, and mortgages, and title-deeds'; that he is considered to be an 'eminently safe man'; that he loves being associated with John Jacob Astor, that he loves Astor's name, which 'hath a rounded and orbicular sound to it, and rings like unto bullion'; that he is proud that John Jacob Astor has named the lawyer's two grand points as prudence and method; that he is greedy about the Court of Chancery and is upset only when easy income from the Master's office is denied him through dissolution of the court—*that* invades his peace if equity and justice do not; that he uses people—his

clerks—selfishly, putting up with their vagaries not out of any really compassionate humanity but only out of his sense that they are 'most valuable' to him; that he is concerned only with the appearances of things and desires decorum and seemliness at all human costs; that he tolerates Bartleby at first not out of real compassion or fraternal feeling, but because to humour Bartleby 'in his strange wilfullness, will cost me little or nothing while I lay up in my soul what will eventually prove a sweet morsel for my conscience'; that he betrays and abandons Bartleby while mouthing pious and/or legalistic rationalizations for refusing responsibility and running away. In short, the lawyer reveals in every way that he is a smug and heartless man of small vision and hypocritical Christianity, that he is respectable, bourgeois cannibal, a conformist to all the surfaces, gentilities, selfishnesses, and human enormities of established values, law, and order. He is mindless of pain, soulless to real suffering, compassionless to any possible vision that sees the establishment's world as a lie. Whether he discloses his consciousness as a factor of political, economic, social, metaphysical, or psychological reality, he is a shallow and complacent man of easy optimism.

In detailing the lawyer there is critical agreement that the world he rules dooms human activity to a walled-in (almost all critics, especially since Leo Marx, have specified the imagery of the walls: that need not be done again) round of alternating acquiescence and frustration (almost all critics have noted the complementary ante- and post-meridian changes in the behaviour and personalities of Turkey and Nippers: that need not be done again). People struggle between desire and submission in the lawyer's world—if Bartleby's opting-out is characterized by 'I prefer not to,' Turkey's key phrase is 'with submission, sir'— and spend half their lives conforming to their lot and half their lives raging against it. Yet, the established world is inhabited by people whose very vision is walled-in for, despite their longings for freedom from their hated rounds of monotonous sameness in which everything and everyone is a copy and a repetition, they uphold the system: what they aspire to is the lawyer's top-dog position in the walled-in world. The narrator is interested only in containing and repressing the periods of resentment in which people do not engage in profit-making labour for the boss, in which they turn against the symbols of their monotonous lives (Turkey blots his papers in steaming fury, Nippers grinds his teeth and fights with his hated desk), and in which people have no real individuality—no real names, but only nicknames—but merely alternatingly duplicate each other with fits that differentiate them only so that they reflect each other. The lawyer wants to see all activity and appearances buttoned up into law, order, decorum, and profitable routine: everyone is to spend his life copying the law indeed. Whenever the lawyer confronts Bartleby in a serious showdown, he buttons things up. 'I buttoned up my coat, balanced myself, advanced slowly towards him. . . .' 'What shall I do? I now said to myself, buttoning up my coat to the last button.' The buttoning is itself an enactment of a contemporary slang phrase, 'button up,' meaning 'shut up,' 'shape up.' The phrase, like the action, is one of repression, suppression, conformity.

If the walled-in workers yearn, like Nippers, 'the truth of

the matter was, Nippers knew not what he wanted. Or, if he wanted anything, it was to be rid of his scrivener's table altogether.' However, Nippers thinks that the way to be rid of his table is by taking on even more of the same, by succeeding, like the lawyer, by continuing the system, not by opting-out of or by destroying it. His twin vices of ambition and indigestion (Turkey's twin characteristics are, similarly, submission and insolence), are indicators of his impatience with how far he has come in a system in which he too wants to be a lawyer. His ambition 'was evinced by a certain impatience at the duties of a mere copyist, an unwarrantable usurpation of strictly professional affairs, such as the original drawing up of legal documents.' Thus Turkey, also, when presented with a token of status—fittingly, the lawyer's cast-off coat 'which buttoned straight up from the knee to the neck'—becomes insolently and snobbishly restive not with the world he lives in but merely with his position within it. And Ginger Nut, the little son of a carter, also plays at being a lawyer with his little desk in the corner. In sum, the ordinary population, in its fits and frustrations and frenzies and alternations, acquiesces, with submission, sir, to the values of the world epitomized by the lawyer. Melville's metaphors for the populace, like Shakespeare's, never give us a picture of a revolutionary mass with class consciousness despite several wistful critical attempts to find in Melville a major literary neo-Marxian voice.

Given the nature of the world's common inhabitants, the snug lawyer becomes even more the enemy of human freedom when he blandly and civilly views the inhabitants of his world not as people but in the way he first views Bartleby—as 'a valuable acquisition.' Committing the unforgivable sin of reducing people to things, he thinks that, like any acquisition, people can be bought. Twice, while trying to get Bartleby out of his life, he gives him money. Commercializing all human relations, he is yet smug enough to feel that Bartleby's 'perverseness seemed ungrateful, considering the undeniable good usage and indulgence he had received from me.' He 'trembled to think' of what might happen to his world if the implications of 'prefer' were to become the basis of human conduct—button up, boy. Contemplating Bartleby's incredible and fantastic plight, the lawyer allows 'necessities connected with my business' to 'tyrannize over all other considerations.' He congratulates himself that his assumptions about Bartleby's departure will get rid of Bartleby in a seemly and decorous way: he can do something that nags at his conscience, but is satisfied as long as appearances and the *status quo* remain undisturbed. He indulges in 'sweet charity's sake' only as a guarantee of his own safety—he continues to buy human beings and human actions. He is constantly concerned that Bartleby is 'scandalizing [his] professional reputation,' and even in the Tombs he tries to placate his conscience by attempting to talk Bartleby into enjoying the sky and the grass—in prison. In sum, that is the case against the lawyer-narrator, and up to this point almost all critics agree.

A quantitative overview of the criticism suggests that this, too, is ground that need not be gone over yet once more, and can be taken as a given in the tale. But just beyond this agreement lies one of the rocks upon which criticism splits, and that is the question of whether or not the narrator changes. Some see that modifications must be made in the condemnation of the lawyer. Generally, the arguments favouring the proposition that the lawyer undergoes a change of vision insist (1) that there is no possibility of salvation for Bartleby, no matter how great his lonely integrity may be, and that there is a possibility of salvation for the narrator, whose increasingly pained awareness of what Bartleby might be gives him a new sense of the connectedness of all humanity no matter how smug and shallow he was at the beginning; (2) that when all is said and done, it is a vast act of sentiment to see Bartleby as a rebel-hero only, for he effects no rebellion. All he does is to commit an ultimate withdrawal. So, too, it is dangerous to see Bartleby as stoic hero for, as we shall see, it is questionable at best that there are positive moral values shoring up Bartleby's bearing of his burden and, in any event, Bartleby does not in any positive way indicate how life may be borne. Just the opposite, in fact. But the narrator comes to feel the agony of the world at last: Melville is as much the lawyer as he is Bartleby, and to divide him into allegiance to only one aspect of himself is to oversimplify Melville's sense of reality by substituting a straw-man for the narrator who actually exists in the story. (3) For all that is wrong with the lawyer, Bartleby, finally, is socially irresponsible: he leads only towards death. All arguments that would modify the agreement about the initial self-presentation of the narrator depend upon the narrator's sympathetic acts and thoughts concerning Bartleby, upon the tone of the narratorial voice when the lawyer describes the Tombs and murmurs, 'with kings and counselors,' upon the section presenting the Dead Letters Office, and upon the tone of the narrator's final cry, 'Ah Bartleby! Ah humanity!'

Those who see the narrator as unredeemable and a total villain all denigrate as maudlin the lawyer's feelings when he begins to react deeply to Bartleby; they dismiss the epilogue as the 'thick Victorianism' of an attempt to furnish a liberal 'hard times' explanation for Bartleby, and refuse to see the narrator's last cry as anything but 'a last sentimental gesture' [Kingsley Widmer, *The Ways of Nihilism*]. It is significant, for instance, that the most uncompromising view of the lawyer as villain [William Bysshe Stein, "Bartleby: The Christian Conscience," *Bartleby the Scrivener, Melville Annual 1965 Symposium*] not only sees him as 'incapable of moral regeneration' but fails to deal with or even mention the narrator's final cry. The Dead Letters epilogue is seen suddenly and somehow as 'Melville's' rather than as the narrator's, for to attribute sensitivity and pained compassion to the narrator would ruin the thesis of unmixed villainy. In fact, all views of the narrator as unchanging villain sweep away every instance in which Melville makes the narrator's villainy problematical without ever distinguishing in terms of tone between the narrator's moments of smugness and his moments of pain.

Well, I find that there is no arguing about tone. If there is any one aspect of literary art that is crucial to comprehension it is tone, and of all aspects of art it is the one most encysted by the Gestalt in which the reader sees the parts. As just one more critic I can only assert that a quick juxtaposition of parts will establish tone. Read the opening passages through the Turkey and Nippers episodes. Then immediately read the entire Sunday morning sequence detailing the narrator's 'overpowering stinging melancholy' as distinct from the mere sentimentality of 'a not unpleasant sadness' and his consequent Melvillean awareness of human fraternity in mortal woe. Then read the episode in the Tombs. Then read the epilogue. The juxtaposition must—should—create at least a sense of uneasiness in the critics who assert that the narrator never changes. There is, I submit, a palpable shift in Melville's presentation of the narrator, and it is discernible at the crucial episode—almost exactly half way through the story—of the narrator's Sunday morning visit to his office. Up to that moment Melville has the narrator disclose only those self-revelatory ironies and pseudo-sympathies that destroy the lawyer's assumed image. He is indeed the bad guy. But for the remaining half of the story Melville has the narrator vacillate between continued self-exposing hypocrisy and puzzled concern and pain, with the power of the sympathetic passages—the Tombs, the epilogue—gaining ascendence over the others. The nature of the narrator's consciousness begins to change. Does he still worry about being scandalized? Does he still try to explain Bartleby away? Is he still self-seeking and self-protective? Does he still fly into a rage? Does he still try to evade Bartleby? Of course. That is the truth. It is nothing but the truth. But it is not the whole truth. In the first half of the story there are no expressions of pain (astonishment, outrage, anger, and bewilderment, yes, but not the pain of his own deepest self's contact with Bartleby) or of confusion deeper than those of the law office proprieties. The last half of the story is full of them, including among them such awarenesses as the fact that 'I might give alms to his body; but his body did not pain him; it was his soul that suffered, and his soul I could not reach.' It is the narrator, after all, who becomes aware of Bartleby as 'alone, absolutely alone in the universe. A bit of wreck in the mid-Atlantic.' Continuing to act the hypocritical burgher, nevertheless, the narrator now has his consciousness focused on the knowledge that he has to wrench himself, almost in tears, 'from him whom I had so longed to be rid of.' Nowhere in the first half is there a physico-psychic jolt of current running between the narrator and Bartleby as there is in the death scene in the Tombs. And in the context of the Tombs the grub-man, fittingly named Mr Cutlets in the original *Putnam's* version, makes even the lawyer's attempt to cheer Bartleby by pointing to grass and sky less a matter of blind smugness than one of pathetic failure. (Food as a pervasive motif in **'Bartleby'** should be the subject of a short critical essay, for the story is filled with instances of food and feeding. The negative relationship of oral gratification to total separation is a psychological rendition of the central question of nourishment and sustenance for human hope, for the ability of the human spirit to bear consciousness and pain and still live and remain human.) The narrator's reply to the grub-man, 'with kings and counselors,' draws the clear and distinct distance in insight, sympathy, and pain between the lawyer and the grub-man. At the beginning the lawyer was to Bartleby as the grub-man now is to the lawyer. One can refuse to recognize a meaningful change in the lawyer only by refusing to recognize that the

second half of the story does prepare for an undeniable difference between the lawyer and the grub-man. Were there no change there could be no difference between the lawyer and the grub-man, for Mr Cutlets is but a meaty, mindless, and relatively moneyless version of what the lawyer was at the beginning. Mr Cutlets is an official grub inhabiting the same world of grubby morality that the lawyer's walled-in office does, and he can no more supply sustenance for Bartleby than can the lifeless bust of Cicero in the lawyer's office—the Cicero, no doubt, of *De officiis*. Yet, at the end of the story the difference between the grub-man and the narrator is a qualitative difference, not a mere difference in manner and education, but a difference in insight and sympathy, which is exactly what is denied by an unmixed view of the narrator. Even before the midpoint of the tale the narrator is not unmixed in his given qualities. Consider the following passage:

> He lives, then, on ginger-nuts, thought I; never eats a dinner, properly speaking; he must be a vegetarian, then; but no; he never eats even vegetables, he eats nothing but ginger-nuts. My mind then ran on in reveries concerning the probable effects upon the human constitution of living entirely on ginger-nuts. Ginger-nuts are so called, because they contain ginger as one of their peculiar constituents, and the final flavoring one. Now, what was ginger? A hot, spicy thing. Was Bartleby hot and spicy? Not at all. Ginger, then, had no effect upon Bartleby. Probably he preferred it should have none.

This passage can be and has been fitted into ideologies that polemicize against the narrator. Yet all such critical ingenuity always misses one humble, simple, tonal, surface fact: the passage is mildly funny. The narrator has a sense of humour. The presentation of the clerks discloses an observer with a sense of humour that makes his paternalistic relationship to their vagaries not totally and solely a matter of selfish exploitation. Scattered throughout the tale on either side of the midpoint are small instances of humour which create the expectation that this same smug narrator might yet be a man with enough sensibilities to recognize a connection with Bartleby. As that metaphysical wanderer-narrator, Ishmael, from the very beginning is hintingly given qualities which will enable him to see the Ahab he admiringly repudiates as an extended aspect of his own human identity, so too that prudentially selfish lawyer-narrator from the very beginning is hintingly given qualities which will enable him to see that the Bartleby he will compassionately leave is inextricably interrelated with his own human identity. Surely there is a tonal difference not only between the narrator and the grub-man but also between the lawyer and all the other inhabitants and landlords and lawyers who do not for a moment see Bartleby as anything but a nuisance to be got rid of. The difference between the lawyer and the successors to his chambers is scanted or ignored by critics who fix the narrator as a single moral quantity, and for the same reasons that make them miss the intermittent humour of the tale.

But, as I say, the tonal aspect of change in the lawyer cannot be argued: either you hear it or you do not. Rather, I would open a question which seems to me quite pertinent. Why has there been so much commentary on

'Bartleby'? Why so much varied and fascinated response beyond the agreement about the preliminary characterization of the lawyer and of Bartleby as his opponent? Clearly one answer must be that there is something about the tale that creates Melvillean nuance; *something* about this story must offer ambiguity and multiplicities of meaning. But what is the effect of a rigid definition of the lawyer as unmixed villain? The effect is to remove ambiguity, multiplicity, and subtlety by reducing the story to a simple tale of good versus evil (defined by whatever Gestalt). Problems of meaning remain in the superimposition of Gestalts upon the story and in conflicts between Gestalts—lots of room for explicators still—but moral ambiguity, moral evaluation is removed as a problem. And is not that problem precisely the central one that remains to puzzle the reader and itch in his mind? Remove shiftings of moral evaluations, and all that is left is the working out of equivalents to hang around the lawyer and Bartleby—which is what, I think, accounts for so much critical cleverness and narrowness in much of the criticism of **'Bartleby.'** To see the lawyer as a fixed value is to remove him as a source of that itch that engages the reader in the first place and that the spate of criticism undeniably announces. And to remove the narrator as a source is to be quite tricky indeed, not only because the narrator is the only source of information we have about Bartleby but also because the narrator is the only continuing source of response to Bartleby. To fix the narrator is to place the burden for *all* the creation of multiple meaning in the story on Bartleby alone. Yet, why do all readers come away from the story with impression that in the narrator they have met a person—whether they scorn him or not—and that in Bartleby they have met—what? —a quality? And embodied in a repetitive cadaver, at that?

There is in this question a serious matter that must be met, but which is all but unmentioned in **'Bartleby'** criticism, and that is the matter of types of characterization. It is neither accidental nor insignificant that all critics confront the story by characterizing the narrator in social, political, religious, and economic, as well as moral, terms, and by characterizing Bartleby in typal or mythic terms. Furthermore, all readers come away from the story with the sense that it is weird. The sense of weirdness is a result of the same factor that accounts for the ways in which critics characterize the lawyer and Bartleby. That is, the lawyer and Bartleby are characters from two distinctly different modes of fiction. The narrator comes from a recognizable world and can be measured in terms of that world: he is the kind of character who inhabits the province of realistic fiction. Bartleby, however, in every way inhabits a world other than the narrator's. He comes from the province of allegorical fiction, or romantic fiction, or both. The narrator is a human character; Bartleby is a metaphor. The narrator is sociologically explicable; Bartleby is no more sociologically explicable than is Ahab. The vehicle for the realistic character is verisimilitude; the lawyer, like his clerks, is given human, peculiar characteristics by which he is recognized, and the verisimilitude of characterizing human peculiarities is the vehicle for individuation, regardless of purpose—sentiment, rebellion, reportage—in realistic fiction. The narrator and his clerks come from the fiction of a writer like Dickens. But the vehicle for the alle-

gorical character is typalism. Bartleby is given metaphoric weightings by which he is recognized, mysterious qualities independent of verisimilitude or realistic statistication. He comes from the fiction of a writer like Bunyan turned into Kafka—the emblematic quality of characterization remains, but all the rubrics have been erased from the labels for which the character is beast of burden. The science-fiction and gothic impingement of alien worlds gives **'Bartleby'** its weirdness. One does not expect the preternatural or the preternaturalistic to be accommodated into simultaneous existence with the realistic or the naturalistic. It is the calm intrusion of one world into another that gives **'Bartleby'** its Kafkan tones and makes it seem so very modern in its techniques and surfaces. In terms of action within the recognizable or naturalistic or Dickensian world the realistic character has dynamic dimensions: his fate and his character may both change along with his insights and experiences. But the inhabitant of the typal world is fixed. In speech, action, and possibility Bartleby *as character* is as rigidly fixed as a corpse. In the problem of moral evaluation, when the question is, what should the character do? Bartleby offers the narrator no world in which to do anything. He offers only the possibility of becoming like Bartleby, which is to say the possibility of leaving altogether the world of reality as it is defined for characterization within the demands of realistic fiction. The very nature of the differences in fictive worlds, fictive methods, and fictive characterization suggests that if either of the characters may undergo change, it is the lawyer, not Bartleby. I submit that in relation to Bartleby, it is the narrator who is not the fixed value. Nor, I should add, does this suggestion make a freak of **'Bartleby the Scrivener'** within the canon of Melville's works. The mixing of characters from different worlds of fictive mode is a constant Melvillean technique and always accounts for the element of weirdness in his fiction. For instance, is not the magnificently created sense of displacement, discontinuity of worlds, and disproportion in the confrontations between Ahab and Starbuck attributable to the fact that they are confrontations between a ranging myth and a man from Nantucket, Massachusetts? And Melville's typal characters are disconnected from the humanity of verisimilitude and the world of its realities. What is Ahab's past? A hint from Elijah. And as for Bartleby, there is only an uncertain rumour about the Dead Letters Office. Consistently and pervasively Melville's typal characters are not of woman born, have no dimensions taken from realistic fiction's world of verisimilitude. They are characters without a past and without social measurements.

In fact, what do we know of Bartleby? Only what the lawyer tells us, and he warns us from the very beginning that Bartleby does not inhabit the same dimensions as other scriveners, about whom he could write some amusing and sentimental vignettes. 'While of other law-copyists I might write the complete life, of Bartleby nothing of that sort can be done. I believe that no materials exist for a full and satisfactory biography of this man. . . . Bartleby was one of those beings of whom nothing is ascertainable, except from the original sources, and in his case, those are very small. What my own astonished eyes saw of Bartleby, *that* is all I know of him, except, indeed, one vague report, which will appear in the sequel.' The appropriate question to ask, since Melville obviously knew he would furnish no sudden world of verisimilitude out of Bartleby's past, is why Melville chose to add the 'sequel' about the Dead Letter Office; and in order to answer that question it becomes necessary to ask what it is we know of Bartleby without the epilogue.

Here again, the body of criticism gives us a solid agreement: Bartleby is the *isolato* who has come to the nadir of pallid despair in which all things are equal ('I am not particular') and all things are pointless ('I prefer not to'). The ordinary world that demands reasonableness is seen by Bartleby to be a dead end of meaninglessness that mocks all attempts to copy a non-existent law and order ('At present I prefer not to be a little reasonable'). There is at least this much preliminary bedrock of agreement. The criticism divides on the identification and evaluation of Bartleby. To some he is entirely heroic; to some he is mixed in his qualities. As is to be expected, those critics who see the lawyer as all villainous tend to see Bartleby as all good; those critics who see the lawyer as a changing quality tend to see unchanging Bartleby as a quality demanding a mixed response. If we are to be thrown on Bartleby as the sole source of ambiguity and multiplicity, we find that the criticism provides ample evidence that we cannot settle on a fixed response to him. Readers who conclude that Bartleby is the type of the hero, the rebel of whatever—art, nihilism, Christian morality, political honesty, metaphysical awareness—never satisfactorily handle those hard stumbling-blocks of facts which are the specifics whereby Bartleby is shown to us.

Would we have him stand as a life-principle, a rebellion against claustrophobic immurement in the dehumanizing world of the respectable lawyer? Would we have him the representative of true Christianity, true art, or the true revolution in his nay-saying to the mechanical world of law-copyists? To do so goes beyond the basic recognition that Bartleby prefers not to participate in any activity whatsoever; to do so assigns meanings to him that are not verifiable in the actual facts of the story. Because Melville is so heavily involved in metaphysical ideas, because Melville makes mirrors, the temptation is great to assign

---

One does not expect the preternatural or the preternaturalistic to be accommodated into simultaneous existence with the realistic or the naturalistic. It is the calm intrusion of one world into another that gives 'Bartleby' its Kafkan tones and makes it seem so very modern in its techniques and surfaces.

—*Milton R. Stern*

---

meanings out of the Gestalt of the critic, but to do that is to reduce criticism to a game of filling in the blanks: the lawyer equals—; Bartleby equals—. But when we look at the specific details through which Bartleby is in fact presented, it becomes a bit difficult to turn our impression of a pallid, sick, corpse-like, motionless, silent fixed being into the life-principle or the humanity-principle or the rebel-principle or the reality-principle or an active body of moral principles. What are the specific terms that actually present Bartleby? In this long short story the catalogue surprisingly is not so long that the salient facts cannot be listed conveniently; and when the concrete instances are precisely isolated, they become quite instructive in the revelation of what is repeated.

Bartleby's movements are most often accompanied by the word 'gliding,' and his voice is most often described as 'mild.' He is 'pallidly neat, pitiably respectable, incurably forlorn'; 'he wrote on silently, palely, mechanically'; his face is 'leanly composed; his gray eye dimly calm'; he has absolutely no 'agitation, uneasiness, anger, or impertinence,' nor is there 'anything ordinarily human about him'; his corner is called a 'hermitage' (four times); he is 'gentle' or totally silent; he appears 'like a very ghost'; he is 'a pale young scrivener'; he is characterized by 'his steadiness, his freedom from all dissipation, his incessant industry (except when [in a] . . . standing revery . . .). his great stillness, his unalterableness of demeanor'; his is a 'lean visage'; he is an 'apparition'; he has a 'cadaverously gentlemanly nonchalance'; he is 'eminently decorous'; he will not be seen in dishabille and would not 'by any singular occupation violate the proprieties' of Sunday; although he has very few belongings, he owns a blacking box and brush to keep his shoes shined; although he does not care for money (he does not touch the conscience money twice given him by the narrator), he frugally saves his salary and keeps it knotted in a handkerchief 'bank' hidden in the recesses of his desk; he has no interest in or apparent need for food or drink; he has a 'pale form' that appears as though 'laid out, among uncaring strangers, in its shivering winding-sheet'; he is 'thin and pale' with an air of 'pallid haughtiness'; his tones are 'mildly cadaverous'; he 'would prefer to be left alone here'; 'he seemed alone, absolutely alone in the universe [like] . . . a bit of wreck in the mid-Atlantic'; his triumph over the narrator is a 'cadaverous triumph'; he becomes both totally silent and totally motionless; he 'silently acquiesced' in 'his pale, unmoving way'; and he is 'prone to a pallid hopelessness.'

It will not do to object that these are only the narrator's vision of Bartleby, for everything we know about Bartleby is given through the narrator's vision, regardless of the meanings we would affix to Bartleby. Melville could have chosen to give us, through the narrator, other kinds of details for constant repetition, but he did not. What he did choose to give was a repetition of details that result in two major categories of impression. One is that of a silent, motionless, emaciated, pale, cadaverous negativism and withdrawal, a suggestion of the implacable stubbornness of a corpse, of death itself. The other is that of a mechanically industrious, mild, and seemly respectability. Just as the details that present the narrator begin to change at that crucial Sunday morning mid-point of the story, so they change for Bartleby, too. On the Tuesday following that Sunday Bartleby announces, 'I have given up copying' and abandons his industry altogether. From that moment the details of presentation begin to emphasize the characteristics of silence, motionlessness, and death much more than those of respectability. In short, just as the narrator's responses begin to be mixed with anguish and sympathy, Bartleby's characteristics begin to be associated with total withdrawal and extinction.

It is also important to note that from the mid-point on, the lawyer's strange sense of private connection with Bartleby also intensifies. 'I never feel so private as when I know you are here,' he says, thinking of Bartleby. The lawyer discovers that it is Bartleby who mysteriously has the unaccounted-for key to his private chambers. The lawyer has to tear himself away from the Bartleby he had longed to be rid of. And, finally, when the lawyer touches the hand of Bartleby's foetally curled corpse, 'a tingling ran up my arm and down my spine to my feet.' Melville has the lawyer supply ample hints that Bartleby has an essential, interior, and intimate connection with him. When one considers that up to the mid-point the lawyer was smugly, snugly, and actively respectable and that Bartleby was pallidly, forlornly, and mechanically respectable, there is an opening for speculation about Bartleby as an inversion, or at least a version, of the narrator. And after the mid-point the more the narrator becomes agonizingly aware of his connection with Bartleby, yet fails to give up his way of life, the more Bartleby repudiates him ('I know you, and I want nothing to say to you'), and retreats into suicide by refusing any of the food of this world. It is as though the lawyer came to learn that in seeing the repressed and negativistic Bartleby he saw himself, the logical, or at least spiritual extension of his very life which offers neither nourishment nor hope for everything within us that is buttoned up beneath the surfaces of conventional acquiescence to forms and values. It is just this possibility that leads some critics to contend that the narrator is changeless, unredeemed, and unredeemable: he does not, after all, give up his life when confronted with the apparition of Bartleby. But when religious or political meanings are affixed to Bartleby, the nagging questions fail to disappear. If Bartleby is the narrator's conscience or the spirit of true Christianity, why should he tend more towards death, isolation, withdrawal, and silence than towards strength, activity, and expression, as the narrator becomes increasingly tortured by the pain of sympathy? If Bartleby is the spirit of rebellion against the culture that is, why should he droop, fail, and withdraw just as the narrator becomes aware in anguish of a strange kind of justice in Bartleby's existence—just as the narrator finds he *cannot* rationalize Bartleby away with charges of vagrancy or any other charges?

I am convinced that the explications that tend towards a one-to-one identification of Bartleby and the critic's political or religious Gestalt fail and will continue to fail to satisfy the logic, the psychological demands, that the story sets up. On the level of metaphysical points of view, there is, at least, a general basic agreement in the critical canon. As the narrator, at least at first, represents the materialis-

tic world of hypocritical and blind bourgeois selfishness, Bartleby is the woebegone representative of a view of existence that denies all the shallow rationality and expectations of predictability, purpose, law, and meaning that the comfortably mindless and selfish commercial world self-justifyingly assumes to be the nature of the universe: God's in his heaven and all's right with the world. On this level there is general agreement that the lawyer, at least at the beginning, and Bartleby are the conflicting and obverse sides of human vision and human experience. If one is a vision of orthodox optimism and institutionalized belonging, the other is a vision of existential absurdity, the vision of the outcast stranger. This vision reduces to absurd meaninglessness all the activities of the lawyer's institutionalized world. On the level of metaphysical vision the psychological expectations are satisfied: as there are no alternatives in the institutionalized world for Bartleby's vision and no point in any kind of action on his part, pallid and silent withdrawal follows.

But when we parallel the level of metaphysical vision with the tempting levels of politics, the psychologics are not satisfied. On this level the narrator is the capitalist boss who exploits those who work for him, denying them full human existence and identity; Bartleby is the nay-sayer who refuses to copy the law-and-order of the narrator's world any longer. But on this level the story must remain psychologically frustrating, especially because there is certainly enough material that 'fits.' One might expect the fury of an Ahab or the activity of a Joe Hill or even the unaware, protesting dissoluteness of the *Lumpenproletariat,* but hardly the ghost of a motionless cadaver. The fictive mode from which Bartleby characterologically comes is not that which satisfies in any way the demands of realistic fiction. On this level **'Bartleby'** criticism becomes confused about the difference between the victim and the victim-rebel. Even if Bartleby were to be seen as victim only, what the story would then need would be something like a Hurstwood, or a Clyde Griffiths, but what we have is—Bartleby. And, on the political level, the story certainly does not psychologically support the view of Bartleby as rebel-hero if the type of pure victim is to be abandoned.

The same is true of the view of Bartleby as hero-artist. One might think of Joyce's silence, exile, and cunning as fitting Bartleby, but the 'fit' squeezes a bit with the cunning, and it does not take too much thinking before one runs into equally tight fits with the differences between Joyce's—or even Stephen Dedalus's—silence and exile and Bartleby's. Again, if Bartleby is to be 'the artist,' he is victim rather than victim-hero-rebel, closer to Kafka's hunger artist than to Dedalus. And, even at that, unlike the hunger artist Bartleby has no art of his own (he is himself either a mail-clerk or a copyist) that is sacrificed: abstemiousness is certainly not treated in Melville's story as it is in Kafka's. All that one can say is that Bartleby finds no food for his sustenance or values worth copying in the established world—and we are back to the one area of agreement, which is on the level of metaphysical vision, and which cannot really be specified in a one-to-one relationship to 'the artist.'

And if the ideologies of Christianity replace those of politics or artistic identity as the something further that is to parallel the level of metaphysical vision, psychological expectations run into further difficulty in the basic question of why Bartleby should choose suicide just as he has begun to make some meaningful impact upon the lawyer. What the specifics of the story and the inflexibly unrelenting characterology of Bartleby suggest in tandem with the strengths and weaknesses of critical commentary is either that there is no really useful particular level with which to parallel the level of metaphysical vision, or that if there is, the fruitful directions are to be found in the psychologics rather than the political logic or Christian logic of the critic's Gestalt. What remains, I suggest, for **'Bartleby'** criticism that will not be merely another repetition of what has already been said too often is not a one-to-one connection between Bartleby and a clinical category of psychopathology, but an exploration of psychological theory concerning various aspects of the self, theory that will provide a parallel to the metaphysical connections between the lawyer and Bartleby as somehow interrelated beings.

The matter of the epilogue bears strongly upon my view of approaches to **'Bartleby.'** For those who see no change in the narrator the epilogue is unsatisfactory because it creates too sympathetic a perspective for the narrator to possess; or, alternatively, the epilogue becomes one more irony in which Melville creates a merely sentimental perspective with which to establish the narrator's shallowness. In fact, the epilogue does sound like any number of sentimental pieces in the gift-book and periodical literature of the nineteenth century. But even if one were to isolate a 'Dead Letters Office' tradition in sentimental literature, the basic question would still remain: how does Melville use it? The fact of the tradition is much less important than its function within this tale, especially when one is cognizant of the fact that in *Pierre,* written only a little more than a year before the writing of **'Bartleby,'** Melville had used various elements of the popular sentimental literary tradition for very unpopular and unsentimental reasons. Let us consider the epilogue for a moment from the point of view of the writer rather than from the desire for interpretation.

What were Melville's necessities by the time he came to the epilogue? He had promised the epilogue at the very beginning of the story, when he obviously had the entire tale clearly in mind. One thing is certain: by the end of the tale Melville has not 'explained' Bartleby. He had planned, from the very beginning of the first instalment, not to say what happened to Bartleby to make him that way. But what could he say to answer this question? What events could he invent which would be horrible enough? And suppose he invented something truly hideous enough so that the character of Bartleby himself were not simply maudlin. In that event, the details of the destruction of all hope, all meaning, and all purpose—all life itself—would demand the writing of another story, something like the day-to-day to day-to-day incremental buildup of the horrors of an Auschwitz, or some other hell. But that was not the story Melville had in mind, and the story he told was the story he wanted to tell. All he could do was suggest, and merely suggest at that, a vision of some sort that

would hint at universal possibilities of dead hopes, closed lives, pointless endeavours, and missed connections. Moreover, he had to avoid a hint so lurid that it would shift the emotional emphasis, dragging the weight of the story and the reader's attention from all that had preceded the epilogue to the epilogue itself. Consciously or not, Melville was evidently aware that a hint that really tried to account for Bartleby's life would defeat the very purpose it was there for: to prevent a shift of the reader's engagement to a demand for seeing *more*. The mild, brief universal so lightly hinted about the affairs of mortal men, the Dead Letters Office, says, in effect, 'there is no more.' That is, the uncertain rumour about the Dead Letter Office at once universalizes Bartleby and keeps the focus exactly where Melville wants it—on the effect of Bartleby's condition, not on the cause of it.

Bartleby as a victim of the established world also comes to seem a victim of existence itself, and this, I think, is at the centre of what I take to be Melville's purpose—a speculation not about stoicism but about victimization. In much of his fiction he is anguished by victimization, compassionate with it, fascinated by it, and yet he also finds that in inexplicable ways the victim acquiesces in his victimization and intensifies the process. It is to ask the question, 'What else could Bartleby do?' Neither the universe nor the established world of the lawyer allowed him any alternatives. He could only assume his victimization and accept the death that is the consequence of it in his uncompromisingly honest view of a world empty of real alternatives—and thereby expose the nature of the world. But if the lawyer is to be attacked as the dehumanized organization man, is not Bartleby presented as dehumanized both explicitly and implicitly throughout the story, saying to the life around him, 'I prefer not to live it'?

My contention is that if one is willing to accept the facts of the story's characterization rather than attempt to fit those facts into an ideology, one has to conclude that Melville found not only heartbreak and terror in human victimization but also something mysteriously acquiescent and repelling about the dehumanized victim. The human possibilities for inhumanity construct rationalizations for the perverse desire to barbarize the victim precisely because of his passive victimization: the smug narrator burns to be rebelled against in order to justify his own sense of *separation* from the victim: the bastard is getting what he deserves. I suggest that Melville's psychological insights are too keen, when he puts them in the lawyer's mind that crucial Sunday morning, to dismiss them as merely more instances of the lawyer's selfishness—especially since those insights occur, as they do, in the context of the true melancholy that the narrator, deeply shaken for the first time in his life, experiences for the first time in his life. 'My first emotions,' he says, 'had been those of pure melancholy and sincerest pity; but just in proportion as the forlornness of Bartleby *grew and grew in my imagination,* did that same melancholy merge into fear, that pity into repulsion. *So true it is, and so terrible, too,* that up to a certain point the thought or sight of misery enlists our best affections; but, in special cases, beyond that point it does not. They err who would assert that invariably this is owing to the inherent selfishness of the human heart. It rather proceeds from a certain hopelessness of remedying excessive and organic ill' [italics added]. The lawyer's naked glimpse of Bartleby is as though one could imagine the anachronistic possibility of the good, Christian, prudent, American businessman doing a thriving, profitable business with the Nazis and suddenly becoming soul-shakingly aware of the death-camps at Auschwitz. The lawyer's speech is partly self-defensive. But it also expresses the horror that goes beyond a defence of one's self in shallow selfishness and becomes a fearful revulsion that includes the victim—take it away, make it not be. Yet what could the victim do but be? Either he must *be,* in the face of the observer's desperate desire for him to go away, not to be, or he himself must also prefer not to be. The first choice can only increase the observer's shock and horror; the second can only increase the observer's guilt and remorse because of his own psychological complicity in the victim's death. The more Bartleby preferred not to, the more the lawyer wished him to vacate the premises. The intimate, interior oneness of Bartleby and lawyer must be contemplated in the intricate and complex context of victimization.

But once a consideration is admitted into evidence, it cannot be used by the prosecution only. If we ask the question, but what else could he do? we must be willing to apply it to the lawyer as well. In the longest and most intelligent attack on the narrator and defence of Bartleby as hero, Kingsley Widmer concludes that the 'narrator never . . . changes his view and way of life.' It is a charge that subsumes within it the many narrower, less thoughtful, and less suggestive attacks on the lawyer and defences of Bartleby. But in terms of Bartleby as the only alternative to the lawyer, what, indeed, could the lawyer do? To apply equal sanctions to Bartleby and narrator is to create no contest. As metaphor Bartleby simply is not subject to the kinds of reality that are inevitable for the lawyer, who is derived from realistic characterology. Arguing from his own political and philosophical Gestalt, Widmer asserts that because culture is the product of the inhuman lawyer's world and serves only to civilize that world's enormities, against which Bartleby rebels, it is a sign of the dehumanizing failure of meliorism. As the lawyer's culture is a lie in human terms, culture up to the total revolution of Bartleby is to be repudiated. Bartleby's naysaying unto death is the truly revolutionary response. In sum, not only is the present to be put to death as a sacrifice to a metaphor of the liberated future, but so is the past as well. (Is it not fitting that Bartleby, who is heroic to Widmer, and who has no emulative present, is a man with no past?) But to me there is a familiar Melvillism in the fact that, being totally committed to his vision and thus isolating himself from all connections with the shallow lee-shore present, Bartleby in his monomania leads not to full life in the future but pallidly to death. It is clear to me that if Melville does not condone the culture of *is,* neither does he advocate a destruction of *was.* Not, at least, the multiple Melville, the mirror-maker, that we know in the totality of his works. One cannot make the corpselike Bartleby a sign of life without wrenching that cadaver out of Melville's presentation of him and into the polemics of one's own Gestalt.

Widmer's charge is extra-literary, for, like all strong art, **'Bartleby the Scrivener'** leads strong readers beyond the literary fact itself, and Widmer is justified in stepping beyond. In my disagreement with his view I wish simply to meet him on his own grounds. True, within the story itself, one can find instances to rebut the charge against the narrator. One instance that is always either slighted or virtually ignored in attacks on the narrator is the moment in which he does offer to open his life to Bartleby, to support him, to stay with him, and to assume responsibility for him: ' "Bartleby," said I, in the kindest tone I could assume under such exciting circumstances, "will you go home with me now—not to my office, but my dwelling—and remain there till we can conclude upon some convenient arrangement for you at our leisure? Come, let us start now, right away." ' At this point it is more than clear that were Bartleby to accompany the narrator, he would never leave for 'some convenient arrangement' elsewhere. The narrator offers no less than a lifelong 'arrangement.' And he does not offer gradualism either; the delays, assumptions, and illusions are gone: 'Come, let us start now, right away.' But even with this evidence those who wish to simplify the story into a totalistic choice of Bartleby-hero versus narrator-villain can argue that the lawyer wishes only to get Bartleby out of the public building and into his private home—as though the connection between public and private, outer and inner, were not the essence of the connection in victimization between the lawyer and Bartleby in the first place.

So we return to the question, what else could the narrator do? What life could the narrator change to, other than Bartleby's? And again Melville gives us no alternatives other than the lawyer and Bartleby. With this inescapable given, then, let us abandon the evidences within the story for a moment and step outside it with Widmer to the arguments beyond. Widmer identifies the true essence of humanity as nihilism, 'that simply recurrent human reality—the vital desire to angrily negate [sic] things as they are.' (Widmer) It is significant that Widmer feels it necessary to intrude that word 'angrily,' for it provides the human and psychologically necessary dimension that the characterologically typal Bartleby most patently lacks. But, given Widmer's premise, the story 'reveals the confession of a decent, prudent, rational "liberal" who finds in his chambers of consciousness the incomprehensible, the perverse, irrational demon of denial, and of his own denied humanity'. (Widmer) 'The attempt to wryly force [sic] benevolent American rationalism to an awareness of our forlorn and walled-in humanity provides the larger purpose of the tale' (Widmer). But if we must assume that the spirit of denial is deeply human, must we assume, then, that it is the only deep or true humanity, much less the total essence of humanity, as Widmer assumes? Is not the need for self-deception as human as the desire for denial? Is not the conscious as *real* as the unconscious? Is not the invention of predictable meaning as human as the nihilistic response to the revelation of cosmic absurdity? By what fiats may critics *assume,* like that man of assumptions, the lawyer, total categories of the really human and the falsely human in human behaviour and in human history and in human perception? What is true is that we wish to identify as human what affirms life rather than what denies it, what enlarges personality rather than what claustrophobically walls it in. It is also true that as a repressive principle the narrator in the first half of the tale is dehumanizing. But can the denials of Bartleby really be held up as a model of what affirms life and enlarges personality? For Widmer Bartleby becomes 'a small wan Ahab' who 'defiantly butts all . . . blind walls' (Widmer). Thus Bartleby becomes an 'abstract personification of the attorney's own humanity' (Widmer), as though, again, the principle of defiance were the totality subsumed under the category 'human.' Will, preference, in and of itself, and not rationality—certainly not rationality—becomes the true human characteristic. The true morality, therefore, is the demonic, not the common morality. 'The scrivener provides the human completion, the rage [and here again, significantly, is Widmer's response to the demands of psychologic and he invents for Bartleby a characteristic of which Bartleby is, in fact, completely devoid] to the restraint, the covert rebellion to the conviction that "the easiest way of life is the best," the assertion of *human* preferences against depersonalized assumptions, and the melancholy pessimism to balance the bland optimism' (Widmer, italics added). For Widmer anything less than Bartleby's willingness to go to death in his denials of the present points away from the true morality on the other side of the nihilistic revolution and is merely meliorism. Again, there is nothing the narrator can do short of becoming Bartleby. But the good world on the other side of Bartleby's pallid and unvarying negations comes from Widmer's Gestalt, not from Melville's story. For not only is Bartleby no small, wan Ahab, he is the complementary opposite of Ahab, and offers none of the Ahabian rage that Widmer consequently has to supply for him. Moreover, the imputation to Melville of millennial views of history is most strange in the context of invoking Ahab's spirit. For surely if Melville saw anything in that context, it was Ahab's murderous miscalculations about the possibilities of experience. If our context is Melville's rather than Widmer's Gestalt, what we have is not the total rebel ushering in the ultimate revolution, but the endless, indeterminate continuations of history, as repetitive and as illuminating of human limitation as the great shroud of the sea that rolls on as it did five thousand years ago. The totalistic critical view makes demands and meanings that entirely subvert and are deaf to the despairing tone of the tale as well as to its indeterminateness.

It is precisely at the point of turning everyone into Bartleby, which for Widmer would be the salvation of the revolution accomplished, that Melville draws back—the same Melville who looks askance at romantic and nihilistic versions of history and the human essence; the same Melville who says that if oysters and champagne are the foods of the body, get you your oysters and champagne; the same Melville who warmly sees the inescapable necessity of the lee shore for all that is kindly to our mortalities even as he urges Bulkington to keep the open independence of his soul's sea from the lee shore's lawyer-like slavish and shallow copy-assumptions; the same Melville who would repudiate the mast-head visions in order to ameliorate the ship's course with the first hint of the hitching tiller; the same Melville who has Ishmael learn that man must eventually learn to lower or at least shift his conceit of attain-

able felicity. He is, to the point, the same Melville who leaves the stage to the lawyer, not to Bartleby. Because he is the Melville who is so gnarledly aware that the only operable human actuality is the despised and limited *now* trapped between absolutes of infinity and eternity, he draws back from the absolutist prescriptions of totalistic literary criticism that would have the world go even unto death for salvation in the future. He will not annihilate the limited human existence within mortal history, the source of realistic fiction, for the triumph of the absolute quality of typalism, even when heroic. Much less does he do so for idea, the bloodless universal, the pallid metaphor. In **'Bartleby'** the problems of fictive characterization *are* the problems of metaphysics and psychology. If Edwards on the will and Priestly on necessity, if Locke and Paley are not justifications of necessity that Melville accepts, the deathlessness of the white whale and the deathfulness of Bartleby are. I take it that the real agony of the story comes from Melville's seeing that man must smash the surfaces of respectable and established vision to become fully human, but that if, in doing so, truth turn out to be the frozen absurd or the new vision become the monomania of totalistic defiance, man is plunged into even more deadly and deathly dehumanization. Both Bartleby and the lawyer are victims of human limitation; both suffer dehumanizations, and **'Bartleby'** is indeed a speculation about the process of victimization. The cosmic truth kills. The comfortable lies blind us and destroy our hearts that should be enlarged by woe. Both the defiant vision and the lee shore are needed, both are inescapable, and to wake from the world of one into the world of the other is mortal despair, overpowering, stinging melancholy. It is this impingement of worlds that is Melville's constant technique in mingling the characters of different fictive modes to suggest his view of the dilemma of men.

Ah, Bartleby! Ah, humanity!

Perhaps it is a deep knowledge that one possible corollary of the total revolution is generational suicide—*that* as a possibility at least as much as the good world that is supposed to lie beyond the revolution of total negation—that continues to make the masses, who desire nothing so much as a secured present, the despair of the total revolutionaries. I do not mean for a moment that Melville endorses the status quo he presents in the narrator's world. I do mean that through his vision of Bartleby the narrator is awakened to the perception of vulnerable nakedness and woe that makes us all monkey-rope brothers. Paradoxically it is 'revolutionary' Bartleby, not the narrator, who is the one-dimensional man.

When I called **'Bartleby'** a speculation, I meant just that. To see it as a polemic rather than as a query is to substitute the Gestalt of the critic for the Gestalt of the story. To reduce the narrator to a fixed moral quantity is to deny the extent to which the story continues to nag and itch after you have read all the criticism that affixes weightings, labels, answers, to what Melville created as lasting question marks. To insist upon ideological equivalents for the details of the story is to lose the suppleness and openness of the story, which is, I think, why critiques of the story always seem to be so much more rigid than the tale itself.

To fix an ideology upon this tale is to substitute a desire for a satisfying *quod erat demonstrandum* in place of the continuing perturbation left by the tale, and which is a mark of its particular art. The substitution of polemical answers for Melville's questions is merely to discover the face in the mirror—it is, finally, to substitute the lesser imagination behind fixed quantities for the greater imagination behind the tale. The paradox, as I see it, is that the critics who dismiss the narrator as merely smug and bad in his narrow solipsism are guilty of exactly the same sin of which they indict him.

I suggest that as a speculation about human victimization **'Bartleby the Scrivener'** is a despairing recognition that neither the lee-shore life nor the truth-piercing total vision that repudiates it provides adequate sustenance for our hungry humanity. Yet, a glimpse of the victim's woe can become the woe that is wisdom, and, given that, a man is on his way to becoming human even in his only present world, for that world will never be the same to him again. Perhaps that is the birth of revolution. (I suspect, in my memory of his works, that Melville would say, 'No, no— that *is* the unending revolution.') When I say, then, that we can declare a blessed moratorium on saying certain kinds of things about Bartleby and the narrator, I do not mean that we can declare a moratorium on speculations that continue to explore the story both within and beyond itself. All readers provide that 'beyond' out of their own times and visions and will continue to know the headache of trying to explore the story in that beyond. On errands of contemplation art speeds to—contemplation, and leaves us—ah, Melville! ah readers! —with our own dead letters offices. And with kings and counsellors.

Michael Murphy   (essay date 1985)

SOURCE: " 'Bartleby the Scrivener': A Simple Reading," in *Arizona Quarterly*, Vol. 41, No. 2, Summer, 1985, pp. 143-51.

[*In the following essay, Murphy contends that "Bartleby, the Scrivener" is a metaphorical story about the inner life of one individual, the lawyer.*]

It is a fact not generally acknowledged that **"Bartleby, the Scrivener"** is a story with only one character—the lawyer who tells it. Bartleby is simply an aspect of The Lawyer's character, long suppressed. Ginger Nut, Nippers, and Turkey are other facets of his personality or stages in his career. Even personages with "walk-on" parts like The Grubman, The Turnkey, and The Landlord are not separate characters, but parts of The Lawyer.

The lawyer is *a* lawyer, of course, but it might be possible to see him as The Writer or The Successful Popular Writer. Certainly some critics have seen him as that, and Bartleby as the serious but less successful writer like Melville himself. No doubt other occupations, though not all, might be read in for The Lawyer. Full Profesor, for example, whose bartlepart would prefer not to teach Freshman Composition with its endless checking of copy. But the author *has* chosen a lawyer and has given him a local habitation if not a name.

The namelessness is important; it has been noticed, but its significance has not been much dwelt upon. The lawyer may not be exactly Everyman, but the reader can fill in appropriately the blank left by the author-allegorist. It is not an accident that the lawyer's underlings do not have real names either, just nicknames—of the schoolboy variety at that, indicating a certain affection even for traits of character or habit not always pleasing but always bearable. Even Bartleby does not have a full name. Is "Bartleby" a first name or a surname, anyway? Between them all they do not have a complete name because, not only are they not several people, but together they do not amount to a complete man, not at any rate to the complete Christian man who can, without qualification, be called by both his surname *and* his Christian name (which we now generally call "first name").

They do amount to a rather pleasant, competent, aging lawyer, attached to his comfortable and remunerative routine, but without any great vices or any great ambition of either the material or spiritual kind; he does not have the kind of excess that makes saint or sinner. No Wall Street Faust, he is the kind of unimaginative man who likes to look upon the face of John Jacob Astor, the man who launched a thousand ships or built a thousand miles of railroad or something splendidly useful like that. From such a man it is a compliment to be assured that one is a useful drudge who does not even have the capacity to sin big like one's employer. This diploma from J. J. Astor, capitalizing the words SAFE, PRUDENCE, METHOD, is his only trophy. The only other thing that decorates his life or his office is the bust of Cicero. The diploma belongs; the bust is comically out of place, for it is the image of a great lawyer who wrote a book about friendship that is still read, and who spoke out with immortal eloquence in great and important causes. It does not fit well in the pokey office of a man who is, by his own admission, a bit of a turkey. One might consider it the remnant of a youthful ideal to serve *pro patria et justitia* were it not that he tells us that he had never really had such an ideal. Perhaps it is his way of acknowledging an ideal he never had the courage to adopt fully but always vaguely admired. It is the image of a secular saint safe on his pedestal and in his grave. Somewhere around but out of sight he has the somewhat faded picture of an even more famous Man who is rumored to be alive if not too well in the neighborhood of Wall Street.

The lawyer *is* alive and well and sixtyish when he encounters Bartleby, the last, not-too-robust incarnation of something (unspecified) other than what he has taken as his ideal—the easiest way of life. One reason that may account for the lawyer's almost comic attachment to this ideal, and hence for his extreme reluctance to give it up, is the possibility that his current ease has been attained with some difficulty. We *know* nothing of his history, for he never wittingly tells us anything of it. But in such "I" narratives we are often expected to surmise some things that we are not explicitly told, as in the stories told by the young captain in Conrad's "Secret Sharer" or James's "Turn of the Screw," for example. Here the trinity of Ginger Nut, Nippers, and Turkey can be seen as stages of the lawyer's career, ghosts of his past who, like the poor, are always with him, unforgettable, unforgotten, as the death notices say. Turkey may also represent the ghost of a possible and feared future (he is the same age as his master). The lawyer, a benevolent Scrooge, has climbed from gingerness, through nipperdom, to turkitude and ease. Hence suggestions that the much-desired goal is something of a dead end are not easy to entertain at the age of sixty. Those who have climbed from teaching assistant to instructor and over the ragged strata of professor may have some sympathy with the feeling.

Why don't I say No to Safe; go out and get drunk once in a while? Why don't I go home and do something else with my declining years besides flunkying for rich men?

With submission, sir. I cannot do that, sir.

Why not?

Well, for one thing, I have no home to go to: no wife, no children. Never had the time. Or maybe it was because I preferred not to be burdened in that way. In any case, I have only my work and the office. Besides, a man who has a good overcoat, but who remembers the time when he did not, is eternally afraid that the time will come again when he will not. He can never really relax in that overcoat, because he knows as well as any Russian that if he does, someone is going to take it away from him.

So I come to work, even in the afternoons which I could probably take off now. I am not J. J. Astor nor was meant to be. Not Jesus Christ either, though I admire both in their degree.

The trinity, always with him because part of his past and present and possible future, are not and never have been quite content with the lot he has chosen. But theirs is and always has been a manageable dissatisfaction, the kind that most people have to deal with. It is when the lawyer takes on the job of Master in Chancery, a not very onerous but quite remunerative position, that the protest within him takes on a new form. Quiet and almost unnoticed at first because of its difference from the noisy but harmless cantankerousness of the trinity, it becomes quietly more insistent and more unmanageable. At first the lawyer pretends that this master's job, so dubious apparently that even nineteenth-century politicians later reform it out of existence, deserves all his attention, and he buries his new misgivings (Bartleby) under a pile of work which blots out unease with industry. But the uneasiness is now in the same room with him, blocked off only by a screen and not by doors which can be shut to keep out the noisy but tolerable objections of Turkey and the others. Bartleby is merely a whisper away, and when the workaholic routine begins to fail, the objection comes through loudly enough to be heard.

This rebellion is of an altogether less manageable kind than the semi-comic antics of his other goblins. This is not comic at all; it is becoming serious now, for he cannot easily shut out the persistent, nagging thought that he would prefer not to do a snug business among rich men's bonds and mortgages and title deeds.

But I can do nothing else. I have no home life, only an office life. I have begotten and bred nothing, and certainly cannot start now, can I? Nippers and the others are not my recalci-

trant but eventually obedient children. They are just parts of me that will die with me. And that may very well occur soon if I give up this work, which is the only life I know. Even if I did not die of that, I should certainly not be at ease. The trinity will not go away; their antics may be different, but they will haunt me with the fear of coatlessness, a fear not to be scoffed at. Prudence and Method may not be theological virtues up there with Faith, Hope, and Charity; but they are the hinge that has enabled me to swing not only a good overcoat, but the regard of a man like John Jacob Astor, a feat to be sneered at only by those who have never had even a back-handed compliment from a robber baron, or those too well-heeled to need him or too unworldly to care. And, sirs, with submission, that am not I.

I work six days a week and, as society prescribes, I rest on the Sabbath—more or less. One Sunday recently, though, when I came downtown to worship at Holy Trinity, I was seduced into paying a visit to my nearby place of work on this holiday—sorry, holy day. There I found my new employee Bartleby in possession, urging me not to come into my own office, if you don't mind; asking me not to violate by such secular occupation the proprieties of the day, as I think he put it. An insubordinate suggestion from one of my own underlings, certainly. Rather insolent, too, the way he picked up on my own turn of phrase. That could become infectious, and bad for discipline in the office.

I'm afraid I listened to him at first, but finally the lawyer in me asserted himself, and I entered. What I found was not very spectacular, really the same office that I occupy the other six days of the week, but I did see it with slightly different eyes—Sabbath eyes, I suppose. At any rate there was the naked evidence of an arid existence, including the pathetic savings in my desk. My *savings?*

Bartleby has no mirror, but the narrator gets a glimpse of himself, and unwittingly paints a self-portrait into his picture of that barren bachelor existence along with his first intimation of its relevance to himself: "For both Bartleby and I were sons of Adam"—a characteristically sentimental touch. But the vision of their "fraternal" relationship is momentary, and clouded by the usual office gloom. It might have been the lawyer's incident on the road to Damascus, but the walls do their work. The lawyer has not kept these chambers for nothing. There can be no dazzling light in there, and the dimness allows him to perceive things more or less as he wills. Splendid visions that knock you off your office chair are reduced to shadowy specters seen as in a glass darkly. You can even turn the glass to the wall if you find what you see disturbing. Our narrator *does*. He attributes to "Bartleby" what the reader sees to be true of the narrator himself:

What miserable friendlessness and loneliness are here revealed. Of a Sunday, Wall Street is as deserted as Petra.

And yet you cannot stay away from it.

But (if you'll allow me a little witticism) super hanc petram aedificabo ecclesiam meam. *It is upon this rock that I shall build, indeed have built, my church. Or, to be more modest, but equally metaphorical, it is there that I occupy a small, unpretentious chapel in the temple built by men like J. J. Astor. It is as dim as an orthodox church like Holy Trinity, only there is no stained glass, just grimy windows and walls that obstruct the light.*

If the likes of Bartleby prevail against us, what will happen? We conduct a useful service to man on six of seven days a week. Some of you may misconstrue that into "a useful service to Mammon six days a week." But laborare est orare, *to work is to pray. That is our antiphon, and it has a long and respectable history, if I mistake not. Even with only half the mind on the job on any given morning or afternoon, we still offer a service acceptable to the law, and always in the past, I thought, not unacceptable unto the Lord.*

Then came this strange acolyte who was an angel of work at first, but now answers our antiphon with the unorthodox response "I would prefer not to." I could understand it a little better if he were less subjunctive about it, if he said plainly "non serviam." Then I should know for certain (I think) where he came from and why.

Reason and bribery, as he frankly calls them, or prayer and sacrifice, as he might have called them, do not work. Something more is being asked for, he knows. So he flees with the desperation of a good man determined to avoid the occasions of sin. For do we not pray "Lead us not into temptation." And is it not often up to us to deliver ourselves from evil, real or apparent? But Bartleby continues to trespass against him even at a distance. The lawyer makes one more effort to exorcise this now-weakened spirit in the only fashion he knows how: there in the desert of Wall Street he makes Bartleby several offers—of work. Do they reveal the lawyer's failure or his refusal to comprehend what is being asked, or do they show a last attempt to compromise about a demand that he understands reasonably well—well enough, at any rate, to feel that he is being asked for too much? Does he know that his final offer, to take Bartleby home, is in fact empty? Bartleby has been there already and has been asked to leave. For the lawyer's home is his office, and as the story shows, he cannot be reached there. To reverse once more the application of his comments about Bartleby: "his soul I could not reach." Earlier communications have remained unanswered, or have been returned unopened to end up in the Dead Letter Office. Now even a personal messenger, a sort of Wall Street runner (in place), has been clumsily but effectively sidestepped, and his message evaded. Mr. Worldy Wiseman is successful and sixty, and will stay comfortably in Vanity Fair, thank you.

Bartleby, a clerk whose speech is short and quick and full of high sentence, a gaunt, sober, threadbare man, does not relate the old story of patient Griselda, but enacts the story of a new Griselda. Unlike the old one, he does not win out in the end, for this is a tale of modern Wall Street or Lombard Street, not a romance of old York or old Lombardy. This Griselda is dead and buried in *New* York. The mettlesome romantic poet Byron is also dead and buried somewhere far away; and romantic Ireland's dead and gone and with O'Leary in the grave. The unblinking eye of common or gorgon sense continues to turn them all stone cold, fit only for monuments to be erected by those who live happily ever after, like the lawyer; to be carved or scrawled upon by those, like us, who criticize ever after both monument and builder.

I did my best. I really did. How many of my detractors could have done better? I think I know St. Matthew's Gospel and the Sermon on the Mount and the Corporal Works of Mercy as well as the next man. I certainly visited Bartleby in prison. At the Tombs I urged Turkey—I mean The Turnkey—to let him remain in as indulgent confinement as possible. I have forgotten the name of The Grubman, which I did ask for. Something resembling Ginger Nut, I think. At any rate he shared that perceptive young fellow's view of Bartleby's sanity. He also performed a function rather like his, so I paid him to see that Bartleby was offered good food. The prison itself was not so bad, I remember. There was grass under foot and sky overhead, though Bartleby did not seem to notice. Difference of mood, I imagine. He was marooned on this not unpleasant island, you might say, with a plentiful supply of food and water, which I had provided. But he spoke and acted almost as if I had made him walk the plank. As you very well know, I had been at pains to avoid that kind of—premature act.

So I turned away, sadly. He wanted too much. He really did. He preferred not to eat our food, which was too coarse for him, as he had preferred not to share our work, which was too crass for him. He was not really of this world. We, fortunately or unfortunately, are.

So he sleeps with Kings and counsellors. Now there is a phrase I have always liked. It hath a round and orbicular sound to it, though it comes from a strange chapter of a strange book about a man who was expected to give up all his possessions with equanimity. It all turned out well in the end, however. They read a good deal of that sort of thing over at Holy Trinity, and it goes well enough with the stained glass. Besides, they are really a rather wellbred lot, who do not like extremes, although I think I can say that we have not reduced it all to mere literature, like some college professors I have heard about.

Ah, Bartleby! Ah, humanity! Ah, well.

"Bartleby" serves as the literary objectification of Melville's intense awareness of the psychological trauma of fragmentation, anxiety, and alienation. And behind it all lies the source of psychic disequilibrium—a dead, blank wall—the void of nothingness.

—*Ted Billy, in the* Arizona Quarterly, *Spring, 1975.*

Graham Nicol Forst   (essay date 1987)

SOURCE: "Up Wall Street towards Broadway: The Narrator's Pilgrimage in Melville's 'Bartleby the Scrivener'," in *Studies in Short Fiction*, Vol. 24, No. 3, Summer, 1987, pp. 263-70.

[*In the following essay, Forst contends that "Bartleby, the*

Scrivener" records a spiritual awakening undergone by the narrator.]

"No materials exist," says Bartleby's worldly employer, for "a full and satisfactory biography of this man."

For nothing is ever "ascertainable" about such men, except what our own "astonished eyes" tell us. Perhaps such men hardly "exist" except deep in our mythic imaginations where, as archetypes, they rest, until their presence is urged forth by the call of touching, sympathetic imaginations, Coleridge's, Melville's, Conrad's. Or the writers of Isaiah, or the Gospels.

But the surprising thing is not that *we* should discover such a mythic presence in this character—after all, we've met Ahab and Billy Budd. The surprising thing is that it should be recognized by an elderly, conservative, "eminently *safe*," prudent, methodical attorney-at-law, whose vision has been long dimmed by unambition and the dolor of pencils and dust in his walled-in quarters in New York's financial district. Exactly what "materials" are missing? Do not the parts make up the whole? Has not everyone by the mid-nineteenth century caught the spirit of Positivism and Scientism?

Apparently not. And yet critics differ quite widely on this question of whether there is any development, or "growth" in the narrator of Melville's **"Bartleby the Scrivener,"** and if there is, of what *kind* of change he undergoes. Most critics are willing to grant that he has at least been "vaguely perturbed" or "temporarily shaken" [Maurice Friedman, "Bartleby and the Modern Exile," in *Melville Annual 1965,* edited by Howard P. Vincent, 1966], but no more, perhaps because, as William Bysshe Stein puts it, he is "incapable of moral regeneration," and therefore unable to exhibit "[any] evidence of contrition" ["Bartleby: The Christian Conscience," in *Melville Annual 1965*]. In fact, Stein actually finds Melville inviting "an association with Judas" in the figure of the lawyer, suggesting perhaps that the lawyer's "change" was not exactly for the best.

At the other extreme, there are those who see the lawyer as almost beatified through his association with Bartleby. Leo Marx, for example, in his well-known and influential article "Melville's Parable of the Walls" [*Melville Annual 1965*], sees in the lawyer's famous peroration ("Ah, Bartleby! Ah, humanity!") neither rhetoric nor self-pity, but rather a "deeply felt and spontaneous . . . expression of human brotherhood as persistent, as magical as the leaves of grass"; and more recently, Donald H. Craver and Patricia R. Plante have described the pusillanimous attorney as "[rising] to heights of nobility every bit as ethereal as those reached by [Bartleby]" ["Bartleby, or the Ambiguities," in *Studies in Short Fiction* 20, Spring-Summer, 1983].

Part of the difficulty in understanding the kind of change, if any, the lawyer experiences lies in the fact that, although he is quite frank about his "snug" life *before* Bartleby arrived, he reveals little about his existence after Bartleby's death: does he return to his new chambers? if so, what is his attitude towards his work, his employees? and if not, what *does* he do now?

Such speculations are not tantamount to asking what becomes, say, of Coleridge's sadder but wiser wedding guest when he arises the morrow morn: after all, we never hear from him again. Melville's narrator, on the other hand, has presented us with a twenty-thousand word "biography" (confession?) he expects us to read, and that in itself should tell us *something* about how he has been affected by his relationship with Bartleby.

To some extent, our understanding of Melville's intentions with regard to the lawyer is aided by the recent turn in **"Bartleby"** criticism which identifies the scrivener as a Christ-figure. For once this connection is made, the role of the timid attorney can be seen as similar to that of the shady night disciple of the Gospel of John: Nicodemus, the wealthy Pharisee who comes to Christ at dusk, and receives the devastating knowledge that he must be "born again." A literalist, he of course misses the metaphor: can one "enter the second time into his mother's womb?" he asks, densely (John 3:4).

Nicodemus leaves, apparently puzzled; and we almost totally lose sight of him, until John 19, where he reappears silently to enact, along with Joseph of Arimathaea, the great redeeming love-labour of the embalming and entombment of the Christ (39-42). Apparently, *something* had entered the good man's soul, and whatever else John wanted us to see in the myth of Nicodemus, we certainly learn from it the transforming (or biblically, cleansing or healing) power of faith brought by the recognition of God's presence.

Something similar, I think, is Melville's intention with the narrator of **"Bartleby,"** that is, to depict an instance of what Joseph Campbell has identified [in his *The Hero with a Thousand Faces*] as the hero-archetype who "refuses the call," because he is "walled in by boredom" or (in Freudian terms) "bound in by the walls of childhood" (i. e., unable to shed the "infantile ego"). Such characters are sometimes unable (Minos, Daphne, Lot's wife) to confront the possibility of their salvation, but there are many examples of characters (Brynhild, Sleeping Beauty) whose "obstinate refusal of the call proves to be the occasion of a providential revelation of some unsuspected principle of release" [*The Hero with a Thousand Faces*].

Such is the case with Nicodemus, and such is the case with Bartleby's hesitant biographer who, like his fellow biblical lawyer, is first presented to us as a literalist, bent on drawing a picture of himself as the epitome of cool dispassion and Latinate formality, determined to avoid the trivial or sentimental yet (now, in any case, if not before his experience with Bartleby) sensitive and literate enough, and apparently at great enough leisure, to consider writing biographies of scriveners he's known. In those pre-Bartleby days, he was an *homme moyen,* a peace-loving, "snug" man who has been deeply shaken by his meeting with this mythical presence for whom no biography can be written—this Cain, this Wandering Jew, this Ancient Mariner, this Christ. His life was gray: like the angel of the church of the Laodiceans in Revelation, he was "neither hot nor cold"; he was a man whom we, like the angel of the Lord, would "spue out of our mouths" (3:16). He has been strictly a man of this world, never thinking beyond the realms of animal, mineral, vegetable, terms reflected by the names of his employees—"Turkey," "Nippers," (which Melville's Webster would have defined as "pliers") and "Ginger Nut" respectively. The four lived perfectly harmoniously in the confines of their office-cum-cell on Wall Street.

Until *He* appeared, in answer to a Help Wanted advertisement. And while the lawyer, like the biblical Nicodemus, has shown a preference for darkness, Bartleby by contrast is immediately associated with light: upon his "advent," he is framed by the light of the open door; and he is soon placed in a corner of the office where "the light came down from far above . . . as from a very small opening in a dome."

The story of the hermit's "ascendance" from the life of copy-clerk, and the narrator's rather hesitant epiphany, begins *tertia die,* "on the third day" of his employment. It begins, of course, with one of literature's most famous refusals to comply, a rebellion which cannot, in terms of this type of myth, end, until the attorney has been shown the way to "come to the light," to quote Christ's challenge to Nicodemus (John 3:20).

Melville presents the stages of the lawyer's growth with care, building gradually towards the story's climax, which occurs on that fateful Sunday morning, when the narrator decides to go to church to hear "a celebrated preacher." Halfway there, he is drawn to his chambers, where he finds "the apparition of Bartleby," who refuses the lawyer entrance. Bartleby says he is "deeply engaged."

Bartleby's presence in the office of a Sunday has "a strange effect" on the lawyer. He finally begins to perceive a certain aura of holiness about his erstwhile tenant: could Bartleby be desecrating God's law by *copying* on a *Sunday*? No: "there was something about Bartleby that forbade the supposition that he would by any secular occupation violate the proprieties of the day." Bit by bit, the lawyer begins to die, painfully, to the world. For "the first time" in his life, as he admits in this his most passionate confession yet, he finds himself in the grip of an "overpowering stinging melancholy." He suddenly feels drawn "irresistibly to gloom," and, more important, begins to realize a new, "fraternal" relation to Bartleby: "For both I and Bartleby were sons of Adam."

Now we are at the dead centre of the story: this experience has obviously been a deeply searching one for the lawyer, so much so that he now sees his past religious life as gesture and empty ritual. As he puts it, he "did not accomplish the purpose of going to Trinity Church that morning," realizing that "the things [he] had seen disqualified [him] for the time from church-going"—a surprising description of the dark he walks in from this benighted somnambulist!

As a further sign of his "enlightening" attitude, the lawyer begins to be genuinely solicitous towards Bartleby. He tries to find out about Bartleby's past, his needs; he even begins to defend him against the tormenting Nippers, just as the gradually awakening Nicodemus finally began to defend Jesus against his detractors (see John, 7:50-52).

Nevertheless the narrator, unable to find in his heart the necessary compassion to reach out to Bartleby, tries to fire him, and then to buy him off. "What earthly right have you to stay here?" demands the lawyer in frustration.

It's a rhetorical question: his being there has nothing, of course, to do with "earthly" rights. Bartleby's mission is divine: to awaken the narrator to his responsibility with regards to the keeping of his brother.

At this point in the story, the narrator drifts into a contemplation of a bloody 1841 Wall Street murder of "the unfortunate Adams" by the "still more unfortunate Colt." At first glance, this allusion hardly seems appropriate for a person who has begun to awaken to his fraternal responsibilities, and who has just admitted to Bartleby's "wondrous ascendency" over him. And in fact many critics, including the most recent and thorough chronicler of the Colt-Adams murder, T. H. Giddings, find in the allusion an incongruous associative leap, i. e. from the mere "nervous resentment" the lawyer felt over Bartleby's recalcitrance, to thoughts of mayhem.

In fact Giddings thinks the association so inapt that he judges it an artistic blemish; he goes so far as to accuse Melville here of "carelessness" in plotting, of poorly "imagining the scene"; and to imply that in any case the allusion was and is too topical to serve the needs of fiction ["Melville, the Colt-Adams Murder, and 'Bartleby,' " in *Studies in American Fiction* 2, Autumn, 1974].

If we regard the event as just another New York homicide, it's hard to disagree with Giddings; it happened eleven years before the appearance in print of **"Bartleby,"** and, obviously, has faded farther and farther into obscurity with each successive generation of readers. And even if, for whatever narrative reason, Melville *did* wish the allusion to the historical case to register at least with his contemporary readers, he gives precious few details of the case to trigger their recollections.

But what if the murder be seen not as just another downtown homicide but as the *archetypal* homicide: the murder of Cain by Abel, an event which figures again and again in Melville's works. Not only do the initials (C, A) fit but we also have the specific allusion to Cain's father in the name "Adams," which is emphasized in the line following this paragraph when the lawyer talks of "the old Adam of resentment" rising in him. Also, this interpretation accounts for the lack of specific details of the New York murder in the allusion, and for the reference to the murderer as being (i. e. like Cain) "more unfortunate" than his victim. As well, it emphatically saves Melville from the charge of poor plotting and imagining.

Indeed, the opposite becomes true; seen in this way, the allusion becomes a master-stroke of plotting, as perfectly placed to develop the theme of the lawyer's moral awakening: for it is immediately after this allusion, with its attendant question of fraternal responsibility, that the narrator suddenly finds himself able to "grapple" and "throw" his old streak of meanness, simply by recalling the redeeming injunction:

" 'A new commandment give I unto you, that ye

love one another.' " "Yes," muses the lawyer, as if to underline this moment of redemptive release, "this it was that saved me."

Gradually, the lawyer begins darkly to perceive that Bartleby was "billeted upon [him] for some mysterious purpose of an all-wise Providence," recalling the verse from John 3 where Nicodemus tells Christ, "we know that thou art a teacher come from God" (2). The lawyer now sees comforting Bartleby as his "mission in this world" and his new frame of mind as "blessed."

Tragically, however, he cannot live up to the demands made on him, and Bartleby ends up being led to prison in a scene "contrived," as Stein says, "to parallel the scenario of the crucifixion." And since the story is set in downtown Manhattan, Melville can build on this line of Christian (Easter) imagery by referring to the name of the prison to which Bartleby has been led, "The Tombs," as it was and still is (appropriately) called. And when the guilt-stricken narrator finally goes to visit Bartleby there, he is greeted with Christ's admonition to the unbelievers in John 5: " 'I know you.' "

This line of imagery comes to a point when, the last time the narrator goes to the Tombs, he is unable to find Bartleby. And although (again like Nicodemus) he does find the martyr's pitiable physical remains (in a position, says [Ray B. Browne in his *Melville's Drive to Humanism*, 1971], "suggestive of the picture of the crucified Christ taken down from the cross"), Bartleby's self, according to the narrator, *has* arisen from the Tombs, to live—and here he quotes from Job, "with kings and counselors."

With this poignant reference to the life-curse of the Old Testament's most exquisite sufferer, we see how much the narrator has grown in his thought and feelings. No longer the *homme moyen* of pre-Bartleby days, the "unambitious," "snug," "cool," and "eminently *safe*" attorney, who breathed, perhaps, but was nonetheless "deficient in life," he now clearly brims with it, having learned about suffering and despair, about human hope and hunger; having clearly heard the cries for compassion and brotherhood. In Melville's clever play on Manhattan street names, he has passed "up Wall Street towards Broadway."

But perhaps the best evidence of the effect Bartleby has had on the lawyer is supplied by the short epilogue attached to Bartleby's "biography." Often skimmed or seriously misread as appended solely to satisfy some supposed interest we may have (according to the narrator) with respect to "who Bartleby was" or "the manner of life he led," clearly the real reason for its inclusion by the narrator is to help himself (and the reader) find out who *he* is and what manner of life *he* lives. Otherwise, there would be no excusing the passage from the charge that it is an "artistic flaw" of the sort that tries to "[take] the reader outside of the confines of the story itself " [Charles G. Hoffman, "The Shorter Fiction of Herman Melville," *South Atlantic Quarterly*, 52, 1953]. For notwithstanding the narrator's assumptions to the contrary, the reader of literature no more *needs* nor wishes such "real" information about literary characters than he needs or wishes fictional information about real people. In literature, the engagement of our moral and aesthetic senses points our interest less towards how characters may exist "outside the confines of the story" than towards the consideration of how such lives affect those which they touch *in* the narrative.

From this point of view, the function of the "sequel" is clearly to confirm how profound and lasting and morally chastening was Bartleby's effect on the lawyer. For, first, we learn from the epilogue that the Bartleby "episode" had occurred perhaps years before this narrative was written: the information about the Dead Letter Office came to the narrator's ear "a few months after the scrivener's decease" and he confesses that he "could never ascertain . . . how true it is." This fact, of course, requires us to ask why he is telling the story at all. And why after all this time? Surely, Melville intends us to see that his narrator is seeking some kind of release here: like Dostoevsky's Underground Man or Lagerkvist's tortured Barabbas, or (once again the analogy is irresistible) Coleridge's Mariner, an agony constantly "burns" within his heart, as it will do until he "teaches his tale."

Second, the power and permanence of Bartleby's effect on the lawyer are demonstrated by his very anxiousness, also revealed here in the sequel, desperately to grasp for scraps of information about Bartleby, an anxiety which has, apparently never diminished over time. And when he *did* learn something, we can't help but notice what a powerful impact it had on him, one which he clearly wants to share with his readers. Nor can his thoughts on the subject of Bartleby in the Dead Letter Office be considered those of a "cool . . . eminently *safe* man": " . . . hardly can I express the emotions which seize me," he exclaims in passion: "Dead letters! does it not sound like dead men?"

And now comes the third point: the narrator clearly shows, in his summing up at the end of the epilogue, that he *has* learned what all our Bartlebys have to teach us: the dread, fatal consequences of human alienation. We cannot, surely, resist the notion which is so powerfully suggested by these concluding sentences that the narrator has truly struggled to arise redemptively to a view of love and charity embraced by the Sermon on the Mount:

> Sometimes from out the folded paper the pale clerk takes a ring—the finger it was meant for, perhaps, moulders in the grave; a banknote sent in swiftest charity—he whom it would relieve, nor eats nor hungers any more; pardon for those who died despairing; hope for those who died unhoping; good tidings for those who died stifled by unrelieved circumstances. On errands of life, these letters speed to death.
>
> Ah Bartleby! Ah humanity!

Are these sentiments, as Hershel Parker has called them [in "The 'Sequel' in 'Bartleby,' " in *Bartleby the Inscrutable*, edited by Thomas M. Inge, 1979], merely "sententious"? Is their expression simply a matter of the narrator allowing himself to "feel a gentle, superior sadness, a delicious melancholy"? Do these concluding words merely serve to "reduce his experience with the strange scrivener to manageable, non-unpleasing terms" in order to "show that he is at last in control?" What textual reason is there to read this passage ironically? Surely, there is far too much evidence both here and in the narrative that the lawyer has undergone a strong spiritual challenge to raise the possibility that Melville would end the story so cynically. For granting that the lawyer *failed* Bartleby in some important way, and that he was in fact the deadest of the dead letters, it is also true that he now *knows* how weak he was. He also knows that his actions, when he *did* act, were just funeral flowers: beautiful, well-meant, but uselessly after the fact. The very telling of the tale attests to such knowledge. And so, although he may, like the magi in Eliot's poem, finally return to his little kingdom, his walled-in life, his triplicate non-existence, his straitened world of Turkeys, Nippers, Ginger-Nuts, he will have been changed greatly by this painfully acquired knowledge.

> "How can a man be born when he is old?"

The question is asked of the Christ by the night-visiting Nicodemus. It is a question Bartleby's elderly biographer will carry with him heavily, as he stumbles in wonderment towards his own dark, private Tombs.

FURTHER READING

Bibliography

Bebb, Bruce. " 'Bartleby': An Annotated Checklist of Criticism." In *Bartleby the Inscrutable: A Collection of Commentary on Herman Melville's Tale "Bartleby the Scrivener,"* edited by M. Thomas Inge, pp. 199-238. Hamden, Conn.: Archon Books, 1979.
   Descriptive catalogue of criticism organized chronologically by publication date.

Newman, Lea Bertani Vozar. "Bartleby, the Scrivener." In her *A Reader's Guide to the Short Stories of Herman Melville,* pp. 19-78. Boston: G. K. Hall, 1986.
   Extended overview of critical perspectives on "Bartleby, the Scrivener," accompanied by a comprehensive list of essays and books containing interpretations of the story. The bibliography is organized alphabetically by critic name.

Criticism

Abcarian, Richard. "The World of Love and the Spheres of Fright: Melville's 'Bartleby the Scrivener.' " *Studies in Short Fiction* 1, No. 3 (Spring 1964): 207-15.
   Studies the development of the relationship of the lawyer to Bartleby in order to reveal the lawyer's growing realization that he is symbolically linked with Bartleby, whose condition represents the human condition.

Abrams, Robert E. " 'Bartleby' and the Fragile Pageantry of the Ego." *ELH* 45, No. 3 (Fall 1978): 488-500.
   Argues that the mystery of the self is evidenced in enigmatic Bartleby, who lacks the social façade that disguises the true self of most individuals.

Anderson, Walter E. "Form and Meaning in 'Bartleby the Scrivener.' " *Studies in Short Fiction* 18, No. 4 (Fall 1981): 383-93.

Explains "Bartleby, the Scrivener" as a Christian parable. According to Anderson, the lawyer represents most people, who (given the same set of circumstances) also would fail to meet their moral obligation to Bartleby.

Billy, Ted. "Eros and Thanatos in 'Bartleby.' " *Arizona Quarterly* 31, No. 1 (Spring 1975): 21-32.
   Proceeding from the premise that Bartleby and the narrator are fictional representations of thanatos and eros, respectively, Billy maintains that the two characters enact a tragic conflict between life and death instincts in the human psyche.

Bollas, Christopher. "Melville's Lost Self: 'Bartleby.' " *American Imago* 31, No. 4 (Winter 1974): 401-11.
   Psychoanalytic study interpreting "Bartleby, the Scrivener" as a metaphor for the relationship between an individual's ego and true self.

Cornwell, Ethel F. "Bartleby the Absurd." *The International Fiction Review* 9, No. 2 (Summer 1982): 93-9.
   Perceives Bartleby as a person who became aware of life as absurd.

Emery, Allan Moore. "The Alternatives of Melville's 'Bartleby.' " *Nineteenth Century Fiction* 31, No. 2 (September 1976): 170-87.
   Explores the influence of the philosophers Jonathan Edwards and Joseph Priestly on the themes of freedom and limitation, free will and determinism in "Bartleby, the Scrivener."

Inge, M. Thomas, ed. *Bartleby the Inscrutable: A Collection of Commentary on Herman Melville's Tale "Bartleby the Scrivener."* Hamden, Conn.: Archon Books, 1979, 238 p.
   Anthology of criticism providing "a representative sampling of some of the most provocative critical essays published on 'Bartleby, the Scrivener,' along with four more recent essays especially commissioned for this book."

Kaplan, Morton, and Kloss, Robert. "Fantasy of Passivity: Melville's 'Bartleby the Scrivener.' " In their *The Unspoken Motive: A Guide to Psychoanalytic Literary Criticism,* pp. 63-79. New York: The Free Press, 1973.
   Diagnose Bartleby manic-depressive and contend that the narrator's veneer of passivity is a neurotic attempt to repress underlying impulses toward aggression and violence.

Marler, Robert F. " 'Bartleby, the Scrivener' and the American Short Story." *Genre* VI, No. 4 (December 1973): 428-47.
   Contends that "Bartleby, the Scrivener" is perhaps the first modern American short story, as distinguished from the type of short fiction known as the tale, because it avoids the moralism, allegory, romantic characterization, and other traits of the tale. Marler concludes that the narrator is the main character and not a villain.

McCall, Dan. *The Silence of Bartleby.* Ithaca, N.Y.: Cornell University Press, 1989, 206 p.
   Book-length study that employs a different critical approach to "Bartleby, the Scrivener" in each chapter. The chapters are entitled "Swimming through Libraries," " 'A Little *Luny*,' " " 'A Passive Resistance,' " " 'Hawthorne: A Problem,' " and "The Reliable Narrator."

Miller, Lewis H., Jr. " 'Bartleby' and the Dead Letter." *Studies in American Fiction* 8, No. 1 (Spring 1980): 1-12.
   Demonstrates that language in "Bartleby, the Scriven-

er" belies the narrator's assessment of the events related by him. Miller further asserts that the story's concluding account of Bartleby's previous position in a dead letter office "provides a definitive ironic perspective from which to view the narrator."

Norman, Liane. "Bartleby and the Reader." *The New England Quarterly* XLIV, No. 1 (March 1971): 22-39.

Contends that the reader is encouraged by Melville to identify with the lawyer until the lawyer's attitudes are revealed to have philosophic shortcomings.

Perry, Dennis R. " 'Ah, Humanity': Compulsion Neuroses in Melville's 'Bartleby.' " *Studies in Short Fiction* 24, No. 4 (Fall 1987): 407-15.

Provides a psychoanalytic interpretation of "Bartleby, the Scrivener," contending that the characters evince varying degrees of compulsion neuroses.

Pribek, Thomas. "Melville's Copyists: The 'Bar-tenders' of Wall Street." *Papers on Language and Literature* 22, No. 2 (Spring 1986): 176-86.

Examines the inequality, disillusionment, and discontent seen in "Bartleby, the Scrivener" as a by-product of the "competitive commercial world."

Reinert, Otto. "Bartleby the Inscrutable: Notes on a Melville Motif." In *Americana Norvegica: Norwegian Contributions to American Studies*, Vol. I, edited by Sigmund Skard and Henry H. Wasser, pp. 180-205. Philadelphia: University of Pennsylvania Press, 1966.

Interpretation focusing on the existentialist dimension of "Bartleby, the Scrivener," particularly as manifested in Bartleby's "passive endurance" and the recognition that the lawyer and Bartleby are "both protagonist and antagonist, both victim and victimizer." Reinert also considers the story in relation to Melville's other works that treat existentialist concerns.

Roundy, Nancy. " *That* Is All I Know of Him . . .': Epistemology and Art in Melville's 'Bartleby.' " *Essays in Arts and Sciences* IX, No. 1 (May 1980): 33-43.

Presents the narrator of "Bartleby, the Scrivener" as an artist who has been positively altered by his creative act, storytelling: "His sympathies have been awakened, his knowledge broadened, and his story is effective because of this change. From mere perception to imaginative vision—this is the lawyer's route, in his achievement of balanced art."

Schechter, Harold. "Bartleby the Chronometer." *Studies in Short Fiction* 19, No. 4 (Fall 1982): 359-66.

Argues that by earthly standards the lawyer in "Bartleby, the Scrivener" is a morally upright man, but his treatment of Bartleby demonstrates that the lawyer falls far short of heavenly standards and adherence to "Christ's precepts."

Shusterman, David. "The 'Reader Fallacy' and 'Bartleby the Scrivener.' " *The New England Quarterly* XLV, No. 1 (March 1972): 118-24.

Contests the critical method of Liane Norman in her essay "Bartleby and the Reader."

Silver, Allan. "The Lawyer and the Scrivener." *Partisan Review* XLVIII, No. 3 (1981): 409-24.

Viewing the lawyer as the "sole center of experience and meaning" in "Bartleby, the Scrivener," Silver focuses on the character's moral, social, and professional obligations to Bartleby.

Vincent, Howard P., ed. *Melville Annual 1965, a Symposium: "Bartleby the Scrivener."* Kent, Ohio: Kent State University Press, 199 p.

Collection of diverse essays on "Bartleby, the Scrivener," including discussions by a psychiatrist, a filmmaker, and a musician whose critical approaches reflect their respective fields of knowledge. A secondary bibliography and a facsimile reprinting of "Bartleby, the Scrivener" are included in the volume.

Widmer, Kingsley. "The Negative Affirmation: Melville's 'Bartleby.' " *Modern Fiction Studies* VIII, No. 3 (Autumn 1962): 276-86.

Perceiving Bartleby as "mutedly demonic," "nihilistic," and "a specter of irrational will" and the narrator-attorney as "pragmatically moral" and "a liberal rationalist," Widmer states: "All the civilized decency of the narrator fails to adequately confront Bartleby, and this indicts the best traditions of moral reasonableness, in Melville's time and in ours."

Wilson, James C. " 'Bartleby': The Walls of Wall Street." *Arizona Quarterly* 37, No. 4 (Winter 1981): 335-46.

Explicating "Bartleby, the Scrivener" as "one of the bitterest indictments of American capitalism ever published," Wilson attempts to show that Bartleby is reduced from a human being to an abstract concept of humanity by the narrator and the world of Wall Street.

Additional coverage of Melville's life and career is contained in the following sources published by Gale Research: *Contemporary Dictionary of American Literary Biography, 1640-1865*; *Dictionary of Literary Biography*, Vols. 3, 74; *DISCovering Authors*; *Nineteenth-Century Literature Criticism*, Vols. 3, 12, 29, 45; *Short Story Criticism*, Vol. 1; *Something about the Author*, Vol. 59; and *World Literature Criticism*.

Appendix:

Select Bibliography of General Sources on Short Fiction

BOOKS OF CRITICISM

Allen, Walter. *The Short Story in English*. New York: Oxford University Press, 1981, 413 p.

Aycock, Wendell M., ed. *The Teller and the Tale: Aspects of the Short Story* (Proceedings of the Comparative Literature Symposium, Texas Tech University, Volume XIII). Lubbock: Texas Tech Press, 1982, 156 p.

Averill, Deborah. *The Irish Short Story from George Moore to Frank O'Connor*. Washington, D.C.: University Press of America, 1982, 329 p.

Bates, H. E. *The Modern Short Story: A Critical Survey*. Boston: Writer, 1941, 231 p.

Bayley, John. *The Short Story: Henry James to Elizabeth Bowen*. Great Britain: The Harvester Press Limited, 1988, 197 p.

Bennett, E. K. *A History of the German Novelle: From Goethe to Thomas Mann*. Cambridge: At the University Press, 1934, 296 p.

Bone, Robert. *Down Home: A History of Afro-American Short Fiction from Its Beginning to the End of the Harlem Renaissance*. Rev. ed. New York: Columbia University Press, 1988, 350 p.

Bruck, Peter. *The Black American Short Story in the Twentieth Century: A Collection of Critical Essays*. Amsterdam: B. R. Grüner Publishing Co., 1977, 209 p.

Burnett, Whit, and Burnett, Hallie. *The Modern Short Story in the Making*. New York: Hawthorn Books, 1964, 405 p.

Canby, Henry Seidel. *The Short Story in English*. New York: Henry Holt and Co., 1909, 386 p.

Current-García, Eugene. *The American Short Story before 1850: A Critical History*. Twayne's Critical History of the Short Story, edited by William Peden. Boston: Twayne Publishers, 1985, 168 p.

Flora, Joseph M., ed. *The English Short Story, 1880-1945: A Critical History*. Twayne's Critical History of the Short Story, edited by William Peden. Boston: Twayne Publishers, 1985, 215 p.

Foster, David William. *Studies in the Contemporary Spanish-American Short Story*. Columbia, Mo.: University of Missouri Press, 1979, 126 p.

George, Albert J. *Short Fiction in France, 1800-1850*. Syracuse, N.Y.: Syracuse University Press, 1964, 245 p.

Gerlach, John. *Toward an End: Closure and Structure in the American Short Story*. University, Ala.: The University of Alabama Press, 1985, 193 p.

Hankin, Cherry, ed. *Critical Essays on the New Zealand Short Story*. Auckland: Heinemann Publishers,

1982, 186 p.

Hanson, Clare, ed. *Re-Reading the Short Story*. London: MacMillan Press, 1989, 137 p.

Harris, Wendell V. *British Short Fiction in the Nineteenth Century*. Detroit: Wayne State University Press, 1979, 209 p.

Huntington, John. *Rationalizing Genius: Ideological Strategies in the Classic American Science Fiction Short Story*. New Brunswick: Rutgers University Press, 1989, 216 p.

Kilroy, James F., ed. *The Irish Short Story: A Critical History*. Twayne's Critical History of the Short Story, edited by William Peden. Boston: Twayne Publishers, 1984, 251 p.

Lee, A. Robert. *The Nineteenth-Century American Short Story*. Totowa, N. J.: Vision / Barnes & Noble, 1986, 196 p.

Leibowitz, Judith. *Narrative Purpose in the Novella*. The Hague: Mouton, 1974, 137 p.

Lohafer, Susan. *Coming to Terms with the Short Story*. Baton Rouge: Louisiana State University Press, 1983, 171 p.

Lohafer, Susan, and Clarey, Jo Ellyn. *Short Story Theory at a Crossroads*. Baton Rouge: Louisiana State University Press, 1989, 352 p.

Mann, Susan Garland. *The Short Story Cycle: A Genre Companion and Reference Guide*. New York: Greenwood Press, 1989, 228 p.

Matthews, Brander. *The Philosophy of the Short Story*. New York, N.Y.: Longmans, Green and Co., 1901, 83 p.

May, Charles E., ed. *Short Story Theories*. Athens, Oh.: Ohio University Press, 1976, 251 p.

McClave, Heather, ed. *Women Writers of the Short Story: A Collection of Critical Essays*. Englewood Cliffs, N. J.: Prentice-Hall, 1980, 171 p.

Moser, Charles, ed. *The Russian Short Story: A Critical History*. Twayne's Critical History of the Short Story, edited by William Peden. Boston: Twayne Publishers, 1986, 232 p.

New, W. H. *Dreams of Speech and Violence: The Art of the Short Story in Canada and New Zealand*. Toronto: The University of Toronto Press, 1987, 302 p.

Newman, Frances. *The Short Story's Mutations: From Petronius to Paul Morand*. New York: B. W. Huebsch, 1925, 332 p.

O'Connor, Frank. *The Lonely Voice: A Study of the Short Story*. Cleveland: World Publishing Co., 1963, 220 p.

O'Faolain, Sean. *The Short Story*. New York: Devin-Adair Co., 1951, 370 p.

Orel, Harold. *The Victorian Short Story: Development and Triumph of a Literary Genre*. Cambridge: Cambridge University Press, 1986, 213 p.

O'Toole, L. Michael. *Structure, Style and Interpretation in the Russian Short Story*. New Haven: Yale University Press, 1982, 272 p.

Pattee, Fred Lewis. *The Development of the American Short Story: An Historical Survey*. New York: Harper and Brothers Publishers, 1923, 388 p.

Peden, Margaret Sayers, ed. *The Latin American Short Story: A Critical History*. Twayne's Critical History of the Short Story, edited by William Peden. Boston: Twayne Publishers, 1983, 160 p.

Peden, William. *The American Short Story: Continuity and Change, 1940-1975*. Rev. ed. Boston: Houghton Mifflin Co., 1975, 215 p.

Reid, Ian. *The Short Story*. The Critical Idiom, edited by John D. Jump. London: Methuen and Co., 1977, 76 p.

Rhode, Robert D. *Setting in the American Short Story of Local Color, 1865-1900*. The Hague: Mouton, 1975, 189 p.

Rohrberger, Mary. *Hawthorne and the Modern Short Story: A Study in Genre*. The Hague: Mouton and Co., 1966, 148 p.

Shaw, Valerie. *The Short Story: A Critical Introduction*. London: Longman, 1983, 294 p.

Stephens, Michael. *The Dramaturgy of Style: Voice in Short Fiction*. Carbondale, Ill.: Southern Illinois University Press, 1986, 281 p.

Stevick, Philip, ed. *The American Short Story, 1900-1945: A Critical History*. Twayne's Critical History of the Short Story, edited by William Peden. Boston: Twayne Publishers, 1984, 209 p.

Summers, Hollis, ed. *Discussion of the Short Story*. Boston: D. C. Heath and Co., 1963, 118 p.

Vannatta, Dennis, ed. *The English Short Story, 1945-1980: A Critical History*. Twayne's Critical History of the Short Story, edited by William Peden. Boston: Twayne Publishers, 1985, 206 p.

Voss, Arthur. *The American Short Story: A Critical Survey*. Norman, Okla.: University of Oklahoma Press, 1973, 399 p.

Walker, Warren S. *Twentieth-Century Short Story Explication: New Series, Vol. 1: 1989-1990*. Hamden, Conn.: Shoe String, 1993, 366 p.

Ward, Alfred C. *Aspects of the Modern Short Story: English and American*. London: University of London Press, 1924, 307 p.

Weaver, Gordon, ed. *The American Short Story, 1945-1980: A Critical History*. Twayne's Critical History of the Short Story, edited by William Peden. Boston: Twayne Publishers, 1983, 150 p.

West, Ray B., Jr. *The Short Story in America, 1900-1950*. Chicago: Henry Regnery Co., 1952, 147 p.

Williams, Blanche Colton. *Our Short Story Writers*. New York: Moffat, Yard and Co., 1920, 357 p.

Wright, Austin McGiffert. *The American Short Story in the Twenties*. Chicago: University of Chicago Press, 1961, 425 p.

CRITICAL ANTHOLOGIES

Atkinson, W. Patterson, ed. *The Short-Story*. Boston: Allyn and Bacon, 1923, 317 p.

Baldwin, Charles Sears, ed. *American Short Stories*. New York, N.Y.: Longmans, Green and Co., 1904, 333 p.

Charters, Ann, ed. *The Story and Its Writer: An Introduction to Short Fiction*. New York: St. Martin's Press, 1983, 1239 p.

Current-García, Eugene, and Patrick, Walton R., eds. *American Short Stories: 1820 to the Present*. Key Editions, edited by John C. Gerber. Chicago: Scott, Foresman and Co., 1952, 633 p.

Fagin, N. Bryllion, ed. *America through the Short Story*. Boston: Little, Brown, and Co., 1936, 508 p.

Frakes, James R., and Traschen, Isadore, eds. *Short Fiction: A Critical Collection*. Prentice-Hall English Literature Series, edited by Maynard Mack. Englewood Cliffs, N.J.: Prentice-Hall, 1959, 459 p.

Gifford, Douglas, ed. *Scottish Short Stories, 1800-1900*. The Scottish Library, edited by Alexander Scott. London: Calder and Boyars, 1971, 350 p.

Gordon, Caroline, and Tate, Allen, eds. *The House of Fiction: An Anthology of the Short Story with Commentary*. Rev. ed. New York: Charles Scribner's Sons, 1960, 469 p.

Greet, T. Y., et. al. *The Worlds of Fiction: Stories in Context*. Boston, Mass.: Houghton Mifflin Co., 1964, 429 p.

Gullason, Thomas A., and Caspar, Leonard, eds. *The World of Short Fiction: An International Collection*. New York: Harper and Row, 1962, 548 p.

Havighurst, Walter, ed. *Masters of the Modern Short Story*. New York: Harcourt, Brace and Co., 1945, 538 p.

Litz, A. Walton, ed. *Major American Short Stories*. New York: Oxford University Press, 1975, 823 p.

Matthews, Brander, ed. *The Short-Story: Specimens Illustrating Its Development*. New York: American Book Co., 1907, 399 p.

Menton, Seymour, ed. *The Spanish American Short Story: A Critical Anthology*. Berkeley and Los Angeles: University of California Press, 1980, 496 p.

Mzamane, Mbulelo Vizikhungo, ed. *Hungry Flames, and Other Black South African Short Stories*. Longman African Classics. Essex: Longman, 1986, 162 p.

Schorer, Mark, ed. *The Short Story: A Critical Anthology*. Rev. ed. Prentice-Hall English Literature Series, edited by Maynard Mack. Englewood Cliffs, N. J.: Prentice-Hall, 1967, 459 p.

Simpson, Claude M., ed. *The Local Colorists: American Short Stories, 1857-1900*. New York: Harper and Brothers Publishers, 1960, 340 p.

Stanton, Robert, ed. *The Short Story and the Reader*. New York: Henry Holt and Co., 1960, 557 p.

West, Ray B., Jr., ed. *American Short Stories*. New York: Thomas Y. Crowell Co., 1959, 267 p.

Short Story
Criticism
Indexes

Literary Criticism Series
Cumulative Author Index

SSC Cumulative Nationality Index
SSC Cumulative Title Index

How to Use This Index

The main references

```
Calvino, Italo
    1923-1985.....CLC 5, 8, 11, 22, 33, 39,
                                  73; SSC 3
```

list all author entries in the following Gale Literary Criticism series:

BLC = *Black Literature Criticism*
CLC = *Contemporary Literary Criticism*
CLR = *Children's Literature Review*
CMLC = *Classical and Medieval Literature Criticism*
DA = *DISCovering Authors*
DC = *Drama Criticism*
HLC = *Hispanic Literature Criticism*
LC = *Literature Criticism from 1400 to 1800*
NCLC = *Nineteenth-Century Literature Criticism*
PC = *Poetry Criticism*
SSC = *Short Story Criticism*
TCLC = *Twentieth-Century Literary Criticism*
WLC = *World Literature Criticism, 1500 to the Present*

The cross-references

```
See also CANR 23; CA 85-88;
    obituary CA 116
```

list all author entries in the following Gale biographical and literary sources:

AAYA = *Authors & Artists for Young Adults*
AITN = *Authors in the News*
BEST = *Bestsellers*
BW = *Black Writers*
CA = *Contemporary Authors*
CAAS = *Contemporary Authors Autobiography Series*
CABS = *Contemporary Authors Bibliographical Series*
CANR = *Contemporary Authors New Revision Series*
CAP = *Contemporary Authors Permanent Series*
CDALB = *Concise Dictionary of American Literary Biography*
CDBLB = *Concise Dictionary of British Literary Biography*
DLB = *Dictionary of Literary Biography*
DLBD = *Dictionary of Literary Biography Documentary Series*
DLBY = *Dictionary of Literary Biography Yearbook*
HW = *Hispanic Writers*
JRDA = *Junior DISCovering Authors*
MAICYA = *Major Authors and Illustrators for Children and Young Adults*
MTCW = *Major 20th-Century Writers*
NNAL = *Native North American Literature*
SAAS = *Something about the Author Autobiography Series*
SATA = *Something about the Author*
YABC = *Yesterday's Authors of Books for Children*

Literary Criticism Series
Cumulative Author Index

Abasiyanik, Sait Faik 1906-1954
See Sait Faik
See also CA 123

Abbey, Edward 1927-1989 ...... **CLC 36, 59**
See also CA 45-48; 128; CANR 2, 41

Abbott, Lee K(ittredge) 1947- ...... **CLC 48**
See also CA 124; DLB 130

Abe, Kobo 1924-1993 ..... **CLC 8, 22, 53, 81**
See also CA 65-68; 140; CANR 24; MTCW

Abelard, Peter c. 1079-c. 1142 ... **CMLC 11**
See also DLB 115

Abell, Kjeld 1901-1961 .... **CLC 15**
See also CA 111

Abish, Walter 1931- .... **CLC 22**
See also CA 101; CANR 37; DLB 130

Abrahams, Peter (Henry) 1919- ..... **CLC 4**
See also BW 1; CA 57-60; CANR 26;
DLB 117; MTCW

Abrams, M(eyer) H(oward) 1912-... **CLC 24**
See also CA 57-60; CANR 13, 33; DLB 67

Abse, Dannie 1923-............ **CLC 7, 29**
See also CA 53-56; CAAS 1; CANR 4;
DLB 27

Achebe, (Albert) Chinua(lumogu)
1930- ..... **CLC 1, 3, 5, 7, 11, 26, 51, 75;**
BLC; DA; WLC
See also BW 2; CA 1-4R; CANR 6, 26;
CLR 20; DLB 117; MAICYA; MTCW;
SATA 38, 40

Acker, Kathy 1948- .... **CLC 45**
See also CA 117; 122

Ackroyd, Peter 1949-.......... **CLC 34, 52**
See also CA 123; 127

Acorn, Milton 1923-............. **CLC 15**
See also CA 103; DLB 53

Adamov, Arthur 1908-1970 ...... **CLC 4, 25**
See also CA 17-18; 25-28R; CAP 2; MTCW

Adams, Alice (Boyd) 1926- ... **CLC 6, 13, 46**
See also CA 81-84; CANR 26; DLBY 86;
MTCW

Adams, Andy 1859-1935......... **TCLC 56**
See also YABC 1

Adams, Douglas (Noel) 1952- ... **CLC 27, 60**
See also AAYA 4; BEST 89:3; CA 106;
CANR 34; DLBY 83; JRDA

Adams, Francis 1862-1893....... **NCLC 33**

Adams, Henry (Brooks)
1838-1918 .... **TCLC 4, 52; DA**
See also CA 104; 133; DLB 12, 47

Adams, Richard (George)
1920- .... **CLC 4, 5, 18**
See also AITN 1, 2; CA 49-52; CANR 3,
35; CLR 20; JRDA; MAICYA; MTCW;
SATA 7, 69

Adamson, Joy(-Friederike Victoria)
1910-1980 .... **CLC 17**
See also CA 69-72; 93-96; CANR 22;
MTCW; SATA 11, 22

Adcock, Fleur 1934-............. **CLC 41**
See also CA 25-28R; CANR 11, 34;
DLB 40

Addams, Charles (Samuel)
1912-1988 .... **CLC 30**
See also CA 61-64; 126; CANR 12

Addison, Joseph 1672-1719 .... **LC 18**
See also CDBLB 1660-1789; DLB 101

Adler, C(arole) S(chwerdtfeger)
1932- .... **CLC 35**
See also AAYA 4; CA 89-92; CANR 19,
40; JRDA; MAICYA; SAAS 15;
SATA 26, 63

Adler, Renata 1938-............ **CLC 8, 31**
See also CA 49-52; CANR 5, 22; MTCW

Ady, Endre 1877-1919 .... **TCLC 11**
See also CA 107

Aeschylus
525B.C.-456B.C. .... **CMLC 11; DA**

Afton, Effie
See Harper, Frances Ellen Watkins

Agapida, Fray Antonio
See Irving, Washington

Agee, James (Rufus)
1909-1955 .... **TCLC 1, 19**
See also AITN 1; CA 108;
CDALB 1941-1968; DLB 2, 26

Aghill, Gordon
See Silverberg, Robert

Agnon, S(hmuel) Y(osef Halevi)
1888-1970 .... **CLC 4, 8, 14**
See also CA 17-18; 25-28R; CAP 2; MTCW

Agrippa von Nettesheim, Henry Cornelius
1486-1535 .... **LC 27**

Aherne, Owen
See Cassill, R(onald) V(erlin)

Ai 1947-................... **CLC 4, 14, 69**
See also CA 85-88; CAAS 13; DLB 120

Aickman, Robert (Fordyce)
1914-1981 .... **CLC 57**
See also CA 5-8R; CANR 3

Aiken, Conrad (Potter)
1889-1973 ... **CLC 1, 3, 5, 10, 52; SSC 9**
See also CA 5-8R; 45-48; CANR 4;
CDALB 1929-1941; DLB 9, 45, 102;
MTCW; SATA 3, 30

Aiken, Joan (Delano) 1924-........ **CLC 35**
See also AAYA 1; CA 9-12R; CANR 4, 23,
34; CLR 1, 19; JRDA; MAICYA;
MTCW; SAAS 1; SATA 2, 30, 73

Ainsworth, William Harrison
1805-1882 .... **NCLC 13**
See also DLB 21; SATA 24

Aitmatov, Chingiz (Torekulovich)
1928-..................... **CLC 71**
See also CA 103; CANR 38; MTCW;
SATA 56

Akers, Floyd
See Baum, L(yman) Frank

Akhmadulina, Bella Akhatovna
1937-..................... **CLC 53**
See also CA 65-68

Akhmatova, Anna
1888-1966 .... **CLC 11, 25, 64; PC 2**
See also CA 19-20; 25-28R; CANR 35;
CAP 1; MTCW

Aksakov, Sergei Timofeyvich
1791-1859 .... **NCLC 2**

Aksenov, Vassily .... **CLC 22**
See also Aksyonov, Vassily (Pavlovich)

Aksyonov, Vassily (Pavlovich)
1932-..................... **CLC 37**
See also Aksenov, Vassily
See also CA 53-56; CANR 12

Akutagawa Ryunosuke
1892-1927 .... **TCLC 16**
See also CA 117

Alain 1868-1951 .... **TCLC 41**

Alain-Fournier .... **TCLC 6**
See also Fournier, Henri Alban
See also DLB 65

Alarcon, Pedro Antonio de
1833-1891 .... **NCLC 1**

Alas (y Urena), Leopoldo (Enrique Garcia)
1852-1901 .... **TCLC 29**
See also CA 113; 131; HW

Albee, Edward (Franklin III)
1928-...... **CLC 1, 2, 3, 5, 9, 11, 13, 25,**
53; DA; WLC
See also AITN 1; CA 5-8R; CABS 3;
CANR 8; CDALB 1941-1968; DLB 7;
MTCW

Alberti, Rafael 1902-............. **CLC 7**
See also CA 85-88; DLB 108

Alcala-Galiano, Juan Valera y
See Valera y Alcala-Galiano, Juan

Alcott, Amos Bronson 1799-1888 .. **NCLC 1**
See also DLB 1

Alcott, Louisa May
1832-1888 .... **NCLC 6; DA; WLC**
See also CDALB 1865-1917; CLR 1;
DLB 1, 42, 79; JRDA; MAICYA;
YABC 1

Aldanov, M. A.
See Aldanov, Mark (Alexandrovich)

Aldanov, Mark (Alexandrovich)
1886(?)-1957 .... **TCLC 23**
See also CA 118

Aldington, Richard 1892-1962...... **CLC 49**
See also CA 85-88; CANR 45; DLB 20, 36,
100

August, John
See De Voto, Bernard (Augustine)

Augustine, St. 354-430 .... **CMLC 6**

Aurelius
See Bourne, Randolph S(illiman)

Austen, Jane
1775-1817 .... **NCLC 1, 13, 19, 33; DA;**
WLC
See also CDBLB 1789-1832; DLB 116

Auster, Paul 1947- .... **CLC 47**
See also CA 69-72; CANR 23

Austin, Frank
See Faust, Frederick (Schiller)

Austin, Mary (Hunter)
1868-1934 .... **TCLC 25**
See also CA 109; DLB 9, 78

Autran Dourado, Waldomiro
See Dourado, (Waldomiro Freitas) Autran

Averroes 1126-1198 .... **CMLC 7**
See also DLB 115

Avison, Margaret 1918- .... **CLC 2, 4**
See also CA 17-20R; DLB 53; MTCW

Axton, David
See Koontz, Dean R(ay)

Ayckbourn, Alan
1939- .... **CLC 5, 8, 18, 33, 74**
See also CA 21-24R; CANR 31; DLB 13;
MTCW

Aydy, Catherine
See Tennant, Emma (Christina)

Ayme, Marcel (Andre) 1902-1967... **CLC 11**
See also CA 89-92; CLR 25; DLB 72

Ayrton, Michael 1921-1975 .... **CLC 7**
See also CA 5-8R; 61-64; CANR 9, 21

Azorin .... **CLC 11**
See also Martinez Ruiz, Jose

Azuela, Mariano
1873-1952 .... **TCLC 3; HLC**
See also CA 104; 131; HW; MTCW

Baastad, Babbis Friis
See Friis-Baastad, Babbis Ellinor

Bab
See Gilbert, W(illiam) S(chwenck)

Babbis, Eleanor
See Friis-Baastad, Babbis Ellinor

Babel, Isaak (Emmanuilovich)
1894-1941(?) ...... **TCLC 2, 13; SSC 16**
See also CA 104

Babits, Mihaly 1883-1941 .... **TCLC 14**
See also CA 114

Babur 1483-1530 .... **LC 18**

Bacchelli, Riccardo 1891-1985 ..... **CLC 19**
See also CA 29-32R; 117

Bach, Richard (David) 1936- .... **CLC 14**
See also AITN 1; BEST 89:2; CA 9-12R;
CANR 18; MTCW; SATA 13

Bachman, Richard
See King, Stephen (Edwin)

Bachmann, Ingeborg 1926-1973..... **CLC 69**
See also CA 93-96; 45-48; DLB 85

Bacon, Francis 1561-1626 .... **LC 18**
See also CDBLB Before 1660

Bacon, Roger 1214(?)-1292 ...... **CMLC 14**
See also DLB 115

Bacovia, George .... **TCLC 24**
See also Vasiliu, Gheorghe

Badanes, Jerome 1937- .... **CLC 59**

Bagehot, Walter 1826-1877 ..... **NCLC 10**
See also DLB 55

Bagnold, Enid 1889-1981 .... **CLC 25**
See also CA 5-8R; 103; CANR 5, 40;
DLB 13; MAICYA; SATA 1, 25

Bagrjana, Elisaveta
See Belcheva, Elisaveta

Bagryana, Elisaveta
See Belcheva, Elisaveta

Bailey, Paul 1937- .... **CLC 45**
See also CA 21-24R; CANR 16; DLB 14

Baillie, Joanna 1762-1851 .... **NCLC 2**
See also DLB 93

Bainbridge, Beryl (Margaret)
1933- .... **CLC 4, 5, 8, 10, 14, 18, 22, 62**
See also CA 21-24R; CANR 24; DLB 14;
MTCW

Baker, Elliott 1922- .... **CLC 8**
See also CA 45-48; CANR 2

Baker, Nicholson 1957- .... **CLC 61**
See also CA 135

Baker, Ray Stannard 1870-1946 ... **TCLC 47**
See also CA 118

Baker, Russell (Wayne) 1925- ...... **CLC 31**
See also BEST 89:4; CA 57-60; CANR 11,
41; MTCW

Bakhtin, M.
See Bakhtin, Mikhail Mikhailovich

Bakhtin, M. M.
See Bakhtin, Mikhail Mikhailovich

Bakhtin, Mikhail
See Bakhtin, Mikhail Mikhailovich

Bakhtin, Mikhail Mikhailovich
1895-1975 .... **CLC 83**
See also CA 128; 113

Bakshi, Ralph 1938(?)- .... **CLC 26**
See also CA 112; 138

Bakunin, Mikhail (Alexandrovich)
1814-1876 .... **NCLC 25**

Baldwin, James (Arthur)
1924-1987 ...... **CLC 1, 2, 3, 4, 5, 8, 13,**
15, 17, 42, 50, 67; BLC; DA; DC 1;
SSC 10; WLC
See also AAYA 4; BW 1; CA 1-4R; 124;
CABS 1; CANR 3, 24;
CDALB 1941-1968; DLB 2, 7, 33;
DLBY 87; MTCW; SATA 9, 54

Ballard, J(ames) G(raham)
1930- .... **CLC 3, 6, 14, 36; SSC 1**
See also AAYA 3; CA 5-8R; CANR 15, 39;
DLB 14; MTCW

Balmont, Konstantin (Dmitriyevich)
1867-1943 .... **TCLC 11**
See also CA 109

Balzac, Honore de
1799-1850 .... **NCLC 5, 35; DA; SSC 5;**
WLC
See also DLB 119

Bambara, Toni Cade
1939- .... **CLC 19; BLC; DA**
See also AAYA 5; BW 2; CA 29-32R;
CANR 24; DLB 38; MTCW

Bamdad, A.
See Shamlu, Ahmad

Banat, D. R.
See Bradbury, Ray (Douglas)

Bancroft, Laura
See Baum, L(yman) Frank

Banim, John 1798-1842 .... **NCLC 13**
See also DLB 116

Banim, Michael 1796-1874 ...... **NCLC 13**

Banks, Iain
See Banks, Iain M(enzies)

Banks, Iain M(enzies) 1954- .... **CLC 34**
See also CA 123; 128

Banks, Lynne Reid .... **CLC 23**
See also Reid Banks, Lynne
See also AAYA 6

Banks, Russell 1940- .... **CLC 37, 72**
See also CA 65-68; CAAS 15; CANR 19;
DLB 130

Banville, John 1945- .... **CLC 46**
See also CA 117; 128; DLB 14

Banville, Theodore (Faullain) de
1832-1891 .... **NCLC 9**

Baraka, Amiri
1934- .... **CLC 1, 2, 3, 5, 10, 14, 33;**
BLC; DA; PC 4
See also Jones, LeRoi
See also BW 2; CA 21-24R; CABS 3;
CANR 27, 38; CDALB 1941-1968;
DLB 5, 7, 16, 38; DLBD 8; MTCW

Barbellion, W. N. P. .... **TCLC 24**
See also Cummings, Bruce F(rederick)

Barbera, Jack (Vincent) 1945- ...... **CLC 44**
See also CA 110; CANR 45

Barbey d'Aurevilly, Jules Amedee
1808-1889 .... **NCLC 1; SSC 17**
See also DLB 119

Barbusse, Henri 1873-1935 .... **TCLC 5**
See also CA 105; DLB 65

Barclay, Bill
See Moorcock, Michael (John)

Barclay, William Ewert
See Moorcock, Michael (John)

Barea, Arturo 1897-1957 .... **TCLC 14**
See also CA 111

Barfoot, Joan 1946- .... **CLC 18**
See also CA 105

Baring, Maurice 1874-1945 .... **TCLC 8**
See also CA 105; DLB 34

Barker, Clive 1952- .... **CLC 52**
See also AAYA 10; BEST 90:3; CA 121;
129; MTCW

Barker, George Granville
1913-1991 .... **CLC 8, 48**
See also CA 9-12R; 135; CANR 7, 38;
DLB 20; MTCW

Barker, Harley Granville
See Granville-Barker, Harley
See also DLB 10

Barker, Howard 1946-............ **CLC 37**
See also CA 102; DLB 13

Barker, Pat 1943-................ **CLC 32**
See also CA 117; 122

Barlow, Joel 1754-1812 .... **NCLC 23**
See also DLB 37

Barnard, Mary (Ethel) 1909-....... **CLC 48**
See also CA 21-22; CAP 2

Barnes, Djuna
1892-1982 ... **CLC 3, 4, 8, 11, 29; SSC 3**
See also CA 9-12R; 107; CANR 16; DLB 4,
9, 45; MTCW

Barnes, Julian 1946-.............. **CLC 42**
See also CA 102; CANR 19; DLBY 93

Barnes, Peter 1931- .... **CLC 5, 56**
See also CA 65-68; CAAS 12; CANR 33,
34; DLB 13; MTCW

Baroja (y Nessi), Pio
1872-1956 .... **TCLC 8; HLC**
See also CA 104

Baron, David
See Pinter, Harold

Baron Corvo
See Rolfe, Frederick (William Serafino
Austin Lewis Mary)

Barondess, Sue K(aufman)
1926-1977 .... **CLC 8**
See also Kaufman, Sue
See also CA 1-4R; 69-72; CANR 1

Baron de Teive
See Pessoa, Fernando (Antonio Nogueira)

Barres, Maurice 1862-1923 .... **TCLC 47**
See also DLB 123

Barreto, Afonso Henrique de Lima
See Lima Barreto, Afonso Henrique de

Barrett, (Roger) Syd 1946- .... **CLC 35**

Barrett, William (Christopher)
1913-1992 .... **CLC 27**
See also CA 13-16R; 139; CANR 11

Barrie, J(ames) M(atthew)
1860-1937 .... **TCLC 2**
See also CA 104; 136; CDBLB 1890-1914;
CLR 16; DLB 10, 141; MAICYA;
YABC 1

Barrington, Michael
See Moorcock, Michael (John)

Barrol, Grady
See Bograd, Larry

Barry, Mike
See Malzberg, Barry N(athaniel)

Barry, Philip 1896-1949 .... **TCLC 11**
See also CA 109; DLB 7

Bart, Andre Schwarz
See Schwarz-Bart, Andre

Barth, John (Simmons)
1930- ...... **CLC 1, 2, 3, 5, 7, 9, 10, 14,
27, 51; SSC 10**
See also AITN 1, 2; CA 1-4R; CABS 1;
CANR 5, 23; DLB 2; MTCW

Barthelme, Donald
1931-1989 ...... **CLC 1, 2, 3, 5, 6, 8, 13,
23, 46, 59; SSC 2**
See also CA 21-24R; 129; CANR 20;
DLB 2; DLBY 80, 89; MTCW; SATA 7,
62

Barthelme, Frederick 1943-........ **CLC 36**
See also CA 114; 122; DLBY 85

Barthes, Roland (Gerard)
1915-1980 .... **CLC 24, 83**
See also CA 130; 97-100; MTCW

Barzun, Jacques (Martin) 1907-.... **CLC 51**
See also CA 61-64; CANR 22

Bashevis, Isaac
See Singer, Isaac Bashevis

Bashkirtseff, Marie 1859-1884 ... **NCLC 27**

Basho
See Matsuo Basho

Bass, Kingsley B., Jr.
See Bullins, Ed

Bass, Rick 1958-................ **CLC 79**
See also CA 126

Bassani, Giorgio 1916-............ **CLC 9**
See also CA 65-68; CANR 33; DLB 128;
MTCW

Bastos, Augusto (Antonio) Roa
See Roa Bastos, Augusto (Antonio)

Bataille, Georges 1897-1962 .... **CLC 29**
See also CA 101; 89-92

Bates, H(erbert) E(rnest)
1905-1974 .... **CLC 46; SSC 10**
See also CA 93-96; 45-48; CANR 34;
MTCW

Bauchart
See Camus, Albert

Baudelaire, Charles
1821-1867 ..... **NCLC 6, 29; DA; PC 1;
WLC**

Baudrillard, Jean 1929-........... **CLC 60**

Baum, L(yman) Frank 1856-1919 ... **TCLC 7**
See also CA 108; 133; CLR 15; DLB 22;
JRDA; MAICYA; MTCW; SATA 18

Baum, Louis F.
See Baum, L(yman) Frank

Baumbach, Jonathan 1933-....... **CLC 6, 23**
See also CA 13-16R; CAAS 5; CANR 12;
DLBY 80; MTCW

Bausch, Richard (Carl) 1945- ...... **CLC 51**
See also CA 101; CAAS 14; CANR 43;
DLB 130

Baxter, Charles 1947-......... **CLC 45, 78**
See also CA 57-60; CANR 40; DLB 130

Baxter, George Owen
See Faust, Frederick (Schiller)

Baxter, James K(eir) 1926-1972 .... **CLC 14**
See also CA 77-80

Baxter, John
See Hunt, E(verette) Howard, Jr.

Bayer, Sylvia
See Glassco, John

Baynton, Barbara 1857-1929 ..... **TCLC 57**

Beagle, Peter S(oyer) 1939-........ **CLC 7**
See also CA 9-12R; CANR 4; DLBY 80;
SATA 60

Bean, Normal
See Burroughs, Edgar Rice

Beard, Charles A(ustin)
1874-1948 .... **TCLC 15**
See also CA 115; DLB 17; SATA 18

Beardsley, Aubrey 1872-1898 ..... **NCLC 6**

Beattie, Ann
1947-.... **CLC 8, 13, 18, 40, 63; SSC 11**
See also BEST 90:2; CA 81-84; DLBY 82;
MTCW

Beattie, James 1735-1803 .... **NCLC 25**
See also DLB 109

Beauchamp, Kathleen Mansfield 1888-1923
See Mansfield, Katherine
See also CA 104; 134; DA

Beaumarchais, Pierre-Augustin Caron de
1732-1799 .... **DC 4**

**Beauvoir, Simone (Lucie Ernestine Marie
Bertrand) de**
1908-1986 .... **CLC 1, 2, 4, 8, 14, 31, 44,
50, 71; DA; WLC**
See also CA 9-12R; 118; CANR 28;
DLB 72; DLBY 86; MTCW

Becker, Jurek 1937-............ **CLC 7, 19**
See also CA 85-88; DLB 75

Becker, Walter 1950-............ **CLC 26**

Beckett, Samuel (Barclay)
1906-1989 ...... **CLC 1, 2, 3, 4, 6, 9, 10,
11, 14, 18, 29, 57, 59, 83; DA; SSC 16;
WLC**
See also CA 5-8R; 130; CANR 33;
CDBLB 1945-1960; DLB 13, 15;
DLBY 90; MTCW

Beckford, William 1760-1844 .... **NCLC 16**
See also DLB 39

Beckman, Gunnel 1910-.......... **CLC 26**
See also CA 33-36R; CANR 15; CLR 25;
MAICYA; SAAS 9; SATA 6

Becque, Henri 1837-1899......... **NCLC 3**

Beddoes, Thomas Lovell
1803-1849 .... **NCLC 3**
See also DLB 96

Bedford, Donald F.
See Fearing, Kenneth (Flexner)

Beecher, Catharine Esther
1800-1878 .... **NCLC 30**
See also DLB 1

Beecher, John 1904-1980.......... **CLC 6**
See also AITN 1; CA 5-8R; 105; CANR 8

Beer, Johann 1655-1700............. **LC 5**

Beer, Patricia 1924-.............. **CLC 58**
See also CA 61-64; CANR 13; DLB 40

Beerbohm, Henry Maximilian
1872-1956 .... **TCLC 1, 24**
See also CA 104; DLB 34, 100

Beerbohm, Max
See Beerbohm, Henry Maximilian

Begiebing, Robert J(ohn) 1946-..... **CLC 70**
See also CA 122; CANR 40

Behan, Brendan
1923-1964 .... **CLC 1, 8, 11, 15, 79**
See also CA 73-76; CANR 33;
CDBLB 1945-1960; DLB 13; MTCW

Behn, Aphra
1640(?)-1689 .... **LC 1; DA; DC 4; WLC**
See also DLB 39, 80, 131

Behrman, S(amuel) N(athaniel)
1893-1973 .... **CLC 40**
See also CA 13-16; 45-48; CAP 1; DLB 7,
44

Besant, Annie (Wood) 1847-1933 ... **TCLC 9**
See also CA 105

Bessie, Alvah 1904-1985.......... **CLC 23**
See also CA 5-8R; 116; CANR 2; DLB 26

Bethlen, T. D.
See Silverberg, Robert

Beti, Mongo................ **CLC 27; BLC**
See also Biyidi, Alexandre

Betjeman, John
1906-1984 .... **CLC 2, 6, 10, 34, 43**
See also CA 9-12R; 112; CANR 33;
CDBLB 1945-1960; DLB 20; DLBY 84;
MTCW

Bettelheim, Bruno 1903-1990 ...... **CLC 79**
See also CA 81-84; 131; CANR 23; MTCW

Betti, Ugo 1892-1953 .... **TCLC 5**
See also CA 104

Betts, Doris (Waugh) 1932-.... **CLC 3, 6, 28**
See also CA 13-16R; CANR 9; DLBY 82

Bevan, Alistair
See Roberts, Keith (John Kingston)

Bialik, Chaim Nachman
1873-1934 .... **TCLC 25**

Bickerstaff, Isaac
See Swift, Jonathan

Bidart, Frank 1939- .... **CLC 33**
See also CA 140

Bienek, Horst 1930-........... **CLC 7, 11**
See also CA 73-76; DLB 75

Bierce, Ambrose (Gwinett)
1842-1914(?) .... **TCLC 1, 7, 44; DA;**
SSC 9; WLC
See also CA 104; 139; CDALB 1865-1917;
DLB 11, 12, 23, 71, 74

Billings, Josh
See Shaw, Henry Wheeler

Billington, (Lady) Rachel (Mary)
1942- .... **CLC 43**
See also AITN 2; CA 33-36R; CANR 44

Binyon, T(imothy) J(ohn) 1936- .... **CLC 34**
See also CA 111; CANR 28

Bioy Casares, Adolfo
1914- ...... **CLC 4, 8, 13; HLC; SSC 17**
See also CA 29-32R; CANR 19, 43;
DLB 113; HW; MTCW

Bird, C.
See Ellison, Harlan

Bird, Cordwainer
See Ellison, Harlan

Bird, Robert Montgomery
1806-1854 .... **NCLC 1**

Birney, (Alfred) Earle
1904- .... **CLC 1, 4, 6, 11**
See also CA 1-4R; CANR 5, 20; DLB 88;
MTCW

Bishop, Elizabeth
1911-1979 ..... **CLC 1, 4, 9, 13, 15, 32;**
DA; PC 3
See also CA 5-8R; 89-92; CABS 2;
CANR 26; CDALB 1968-1988; DLB 5;
MTCW; SATA 24

Bishop, John 1935-.............. **CLC 10**
See also CA 105

Bissett, Bill 1939-................ **CLC 18**
See also CA 69-72; CAAS 19; CANR 15;
DLB 53; MTCW

Bitov, Andrei (Georgievich) 1937-... **CLC 57**
See also CA 142

Biyidi, Alexandre 1932-
See Beti, Mongo
See also BW 1; CA 114; 124; MTCW

Bjarme, Brynjolf
See Ibsen, Henrik (Johan)

Bjornson, Bjornstjerne (Martinius)
1832-1910 .... **TCLC 7, 37**
See also CA 104

Black, Robert
See Holdstock, Robert P.

Blackburn, Paul 1926-1971 ...... **CLC 9, 43**
See also CA 81-84; 33-36R; CANR 34;
DLB 16; DLBY 81

Black Elk 1863-1950 .... **TCLC 33**
See also CA 144

Black Hobart
See Sanders, (James) Ed(ward)

Blacklin, Malcolm
See Chambers, Aidan

Blackmore, R(ichard) D(oddridge)
1825-1900 .... **TCLC 27**
See also CA 120; DLB 18

Blackmur, R(ichard) P(almer)
1904-1965 .... **CLC 2, 24**
See also CA 11-12; 25-28R; CAP 1; DLB 63

Black Tarantula, The
See Acker, Kathy

Blackwood, Algernon (Henry)
1869-1951 .... **TCLC 5**
See also CA 105

Blackwood, Caroline 1931- .... **CLC 6, 9**
See also CA 85-88; CANR 32; DLB 14;
MTCW

Blade, Alexander
See Hamilton, Edmond; Silverberg, Robert

Blaga, Lucian 1895-1961 .... **CLC 75**

Blair, Eric (Arthur) 1903-1950
See Orwell, George
See also CA 104; 132; DA; MTCW;
SATA 29

Blais, Marie-Claire
1939- .... **CLC 2, 4, 6, 13, 22**
See also CA 21-24R; CAAS 4; CANR 38;
DLB 53; MTCW

Blaise, Clark 1940-............... **CLC 29**
See also AITN 2; CA 53-56; CAAS 3;
CANR 5; DLB 53

Blake, Nicholas
See Day Lewis, C(ecil)
See also DLB 77

Blake, William
1757-1827 ..... **NCLC 13, 37; DA; WLC**
See also CDBLB 1789-1832; DLB 93;
MAICYA; SATA 30

Blasco Ibanez, Vicente
1867-1928 .... **TCLC 12**
See also CA 110; 131; HW; MTCW

Blatty, William Peter 1928-......... **CLC 2**
See also CA 5-8R; CANR 9

Bleeck, Oliver
See Thomas, Ross (Elmore)

Blessing, Lee 1949-.............. **CLC 54**

Blish, James (Benjamin)
1921-1975 .... **CLC 14**
See also CA 1-4R; 57-60; CANR 3; DLB 8;
MTCW; SATA 66

Bliss, Reginald
See Wells, H(erbert) G(eorge)

Blixen, Karen (Christentze Dinesen)
1885-1962
See Dinesen, Isak
See also CA 25-28; CANR 22; CAP 2;
MTCW; SATA 44

Bloch, Robert (Albert) 1917-....... **CLC 33**
See also CA 5-8R; CANR 5; DLB 44;
SATA 12

Blok, Alexander (Alexandrovich)
1880-1921 .... **TCLC 5**
See also CA 104

Blom, Jan
See Breytenbach, Breyten

Bloom, Harold 1930- .... **CLC 24**
See also CA 13-16R; CANR 39; DLB 67

Bloomfield, Aurelius
See Bourne, Randolph S(illiman)

Blount, Roy (Alton), Jr. 1941- ..... **CLC 38**
See also CA 53-56; CANR 10, 28; MTCW

Bloy, Leon 1846-1917............ **TCLC 22**
See also CA 121; DLB 123

Blume, Judy (Sussman) 1938-... **CLC 12, 30**
See also AAYA 3; CA 29-32R; CANR 13,
37; CLR 2, 15; DLB 52; JRDA;
MAICYA; MTCW; SATA 2, 31, 79

Blunden, Edmund (Charles)
1896-1974 .... **CLC 2, 56**
See also CA 17-18; 45-48; CAP 2; DLB 20,
100; MTCW

Bly, Robert (Elwood)
1926- .... **CLC 1, 2, 5, 10, 15, 38**
See also CA 5-8R; CANR 41; DLB 5;
MTCW

Boas, Franz 1858-1942.......... **TCLC 56**
See also CA 115

Bobette
See Simenon, Georges (Jacques Christian)

Boccaccio, Giovanni
1313-1375 .... **CMLC 13; SSC 10**

Bochco, Steven 1943-............. **CLC 35**
See also AAYA 11; CA 124; 138

Bodenheim, Maxwell 1892-1954 ... **TCLC 44**
See also CA 110; DLB 9, 45

Bodker, Cecil 1927-.............. **CLC 21**
See also CA 73-76; CANR 13, 44; CLR 23;
MAICYA; SATA 14

Boell, Heinrich (Theodor)
1917-1985 .... **CLC 2, 3, 6, 9, 11, 15, 27,**
32, 72; DA; WLC
See also CA 21-24R; 116; CANR 24;
DLB 69; DLBY 85; MTCW

Boerne, Alfred
See Doeblin, Alfred

Bogan, Louise 1897-1970..... **CLC 4, 39, 46**
See also CA 73-76; 25-28R; CANR 33;
DLB 45; MTCW

Browning, Robert
1812-1889 .... **NCLC 19; DA; PC 2**
See also CDBLB 1832-1890; DLB 32;
YABC 1

Browning, Tod 1882-1962 .... **CLC 16**
See also CA 141; 117

Bruccoli, Matthew J(oseph) 1931- .. **CLC 34**
See also CA 9-12R; CANR 7; DLB 103

Bruce, Lenny .... **CLC 21**
See also Schneider, Leonard Alfred

Bruin, John
See Brutus, Dennis

Brulard, Henri
See Stendhal

Brulls, Christian
See Simenon, Georges (Jacques Christian)

Brunner, John (Kilian Houston)
1934- .... **CLC 8, 10**
See also CA 1-4R; CAAS 8; CANR 2, 37;
MTCW

Bruno, Giordano 1548-1600 .... **LC 27**

Brutus, Dennis 1924- .... **CLC 43; BLC**
See also BW 2; CA 49-52; CAAS 14;
CANR 2, 27, 42; DLB 117

Bryan, C(ourtlandt) D(ixon) B(arnes)
1936- .... **CLC 29**
See also CA 73-76; CANR 13

Bryan, Michael
See Moore, Brian

Bryant, William Cullen
1794-1878 .... **NCLC 6, 46; DA**
See also CDALB 1640-1865; DLB 3, 43, 59

Bryusov, Valery Yakovlevich
1873-1924 .... **TCLC 10**
See also CA 107

Buchan, John 1875-1940 .... **TCLC 41**
See also CA 108; 145; DLB 34, 70; YABC 2

Buchanan, George 1506-1582 .... **LC 4**

Buchheim, Lothar-Guenther 1918- ... **CLC 6**
See also CA 85-88

Buchner, (Karl) Georg
1813-1837 .... **NCLC 26**

Buchwald, Art(hur) 1925-.......... **CLC 33**
See also AITN 1; CA 5-8R; CANR 21;
MTCW; SATA 10

Buck, Pearl S(ydenstricker)
1892-1973 .... **CLC 7, 11, 18; DA**
See also AITN 1; CA 1-4R; 41-44R;
CANR 1, 34; DLB 9, 102; MTCW;
SATA 1, 25

Buckler, Ernest 1908-1984......... **CLC 13**
See also CA 11-12; 114; CAP 1; DLB 68;
SATA 47

Buckley, Vincent (Thomas)
1925-1988 .... **CLC 57**
See also CA 101

Buckley, William F(rank), Jr.
1925- .... **CLC 7, 18, 37**
See also AITN 1; CA 1-4R; CANR 1, 24;
DLB 137; DLBY 80; MTCW

Buechner, (Carl) Frederick
1926- .... **CLC 2, 4, 6, 9**
See also CA 13-16R; CANR 11, 39;
DLBY 80; MTCW

Buell, John (Edward) 1927-........ **CLC 10**
See also CA 1-4R; DLB 53

Buero Vallejo, Antonio 1916- ... **CLC 15, 46**
See also CA 106; CANR 24; HW; MTCW

Bufalino, Gesualdo 1920(?)-........ **CLC 74**

Bugayev, Boris Nikolayevich 1880-1934
See Bely, Andrey
See also CA 104

Bukowski, Charles
1920-1994 .... **CLC 2, 5, 9, 41, 82**
See also CA 17-20R; 144; CANR 40;
DLB 5, 130; MTCW

Bulgakov, Mikhail (Afanas'evich)
1891-1940 .... **TCLC 2, 16**
See also CA 105

Bulgya, Alexander Alexandrovich
1901-1956 .... **TCLC 53**
See also Fadeyev, Alexander
See also CA 117

Bullins, Ed 1935- .... **CLC 1, 5, 7; BLC**
See also BW 2; CA 49-52; CAAS 16;
CANR 24; DLB 7, 38; MTCW

Bulwer-Lytton, Edward (George Earle Lytton)
1803-1873 .... **NCLC 1, 45**
See also DLB 21

Bunin, Ivan Alexeyevich
1870-1953 .... **TCLC 6; SSC 5**
See also CA 104

Bunting, Basil 1900-1985.... **CLC 10, 39, 47**
See also CA 53-56; 115; CANR 7; DLB 20

Bunuel, Luis 1900-1983 .. **CLC 16, 80; HLC**
See also CA 101; 110; CANR 32; HW

Bunyan, John 1628-1688 .. **LC 4; DA; WLC**
See also CDBLB 1660-1789; DLB 39

Burford, Eleanor
See Hibbert, Eleanor Alice Burford

Burgess, Anthony
. **CLC 1, 2, 4, 5, 8, 10, 13, 15, 22, 40, 62,
81**
See also Wilson, John (Anthony) Burgess
See also AITN 1; CDBLB 1960 to Present;
DLB 14

Burke, Edmund
1729(?)-1797 .... **LC 7; DA; WLC**
See also DLB 104

Burke, Kenneth (Duva)
1897-1993 .... **CLC 2, 24**
See also CA 5-8R; 143; CANR 39; DLB 45,
63; MTCW

Burke, Leda
See Garnett, David

Burke, Ralph
See Silverberg, Robert

Burney, Fanny 1752-1840 .... **NCLC 12**
See also DLB 39

Burns, Robert
1759-1796 ...... **LC 3; DA; PC 6; WLC**
See also CDBLB 1789-1832; DLB 109

Burns, Tex
See L'Amour, Louis (Dearborn)

Burnshaw, Stanley 1906- ..... **CLC 3, 13, 44**
See also CA 9-12R; DLB 48

Burr, Anne 1937- .... **CLC 6**
See also CA 25-28R

Burroughs, Edgar Rice
1875-1950 .... **TCLC 2, 32**
See also AAYA 11; CA 104; 132; DLB 8;
MTCW; SATA 41

Burroughs, William S(eward)
1914- .... **CLC 1, 2, 5, 15, 22, 42, 75;
DA; WLC**
See also AITN 2; CA 9-12R; CANR 20;
DLB 2, 8, 16; DLBY 81; MTCW

Burton, Richard F. 1821-1890.... **NCLC 42**
See also DLB 55

Busch, Frederick 1941- ... **CLC 7, 10, 18, 47**
See also CA 33-36R; CAAS 1; CANR 45;
DLB 6

Bush, Ronald 1946- .... **CLC 34**
See also CA 136

Bustos, F(rancisco)
See Borges, Jorge Luis

Bustos Domecq, H(onorio)
See Bioy Casares, Adolfo; Borges, Jorge
Luis

Butler, Octavia E(stelle) 1947- ..... **CLC 38**
See also BW 2; CA 73-76; CANR 12, 24,
38; DLB 33; MTCW

Butler, Robert Olen (Jr.) 1945-..... **CLC 81**
See also CA 112

Butler, Samuel 1612-1680 .... **LC 16**
See also DLB 101, 126

Butler, Samuel
1835-1902 ...... **TCLC 1, 33; DA; WLC**
See also CA 143; CDBLB 1890-1914;
DLB 18, 57

Butler, Walter C.
See Faust, Frederick (Schiller)

Butor, Michel (Marie Francois)
1926- .... **CLC 1, 3, 8, 11, 15**
See also CA 9-12R; CANR 33; DLB 83;
MTCW

Buzo, Alexander (John) 1944-...... **CLC 61**
See also CA 97-100; CANR 17, 39

Buzzati, Dino 1906-1972 .... **CLC 36**
See also CA 33-36R

Byars, Betsy (Cromer) 1928-....... **CLC 35**
See also CA 33-36R; CANR 18, 36; CLR 1,
16; DLB 52; JRDA; MAICYA; MTCW;
SAAS 1; SATA 4, 46

Byatt, A(ntonia) S(usan Drabble)
1936- .... **CLC 19, 65**
See also CA 13-16R; CANR 13, 33;
DLB 14; MTCW

Byrne, David 1952-.............. **CLC 26**
See also CA 127

Byrne, John Keyes 1926-
See Leonard, Hugh
See also CA 102

Byron, George Gordon (Noel)
1788-1824 ...... **NCLC 2, 12; DA; WLC**
See also CDBLB 1789-1832; DLB 96, 110

C. 3. 3.
See Wilde, Oscar (Fingal O'Flahertie Wills)

Caballero, Fernan 1796-1877..... **NCLC 10**

Cabell, James Branch 1879-1958 ... **TCLC 6**
See also CA 105; DLB 9, 78

Cable, George Washington
1844-1925 . . . . **TCLC 4; SSC 4**
See also CA 104; DLB 12, 74

Cabral de Melo Neto, Joao 1920-. . . **CLC 76**

Cabrera Infante, G(uillermo)
1929- . . . . **CLC 5, 25, 45; HLC**
See also CA 85-88; CANR 29; DLB 113;
HW; MTCW

Cade, Toni
See Bambara, Toni Cade

Cadmus and Harmonia
See Buchan, John

Caedmon fl. 658-680 . . . . **CMLC 7**

Caeiro, Alberto
See Pessoa, Fernando (Antonio Nogueira)

Cage, John (Milton, Jr.) 1912- . . . . . **CLC 41**
See also CA 13-16R; CANR 9

Cain, G.
See Cabrera Infante, G(uillermo)

Cain, Guillermo
See Cabrera Infante, G(uillermo)

Cain, James M(allahan)
1892-1977 . . . . **CLC 3, 11, 28**
See also AITN 1; CA 17-20R; 73-76;
CANR 8, 34; MTCW

Caine, Mark
See Raphael, Frederic (Michael)

Calasso, Roberto 1941- . . . . **CLC 81**
See also CA 143

Calderon de la Barca, Pedro
1600-1681 . . . . **LC 23; DC 3**

Caldwell, Erskine (Preston)
1903-1987 . . . . **CLC 1, 8, 14, 50, 60**
See also AITN 1; CA 1-4R; 121; CAAS 1;
CANR 2, 33; DLB 9, 86; MTCW

Caldwell, (Janet Miriam) Taylor (Holland)
1900-1985 . . . . **CLC 2, 28, 39**
See also CA 5-8R; 116; CANR 5

Calhoun, John Caldwell
1782-1850 . . . . **NCLC 15**
See also DLB 3

Calisher, Hortense
1911- . . . . **CLC 2, 4, 8, 38; SSC 15**
See also CA 1-4R; CANR 1, 22; DLB 2;
MTCW

Callaghan, Morley Edward
1903-1990 . . . . **CLC 3, 14, 41, 65**
See also CA 9-12R; 132; CANR 33;
DLB 68; MTCW

Calvino, Italo
1923-1985 . . . . . **CLC 5, 8, 11, 22, 33, 39,
73; SSC 3**
See also CA 85-88; 116; CANR 23; MTCW

Cameron, Carey 1952- . . . . **CLC 59**
See also CA 135

Cameron, Peter 1959-. . . . . **CLC 44**
See also CA 125

Campana, Dino 1885-1932. . . . . . . **TCLC 20**
See also CA 117; DLB 114

Campbell, John W(ood, Jr.)
1910-1971 . . . . **CLC 32**
See also CA 21-22; 29-32R; CANR 34;
CAP 2; DLB 8; MTCW

Campbell, Joseph 1904-1987 . . . . . . **CLC 69**
See also AAYA 3; BEST 89:2; CA 1-4R;
124; CANR 3, 28; MTCW

Campbell, Maria 1940-. . . . . **CLC 85**
See also CA 102; NNAL

Campbell, (John) Ramsey 1946- . . . . **CLC 42**
See also CA 57-60; CANR 7

Campbell, (Ignatius) Roy (Dunnachie)
1901-1957 . . . . **TCLC 5**
See also CA 104; DLB 20

Campbell, Thomas 1777-1844 . . . . **NCLC 19**
See also DLB 93; 144

Campbell, Wilfred . . . . **TCLC 9**
See also Campbell, William

Campbell, William 1858(?)-1918
See Campbell, Wilfred
See also CA 106; DLB 92

Campos, Alvaro de
See Pessoa, Fernando (Antonio Nogueira)

Camus, Albert
1913-1960 . . . . **CLC 1, 2, 4, 9, 11, 14, 32,
63, 69; DA; DC 2; SSC 9; WLC**
See also CA 89-92; DLB 72; MTCW

Canby, Vincent 1924- . . . . **CLC 13**
See also CA 81-84

Cancale
See Desnos, Robert

Canetti, Elias 1905- . . . . . . **CLC 3, 14, 25, 75**
See also CA 21-24R; CANR 23; DLB 85,
124; MTCW

Canin, Ethan 1960-. . . . . **CLC 55**
See also CA 131; 135

Cannon, Curt
See Hunter, Evan

Cape, Judith
See Page, P(atricia) K(athleen)

Capek, Karel
1890-1938 . . . . . **TCLC 6, 37; DA; DC 1;
WLC**
See also CA 104; 140

Capote, Truman
1924-1984 . . . . . **CLC 1, 3, 8, 13, 19, 34,
38, 58; DA; SSC 2; WLC**
See also CA 5-8R; 113; CANR 18;
CDALB 1941-1968; DLB 2; DLBY 80,
84; MTCW

Capra, Frank 1897-1991. . . . . **CLC 16**
See also CA 61-64; 135

Caputo, Philip 1941-. . . . . **CLC 32**
See also CA 73-76; CANR 40

Card, Orson Scott 1951- . . . . **CLC 44, 47, 50**
See also AAYA 11; CA 102; CANR 27;
MTCW

Cardenal (Martinez), Ernesto
1925- . . . . **CLC 31; HLC**
See also CA 49-52; CANR 2, 32; HW;
MTCW

Carducci, Giosue 1835-1907. . . . . . . **TCLC 32**

Carew, Thomas 1595(?)-1640 . . . . **LC 13**
See also DLB 126

Carey, Ernestine Gilbreth 1908- . . . . **CLC 17**
See also CA 5-8R; SATA 2

Carey, Peter 1943- . . . . **CLC 40, 55**
See also CA 123; 127; MTCW

Carleton, William 1794-1869 . . . . . . **NCLC 3**

Carlisle, Henry (Coffin) 1926- . . . . . . **CLC 33**
See also CA 13-16R; CANR 15

Carlsen, Chris
See Holdstock, Robert P.

Carlson, Ron(ald F.) 1947-. . . . . **CLC 54**
See also CA 105; CANR 27

Carlyle, Thomas 1795-1881 . . **NCLC 22; DA**
See also CDBLB 1789-1832; DLB 55; 144

Carman, (William) Bliss
1861-1929 . . . . **TCLC 7**
See also CA 104; DLB 92

Carnegie, Dale 1888-1955 . . . . **TCLC 53**

Carossa, Hans 1878-1956. . . . . **TCLC 48**
See also DLB 66

Carpenter, Don(ald Richard)
1931- . . . . **CLC 41**
See also CA 45-48; CANR 1

Carpentier (y Valmont), Alejo
1904-1980 . . . . **CLC 8, 11, 38; HLC**
See also CA 65-68; 97-100; CANR 11;
DLB 113; HW

Carr, Emily 1871-1945. . . . . **TCLC 32**
See also DLB 68

Carr, John Dickson 1906-1977 . . . . . . **CLC 3**
See also CA 49-52; 69-72; CANR 3, 33;
MTCW

Carr, Philippa
See Hibbert, Eleanor Alice Burford

Carr, Virginia Spencer 1929-. . . . . . . **CLC 34**
See also CA 61-64; DLB 111

Carrier, Roch 1937- . . . . **CLC 13, 78**
See also CA 130; DLB 53

Carroll, James P. 1943(?)-. . . . . **CLC 38**
See also CA 81-84

Carroll, Jim 1951- . . . . **CLC 35**
See also CA 45-48; CANR 42

Carroll, Lewis . . . . **NCLC 2; WLC**
See also Dodgson, Charles Lutwidge
See also CDBLB 1832-1890; CLR 2, 18;
DLB 18; JRDA

Carroll, Paul Vincent 1900-1968. . . . **CLC 10**
See also CA 9-12R; 25-28R; DLB 10

Carruth, Hayden
1921- . . . . . . **CLC 4, 7, 10, 18, 84; PC 10**
See also CA 9-12R; CANR 4, 38; DLB 5;
MTCW; SATA 47

Carson, Rachel Louise 1907-1964 . . . **CLC 71**
See also CA 77-80; CANR 35; MTCW;
SATA 23

Carter, Angela (Olive)
1940-1992 . . . . . . **CLC 5, 41, 76; SSC 13**
See also CA 53-56; 136; CANR 12, 36;
DLB 14; MTCW; SATA 66;
SATA-Obit 70

Carter, Nick
See Smith, Martin Cruz

Carver, Raymond
1938-1988 . . . **CLC 22, 36, 53, 55; SSC 8**
See also CA 33-36R; 126; CANR 17, 34;
DLB 130; DLBY 84, 88; MTCW

Cary, (Arthur) Joyce (Lunel)
1888-1957 . . . . **TCLC 1, 29**
See also CA 104; CDBLB 1914-1945;
DLB 15, 100

Casanova de Seingalt, Giovanni Jacopo
1725-1798 . . . . **LC 13**

Casares, Adolfo Bioy
See Bioy Casares, Adolfo

Casely-Hayford, J(oseph) E(phraim)
1866-1930 . . . . **TCLC 24; BLC**
See also BW 2; CA 123

Casey, John (Dudley) 1939- . . . . **CLC 59**
See also BEST 90:2; CA 69-72; CANR 23

Casey, Michael 1947- . . . . **CLC 2**
See also CA 65-68; DLB 5

Casey, Patrick
See Thurman, Wallace (Henry)

Casey, Warren (Peter) 1935-1988 . . . **CLC 12**
See also CA 101; 127

Casona, Alejandro . . . . **CLC 49**
See also Alvarez, Alejandro Rodriguez

Cassavetes, John 1929-1989 . . . . **CLC 20**
See also CA 85-88; 127

Cassill, R(onald) V(erlin) 1919- . . . **CLC 4, 23**
See also CA 9-12R; CAAS 1; CANR 7, 45;
DLB 6

Cassity, (Allen) Turner 1929- . . . . **CLC 6, 42**
See also CA 17-20R; CAAS 8; CANR 11;
DLB 105

Castaneda, Carlos 1931(?)- . . . . **CLC 12**
See also CA 25-28R; CANR 32; HW;
MTCW

Castedo, Elena 1937- . . . . **CLC 65**
See also CA 132

Castedo-Ellerman, Elena
See Castedo, Elena

Castellanos, Rosario
1925-1974 . . . . **CLC 66; HLC**
See also CA 131; 53-56; DLB 113; HW

Castelvetro, Lodovico 1505-1571 . . . . . **LC 12**

Castiglione, Baldassare 1478-1529 . . . **LC 12**

Castle, Robert
See Hamilton, Edmond

Castro, Guillen de 1569-1631 . . . . **LC 19**

Castro, Rosalia de 1837-1885 . . . . . **NCLC 3**

Cather, Willa
See Cather, Willa Sibert

Cather, Willa Sibert
1873-1947 . . . . **TCLC 1, 11, 31; DA;
SSC 2; WLC**
See also CA 104; 128; CDALB 1865-1917;
DLB 9, 54, 78; DLBD 1; MTCW;
SATA 30

Catton, (Charles) Bruce
1899-1978 . . . . **CLC 35**
See also AITN 1; CA 5-8R; 81-84;
CANR 7; DLB 17; SATA 2, 24

Cauldwell, Frank
See King, Francis (Henry)

Caunitz, William J. 1933- . . . . **CLC 34**
See also BEST 89:3; CA 125; 130

Causley, Charles (Stanley) 1917- . . . . . **CLC 7**
See also CA 9-12R; CANR 5, 35; CLR 30;
DLB 27; MTCW; SATA 3, 66

Caute, David 1936- . . . . **CLC 29**
See also CA 1-4R; CAAS 4; CANR 1, 33;
DLB 14

Cavafy, C(onstantine) P(eter) . . . . . **TCLC 2, 7**
See also Kavafis, Konstantinos Petrou

Cavallo, Evelyn
See Spark, Muriel (Sarah)

Cavanna, Betty . . . . **CLC 12**
See also Harrison, Elizabeth Cavanna
See also JRDA; MAICYA; SAAS 4;
SATA 1, 30

Caxton, William 1421(?)-1491(?) . . . . . **LC 17**

Cayrol, Jean 1911- . . . . **CLC 11**
See also CA 89-92; DLB 83

Cela, Camilo Jose
1916- . . . . **CLC 4, 13, 59; HLC**
See also BEST 90:2; CA 21-24R; CAAS 10;
CANR 21, 32; DLBY 89; HW; MTCW

Celan, Paul . . . . . . **CLC 10, 19, 53, 82; PC 10**
See also Antschel, Paul
See also DLB 69

Celine, Louis-Ferdinand
. . . . **CLC 1, 3, 4, 7, 9, 15, 47**
See also Destouches, Louis-Ferdinand
See also DLB 72

Cellini, Benvenuto 1500-1571 . . . . **LC 7**

Cendrars, Blaise
See Sauser-Hall, Frederic

Cernuda (y Bidon), Luis
1902-1963 . . . . **CLC 54**
See also CA 131; 89-92; DLB 134; HW

Cervantes (Saavedra), Miguel de
1547-1616 . . . . . . **LC 6, 23; DA; SSC 12;
WLC**

Cesaire, Aime (Fernand)
1913- . . . . **CLC 19, 32; BLC**
See also BW 2; CA 65-68; CANR 24, 43;
MTCW

Chabon, Michael 1965(?)- . . . . **CLC 55**
See also CA 139

Chabrol, Claude 1930- . . . . **CLC 16**
See also CA 110

Challans, Mary 1905-1983
See Renault, Mary
See also CA 81-84; 111; SATA 23, 36

Challis, George
See Faust, Frederick (Schiller)

Chambers, Aidan 1934- . . . . **CLC 35**
See also CA 25-28R; CANR 12, 31; JRDA;
MAICYA; SAAS 12; SATA 1, 69

Chambers, James 1948-
See Cliff, Jimmy
See also CA 124

Chambers, Jessie
See Lawrence, D(avid) H(erbert Richards)

Chambers, Robert W. 1865-1933 . . . **TCLC 41**

Chandler, Raymond (Thornton)
1888-1959 . . . . **TCLC 1, 7**
See also CA 104; 129; CDALB 1929-1941;
DLBD 6; MTCW

Chang, Jung 1952- . . . . **CLC 71**
See also CA 142

Channing, William Ellery
1780-1842 . . . . **NCLC 17**
See also DLB 1, 59

Chaplin, Charles Spencer
1889-1977 . . . . **CLC 16**
See also Chaplin, Charlie
See also CA 81-84; 73-76

Chaplin, Charlie
See Chaplin, Charles Spencer
See also DLB 44

Chapman, George 1559(?)-1634 . . . . . . **LC 22**
See also DLB 62, 121

Chapman, Graham 1941-1989 . . . . . . **CLC 21**
See also Monty Python
See also CA 116; 129; CANR 35

Chapman, John Jay 1862-1933 . . . . . **TCLC 7**
See also CA 104

Chapman, Walker
See Silverberg, Robert

Chappell, Fred (Davis) 1936- . . . . **CLC 40, 78**
See also CA 5-8R; CAAS 4; CANR 8, 33;
DLB 6, 105

Char, Rene(-Emile)
1907-1988 . . . . **CLC 9, 11, 14, 55**
See also CA 13-16R; 124; CANR 32;
MTCW

Charby, Jay
See Ellison, Harlan

Chardin, Pierre Teilhard de
See Teilhard de Chardin, (Marie Joseph)
Pierre

Charles I 1600-1649 . . . . **LC 13**

Charyn, Jerome 1937- . . . . **CLC 5, 8, 18**
See also CA 5-8R; CAAS 1; CANR 7;
DLBY 83; MTCW

Chase, Mary (Coyle) 1907-1981 . . . . . . **DC 1**
See also CA 77-80; 105; SATA 17, 29

Chase, Mary Ellen 1887-1973 . . . . **CLC 2**
See also CA 13-16; 41-44R; CAP 1;
SATA 10

Chase, Nicholas
See Hyde, Anthony

Chateaubriand, Francois Rene de
1768-1848 . . . . **NCLC 3**
See also DLB 119

Chatterje, Sarat Chandra 1876-1936(?)
See Chatterji, Saratchandra
See also CA 109

Chatterji, Bankim Chandra
1838-1894 . . . . **NCLC 19**

Chatterji, Saratchandra . . . . **TCLC 13**
See also Chatterje, Sarat Chandra

Chatterton, Thomas 1752-1770 . . . . **LC 3**
See also DLB 109

Chatwin, (Charles) Bruce
1940-1989 . . . . **CLC 28, 57, 59**
See also AAYA 4; BEST 90:1; CA 85-88;
127

Chaucer, Daniel
See Ford, Ford Madox

Chaucer, Geoffrey
1340(?)-1400 . . . . **LC 17; DA**
See also CDBLB Before 1660

Clerihew, E.
See Bentley, E(dmund) C(lerihew)

Clerk, N. W.
See Lewis, C(live) S(taples)

Cliff, Jimmy.................... **CLC 21**
See also Chambers, James

Clifton, (Thelma) Lucille
1936- .... **CLC 19, 66; BLC**
See also BW 2; CA 49-52; CANR 2, 24, 42;
CLR 5; DLB 5, 41; MAICYA; MTCW;
SATA 20, 69

Clinton, Dirk
See Silverberg, Robert

Clough, Arthur Hugh 1819-1861.. **NCLC 27**
See also DLB 32

Clutha, Janet Paterson Frame 1924-
See Frame, Janet
See also CA 1-4R; CANR 2, 36; MTCW

Clyne, Terence
See Blatty, William Peter

Cobalt, Martin
See Mayne, William (James Carter)

Coburn, D(onald) L(ee) 1938- ...... **CLC 10**
See also CA 89-92

Cocteau, Jean (Maurice Eugene Clement)
1889-1963 .... **CLC 1, 8, 15, 16, 43; DA;**
WLC
See also CA 25-28; CANR 40; CAP 2;
DLB 65; MTCW

Codrescu, Andrei 1946- .... **CLC 46**
See also CA 33-36R; CAAS 19; CANR 13,
34

Coe, Max
See Bourne, Randolph S(illiman)

Coe, Tucker
See Westlake, Donald E(dwin)

Coetzee, J(ohn) M(ichael)
1940- .... **CLC 23, 33, 66**
See also CA 77-80; CANR 41; MTCW

Coffey, Brian
See Koontz, Dean R(ay)

Cohen, Arthur A(llen)
1928-1986 .... **CLC 7, 31**
See also CA 1-4R; 120; CANR 1, 17, 42;
DLB 28

Cohen, Leonard (Norman)
1934- .... **CLC 3, 38**
See also CA 21-24R; CANR 14; DLB 53;
MTCW

Cohen, Matt 1942- .... **CLC 19**
See also CA 61-64; CAAS 18; CANR 40;
DLB 53

Cohen-Solal, Annie 19(?)- .... **CLC 50**

Colegate, Isabel 1931- .... **CLC 36**
See also CA 17-20R; CANR 8, 22; DLB 14;
MTCW

Coleman, Emmett
See Reed, Ishmael

Coleridge, Samuel Taylor
1772-1834 ....**NCLC 9; DA; WLC**
See also CDBLB 1789-1832; DLB 93, 107

Coleridge, Sara 1802-1852....... **NCLC 31**

Coles, Don 1928- .... **CLC 46**
See also CA 115; CANR 38

Colette, (Sidonie-Gabrielle)
1873-1954 ...... **TCLC 1, 5, 16; SSC 10**
See also CA 104; 131; DLB 65; MTCW

Collett, (Jacobine) Camilla (Wergeland)
1813-1895 .... **NCLC 22**

Collier, Christopher 1930-........ **CLC 30**
See also CA 33-36R; CANR 13, 33; JRDA;
MAICYA; SATA 16, 70

Collier, James L(incoln) 1928- ..... **CLC 30**
See also CA 9-12R; CANR 4, 33; CLR 3;
JRDA; MAICYA; SATA 8, 70

Collier, Jeremy 1650-1726.......... **LC 6**

Collins, Hunt
See Hunter, Evan

Collins, Linda 1931-.............. **CLC 44**
See also CA 125

Collins, (William) Wilkie
1824-1889 .... **NCLC 1, 18**
See also CDBLB 1832-1890; DLB 18, 70

Collins, William 1721-1759 .... **LC 4**
See also DLB 109

Colman, George
See Glassco, John

Colt, Winchester Remington
See Hubbard, L(afayette) Ron(ald)

Colter, Cyrus 1910- .... **CLC 58**
See also BW 1; CA 65-68; CANR 10;
DLB 33

Colton, James
See Hansen, Joseph

Colum, Padraic 1881-1972........ **CLC 28**
See also CA 73-76; 33-36R; CANR 35;
MAICYA; MTCW; SATA 15

Colvin, James
See Moorcock, Michael (John)

Colwin, Laurie (E.)
1944-1992 .... **CLC 5, 13, 23, 84**
See also CA 89-92; 139; CANR 20;
DLBY 80; MTCW

Comfort, Alex(ander) 1920-........ **CLC 7**
See also CA 1-4R; CANR 1, 45

Comfort, Montgomery
See Campbell, (John) Ramsey

Compton-Burnett, I(vy)
1884(?)-1969 ...... **CLC 1, 3, 10, 15, 34**
See also CA 1-4R; 25-28R; CANR 4;
DLB 36; MTCW

Comstock, Anthony 1844-1915 .... **TCLC 13**
See also CA 110

Conan Doyle, Arthur
See Doyle, Arthur Conan

Conde, Maryse 1937-............. **CLC 52**
See also Boucolon, Maryse
See also BW 2

Condillac, Etienne Bonnot de
1714-1780 .... **LC 26**

Condon, Richard (Thomas)
1915- .... **CLC 4, 6, 8, 10, 45**
See also BEST 90:3; CA 1-4R; CAAS 1;
CANR 2, 23; MTCW

Congreve, William
1670-1729 ... **LC 5, 21; DA; DC 2; WLC**
See also CDBLB 1660-1789; DLB 39, 84

Connell, Evan S(helby), Jr.
1924- .... **CLC 4, 6, 45**
See also AAYA 7; CA 1-4R; CAAS 2;
CANR 2, 39; DLB 2; DLBY 81; MTCW

Connelly, Marc(us Cook)
1890-1980 .... **CLC 7**
See also CA 85-88; 102; CANR 30; DLB 7;
DLBY 80; SATA 25

Connor, Ralph .... **TCLC 31**
See also Gordon, Charles William
See also DLB 92

Conrad, Joseph
1857-1924 .... **TCLC 1, 6, 13, 25, 43, 57;**
DA; SSC 9; WLC
See also CA 104; 131; CDBLB 1890-1914;
DLB 10, 34, 98; MTCW; SATA 27

Conrad, Robert Arnold
See Hart, Moss

Conroy, Pat 1945-............. **CLC 30, 74**
See also AAYA 8; AITN 1; CA 85-88;
CANR 24; DLB 6; MTCW

Constant (de Rebecque), (Henri) Benjamin
1767-1830 .... **NCLC 6**
See also DLB 119

Conybeare, Charles Augustus
See Eliot, T(homas) S(tearns)

Cook, Michael 1933- .... **CLC 58**
See also CA 93-96; DLB 53

Cook, Robin 1940- .... **CLC 14**
See also BEST 90:2; CA 108; 111;
CANR 41

Cook, Roy
See Silverberg, Robert

Cooke, Elizabeth 1948- .... **CLC 55**
See also CA 129

Cooke, John Esten 1830-1886..... **NCLC 5**
See also DLB 3

Cooke, John Estes
See Baum, L(yman) Frank

Cooke, M. E.
See Creasey, John

Cooke, Margaret
See Creasey, John

Cooney, Ray .... **CLC 62**

Cooper, Henry St. John
See Creasey, John

Cooper, J. California............... **CLC 56**
See also AAYA 12; BW 1; CA 125

Cooper, James Fenimore
1789-1851 .... **NCLC 1, 27**
See also CDALB 1640-1865; DLB 3;
SATA 19

Coover, Robert (Lowell)
1932- ..... **CLC 3, 7, 15, 32, 46; SSC 15**
See also CA 45-48; CANR 3, 37; DLB 2;
DLBY 81; MTCW

Copeland, Stewart (Armstrong)
1952- .... **CLC 26**

Coppard, A(lfred) E(dgar)
1878-1957 .... **TCLC 5**
See also CA 114; YABC 1

Coppee, Francois 1842-1908 ...... **TCLC 25**

Coppola, Francis Ford 1939-....... **CLC 16**
See also CA 77-80; CANR 40; DLB 44

Corbiere, Tristan 1845-1875 ..... **NCLC 43**

Corcoran, Barbara 1911- .... **CLC 17**
See also CA 21-24R; CAAS 2; CANR 11,
28; DLB 52; JRDA; SATA 3, 77

Cordelier, Maurice
See Giraudoux, (Hippolyte) Jean

Corelli, Marie 1855-1924........ **TCLC 51**
See also Mackay, Mary
See also DLB 34

Corman, Cid..................... **CLC 9**
See also Corman, Sidney
See also CAAS 2; DLB 5

Corman, Sidney 1924-
See Corman, Cid
See also CA 85-88; CANR 44

Cormier, Robert (Edmund)
1925- .... **CLC 12, 30; DA**
See also AAYA 3; CA 1-4R; CANR 5, 23;
CDALB 1968-1988; CLR 12; DLB 52;
JRDA; MAICYA; MTCW; SATA 10, 45

Corn, Alfred (DeWitt III) 1943- .... **CLC 33**
See also CA 104; CANR 44; DLB 120;
DLBY 80

Cornwell, David (John Moore)
1931- .... **CLC 9, 15**
See also le Carre, John
See also CA 5-8R; CANR 13, 33; MTCW

Corso, (Nunzio) Gregory 1930- ... **CLC 1, 11**
See also CA 5-8R; CANR 41; DLB 5, 16;
MTCW

Cortazar, Julio
1914-1984 ...... **CLC 2, 3, 5, 10, 13, 15,
33, 34; HLC; SSC 7**
See also CA 21-24R; CANR 12, 32;
DLB 113; HW; MTCW

Corwin, Cecil
See Kornbluth, C(yril) M.

Cosic, Dobrica 1921- .... **CLC 14**
See also CA 122; 138

Costain, Thomas B(ertram)
1885-1965 .... **CLC 30**
See also CA 5-8R; 25-28R; DLB 9

Costantini, Humberto
1924(?)-1987 .... **CLC 49**
See also CA 131; 122; HW

Costello, Elvis 1955-............. **CLC 21**

Cotter, Joseph Seamon Sr.
1861-1949 .... **TCLC 28; BLC**
See also BW 1; CA 124; DLB 50

Couch, Arthur Thomas Quiller
See Quiller-Couch, Arthur Thomas

Coulton, James
See Hansen, Joseph

Couperus, Louis (Marie Anne)
1863-1923 .... **TCLC 15**
See also CA 115

Coupland, Douglas 1961- .... **CLC 85**
See also CA 142

Court, Wesli
See Turco, Lewis (Putnam)

Courtenay, Bryce 1933- .... **CLC 59**
See also CA 138

Courtney, Robert
See Ellison, Harlan

Cousteau, Jacques-Yves 1910-...... **CLC 30**
See also CA 65-68; CANR 15; MTCW;
SATA 38

Coward, Noel (Peirce)
1899-1973 .... **CLC 1, 9, 29, 51**
See also AITN 1; CA 17-18; 41-44R;
CANR 35; CAP 2; CDBLB 1914-1945;
DLB 10; MTCW

Cowley, Malcolm 1898-1989 .... **CLC 39**
See also CA 5-8R; 128; CANR 3; DLB 4,
48; DLBY 81, 89; MTCW

Cowper, William 1731-1800....... **NCLC 8**
See also DLB 104, 109

Cox, William Trevor 1928- ... **CLC 9, 14, 71**
See also Trevor, William
See also CA 9-12R; CANR 4, 37; DLB 14;
MTCW

Cozzens, James Gould
1903-1978 .... **CLC 1, 4, 11**
See also CA 9-12R; 81-84; CANR 19;
CDALB 1941-1968; DLB 9; DLBD 2;
DLBY 84; MTCW

Crabbe, George 1754-1832....... **NCLC 26**
See also DLB 93

Craig, A. A.
See Anderson, Poul (William)

Craik, Dinah Maria (Mulock)
1826-1887 .... **NCLC 38**
See also DLB 35; MAICYA; SATA 34

Cram, Ralph Adams 1863-1942.... **TCLC 45**

Crane, (Harold) Hart
1899-1932 .... **TCLC 2, 5; DA; PC 3;
WLC**
See also CA 104; 127; CDALB 1917-1929;
DLB 4, 48; MTCW

Crane, R(onald) S(almon)
1886-1967 .... **CLC 27**
See also CA 85-88; DLB 63

Crane, Stephen (Townley)
1871-1900 .... **TCLC 11, 17, 32; DA;
SSC 7; WLC**
See also CA 109; 140; CDALB 1865-1917;
DLB 12, 54, 78; YABC 2

Crase, Douglas 1944- .... **CLC 58**
See also CA 106

Crashaw, Richard 1612(?)-1649...... **LC 24**
See also DLB 126

Craven, Margaret 1901-1980....... **CLC 17**
See also CA 103

Crawford, F(rancis) Marion
1854-1909 .... **TCLC 10**
See also CA 107; DLB 71

Crawford, Isabella Valancy
1850-1887 .... **NCLC 12**
See also DLB 92

Crayon, Geoffrey
See Irving, Washington

Creasey, John 1908-1973......... **CLC 11**
See also CA 5-8R; 41-44R; CANR 8;
DLB 77; MTCW

Crebillon, Claude Prosper Jolyot de (fils)
1707-1777 .... **LC 1**

Credo
See Creasey, John

Creeley, Robert (White)
1926- ..... **CLC 1, 2, 4, 8, 11, 15, 36, 78**
See also CA 1-4R; CAAS 10; CANR 23, 43;
DLB 5, 16; MTCW

Crews, Harry (Eugene)
1935- .... **CLC 6, 23, 49**
See also AITN 1; CA 25-28R; CANR 20;
DLB 6, 143; MTCW

Crichton, (John) Michael
1942- .... **CLC 2, 6, 54**
See also AAYA 10; AITN 2; CA 25-28R;
CANR 13, 40; DLBY 81; JRDA;
MTCW; SATA 9

Crispin, Edmund .... **CLC 22**
See also Montgomery, (Robert) Bruce
See also DLB 87

Cristofer, Michael 1945(?)- .... **CLC 28**
See also CA 110; DLB 7

Croce, Benedetto 1866-1952 ...... **TCLC 37**
See also CA 120

Crockett, David 1786-1836 .... **NCLC 8**
See also DLB 3, 11

Crockett, Davy
See Crockett, David

Crofts, Freeman Wills
1879-1957 .... **TCLC 55**
See also CA 115; DLB 77

Croker, John Wilson 1780-1857 .. **NCLC 10**
See also DLB 110

Crommelynck, Fernand 1885-1970 .. **CLC 75**
See also CA 89-92

Cronin, A(rchibald) J(oseph)
1896-1981 .... **CLC 32**
See also CA 1-4R; 102; CANR 5; SATA 25,
47

Cross, Amanda
See Heilbrun, Carolyn G(old)

Crothers, Rachel 1878(?)-1958..... **TCLC 19**
See also CA 113; DLB 7

Croves, Hal
See Traven, B.

Crowfield, Christopher
See Stowe, Harriet (Elizabeth) Beecher

Crowley, Aleister................. **TCLC 7**
See also Crowley, Edward Alexander

Crowley, Edward Alexander 1875-1947
See Crowley, Aleister
See also CA 104

Crowley, John 1942-............. **CLC 57**
See also CA 61-64; CANR 43; DLBY 82;
SATA 65

Crud
See Crumb, R(obert)

Crumarums
See Crumb, R(obert)

Crumb, R(obert) 1943-............ **CLC 17**
See also CA 106

Crumbum
See Crumb, R(obert)

Crumski
See Crumb, R(obert)

Crum the Bum
See Crumb, R(obert)

de Beauvoir, Simone (Lucie Ernestine Marie Bertrand)
See Beauvoir, Simone (Lucie Ernestine Marie Bertrand) de

de Brissac, Malcolm
See Dickinson, Peter (Malcolm)

de Chardin, Pierre Teilhard
See Teilhard de Chardin, (Marie Joseph) Pierre

Dee, John 1527-1608 . . . . **LC 20**

Deer, Sandra 1940- . . . . **CLC 45**

De Ferrari, Gabriella . . . . **CLC 65**

Defoe, Daniel
1660(?)-1731 . . . . **LC 1; DA; WLC**
See also CDBLB 1660-1789; DLB 39, 95, 101; JRDA; MAICYA; SATA 22

de Gourmont, Remy
See Gourmont, Remy de

de Hartog, Jan 1914- . . . . **CLC 19**
See also CA 1-4R; CANR 1

de Hostos, E. M.
See Hostos (y Bonilla), Eugenio Maria de

de Hostos, Eugenio M.
See Hostos (y Bonilla), Eugenio Maria de

Deighton, Len . . . . **CLC 4, 7, 22, 46**
See also Deighton, Leonard Cyril
See also AAYA 6; BEST 89:2; CDBLB 1960 to Present; DLB 87

Deighton, Leonard Cyril 1929-
See Deighton, Len
See also CA 9-12R; CANR 19, 33; MTCW

Dekker, Thomas 1572(?)-1632 . . . . . . **LC 22**
See also CDBLB Before 1660; DLB 62

de la Mare, Walter (John)
1873-1956 . . **TCLC 4, 53; SSC 14; WLC**
See also CDBLB 1914-1945; CLR 23; DLB 19; SATA 16

Delaney, Franey
See O'Hara, John (Henry)

Delaney, Shelagh 1939- . . . . **CLC 29**
See also CA 17-20R; CANR 30; CDBLB 1960 to Present; DLB 13; MTCW

Delany, Mary (Granville Pendarves)
1700-1788 . . . . **LC 12**

Delany, Samuel R(ay, Jr.)
1942- . . . . **CLC 8, 14, 38; BLC**
See also BW 2; CA 81-84; CANR 27, 43; DLB 8, 33; MTCW

De La Ramee, (Marie) Louise 1839-1908
See Ouida
See also SATA 20

de la Roche, Mazo 1879-1961 . . . . . **CLC 14**
See also CA 85-88; CANR 30; DLB 68; SATA 64

Delbanco, Nicholas (Franklin)
1942- . . . . **CLC 6, 13**
See also CA 17-20R; CAAS 2; CANR 29; DLB 6

del Castillo, Michel 1933- . . . . **CLC 38**
See also CA 109

Deledda, Grazia (Cosima)
1875(?)-1936 . . . . **TCLC 23**
See also CA 123

Delibes, Miguel . . . . **CLC 8, 18**
See also Delibes Setien, Miguel

Delibes Setien, Miguel 1920-
See Delibes, Miguel
See also CA 45-48; CANR 1, 32; HW; MTCW

DeLillo, Don
1936- . . . . . **CLC 8, 10, 13, 27, 39, 54, 76**
See also BEST 89:1; CA 81-84; CANR 21; DLB 6; MTCW

de Lisser, H. G.
See De Lisser, Herbert George
See also DLB 117

De Lisser, Herbert George
1878-1944 . . . . **TCLC 12**
See also de Lisser, H. G.
See also BW 2; CA 109

Deloria, Vine (Victor), Jr. 1933- . . . . **CLC 21**
See also CA 53-56; CANR 5, 20; MTCW; SATA 21

Del Vecchio, John M(ichael)
1947- . . . . **CLC 29**
See also CA 110; DLBD 9

de Man, Paul (Adolph Michel)
1919-1983 . . . . **CLC 55**
See also CA 128; 111; DLB 67; MTCW

De Marinis, Rick 1934- . . . . **CLC 54**
See also CA 57-60; CANR 9, 25

Demby, William 1922- . . . . **CLC 53; BLC**
See also BW 1; CA 81-84; DLB 33

Demijohn, Thom
See Disch, Thomas M(ichael)

de Montherlant, Henry (Milon)
See Montherlant, Henry (Milon) de

Demosthenes 384B.C.-322B.C. . . . **CMLC 13**

de Natale, Francine
See Malzberg, Barry N(athaniel)

Denby, Edwin (Orr) 1903-1983 . . . . . **CLC 48**
See also CA 138; 110

Denis, Julio
See Cortazar, Julio

Denmark, Harrison
See Zelazny, Roger (Joseph)

Dennis, John 1658-1734 . . . . **LC 11**
See also DLB 101

Dennis, Nigel (Forbes) 1912-1989 . . . . **CLC 8**
See also CA 25-28R; 129; DLB 13, 15; MTCW

De Palma, Brian (Russell) 1940- . . . . **CLC 20**
See also CA 109

De Quincey, Thomas 1785-1859 . . . **NCLC 4**
See also CDBLB 1789-1832; DLB 110; 144

Deren, Eleanora 1908(?)-1961
See Deren, Maya
See also CA 111

Deren, Maya . . . . **CLC 16**
See also Deren, Eleanora

Derleth, August (William)
1909-1971 . . . . **CLC 31**
See also CA 1-4R; 29-32R; CANR 4; DLB 9; SATA 5

Der Nister 1884-1950 . . . . **TCLC 56**

de Routisie, Albert
See Aragon, Louis

Derrida, Jacques 1930- . . . . **CLC 24**
See also CA 124; 127

Derry Down Derry
See Lear, Edward

Dersonnes, Jacques
See Simenon, Georges (Jacques Christian)

Desai, Anita 1937- . . . . **CLC 19, 37**
See also CA 81-84; CANR 33; MTCW; SATA 63

de Saint-Luc, Jean
See Glassco, John

de Saint Roman, Arnaud
See Aragon, Louis

Descartes, Rene 1596-1650 . . . . **LC 20**

De Sica, Vittorio 1901(?)-1974 . . . . . **CLC 20**
See also CA 117

Desnos, Robert 1900-1945 . . . . **TCLC 22**
See also CA 121

Destouches, Louis-Ferdinand
1894-1961 . . . . **CLC 9, 15**
See also Celine, Louis-Ferdinand
See also CA 85-88; CANR 28; MTCW

Deutsch, Babette 1895-1982 . . . . **CLC 18**
See also CA 1-4R; 108; CANR 4; DLB 45; SATA 1, 33

Devenant, William 1606-1649 . . . . . . **LC 13**

Devkota, Laxmiprasad
1909-1959 . . . . **TCLC 23**
See also CA 123

De Voto, Bernard (Augustine)
1897-1955 . . . . **TCLC 29**
See also CA 113; DLB 9

De Vries, Peter
1910-1993 . . . . **CLC 1, 2, 3, 7, 10, 28, 46**
See also CA 17-20R; 142; CANR 41; DLB 6; DLBY 82; MTCW

Dexter, Martin
See Faust, Frederick (Schiller)

Dexter, Pete 1943- . . . . **CLC 34, 55**
See also BEST 89:2; CA 127; 131; MTCW

Diamano, Silmang
See Senghor, Leopold Sedar

Diamond, Neil 1941- . . . . **CLC 30**
See also CA 108

di Bassetto, Corno
See Shaw, George Bernard

Dick, Philip K(indred)
1928-1982 . . . . **CLC 10, 30, 72**
See also CA 49-52; 106; CANR 2, 16; DLB 8; MTCW

Dickens, Charles (John Huffam)
1812-1870 . . . . . **NCLC 3, 8, 18, 26; DA; SSC 17; WLC**
See also CDBLB 1832-1890; DLB 21, 55, 70; JRDA; MAICYA; SATA 15

Dickey, James (Lafayette)
1923- . . . . **CLC 1, 2, 4, 7, 10, 15, 47**
See also AITN 1, 2; CA 9-12R; CABS 2; CANR 10; CDALB 1968-1988; DLB 5; DLBD 7; DLBY 82, 93; MTCW

Dickey, William 1928-1994 . . . . . . **CLC 3, 28**
See also CA 9-12R; 145; CANR 24; DLB 5

Dickinson, Charles 1951- . . . . **CLC 49**
See also CA 128

Dickinson, Emily (Elizabeth)
1830-1886 .. **NCLC 21; DA; PC 1; WLC**
See also CDALB 1865-1917; DLB 1;
SATA 29

Dickinson, Peter (Malcolm)
1927- .... **CLC 12, 35**
See also AAYA 9; CA 41-44R; CANR 31;
CLR 29; DLB 87; JRDA; MAICYA;
SATA 5, 62

Dickson, Carr
See Carr, John Dickson

Dickson, Carter
See Carr, John Dickson

Diderot, Denis 1713-1784 .... **LC 26**

Didion, Joan 1934- ..... **CLC 1, 3, 8, 14, 32**
See also AITN 1; CA 5-8R; CANR 14;
CDALB 1968-1988; DLB 2; DLBY 81,
86; MTCW

Dietrich, Robert
See Hunt, E(verette) Howard, Jr.

Dillard, Annie 1945- .... **CLC 9, 60**
See also AAYA 6; CA 49-52; CANR 3, 43;
DLBY 80; MTCW; SATA 10

Dillard, R(ichard) H(enry) W(ilde)
1937- .... **CLC 5**
See also CA 21-24R; CAAS 7; CANR 10;
DLB 5

Dillon, Eilis 1920- .... **CLC 17**
See also CA 9-12R; CAAS 3; CANR 4, 38;
CLR 26; MAICYA; SATA 2, 74

Dimont, Penelope
See Mortimer, Penelope (Ruth)

Dinesen, Isak .... **CLC 10, 29; SSC 7**
See also Blixen, Karen (Christentze
Dinesen)

Ding Ling .... **CLC 68**
See also Chiang Pin-chin

Disch, Thomas M(ichael) 1940- ... **CLC 7, 36**
See also CA 21-24R; CAAS 4; CANR 17,
36; CLR 18; DLB 8; MAICYA; MTCW;
SAAS 15; SATA 54

Disch, Tom
See Disch, Thomas M(ichael)

d'Isly, Georges
See Simenon, Georges (Jacques Christian)

Disraeli, Benjamin 1804-1881 .. **NCLC 2, 39**
See also DLB 21, 55

Ditcum, Steve
See Crumb, R(obert)

Dixon, Paige
See Corcoran, Barbara

Dixon, Stephen 1936- ..... **CLC 52; SSC 16**
See also CA 89-92; CANR 17, 40; DLB 130

Dobell, Sydney Thompson
1824-1874 .... **NCLC 43**
See also DLB 32

Doblin, Alfred .... **TCLC 13**
See also Doeblin, Alfred

Dobrolyubov, Nikolai Alexandrovich
1836-1861 .... **NCLC 5**

Dobyns, Stephen 1941- .... **CLC 37**
See also CA 45-48; CANR 2, 18

Doctorow, E(dgar) L(aurence)
1931- ..... **CLC 6, 11, 15, 18, 37, 44, 65**
See also AITN 2; BEST 89:3; CA 45-48;
CANR 2, 33; CDALB 1968-1988; DLB 2,
28; DLBY 80; MTCW

Dodgson, Charles Lutwidge 1832-1898
See Carroll, Lewis
See also CLR 2; DA; MAICYA; YABC 2

Dodson, Owen (Vincent)
1914-1983 .... **CLC 79; BLC**
See also BW 1; CA 65-68; 110; CANR 24;
DLB 76

Doeblin, Alfred 1878-1957 .... **TCLC 13**
See also Doblin, Alfred
See also CA 110; 141; DLB 66

Doerr, Harriet 1910- .... **CLC 34**
See also CA 117; 122

Domecq, H(onorio) Bustos
See Bioy Casares, Adolfo; Borges, Jorge
Luis

Domini, Rey
See Lorde, Audre (Geraldine)

Dominique
See Proust, (Valentin-Louis-George-Eugene-)
Marcel

Don, A
See Stephen, Leslie

Donaldson, Stephen R. 1947- .... **CLC 46**
See also CA 89-92; CANR 13

Donleavy, J(ames) P(atrick)
1926- .... **CLC 1, 4, 6, 10, 45**
See also AITN 2; CA 9-12R; CANR 24;
DLB 6; MTCW

Donne, John
1572-1631 .... **LC 10, 24; DA; PC 1**
See also CDBLB Before 1660; DLB 121

Donnell, David 1939(?)- .... **CLC 34**

Donoso (Yanez), Jose
1924- .... **CLC 4, 8, 11, 32; HLC**
See also CA 81-84; CANR 32; DLB 113;
HW; MTCW

Donovan, John 1928-1992 .... **CLC 35**
See also CA 97-100; 137; CLR 3;
MAICYA; SATA 29

Don Roberto
See Cunninghame Graham, R(obert)
B(ontine)

Doolittle, Hilda
1886-1961 ..... **CLC 3, 8, 14, 31, 34, 73;**
DA; PC 5; WLC
See also H. D.
See also CA 97-100; CANR 35; DLB 4, 45;
MTCW

Dorfman, Ariel 1942- .... **CLC 48, 77; HLC**
See also CA 124; 130; HW

Dorn, Edward (Merton) 1929- ... **CLC 10, 18**
See also CA 93-96; CANR 42; DLB 5

Dorsan, Luc
See Simenon, Georges (Jacques Christian)

Dorsange, Jean
See Simenon, Georges (Jacques Christian)

Dos Passos, John (Roderigo)
1896-1970 ...... **CLC 1, 4, 8, 11, 15, 25,**
34, 82; DA; WLC
See also CA 1-4R; 29-32R; CANR 3;
CDALB 1929-1941; DLB 4, 9; DLBD 1;
MTCW

Dossage, Jean
See Simenon, Georges (Jacques Christian)

Dostoevsky, Fedor Mikhailovich
1821-1881 ...... **NCLC 2, 7, 21, 33, 43;**
DA; SSC 2; WLC

Doughty, Charles M(ontagu)
1843-1926 .... **TCLC 27**
See also CA 115; DLB 19, 57

Douglas, Ellen .... **CLC 73**
See also Haxton, Josephine Ayres;
Williamson, Ellen Douglas

Douglas, Gavin 1475(?)-1522 .... **LC 20**

Douglas, Keith 1920-1944 .... **TCLC 40**
See also DLB 27

Douglas, Leonard
See Bradbury, Ray (Douglas)

Douglas, Michael
See Crichton, (John) Michael

Douglass, Frederick
1817(?)-1895 .... **NCLC 7; BLC; DA;**
WLC
See also CDALB 1640-1865; DLB 1, 43, 50,
79; SATA 29

Dourado, (Waldomiro Freitas) Autran
1926- .... **CLC 23, 60**
See also CA 25-28R; CANR 34

Dourado, Waldomiro Autran
See Dourado, (Waldomiro Freitas) Autran

Dove, Rita (Frances)
1952- .... **CLC 50, 81; PC 6**
See also BW 2; CA 109; CAAS 19;
CANR 27, 42; DLB 120

Dowell, Coleman 1925-1985........ **CLC 60**
See also CA 25-28R; 117; CANR 10;
DLB 130

Dowson, Ernest Christopher
1867-1900 .... **TCLC 4**
See also CA 105; DLB 19, 135

Doyle, A. Conan
See Doyle, Arthur Conan

Doyle, Arthur Conan
1859-1930 .... **TCLC 7; DA; SSC 12;**
WLC
See also CA 104; 122; CDBLB 1890-1914;
DLB 18, 70; MTCW; SATA 24

Doyle, Conan
See Doyle, Arthur Conan

Doyle, John
See Graves, Robert (von Ranke)

Doyle, Roddy 1958(?)- .... **CLC 81**
See also CA 143

Doyle, Sir A. Conan
See Doyle, Arthur Conan

Doyle, Sir Arthur Conan
See Doyle, Arthur Conan

Dr. A
See Asimov, Isaac; Silverstein, Alvin

Drabble, Margaret
　　1939- .... **CLC 2, 3, 5, 8, 10, 22, 53**
　　See also CA 13-16R; CANR 18, 35;
　　CDBLB 1960 to Present; DLB 14;
　　MTCW; SATA 48

Drapier, M. B.
　　See Swift, Jonathan

Drayham, James
　　See Mencken, H(enry) L(ouis)

Drayton, Michael 1563-1631 .... **LC 8**

Dreadstone, Carl
　　See Campbell, (John) Ramsey

Dreiser, Theodore (Herman Albert)
　　1871-1945 ...... **TCLC 10, 18, 35; DA;**
　　　　　　　　　　　　　　　　　　WLC
　　See also CA 106; 132; CDALB 1865-1917;
　　DLB 9, 12, 102, 137; DLBD 1; MTCW

Drexler, Rosalyn 1926- .... **CLC 2, 6**
　　See also CA 81-84

Dreyer, Carl Theodor 1889-1968.... **CLC 16**
　　See also CA 116

Drieu la Rochelle, Pierre(-Eugene)
　　1893-1945 .... **TCLC 21**
　　See also CA 117; DLB 72

Drinkwater, John 1882-1937 ...... **TCLC 57**
　　See also CA 109; DLB 10, 19

Drop Shot
　　See Cable, George Washington

Droste-Hulshoff, Annette Freiin von
　　1797-1848 .... **NCLC 3**
　　See also DLB 133

Drummond, Walter
　　See Silverberg, Robert

Drummond, William Henry
　　1854-1907 .... **TCLC 25**
　　See also DLB 92

Drummond de Andrade, Carlos
　　1902-1987 .... **CLC 18**
　　See also Andrade, Carlos Drummond de
　　See also CA 132; 123

Drury, Allen (Stuart) 1918- .... **CLC 37**
　　See also CA 57-60; CANR 18

Dryden, John
　　1631-1700 ... **LC 3, 21; DA; DC 3; WLC**
　　See also CDBLB 1660-1789; DLB 80, 101,
　　131

Duberman, Martin 1930- .... **CLC 8**
　　See also CA 1-4R; CANR 2

Dubie, Norman (Evans) 1945- ...... **CLC 36**
　　See also CA 69-72; CANR 12; DLB 120

Du Bois, W(illiam) E(dward) B(urghardt)
　　1868-1963 ...... **CLC 1, 2, 13, 64; BLC;**
　　　　　　　　　　　　　　　　　DA; WLC
　　See also BW 1; CA 85-88; CANR 34;
　　CDALB 1865-1917; DLB 47, 50, 91;
　　MTCW; SATA 42

Dubus, Andre 1936- ... **CLC 13, 36; SSC 15**
　　See also CA 21-24R; CANR 17; DLB 130

Duca Minimo
　　See D'Annunzio, Gabriele

Ducharme, Rejean 1941- .... **CLC 74**
　　See also DLB 60

Duclos, Charles Pinot 1704-1772 ..... **LC 1**

Dudek, Louis 1918- .... **CLC 11, 19**
　　See also CA 45-48; CAAS 14; CANR 1;
　　DLB 88

Duerrenmatt, Friedrich
　　1921-1990 ..... **CLC 1, 4, 8, 11, 15, 43**
　　See also CA 17-20R; CANR 33; DLB 69,
　　124; MTCW

Duffy, Bruce (?)- .... **CLC 50**

Duffy, Maureen 1933- .... **CLC 37**
　　See also CA 25-28R; CANR 33; DLB 14;
　　MTCW

Dugan, Alan 1923- .... **CLC 2, 6**
　　See also CA 81-84; DLB 5

du Gard, Roger Martin
　　See Martin du Gard, Roger

Duhamel, Georges 1884-1966 .... **CLC 8**
　　See also CA 81-84; 25-28R; CANR 35;
　　DLB 65; MTCW

Dujardin, Edouard (Emile Louis)
　　1861-1949 .... **TCLC 13**
　　See also CA 109; DLB 123

Dumas, Alexandre (Davy de la Pailleterie)
　　1802-1870 .... **NCLC 11; DA; WLC**
　　See also DLB 119; SATA 18

Dumas, Alexandre
　　1824-1895 .... **NCLC 9; DC 1**

Dumas, Claudine
　　See Malzberg, Barry N(athaniel)

Dumas, Henry L. 1934-1968 ..... **CLC 6, 62**
　　See also BW 1; CA 85-88; DLB 41

du Maurier, Daphne
　　1907-1989 .... **CLC 6, 11, 59**
　　See also CA 5-8R; 128; CANR 6; MTCW;
　　SATA 27, 60

Dunbar, Paul Laurence
　　1872-1906 ...... **TCLC 2, 12; BLC; DA;**
　　　　　　　　　　　　PC 5; SSC 8; WLC
　　See also BW 1; CA 104; 124;
　　CDALB 1865-1917; DLB 50, 54, 78;
　　SATA 34

Dunbar, William 1460(?)-1530(?) .... **LC 20**

Duncan, Lois 1934- .... **CLC 26**
　　See also AAYA 4; CA 1-4R; CANR 2, 23,
　　36; CLR 29; JRDA; MAICYA; SAAS 2;
　　SATA 1, 36, 75

Duncan, Robert (Edward)
　　1919-1988 .... **CLC 1, 2, 4, 7, 15, 41, 55;**
　　　　　　　　　　　　　　　　　　PC 2
　　See also CA 9-12R; 124; CANR 28; DLB 5,
　　16; MTCW

Dunlap, William 1766-1839 .... **NCLC 2**
　　See also DLB 30, 37, 59

Dunn, Douglas (Eaglesham)
　　1942- .... **CLC 6, 40**
　　See also CA 45-48; CANR 2, 33; DLB 40;
　　MTCW

Dunn, Katherine (Karen) 1945- ..... **CLC 71**
　　See also CA 33-36R

Dunn, Stephen 1939- .... **CLC 36**
　　See also CA 33-36R; CANR 12; DLB 105

Dunne, Finley Peter 1867-1936.... **TCLC 28**
　　See also CA 108; DLB 11, 23

Dunne, John Gregory 1932- .... **CLC 28**
　　See also CA 25-28R; CANR 14; DLBY 80

Dunsany, Edward John Moreton Drax
　　　Plunkett 1878-1957
　　See Dunsany, Lord
　　See also CA 104; DLB 10

Dunsany, Lord .... **TCLC 2**
　　See also Dunsany, Edward John Moreton
　　Drax Plunkett
　　See also DLB 77

du Perry, Jean
　　See Simenon, Georges (Jacques Christian)

Durang, Christopher (Ferdinand)
　　1949- .... **CLC 27, 38**
　　See also CA 105

Duras, Marguerite
　　1914- ...... **CLC 3, 6, 11, 20, 34, 40, 68**
　　See also CA 25-28R; DLB 83; MTCW

Durban, (Rosa) Pam 1947-......... **CLC 39**
　　See also CA 123

Durcan, Paul 1944-............. **CLC 43, 70**
　　See also CA 134

Durkheim, Emile 1858-1917 ...... **TCLC 55**

Durrell, Lawrence (George)
　　1912-1990 .... **CLC 1, 4, 6, 8, 13, 27, 41**
　　See also CA 9-12R; 132; CANR 40;
　　CDBLB 1945-1960; DLB 15, 27;
　　DLBY 90; MTCW

Durrenmatt, Friedrich
　　See Duerrenmatt, Friedrich

Dutt, Toru 1856-1877.......... **NCLC 29**

Dwight, Timothy 1752-1817...... **NCLC 13**
　　See also DLB 37

Dworkin, Andrea 1946- .... **CLC 43**
　　See also CA 77-80; CANR 16, 39; MTCW

Dwyer, Deanna
　　See Koontz, Dean R(ay)

Dwyer, K. R.
　　See Koontz, Dean R(ay)

Dylan, Bob 1941- ...... **CLC 3, 4, 6, 12, 77**
　　See also CA 41-44R; DLB 16

Eagleton, Terence (Francis) 1943-
　　See Eagleton, Terry
　　See also CA 57-60; CANR 7, 23; MTCW

Eagleton, Terry .... **CLC 63**
　　See also Eagleton, Terence (Francis)

Early, Jack
　　See Scoppettone, Sandra

East, Michael
　　See West, Morris L(anglo)

Eastaway, Edward
　　See Thomas, (Philip) Edward

Eastlake, William (Derry) 1917-..... **CLC 8**
　　See also CA 5-8R; CAAS 1; CANR 5;
　　DLB 6

Eastman, Charles A(lexander)
　　1858-1939 .... **TCLC 55**
　　See also YABC 1

Eberhart, Richard (Ghormley)
　　1904- .... **CLC 3, 11, 19, 56**
　　See also CA 1-4R; CANR 2;
　　CDALB 1941-1968; DLB 48; MTCW

Eberstadt, Fernanda 1960-........ **CLC 39**
　　See also CA 136

Echegaray (y Eizaguirre), Jose (Maria Waldo)
　　1832-1916 . . . . **TCLC 4**
　See also CA 104; CANR 32; HW; MTCW

Echeverria, (Jose) Esteban (Antonino)
　　1805-1851 . . . . **NCLC 18**

Echo
　See Proust, (Valentin-Louis-George-Eugene-)
　　Marcel

Eckert, Allan W. 1931- . . . . **CLC 17**
　See also CA 13-16R; CANR 14, 45;
　　SATA 27, 29

Eckhart, Meister 1260(?)-1328(?) . . **CMLC 9**
　See also DLB 115

Eckmar, F. R.
　See de Hartog, Jan

Eco, Umberto 1932- . . . . **CLC 28, 60**
　See also BEST 90:1; CA 77-80; CANR 12,
　　33; MTCW

Eddison, E(ric) R(ucker)
　　1882-1945 . . . . **TCLC 15**
　See also CA 109

Edel, (Joseph) Leon 1907- . . . . . . **CLC 29, 34**
　See also CA 1-4R; CANR 1, 22; DLB 103

Eden, Emily 1797-1869 . . . . **NCLC 10**

Edgar, David 1948- . . . . **CLC 42**
　See also CA 57-60; CANR 12; DLB 13;
　　MTCW

Edgerton, Clyde (Carlyle) 1944- . . . . **CLC 39**
　See also CA 118; 134

Edgeworth, Maria 1767-1849 . . . . . . **NCLC 1**
　See also DLB 116; SATA 21

Edmonds, Paul
　See Kuttner, Henry

Edmonds, Walter D(umaux) 1903- . . **CLC 35**
　See also CA 5-8R; CANR 2; DLB 9;
　　MAICYA; SAAS 4; SATA 1, 27

Edmondson, Wallace
　See Ellison, Harlan

Edson, Russell . . . . **CLC 13**
　See also CA 33-36R

Edwards, Bronwen Elizabeth
　See Rose, Wendy

Edwards, G(erald) B(asil)
　　1899-1976 . . . . **CLC 25**
　See also CA 110

Edwards, Gus 1939- . . . . **CLC 43**
　See also CA 108

Edwards, Jonathan 1703-1758 . . . . **LC 7; DA**
　See also DLB 24

Efron, Marina Ivanovna Tsvetaeva
　See Tsvetaeva (Efron), Marina (Ivanovna)

Ehle, John (Marsden, Jr.) 1925- . . . . **CLC 27**
　See also CA 9-12R

Ehrenbourg, Ilya (Grigoryevich)
　See Ehrenburg, Ilya (Grigoryevich)

Ehrenburg, Ilya (Grigoryevich)
　　1891-1967 . . . . **CLC 18, 34, 62**
　See also CA 102; 25-28R

Ehrenburg, Ilyo (Grigoryevich)
　See Ehrenburg, Ilya (Grigoryevich)

Eich, Guenter 1907-1972 . . . . **CLC 15**
　See also CA 111; 93-96; DLB 69, 124

Eichendorff, Joseph Freiherr von
　　1788-1857 . . . . **NCLC 8**
　See also DLB 90

Eigner, Larry . . . . **CLC 9**
　See also Eigner, Laurence (Joel)
　See also DLB 5

Eigner, Laurence (Joel) 1927-
　See Eigner, Larry
　See also CA 9-12R; CANR 6

Eiseley, Loren Corey 1907-1977 . . . . . **CLC 7**
　See also AAYA 5; CA 1-4R; 73-76;
　　CANR 6

Eisenstadt, Jill 1963- . . . . **CLC 50**
　See also CA 140

Eisenstein, Sergei (Mikhailovich)
　　1898-1948 . . . . **TCLC 57**
　See also CA 114

Eisner, Simon
　See Kornbluth, C(yril) M.

Ekeloef, (Bengt) Gunnar
　　1907-1968 . . . . **CLC 27**
　See also Ekelof, (Bengt) Gunnar
　See also CA 123; 25-28R

Ekelof, (Bengt) Gunnar . . . . **CLC 27**
　See also Ekeloef, (Bengt) Gunnar

Ekwensi, C. O. D.
　See Ekwensi, Cyprian (Odiatu Duaka)

Ekwensi, Cyprian (Odiatu Duaka)
　　1921- . . . . **CLC 4; BLC**
　See also BW 2; CA 29-32R; CANR 18, 42;
　　DLB 117; MTCW; SATA 66

Elaine . . . . **TCLC 18**
　See also Leverson, Ada

El Crummo
　See Crumb, R(obert)

Elia
　See Lamb, Charles

Eliade, Mircea 1907-1986 . . . . **CLC 19**
　See also CA 65-68; 119; CANR 30; MTCW

Eliot, A. D.
　See Jewett, (Theodora) Sarah Orne

Eliot, Alice
　See Jewett, (Theodora) Sarah Orne

Eliot, Dan
　See Silverberg, Robert

Eliot, George
　　1819-1880 . . . . **NCLC 4, 13, 23, 41; DA;
　　　　　　　　　　　　　　　　　　　　WLC**
　See also CDBLB 1832-1890; DLB 21, 35, 55

Eliot, John 1604-1690 . . . . **LC 5**
　See also DLB 24

Eliot, T(homas) S(tearns)
　　1888-1965 . . . . . **CLC 1, 2, 3, 6, 9, 10, 13,
　　　15, 24, 34, 41, 55, 57; DA; PC 5; WLC 2**
　See also CA 5-8R; 25-28R; CANR 41;
　　CDALB 1929-1941; DLB 7, 10, 45, 63;
　　DLBY 88; MTCW

Elizabeth 1866-1941 . . . . **TCLC 41**

Elkin, Stanley L(awrence)
　　1930- . . . **CLC 4, 6, 9, 14, 27, 51; SSC 12**
　See also CA 9-12R; CANR 8; DLB 2, 28;
　　DLBY 80; MTCW

Elledge, Scott . . . . **CLC 34**

Elliott, Don
　See Silverberg, Robert

Elliott, George P(aul) 1918-1980 . . . . . **CLC 2**
　See also CA 1-4R; 97-100; CANR 2

Elliott, Janice 1931- . . . . **CLC 47**
　See also CA 13-16R; CANR 8, 29; DLB 14

Elliott, Sumner Locke 1917-1991 . . . **CLC 38**
　See also CA 5-8R; 134; CANR 2, 21

Elliott, William
　See Bradbury, Ray (Douglas)

Ellis, A. E. . . . . **CLC 7**

Ellis, Alice Thomas . . . . **CLC 40**
　See also Haycraft, Anna

Ellis, Bret Easton 1964- . . . . . . **CLC 39, 71**
　See also AAYA 2; CA 118; 123

Ellis, (Henry) Havelock
　　1859-1939 . . . . **TCLC 14**
　See also CA 109

Ellis, Landon
　See Ellison, Harlan

Ellis, Trey 1962- . . . . **CLC 55**

Ellison, Harlan
　　1934- . . . . **CLC 1, 13, 42; SSC 14**
　See also CA 5-8R; CANR 5; DLB 8;
　　MTCW

Ellison, Ralph (Waldo)
　　1914-1994 . . . . . . **CLC 1, 3, 11, 54; BLC;
　　　　　　　　　　　　　　　　　　　　DA; WLC**
　See also BW 1; CA 9-12R; 145; CANR 24;
　　CDALB 1941-1968; DLB 2, 76; MTCW

Ellmann, Lucy (Elizabeth) 1956- . . . . **CLC 61**
　See also CA 128

Ellmann, Richard (David)
　　1918-1987 . . . . **CLC 50**
　See also BEST 89:2; CA 1-4R; 122;
　　CANR 2, 28; DLB 103; DLBY 87;
　　MTCW

Elman, Richard 1934- . . . . **CLC 19**
　See also CA 17-20R; CAAS 3

Elron
　See Hubbard, L(afayette) Ron(ald)

Eluard, Paul . . . . **TCLC 7, 41**
　See also Grindel, Eugene

Elyot, Sir Thomas 1490(?)-1546 . . . . . **LC 11**

Elytis, Odysseus 1911- . . . . **CLC 15, 49**
　See also CA 102; MTCW

Emecheta, (Florence Onye) Buchi
　　1944- . . . . **CLC 14, 48; BLC**
　See also BW 2; CA 81-84; CANR 27;
　　DLB 117; MTCW; SATA 66

Emerson, Ralph Waldo
　　1803-1882 . . . . . . **NCLC 1, 38; DA; WLC**
　See also CDALB 1640-1865; DLB 1, 59, 73

Eminescu, Mihail 1850-1889 . . . . . **NCLC 33**

Empson, William
　　1906-1984 . . . . **CLC 3, 8, 19, 33, 34**
　See also CA 17-20R; 112; CANR 31;
　　DLB 20; MTCW

Enchi Fumiko (Ueda) 1905-1986 . . . . **CLC 31**
　See also CA 129; 121

Ende, Michael (Andreas Helmuth)
　　1929- . . . . **CLC 31**
　See also CA 118; 124; CANR 36; CLR 14;
　　DLB 75; MAICYA; SATA 42, 61

Endo, Shusaku 1923- ..... **CLC 7, 14, 19, 54**
See also CA 29-32R; CANR 21; MTCW

Engel, Marian 1933-1985......... **CLC 36**
See also CA 25-28R; CANR 12; DLB 53

Engelhardt, Frederick
See Hubbard, L(afayette) Ron(ald)

Enright, D(ennis) J(oseph)
1920- .... **CLC 4, 8, 31**
See also CA 1-4R; CANR 1, 42; DLB 27;
SATA 25

Enzensberger, Hans Magnus
1929- .... **CLC 43**
See also CA 116; 119

Ephron, Nora 1941- .... **CLC 17, 31**
See also AITN 2; CA 65-68; CANR 12, 39

Epsilon
See Betjeman, John

Epstein, Daniel Mark 1948- .... **CLC 7**
See also CA 49-52; CANR 2

Epstein, Jacob 1956- .... **CLC 19**
See also CA 114

Epstein, Joseph 1937-............. **CLC 39**
See also CA 112; 119

Epstein, Leslie 1938- .... **CLC 27**
See also CA 73-76; CAAS 12; CANR 23

Equiano, Olaudah
1745(?)-1797 .... **LC 16; BLC**
See also DLB 37, 50

Erasmus, Desiderius 1469(?)-1536.... **LC 16**

Erdman, Paul E(mil) 1932- .... **CLC 25**
See also AITN 1; CA 61-64; CANR 13, 43

Erdrich, Louise 1954-......... **CLC 39, 54**
See also AAYA 10; BEST 89:1; CA 114;
CANR 41; MTCW

Erenburg, Ilya (Grigoryevich)
See Ehrenburg, Ilya (Grigoryevich)

Erickson, Stephen Michael 1950-
See Erickson, Steve
See also CA 129

Erickson, Steve .... **CLC 64**
See also Erickson, Stephen Michael

Ericson, Walter
See Fast, Howard (Melvin)

Eriksson, Buntel
See Bergman, (Ernst) Ingmar

Eschenbach, Wolfram von
See Wolfram von Eschenbach

Eseki, Bruno
See Mphahlele, Ezekiel

Esenin, Sergei (Alexandrovich)
1895-1925 .... **TCLC 4**
See also CA 104

Eshleman, Clayton 1935-........... **CLC 7**
See also CA 33-36R; CAAS 6; DLB 5

Espriella, Don Manuel Alvarez
See Southey, Robert

Espriu, Salvador 1913-1985........ **CLC 9**
See also CA 115; DLB 134

Espronceda, Jose de 1808-1842... **NCLC 39**

Esse, James
See Stephens, James

Esterbrook, Tom
See Hubbard, L(afayette) Ron(ald)

Estleman, Loren D. 1952- .... **CLC 48**
See also CA 85-88; CANR 27; MTCW

Eugenides, Jeffrey 1960(?)- .... **CLC 81**
See also CA 144

Euripides c. 485B.C.-406B.C. .... **DC 4**
See also DA

Evan, Evin
See Faust, Frederick (Schiller)

Evans, Evan
See Faust, Frederick (Schiller)

Evans, Marian
See Eliot, George

Evans, Mary Ann
See Eliot, George

Evarts, Esther
See Benson, Sally

Everett, Percival L. 1956- .... **CLC 57**
See also BW 2; CA 129

Everson, R(onald) G(ilmour)
1903- .... **CLC 27**
See also CA 17-20R; DLB 88

Everson, William (Oliver)
1912-1994............ **CLC 1, 5, 14**
See also CA 9-12R; 145; CANR 20; DLB 5,
16; MTCW

Evtushenko, Evgenii Aleksandrovich
See Yevtushenko, Yevgeny (Alexandrovich)

Ewart, Gavin (Buchanan)
1916- .... **CLC 13, 46**
See also CA 89-92; CANR 17; DLB 40;
MTCW

Ewers, Hanns Heinz 1871-1943 ... **TCLC 12**
See also CA 109

Ewing, Frederick R.
See Sturgeon, Theodore (Hamilton)

Exley, Frederick (Earl)
1929-1992 .... **CLC 6, 11**
See also AITN 2; CA 81-84; 138; DLB 143;
DLBY 81

Eynhardt, Guillermo
See Quiroga, Horacio (Sylvestre)

Ezekiel, Nissim 1924-............. **CLC 61**
See also CA 61-64

Ezekiel, Tish O'Dowd 1943- .... **CLC 34**
See also CA 129

Fadeyev, A.
See Bulgya, Alexander Alexandrovich

Fadeyev, Alexander .... **TCLC 53**
See also Bulgya, Alexander Alexandrovich

Fagen, Donald 1948-............. **CLC 26**

Fainzilberg, Ilya Arnoldovich 1897-1937
See Ilf, Ilya
See also CA 120

Fair, Ronald L. 1932-............. **CLC 18**
See also BW 1; CA 69-72; CANR 25;
DLB 33

Fairbairns, Zoe (Ann) 1948- .... **CLC 32**
See also CA 103; CANR 21

Falco, Gian
See Papini, Giovanni

Falconer, James
See Kirkup, James

Falconer, Kenneth
See Kornbluth, C(yril) M.

Falkland, Samuel
See Heijermans, Herman

Fallaci, Oriana 1930-............. **CLC 11**
See also CA 77-80; CANR 15; MTCW

Faludy, George 1913-............. **CLC 42**
See also CA 21-24R

Faludy, Gyoergy
See Faludy, George

Fanon, Frantz 1925-1961..... **CLC 74; BLC**
See also BW 1; CA 116; 89-92

Fanshawe, Ann 1625-1680 .... **LC 11**

Fante, John (Thomas) 1911-1983 ... **CLC 60**
See also CA 69-72; 109; CANR 23;
DLB 130; DLBY 83

Farah, Nuruddin 1945-....... **CLC 53; BLC**
See also BW 2; CA 106; DLB 125

Fargue, Leon-Paul 1876(?)-1947 ... **TCLC 11**
See also CA 109

Farigoule, Louis
See Romains, Jules

Farina, Richard 1936(?)-1966 .... **CLC 9**
See also CA 81-84; 25-28R

Farley, Walter (Lorimer)
1915-1989 .... **CLC 17**
See also CA 17-20R; CANR 8, 29; DLB 22;
JRDA; MAICYA; SATA 2, 43

Farmer, Philip Jose 1918-....... **CLC 1, 19**
See also CA 1-4R; CANR 4, 35; DLB 8;
MTCW

Farquhar, George 1677-1707........ **LC 21**
See also DLB 84

Farrell, J(ames) G(ordon)
1935-1979 .... **CLC 6**
See also CA 73-76; 89-92; CANR 36;
DLB 14; MTCW

Farrell, James T(homas)
1904-1979 .... **CLC 1, 4, 8, 11, 66**
See also CA 5-8R; 89-92; CANR 9; DLB 4,
9, 86; DLBD 2; MTCW

Farren, Richard J.
See Betjeman, John

Farren, Richard M.
See Betjeman, John

Fassbinder, Rainer Werner
1946-1982 .... **CLC 20**
See also CA 93-96; 106; CANR 31

Fast, Howard (Melvin) 1914- ...... **CLC 23**
See also CA 1-4R; CAAS 18; CANR 1, 33;
DLB 9; SATA 7

Faulcon, Robert
See Holdstock, Robert P.

Faulkner, William (Cuthbert)
1897-1962 ..... **CLC 1, 3, 6, 8, 9, 11, 14,
18, 28, 52, 68; DA; SSC 1; WLC**
See also AAYA 7; CA 81-84; CANR 33;
CDALB 1929-1941; DLB 9, 11, 44, 102;
DLBD 2; DLBY 86; MTCW

Fauset, Jessie Redmon
1884(?)-1961 .... **CLC 19, 54; BLC**
See also BW 1; CA 109; DLB 51

Forche, Carolyn (Louise)
1950- . . . . **CLC 25, 83; PC 10**
See also CA 109; 117; DLB 5

Ford, Elbur
See Hibbert, Eleanor Alice Burford

Ford, Ford Madox
1873-1939 . . . . **TCLC 1, 15, 39, 57**
See also CA 104; 132; CDBLB 1914-1945;
DLB 34, 98; MTCW

Ford, John 1895-1973. . . . . **CLC 16**
See also CA 45-48

Ford, Richard 1944- . . . . **CLC 46**
See also CA 69-72; CANR 11

Ford, Webster
See Masters, Edgar Lee

Foreman, Richard 1937-. . . . . **CLC 50**
See also CA 65-68; CANR 32

Forester, C(ecil) S(cott)
1899-1966 . . . . **CLC 35**
See also CA 73-76; 25-28R; SATA 13

Forez
See Mauriac, Francois (Charles)

Forman, James Douglas 1932-. . . . . . **CLC 21**
See also CA 9-12R; CANR 4, 19, 42;
JRDA; MAICYA; SATA 8, 70

Fornes, Maria Irene 1930-. . . . . . **CLC 39, 61**
See also CA 25-28R; CANR 28; DLB 7;
HW; MTCW

Forrest, Leon 1937- . . . . **CLC 4**
See also BW 2; CA 89-92; CAAS 7;
CANR 25; DLB 33

Forster, E(dward) M(organ)
1879-1970 . . . . . **CLC 1, 2, 3, 4, 9, 10, 13,**
15, 22, 45, 77; DA; WLC
See also AAYA 2; CA 13-14; 25-28R;
CANR 45; CAP 1; CDBLB 1914-1945;
DLB 34, 98; DLBD 10; MTCW;
SATA 57

Forster, John 1812-1876 . . . . **NCLC 11**
See also DLB 144

Forsyth, Frederick 1938-. . . . . . **CLC 2, 5, 36**
See also BEST 89:4; CA 85-88; CANR 38;
DLB 87; MTCW

Forten, Charlotte L. . . . . **TCLC 16; BLC**
See also Grimke, Charlotte L(ottie) Forten
See also DLB 50

Foscolo, Ugo 1778-1827 . . . . **NCLC 8**

Fosse, Bob . . . . **CLC 20**
See also Fosse, Robert Louis

Fosse, Robert Louis 1927-1987
See Fosse, Bob
See also CA 110; 123

Foster, Stephen Collins
1826-1864 . . . . **NCLC 26**

Foucault, Michel
1926-1984 . . . . **CLC 31, 34, 69**
See also CA 105; 113; CANR 34; MTCW

Fouque, Friedrich (Heinrich Karl) de la Motte
1777-1843 . . . . **NCLC 2**
See also DLB 90

Fournier, Henri Alban 1886-1914
See Alain-Fournier
See also CA 104

Fournier, Pierre 1916- . . . . **CLC 11**
See also Gascar, Pierre
See also CA 89-92; CANR 16, 40

Fowles, John
1926- . . . . **CLC 1, 2, 3, 4, 6, 9, 10, 15, 33**
See also CA 5-8R; CANR 25; CDBLB 1960
to Present; DLB 14, 139; MTCW;
SATA 22

Fox, Paula 1923-. . . . . **CLC 2, 8**
See also AAYA 3; CA 73-76; CANR 20,
36; CLR 1; DLB 52; JRDA; MAICYA;
MTCW; SATA 17, 60

Fox, William Price (Jr.) 1926- . . . . . **CLC 22**
See also CA 17-20R; CAAS 19; CANR 11;
DLB 2; DLBY 81

Foxe, John 1516(?)-1587 . . . . **LC 14**

Frame, Janet . . . . **CLC 2, 3, 6, 22, 66**
See also Clutha, Janet Paterson Frame

France, Anatole . . . . **TCLC 9**
See also Thibault, Jacques Anatole Francois
See also DLB 123

Francis, Claude 19(?)- . . . . **CLC 50**

Francis, Dick 1920- . . . . **CLC 2, 22, 42**
See also AAYA 5; BEST 89:3; CA 5-8R;
CANR 9, 42; CDBLB 1960 to Present;
DLB 87; MTCW

Francis, Robert (Churchill)
1901-1987 . . . . **CLC 15**
See also CA 1-4R; 123; CANR 1

Frank, Anne(lies Marie)
1929-1945 . . . . **TCLC 17; DA; WLC**
See also AAYA 12; CA 113; 133; MTCW;
SATA 42

Frank, Elizabeth 1945-. . . . . **CLC 39**
See also CA 121; 126

Franklin, Benjamin
See Hasek, Jaroslav (Matej Frantisek)

Franklin, Benjamin 1706-1790. . . **LC 25; DA**
See also CDALB 1640-1865; DLB 24, 43,
73

Franklin, (Stella Maraia Sarah) Miles
1879-1954 . . . . **TCLC 7**
See also CA 104

Fraser, (Lady) Antonia (Pakenham)
1932- . . . . **CLC 32**
See also CA 85-88; CANR 44; MTCW;
SATA 32

Fraser, George MacDonald 1925-. . . . **CLC 7**
See also CA 45-48; CANR 2

Fraser, Sylvia 1935-. . . . . **CLC 64**
See also CA 45-48; CANR 1, 16

Frayn, Michael 1933-. . . . . . . **CLC 3, 7, 31, 47**
See also CA 5-8R; CANR 30; DLB 13, 14;
MTCW

Fraze, Candida (Merrill) 1945-. . . . . . **CLC 50**
See also CA 126

Frazer, J(ames) G(eorge)
1854-1941 . . . . **TCLC 32**
See also CA 118

Frazer, Robert Caine
See Creasey, John

Frazer, Sir James George
See Frazer, J(ames) G(eorge)

Frazier, Ian 1951-. . . . . **CLC 46**
See also CA 130

Frederic, Harold 1856-1898. . . . . . **NCLC 10**
See also DLB 12, 23

Frederick, John
See Faust, Frederick (Schiller)

Frederick the Great 1712-1786 . . . . . . **LC 14**

Fredro, Aleksander 1793-1876. . . . . **NCLC 8**

Freeling, Nicolas 1927- . . . . **CLC 38**
See also CA 49-52; CAAS 12; CANR 1, 17;
DLB 87

Freeman, Douglas Southall
1886-1953 . . . . **TCLC 11**
See also CA 109; DLB 17

Freeman, Judith 1946-. . . . . **CLC 55**

Freeman, Mary Eleanor Wilkins
1852-1930 . . . . **TCLC 9; SSC 1**
See also CA 106; DLB 12, 78

Freeman, R(ichard) Austin
1862-1943 . . . . **TCLC 21**
See also CA 113; DLB 70

French, Marilyn 1929-. . . . . . . **CLC 10, 18, 60**
See also CA 69-72; CANR 3, 31; MTCW

French, Paul
See Asimov, Isaac

Freneau, Philip Morin 1752-1832 . . **NCLC 1**
See also DLB 37, 43

Freud, Sigmund 1856-1939 . . . . **TCLC 52**
See also CA 115; 133; MTCW

Friedan, Betty (Naomi) 1921-. . . . . . **CLC 74**
See also CA 65-68; CANR 18, 45; MTCW

Friedman, B(ernard) H(arper)
1926- . . . . **CLC 7**
See also CA 1-4R; CANR 3

Friedman, Bruce Jay 1930-. . . . **CLC 3, 5, 56**
See also CA 9-12R; CANR 25; DLB 2, 28

Friel, Brian 1929-. . . . . **CLC 5, 42, 59**
See also CA 21-24R; CANR 33; DLB 13;
MTCW

Friis-Baastad, Babbis Ellinor
1921-1970 . . . . **CLC 12**
See also CA 17-20R; 134; SATA 7

Frisch, Max (Rudolf)
1911-1991 . . . . . . **CLC 3, 9, 14, 18, 32, 44**
See also CA 85-88; 134; CANR 32;
DLB 69, 124; MTCW

Fromentin, Eugene (Samuel Auguste)
1820-1876 . . . . **NCLC 10**
See also DLB 123

Frost, Frederick
See Faust, Frederick (Schiller)

Frost, Robert (Lee)
1874-1963 . . . . **CLC 1, 3, 4, 9, 10, 13, 15,**
26, 34, 44; DA; PC 1; WLC
See also CA 89-92; CANR 33;
CDALB 1917-1929; DLB 54; DLBD 7;
MTCW; SATA 14

Froude, James Anthony
1818-1894 . . . . **NCLC 43**
See also DLB 18, 57, 144

Froy, Herald
See Waterhouse, Keith (Spencer)

Fry, Christopher 1907-. . . . . . . **CLC 2, 10, 14**
See also CA 17-20R; CANR 9, 30; DLB 13;
MTCW; SATA 66

Frye, (Herman) Northrop
1912-1991 . . . . **CLC 24, 70**
See also CA 5-8R; 133; CANR 8, 37;
DLB 67, 68; MTCW

Fuchs, Daniel 1909-1993 . . . . **CLC 8, 22**
See also CA 81-84; 142; CAAS 5;
CANR 40; DLB 9, 26, 28; DLBY 93

Fuchs, Daniel 1934- . . . . **CLC 34**
See also CA 37-40R; CANR 14

Fuentes, Carlos
1928- . . . . . . **CLC 3, 8, 10, 13, 22, 41, 60;**
DA; HLC; WLC
See also AAYA 4; AITN 2; CA 69-72;
CANR 10, 32; DLB 113; HW; MTCW

Fuentes, Gregorio Lopez y
See Lopez y Fuentes, Gregorio

Fugard, (Harold) Athol
1932- . . . . **CLC 5, 9, 14, 25, 40, 80; DC 3**
See also CA 85-88; CANR 32; MTCW

Fugard, Sheila 1932- . . . . **CLC 48**
See also CA 125

Fuller, Charles (H., Jr.)
1939- . . . . **CLC 25; BLC; DC 1**
See also BW 2; CA 108; 112; DLB 38;
MTCW

Fuller, John (Leopold) 1937- . . . . **CLC 62**
See also CA 21-24R; CANR 9, 44; DLB 40

Fuller, Margaret . . . . **NCLC 5**
See also Ossoli, Sarah Margaret (Fuller
marchesa d')

Fuller, Roy (Broadbent)
1912-1991 . . . . **CLC 4, 28**
See also CA 5-8R; 135; CAAS 10; DLB 15,
20

Fulton, Alice 1952- . . . . **CLC 52**
See also CA 116

Furphy, Joseph 1843-1912 . . . . **TCLC 25**

Fussell, Paul 1924- . . . . **CLC 74**
See also BEST 90:1; CA 17-20R; CANR 8,
21, 35; MTCW

Futabatei, Shimei 1864-1909 . . . . . . **TCLC 44**

Futrelle, Jacques 1875-1912 . . . . . . **TCLC 19**
See also CA 113

Gaboriau, Emile 1835-1873 . . . . . . **NCLC 14**

Gadda, Carlo Emilio 1893-1973 . . . . **CLC 11**
See also CA 89-92

Gaddis, William
1922- . . . . **CLC 1, 3, 6, 8, 10, 19, 43**
See also CA 17-20R; CANR 21; DLB 2;
MTCW

Gaines, Ernest J(ames)
1933- . . . . **CLC 3, 11, 18; BLC**
See also AITN 1; BW 2; CA 9-12R;
CANR 6, 24, 42; CDALB 1968-1988;
DLB 2, 33; DLBY 80; MTCW

Gaitskill, Mary 1954- . . . . **CLC 69**
See also CA 128

Galdos, Benito Perez
See Perez Galdos, Benito

Gale, Zona 1874-1938 . . . . **TCLC 7**
See also CA 105; DLB 9, 78

Galeano, Eduardo (Hughes) 1940- . . . **CLC 72**
See also CA 29-32R; CANR 13, 32; HW

Galiano, Juan Valera y Alcala
See Valera y Alcala-Galiano, Juan

Gallagher, Tess 1943- . . . . **CLC 18, 63; PC 9**
See also CA 106; DLB 120

Gallant, Mavis
1922- . . . . **CLC 7, 18, 38; SSC 5**
See also CA 69-72; CANR 29; DLB 53;
MTCW

Gallant, Roy A(rthur) 1924- . . . . **CLC 17**
See also CA 5-8R; CANR 4, 29; CLR 30;
MAICYA; SATA 4, 68

Gallico, Paul (William) 1897-1976 . . . **CLC 2**
See also AITN 1; CA 5-8R; 69-72;
CANR 23; DLB 9; MAICYA; SATA 13

Gallup, Ralph
See Whitemore, Hugh (John)

Galsworthy, John
1867-1933 . . . . **TCLC 1, 45; DA; WLC 2**
See also CA 104; 141; CDBLB 1890-1914;
DLB 10, 34, 98

Galt, John 1779-1839 . . . . **NCLC 1**
See also DLB 99, 116

Galvin, James 1951- . . . . **CLC 38**
See also CA 108; CANR 26

Gamboa, Federico 1864-1939 . . . . . **TCLC 36**

Gann, Ernest Kellogg 1910-1991 . . . . **CLC 23**
See also AITN 1; CA 1-4R; 136; CANR 1

Garcia, Cristina 1958- . . . . **CLC 76**
See also CA 141

Garcia Lorca, Federico
1898-1936 . . . . **TCLC 1, 7, 49; DA;**
DC 2; HLC; PC 3; WLC
See also CA 104; 131; DLB 108; HW;
MTCW

Garcia Marquez, Gabriel (Jose)
1928- . . . . **CLC 2, 3, 8, 10, 15, 27, 47, 55,**
68; DA; HLC; SSC 8; WLC
See also AAYA 3; BEST 89:1, 90:4;
CA 33-36R; CANR 10, 28; DLB 113;
HW; MTCW

Gard, Janice
See Latham, Jean Lee

Gard, Roger Martin du
See Martin du Gard, Roger

Gardam, Jane 1928- . . . . **CLC 43**
See also CA 49-52; CANR 2, 18, 33;
CLR 12; DLB 14; MAICYA; MTCW;
SAAS 9; SATA 28, 39, 76

Gardner, Herb . . . . **CLC 44**

Gardner, John (Champlin), Jr.
1933-1982 . . . . . **CLC 2, 3, 5, 7, 8, 10, 18,**
28, 34; SSC 7
See also AITN 1; CA 65-68; 107;
CANR 33; DLB 2; DLBY 82; MTCW;
SATA 31, 40

Gardner, John (Edmund) 1926- . . . . . **CLC 30**
See also CA 103; CANR 15; MTCW

Gardner, Noel
See Kuttner, Henry

Gardons, S. S.
See Snodgrass, W(illiam) D(e Witt)

Garfield, Leon 1921- . . . . **CLC 12**
See also AAYA 8; CA 17-20R; CANR 38,
41; CLR 21; JRDA; MAICYA; SATA 1,
32, 76

Garland, (Hannibal) Hamlin
1860-1940 . . . . **TCLC 3**
See also CA 104; DLB 12, 71, 78

Garneau, (Hector de) Saint-Denys
1912-1943 . . . . **TCLC 13**
See also CA 111; DLB 88

Garner, Alan 1934- . . . . **CLC 17**
See also CA 73-76; CANR 15; CLR 20;
MAICYA; MTCW; SATA 18, 69

Garner, Hugh 1913-1979 . . . . **CLC 13**
See also CA 69-72; CANR 31; DLB 68

Garnett, David 1892-1981 . . . . **CLC 3**
See also CA 5-8R; 103; CANR 17; DLB 34

Garos, Stephanie
See Katz, Steve

Garrett, George (Palmer)
1929- . . . . **CLC 3, 11, 51**
See also CA 1-4R; CAAS 5; CANR 1, 42;
DLB 2, 5, 130; DLBY 83

Garrick, David 1717-1779 . . . . **LC 15**
See also DLB 84

Garrigue, Jean 1914-1972 . . . . **CLC 2, 8**
See also CA 5-8R; 37-40R; CANR 20

Garrison, Frederick
See Sinclair, Upton (Beall)

Garth, Will
See Hamilton, Edmond; Kuttner, Henry

Garvey, Marcus (Moziah, Jr.)
1887-1940 . . . . **TCLC 41; BLC**
See also BW 1; CA 120; 124

Gary, Romain . . . . **CLC 25**
See also Kacew, Romain
See also DLB 83

Gascar, Pierre . . . . **CLC 11**
See also Fournier, Pierre

Gascoyne, David (Emery) 1916- . . . . **CLC 45**
See also CA 65-68; CANR 10, 28; DLB 20;
MTCW

Gaskell, Elizabeth Cleghorn
1810-1865 . . . . **NCLC 5**
See also CDBLB 1832-1890; DLB 21, 144

Gass, William H(oward)
1924- . . . **CLC 1, 2, 8, 11, 15, 39; SSC 12**
See also CA 17-20R; CANR 30; DLB 2;
MTCW

Gasset, Jose Ortega y
See Ortega y Gasset, Jose

Gates, Henry Louis, Jr. 1950- . . . . . . **CLC 65**
See also BW 2; CA 109; CANR 25; DLB 67

Gautier, Theophile 1811-1872 . . . . . **NCLC 1**
See also DLB 119

Gawsworth, John
See Bates, H(erbert) E(rnest)

Gaye, Marvin (Penze) 1939-1984 . . . **CLC 26**
See also CA 112

Gebler, Carlo (Ernest) 1954- . . . . **CLC 39**
See also CA 119; 133

Gee, Maggie (Mary) 1948- . . . . **CLC 57**
See also CA 130

Gee, Maurice (Gough) 1931- . . . . **CLC 29**
See also CA 97-100; SATA 46

Gelbart, Larry (Simon) 1923- . . . **CLC 21, 61**
See also CA 73-76; CANR 45

Gelber, Jack 1932-........ CLC 1, 6, 14, 79
See also CA 1-4R; CANR 2; DLB 7

Gellhorn, Martha (Ellis) 1908-.. CLC 14, 60
See also CA 77-80; CANR 44; DLBY 82

Genet, Jean
1910-1986 ... CLC 1, 2, 5, 10, 14, 44, 46
See also CA 13-16R; CANR 18; DLB 72;
DLBY 86; MTCW

Gent, Peter 1942-............... CLC 29
See also AITN 1; CA 89-92; DLBY 82

Gentlewoman in New England, A
See Bradstreet, Anne

Gentlewoman in Those Parts, A
See Bradstreet, Anne

George, Jean Craighead 1919-...... CLC 35
See also AAYA 8; CA 5-8R; CANR 25;
CLR 1; DLB 52; JRDA; MAICYA;
SATA 2, 68

George, Stefan (Anton)
1868-1933 .... TCLC 2, 14
See also CA 104

Georges, Georges Martin
See Simenon, Georges (Jacques Christian)

Gerhardi, William Alexander
See Gerhardie, William Alexander

Gerhardie, William Alexander
1895-1977 .... CLC 5
See also CA 25-28R; 73-76; CANR 18;
DLB 36

Gerstler, Amy 1956-.............. CLC 70

Gertler, T. .... CLC 34
See also CA 116; 121

Ghalib 1797-1869 .... NCLC 39

Ghelderode, Michel de
1898-1962 .... CLC 6, 11
See also CA 85-88; CANR 40

Ghiselin, Brewster 1903-........ CLC 23
See also CA 13-16R; CAAS 10; CANR 13

Ghose, Zulfikar 1935-............ CLC 42
See also CA 65-68

Ghosh, Amitav 1956-............. CLC 44

Giacosa, Giuseppe 1847-1906 ...... TCLC 7
See also CA 104

Gibb, Lee
See Waterhouse, Keith (Spencer)

Gibbon, Lewis Grassic .... TCLC 4
See also Mitchell, James Leslie

Gibbons, Kaye 1960- .... CLC 50

Gibran, Kahlil
1883-1931 .... TCLC 1, 9; PC 9
See also CA 104

Gibson, William 1914-........ CLC 23; DA
See also CA 9-12R; CANR 9, 42; DLB 7;
SATA 66

Gibson, William (Ford) 1948-... CLC 39, 63
See also AAYA 12; CA 126; 133

Gide, Andre (Paul Guillaume)
1869-1951 .... TCLC 5, 12, 36; DA;
SSC 13; WLC
See also CA 104; 124; DLB 65; MTCW

Gifford, Barry (Colby) 1946-...... CLC 34
See also CA 65-68; CANR 9, 30, 40

Gilbert, W(illiam) S(chwenck)
1836-1911 .... TCLC 3
See also CA 104; SATA 36

Gilbreth, Frank B., Jr. 1911-....... CLC 17
See also CA 9-12R; SATA 2

Gilchrist, Ellen 1935-.. CLC 34, 48; SSC 14
See also CA 113; 116; CANR 41; DLB 130;
MTCW

Giles, Molly 1942-............... CLC 39
See also CA 126

Gill, Patrick
See Creasey, John

Gilliam, Terry (Vance) 1940-....... CLC 21
See also Monty Python
See also CA 108; 113; CANR 35

Gillian, Jerry
See Gilliam, Terry (Vance)

Gilliatt, Penelope (Ann Douglass)
1932-1993 .... CLC 2, 10, 13, 53
See also AITN 2; CA 13-16R; 141; DLB 14

Gilman, Charlotte (Anna) Perkins (Stetson)
1860-1935 .... TCLC 9, 37; SSC 13
See also CA 106

Gilmour, David 1949-............. CLC 35
See also CA 138

Gilpin, William 1724-1804....... NCLC 30

Gilray, J. D.
See Mencken, H(enry) L(ouis)

Gilroy, Frank D(aniel) 1925-........ CLC 2
See also CA 81-84; CANR 32; DLB 7

Ginsberg, Allen
1926- ...... CLC 1, 2, 3, 4, 6, 13, 36, 69;
DA; PC 4; WLC 3
See also AITN 1; CA 1-4R; CANR 2, 41;
CDALB 1941-1968; DLB 5, 16; MTCW

Ginzburg, Natalia
1916-1991 .... CLC 5, 11, 54, 70
See also CA 85-88; 135; CANR 33; MTCW

Giono, Jean 1895-1970......... CLC 4, 11
See also CA 45-48; 29-32R; CANR 2, 35;
DLB 72; MTCW

Giovanni, Nikki
1943- ...... CLC 2, 4, 19, 64; BLC; DA
See also AITN 1; BW 2; CA 29-32R;
CAAS 6; CANR 18, 41; CLR 6; DLB 5,
41; MAICYA; MTCW; SATA 24

Giovene, Andrea 1904-............. CLC 7
See also CA 85-88

Gippius, Zinaida (Nikolayevna) 1869-1945
See Hippius, Zinaida
See also CA 106

Giraudoux, (Hippolyte) Jean
1882-1944 .... TCLC 2, 7
See also CA 104; DLB 65

Gironella, Jose Maria 1917-....... CLC 11
See also CA 101

Gissing, George (Robert)
1857-1903 .... TCLC 3, 24, 47
See also CA 105; DLB 18, 135

Giurlani, Aldo
See Palazzeschi, Aldo

Gladkov, Fyodor (Vasilyevich)
1883-1958 .... TCLC 27

Glanville, Brian (Lester) 1931-...... CLC 6
See also CA 5-8R; CAAS 9; CANR 3;
DLB 15, 139; SATA 42

Glasgow, Ellen (Anderson Gholson)
1873(?)-1945 .... TCLC 2, 7
See also CA 104; DLB 9, 12

Glaspell, Susan (Keating)
1882(?)-1948 .... TCLC 55
See also CA 110; DLB 7, 9, 78; YABC 2

Glassco, John 1909-1981 .... CLC 9
See also CA 13-16R; 102; CANR 15;
DLB 68

Glasscock, Amnesia
See Steinbeck, John (Ernst)

Glasser, Ronald J. 1940(?)-........ CLC 37

Glassman, Joyce
See Johnson, Joyce

Glendinning, Victoria 1937-........ CLC 50
See also CA 120; 127

Glissant, Edouard 1928-........ CLC 10, 68

Gloag, Julian 1930- .... CLC 40
See also AITN 1; CA 65-68; CANR 10

Glowacki, Aleksander
See Prus, Boleslaw

Glueck, Louise (Elisabeth)
1943- .... CLC 7, 22, 44, 81
See also CA 33-36R; CANR 40; DLB 5

Gobineau, Joseph Arthur (Comte) de
1816-1882 .... NCLC 17
See also DLB 123

Godard, Jean-Luc 1930-.......... CLC 20
See also CA 93-96

Godden, (Margaret) Rumer 1907-... CLC 53
See also AAYA 6; CA 5-8R; CANR 4, 27,
36; CLR 20; MAICYA; SAAS 12;
SATA 3, 36

Godoy Alcayaga, Lucila 1889-1957
See Mistral, Gabriela
See also BW 2; CA 104; 131; HW; MTCW

Godwin, Gail (Kathleen)
1937- .... CLC 5, 8, 22, 31, 69
See also CA 29-32R; CANR 15, 43; DLB 6;
MTCW

Godwin, William 1756-1836...... NCLC 14
See also CDBLB 1789-1832; DLB 39, 104,
142

Goethe, Johann Wolfgang von
1749-1832 .... NCLC 4, 22, 34; DA;
PC 5; WLC 3
See also DLB 94

Gogarty, Oliver St. John
1878-1957 .... TCLC 15
See also CA 109; DLB 15, 19

Gogol, Nikolai (Vasilyevich)
1809-1852 .... NCLC 5, 15, 31; DA;
DC 1; SSC 4; WLC
See also AITN 1; BW 1; CA 124; 114;
DLB 33

Goines, Donald
1937(?)-1974 .... CLC 80; BLC
See also AITN 1; BW 1; CA 124; 114;
DLB 33

Gold, Herbert 1924-....... CLC 4, 7, 14, 42
See also CA 9-12R; CANR 17, 45; DLB 2;
DLBY 81

Goldbarth, Albert 1948-.......... CLC 5, 38
See also CA 53-56; CANR 6, 40; DLB 120

Goldberg, Anatol 1910-1982 . . . . **CLC 34**
See also CA 131; 117

Goldemberg, Isaac 1945- . . . . **CLC 52**
See also CA 69-72; CAAS 12; CANR 11, 32; HW

Golding, William (Gerald)
1911-1993 . . . . **CLC 1, 2, 3, 8, 10, 17, 27, 58, 81; DA; WLC**
See also AAYA 5; CA 5-8R; 141; CANR 13, 33; CDBLB 1945-1960; DLB 15, 100; MTCW

Goldman, Emma 1869-1940 . . . . . . **TCLC 13**
See also CA 110

Goldman, Francisco 1955- . . . . **CLC 76**

Goldman, William (W.) 1931- . . . . **CLC 1, 48**
See also CA 9-12R; CANR 29; DLB 44

Goldmann, Lucien 1913-1970 . . . . . . **CLC 24**
See also CA 25-28; CAP 2

Goldoni, Carlo 1707-1793 . . . . **LC 4**

Goldsberry, Steven 1949- . . . . **CLC 34**
See also CA 131

Goldsmith, Oliver
1728-1774 . . . . **LC 2; DA; WLC**
See also CDBLB 1660-1789; DLB 39, 89, 104, 109, 142; SATA 26

Goldsmith, Peter
See Priestley, J(ohn) B(oynton)

Gombrowicz, Witold
1904-1969 . . . . **CLC 4, 7, 11, 49**
See also CA 19-20; 25-28R; CAP 2

Gomez de la Serna, Ramon
1888-1963 . . . . **CLC 9**
See also CA 116; HW

Goncharov, Ivan Alexandrovich
1812-1891 . . . . **NCLC 1**

Goncourt, Edmond (Louis Antoine Huot) de
1822-1896 . . . . **NCLC 7**
See also DLB 123

Goncourt, Jules (Alfred Huot) de
1830-1870 . . . . **NCLC 7**
See also DLB 123

Gontier, Fernande 19(?)- . . . . **CLC 50**

Goodman, Paul 1911-1972 . . . . **CLC 1, 2, 4, 7**
See also CA 19-20; 37-40R; CANR 34; CAP 2; DLB 130; MTCW

Gordimer, Nadine
1923- . . . . **CLC 3, 5, 7, 10, 18, 33, 51, 70; DA; SSC 17**
See also CA 5-8R; CANR 3, 28; MTCW

Gordon, Adam Lindsay
1833-1870 . . . . **NCLC 21**

Gordon, Caroline
1895-1981 . . . **CLC 6, 13, 29, 83; SSC 15**
See also CA 11-12; 103; CANR 36; CAP 1; DLB 4, 9, 102; DLBY 81; MTCW

Gordon, Charles William 1860-1937
See Connor, Ralph
See also CA 109

Gordon, Mary (Catherine)
1949- . . . . **CLC 13, 22**
See also CA 102; CANR 44; DLB 6; DLBY 81; MTCW

Gordon, Sol 1923- . . . . **CLC 26**
See also CA 53-56; CANR 4; SATA 11

Gordone, Charles 1925- . . . . **CLC 1, 4**
See also BW 1; CA 93-96; DLB 7; MTCW

Gorenko, Anna Andreevna
See Akhmatova, Anna

Gorky, Maxim . . . . **TCLC 8; WLC**
See also Peshkov, Alexei Maximovich

Goryan, Sirak
See Saroyan, William

Gosse, Edmund (William)
1849-1928 . . . . **TCLC 28**
See also CA 117; DLB 57, 144

Gotlieb, Phyllis Fay (Bloom)
1926- . . . . **CLC 18**
See also CA 13-16R; CANR 7; DLB 88

Gottesman, S. D.
See Kornbluth, C(yril) M.; Pohl, Frederik

Gottfried von Strassburg
fl. c. 1210- . . . . **CMLC 10**
See also DLB 138

Gould, Lois . . . . **CLC 4, 10**
See also CA 77-80; CANR 29; MTCW

Gourmont, Remy de 1858-1915 . . . . **TCLC 17**
See also CA 109

Govier, Katherine 1948- . . . . **CLC 51**
See also CA 101; CANR 18, 40

Goyen, (Charles) William
1915-1983 . . . . **CLC 5, 8, 14, 40**
See also AITN 2; CA 5-8R; 110; CANR 6; DLB 2; DLBY 83

Goytisolo, Juan
1931- . . . . **CLC 5, 10, 23; HLC**
See also CA 85-88; CANR 32; HW; MTCW

Gozzano, Guido 1883-1916 . . . . **PC 10**
See also DLB 114

Gozzi, (Conte) Carlo 1720-1806 . . **NCLC 23**

Grabbe, Christian Dietrich
1801-1836 . . . . **NCLC 2**
See also DLB 133

Grace, Patricia 1937- . . . . **CLC 56**

Gracian y Morales, Baltasar
1601-1658 . . . . **LC 15**

Gracq, Julien . . . . **CLC 11, 48**
See also Poirier, Louis
See also DLB 83

Grade, Chaim 1910-1982 . . . . **CLC 10**
See also CA 93-96; 107

Graduate of Oxford, A
See Ruskin, John

Graham, John
See Phillips, David Graham

Graham, Jorie 1951- . . . . **CLC 48**
See also CA 111; DLB 120

Graham, R(obert) B(ontine) Cunninghame
See Cunninghame Graham, R(obert) B(ontine)
See also DLB 98, 135

Graham, Robert
See Haldeman, Joe (William)

Graham, Tom
See Lewis, (Harry) Sinclair

Graham, W(illiam) S(ydney)
1918-1986 . . . . **CLC 29**
See also CA 73-76; 118; DLB 20

Graham, Winston (Mawdsley)
1910- . . . . **CLC 23**
See also CA 49-52; CANR 2, 22, 45; DLB 77

Grant, Skeeter
See Spiegelman, Art

Granville-Barker, Harley
1877-1946 . . . . **TCLC 2**
See also Barker, Harley Granville
See also CA 104

Grass, Guenter (Wilhelm)
1927- . . . . . **CLC 1, 2, 4, 6, 11, 15, 22, 32, 49; DA; WLC**
See also CA 13-16R; CANR 20; DLB 75, 124; MTCW

Gratton, Thomas
See Hulme, T(homas) E(rnest)

Grau, Shirley Ann
1929- . . . . **CLC 4, 9; SSC 15**
See also CA 89-92; CANR 22; DLB 2; MTCW

Gravel, Fern
See Hall, James Norman

Graver, Elizabeth 1964- . . . . **CLC 70**
See also CA 135

Graves, Richard Perceval 1945- . . . . **CLC 44**
See also CA 65-68; CANR 9, 26

Graves, Robert (von Ranke)
1895-1985 . . . . . . **CLC 1, 2, 6, 11, 39, 44, 45; PC 6**
See also CA 5-8R; 117; CANR 5, 36; CDBLB 1914-1945; DLB 20, 100; DLBY 85; MTCW; SATA 45

Gray, Alasdair 1934- . . . . **CLC 41**
See also CA 126; MTCW

Gray, Amlin 1946- . . . . **CLC 29**
See also CA 138

Gray, Francine du Plessix 1930- . . . . **CLC 22**
See also BEST 90:3; CA 61-64; CAAS 2; CANR 11, 33; MTCW

Gray, John (Henry) 1866-1934 . . . . **TCLC 19**
See also CA 119

Gray, Simon (James Holliday)
1936- . . . . **CLC 9, 14, 36**
See also AITN 1; CA 21-24R; CAAS 3; CANR 32; DLB 13; MTCW

Gray, Spalding 1941- . . . . **CLC 49**
See also CA 128

Gray, Thomas
1716-1771 . . . . . . **LC 4; DA; PC 2; WLC**
See also CDBLB 1660-1789; DLB 109

Grayson, David
See Baker, Ray Stannard

Grayson, Richard (A.) 1951- . . . . **CLC 38**
See also CA 85-88; CANR 14, 31

Greeley, Andrew M(oran) 1928- . . . . **CLC 28**
See also CA 5-8R; CAAS 7; CANR 7, 43; MTCW

Green, Brian
See Card, Orson Scott

Green, Hannah
See Greenberg, Joanne (Goldenberg)

Green, Hannah . . . . **CLC 3**
See also CA 73-76

Harrison, Elizabeth Cavanna 1909-
See Cavanna, Betty
See also CA 9-12R; CANR 6, 27

Harrison, Harry (Max) 1925- ...... **CLC 42**
See also CA 1-4R; CANR 5, 21; DLB 8;
SATA 4

Harrison, James (Thomas)
1937- .... **CLC 6, 14, 33, 66**
See also CA 13-16R; CANR 8; DLBY 82

Harrison, Jim
See Harrison, James (Thomas)

Harrison, Kathryn 1961- .... **CLC 70**
See also CA 144

Harrison, Tony 1937-............. **CLC 43**
See also CA 65-68; CANR 44; DLB 40;
MTCW

Harriss, Will(ard Irvin) 1922- ...... **CLC 34**
See also CA 111

Harson, Sley
See Ellison, Harlan

Hart, Ellis
See Ellison, Harlan

Hart, Josephine 1942(?)- .... **CLC 70**
See also CA 138

Hart, Moss 1904-1961 .... **CLC 66**
See also CA 109; 89-92; DLB 7

Harte, (Francis) Bret(t)
1836(?)-1902 .... **TCLC 1, 25; DA;**
                                      SSC 8; WLC
See also CA 104; 140; CDALB 1865-1917;
DLB 12, 64, 74, 79; SATA 26

Hartley, L(eslie) P(oles)
1895-1972 .... **CLC 2, 22**
See also CA 45-48; 37-40R; CANR 33;
DLB 15, 139; MTCW

Hartman, Geoffrey H. 1929- .... **CLC 27**
See also CA 117; 125; DLB 67

Haruf, Kent 19(?)- .... **CLC 34**

Harwood, Ronald 1934- .... **CLC 32**
See also CA 1-4R; CANR 4; DLB 13

Hasek, Jaroslav (Matej Frantisek)
1883-1923 .... **TCLC 4**
See also CA 104; 129; MTCW

Hass, Robert 1941-............. **CLC 18, 39**
See also CA 111; CANR 30; DLB 105

Hastings, Hudson
See Kuttner, Henry

Hastings, Selina.................. **CLC 44**

Hatteras, Amelia
See Mencken, H(enry) L(ouis)

Hatteras, Owen................. **TCLC 18**
See also Mencken, H(enry) L(ouis); Nathan,
George Jean

Hauptmann, Gerhart (Johann Robert)
1862-1946 .... **TCLC 4**
See also CA 104; DLB 66, 118

Havel, Vaclav 1936-........ **CLC 25, 58, 65**
See also CA 104; CANR 36; MTCW

Haviaras, Stratis................. **CLC 33**
See also Chaviaras, Strates

Hawes, Stephen 1475(?)-1523(?) ..... **LC 17**

Hawkes, John (Clendennin Burne, Jr.)
1925- ...... **CLC 1, 2, 3, 4, 7, 9, 14, 15,**
                                      27, 49
See also CA 1-4R; CANR 2; DLB 2, 7;
DLBY 80; MTCW

Hawking, S. W.
See Hawking, Stephen W(illiam)

Hawking, Stephen W(illiam)
1942- .... **CLC 63**
See also BEST 89:1; CA 126; 129

Hawthorne, Julian 1846-1934 ..... **TCLC 25**

Hawthorne, Nathaniel
1804-1864 ...... **NCLC 39; DA; SSC 3;**
                                      WLC
See also CDALB 1640-1865; DLB 1, 74;
YABC 2

Haxton, Josephine Ayres 1921-
See Douglas, Ellen
See also CA 115; CANR 41

Hayaseca y Eizaguirre, Jorge
See Echegaray (y Eizaguirre), Jose (Maria
Waldo)

Hayashi Fumiko 1904-1951....... **TCLC 27**

Haycraft, Anna
See Ellis, Alice Thomas
See also CA 122

Hayden, Robert E(arl)
1913-1980 ...... **CLC 5, 9, 14, 37; BLC;**
                                      DA; PC 6
See also BW 1; CA 69-72; 97-100; CABS 2;
CANR 24; CDALB 1941-1968; DLB 5,
76; MTCW; SATA 19, 26

Hayford, J(oseph) E(phraim) Casely
See Casely-Hayford, J(oseph) E(phraim)

Hayman, Ronald 1932-............ **CLC 44**
See also CA 25-28R; CANR 18

Haywood, Eliza (Fowler)
1693(?)-1756 .... **LC 1**

Hazlitt, William 1778-1830...... **NCLC 29**
See also DLB 110

Hazzard, Shirley 1931- .... **CLC 18**
See also CA 9-12R; CANR 4; DLBY 82;
MTCW

Head, Bessie 1937-1986... **CLC 25, 67; BLC**
See also BW 2; CA 29-32R; 119; CANR 25;
DLB 117; MTCW

Headon, (Nicky) Topper 1956(?)- ... **CLC 30**

Heaney, Seamus (Justin)
1939- .... **CLC 5, 7, 14, 25, 37, 74**
See also CA 85-88; CANR 25;
CDBLB 1960 to Present; DLB 40;
MTCW

Hearn, (Patricio) Lafcadio (Tessima Carlos)
1850-1904 .... **TCLC 9**
See also CA 105; DLB 12, 78

Hearne, Vicki 1946-.............. **CLC 56**
See also CA 139

Hearon, Shelby 1931-............. **CLC 63**
See also AITN 2; CA 25-28R; CANR 18

Heat-Moon, William Least......... **CLC 29**
See also Trogdon, William (Lewis)
See also AAYA 9

Hebbel, Friedrich 1813-1863 ..... **NCLC 43**
See also DLB 129

Hebert, Anne 1916- .... **CLC 4, 13, 29**
See also CA 85-88; DLB 68; MTCW

Hecht, Anthony (Evan)
1923- .... **CLC 8, 13, 19**
See also CA 9-12R; CANR 6; DLB 5

Hecht, Ben 1894-1964 .... **CLC 8**
See also CA 85-88; DLB 7, 9, 25, 26, 28, 86

Hedayat, Sadeq 1903-1951....... **TCLC 21**
See also CA 120

Hegel, Georg Wilhelm Friedrich
1770-1831 .... **NCLC 46**
See also DLB 90

Heidegger, Martin 1889-1976 ...... **CLC 24**
See also CA 81-84; 65-68; CANR 34;
MTCW

Heidenstam, (Carl Gustaf) Verner von
1859-1940 .... **TCLC 5**
See also CA 104

Heifner, Jack 1946-.............. **CLC 11**
See also CA 105

Heijermans, Herman 1864-1924 ... **TCLC 24**
See also CA 123

Heilbrun, Carolyn G(old) 1926-..... **CLC 25**
See also CA 45-48; CANR 1, 28

Heine, Heinrich 1797-1856 .... **NCLC 4**
See also DLB 90

Heinemann, Larry (Curtiss) 1944- .. **CLC 50**
See also CA 110; CANR 31; DLBD 9

Heiney, Donald (William) 1921-1993
See Harris, MacDonald
See also CA 1-4R; 142; CANR 3

Heinlein, Robert A(nson)
1907-1988 ...... **CLC 1, 3, 8, 14, 26, 55**
See also CA 1-4R; 125; CANR 1, 20;
DLB 8; JRDA; MAICYA; MTCW;
SATA 9, 56, 69

Helforth, John
See Doolittle, Hilda

Hellenhofferu, Vojtech Kapristian z
See Hasek, Jaroslav (Matej Frantisek)

Heller, Joseph
1923- .... **CLC 1, 3, 5, 8, 11, 36, 63; DA;**
                                      WLC
See also AITN 1; CA 5-8R; CABS 1;
CANR 8, 42; DLB 2, 28; DLBY 80;
MTCW

Hellman, Lillian (Florence)
1906-1984 ...... **CLC 2, 4, 8, 14, 18, 34,**
                                      44, 52; DC 1
See also AITN 1, 2; CA 13-16R; 112;
CANR 33; DLB 7; DLBY 84; MTCW

Helprin, Mark 1947- ..... **CLC 7, 10, 22, 32**
See also CA 81-84; DLBY 85; MTCW

Helvetius, Claude-Adrien
1715-1771 .... **LC 26**

Helyar, Jane Penelope Josephine 1933-
See Poole, Josephine
See also CA 21-24R; CANR 10, 26

Hemans, Felicia 1793-1835 ...... **NCLC 29**
See also DLB 96

Hemingway, Ernest (Miller)
1899-1961 .... CLC 1, 3, 6, 8, 10, 13, 19,
30, 34, 39, 41, 44, 50, 61, 80; DA; SSC 1;
WLC
See also CA 77-80; CANR 34;
CDALB 1917-1929; DLB 4, 9, 102;
DLBD 1; DLBY 81, 87; MTCW

Hempel, Amy 1951- .... CLC 39
See also CA 118; 137

Henderson, F. C.
See Mencken, H(enry) L(ouis)

Henderson, Sylvia
See Ashton-Warner, Sylvia (Constance)

Henley, Beth .... CLC 23
See also Henley, Elizabeth Becker
See also CABS 3; DLBY 86

Henley, Elizabeth Becker 1952-
See Henley, Beth
See also CA 107; CANR 32; MTCW

Henley, William Ernest
1849-1903 .... TCLC 8
See also CA 105; DLB 19

Hennissart, Martha
See Lathen, Emma
See also CA 85-88

Henry, O. .... TCLC 1, 19; SSC 5; WLC
See also Porter, William Sydney

Henry, Patrick 1736- .... LC 25
See also CA 145

Henryson, Robert 1430(?)-1506(?).... LC 20

Henry VIII 1491-1547 .... LC 10

Henschke, Alfred
See Klabund

Hentoff, Nat(han Irving) 1925- ..... CLC 26
See also AAYA 4; CA 1-4R; CAAS 6;
CANR 5, 25; CLR 1; JRDA; MAICYA;
SATA 27, 42, 69

Heppenstall, (John) Rayner
1911-1981 .... CLC 10
See also CA 1-4R; 103; CANR 29

Herbert, Frank (Patrick)
1920-1986 ...... CLC 12, 23, 35, 44, 85
See also CA 53-56; 118; CANR 5, 43;
DLB 8; MTCW; SATA 9, 37, 47

Herbert, George 1593-1633 .... LC 24; PC 4
See also CDBLB Before 1660; DLB 126

Herbert, Zbigniew 1924- .... CLC 9, 43
See also CA 89-92; CANR 36; MTCW

Herbst, Josephine (Frey)
1897-1969 .... CLC 34
See also CA 5-8R; 25-28R; DLB 9

Hergesheimer, Joseph
1880-1954 .... TCLC 11
See also CA 109; DLB 102, 9

Herlihy, James Leo 1927-1993 ...... CLC 6
See also CA 1-4R; 143; CANR 2

Hermogenes fl. c. 175- .... CMLC 6

Hernandez, Jose 1834-1886 ...... NCLC 17

Herrick, Robert
1591-1674 .... LC 13; DA; PC 9
See also DLB 126

Herring, Guilles
See Somerville, Edith

Herriot, James 1916- .... CLC 12
See also Wight, James Alfred
See also AAYA 1; CANR 40

Herrmann, Dorothy 1941- .... CLC 44
See also CA 107

Herrmann, Taffy
See Herrmann, Dorothy

Hersey, John (Richard)
1914-1993 ...... CLC 1, 2, 7, 9, 40, 81
See also CA 17-20R; 140; CANR 33;
DLB 6; MTCW; SATA 25;
SATA-Obit 76

Herzen, Aleksandr Ivanovich
1812-1870 .... NCLC 10

Herzl, Theodor 1860-1904 .... TCLC 36

Herzog, Werner 1942- .... CLC 16
See also CA 89-92

Hesiod c. 8th cent. B.C.- .... CMLC 5

Hesse, Hermann
1877-1962 .... CLC 1, 2, 3, 6, 11, 17, 25,
69; DA; SSC 9; WLC
See also CA 17-18; CAP 2; DLB 66;
MTCW; SATA 50

Hewes, Cady
See De Voto, Bernard (Augustine)

Heyen, William 1940- .... CLC 13, 18
See also CA 33-36R; CAAS 9; DLB 5

Heyerdahl, Thor 1914- .... CLC 26
See also CA 5-8R; CANR 5, 22; MTCW;
SATA 2, 52

Heym, Georg (Theodor Franz Arthur)
1887-1912 .... TCLC 9
See also CA 106

Heym, Stefan 1913- .... CLC 41
See also CA 9-12R; CANR 4; DLB 69

Heyse, Paul (Johann Ludwig von)
1830-1914 .... TCLC 8
See also CA 104; DLB 129

Hibbert, Eleanor Alice Burford
1906-1993 .... CLC 7
See also BEST 90:4; CA 17-20R; 140;
CANR 9, 28; SATA 2; SATA-Obit 74

Higgins, George V(incent)
1939- .... CLC 4, 7, 10, 18
See also CA 77-80; CAAS 5; CANR 17;
DLB 2; DLBY 81; MTCW

Higginson, Thomas Wentworth
1823-1911 .... TCLC 36
See also DLB 1, 64

Highet, Helen
See MacInnes, Helen (Clark)

Highsmith, (Mary) Patricia
1921- .... CLC 2, 4, 14, 42
See also CA 1-4R; CANR 1, 20; MTCW

Highwater, Jamake (Mamake)
1942(?)- .... CLC 12
See also AAYA 7; CA 65-68; CAAS 7;
CANR 10, 34; CLR 17; DLB 52;
DLBY 85; JRDA; MAICYA; SATA 30,
32, 69

Hijuelos, Oscar 1951- ...... CLC 65; HLC
See also BEST 90:1; CA 123; HW

Hikmet, Nazim 1902(?)-1963....... CLC 40
See also CA 141; 93-96

Hildesheimer, Wolfgang
1916-1991 .... CLC 49
See also CA 101; 135; DLB 69, 124

Hill, Geoffrey (William)
1932- .... CLC 5, 8, 18, 45
See also CA 81-84; CANR 21;
CDBLB 1960 to Present; DLB 40;
MTCW

Hill, George Roy 1921- .... CLC 26
See also CA 110; 122

Hill, John
See Koontz, Dean R(ay)

Hill, Susan (Elizabeth) 1942- .... CLC 4
See also CA 33-36R; CANR 29; DLB 14,
139; MTCW

Hillerman, Tony 1925- .... CLC 62
See also AAYA 6; BEST 89:1; CA 29-32R;
CANR 21, 42; SATA 6

Hillesum, Etty 1914-1943 .... TCLC 49
See also CA 137

Hilliard, Noel (Harvey) 1929- ...... CLC 15
See also CA 9-12R; CANR 7

Hillis, Rick 1956- .... CLC 66
See also CA 134

Hilton, James 1900-1954......... TCLC 21
See also CA 108; DLB 34, 77; SATA 34

Himes, Chester (Bomar)
1909-1984 .... CLC 2, 4, 7, 18, 58; BLC
See also BW 2; CA 25-28R; 114; CANR 22;
DLB 2, 76, 143; MTCW

Hinde, Thomas .... CLC 6, 11
See also Chitty, Thomas Willes

Hindin, Nathan
See Bloch, Robert (Albert)

Hine, (William) Daryl 1936- .... CLC 15
See also CA 1-4R; CAAS 15; CANR 1, 20;
DLB 60

Hinkson, Katharine Tynan
See Tynan, Katharine

Hinton, S(usan) E(loise)
1950- .... CLC 30; DA
See also AAYA 2; CA 81-84; CANR 32;
CLR 3, 23; JRDA; MAICYA; MTCW;
SATA 19, 58

Hippius, Zinaida .... TCLC 9
See also Gippius, Zinaida (Nikolayevna)

Hiraoka, Kimitake 1925-1970
See Mishima, Yukio
See also CA 97-100; 29-32R; MTCW

Hirsch, E(ric) D(onald), Jr. 1928-... CLC 79
See also CA 25-28R; CANR 27; DLB 67;
MTCW

Hirsch, Edward 1950- .... CLC 31, 50
See also CA 104; CANR 20, 42; DLB 120

Hitchcock, Alfred (Joseph)
1899-1980 .... CLC 16
See also CA 97-100; SATA 24, 27

Hitler, Adolf 1889-1945......... TCLC 53
See also CA 117

Hoagland, Edward 1932- .... CLC 28
See also CA 1-4R; CANR 2, 31; DLB 6;
SATA 51

Hoban, Russell (Conwell) 1925- .. **CLC 7, 25**
See also CA 5-8R; CANR 23, 37; CLR 3;
DLB 52; MAICYA; MTCW; SATA 1,
40, 78

Hobbs, Perry
See Blackmur, R(ichard) P(almer)

Hobson, Laura Z(ametkin)
1900-1986 .... **CLC 7, 25**
See also CA 17-20R; 118; DLB 28;
SATA 52

Hochhuth, Rolf 1931- .... **CLC 4, 11, 18**
See also CA 5-8R; CANR 33; DLB 124;
MTCW

Hochman, Sandra 1936- .... **CLC 3, 8**
See also CA 5-8R; DLB 5

Hochwaelder, Fritz 1911-1986...... **CLC 36**
See also CA 29-32R; 120; CANR 42;
MTCW

Hochwalder, Fritz
See Hochwaelder, Fritz

Hocking, Mary (Eunice) 1921- ..... **CLC 13**
See also CA 101; CANR 18, 40

Hodgins, Jack 1938- .... **CLC 23**
See also CA 93-96; DLB 60

Hodgson, William Hope
1877(?)-1918 .... **TCLC 13**
See also CA 111; DLB 70

Hoffman, Alice 1952- .... **CLC 51**
See also CA 77-80; CANR 34; MTCW

Hoffman, Daniel (Gerard)
1923- .... **CLC 6, 13, 23**
See also CA 1-4R; CANR 4; DLB 5

Hoffman, Stanley 1944- .... **CLC 5**
See also CA 77-80

Hoffman, William M(oses) 1939- ... **CLC 40**
See also CA 57-60; CANR 11

Hoffmann, E(rnst) T(heodor) A(madeus)
1776-1822 .... **NCLC 2; SSC 13**
See also DLB 90; SATA 27

Hofmann, Gert 1931- .... **CLC 54**
See also CA 128

Hofmannsthal, Hugo von
1874-1929 .... **TCLC 11; DC 4**
See also CA 106; DLB 81, 118

Hogan, Linda 1947- .... **CLC 73**
See also CA 120; CANR 45

Hogarth, Charles
See Creasey, John

Hogg, James 1770-1835 .... **NCLC 4**
See also DLB 93, 116

Holbach, Paul Henri Thiry Baron
1723-1789 .... **LC 14**

Holberg, Ludvig 1684-1754 .... **LC 6**

Holden, Ursula 1921- .... **CLC 18**
See also CA 101; CAAS 8; CANR 22

Holderlin, (Johann Christian) Friedrich
1770-1843 .... **NCLC 16; PC 4**

Holdstock, Robert
See Holdstock, Robert P.

Holdstock, Robert P. 1948- .... **CLC 39**
See also CA 131

Holland, Isabelle 1920- .... **CLC 21**
See also AAYA 11; CA 21-24R; CANR 10,
25; JRDA; MAICYA; SATA 8, 70

Holland, Marcus
See Caldwell, (Janet Miriam) Taylor
(Holland)

Hollander, John 1929- ...... **CLC 2, 5, 8, 14**
See also CA 1-4R; CANR 1; DLB 5;
SATA 13

Hollander, Paul
See Silverberg, Robert

Holleran, Andrew 1943(?)- .... **CLC 38**
See also CA 144

Hollinghurst, Alan 1954- .... **CLC 55**
See also CA 114

Hollis, Jim
See Summers, Hollis (Spurgeon, Jr.)

Holmes, John
See Souster, (Holmes) Raymond

Holmes, John Clellon 1926-1988.... **CLC 56**
See also CA 9-12R; 125; CANR 4; DLB 16

Holmes, Oliver Wendell
1809-1894 .... **NCLC 14**
See also CDALB 1640-1865; DLB 1;
SATA 34

Holmes, Raymond
See Souster, (Holmes) Raymond

Holt, Victoria
See Hibbert, Eleanor Alice Burford

Holub, Miroslav 1923- .... **CLC 4**
See also CA 21-24R; CANR 10

Homer c. 8th cent. B.C.- ..... **CMLC 1; DA**

Honig, Edwin 1919- .... **CLC 33**
See also CA 5-8R; CAAS 8; CANR 4, 45;
DLB 5

Hood, Hugh (John Blagdon)
1928- .... **CLC 15, 28**
See also CA 49-52; CAAS 17; CANR 1, 33;
DLB 53

Hood, Thomas 1799-1845........ **NCLC 16**
See also DLB 96

Hooker, (Peter) Jeremy 1941- ...... **CLC 43**
See also CA 77-80; CANR 22; DLB 40

Hope, A(lec) D(erwent) 1907- .... **CLC 3, 51**
See also CA 21-24R; CANR 33; MTCW

Hope, Brian
See Creasey, John

Hope, Christopher (David Tully)
1944- .... **CLC 52**
See also CA 106; SATA 62

Hopkins, Gerard Manley
1844-1889 .... **NCLC 17; DA; WLC**
See also CDBLB 1890-1914; DLB 35, 57

Hopkins, John (Richard) 1931- ...... **CLC 4**
See also CA 85-88

Hopkins, Pauline Elizabeth
1859-1930 .... **TCLC 28; BLC**
See also BW 2; CA 141; DLB 50

Hopkinson, Francis 1737-1791 ...... **LC 25**
See also DLB 31

Hopley-Woolrich, Cornell George 1903-1968
See Woolrich, Cornell
See also CA 13-14; CAP 1

Horatio
See Proust, (Valentin-Louis-George-Eugene-)
Marcel

Horgan, Paul 1903- .... **CLC 9, 53**
See also CA 13-16R; CANR 9, 35;
DLB 102; DLBY 85; MTCW; SATA 13

Horn, Peter
See Kuttner, Henry

Hornem, Horace Esq.
See Byron, George Gordon (Noel)

Horovitz, Israel 1939- .... **CLC 56**
See also CA 33-36R; DLB 7

Horvath, Odon von
See Horvath, Oedoen von
See also DLB 85, 124

Horvath, Oedoen von 1901-1938... **TCLC 45**
See also Horvath, Odon von
See also CA 118

Horwitz, Julius 1920-1986......... **CLC 14**
See also CA 9-12R; 119; CANR 12

Hospital, Janette Turner 1942-..... **CLC 42**
See also CA 108

Hostos, E. M. de
See Hostos (y Bonilla), Eugenio Maria de

Hostos, Eugenio M. de
See Hostos (y Bonilla), Eugenio Maria de

Hostos, Eugenio Maria
See Hostos (y Bonilla), Eugenio Maria de

Hostos (y Bonilla), Eugenio Maria de
1839-1903 .... **TCLC 24**
See also CA 123; 131; HW

Houdini
See Lovecraft, H(oward) P(hillips)

Hougan, Carolyn 1943- .... **CLC 34**
See also CA 139

Household, Geoffrey (Edward West)
1900-1988 .... **CLC 11**
See also CA 77-80; 126; DLB 87; SATA 14,
59

Housman, A(lfred) E(dward)
1859-1936 ...... **TCLC 1, 10; DA; PC 2**
See also CA 104; 125; DLB 19; MTCW

Housman, Laurence 1865-1959 ..... **TCLC 7**
See also CA 106; DLB 10; SATA 25

Howard, Elizabeth Jane 1923- ... **CLC 7, 29**
See also CA 5-8R; CANR 8

Howard, Maureen 1930- ..... **CLC 5, 14, 46**
See also CA 53-56; CANR 31; DLBY 83;
MTCW

Howard, Richard 1929- ...... **CLC 7, 10, 47**
See also AITN 1; CA 85-88; CANR 25;
DLB 5

Howard, Robert Ervin 1906-1936... **TCLC 8**
See also CA 105

Howard, Warren F.
See Pohl, Frederik

Howe, Fanny 1940- .... **CLC 47**
See also CA 117; SATA 52

Howe, Irving 1920-1993.......... **CLC 85**
See also CA 9-12R; 141; CANR 21;
DLB 67; MTCW

Howe, Julia Ward 1819-1910 ..... **TCLC 21**
See also CA 117; DLB 1

Howe, Susan 1937- .... **CLC 72**
See also DLB 120

Howe, Tina 1937- .... **CLC 48**
See also CA 109

Irving, John (Winslow)
1942- . . . . **CLC 13, 23, 38**
See also AAYA 8; BEST 89:3; CA 25-28R;
CANR 28; DLB 6; DLBY 82; MTCW

Irving, Washington
1783-1859 . . . . **NCLC 2, 19; DA; SSC 2;**
WLC
See also CDALB 1640-1865; DLB 3, 11, 30,
59, 73, 74; YABC 2

Irwin, P. K.
See Page, P(atricia) K(athleen)

Isaacs, Susan 1943- . . . . **CLC 32**
See also BEST 89:1; CA 89-92; CANR 20,
41; MTCW

Isherwood, Christopher (William Bradshaw)
1904-1986 . . . . **CLC 1, 9, 11, 14, 44**
See also CA 13-16R; 117; CANR 35;
DLB 15; DLBY 86; MTCW

Ishiguro, Kazuo 1954- . . . . . . **CLC 27, 56, 59**
See also BEST 90:2; CA 120; MTCW

Ishikawa Takuboku
1886(?)-1912 . . . . **TCLC 15; PC 10**
See also CA 113

Iskander, Fazil 1929- . . . . **CLC 47**
See also CA 102

Ivan IV 1530-1584 . . . . **LC 17**

Ivanov, Vyacheslav Ivanovich
1866-1949 . . . . **TCLC 33**
See also CA 122

Ivask, Ivar Vidrik 1927-1992 . . . . **CLC 14**
See also CA 37-40R; 139; CANR 24

Jackson, Daniel
See Wingrove, David (John)

Jackson, Jesse 1908-1983 . . . . **CLC 12**
See also BW 1; CA 25-28R; 109; CANR 27;
CLR 28; MAICYA; SATA 2, 29, 48

Jackson, Laura (Riding) 1901-1991
See Riding, Laura
See also CA 65-68; 135; CANR 28; DLB 48

Jackson, Sam
See Trumbo, Dalton

Jackson, Sara
See Wingrove, David (John)

Jackson, Shirley
1919-1965 . . . . . **CLC 11, 60; DA; SSC 9;**
WLC
See also AAYA 9; CA 1-4R; 25-28R;
CANR 4; CDALB 1941-1968; DLB 6;
SATA 2

Jacob, (Cyprien-)Max 1876-1944 . . . **TCLC 6**
See also CA 104

Jacobs, Jim 1942- . . . . **CLC 12**
See also CA 97-100

Jacobs, W(illiam) W(ymark)
1863-1943 . . . . **TCLC 22**
See also CA 121; DLB 135

Jacobsen, Jens Peter 1847-1885 . . **NCLC 34**

Jacobsen, Josephine 1908- . . . . **CLC 48**
See also CA 33-36R; CAAS 18; CANR 23

Jacobson, Dan 1929- . . . . **CLC 4, 14**
See also CA 1-4R; CANR 2, 25; DLB 14;
MTCW

Jacqueline
See Carpentier (y Valmont), Alejo

Jagger, Mick 1944- . . . . **CLC 17**

Jakes, John (William) 1932- . . . . **CLC 29**
See also BEST 89:4; CA 57-60; CANR 10,
43; DLBY 83; MTCW; SATA 62

James, Andrew
See Kirkup, James

James, C(yril) L(ionel) R(obert)
1901-1989 . . . . **CLC 33**
See also BW 2; CA 117; 125; 128; DLB 125;
MTCW

James, Daniel (Lewis) 1911-1988
See Santiago, Danny
See also CA 125

James, Dynely
See Mayne, William (James Carter)

James, Henry
1843-1916 . . . . . **TCLC 2, 11, 24, 40, 47;**
DA; SSC 8; WLC
See also CA 104; 132; CDALB 1865-1917;
DLB 12, 71, 74; MTCW

James, M. R.
See James, Montague (Rhodes)

James, Montague (Rhodes)
1862-1936 . . . . **TCLC 6; SSC 16**
See also CA 104

James, P. D. . . . . **CLC 18, 46**
See also White, Phyllis Dorothy James
See also BEST 90:2; CDBLB 1960 to
Present; DLB 87

James, Philip
See Moorcock, Michael (John)

James, William 1842-1910 . . . . . **TCLC 15, 32**
See also CA 109

James I 1394-1437 . . . . **LC 20**

Jameson, Anna 1794-1860 . . . . **NCLC 43**
See also DLB 99

Jami, Nur al-Din 'Abd al-Rahman
1414-1492 . . . . **LC 9**

Jandl, Ernst 1925- . . . . **CLC 34**

Janowitz, Tama 1957- . . . . **CLC 43**
See also CA 106

Jarrell, Randall
1914-1965 . . . . . . **CLC 1, 2, 6, 9, 13, 49**
See also CA 5-8R; 25-28R; CABS 2;
CANR 6, 34; CDALB 1941-1968; CLR 6;
DLB 48, 52; MAICYA; MTCW; SATA 7

Jarry, Alfred 1873-1907 . . . . **TCLC 2, 14**
See also CA 104

Jarvis, E. K.
See Bloch, Robert (Albert); Ellison, Harlan;
Silverberg, Robert

Jeake, Samuel, Jr.
See Aiken, Conrad (Potter)

Jean Paul 1763-1825 . . . . **NCLC 7**

Jefferies, (John) Richard
1848-1887 . . . . **NCLC 47**
See also DLB 98, 141; SATA 16

Jeffers, (John) Robinson
1887-1962 . . . . **CLC 2, 3, 11, 15, 54; DA;**
WLC
See also CA 85-88; CANR 35;
CDALB 1917-1929; DLB 45; MTCW

Jefferson, Janet
See Mencken, H(enry) L(ouis)

Jefferson, Thomas 1743-1826 . . . . **NCLC 11**
See also CDALB 1640-1865; DLB 31

Jeffrey, Francis 1773-1850 . . . . . . **NCLC 33**
See also DLB 107

Jelakowitch, Ivan
See Heijermans, Herman

Jellicoe, (Patricia) Ann 1927- . . . . . . **CLC 27**
See also CA 85-88; DLB 13

Jen, Gish . . . . **CLC 70**
See also Jen, Lillian

Jen, Lillian 1956(?)-
See Jen, Gish
See also CA 135

Jenkins, (John) Robin 1912- . . . . **CLC 52**
See also CA 1-4R; CANR 1; DLB 14

Jennings, Elizabeth (Joan)
1926- . . . . **CLC 5, 14**
See also CA 61-64; CAAS 5; CANR 8, 39;
DLB 27; MTCW; SATA 66

Jennings, Waylon 1937- . . . . **CLC 21**

Jensen, Johannes V. 1873-1950 . . . . **TCLC 41**

Jensen, Laura (Linnea) 1948- . . . . . . **CLC 37**
See also CA 103

Jerome, Jerome K(lapka)
1859-1927 . . . . **TCLC 23**
See also CA 119; DLB 10, 34, 135

Jerrold, Douglas William
1803-1857 . . . . **NCLC 2**

Jewett, (Theodora) Sarah Orne
1849-1909 . . . . **TCLC 1, 22; SSC 6**
See also CA 108; 127; DLB 12, 74;
SATA 15

Jewsbury, Geraldine (Endsor)
1812-1880 . . . . **NCLC 22**
See also DLB 21

Jhabvala, Ruth Prawer
1927- . . . . **CLC 4, 8, 29**
See also CA 1-4R; CANR 2, 29; DLB 139;
MTCW

Jiles, Paulette 1943- . . . . **CLC 13, 58**
See also CA 101

Jimenez (Mantecon), Juan Ramon
1881-1958 . . . . **TCLC 4; HLC; PC 7**
See also CA 104; 131; DLB 134; HW;
MTCW

Jimenez, Ramon
See Jimenez (Mantecon), Juan Ramon

Jimenez Mantecon, Juan
See Jimenez (Mantecon), Juan Ramon

Joel, Billy . . . . **CLC 26**
See also Joel, William Martin

Joel, William Martin 1949-
See Joel, Billy
See also CA 108

John of the Cross, St. 1542-1591 . . . . **LC 18**

Johnson, B(ryan) S(tanley William)
1933-1973 . . . . **CLC 6, 9**
See also CA 9-12R; 53-56; CANR 9;
DLB 14, 40

Johnson, Benj. F. of Boo
See Riley, James Whitcomb

Johnson, Benjamin F. of Boo
See Riley, James Whitcomb

Johnson, Charles (Richard)
1948- . . . . CLC 7, 51, 65; BLC
See also BW 2; CA 116; CAAS 18;
CANR 42; DLB 33

Johnson, Denis 1949- . . . . CLC 52
See also CA 117; 121; DLB 120

Johnson, Diane 1934- . . . . CLC 5, 13, 48
See also CA 41-44R; CANR 17, 40;
DLBY 80; MTCW

Johnson, Eyvind (Olof Verner)
1900-1976 . . . . CLC 14
See also CA 73-76; 69-72; CANR 34

Johnson, J. R.
See James, C(yril) L(ionel) R(obert)

Johnson, James Weldon
1871-1938 . . . . TCLC 3, 19; BLC
See also BW 1; CA 104; 125;
CDALB 1917-1929; CLR 32; DLB 51;
MTCW; SATA 31

Johnson, Joyce 1935- . . . . CLC 58
See also CA 125; 129

Johnson, Lionel (Pigot)
1867-1902 . . . . TCLC 19
See also CA 117; DLB 19

Johnson, Mel
See Malzberg, Barry N(athaniel)

Johnson, Pamela Hansford
1912-1981 . . . . CLC 1, 7, 27
See also CA 1-4R; 104; CANR 2, 28;
DLB 15; MTCW

Johnson, Samuel
1709-1784 . . . . LC 15; DA; WLC
See also CDBLB 1660-1789; DLB 39, 95,
104, 142

Johnson, Uwe
1934-1984 . . . . CLC 5, 10, 15, 40
See also CA 1-4R; 112; CANR 1, 39;
DLB 75; MTCW

Johnston, George (Benson) 1913- . . . CLC 51
See also CA 1-4R; CANR 5, 20; DLB 88

Johnston, Jennifer 1930- . . . . CLC 7
See also CA 85-88; DLB 14

Jolley, (Monica) Elizabeth 1923- . . . CLC 46
See also CA 127; CAAS 13

Jones, Arthur Llewellyn 1863-1947
See Machen, Arthur
See also CA 104

Jones, D(ouglas) G(ordon) 1929- . . . . CLC 10
See also CA 29-32R; CANR 13; DLB 53

Jones, David (Michael)
1895-1974 . . . . CLC 2, 4, 7, 13, 42
See also CA 9-12R; 53-56; CANR 28;
CDBLB 1945-1960; DLB 20, 100; MTCW

Jones, David Robert 1947-
See Bowie, David
See also CA 103

Jones, Diana Wynne 1934- . . . . CLC 26
See also AAYA 12; CA 49-52; CANR 4,
26; CLR 23; JRDA; MAICYA; SAAS 7;
SATA 9, 70

Jones, Edward P. 1950- . . . . CLC 76
See also BW 2; CA 142

Jones, Gayl 1949- . . . . CLC 6, 9; BLC
See also BW 2; CA 77-80; CANR 27;
DLB 33; MTCW

Jones, James 1921-1977. . . . CLC 1, 3, 10, 39
See also AITN 1, 2; CA 1-4R; 69-72;
CANR 6; DLB 2, 143; MTCW

Jones, John J.
See Lovecraft, H(oward) P(hillips)

Jones, LeRoi . . . . CLC 1, 2, 3, 5, 10, 14
See also Baraka, Amiri

Jones, Louis B. . . . . CLC 65
See also CA 141

Jones, Madison (Percy, Jr.) 1925- . . . CLC 4
See also CA 13-16R; CAAS 11; CANR 7

Jones, Mervyn 1922- . . . . CLC 10, 52
See also CA 45-48; CAAS 5; CANR 1;
MTCW

Jones, Mick 1956(?)- . . . . CLC 30

Jones, Nettie (Pearl) 1941- . . . . CLC 34
See also BW 2; CA 137

Jones, Preston 1936-1979 . . . . CLC 10
See also CA 73-76; 89-92; DLB 7

Jones, Robert F(rancis) 1934- . . . . . . CLC 7
See also CA 49-52; CANR 2

Jones, Rod 1953- . . . . CLC 50
See also CA 128

Jones, Terence Graham Parry
1942- . . . . CLC 21
See also Jones, Terry; Monty Python
See also CA 112; 116; CANR 35; SATA 51

Jones, Terry
See Jones, Terence Graham Parry
See also SATA 67

Jones, Thom 1945(?)- . . . . CLC 81

Jong, Erica 1942- . . . . . . CLC 4, 6, 8, 18, 83
See also AITN 1; BEST 90:2; CA 73-76;
CANR 26; DLB 2, 5, 28; MTCW

Jonson, Ben(jamin)
1572(?)-1637 . . . . LC 6; DA; DC 4; WLC
See also CDBLB Before 1660; DLB 62, 121

Jordan, June 1936- . . . . CLC 5, 11, 23
See also AAYA 2; BW 2; CA 33-36R;
CANR 25; CLR 10; DLB 38; MAICYA;
MTCW; SATA 4

Jordan, Pat(rick M.) 1941- . . . . CLC 37
See also CA 33-36R

Jorgensen, Ivar
See Ellison, Harlan

Jorgenson, Ivar
See Silverberg, Robert

Josephus, Flavius c. 37-100 . . . . . . CMLC 13

Josipovici, Gabriel 1940- . . . . CLC 6, 43
See also CA 37-40R; CAAS 8; DLB 14

Joubert, Joseph 1754-1824 . . . . NCLC 9

Jouve, Pierre Jean 1887-1976 . . . . . . CLC 47
See also CA 65-68

Joyce, James (Augustine Aloysius)
1882-1941 . . . . . . TCLC 3, 8, 16, 35; DA;
SSC 3; WLC
See also CA 104; 126; CDBLB 1914-1945;
DLB 10, 19, 36; MTCW

Jozsef, Attila 1905-1937 . . . . TCLC 22
See also CA 116

Juana Ines de la Cruz 1651(?)-1695 . . . LC 5

Judd, Cyril
See Kornbluth, C(yril) M.; Pohl, Frederik

Julian of Norwich 1342(?)-1416(?) . . . . LC 6

Just, Ward (Swift) 1935- . . . . CLC 4, 27
See also CA 25-28R; CANR 32

Justice, Donald (Rodney) 1925- . . CLC 6, 19
See also CA 5-8R; CANR 26; DLBY 83

Juvenal c. 55-c. 127 . . . . CMLC 8

Juvenis
See Bourne, Randolph S(illiman)

Kacew, Romain 1914-1980
See Gary, Romain
See also CA 108; 102

Kadare, Ismail 1936- . . . . CLC 52

Kadohata, Cynthia . . . . CLC 59
See also CA 140

Kafka, Franz
1883-1924 . . . . TCLC 2, 6, 13, 29, 47, 53;
DA; SSC 5; WLC
See also CA 105; 126; DLB 81; MTCW

Kahanovitsch, Pinkhes
See Der Nister

Kahn, Roger 1927- . . . . CLC 30
See also CA 25-28R; CANR 44; SATA 37

Kain, Saul
See Sassoon, Siegfried (Lorraine)

Kaiser, Georg 1878-1945 . . . . TCLC 9
See also CA 106; DLB 124

Kaletski, Alexander 1946- . . . . CLC 39
See also CA 118; 143

Kalidasa fl. c. 400- . . . . CMLC 9

Kallman, Chester (Simon)
1921-1975 . . . . CLC 2
See also CA 45-48; 53-56; CANR 3

Kaminsky, Melvin 1926-
See Brooks, Mel
See also CA 65-68; CANR 16

Kaminsky, Stuart M(elvin) 1934- . . . CLC 59
See also CA 73-76; CANR 29

Kane, Paul
See Simon, Paul

Kane, Wilson
See Bloch, Robert (Albert)

Kanin, Garson 1912- . . . . CLC 22
See also AITN 1; CA 5-8R; CANR 7;
DLB 7

Kaniuk, Yoram 1930- . . . . CLC 19
See also CA 134

Kant, Immanuel 1724-1804 . . . . . . NCLC 27
See also DLB 94

Kantor, MacKinlay 1904-1977 . . . . . . CLC 7
See also CA 61-64; 73-76; DLB 9, 102

Kaplan, David Michael 1946- . . . . . . CLC 50

Kaplan, James 1951- . . . . CLC 59
See also CA 135

Karageorge, Michael
See Anderson, Poul (William)

Karamzin, Nikolai Mikhailovich
1766-1826 . . . . NCLC 3

Karapanou, Margarita 1946- . . . . CLC 13
See also CA 101

Karinthy, Frigyes 1887-1938 . . . . . . TCLC 47

Karl, Frederick R(obert) 1927- . . . . . CLC 34
See also CA 5-8R; CANR 3, 44

Kastel, Warren
  See Silverberg, Robert

Kataev, Evgeny Petrovich 1903-1942
  See Petrov, Evgeny
  See also CA 120

Kataphusin
  See Ruskin, John

Katz, Steve 1935- . . . . CLC **47**
  See also CA 25-28R; CAAS 14; CANR 12;
  DLBY 83

Kauffman, Janet 1945- . . . . CLC **42**
  See also CA 117; CANR 43; DLBY 86

Kaufman, Bob (Garnell)
  1925-1986 . . . . CLC **49**
  See also BW 1; CA 41-44R; 118; CANR 22;
  DLB 16, 41

Kaufman, George S. 1889-1961 . . . . . CLC **38**
  See also CA 108; 93-96; DLB 7

Kaufman, Sue . . . . CLC **3, 8**
  See also Barondess, Sue K(aufman)

Kavafis, Konstantinos Petrou 1863-1933
  See Cavafy, C(onstantine) P(eter)
  See also CA 104

Kavan, Anna 1901-1968 . . . . . . CLC **5, 13, 82**
  See also CA 5-8R; CANR 6; MTCW

Kavanagh, Dan
  See Barnes, Julian

Kavanagh, Patrick (Joseph)
  1904-1967 . . . . CLC **22**
  See also CA 123; 25-28R; DLB 15, 20;
  MTCW

Kawabata, Yasunari
  1899-1972 . . . . . CLC **2, 5, 9, 18;** SSC **17**
  See also CA 93-96; 33-36R

Kaye, M(ary) M(argaret) 1909- . . . . . CLC **28**
  See also CA 89-92; CANR 24; MTCW;
  SATA 62

Kaye, Mollie
  See Kaye, M(ary) M(argaret)

Kaye-Smith, Sheila 1887-1956 . . . . . TCLC **20**
  See also CA 118; DLB 36

Kaymor, Patrice Maguilene
  See Senghor, Leopold Sedar

Kazan, Elia 1909- . . . . CLC **6, 16, 63**
  See also CA 21-24R; CANR 32

Kazantzakis, Nikos
  1883(?)-1957 . . . . TCLC **2, 5, 33**
  See also CA 105; 132; MTCW

Kazin, Alfred 1915- . . . . CLC **34, 38**
  See also CA 1-4R; CAAS 7; CANR 1, 45;
  DLB 67

Keane, Mary Nesta (Skrine) 1904-
  See Keane, Molly
  See also CA 108; 114

Keane, Molly . . . . CLC **31**
  See also Keane, Mary Nesta (Skrine)

Keates, Jonathan 19(?)- . . . . CLC **34**

Keaton, Buster 1895-1966 . . . . CLC **20**

Keats, John
  1795-1821 . . . NCLC **8;** DA; PC **1;** WLC
  See also CDBLB 1789-1832; DLB 96, 110

Keene, Donald 1922- . . . . CLC **34**
  See also CA 1-4R; CANR 5

Keillor, Garrison . . . . CLC **40**
  See also Keillor, Gary (Edward)
  See also AAYA 2; BEST 89:3; DLBY 87;
  SATA 58

Keillor, Gary (Edward) 1942-
  See Keillor, Garrison
  See also CA 111; 117; CANR 36; MTCW

Keith, Michael
  See Hubbard, L(afayette) Ron(ald)

Keller, Gottfried 1819-1890 . . . . . . NCLC **2**
  See also DLB 129

Kellerman, Jonathan 1949- . . . . CLC **44**
  See also BEST 90:1; CA 106; CANR 29

Kelley, William Melvin 1937- . . . . . . CLC **22**
  See also BW 1; CA 77-80; CANR 27;
  DLB 33

Kellogg, Marjorie 1922- . . . . CLC **2**
  See also CA 81-84

Kellow, Kathleen
  See Hibbert, Eleanor Alice Burford

Kelly, M(ilton) T(erry) 1947- . . . . CLC **55**
  See also CA 97-100; CANR 19, 43

Kelman, James 1946- . . . . CLC **58**

Kemal, Yashar 1923- . . . . CLC **14, 29**
  See also CA 89-92; CANR 44

Kemble, Fanny 1809-1893 . . . . NCLC **18**
  See also DLB 32

Kemelman, Harry 1908- . . . . CLC **2**
  See also AITN 1; CA 9-12R; CANR 6;
  DLB 28

Kempe, Margery 1373(?)-1440(?) . . . . . LC **6**

Kempis, Thomas a 1380-1471 . . . . LC **11**

Kendall, Henry 1839-1882 . . . . NCLC **12**

Keneally, Thomas (Michael)
  1935- . . . . . . CLC **5, 8, 10, 14, 19, 27, 43**
  See also CA 85-88; CANR 10; MTCW

Kennedy, Adrienne (Lita)
  1931- . . . . CLC **66;** BLC
  See also BW 2; CA 103; CABS 3;
  CANR 26; DLB 38

Kennedy, John Pendleton
  1795-1870 . . . . NCLC **2**
  See also DLB 3

Kennedy, Joseph Charles 1929-
  See Kennedy, X. J.
  See also CA 1-4R; CANR 4, 30, 40;
  SATA 14

Kennedy, William 1928- . . . CLC **6, 28, 34, 53**
  See also AAYA 1; CA 85-88; CANR 14,
  31; DLB 143; DLBY 85; MTCW;
  SATA 57

Kennedy, X. J. . . . . CLC **8, 42**
  See also Kennedy, Joseph Charles
  See also CAAS 9; CLR 27; DLB 5

Kent, Kelvin
  See Kuttner, Henry

Kenton, Maxwell
  See Southern, Terry

Kenyon, Robert O.
  See Kuttner, Henry

Kerouac, Jack . . . . . CLC **1, 2, 3, 5, 14, 29, 61**
  See also Kerouac, Jean-Louis Lebris de
  See also CDALB 1941-1968; DLB 2, 16;
  DLBD 3

Kerouac, Jean-Louis Lebris de 1922-1969
  See Kerouac, Jack
  See also AITN 1; CA 5-8R; 25-28R;
  CANR 26; DA; MTCW; WLC

Kerr, Jean 1923- . . . . CLC **22**
  See also CA 5-8R; CANR 7

Kerr, M. E. . . . . CLC **12, 35**
  See also Meaker, Marijane (Agnes)
  See also AAYA 2; CLR 29; SAAS 1

Kerr, Robert . . . . CLC **55**

Kerrigan, (Thomas) Anthony
  1918- . . . . CLC **4, 6**
  See also CA 49-52; CAAS 11; CANR 4

Kerry, Lois
  See Duncan, Lois

Kesey, Ken (Elton)
  1935- . . . . . . CLC **1, 3, 6, 11, 46, 64;** DA;
  WLC
  See also CA 1-4R; CANR 22, 38;
  CDALB 1968-1988; DLB 2, 16; MTCW;
  SATA 66

Kesselring, Joseph (Otto)
  1902-1967 . . . . CLC **45**

Kessler, Jascha (Frederick) 1929- . . . . CLC **4**
  See also CA 17-20R; CANR 8

Kettelkamp, Larry (Dale) 1933- . . . . CLC **12**
  See also CA 29-32R; CANR 16; SAAS 3;
  SATA 2

Keyber, Conny
  See Fielding, Henry

Keyes, Daniel 1927- . . . . CLC **80;** DA
  See also CA 17-20R; CANR 10, 26;
  SATA 37

Khanshendel, Chiron
  See Rose, Wendy

Khayyam, Omar
  1048-1131 . . . . CMLC **11;** PC **8**

Kherdian, David 1931- . . . . CLC **6, 9**
  See also CA 21-24R; CAAS 2; CANR 39;
  CLR 24; JRDA; MAICYA; SATA 16, 74

Khlebnikov, Velimir . . . . TCLC **20**
  See also Khlebnikov, Viktor Vladimirovich

Khlebnikov, Viktor Vladimirovich 1885-1922
  See Khlebnikov, Velimir
  See also CA 117

Khodasevich, Vladislav (Felitsianovich)
  1886-1939 . . . . TCLC **15**
  See also CA 115

Kielland, Alexander Lange
  1849-1906 . . . . TCLC **5**
  See also CA 104

Kiely, Benedict 1919- . . . . CLC **23, 43**
  See also CA 1-4R; CANR 2; DLB 15

Kienzle, William X(avier) 1928- . . . . CLC **25**
  See also CA 93-96; CAAS 1; CANR 9, 31;
  MTCW

Kierkegaard, Soren 1813-1855 . . . . NCLC **34**

Killens, John Oliver 1916-1987 . . . . . CLC **10**
  See also BW 2; CA 77-80; 123; CAAS 2;
  CANR 26; DLB 33

Killigrew, Anne 1660-1685 . . . . LC **4**
  See also DLB 131

Kim
  See Simenon, Georges (Jacques Christian)

Kincaid, Jamaica 1949- ... **CLC 43, 68; BLC**
See also BW 2; CA 125

King, Francis (Henry) 1923- ..... **CLC 8, 53**
See also CA 1-4R; CANR 1, 33; DLB 15,
139; MTCW

King, Martin Luther, Jr.
1929-1968 .... **CLC 83; BLC; DA**
See also BW 2; CA 25-28; CANR 27, 44;
CAP 2; MTCW; SATA 14

King, Stephen (Edwin)
1947- ..... **CLC 12, 26, 37, 61; SSC 17**
See also AAYA 1; BEST 90:1; CA 61-64;
CANR 1, 30; DLB 143; DLBY 80;
JRDA; MTCW; SATA 9, 55

King, Steve
See King, Stephen (Edwin)

Kingman, Lee .... **CLC 17**
See also Natti, (Mary) Lee
See also SAAS 3; SATA 1, 67

Kingsley, Charles 1819-1875 ..... **NCLC 35**
See also DLB 21, 32; YABC 2

Kingsley, Sidney 1906- .... **CLC 44**
See also CA 85-88; DLB 7

Kingsolver, Barbara 1955- ...... **CLC 55, 81**
See also CA 129; 134

Kingston, Maxine (Ting Ting) Hong
1940- .... **CLC 12, 19, 58**
See also AAYA 8; CA 69-72; CANR 13,
38; DLBY 80; MTCW; SATA 53

Kinnell, Galway
1927- .... **CLC 1, 2, 3, 5, 13, 29**
See also CA 9-12R; CANR 10, 34; DLB 5;
DLBY 87; MTCW

Kinsella, Thomas 1928- .... **CLC 4, 19**
See also CA 17-20R; CANR 15; DLB 27;
MTCW

Kinsella, W(illiam) P(atrick)
1935- .... **CLC 27, 43**
See also AAYA 7; CA 97-100; CAAS 7;
CANR 21, 35; MTCW

Kipling, (Joseph) Rudyard
1865-1936 ...... **TCLC 8, 17; DA; PC 3;**
SSC 5; WLC
See also CA 105; 120; CANR 33;
CDBLB 1890-1914; DLB 19, 34, 141;
MAICYA; MTCW; YABC 2

Kirkup, James 1918- .... **CLC 1**
See also CA 1-4R; CAAS 4; CANR 2;
DLB 27; SATA 12

Kirkwood, James 1930(?)-1989 ...... **CLC 9**
See also AITN 2; CA 1-4R; 128; CANR 6,
40

Kis, Danilo 1935-1989 .... **CLC 57**
See also CA 109; 118; 129; MTCW

Kivi, Aleksis 1834-1872 .... **NCLC 30**

Kizer, Carolyn (Ashley)
1925- .... **CLC 15, 39, 80**
See also CA 65-68; CAAS 5; CANR 24;
DLB 5

Klabund 1890-1928 .... **TCLC 44**
See also DLB 66

Klappert, Peter 1942- .... **CLC 57**
See also CA 33-36R; DLB 5

Klein, A(braham) M(oses)
1909-1972 .... **CLC 19**
See also CA 101; 37-40R; DLB 68

Klein, Norma 1938-1989 .... **CLC 30**
See also AAYA 2; CA 41-44R; 128;
CANR 15, 37; CLR 2, 19; JRDA;
MAICYA; SAAS 1; SATA 7, 57

Klein, T(heodore) E(ibon) D(onald)
1947- .... **CLC 34**
See also CA 119; CANR 44

Kleist, Heinrich von
1777-1811 .... **NCLC 2, 37**
See also DLB 90

Klima, Ivan 1931- .... **CLC 56**
See also CA 25-28R; CANR 17

Klimentov, Andrei Platonovich 1899-1951
See Platonov, Andrei
See also CA 108

Klinger, Friedrich Maximilian von
1752-1831 .... **NCLC 1**
See also DLB 94

Klopstock, Friedrich Gottlieb
1724-1803 .... **NCLC 11**
See also DLB 97

Knebel, Fletcher 1911-1993 .... **CLC 14**
See also AITN 1; CA 1-4R; 140; CAAS 3;
CANR 1, 36; SATA 36; SATA-Obit 75

Knickerbocker, Diedrich
See Irving, Washington

Knight, Etheridge
1931-1991 .... **CLC 40; BLC**
See also BW 1; CA 21-24R; 133; CANR 23;
DLB 41

Knight, Sarah Kemble 1666-1727 ..... **LC 7**
See also DLB 24

Knister, Raymond 1899-1932 ...... **TCLC 56**
See also DLB 68

Knowles, John
1926- .... **CLC 1, 4, 10, 26; DA**
See also AAYA 10; CA 17-20R; CANR 40;
CDALB 1968-1988; DLB 6; MTCW;
SATA 8

Knox, Calvin M.
See Silverberg, Robert

Knye, Cassandra
See Disch, Thomas M(ichael)

Koch, C(hristopher) J(ohn) 1932- ... **CLC 42**
See also CA 127

Koch, Christopher
See Koch, C(hristopher) J(ohn)

Koch, Kenneth 1925- .... **CLC 5, 8, 44**
See also CA 1-4R; CANR 6, 36; DLB 5;
SATA 65

Kochanowski, Jan 1530-1584 .... **LC 10**

Kock, Charles Paul de
1794-1871 .... **NCLC 16**

Koda Shigeyuki 1867-1947
See Rohan, Koda
See also CA 121

Koestler, Arthur
1905-1983 ...... **CLC 1, 3, 6, 8, 15, 33**
See also CA 1-4R; 109; CANR 1, 33;
CDBLB 1945-1960; DLBY 83; MTCW

Kogawa, Joy Nozomi 1935- .... **CLC 78**
See also CA 101; CANR 19

Kohout, Pavel 1928- .... **CLC 13**
See also CA 45-48; CANR 3

Koizumi, Yakumo
See Hearn, (Patricio) Lafcadio (Tessima
Carlos)

Kolmar, Gertrud 1894-1943 .... **TCLC 40**

Konrad, George
See Konrad, Gyoergy

Konrad, Gyoergy 1933- ...... **CLC 4, 10, 73**
See also CA 85-88

Konwicki, Tadeusz 1926- ..... **CLC 8, 28, 54**
See also CA 101; CAAS 9; CANR 39;
MTCW

Koontz, Dean R(ay) 1945- .... **CLC 78**
See also AAYA 9; BEST 89:3, 90:2;
CA 108; CANR 19, 36; MTCW

Kopit, Arthur (Lee) 1937- .... **CLC 1, 18, 33**
See also AITN 1; CA 81-84; CABS 3;
DLB 7; MTCW

Kops, Bernard 1926- .... **CLC 4**
See also CA 5-8R; DLB 13

Kornbluth, C(yril) M. 1923-1958 .... **TCLC 8**
See also CA 105; DLB 8

Korolenko, V. G.
See Korolenko, Vladimir Galaktionovich

Korolenko, Vladimir
See Korolenko, Vladimir Galaktionovich

Korolenko, Vladimir G.
See Korolenko, Vladimir Galaktionovich

Korolenko, Vladimir Galaktionovich
1853-1921 .... **TCLC 22**
See also CA 121

Kosinski, Jerzy (Nikodem)
1933-1991 .... **CLC 1, 2, 3, 6, 10, 15, 53,**
70
See also CA 17-20R; 134; CANR 9; DLB 2;
DLBY 82; MTCW

Kostelanetz, Richard (Cory) 1940- .. **CLC 28**
See also CA 13-16R; CAAS 8; CANR 38

Kostrowitzki, Wilhelm Apollinaris de
1880-1918
See Apollinaire, Guillaume
See also CA 104

Kotlowitz, Robert 1924- .... **CLC 4**
See also CA 33-36R; CANR 36

Kotzebue, August (Friedrich Ferdinand) von
1761-1819 .... **NCLC 25**
See also DLB 94

Kotzwinkle, William 1938- ... **CLC 5, 14, 35**
See also CA 45-48; CANR 3, 44; CLR 6;
MAICYA; SATA 24, 70

Kozol, Jonathan 1936- .... **CLC 17**
See also CA 61-64; CANR 16, 45

Kozoll, Michael 1940(?)- .... **CLC 35**

Kramer, Kathryn 19(?)- .... **CLC 34**

Kramer, Larry 1935- .... **CLC 42**
See also CA 124; 126

Krasicki, Ignacy 1735-1801 .... **NCLC 8**

Krasinski, Zygmunt 1812-1859 .... **NCLC 4**

Kraus, Karl 1874-1936 .... **TCLC 5**
See also CA 104; DLB 118

Kreve (Mickevicius), Vincas
1882-1954 .... **TCLC 27**

Laredo, Betty
See Codrescu, Andrei

Larkin, Maia
See Wojciechowska, Maia (Teresa)

Larkin, Philip (Arthur)
1922-1985 .... **CLC 3, 5, 8, 9, 13, 18, 33,**
39, 64
See also CA 5-8R; 117; CANR 24;
CDBLB 1960 to Present; DLB 27;
MTCW

Larra (y Sanchez de Castro), Mariano Jose de
1809-1837 .... **NCLC 17**

Larsen, Eric 1941- .... **CLC 55**
See also CA 132

Larsen, Nella 1891-1964 ..... **CLC 37; BLC**
See also BW 1; CA 125; DLB 51

Larson, Charles R(aymond) 1938-... **CLC 31**
See also CA 53-56; CANR 4

Lasker-Schueler, Else 1869-1945 .. **TCLC 57**
See also DLB 66, 124

Latham, Jean Lee 1902-........... **CLC 12**
See also AITN 1; CA 5-8R; CANR 7;
MAICYA; SATA 2, 68

Latham, Mavis
See Clark, Mavis Thorpe

Lathen, Emma.................... **CLC 2**
See also Hennissart, Martha; Latsis, Mary
J(ane)

Lathrop, Francis
See Leiber, Fritz (Reuter, Jr.)

Latsis, Mary J(ane)
See Lathen, Emma
See also CA 85-88

Lattimore, Richmond (Alexander)
1906-1984 .... **CLC 3**
See also CA 1-4R; 112; CANR 1

Laughlin, James 1914-........... **CLC 49**
See also CA 21-24R; CANR 9; DLB 48

Laurence, (Jean) Margaret (Wemyss)
1926-1987 .. **CLC 3, 6, 13, 50, 62; SSC 7**
See also CA 5-8R; 121; CANR 33; DLB 53;
MTCW; SATA 50

Laurent, Antoine 1952- .... **CLC 50**

Lauscher, Hermann
See Hesse, Hermann

Lautreamont, Comte de
1846-1870 .... **NCLC 12; SSC 14**

Laverty, Donald
See Blish, James (Benjamin)

Lavin, Mary 1912- ...... **CLC 4, 18; SSC 4**
See also CA 9-12R; CANR 33; DLB 15;
MTCW

Lavond, Paul Dennis
See Kornbluth, C(yril) M.; Pohl, Frederik

Lawler, Raymond Evenor 1922- .... **CLC 58**
See also CA 103

Lawrence, D(avid) H(erbert Richards)
1885-1930 ...... **TCLC 2, 9, 16, 33, 48;**
DA; SSC 4; WLC
See also CA 104; 121; CDBLB 1914-1945;
DLB 10, 19, 36, 98; MTCW

Lawrence, T(homas) E(dward)
1888-1935 .... **TCLC 18**
See also Dale, Colin
See also CA 115

Lawrence of Arabia
See Lawrence, T(homas) E(dward)

Lawson, Henry (Archibald Hertzberg)
1867-1922 .... **TCLC 27**
See also CA 120

Lawton, Dennis
See Faust, Frederick (Schiller)

Laxness, Halldor.................. **CLC 25**
See also Gudjonsson, Halldor Kiljan

Layamon fl. c. 1200-........... **CMLC 10**

Laye, Camara 1928-1980 ... **CLC 4, 38; BLC**
See also BW 1; CA 85-88; 97-100;
CANR 25; MTCW

Layton, Irving (Peter) 1912-..... **CLC 2, 15**
See also CA 1-4R; CANR 2, 33, 43;
DLB 88; MTCW

Lazarus, Emma 1849-1887........ **NCLC 8**

Lazarus, Felix
See Cable, George Washington

Lazarus, Henry
See Slavitt, David R(ytman)

Lea, Joan
See Neufeld, John (Arthur)

Leacock, Stephen (Butler)
1869-1944 .... **TCLC 2**
See also CA 104; 141; DLB 92

Lear, Edward 1812-1888 .... **NCLC 3**
See also CLR 1; DLB 32; MAICYA;
SATA 18

Lear, Norman (Milton) 1922- ...... **CLC 12**
See also CA 73-76

Leavis, F(rank) R(aymond)
1895-1978 .... **CLC 24**
See also CA 21-24R; 77-80; CANR 44;
MTCW

Leavitt, David 1961-............. **CLC 34**
See also CA 116; 122; DLB 130

Leblanc, Maurice (Marie Emile)
1864-1941 .... **TCLC 49**
See also CA 110

Lebowitz, Fran(ces Ann)
1951(?)-.................. **CLC 11, 36**
See also CA 81-84; CANR 14; MTCW

Lebrecht, Peter
See Tieck, (Johann) Ludwig

le Carre, John .... **CLC 3, 5, 9, 15, 28**
See also Cornwell, David (John Moore)
See also BEST 89:4; CDBLB 1960 to
Present; DLB 87

Le Clezio, J(ean) M(arie) G(ustave)
1940-................... **CLC 31**
See also CA 116; 128; DLB 83

Leconte de Lisle, Charles-Marie-Rene
1818-1894 .... **NCLC 29**

Le Coq, Monsieur
See Simenon, Georges (Jacques Christian)

Leduc, Violette 1907-1972........ **CLC 22**
See also CA 13-14; 33-36R; CAP 1

Ledwidge, Francis 1887(?)-1917 ... **TCLC 23**
See also CA 123; DLB 20

Lee, Andrea 1953- .... **CLC 36; BLC**
See also BW 1; CA 125

Lee, Andrew
See Auchincloss, Louis (Stanton)

Lee, Don L....................... **CLC 2**
See also Madhubuti, Haki R.

Lee, George W(ashington)
1894-1976 .... **CLC 52; BLC**
See also BW 1; CA 125; DLB 51

Lee, (Nelle) Harper
1926- .... **CLC 12, 60; DA; WLC**
See also CA 13-16R; CDALB 1941-1968;
DLB 6; MTCW; SATA 11

Lee, Julian
See Latham, Jean Lee

Lee, Larry
See Lee, Lawrence

Lee, Lawrence 1941-1990......... **CLC 34**
See also CA 131; CANR 43

Lee, Manfred B(ennington)
1905-1971 .... **CLC 11**
See also Queen, Ellery
See also CA 1-4R; 29-32R; CANR 2;
DLB 137

Lee, Stan 1922-................. **CLC 17**
See also AAYA 5; CA 108; 111

Lee, Tanith 1947-................ **CLC 46**
See also CA 37-40R; SATA 8

Lee, Vernon...................... **TCLC 5**
See also Paget, Violet
See also DLB 57

Lee, William
See Burroughs, William S(eward)

Lee, Willy
See Burroughs, William S(eward)

Lee-Hamilton, Eugene (Jacob)
1845-1907 .... **TCLC 22**
See also CA 117

Leet, Judith 1935- .... **CLC 11**

Le Fanu, Joseph Sheridan
1814-1873 .... **NCLC 9; SSC 14**
See also DLB 21, 70

Leffland, Ella 1931-............. **CLC 19**
See also CA 29-32R; CANR 35; DLBY 84;
SATA 65

Leger, Alexis
See Leger, (Marie-Rene Auguste) Alexis
Saint-Leger

Leger, (Marie-Rene Auguste) Alexis
Saint-Leger 1887-1975....... **CLC 11**
See also Perse, St.-John
See also CA 13-16R; 61-64; CANR 43;
MTCW

Leger, Saintleger
See Leger, (Marie-Rene Auguste) Alexis
Saint-Leger

Le Guin, Ursula K(roeber)
1929- .... **CLC 8, 13, 22, 45, 71; SSC 12**
See also AAYA 9; AITN 1; CA 21-24R;
CANR 9, 32; CDALB 1968-1988; CLR 3,
28; DLB 8, 52; JRDA; MAICYA;
MTCW; SATA 4, 52

Lehmann, Rosamond (Nina)
1901-1990 .... **CLC 5**
See also CA 77-80; 131; CANR 8; DLB 15

Leiber, Fritz (Reuter, Jr.)
1910-1992 . . . . **CLC 25**
See also CA 45-48; 139; CANR 2, 40;
DLB 8; MTCW; SATA 45;
SATA-Obit 73

Leimbach, Martha   1963-
See Leimbach, Marti
See also CA 130

Leimbach, Marti . . . . **CLC 65**
See also Leimbach, Martha

Leino, Eino . . . . **TCLC 24**
See also Loennbohm, Armas Eino Leopold

Leiris, Michel (Julien)   1901-1990 . . . **CLC 61**
See also CA 119; 128; 132

Leithauser, Brad   1953- . . . . **CLC 27**
See also CA 107; CANR 27; DLB 120

Lelchuk, Alan   1938- . . . . **CLC 5**
See also CA 45-48; CANR 1

Lem, Stanislaw   1921- . . . . **CLC 8, 15, 40**
See also CA 105; CAAS 1; CANR 32;
MTCW

Lemann, Nancy   1956- . . . . **CLC 39**
See also CA 118; 136

Lemonnier, (Antoine Louis) Camille
1844-1913 . . . . **TCLC 22**
See also CA 121

Lenau, Nikolaus   1802-1850 . . . . . . **NCLC 16**

L'Engle, Madeleine (Camp Franklin)
1918- . . . . **CLC 12**
See also AAYA 1; AITN 2; CA 1-4R;
CANR 3, 21, 39; CLR 1, 14; DLB 52;
JRDA; MAICYA; MTCW; SAAS 15;
SATA 1, 27, 75

Lengyel, Jozsef   1896-1975 . . . . **CLC 7**
See also CA 85-88; 57-60

Lennon, John (Ono)
1940-1980 . . . . **CLC 12, 35**
See also CA 102

Lennox, Charlotte Ramsay
1729(?)-1804 . . . . **NCLC 23**
See also DLB 39

Lentricchia, Frank (Jr.)   1940- . . . . . . **CLC 34**
See also CA 25-28R; CANR 19

Lenz, Siegfried   1926- . . . . **CLC 27**
See also CA 89-92; DLB 75

Leonard, Elmore (John, Jr.)
1925- . . . . **CLC 28, 34, 71**
See also AITN 1; BEST 89:1, 90:4;
CA 81-84; CANR 12, 28; MTCW

Leonard, Hugh . . . . **CLC 19**
See also Byrne, John Keyes
See also DLB 13

Leopardi, (Conte) Giacomo (Talegardo
Francesco di Sales Save
1798-1837 . . . . **NCLC 22**

Le Reveler
See Artaud, Antonin

Lerman, Eleanor   1952- . . . . **CLC 9**
See also CA 85-88

Lerman, Rhoda   1936- . . . . **CLC 56**
See also CA 49-52

Lermontov, Mikhail Yuryevich
1814-1841 . . . . **NCLC 47**

Leroux, Gaston   1868-1927 . . . . **TCLC 25**
See also CA 108; 136; SATA 65

Lesage, Alain-Rene   1668-1747 . . . . **LC 2**

Leskov, Nikolai (Semyonovich)
1831-1895 . . . . **NCLC 25**

Lessing, Doris (May)
1919- . . . . . **CLC 1, 2, 3, 6, 10, 15, 22, 40;
DA; SSC 6**
See also CA 9-12R; CAAS 14; CANR 33;
CDBLB 1960 to Present; DLB 15, 139;
DLBY 85; MTCW

Lessing, Gotthold Ephraim
1729-1781 . . . . **LC 8**
See also DLB 97

Lester, Richard   1932- . . . . **CLC 20**

Lever, Charles (James)
1806-1872 . . . . **NCLC 23**
See also DLB 21

Leverson, Ada   1865(?)-1936(?) . . . . **TCLC 18**
See also Elaine
See also CA 117

Levertov, Denise
1923- . . . . . . **CLC 1, 2, 3, 5, 8, 15, 28, 66**
See also CA 1-4R; CAAS 19; CANR 3, 29;
DLB 5; MTCW

Levi, Jonathan . . . . **CLC 76**

Levi, Peter (Chad Tigar)   1931- . . . . . **CLC 41**
See also CA 5-8R; CANR 34; DLB 40

Levi, Primo
1919-1987 . . . . **CLC 37, 50; SSC 12**
See also CA 13-16R; 122; CANR 12, 33;
MTCW

Levin, Ira   1929- . . . . **CLC 3, 6**
See also CA 21-24R; CANR 17, 44;
MTCW; SATA 66

Levin, Meyer   1905-1981 . . . . **CLC 7**
See also AITN 1; CA 9-12R; 104;
CANR 15; DLB 9, 28; DLBY 81;
SATA 21, 27

Levine, Norman   1924- . . . . **CLC 54**
See also CA 73-76; CANR 14; DLB 88

Levine, Philip   1928- . . **CLC 2, 4, 5, 9, 14, 33**
See also CA 9-12R; CANR 9, 37; DLB 5

Levinson, Deirdre   1931- . . . . **CLC 49**
See also CA 73-76

Levi-Strauss, Claude   1908- . . . . **CLC 38**
See also CA 1-4R; CANR 6, 32; MTCW

Levitin, Sonia (Wolff)   1934- . . . . **CLC 17**
See also CA 29-32R; CANR 14, 32; JRDA;
MAICYA; SAAS 2; SATA 4, 68

Levon, O. U.
See Kesey, Ken (Elton)

Lewes, George Henry
1817-1878 . . . . **NCLC 25**
See also DLB 55, 144

Lewis, Alun   1915-1944 . . . . **TCLC 3**
See also CA 104; DLB 20

Lewis, C. Day
See Day Lewis, C(ecil)

Lewis, C(live) S(taples)
1898-1963 . . . . . **CLC 1, 3, 6, 14, 27; DA;
WLC**
See also AAYA 3; CA 81-84; CANR 33;
CDBLB 1945-1960; CLR 3, 27; DLB 15,
100; JRDA; MAICYA; MTCW;
SATA 13

Lewis, Janet   1899- . . . . **CLC 41**
See also Winters, Janet Lewis
See also CA 9-12R; CANR 29; CAP 1;
DLBY 87

Lewis, Matthew Gregory
1775-1818 . . . . **NCLC 11**
See also DLB 39

Lewis, (Harry) Sinclair
1885-1951 . . . . . **TCLC 4, 13, 23, 39; DA;
WLC**
See also CA 104; 133; CDALB 1917-1929;
DLB 9, 102; DLBD 1; MTCW

Lewis, (Percy) Wyndham
1884(?)-1957 . . . . **TCLC 2, 9**
See also CA 104; DLB 15

Lewisohn, Ludwig   1883-1955 . . . . . . **TCLC 19**
See also CA 107; DLB 4, 9, 28, 102

Lezama Lima, Jose   1910-1976 . . . **CLC 4, 10**
See also CA 77-80; DLB 113; HW

L'Heureux, John (Clarke)   1934- . . . . **CLC 52**
See also CA 13-16R; CANR 23, 45

Liddell, C. H.
See Kuttner, Henry

Lie, Jonas (Lauritz Idemil)
1833-1908(?) . . . . **TCLC 5**
See also CA 115

Lieber, Joel   1937-1971 . . . . **CLC 6**
See also CA 73-76; 29-32R

Lieber, Stanley Martin
See Lee, Stan

Lieberman, Laurence (James)
1935- . . . . **CLC 4, 36**
See also CA 17-20R; CANR 8, 36

Lieksman, Anders
See Haavikko, Paavo Juhani

Li Fei-kan   1904-
See Pa Chin
See also CA 105

Lifton, Robert Jay   1926- . . . . **CLC 67**
See also CA 17-20R; CANR 27; SATA 66

Lightfoot, Gordon   1938- . . . . **CLC 26**
See also CA 109

Lightman, Alan P.   1948- . . . . **CLC 81**
See also CA 141

Ligotti, Thomas   1953- . . . . **CLC 44; SSC 16**
See also CA 123

Liliencron, (Friedrich Adolf Axel) Detlev von
1844-1909 . . . . **TCLC 18**
See also CA 117

Lilly, William   1602-1681 . . . . **LC 27**

Lima, Jose Lezama
See Lezama Lima, Jose

Lima Barreto, Afonso Henrique de
1881-1922 . . . . **TCLC 23**
See also CA 117

Limonov, Eduard . . . . **CLC 67**

Lucas, Craig 1951- . . . . **CLC 64**
  See also CA 137

Lucas, George 1944- . . . . **CLC 16**
  See also AAYA 1; CA 77-80; CANR 30;
  SATA 56

Lucas, Hans
  See Godard, Jean-Luc

Lucas, Victoria
  See Plath, Sylvia

Ludlam, Charles 1943-1987 . . . . . **CLC 46, 50**
  See also CA 85-88; 122

Ludlum, Robert 1927- . . . . **CLC 22, 43**
  See also AAYA 10; BEST 89:1, 90:3;
  CA 33-36R; CANR 25, 41; DLBY 82;
  MTCW

Ludwig, Ken . . . . **CLC 60**

Ludwig, Otto 1813-1865 . . . . **NCLC 4**
  See also DLB 129

Lugones, Leopoldo 1874-1938 . . . . . **TCLC 15**
  See also CA 116; 131; HW

Lu Hsun 1881-1936 . . . . **TCLC 3**

Lukacs, George . . . . **CLC 24**
  See also Lukacs, Gyorgy (Szegeny von)

Lukacs, Gyorgy (Szegeny von) 1885-1971
  See Lukacs, George
  See also CA 101; 29-32R

Luke, Peter (Ambrose Cyprian)
  1919- . . . . **CLC 38**
  See also CA 81-84; DLB 13

Lunar, Dennis
  See Mungo, Raymond

Lurie, Alison 1926- . . . . **CLC 4, 5, 18, 39**
  See also CA 1-4R; CANR 2, 17; DLB 2;
  MTCW; SATA 46

Lustig, Arnost 1926- . . . . **CLC 56**
  See also AAYA 3; CA 69-72; SATA 56

Luther, Martin 1483-1546 . . . . **LC 9**

Luzi, Mario 1914- . . . . **CLC 13**
  See also CA 61-64; CANR 9; DLB 128

Lynch, B. Suarez
  See Bioy Casares, Adolfo; Borges, Jorge
  Luis

Lynch, David (K.) 1946- . . . . **CLC 66**
  See also CA 124; 129

Lynch, James
  See Andreyev, Leonid (Nikolaevich)

Lynch Davis, B.
  See Bioy Casares, Adolfo; Borges, Jorge
  Luis

Lyndsay, Sir David 1490-1555 . . . . . . **LC 20**

Lynn, Kenneth S(chuyler) 1923- . . . . **CLC 50**
  See also CA 1-4R; CANR 3, 27

Lynx
  See West, Rebecca

Lyons, Marcus
  See Blish, James (Benjamin)

Lyre, Pinchbeck
  See Sassoon, Siegfried (Lorraine)

Lytle, Andrew (Nelson) 1902- . . . . . **CLC 22**
  See also CA 9-12R; DLB 6

Lyttelton, George 1709-1773 . . . . **LC 10**

Maas, Peter 1929- . . . . **CLC 29**
  See also CA 93-96

Macaulay, Rose 1881-1958 . . . . . **TCLC 7, 44**
  See also CA 104; DLB 36

Macaulay, Thomas Babington
  1800-1859 . . . . **NCLC 42**
  See also CDBLB 1832-1890; DLB 32, 55

MacBeth, George (Mann)
  1932-1992 . . . . **CLC 2, 5, 9**
  See also CA 25-28R; 136; DLB 40; MTCW;
  SATA 4; SATA-Obit 70

MacCaig, Norman (Alexander)
  1910- . . . . **CLC 36**
  See also CA 9-12R; CANR 3, 34; DLB 27

MacCarthy, (Sir Charles Otto) Desmond
  1877-1952 . . . . **TCLC 36**

MacDiarmid, Hugh
  . . . . **CLC 2, 4, 11, 19, 63; PC 9**
  See also Grieve, C(hristopher) M(urray)
  See also CDBLB 1945-1960; DLB 20

MacDonald, Anson
  See Heinlein, Robert A(nson)

Macdonald, Cynthia 1928- . . . . . . **CLC 13, 19**
  See also CA 49-52; CANR 4, 44; DLB 105

MacDonald, George 1824-1905 . . . . . **TCLC 9**
  See also CA 106; 137; DLB 18; MAICYA;
  SATA 33

Macdonald, John
  See Millar, Kenneth

MacDonald, John D(ann)
  1916-1986 . . . . **CLC 3, 27, 44**
  See also CA 1-4R; 121; CANR 1, 19;
  DLB 8; DLBY 86; MTCW

Macdonald, John Ross
  See Millar, Kenneth

Macdonald, Ross . . . . . **CLC 1, 2, 3, 14, 34, 41**
  See also Millar, Kenneth
  See also DLBD 6

MacDougal, John
  See Blish, James (Benjamin)

MacEwen, Gwendolyn (Margaret)
  1941-1987 . . . . **CLC 13, 55**
  See also CA 9-12R; 124; CANR 7, 22;
  DLB 53; SATA 50, 55

Macha, Karel Hynek 1810-1846 . . **NCLC 46**

Machado (y Ruiz), Antonio
  1875-1939 . . . . **TCLC 3**
  See also CA 104; DLB 108

Machado de Assis, Joaquim Maria
  1839-1908 . . . . **TCLC 10; BLC**
  See also CA 107

Machen, Arthur . . . . **TCLC 4**
  See also Jones, Arthur Llewellyn
  See also DLB 36

Machiavelli, Niccolo 1469-1527 . . **LC 8; DA**

MacInnes, Colin 1914-1976 . . . . . . **CLC 4, 23**
  See also CA 69-72; 65-68; CANR 21;
  DLB 14; MTCW

MacInnes, Helen (Clark)
  1907-1985 . . . . **CLC 27, 39**
  See also CA 1-4R; 117; CANR 1, 28;
  DLB 87; MTCW; SATA 22, 44

Mackay, Mary 1855-1924
  See Corelli, Marie
  See also CA 118

Mackenzie, Compton (Edward Montague)
  1883-1972 . . . . **CLC 18**
  See also CA 21-22; 37-40R; CAP 2;
  DLB 34, 100

Mackenzie, Henry 1745-1831 . . . . **NCLC 41**
  See also DLB 39

Mackintosh, Elizabeth 1896(?)-1952
  See Tey, Josephine
  See also CA 110

MacLaren, James
  See Grieve, C(hristopher) M(urray)

Mac Laverty, Bernard 1942- . . . . **CLC 31**
  See also CA 116; 118; CANR 43

MacLean, Alistair (Stuart)
  1922-1987 . . . . **CLC 3, 13, 50, 63**
  See also CA 57-60; 121; CANR 28; MTCW;
  SATA 23, 50

Maclean, Norman (Fitzroy)
  1902-1990 . . . . **CLC 78; SSC 13**
  See also CA 102; 132

MacLeish, Archibald
  1892-1982 . . . . **CLC 3, 8, 14, 68**
  See also CA 9-12R; 106; CANR 33; DLB 4,
  7, 45; DLBY 82; MTCW

MacLennan, (John) Hugh
  1907-1990 . . . . **CLC 2, 14**
  See also CA 5-8R; 142; CANR 33; DLB 68;
  MTCW

MacLeod, Alistair 1936- . . . . **CLC 56**
  See also CA 123; DLB 60

MacNeice, (Frederick) Louis
  1907-1963 . . . . **CLC 1, 4, 10, 53**
  See also CA 85-88; DLB 10, 20; MTCW

MacNeill, Dand
  See Fraser, George MacDonald

Macpherson, (Jean) Jay 1931- . . . . . . **CLC 14**
  See also CA 5-8R; DLB 53

MacShane, Frank 1927- . . . . **CLC 39**
  See also CA 9-12R; CANR 3, 33; DLB 111

Macumber, Mari
  See Sandoz, Mari(e Susette)

Madach, Imre 1823-1864 . . . . **NCLC 19**

Madden, (Jerry) David 1933- . . . . **CLC 5, 15**
  See also CA 1-4R; CAAS 3; CANR 4, 45;
  DLB 6; MTCW

Maddern, Al(an)
  See Ellison, Harlan

Madhubuti, Haki R.
  1942- . . . . **CLC 6, 73; BLC; PC 5**
  See also Lee, Don L.
  See also BW 2; CA 73-76; CANR 24;
  DLB 5, 41; DLBD 8

Maepenn, Hugh
  See Kuttner, Henry

Maepenn, K. H.
  See Kuttner, Henry

Maeterlinck, Maurice 1862-1949 . . . **TCLC 3**
  See also CA 104; 136; SATA 66

Maginn, William 1794-1842 . . . . **NCLC 8**
  See also DLB 110

Mahapatra, Jayanta 1928- . . . . **CLC 33**
  See also CA 73-76; CAAS 9; CANR 15, 33

Marsden, James
See Creasey, John

Marsh, (Edith) Ngaio
1899-1982 .... CLC 7, 53
See also CA 9-12R; CANR 6; DLB 77;
MTCW

Marshall, Garry 1934-........... CLC 17
See also AAYA 3; CA 111; SATA 60

Marshall, Paule
1929- .... CLC 27, 72; BLC; SSC 3
See also BW 2; CA 77-80; CANR 25;
DLB 33; MTCW

Marsten, Richard
See Hunter, Evan

Martha, Henry
See Harris, Mark

Martial 40-104 .... PC 10

Martin, Ken
See Hubbard, L(afayette) Ron(ald)

Martin, Richard
See Creasey, John

Martin, Steve 1945-............. CLC 30
See also CA 97-100; CANR 30; MTCW

Martin, Violet Florence
1862-1915 .... TCLC 51

Martin, Webber
See Silverberg, Robert

Martindale, Patrick Victor
See White, Patrick (Victor Martindale)

Martin du Gard, Roger
1881-1958 .... TCLC 24
See also CA 118; DLB 65

Martineau, Harriet 1802-1876.... NCLC 26
See also DLB 21, 55; YABC 2

Martines, Julia
See O'Faolain, Julia

Martinez, Jacinto Benavente y
See Benavente (y Martinez), Jacinto

Martinez Ruiz, Jose 1873-1967
See Azorin; Ruiz, Jose Martinez
See also CA 93-96; HW

Martinez Sierra, Gregorio
1881-1947 .... TCLC 6
See also CA 115

Martinez Sierra, Maria (de la O'LeJarraga)
1874-1974 .... TCLC 6
See also CA 115

Martinsen, Martin
See Follett, Ken(neth Martin)

Martinson, Harry (Edmund)
1904-1978 .... CLC 14
See also CA 77-80; CANR 34

Marut, Ret
See Traven, B.

Marut, Robert
See Traven, B.

Marvell, Andrew
1621-1678 ..... LC 4; DA; PC 10; WLC
See also CDBLB 1660-1789; DLB 131

Marx, Karl (Heinrich)
1818-1883 .... NCLC 17
See also DLB 129

Masaoka Shiki. .... TCLC 18
See also Masaoka Tsunenori

Masaoka Tsunenori 1867-1902
See Masaoka Shiki
See also CA 117

Masefield, John (Edward)
1878-1967 .... CLC 11, 47
See also CA 19-20; 25-28R; CANR 33;
CAP 2; CDBLB 1890-1914; DLB 10;
MTCW; SATA 19

Maso, Carole 19(?)- .... CLC 44

Mason, Bobbie Ann
1940- .... CLC 28, 43, 82; SSC 4
See also AAYA 5; CA 53-56; CANR 11,
31; DLBY 87; MTCW

Mason, Ernst
See Pohl, Frederik

Mason, Lee W.
See Malzberg, Barry N(athaniel)

Mason, Nick 1945-.............. CLC 35

Mason, Tally
See Derleth, August (William)

Mass, William
See Gibson, William

Masters, Edgar Lee
1868-1950 ...... TCLC 2, 25; DA; PC 1
See also CA 104; 133; CDALB 1865-1917;
DLB 54; MTCW

Masters, Hilary 1928-........... CLC 48
See also CA 25-28R; CANR 13

Mastrosimone, William 19(?)-...... CLC 36

Mathe, Albert
See Camus, Albert

Matheson, Richard Burton 1926-... CLC 37
See also CA 97-100; DLB 8, 44

Mathews, Harry 1930-.......... CLC 6, 52
See also CA 21-24R; CAAS 6; CANR 18,
40

Mathews, John Joseph 1894-1979... CLC 84
See also CA 19-20; 142; CANR 45; CAP 2

Mathias, Roland (Glyn) 1915-...... CLC 45
See also CA 97-100; CANR 19, 41; DLB 27

Matsuo Basho 1644-1694........... PC 3

Mattheson, Rodney
See Creasey, John

Matthews, Greg 1949- .... CLC 45
See also CA 135

Matthews, William 1942-......... CLC 40
See also CA 29-32R; CAAS 18; CANR 12;
DLB 5

Matthias, John (Edward) 1941-..... CLC 9
See also CA 33-36R

Matthiessen, Peter
1927- .... CLC 5, 7, 11, 32, 64
See also AAYA 6; BEST 90:4; CA 9-12R;
CANR 21; DLB 6; MTCW; SATA 27

Maturin, Charles Robert
1780(?)-1824 .... NCLC 6

Matute (Ausejo), Ana Maria
1925- .... CLC 11
See also CA 89-92; MTCW

Maugham, W. S.
See Maugham, W(illiam) Somerset

Maugham, W(illiam) Somerset
1874-1965 ...... CLC 1, 11, 15, 67; DA;
SSC 8; WLC
See also CA 5-8R; 25-28R; CANR 40;
CDBLB 1914-1945; DLB 10, 36, 77, 100;
MTCW; SATA 54

Maugham, William Somerset
See Maugham, W(illiam) Somerset

Maupassant, (Henri Rene Albert) Guy de
1850-1893 .... NCLC 1, 42; DA; SSC 1;
WLC
See also DLB 123

Maurhut, Richard
See Traven, B.

Mauriac, Claude 1914-............ CLC 9
See also CA 89-92; DLB 83

Mauriac, Francois (Charles)
1885-1970 .... CLC 4, 9, 56
See also CA 25-28; CAP 2; DLB 65;
MTCW

Mavor, Osborne Henry 1888-1951
See Bridie, James
See also CA 104

Maxwell, William (Keepers, Jr.)
1908- .... CLC 19
See also CA 93-96; DLBY 80

May, Elaine 1932- .... CLC 16
See also CA 124; 142; DLB 44

Mayakovski, Vladimir (Vladimirovich)
1893-1930 .... TCLC 4, 18
See also CA 104

Mayhew, Henry 1812-1887 ...... NCLC 31
See also DLB 18, 55

Maynard, Joyce 1953-............ CLC 23
See also CA 111; 129

Mayne, William (James Carter)
1928- .... CLC 12
See also CA 9-12R; CANR 37; CLR 25;
JRDA; MAICYA; SAAS 11; SATA 6, 68

Mayo, Jim
See L'Amour, Louis (Dearborn)

Maysles, Albert 1926- .... CLC 16
See also CA 29-32R

Maysles, David 1932-............ CLC 16

Mazer, Norma Fox 1931- .... CLC 26
See also AAYA 5; CA 69-72; CANR 12,
32; CLR 23; JRDA; MAICYA; SAAS 1;
SATA 24, 67

Mazzini, Guiseppe 1805-1872 .... NCLC 34

McAuley, James Phillip
1917-1976 .... CLC 45
See also CA 97-100

McBain, Ed
See Hunter, Evan

McBrien, William Augustine
1930- .... CLC 44
See also CA 107

McCaffrey, Anne (Inez) 1926-...... CLC 17
See also AAYA 6; AITN 2; BEST 89:2;
CA 25-28R; CANR 15, 35; DLB 8;
JRDA; MAICYA; MTCW; SAAS 11;
SATA 8, 70

McCann, Arthur
See Campbell, John W(ood, Jr.)

Merritt, E. B.
See Waddington, Miriam

Merton, Thomas
1915-1968 .. **CLC 1, 3, 11, 34, 83; PC 10**
See also CA 5-8R; 25-28R; CANR 22;
DLB 48; DLBY 81; MTCW

Merwin, W(illiam) S(tanley)
1927- ...... **CLC 1, 2, 3, 5, 8, 13, 18, 45**
See also CA 13-16R; CANR 15; DLB 5;
MTCW

Metcalf, John 1938-............. **CLC 37**
See also CA 113; DLB 60

Metcalf, Suzanne
See Baum, L(yman) Frank

Mew, Charlotte (Mary)
1870-1928 .... **TCLC 8**
See also CA 105; DLB 19, 135

Mewshaw, Michael 1943-.......... **CLC 9**
See also CA 53-56; CANR 7; DLBY 80

Meyer, June
See Jordan, June

Meyer, Lynn
See Slavitt, David R(ytman)

Meyer-Meyrink, Gustav 1868-1932
See Meyrink, Gustav
See also CA 117

Meyers, Jeffrey 1939- .... **CLC 39**
See also CA 73-76; DLB 111

Meynell, Alice (Christina Gertrude Thompson)
1847-1922 .... **TCLC 6**
See also CA 104; DLB 19, 98

Meyrink, Gustav .... **TCLC 21**
See also Meyer-Meyrink, Gustav
See also DLB 81

Michaels, Leonard
1933- .... **CLC 6, 25; SSC 16**
See also CA 61-64; CANR 21; DLB 130;
MTCW

Michaux, Henri 1899-1984 ...... **CLC 8, 19**
See also CA 85-88; 114

Michelangelo 1475-1564............ **LC 12**

Michelet, Jules 1798-1874....... **NCLC 31**

Michener, James A(lbert)
1907(?)-.......... **CLC 1, 5, 11, 29, 60**
See also AITN 1; BEST 90:1; CA 5-8R;
CANR 21, 45; DLB 6; MTCW

Mickiewicz, Adam 1798-1855 ..... **NCLC 3**

Middleton, Christopher 1926-...... **CLC 13**
See also CA 13-16R; CANR 29; DLB 40

Middleton, Richard (Barham)
1882-1911 .... **TCLC 56**

Middleton, Stanley 1919-....... **CLC 7, 38**
See also CA 25-28R; CANR 21; DLB 14

Migueis, Jose Rodrigues 1901-..... **CLC 10**

Mikszath, Kalman 1847-1910 ..... **TCLC 31**

Miles, Josephine
1911-1985 .... **CLC 1, 2, 14, 34, 39**
See also CA 1-4R; 116; CANR 2; DLB 48

Militant
See Sandburg, Carl (August)

Mill, John Stuart 1806-1873 ..... **NCLC 11**
See also CDBLB 1832-1890; DLB 55

Millar, Kenneth 1915-1983 .... **CLC 14**
See also Macdonald, Ross
See also CA 9-12R; 110; CANR 16; DLB 2;
DLBD 6; DLBY 83; MTCW

Millay, E. Vincent
See Millay, Edna St. Vincent

Millay, Edna St. Vincent
1892-1950 ...... **TCLC 4, 49; DA; PC 6**
See also CA 104; 130; CDALB 1917-1929;
DLB 45; MTCW

Miller, Arthur
1915- .... **CLC 1, 2, 6, 10, 15, 26, 47, 78;
DA; DC 1; WLC**
See also AITN 1; CA 1-4R; CABS 3;
CANR 2, 30; CDALB 1941-1968; DLB 7;
MTCW

Miller, Henry (Valentine)
1891-1980 .... **CLC 1, 2, 4, 9, 14, 43, 84;
DA; WLC**
See also CA 9-12R; 97-100; CANR 33;
CDALB 1929-1941; DLB 4, 9; DLBY 80;
MTCW

Miller, Jason 1939(?)- .... **CLC 2**
See also AITN 1; CA 73-76; DLB 7

Miller, Sue 1943- .... **CLC 44**
See also BEST 90:3; CA 139; DLB 143

Miller, Walter M(ichael, Jr.)
1923- .... **CLC 4, 30**
See also CA 85-88; DLB 8

Millett, Kate 1934-............... **CLC 67**
See also AITN 1; CA 73-76; CANR 32;
MTCW

Millhauser, Steven 1943-...... **CLC 21, 54**
See also CA 110; 111; DLB 2

Millin, Sarah Gertrude 1889-1968 .. **CLC 49**
See also CA 102; 93-96

Milne, A(lan) A(lexander)
1882-1956 .... **TCLC 6**
See also CA 104; 133; CLR 1, 26; DLB 10,
77, 100; MAICYA; MTCW; YABC 1

Milner, Ron(ald) 1938-....... **CLC 56; BLC**
See also AITN 1; BW 1; CA 73-76;
CANR 24; DLB 38; MTCW

Milosz, Czeslaw
1911- ... **CLC 5, 11, 22, 31, 56, 82; PC 8**
See also CA 81-84; CANR 23; MTCW

Milton, John 1608-1674... **LC 9; DA; WLC**
See also CDBLB 1660-1789; DLB 131

Minehaha, Cornelius
See Wedekind, (Benjamin) Frank(lin)

Miner, Valerie 1947- .... **CLC 40**
See also CA 97-100

Minimo, Duca
See D'Annunzio, Gabriele

Minot, Susan 1956- .... **CLC 44**
See also CA 134

Minus, Ed 1938-................. **CLC 39**

Miranda, Javier
See Bioy Casares, Adolfo

Mirbeau, Octave 1848-1917...... **TCLC 55**
See also DLB 123

Miro (Ferrer), Gabriel (Francisco Victor)
1879-1930 .... **TCLC 5**
See also CA 104

Mishima, Yukio
.... **CLC 2, 4, 6, 9, 27; DC 1; SSC 4**
See also Hiraoka, Kimitake

Mistral, Frederic 1830-1914 ...... **TCLC 51**
See also CA 122

Mistral, Gabriela........... **TCLC 2; HLC**
See also Godoy Alcayaga, Lucila

Mistry, Rohinton 1952- .... **CLC 71**
See also CA 141

Mitchell, Clyde
See Ellison, Harlan; Silverberg, Robert

Mitchell, James Leslie 1901-1935
See Gibbon, Lewis Grassic
See also CA 104; DLB 15

Mitchell, Joni 1943-............. **CLC 12**
See also CA 112

Mitchell, Margaret (Munnerlyn)
1900-1949 .... **TCLC 11**
See also CA 109; 125; DLB 9; MTCW

Mitchell, Peggy
See Mitchell, Margaret (Munnerlyn)

Mitchell, S(ilas) Weir 1829-1914 .. **TCLC 36**

Mitchell, W(illiam) O(rmond)
1914-...................... **CLC 25**
See also CA 77-80; CANR 15, 43; DLB 88

Mitford, Mary Russell 1787-1855.. **NCLC 4**
See also DLB 110, 116

Mitford, Nancy 1904-1973........ **CLC 44**
See also CA 9-12R

Miyamoto, Yuriko 1899-1951 ..... **TCLC 37**

Mo, Timothy (Peter) 1950(?)-...... **CLC 46**
See also CA 117; MTCW

Modarressi, Taghi (M.) 1931-...... **CLC 44**
See also CA 121; 134

Modiano, Patrick (Jean) 1945-...... **CLC 18**
See also CA 85-88; CANR 17, 40; DLB 83

Moerck, Paal
See Roelvaag, O(le) E(dvart)

Mofolo, Thomas (Mokopu)
1875(?)-1948 .... **TCLC 22; BLC**
See also CA 121

Mohr, Nicholasa 1935-...... **CLC 12; HLC**
See also AAYA 8; CA 49-52; CANR 1, 32;
CLR 22; HW; JRDA; SAAS 8; SATA 8

Mojtabai, A(nn) G(race)
1938-............... **CLC 5, 9, 15, 29**
See also CA 85-88

Moliere 1622-1673 .... **LC 10; DA; WLC**

Molin, Charles
See Mayne, William (James Carter)

Molnar, Ferenc 1878-1952........ **TCLC 20**
See also CA 109

Momaday, N(avarre) Scott
1934-.............. **CLC 2, 19, 85; DA**
See also AAYA 11; CA 25-28R; CANR 14,
34; DLB 143; MTCW; NNAL; SATA 30,
48

Monette, Paul 1945-.............. **CLC 82**
See also CA 139

Monroe, Harriet 1860-1936....... **TCLC 12**
See also CA 109; DLB 54, 91

Monroe, Lyle
See Heinlein, Robert A(nson)

Montagu, Elizabeth 1917- .... **NCLC 7**
See also CA 9-12R

Montagu, Mary (Pierrepont) Wortley
    1689-1762 .... **LC 9**
See also DLB 95, 101

Montagu, W. H.
See Coleridge, Samuel Taylor

Montague, John (Patrick)
    1929- .... **CLC 13, 46**
See also CA 9-12R; CANR 9; DLB 40;
MTCW

Montaigne, Michel (Eyquem) de
    1533-1592 .... **LC 8; DA; WLC**

Montale, Eugenio 1896-1981 ... **CLC 7, 9, 18**
See also CA 17-20R; 104; CANR 30;
DLB 114; MTCW

Montesquieu, Charles-Louis de Secondat
    1689-1755 .... **LC 7**

Montgomery, (Robert) Bruce 1921-1978
See Crispin, Edmund
See also CA 104

Montgomery, L(ucy) M(aud)
    1874-1942 .... **TCLC 51**
See also AAYA 12; CA 108; 137; CLR 8;
DLB 92; JRDA; MAICYA; YABC 1

Montgomery, Marion H., Jr. 1925- .. **CLC 7**
See also AITN 1; CA 1-4R; CANR 3;
DLB 6

Montgomery, Max
See Davenport, Guy (Mattison, Jr.)

Montherlant, Henry (Milon) de
    1896-1972 .... **CLC 8, 19**
See also CA 85-88; 37-40R; DLB 72;
MTCW

Monty Python
See Chapman, Graham; Cleese, John
(Marwood); Gilliam, Terry (Vance); Idle,
Eric; Jones, Terence Graham Parry; Palin,
Michael (Edward)
See also AAYA 7

Moodie, Susanna (Strickland)
    1803-1885 .... **NCLC 14**
See also DLB 99

Mooney, Edward 1951-
See Mooney, Ted
See also CA 130

Mooney, Ted .... **CLC 25**
See also Mooney, Edward

Moorcock, Michael (John)
    1939- .... **CLC 5, 27, 58**
See also CA 45-48; CAAS 5; CANR 2, 17,
38; DLB 14; MTCW

Moore, Brian
    1921- .... **CLC 1, 3, 5, 7, 8, 19, 32**
See also CA 1-4R; CANR 1, 25, 42; MTCW

Moore, Edward
See Muir, Edwin

Moore, George Augustus
    1852-1933 .... **TCLC 7**
See also CA 104; DLB 10, 18, 57, 135

Moore, Lorrie .... **CLC 39, 45, 68**
See also Moore, Marie Lorena

Moore, Marianne (Craig)
    1887-1972 .... **CLC 1, 2, 4, 8, 10, 13, 19,**
                                        47; DA; PC 4
See also CA 1-4R; 33-36R; CANR 3;
CDALB 1929-1941; DLB 45; DLBD 7;
MTCW; SATA 20

Moore, Marie Lorena 1957-
See Moore, Lorrie
See also CA 116; CANR 39

Moore, Thomas 1779-1852 .... **NCLC 6**
See also DLB 96, 144

Morand, Paul 1888-1976 .... **CLC 41**
See also CA 69-72; DLB 65

Morante, Elsa 1918-1985 .... **CLC 8, 47**
See also CA 85-88; 117; CANR 35; MTCW

Moravia, Alberto .... **CLC 2, 7, 11, 27, 46**
See also Pincherle, Alberto

More, Hannah 1745-1833 .... **NCLC 27**
See also DLB 107, 109, 116

More, Henry 1614-1687 .... **LC 9**
See also DLB 126

More, Sir Thomas 1478-1535 ...... **LC 10**

Moreas, Jean .... **TCLC 18**
See also Papadiamantopoulos, Johannes

Morgan, Berry 1919- .... **CLC 6**
See also CA 49-52; DLB 6

Morgan, Claire
See Highsmith, (Mary) Patricia

Morgan, Edwin (George) 1920- ..... **CLC 31**
See also CA 5-8R; CANR 3, 43; DLB 27

Morgan, (George) Frederick
    1922- .... **CLC 23**
See also CA 17-20R; CANR 21

Morgan, Harriet
See Mencken, H(enry) L(ouis)

Morgan, Jane
See Cooper, James Fenimore

Morgan, Janet 1945- .... **CLC 39**
See also CA 65-68

Morgan, Lady 1776(?)-1859 ...... **NCLC 29**
See also DLB 116

Morgan, Robin 1941- .... **CLC 2**
See also CA 69-72; CANR 29; MTCW

Morgan, Scott
See Kuttner, Henry

Morgan, Seth 1949(?)-1990 .... **CLC 65**
See also CA 132

Morgenstern, Christian
    1871-1914 .... **TCLC 8**
See also CA 105

Morgenstern, S.
See Goldman, William (W.)

Moricz, Zsigmond 1879-1942 ..... **TCLC 33**

Morike, Eduard (Friedrich)
    1804-1875 .... **NCLC 10**
See also DLB 133

Mori Ogai .... **TCLC 14**
See also Mori Rintaro

Mori Rintaro 1862-1922
See Mori Ogai
See also CA 110

Moritz, Karl Philipp 1756-1793 ...... **LC 2**
See also DLB 94

Morland, Peter Henry
See Faust, Frederick (Schiller)

Morren, Theophil
See Hofmannsthal, Hugo von

Morris, Bill 1952- .... **CLC 76**

Morris, Julian
See West, Morris L(anglo)

Morris, Steveland Judkins 1950(?)-
See Wonder, Stevie
See also CA 111

Morris, William 1834-1896 .... **NCLC 4**
See also CDBLB 1832-1890; DLB 18, 35, 57

Morris, Wright 1910-... **CLC 1, 3, 7, 18, 37**
See also CA 9-12R; CANR 21; DLB 2;
DLBY 81; MTCW

Morrison, Chloe Anthony Wofford
See Morrison, Toni

Morrison, James Douglas 1943-1971
See Morrison, Jim
See also CA 73-76; CANR 40

Morrison, Jim .... **CLC 17**
See also Morrison, James Douglas

Morrison, Toni
    1931- .. **CLC 4, 10, 22, 55, 81; BLC; DA**
See also AAYA 1; BW 2; CA 29-32R;
CANR 27, 42; CDALB 1968-1988;
DLB 6, 33, 143; DLBY 81; MTCW;
SATA 57

Morrison, Van 1945- .... **CLC 21**
See also CA 116

Mortimer, John (Clifford)
    1923- .... **CLC 28, 43**
See also CA 13-16R; CANR 21;
CDBLB 1960 to Present; DLB 13;
MTCW

Mortimer, Penelope (Ruth) 1918-.... **CLC 5**
See also CA 57-60; CANR 45

Morton, Anthony
See Creasey, John

Mosher, Howard Frank 1943-...... **CLC 62**
See also CA 139

Mosley, Nicholas 1923-......... **CLC 43, 70**
See also CA 69-72; CANR 41; DLB 14

Moss, Howard
    1922-1987 .... **CLC 7, 14, 45, 50**
See also CA 1-4R; 123; CANR 1, 44;
DLB 5

Mossgiel, Rab
See Burns, Robert

Motion, Andrew 1952-........... **CLC 47**
See also DLB 40

Motley, Willard (Francis)
    1909-1965 .... **CLC 18**
See also BW 1; CA 117; 106; DLB 76, 143

Motoori, Norinaga 1730-1801 .... **NCLC 45**

Mott, Michael (Charles Alston)
    1930- .... **CLC 15, 34**
See also CA 5-8R; CAAS 7; CANR 7, 29

Mowat, Farley (McGill) 1921- ..... **CLC 26**
See also AAYA 1; CA 1-4R; CANR 4, 24,
42; CLR 20; DLB 68; JRDA; MAICYA;
MTCW; SATA 3, 55

Moyers, Bill 1934-............... **CLC 74**
See also AITN 2; CA 61-64; CANR 31

Mphahlele, Es'kia
See Mphahlele, Ezekiel
See also DLB 125

Mphahlele, Ezekiel 1919-..... CLC 25; BLC
See also Mphahlele, Es'kia
See also BW 2; CA 81-84; CANR 26

Mqhayi, S(amuel) E(dward) K(rune Loliwe)
1875-1945 .... TCLC 25; BLC

Mr. Martin
See Burroughs, William S(eward)

Mrozek, Slawomir 1930-........ CLC 3, 13
See also CA 13-16R; CAAS 10; CANR 29;
MTCW

Mrs. Belloc-Lowndes
See Lowndes, Marie Adelaide (Belloc)

Mtwa, Percy (?)-................ CLC 47

Mueller, Lisel 1924-........... CLC 13, 51
See also CA 93-96; DLB 105

Muir, Edwin 1887-1959 .... TCLC 2
See also CA 104; DLB 20, 100

Muir, John 1838-1914 .... TCLC 28

Mujica Lainez, Manuel
1910-1984 .... CLC 31
See also Lainez, Manuel Mujica
See also CA 81-84; 112; CANR 32; HW

Mukherjee, Bharati 1940-......... CLC 53
See also BEST 89:2; CA 107; CANR 45;
DLB 60; MTCW

Muldoon, Paul 1951-.......... CLC 32, 72
See also CA 113; 129; DLB 40

Mulisch, Harry 1927-............ CLC 42
See also CA 9-12R; CANR 6, 26

Mull, Martin 1943-.............. CLC 17
See also CA 105

Mulock, Dinah Maria
See Craik, Dinah Maria (Mulock)

Munford, Robert 1737(?)-1783 .... LC 5
See also DLB 31

Mungo, Raymond 1946-.......... CLC 72
See also CA 49-52; CANR 2

Munro, Alice
1931-........ CLC 6, 10, 19, 50; SSC 3
See also AITN 2; CA 33-36R; CANR 33;
DLB 53; MTCW; SATA 29

Munro, H(ector) H(ugh) 1870-1916
See Saki
See also CA 104; 130; CDBLB 1890-1914;
DA; DLB 34; MTCW; WLC

Murasaki, Lady................ CMLC 1

Murdoch, (Jean) Iris
1919- ...... CLC 1, 2, 3, 4, 6, 8, 11, 15,
22, 31, 51
See also CA 13-16R; CANR 8, 43;
CDBLB 1960 to Present; DLB 14;
MTCW

Murnau, Friedrich Wilhelm
See Plumpe, Friedrich Wilhelm

Murphy, Richard 1927-........... CLC 41
See also CA 29-32R; DLB 40

Murphy, Sylvia 1937-............ CLC 34
See also CA 121

Murphy, Thomas (Bernard) 1935-... CLC 51
See also CA 101

Murray, Albert L. 1916-.......... CLC 73
See also BW 2; CA 49-52; CANR 26;
DLB 38

Murray, Les(lie) A(llan) 1938- ..... CLC 40
See also CA 21-24R; CANR 11, 27

Murry, J. Middleton
See Murry, John Middleton

Murry, John Middleton
1889-1957 .... TCLC 16
See also CA 118

Musgrave, Susan 1951- .... CLC 13, 54
See also CA 69-72; CANR 45

Musil, Robert (Edler von)
1880-1942 .... TCLC 12
See also CA 109; DLB 81, 124

Musset, (Louis Charles) Alfred de
1810-1857 .... NCLC 7

My Brother's Brother
See Chekhov, Anton (Pavlovich)

Myers, Walter Dean 1937- ... CLC 35; BLC
See also AAYA 4; BW 2; CA 33-36R;
CANR 20, 42; CLR 4, 16, 35; DLB 33;
JRDA; MAICYA; SAAS 2; SATA 27, 41,
71

Myers, Walter M.
See Myers, Walter Dean

Myles, Symon
See Follett, Ken(neth Martin)

Nabokov, Vladimir (Vladimirovich)
1899-1977 ..... CLC 1, 2, 3, 6, 8, 11, 15,
23, 44, 46, 64; DA; SSC 11; WLC
See also CA 5-8R; 69-72; CANR 20;
CDALB 1941-1968; DLB 2; DLBD 3;
DLBY 80, 91; MTCW

Nagai Kafu.................... TCLC 51
See also Nagai Sokichi

Nagai Sokichi 1879-1959
See Nagai Kafu
See also CA 117

Nagy, Laszlo 1925-1978........... CLC 7
See also CA 129; 112

Naipaul, Shiva(dhar Srinivasa)
1945-1985 .... CLC 32, 39
See also CA 110; 112; 116; CANR 33;
DLBY 85; MTCW

Naipaul, V(idiadhar) S(urajprasad)
1932- .... CLC 4, 7, 9, 13, 18, 37
See also CA 1-4R; CANR 1, 33;
CDBLB 1960 to Present; DLB 125;
DLBY 85; MTCW

Nakos, Lilika 1899(?)-............ CLC 29

Narayan, R(asipuram) K(rishnaswami)
1906- .... CLC 7, 28, 47
See also CA 81-84; CANR 33; MTCW;
SATA 62

Nash, (Frediric) Ogden 1902-1971 .. CLC 23
See also CA 13-14; 29-32R; CANR 34;
CAP 1; DLB 11; MAICYA; MTCW;
SATA 2, 46

Nathan, Daniel
See Dannay, Frederic

Nathan, George Jean 1882-1958 ... TCLC 18
See also Hatteras, Owen
See also CA 114; DLB 137

Natsume, Kinnosuke 1867-1916
See Natsume, Soseki
See also CA 104

Natsume, Soseki .... TCLC 2, 10
See also Natsume, Kinnosuke

Natti, (Mary) Lee 1919-
See Kingman, Lee
See also CA 5-8R; CANR 2

Naylor, Gloria
1950-........... CLC 28, 52; BLC; DA
See also AAYA 6; BW 2; CA 107;
CANR 27; MTCW

Neihardt, John Gneisenau
1881-1973 .... CLC 32
See also CA 13-14; CAP 1; DLB 9, 54

Nekrasov, Nikolai Alekseevich
1821-1878 .... NCLC 11

Nelligan, Emile 1879-1941....... TCLC 14
See also CA 114; DLB 92

Nelson, Willie 1933-.............. CLC 17
See also CA 107

Nemerov, Howard (Stanley)
1920-1991 .... CLC 2, 6, 9, 36
See also CA 1-4R; 134; CABS 2; CANR 1,
27; DLB 6; DLBY 83; MTCW

Neruda, Pablo
1904-1973 ..... CLC 1, 2, 5, 7, 9, 28, 62;
DA; HLC; PC 4; WLC
See also CA 19-20; 45-48; CAP 2; HW;
MTCW

Nerval, Gerard de 1808-1855...... NCLC 1

Nervo, (Jose) Amado (Ruiz de)
1870-1919 .... TCLC 11
See also CA 109; 131; HW

Nessi, Pio Baroja y
See Baroja (y Nessi), Pio

Nestroy, Johann 1801-1862...... NCLC 42
See also DLB 133

Neufeld, John (Arthur) 1938- ...... CLC 17
See also AAYA 11; CA 25-28R; CANR 11,
37; MAICYA; SAAS 3; SATA 6

Neville, Emily Cheney 1919-....... CLC 12
See also CA 5-8R; CANR 3, 37; JRDA;
MAICYA; SAAS 2; SATA 1

Newbound, Bernard Slade 1930-
See Slade, Bernard
See also CA 81-84

Newby, P(ercy) H(oward)
1918-.................... CLC 2, 13
See also CA 5-8R; CANR 32; DLB 15;
MTCW

Newlove, Donald 1928- .... CLC 6
See also CA 29-32R; CANR 25

Newlove, John (Herbert) 1938-..... CLC 14
See also CA 21-24R; CANR 9, 25

Newman, Charles 1938-.......... CLC 2, 8
See also CA 21-24R

Newman, Edwin (Harold) 1919- .... CLC 14
See also AITN 1; CA 69-72; CANR 5

Newman, John Henry
1801-1890 .... NCLC 38
See also DLB 18, 32, 55

Newton, Suzanne 1936-.......... CLC 35
See also CA 41-44R; CANR 14; JRDA;
SATA 5, 77

O'Donovan, Michael John
1903-1966 .... **CLC 14**
See also O'Connor, Frank
See also CA 93-96

Oe, Kenzaburo 1935- .... **CLC 10, 36**
See also CA 97-100; CANR 36; MTCW

O'Faolain, Julia 1932- .... **CLC 6, 19, 47**
See also CA 81-84; CAAS 2; CANR 12;
DLB 14; MTCW

O'Faolain, Sean
1900-1991 .... **CLC 1, 7, 14, 32, 70;**
SSC 13
See also CA 61-64; 134; CANR 12;
DLB 15; MTCW

O'Flaherty, Liam
1896-1984 .... **CLC 5, 34; SSC 6**
See also CA 101; 113; CANR 35; DLB 36;
DLBY 84; MTCW

Ogilvy, Gavin
See Barrie, J(ames) M(atthew)

O'Grady, Standish James
1846-1928 .... **TCLC 5**
See also CA 104

O'Grady, Timothy 1951- .... **CLC 59**
See also CA 138

O'Hara, Frank
1926-1966 .... **CLC 2, 5, 13, 78**
See also CA 9-12R; 25-28R; CANR 33;
DLB 5, 16; MTCW

O'Hara, John (Henry)
1905-1970 .... **CLC 1, 2, 3, 6, 11, 42;**
SSC 15
See also CA 5-8R; 25-28R; CANR 31;
CDALB 1929-1941; DLB 9, 86; DLBD 2;
MTCW

O Hehir, Diana 1922- .... **CLC 41**
See also CA 93-96

Okigbo, Christopher (Ifenayichukwu)
1932-1967 ..... **CLC 25, 84; BLC; PC 7**
See also BW 1; CA 77-80; DLB 125;
MTCW

Olds, Sharon 1942- .... **CLC 32, 39, 85**
See also CA 101; CANR 18, 41; DLB 120

Oldstyle, Jonathan
See Irving, Washington

Olesha, Yuri (Karlovich)
1899-1960 .... **CLC 8**
See also CA 85-88

Oliphant, Laurence
1829(?)-1888 .... **NCLC 47**
See also DLB 18

Oliphant, Margaret (Oliphant Wilson)
1828-1897 .... **NCLC 11**
See also DLB 18

Oliver, Mary 1935- .... **CLC 19, 34**
See also CA 21-24R; CANR 9, 43; DLB 5

Olivier, Laurence (Kerr)
1907-1989 .... **CLC 20**
See also CA 111; 129

Olsen, Tillie
1913- .... **CLC 4, 13; DA; SSC 11**
See also CA 1-4R; CANR 1, 43; DLB 28;
DLBY 80; MTCW

Olson, Charles (John)
1910-1970 ..... **CLC 1, 2, 5, 6, 9, 11, 29**
See also CA 13-16; 25-28R; CABS 2;
CANR 35; CAP 1; DLB 5, 16; MTCW

Olson, Toby 1937- .... **CLC 28**
See also CA 65-68; CANR 9, 31

Olyesha, Yuri
See Olesha, Yuri (Karlovich)

Ondaatje, (Philip) Michael
1943- .... **CLC 14, 29, 51, 76**
See also CA 77-80; CANR 42; DLB 60

Oneal, Elizabeth 1934-
See Oneal, Zibby
See also CA 106; CANR 28; MAICYA;
SATA 30

Oneal, Zibby .... **CLC 30**
See also Oneal, Elizabeth
See also AAYA 5; CLR 13; JRDA

O'Neill, Eugene (Gladstone)
1888-1953 ...... **TCLC 1, 6, 27, 49; DA;**
WLC
See also AITN 1; CA 110; 132;
CDALB 1929-1941; DLB 7; MTCW

Onetti, Juan Carlos 1909-1994 ... **CLC 7, 10**
See also CA 85-88; 145; CANR 32;
DLB 113; HW; MTCW

O Nuallain, Brian 1911-1966
See O'Brien, Flann
See also CA 21-22; 25-28R; CAP 2

Oppen, George 1908-1984 .... **CLC 7, 13, 34**
See also CA 13-16R; 113; CANR 8; DLB 5

Oppenheim, E(dward) Phillips
1866-1946 .... **TCLC 45**
See also CA 111; DLB 70

Orlovitz, Gil 1918-1973 .... **CLC 22**
See also CA 77-80; 45-48; DLB 2, 5

Orris
See Ingelow, Jean

Ortega y Gasset, Jose
1883-1955 .... **TCLC 9; HLC**
See also CA 106; 130; HW; MTCW

Ortiz, Simon J(oseph) 1941- .... **CLC 45**
See also CA 134; DLB 120

Orton, Joe .... **CLC 4, 13, 43; DC 3**
See also Orton, John Kingsley
See also CDBLB 1960 to Present; DLB 13

Orton, John Kingsley 1933-1967
See Orton, Joe
See also CA 85-88; CANR 35; MTCW

Orwell, George
.... **TCLC 2, 6, 15, 31, 51; WLC**
See also Blair, Eric (Arthur)
See also CDBLB 1945-1960; DLB 15, 98

Osborne, David
See Silverberg, Robert

Osborne, George
See Silverberg, Robert

Osborne, John (James)
1929- .... **CLC 1, 2, 5, 11, 45; DA; WLC**
See also CA 13-16R; CANR 21;
CDBLB 1945-1960; DLB 13; MTCW

Osborne, Lawrence 1958- .... **CLC 50**

Oshima, Nagisa 1932- .... **CLC 20**
See also CA 116; 121

Oskison, John Milton
1874-1947 .... **TCLC 35**
See also CA 144

Ossoli, Sarah Margaret (Fuller marchesa d')
1810-1850
See Fuller, Margaret
See also SATA 25

Ostrovsky, Alexander
1823-1886 .... **NCLC 30**

Otero, Blas de 1916-1979......... **CLC 11**
See also CA 89-92; DLB 134

Otto, Whitney 1955-............. **CLC 70**
See also CA 140

Ouida .... **TCLC 43**
See also De La Ramee, (Marie) Louise
See also DLB 18

Ousmane, Sembene 1923- .... **CLC 66; BLC**
See also BW 1; CA 117; 125; MTCW

Ovid 43B.C.-18(?) .... **CMLC 7; PC 2**

Owen, Hugh
See Faust, Frederick (Schiller)

Owen, Wilfred (Edward Salter)
1893-1918 ...... **TCLC 5, 27; DA; WLC**
See also CA 104; 141; CDBLB 1914-1945;
DLB 20

Owens, Rochelle 1936-............ **CLC 8**
See also CA 17-20R; CAAS 2; CANR 39

Oz, Amos 1939- ... **CLC 5, 8, 11, 27, 33, 54**
See also CA 53-56; CANR 27; MTCW

Ozick, Cynthia
1928- .... **CLC 3, 7, 28, 62; SSC 15**
See also BEST 90:1; CA 17-20R; CANR 23;
DLB 28; DLBY 82; MTCW

Ozu, Yasujiro 1903-1963........ **CLC 16**
See also CA 112

Pacheco, C.
See Pessoa, Fernando (Antonio Nogueira)

Pa Chin .... **CLC 18**
See also Li Fei-kan

Pack, Robert 1929-............. **CLC 13**
See also CA 1-4R; CANR 3, 44; DLB 5

Padgett, Lewis
See Kuttner, Henry

Padilla (Lorenzo), Heberto 1932-... **CLC 38**
See also AITN 1; CA 123; 131; HW

Page, Jimmy 1944-.............. **CLC 12**

Page, Louise 1955-.............. **CLC 40**
See also CA 140

Page, P(atricia) K(athleen)
1916- .... **CLC 7, 18**
See also CA 53-56; CANR 4, 22; DLB 68;
MTCW

Paget, Violet 1856-1935
See Lee, Vernon
See also CA 104

Paget-Lowe, Henry
See Lovecraft, H(oward) P(hillips)

Paglia, Camille (Anna) 1947-....... **CLC 68**
See also CA 140

Paige, Richard
See Koontz, Dean R(ay)

Pakenham, Antonia
See Fraser, (Lady) Antonia (Pakenham)

Palamas, Kostes 1859-1943 .... **TCLC 5**
See also CA 105

Palazzeschi, Aldo 1885-1974 ...... **CLC 11**
See also CA 89-92; 53-56; DLB 114

Paley, Grace 1922-.... **CLC 4, 6, 37; SSC 8**
See also CA 25-28R; CANR 13; DLB 28;
MTCW

Palin, Michael (Edward) 1943- ..... **CLC 21**
See also Monty Python
See also CA 107; CANR 35; SATA 67

Palliser, Charles 1947-........... **CLC 65**
See also CA 136

Palma, Ricardo 1833-1919 .... **TCLC 29**

Pancake, Breece Dexter 1952-1979
See Pancake, Breece D'J
See also CA 123; 109

Pancake, Breece D'J .... **CLC 29**
See also Pancake, Breece Dexter
See also DLB 130

Panko, Rudy
See Gogol, Nikolai (Vasilyevich)

Papadiamantis, Alexandros
1851-1911 .... **TCLC 29**

Papadiamantopoulos, Johannes 1856-1910
See Moreas, Jean
See also CA 117

Papini, Giovanni 1881-1956 ...... **TCLC 22**
See also CA 121

Paracelsus 1493-1541 .... **LC 14**

Parasol, Peter
See Stevens, Wallace

Parfenie, Maria
See Codrescu, Andrei

Parini, Jay (Lee) 1948- .... **CLC 54**
See also CA 97-100; CAAS 16; CANR 32

Park, Jordan
See Kornbluth, C(yril) M.; Pohl, Frederik

Parker, Bert
See Ellison, Harlan

Parker, Dorothy (Rothschild)
1893-1967 .... **CLC 15, 68; SSC 2**
See also CA 19-20; 25-28R; CAP 2;
DLB 11, 45, 86; MTCW

Parker, Robert B(rown) 1932-...... **CLC 27**
See also BEST 89:4; CA 49-52; CANR 1,
26; MTCW

Parkin, Frank 1940-.............. **CLC 43**

Parkman, Francis, Jr.
1823-1893 .... **NCLC 12**
See also DLB 1, 30

Parks, Gordon (Alexander Buchanan)
1912- .... **CLC 1, 16; BLC**
See also AITN 2; BW 2; CA 41-44R;
CANR 26; DLB 33; SATA 8

Parnell, Thomas 1679-1718 .... **LC 3**
See also DLB 94

Parra, Nicanor 1914-....... **CLC 2; HLC**
See also CA 85-88; CANR 32; HW; MTCW

Parrish, Mary Frances
See Fisher, M(ary) F(rances) K(ennedy)

Parson
See Coleridge, Samuel Taylor

Parson Lot
See Kingsley, Charles

Partridge, Anthony
See Oppenheim, E(dward) Phillips

Pascoli, Giovanni 1855-1912 ..... **TCLC 45**

Pasolini, Pier Paolo
1922-1975 .... **CLC 20, 37**
See also CA 93-96; 61-64; DLB 128;
MTCW

Pasquini
See Silone, Ignazio

Pastan, Linda (Olenik) 1932- ...... **CLC 27**
See also CA 61-64; CANR 18, 40; DLB 5

Pasternak, Boris (Leonidovich)
1890-1960 ...... **CLC 7, 10, 18, 63; DA;**
PC 6; WLC
See also CA 127; 116; MTCW

Patchen, Kenneth 1911-1972 ... **CLC 1, 2, 18**
See also CA 1-4R; 33-36R; CANR 3, 35;
DLB 16, 48; MTCW

Pater, Walter (Horatio)
1839-1894 .... **NCLC 7**
See also CDBLB 1832-1890; DLB 57

Paterson, A(ndrew) B(arton)
1864-1941 .... **TCLC 32**

Paterson, Katherine (Womeldorf)
1932-.................... **CLC 12, 30**
See also AAYA 1; CA 21-24R; CANR 28;
CLR 7; DLB 52; JRDA; MAICYA;
MTCW; SATA 13, 53

Patmore, Coventry Kersey Dighton
1823-1896 .... **NCLC 9**
See also DLB 35, 98

Paton, Alan (Stewart)
1903-1988 ...... **CLC 4, 10, 25, 55; DA;**
WLC
See also CA 13-16; 125; CANR 22; CAP 1;
MTCW; SATA 11, 56

Paton Walsh, Gillian 1937-
See Walsh, Jill Paton
See also CANR 38; JRDA; MAICYA;
SAAS 3; SATA 4, 72

Paulding, James Kirke 1778-1860.. **NCLC 2**
See also DLB 3, 59, 74

Paulin, Thomas Neilson 1949-
See Paulin, Tom
See also CA 123; 128

Paulin, Tom.................... **CLC 37**
See also Paulin, Thomas Neilson
See also DLB 40

Paustovsky, Konstantin (Georgievich)
1892-1968 .... **CLC 40**
See also CA 93-96; 25-28R

Pavese, Cesare 1908-1950 .... **TCLC 3**
See also CA 104; DLB 128

Pavic, Milorad 1929-.............. **CLC 60**
See also CA 136

Payne, Alan
See Jakes, John (William)

Paz, Gil
See Lugones, Leopoldo

Paz, Octavio
1914- .... **CLC 3, 4, 6, 10, 19, 51, 65;**
DA; HLC; PC 1; WLC
See also CA 73-76; CANR 32; DLBY 90;
HW; MTCW

Peacock, Molly 1947-............. **CLC 60**
See also CA 103; DLB 120

Peacock, Thomas Love
1785-1866 .... **NCLC 22**
See also DLB 96, 116

Peake, Mervyn 1911-1968 .... **CLC 7, 54**
See also CA 5-8R; 25-28R; CANR 3;
DLB 15; MTCW; SATA 23

Pearce, Philippa .... **CLC 21**
See also Christie, (Ann) Philippa
See also CLR 9; MAICYA; SATA 1, 67

Pearl, Eric
See Elman, Richard

Pearson, T(homas) R(eid) 1956- .... **CLC 39**
See also CA 120; 130

Peck, Dale 1968(?)- .... **CLC 81**

Peck, John 1941-................. **CLC 3**
See also CA 49-52; CANR 3

Peck, Richard (Wayne) 1934-...... **CLC 21**
See also AAYA 1; CA 85-88; CANR 19,
38; CLR 15; JRDA; MAICYA; SAAS 2;
SATA 18, 55

Peck, Robert Newton 1928-.... **CLC 17; DA**
See also AAYA 3; CA 81-84; CANR 31;
JRDA; MAICYA; SAAS 1; SATA 21, 62

Peckinpah, (David) Sam(uel)
1925-1984 .... **CLC 20**
See also CA 109; 114

Pedersen, Knut 1859-1952
See Hamsun, Knut
See also CA 104; 119; MTCW

Peeslake, Gaffer
See Durrell, Lawrence (George)

Peguy, Charles Pierre
1873-1914 .... **TCLC 10**
See also CA 107

Pena, Ramon del Valle y
See Valle-Inclan, Ramon (Maria) del

Pendennis, Arthur Esquir
See Thackeray, William Makepeace

Penn, William 1644-1718........... **LC 25**
See also DLB 24

Pepys, Samuel
1633-1703 .... **LC 11; DA; WLC**
See also CDBLB 1660-1789; DLB 101

Percy, Walker
1916-1990 .... **CLC 2, 3, 6, 8, 14, 18, 47,**
65
See also CA 1-4R; 131; CANR 1, 23;
DLB 2; DLBY 80, 90; MTCW

Perec, Georges 1936-1982 .... **CLC 56**
See also CA 141; DLB 83

Pereda (y Sanchez de Porrua), Jose Maria de
1833-1906 .... **TCLC 16**
See also CA 117

Pereda y Porrua, Jose Maria de
See Pereda (y Sanchez de Porrua), Jose
Maria de

Peregoy, George Weems
See Mencken, H(enry) L(ouis)

Police, The
See Copeland, Stewart (Armstrong);
Summers, Andrew James; Sumner,
Gordon Matthew

Pollitt, Katha 1949- .... CLC 28
See also CA 120; 122; MTCW

Pollock, (Mary) Sharon 1936- ...... CLC 50
See also CA 141; DLB 60

Pomerance, Bernard 1940- .... CLC 13
See also CA 101

Ponge, Francis (Jean Gaston Alfred)
1899-1988 .... CLC 6, 18
See also CA 85-88; 126; CANR 40

Pontoppidan, Henrik 1857-1943 ... TCLC 29

Poole, Josephine .... CLC 17
See also Helyar, Jane Penelope Josephine
See also SAAS 2; SATA 5

Popa, Vasko 1922- .... CLC 19
See also CA 112

Pope, Alexander
1688-1744 .... LC 3; DA; WLC
See also CDBLB 1660-1789; DLB 95, 101

Porter, Connie (Rose) 1959(?)- ..... CLC 70
See also BW 2; CA 142

Porter, Gene(va Grace) Stratton
1863(?)-1924 .... TCLC 21
See also CA 112

Porter, Katherine Anne
1890-1980 ...... CLC 1, 3, 7, 10, 13, 15,
27; DA; SSC 4
See also AITN 2; CA 1-4R; 101; CANR 1;
DLB 4, 9, 102; DLBY 80; MTCW;
SATA 23, 39

Porter, Peter (Neville Frederick)
1929- .... CLC 5, 13, 33
See also CA 85-88; DLB 40

Porter, William Sydney 1862-1910
See Henry, O.
See also CA 104; 131; CDALB 1865-1917;
DA; DLB 12, 78, 79; MTCW; YABC 2

Portillo (y Pacheco), Jose Lopez
See Lopez Portillo (y Pacheco), Jose

Post, Melville Davisson
1869-1930 .... TCLC 39
See also CA 110

Potok, Chaim 1929- .... CLC 2, 7, 14, 26
See also AITN 1, 2; CA 17-20R; CANR 19,
35; DLB 28; MTCW; SATA 33

Potter, Beatrice
See Webb, (Martha) Beatrice (Potter)
See also MAICYA

Potter, Dennis (Christopher George)
1935-1994 .... CLC 58
See also CA 107; 145; CANR 33; MTCW

Pound, Ezra (Weston Loomis)
1885-1972 ...... CLC 1, 2, 3, 4, 5, 7, 10,
13, 18, 34, 48, 50; DA; PC 4; WLC
See also CA 5-8R; 37-40R; CANR 40;
CDALB 1917-1929; DLB 4, 45, 63;
MTCW

Povod, Reinaldo 1959- .... CLC 44
See also CA 136

Powell, Anthony (Dymoke)
1905- .... CLC 1, 3, 7, 9, 10, 31
See also CA 1-4R; CANR 1, 32;
CDBLB 1945-1960; DLB 15; MTCW

Powell, Dawn 1897-1965 .... CLC 66
See also CA 5-8R

Powell, Padgett 1952- .... CLC 34
See also CA 126

Powers, J(ames) F(arl)
1917- .... CLC 1, 4, 8, 57; SSC 4
See also CA 1-4R; CANR 2; DLB 130;
MTCW

Powers, John J(ames) 1945-
See Powers, John R.
See also CA 69-72

Powers, John R. .... CLC 66
See also Powers, John J(ames)

Pownall, David 1938- .... CLC 10
See also CA 89-92; CAAS 18; DLB 14

Powys, John Cowper
1872-1963 .... CLC 7, 9, 15, 46
See also CA 85-88; DLB 15; MTCW

Powys, T(heodore) F(rancis)
1875-1953 .... TCLC 9
See also CA 106; DLB 36

Prager, Emily 1952- .... CLC 56

Pratt, E(dwin) J(ohn)
1883(?)-1964 .... CLC 19
See also CA 141; 93-96; DLB 92

Premchand .... TCLC 21
See also Srivastava, Dhanpat Rai

Preussler, Otfried 1923- .... CLC 17
See also CA 77-80; SATA 24

Prevert, Jacques (Henri Marie)
1900-1977 .... CLC 15
See also CA 77-80; 69-72; CANR 29;
MTCW; SATA 30

Prevost, Abbe (Antoine Francois)
1697-1763 .... LC 1

Price, (Edward) Reynolds
1933- .... CLC 3, 6, 13, 43, 50, 63
See also CA 1-4R; CANR 1, 37; DLB 2

Price, Richard 1949- .... CLC 6, 12
See also CA 49-52; CANR 3; DLBY 81

Prichard, Katharine Susannah
1883-1969 .... CLC 46
See also CA 11-12; CANR 33; CAP 1;
MTCW; SATA 66

Priestley, J(ohn) B(oynton)
1894-1984 .... CLC 2, 5, 9, 34
See also CA 9-12R; 113; CANR 33;
CDBLB 1914-1945; DLB 10, 34, 77, 100,
139; DLBY 84; MTCW

Prince 1958(?)- .... CLC 35

Prince, F(rank) T(empleton) 1912- .. CLC 22
See also CA 101; CANR 43; DLB 20

Prince Kropotkin
See Kropotkin, Peter (Aleksieevich)

Prior, Matthew 1664-1721.......... LC 4
See also DLB 95

Pritchard, William H(arrison)
1932- .... CLC 34
See also CA 65-68; CANR 23; DLB 111

Pritchett, V(ictor) S(awdon)
1900- .... CLC 5, 13, 15, 41; SSC 14
See also CA 61-64; CANR 31; DLB 15,
139; MTCW

Private 19022
See Manning, Frederic

Probst, Mark 1925- .... CLC 59
See also CA 130

Prokosch, Frederic 1908-1989.... CLC 4, 48
See also CA 73-76; 128; DLB 48

Prophet, The
See Dreiser, Theodore (Herman Albert)

Prose, Francine 1947- .... CLC 45
See also CA 109; 112

Proudhon
See Cunha, Euclides (Rodrigues Pimenta) da

Proulx, E. Annie 1935- .... CLC 81

**Proust, (Valentin-Louis-George-Eugene-)
Marcel**
1871-1922 ... TCLC 7, 13, 33; DA; WLC
See also CA 104; 120; DLB 65; MTCW

Prowler, Harley
See Masters, Edgar Lee

Prus, Boleslaw 1845-1912 .... TCLC 48

Pryor, Richard (Franklin Lenox Thomas)
1940- .... CLC 26
See also CA 122

Przybyszewski, Stanislaw
1868-1927 .... TCLC 36
See also DLB 66

Pteleon
See Grieve, C(hristopher) M(urray)

Puckett, Lute
See Masters, Edgar Lee

Puig, Manuel
1932-1990 ... CLC 3, 5, 10, 28, 65; HLC
See also CA 45-48; CANR 2, 32; DLB 113;
HW; MTCW

Purdy, Al(fred Wellington)
1918- .... CLC 3, 6, 14, 50
See also CA 81-84; CAAS 17; CANR 42;
DLB 88

Purdy, James (Amos)
1923- .... CLC 2, 4, 10, 28, 52
See also CA 33-36R; CAAS 1; CANR 19;
DLB 2; MTCW

Pure, Simon
See Swinnerton, Frank Arthur

Pushkin, Alexander (Sergeyevich)
1799-1837 .... NCLC 3, 27; DA; PC 10;
WLC
See also SATA 61

P'u Sung-ling 1640-1715 .... LC 3

Putnam, Arthur Lee
See Alger, Horatio, Jr.

Puzo, Mario 1920- .... CLC 1, 2, 6, 36
See also CA 65-68; CANR 4, 42; DLB 6;
MTCW

Pym, Barbara (Mary Crampton)
1913-1980 .... CLC 13, 19, 37
See also CA 13-14; 97-100; CANR 13, 34;
CAP 1; DLB 14; DLBY 87; MTCW

Pynchon, Thomas (Ruggles, Jr.)
1937- ..... **CLC 2, 3, 6, 9, 11, 18, 33, 62, 72; DA; SSC 14; WLC**
See also BEST 90:2; CA 17-20R; CANR 22; DLB 2; MTCW

Qian Zhongshu
See Ch'ien Chung-shu

Qroll
See Dagerman, Stig (Halvard)

Quarrington, Paul (Lewis) 1953- .... **CLC 65**
See also CA 129

Quasimodo, Salvatore 1901-1968 ... **CLC 10**
See also CA 13-16; 25-28R; CAP 1; DLB 114; MTCW

Queen, Ellery. .... **CLC 3, 11**
See also Dannay, Frederic; Davidson, Avram; Lee, Manfred B(ennington); Sturgeon, Theodore (Hamilton); Vance, John Holbrook

Queen, Ellery, Jr.
See Dannay, Frederic; Lee, Manfred B(ennington)

Queneau, Raymond
1903-1976 .... **CLC 2, 5, 10, 42**
See also CA 77-80; 69-72; CANR 32; DLB 72; MTCW

Quevedo, Francisco de 1580-1645.... **LC 23**

Quiller-Couch, Arthur Thomas
1863-1944 .... **TCLC 53**
See also CA 118; DLB 135

Quin, Ann (Marie) 1936-1973 .... **CLC 6**
See also CA 9-12R; 45-48; DLB 14

Quinn, Martin
See Smith, Martin Cruz

Quinn, Simon
See Smith, Martin Cruz

Quiroga, Horacio (Sylvestre)
1878-1937 .... **TCLC 20; HLC**
See also CA 117; 131; HW; MTCW

Quoirez, Francoise 1935- .... **CLC 9**
See also Sagan, Francoise
See also CA 49-52; CANR 6, 39; MTCW

Raabe, Wilhelm 1831-1910 .... **TCLC 45**
See also DLB 129

Rabe, David (William) 1940-... **CLC 4, 8, 33**
See also CA 85-88; CABS 3; DLB 7

Rabelais, Francois
1483-1553 .... **LC 5; DA; WLC**

Rabinovitch, Sholem 1859-1916
See Aleichem, Sholom
See also CA 104

Radcliffe, Ann (Ward) 1764-1823 .. **NCLC 6**
See also DLB 39

Radiguet, Raymond 1903-1923 .... **TCLC 29**
See also DLB 65

Radnoti, Miklos 1909-1944 .... **TCLC 16**
See also CA 118

Rado, James 1939- .... **CLC 17**
See also CA 105

Radvanyi, Netty 1900-1983
See Seghers, Anna
See also CA 85-88; 110

Rae, Ben
See Griffiths, Trevor

Raeburn, John (Hay) 1941-........ **CLC 34**
See also CA 57-60

Ragni, Gerome 1942-1991 .... **CLC 17**
See also CA 105; 134

Rahv, Philip 1908-1973 .... **CLC 24**
See also Greenberg, Ivan
See also DLB 137

Raine, Craig 1944- .... **CLC 32**
See also CA 108; CANR 29; DLB 40

Raine, Kathleen (Jessie) 1908- ... **CLC 7, 45**
See also CA 85-88; DLB 20; MTCW

Rainis, Janis 1865-1929 .... **TCLC 29**

Rakosi, Carl .... **CLC 47**
See also Rawley, Callman
See also CAAS 5

Raleigh, Richard
See Lovecraft, H(oward) P(hillips)

Rallentando, H. P.
See Sayers, Dorothy L(eigh)

Ramal, Walter
See de la Mare, Walter (John)

Ramon, Juan
See Jimenez (Mantecon), Juan Ramon

Ramos, Graciliano 1892-1953 ..... **TCLC 32**

Rampersad, Arnold 1941-.......... **CLC 44**
See also BW 2; CA 127; 133; DLB 111

Rampling, Anne
See Rice, Anne

Ramuz, Charles-Ferdinand
1878-1947 .... **TCLC 33**

Rand, Ayn
1905-1982 ...... **CLC 3, 30, 44, 79; DA; WLC**
See also AAYA 10; CA 13-16R; 105; CANR 27; MTCW

Randall, Dudley (Felker)
1914- .... **CLC 1; BLC**
See also BW 1; CA 25-28R; CANR 23; DLB 41

Randall, Robert
See Silverberg, Robert

Ranger, Ken
See Creasey, John

Ransom, John Crowe
1888-1974 .... **CLC 2, 4, 5, 11, 24**
See also CA 5-8R; 49-52; CANR 6, 34; DLB 45, 63; MTCW

Rao, Raja 1909- .... **CLC 25, 56**
See also CA 73-76; MTCW

Raphael, Frederic (Michael)
1931- .... **CLC 2, 14**
See also CA 1-4R; CANR 1; DLB 14

Ratcliffe, James P.
See Mencken, H(enry) L(ouis)

Rathbone, Julian 1935- .... **CLC 41**
See also CA 101; CANR 34

Rattigan, Terence (Mervyn)
1911-1977 .... **CLC 7**
See also CA 85-88; 73-76; CDBLB 1945-1960; DLB 13; MTCW

Ratushinskaya, Irina 1954- .... **CLC 54**
See also CA 129

Raven, Simon (Arthur Noel)
1927- .... **CLC 14**
See also CA 81-84

Rawley, Callman 1903-
See Rakosi, Carl
See also CA 21-24R; CANR 12, 32

Rawlings, Marjorie Kinnan
1896-1953 .... **TCLC 4**
See also CA 104; 137; DLB 9, 22, 102; JRDA; MAICYA; YABC 1

Ray, Satyajit 1921-1992........ **CLC 16, 76**
See also CA 114; 137

Read, Herbert Edward 1893-1968.... **CLC 4**
See also CA 85-88; 25-28R; DLB 20

Read, Piers Paul 1941- ...... **CLC 4, 10, 25**
See also CA 21-24R; CANR 38; DLB 14; SATA 21

Reade, Charles 1814-1884 .... **NCLC 2**
See also DLB 21

Reade, Hamish
See Gray, Simon (James Holliday)

Reading, Peter 1946- .... **CLC 47**
See also CA 103; DLB 40

Reaney, James 1926- .... **CLC 13**
See also CA 41-44R; CAAS 15; CANR 42; DLB 68; SATA 43

Rebreanu, Liviu 1885-1944 .... **TCLC 28**

Rechy, John (Francisco)
1934- .... **CLC 1, 7, 14, 18; HLC**
See also CA 5-8R; CAAS 4; CANR 6, 32; DLB 122; DLBY 82; HW

Redcam, Tom 1870-1933 .... **TCLC 25**

Reddin, Keith. .... **CLC 67**

Redgrove, Peter (William)
1932- .... **CLC 6, 41**
See also CA 1-4R; CANR 3, 39; DLB 40

Redmon, Anne .... **CLC 22**
See also Nightingale, Anne Redmon
See also DLBY 86

Reed, Eliot
See Ambler, Eric

Reed, Ishmael
1938- ... **CLC 2, 3, 5, 6, 13, 32, 60; BLC**
See also BW 2; CA 21-24R; CANR 25; DLB 2, 5, 33; DLBD 8; MTCW

Reed, John (Silas) 1887-1920 ...... **TCLC 9**
See also CA 106

Reed, Lou. .... **CLC 21**
See also Firbank, Louis

Reeve, Clara 1729-1807 .... **NCLC 19**
See also DLB 39

Reich, Wilhelm 1897-1957........ **TCLC 57**

Reid, Christopher (John) 1949-..... **CLC 33**
See also CA 140; DLB 40

Reid, Desmond
See Moorcock, Michael (John)

Reid Banks, Lynne 1929-
See Banks, Lynne Reid
See also CA 1-4R; CANR 6, 22, 38; CLR 24; JRDA; MAICYA; SATA 22, 75

Reilly, William K.
See Creasey, John

Reiner, Max
See Caldwell, (Janet Miriam) Taylor
(Holland)

Reis, Ricardo
See Pessoa, Fernando (Antonio Nogueira)

Remarque, Erich Maria
1898-1970 . . . . **CLC 21; DA**
See also CA 77-80; 29-32R; DLB 56;
MTCW

Remizov, A.
See Remizov, Aleksei (Mikhailovich)

Remizov, A. M.
See Remizov, Aleksei (Mikhailovich)

Remizov, Aleksei (Mikhailovich)
1877-1957 . . . . **TCLC 27**
See also CA 125; 133

Renan, Joseph Ernest
1823-1892 . . . . **NCLC 26**

Renard, Jules 1864-1910 . . . . **TCLC 17**
See also CA 117

Renault, Mary . . . . **CLC 3, 11, 17**
See also Challans, Mary
See also DLBY 83

Rendell, Ruth (Barbara) 1930- . . **CLC 28, 48**
See also Vine, Barbara
See also CA 109; CANR 32; DLB 87;
MTCW

Renoir, Jean 1894-1979 . . . . **CLC 20**
See also CA 129; 85-88

Resnais, Alain 1922- . . . . **CLC 16**

Reverdy, Pierre 1889-1960 . . . . **CLC 53**
See also CA 97-100; 89-92

Rexroth, Kenneth
1905-1982 . . . . . . **CLC 1, 2, 6, 11, 22, 49**
See also CA 5-8R; 107; CANR 14, 34;
CDALB 1941-1968; DLB 16, 48;
DLBY 82; MTCW

Reyes, Alfonso 1889-1959 . . . . **TCLC 33**
See also CA 131; HW

Reyes y Basoalto, Ricardo Eliecer Neftali
See Neruda, Pablo

Reymont, Wladyslaw (Stanislaw)
1868(?)-1925 . . . . **TCLC 5**
See also CA 104

Reynolds, Jonathan 1942- . . . . **CLC 6, 38**
See also CA 65-68; CANR 28

Reynolds, Joshua 1723-1792 . . . . **LC 15**
See also DLB 104

Reynolds, Michael Shane 1937- . . . . **CLC 44**
See also CA 65-68; CANR 9

Reznikoff, Charles 1894-1976 . . . . **CLC 9**
See also CA 33-36; 61-64; CAP 2; DLB 28,
45

Rezzori (d'Arezzo), Gregor von
1914- . . . . **CLC 25**
See also CA 122; 136

Rhine, Richard
See Silverstein, Alvin

Rhodes, Eugene Manlove
1869-1934 . . . . **TCLC 53**

R'hoone
See Balzac, Honore de

Rhys, Jean
1890(?)-1979 . . . . **CLC 2, 4, 6, 14, 19, 51**
See also CA 25-28R; 85-88; CANR 35;
CDBLB 1945-1960; DLB 36, 117; MTCW

Ribeiro, Darcy 1922- . . . . **CLC 34**
See also CA 33-36R

Ribeiro, Joao Ubaldo (Osorio Pimentel)
1941- . . . . **CLC 10, 67**
See also CA 81-84

Ribman, Ronald (Burt) 1932- . . . . . . **CLC 7**
See also CA 21-24R

Ricci, Nino 1959- . . . . **CLC 70**
See also CA 137

Rice, Anne 1941- . . . . **CLC 41**
See also AAYA 9; BEST 89:2; CA 65-68;
CANR 12, 36

Rice, Elmer (Leopold)
1892-1967 . . . . **CLC 7, 49**
See also CA 21-22; 25-28R; CAP 2; DLB 4,
7; MTCW

Rice, Tim 1944- . . . . **CLC 21**
See also CA 103

Rich, Adrienne (Cecile)
1929- . . . . **CLC 3, 6, 7, 11, 18, 36, 73, 76;
PC 5**
See also CA 9-12R; CANR 20; DLB 5, 67;
MTCW

Rich, Barbara
See Graves, Robert (von Ranke)

Rich, Robert
See Trumbo, Dalton

Richards, David Adams 1950- . . . . . . **CLC 59**
See also CA 93-96; DLB 53

Richards, I(vor) A(rmstrong)
1893-1979 . . . . **CLC 14, 24**
See also CA 41-44R; 89-92; CANR 34;
DLB 27

Richardson, Anne
See Roiphe, Anne (Richardson)

Richardson, Dorothy Miller
1873-1957 . . . . **TCLC 3**
See also CA 104; DLB 36

Richardson, Ethel Florence (Lindesay)
1870-1946
See Richardson, Henry Handel
See also CA 105

Richardson, Henry Handel . . . . **TCLC 4**
See also Richardson, Ethel Florence
(Lindesay)

Richardson, Samuel
1689-1761 . . . . **LC 1; DA; WLC**
See also CDBLB 1660-1789; DLB 39

Richler, Mordecai
1931- . . . . **CLC 3, 5, 9, 13, 18, 46, 70**
See also AITN 1; CA 65-68; CANR 31;
CLR 17; DLB 53; MAICYA; MTCW;
SATA 27, 44

Richter, Conrad (Michael)
1890-1968 . . . . **CLC 30**
See also CA 5-8R; 25-28R; CANR 23;
DLB 9; MTCW; SATA 3

Riddell, J. H. 1832-1906 . . . . **TCLC 40**

Riding, Laura . . . . **CLC 3, 7**
See also Jackson, Laura (Riding)

Riefenstahl, Berta Helene Amalia 1902-
See Riefenstahl, Leni
See also CA 108

Riefenstahl, Leni . . . . **CLC 16**
See also Riefenstahl, Berta Helene Amalia

Riffe, Ernest
See Bergman, (Ernst) Ingmar

Riggs, (Rolla) Lynn 1899-1954 . . . . **TCLC 56**
See also CA 144

Riley, James Whitcomb
1849-1916 . . . . **TCLC 51**
See also CA 118; 137; MAICYA; SATA 17

Riley, Tex
See Creasey, John

Rilke, Rainer Maria
1875-1926 . . . . **TCLC 1, 6, 19; PC 2**
See also CA 104; 132; DLB 81; MTCW

Rimbaud, (Jean Nicolas) Arthur
1854-1891 . . . . . **NCLC 4, 35; DA; PC 3;
WLC**

Rinehart, Mary Roberts
1876-1958 . . . . **TCLC 52**
See also CA 108

Ringmaster, The
See Mencken, H(enry) L(ouis)

Ringwood, Gwen(dolyn Margaret) Pharis
1910-1984 . . . . **CLC 48**
See also CA 112; DLB 88

Rio, Michel 19(?)- . . . . **CLC 43**

Ritsos, Giannes
See Ritsos, Yannis

Ritsos, Yannis 1909-1990 . . . . . **CLC 6, 13, 31**
See also CA 77-80; 133; CANR 39; MTCW

Ritter, Erika 1948(?)- . . . . **CLC 52**

Rivera, Jose Eustasio 1889-1928 . . . **TCLC 35**
See also HW

Rivers, Conrad Kent 1933-1968 . . . . . . **CLC 1**
See also BW 1; CA 85-88; DLB 41

Rivers, Elfrida
See Bradley, Marion Zimmer

Riverside, John
See Heinlein, Robert A(nson)

Rizal, Jose 1861-1896 . . . . **NCLC 27**

Roa Bastos, Augusto (Antonio)
1917- . . . . **CLC 45; HLC**
See also CA 131; DLB 113; HW

Robbe-Grillet, Alain
1922- . . . . . . **CLC 1, 2, 4, 6, 8, 10, 14, 43**
See also CA 9-12R; CANR 33; DLB 83;
MTCW

Robbins, Harold 1916- . . . . **CLC 5**
See also CA 73-76; CANR 26; MTCW

Robbins, Thomas Eugene 1936-
See Robbins, Tom
See also CA 81-84; CANR 29; MTCW

Robbins, Tom . . . . **CLC 9, 32, 64**
See also Robbins, Thomas Eugene
See also BEST 90:3; DLBY 80

Robbins, Trina 1938- . . . . **CLC 21**
See also CA 128

Roberts, Charles G(eorge) D(ouglas)
1860-1943 . . . . **TCLC 8**
See also CA 105; CLR 33; DLB 92;
SATA 29

Rudkin, (James) David 1936- ...... **CLC 14**
See also CA 89-92; DLB 13

Rudnik, Raphael 1933-............. **CLC 7**
See also CA 29-32R

Ruffian, M.
See Hasek, Jaroslav (Matej Frantisek)

Ruiz, Jose Martinez .... **CLC 11**
See also Martinez Ruiz, Jose

Rukeyser, Muriel
1913-1980 .... **CLC 6, 10, 15, 27**
See also CA 5-8R; 93-96; CANR 26;
DLB 48; MTCW; SATA 22

Rule, Jane (Vance) 1931-.......... **CLC 27**
See also CA 25-28R; CAAS 18; CANR 12;
DLB 60

Rulfo, Juan 1918-1986.... **CLC 8, 80; HLC**
See also CA 85-88; 118; CANR 26;
DLB 113; HW; MTCW

Runeberg, Johan 1804-1877...... **NCLC 41**

Runyon, (Alfred) Damon
1884(?)-1946 .... **TCLC 10**
See also CA 107; DLB 11, 86

Rush, Norman 1933-.............. **CLC 44**
See also CA 121; 126

Rushdie, (Ahmed) Salman
1947- .... **CLC 23, 31, 55**
See also BEST 89:3; CA 108; 111;
CANR 33; MTCW

Rushforth, Peter (Scott) 1945- ..... **CLC 19**
See also CA 101

Ruskin, John 1819-1900......... **TCLC 20**
See also CA 114; 129; CDBLB 1832-1890;
DLB 55; SATA 24

Russ, Joanna 1937-.............. **CLC 15**
See also CA 25-28R; CANR 11, 31; DLB 8;
MTCW

Russell, (Henry) Ken(neth Alfred)
1927- .... **CLC 16**
See also CA 105

Russell, Willy 1947-.............. **CLC 60**

Rutherford, Mark .... **TCLC 25**
See also White, William Hale
See also DLB 18

Ryan, Cornelius (John) 1920-1974 ... **CLC 7**
See also CA 69-72; 53-56; CANR 38

Ryan, Michael 1946- .... **CLC 65**
See also CA 49-52; DLBY 82

Rybakov, Anatoli (Naumovich)
1911- .... **CLC 23, 53**
See also CA 126; 135; SATA 79

Ryder, Jonathan
See Ludlum, Robert

Ryga, George 1932-1987 .... **CLC 14**
See also CA 101; 124; CANR 43; DLB 60

S. S.
See Sassoon, Siegfried (Lorraine)

Saba, Umberto 1883-1957 .... **TCLC 33**
See also CA 144; DLB 114

Sabatini, Rafael 1875-1950 .... **TCLC 47**

Sabato, Ernesto (R.)
1911- .... **CLC 10, 23; HLC**
See also CA 97-100; CANR 32; HW;
MTCW

Sacastru, Martin
See Bioy Casares, Adolfo

Sacher-Masoch, Leopold von
1836(?)-1895 .... **NCLC 31**

Sachs, Marilyn (Stickle) 1927- ..... **CLC 35**
See also AAYA 2; CA 17-20R; CANR 13;
CLR 2; JRDA; MAICYA; SAAS 2;
SATA 3, 68

Sachs, Nelly 1891-1970 .... **CLC 14**
See also CA 17-18; 25-28R; CAP 2

Sackler, Howard (Oliver)
1929-1982 .... **CLC 14**
See also CA 61-64; 108; CANR 30; DLB 7

Sacks, Oliver (Wolf) 1933- .... **CLC 67**
See also CA 53-56; CANR 28; MTCW

Sade, Donatien Alphonse Francois Comte
1740-1814 .... **NCLC 47**

Sadoff, Ira 1945-................. **CLC 9**
See also CA 53-56; CANR 5, 21; DLB 120

Saetone
See Camus, Albert

Safire, William 1929-............. **CLC 10**
See also CA 17-20R; CANR 31

Sagan, Carl (Edward) 1934-....... **CLC 30**
See also AAYA 2; CA 25-28R; CANR 11,
36; MTCW; SATA 58

Sagan, Francoise .... **CLC 3, 6, 9, 17, 36**
See also Quoirez, Francoise
See also DLB 83

Sahgal, Nayantara (Pandit) 1927-... **CLC 41**
See also CA 9-12R; CANR 11

Saint, H(arry) F. 1941- .... **CLC 50**
See also CA 127

St. Aubin de Teran, Lisa 1953-
See Teran, Lisa St. Aubin de
See also CA 118; 126

Sainte-Beuve, Charles Augustin
1804-1869 .... **NCLC 5**

Saint-Exupery, Antoine (Jean Baptiste Marie Roger) de
1900-1944 .... **TCLC 2, 56; WLC**
See also CA 108; 132; CLR 10; DLB 72;
MAICYA; MTCW; SATA 20

St. John, David
See Hunt, E(verette) Howard, Jr.

Saint-John Perse
See Leger, (Marie-Rene Auguste) Alexis
Saint-Leger

Saintsbury, George (Edward Bateman)
1845-1933 .... **TCLC 31**
See also DLB 57

Sait Faik .... **TCLC 23**
See also Abasiyanik, Sait Faik

Saki .... **TCLC 3; SSC 12**
See also Munro, H(ector) H(ugh)

Sala, George Augustus .... **NCLC 46**

Salama, Hannu 1936-............. **CLC 18**

Salamanca, J(ack) R(ichard)
1922- .... **CLC 4, 15**
See also CA 25-28R

Sale, J. Kirkpatrick
See Sale, Kirkpatrick

Sale, Kirkpatrick 1937- .... **CLC 68**
See also CA 13-16R; CANR 10

Salinas (y Serrano), Pedro
1891(?)-1951 .... **TCLC 17**
See also CA 117; DLB 134

Salinger, J(erome) D(avid)
1919- ...... **CLC 1, 3, 8, 12, 55, 56; DA;
SSC 2; WLC**
See also AAYA 2; CA 5-8R; CANR 39;
CDALB 1941-1968; CLR 18; DLB 2, 102;
MAICYA; MTCW; SATA 67

Salisbury, John
See Caute, David

Salter, James 1925- .... **CLC 7, 52, 59**
See also CA 73-76; DLB 130

Saltus, Edgar (Everton)
1855-1921 .... **TCLC 8**
See also CA 105

Saltykov, Mikhail Evgrafovich
1826-1889 .... **NCLC 16**

Samarakis, Antonis 1919- .... **CLC 5**
See also CA 25-28R; CAAS 16; CANR 36

Sanchez, Florencio 1875-1910..... **TCLC 37**
See also HW

Sanchez, Luis Rafael 1936-........ **CLC 23**
See also CA 128; HW

Sanchez, Sonia 1934-... **CLC 5; BLC; PC 9**
See also BW 2; CA 33-36R; CANR 24;
CLR 18; DLB 41; DLBD 8; MAICYA;
MTCW; SATA 22

Sand, George
1804-1876 ...... **NCLC 2, 42; DA; WLC**
See also DLB 119

Sandburg, Carl (August)
1878-1967 .... **CLC 1, 4, 10, 15, 35; DA;
PC 2; WLC**
See also CA 5-8R; 25-28R; CANR 35;
CDALB 1865-1917; DLB 17, 54;
MAICYA; MTCW; SATA 8

Sandburg, Charles
See Sandburg, Carl (August)

Sandburg, Charles A.
See Sandburg, Carl (August)

Sanders, (James) Ed(ward) 1939- ... **CLC 53**
See also CA 13-16R; CANR 13, 44;
DLB 16

Sanders, Lawrence 1920-.......... **CLC 41**
See also BEST 89:4; CA 81-84; CANR 33;
MTCW

Sanders, Noah
See Blount, Roy (Alton), Jr.

Sanders, Winston P.
See Anderson, Poul (William)

Sandoz, Mari(e Susette)
1896-1966 .... **CLC 28**
See also CA 1-4R; 25-28R; CANR 17;
DLB 9; MTCW; SATA 5

Saner, Reg(inald Anthony) 1931- .... **CLC 9**
See also CA 65-68

Sannazaro, Jacopo 1456(?)-1530 ...... **LC 8**

Sansom, William 1912-1976....... **CLC 2, 6**
See also CA 5-8R; 65-68; CANR 42;
DLB 139; MTCW

Santayana, George 1863-1952..... **TCLC 40**
See also CA 115; DLB 54, 71

Santiago, Danny .... **CLC 33**
See also James, Daniel (Lewis); James,
Daniel (Lewis)
See also DLB 122

Santmyer, Helen Hoover
1895-1986 .... **CLC 33**
See also CA 1-4R; 118; CANR 15, 33;
DLBY 84; MTCW

Santos, Bienvenido N(uqui) 1911-... **CLC 22**
See also CA 101; CANR 19

Sapper .... **TCLC 44**
See also McNeile, Herman Cyril

Sappho fl. 6th cent. B.C.-... **CMLC 3; PC 5**

Sarduy, Severo 1937-1993 .... **CLC 6**
See also CA 89-92; 142; DLB 113; HW

Sargeson, Frank 1903-1982 .... **CLC 31**
See also CA 25-28R; 106; CANR 38

Sarmiento, Felix Ruben Garcia
See Dario, Ruben

Saroyan, William
1908-1981 ..... **CLC 1, 8, 10, 29, 34, 56;**
DA; WLC
See also CA 5-8R; 103; CANR 30; DLB 7,
9, 86; DLBY 81; MTCW; SATA 23, 24

Sarraute, Nathalie
1900- .... **CLC 1, 2, 4, 8, 10, 31, 80**
See also CA 9-12R; CANR 23; DLB 83;
MTCW

Sarton, (Eleanor) May
1912- .... **CLC 4, 14, 49**
See also CA 1-4R; CANR 1, 34; DLB 48;
DLBY 81; MTCW; SATA 36

Sartre, Jean-Paul
1905-1980 .... **CLC 1, 4, 7, 9, 13, 18, 24,**
44, 50, 52; DA; DC 3; WLC
See also CA 9-12R; 97-100; CANR 21;
DLB 72; MTCW

Sassoon, Siegfried (Lorraine)
1886-1967 .... **CLC 36**
See also CA 104; 25-28R; CANR 36;
DLB 20; MTCW

Satterfield, Charles
See Pohl, Frederik

Saul, John (W. III) 1942- .... **CLC 46**
See also AAYA 10; BEST 90:4; CA 81-84;
CANR 16, 40

Saunders, Caleb
See Heinlein, Robert A(nson)

Saura (Atares), Carlos 1932-....... **CLC 20**
See also CA 114; 131; HW

Sauser-Hall, Frederic 1887-1961.... **CLC 18**
See also CA 102; 93-96; CANR 36; MTCW

Saussure, Ferdinand de
1857-1913 .... **TCLC 49**

Savage, Catharine
See Brosman, Catharine Savage

Savage, Thomas 1915- .... **CLC 40**
See also CA 126; 132; CAAS 15

Savan, Glenn 19(?)- .... **CLC 50**

Sayers, Dorothy L(eigh)
1893-1957 .... **TCLC 2, 15**
See also CA 104; 119; CDBLB 1914-1945;
DLB 10, 36, 77, 100; MTCW

Sayers, Valerie 1952- .... **CLC 50**
See also CA 134

Sayles, John (Thomas)
1950- .... **CLC 7, 10, 14**
See also CA 57-60; CANR 41; DLB 44

Scammell, Michael .... **CLC 34**

Scannell, Vernon 1922- .... **CLC 49**
See also CA 5-8R; CANR 8, 24; DLB 27;
SATA 59

Scarlett, Susan
See Streatfeild, (Mary) Noel

Schaeffer, Susan Fromberg
1941- .... **CLC 6, 11, 22**
See also CA 49-52; CANR 18; DLB 28;
MTCW; SATA 22

Schary, Jill
See Robinson, Jill

Schell, Jonathan 1943-............ **CLC 35**
See also CA 73-76; CANR 12

Schelling, Friedrich Wilhelm Joseph von
1775-1854 .... **NCLC 30**
See also DLB 90

Schendel, Arthur van 1874-1946... **TCLC 56**

Scherer, Jean-Marie Maurice 1920-
See Rohmer, Eric
See also CA 110

Schevill, James (Erwin) 1920-....... **CLC 7**
See also CA 5-8R; CAAS 12

Schiller, Friedrich 1759-1805 .... **NCLC 39**
See also DLB 94

Schisgal, Murray (Joseph) 1926-..... **CLC 6**
See also CA 21-24R

Schlee, Ann 1934-................ **CLC 35**
See also CA 101; CANR 29; SATA 36, 44

Schlegel, August Wilhelm von
1767-1845 .... **NCLC 15**
See also DLB 94

Schlegel, Friedrich 1772-1829 .... **NCLC 45**
See also DLB 90

Schlegel, Johann Elias (von)
1719(?)-1749 .... **LC 5**

Schlesinger, Arthur M(eier), Jr.
1917- .... **CLC 84**
See also AITN 1; CA 1-4R; CANR 1, 28;
DLB 17; MTCW; SATA 61

Schmidt, Arno (Otto) 1914-1979.... **CLC 56**
See also CA 128; 109; DLB 69

Schmitz, Aron Hector 1861-1928
See Svevo, Italo
See also CA 104; 122; MTCW

Schnackenberg, Gjertrud 1953-..... **CLC 40**
See also CA 116; DLB 120

Schneider, Leonard Alfred 1925-1966
See Bruce, Lenny
See also CA 89-92

Schnitzler, Arthur
1862-1931 .... **TCLC 4; SSC 15**
See also CA 104; DLB 81, 118

Schor, Sandra (M.) 1932(?)-1990 ... **CLC 65**
See also CA 132

Schorer, Mark 1908-1977 .... **CLC 9**
See also CA 5-8R; 73-76; CANR 7;
DLB 103

Schrader, Paul (Joseph) 1946-...... **CLC 26**
See also CA 37-40R; CANR 41; DLB 44

Schreiner, Olive (Emilie Albertina)
1855-1920 .... **TCLC 9**
See also CA 105; DLB 18

Schulberg, Budd (Wilson)
1914- .... **CLC 7, 48**
See also CA 25-28R; CANR 19; DLB 6, 26,
28; DLBY 81

Schulz, Bruno
1892-1942 .... **TCLC 5, 51; SSC 13**
See also CA 115; 123

Schulz, Charles M(onroe) 1922- .... **CLC 12**
See also CA 9-12R; CANR 6; SATA 10

Schumacher, E(rnst) F(riedrich)
1911-1977 .... **CLC 80**
See also CA 81-84; 73-76; CANR 34

Schuyler, James Marcus
1923-1991 .... **CLC 5, 23**
See also CA 101; 134; DLB 5

Schwartz, Delmore (David)
1913-1966 ...... **CLC 2, 4, 10, 45; PC 8**
See also CA 17-18; 25-28R; CANR 35;
CAP 2; DLB 28, 48; MTCW

Schwartz, Ernst
See Ozu, Yasujiro

Schwartz, John Burnham 1965- .... **CLC 59**
See also CA 132

Schwartz, Lynne Sharon 1939-..... **CLC 31**
See also CA 103; CANR 44

Schwartz, Muriel A.
See Eliot, T(homas) S(tearns)

Schwarz-Bart, Andre 1928-....... **CLC 2, 4**
See also CA 89-92

Schwarz-Bart, Simone 1938-........ **CLC 7**
See also BW 2; CA 97-100

Schwob, (Mayer Andre) Marcel
1867-1905 .... **TCLC 20**
See also CA 117; DLB 123

Sciascia, Leonardo
1921-1989 .... **CLC 8, 9, 41**
See also CA 85-88; 130; CANR 35; MTCW

Scoppettone, Sandra 1936-........ **CLC 26**
See also AAYA 11; CA 5-8R; CANR 41;
SATA 9

Scorsese, Martin 1942- .... **CLC 20**
See also CA 110; 114

Scotland, Jay
See Jakes, John (William)

Scott, Duncan Campbell
1862-1947 .... **TCLC 6**
See also CA 104; DLB 92

Scott, Evelyn 1893-1963........... **CLC 43**
See also CA 104; 112; DLB 9, 48

Scott, F(rancis) R(eginald)
1899-1985 .... **CLC 22**
See also CA 101; 114; DLB 88

Scott, Frank
See Scott, F(rancis) R(eginald)

Scott, Joanna 1960- .... **CLC 50**
See also CA 126

Scott, Paul (Mark) 1920-1978.... **CLC 9, 60**
See also CA 81-84; 77-80; CANR 33;
DLB 14; MTCW

Scott, Walter
1771-1832 . . . . **NCLC 15; DA; WLC**
See also CDBLB 1789-1832; DLB 93, 107, 116, 144; YABC 2

Scribe, (Augustin) Eugene
1791-1861 . . . . **NCLC 16**

Scrum, R.
See Crumb, R(obert)

Scudery, Madeleine de 1607-1701 . . . . . **LC 2**

Scum
See Crumb, R(obert)

Scumbag, Little Bobby
See Crumb, R(obert)

Seabrook, John
See Hubbard, L(afayette) Ron(ald)

Sealy, I. Allan 1951- . . . . **CLC 55**

Search, Alexander
See Pessoa, Fernando (Antonio Nogueira)

Sebastian, Lee
See Silverberg, Robert

Sebastian Owl
See Thompson, Hunter S(tockton)

Sebestyen, Ouida 1924- . . . . **CLC 30**
See also AAYA 8; CA 107; CANR 40; CLR 17; JRDA; MAICYA; SAAS 10; SATA 39

Secundus, H. Scriblerus
See Fielding, Henry

Sedges, John
See Buck, Pearl S(ydenstricker)

Sedgwick, Catharine Maria
1789-1867 . . . . **NCLC 19**
See also DLB 1, 74

Seelye, John 1931- . . . . **CLC 7**

Seferiades, Giorgos Stylianou 1900-1971
See Seferis, George
See also CA 5-8R; 33-36R; CANR 5, 36; MTCW

Seferis, George . . . . **CLC 5, 11**
See also Seferiades, Giorgos Stylianou

Segal, Erich (Wolf) 1937- . . . . **CLC 3, 10**
See also BEST 89:1; CA 25-28R; CANR 20, 36; DLBY 86; MTCW

Seger, Bob 1945- . . . . **CLC 35**

Seghers, Anna . . . . **CLC 7**
See also Radvanyi, Netty
See also DLB 69

Seidel, Frederick (Lewis) 1936- . . . . **CLC 18**
See also CA 13-16R; CANR 8; DLBY 84

Seifert, Jaroslav 1901-1986 . . . . . **CLC 34, 44**
See also CA 127; MTCW

Sei Shonagon c. 966-1017(?) . . . . . . **CMLC 6**

Selby, Hubert, Jr. 1928- . . . . . **CLC 1, 2, 4, 8**
See also CA 13-16R; CANR 33; DLB 2

Selzer, Richard 1928- . . . . **CLC 74**
See also CA 65-68; CANR 14

Sembene, Ousmane
See Ousmane, Sembene

Senancour, Etienne Pivert de
1770-1846 . . . . **NCLC 16**
See also DLB 119

Sender, Ramon (Jose)
1902-1982 . . . . **CLC 8; HLC**
See also CA 5-8R; 105; CANR 8; HW; MTCW

Seneca, Lucius Annaeus
4B.C.-65 . . . . **CMLC 6**

Senghor, Leopold Sedar
1906- . . . . **CLC 54; BLC**
See also BW 2; CA 116; 125; MTCW

Serling, (Edward) Rod(man)
1924-1975 . . . . **CLC 30**
See also AITN 1; CA 65-68; 57-60; DLB 26

Serna, Ramon Gomez de la
See Gomez de la Serna, Ramon

Serpieres
See Guillevic, (Eugene)

Service, Robert
See Service, Robert W(illiam)
See also DLB 92

Service, Robert W(illiam)
1874(?)-1958 . . . . . . **TCLC 15; DA; WLC**
See also Service, Robert
See also CA 115; 140; SATA 20

Seth, Vikram 1952- . . . . **CLC 43**
See also CA 121; 127; DLB 120

Seton, Cynthia Propper
1926-1982 . . . . **CLC 27**
See also CA 5-8R; 108; CANR 7

Seton, Ernest (Evan) Thompson
1860-1946 . . . . **TCLC 31**
See also CA 109; DLB 92; JRDA; SATA 18

Seton-Thompson, Ernest
See Seton, Ernest (Evan) Thompson

Settle, Mary Lee 1918- . . . . **CLC 19, 61**
See also CA 89-92; CAAS 1; CANR 44; DLB 6

Seuphor, Michel
See Arp, Jean

Sevigne, Marie (de Rabutin-Chantal) Marquise de 1626-1696 . . . . **LC 11**

Sexton, Anne (Harvey)
1928-1974 . . . . **CLC 2, 4, 6, 8, 10, 15, 53; DA; PC 2; WLC**
See also CA 1-4R; 53-56; CABS 2; CANR 3, 36; CDALB 1941-1968; DLB 5; MTCW; SATA 10

Shaara, Michael (Joseph Jr.)
1929-1988 . . . . **CLC 15**
See also AITN 1; CA 102; DLBY 83

Shackleton, C. C.
See Aldiss, Brian W(ilson)

Shacochis, Bob . . . . **CLC 39**
See also Shacochis, Robert G.

Shacochis, Robert G. 1951-
See Shacochis, Bob
See also CA 119; 124

Shaffer, Anthony (Joshua) 1926- . . . . **CLC 19**
See also CA 110; 116; DLB 13

Shaffer, Peter (Levin)
1926- . . . . **CLC 5, 14, 18, 37, 60**
See also CA 25-28R; CANR 25; CDBLB 1960 to Present; DLB 13; MTCW

Shakey, Bernard
See Young, Neil

Shalamov, Varlam (Tikhonovich)
1907(?)-1982 . . . . **CLC 18**
See also CA 129; 105

Shamlu, Ahmad 1925- . . . . **CLC 10**

Shammas, Anton 1951- . . . . **CLC 55**

Shange, Ntozake
1948- . . . . **CLC 8, 25, 38, 74; BLC; DC 3**
See also AAYA 9; BW 2; CA 85-88; CABS 3; CANR 27; DLB 38; MTCW

Shanley, John Patrick 1950- . . . . **CLC 75**
See also CA 128; 133

Shapcott, Thomas William 1935- . . . **CLC 38**
See also CA 69-72

Shapiro, Jane . . . . **CLC 76**

Shapiro, Karl (Jay) 1913- . . **CLC 4, 8, 15, 53**
See also CA 1-4R; CAAS 6; CANR 1, 36; DLB 48; MTCW

Sharp, William 1855-1905 . . . . **TCLC 39**

Sharpe, Thomas Ridley 1928-
See Sharpe, Tom
See also CA 114; 122

Sharpe, Tom . . . . **CLC 36**
See also Sharpe, Thomas Ridley
See also DLB 14

Shaw, Bernard . . . . **TCLC 45**
See also Shaw, George Bernard
See also BW 1

Shaw, G. Bernard
See Shaw, George Bernard

Shaw, George Bernard
1856-1950 . . . . **TCLC 3, 9, 21; DA; WLC**
See also Shaw, Bernard
See also CA 104; 128; CDBLB 1914-1945; DLB 10, 57; MTCW

Shaw, Henry Wheeler
1818-1885 . . . . **NCLC 15**
See also DLB 11

Shaw, Irwin 1913-1984 . . . . . . **CLC 7, 23, 34**
See also AITN 1; CA 13-16R; 112; CANR 21; CDALB 1941-1968; DLB 6, 102; DLBY 84; MTCW

Shaw, Robert 1927-1978 . . . . **CLC 5**
See also AITN 1; CA 1-4R; 81-84; CANR 4; DLB 13, 14

Shaw, T. E.
See Lawrence, T(homas) E(dward)

Shawn, Wallace 1943- . . . . **CLC 41**
See also CA 112

Sheed, Wilfrid (John Joseph)
1930- . . . . **CLC 2, 4, 10, 53**
See also CA 65-68; CANR 30; DLB 6; MTCW

Sheldon, Alice Hastings Bradley
1915(?)-1987
See Tiptree, James, Jr.
See also CA 108; 122; CANR 34; MTCW

Sheldon, John
See Bloch, Robert (Albert)

Shelley, Mary Wollstonecraft (Godwin)
1797-1851 . . . . **NCLC 14; DA; WLC**
See also CDBLB 1789-1832; DLB 110, 116; SATA 29

Shelley, Percy Bysshe
1792-1822 . . . . **NCLC 18; DA; WLC**
See also CDBLB 1789-1832; DLB 96, 110

Souster, (Holmes) Raymond
1921- .... **CLC 5, 14**
See also CA 13-16R; CAAS 14; CANR 13,
29; DLB 88; SATA 63

Southern, Terry 1926- .... **CLC 7**
See also CA 1-4R; CANR 1; DLB 2

Southey, Robert 1774-1843 .... **NCLC 8**
See also DLB 93, 107, 142; SATA 54

Southworth, Emma Dorothy Eliza Nevitte
1819-1899 .... **NCLC 26**

Souza, Ernest
See Scott, Evelyn

Soyinka, Wole
1934- .... **CLC 3, 5, 14, 36, 44; BLC;
DA; DC 2; WLC**
See also BW 2; CA 13-16R; CANR 27, 39;
DLB 125; MTCW

Spackman, W(illiam) M(ode)
1905-1990 .... **CLC 46**
See also CA 81-84; 132

Spacks, Barry 1931- .... **CLC 14**
See also CA 29-32R; CANR 33; DLB 105

Spanidou, Irini 1946- .... **CLC 44**

Spark, Muriel (Sarah)
1918- .... **CLC 2, 3, 5, 8, 13, 18, 40;
SSC 10**
See also CA 5-8R; CANR 12, 36;
CDBLB 1945-1960; DLB 15, 139; MTCW

Spaulding, Douglas
See Bradbury, Ray (Douglas)

Spaulding, Leonard
See Bradbury, Ray (Douglas)

Spence, J. A. D.
See Eliot, T(homas) S(tearns)

Spencer, Elizabeth 1921- .... **CLC 22**
See also CA 13-16R; CANR 32; DLB 6;
MTCW; SATA 14

Spencer, Leonard G.
See Silverberg, Robert

Spencer, Scott 1945- .... **CLC 30**
See also CA 113; DLBY 86

Spender, Stephen (Harold)
1909- .... **CLC 1, 2, 5, 10, 41**
See also CA 9-12R; CANR 31;
CDBLB 1945-1960; DLB 20; MTCW

Spengler, Oswald (Arnold Gottfried)
1880-1936 .... **TCLC 25**
See also CA 118

Spenser, Edmund
1552(?)-1599 .... **LC 5; DA; PC 8; WLC**
See also CDBLB Before 1660

Spicer, Jack 1925-1965 ...... **CLC 8, 18, 72**
See also CA 85-88; DLB 5, 16

Spiegelman, Art 1948- .... **CLC 76**
See also AAYA 10; CA 125; CANR 41

Spielberg, Peter 1929- .... **CLC 6**
See also CA 5-8R; CANR 4; DLBY 81

Spielberg, Steven 1947- .... **CLC 20**
See also AAYA 8; CA 77-80; CANR 32;
SATA 32

Spillane, Frank Morrison 1918-
See Spillane, Mickey
See also CA 25-28R; CANR 28; MTCW;
SATA 66

Spillane, Mickey .... **CLC 3, 13**
See also Spillane, Frank Morrison

Spinoza, Benedictus de 1632-1677 .... **LC 9**

Spinrad, Norman (Richard) 1940-... **CLC 46**
See also CA 37-40R; CAAS 19; CANR 20;
DLB 8

Spitteler, Carl (Friedrich Georg)
1845-1924 .... **TCLC 12**
See also CA 109; DLB 129

Spivack, Kathleen (Romola Drucker)
1938- .... **CLC 6**
See also CA 49-52

Spoto, Donald 1941-............. **CLC 39**
See also CA 65-68; CANR 11

Springsteen, Bruce (F.) 1949- ...... **CLC 17**
See also CA 111

Spurling, Hilary 1940-............ **CLC 34**
See also CA 104; CANR 25

Squires, (James) Radcliffe
1917-1993 .... **CLC 51**
See also CA 1-4R; 140; CANR 6, 21

Srivastava, Dhanpat Rai 1880(?)-1936
See Premchand
See also CA 118

Stacy, Donald
See Pohl, Frederik

Stael, Germaine de
See Stael-Holstein, Anne Louise Germaine
Necker Baronn
See also DLB 119

**Stael-Holstein, Anne Louise Germaine Necker
Baronn** 1766-1817 .... **NCLC 3**
See also Stael, Germaine de

Stafford, Jean 1915-1979 ... **CLC 4, 7, 19, 68**
See also CA 1-4R; 85-88; CANR 3; DLB 2;
MTCW; SATA 22

Stafford, William (Edgar)
1914-1993 .... **CLC 4, 7, 29**
See also CA 5-8R; 142; CAAS 3; CANR 5,
22; DLB 5

Staines, Trevor
See Brunner, John (Kilian Houston)

Stairs, Gordon
See Austin, Mary (Hunter)

Stannard, Martin 1947- .... **CLC 44**
See also CA 142

Stanton, Maura 1946- .... **CLC 9**
See also CA 89-92; CANR 15; DLB 120

Stanton, Schuyler
See Baum, L(yman) Frank

Stapledon, (William) Olaf
1886-1950 .... **TCLC 22**
See also CA 111; DLB 15

Starbuck, George (Edwin) 1931-.... **CLC 53**
See also CA 21-24R; CANR 23

Stark, Richard
See Westlake, Donald E(dwin)

Staunton, Schuyler
See Baum, L(yman) Frank

Stead, Christina (Ellen)
1902-1983 .... **CLC 2, 5, 8, 32, 80**
See also CA 13-16R; 109; CANR 33, 40;
MTCW

Stead, William Thomas
1849-1912 .... **TCLC 48**

Steele, Richard 1672-1729 .... **LC 18**
See also CDBLB 1660-1789; DLB 84, 101

Steele, Timothy (Reid) 1948-....... **CLC 45**
See also CA 93-96; CANR 16; DLB 120

Steffens, (Joseph) Lincoln
1866-1936 .... **TCLC 20**
See also CA 117

Stegner, Wallace (Earle)
1909-1993 .... **CLC 9, 49, 81**
See also AITN 1; BEST 90:3; CA 1-4R;
141; CAAS 9; CANR 1, 21; DLB 9;
DLBY 93; MTCW

Stein, Gertrude
1874-1946 ...... **TCLC 1, 6, 28, 48; DA;
WLC**
See also CA 104; 132; CDALB 1917-1929;
DLB 4, 54, 86; MTCW

Steinbeck, John (Ernst)
1902-1968 ...... **CLC 1, 5, 9, 13, 21, 34,
45, 75; DA; SSC 11; WLC**
See also AAYA 12; CA 1-4R; 25-28R;
CANR 1, 35; CDALB 1929-1941; DLB 7,
9; DLBD 2; MTCW; SATA 9

Steinem, Gloria 1934-............. **CLC 63**
See also CA 53-56; CANR 28; MTCW

Steiner, George 1929-............. **CLC 24**
See also CA 73-76; CANR 31; DLB 67;
MTCW; SATA 62

Steiner, K. Leslie
See Delany, Samuel R(ay, Jr.)

Steiner, Rudolf 1861-1925 .... **TCLC 13**
See also CA 107

Stendhal
1783-1842 ..... **NCLC 23, 46; DA; WLC**
See also DLB 119

Stephen, Leslie 1832-1904 .... **TCLC 23**
See also CA 123; DLB 57, 144

Stephen, Sir Leslie
See Stephen, Leslie

Stephen, Virginia
See Woolf, (Adeline) Virginia

Stephens, James 1882(?)-1950 ...... **TCLC 4**
See also CA 104; DLB 19

Stephens, Reed
See Donaldson, Stephen R.

Steptoe, Lydia
See Barnes, Djuna

Sterchi, Beat 1949-............... **CLC 65**

Sterling, Brett
See Bradbury, Ray (Douglas); Hamilton,
Edmond

Sterling, Bruce 1954-............. **CLC 72**
See also CA 119; CANR 44

Sterling, George 1869-1926 .... **TCLC 20**
See also CA 117; DLB 54

Stern, Gerald 1925- .... **CLC 40**
See also CA 81-84; CANR 28; DLB 105

Stern, Richard (Gustave) 1928-... **CLC 4, 39**
See also CA 1-4R; CANR 1, 25; DLBY 87

Sternberg, Josef von 1894-1969..... **CLC 20**
See also CA 81-84

Suskind, Patrick
See Sueskind, Patrick
See also CA 145

Sutcliff, Rosemary 1920-1992 ...... **CLC 26**
See also AAYA 10; CA 5-8R; 139;
CANR 37; CLR 1; JRDA; MAICYA;
SATA 6, 44, 78; SATA-Obit 73

Sutro, Alfred 1863-1933 .... **TCLC 6**
See also CA 105; DLB 10

Sutton, Henry
See Slavitt, David R(ytman)

Svevo, Italo .... **TCLC 2, 35**
See also Schmitz, Aron Hector

Swados, Elizabeth 1951- .... **CLC 12**
See also CA 97-100

Swados, Harvey 1920-1972 .... **CLC 5**
See also CA 5-8R; 37-40R; CANR 6;
DLB 2

Swan, Gladys 1934- .... **CLC 69**
See also CA 101; CANR 17, 39

Swarthout, Glendon (Fred)
1918-1992 .... **CLC 35**
See also CA 1-4R; 139; CANR 1; SATA 26

Sweet, Sarah C.
See Jewett, (Theodora) Sarah Orne

Swenson, May
1919-1989 .... **CLC 4, 14, 61; DA**
See also CA 5-8R; 130; CANR 36; DLB 5;
MTCW; SATA 15

Swift, Augustus
See Lovecraft, H(oward) P(hillips)

Swift, Graham 1949- .... **CLC 41**
See also CA 117; 122

Swift, Jonathan
1667-1745 ..... **LC 1; DA; PC 9; WLC**
See also CDBLB 1660-1789; DLB 39, 95,
101; SATA 19

Swinburne, Algernon Charles
1837-1909 ...... **TCLC 8, 36; DA; WLC**
See also CA 105; 140; CDBLB 1832-1890;
DLB 35, 57

Swinfen, Ann .... **CLC 34**

Swinnerton, Frank Arthur
1884-1982 .... **CLC 31**
See also CA 108; DLB 34

Swithen, John
See King, Stephen (Edwin)

Sylvia
See Ashton-Warner, Sylvia (Constance)

Symmes, Robert Edward
See Duncan, Robert (Edward)

Symonds, John Addington
1840-1893 .... **NCLC 34**
See also DLB 57, 144

Symons, Arthur 1865-1945 .... **TCLC 11**
See also CA 107; DLB 19, 57

Symons, Julian (Gustave)
1912- .... **CLC 2, 14, 32**
See also CA 49-52; CAAS 3; CANR 3, 33;
DLB 87; DLBY 92; MTCW

Synge, (Edmund) J(ohn) M(illington)
1871-1909 .... **TCLC 6, 37; DC 2**
See also CA 104; 141; CDBLB 1890-1914;
DLB 10, 19

Syruc, J.
See Milosz, Czeslaw

Szirtes, George 1948- .... **CLC 46**
See also CA 109; CANR 27

Tabori, George 1914- .... **CLC 19**
See also CA 49-52; CANR 4

Tagore, Rabindranath
1861-1941 .... **TCLC 3, 53; PC 8**
See also CA 104; 120; MTCW

Taine, Hippolyte Adolphe
1828-1893 .... **NCLC 15**

Talese, Gay 1932- .... **CLC 37**
See also AITN 1; CA 1-4R; CANR 9;
MTCW

Tallent, Elizabeth (Ann) 1954- ..... **CLC 45**
See also CA 117; DLB 130

Tally, Ted 1952- .... **CLC 42**
See also CA 120; 124

Tamayo y Baus, Manuel
1829-1898 .... **NCLC 1**

Tammsaare, A(nton) H(ansen)
1878-1940 .... **TCLC 27**

Tan, Amy 1952- .... **CLC 59**
See also AAYA 9; BEST 89:3; CA 136;
SATA 75

Tandem, Felix
See Spitteler, Carl (Friedrich Georg)

Tanizaki, Jun'ichiro
1886-1965 .... **CLC 8, 14, 28**
See also CA 93-96; 25-28R

Tanner, William
See Amis, Kingsley (William)

Tao Lao
See Storni, Alfonsina

Tarassoff, Lev
See Troyat, Henri

Tarbell, Ida M(inerva)
1857-1944 .... **TCLC 40**
See also CA 122; DLB 47

Tarkington, (Newton) Booth
1869-1946 .... **TCLC 9**
See also CA 110; 143; DLB 9, 102;
SATA 17

Tarkovsky, Andrei (Arsenyevich)
1932-1986 .... **CLC 75**
See also CA 127

Tartt, Donna 1964(?)- .... **CLC 76**
See also CA 142

Tasso, Torquato 1544-1595 .... **LC 5**

Tate, (John Orley) Allen
1899-1979 .... **CLC 2, 4, 6, 9, 11, 14, 24**
See also CA 5-8R; 85-88; CANR 32;
DLB 4, 45, 63; MTCW

Tate, Ellalice
See Hibbert, Eleanor Alice Burford

Tate, James (Vincent) 1943- ... **CLC 2, 6, 25**
See also CA 21-24R; CANR 29; DLB 5

Tavel, Ronald 1940- .... **CLC 6**
See also CA 21-24R; CANR 33

Taylor, Cecil Philip 1929-1981 ..... **CLC 27**
See also CA 25-28R; 105

Taylor, Edward 1642(?)-1729.... **LC 11; DA**
See also DLB 24

Taylor, Eleanor Ross 1920- .... **CLC 5**
See also CA 81-84

Taylor, Elizabeth 1912-1975 ... **CLC 2, 4, 29**
See also CA 13-16R; CANR 9; DLB 139;
MTCW; SATA 13

Taylor, Henry (Splawn) 1942-...... **CLC 44**
See also CA 33-36R; CAAS 7; CANR 31;
DLB 5

Taylor, Kamala (Purnaiya) 1924-
See Markandaya, Kamala
See also CA 77-80

Taylor, Mildred D. .... **CLC 21**
See also AAYA 10; BW 1; CA 85-88;
CANR 25; CLR 9; DLB 52; JRDA;
MAICYA; SAAS 5; SATA 15, 70

Taylor, Peter (Hillsman)
1917- ...... **CLC 1, 4, 18, 37, 44, 50, 71;**
SSC 10
See also CA 13-16R; CANR 9; DLBY 81;
MTCW

Taylor, Robert Lewis 1912- .... **CLC 14**
See also CA 1-4R; CANR 3; SATA 10

Tchekhov, Anton
See Chekhov, Anton (Pavlovich)

Teasdale, Sara 1884-1933 .... **TCLC 4**
See also CA 104; DLB 45; SATA 32

Tegner, Esaias 1782-1846 .... **NCLC 2**

Teilhard de Chardin, (Marie Joseph) Pierre
1881-1955 .... **TCLC 9**
See also CA 105

Temple, Ann
See Mortimer, Penelope (Ruth)

Tennant, Emma (Christina)
1937- .... **CLC 13, 52**
See also CA 65-68; CAAS 9; CANR 10, 38;
DLB 14

Tenneshaw, S. M.
See Silverberg, Robert

Tennyson, Alfred
1809-1892 .. **NCLC 30; DA; PC 6; WLC**
See also CDBLB 1832-1890; DLB 32

Teran, Lisa St. Aubin de .... **CLC 36**
See also St. Aubin de Teran, Lisa

Terence 195(?)B.C.-159B.C...... **CMLC 14**

Teresa de Jesus, St. 1515-1582 ...... **LC 18**

Terkel, Louis 1912-
See Terkel, Studs
See also CA 57-60; CANR 18, 45; MTCW

Terkel, Studs .... **CLC 38**
See also Terkel, Louis
See also AITN 1

Terry, C. V.
See Slaughter, Frank G(ill)

Terry, Megan 1932- .... **CLC 19**
See also CA 77-80; CABS 3; CANR 43;
DLB 7

Tertz, Abram
See Sinyavsky, Andrei (Donatevich)

Tesich, Steve 1943(?)-.......... **CLC 40, 69**
See also CA 105; DLBY 83

Teternikov, Fyodor Kuzmich 1863-1927
See Sologub, Fyodor
See also CA 104

Torsvan, Traven
See Traven, B.

Tournier, Michel (Edouard)
1924- .... CLC 6, 23, 36
See also CA 49-52; CANR 3, 36; DLB 83;
MTCW; SATA 23

Tournimparte, Alessandra
See Ginzburg, Natalia

Towers, Ivar
See Kornbluth, C(yril) M.

Townsend, Sue 1946- .... CLC 61
See also CA 119; 127; MTCW; SATA 48,
55

Townshend, Peter (Dennis Blandford)
1945- .... CLC 17, 42
See also CA 107

Tozzi, Federigo 1883-1920....... TCLC 31

Traill, Catharine Parr
1802-1899 .... NCLC 31
See also DLB 99

Trakl, Georg 1887-1914.......... TCLC 5
See also CA 104

Transtroemer, Tomas (Goesta)
1931- .... CLC 52, 65
See also CA 117; 129; CAAS 17

Transtromer, Tomas Gosta
See Transtroemer, Tomas (Goesta)

Traven, B. (?)-1969............. CLC 8, 11
See also CA 19-20; 25-28R; CAP 2; DLB 9,
56; MTCW

Treitel, Jonathan 1959- .... CLC 70

Tremain, Rose 1943-............. CLC 42
See also CA 97-100; CANR 44; DLB 14

Tremblay, Michel 1942-.......... CLC 29
See also CA 116; 128; DLB 60; MTCW

Trevanian....................... CLC 29
See also Whitaker, Rod(ney)

Trevor, Glen
See Hilton, James

Trevor, William
1928- .... CLC 7, 9, 14, 25, 71
See also Cox, William Trevor
See also DLB 14, 139

Trifonov, Yuri (Valentinovich)
1925-1981 .... CLC 45
See also CA 126; 103; MTCW

Trilling, Lionel 1905-1975 .... CLC 9, 11, 24
See also CA 9-12R; 61-64; CANR 10;
DLB 28, 63; MTCW

Trimball, W. H.
See Mencken, H(enry) L(ouis)

Tristan
See Gomez de la Serna, Ramon

Tristram
See Housman, A(lfred) E(dward)

Trogdon, William (Lewis) 1939-
See Heat-Moon, William Least
See also CA 115; 119

Trollope, Anthony
1815-1882 ..... NCLC 6, 33; DA; WLC
See also CDBLB 1832-1890; DLB 21, 57;
SATA 22

Trollope, Frances 1779-1863 ..... NCLC 30
See also DLB 21

Trotsky, Leon 1879-1940........ TCLC 22
See also CA 118

Trotter (Cockburn), Catharine
1679-1749 .... LC 8
See also DLB 84

Trout, Kilgore
See Farmer, Philip Jose

Trow, George W. S. 1943-........ CLC 52
See also CA 126

Troyat, Henri 1911-............. CLC 23
See also CA 45-48; CANR 2, 33; MTCW

Trudeau, G(arretson) B(eekman) 1948-
See Trudeau, Garry B.
See also CA 81-84; CANR 31; SATA 35

Trudeau, Garry B................ CLC 12
See also Trudeau, G(arretson) B(eekman)
See also AAYA 10; AITN 2

Truffaut, Francois 1932-1984....... CLC 20
See also CA 81-84; 113; CANR 34

Trumbo, Dalton 1905-1976 .... CLC 19
See also CA 21-24R; 69-72; CANR 10;
DLB 26

Trumbull, John 1750-1831...... NCLC 30
See also DLB 31

Trundlett, Helen B.
See Eliot, T(homas) S(tearns)

Tryon, Thomas 1926-1991 ...... CLC 3, 11
See also AITN 1; CA 29-32R; 135;
CANR 32; MTCW

Tryon, Tom
See Tryon, Thomas

Ts'ao Hsueh-ch'in 1715(?)-1763....... LC 1

Tsushima, Shuji 1909-1948
See Dazai, Osamu
See also CA 107

Tsvetaeva (Efron), Marina (Ivanovna)
1892-1941 .... TCLC 7, 35
See also CA 104; 128; MTCW

Tuck, Lily 1938-................ CLC 70
See also CA 139

Tu Fu 712-770.................... PC 9

Tunis, John R(oberts) 1889-1975 ... CLC 12
See also CA 61-64; DLB 22; JRDA;
MAICYA; SATA 30, 37

Tuohy, Frank.................... CLC 37
See also Tuohy, John Francis
See also DLB 14, 139

Tuohy, John Francis 1925-
See Tuohy, Frank
See also CA 5-8R; CANR 3

Turco, Lewis (Putnam) 1934- ... CLC 11, 63
See also CA 13-16R; CANR 24; DLBY 84

Turgenev, Ivan
1818-1883 ...... NCLC 21; DA; SSC 7;
WLC

Turgot, Anne-Robert-Jacques
1727-1781 .... LC 26

Turner, Frederick 1943-.......... CLC 48
See also CA 73-76; CAAS 10; CANR 12,
30; DLB 40

Tutu, Desmond M(pilo)
1931- .... CLC 80; BLC
See also BW 1; CA 125

Tutuola, Amos 1920- ... CLC 5, 14, 29; BLC
See also BW 2; CA 9-12R; CANR 27;
DLB 125; MTCW

Twain, Mark
... TCLC 6, 12, 19, 36, 48; SSC 6; WLC
See also Clemens, Samuel Langhorne
See also DLB 11, 12, 23, 64, 74

Tyler, Anne
1941- .... CLC 7, 11, 18, 28, 44, 59
See also BEST 89:1; CA 9-12R; CANR 11,
33; DLB 6, 143; DLBY 82; MTCW;
SATA 7

Tyler, Royall 1757-1826.......... NCLC 3
See also DLB 37

Tynan, Katharine 1861-1931 .... TCLC 3
See also CA 104

Tyutchev, Fyodor 1803-1873 ..... NCLC 34

Tzara, Tristan .... CLC 47
See also Rosenfeld, Samuel

Uhry, Alfred 1936-.............. CLC 55
See also CA 127; 133

Ulf, Haerved
See Strindberg, (Johan) August

Ulf, Harved
See Strindberg, (Johan) August

Ulibarri, Sabine R(eyes) 1919- ..... CLC 83
See also CA 131; DLB 82; HW

Unamuno (y Jugo), Miguel de
1864-1936 .... TCLC 2, 9; HLC; SSC 11
See also CA 104; 131; DLB 108; HW;
MTCW

Undercliffe, Errol
See Campbell, (John) Ramsey

Underwood, Miles
See Glassco, John

Undset, Sigrid
1882-1949 .... TCLC 3; DA; WLC
See also CA 104; 129; MTCW

Ungaretti, Giuseppe
1888-1970 .... CLC 7, 11, 15
See also CA 19-20; 25-28R; CAP 2;
DLB 114

Unger, Douglas 1952-............. CLC 34
See also CA 130

Unsworth, Barry (Forster) 1930-.... CLC 76
See also CA 25-28R; CANR 30

Updike, John (Hoyer)
1932- ...... CLC 1, 2, 3, 5, 7, 9, 13, 15,
23, 34, 43, 70; DA; SSC 13; WLC
See also CA 1-4R; CABS 1; CANR 4, 33;
CDALB 1968-1988; DLB 2, 5, 143;
DLBD 3; DLBY 80, 82; MTCW

Upshaw, Margaret Mitchell
See Mitchell, Margaret (Munnerlyn)

Upton, Mark
See Sanders, Lawrence

Urdang, Constance (Henriette)
1922- .... CLC 47
See also CA 21-24R; CANR 9, 24

Uriel, Henry
See Faust, Frederick (Schiller)

Uris, Leon (Marcus) 1924-....... CLC 7, 32
See also AITN 1, 2; BEST 89:2; CA 1-4R;
CANR 1, 40; MTCW; SATA 49

Urmuz
    See Codrescu, Andrei

Ustinov, Peter (Alexander) 1921- .... **CLC 1**
    See also AITN 1; CA 13-16R; CANR 25;
    DLB 13

Vaculik, Ludvik 1926- .... **CLC 7**
    See also CA 53-56

Valdez, Luis (Miguel)
    1940- .... **CLC 84; HLC**
    See also CA 101; CANR 32; DLB 122; HW

Valenzuela, Luisa 1938- ... **CLC 31; SSC 14**
    See also CA 101; CANR 32; DLB 113; HW

Valera y Alcala-Galiano, Juan
    1824-1905 .... **TCLC 10**
    See also CA 106

Valery, (Ambroise) Paul (Toussaint Jules)
    1871-1945 .... **TCLC 4, 15; PC 9**
    See also CA 104; 122; MTCW

Valle-Inclan, Ramon (Maria) del
    1866-1936 .... **TCLC 5; HLC**
    See also CA 106; DLB 134

Vallejo, Antonio Buero
    See Buero Vallejo, Antonio

Vallejo, Cesar (Abraham)
    1892-1938 .... **TCLC 3, 56; HLC**
    See also CA 105; HW

Valle Y Pena, Ramon del
    See Valle-Inclan, Ramon (Maria) del

Van Ash, Cay 1918- .... **CLC 34**

Vanbrugh, Sir John 1664-1726 ...... **LC 21**
    See also DLB 80

Van Campen, Karl
    See Campbell, John W(ood, Jr.)

Vance, Gerald
    See Silverberg, Robert

Vance, Jack .... **CLC 35**
    See also Vance, John Holbrook
    See also DLB 8

Vance, John Holbrook 1916-
    See Queen, Ellery; Vance, Jack
    See also CA 29-32R; CANR 17; MTCW

Van Den Bogarde, Derek Jules Gaspard Ulric
    Niven 1921-
    See Bogarde, Dirk
    See also CA 77-80

Vandenburgh, Jane .... **CLC 59**

Vanderhaeghe, Guy 1951- .... **CLC 41**
    See also CA 113

van der Post, Laurens (Jan) 1906- ... **CLC 5**
    See also CA 5-8R; CANR 35

van de Wetering, Janwillem 1931- .. **CLC 47**
    See also CA 49-52; CANR 4

Van Dine, S. S. .... **TCLC 23**
    See also Wright, Willard Huntington

Van Doren, Carl (Clinton)
    1885-1950 .... **TCLC 18**
    See also CA 111

Van Doren, Mark 1894-1972..... **CLC 6, 10**
    See also CA 1-4R; 37-40R; CANR 3;
    DLB 45; MTCW

Van Druten, John (William)
    1901-1957 .... **TCLC 2**
    See also CA 104; DLB 10

Van Duyn, Mona (Jane)
    1921- .... **CLC 3, 7, 63**
    See also CA 9-12R; CANR 7, 38; DLB 5

Van Dyne, Edith
    See Baum, L(yman) Frank

van Itallie, Jean-Claude 1936- .... **CLC 3**
    See also CA 45-48; CAAS 2; CANR 1;
    DLB 7

van Ostaijen, Paul 1896-1928 ..... **TCLC 33**

Van Peebles, Melvin 1932- ...... **CLC 2, 20**
    See also BW 2; CA 85-88; CANR 27

Vansittart, Peter 1920-............ **CLC 42**
    See also CA 1-4R; CANR 3

Van Vechten, Carl 1880-1964 ...... **CLC 33**
    See also CA 89-92; DLB 4, 9, 51

Van Vogt, A(lfred) E(lton) 1912-..... **CLC 1**
    See also CA 21-24R; CANR 28; DLB 8;
    SATA 14

Varda, Agnes 1928- .... **CLC 16**
    See also CA 116; 122

Vargas Llosa, (Jorge) Mario (Pedro)
    1936- .... **CLC 3, 6, 9, 10, 15, 31, 42, 85;**
                                    DA; HLC
    See also CA 73-76; CANR 18, 32, 42; HW;
    MTCW

Vasiliu, Gheorghe 1881-1957
    See Bacovia, George
    See also CA 123

Vassa, Gustavus
    See Equiano, Olaudah

Vassilikos, Vassilis 1933-........ **CLC 4, 8**
    See also CA 81-84

Vaughan, Henry 1621-1695 .... **LC 27**
    See also DLB 131

Vaughn, Stephanie................ **CLC 62**

Vazov, Ivan (Minchov)
    1850-1921 .... **TCLC 25**
    See also CA 121

Veblen, Thorstein (Bunde)
    1857-1929 .... **TCLC 31**
    See also CA 115

Vega, Lope de 1562-1635 .... **LC 23**

Venison, Alfred
    See Pound, Ezra (Weston Loomis)

Verdi, Marie de
    See Mencken, H(enry) L(ouis)

Verdu, Matilde
    See Cela, Camilo Jose

Verga, Giovanni (Carmelo)
    1840-1922 .... **TCLC 3**
    See also CA 104; 123

Vergil 70B.C.-19B.C. .... **CMLC 9; DA**

Verhaeren, Emile (Adolphe Gustave)
    1855-1916 .... **TCLC 12**
    See also CA 109

Verlaine, Paul (Marie)
    1844-1896 .... **NCLC 2; PC 2**

Verne, Jules (Gabriel)
    1828-1905 .... **TCLC 6, 52**
    See also CA 110; 131; DLB 123; JRDA;
    MAICYA; SATA 21

Very, Jones 1813-1880 .... **NCLC 9**
    See also DLB 1

Vesaas, Tarjei 1897-1970 .... **CLC 48**
    See also CA 29-32R

Vialis, Gaston
    See Simenon, Georges (Jacques Christian)

Vian, Boris 1920-1959 .... **TCLC 9**
    See also CA 106; DLB 72

Viaud, (Louis Marie) Julien 1850-1923
    See Loti, Pierre
    See also CA 107

Vicar, Henry
    See Felsen, Henry Gregor

Vicker, Angus
    See Felsen, Henry Gregor

Vidal, Gore
    1925- ..... **CLC 2, 4, 6, 8, 10, 22, 33, 72**
    See also AITN 1; BEST 90:2; CA 5-8R;
    CANR 13, 45; DLB 6; MTCW

Viereck, Peter (Robert Edwin)
    1916-........................ **CLC 4**
    See also CA 1-4R; CANR 1; DLB 5

Vigny, Alfred (Victor) de
    1797-1863 .... **NCLC 7**
    See also DLB 119

Vilakazi, Benedict Wallet
    1906-1947 .... **TCLC 37**

Villiers de l'Isle Adam, Jean Marie Mathias
    Philippe Auguste Comte
    1838-1889 .... **NCLC 3; SSC 14**
    See also DLB 123

Vinci, Leonardo da 1452-1519....... **LC 12**

Vine, Barbara .... **CLC 50**
    See also Rendell, Ruth (Barbara)
    See also BEST 90:4

Vinge, Joan D(ennison) 1948-...... **CLC 30**
    See also CA 93-96; SATA 36

Violis, G.
    See Simenon, Georges (Jacques Christian)

Visconti, Luchino 1906-1976....... **CLC 16**
    See also CA 81-84; 65-68; CANR 39

Vittorini, Elio 1908-1966 ...... **CLC 6, 9, 14**
    See also CA 133; 25-28R

Vizinczey, Stephen 1933-.......... **CLC 40**
    See also CA 128

Vliet, R(ussell) G(ordon)
    1929-1984 .... **CLC 22**
    See also CA 37-40R; 112; CANR 18

Vogau, Boris Andreyevich 1894-1937(?)
    See Pilnyak, Boris
    See also CA 123

Vogel, Paula A(nne) 1951-........ **CLC 76**
    See also CA 108

Voight, Ellen Bryant 1943- .... **CLC 54**
    See also CA 69-72; CANR 11, 29; DLB 120

Voigt, Cynthia 1942- .... **CLC 30**
    See also AAYA 3; CA 106; CANR 18, 37,
    40; CLR 13; JRDA; MAICYA;
    SATA 33, 48, 79

Voinovich, Vladimir (Nikolaevich)
    1932- .... **CLC 10, 49**
    See also CA 81-84; CAAS 12; CANR 33;
    MTCW

Voloshinov, V. N.
    See Bakhtin, Mikhail Mikhailovich

Voltaire
1694-1778 . . . **LC 14; DA; SSC 12; WLC**

von Daeniken, Erich 1935- . . . . **CLC 30**
See also AITN 1; CA 37-40R; CANR 17,
44

von Daniken, Erich
See von Daeniken, Erich

von Heidenstam, (Carl Gustaf) Verner
See Heidenstam, (Carl Gustaf) Verner von

von Heyse, Paul (Johann Ludwig)
See Heyse, Paul (Johann Ludwig von)

von Hofmannsthal, Hugo
See Hofmannsthal, Hugo von

von Horvath, Odon
See Horvath, Oedoen von

von Horvath, Oedoen
See Horvath, Oedoen von

von Liliencron, (Friedrich Adolf Axel) Detlev
See Liliencron, (Friedrich Adolf Axel)
Detlev von

Vonnegut, Kurt, Jr.
1922- . . . . . . **CLC 1, 2, 3, 4, 5, 8, 12, 22,**
40, 60; DA; SSC 8; WLC
See also AAYA 6; AITN 1; BEST 90:4;
CA 1-4R; CANR 1, 25;
CDALB 1968-1988; DLB 2, 8; DLBD 3;
DLBY 80; MTCW

Von Rachen, Kurt
See Hubbard, L(afayette) Ron(ald)

von Rezzori (d'Arezzo), Gregor
See Rezzori (d'Arezzo), Gregor von

von Sternberg, Josef
See Sternberg, Josef von

Vorster, Gordon 1924- . . . . **CLC 34**
See also CA 133

Vosce, Trudie
See Ozick, Cynthia

Voznesensky, Andrei (Andreievich)
1933- . . . . **CLC 1, 15, 57**
See also CA 89-92; CANR 37; MTCW

Waddington, Miriam 1917- . . . . **CLC 28**
See also CA 21-24R; CANR 12, 30;
DLB 68

Wagman, Fredrica 1937- . . . . **CLC 7**
See also CA 97-100

Wagner, Richard 1813-1883 . . . . **NCLC 9**
See also DLB 129

Wagner-Martin, Linda 1936- . . . . **CLC 50**

Wagoner, David (Russell)
1926- . . . . **CLC 3, 5, 15**
See also CA 1-4R; CAAS 3; CANR 2;
DLB 5; SATA 14

Wah, Fred(erick James) 1939- . . . . . . **CLC 44**
See also CA 107; 141; DLB 60

Wahloo, Per 1926-1975 . . . . **CLC 7**
See also CA 61-64

Wahloo, Peter
See Wahloo, Per

Wain, John (Barrington)
1925-1994 . . . . **CLC 2, 11, 15, 46**
See also CA 5-8R; 145; CAAS 4; CANR 23;
CDBLB 1960 to Present; DLB 15, 27,
139; MTCW

Wajda, Andrzej 1926- . . . . **CLC 16**
See also CA 102

Wakefield, Dan 1932- . . . . **CLC 7**
See also CA 21-24R; CAAS 7

Wakoski, Diane
1937- . . . . **CLC 2, 4, 7, 9, 11, 40**
See also CA 13-16R; CAAS 1; CANR 9;
DLB 5

Wakoski-Sherbell, Diane
See Wakoski, Diane

Walcott, Derek (Alton)
1930- . . . . **CLC 2, 4, 9, 14, 25, 42, 67, 76;**
BLC
See also BW 2; CA 89-92; CANR 26;
DLB 117; DLBY 81; MTCW

Waldman, Anne 1945- . . . . **CLC 7**
See also CA 37-40R; CAAS 17; CANR 34;
DLB 16

Waldo, E. Hunter
See Sturgeon, Theodore (Hamilton)

Waldo, Edward Hamilton
See Sturgeon, Theodore (Hamilton)

Walker, Alice (Malsenior)
1944- . . . . **CLC 5, 6, 9, 19, 27, 46, 58;**
BLC; DA; SSC 5
See also AAYA 3; BEST 89:4; BW 2;
CA 37-40R; CANR 9, 27;
CDALB 1968-1988; DLB 6, 33, 143;
MTCW; SATA 31

Walker, David Harry 1911-1992 . . . . **CLC 14**
See also CA 1-4R; 137; CANR 1; SATA 8;
SATA-Obit 71

Walker, Edward Joseph 1934-
See Walker, Ted
See also CA 21-24R; CANR 12, 28

Walker, George F. 1947- . . . . **CLC 44, 61**
See also CA 103; CANR 21, 43; DLB 60

Walker, Joseph A. 1935- . . . . **CLC 19**
See also BW 1; CA 89-92; CANR 26;
DLB 38

Walker, Margaret (Abigail)
1915- . . . . **CLC 1, 6; BLC**
See also BW 2; CA 73-76; CANR 26;
DLB 76; MTCW

Walker, Ted . . . . **CLC 13**
See also Walker, Edward Joseph
See also DLB 40

Wallace, David Foster 1962- . . . . **CLC 50**
See also CA 132

Wallace, Dexter
See Masters, Edgar Lee

Wallace, (Richard Horatio) Edgar
1875-1932 . . . . **TCLC 57**
See also CA 115; DLB 70

Wallace, Irving 1916-1990 . . . . . . **CLC 7, 13**
See also AITN 1; CA 1-4R; 132; CAAS 1;
CANR 1, 27; MTCW

Wallant, Edward Lewis
1926-1962 . . . . **CLC 5, 10**
See also CA 1-4R; CANR 22; DLB 2, 28,
143; MTCW

Walpole, Horace 1717-1797 . . . . **LC 2**
See also DLB 39, 104

Walpole, Hugh (Seymour)
1884-1941 . . . . **TCLC 5**
See also CA 104; DLB 34

Walser, Martin 1927- . . . . **CLC 27**
See also CA 57-60; CANR 8; DLB 75, 124

Walser, Robert 1878-1956 . . . . **TCLC 18**
See also CA 118; DLB 66

Walsh, Jill Paton . . . . **CLC 35**
See also Paton Walsh, Gillian
See also AAYA 11; CLR 2; SAAS 3

Walter, Villiam Christian
See Andersen, Hans Christian

Wambaugh, Joseph (Aloysius, Jr.)
1937- . . . . **CLC 3, 18**
See also AITN 1; BEST 89:3; CA 33-36R;
CANR 42; DLB 6; DLBY 83; MTCW

Ward, Arthur Henry Sarsfield 1883-1959
See Rohmer, Sax
See also CA 108

Ward, Douglas Turner 1930- . . . . **CLC 19**
See also BW 1; CA 81-84; CANR 27;
DLB 7, 38

Ward, Mary Augusta
See Ward, Mrs. Humphry

Ward, Mrs. Humphry
1851-1920 . . . . **TCLC 55**
See also DLB 18

Ward, Peter
See Faust, Frederick (Schiller)

Warhol, Andy 1928(?)-1987 . . . . **CLC 20**
See also AAYA 12; BEST 89:4; CA 89-92;
121; CANR 34

Warner, Francis (Robert le Plastrier)
1937- . . . . **CLC 14**
See also CA 53-56; CANR 11

Warner, Marina 1946- . . . . **CLC 59**
See also CA 65-68; CANR 21

Warner, Rex (Ernest) 1905-1986 . . . . **CLC 45**
See also CA 89-92; 119; DLB 15

Warner, Susan (Bogert)
1819-1885 . . . . **NCLC 31**
See also DLB 3, 42

Warner, Sylvia (Constance) Ashton
See Ashton-Warner, Sylvia (Constance)

Warner, Sylvia Townsend
1893-1978 . . . . **CLC 7, 19**
See also CA 61-64; 77-80; CANR 16;
DLB 34, 139; MTCW

Warren, Mercy Otis 1728-1814 . . . **NCLC 13**
See also DLB 31

Warren, Robert Penn
1905-1989 . . . . **CLC 1, 4, 6, 8, 10, 13, 18,**
39, 53, 59; DA; SSC 4; WLC
See also AITN 1; CA 13-16R; 129;
CANR 10; CDALB 1968-1988; DLB 2,
48; DLBY 80, 89; MTCW; SATA 46, 63

Warshofsky, Isaac
See Singer, Isaac Bashevis

Warton, Thomas 1728-1790 . . . . **LC 15**
See also DLB 104, 109

Waruk, Kona
See Harris, (Theodore) Wilson

Warung, Price 1855-1911 . . . . **TCLC 45**

Westall, Robert (Atkinson)
1929-1993 .... **CLC 17**
See also AAYA 12; CA 69-72; 141;
CANR 18; CLR 13; JRDA; MAICYA;
SAAS 2; SATA 23, 69; SATA-Obit 75

Westlake, Donald E(dwin)
1933- .... **CLC 7, 33**
See also CA 17-20R; CAAS 13; CANR 16,
44

Westmacott, Mary
See Christie, Agatha (Mary Clarissa)

Weston, Allen
See Norton, Andre

Wetcheek, J. L.
See Feuchtwanger, Lion

Wetering, Janwillem van de
See van de Wetering, Janwillem

Wetherell, Elizabeth
See Warner, Susan (Bogert)

Whalen, Philip 1923- .... **CLC 6, 29**
See also CA 9-12R; CANR 5, 39; DLB 16

Wharton, Edith (Newbold Jones)
1862-1937 ...... **TCLC 3, 9, 27, 53; DA;
SSC 6; WLC**
See also CA 104; 132; CDALB 1865-1917;
DLB 4, 9, 12, 78; MTCW

Wharton, James
See Mencken, H(enry) L(ouis)

Wharton, William (a pseudonym)
.... **CLC 18, 37**
See also CA 93-96; DLBY 80

Wheatley (Peters), Phillis
1754(?)-1784 .... **LC 3; BLC; DA; PC 3;
WLC**
See also CDALB 1640-1865; DLB 31, 50

Wheelock, John Hall 1886-1978 .... **CLC 14**
See also CA 13-16R; 77-80; CANR 14;
DLB 45

White, E(lwyn) B(rooks)
1899-1985 .... **CLC 10, 34, 39**
See also AITN 2; CA 13-16R; 116;
CANR 16, 37; CLR 1, 21; DLB 11, 22;
MAICYA; MTCW; SATA 2, 29, 44

White, Edmund (Valentine III)
1940- .... **CLC 27**
See also AAYA 7; CA 45-48; CANR 3, 19,
36; MTCW

White, Patrick (Victor Martindale)
1912-1990 .. **CLC 3, 4, 5, 7, 9, 18, 65, 69**
See also CA 81-84; 132; CANR 43; MTCW

White, Phyllis Dorothy James 1920-
See James, P. D.
See also CA 21-24R; CANR 17, 43; MTCW

White, T(erence) H(anbury)
1906-1964 .... **CLC 30**
See also CA 73-76; CANR 37; JRDA;
MAICYA; SATA 12

White, Terence de Vere
1912-1994 .... **CLC 49**
See also CA 49-52; 145; CANR 3

White, Walter F(rancis)
1893-1955 .... **TCLC 15**
See also White, Walter
See also BW 1; CA 115; 124; DLB 51

White, William Hale 1831-1913
See Rutherford, Mark
See also CA 121

Whitehead, E(dward) A(nthony)
1933- .... **CLC 5**
See also CA 65-68

Whitemore, Hugh (John) 1936-..... **CLC 37**
See also CA 132

Whitman, Sarah Helen (Power)
1803-1878 .... **NCLC 19**
See also DLB 1

Whitman, Walt(er)
1819-1892 ..... **NCLC 4, 31; DA; PC 3;
WLC**
See also CDALB 1640-1865; DLB 3, 64;
SATA 20

Whitney, Phyllis A(yame) 1903-.... **CLC 42**
See also AITN 2; BEST 90:3; CA 1-4R;
CANR 3, 25, 38; JRDA; MAICYA;
SATA 1, 30

Whittemore, (Edward) Reed (Jr.)
1919- .... **CLC 4**
See also CA 9-12R; CAAS 8; CANR 4;
DLB 5

Whittier, John Greenleaf
1807-1892 .... **NCLC 8**
See also CDALB 1640-1865; DLB 1

Whittlebot, Hernia
See Coward, Noel (Peirce)

Wicker, Thomas Grey 1926-
See Wicker, Tom
See also CA 65-68; CANR 21

Wicker, Tom .... **CLC 7**
See also Wicker, Thomas Grey

Wideman, John Edgar
1941- .... **CLC 5, 34, 36, 67; BLC**
See also BW 2; CA 85-88; CANR 14, 42;
DLB 33, 143

Wiebe, Rudy (Henry) 1934-... **CLC 6, 11, 14**
See also CA 37-40R; CANR 42; DLB 60

Wieland, Christoph Martin
1733-1813 .... **NCLC 17**
See also DLB 97

Wiene, Robert 1881-1938........ **TCLC 56**

Wieners, John 1934-.............. **CLC 7**
See also CA 13-16R; DLB 16

Wiesel, Elie(zer)
1928- .... **CLC 3, 5, 11, 37; DA**
See also AAYA 7; AITN 1; CA 5-8R;
CAAS 4; CANR 8, 40; DLB 83;
DLBY 87; MTCW; SATA 56

Wiggins, Marianne 1947-......... **CLC 57**
See also BEST 89:3; CA 130

Wight, James Alfred 1916-
See Herriot, James
See also CA 77-80; SATA 44, 55

Wilbur, Richard (Purdy)
1921- .... **CLC 3, 6, 9, 14, 53; DA**
See also CA 1-4R; CABS 2; CANR 2, 29;
DLB 5; MTCW; SATA 9

Wild, Peter 1940-................ **CLC 14**
See also CA 37-40R; DLB 5

Wilde, Oscar (Fingal O'Flahertie Wills)
1854(?)-1900 .... **TCLC 1, 8, 23, 41; DA;
SSC 11; WLC**
See also CA 104; 119; CDBLB 1890-1914;
DLB 10, 19, 34, 57, 141; SATA 24

Wilder, Billy .... **CLC 20**
See also Wilder, Samuel
See also DLB 26

Wilder, Samuel 1906-
See Wilder, Billy
See also CA 89-92

Wilder, Thornton (Niven)
1897-1975 ...... **CLC 1, 5, 6, 10, 15, 35,
82; DA; DC 1; WLC**
See also AITN 2; CA 13-16R; 61-64;
CANR 40; DLB 4, 7, 9; MTCW

Wilding, Michael 1942-........... **CLC 73**
See also CA 104; CANR 24

Wiley, Richard 1944-............. **CLC 44**
See also CA 121; 129

Wilhelm, Kate .... **CLC 7**
See also Wilhelm, Katie Gertrude
See also CAAS 5; DLB 8

Wilhelm, Katie Gertrude 1928-
See Wilhelm, Kate
See also CA 37-40R; CANR 17, 36; MTCW

Wilkins, Mary
See Freeman, Mary Eleanor Wilkins

Willard, Nancy 1936-.......... **CLC 7, 37**
See also CA 89-92; CANR 10, 39; CLR 5;
DLB 5, 52; MAICYA; MTCW;
SATA 30, 37, 71

Williams, C(harles) K(enneth)
1936- .... **CLC 33, 56**
See also CA 37-40R; DLB 5

Williams, Charles
See Collier, James L(incoln)

Williams, Charles (Walter Stansby)
1886-1945 .... **TCLC 1, 11**
See also CA 104; DLB 100

Williams, (George) Emlyn
1905-1987 .... **CLC 15**
See also CA 104; 123; CANR 36; DLB 10,
77; MTCW

Williams, Hugo 1942-............. **CLC 42**
See also CA 17-20R; CANR 45; DLB 40

Williams, J. Walker
See Wodehouse, P(elham) G(renville)

Williams, John A(lfred)
1925- .... **CLC 5, 13; BLC**
See also BW 2; CA 53-56; CAAS 3;
CANR 6, 26; DLB 2, 33

Williams, Jonathan (Chamberlain)
1929- .... **CLC 13**
See also CA 9-12R; CAAS 12; CANR 8;
DLB 5

Williams, Joy 1944-.............. **CLC 31**
See also CA 41-44R; CANR 22

Williams, Norman 1952-.......... **CLC 39**
See also CA 118

Williams, Tennessee
1911-1983 ..... **CLC 1, 2, 5, 7, 8, 11, 15,
19, 30, 39, 45, 71; DA; DC 4; WLC**
See also AITN 1, 2; CA 5-8R; 108;
CABS 3; CANR 31; CDALB 1941-1968;
DLB 7; DLBD 4; DLBY 83; MTCW

Williams, Thomas (Alonzo)
1926-1990 .... CLC 14
See also CA 1-4R; 132; CANR 2

Williams, William C.
See Williams, William Carlos

Williams, William Carlos
1883-1963 .... CLC 1, 2, 5, 9, 13, 22, 42,
67; DA; PC 7
See also CA 89-92; CANR 34;
CDALB 1917-1929; DLB 4, 16, 54, 86;
MTCW

Williamson, David (Keith) 1942-.... CLC 56
See also CA 103; CANR 41

Williamson, Ellen Douglas 1905-1984
See Douglas, Ellen
See also CA 17-20R; 114; CANR 39

Williamson, Jack................. CLC 29
See also Williamson, John Stewart
See also CAAS 8; DLB 8

Williamson, John Stewart 1908-
See Williamson, Jack
See also CA 17-20R; CANR 23

Willie, Frederick
See Lovecraft, H(oward) P(hillips)

Willingham, Calder (Baynard, Jr.)
1922- .... CLC 5, 51
See also CA 5-8R; CANR 3; DLB 2, 44;
MTCW

Willis, Charles
See Clarke, Arthur C(harles)

Willy
See Colette, (Sidonie-Gabrielle)

Willy, Colette
See Colette, (Sidonie-Gabrielle)

Wilson, A(ndrew) N(orman) 1950- .. CLC 33
See also CA 112; 122; DLB 14

Wilson, Angus (Frank Johnstone)
1913-1991 .... CLC 2, 3, 5, 25, 34
See also CA 5-8R; 134; CANR 21; DLB 15,
139; MTCW

Wilson, August
1945- .. CLC 39, 50, 63; BLC; DA; DC 2
See also BW 2; CA 115; 122; CANR 42;
MTCW

Wilson, Brian 1942-.............. CLC 12

Wilson, Colin 1931- .... CLC 3, 14
See also CA 1-4R; CAAS 5; CANR 1, 22,
33; DLB 14; MTCW

Wilson, Dirk
See Pohl, Frederik

Wilson, Edmund
1895-1972 .... CLC 1, 2, 3, 8, 24
See also CA 1-4R; 37-40R; CANR 1;
DLB 63; MTCW

Wilson, Ethel Davis (Bryant)
1888(?)-1980 .... CLC 13
See also CA 102; DLB 68; MTCW

Wilson, John 1785-1854.......... NCLC 5

Wilson, John (Anthony) Burgess 1917-1993
See Burgess, Anthony
See also CA 1-4R; 143; CANR 2; MTCW

Wilson, Lanford 1937-....... CLC 7, 14, 36
See also CA 17-20R; CABS 3; CANR 45;
DLB 7

Wilson, Robert M. 1944-........ CLC 7, 9
See also CA 49-52; CANR 2, 41; MTCW

Wilson, Robert McLiam 1964- ..... CLC 59
See also CA 132

Wilson, Sloan 1920-............. CLC 32
See also CA 1-4R; CANR 1, 44

Wilson, Snoo 1948-.............. CLC 33
See also CA 69-72

Wilson, William S(mith) 1932- ..... CLC 49
See also CA 81-84

Winchilsea, Anne (Kingsmill) Finch Counte
1661-1720 .... LC 3

Windham, Basil
See Wodehouse, P(elham) G(renville)

Wingrove, David (John) 1954-...... CLC 68
See also CA 133

Winters, Janet Lewis .... CLC 41
See also Lewis, Janet
See also DLBY 87

Winters, (Arthur) Yvor
1900-1968 .... CLC 4, 8, 32
See also CA 11-12; 25-28R; CAP 1;
DLB 48; MTCW

Winterson, Jeanette 1959-........ CLC 64
See also CA 136

Wiseman, Frederick 1930-........ CLC 20

Wister, Owen 1860-1938 .... TCLC 21
See also CA 108; DLB 9, 78; SATA 62

Witkacy
See Witkiewicz, Stanislaw Ignacy

Witkiewicz, Stanislaw Ignacy
1885-1939 .... TCLC 8
See also CA 105

Wittig, Monique 1935(?)-.......... CLC 22
See also CA 116; 135; DLB 83

Wittlin, Jozef 1896-1976 .... CLC 25
See also CA 49-52; 65-68; CANR 3

Wodehouse, P(elham) G(renville)
1881-1975 ... CLC 1, 2, 5, 10, 22; SSC 2
See also AITN 2; CA 45-48; 57-60;
CANR 3, 33; CDBLB 1914-1945;
DLB 34; MTCW; SATA 22

Woiwode, L.
See Woiwode, Larry (Alfred)

Woiwode, Larry (Alfred) 1941-.... CLC 6, 10
See also CA 73-76; CANR 16; DLB 6

Wojciechowska, Maia (Teresa)
1927- .... CLC 26
See also AAYA 8; CA 9-12R; CANR 4, 41;
CLR 1; JRDA; MAICYA; SAAS 1;
SATA 1, 28

Wolf, Christa 1929- .... CLC 14, 29, 58
See also CA 85-88; CANR 45; DLB 75;
MTCW

Wolfe, Gene (Rodman) 1931-....... CLC 25
See also CA 57-60; CAAS 9; CANR 6, 32;
DLB 8

Wolfe, George C. 1954- .... CLC 49

Wolfe, Thomas (Clayton)
1900-1938 ... TCLC 4, 13, 29; DA; WLC
See also CA 104; 132; CDALB 1929-1941;
DLB 9, 102; DLBD 2; DLBY 85; MTCW

Wolfe, Thomas Kennerly, Jr. 1931-
See Wolfe, Tom
See also CA 13-16R; CANR 9, 33; MTCW

Wolfe, Tom .... CLC 1, 2, 9, 15, 35, 51
See also Wolfe, Thomas Kennerly, Jr.
See also AAYA 8; AITN 2; BEST 89:1

Wolff, Geoffrey (Ansell) 1937- ..... CLC 41
See also CA 29-32R; CANR 29, 43

Wolff, Sonia
See Levitin, Sonia (Wolff)

Wolff, Tobias (Jonathan Ansell)
1945- .... CLC 39, 64
See also BEST 90:2; CA 114; 117; DLB 130

Wolfram von Eschenbach
c. 1170-c. 1220 .... CMLC 5
See also DLB 138

Wolitzer, Hilma 1930-............ CLC 17
See also CA 65-68; CANR 18, 40; SATA 31

Wollstonecraft, Mary 1759-1797...... LC 5
See also CDBLB 1789-1832; DLB 39, 104

Wonder, Stevie .... CLC 12
See also Morris, Steveland Judkins

Wong, Jade Snow 1922-.......... CLC 17
See also CA 109

Woodcott, Keith
See Brunner, John (Kilian Houston)

Woodruff, Robert W.
See Mencken, H(enry) L(ouis)

Woolf, (Adeline) Virginia
1882-1941 .... TCLC 1, 5, 20, 43, 56;
DA; SSC 7; WLC
See also CA 104; 130; CDBLB 1914-1945;
DLB 36, 100; DLBD 10; MTCW

Woollcott, Alexander (Humphreys)
1887-1943 .... TCLC 5
See also CA 105; DLB 29

Woolrich, Cornell 1903-1968...... CLC 77
See also Hopley-Woolrich, Cornell George

Wordsworth, Dorothy
1771-1855 .... NCLC 25
See also DLB 107

Wordsworth, William
1770-1850 .... NCLC 12, 38; DA; PC 4;
WLC
See also CDBLB 1789-1832; DLB 93, 107

Wouk, Herman 1915-........... CLC 1, 9, 38
See also CA 5-8R; CANR 6, 33; DLBY 82;
MTCW

Wright, Charles (Penzel, Jr.)
1935- .... CLC 6, 13, 28
See also CA 29-32R; CAAS 7; CANR 23,
36; DLBY 82; MTCW

Wright, Charles Stevenson
1932- .... CLC 49; BLC 3
See also BW 1; CA 9-12R; CANR 26;
DLB 33

Wright, Jack R.
See Harris, Mark

Wright, James (Arlington)
1927-1980 .... CLC 3, 5, 10, 28
See also AITN 2; CA 49-52; 97-100;
CANR 4, 34; DLB 5; MTCW

SSC Cumulative Nationality Index

SSC Cumulative Title Index

Title Index

Title Index

Title Index

ISBN 0-8103-9281-X